ORDNANCE SURVEY

STREET ATLAS

Cheshire

Contents

IV *Key to maps*

VI *Administrative boundaries*

1 *Street maps*

238 *Index explanation and abbreviations*

239 *Index of towns, villages and rural localities*

240 *Index of street names*

CANDLE WORKSHOP p184

32 HULME HALL AVE p35

PHILIP'S

First edition published 1995
Reprinted 1996 by

Ordnance Survey	and	Philip's
Romsey Road		an imprint of Reed Consumer Books Limited
Maybush		Michelin House, 81 Fulham Road, London, SW3 6RB
Southampton SO16 4GU		and Auckland, Melbourne, Singapore and Toronto

ISBN 0-540-06143-3 (Philip's, hardback)
ISBN 0-540-06144-1 (Philip's, softback)
ISBN 0-319-00562-3 (Ordnance Survey, hardback)
ISBN 0-319-00563-1 (Ordnance Survey, softback)

To the best of the Publishers' knowledge, the information in this atlas was correct at the time of going to press. No responsibility can be accepted for any errors or their consequences.

The representation in this atlas of a road, track or path is no evidence of the existence of a right of way.

Printed and bound in Great Britain by
Butler & Tanner Ltd, Frome and London

Key to map symbols

British Rail station

Private railway station

Bus or coach station

Heliport

Police station (may not be open 24 hours)

Hospital with casualty facilities
(may not be open 24 hours)

Post office

Place of worship

Important building

Parking

174 **Adjoining page indicator**

No adjoining page

Motorway

Dual carriageway

Main or through road

A27 **Road numbers** (Department of Transport)

Gate or obstruction to traffic (restrictions may not apply at all times or to all vehicles)

All paths, bridleways, BOAT's, RUPP's, dismantled railways, etc.

Track

The representation in this atlas of a road, track or path is no evidence of the existence of a right of way

Amb Sta	**Ambulance station**	LC	**Level crossing**
Coll	**College**	Liby	**Library**
FB	**Footbridge**	Mus	**Museum**
F Sta	**Fire station**	Sch	**School**
Hospl	**Hospital**	TH	**Town hall**

0 | 1/4 | 1/2 | 3/4 | 1 mile

0 | 250m | 500m | 250m | 1 Kilometre

The scale of the maps is 3½ inches to 1 mile (1:18103)

The small numbers around the edges of the maps identify the 1 kilometre National Grid lines

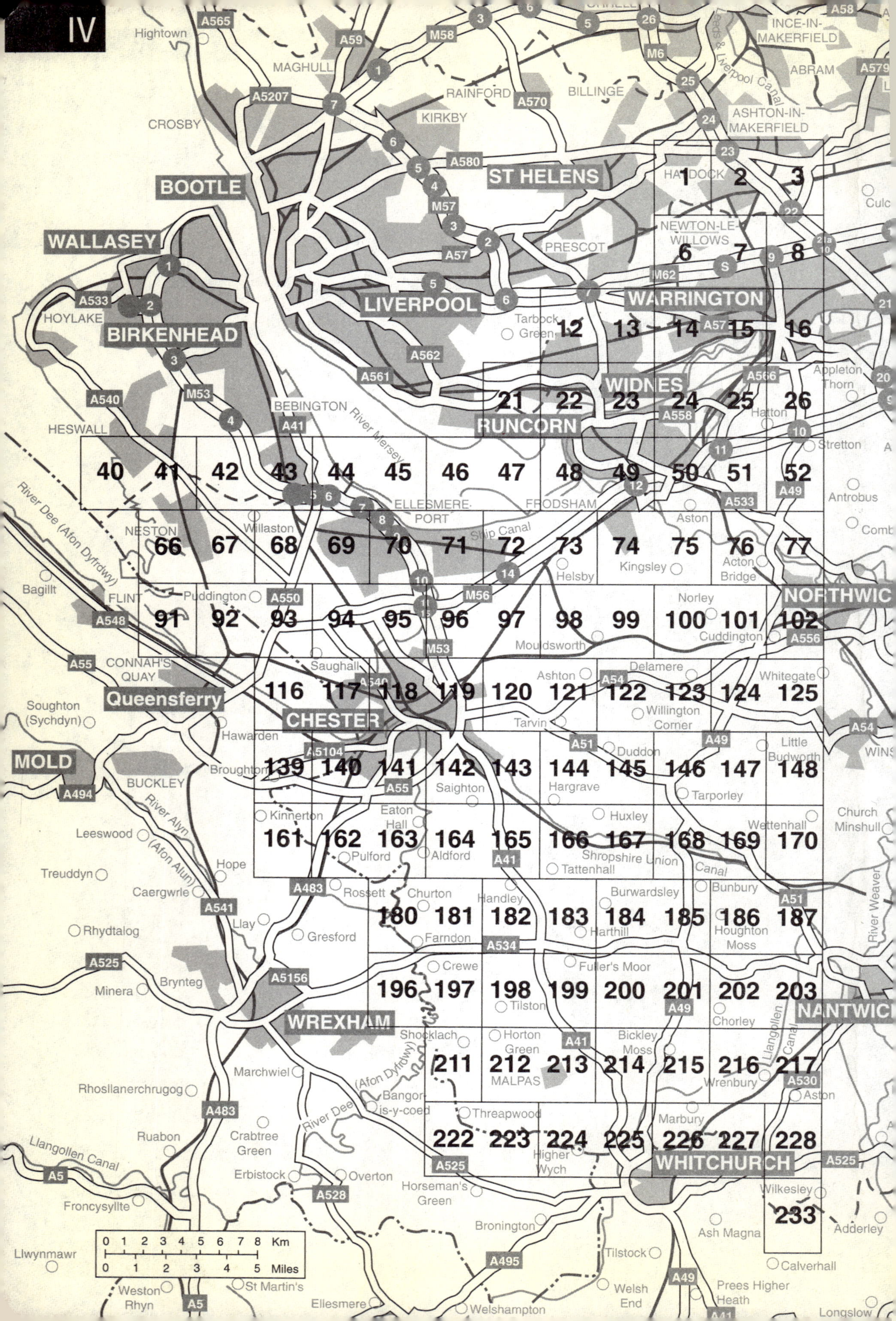

Hightown
A565
A59
M58
MAGHULL
A5207
RAINFORD
A570
BILLINGE
M6
Leeds & Liverpool Canal
INCE-IN-MAKERFIELD
ABRAM
A58
A579
ASHTON-IN-MAKERFIELD
CROSBY
KIRKBY
A580
ST HELENS
BOOTLE
HAYDOCK
1
2
3
Culc
M57
NEWTON-LE-WILLOWS
6
7
8
WALLASEY
A57
PRESCOT
M62
WARRINGTON
A533
HOYLAKE
BIRKENHEAD
LIVERPOOL
Tarbock Green
12
13
14
15
16
A562
A561
A566
Appleton Thorn
M53
WIDNES
21
22
23
24
25
26
A540
BEBINGTON
A41
River Mersey
RUNCORN
A558
Hatton
HESWALL
Stretton
40
41
42
43
44
45
46
47
48
49
50
51
52
A49
River Dee (Afon Dyfrdwy)
ELLESMERE PORT
FRODSHAM
A533
Antrobus
NESTON
Willaston
Ship Canal
Aston
66
67
68
69
70
71
72
73
74
75
76
77
Bagillt
Helsby
Kingsley
Acton Bridge
FLINT
Puddington
A550
M56
Norley
NORTHWICH
A548
91
92
93
94
95
96
97
98
99
100
101
102
M53
Mouldsworth
Cuddington
A556
A55
CONNAH'S QUAY
Saughall
A540
Ashton
Delamere
Whitegate
Queensferry
116
117
118
119
120
121
122
123
124
125
Soughton (Sychdyn)
CHESTER
A54
Tarvin
Willington Corner
Hawarden
A51
A49
Little Budworth
A54
MOLD
A5104
Duddon
Broughton
139
140
141
142
143
144
145
146
147
148
A494
BUCKLEY
A55
Saighton
Hargrave
Tarporley
River Alyn (Afon Alun)
Kinnerton
Eaton Hall
Huxley
Church Minshull
Wettenhall
Leeswood
161
162
163
164
165
166
167
168
169
170
Pulford
Aldford
A41
Shropshire Union Canal
Treuddyn
Hope
Tattenhall
Caergwrle
A483
Rossett
Churton
Handley
Burwardsley
Bunbury
A51
A541
180
181
182
183
184
185
186
187
Llay
Harthill
Houghton Moss
River Weaver
Rhydtalog
Gresford
Farndon
A534
A525
Crewe
Fuller's Moor
Brynteg
A5156
Minera
196
197
198
199
200
201
202
203
Tilston
A49
WREXHAM
Chorley
NANTWICH
Shocklach
Horton Green
A41
Bickley Moss
Llangollen Canal
Marchwiel
211
212
213
214
215
216
217
Rhosllanerchrugog
(Afon Dyfrdwy)
MALPAS
Wrenbury
A530
Aston
Bangor-is-y-coed
A483
River Dee
Threapwood
Marbury
Ruabon
Crabtree Green
222
223
224
225
226
227
228
Llangollen Canal
Higher Wych
WHITCHURCH
A525
A5
Erbistock
Overton
A525
A528
Horseman's Green
Wilkesley
Froncysyllte
233
Ash Magna
Adderley
Bronington
Llwynmawr
0 1 2 3 4 5 6 7 8 Km
0 1 2 3 4 5 Miles
Tilstock
A495
Calverhall
Weston Rhyn
St Martin's
A49
A5
Welsh End
Prees Higher Heath
Ellesmere
Welshampton
A41
Longslow

Key to map pages

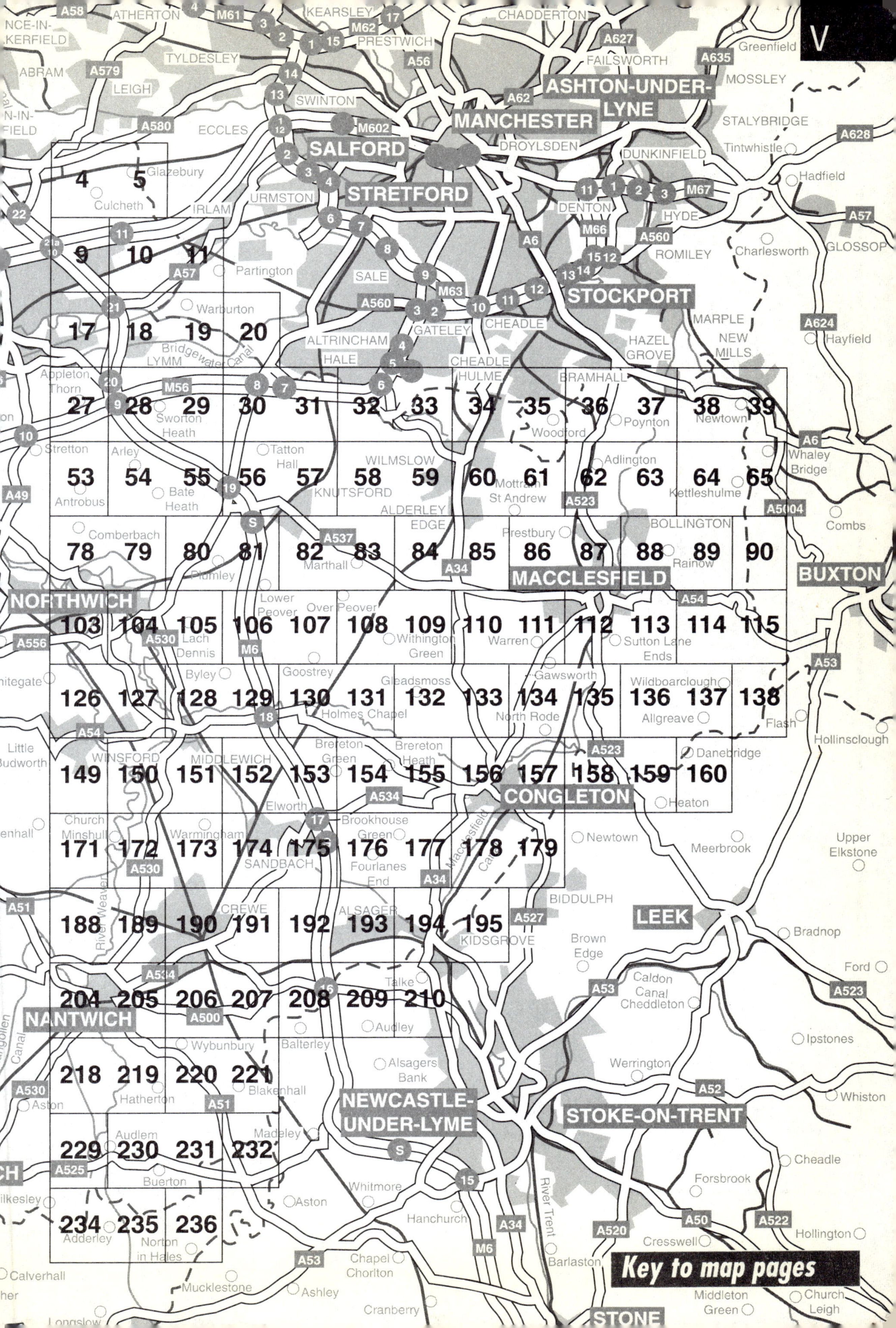

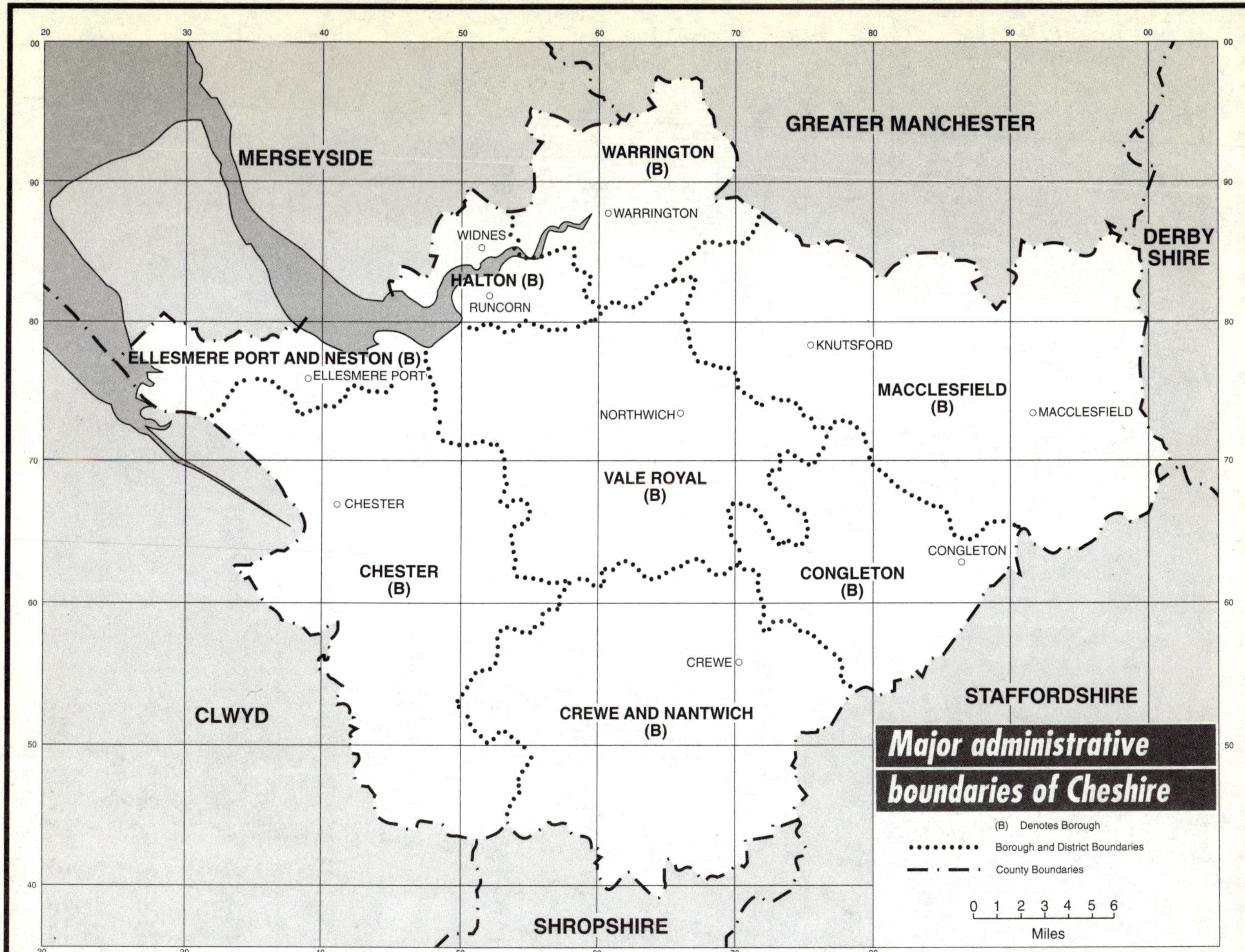
Major administrative boundaries of Cheshire
(B) Denotes Borough
Borough and District Boundaries
County Boundaries
0 1 2 3 4 5 6
Miles
MERSEYSIDE
GREATER MANCHESTER
DERBY SHIRE
STAFFORDSHIRE
SHROPSHIRE
CLWYD
WARRINGTON (B)
WARRINGTON
WIDNES
HALTON (B)
RUNCORN
ELLESMERE PORT AND NESTON (B)
ELLESMERE PORT
KNUTSFORD
MACCLESFIELD (B)
MACCLESFIELD
NORTHWICH
VALE ROYAL (B)
CHESTER
CHESTER (B)
CONGLETON
CONGLETON (B)
CREWE
CREWE AND NANTWICH (B)

2

A
B
C
A580
EAST LANCASHIRE RD
A58
LIVERPOOL RD
Garswood Gates Farm
Icehouse Plantation
Works
Florida Farm
Vicarage
Stanley Bank
Clipsley Brook
VICARAGE RD
WEST END RD
A599
CLIPSLEY LA
Works
HAYDOCK LA
Clipsley Brook
Haydock Lane Industrial Estate
North Florida
MILLFIELD LA
Oil Depot
Dismantled Railway
Yew Tree Farm Trading Estate
KILBUCK LA
KENYON'S LA
PIELE RD
1 ELM RD
2 LARCH RD
3 BISHOP REEVES RD
4 WESLEY AVE
5 GORDON AVE
6 GAYNOR AVE
7 WINSFORD CL
PEACH GR
BLUEBELL AVE
PRIMROSE GR
1 LENFIELD DR
2 WEST END GR
3 WEST SIDE AVE
4 RUNNYMEDE DR
5 BURROWS ST
6 PLATTS ST
New Boston
PENNY LA
CHURCH RD
Liby
Sch
Schs
Works
Dismantled Railway
HAYDOCK
Sch
Blackbrook
Cooper Lane
Wagon Lane
Old Whint Road
GRANGE RD
Grange Farm
Fox Covert
Woodside Farm
Tip (disused)
Hall House Farm
St Helens Canal (disused)
Cloghe Brook
Sankey Brook
CROW LA E
A572
Ashton's Green
A572
NEWTON RD
Newton Common
Sankey Valley Park
COMMON RD
Pennington Lane Farm
PENNINGTON LA
Schs
Sch
DERBYSHIRE HILL RD
WARING AVE
FLEET LA
Recreation Ground
ST HELENS
Parr Flat
Parr Moss
Tip (disused)
Tip (disused)
Mine (disused)
BROAD LA
Moss Hall Farm
Collins Green Farm
PENKFORD LA
B5204
Penkford Bridge
Collins Green
EARLE ST
WHARF RD
Sankey Viaduct
Mill Farm
4
97
3
96
2
95
1
94
54
55
56

6

2

1

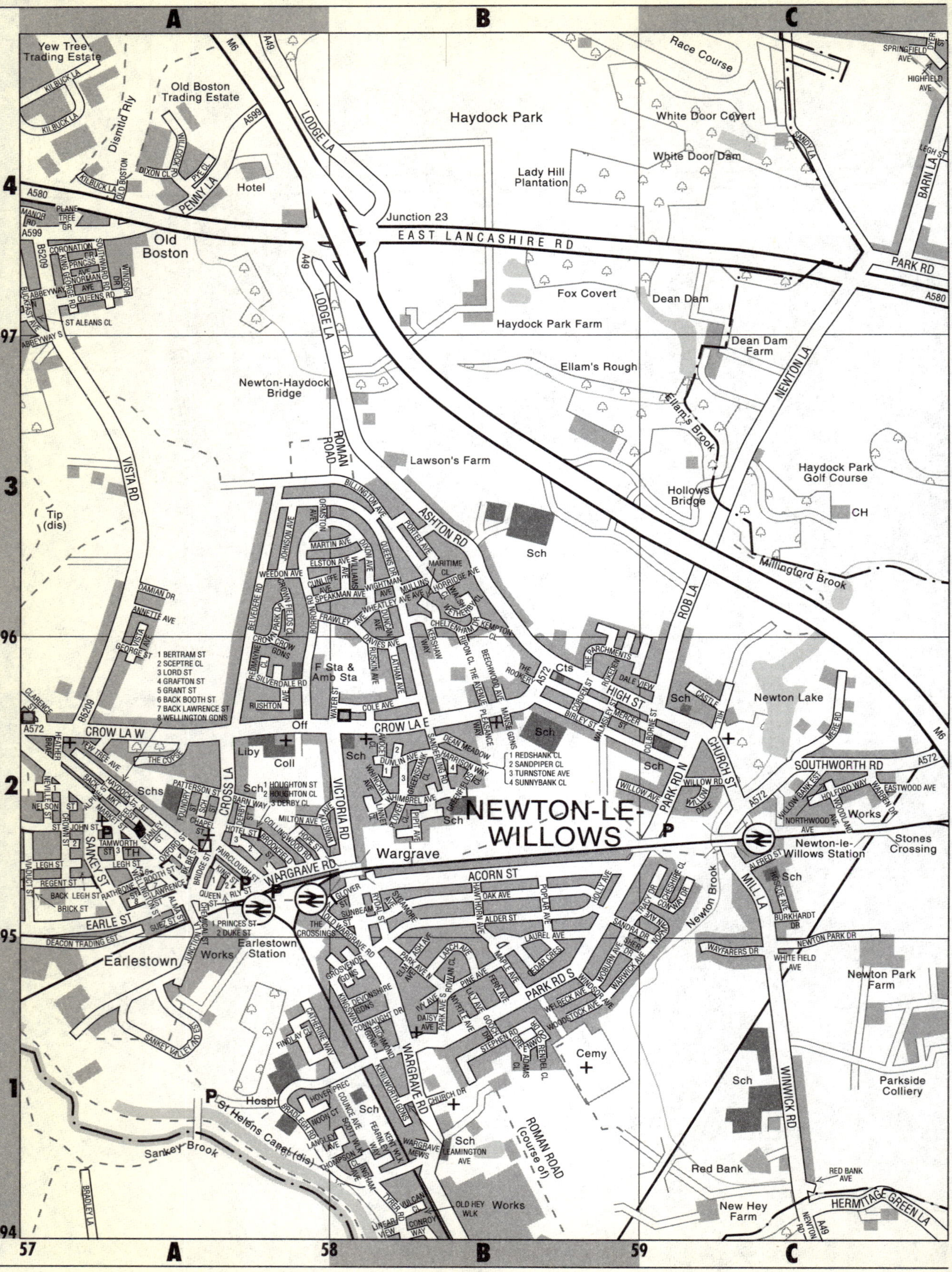

A
B
C
Yew Tree Trading Estate
Old Boston Trading Estate
Dismtld Rly
Haydock Park
Race Course
White Door Covert
White Door Dam
Lady Hill Plantation
Hotel
Junction 23
EAST LANCASHIRE RD
PARK RD
A580
Old Boston
Fox Covert
Dean Dam
Haydock Park Farm
Dean Dam Farm
Ellam's Rough
Newton-Haydock Bridge
Ellam's Brook
NEWTON LA
Lawson's Farm
Haydock Park Golf Course
CH
Hollows Bridge
Tip (dis)
VISTA RD
ROMAN ROAD
LODGE LA
ASHTON RD
Sch
Millingford Brook
M6
A49
A599
A572
B5209
ROB LA
1 BERTRAM ST
2 SCEPTRE CL
3 LORD ST
4 GRAFTON ST
5 GRANT ST
6 BACK BOOTH ST
7 BACK LAWRENCE ST
8 WELLINGTON GDNS
F Sta & Amb Sta
Cts
HIGH ST
Newton Lake
CROW LA W
CROW LA E
Off
Liby
Coll
Schs
Sch
1 HOUGHTON ST
2 HOUGHTON CL
3 DERBY CL
1 REDSHANK CL
2 SANDPIPER CL
3 TURNSTONE AVE
4 SUNNYBANK CL
SOUTHWORTH RD
NEWTON-LE-WILLOWS
CHURCH ST
Works
Newton-le-Willows Station
Stones Crossing
Wargrave
VICTORIA RD
CROSS LA
WARGRAVE RD
ACORN ST
MILL LA
Newton Brook
1 PRINCES ST
2 DUKE ST
Earlestown Station
Earlestown
EARLE ST
SANKEY ST
DEACON TRADING EST
PARK RD S
Newton Park Farm
Cemy
Parkside Colliery
Hospl
St Helens Canal (dis)
Sankey Brook
ROMAN ROAD (course of)
WINWICK RD
Red Bank
New Hey Farm
HERMITAGE GREEN LA
BRADLEY LA
4
3
2
1
97
96
95
94
57
58
59

1
7

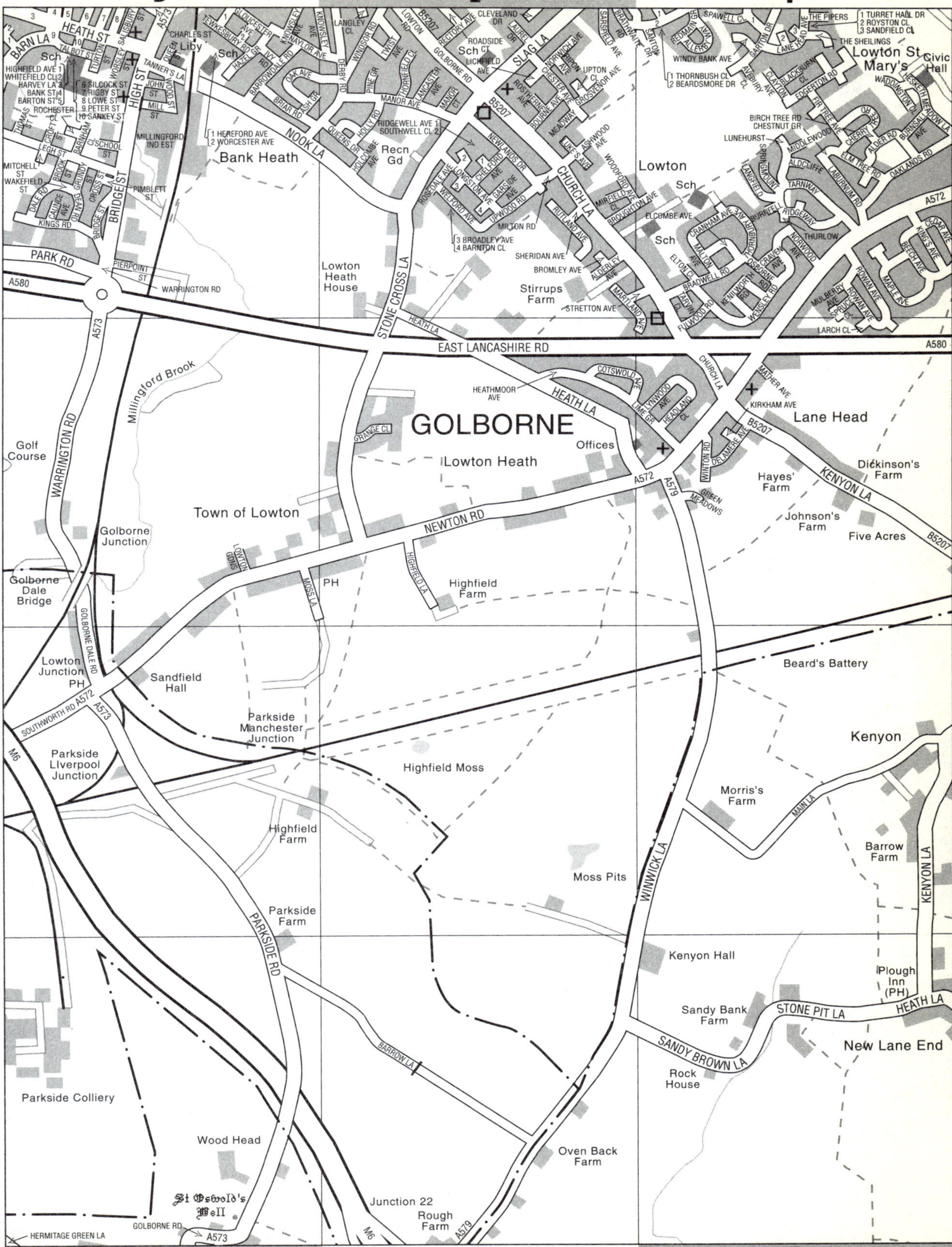
D
E
F
GOLBORNE
Lowton St Mary's
Civic Hall
Lowton
Bank Heath
Recn Gd
Lowton Heath House
Stirrups Farm
Lane Head
Lowton Heath
Offices
Town of Lowton
Golborne Junction
Golborne Dale Bridge
Golf Course
Lowton Junction
PH
Sandfield Hall
Parkside Manchester Junction
Parkside Liverpool Junction
Highfield Moss
Highfield Farm
Parkside Farm
Moss Pits
Kenyon Hall
Kenyon
Morris's Farm
Barrow Farm
Beard's Battery
Hayes' Farm
Dickinson's Farm
Johnson's Farm
Five Acres
Sandy Bank Farm
Plough Inn (PH)
New Lane End
Rock House
Oven Back Farm
Junction 22
Rough Farm
Wood Head
Parkside Colliery
St Oswold's Well
Millingford Brook
Sch
Liby
EAST LANCASHIRE RD
A580
PARK RD
WARRINGTON RD
WARRINGTON RD
A573
STONE CROSS LA
HEATH LA
NEWTON RD
A572
A579
WINWICK LA
PARKSIDE RD
BARROW LA
SANDY BROWN LA
STONE PIT LA
HEATH LA
KENYON LA
MAIN LA
B5207
CHURCH LA
SLAG LA
NOOK LA
GOLBORNE RD
HIGHFIELD LA
MOSS LA
GOLBORNE DALE RD
SOUTHWORTH RD
HERMITAGE GREEN LA
M6
HEATH ST
HIGH ST
BRIDGE ST
BARN LA
1 TURRET HALL DR
2 ROYSTON CL
3 SANDFIELD CL
1 HEREFORD AVE
2 WORCESTER AVE
1 THORNBUSH CL
2 BEARDSMORE DR
3 BROADLEY AVE
4 BARNTON CL
RIDGEWELL AVE 1
SOUTHWELL CL 2
HIGHFIELD AVE 1
WHITEFIELD CL 2
HARVEY LA 3
BANK ST 4
BARTON ST 5
6 SILCOCK ST
7 RIGBY ST
8 LOWE ST
9 PETER ST
10 SANKEY ST
60
61
62
94
95
96
97
1
2
3
4

A
B
C
4
3
2
1
97
96
95
94
63
64
65
Pennington Flash
Country Park
NEWTON RD
ST NICHOLAS RD
POND ST
ALFRED RD
SANDY LA
CHPL WLK
ASTBURY CL
MILLDALE RD
ST HELENS RD
A572
BELGRAVE CL
THE POPLARS
FIELDSEND CL
DALESFORD CL
ARLINGTON DR
MEDWAY CL
LINCOLN CL
CANAAN
GREENACRES CL
MAYFIELD DR
BERKELEY CL
REEVE ST
SILSDEN AVE
Schs
Wash
End
Lowton
Common
Sch
BARFORD DR
ADWELL CL
FOUNTAINS WLK
FINCHDALE GDNS
BOLTON CL
STONEBURY AVE
LINDISFARNE AVE
ABBEY RD
HESKETH MEADOW LA
Fairhouse
Farm
Pocket
Nook
POCKET NOOK LA
MOORFIELD CRES
CARR LA
A572
Sch
CEDAR AVE
A579
Carr Brook
Yates'
Farm
Yew Tree
Farm
Carr Lane
A580
Wood's
Farm
EAST LANCASHIRE RD
Depot
Culcheth
Carrs
A580
Diggle Green
Farm
B5207
Carr
Bridge
LC
WILTON LA
Birchall's
Farm
B5207
Broseley
Bridge
Leigh Golf
Course
Jibcroft Brook
Broseley Hall
Farm
BROSELEY LA
Dismantled Railway
HUTTON CL
DORFORD CL
Leatherbarrow
Farm
Hospl
The Covert
Wilton
Grange
KENYON LA
Twiss
Green
Sch
TWISS GREEN DR
BIRCHALL AVE
LAYLAND AVE
TWISS GREEN LA
CAWLEY AVE
SUTTON AVE
BOSTON CL
CHILTERN RD
BURNHAM CL
BOWDEN CL
MARTIN CL
COLECLOUGH PL
LOWTHER AVE
CULCHETH HILL DR
CRANWELL AVE
CHATSWORTH AVE
CH
Leigh Golf Course
BROSELEY AVE
BEECHWOOD LA
CLAREMONT RD
RICHMOND CL
BARNWELL AVE
ROUGHLEA AVE
BROOKFIELD RD
THE LIMES
HOB HEY LA
COMMON LA
WELLFIELD RD
SANDOWN CL
WIRRAL CL
HESWALL AVE
ELLESMERE RD
BURTON CL
KIRKBY RD
WITHINS RD
RILSTON AVE
CLIFTON AVE
BEECHMILL DR
RADCLIFFE AVE
PRESTWICH AVE
SEPHTON AVE
LODGE DR
Liby
A574
B5207
THOMPSON AVE
CHARNOCK RD
NEWSHOLME CL
CHURCH LA
WALTON RD
WIGSHAW LA
RIMINGTON CL
JACKSON AVE
LANGCLIFFE CL
CROFTON GDNS
RATHMELL CL
LANSDOWNE
GILBERLAND
KAYE AVE
HAMPSON AVE
POPLAR AVE
CHATBURN CT
BROADHURST AVE
WIGSHAW LA
Blakeley
Farm
Kenyon
Farm
ROBINS LA
WARRINGTON RD
Sch
GATE AVE
WHITE CT
YORK AVE
NEWCHURCH LA
CROSSFIELD AVE
WINHAM AVE
THAMES RD
SEVERN RD
RIBBLE CL
Glaziers Lane
Farm
Wigshaw
GLAZIERS LA
Taylor
Industrial
Estate
WHITEFIELD DR
GREENWOOD CL
CEDAR CT
BEECH CT
HEATH LA
Sch
MUSTARD LA
LADY LA
Little
Town
Oaklands
Farm
Yew Tree
Farm
NEW HALL LA
New Hall Lane
Bates
Farm
A574

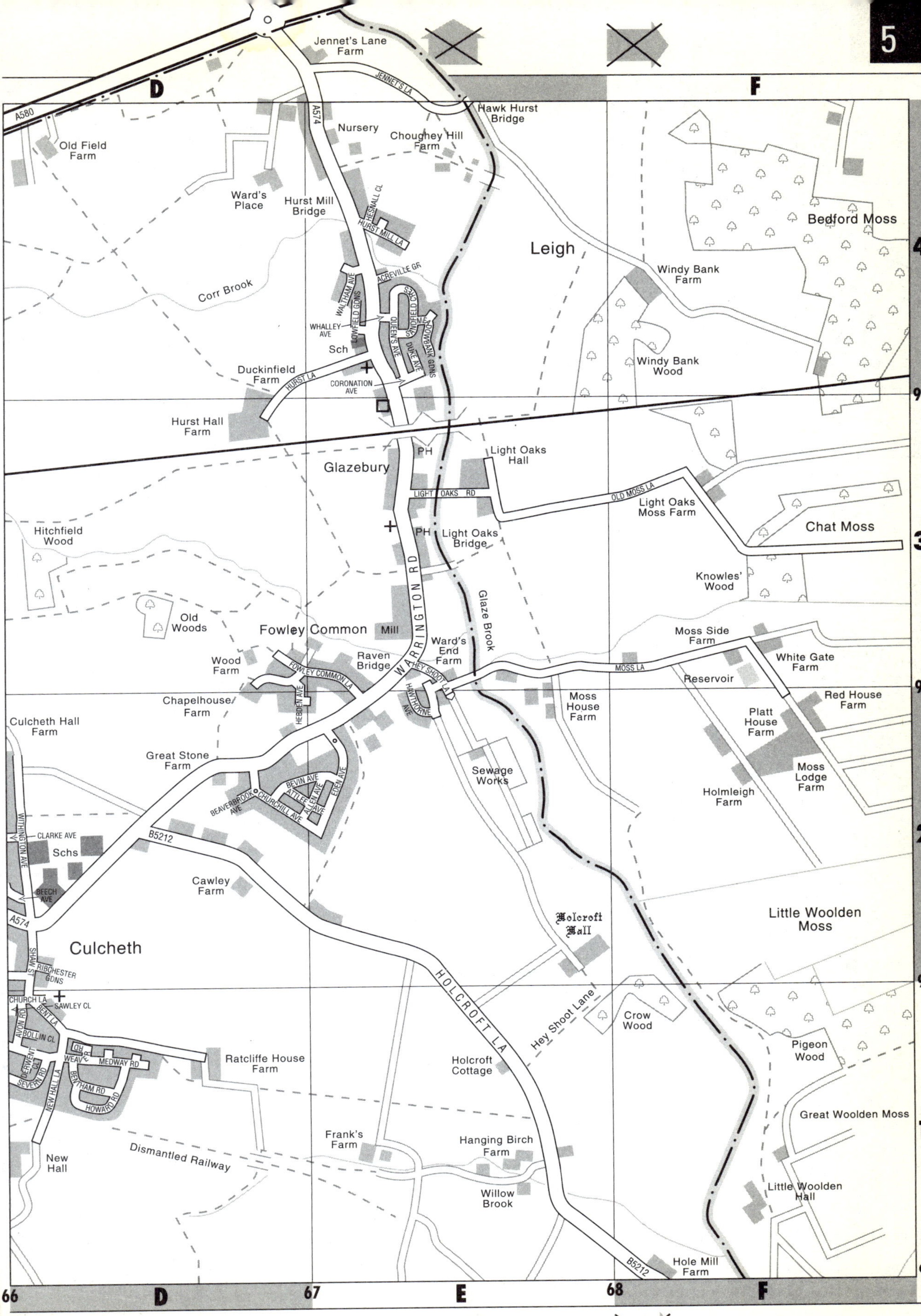

Jennet's Lane Farm
JENNET'S LA
D
F
A580
A574
Hawk Hurst Bridge
Nursery
Choughey Hill Farm
Old Field Farm
Ward's Place
Hurst Mill Bridge
HESNALL CL
HURST MILL LA
Bedford Moss
Leigh
4
Windy Bank Farm
ACREVILLE GR
WALTHAM AVE
Corr Brook
LOWFIELD GDNS
QUEEN'S AVE
DUKE AVE
DOWBANK GDNS
WHALLEY AVE
Sch
Windy Bank Wood
Duckinfield Farm
HURST LA
CORONATION AVE
97
Hurst Hall Farm
PH
Light Oaks Hall
Glazebury
LIGHT OAKS RD
OLD MOSS LA
Light Oaks Moss Farm
Chat Moss
Hitchfield Wood
PH
Light Oaks Bridge
3
WARRINGTON RD
Knowles' Wood
Glaze Brook
Old Woods
Fowley Common
Mill
Moss Side Farm
Ward's End Farm
White Gate Farm
Wood Farm
Raven Bridge
FOWLEY COMMON LA
HEY SHOOT LA
MOSS LA
Reservoir
HEBDEN AVE
HAWTHORNE AVE
Moss House Farm
96
Red House Farm
Chapelhouse Farm
Culcheth Hall Farm
Platt House Farm
Great Stone Farm
Sewage Works
Moss Lodge Farm
BEVIN AVE
ATTLEE AVE
ALLEN AVE
EDEN AVE
BEAVERBROOK AVE
CHURCHILL AVE
Holmleigh Farm
WITHINGTON AVE
CLARKE AVE
B5212
2
Schs
Cawley Farm
BEECH AVE
A574
Holcroft Hall
Little Woolden Moss
Culcheth
SHAW ST
RIBCHESTER GDNS
95
CHURCH LA
SAWLEY CL
HOLCROFT LA
Hey Shoot Lane
Crow Wood
AVON RD
BENT LA
BOLLIN CL
Pigeon Wood
DERWENT CL
WEAVER RD
MEDWAY RD
Ratcliffe House Farm
SEVERN RD
Holcroft Cottage
BENTHAM RD
HOWARD RD
NEW HALL LA
Great Woolden Moss
1
Frank's Farm
Hanging Birch Farm
New Hall
Dismantled Railway
Willow Brook
Little Woolden Hall
Hole Mill Farm
B5212
94
66
D
67
E
68
F

1

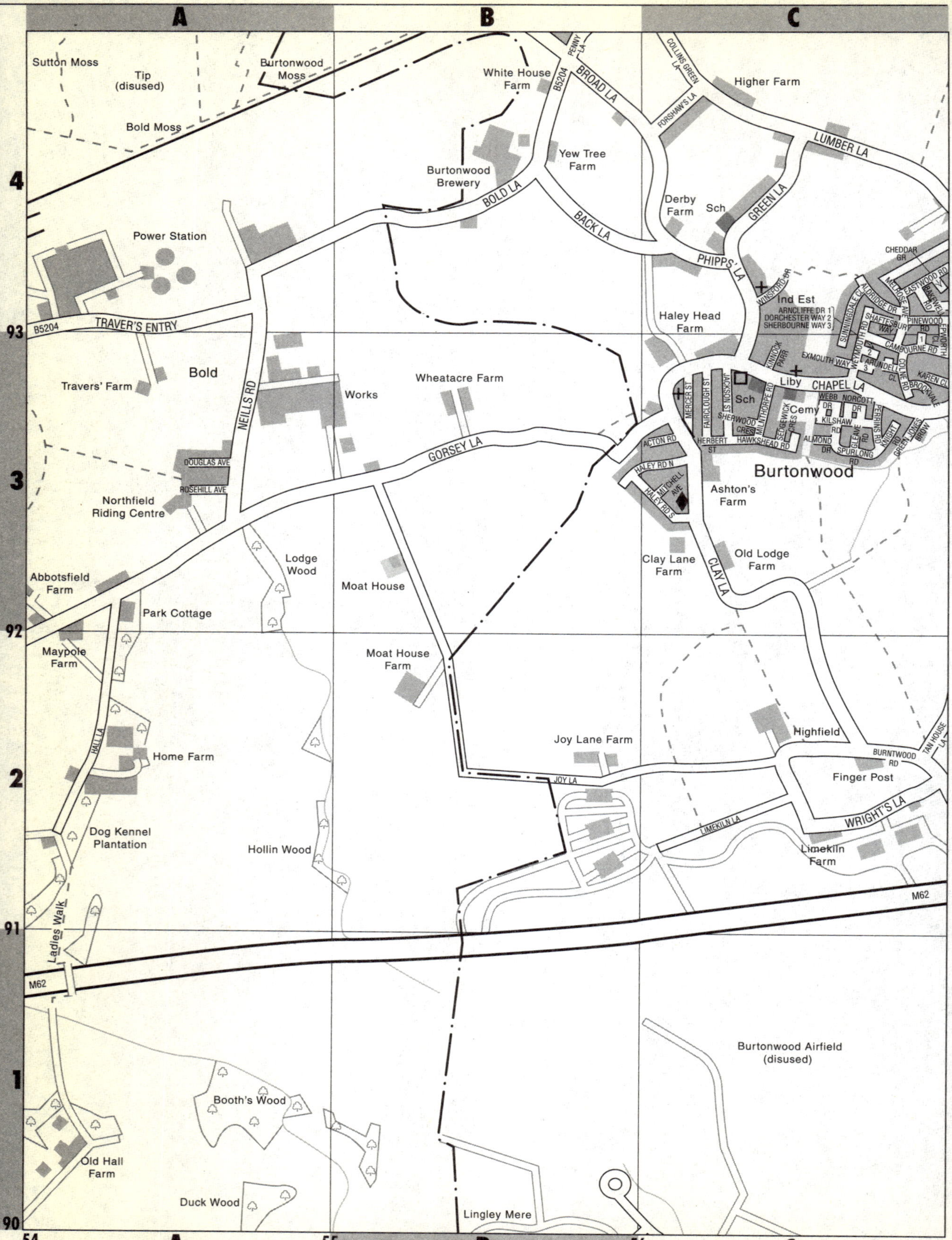
A
B
C
Sutton Moss
Tip
(disused)
Burtonwood
Moss
Bold Moss
White House
Farm
PENNY LA
B5204
BROAD LA
COLLINS GREEN LA
FORSHAW'S LA
Higher Farm
LUMBER LA
Yew Tree
Farm
Burtonwood
Brewery
BOLD LA
BACK LA
Derby
Farm
Sch
GREEN LA
Power Station
PHIPPS' LA
CHEDDAR GR
WINSFORD DR
Ind Est
ARNCLIFFE DR 1
DORCHESTER WAY 2
SHERBOURNE WAY 3
SUNNINGDALE CL
ALDRIDGE DR
MELROSE AVE
EASTWOOD RD
BAKEWELL RD
SHAFTESBURY WAY
PINEWOOD RD
EPWORTH CL
CAMBOURNE RD
WEYMOUTH RD
EXMOUTH WAY
ARUNDELL CL
COLNE RD
KAREN CL
BROOKVALE
KINNOCK PARK
Haley Head
Farm
B5204
TRAVER'S ENTRY
Bold
Travers' Farm
NEILLS RD
Works
Wheatacre Farm
Liby
CHAPEL LA
MERCER ST
FAIRCLOUGH ST
JACKSON ST
MILNTHORPE RD
Sch
SEDGEWICK CRES
Cemy
WEBB DR
NORCOTT DR
KILSHAW RD
PERRINS RD
SHERWOOD CRES
HAWKSHEAD RD
ALMOND DR
GLEAVE RD
SPURLONG RD
KNIGHT RD
GREEN JONES BROW
ACTON RD
HERBERT ST
GORSEY LA
DOUGLAS AVE
ROSEHILL AVE
HALEY RD N
MITCHELL AVE
HALEY RD S
Burtonwood
Ashton's
Farm
Northfield
Riding Centre
Lodge
Wood
Clay Lane
Farm
CLAY LA
Old Lodge
Farm
Abbotsfield
Farm
Moat House
Park Cottage
Maypole
Farm
Moat House
Farm
Joy Lane Farm
Highfield
TAN HOUSE LA
BURNTWOOD RD
HALL LA
Home Farm
JOY LA
Finger Post
WRIGHT'S LA
LIMEKILN LA
Dog Kennel
Plantation
Hollin Wood
Limekiln
Farm
M62
Ladies Walk
M62
Burtonwood Airfield
(disused)
Booth's Wood
Old Hall
Farm
Duck Wood
Lingley Mere
4
93
3
92
2
91
1
90
54
55
56
A
B
C

14

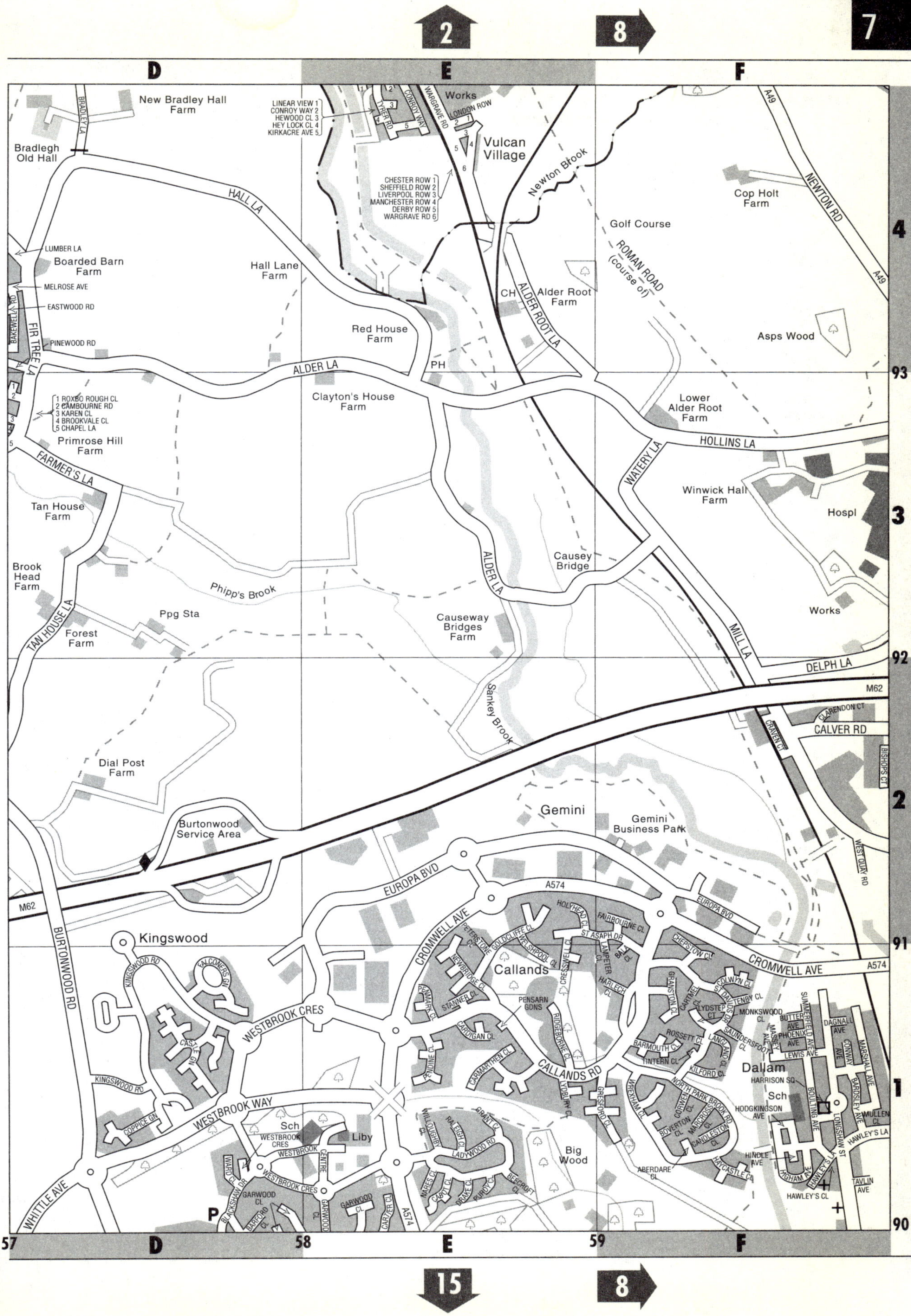
2
8
D
E
F
New Bradley Hall Farm
Bradlegh Old Hall
Works
Vulcan Village
Newton Brook
Cop Holt Farm
NEWTON RD
Golf Course
ROMAN ROAD (course of)
Boarded Barn Farm
Hall Lane Farm
Red House Farm
Alder Root Farm
Asps Wood
ALDER LA
Clayton's House Farm
Lower Alder Root Farm
HOLLINS LA
Primrose Hill Farm
Winwick Hall Farm
Hospl
Tan House Farm
Brook Head Farm
Phipp's Brook
Ppg Sta
Causey Bridge
Forest Farm
Causeway Bridges Farm
DELPH LA
M62
Sankey Brook
CALVER RD
Dial Post Farm
Gemini
Gemini Business Park
Burtonwood Service Area
EUROPA BVD
A574
Kingswood
CROMWELL AVE
Callands
WESTBROOK CRES
CALLANDS RD
Dallam
WESTBROOK WAY
Sch
Liby
Big Wood
BURTONWOOD RD
WHITTLE AVE
57
58
59
90
91
92
93
1
2
3
4
15
8

7 3

A
B
C
HERMITAGE GREEN LA
Hermitage Green
A573
GEROSA AVE
PH
M6
A579
WINWICK LA
Junction 22
Sand Pit
Island Plantation
Cockshot Brook
Southworth Hall
Cockshot Farm
SMITHY BROW
Smithy Brow
Cockshot Bridge
Highfields
WATERWORKS LA
HIGHFIELD LA
A49
GOLBORNE RD
SOUTHWORTH LA
DAM LA
Mill Brow House
GREEN LA
GREEN LA CL
OLD SCHOOL HOUSE LA
THE PRIORY
NEWTON RD
MYDDLETON LA
Myddleton Hall
ILEX AVE
HORNBY LA
ASH RD
MAPLE RD
WINWICK LINK RD
ARBURY LA
HOLLINS LA
CHURCH WK
Sch
ST OSWALDS CL
PILGRIM CL
DALE RD
Winwick
Delph Farm
Arbury
HOLLINS DR
FARINGDON RD
LINKSIDE A
Pumping Station
DELPH LA
Hospital
A49
Mainfield
Spa Well House
Junction 10
M6
Delph Farm
NEWTON RD A49
DELPH LA
Midhops Farm
M62
Hospital
Golf Course
M62
Junction 9
Peel Hall
MILL LA
PH
SOLWAY CL
KINROSS CL
BISHOPS CT
ELM RD
BOWOOD CT
BIRCH AVE
BEXHILL AVE
NEWHAVEN RD
Houghton Green
DUNDEE CL
ENFIELD PARK RD
SHETLAND CL
Winwick Quay
POPLARS AVE
HASTINGS AVE
RADLEY LA
GAIRLOCH CL
KILSYTH CL
CAMERON CT
GRISEDALE AVE
Radley Plantation
BALLATER DR
HARVARD CT
CALVER RD
MILL LA
ULVERSTON AVE
LANCING AVE
COTSWOLD RD
EMMERDALE AVE
LOCKERBIE CL
COLDSTREAM CL
MONTROSE CL
MILL CL
CINNAMON LA N
PERTH CT
WAYWELL CL
COLVILLE CT
TOLL BAR RD
CHILTERN AVE
OXENHAM RD
PENTLAND AVE
CLEVELAND RD
PETWORTH AVE
Sch
Hulme
THIRLMERE AVE
WINDERMERE AVE
HORSESHOE CRES
HILL FARM CL
PERTH CL
GABLES CL
CINNAMON BROW
BRIERS CL
DELAFIELD CL
CROPPERS RD
ACCERLEY CL
Sch
Mill Brook
CHETHAM CT
CHEVIOT AVE
CHILTERN CR
MENDIP AVE
ESKDALE AVE
SCAFELL AVE
CARTMEL AVE
ULLSWATER AVE
BUTTERMERE AVE
CANBERRA AVE
BUTTERMERE CRES
OSPREY CL
GRASMERE AVE
TEAL CL
FOXFIELD CL
MORVEN CL
WELSBY CL
NEWTON RD
ENFIELD PARK RD
ISHERWOOD CL
WASLEY CL
BICKLEY CL
BROMLEY CL
Sch
SANDY LA W
ST STEPHEN'S AVE
HUNTER AV
PC
BORROWDALE AVE
MARDALE AVE
BENTHAM AVE
AMBLESIDE CL
POPLARS AVE
HONISTER AVE
MALLARD CL
CONCORD PL
AVOCET CL
QUAIL CL
BITTERN CL
LINNET CL
SWIFT CL
DUNLIN CL
ST BRIDGETS CL
A574
CROWE AVE
AJAX AVE
HOWSON RD
APPLEBY RD
KESWICK AVE
KIRKSTONE AVE
KENDAL AV
BOWNESS AVE
CANBERRA SQ
METEOR CRES
HALIFAX CL
GREENWOOD CRES
TROSSACH CL
TYNE CL
THAMES CL
Sch
Blackbrook
PARKFIELDS CL
VULCAN CL
CHILTERN PL 1
BRENDON AVE 2
WANSFELL PL 3
KENTMERE PL 4
CHILTERN RD 5
CRAWLEY AVE 6
SEAFORD PL 7
ACHILLES AV
SINCLAIR AVE
COOPER AVE
LOCKER AVE
POOLE AVE
PATTERDALE AVE
THE KESWICK CR
THE COPPINS
WHITTAKER A
CATTERALL AVE
CAPESTHORNE RD
ORANGE GR
AVERY CL
BRANTFIELD CT
VULCAN CL
VALIANT CL
STATHAM AVE
WINWICK RD
GOUGH AVE
MARRON AV
DEAN CT
Longford
BYRON CT
SMALL CL
SMALL AVE
HUGHES PL
HUGHES AVE
FAIRBROTHER CRES
Liby
1 LANGDALE CL
2 PENNINE RD
3 REDESDALE CL
4 SEVERN CL
5 HUMBER RD
6 MEDWAY CL
Liby
INSALL RD
CURRANS RD
DENSHAM AVE
NORTHWAY
ARMOUR AVE
CLOUGH AVE
WALPOLE G
KEATS GR
BURNS GR
TENNYSON DR
DRYDEN PL
RUSKIN AVE
SANDY LA
FESTIVAL AVE
FESTIVAL CRES
CALDBECK A
BLENHEIM CL
MARTIN AVE
ANTRIM RD
FISHER AVE
SHAKESPEARE GR
KIPLING AVE
Sch
PRIMROSE CL
ST MAWGAN CT
BLACKBROOKE AVE
GAYHURST AVE
APPLETREE GR
Sch
WADDINGTON CL
ALBAN RETAIL PARK
COSSACK AVE
Sch
CLIVE AVE
FIELDVIEW DR
CAPESTHORNE RD
POVEY RD
NEVILLE AVE
POPLARS AVE
DEREK AVE
BOYLE AVE
HARDING AVE
Padgate Brook
ANSON CL
JURBY CT
RUISLIP CT
GOSPORT DR
HAWLEY'S LA
WINWICK RD
A50
MILVAIN DR
BEATTY A
MARINA DR
Sch
PARK RD
WOODCOTE CL
BURTON RD
WARREN RD
BRUCE AVE
Sch
HILDEN RD
CATTERICK CT
BIGGIN CT
VALLEY CT
RUDLOE CT
A574
Dallam Brook
LONG LA
WINSTANLEY IND EST
FIELD RD
PC
BIRTLES RD
OSBORNE AVE
BAWTRY CT
DUXFORD CT
BIRCHWOOD WAY
Padgate
ATHLONE RD
Coll
Sch
LONGFIELD
HALLFIELDS RD 1
HALLOWS AVE 2
VALE OWEN RD 3
MALCOLM AVE 4
FERGUSON DR 5
SYLVIA CRES 6
ORFORD GREEN
ST MARGARET'S A
ANDOVER CL
A574
WOODVALE CL
1 POCKLINGTON CT
2 NORTHOLT CT
3 FINNINGLEY CT
Rcn Gd
PC
P
A49
Sch
A50
HILDEN PL
4
93
3
92
2
91
1
90
60
61
62

7 16

4
10

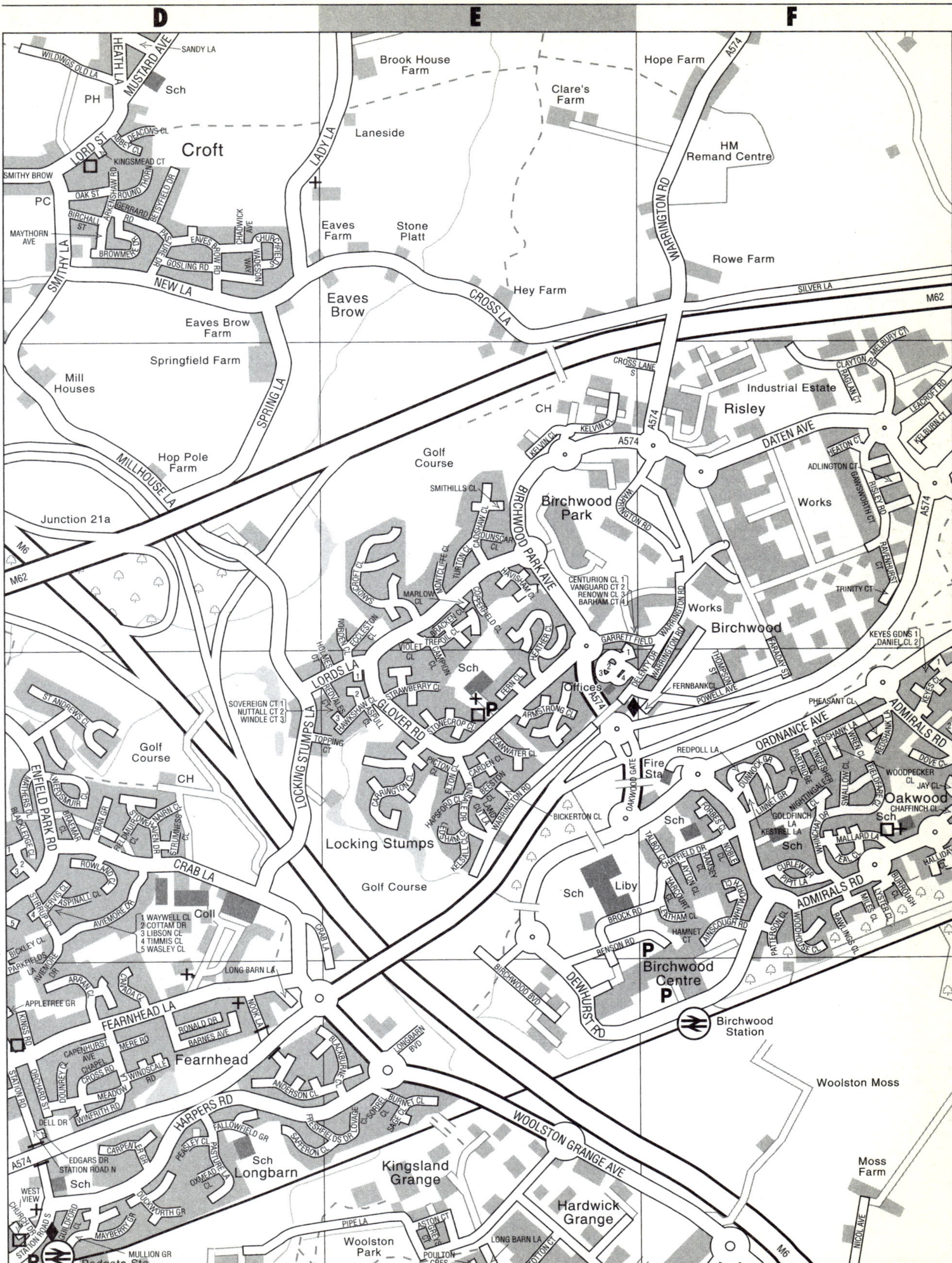
D
E
F
4
3
2
1
93
92
91
90
63
64
65
Croft
Sch
PH
PC
SANDY LA
WILDINGS OLD LA
HEATH LA
MUSTARD AVE
DEACONS CL
ABBEY CL
LORD ST
KINGSMEAD CT
SMITHY BROW
OAK ST
ARKENSHAW RD
ROUND THORN
BEYSFIELD DR
GERRARD RD
BIRCHALL ST
MAYTHORN AVE
CHADWICK AVE
CHURCHFIELDS
EAVES BROW RD
WADESON WAY
BROWMERE DR
PASTURE DR
GOSLING RD
SMITHY LA
NEW LA
Brook House Farm
Laneside
LADY LA
Eaves Farm
Stone Platt
Eaves Brow
Eaves Brow Farm
Springfield Farm
Mill Houses
SPRING LA
Hop Pole Farm
MILLHOUSE LA
Junction 21a
M6
M62
Clare's Farm
Hope Farm
A574
HM Remand Centre
WARRINGTON RD
Rowe Farm
Hey Farm
CROSS LA
SILVER LA
CROSS LANE S
CH
KELVIN CL
Golf Course
Industrial Estate
Risley
DATEN AVE
CLAYTON RD
MELBURY CT
RAGLAN CT
LEACROFT RD
KELBURN CT
HEATON CT
ADLINGTON CT
GAWSWORTH CT
RISLEY RD
Works
Birchwood Park
SMITHILLS CL
BIRCHWOOD PARK AVE
CADSHAW CL
DUNSCAR CL
TURTON CL
MONTCLIFFE CL
SANDYCROFT CL
MARLOW CL
HAVISHAM CL
COPPERFIELD CL
BRACKEN CL
TREFOIL CL
CAMPION CL
VIOLET CL
NORDEN CL
ECCLESTON CL
HOLMES CL
LORDS LA
HEATHER CL
CENTURION CL 1
VANGUARD CT 2
RENOWN CL 3
BARHAM CT 4
GARRETT FIELD
RAVENHURST CT
TRINITY CT
Birchwood
FARADAY ST
THOMPSON ST
Offices
DELENTY DR
FERNBANK CL
POWELL AVE
KEYES GDNS 1
DANIEL CL 2
Sch
FERN CL
ARMSTRONG CL
STRAWBERRY CL
GLOVER RD
HAWKSHAW CL
REDVALES CL
ASPULL CL
STONECROP CL
SOVEREIGN CT 1
NUTTALL CT 2
WINDLE CT 3
TOPPING CT
LOCKING STUMPS LA
DEANWATER CL
PHEASANT CL
ADMIRALS RD
ORDNANCE AVE
REDSHANK LA
WREN CL
REDPOLL LA
DUNNOCK GR
PARTRIDGE CL
KINGFISHER CL
SWALLOW CL
FIELDFARE CL
WOODPECKER CL
JAY CL
Oakwood
CHAFFINCH CL
DOVE CL
KEYES CL
Fire Sta
OAKWOOD GATE
PICTON CL
CARDEN CL
BEESTON CL
CARRINGTON CL
ELTON CL
HAPSFORD CL
WINSFORD DR
UTTA CL
LANDS CL
WARRINGTON RD
BICKERTON CL
Locking Stumps
Golf Course
LINNET GR
GOLDFINCH LA
NIGHTINGALE CL
KESTREL LA
WHINCHAT DR
MALLARD LA
TEAL CL
HALLIDAY CL
CURLEW GR
PIPIT LA
ADMIRALS RD
BURROUGH CL
LYSTER CL
MILES CL
RAWLINGS CL
WOODHOUSE CL
PATTERSON CL
FORBES CL
NOBLE CL
TALBOT CL
CHATFIELD DR
RAMSEY CL
LAYTON CL
HARCOURT CL
WHITWORTH CL
AINSCOUGH RD
LEATHAM CL
HAMNET CT
Liby
BROCK RD
BENSON RD
P
Birchwood Centre
DEWHURST RD
BIRCHWOOD BVD
Birchwood Station
Woolston Moss
Moss Farm
NICOL AVE
ST ANDREWS CL
ENFIELD PARK RD
WEEDSMUIR CL
MATHERS CL
BLACKLEDGE CL
BRAEMAR CL
OBAN GR
STONEHAVEN DR
NAIRN CL
ELLIMUIR CL
STRUMNESS CL
ROWLAND CL
CRAB LA
ASPINALL CL
JERVIS CL
STIRRUP CL
AVIEMORE DR
1 WAYWELL CL
2 COTTAM DR
3 LIBSON CL
4 TIMMIS CL
5 WASLEY CL
Coll
BICKLEY CL
PARKFIELDS LA
LONG BARN LA
NOOK LA
ARRAN CL
CANADA CL
APPLETREE GR
FEARNHEAD LA
RONALD DR
BARNES AVE
KINGS RD
CAPENHURST AVE
MERE RD
CHAPEL CROSS RD
WINDSCALE RD
Fearnhead
DUNDREY CL
STATION RD
ORCHARD ST
MEADOW LA
WINFRITH RD
DELL DR
BLACKBURNE CL
LONGBARN BVD
ANDERSON CL
HARPERS RD
BURNET CL
SORREL CL
LOVAGE CL
SAGE CL
FRESHFIELDS DR
SAFFRON CL
FALLOWFIELD GR
PEASLEY CL
PASTURE LA
CARPENTER GR
OXMEAD CL
Sch
Longbarn
EDGARS DR
STATION ROAD N
A574
WEST VIEW
Sch
CHURCH DR
STATION ROAD S
GUILDFORD CL
MAYBERRY GR
DUCKWORTH GR
MULLION GR
Padgate Sta
Kingsland Grange
WOOLSTON GRANGE AVE
Hardwick Grange
PIPE LA
ASTON CT
Woolston Park
POULTON CRES
LONG BARN LA
TOTTON CT
M6

17
10

9
5

A
B
C
B5212
Keeper's Cottage
Glaze Brook
Aikin Knowle's Bridge
HOLCROFT LA
M62
Old Abbey Farm
Moss Side Farm
Junction 11
Ferndale Nurseries
SILVER LA
Holcroft Moss
M62
PRESTWOOD CT
A574
Pestfurlong Hill
LEACROFT RD
Industrial Estate
Pestfurlong Moss
BIRCHWOOD WAY
SILVER LA
Glazebrook Moss
HAMSTERLEY CL
ALDERWOOD CL
ARDEN CL
GORSE COVERT RD
A574
PERCROSS CL
STANMORE CL
DARNAWAY CL
RENDLESHAM CL
WOOLMER CL
ROCKINGHAM CL
Hoyle's Moss Farm
BRAMSHILL CL
FISHERFIELD DR
Sch
HAZELBOROUGH CL
MOSS
GORSE COVERT RD
WHITTLEWOOD CL
RINGWOOD CL
BOWLAND CL
ASHDOWN LA
GILDERDALE CL
SCHOOL LA
New Hall Farm
Milverton Farm
MOSS LA
WESTWAY CRES 1
WIGMORE CL 2
DUNLEY CL 3
ROSENDALE DR 4
CULBIN CL 5
GATE
P
Gorse Covert
Birchwood Forest Park
KILLINGWORTH LA
DALBY CL
CHARNWOOD CL
Omrod Farm
ORDNANCE AVE
P
Visitors Centre
Risley Moss
KEYES CL
DAM LA
Bridge Farm
DAM HEAD LA
DANIEL CL
Birchwood Brook
Risley Moss Country Park
Hollingreave Farm
Land Fill Site
Moss Hall Farm
MANSFIELD CL
COLEBROOK CL
ADMIRALS RD
McCARTHY CL
PALLISER CL
PENNANT
FISHMORE
Moss Side
Prospect Farm
PROSPECT LA
Moss Side Farm No.2
Ash Tree Farm
Moss Side Farm
MOSS SIDE LA
Rixton Moss
Brick Works
WOODEND LA
Woodend Farm
HOLLY BUSH LA
Woolston Moss
Works
Rixton Clay Pits Nature Reserve
MOAT LA
Gas Compressor Station
CHAPEL LA
Moss Head
Rixton Firs
Marshall's Farm
MANCHESTER RD
BROOK LA
Moss Farm
A57
4
93
3
92
2
91
1
90
66
67
68
A
B
C

9
18

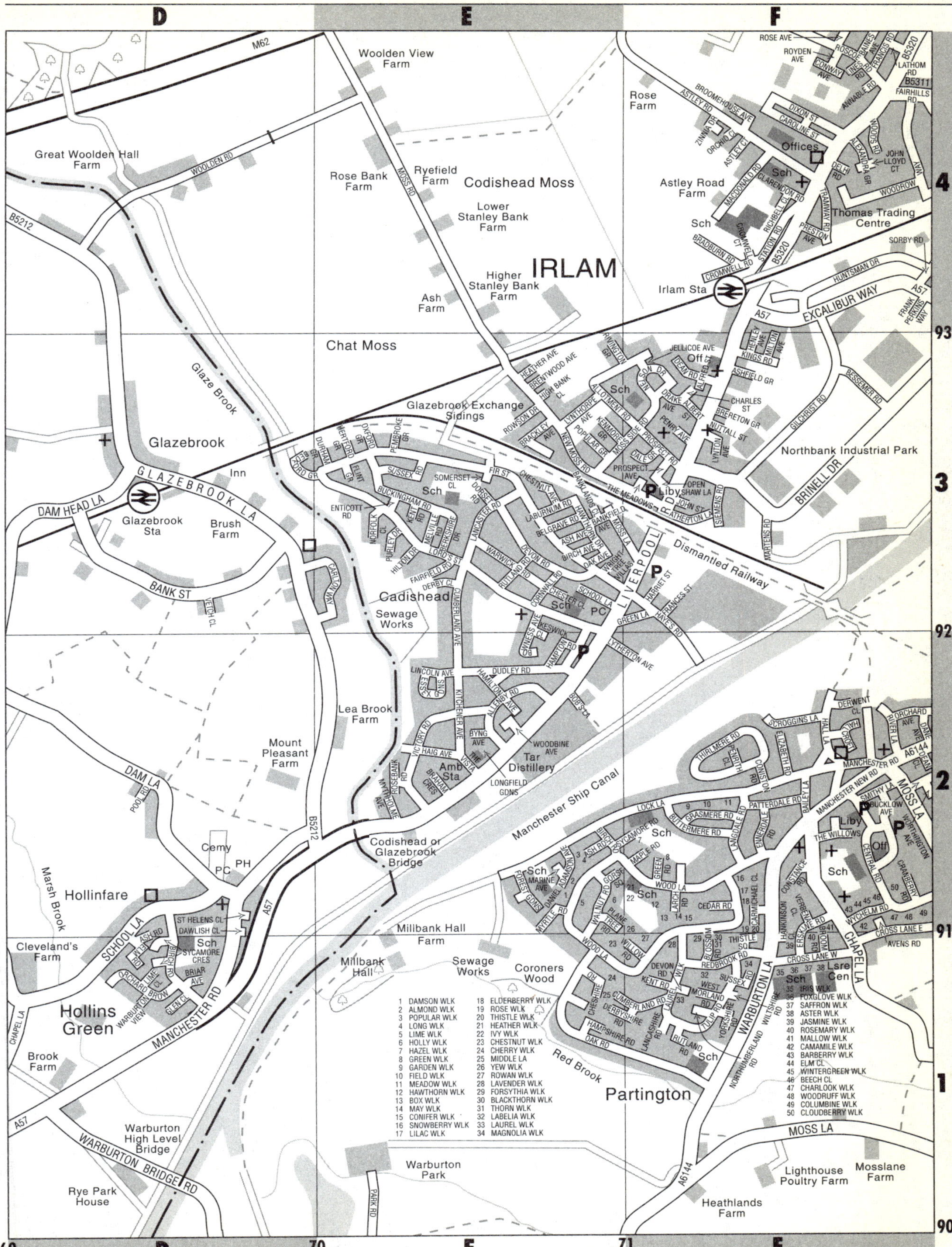

D
E
F
4
93
3
92
2
91
1
90
69
70
71
M62
Woolden View Farm
Great Woolden Hall Farm
WOOLDEN RD
B5212
Rose Bank Farm
Ryefield Farm
MOSS RD
Codishead Moss
Lower Stanley Bank Farm
Higher Stanley Bank Farm
Ash Farm
IRLAM
Chat Moss
Rose Farm
Astley Road Farm
Offices
Sch
Thomas Trading Centre
Irlam Sta
EXCALIBUR WAY
A57
Northbank Industrial Park
BRINELL DR
Glaze Brook
Glazebrook
Glazebrook Exchange Sidings
GLAZEBROOK LA
DAM HEAD LA
Glazebrook Sta
Inn
Brush Farm
BANK ST
Cadishead
Sewage Works
LIVERPOOL RD
Dismantled Railway
Lea Brook Farm
Mount Pleasant Farm
Tar Distillery
Amb Sta
Manchester Ship Canal
Codishead or Glazebrook Bridge
DAM LA
Cemy
PC
PH
Marsh Brook
Hollinfare
Cleveland's Farm
SCHOOL LA
Hollins Green
MANCHESTER RD
B5212
Millbank Hall Farm
Millbank Hall
Sewage Works
Coroners Wood
Brook Farm
A57
Warburton High Level Bridge
WARBURTON BRIDGE RD
Rye Park House
Warburton Park
PARK RD
Red Brook
Partington
WARBURTON LA
MOSS LA
A6144
Lighthouse Poultry Farm
Mosslane Farm
Heathlands Farm
CHAPEL LA
MANCHESTER NEW RD
Lsre Cen
1 DAMSON WLK
2 ALMOND WLK
3 POPULAR WLK
4 LONG WLK
5 LIME WLK
6 HOLLY WLK
7 HAZEL WLK
8 GREEN WLK
9 GARDEN WLK
10 FIELD WLK
11 MEADOW WLK
12 HAWTHORN WLK
13 BOX WLK
14 MAY WLK
15 CONIFER WLK
16 SNOWBERRY WLK
17 LILAC WLK
18 ELDERBERRY WLK
19 ROSE WLK
20 THISTLE WLK
21 HEATHER WLK
22 IVY WLK
23 CHESTNUT WLK
24 CHERRY WLK
25 MIDDLE LA
26 YEW WLK
27 ROWAN WLK
28 LAVENDER WLK
29 FORSYTHIA WLK
30 BLACKTHORN WLK
31 THORN WLK
32 LABELIA WLK
33 LAUREL WLK
34 MAGNOLIA WLK
35 IRIS WLK
36 FOXGLOVE WLK
37 SAFFRON WLK
38 ASTER WLK
39 JASMINE WLK
40 ROSEMARY WLK
41 MALLOW WLK
42 CAMAMILE WLK
43 BARBERRY WLK
44 ELM CL
45 WINTERGREEN WLK
46 BEECH CL
47 CHARLOOK WLK
48 WOODRUFF WLK
49 COLUMBINE WLK
50 CLOUDBERRY WLK

Mill Wood
Cronton Lane
M62
Junction 7
WARRINGTON RD
Sandhill Farm
A57
A569
LOYOLA HEY
Higher Shaw Farm
Rough Head
HALL LA
Cronton Wood
NORLAND'S LA
Fox's Bank Brook
PENNY LA
Penny Lane Farm
Norland's House
Pex Hill
Town End
Mill Lane
Norland's Farm
A5080
TILE LA
Gorse Lodge Nursery
SMITHY LA
Sch
Cronton
The Hillcrest Hotel
Cronton Farm
CRONTON RD
CRONTON LA
Coll
Smaller Gorse Farm
Caxton Lodge
ALDER LA
SANDY LA
CHAPEL LA
LODGE LA
Rose Farm
Upton Rocks
Holly Farm
UPTON LA
Stock's Well Pumping Station
Stock's Well House
STOCKSWELL RD
Rock Lane
ROCK LA
Linacre House
NORTHERN LA
Schs
HOUGH GREEN RD
Cemy
The Topped Oak (PH)
Upton
Playing Field
Rugby Football Ground
Golf Course
Hough Green
Hough Green Station
NETHERLEY RD
B5178
PRESCOT RD
Ball o' Ditton
LIVERPOOL RD
HALE RD
DITCHFIELD RD
HIGHFIELD RD
LOWER HOUSE LA
CH
A
B
C
1
2
3
4
86
87
88
89
48
49
50

14

D
E
F
Union Bank Farm Cottage
Tibb's Cross Farm
TIBBS CROSS LA
JUBITS LA
A568
A569
CLOCK FACE RD
Old Brook Hall
A57
Rainhill Place Farm
Wilmere House
WARRINGTON RD
Bold Bridge
Bank Head
Nursery Farm
Bold Heath
SCHOOL LA
BOLD CROSS
Bridge Farm
Griffin Inn (PH)
Works
WILMERE LA
TWYFORD LA
Dismantled Railway
MILL LA
Willow Farm
Cranshaw Hall
CRANSHAW LA
Glebe Farm
A5080
LUNTS HEATH RD
Club
Lunt's Bridge Farm
Garden Centre
Lunt Bridge
Mill Green Farm
MILL GREEN LA
South Lane Farm
SOUTH LANE ENTRY
Lunts Heath
SOUTH LA
Boundary Farm
DERBY RD
Abbey Farm
Schs
PIT LA
FARNWORTH ST
Works
Farnworth
Barrow's Green
BIRCHFIELD RD
Crematorium
Cemetery
MOORFIELD RD
BARROW'S GREEN LA
DYKIN RD
1 LAMPORT CL
2 FAIRBURN CL
3 ELTHAM WLK
4 BELGRAVE CL
5 SHEVINGTON WLK
6 SOMERFORD WLK
7 CHALGRAVE CL
8 SHELTON CL
Clock Lane
Widnes North Station
Bower's Brook
Clock Lane Farm
LOCKETT RD
VICTORIA RD
Sch
Crow Wood
CROW WOOD LA
WIDNES RD
A562
DANS RD
Victoria Park
PEEL HOUSE LA
Appleton
Shell Green
1 TAYLOR ST
2 CLIFFE ST
3 HENRY ST
1 RABY CL
2 HADFIELD CL
3 NORBURY CL
HALTON VIEW RD
BENNETT'S LA
GORSEY LA
KINGSWAY
LEIGH AVE
DEACON RD
ALBERT RD
B5178
1 ASHFORD WAY
2 MELVILLE CL
3 KINGHAM CL
4 WILSON CL
FIDDLER'S FERRY RD
WARRINGTON RD
Halton View
PAGE LA
Works
Power Station
JOHNSON'S LA
89
88
87
86
4
3
2
1
51
52
53

23

14

13
6

A
B
C
4
89
3
88
2
87
1
86
54
55
56
Lingley Mere
Finch's Plantation
South Park Plantation
Eccles Plantation
Whittle Brook
LINGLEY GREEN AVE
Sports Centre
Schs
BARROW HALL LA
Brow Farm
WHITTLE AVE
AIREDALE CL
KINGSDALE RD
BISHOPDALE CL
BARONDALE CL
COVERDALE CL
SWALEDALE CL
Park Farm
Bargyloo
A57
WARRINGTON RD
SOUTH LA ENTRY
Dawson House
LEON CL
FRESHWATER CL
VENTNOR CL
SHANKLIN CL
MAYFAIR CL
RUSCOLM CL
MURIEL CL
AUDRE CL
PYECROFT CL
PYECROFT RD
FRASER RD
LINGLEY RD
HILARY CL
PAUL CL
SANDERSON CL
WARWICK AVE
STANLEY AVE
YORK AVE
PRINCESS AVE
CRONULLA DR
1 CODGEE AVE
2 CLOVELLY AVE
MILL AVE
GREENWAY
NORTH VIEW
HALL TERR
PHILIPS DR
SUNNYSIDE
CHESTNUT AVE
CONIFER GR
ROWAN CL
CEDAR CL
WOODSIDE RD
VINE CRES
CHARLES AVE
HALTON RD
LILFORD DR
WILMOT AVE
WHITTLE HALL LA
WROXHAM RD
KIRCALDY AVE
CROMDALE WAY
KINTORE DR
Sch
PARK RD
PH
Hayfield Farm
SANDY LA
Greenside Farm
KEITH AVE
RHONA DR
DUNCANSBY CRES
VICTORIA AVE
THE FORD RD
RANWORTH RD
NORFOLK DR
SHERINGHAM RD
YARMOUTH RD
WEDNESBURY DR
LINGWOOD RD
CONWAY AVE
CAMPBELL CRES
STATION RD
Laburnum Farm
LIVERPOOL RD
HENDERSON CL
EDWARD RD
FRIENDS LA
LABURNUM LA
BEECHWOOD AVE
Sankey Sta
FORGE RD
CUNNINGHAM CL
1 KINGSTON AVE
2 SOUTHFIELDS AVE
Sandy Lane Farm
ST VINCENT RD
FRIARS AVE
ST STEPHEN RD
ST ALBAN RD
ST JOSEPH'S CL
WALTON AVE
HOLLY RD
WALSINGHAM RD
SOUTHDALE
ST MARY'S RD
THE DALE
WHITETHORN AVE
SUSAN DR
GROARKE DR
DENISE AVE
NORTON AVE
KENYON AVE
LARCH AVE
WINDMILL LA
1 HELSTON CL
2 WILLIAM PENN CL
BURNHAM CL
UPTON DR
HOLLY TERR
STOCKS LA
MEETING LA
HEATH RD
CONISTON AVE
WITHYCOMBE RD
BABBACOMBE RD
PAIGNTON CL
BIDEFORD RD
SIDMOUTH CL
JUBILEE AVE
TIVERTON CL
HONITON WAY
Liby
GREYSTONE RD
HILLSIDE GR
CHERRY TREE AVE
PHYTHIAN CRES
FORMBY CL
AINSDALE CL
HESKETH CL
CORONATION DR
THE GROVE
A5080
SOUTH LA
LYNTON CL
BARNSTAPLE WAY
PORLOCK CL
AVON AVE
BROAD OAK AVE
DAISY BANK RD
Recn Gd
A562
ARLINGTON DR
TAVISTOCK RD
HASLEMERE DR
BANK GDNS
Four Top'd Oak
GREENALL AVE
VICTORIA RD
WARRINGTON RD
INGLENOOK RD
ASH RD
LYONS RD
VAUXHALL CL
Brook Farm
FARNWORTH RD
WIDNES RD
PADSTOW CL
PENRYN CL
FENHAM DR
BEADNELL DR
POPLAR AVE
WOODLEY RD
HALL NOOK
ELM RD
OAK RD
OAKMERE DR
MAPLE CRES
THORN CL
BEECH AVE
CUERDLEY RD
Doe Green
TREGARON DR
STATION RD
LAUNCESTON DR
ST AUSTELL CL
WELL LA
ST BRIDES CL
BRAMBLE CL
SOUTHLANDS AVE
STANSTEAD AVE
MANSTON RD
HAMBLE DR
NEWLYN GDNS
THE PARK
Works
ROTHAY DR
ROEBURN WAY
CHAPEL RD
RADLETT CL
FALMOUTH DR
BRIMELOW CRES
DITCHFIELD RD
Sch
Hall Nook
MOWCROFT LA
TANNERY LA
POLPERRO CL
WALKER CL
Penketh
LC
1 CALSTOCK CL
2 BUCKFAST CL
SHAFTESBURY AVE
BACK LA
Cuerdley Cross
CUERDLEY GREEN
TAYLOR'S LANE
WRIGHTS LANE
Marsh End Farm
MARSH LANE
Fiddler's Ferry
St Helens Canal (dis)
River Mersey
Mersey Way
Fiddler's Ferry Reach
Power Station

13
24

7
16

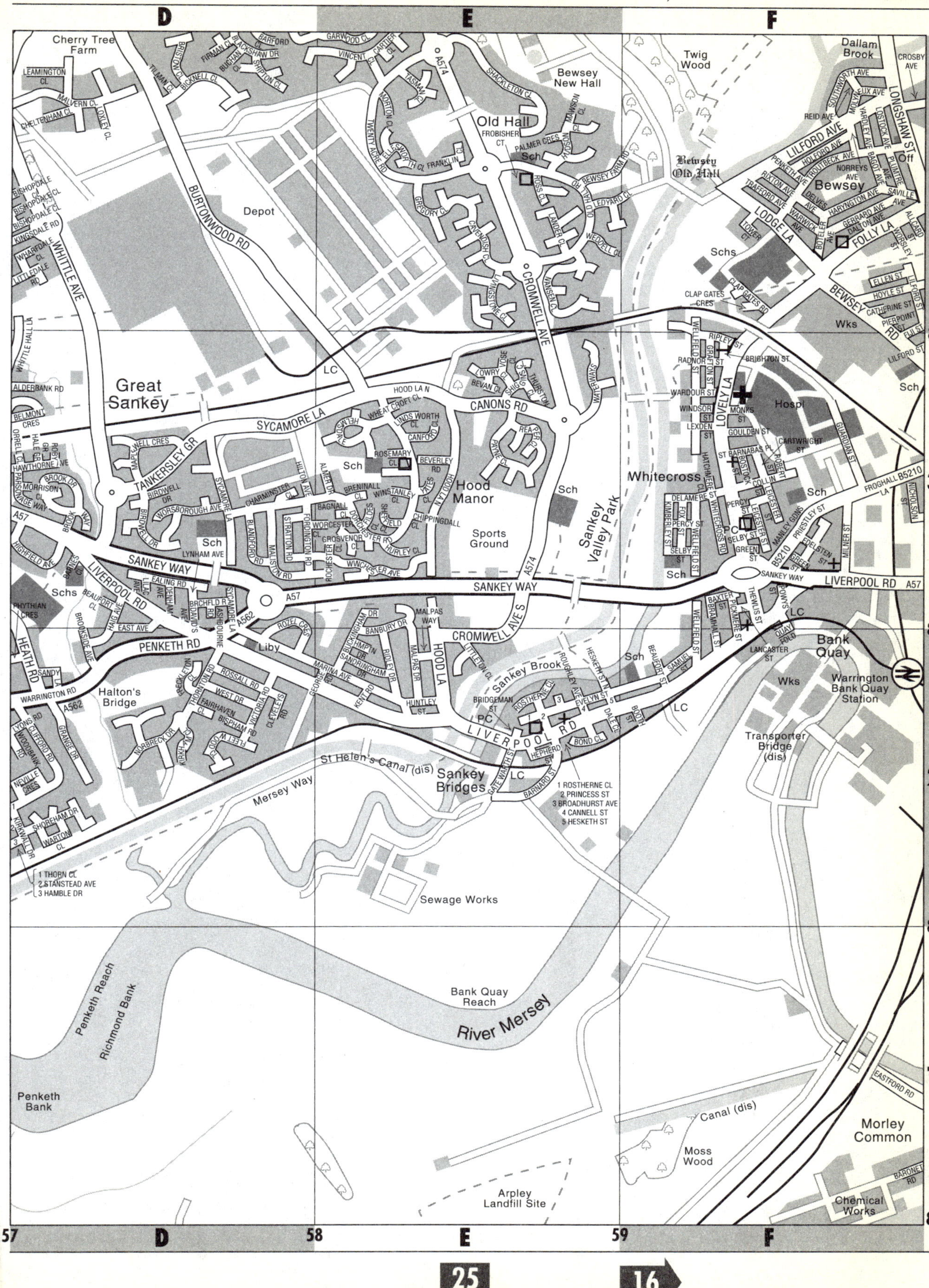
D
E
F
Cherry Tree Farm
Twig Wood
Bewsey New Hall
Dallam Brook
Old Hall
Bewsey Old Hall
Bewsey
Depot
BURTONWOOD RD
WHITTLE AVE
CROMWELL AVE
A574
LILFORD AVE
LONGSHAW ST
LODGE LA
FOLLY LA
BEWSEY RD
Schs
Wks
Sch
Hospl
LOVELY LA
Great Sankey
SYCAMORE LA
HOOD LA N
CANONS RD
TANKERSLEY GR
Hood Manor
Sports Ground
Sankey Valley Park
Whitecross
FROGHALL LA
B5210
SANKEY WAY
LIVERPOOL RD
A57
A562
PENKETH RD
CROMWELL AVE S
HOOD LA
Liby
Halton's Bridge
HEATH RD
WARRINGTON RD
Sankey Brook
Bank Quay
Warrington Bank Quay Station
LC
PC
Transporter Bridge (dis)
St Helen's Canal (dis)
Sankey Bridges
Mersey Way
Sewage Works
1 ROSTHERNE CL
2 PRINCESS ST
3 BROADHURST AVE
4 CANNELL ST
5 HESKETH ST
1 THORN CL
2 STANSTEAD AVE
3 HAMBLE DR
Penketh Reach
Richmond Bank
Bank Quay Reach
River Mersey
Penketh Bank
Canal (dis)
Moss Wood
Arpley Landfill Site
Morley Common
Chemical Works
EASTFORD RD
BARONET RD
4
89
3
88
2
87
1
86
57
58
59

25
16

15
8

A
B
C
Padgate
Kerfoot Business Park
Hawthorne Business Park
Dsmtd Rly
Works
WARRINGTON
Cemy
Bruche
Padgate Brook
Mersey Way
Rd under con
Town Hall
Golden Sq
Market Gate
Mkt
Mus Liby
Amb Sta
River Mersey
Howley
Kingsway Bridge
Westy
Victoria Park
Howley Lock
Parkdale Ind Est
Brian Bevan Island
Centre Park
Arpley Meadows
Coll
Latchford
Wilderspool
Schs
Manchester Ship Canal
Runcorn & Latchford Canal
Walton Lock
Bridgewater Canal
Cheshire Ring Canal Walk
Stockton Heath
Mountain Farm
WINWICK RD
ORFORD RD
MANCHESTER RD
KINGSWAY N
KINGSWAY S
CHURCH ST
MERSEY ST
WILSON PATTEN ST
KNUTSFORD RD
WILDERSPOOL CSWY
LOUSHERS LA
STATION RD
CHESTER RD
GAINSBOROUGH RD
ELLESMERE RD
STOCKTON LA
ACKERS RD
FAIRFIELD RD
THELWALL LA
MARSH HOUSE LA
FOLLY LA
KERFOOT ST
PADGATE LA
A49
A50
A57
A574
A5060
B5156
B5210
B5157
60
61
62
86
87
88
89
1
2
3
4

15
26

D
E
F
Grange
Martinscroft Moss
Sch
Spittle Brook
Woolston
HARDWICK GRANGE
WOOLSTON GRANGE AVE
M6
NICOL AVE
POULTON CRES
POULTON CT
TOTTON CT
LONG BARN LA
MELFORD CT
RUFFORD CT
RIVINGTON CT
CRANFORD CT
CHESFORD GRANGE
GREEN LA
HOLES LA
HILLOCK LA
GIG LA
DAM LA
WARREN LA
EPPING DR
ELIZABETH CR
REGENT AVE
BARWICK CL
FIRTREE AVE
LIMETREE AVE
SPRINGFIELD AVE
MEAD RD
BRUCHE HEATH GDNS
PRINCESS AVE
QUEENS CRES
NORTHDALE RD
THORN RD
PINE GR
CEDAR GR
BIRCHDALE RD
EASTDALE RD
WESTDALE RD
ASPEN GR
RUSHMORE GR
HEATHWOOD GR
ROYSTON AVE
MANCHESTER RD
A57
NEW MANCHESTER RD
LARKFIELD AVE
WILKINSON AVE
Paddington
Sch
Liby
ALMOND GR
WILDWOOD GR
MARGARET AVE
GORDON AVE
WENTWORTH AVE
BRICKHURST WAY
DORSET WAY
SOMERSET WAY
MONROE CL
HAYFIELD RD
HALL RD
GREENFIELDS CL
AUSTRAL AVE
FERNDALE CL
OAKDENE AVE
HILL TOP RD
RYDER RD
ROSEDALE AVE
LABURNUM AVE
Leisure Centre
P
BARON CL
MANOR CL
LAUREL AVE
ALDER RD
ASCOT CL
IVY RD
WHITE HOUSE
MAPLE
SUNCROFT
MAWDSLEY AVE
ABINGDON
LADYCROFT
CLARES FARM CL
Martinscroft
HAWTHORNE AVE
NEW CUT LA
BRIDGE RD
BRIDGE LA
CLIFTON
PARKSWAY
RUNNYMEDE
FITZ WALTER RD
LANGTON
MARSHALL RD
CLIFTONVILLE RD
REEL CL
GLOUCESTER CL
HEREFORD CL
HERTFORD CL
WESSEX CL
NOTTINGHAM CL
HICKORY CL
LAWSON CL
SPRUCE CL
REDWOOD CL
MULBERRY CL
DENNETT CL
WALNUT CL
MAGNOLIA CL
CROFTSIDE
BATTERY LA
RIVERSDALE
TARN CT
EDWARD GDNS
LINCOLN CL
SHROPSHIRE CL
TIMBERSCOMBE GDNS
WEIR LA
DURHAM CL
BERWICK CL
Grey Mist
Mersey Way
River Mersey
Woolston New Weir
Woolston Weir
The Eyes
89
4
3
88
MERSEY WLK
1 WARING AVE
2 BRYANT AVE
BRIDGEWATER AVE
MORRIS AVE
GARNETT AVE
BARRYMORE AVE
TIMBERLEY AVE
RICHMOND AVE
TILSTON AVE
HENSHALL AVE
BROADBENT AVE
PICHAEL NOOK
PARKFIELD AVE
MOSELEY AVE
REYNOLDS ST
GASKELL AVE
BRUNTLEIGH AVE
RICHMOND ST
DOVER RD
SELKIRK AVE
LATCHFORD ST
Works
Thelwall Ferry P
Laskey Lane Farm
LASKEY LA
VILLAGE CL
FERRY LA
ALDERLEY RD
WILMSLOW CRES
PRESTBURY DR
MOBBERLEY CL
HANDFORTH CL
Ind Est
WOODFORD CL
Sch
LYMM RD
B5157
A56
2
THELWALL LA
Latchford Locks
THELWALL NEW RD
BUNTINGFORD RD
PELHAM RD
BEECH AVE
SELWORTHY DR
MOORE AVE
PICKERING CRES
ALL SAINTS DR
PARRY DR
Thelwall
BELL LA
DEANS LA
WOODLANDS DR
STOCKPORT RD
BALDOCK CL
DUNMOW RD
WATTON CL
BARLEY RD
RICHMOND AVE
ASHLEY CL
STANTON RD
WILSON CL
BRADSHAW LA
QUEENS DR
B5157
MARTHAM CL
BARTON AVE
CROSS LA
SPRINGFIELD AVE
CAWTHORNE AVE
KNUTSFORD OLD RD
MAYFIELD RD
WINDSOR DR
KENSINGTON AVE
KNIGHTSBRIDGE AVE
WESTMINSTER
ASCOT AVE
CORONATION AVE
87
Dsmtld Rlwy
HALFACRE LA
A50
ADAMSON CT
MEREDITH AVE
NICHOLLS ST
GEORGES CRES
MARESFIELD AVE
EAST VIEW
HEATHFIELD PARK
MARLFIELD RD
BROOKFIELD PARK
MIDDLEHURST RD
SHIRLEY DR
ALDONNAN RD
CLARENCE RD
EUCLID AVE
ST ANNES AVE
ST ANNES AVE E
Thelwall Heys
Cheshire Ring Canal Walk
Bridgewater Canal
Oak House
TUDOR CL
HALLCROFT PL
YORK DR
YORK RD
HARWOOD RD
VICTORIA AVE
ALBERT RD
Liby
BEECHFIELD RD
CHESTER RD
SHADEWOOD RD
BOYDELL AVE
LINDI AVE
PORTOLA CL
BARNSWOOD CL
KNUTSFORD RD
WEASTE LA
1
Highfields Farm
Thelwall Grange
BARRYMORE RD
A56
STOCKTON LA
Grappenhall
Sch
PH
WILFREDS DR
GLEBE AVE
MENLOW CL
LAUREL BANK
BELLHOUSE LA
CLIFF LA
COPPICE DR
MARIE DR
STONELEIGH GDNS
CHURCH LA
BROAD LA
BRACKENWOOD MEWS
HAZELWOOD MEWS
CANAL SIDE
AUSTRALIA LA
Canal Bank Farm
Sch
CINDER LA
A50
86
63
64
65

17
10

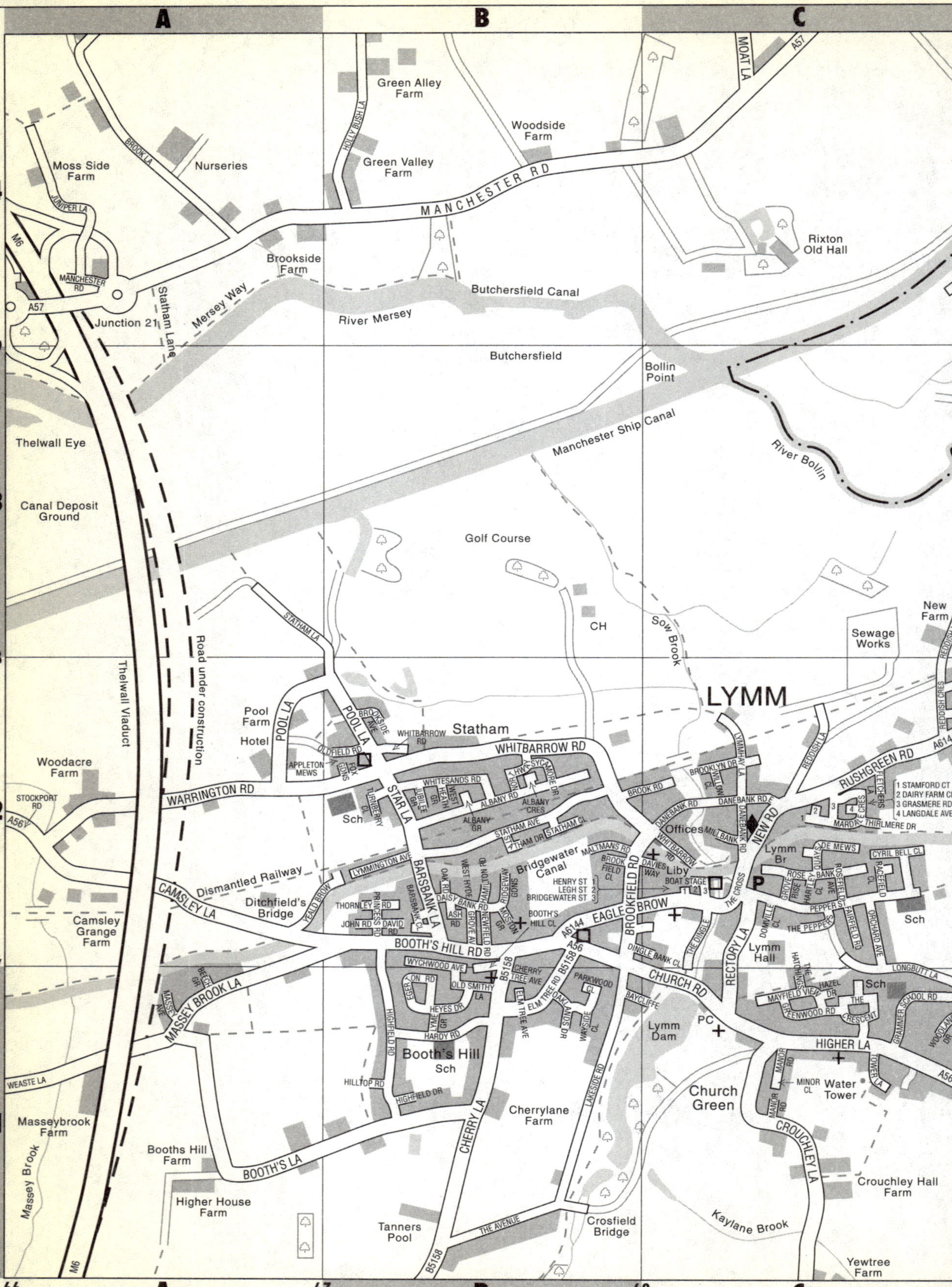
A
B
C
4
3
2
1
89
88
87
86
66
67
68
Green Alley Farm
Woodside Farm
Moss Side Farm
Nurseries
Green Valley Farm
MANCHESTER RD
MOAT LA
A57
BROOK LA
HOLLY BUSH LA
JUNIPER LA
M6
MANCHESTER RD
A57
Junction 21
Statham Lane
Mersey Way
Brookside Farm
Butchersfield Canal
River Mersey
Rixton Old Hall
Butchersfield
Bollin Point
Thelwall Eye
Manchester Ship Canal
River Bollin
Canal Deposit Ground
Golf Course
CH
Sow Brook
New Farm
Sewage Works
STATHAM LA
Road under construction
Thelwall Viaduct
LYMM
Statham
Pool Farm
Hotel
POOL LA
WHITBARROW RD
WHITBARROW RD
Woodacre Farm
APPLETON MEWS
OLDFIELD RD
FOX GDNS
STAR LA
WARRINGTON RD
WHITESANDS RD
ALBANY RD
ALBANY CRES
SYCAMORE DR
STOCKPORT RD
A56
Sch
TURNBERRY CL
STATHAM AVE
STATHAM DR
STATHAM CL
BROOK RD
DANEBANK RD
BROOKLYN DR
DANEBANK RD
NEW RD
RUSHGREEN RD
A6144
REDDISH LA
REDDISH CRES
1 STAMFORD CT
2 DAIRY FARM CL
3 GRASMERE RD
4 LANGDALE AVE
THIRLMERE DR
Offices
MILLBANK RD
Dismantled Railway
LYMMINGTON AVE
BARSBANK LA
Bridgewater Canal
MALTMANS RD
BROOKFIELD RD
DAVIES WAY
Liby
BOAT STAGE
HENRY ST
LEGH ST
BRIDGEWATER ST
Lymm Br
DE MEWS
CYRIL BELL CL
ROSE
BANK
CAMSLEY LA
Ditchfield's Bridge
THORNLEY RD
JOHN RD
DAVID RD
BARSBANK CL
DAISY BANK RD
ASH RD
OAK RD
BOOTH'S HILL CL
A6144
EAGLE BROW
THE CROSS
THE DINGLE
RECTORY LA
PEPPER ST
THE PEPPER
FAIRFIELD RD
ORCHARD AVE
Sch
Camsley Grange Farm
BOOTH'S HILL RD
A56
DINGLE BANK CL
Lymm Hall
LONGBUTT LA
WYCHWOOD AVE
B5158
CHERRY TREE AVE
B5158
PARKWOOD CL
CHURCH RD
Sch
OLD SMITHY LA
HEYES DR
HARDY RD
ELM TREE RD
ELM TREE AVE
OAKLANDS DR
WAYSIDE CL
BAYCLIFFE
MAYFIELD VIEW
HAZEL DR
THE CRESCENT
GREENWOOD RD
GRAMMER SCHOOL RD
MASSEY BROOK LA
HIGHFIELD RD
Booth's Hill
Sch
Lymm Dam
PC
HIGHER LA
A56
WEASTE LA
HILLTOP RD
HIGHFIELD DR
LAKESIDE RD
Church Green
MINOR CL
MANOR RD
Water Tower
Masseybrook Farm
Cherrylane Farm
CHERRY LA
CROUCHLEY LA
Massey Brook
Booths Hill Farm
BOOTH'S LA
Crouchley Hall Farm
Higher House Farm
THE AVENUE
Tanners Pool
Crosfield Bridge
Kaylane Brook
Yewtree Farm
B5158
M6

11
20

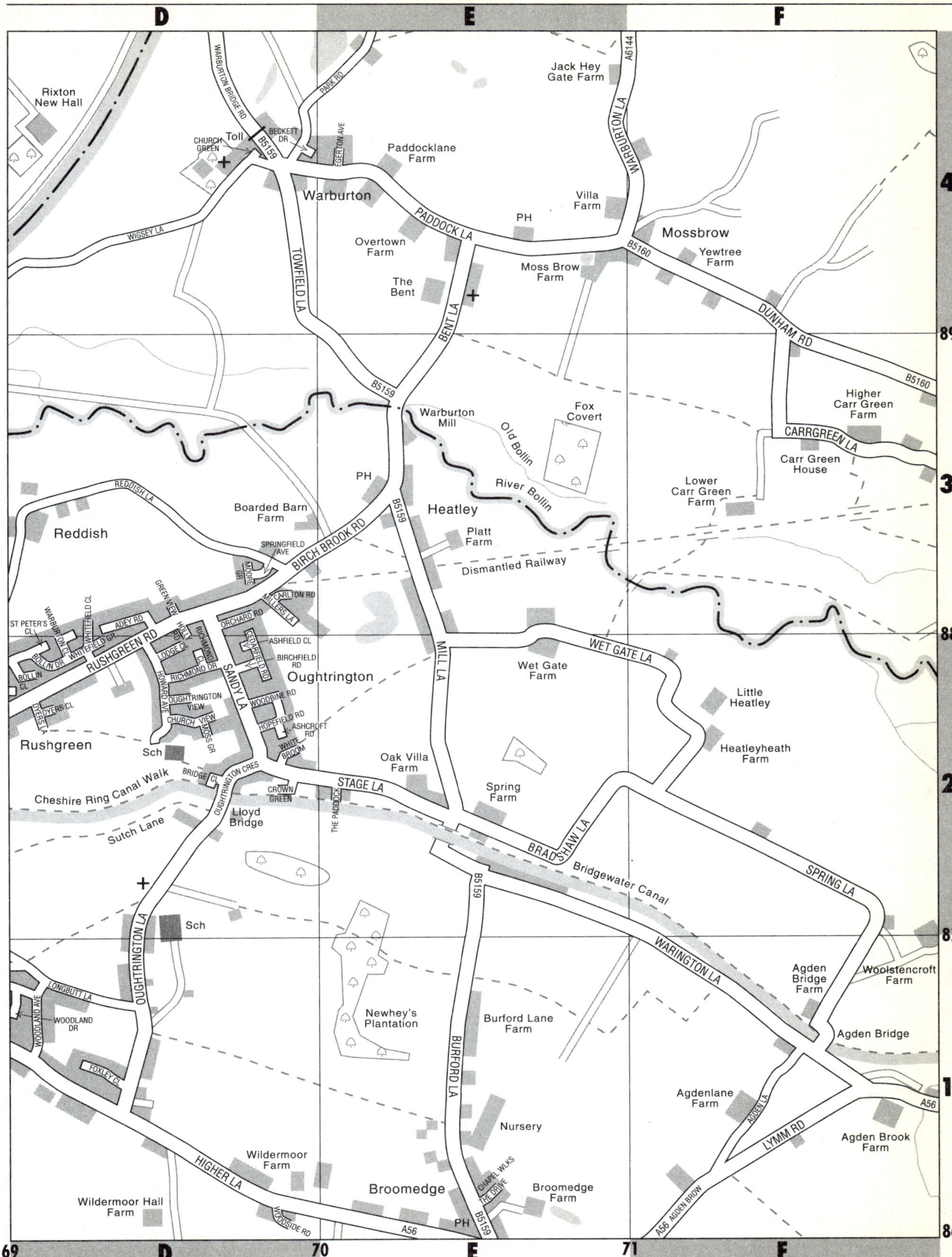
D
E
F
Rixton New Hall
WARBURTON BRIDGE RD
PARK RD
Jack Hey Gate Farm
A6144
CHURCH GREEN
Toll
BECKETT DR
B5159
EGERTON AVE
Paddocklane Farm
WARBURTON LA
Warburton
Villa Farm
PH
WIGSEY LA
PADDOCK LA
Mossbrow
Overtown Farm
B5160
Yewtree Farm
Moss Brow Farm
TOWFIELD LA
The Bent
BENT LA
DUNHAM RD
4
89
B5159
B5160
Higher Carr Green Farm
Warburton Mill
Fox Covert
Old Bollin
CARRGREEN LA
Carr Green House
PH
River Bollin
Lower Carr Green Farm
3
REDDISH LA
Boarded Barn Farm
B5159
Heatley
Reddish
Platt Farm
SPRINGFIELD AVE
BIRCH BROOK RD
Dismantled Railway
MOORE GR
GREEN VIEW
CARLTON RD
WHITEFIELD CL
MILLERS LA
ST PETER'S CL
WARBURTON CL
ADEY RD
ORCHARD RD
HOLLY RD
RICHMOND CL
ASHFIELD CL
88
WHITEFIELD GR
BOLLIN DR
RUSHGREEN RD
LODGE CL
CEDARFIELD RD
WET GATE LA
BIRCHFIELD RD
MILL LA
Wet Gate Farm
BOLLIN CL
RICHMOND DR
SANDY LA
Oughtrington
HOWARD AVE
Little Heatley
DYERS CL
OUGHTRINGTON VIEW
WOODBINE RD
DYERS LA
CHURCH VIEW
HOPEFIELD RD
ASHCROFT RD
Rushgreen
MOSS GR
Heatleyheath Farm
Sch
WHITE BROOM
Oak Villa Farm
BRIDGE CL
OUGHTRINGTON CRES
Cheshire Ring Canal Walk
STAGE LA
Spring Farm
2
CROWN GREEN
Lloyd Bridge
THE PADDOCK
Sutch Lane
BRADSHAW LA
Bridgewater Canal
SPRING LA
B5159
Sch
87
OUGHTRINGTON LA
WARINGTON LA
Agden Bridge Farm
Woolstencroft Farm
LONGBUTT LA
Newhey's Plantation
Burford Lane Farm
WOODLAND AVE
WOODLAND DR
Agden Bridge
FOXLEY CL
BURFORD LA
1
Agdenlane Farm
A56
AGDEN LA
Nursery
LYMM RD
Agden Brook Farm
Wildermoor Farm
HIGHER LA
CHAPEL WLKS
THE DRIVE
Broomedge
Broomedge Farm
Wildermoor Hall Farm
WOODSIDE RD
A56
PH
B5159
A56 AGDEN BROW
86
69
70
71
D
E
F

29
20

19

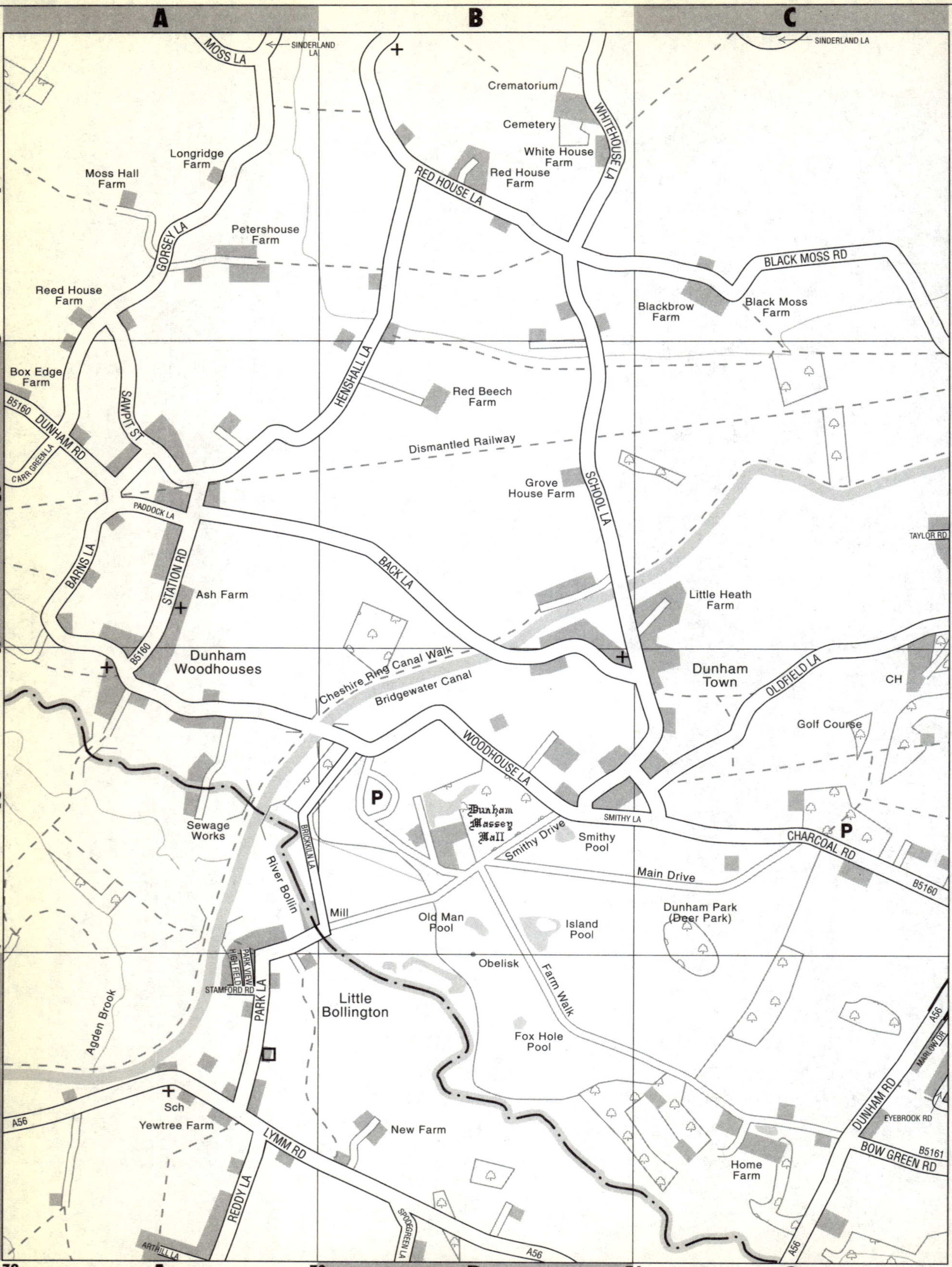
A
B
C
4
3
2
1
89
88
87
86
72
73
74
MOSS LA
SINDERLAND LA
Crematorium
Cemetery
WHITEHOUSE LA
White House Farm
Red House Farm
RED HOUSE LA
Longridge Farm
Moss Hall Farm
Petershouse Farm
GORSEY LA
Reed House Farm
BLACK MOSS RD
Blackbrow Farm
Black Moss Farm
Box Edge Farm
SAWPIT ST
HENSHALL LA
Red Beech Farm
B5160
DUNHAM RD
CARR GREEN LA
Dismantled Railway
Grove House Farm
SCHOOL LA
PADDOCK LA
TAYLOR RD
BARNS LA
STATION RD
BACK LA
Ash Farm
Little Heath Farm
Dunham Woodhouses
Cheshire Ring Canal Walk
Bridgewater Canal
Dunham Town
OLDFIELD LA
CH
Golf Course
WOODHOUSE LA
P
Dunham Massey Hall
Smithy Drive
SMITHY LA
Smithy Pool
CHARCOAL RD
Sewage Works
BRICKKILN LA
River Bollin
Main Drive
Mill
Old Man Pool
Island Pool
Dunham Park (Deer Park)
Obelisk
Farm Walk
PARK VIEW
HIGH FIELD
STAMFORD RD
PARK LA
Little Bollington
Agden Brook
Fox Hole Pool
A56
MARLOW DR
DUNHAM RD
Sch
Yewtree Farm
New Farm
EYEBROOK RD
LYMM RD
BOW GREEN RD
B5161
Home Farm
REDDY LA
SPODEGREEN LA
ARTHILL LA

19

30

D
E
F
1 GREENSBRIDGE LA
2 HALEWOOD LA ENDS
OXFORD DR
RUTLAND AVE
CHURCH RD
LUSCOMBE CL
ELWYN DR
RONALDSWAY
LOWER CL
RAWLINSON CRES
3 HOLLIES RD
4 GRAHAM DR
Yew Tree Farm
Halewood
Sch
FIR CL
FIR AVE
PENMANN CRES
LEATHERS LA
BIRCHEN RD
HORNBEAM RD
BAILEYS LA
Sch
1 KENTON RD
2 HILLINGDEN AVE
3 KINLOCH CL
BARN CROFT RD
Sports Centre
KEMPSELL WAY
ROSEHEATH DR
ANTONS RD
KNOWL HEY RD
BLAKEACRE RD
RUSHOLME CL
A562
Highfield Farm
OLD HUTTE LA
NORTH RD
Ford Sidings
EAST RD
Motor Works
SOUTH RD
SPEKE BVD
A561
FINCH LA
Finch Farm
RSPCA Home
HIGHER RD
A562
A561
Caravan Site
Ireland's Farm
LOWER RD
Ditton Fold Farm
Wellbrook Farm
Ditton Brook
Tarbock Green
Road under construction
New Farm Bungalows
ASH LA
Bosco Hall Farm
A562
SPEKE RD
Brook House Farm
Newstead Farm
Works
Manor Farm
OLD HIGHER RD
HIGHER RD
HALE BANK RD
Linner Farm
The Beehive Inn (PH)
POTTERS LA
Ramsbrook Farm
Burnt Mill Lane
Burnt Mill Farm
Sewage Works
Ramsbrook Bridge
1 MILLWOOD CT
2 RAMSFIELD RD
Mill Wood
A561
HUTFIELD RD
EAST MILLWOOD RD
MAINTREE CRES
SANDHAM RD
WEST MAINS
EAST MAINS
CASSLEY RD
ELLOWAY RD
MINERS WAY
ALDER WOOD AVE
CROYDE RD
CLAMLEY CT
LEVERET RD
ALDERFIELD DR
CRITCHLEY RD
GREENWAY RD
CATFORD GREEN
Sch
EASTDAM WOOD RD
RINGSFIELD
Sch
Alder Plantation
HEATHGATE AVE
CHURCHWAY RD
DANESWELL RD
ALMEDA RD
RAMSBROOK LA
CARR LA
Ram's Brook
Clamley Park Plantation
Little Boar's Wood
Big Boar's Wood
Hoghton Towers Farm
Marsh Bridge
HALE GATE RD
Ciss Green
1 BANDON CL
2 GREENORE DR
CARLOW CL
ARKLOW DR
WEXFORD AVE
KILDARE CL
ARAN CL
MALIN CL
ENNIS CL
ERRWOOD CL
TOWN LA
PH
CURLENDER WAY
BROCK GDNS
HOGHTON RD
HESKETH RD
IRELAND RD
1 ROSSALL CL
2 MEOLS CL
3 ORFORD CL
4 ST MARYS CL
5 JOHN MIDDLETON CL
6 TURTON CL
7 ASSHETON WLK
8 CLOMLEY GDNS
9 LUMLEY WLK
10 CRAB TREE CL
11 PEACH TREE CL
12 THORN TREE CL
13 ALMOND TREE CL
14 CHERRY TREE CL
15 APPLE TREE CL
16 PEAR TREE CL
Decoy Marsh
Brook Farm
LANGFORD
PHEASANT FIELD
LADYPOOL
HALE RD
COCKSHEAD LA
HOLLY CL
PEPPER ST
HIGH ST
Schs
WELLINGTON GATE
VICARAGE CL
Manor Farm
Hale
Hale Heath
BAILEY'S LA
Old Plantation
Recn Gd
CHURCH END
CHURCH RD
WITHIN WAY
Mersey Way
OGLET LA
Hale Cliff
P
4
85
3
84
2
83
1
82
46
47

21
12

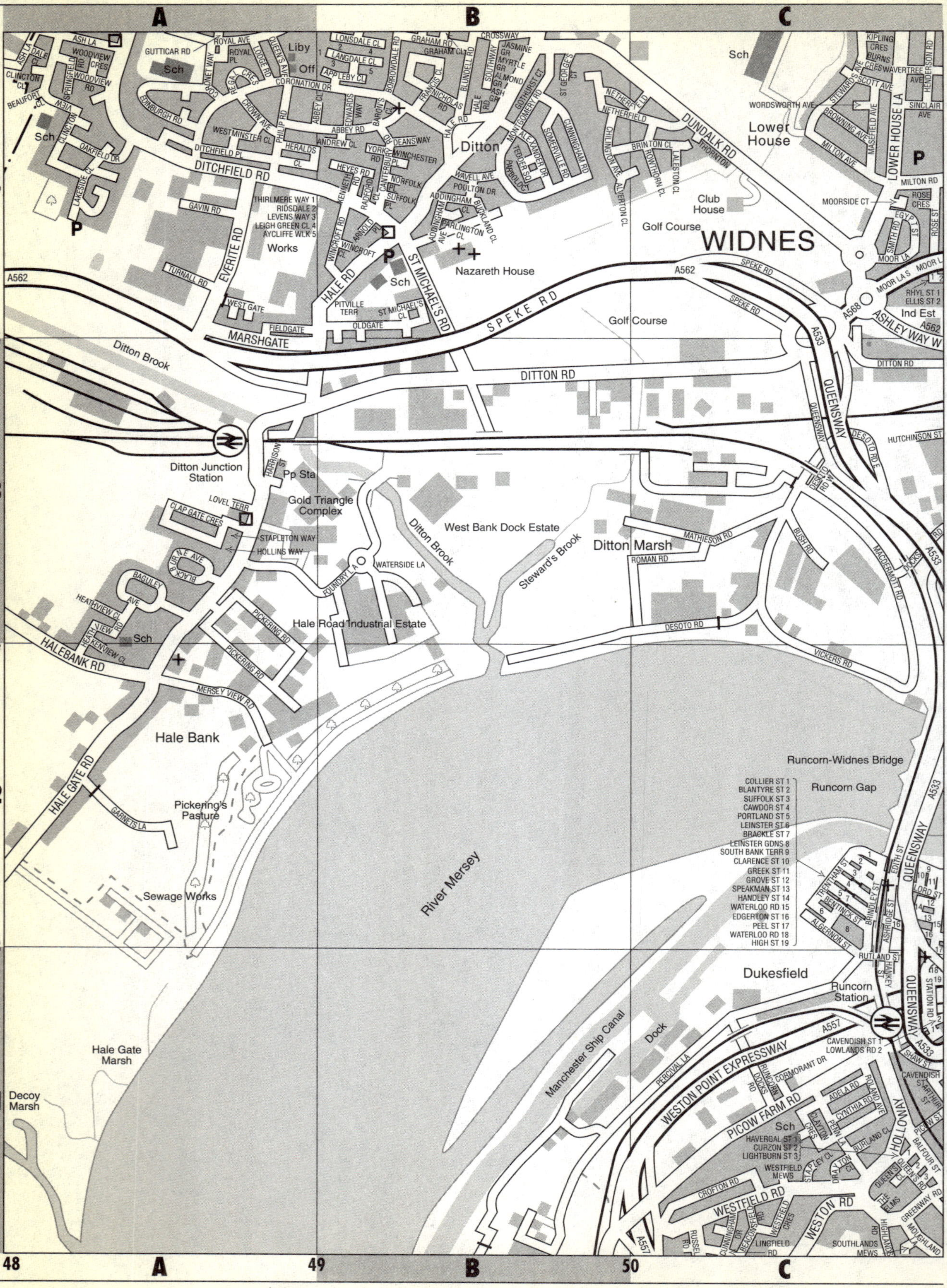
WIDNES
Ditton
Ditton Junction Station
Gold Triangle Complex
West Bank Dock Estate
Ditton Marsh
Hale Road Industrial Estate
Hale Bank
Pickering's Pasture
Sewage Works
River Mersey
Hale Gate Marsh
Decoy Marsh
Runcorn-Widnes Bridge
Runcorn Gap
Dukesfield
Runcorn Station
Manchester Ship Canal
Dock
Lower House
Golf Course
Club House
Nazareth House
SPEKE RD
DITTON RD
QUEENSWAY
WESTON POINT EXPRESSWAY
HALEBANK RD
HALE GATE RD
DITCHFIELD RD
MARSHGATE
COLLIER ST 1
BLANTYRE ST 2
SUFFOLK ST 3
CAWDOR ST 4
PORTLAND ST 5
LEINSTER ST 6
BRACKLE ST 7
LEINSTER GDNS 8
SOUTH BANK TERR 9
CLARENCE ST 10
GREEK ST 11
GROVE ST 12
SPEAKMAN ST 13
HANDLEY ST 14
WATERLOO RD 15
EDGERTON ST 16
PEEL ST 17
WATERLOO RD 18
HIGH ST 19
THIRLMERE WAY 1
RIDSDALE 2
LEVENS WAY 3
LEIGH GREEN CL 4
AYCLIFFE WLK 5

21
48

13
24

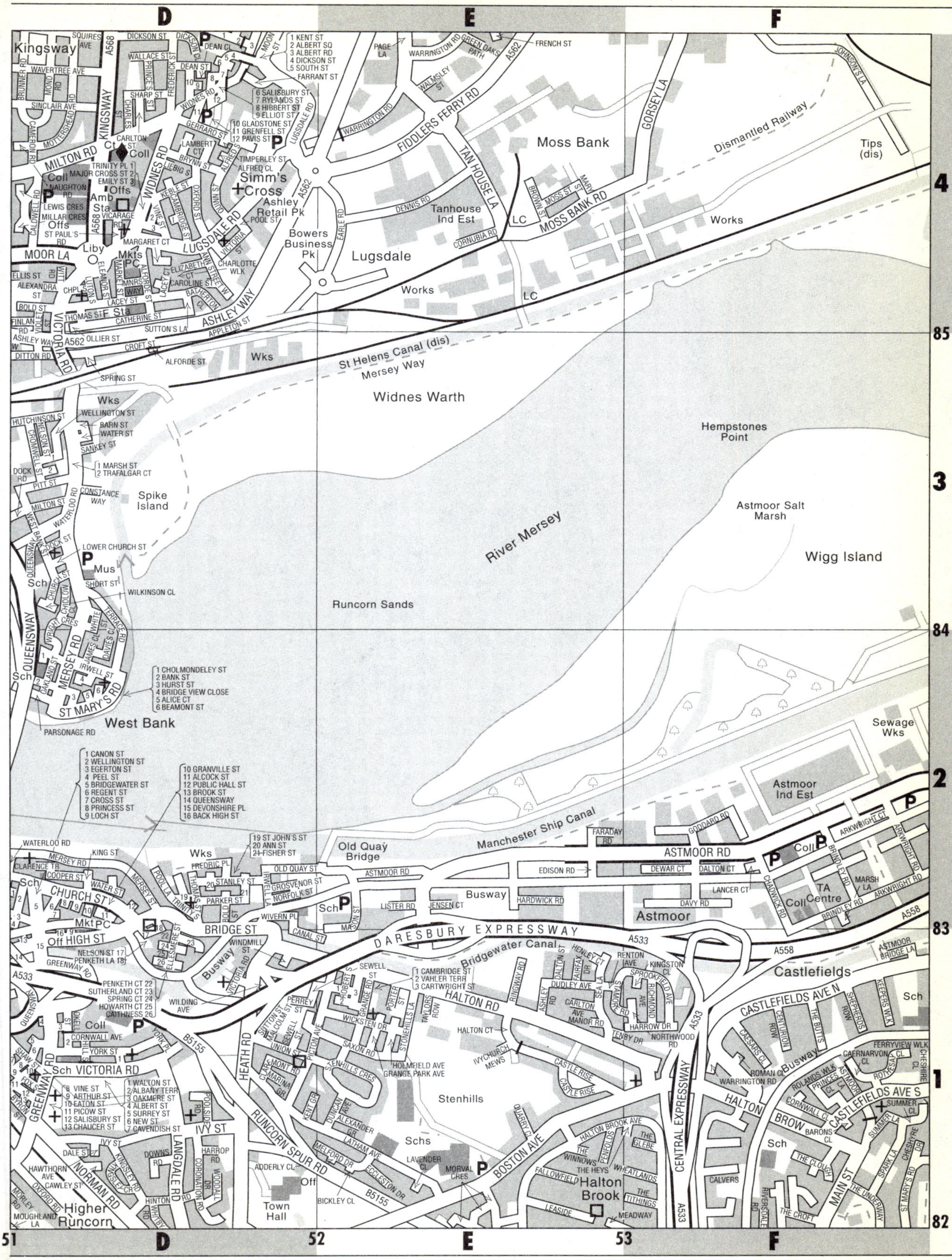
D
E
F
4
85
3
84
2
83
1
82
51
52
53
Kingsway
Moss Bank
Dismantled Railway
Tips (dis)
Simm's Cross
Ashley Retail Pk
Bowers Business Pk
Tanhouse Ind Est
Lugsdale
Works
Wks
St Helens Canal (dis)
Mersey Way
Widnes Warth
Hempstones Point
Spike Island
Astmoor Salt Marsh
Wigg Island
River Mersey
Runcorn Sands
West Bank
Sewage Wks
Astmoor Ind Est
Manchester Ship Canal
Old Quay Bridge
ASTMOOR RD
Busway
Astmoor
DARESBURY EXPRESSWAY
Bridgewater Canal
Castlefields
HALTON RD
Stenhills
Schs
CENTRAL EXPRESSWAY
HALTON BROW
Halton Brook
Town Hall
Higher Runcorn
RUNCORN SPUR RD
BOSTON AVE
MOSS BANK RD
FIDDLERS FERRY RD
TAN HOUSE LA
GORSEY LA
LUGSDALE RD
ASHLEY WAY
WIDNES RD
KINGSWAY
MILTON RD
MOOR LA
VICTORIA RD
QUEENSWAY
MERSEY RD
ST MARY'S RD
CHURCH ST
HIGH ST
BRIDGE ST
VICTORIA RD
GREENWAY RD
LANGDALE RD
IVY ST
NORMAN RD
HEATH RD
CASTLEFIELDS AVE N
CASTLEFIELDS AVE S
MAIN ST
A562
A568
A533
A558
B5155

49
24

23
14

A
B
C
4
85
3
84
2
83
1
82
54
55
56
Fiddlers Ferry Power Station
St Helens Canal (disused)
Mersey Way
Cuerdley Marsh
Norton Marsh
Moss Side Farm
Moss Side
Upper Moss-Side Farm
MOSS SIDE LA
LAPWING LA
River Mersey
Manchester Ship Canal
Halton Moss
Wigg Island
Stonedelph Dock
PEMBROKE CT
ROKEBY CT
Green Wood
WARRINGTON RD
BEESTON CT
CHRISTLETON CT
STUART RD
BERKELEY CT
Lodge Plantation
Manor Farm
KINGS CT
MANOR FARM RD
A558
KECKWICK LA
Sewage Works
Busway
Priory Cottages
Offices
HOWARD CT
HAMPTON CT
MANOR PARK AVE
SEYMOUR CT
ARAGON CT
Manor Park
TUDOR RD
BOLEYN CT
DARESBURY EXPRESSWAY
STEVENTON
NEWMOORE LA
GLASTONBURY CL
SHERBORNE CL
DORCHESTER PARK
SANDY MOOR LA
Keckwick Brook
Astmoor Ind Est
ARKWRIGHT RD
ASTMOOR EAST INTERCHANGE
P
Norton Priory (remains of)
Museum
Big Wood
WINDMILL HILL AVE N
Popular Farm
Haddock's Wood
CASTLEFIELDS AVE N
KINGSHEAD CL
Bridgewater Canal
CANAL REACH
LOCKGATE EAST
BRIDGEWAY EAST
PRIORY RD
TOWNFIELD VIEW
WINDMILL HILL AVE W
North Townfield Bridge
SOUTHWOOD AVE
LOCKGATE WEST
BRIDGEWAY WEST
Schs
FITZWILLIAM WLK
DE LACY ROW
NIGEL WLK
CASTLEFIELDS AVE E
GREENBRIDGE RD
STONELEA
EASTWOOD
SOUTHWOOD AVE
Sch
NORTON HILL AVE
WINDMILL HILL AVE
SWINDEN CL
HARVARD CL
Norton Bridge
CHESTER CL
RICHARD CL
HEDGE HEY
GREEN BRIDGE CL
PLANTATION CL
WESTWOOD AVE
WOODRIDGE
Windmill Hill
CULFORD CL
FARNLEY CL
NEWBURGH CL
CHORLTON CL
LEDSTON CL
ELMORE CL
FIRBANK CL
Bog Wood
1 CONSTABLES CL
2 SUMMER CL
3 ST MARY'S RD
CASTLEFIELDS AVE S
WINDMILL HILL AVE E
SPINNEY WLK
MEADOW ROW
PRIORY CL
PRIMROSE CL
WOODLAND WLK
MERLIN CL
COPPICE CL
KING ARTHUR'S WLK
Pickerings Rough
WHITEBEAM CL
HORNBEAM CL
NORTONWOOD LA
NORTON VILLAGE
Norton
1 WOLVERTON DR
2 MELLOR CL
3 SEAFORD CL
Bridgewater Canal

23
50

15
26

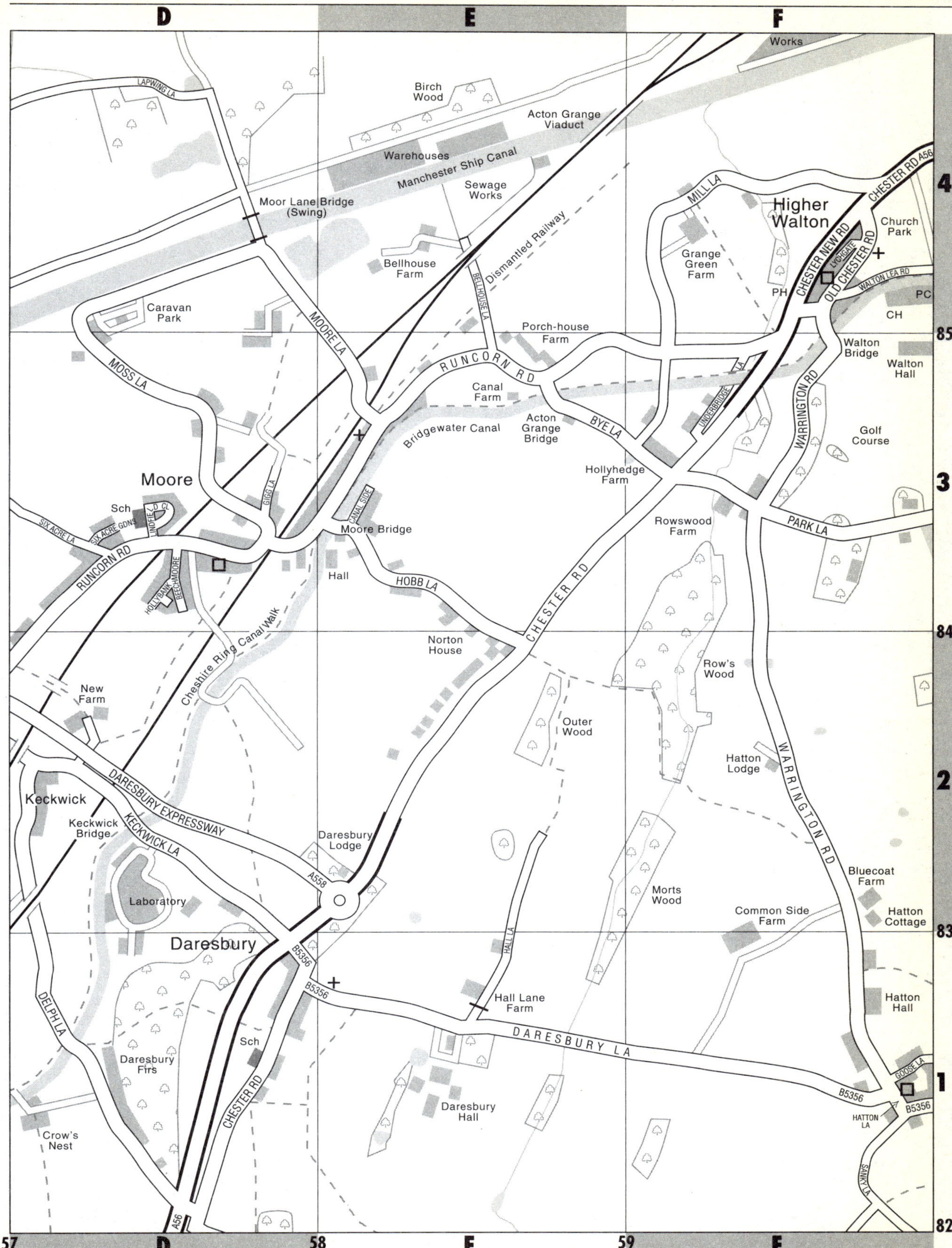
D
E
F
Works
Birch Wood
LAPWING LA
Acton Grange Viaduct
Warehouses
Manchester Ship Canal
Sewage Works
Moor Lane Bridge (Swing)
MILL LA
Higher Walton
CHESTER RD A56
Church Park
Grange Green Farm
CHESTER NEW RD
LYCHGATE
OLD CHESTER RD
WALTON LEA RD
Dismantled Railway
Bellhouse Farm
BELLHOUSE LA
Caravan Park
MOORE LA
PH
PC
CH
Porch-house Farm
RUNCORN RD
MOSS LA
Walton Bridge
Walton Hall
Canal Farm
UNDERBRIDGE LA
WARRINGTON RD
Acton Grange Bridge
Bridgewater Canal
BYE LA
Golf Course
Hollyhedge Farm
Moore
Sch
LINDFIELD CL
GIGG LA
SIX ACRE LA
SIX ACRE GDNS
CANAL SIDE
Moore Bridge
Rowswood Farm
PARK LA
RUNCORN RD
HOLLYBANK
BEECHMOORE
Hall
HOBB LA
CHESTER RD
Cheshire Ring Canal Walk
Norton House
Row's Wood
New Farm
Outer Wood
Hatton Lodge
Keckwick
DARESBURY EXPRESSWAY
Keckwick Bridge
KECKWICK LA
Daresbury Lodge
A558
Morts Wood
Bluecoat Farm
Laboratory
Common Side Farm
Hatton Cottage
Daresbury
B5356
HALL LA
Hatton Hall
Hall Lane Farm
DELPH LA
DARESBURY LA
Sch
Daresbury Firs
GOOSE LA
CHESTER RD
B5356
HATTON LA
Daresbury Hall
Crow's Nest
SANKY LA
A56
4
85
3
84
2
83
1
82
57
58
59

51
26

A
B
C
4
3
2
1
85
84
83
82
60
61
62
Lower Walton
Hillcliffe
Cobbs
Sch
Witherwin Farm
Crematorium
P
Cheshire Ring Canal Walk
Bridgewater Canal
Burial Ground
Sch
Hillfoot Farm
Walton Hall
Golf Course
High Warren
Bellfield Farm
Appleton Reservoir
Dudlow's Green
Appleton Park
Hurst Farm
Delamere Way
Hillside Farm
Great Shepcroft Farm
Goose Lane
Mosswood Hall
Hotel
Stretton
Hatton
Oaktree Farm
Spark Hall
Hospl
Hatton Lane Farm
Fir Tree Farm
Junction 10
CHESTER RD
A 56
WALTON NEW RD
OSBOURNE RD
DERBY RD
KIMBERLEY DR
HAWTHORNE RD
WALTON RD
A 56
A 49
SANDY LA
BRIDGEWATER MEWS
CARLISLE ST
GREENFIELDS AVE
WATERSIDE
HILL CLIFFE RD
RUTLAND AVE
GRANTHAM AVE
GRANBY RD
BELVOIR RD
MELTON AVE
BROOKWOOD CL
CALDERFIELD CL
WHITEFIELD RD
OLD HALL CL
WALTON LEA RD
RED LA
BIRCHDALE RD
BIRCHDALE CRES
WARREN DR
KINGSLEY DR
SNAEFELL RISE
WARREN RD
CLIFFE RD
DELPHFIELDS RD
HIGHWOOD RD
BURFIELD DR
ST MATHEWS CL
ST MARY'S CL
WINDMILL LA
WINDMILL CL
FIELD LA
CAMBRIDGE GDNS
QUARRY LA
LINNWOOD AVE
FIRS LA
PARK LA
HOUGH'S LA
LONDON RD
ROMAN ROAD
GREENWAY
SOUTHWAY AVE
DINGLEWAY
BROOMFIELDS RD
ST MONICAS CL
BRIDGE LA
DALE LA
ASH LA
WOOD LA
HINTON CRES
COBBS LA
FARM LA
HEYES LA
LUMB BROOK RD
MELROSE AVE
BEVERLEY AVE
GUERNSEY CL
CLYDESDALE RD
BERNARD AVE
CAVERSHAM CL
EPSOM GDNS
BROOM AVE
LYON'S LA
CHALFONT CL
HARROW CL
WEYBRIDGE CL
SUNBURY GDNS
HENLEY CL
CHESSINGTON CL
CHISWICK GDNS
DINGLE LA
PANGBOURNE CL
TAPLOW CL
DORNEY CL
PARK CRES
HALL DR
Sch
SHEPPERTON CL
APPLETON HALL GDNS
ABBOTSFIELD CL
LAKESTOKE CL
STAINES CL
MENTMORE GDNS
CANN LA
GREEN LA
CHATWELL GDNS
SHILLINGFORD CL
LONGWOOD RD
EVERSLEY CL
FAIRWAYS
BEECHWAYS
PINEWAYS
LARCHWAYS
DUDLOW GREEN RD
BIRCHWAYS
PETERSHAM DR
TEDDINGTON CL
ROSEMOOR GDNS
CANN LA
HIGHFIELD AVE
PEMBROKE GDNS
LINTON GDNS
WILLOW LA
PEWTERSPEAR LA
STONEHILL CL
HILLSIDE RD
SPRINGHOLM DR
ACTON AVE
LITTLECOTE AVE
FOXHILLS CL
SHEPCROFT LA
STRETTON RD
B 5356
BOWER CRES
TARPORLEY RD
SPARK HALL CL
FIR TREE CL
HATTON LA
GOOSE LA
GOSLING CL
B 5356
M 56
QUEASTEYBIRCH LA
PILLMOSS LA
A 49
A 559
SUMMIT CL
WELL LA
MOSSHALL LA

17
28

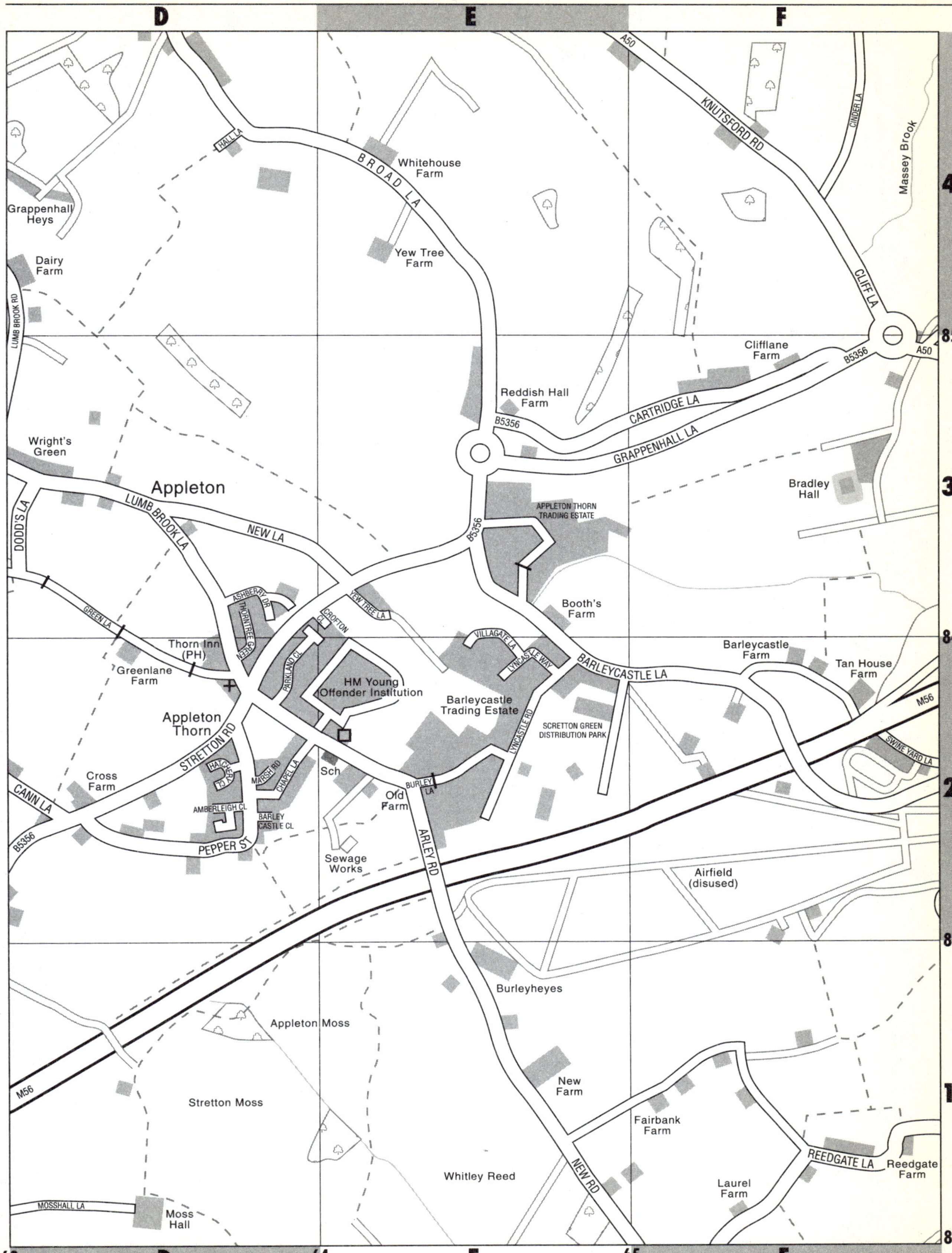
D
E
F
A50
KNUTSFORD RD
CINDER LA
Massey Brook
HALL LA
BROAD LA
Whitehouse Farm
Grappenhall Heys
Dairy Farm
Yew Tree Farm
LUMB BROOK RD
CLIFF LA
Clifflane Farm
B5356
A50
Reddish Hall Farm
B5356
CARTRIDGE LA
GRAPPENHALL LA
Wright's Green
Appleton
Bradley Hall
DODD'S LA
LUMB BROOK LA
NEW LA
B5356
APPLETON THORN TRADING ESTATE
Booth's Farm
ASHBERRY DR
THORNTREE GREEN
YEW TREE LA
CROFTON CL
GREEN LA
Thorn Inn (PH)
VILLAGATE LA
LYNCASTLE WAY
BARLEYCASTLE LA
Barleycastle Farm
Tan House Farm
Greenlane Farm
PARKLAND CL
HM Young Offender Institution
Barleycastle Trading Estate
M56
Appleton Thorn
STRETTON RD
SCRETTON GREEN DISTRIBUTION PARK
LYNCASTLE RD
SWINE YARD LA
Cross Farm
HATCHER CL
MARSH RD
CHAPEL LA
Sch
BURLEY LA
CANN LA
AMBERLEIGH CL
Old Farm
BARLEY CASTLE CL
B5356
PEPPER ST
Sewage Works
ARLEY RD
Airfield (disused)
Burleyheyes
Appleton Moss
M56
New Farm
Stretton Moss
Fairbank Farm
REEDGATE LA
Reedgate Farm
Whitley Reed
NEW RD
Laurel Farm
MOSSHALL LA
Moss Hall
4
85
3
84
2
83
1
82
63
64
65
D
E
F

53
28

27
18

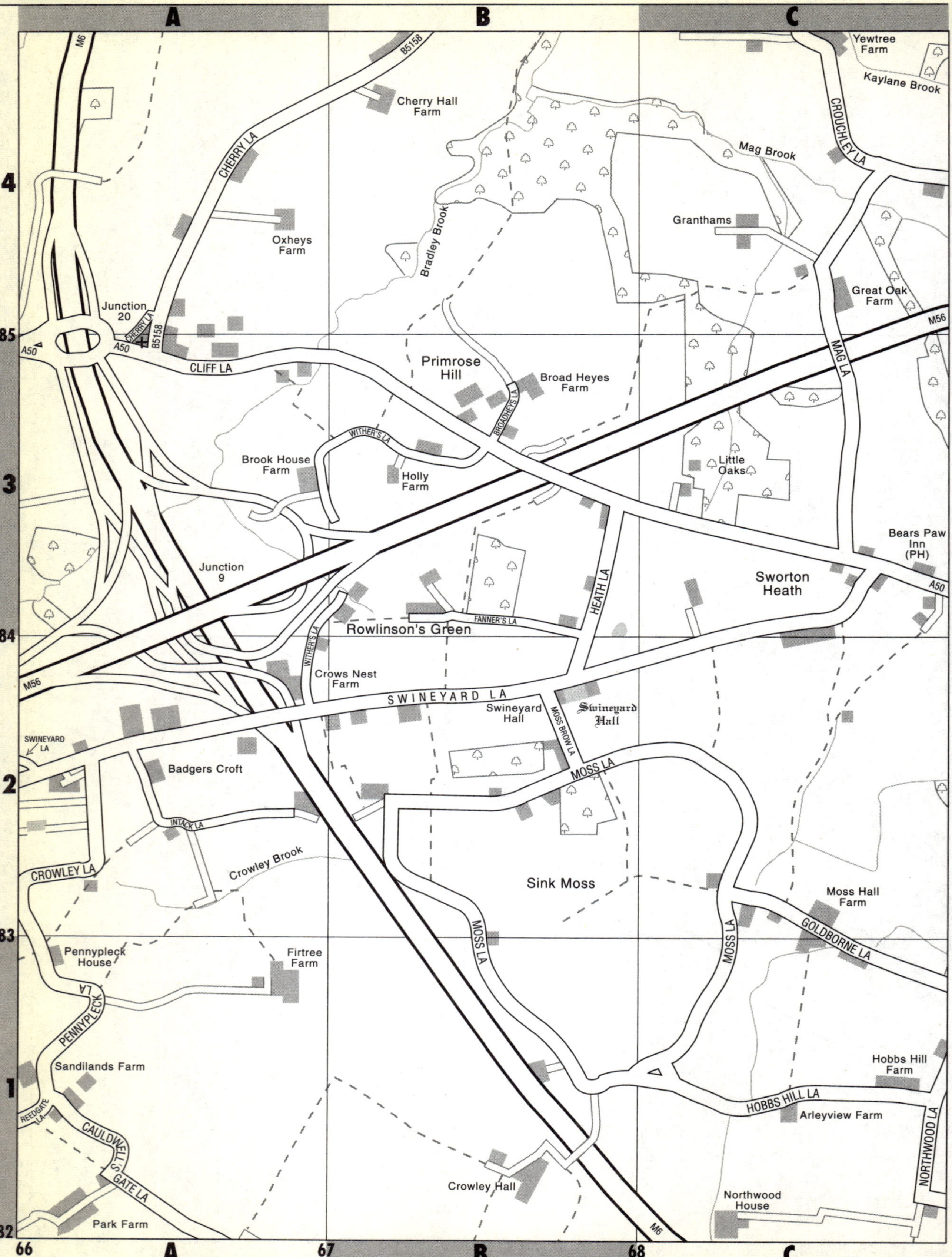

A
B
C
4
85
3
84
2
83
1
82
66
67
68
M6
B5158
Cherry Hall Farm
Yewtree Farm
Kaylane Brook
CROUCHLEY LA
Mag Brook
CHERRY LA
Oxheys Farm
Bradley Brook
Granthams
Great Oak Farm
Junction 20
CHERRY LA
B5158
A50
A50
CLIFF LA
Primrose Hill
Broad Heyes Farm
M56
MAG LA
BROADHEYS LA
WITHER'S LA
Brook House Farm
Holly Farm
Little Oaks
Bears Paw Inn (PH)
Junction 9
HEATH LA
Sworton Heath
A50
FANNER'S LA
Rowlinson's Green
WITHER'S LA
Crows Nest Farm
M56
SWINEYARD LA
Swineyard Hall
MOSS BROW LA
Swineyard Hall
SWINEYARD LA
Badgers Croft
MOSS LA
INTACK LA
CROWLEY LA
Crowley Brook
Sink Moss
Moss Hall Farm
MOSS LA
MOSS LA
GOLDBORNE LA
Pennypleck House
Firtree Farm
PENNYPLECK LA
Sandilands Farm
Hobbs Hill Farm
HOBBS HILL LA
Arleyview Farm
REEDGATE LA
CAULDWELL'S GATE LA
NORTHWOOD LA
Crowley Hall
Northwood House
Park Farm
M6

27
54

19
30

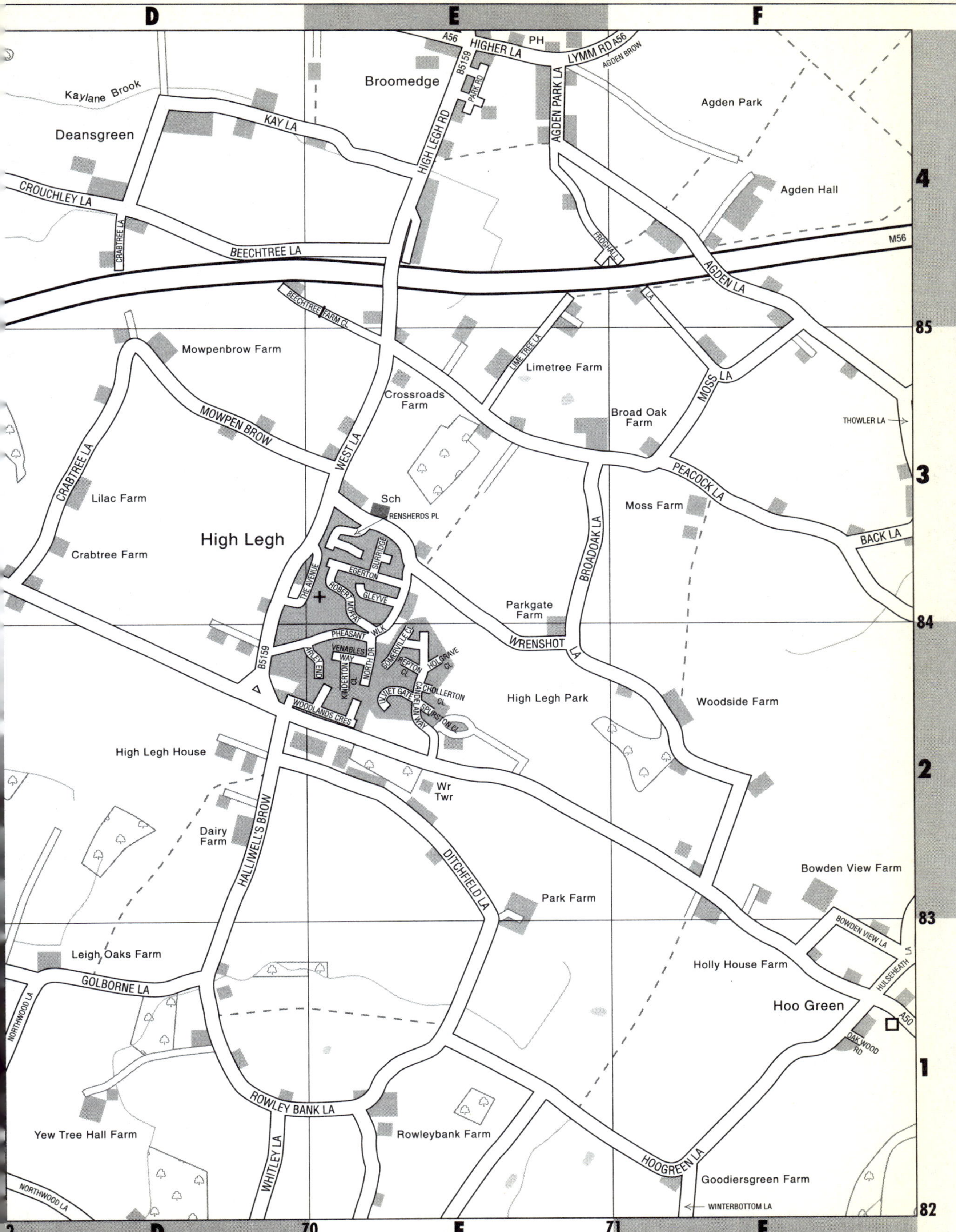
D
E
F
A56
HIGHER LA
PH
LYMM RD A56
AGDEN BROW
B5159
PARK RD
Broomedge
Kaylane Brook
KAY LA
Deansgreen
HIGH LEGH RD
AGDEN PARK LA
Agden Park
Agden Hall
4
CROUCHLEY LA
CRABTREE LA
BEECHTREE LA
FROGHALL
M56
AGDEN LA
BEECHTREE FARM CL
LA
85
Mowpenbrow Farm
LIME TREE LA
Limetree Farm
MOSS LA
Crossroads Farm
Broad Oak Farm
THOWLER LA
MOWPEN BROW
WEST LA
PEACOCK LA
3
CRABTREE LA
Lilac Farm
Sch
RENSHERDS PL
Moss Farm
High Legh
SURRIDGE
BROADOAK LA
BACK LA
Crabtree Farm
EGERTON
THE AVENUE
ROBERT MOFFAT
GLEYVE
Parkgate Farm
84
PHEASANT WLK
SOMERVILLE CL
WRENSHOT LA
VENABLES WAY
ARLEY END
NORTH DR
REPTON CL
HOLGRAVE CL
B5159
KINDERTON CL
LYMVIET GATE
CHOLLERTON CL
CANDELAN WAY
High Legh Park
Woodside Farm
WOODLANDS CRES
SPURSTON CL
High Legh House
2
Wr Twr
Dairy Farm
HALLIWELL'S BROW
DITCHFIELD LA
Bowden View Farm
Park Farm
83
BOWDEN VIEW LA
Leigh Oaks Farm
Holly House Farm
HULSEHEATH LA
GOLBORNE LA
Hoo Green
NORTHWOOD LA
A50
OAKWOOD RD
1
ROWLEY BANK LA
Rowleybank Farm
Yew Tree Hall Farm
WHITLEY LA
HOOGREEN LA
Goodiersgreen Farm
NORTHWOOD LA
WINTERBOTTOM LA
82
70
71

55
30

29
20

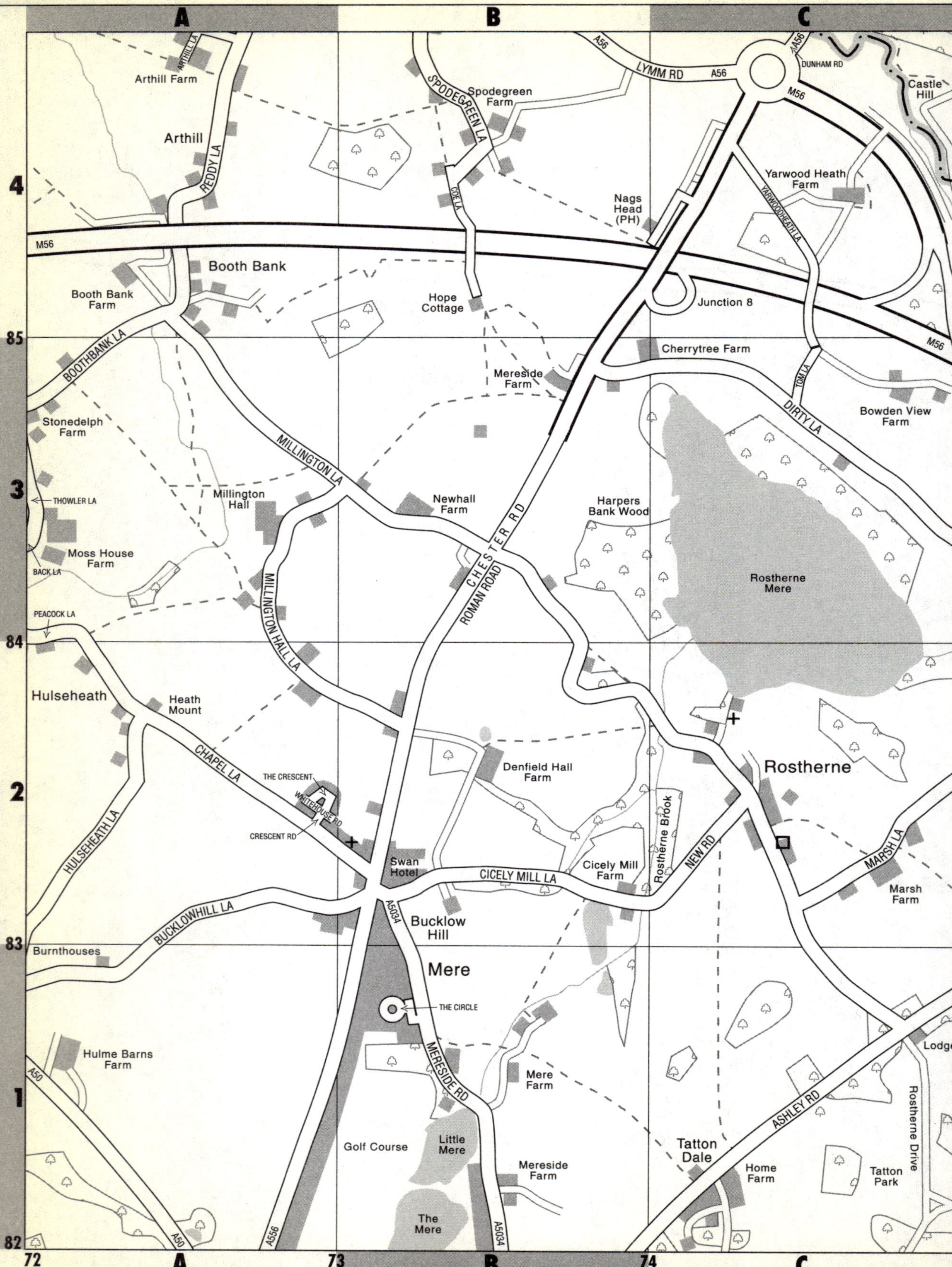
A
B
C
A56
LYMM RD
A56
A56
DUNHAM RD
Castle Hill
M56
ARTHILL LA
Arthill Farm
SPODEGREEN LA
Spodegreen Farm
Arthill
REDDY LA
COE LA
Yarwood Heath Farm
YARWOODHEATH LA
4
Nags Head (PH)
M56
Booth Bank
Booth Bank Farm
Hope Cottage
Junction 8
85
BOOTHBANK LA
Cherrytree Farm
M56
Mereside Farm
TOM LA
Stonedelph Farm
DIRTY LA
Bowden View Farm
MILLINGTON LA
3
THOWLER LA
Millington Hall
Newhall Farm
Harpers Bank Wood
CHESTER RD
Moss House Farm
BACK LA
ROMAN ROAD
MILLINGTON HALL LA
Rostherne Mere
PEACOCK LA
84
Hulseheath
Heath Mount
Rostherne
CHAPEL LA
Denfield Hall Farm
THE CRESCENT
2
WHITEHOUSE RD
CRESCENT RD
HULSEHEATH LA
Rostherne Brook
NEW RD
MARSH LA
Swan Hotel
CICELY MILL LA
Cicely Mill Farm
Marsh Farm
BUCKLOWHILL LA
A5034
Bucklow Hill
83
Burnthouses
Mere
THE CIRCLE
Lodge
Hulme Barns Farm
MERESIDE RD
A50
Mere Farm
1
Rostherne Drive
ASHLEY RD
Little Mere
Golf Course
Tatton Dale
Mereside Farm
Home Farm
Tatton Park
The Mere
A50
A556
A5034
82
72
73
74

29
56

32

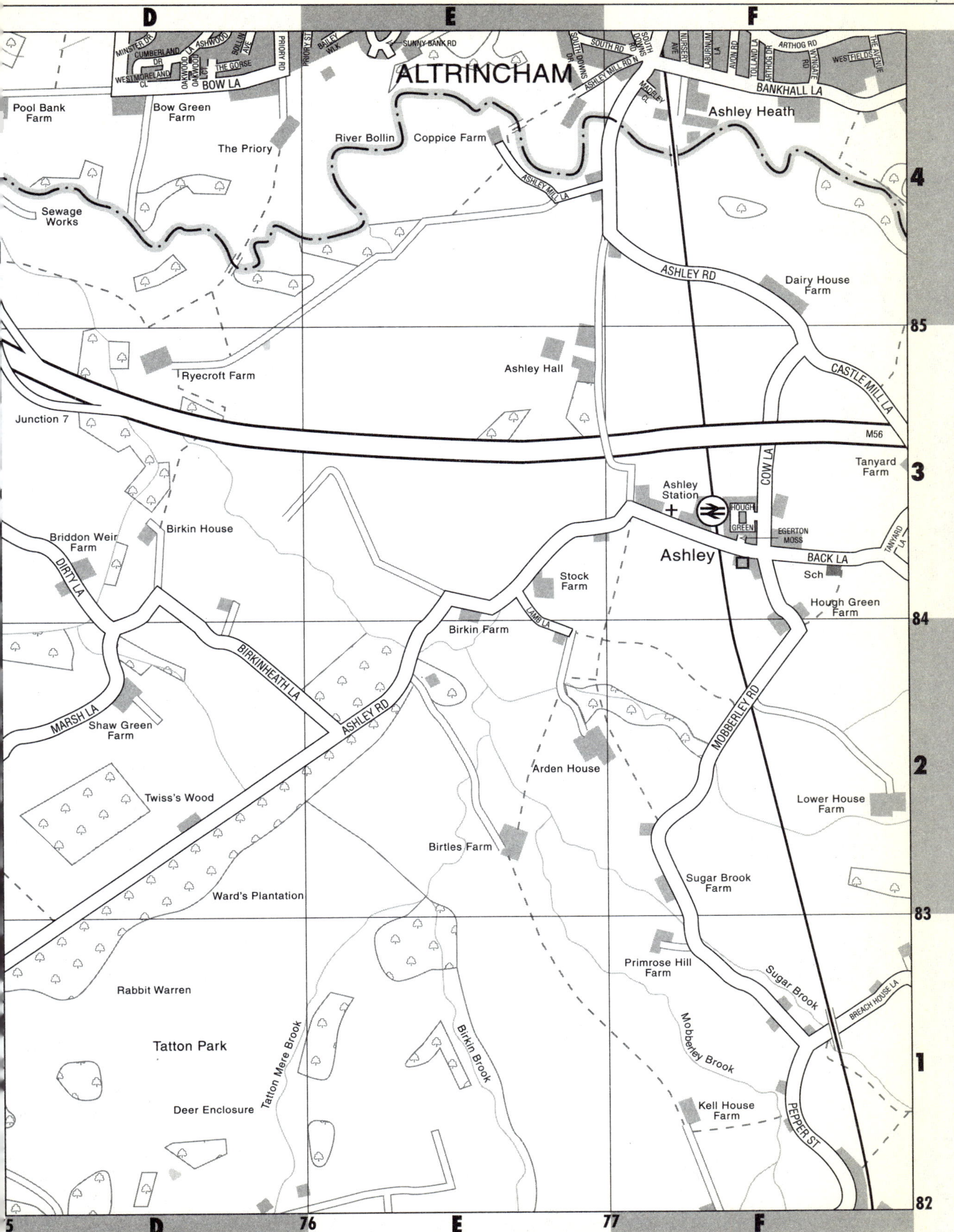

D
E
F
ALTRINCHAM
MINSTER DR
CUMBERLAND DR
ASHWOOD
BOLLIN AVE
PRIORY RD
PRIORY ST
BAILEY WLK
SUNNY BANK RD
SOUTH RD
SOUTH DOWNS DR
SOUTH DOWNS RD
ASHLEY MILL RD N
MADELEY CL
NURSERY AVE
LABURNUM LA
AVON RD
TOLLAND LA
ARTHOG DR
ARTHOG RD
WYNGATE RD
WESTFIELDS
THE AVENUE
WESTMORELAND CL
OAKWOOD LA
THE GORSE
BOW LA
BANKHALL LA
Pool Bank Farm
Bow Green Farm
Ashley Heath
River Bollin
Coppice Farm
The Priory
ASHLEY MILL LA
Sewage Works
ASHLEY RD
Dairy House Farm
Ryecroft Farm
Ashley Hall
CASTLE MILL LA
Junction 7
M56
COW LA
Tanyard Farm
Ashley Station
HOUGH GREEN
EGERTON MOSS
Briddon Weir Farm
Birkin House
DIRTY LA
Ashley
BACK LA
TANYARD LA
Stock Farm
Sch
Hough Green Farm
LAMB LA
Birkin Farm
BIRKINHEATH LA
MARSH LA
Shaw Green Farm
ASHLEY RD
MOBBERLEY RD
Arden House
Twiss's Wood
Lower House Farm
Birtles Farm
Sugar Brook Farm
Ward's Plantation
Primrose Hill Farm
Sugar Brook
BREACH HOUSE LA
Rabbit Warren
Mobberley Brook
Tatton Park
Tatton Mere Brook
Birkin Brook
Kell House Farm
PEPPER ST
Deer Enclosure
4
85
3
84
2
83
1
82
5
76
77

57

32

31

A
B
C
4
3
2
1
85
84
83
82
78
79
80
College
Golf Course
Halebarns
Sch
Flaxhigh Covert
Cricket Ground
M56
BANKHALL LA
BROAD LA
BROADWAY
HAWLEY LA
WICKER LA
A538
DIAL RD
COTTESMORE GDNS
THE MOUNT
KNUTSFORD VIEW
RYDAL DR
BROOKS DR
RUNGER LA
HASTY LA
THE COPPICE
WHITEHOUSE DR
AMBERLEY DR
HAWLEY DR
ELMSWAY
BOLLINWAY
BARROW LA
THE MERRIDALE
RAPPAX RD
LYNWOOD
NORTH RD
CRAMPTON DR
BARNS PL
TITHEBARN RD
ELM RIDGE DR
WILTON DR
HIGH ELM DR
THE DRIVE
PROSPECT DR
HALE RD
WINMARITH DR
CH
Golf Course
CASTLE WAY
MILLWAY
CHAPEL DR
LONGSIDES RD
RAVENWOOD DR
HIGH ELM RD
WARREN DR
Manchester Airport
ROSSMILL LA
CARRWOOD
GORSE BANK RD
STONE MEAD AVE
CHAPEL LA
LONGACRES RD
THE COPSE
BURNSIDE
COTTRELL RD
CRABTREE AVE
RUSHEY CL
MARLFIELD RD
RIVERMEAD AVE
GORSE BANK RD
WEY GATES DR
TANYARD DR
CROFT CL
BUTTERMERE DR
PINFOLD CL
GREENGATE
WARBURTON CL
WARBURTON DR
Warburton Green
A538
Mast
AVRO WAY
1 WESTGATE RD
PINFOLD LA
BOBB HEDGE CL
HASLEMERE AVE
BRIDGE AVE
SANDOWN DR
RIVERSHILL GDNS
BANKSIDE
Oak Farm
SUNBANK LA
PH
WILMSLOW OLD RD
M56
Keepers Cottage
TANYARD LA
Halebank
CASTLE MILL LA
Thorns Green
River Bollin
Back Lane Farm
BACK LA
Cotteril Clough
Chapel House Farm
Castle Mill Farm
BRICKHILL LA
MILL LA
WILMSLOW RD
Castle Hill Farm
Castle Hill
Middle House
Higher House Farm
Meadowlands
Castle Hill Farm
A538
Blackshaw Heys Farm
Breach House Farm
BEACH HOUSE LA
Stock-in-Hey Farm
Bollinhouse Farm
Woodend
Beehive Farm
Woodend Farm
Yarwood House Farm
Cherry Tree Farm
WOOD LA
WOODEND LA

31
58

34

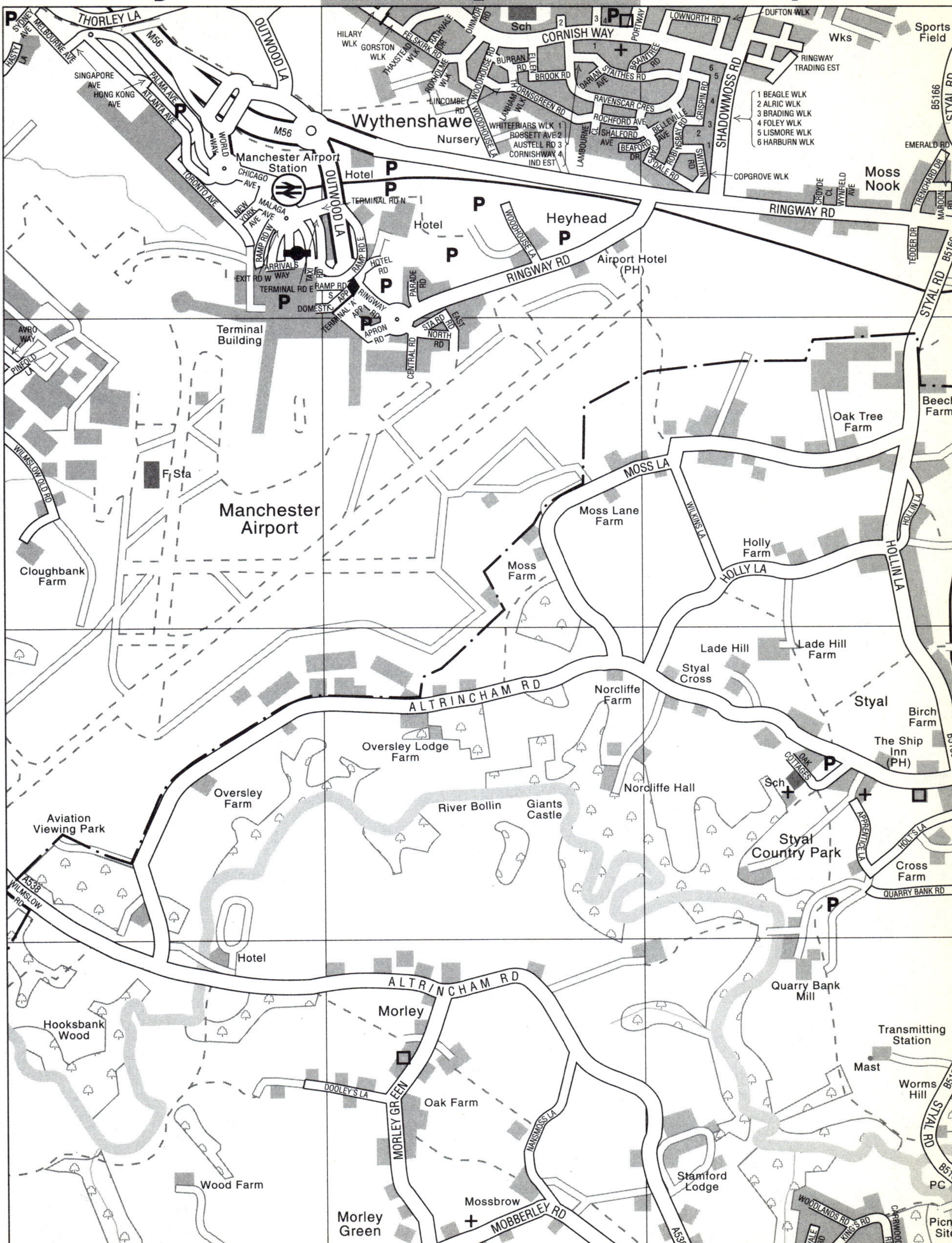
D
E
F
THORLEY LA
SYDNEY AVE
MELBOURNE AVE
HASTY LA
M56
SINGAPORE AVE
HONG KONG AVE
PALMA AVE
ATLANTA AVE
OUTWOOD LA
HILARY WLK
GORSTON WLK
THAXSTEAD WLK
FELSKIRK RD
RATHVALE DR
DINMOR RD
Sch
CORNISH WAY
PORTWAY
LOWNORTH RD
DUFTON WLK
Sports Field
Wks
BURRAN RD
ELLEN
BROOK RD
STAITHES RD
BRANTREE RD
SHADOWMOSS RD
RINGWAY TRADING EST
1 BEAGLE WLK
2 ALRIC WLK
3 BRADING WLK
4 FOLEY WLK
5 LISMORE WLK
6 HARBURN WLK
B5166
STYAL RD
ROKHOLME WLK
WOODHOUSE RD
THORNSGREEN RD
LINCOMBE RD
RAVENSCAR CRES
ROCHFORD AVE
CRISPIN RD
Wythenshawe
Nursery
WHITEFRIARS WLK 1
ROSSETT AVE 2
AUSTELL RD 3
CORNISHWAY 4
IND EST
LAMBOURNE CL
SHALFORD AVE
BEAFORD DR
BELLEVILLE AVE
ROBINSBAY RD
SWITHIN RD
COPGROVE WLK
EMERALD RD
Moss Nook
TRENCHARD DR
MAROON RD
M56
WORLD WAY
Manchester Airport Station
CHICAGO AVE
TORONTO AVE
NEW YORK AVE
MALAGA AVE
Hotel
TERMINAL RD N
CROYDE CL
WYNFIELD AVE
RINGWAY RD
Hotel
P
Heyhead
WOODHOUSE LA
RAMP RD W
ARRIVALS WAY
TAXI RD
RAMP RD E
EXIT RD W
TERMINAL RD E
RAMP RD
DOMESTIC APP
TERMINAL 'A' APP
HOTEL RD
RINGWAY RD
PARADE RD
RINGWAY RD
Airport Hotel (PH)
TEDDER DR
B5166
STYAL RD
AVRO WAY
PINFOLD LA
Terminal Building
APRON RD
STA RD
CENTRAL RD
NORTH RD
EAST RD
85
Beech Farm
Oak Tree Farm
WILMSLOW OLD RD
F Sta
Manchester Airport
MOSS LA
Moss Lane Farm
WILKINS LA
HOLLIN LA
3
Holly Farm
HOLLY LA
HOLLIN LA
Cloughbank Farm
Moss Farm
84
Lade Hill
Lade Hill Farm
Styal Cross
Styal
ALTRINCHAM RD
Norcliffe Farm
Birch Farm
The Ship Inn (PH)
B5166
Oversley Lodge Farm
OAK COTTAGES
Sch
2
Oversley Farm
Norcliffe Hall
Aviation Viewing Park
River Bollin
Giants Castle
Styal Country Park
APPRENTICE LA
HOLT'S LA
Cross Farm
QUARRY BANK RD
A538
WILMSLOW RD
83
Hotel
ALTRINCHAM RD
Quarry Bank Mill
Morley
Hooksbank Wood
Transmitting Station
Mast
Worms Hill
B5166
STYAL RD
1
DOOLEY'S LA
Oak Farm
MORLEY GREEN
NANSMOSS LA
Stamford Lodge
B5166
PC
Wood Farm
Mossbrow
MOBBERLEY RD
A538
WOODLANDS RD
KING'S RD
CARRWOOD RD
VALE RD
Picnic Site
Morley Green
82
81
D
82
E
83
F

59

34

33

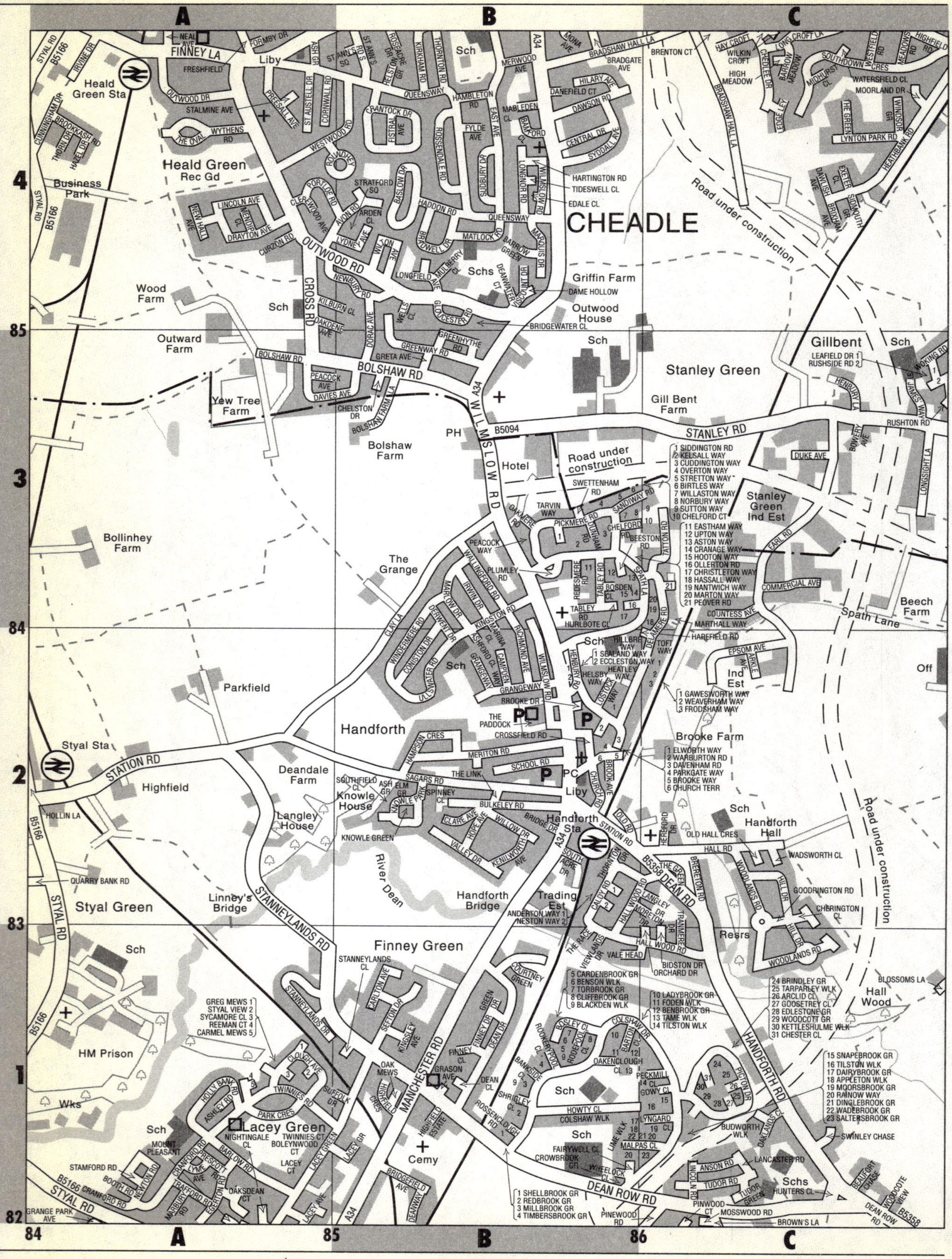
A
B
C
4
85
3
84
2
83
1
82
84
85
86
CHEADLE
Heald Green Sta
Heald Green Rec Gd
Business Park
Wood Farm
Outward Farm
Yew Tree Farm
Bolshaw Farm
Bollinhey Farm
The Grange
Parkfield
Handforth
Styal Sta
Highfield
Deandale Farm
Knowle House
Langley House
Styal Green
Linney's Bridge
River Dean
Handforth Bridge
Finney Green
HM Prison
Wks
Lacey Green
Mount Pleasant
Cemy
Griffin Farm
Outwood House
Stanley Green
Gill Bent Farm
Gillbent
Stanley Green Ind Est
Beech Farm
Spath Lane
Ind Est
Brooke Farm
Handforth Hall
Handforth Sta
Trading Est
Resrs
Hall Wood
Road under construction
Hotel
Schs
Sch
PH
PC
Liby
Off
FINNEY LA
OUTWOOD RD
CROSS RD
BOLSHAW RD
WILMSLOW RD
STANLEY RD
STATION RD
STYAL RD
STANNEYLANDS RD
MANCHESTER RD
DEAN ROW RD
DEAN RD
HANDFORTH RD
COMMERCIAL AVE
QUEENSWAY
B5094
B5166
B5358
A34
1 SIDDINGTON RD
2 KELSALL WAY
3 CUDDINGTON WAY
4 OVERTON WAY
5 STRETTON WAY
6 BIRTLES WAY
7 WILLASTON WAY
8 NORBURY WAY
9 SUTTON WAY
10 CHELFORD CT
11 EASTHAM WAY
12 UPTON WAY
13 ASTON WAY
14 CRANAGE WAY
15 HOOTON WAY
16 OLLERTON RD
17 CHRISTLETON WAY
18 HASSALL WAY
19 NANTWICH WAY
20 MARTON WAY
21 PEOVER RD
1 SEALAND WAY
2 ECCLESTON WAY
1 GAWESWORTH WAY
2 WEAVERHAM WAY
3 FRODSHAM WAY
1 ELWORTH WAY
2 WARBURTON RD
3 DAVENHAM RD
4 PARKGATE WAY
5 BROOKE WAY
6 CHURCH TERR
5 CARDENBROOK GR
6 BENSON WLK
7 TORBROOK GR
8 CLIFFBROOK GR
9 BLACKDEN WLK
10 LADYBROOK GR
11 FODEN WLK
12 BENBROOK GR
13 TAME WLK
14 TILSTON WLK
24 BRINDLEY GR
25 TARPARLEY WLK
26 ARCLID CL
27 GOOSETREY CL
28 EDLESTONE GR
29 WOODCOTT GR
30 KETTLESHULME WLK
31 CHESTER CL
15 SNAPEBROOK GR
16 TILSTON WLK
17 DAIRYBROOK GR
18 APPLETON WLK
19 MOORSBROOK GR
20 RAINOW WAY
21 DINGLEBROOK GR
22 WADEBROOK GR
23 SALTERSBROOK GR
1 SHELLBROOK GR
2 REDBROOK GR
3 MILLBROOK GR
4 TIMBERSBROOK GR
GREG MEWS 1
STYAL VIEW 2
SYCAMORE CL 3
REEMAN CT 4
CARMEL MEWS 5
LEAFIELD DR 1
RUSHSIDE RD 2
ANDERTON WAY 1
NESTON WAY 2

33

60

36

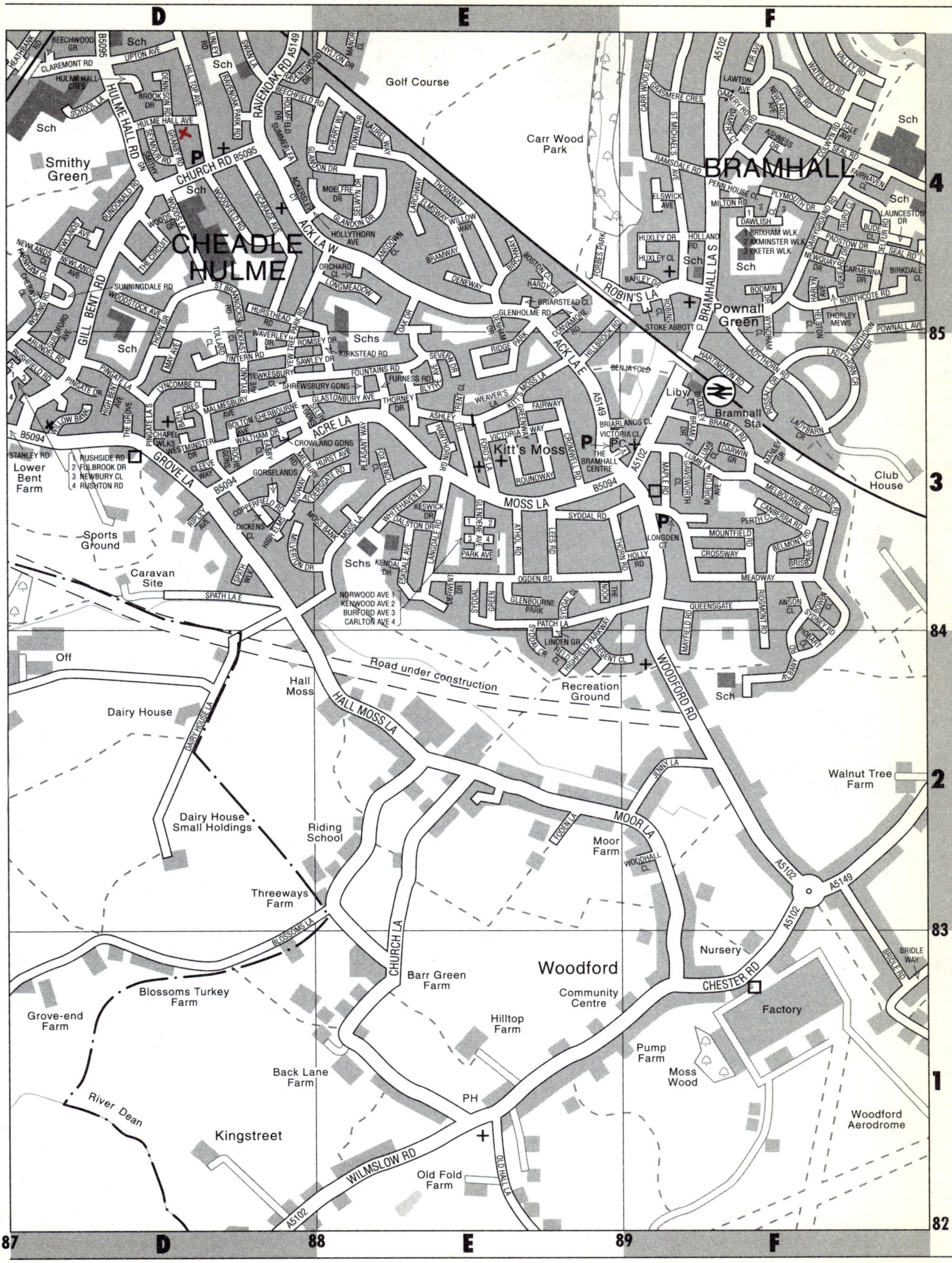

D
E
F
4
3
2
1
85
84
83
82
87
88
89
CHEADLE HULME
BRAMHALL
Golf Course
Carr Wood Park
Smithy Green
Pownall Green
Kitt's Moss
Bramhall Sta
Club House
Lower Bent Farm
Sports Ground
Caravan Site
Off
Hall Moss
Road under construction
Recreation Ground
Dairy House
Dairy House Small Holdings
Riding School
Threeways Farm
Walnut Tree Farm
Moor Farm
Nursery
Woodford
Community Centre
Barr Green Farm
Blossoms Turkey Farm
Grove-end Farm
Hilltop Farm
Factory
Pump Farm
Moss Wood
Back Lane Farm
PH
River Dean
Kingstreet
Old Fold Farm
Woodford Aerodrome
CHURCH RD B5095
ACK LANE
ACRE LA
MOSS LA
GROVE LA
HALL MOSS LA
MOOR LA
CHURCH LA
WILMSLOW RD
CHESTER RD
WOODFORD RD
OLD HALL LA
DAIRY HOUSE LA
BLOSSOMS LA
JENNY LA
SPATH LA E
BRAMHALL LA S
RAVENOAK RD A5149
HULME HALL RD
GILL BENT RD
ROBIN'S LA
A5102
A5149
B5094
1 RUSHSIDE RD
2 FULBROOK DR
3 NEWBURY CL
4 RUSHTON RD
NORWOOD AVE 1
KENWOOD AVE 2
BURFORD AVE 3
CARLTON AVE 4
1 BRIXHAM WLK
2 AXMINSTER WLK
3 EXETER WLK

61

36

35

A
B
C
Wall Bank Farm
Dingle Farm
Schs
BEAUMARIS CRES
SKIPTON CL
PENRHYN CRES
DENBIGH CL
BLAIR CL
TAMWORTH CL
ARUNDEL AVE
KENILWORTH DR
WARWICK CL
LANCASTER CL
A523
SHEPLEY CL
BOWERFIELD AV
A5143
JACKSON'S LA
LAVENHAM CL
ROWLEY RD
EYAM RD
DEHISON RD
CAVENDISH RD
TIDESWELL RD
RUTLAND RD
BAKEWELL RD
MACCLESFIELD RD
DEVONSHIRE RD
MERTON AVE
CHATSWORTH RD
PEVERIL DR
CHERRY TREE DR
Norbury House Farm
HAZEL GROVE
CHARNWOOD CRES
Denbigh Farm
DEAN LA
FIVEWAYS PAR
ALDERLEY CL
MILL LA
WINSFIELD RD
HARTINGTON D
BRADWELL RD
MATLOCK DR
SUDBURY RD
BELVOIR AVE
ELTON DR
LONGNOR RD
SHELDON RD
RIPLEY CL
ASHBOURNE RD
DARLEY RD
BASLOW DR
Norbury Hall
CAPESTHORNE CL 1
CAPESTHORNE RD 2
Lady Brook
1 AINSDALE CL
2 PRINCESS WLK
3 CHEVIN GDNS
4 HILLSIDE CL
Sch
GLENEAGLES CL
NEVIN CL
WESTBY CL
WARTON CL
LYTHAM DR
SEAL RD
CAMBERLEY CL
SUNNINGDALE D
WENTWORTH DR
POWNALL A
Further Dairyground
Dairyground
CHESTER RD
WENSLEY DR
MALTON DR
Millhill Bridge
Norbury Brook
Towers Farm
MILL HILL RD
MILL HILL AVE
Barlowfold
Serpentine Wood
Mill Hill Farm
LOWER PARK CR
ANGLESEY WATER
REDACRE
P
Golf Course
Birch Hall
WOODFORD RD
Hill Green Farm
Park House Farm
LONDON RD N
ANGLESEY DR
PADDOCK CHASE
Poynton Lake
Poynton Park
TOWERS CL
TOWERS RD
Reservoir
Phillip's Bridge
Lower Park Road
GLASTONBURY DR
DUNDRENNAN CL
NEWSTEAD CL
MEATH CL
ABBOTSBURY CL
LOWER PARK RD
Lower Park Lodge
HARTLAND CL
SELBY CL
TINTERN CL
BUCKFAST CL
LINDISFARNE DR
VICARAGE LA
HASELEY CL
COVELL RD
TUTWORTH RD
MALMESBURY CL
SOUTH PARK DR
LAKESIDE DR
WATERS REACH
WARREN LEA
MILLSTONE CL
Towers Yard Farm
Distaff Farm
SOUTH MEAD
DISTAFF RD
WARREN RD
MERTON RD
TEWKESBURY CL 1
BYLANDS CL 2
LAMBOURN CL 3
WHITBY CL
EASBY CL
FURNESS CL
Poynton Station
Sch
BOLTON CL
MILTON DR
OAK GR
KIRKSTALL DR
HAZELBADGE RD
HAZEL BADGE CL
MILTON GR
BURTON DR
WOODSIDE LA
KINGSWOOD
Prince's Incline
Lady's Incline
LADYS CL
BEECH CRES
CHARLECOTE RD
HOLKER CL
SULGRAVE AVE
NORTON DR
KNOLE AVE
HARDWICK RD
RAGLEY CL
BLENHEIM CL
OAKFIELD RD
Poynton
DEVA CL
WAYSIDE DR
CHESTER RD
HIGHFIELD RD
POCHARD DR
MALLARD CRES
TERN DR
BRENT CL
GREBE CL
WIDGEON CL
TEAL AV
PETREL A
SWAN CL
LOSTOCK AVE
PUFFIN AVE
DUNLIN CL
SNIPE CL
WEST PARK AVE
BITTERN CL
FULMAR DR
HERON DR
A5149
PARK AVE
Liby
Civic Hall
SCHOOL LA
SCHOOL CL
PARKLANDS WAY
SCHOOL LA
Sta
BRECON CL
WOBURN CT
Hockley
PARK LA
WINDSOR CL
FOUNTAIN CL
GEORGE'S RD W
GEORGE'S RD E
BULKELEY RD
CLUMBER RD
ORCHARD CL
WILLOW CL
MAPLE AVE
LARCH
CHESTNUT
GLOUCESTER RD
BALMORAL DR
BUCKINGHAM RD
QUEENSWAY
SANDRINGHAM DR
CLIFFORD RD
BROOKFIELD AVE
WIGWAM CL
Wigwam Wood
Sch
GULL CL
LOSTOCK HALL RD
Nursery
Poynton Brook
PICKWICK R
NICKLEBY RD
Schs
LONDON RD S
CLUMBER RD
CLUMBER CL
HOLLY RD
CEDAR RD
BROOKSIDE AVE
ALDER AVE
CHERRY TREE
IVY RD
FIR CL
ASH RD
HAZEL DR
ELM CL
YEWTREE LA
PINE RD
HOCKLEY RD
Sch
BIRCH RD
GROSVENOR DR
ARLINGTON DR
GLENFIELD DR
BRIDLE WAY
Upper Swineseye Farm
Lostockhall Farm
WOOLLEY AVE
Midway
BARNABY RD
DOMBEY RD
VARDEN RD
BARDELL CL
COPPERFIELD RD
MARLEY RD
TAPLEY AVE
ADAMS CL
BAGSTOCK AVE
BROWNLOW CL
DICKENS LA
KETTLESHULME WAY
SUTTON RD
ADLINGTON CL
GAWSWORTH CL
Sch
LAWRENCE PL
WELLER CL
WELLER AVE
HALE AVE
Sch
CURZON RD
MICAWBER RD
FIELDING AVE
BARCLAY RD
VERNON CL
DORRIT CL
GREYMARSH DR
VERNON RD
SPRING RD
SIDDINGTON RD
Woodford Aerodrome
BRIDLE RD
LOSTOCK RD
CALDER CL
THIRD AVE
HOPE GREEN WAY
Sprink Farm
ALDERLEY CL
WINCLE AVE
Industrial Estate
FIRST AVE
SPRINGWELL CL
Wks
Shirdfold Farm
SECOND AVE
Industrial Estate
HOPE LA
ADLINGTON PARK
Hope Green Farm
LONDON RD
Hope Green
Hope Lane
Clayton Greaves Farm
HOPE LA
A523
Brookside Farm
4
85
3
84
2
83
1
82
90
91
92

38

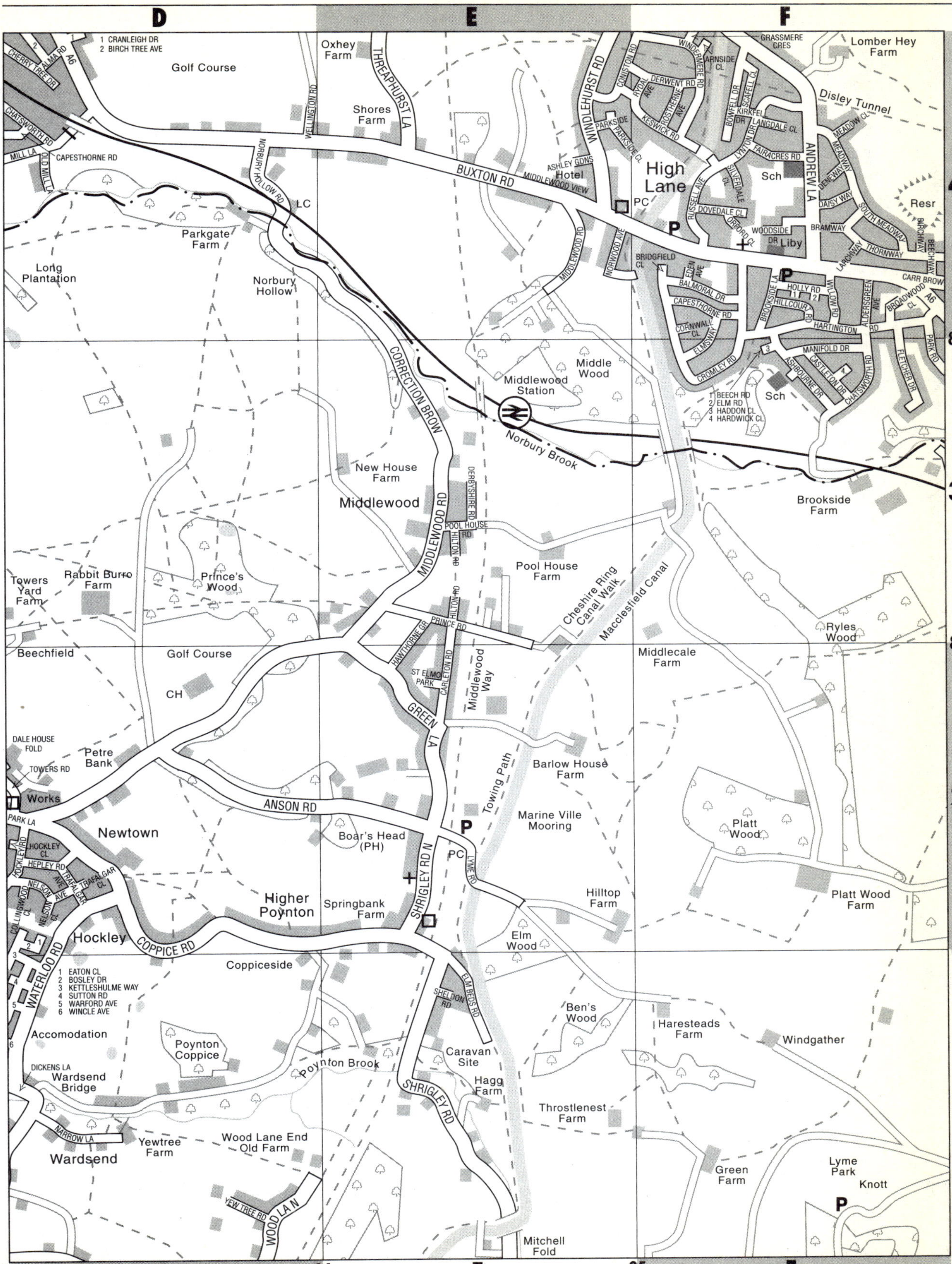
D
E
F
1 CRANLEIGH DR
2 BIRCH TREE AVE
Golf Course
Oxhey Farm
THREAPHURST LA
Shores Farm
WELLINGTON RD
ALMA RD
A6
CHERRY TREE DR
CHATSWORTH RD
MILL LA
OLD MILL LA
CAPESTHORNE RD
NORBURY HOLLOW RD
LC
BUXTON RD
ASHLEY GDNS
Hotel
MIDDLEWOOD VIEW
WINDLEHURST RD
CONISTON RD
RYDAL AVE
DERWENT RD
WINDERMERE RD
ARNSIDE CL
GRASSMERE CRES
Lomber Hey Farm
Disley Tunnel
BOWFELL DR
SCAFELL CL
KIRKFELL DR
LANGDALE CL
KESWICK RD
BORROWDALE AVE
PARKSIDE
PARKSIDE CL
High Lane
PC
LYNTON DR
FAIRACRES RD
Sch
ANDREW LA
MEADOW CL
MEADWAY
DENEWAY
DAISY WAY
SOUTH MEADWAY
Resr
BIRCHWAY
BRAMWAY
THORNWAY
LARCHWAY
BEECHWAY
CARR BROW
RUSSELL AVE
SILVERDALE CL
DOVEDALE CL
ORFORD CL
WOODSIDE DR
Liby
P
Parkgate Farm
Long Plantation
Norbury Hollow
MIDDLEWOOD RD
NORWOOD AVE
BRIDGFIELD CL
EDEN AVE
BALMORAL DR
CAPESTHORNE RD
CORNWALL CL
ELMSWAY
CROMLEY RD
BROOKSIDE LA
HOLLY RD
HILLCOURT RD
WILLOW RD
ALDERSGREEN AVE
BROADWOOD CL
A6
HARTINGTON RD
MANIFOLD DR
ASHBOURNE DR
CASTLETON DR
CHATSWORTH RD
FLETCHER DR
PARK RD
1 BEECH RD
2 ELM RD
3 HADDON CL
4 HARDWICK CL
Sch
CORRECTION BROW
Middlewood Station
Middle Wood
Norbury Brook
Brookside Farm
New House Farm
Middlewood
DERBYSHIRE RD
POOL HOUSE RD
HILTON RD
Pool House Farm
Cheshire Ring Canal Walk
Macclesfield Canal
Towers Yard Farm
Rabbit Burro Farm
Prince's Wood
PRINCE RD
HAWTHORNE GR
Ryles Wood
Beechfield
Golf Course
CH
ST ELMO PARK
CARLETON RD
Middlewood Way
Middlecale Farm
GREEN LA
DALE HOUSE FOLD
TOWERS RD
Petre Bank
Works
PARK LA
Newtown
ANSON RD
Towing Path
Barlow House Farm
Marine Ville Mooring
Platt Wood
Boar's Head (PH)
HOCKLEY CL
HEPLEY RD
NELSON AVE
TRAFALGAR CL
COLLINGWOOD CL
NELSON CL
Higher Poynton
Springbank Farm
SHRIGLEY RD N
PC
LYME RD
Hilltop Farm
Platt Wood Farm
Hockley
COPPICE RD
Elm Wood
WATERLOO RD
Coppiceside
1 EATON CL
2 BOSLEY DR
3 KETTLESHULME WAY
4 SUTTON RD
5 WARFORD AVE
6 WINCLE AVE
SHELDON RD
ELM BEDS RD
Ben's Wood
Haresteads Farm
Windgather
Accomodation
Poynton Coppice
Caravan Site
DICKENS LA
Wardsend Bridge
Poynton Brook
SHRIGLEY RD
Hagg Farm
Throstlenest Farm
NARROW LA
Yewtree Farm
Wood Lane End Old Farm
Wardsend
Green Farm
Lyme Park
Knott
YEW TREE RD
WOOD LA N
Mitchell Fold
4
85
3
84
2
83
1
82
93
94
95

63
38

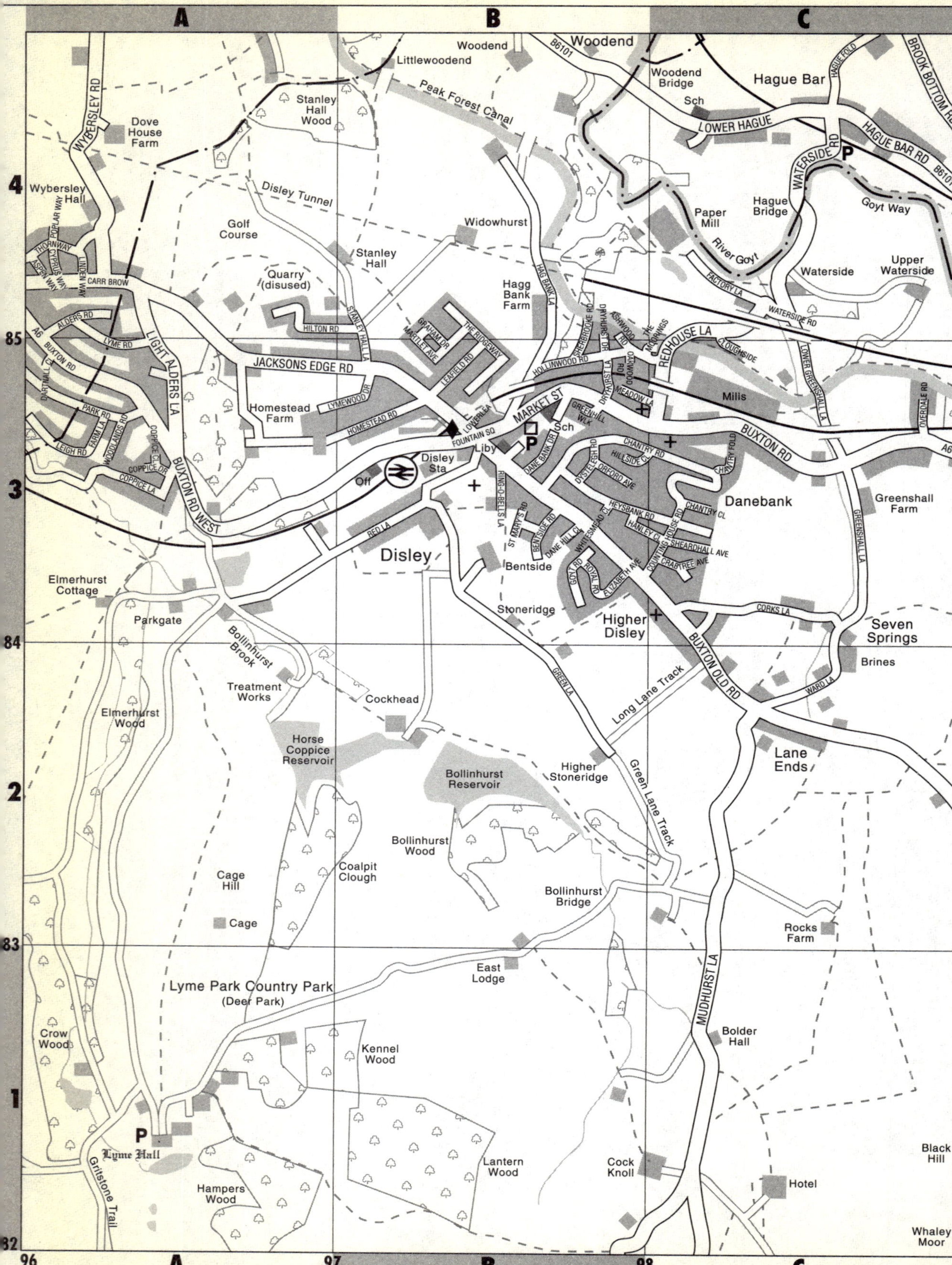
A
B
C
4
85
3
84
2
83
1
82
96
97
98
Woodend
Woodend
B6101
Littlewoodend
Peak Forest Canal
Woodend Bridge
Hague Bar
HAGUE FOLD
BROOK BOTTOM RD
Sch
LOWER HAGUE
HAGUE BAR RD
B6101
WATERSIDE RD
P
Goyt Way
Hague Bridge
Paper Mill
River Goyt
Waterside
Upper Waterside
FACTORY LA
WATERSIDE RD
Stanley Hall Wood
Dove House Farm
WYBERSLEY RD
Wybersley Hall
Disley Tunnel
Golf Course
Widowhurst
Stanley Hall
Quarry (disused)
Hagg Bank Farm
HAGG BANK LA
THORNWAY
POPLAR WAY
CYPRUS WAY
ASPEN WAY
LINDEN WAY
CARR BROW
ALDERS RD
LYME RD
LIGHT ALDERS LA
A6
BUXTON RD
DARTMILL CL
PARK RD
FARM LA
WOODLANDS RD
LEIGH RD
COPPICE CL
COPPICE DR
COPPICE LA
HILTON RD
STANLEY HALL LA
GRAHAM DR
MARTLET AVE
THE RIDGEWAY
LEAFIELD RD
JACKSONS EDGE RD
Homestead Farm
LYMEWOOD DR
HOMESTEAD RD
LOWERLEA
FOUNTAIN SQ
MARKET ST
Sch
P
GREENHILL WLK
HOLLINWOOD RD
HERBROOKE RD
DRYHURST DR
ASHWOOD RD
OAKWOOD RD
THE MOORINGS
REDHOUSE LA
CLOUGHSIDE
DRYHURST LA
MEADOW LA
Mills
LOWER GREENSHALL LA
OVERDALE RD
BUXTON RD
A6
CHANTRY RD
HILLSIDE CL
ORFORD AVE
DYSTELEGH RD
CHANTRY FOLD
Liby
Disley Sta
Off
DANE BANK DR
RING-O-BELLS LA
Danebank
CHANTRY CL
HEYSBANK RD
HANLEY CL
COUNTING HOUSE RD
SHEARDHALL AVE
CRABTREE AVE
Greenshall Farm
GREENSHALL LA
BUXTON RD WEST
RED LA
Disley
ST MARY'S RD
BENTSIDE RD
DANE HILL CL
WHITESMEAD CL
GOYT RD
ROYAL RD
ELIZABETH AVE
Bentside
Elmerhurst Cottage
Stoneridge
Higher Disley
CORKS LA
Seven Springs
Brines
Parkgate
Bollinhurst Brook
Treatment Works
Cockhead
GREEN LA
Long Lane Track
BUXTON OLD RD
WARD LA
Elmerhurst Wood
Horse Coppice Reservoir
Bollinhurst Reservoir
Higher Stoneridge
Green Lane Track
Lane Ends
Bollinhurst Wood
Coalpit Clough
Cage Hill
Cage
Bollinhurst Bridge
Rocks Farm
East Lodge
Lyme Park Country Park
(Deer Park)
MUDHURST LA
Crow Wood
Kennel Wood
Bolder Hall
P
Lyme Hall
Gritstone Trail
Lantern Wood
Cock Knoll
Black Hill
Hampers Wood
Hotel
Whaley Moor

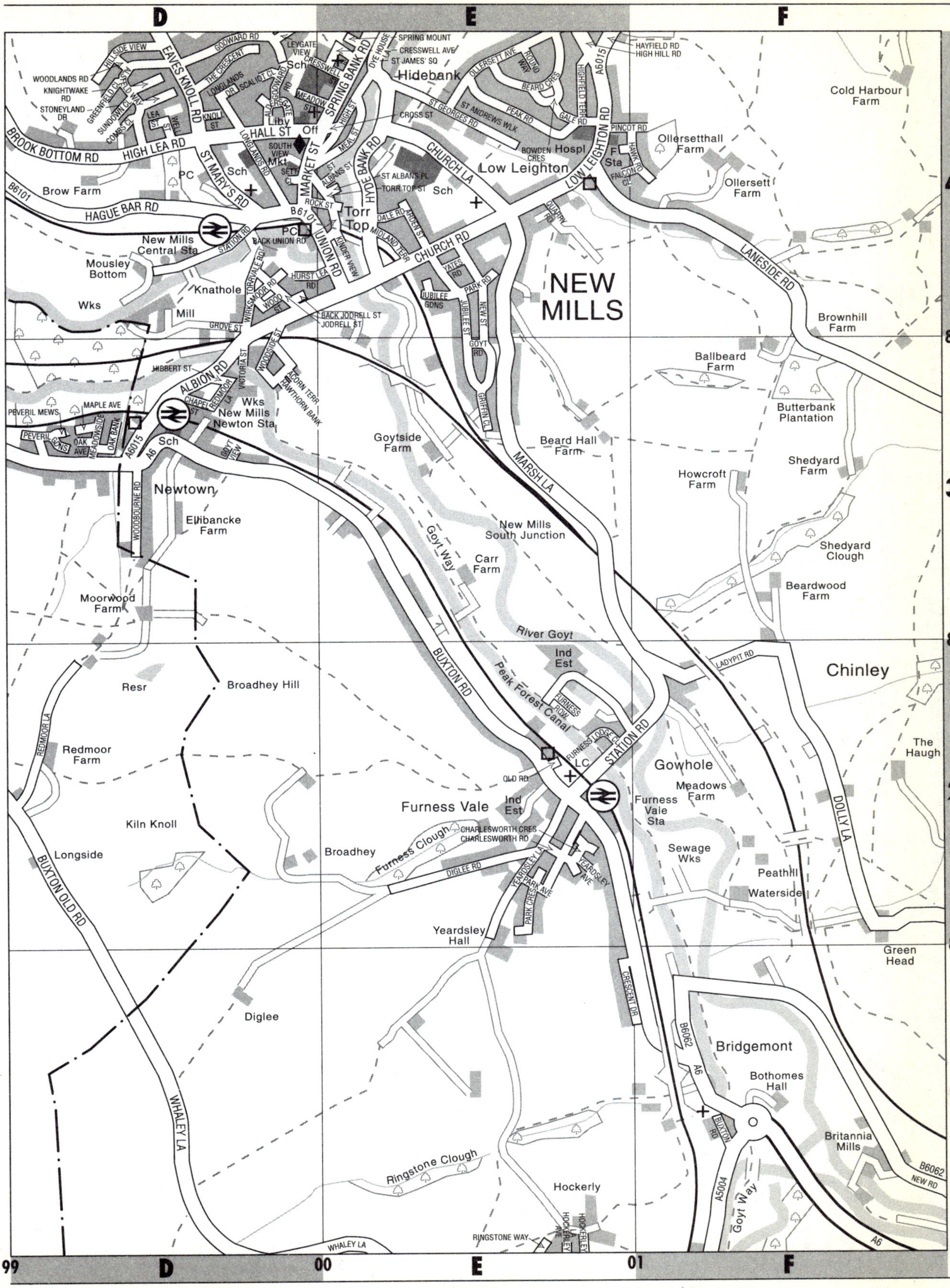
D
E
F
NEW MILLS
Hidebank
Low Leighton
Torr Top
Brow Farm
Mousley Bottom
Knathole
Wks
Mill
New Mills Central Sta
New Mills Newton Sta
Newtown
Ellibancke Farm
Moorwood Farm
Resr
Broadhey Hill
Redmoor Farm
Kiln Knoll
Longside
Broadhey
Diglee
Ringstone Clough
Hockerly
Yeardsley Hall
Furness Vale
Furness Clough
Ind Est
Furness Vale Sta
Gowhole
Meadows Farm
Sewage Wks
Peathill
Waterside
Bridgemont
Bothomes Hall
Britannia Mills
Green Head
The Haugh
Chinley
Beardwood Farm
Shedyard Clough
Shedyard Farm
Howcroft Farm
Butterbank Plantation
Ballbeard Farm
Brownhill Farm
Ollersett Farm
Ollersetthall Farm
Cold Harbour Farm
Beard Hall Farm
Goytside Farm
New Mills South Junction
Carr Farm
River Goyt
Goyt Way
Peak Forest Canal
BUXTON RD
MARSH LA
STATION RD
DOLLY LA
LADYPIT RD
LANESIDE RD
LOW LEIGHTON RD
CHURCH RD
CHURCH LA
HAGUE BAR RD
BROOK BOTTOM RD
HIGH LEA RD
ALBION RD
WHALEY LA
BUXTON OLD RD
REDMOOR LA
WOODBOURNE RD
CRESCENT DR
DIGLEE RD
HAYFIELD RD
HIGH HILL RD
A6
A6015
A5004
B6062
B6101
NEW RD
99
00
01
85
84
83
4
3
2
1

65

A
B
C
4
3
2
1
81
80
79
78
24
25
26
DEE SIDE
TARGET RD
Sewage Works
BROAD LA
MOSTYN AVE
THE MOORINGS
BANKS RD
P
PC
PIPER'S END
PIPER'S CL
WARREN AVE
SANDFIELD PARK
PIPER'S LA
CROSSLEY DR
CROFTSWAY
BUSHWAY
PIPER'S LA
DALESWAY
DELAVOR RD
TEALS WAY
HAWKS WAY
DELAVOR CL
ROOKS WAY
LINNETS WAY
GULLS WAY
WITTERING LA
QUEENS DR
PHILIPS WAY
BROOMLANDS
FEATHER LA
A540
Feather Lane
THURSTASTON RD
TELEGRAPH RD
PENSBY RD
CASTLE DR
THE MOUNT
MOUNT AVE
MOUNT HALL MEWS
ROCKY LA
DEE VIEW RD
WEST GR
Herberts La
Sch
THE HERMITAGE
FARR HILL RD
FARR HILL DR
Brow La
SCHOOL HILL
DAWSTONE RD
CHURCH MEADOW LA
CHURCH FARM CT
ST PETER'S CL
TITHEBARN
THE ROSCOTE
Wirral Way
DAVENPORT RD
PARK WEST
MARINE DR
RECTORY LA
RECTORY CL
RABY CL
THE LYDIATE
VILLAGE RD
ROSCOTE CL
WALLRAKE
HESSLE DR
BEECHFIELD CL
STRATHEARN RD
BROMLEY CL
STATION RD
RONALDSWAY
GAYTON RD
MEADWAY
WESTWAY
MANNERS LA
SEAFIELD AVE
HILBRE AVE
CLOSEBURN AVE
SEABANK RD
HESWALL
RIVERBANK CL
RIVERBANK RD
HINDERTON DR
VICTORIA AVE
WOODBURN DR
LONG MEADOW
LILLYFIELD
COTTAGE DR WEST
COTTAGE LA
COTTAGE DR EAST
River Dee
Gayton Sands

42

Heswall Sta
Hilldene
Thornton Manor
Manor Wood
The Beacons
Windmill (dis)
Sch
Gayton
New Hall Farm
Club House
Gayton Wood
Golf Course
Hotel
Westwood Farm
Westwood Grange Country Club
Backwood Hall Farm
Backwood Hall
Leighton Hall Farm
Ashfield Farm
Ashfield Hall Farm
Fiveways
Cedar Court
Wirral Way
Oakland Farm
Brook House
Clayhill Light Industrial Park
Sch
Parkgate
Schs
MILNER RD
TELEGRAPH RD
DAWSTONE RD
BASKERVYLE RD
WELL LA
GAYTON LA
GAYTON RD
CHESTER RD
CHESTER HIGH RD
PARKGATE LA
NESTON RD
LIVERPOOL RD
BOATHOUSE LA
THE RUNNELL
LEIGHTON RD
NORTH PARADE
THE PARADE
BARNSTON RD
BRIMSTAGE RD
GAYTON PARKWAY
WOOD LA
EARLE DR
A540
A551
A5137
B5135
B5136
4
3
2
1
81
80
79
78

66

42

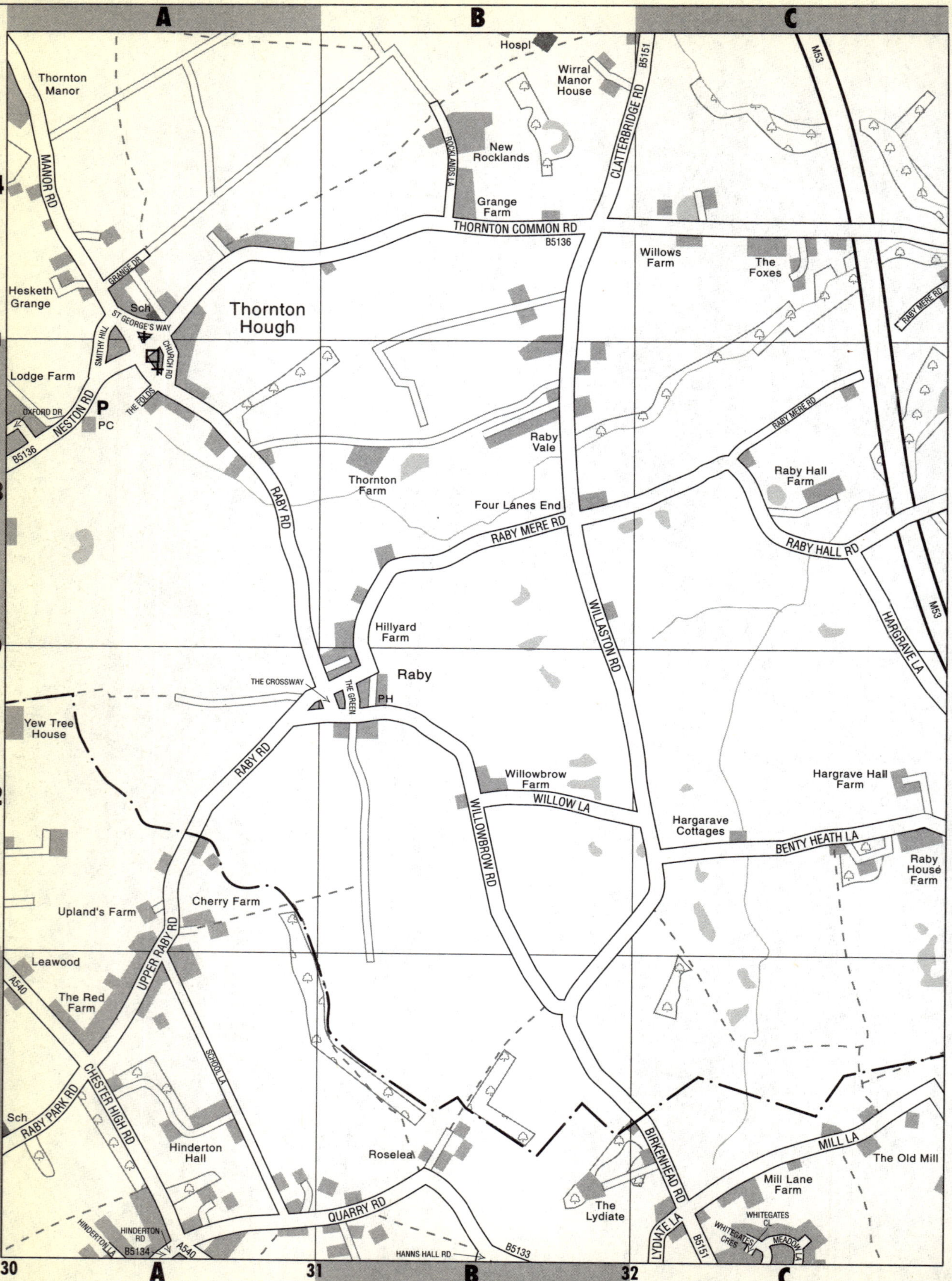
A
B
C
Hospl
Thornton Manor
Wirral Manor House
B5151
M53
MANOR RD
ROCKLANDS LA
New Rocklands
CLATTERBRIDGE RD
4
Grange Farm
THORNTON COMMON RD
B5136
Willows Farm
The Foxes
GRANGE DR
Hesketh Grange
Sch
Thornton Hough
ST GEORGE'S WAY
SMITHY HILL
CHURCH RD
RABY MERE RD
81
Lodge Farm
THE FOLDS
NESTON RD
P
OXFORD DR
PC
B5136
Raby Vale
RABY MERE RD
3
Thornton Farm
Raby Hall Farm
Four Lanes End
RABY RD
RABY MERE RD
RABY HALL RD
WILLASTON RD
Hillyard Farm
HARGRAVE LA
M53
80
Raby
THE CROSSWAY
THE GREEN
PH
Yew Tree House
RABY RD
Willowbrow Farm
Hargrave Hall Farm
2
WILLOW LA
Hargarave Cottages
BENTY HEATH LA
Raby House Farm
WILLOWBROW RD
Cherry Farm
Upland's Farm
UPPER RABY RD
79
Leawood
A540
The Red Farm
SCHOOL LA
1
CHESTER HIGH RD
RABY PARK RD
Sch
Hinderton Hall
Roselea
BIRKENHEAD RD
MILL LA
The Old Mill
Mill Lane Farm
QUARRY RD
The Lydiate
WHITEGATES CL
HINDERTON LA
HINDERTON RD
B5134
A540
HANNS HALL RD
B5133
LYDIATE LA
B5151
WHITEGATES CRES
MEADOW LA
78
30
A
31
B
32
C

44

D
E
F
Lancelyn Farm
The Vineyard Farm
Bromborough Rake Sta
1 BROTHERTON CL
2 WOODLAND WALK
3 ECCLESTON AVE
4 HADLEY AVE
THE RAKE
PARK VIEW
CHESTNUT GR
THE OAKS
THE AVENUE
MAPLE GR
BEECHWOOD RD
ASHFIELD RD
OAKFIELD RD
ASHFIELD CRES
ACRE LA
MARK RAKE
BRADMOOR RD
VALLEY RD
DALE AVE
OTELEY AVE
MAINWARING RD
FORWOOD RD
MOSSLEY AVE
Civic Hall
Liby
ALLPORT LA
GRATRIX RD
HEYS AVE
HAWTHORNE LA
MEADOWSIDE RD
ALLPORT LA
HOWARD AVE
PARKWOOD CL
JUNE AVE
HARROW GR
CAMBRIDGE RD
MENDELL CL
BROMBOROUGH VILLAGE
A41
1 GRASSMOOR CL
2 SHETLAND DR
WRYNOSE RD
HARDKNOTT RD
GRISEDALE RD
TEBAY RD
Green Lane
Sch
NEVILLE RD
AMBLESIDE CL
GLYN AVE
GORDON AVE
Sch
POULTON RD
POULTON HILL RD
Poulton Hall
THORNTON COMMON RD
Raby Mere
Clatter Brook
RABY MERE RD
KENT CL
MEADOW
RICKABY CL
GREENACRE DR
Acre Lane
CUNNINGHAM DR
GREENVILLE CRES
BLYTH RD
MARFORDS AVE
MARTEN AVE
MARLINE AVE
GREENFIELDS CRES
GREENFIELDS AVE
DAVPOOL DR
CALDICOTT AVE
BRANCOTE GDNS
ALLPORTS
THE PORTS
WOODYEAR RD
BRIDLE PARK
BRIDLE CL
WESTMINSTER DR
ALLPORT RD
DIBBINSDALE RD
DIBBINS GREEN
BARRYMORE WAY
MAELOR CL
DELL CL
ALDFORD CL
RABY CL
BLAKELEY CT
BLAKELEY DENE
RABY DR
ORMESBY GR
BLAKELEY BROW
BLAKELEY RD
FAIRLAWN CL
RABY AVE
LAWNS AVE
LINKS CL
MERE AVE
Bromborough Sta
P
ANDERSON CT
LIMEHURST GR
THE WOODCOTES
MORLAND AVE
Sch
MANOR RD
PRINCES AVE
KILBURN AVE
PCs
Cemy
BEBINGTON
Golf Course
BRIDLE RD
Raby Hall
RABY HALL RD
SOMERVILLE CL
BIRKDALE AVE
BRUCE CRES
ANGUS RD
Sch
ALISTAIR DR
SANDIWAY
AINSDALE CL
BROOKHURST RD
MALCOLM CRES
TAVENER CL
FAIRHAVEN DR
WENTWORTH DR
TROON CL
COTTAGE CL
WESTHOUSE CL
THE CHASE
Brookhurst
BROOKHURST CL
BROOKHURST AVE
BOWNESS AVE
CONISTON AVE
KESWICK AVE
KINTORE CL
TURRIFF DR
CULLEN CL
DUNCANSBY DR
NAIRN CL
CROSSDALE RD
DALE RD
GORSEFIELD CL
PORTREE AVE
BANFF AVE
KEITH DR
PLYMYARD CL
PLYMYARD AVE
PLYMYARD COPSE
CHESTERFIELD RD
REDCAR DR
HARROGATE RD
HARROGATE CL
SPRINGHILL AVE
DEARNFORD AVE
DEARNFORD CL
BRONINGTON AVE
REDBROOK
BETTISFIELD AVE
BRINLEY CL
LANGFIELD GR
OAKDENE CL
WOODLEE
EDGEWOOD DR
WHITE LODGE CL
HILARY RD
WINGATE RD
RAEBURN AVE
Eastham
ELGAR AVE
Sch
CH
Bromborough Golf Course
Dibbinsdale Brook
RIBBLESDALE CL
WHARFDALE DR
MILLERSDALE
PARK RD
ST DAVID RD
NEW CHESTER RD
CARLETT BVD
EASTHAM VILLAGE RD
HANDFORD AVE
MALLOWDALE CL
SWALEDALE CL
DARLEYDALE DR
HEYGARTH RD
EDALE CL
WENSLEYDALE AVE
AVONDALE AVE
Sch
ATHOL CL
ATHOL DR
RENFREW AVE
LONSDALE AVE
LINDALE AVE
SELKIRK AVE
PAISLEY AVE
GLENBURN AVE
ADASTON AVE
BERWICK AVE
GRAMPIAN WAY
Liby
P
STANLEY LA
CRANFORD CL
Sch
ROTHESAY DR
ARGYLL AVE
SUTHERLAND DR
AIRDRIE CL
BOWFELL CL
SCAFELL CL
EASTHAM RAKE
CALVELEY AVE
ENNERDALE AVE
DELEMERE AVE
STRETTON CL
Schs
CROSTHWAITE AVE
CRAIGLEIGH GR
BRAMHALL DR
THORNLEIGH AVE
DUNHAM CL
PICKMERE DR
A41
WELLINGTON AVE
HILL PARK DR
LARVIN RD
HELSBY AVE
KELSALL AVE
HORNLEIGH AVE
CLIFTON AVE
HATTON AVE
ASHTON CL
STOKE CL
PICTON CL
INCE AVE
PCs
BELTON CL
SUTTON CL
NORLEY AVE
KINGSLEY AVE
LOWFIELDS CL
LOWFIELDS AVE
M53
Hargrave House Farm
HARGRAVE LA
BENTY HEATH LA
M53
VERNON AVE
Hooton
HOOTON WAY
B5133
Street Hey
STREET HEY LA
DALE HEY
Hooton Bridge
SCHOOL LA
Hooton Farm
MILL LA
OAK RD
HOOTON RD
Hooton Sta
ROFTEN IND EST
WATERWORKS LA
FIELD HEY LA
BEECH HEY LA
LAUREL DR
HAWTHORNE DR
FIELD HEY LA
OVERDALE RD
WOOD LA
BRIARDALE RD
B5133
CROSBY GR
HEATH LA
4
81
3
80
2
79
1
78
33
34
35

68
44

43

A B C

A B C

43

69

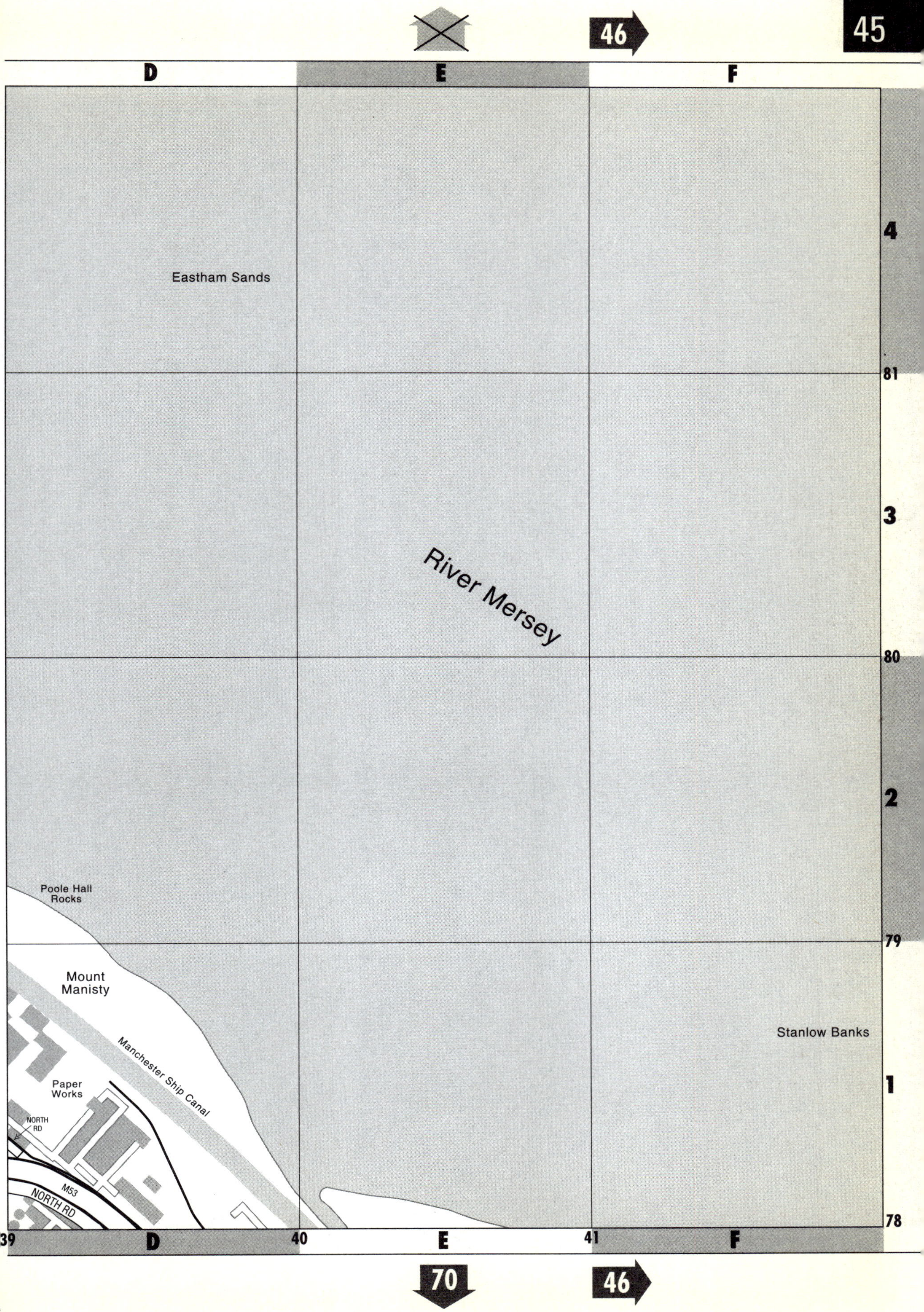
46
D
E
F
4
Eastham Sands
81
3
River Mersey
80
2
Poole Hall
Rocks
79
Mount
Manisty
Manchester Ship Canal
Stanlow Banks
Paper
Works
NORTH
RD
1
M53
NORTH RD
78
39
D
40
E
41
F
70
46

45

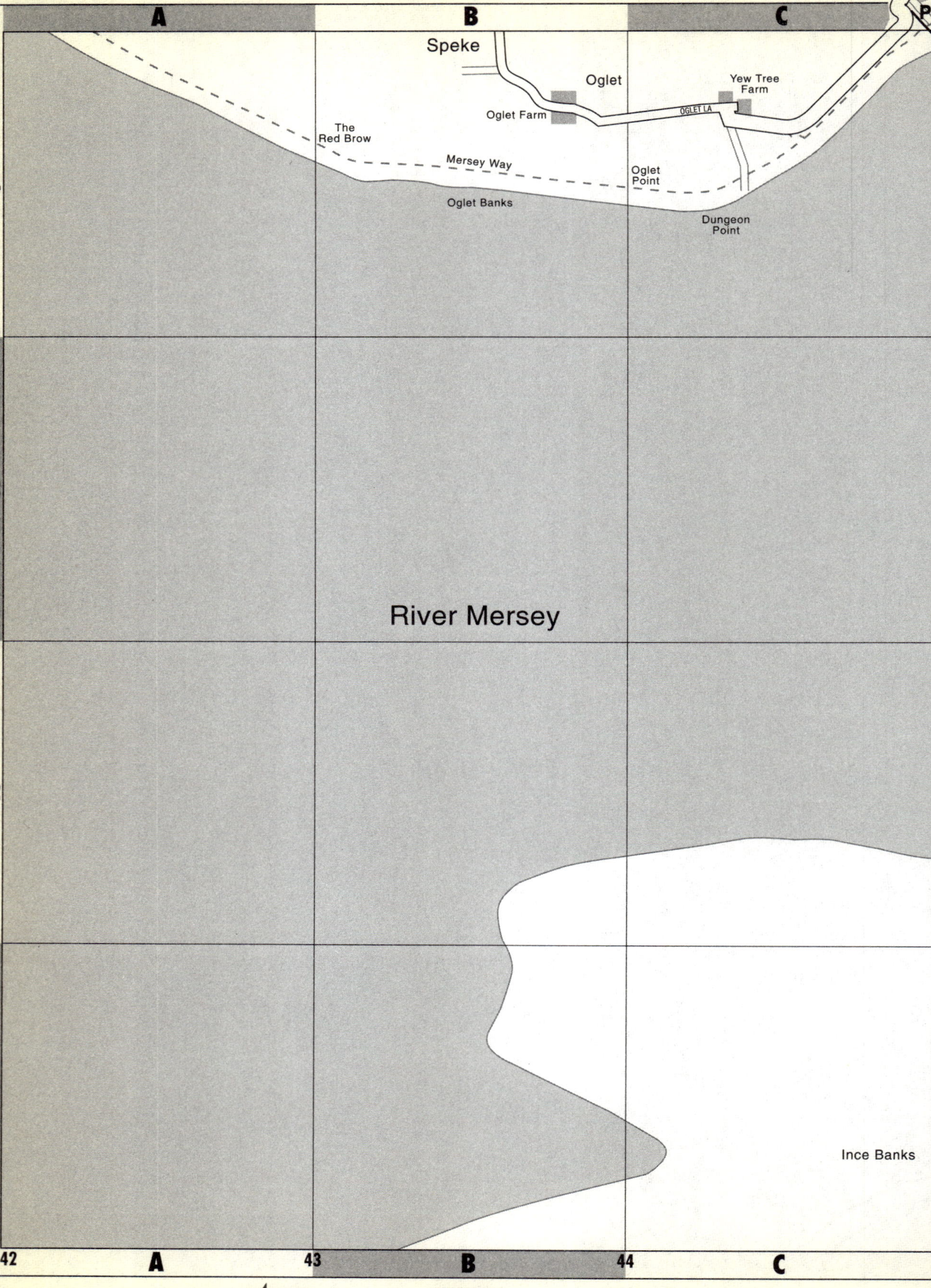
A
B
C
BAILEY'S L
P
Speke
Oglet
Yew Tree
Farm
Oglet Farm
OGLET LA
The
Red Brow
Mersey Way
Oglet
Point
Oglet Banks
Dungeon
Point
4
81
3
River Mersey
80
2
79
1
Ince Banks
78
42
43
44

45
71

21
48

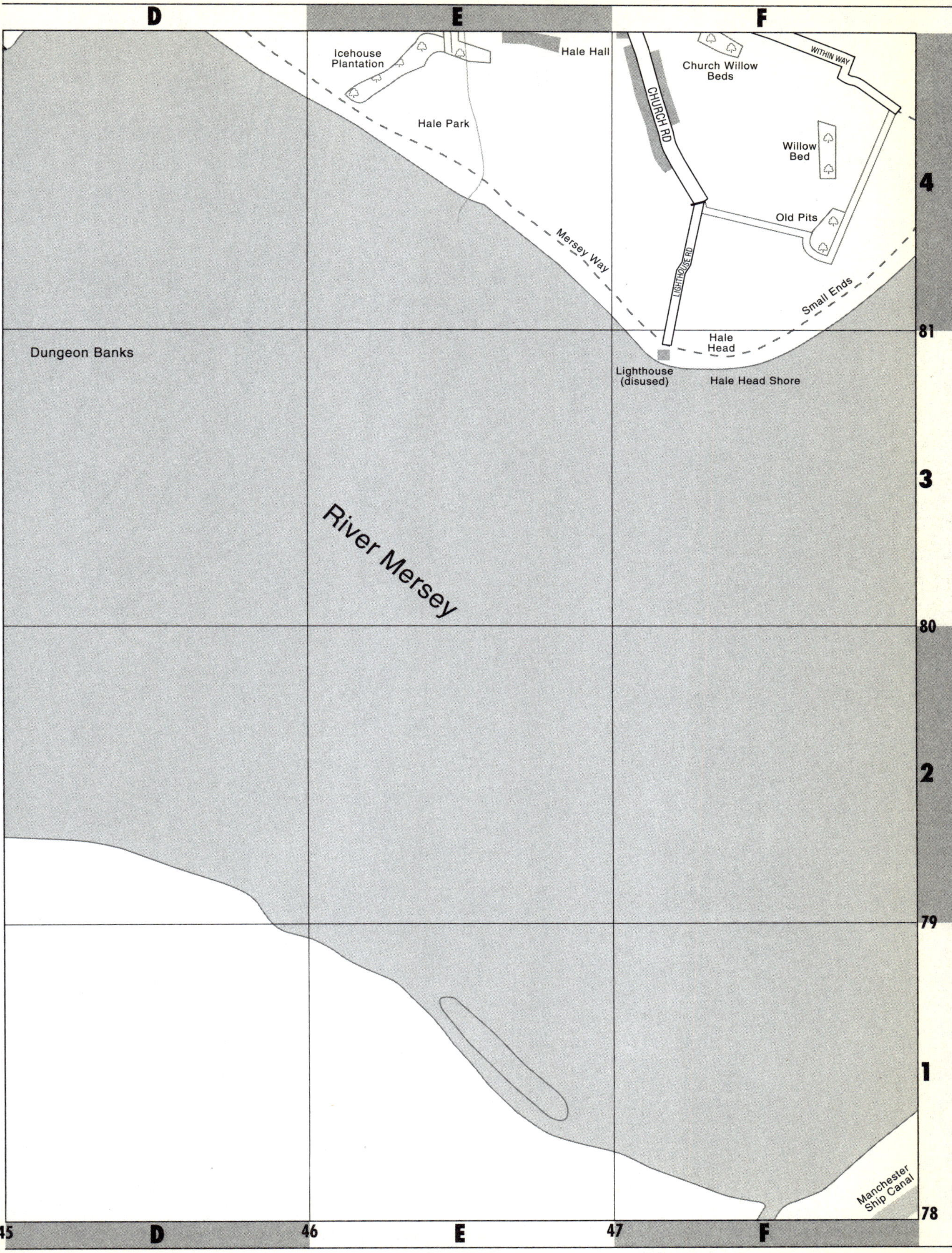
D
E
F
Icehouse Plantation
Hale Hall
Church Willow Beds
WITHIN WAY
CHURCH RD
Hale Park
Willow Bed
Old Pits
Mersey Way
LIGHTHOUSE RD
Small Ends
Hale Head
Lighthouse (disused)
Hale Head Shore
Dungeon Banks
River Mersey
Manchester Ship Canal
4
81
3
80
2
79
1
78
45
46
47

72
48

47
22

A
B
C
4
81
3
80
2
79
1
78
48
49
50
River Mersey
Docks
Runcorn & Western Canal (disused)
Works
PICOW FARM RD
A557
RUSSELL RD
LINGEFIELD RD
BEACONSFIELD RD
CUNNINGHAM DR
HALE VIEW
HILLSIDE AVE
CAMERON AVE
HAZEL AVE
PERRIN AVE
LANCASTER AVE
MINSTER CT
Beacon Hill
JOHNS AVE
Runcorn Hill (Public Park)
HIGHLANDS RD
ROYDEN AVE
COOMBE DR
PARK RD
Recn Gd
MERSEY VIEW
CLARKS TERR
BEACON HILL VIEW
SOUTH RD
LC
SANDY LA
POST OFFICE LA
WEST RD
BAKER RD
CULLEN RD
ALLEN RD
LEONARD ST
SYDNEY ST
ROSCOE CRES
CASTNER AVE
MATHER AVE
WESTON POINT EXPRESSWAY
WESTON RD
Sch
Weston Mersey Locks
Swing Bridge
CANAL SIDE
SOUTH PAR
Weston Point
LYDIATE LA
CHESHYRE'S LA
COLLIER'S ROW
WESTON CT
Sewage Works
ASHTON CL 1
CRESTA DR 2
COMPANY'S CL 3
MONTPELIER AVE 4
LAMBSICKLE CL 5
HEATH RD S
WESTON CRES
MARION DR
LAMBSICKLE LA
TILDSLEY CRES
BANKES' LA
Weston
Manchester Ship Canal
Works
Weaver Navigation
Weaver Sluices
Works
Weston Marsh Lock
River Weaver
ALDER LA
Frodsham Marsh Farm
Frodsham Marsh
BROOK FURLONG
Frodsham Score
Manchester Ship Canal
Canal Deposit Dump
Jetties
MOORDITCH LA
TADGERS LA
MOORDITCH LA

47
73

23
50

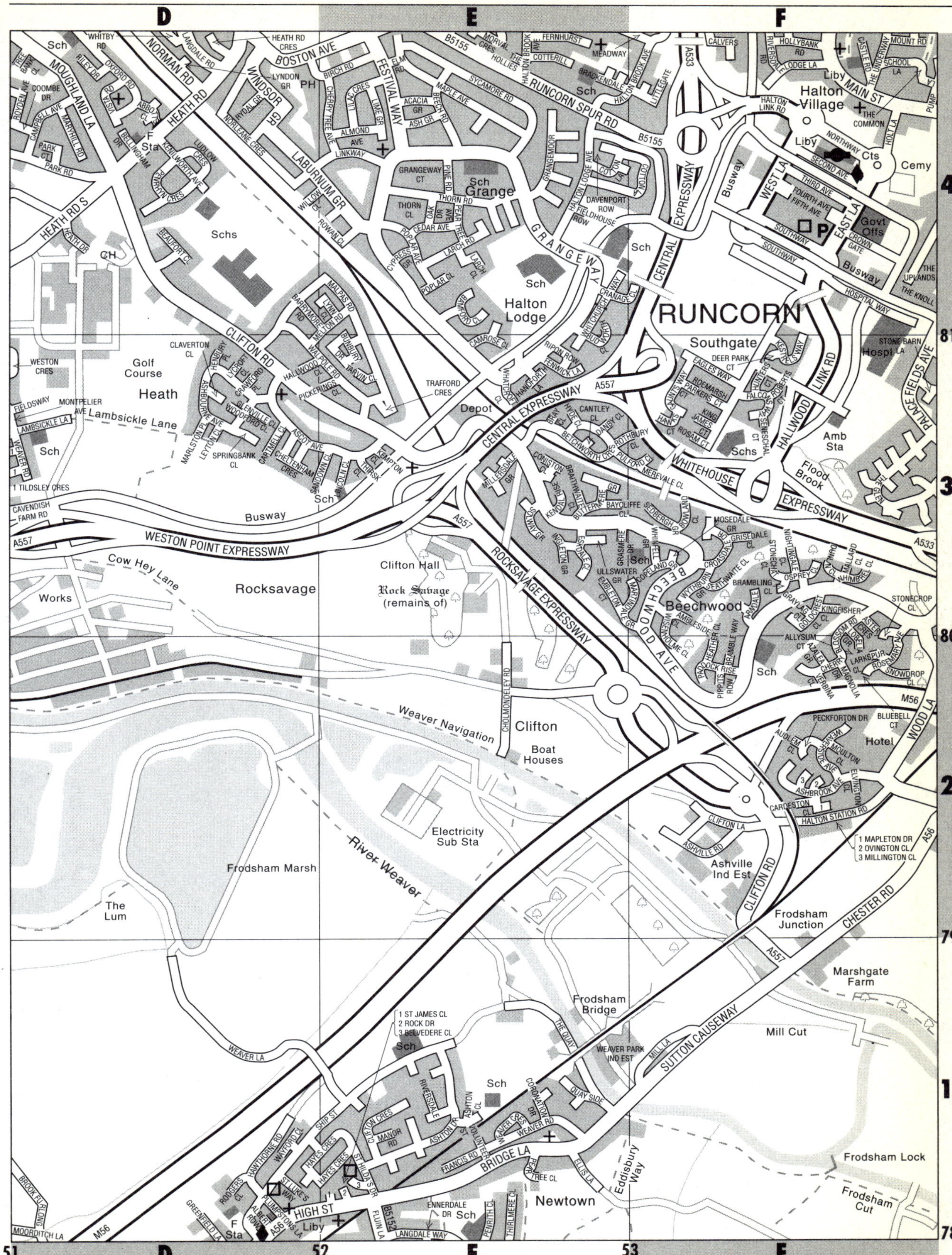
D
E
F
RUNCORN
Halton Village
Halton Lodge
Grange
Southgate
Heath
Golf Course
Rocksavage
Clifton Hall
Rock Savage (remains of)
Beechwood
Clifton
Boat Houses
Weaver Navigation
River Weaver
Frodsham Marsh
The Lum
Electricity Sub Sta
Ashville Ind Est
Frodsham Junction
Marshgate Farm
Mill Cut
Frodsham Bridge
Weaver Park Ind Est
Frodsham Lock
Frodsham Cut
Newtown
Works
Depot
Hospl
Hotel
Amb Sta
Flood Brook
Cemy
Govt Offs
Cts
Liby
Schs
Sch
PH
CH
F Sta
CENTRAL EXPRESSWAY
WESTON POINT EXPRESSWAY
ROCKSAVAGE EXPRESSWAY
WHITEHOUSE EXPRESSWAY
RUNCORN SPUR RD
Busway
Cow Hey Lane
Lambsickle Lane
HEATH RD
HEATH RD S
CLIFTON RD
NORMAN RD
MOUGHLAND LA
BOSTON AVE
WINDSOR GR
LABURNUM GR
FESTIVAL WAY
GRANGEWAY
BEECHWOOD AVE
HALLWOOD LINK RD
PALACE FIELDS AVE
SUTTON CAUSEWAY
CHESTER RD
WOOD LA
HALTON STATION RD
HIGH ST
BRIDGE LA
WEAVER LA
CHOLMONDELEY RD
MAIN ST
Eddisbury Way
A557
A533
A56
M56
B5155
B5152
1 TILDSLEY CRES
1 MAPLETON DR
2 OVINGTON CL
3 MILLINGTON CL
1 ST JAMES CL
2 ROCK DR
3 BELVEDERE CL
4
3
2
1
81
80
79
78
51
52
53

74
50

49
24

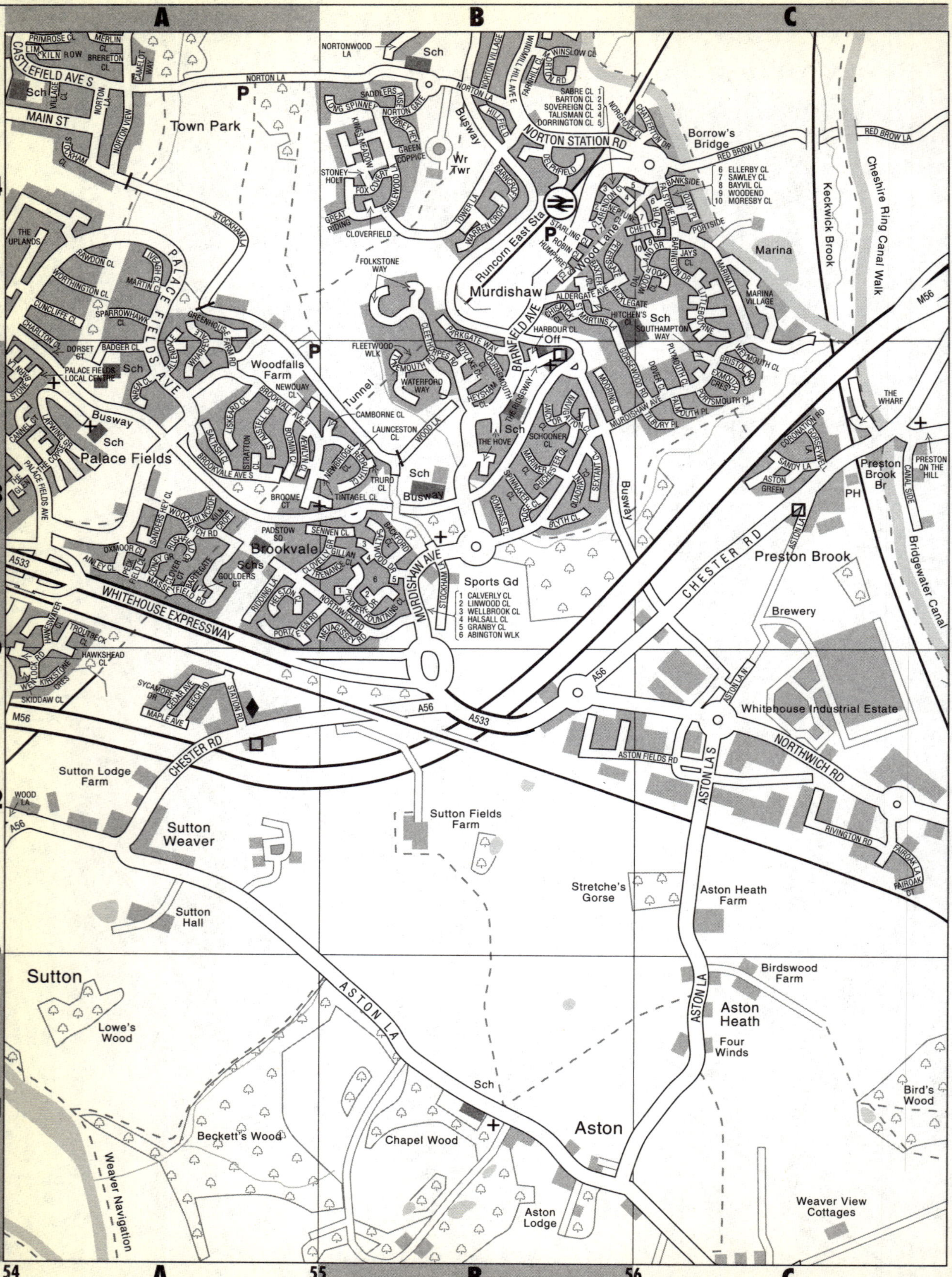

A
B
C
4
81
3
80
2
79
1
78
54
55
56
Town Park
Murdishaw
Woodfalls Farm
Palace Fields
Brookvale
Borrow's Bridge
Marina
Marina Village
Preston Brook
Preston Brook Br
Brewery
Whitehouse Industrial Estate
Sutton Lodge Farm
Sutton Weaver
Sutton Hall
Sutton Fields Farm
Stretche's Gorse
Aston Heath Farm
Birdswood Farm
Aston Heath
Four Winds
Sutton
Lowe's Wood
Beckett's Wood
Chapel Wood
Aston
Aston Lodge
Weaver View Cottages
Bird's Wood
Weaver Navigation
Keckwick Brook
Cheshire Ring Canal Walk
Bridgewater Canal
Sports Gd
Runcorn East Sta
Wood Lane
Busway
Tunnel
Wr Twr
NORTON LA
NORTON STATION RD
MAIN ST
CASTLEFIELD AVE S
PALACE FIELDS AVE
STOCKHAM LA
BARNFIELD AVE
MURDISHAW AVE
WHITEHOUSE EXPRESSWAY
CHESTER RD
ASTON LA
ASTON LA S
NORTHWICH RD
ASTON FIELDS RD
RIVINGTON RD
RED BROW LA
M56
A56
A533
SABRE CL 1
BARTON CL 2
SOVEREIGN CL 3
TALISMAN CL 4
DORRINGTON CL 5
6 ELLERBY CL
7 SAWLEY CL
8 BAYVIL CL
9 WOODEND
10 MORESBY CL
1 CALVERLY CL
2 LINWOOD CL
3 WELLBROOK CL
4 HALSALL CL
5 GRANBY CL
6 ABINGTON WLK

25
52

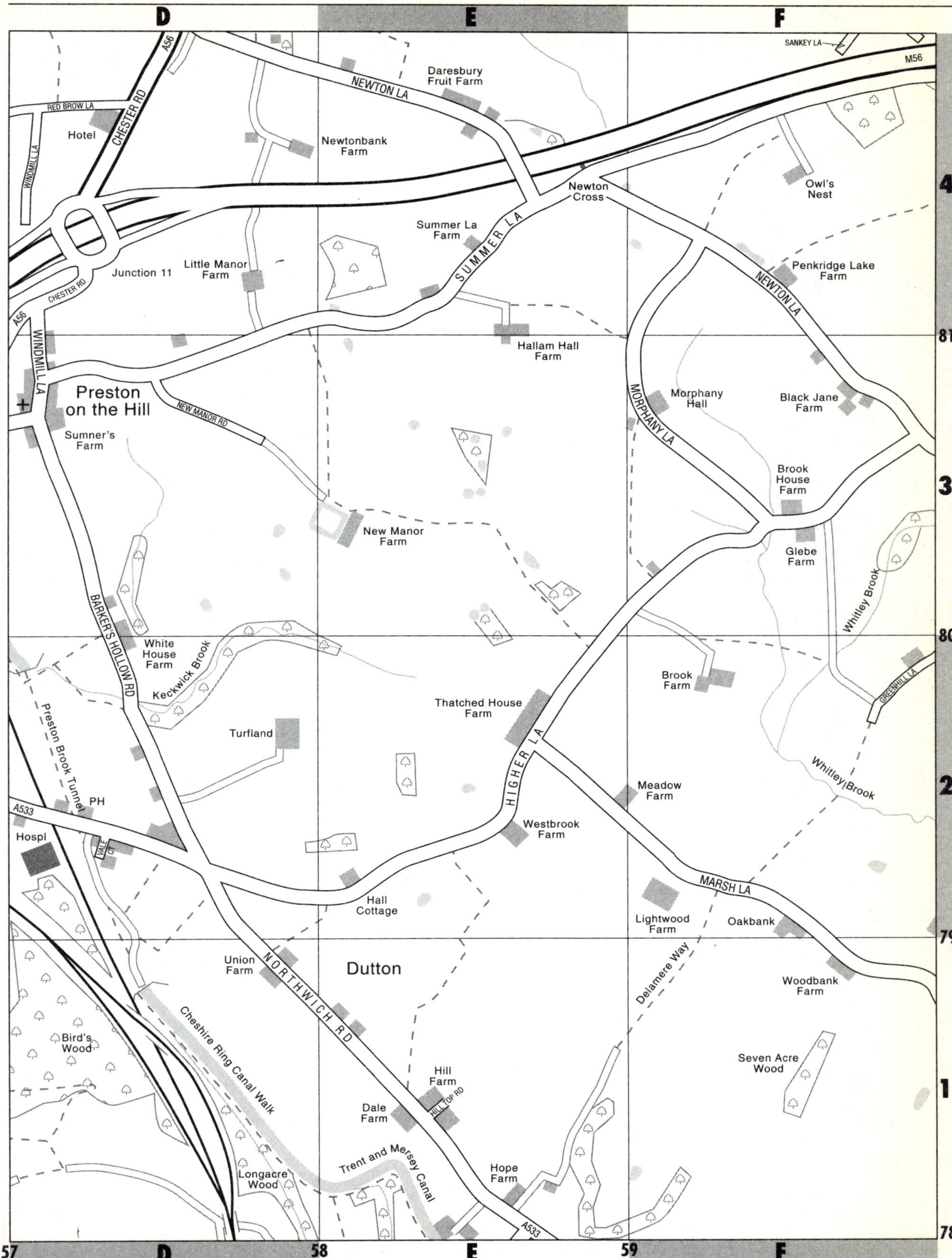
D
E
F
4
81
3
80
2
79
1
78
57
58
59
SANKEY LA
M56
Daresbury
Fruit Farm
NEWTON LA
A56
RED BROW LA
Hotel
CHESTER RD
WINDMILL LA
Newtonbank
Farm
Newton
Cross
Owl's
Nest
Summer La
Farm
SUMMER LA
Junction 11
Little Manor
Farm
CHESTER RD
A56
Penkridge Lake
Farm
NEWTON LA
WINDMILL LA
Hallam Hall
Farm
Preston
on the Hill
NEW MANOR RD
Sumner's
Farm
MORPHANY LA
Morphany
Hall
Black Jane
Farm
Brook
House
Farm
New Manor
Farm
Glebe
Farm
Whitley Brook
BARKER'S HOLLOW RD
White
House
Farm
Keckwick Brook
Preston Brook Tunnel
Brook
Farm
GREENHILL LA
Thatched House
Farm
Turfland
HIGHER LA
Whitley Brook
Meadow
Farm
A533
PH
Hospl
VALE CT
Westbrook
Farm
MARSH LA
Hall
Cottage
Lightwood
Farm
Oakbank
Union
Farm
NORTHWICH RD
Dutton
Delamere Way
Woodbank
Farm
Cheshire Ring Canal Walk
Bird's
Wood
Seven Acre
Wood
Hill
Farm
HILL TOP RD
Dale
Farm
Trent and Mersey Canal
Longacre
Wood
Hope
Farm
A533

76
52

51
26

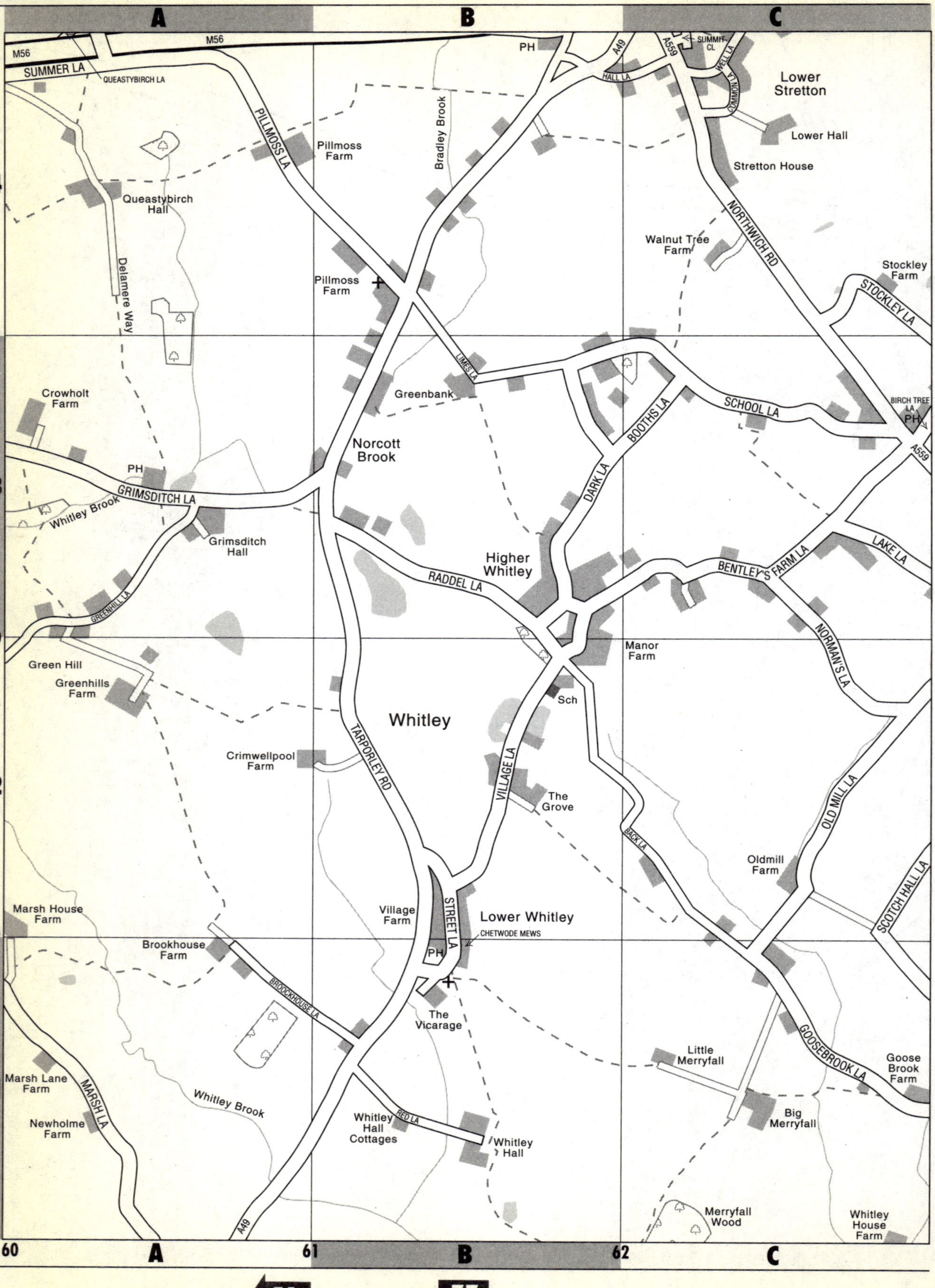
A
B
C
M56
SUMMER LA
QUEASTYBIRCH LA
PH
A49
A559
SUMMIT CL
HALL LA
WELL LA
COMMON LA
Lower Stretton
Lower Hall
Stretton House
PILLMOSS LA
Pillmoss Farm
Bradley Brook
Queastybirch Hall
NORTHWICH RD
Walnut Tree Farm
Stockley Farm
STOCKLEY LA
Delamere Way
Pillmoss Farm
4
81
LIMES LA
Greenbank
Crowholt Farm
SCHOOL LA
BIRCH TREE LA
PH
A559
BOOTHS LA
Norcott Brook
PH
GRIMSDITCH LA
DARK LA
3
Whitley Brook
Grimsditch Hall
Higher Whitley
LAKE LA
BENTLEY'S FARM LA
RADDEL LA
GREENHILL LA
80
Manor Farm
NORMAN'S LA
Green Hill
Greenhills Farm
Sch
Whitley
Crimwellpool Farm
TARPORLEY RD
VILLAGE LA
2
The Grove
OLD MILL LA
BACK LA
Oldmill Farm
SCOTCH HALL LA
Marsh House Farm
Village Farm
STREET LA
Lower Whitley
79
Brookhouse Farm
CHETWODE MEWS
PH
BROOKHOUSE LA
The Vicarage
GOOSEBROOK LA
Little Merryfall
Goose Brook Farm
1
Marsh Lane Farm
MARSH LA
Whitley Brook
Newholme Farm
Whitley Hall Cottages
RED LA
Whitley Hall
Big Merryfall
Merryfall Wood
Whitley House Farm
A49
78
60
61
62

51
77

D E F

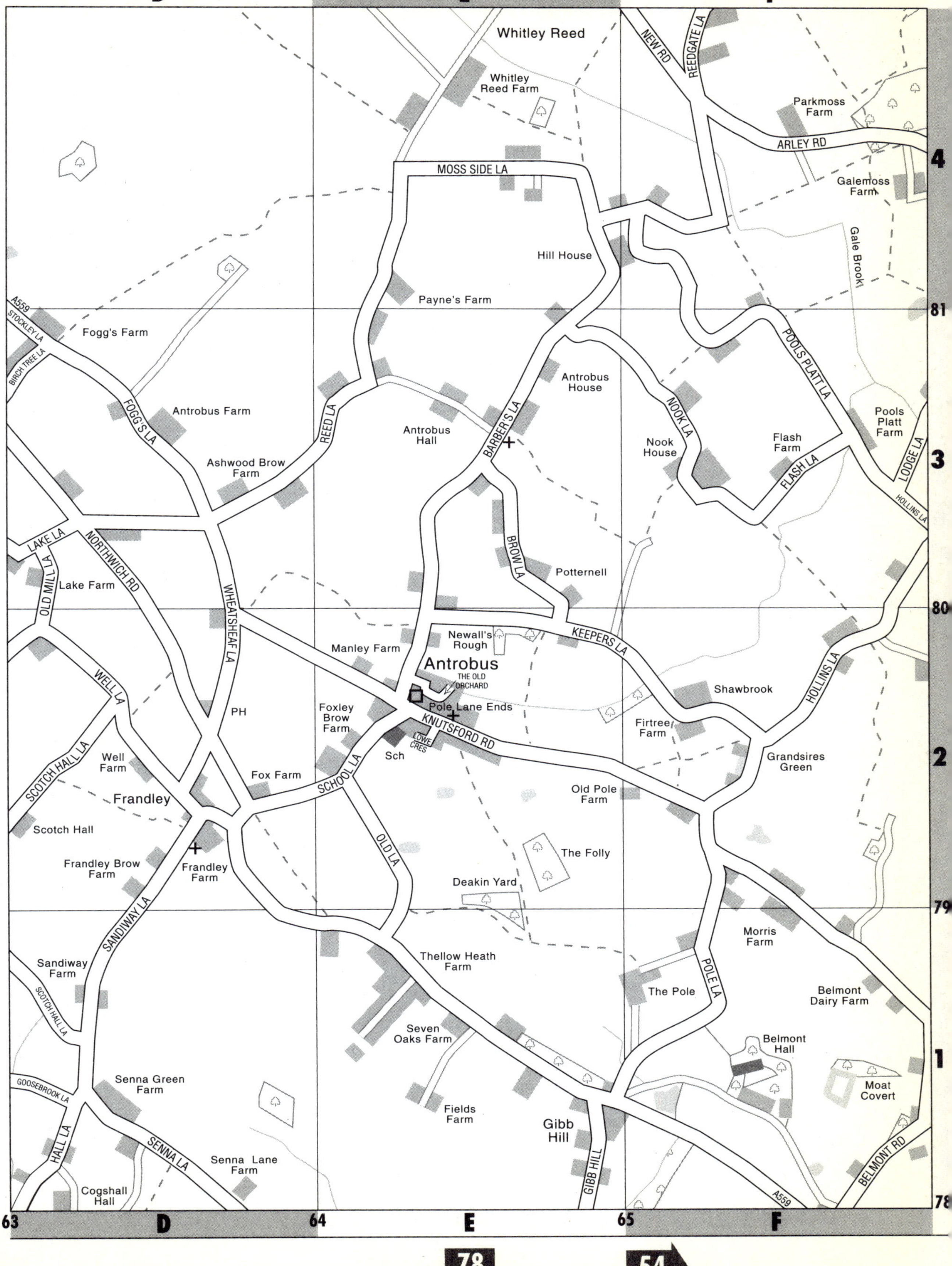
Whitley Reed
Whitley Reed Farm
NEW RD
REEDGATE LA
Parkmoss Farm
ARLEY RD
Galemoss Farm
MOSS SIDE LA
Hill House
Gale Brook
Payne's Farm
A559
STOCKLEY LA
BIRCH TREE LA
Fogg's Farm
Antrobus House
POOLS PLATT LA
FOGG'S LA
Antrobus Farm
Antrobus Hall
BARBER'S LA
NOOK LA
Nook House
Flash Farm
Pools Platt Farm
REED LA
Ashwood Brow Farm
FLASH LA
LODGE LA
HOLLINS LA
LAKE LA
NORTHWICH RD
OLD MILL LA
Lake Farm
WHEATSHEAF LA
BROW LA
Potternell
Newall's Rough
KEEPERS LA
Manley Farm
Antrobus
THE OLD ORCHARD
Shawbrook
HOLLINS LA
WELL LA
PH
Foxley Brow Farm
Pole Lane Ends
KNUTSFORD RD
LOWE CRES
Sch
Firtree Farm
SCOTCH HALL LA
Well Farm
Fox Farm
SCHOOL LA
Grandsires Green
Frandley
Old Pole Farm
Scotch Hall
OLD LA
The Folly
Frandley Brow Farm
Frandley Farm
Deakin Yard
SANDIWAY LA
Morris Farm
Thellow Heath Farm
Sandiway Farm
SCOTCH HALL LA
The Pole
POLE LA
Belmont Dairy Farm
Seven Oaks Farm
Belmont Hall
GOOSEBROOK LA
Senna Green Farm
Moat Covert
Fields Farm
Gibb Hill
HALL LA
SENNA LA
Senna Lane Farm
GIBB HILL
BELMONT RD
A559
Cogshall Hall
4
81
3
80
2
79
1
78
63
64
65

D E F

53
28

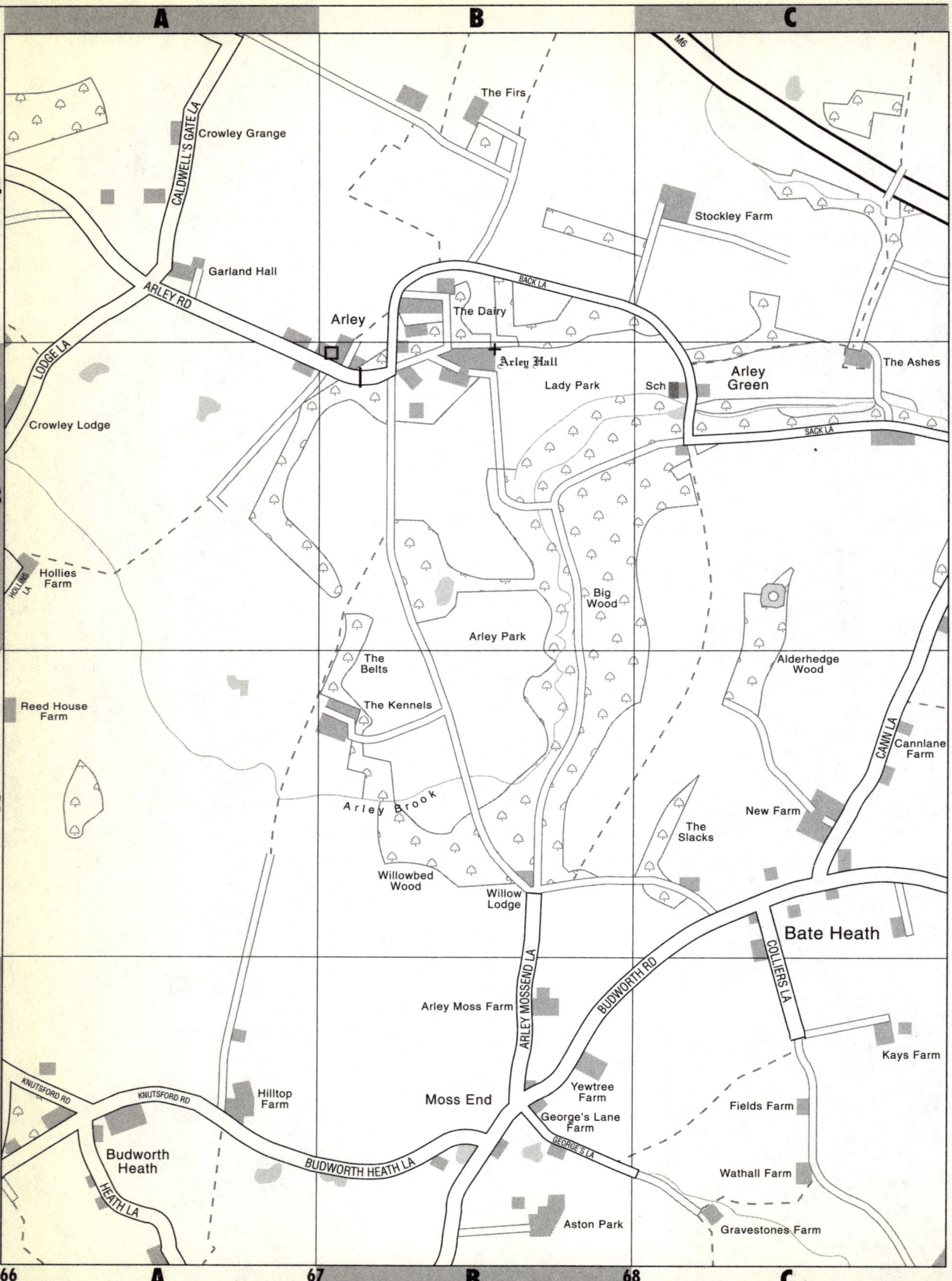
A
B
C
M6
The Firs
Crowley Grange
CALDWELL'S GATE LA
4
Stockley Farm
Garland Hall
ARLEY RD
BACK LA
Arley
The Dairy
81
LODGE LA
Arley Hall
Lady Park
Sch
Arley Green
The Ashes
Crowley Lodge
SACK LA
3
Hollies Farm
HOLLINS LA
Big Wood
Arley Park
80
The Belts
Alderhedge Wood
Reed House Farm
The Kennels
CANN LA
Cannlane Farm
2
Arley Brook
New Farm
The Slacks
Willowbed Wood
Willow Lodge
Bate Heath
79
COLLIERS LA
ARLEY MOSSEND LA
BUDWORTH RD
Arley Moss Farm
Kays Farm
KNUTSFORD RD
KNUTSFORD RD
Hilltop Farm
Yewtree Farm
Moss End
1
Fields Farm
George's Lane Farm
Budworth Heath
GEORGE'S LA
BUDWORTH HEATH LA
Wathall Farm
HEATH LA
Aston Park
Gravestones Farm
78
66
A
67
B
68
C

53
79

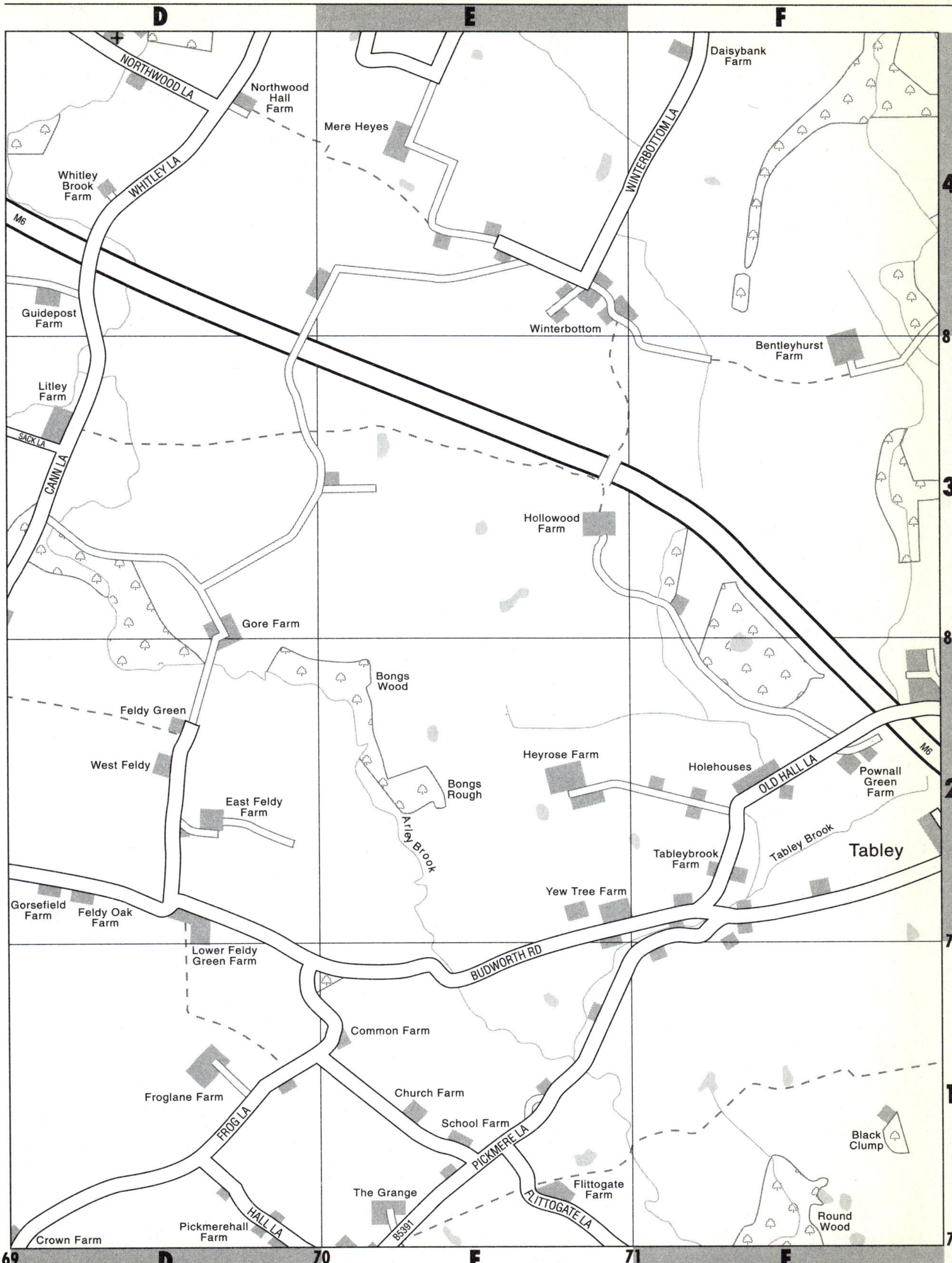
D
E
F
NORTHWOOD LA
Northwood Hall Farm
Mere Heyes
Daisybank Farm
WINTERBOTTOM LA
Whitley Brook Farm
WHITLEY LA
M6
Guidepost Farm
Winterbottom
Bentleyhurst Farm
Litley Farm
SACK LA
CANN LA
Hollowood Farm
Gore Farm
Bongs Wood
Feldy Green
West Feldy
Heyrose Farm
Holehouses
OLD HALL LA
Pownall Green Farm
M6
Bongs Rough
East Feldy Farm
Arley Brook
Tabley Brook
Tabley
Tableybrook Farm
Yew Tree Farm
Gorsefield Farm
Feldy Oak Farm
Lower Feldy Green Farm
BUDWORTH RD
Common Farm
Froglane Farm
Church Farm
School Farm
FROG LA
PICKMERE LA
Black Clump
The Grange
Flittogate Farm
FLITTOGATE LA
HALL LA
Pickmerehall Farm
B5391
Round Wood
Crown Farm
4
81
3
80
2
79
1
78
69
70
71
D
E
F

55
30

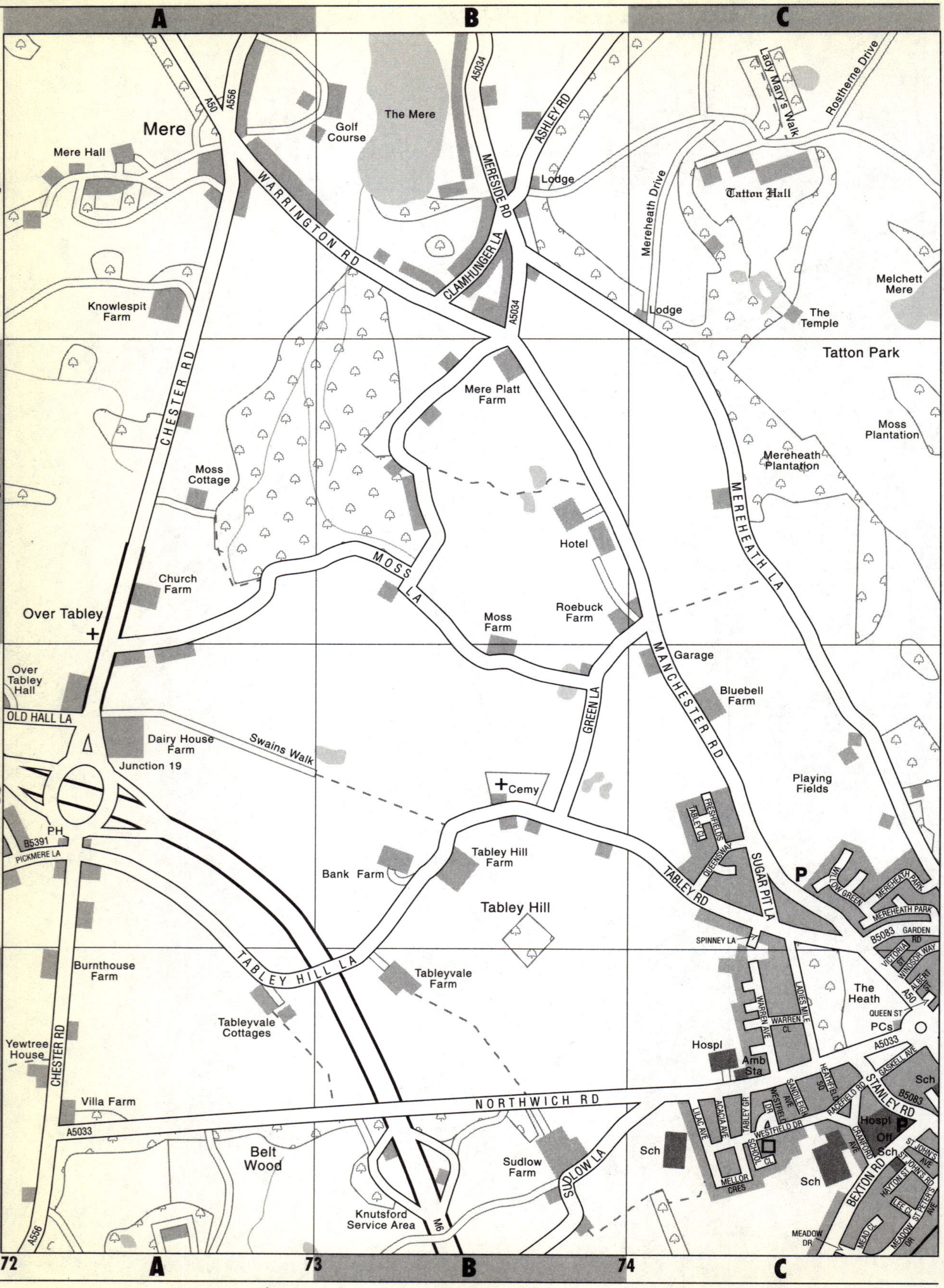
A
B
C
Mere
Mere Hall
Golf Course
The Mere
A50
A556
A5034
ASHLEY RD
MERESIDE RD
WARRINGTON RD
CLAMHUNGER LA
Lodge
Lady Mary's Walk
Rostherne Drive
Mereheath Drive
Tatton Hall
Melchett Mere
The Temple
Lodge
Tatton Park
Knowlespit Farm
CHESTER RD
Mere Platt Farm
Moss Plantation
Mereheath Plantation
Moss Cottage
MERHEATH LA
Hotel
MOSS LA
Church Farm
Over Tabley
Moss Farm
Roebuck Farm
Over Tabley Hall
Garage
Bluebell Farm
OLD HALL LA
Dairy House Farm
Swains Walk
GREEN LA
MANCHESTER RD
Junction 19
Cemy
Playing Fields
PH
B5391
PICKMERE LA
FRESHFIELDS
TABLEY CL
QUEENSWAY
SUGAR PIT LA
P
WILLOW GREEN
MEREHEATH PARK
MEREHEATH PARK
Tabley Hill Farm
Bank Farm
TABLEY RD
Tabley Hill
B5083
GARDEN RD
SPINNEY LA
VICTORIA ST
WINDSOR WAY
TABLEY HILL LA
Burnthouse Farm
Tableyvale Farm
LADIES MILE
WARREN AVE
The Heath
ALBERT ST
A50
QUEEN ST
WARREN CL
Tableyvale Cottages
PCs
A5033
Yewtree House
CHESTER RD
Hospl
Amb Sta
GASKELL AVE
HEATHFIELD SQ
SANDILEIGH AVE
Sch
STANLEY RD
B5083
Villa Farm
NORTHWICH RD
LILAC AVE
ACACIA AVE
TABLEY GR
DR
WESTFIELD
WESTFIELD DR
RACEFIELD RD
CRANFORD AVE
Hospl
P
Off
A5033
Belt Wood
SCHOOL CL
Sch
ST JOHN'S AVE
Sudlow Farm
SUDLOW LA
Sch
MELLOR CRES
Sch
BEXTON RD
HAYTON ST
ST JOHN'S RD
LEE CL
ST PETER'S AVE
MEADOW DR
Knutsford Service Area
M6
A556
MEADOW DR
MEAD CL
4
81
3
80
2
79
1
78
72
73
74
A
B
C

55
81

31
58

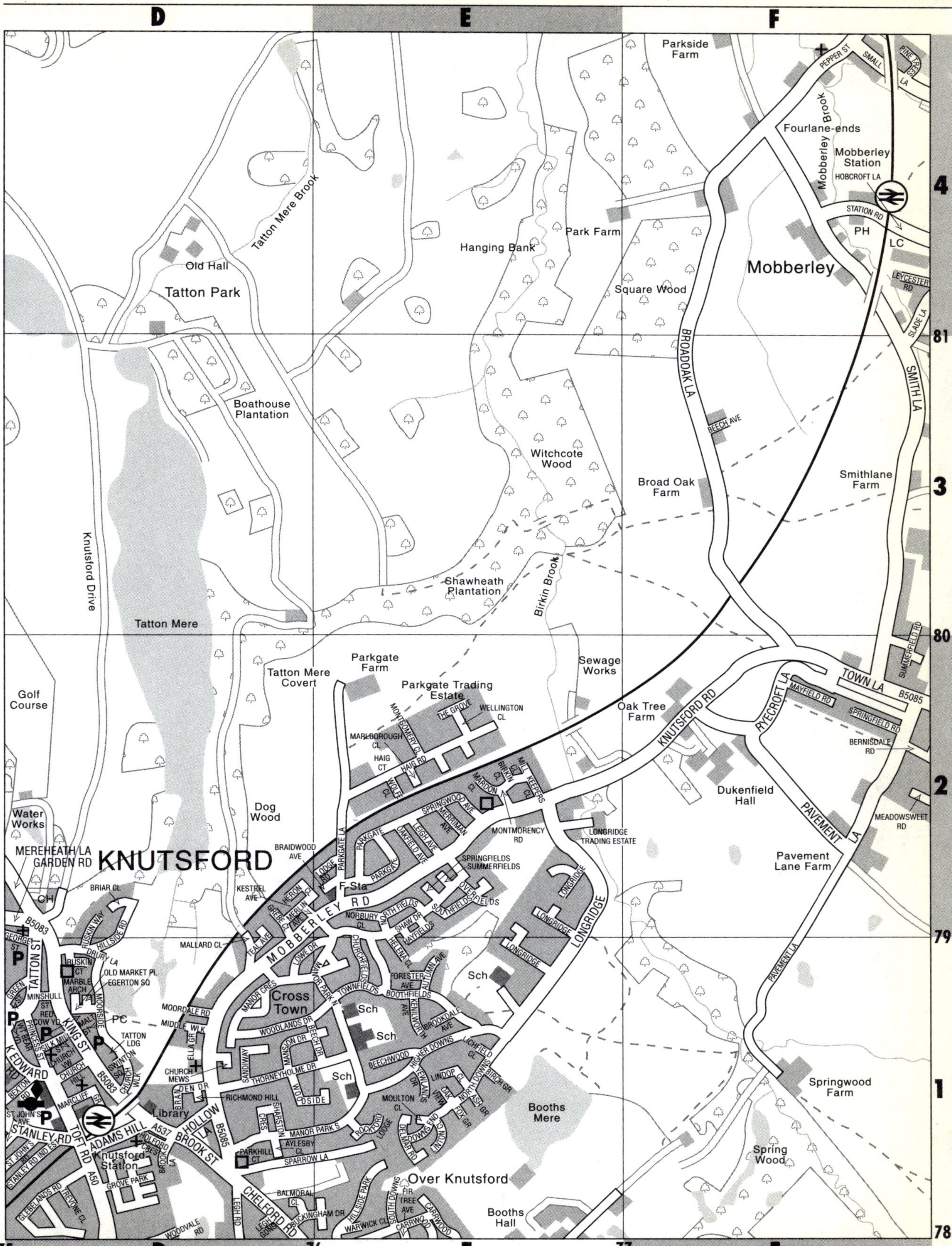
D
E
F
Parkside Farm
Fourlane-ends
Mobberley Brook
Mobberley Station
HOBCROFT LA
STATION RD
PEPPER ST
SMALL
PINE TREES
PH
LC
Mobberley
LEYCESTER RD
SLADE LA
SMITH LA
Tatton Mere Brook
Old Hall
Tatton Park
Hanging Bank
Park Farm
Square Wood
BROADOAK LA
BEECH AVE
Boathouse Plantation
Witchcote Wood
Broad Oak Farm
Smithlane Farm
Knutsford Drive
Shawheath Plantation
Birkin Brook
Tatton Mere
SUMMERFIELDS RD
Golf Course
Parkgate Farm
Tatton Mere Covert
Parkgate Trading Estate
Sewage Works
TOWN LA
B5085
MAYFIELD RD
SPRINGFIELD RD
BERNISDALE RD
Oak Tree Farm
KNUTSFORD RD
RYECROFT LA
WELLINGTON CL
THE GROVE
MONTGOMERY CL
MARLBOROUGH CL
HAIG CT
HAIG RD
WOLFE CL
MILL KEEPERS
BIRKIN CL
MARDON CL
Dukenfield Hall
PAVEMENT LA
MEADOWSWEET RD
Water Works
Dog Wood
SPRINGWOOD AVE
MERRIMAN AVE
MONTMORENCY RD
LONGRIDGE TRADING ESTATE
MEREHEATH LA
GARDEN RD
KNUTSFORD
BRAIDWOOD AVE
PARKGATE LA
LODGE RD
PARKGATE
OAKFIELD AVE
LEIGH AVE
SPRINGFIELDS
SUMMERFIELDS
Pavement Lane Farm
BRIAR CL
KESTREL AVE
HERON CL
MERLIN AVE
GREBE CL
F Sta
MOBBERLEY RD
NORBURY CL
NORTHFIELDS
SOUTHFIELDS
OVERFIELDS
LONGRIDGE
CH
B5083
GEORGE ST
TATTON ST
RUSKIN WY
HILLSIDE RD
DRURY LA
MALLARD CL
TEAL AVE
LOWE DR
CHURCHFIELDS
SHAW DR
HAYFIELDS
HELENA CL
FORESTER AVE
AUTUMN AVE
Sch
RUSKIN CT
OLD MARKET PL
EGERTON SQ
MARBLE ARCH
MOORSIDE
MINSHULL ST
RED COW YD
PRINCESS ST
KING ST
SILK MILL ST
CHURCH VW
CHURCH HILL
MARCLIFF GR
TATTON LDG
B5083
SWINTON SQ
CHURCH WLK
PC
MOORDALE RD
MIDDLE WLK
ELLA GR
CHURCH MEWS
BRAN
DEN DR
Library
MANOR CRES
Cross Town
MANOR PARK N
TOWNFIELDS
BOOTHFIELDS
KENILWORTH AVE
BROOKDALE AVE
WOODLANDS DR
MANSION DR
BEECH DR
SANDIWAY
THORNEYHOLME DR
BEECHWOOD
HIGHER DOWNS
LICHFIELD CT
LINDOP CL
OAK VIEW
YEWLANDS DR
NORTH DOWNS
BIRCH GR
ASH GR
FOX GR
RICHMOND HILL
WOODSIDE
SHARSTON CRES
MOULTON CL
Booths Mere
Springwood Farm
KEDWARD
BEXTON RD
ST JOHN'S AVE
P
STANLEY RD
TOFT RD
ADAMS HILL
A537
HOLLOW LA
BROOK ST
B5085
MANOR PARK S
ROCKFORD LODGE
DOWNS END
DELAMERE RD
LINTON CL
AYLESBY CL
PARKHILL CT
SPARROW LA
Spring Wood
ST JOHN'S RD
STANLEY RD IND EST
Knutsford Station
A50
GROVE PARK
BROOK
Over Knutsford
GLEBELANDS RD
REVONE CL
CHELFORD RD
BALMORAL CL
BUCKINGHAM DR
HILLSIDE PARK
SOUTH DOWNS
FIR TREE AVE
Booths Hall
WOODVALE RD
LEGH RD
LEGH GDNS
WARWICK CL
CARRWOOD
4
81
3
80
2
79
1
78
75
76
77

82
58

57
32

A
B
C
4
3
2
1
81
80
79
78
78
79
80
WOOD LA
Hanson House
Hill House
Oak Farm
WOODEND LA
Owen House Farm
SMALL LA
Mere House Farm
The Oaks
Orrell House Farm
OSTLER'S LA
BLAKELEY LA
Blakeley Farm
SLADE LA
Sunny Bank Farm
LADY LANE
HOBCROFT LA
Greenbank
Hazelhurst Farm
Holt House
Wee Bridge Farm
Benkeyhurst Farm
DAVENPORT LA
BURLEYHURST LA
BURLEYHURST LA
Wayside Farm
Valewood Farm
Dairy Farm
Graveyard Farm
GRAVEYARD LA
Sch
Church Inn (PH)
Works
Sewage Works
Park Farm
Mobberley Hall Farm
NEWTON HALL LA
Mobberley
CHURCH LA
STUBBS LA
Stubbs Farm
OLDFIELD DR
CARLISLE CL
Old Hall
Park Farm
Newton Hall
Yewtree Farm
BUCKLOW AVE
B5085
TOWN LA
SPOUT LA
MOSS LA
PADDOCKHILL LA
1 BURNISDALE RD
2 TATTON STILE
MILL LA
Lodge
HALL LA
EDENFIELD RD
TOWNFIELD RD
Town Lane Farm
DAMSON LA
EDENFIELD CL
DAM LA
Clayhouse Farm
MEADOWSWEET RD
Dam Head Farm
Knolls Green
Clay Lane
KNUTSFORD RD
Coppock House
Antrobus Hall
Hillfield Farm
B5085
Glevehouse Farm
FAULKNER'S LA
Antrobus Bridge
PH
Sch
Warford House
Pedley Brook
Noonsun Farm
ANCOATS RD
PEDLEY HOUSE LA
Bostock Barns Farm
NOAHS ARK LA
Mountpleasant Farm
Sewage Works

57
83

33
60

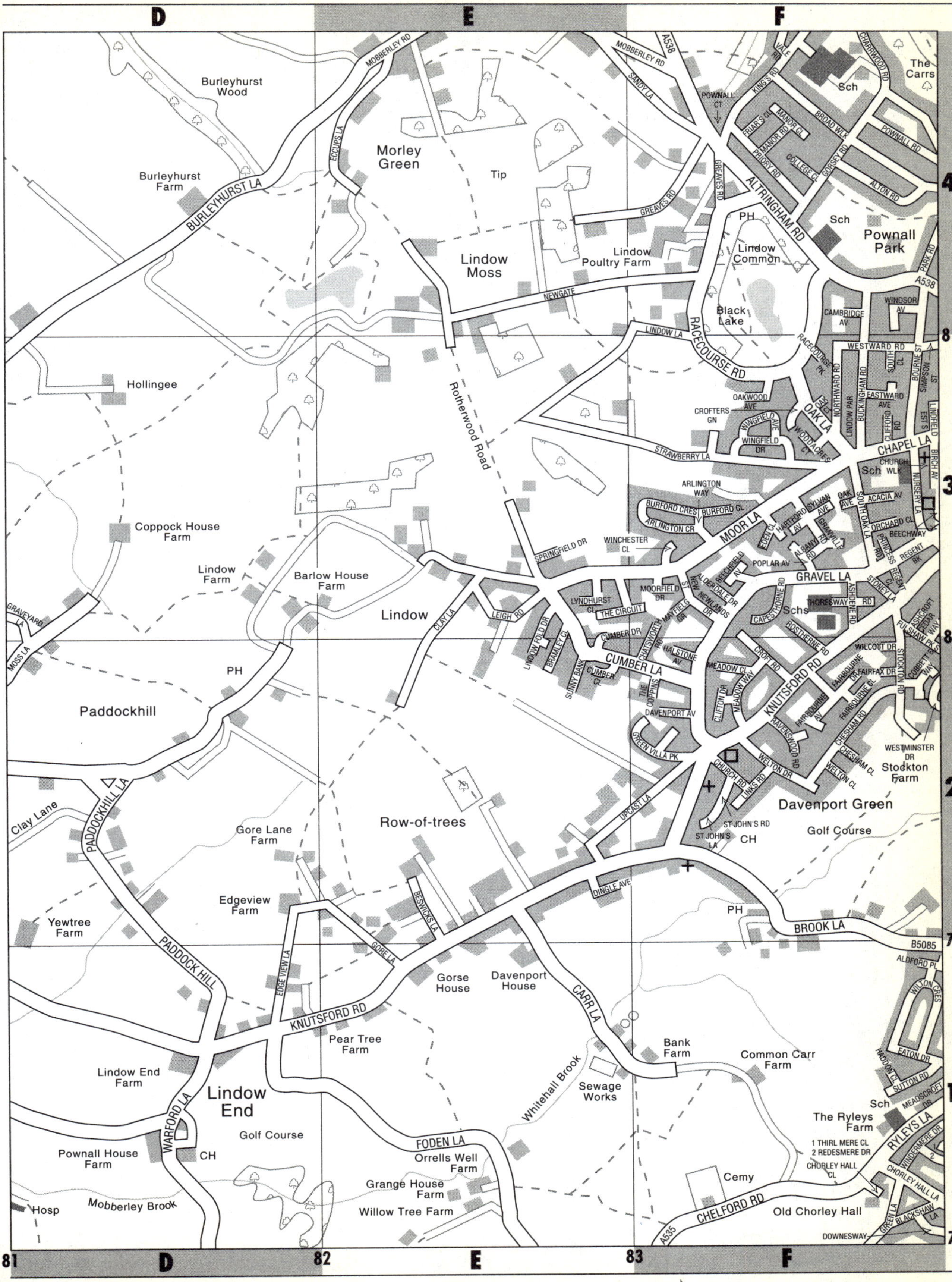
D
E
F
Burleyhurst Wood
Burleyhurst Farm
BURLEYHURST LA
MOBBERLEY RD
ECCUPS LA
Morley Green
Tip
Lindow Moss
NEWGATE
GREAVES RD
Lindow Poultry Farm
SANDY LA
A538
POWNALL CT
GREAVES RD
ALTRINGHAM RD
PH
Lindow Common
Black Lake
RACECOURSE RD
LINDOW LA
VALE RD
KING'S RD
FRIAR'S CL
MANOR CL
MANOR RD
PRIORY RD
COLLEGE CL
BROAD WLK
GORSEY RD
CHARRWOOD RD
POWNALL RD
ALTON RD
Sch
The Carrs
Pownall Park
PARK RD
A538
CAMBRIDGE AV
WINDSOR AV
WESTWARD RD
RACECOURSE PK
NORTHWARD RD
LINDOW PAR
BUCKINGHAM RD
SOUTH CL
BOURNE ST
SIMPSON ST
EASTWARD AVE
CLIFFORD RD
EST S
LINDFIELD
OAKWOOD AVE
CROFTERS GN
WINGFIELD AVE
WINGFIELD DR
OAK LA
WOODACRES CT
STRAWBERRY LA
CHAPEL LA
CHURCH WLK
BIRCH AV
NURSERY LA
Hollingee
Rotherwood Road
Coppock House Farm
Lindow Farm
Barlow House Farm
Lindow
CLAY LA
LEIGH RD
SPRINGFIELD DR
ARLINGTON WAY
BURFORD CRES
BURFORD CL
ARLINGTON CR
MOOR LA
WINCHESTER CL
EDEN CL
HARTFORD AV
SYLVAN AVE
OAK AVE
SOUTH OAK LA
ACACIA AV
GRANVILLE RD
ALBANY RD
ORCHARD CL
BEECHWAY
PRINCESS RD
REGENT BK
POPLAR AV
GRAVEL LA
REGENT CL
STONEY LA
BEECHFIELD AV
ALDERDALE DR
NEW NEWLANDS DR
MOORFIELD DR
LYNDHURST CL
THE CIRCUIT
MAYFIELD GR
CHATSWORTH RD
CUMBER DR
HALSTONE AV
CUMBER LA
CUMBER CL
SUNNY BANK
LINDOW FOLD DR
BRAMLEY CL
THE COPPINS
DAVENPORT AV
GREEN VILLA PK
CAPESTHORNE RD
THORESWAY RD
ASHDENE RD
Schs
ROSTHERNE RD
CROFT RD
MEADOW CL
MEADOW WAY
CLIFTON DR
KNUTSFORD RD
ASHCROFT
CEDAR WAY
FULSHAW PK S
WILCOTT DR
FAIRBOURNE DR
FAIRFAX DR
FAIRBOURNE AV
FAIRBOURNE CL
STOCKTON RD
CORBETT WAY
RAVENSWOOD RD
CHESHAM RD
CHESHAM CL
WELTON CL
WELTON DR
WESTMINSTER DR
Stockton Farm
CHURCH RD
LINKS RD
UPCAST LA
ST JOHN'S RD
ST JOHN'S LA
CH
Davenport Green
Golf Course
GRAVEYARD LA
MOSS LA
PH
Paddockhill
PADDOCKHILL LA
Clay Lane
Gore Lane Farm
Row-of-trees
Edgeview Farm
Yewtree Farm
BESWICKS LA
GORE LA
DINGLE AVE
PH
BROOK LA
B5085
ALDFORD PL
WILSON CRES
PADDOCK HILL
EDGE VIEW LA
KNUTSFORD RD
Gorse House
Davenport House
CARR LA
Pear Tree Farm
Bank Farm
Common Carr Farm
EATON DR
HADDON CL
SUTTON RD
MEADSCROFT DR
Lindow End Farm
Lindow End
WARFORD LA
Whitehall Brook
Sewage Works
Sch
The Ryleys Farm
RYLEYS LA
WINDERMERE DR
1 THIRL MERE CL
2 REDESMERE DR
CHORLEY HALL CL
CHORLEY HALL LA
Golf Course
CH
Pownall House Farm
FODEN LA
Orrells Well Farm
Grange House Farm
Willow Tree Farm
Cemy
CHELFORD RD
A535
Old Chorley Hall
GREEN LA
BLACKSHAW LA
DOWNESWAY
Hosp
Mobberley Brook
4
81
3
80
2
79
1
78
81
D
82
E
83
F

84
60

59
34

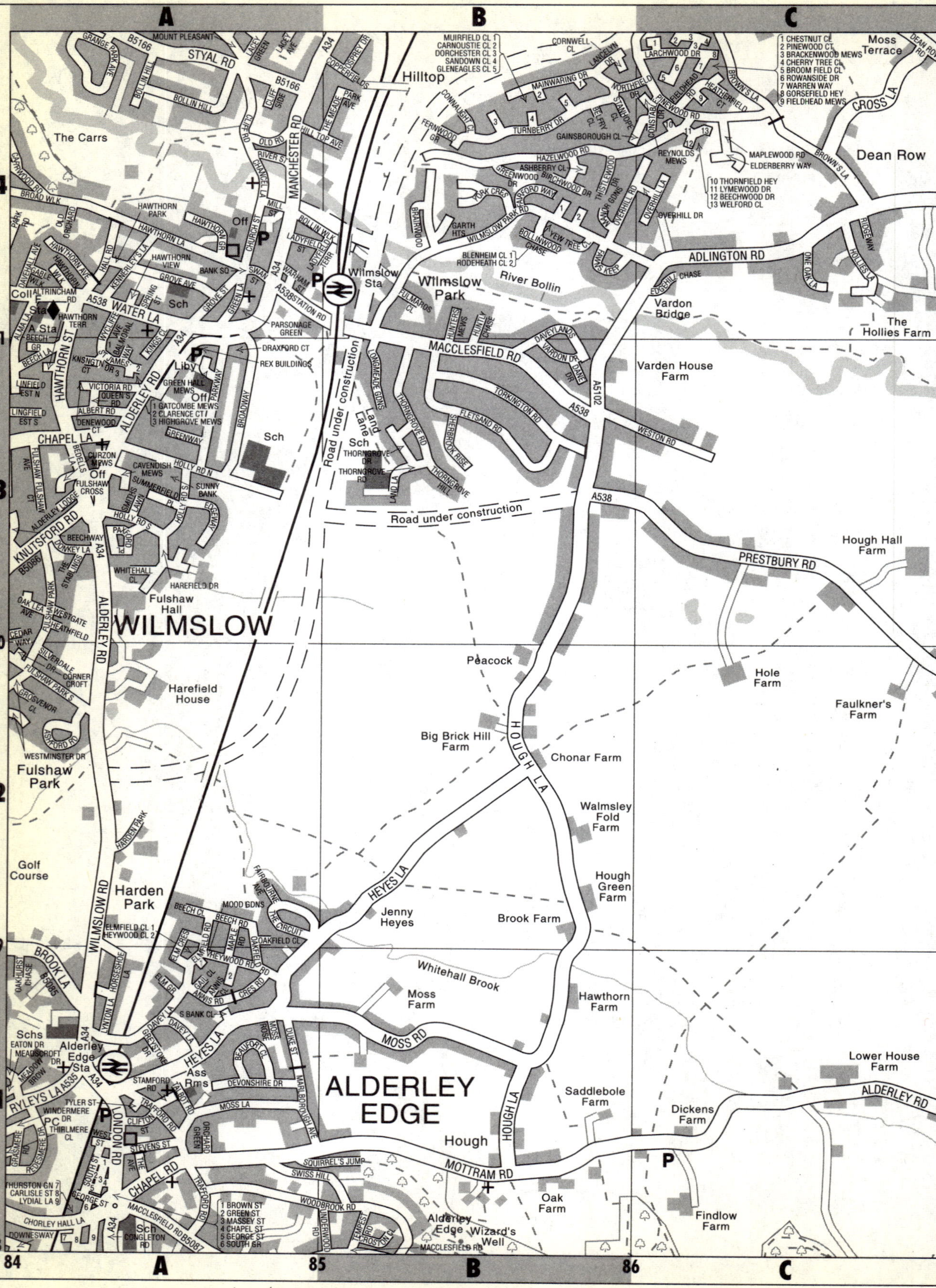
A
B
C
4
3
2
1
81
80
79
78
84
85
86
WILMSLOW
ALDERLEY EDGE
The Carrs
Hilltop
Moss Terrace
Dean Row
Wilmslow Sta
Wilmslow Park
River Bollin
Vardon Bridge
The Hollies Farm
Varden House Farm
Road under construction
Land Lane
Sch
Hough Hall Farm
Fulshaw Hall
Fulshaw Park
Harefield House
Peacock
Hole Farm
Faulkner's Farm
Big Brick Hill Farm
Chonar Farm
Walmsley Fold Farm
Golf Course
Harden Park
Hough Green Farm
Jenny Heyes
Brook Farm
Whitehall Brook
Moss Farm
Hawthorn Farm
Lower House Farm
Saddlebole Farm
Dickens Farm
Hough
Oak Farm
Findlow Farm
Alderley Edge
Wizard's Well
Alderley Edge Sta
Ass Rms
STYAL RD
MANCHESTER RD
ADLINGTON RD
MACCLESFIELD RD
PRESTBURY RD
ALDERLEY RD
WILMSLOW RD
HOUGH LA
HEYES LA
MOSS RD
MOTTRAM RD
LONDON RD
KNUTSFORD RD
WATER LA
CHAPEL LA
BROOK LA
ALDERLEY RD
CROSS LA
BROWN'S LA
A34
A538
A5102
B5166
B5086
B5087

59
85

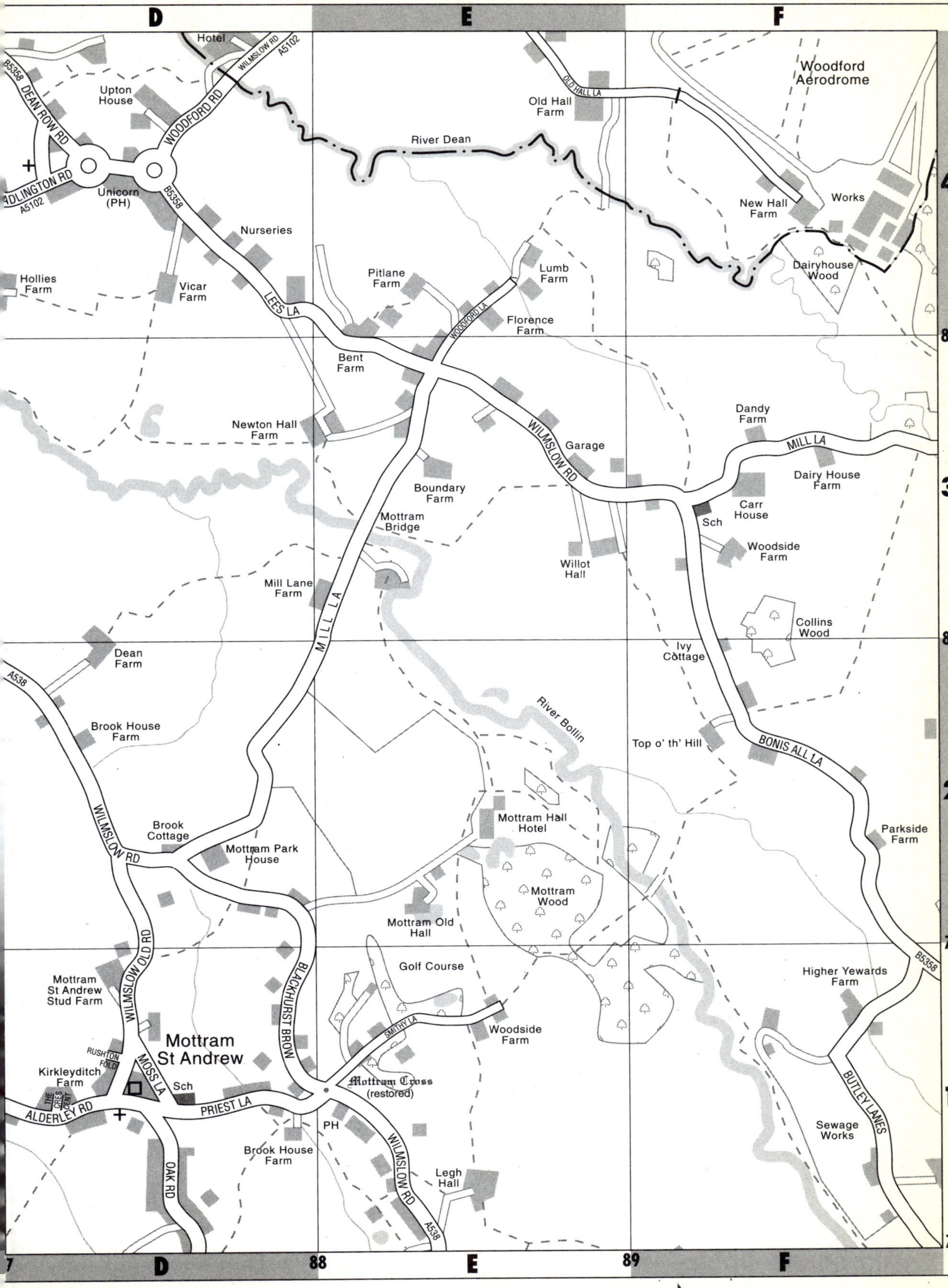
D
E
F
Hotel
WILMSLOW RD
A5102
B5358
DEAN ROW RD
Upton House
WOODFORD RD
ADLINGTON RD
A5102
Unicorn (PH)
B5358
Nurseries
Hollies Farm
Vicar Farm
LEES LA
OLD HALL LA
Old Hall Farm
River Dean
Woodford Aerodrome
New Hall Farm
Works
Dairyhouse Wood
Pitlane Farm
Lumb Farm
WOODFORD LA
Florence Farm
Bent Farm
Newton Hall Farm
WILMSLOW RD
Garage
Dandy Farm
MILL LA
Dairy House Farm
Boundary Farm
Carr House
Sch
Mottram Bridge
Woodside Farm
Willot Hall
Mill Lane Farm
MILL LA
Collins Wood
Dean Farm
Ivy Cottage
A538
River Bollin
Brook House Farm
Top o' th' Hill
BONIS ALL LA
Mottram Hall Hotel
Parkside Farm
Brook Cottage
WILMSLOW RD
Mottram Park House
Mottram Wood
Mottram Old Hall
Golf Course
Higher Yewards Farm
B5358
Mottram St Andrew Stud Farm
WILMSLOW OLD RD
BLACKHURST BROW
SMITHY LA
Woodside Farm
Mottram St Andrew
RUSHTON FOLD
MOSS LA
Kirkleyditch Farm
Sch
Mottram Cross (restored)
BUTLEY LANES
THE CRESCENT
ALDERLEY RD
PRIEST LA
PH
Sewage Works
Brook House Farm
OAK RD
WILMSLOW RD
Legh Hall
A538
4
81
3
80
2
79
1
78
7
88
89
D
E
F

61
36

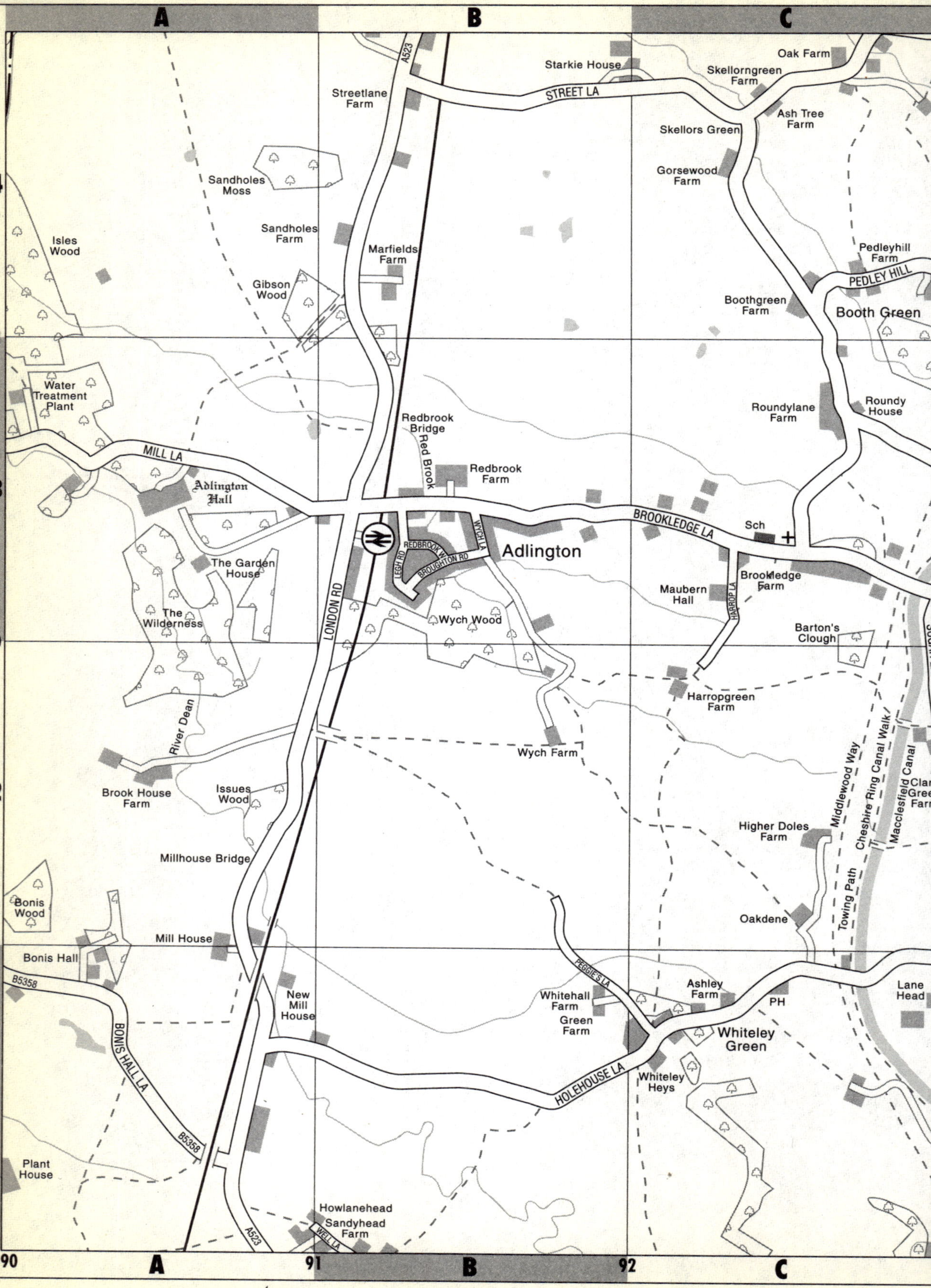
A
B
C
4
3
2
1
81
80
79
78
90
91
92
A523
Starkie House
Oak Farm
Skellorngreen Farm
STREET LA
Streetlane Farm
Ash Tree Farm
Skellors Green
Gorsewood Farm
Sandholes Moss
Sandholes Farm
Isles Wood
Marfields Farm
Gibson Wood
Pedleyhill Farm
PEDLEY HILL
Boothgreen Farm
Booth Green
Water Treatment Plant
Redbrook Bridge
Red Brook
Roundylane Farm
Roundy House
MILL LA
Adlington Hall
Redbrook Farm
BROOKLEDGE LA
Sch
WYCH LA
REDBROOK W
LEGH RD
BROUGHTON RD
Adlington
The Garden House
Maubern Hall
Brookledge Farm
HARROP LA
LONDON RD
The Wilderness
Wych Wood
Barton's Clough
SUGAR LA
Harropgreen Farm
River Dean
Wych Farm
Middlewood Way
Cheshire Ring Canal Walk
Macclesfield Canal
Clark Green Farm
Brook House Farm
Issues Wood
Higher Doles Farm
Millhouse Bridge
Bonis Wood
Oakdene
Towing Path
Mill House
Bonis Hall
B5358
PEGGIE'S LA
Ashley Farm
Lane Head
New Mill House
Whitehall Farm
PH
Green Farm
Whiteley Green
BONIS HALL LA
HOLEHOUSE LA
Whiteley Heys
B5358
Plant House
Howlanehead
Sandyhead Farm
WELL LA
A523

61
87

37
64

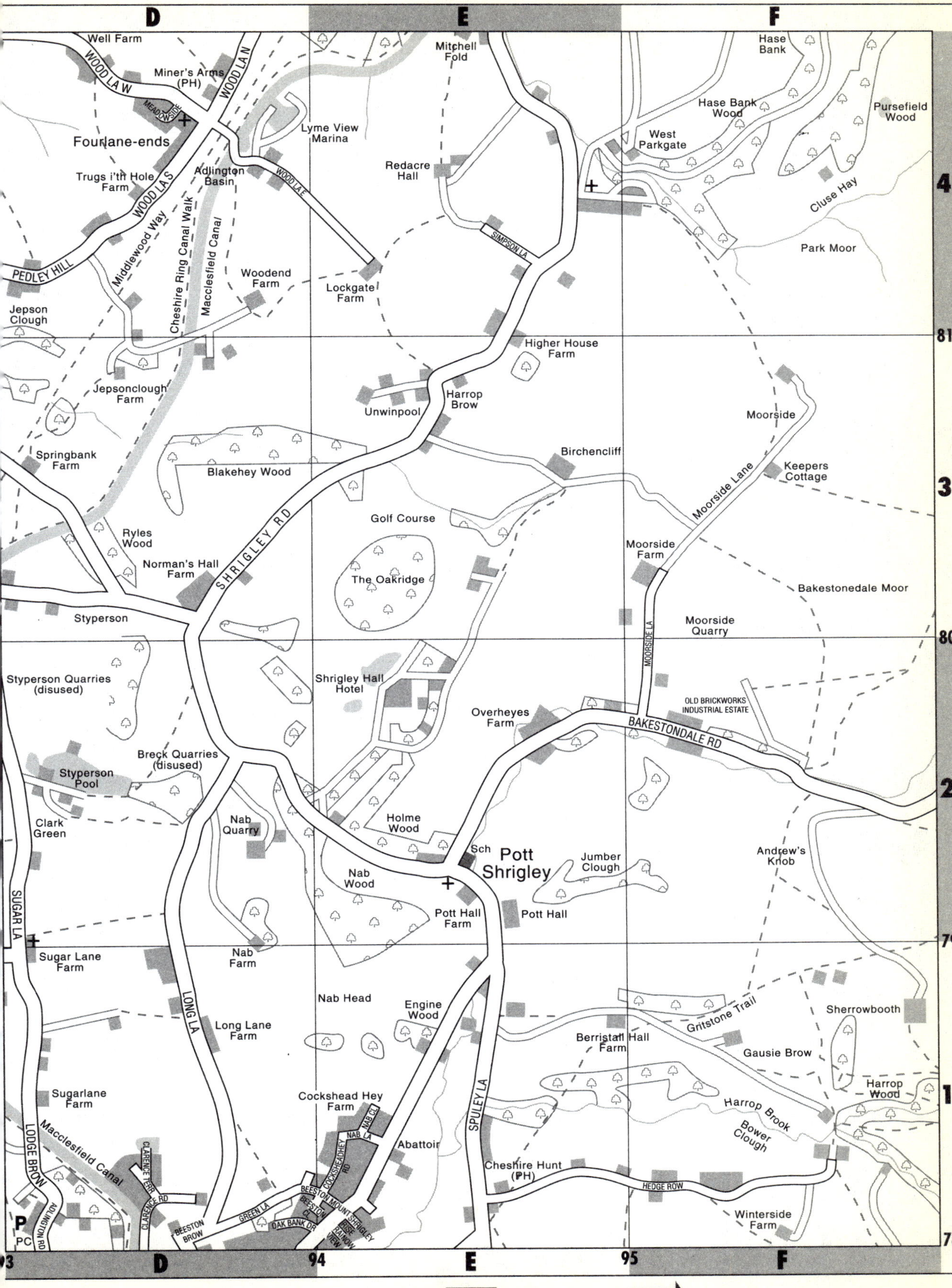
D
E
F
Well Farm
WOOD LA W
Miner's Arms (PH)
WOOD LA N
MEADOWSIDE
Fourlane-ends
Lyme View Marina
Mitchell Fold
Hase Bank
Hase Bank Wood
West Parkgate
Pursefield Wood
Trugs i'th Hole Farm
WOOD LA S
Adlington Basin
WOOD LA E
Redacre Hall
Cluse Hay
Park Moor
SIMPSON LA
PEDLEY HILL
Middlewood Way
Cheshire Ring Canal Walk
Macclesfield Canal
Woodend Farm
Lockgate Farm
Jepson Clough
81
Higher House Farm
Jepsonclough Farm
Harrop Brow
Unwinpool
Moorside
Springbank Farm
Blakehey Wood
Birchencliff
Keepers Cottage
Moorside Lane
3
Golf Course
Ryles Wood
Norman's Hall Farm
SHRIGLEY RD
The Oakridge
Moorside Farm
Bakestonedale Moor
Styperson
Moorside Quarry
80
MOORSIDE LA
Styperson Quarries (disused)
Shrigley Hall Hotel
OLD BRICKWORKS INDUSTRIAL ESTATE
Overheyes Farm
BAKESTONDALE RD
Breck Quarries (disused)
Styperson Pool
2
Clark Green
Nab Quarry
Holme Wood
Sch
Pott Shrigley
Jumber Clough
Andrew's Knob
Nab Wood
Pott Hall Farm
Pott Hall
SUGAR LA
79
Sugar Lane Farm
Nab Farm
Nab Head
Engine Wood
Gritstone Trail
Sherrowbooth
LONG LA
Long Lane Farm
Berristall Hall Farm
Gausie Brow
Sugarlane Farm
Harrop Wood
1
Cockshead Hey Farm
Harrop Brook
Bower Clough
Macclesfield Canal
SPULEY LA
NAB CL
NAB LA
COCKSHEADHEY RD
Abattoir
CLARENCE TERR
Cheshire Hunt (PH)
LODGE BROW
CLARENCE RD
BEESTON MOUNT
HEDGE ROW
BEESTON CL
SHRIGLEY RISE
Winterside Farm
BEESTON BROW
GREEN LA
OAK BANK DR
RAINOW VIEW
ADLINGTON RD
P
PC
78
93
D
94
E
95
F

88
64

63
38

A
B
C
Lyme Park
Higher Moor
Whaley Moor
Knightslow Wood
Handleybarn Farm
Knights Low
Cliff
Bow Stones
Bowstonegate
Lyme Handley
Bailey's Farm
Browside Farm
Holme Wood
Cornfield Farm
Park Moor
Hale House
Sweet Hill
Handley Fold Farm
Sponds Hill
Gritstone Trail
HIGHER LA
Lower Cliff Farm
Hollow Sponds
Higher Cliff Farm
KISHFIELD LA
Sponds
Reed Hill
PADDOCK LA
B5470
FLATTS LA
Kettleshulme
Back Sponds
Sch
Spout House Farm
Manor Farm
The Reed Farm
Ellis Bank
BAKESTONEDALE RD
MACCLESFIELD RD
SIDE END LA
Slaters Green Farm
Brink Farm
Gnathole Brook
Side End Farm
Charles Head
Midfield
Thorneycroft Farm
Brink Brow
Whitelands
Neighbourway Farm
Carr Clough
Charles Head Farm
Near Carr Farm
Todd Brook
Harrop Wood
Further Harrop Farm
Harrop House Farm
Tunstead Knoll Farm
Harrop Brook
Black Brook
Harrop Fold Farm
Dunge Clough
B5470
4
81
3
80
2
79
1
78
96
97
98
A
B
C

63
89

39

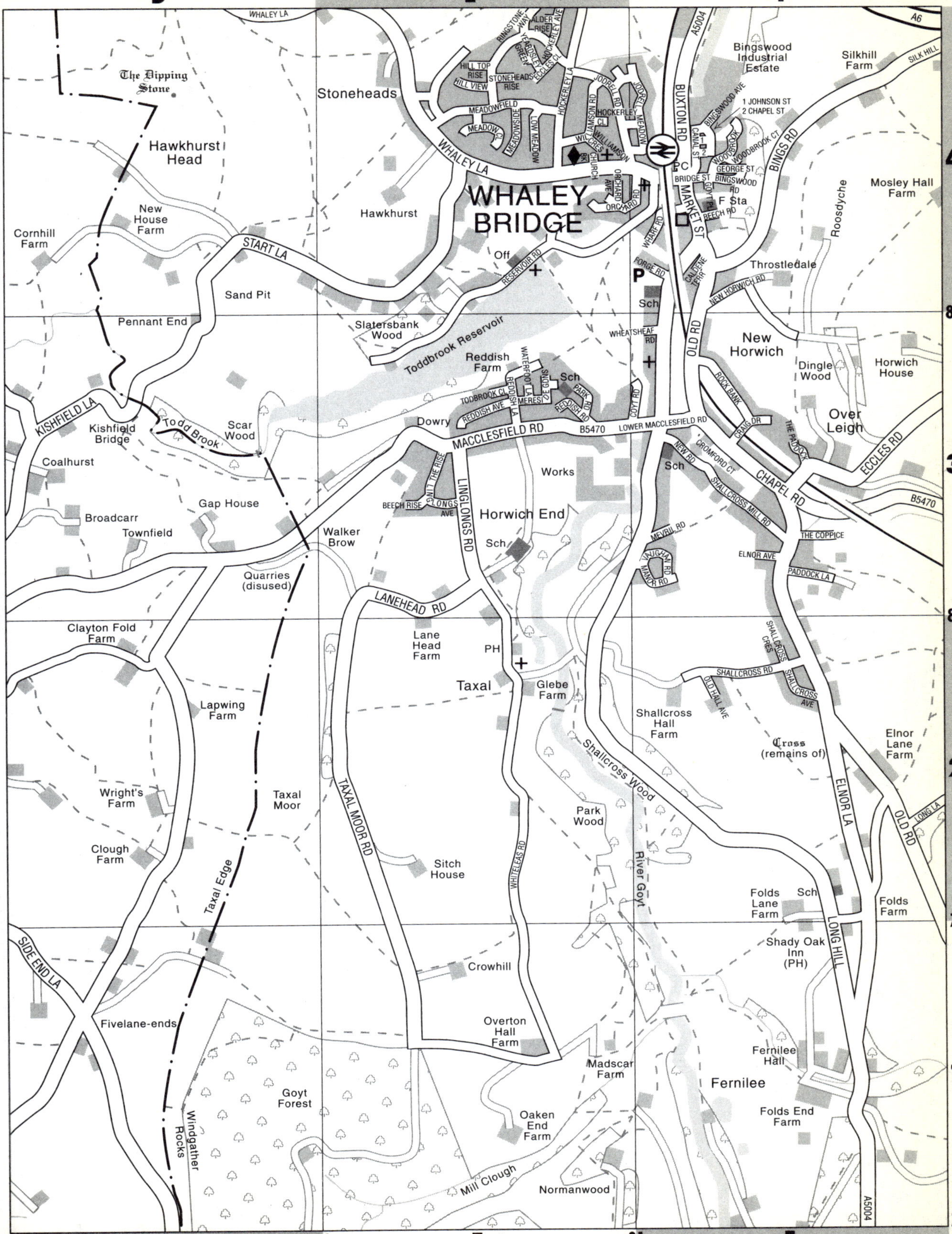

D
E
F
WHALEY LA
The Dipping Stone
Hawkhurst Head
Stoneheads
Bingswood Industrial Estate
Silkhill Farm
SILK HILL
A6
A5004
BUXTON RD
RINGSTONE WAY
ALDER RISE
YEARDSLEY GREEN
HOCKERLEY AVE
ECCLES CL
HILL TOP RISE
HILL VIEW
STONEHEADS RISE
JODRELL RD
HOCKERLEY LA
WILLIAMSON RD
HOCKERLEY CL
MEADOWFIELD
MEADOW CL
MEADOWSIDE
LOW MEADOW
WILLIAMSON CRES
CHURCH AVE
ORCHARD AVE
ORCHARD RD
MEADOW
BINGSWOOD AVE
1 JOHNSON ST
2 CHAPEL ST
CANAL ST
WOODBROOK
WOODBROOK CT
BINGS RD
GEORGE ST
BRIDGE ST
BINGSWOOD RD
GOYT PL
BEECH RD
MARKET ST
PC
F Sta
WHALEY LA
WHALEY BRIDGE
4
Mosley Hall Farm
Roosdyche
Hawkhurst
New House Farm
Cornhill Farm
START LA
Off
RESERVOIR RD
WHARF RD
FORGE RD
CALDENE TERR
Throstledale
NEW HORWICH RD
Sand Pit
P
Sch
Slatersbank Wood
Pennant End
81
WHEATSHEAF RD
OLD RD
New Horwich
Toddbrook Reservoir
Reddish Farm
WATERFOOT LA
SHOPS LA
Sch
PARK RD
Dingle Wood
Horwich House
ROCK BANK
Scar Wood
KISHFIELD LA
Kishfield Bridge
Todd Brook
TODBROOK CL
REDDISH AVE
REDDISH LA
MERES
REDDISH RD
GOYT RD
Dowry
MACCLESFIELD RD
B5470
LOWER MACCLESFIELD RD
CRAIG DR
THE PADDOCK
Over Leigh
ECCLES RD
Coalhurst
NEW RD
CROMFORD CT
Sch
Works
CHAPEL RD
3
SHALLCROSS MILL RD
LINGLONGS RD
LIN THE RISE
BEECH RISE
LONGS AVE
Horwich End
B5470
Gap House
Broadcarr
Townfield
Walker Brow
MEVRIL RD
THE COPPICE
Sch
VAUGHAN RD
MANOR RD
ELNOR AVE
PADDOCK LA
Quarries (disused)
LANEHEAD RD
80
Clayton Fold Farm
Lane Head Farm
PH
SHALLCROSS CRES
Taxal
Glebe Farm
SHALLCROSS RD
OLD HALL AVE
SHALLCROSS AVE
Lapwing Farm
Shallcross Hall Farm
Cross (remains of)
Elnor Lane Farm
Shallcross Wood
2
Wright's Farm
Taxal Moor
TAXAL MOOR RD
Park Wood
ELNOR LA
OLD RD
LONG LA
Clough Farm
WHITELEAS RD
Sitch House
River Goyt
Taxal Edge
Folds Lane Farm
Sch
Folds Farm
79
SIDE END LA
Shady Oak Inn (PH)
LONG HILL
Crowhill
Fivelane-ends
Overton Hall Farm
Fernilee Hall
Madscar Farm
1
Fernilee
Goyt Forest
Oaken End Farm
Folds End Farm
Windgather Rocks
Mill Clough
Normanwood
A5004
78
99
D
00
E
01
F

90

41

NESTON
Moorside
Little Neston
Ness Holt
Sewage Works
Wirral Way
Neston Sta
Cemy
Danger Area
Danger Area
WT Station
Masts
PH
Sch
Schs
Liby
STATION RD
PARKGATE RD
BUGGEN LA
LEIGHTON RD
EARLE DR
HIGH ST
BRIDGE ST
RABY PARK RD
HINDERTON RD
BUSHELL RD
MELLOCK LA
BADGER BAIT
BURTON RD
SCHOOL LA
WELL LA
MARSHLANDS RD
QUAYSIDE
OLD QUAY LA
B5135
B5134
1 MARLOWE RD
2 SHAKESPEARE RD
1 ROMNEY CL
2 ROMNEY WAY
3 ROMNEY CROFT
1 FLINT MEADOW
2 FLINT DR
3 FLINT CL
1 COLLIERY GREEN CT
2 GRAMPIAN WAY
3 TURROCKS CL
4 CROFTEN DR
5 BATHWOOD DR
6 PEERSWOOD CT
WOODFALL LA 1
SCHOOL AVE 2
DAWN CL 3
NESTON RD 4
A
B
C
4
77
3
76
2
75
1
74
27
28
29

91

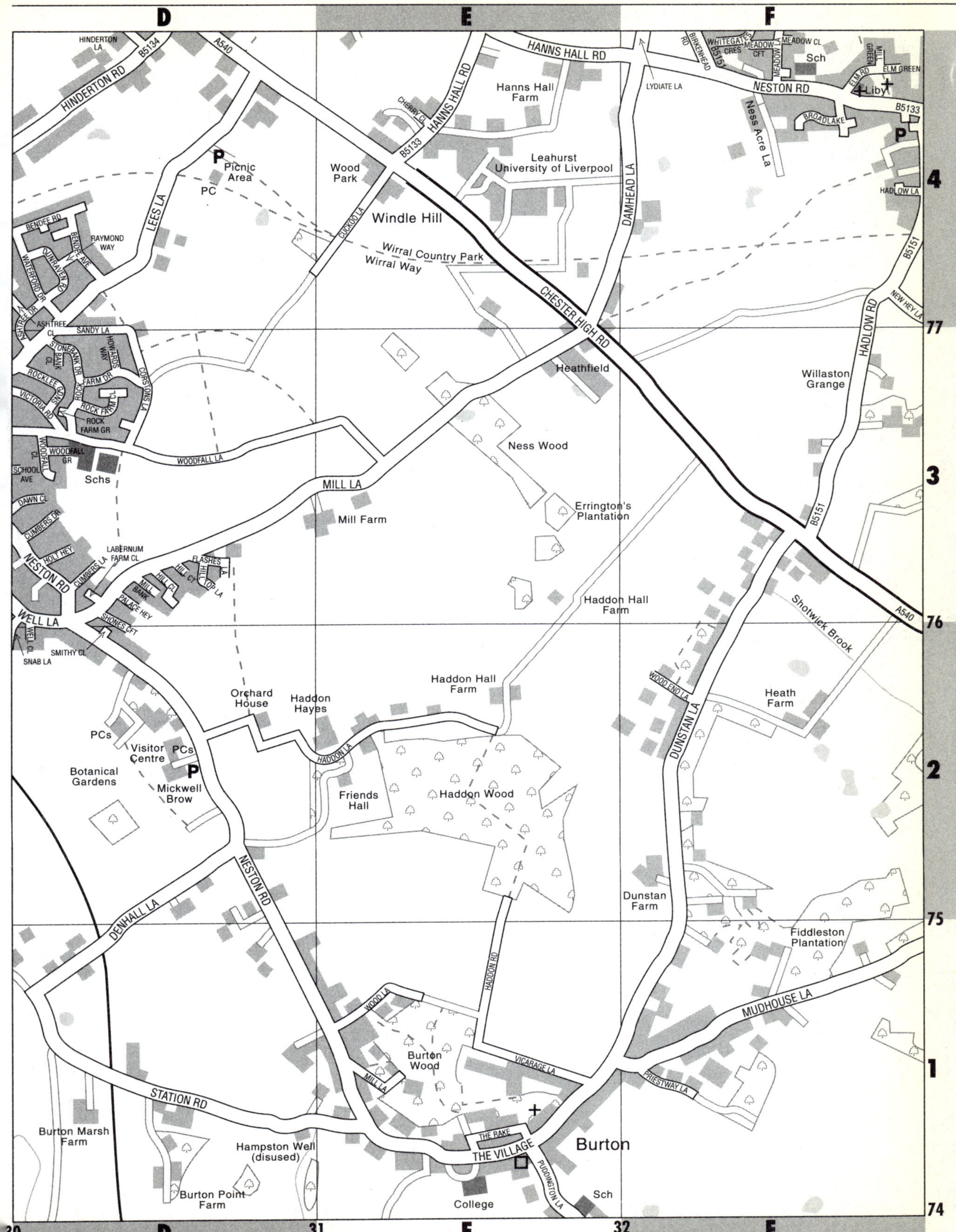
D
E
F
HINDERTON LA
B5134
HINDERTON RD
A540
HANNS HALL RD
BIRKENHEAD RD
WHITEGATES CRES
MEADOW CFT
MEADOW LA
MEADOW CL
Sch
MILL GREEN
ELM GREEN
ELM RD
LYDIATE LA
NESTON RD
Liby
B5133
Ness Acre La
BROADLAKE
P
Hanns Hall Farm
CHERRY CL
HANNS HALL RD
B5133
Leahurst
University of Liverpool
Wood Park
P
Picnic Area
PC
LEES LA
Windle Hill
CUCKOO LA
DAMHEAD LA
HADLOW LA
4
Wirral Country Park
Wirral Way
BENDEE RD
BENDEE AVE
RAYMOND WAY
DUNRAVEN RD
WATERFORD DR
ASHTREE DR
ASHTREE CL
SANDY LA
STONEBANK DR
HOWARDS WAY
ROCKLEE GDNS
ROCK FARM DR
ROCK FARM CL
ROCK FARM GR
VICTORIA RD
CORSONS LA
CHESTER HIGH RD
B5151
NEW HEY LA
HADLOW RD
77
Heathfield
Willaston Grange
WOODFALL CL
WOODFALL GR
WOODFALL LA
SCHOOL AVE
Schs
Ness Wood
MILL LA
3
DAWN CL
CUMBERS DR
Mill Farm
Errington's Plantation
B5151
HOLT HEY
LABERNUM FARM CL
CUMBERS LA
FLASHES LA
HILL CT
HILL TOP LA
HILL CL
MILL BANK
PALACE HEY
NESTON RD
Haddon Hall Farm
A540
WELL LA
WELL CL
SNAB LA
SHONES CFT
SMITHY CL
76
Shotwick Brook
WOOD END LA
Haddon Hall Farm
Heath Farm
Orchard House
Haddon Hayes
PCs
Visitor Centre
PCs
DUNSTAN LA
HADDON LA
Botanical Gardens
P
Mickwell Brow
Friends Hall
Haddon Wood
2
NESTON RD
Dunstan Farm
DENHALL LA
75
Fiddleston Plantation
HADDON RD
WOOD LA
MUDHOUSE LA
Burton Wood
VICARAGE LA
1
MILL LA
PRIESTWAY LA
STATION RD
Burton Marsh Farm
THE RAKE
THE VILLAGE
Burton
Hampston Well (disused)
PUDDINGTON LA
Burton Point Farm
College
Sch
74
30
D
31
E
32
F

67
43

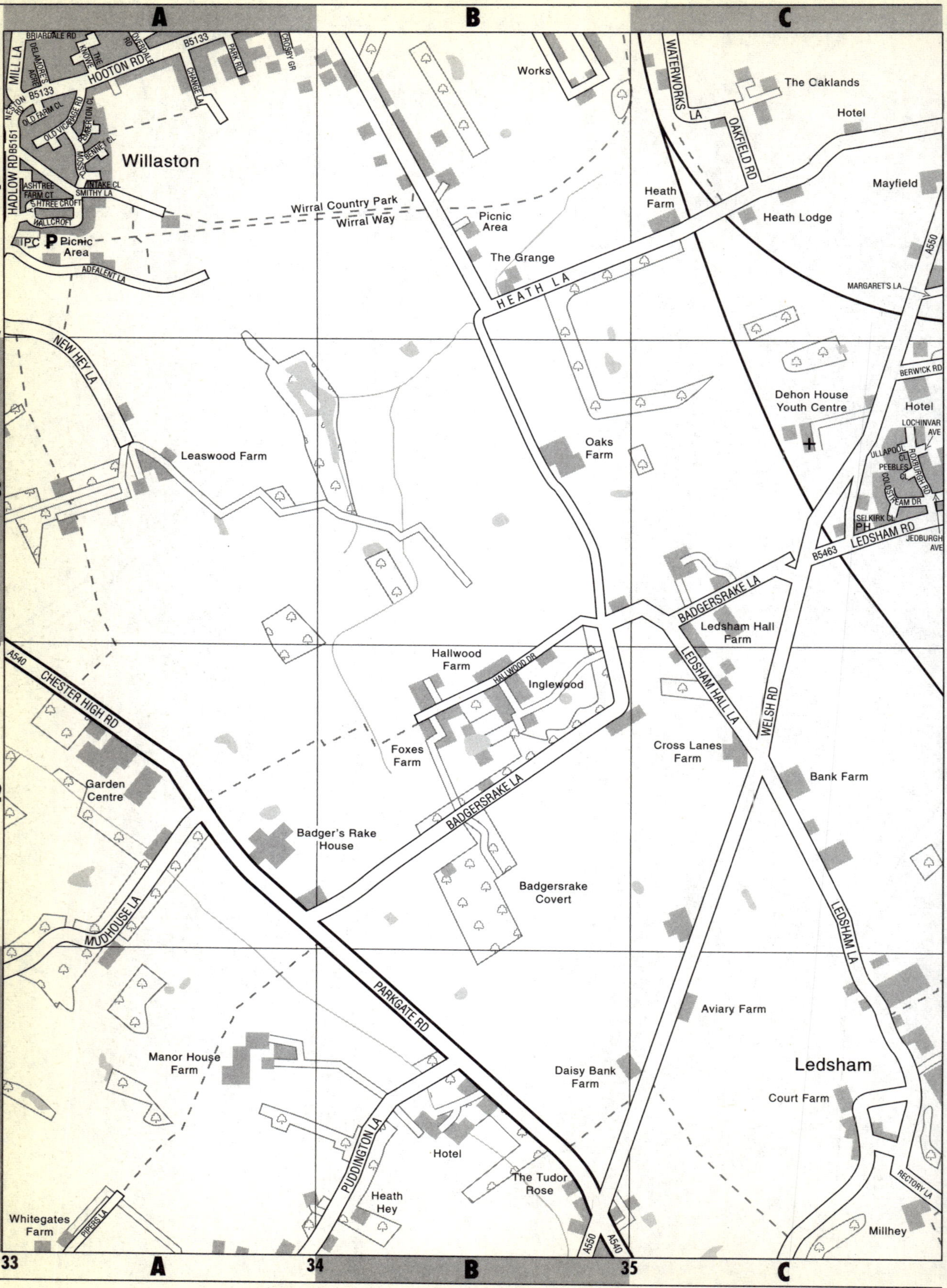
A
B
C
Willaston
Mill La
Hadlow Rd
Hooton Rd
B5133
Wirral Country Park
Wirral Way
Picnic Area
Adfalent La
New Hey La
Leaswood Farm
Works
Picnic Area
The Grange
Heath La
Waterworks La
Oakfield Rd
The Oaklands
Hotel
Heath Farm
Heath Lodge
Mayfield
A550
Margaret's La
Berwick Rd
Dehon House
Youth Centre
Hotel
Oaks Farm
Ledsham Rd
B5463
PH
Badgersrake La
Ledsham Hall Farm
Hallwood Farm
Hallwood Dr
Inglewood
Ledsham Hall La
Welsh Rd
Cross Lanes Farm
Bank Farm
A540
Chester High Rd
Garden Centre
Foxes Farm
Badger's Rake House
Badgersrake Covert
Mudhouse La
Parkgate Rd
Manor House Farm
Aviary Farm
Ledsham La
Ledsham
Daisy Bank Farm
Court Farm
Puddington La
Hotel
The Tudor Rose
Heath Hey
Whitegates Farm
Pipers La
Rectory La
Millhey
A550
A540
77
76
75
74
4
3
2
1
33
34
35

67
93

44
70

D E F

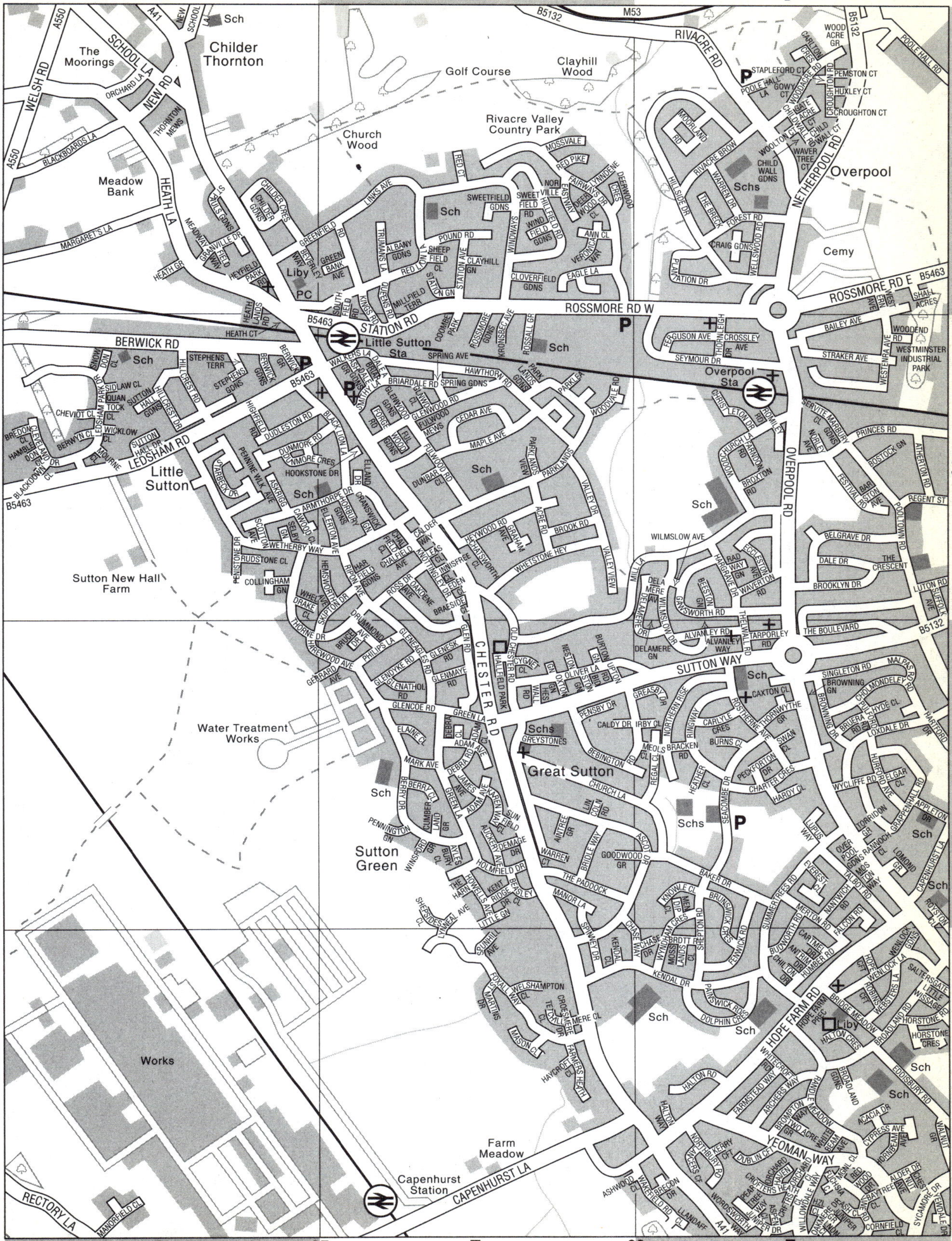

4
3
2
1
77
76
75
74
36 37 38

D E F

94
70

69
45

A
B
C
4
77
3
76
2
75
1
74
39
40
41
River Mersey
Manchester Ship Canal
Oil Storage Depot
Tanks
Junction 8
M53
NORTH RD
LCs
CANAL CT TRADING EST
A5032
MERSEYTON RD
Custom House
POOLE HALL RD
ROSSMORE RD E
B5463
ROSSBANK RD
Rossmore Business Park
UPPER MERSEY ST
ALEXANDRA ST
Mus
DOCK ST
QUEEN ST
Junction 9
Powell's Bridge
Jetties
Works
DOCK YARD RD
OIL SITES RD
ELLESMERE PORT
Sch
Offs
PENN GDNS 1
STAFFORD GDNS 2
HOLLYFIELD GDNS 3
WILLIAM JOHNSON GDNS
HORACE BLACK GDNS
PC
ELEANOR ST
MEADOW LA
Ellesmere Port Station
1 HIGHFIELD RD N
2 ASHFIELD RD N
3 WOODFIELD RD N
PRINCES RD
LC
THE ARCADE
REGENT ST
Coll
WHITBY RD
CROMWELL RD
WATERLOO CL
BRIDGES RD
LUTON RD
SUTTON WAY
B5132
Job Centre
Civic Hall
Whitby
Ct
Off
Mkt
Liby
F Sta & Amb Sta
McGARVA WAY
CAMBRIDGE RD
Works
Shropshire Union Canal
LOXDALE DR
POOLTOWN RD
CAVENDISH GDNS
HARTFORD DR
TA Centre
Wolverham
Stadium
Sports Complex
Weaver's Bridge
SHELLWAY RD
DALE GDNS
Whitby Hall
STANNEY LA
Schs
Hospl
CHESTER RD
OVERPOOL RD
1 HORSTONE RD
2 SALTERSGATE
WOODSIDE
Schs
Stanney Mill Bridge
STANNEY MILL RD
Little Stanney
KINSEY RD
LONGLOOMS RD
A5117
Junction 10
Stanney Woods Country Park
Lime Tree Farm
B5132
SYCAMORE DR
1 YEWDALE DR
2 WILLOW GR
Sports Gnd
Whitbyheath
M53

46
72

D
E
F
Ince Banks
Stanlow Point
Docks
The Bungalow
Manchester Ship Canal
Ferry P
River Gowy
Wood Farm
Hall Farm
Ince
KINSEY'S LA
MARSH LA
Tanks
CORIDOR RD
Chy
THE SQUARE
OIL SITES RD
Stanlow
BRIDGES RD
Stanlow & Thornton Station
Works
Research Centre
POOL LA
Oil Refinery
SHELLWAY RD
Chys
A5117
Church Farm
Thornton Hall
YEW TREE CL
Thornton-le-Moors
THORNTON GREEN LANE
YATES RD
PARK RD
THORNTON GREEN LA
Sewage Works
Thornton Brook
Shropshire Union Canal
Mason's Bridge
B5132
CRYERS LA
4
77
3
76
2
75
1
74
42
43
44
96
72

71
47

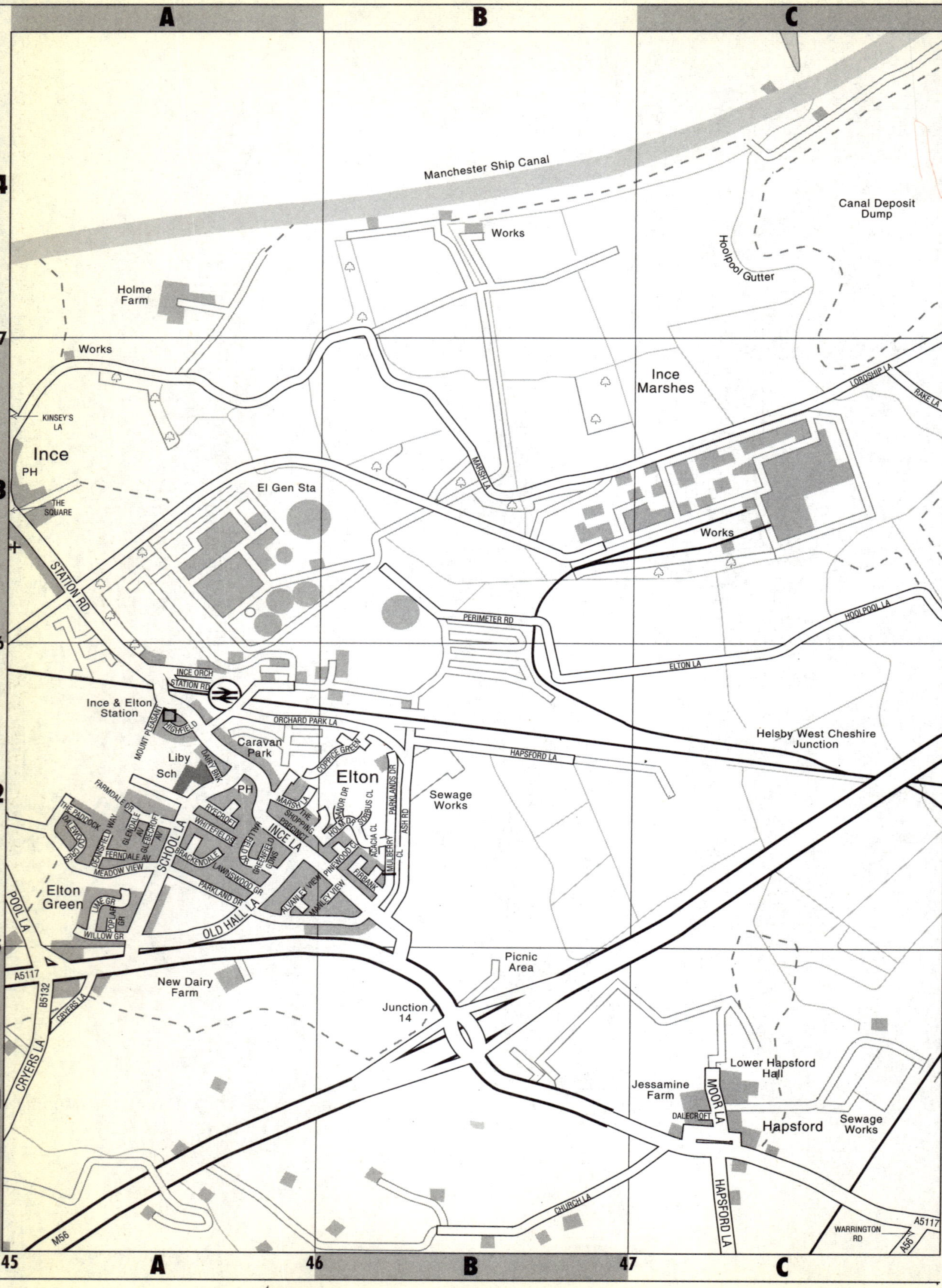
A
B
C
4
77
3
76
2
75
1
74
45
46
47
Manchester Ship Canal
Works
Canal Deposit Dump
Hoolpool Gutter
Holme Farm
Works
KINSEY'S LA
Ince
PH
THE SQUARE
Ince Marshes
LORDSHIP LA
RAKE LA
MARSH LA
El Gen Sta
Works
STATION RD
PERIMETER RD
HOOLPOOL LA
ELTON LA
INCE ORCH
STATION RD
Ince & Elton Station
ORCHARD PARK LA
HAPSFORD LA
Helsby West Cheshire Junction
MOUNT PLEASANT
HIGHFIELD
Caravan Park
Liby
Sch
DAIRY BNK
COPPICE GREEN
Elton
PH
Sewage Works
FARMDALE DR
THE PADDOCK
DALEWOOD CRES
DEANSFIELD WAY
GLENDALE AV
GLEBECROFT AV
FERNDALE AV
MEADOW VIEW
SCHOOL LA
RYECROFT
WHITEFIELDS
BRACKENDALE
HALLFIELD DR
GREENFIELD GDNS
LAWNSWOOD GR
PARKLAND DR
MARSH LA
THE SHOPPING PRECINCT
INCE LA
MANOR DR
HOLLY DR
SORBUS CL
ACACIA CL
PARKLANDS DR
ASH RD
MULBERRY CL
PINEWOOD GR
FIRBANK
ALVANLEY VIEW
MANLEY VIEW
OLD HALL LA
Elton Green
LIME GR
POPLAR GR
WILLOW GR
POOL LA
A5117
B5132
CRYERS LA
CRYERS LA
New Dairy Farm
Picnic Area
Junction 14
Lower Hapsford Hall
Jessamine Farm
MOOR LA
DALECROFT
Hapsford
Sewage Works
HAPSFORD LA
CHURCH LA
M56
A5117
WARRINGTON RD
A56

71
97

48
74

D
E
F
Frodsham Marsh
Canal Deposit Dump
MOORDITCH LA
CROSS LA
TADGERS LA
M56
4
Lordship Marsh
LORDSHIP LA
HARE'S LA
Ppg Sta
STRAIGHT LENGTH
Grassy Lane
HATLEY LA
ELTON LORDSHIP LA
77
Godscroft Hall
GODSCROFT LA
A56
B5393
RAKE LA
Hill View Farm
3
Helsby Marsh
Sch
HOOLPOOL LA
Spring Farm
76
Woodhouses
Meadow Farm
Helsby Station
LOWER RAKE LA
CHESTNUT LA
TARVIN RD
Covertside
Foxhill
2
Helsby
Helsby Hill
Foxhill Wood
OLD CHESTER RD
BATES LA
Wks
Liby
Hornsmill Brook
Firs Farm
HILL RD NORTH
HILL RD SOUTH
FRESHMEADOW LA
75
Longster Trail
Works
P
ALVANLEY RD
Alderhall
RIDGEWAY
Ppg Sta
ROBIN HOOD LA
THE ROCK
Rock Farm
BACK LA
1
COMMONSIDE
Walnut Tree Farm
Poplar Tree Farm
HELSBY RD
FRODSHAM RD
Commonside Farm
Bowlingalley Farm
Cliff Farm
BRAMLEY WLK 1
RUTHIN WLK 2
PH
Sch
A56
WARRINGTON RD
PRIMROSE LA
Alvanley
Sch
74
48
49
50

98
74

73
49

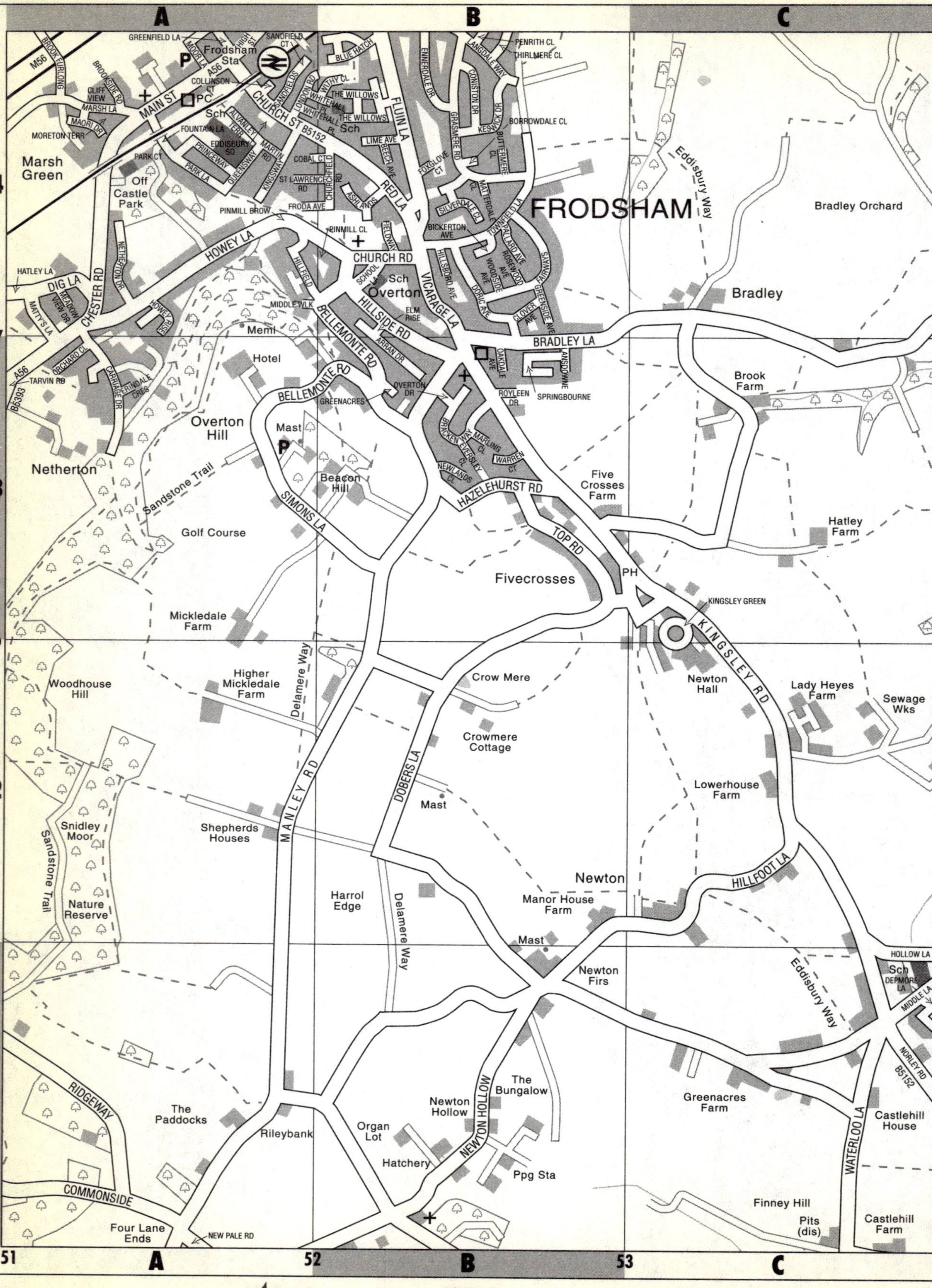
A
B
C
4
77
3
76
2
75
1
74
51
52
53
M56
BROOK FURLONG
GREENFIELD LA
MOOR LA
HIGH ST
Frodsham Sta
SANDFIELD CT
BROOKSIDE RD
CLIFF VIEW
MARSH LA
MAORI DR
MORETON TERR
MAIN ST
A56
COLLINSON CT
PC
Sch
FOUNTAIN LA
ALVANLEY TERR
EDDISBURY SQ
PRINCEWAY
QUEENSWAY
PARK LA
PARK CT
MARTIN RD
KINGSWAY
CHURCH ST B5152
SANDFIELDS
LONDON RD
WITHY CL
WHITEHALL
WHITEHALL PL
BLUE HATCH
THE WILLOWS
FLUIN LA
ENNERDALE DR
LANGDALE WAY
CONISTON DR
GRASMERE RD
PENRITH CL
THIRLMERE CL
KESWICK DR
BUTTERMERE CL
BORROWDALE CL
LIME AVE
BEECH AVE
COBAL CT
ST LAWRENCE RD
CHURCHFIELD RD
ASHLANDS
RED LA
FOXGLOVE CT
MATERDALE CL
SILVERDALE CL
TOWNFIELD LA
BICKERTON AVE
PALLARD AVE
ROSEWOOD AVE
WOODSIDE AVE
FAIRWAYS
SANDYLANE
HILLSBORO AVE
DORIC AVE
GREENSIDE DR
CLOVER AVE
FRODSHAM
Eddisbury Way
Bradley Orchard
Marsh Green
Off Castle Park
PINMILL BROW
FRODA AVE
PINMILL CL
FIELDWAY
CHURCH RD
SCHOOL LA
Sch
Overton
HOWEY LA
NETHERTON DR
HILLFIELD
HATLEY LA
DIG LA
MEADOW VIEW DR
MATTY'S LA
CHESTER RD
HOWEY RISE
MIDDLE WLK
BELLEMONTE RD
HILLSIDE RD
ELM RISE
VICARAGE LA
Bradley
BRADLEY LA
Meml
Hotel
ARRAN DR
OAKDALE AVE
LANSDOWNE
ROYLEEN DR
SPRINGBOURNE
Brook Farm
A56
TARVIN RD
ORCHARD CL
CARRIAGE DR
FERNDALE CRES
B5393
BELLEMONTE RD
GREENACRES
OVERTON DR
Overton Hill
Mast
BRACKEN WAY
MARLING CL
EVERSLEY CL
WARREN CT
NEWLANDS CL
Netherton
Sandstone Trail
Beacon Hill
HAZELEHURST RD
Five Crosses Farm
SIMONS LA
Golf Course
TOP RD
Hatley Farm
Fivecrosses
PH
KINGSLEY GREEN
Mickledale Farm
KINGSLEY RD
Woodhouse Hill
Higher Mickledale Farm
Delamere Way
Crow Mere
Newton Hall
Lady Heyes Farm
Sewage Wks
Crowmere Cottage
DOBERS LA
Lowerhouse Farm
Mast
Snidley Moor
Shepherds Houses
MANLEY RD
Sandstone Trail
Nature Reserve
Harrol Edge
Delamere Way
Newton
HILLFOOT LA
Manor House Farm
Mast
Newton Firs
HOLLOW LA
Sch
DEPMORE LA
MIDDLE LA
Eddisbury Way
NORLEY RD
B5152
RIDGEWAY
The Bungalow
NEWTON HOLLOW
Newton Hollow
Greenacres Farm
WATERLOO LA
Castlehill House
The Paddocks
Rileybank
Organ Lot
Hatchery
Ppg Sta
COMMONSIDE
Finney Hill
Pits (dis)
Castlehill Farm
Four Lane Ends
NEW PALE RD

73
99

50
76

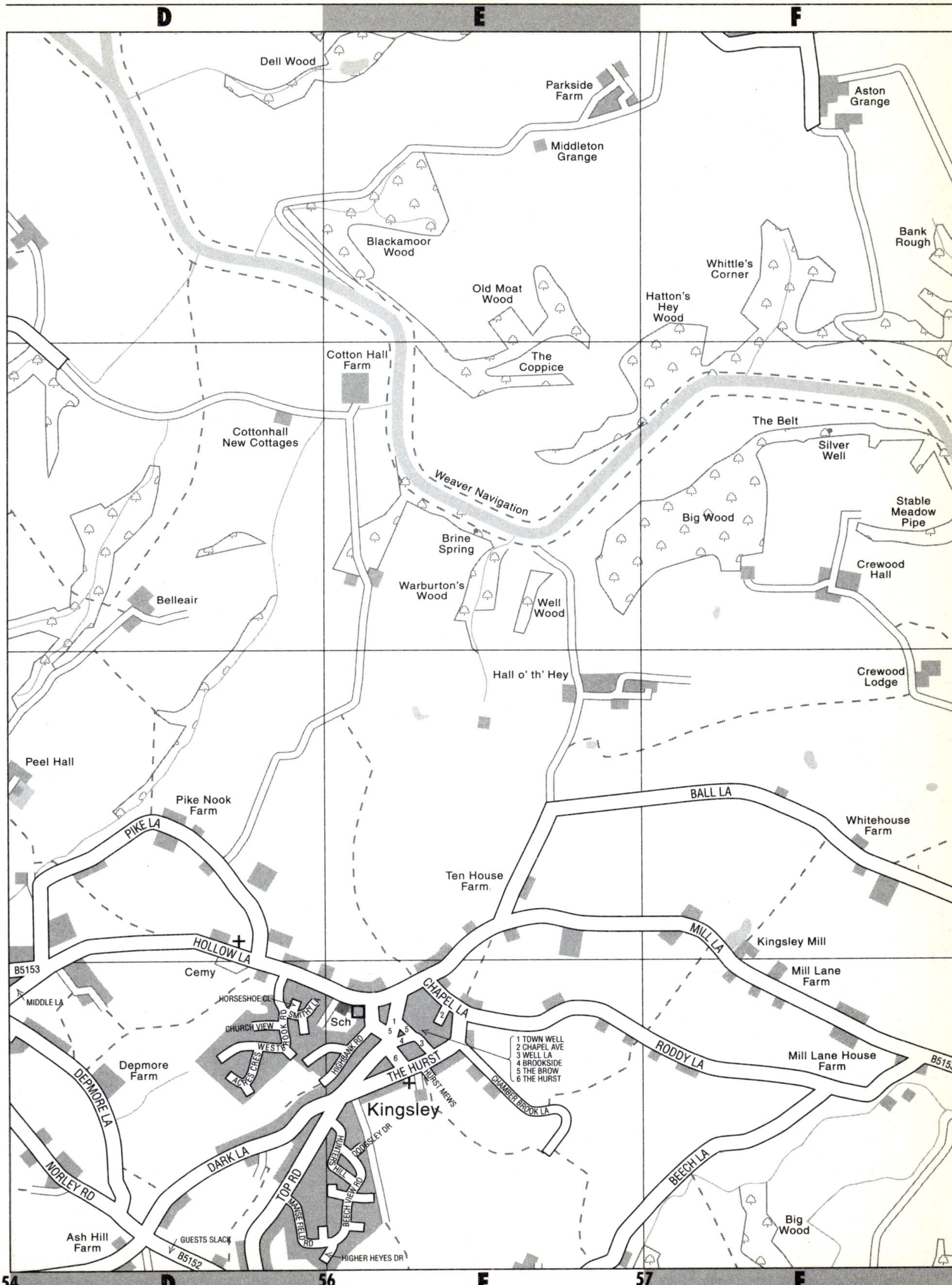
D
E
F
Dell Wood
Parkside Farm
Aston Grange
Middleton Grange
4
Blackamoor Wood
Bank Rough
Whittle's Corner
Old Moat Wood
Hatton's Hey Wood
77
Cotton Hall Farm
The Coppice
Cottonhall New Cottages
The Belt
Silver Well
Weaver Navigation
3
Stable Meadow Pipe
Big Wood
Brine Spring
Crewood Hall
Warburton's Wood
Belleair
Well Wood
76
Hall o' th' Hey
Crewood Lodge
Peel Hall
BALL LA
Pike Nook Farm
2
PIKE LA
Whitehouse Farm
Ten House Farm
MILL LA
Kingsley Mill
HOLLOW LA
75
B5153
Cemy
Mill Lane Farm
CHAPEL LA
MIDDLE LA
HORSESHOE CL
SMITHY LA
Sch
CHURCH VIEW
BROOK RD
1 TOWN WELL
2 CHAPEL AVE
3 WELL LA
4 BROOKSIDE
5 THE BROW
6 THE HURST
RODDY LA
WESTS
HIGHBANK RD
Mill Lane House Farm
B5153
Depmore Farm
ACRES CRES
THE HURST
HURST MEWS
CHAMBER BROOK LA
DEPMORE LA
Kingsley
1
DODGSLEY DR
HUNTERS HILL
DARK LA
BEECH LA
NORLEY RD
TOP RD
BEECH VIEW RD
MANSE FIELD RD
Big Wood
Ash Hill Farm
GUESTS SLACK
HIGHER HEYES DR
B5152
74
54
D
56
E
57
F

100
76

75
51

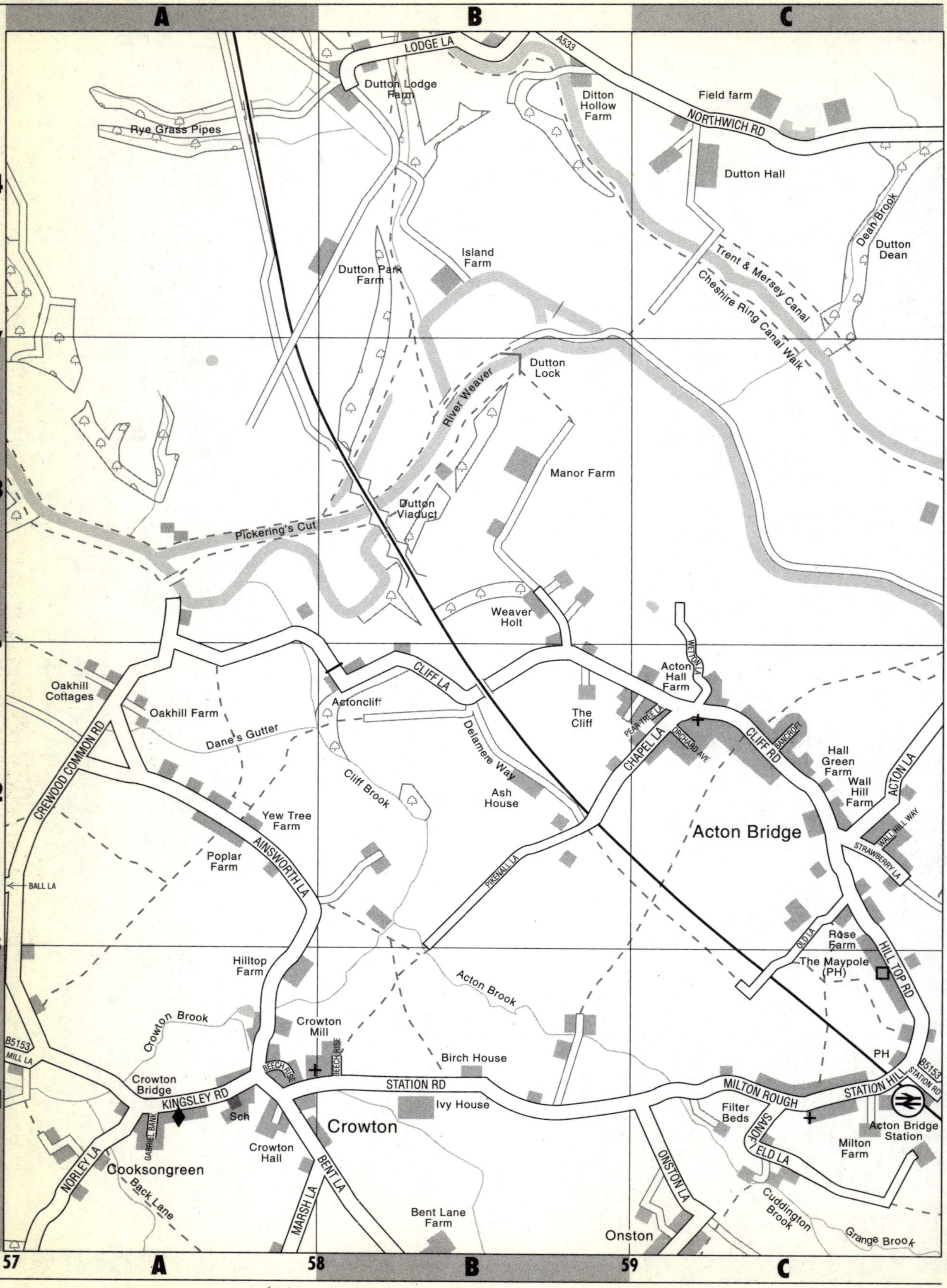
A
B
C
4
77
3
76
2
75
1
74
57
58
59
LODGE LA
A533
Dutton Lodge Farm
Ditton Hollow Farm
Field farm
NORTHWICH RD
Rye Grass Pipes
Dutton Hall
Dean Brook
Dutton Dean
Island Farm
Dutton Park Farm
Trent & Mersey Canal
Cheshire Ring Canal Walk
Dutton Lock
River Weaver
Manor Farm
Dutton Viaduct
Pickering's Cut
Weaver Holt
WETTON LA
Acton Hall Farm
CLIFF LA
Oakhill Cottages
Oakhill Farm
Actoncliff
The Cliff
PEAR TREE LA
ORCHARD AVE
CLIFF RD
BANCROFT
Hall Green Farm
Wall Hill Farm
ACTON LA
WALL HILL WAY
Dane's Gutter
Delamere Way
CHAPEL LA
CREWOOD COMMON RD
Cliff Brook
Ash House
Acton Bridge
STRAWBERRY LA
Yew Tree Farm
Poplar Farm
AINSWORTH LA
PIKENALL LA
BALL LA
OLD LA
Rose Farm
HILL TOP RD
The Maypole (PH)
Hilltop Farm
Acton Brook
Crowton Brook
Crowton Mill
B5153
MILL LA
BEECH RISE
Birch House
PH
B5153
STATION RD
STATION HILL
Crowton Bridge
KINGSLEY RD
STATION RD
MILTON ROUGH
Ivy House
Filter Beds
SANDFIELD LA
Acton Bridge Station
Sch
GABRIEL BANK
Crowton
Crowton Hall
Milton Farm
NORLEY LA
Cooksongreen
BENT LA
ONSTON LA
Back Lane
MARSH LA
Cuddington Brook
Bent Lane Farm
Onston
Grange Brook

75
101

52
78

D
E
F
4
3
2
1
77
76
75
74
61
62
Meadow Farm
MARSH LA
A49
Nook Farm
TARPORLEY RD
Redstocks
Dones Green Farm
Heath Hall Farm
Hotel
Whitley Brook
Dane Farm
NORTHWICH RD
Dones Green
HEATH LA
Dones View Farm
A533
Ash Tree Farm
ASH HOUSE LA
Clatterwick Farm
COGSHALL LA
HALL LA
Whitley Brook
Deslay Heath Farm
Cogshall Farm
CHAPEL LA
Hill Farm
PH
SMITHY LA
Crumleyheath Farm
HOUGH LA
SHUTLEY LA
Heath Lodge
Willowgreen Farm
Willow Green
RUNCORN RD
WARRINGTON RD
Easy Heath Farm
Stoneheys Farm
STONE HEYES LA
WILLOWGREEN LA
LEIGH LA
ORCHARD DR
ST MICHAEL'S CL
CHURCH MEADOWS
SHUTLEY LA
Sch
Shutley Farm
Valley Farm
BRAKELEY RD
CHURCH RD
Stone Leigh House Farm
ACTON LA
Little Leigh
Brakeley Rough
1 HAWTHORNE GR
2 BROOMSFIELD LA
3 WESTFIELD GR
4 ALAMEIN RD
Brakeley Bank Farm
Hawton Clough
Little Leigh Pond
Caravan Site
Trent & Mersey Canal
HOLE HOUSE LA
SPRINGFIELD CRES
WADE CRES
WOODLANDS GR
SNOWDON ST
A533
Cheshire Ring Canal Walk
Daleford House
Saltersford Tunnel
BEECH LA
FAIR VIEW CL
LEIGH'S BROW
River Weaver
Strawberry Lane
Weaver Navigation
B5142
SANDY LA
Sewage Works
Merebrow
Merebank
Weaverham Wood Farm
Mere House Farm
The Woodlands
WELL LA
SHADY BROOK LA
River Weaver
Barnton Cut
ST MARY'S AVE
Owley Wood
STATION RD
PH
B5142
VALLEY RD
HUNTERS HILL
FARM RD
WEAVER VIEW
GERRARD DR
THE CRES
MERVYN RD
OWLEY WOOD RD
AINSWORTH RD
LONG ACRE
LEIGH WAY
PARK AVE
PINFOLD WAY
1 MOSS ST
2 WOODWARD ST
3 LAKE HOUSE CL
CLEAVE RD
HIGH ST
SMITH'S LA
P
CHURCH ST
FARM CL
GREENWOOD CL
ORCHARD CL
MORRIS DR
CLITHEROE RD
BARRYMORE RD
WILBRAHAM RD
WEST RD
TOWER LA
RUTLAND DR
BANK SIDE
B5153
CHAPEL ST
FOREST ST
NORTHWICH RD
CHURCH CL
CHURCH LA
ST BEDE'S AVE
HEATH RD
1 LONGMEADOW
2 BROOK SIDE
FIELDWAY
FERN WAY
WITHEN'S LA
Sch
NICHOLAS RD
WALLERSCOTE RD
A49

102
78

77
53

A
B
C
4
77
3
76
2
75
1
74
63
64
65
Cogshall Hall
Bogs Wood
Brook Farm
Comberbach
Sch
Avenue Farm
PH
Brownslow Farm
BELMONT RD
A559
NORTHWICH RD
COCK LA
Cocklane Farm
Sandicroft
BUDWORTH LA
Brownslow House
GIBB HILL
THE AVENUE
CROWNEST LA
BARRYMORE CRES
BURGAMOT LA
GOOSEBROOK CL
REEDSMERE WALK
MATHER CL
BROOKFIELD RD
SPINNER CRES
CHAPEL CL
WARRINGTON RD
SENNA LA
COGSHALL LA
Brook House Farm
HOUGH LA
FRESHFIELDS
BRACKEN WAY
KENNEL WOOD
FOXLEA RD
THE MOSS
BROADACRE
Marbury Home Farm
Reed Bed
Budworth Mere
Boat House
Kennel Wood
Cogshall Brook
MARBURY RD
STONE HEYES LA
Houghlane Farm
Claycroft Farm
P
Marbury Country Park
Big Wood
Mill
MARBURY LA
Hopyards
1 SWEET BRIER CL
2 FIRTREE CL
3 MAPLE GR
4 LARCHTREE CL
Barnton
Marina
UPLANDS RD
Anderton
NEW RD
OLD RD
Uplands Farm
Witton Flashes
Trent and Mersey Canal
Cheshire Ring Canal Walk
Lift
DAISY BANK LA
SOOT HILL
Cemy
WHITEHALL CL
CORONATION GR
BROOMSFIELD LA
Sch
LAUREL CL
CHERRY TREE AVE
CEDAR DR
WILLOW GR
ASHWOOD CL
REDWOOD CL
PINETREE CL
ELMWOOD
SYCAMORE CRES
HAZELWOOD RD
CHESTNUT GR
OAKTREE CL
LIMEWOOD GR
LIMEWOOD CRES
CHERRY WOOD CRES
YEW TREE DR
LABURNUM CRES
THE DINGLE
GOODWOOD CL
HIGHBANK CL
ORCHARD CL
ASHWOOD CRES
CROCUS ST
ASTBURY DR
ALAMEIN RD
WADE CRES
BEECH LA
TOWNFIELD LA
TOWNFIELD CT
ROSEBANK WALK
ROMAN RISE
Liby
MEADOW DR
GREEN AVE
CENTRAL DR
GRANGE RD
GRANGE AVE
A533
WHEATFIELD CL
EMMETT ST
HICKSON ST
WHITLEY AVE
LYDYETT LA
CHURCHFIELD
HAYES DR
BRACKEN WAY
NURSERY RD
BROADWAY
SPENCER ST
GEORGE ST
CROSS ST
HILL TOP
MONDS ST
LYDYETT LA
THE MEWS
MANOR DR
RUNCORN RD
CHURCH RD
RAYS BROW
PRINCES PARK
PLUMBS FOLD
BLACKCROFT AVE
OAKWOOD LA
Tunnel
TUNNEL RD
CANAL SIDE
Ropery Farm
Sewage Works
Sewage Works
Barnton Cut
Weaver Navigation
Works
River Weaver
SOLWAY RD
BRUNNER BSNS CENTRE
Winnington
SANDYBANK
PARK RD
HEMMING ST
DYAR TERR
WINNINGTON ST
MOSS TERR
WINNINGTON AVE
BOND ST
NORTHWAY
BARN MEADOW
HILLVIEW RISE
CLARY MEADOW
SPRING MEADOW
OAKLEIGH RISE
FOXES FOLD
MOSS RD
B5374
MORETON ST
APPLETON ST
THE WOODLANDS
A533
Hospl
BOWLING GREEN CT
BESWICKS RD
VICTORIA PARK
VERDIN AVE
OLDHAMS HILL
BARONS QUAY RD
LEICESTER ST
WEAVER WAY
WITTON ST
PC

77
103

54
80

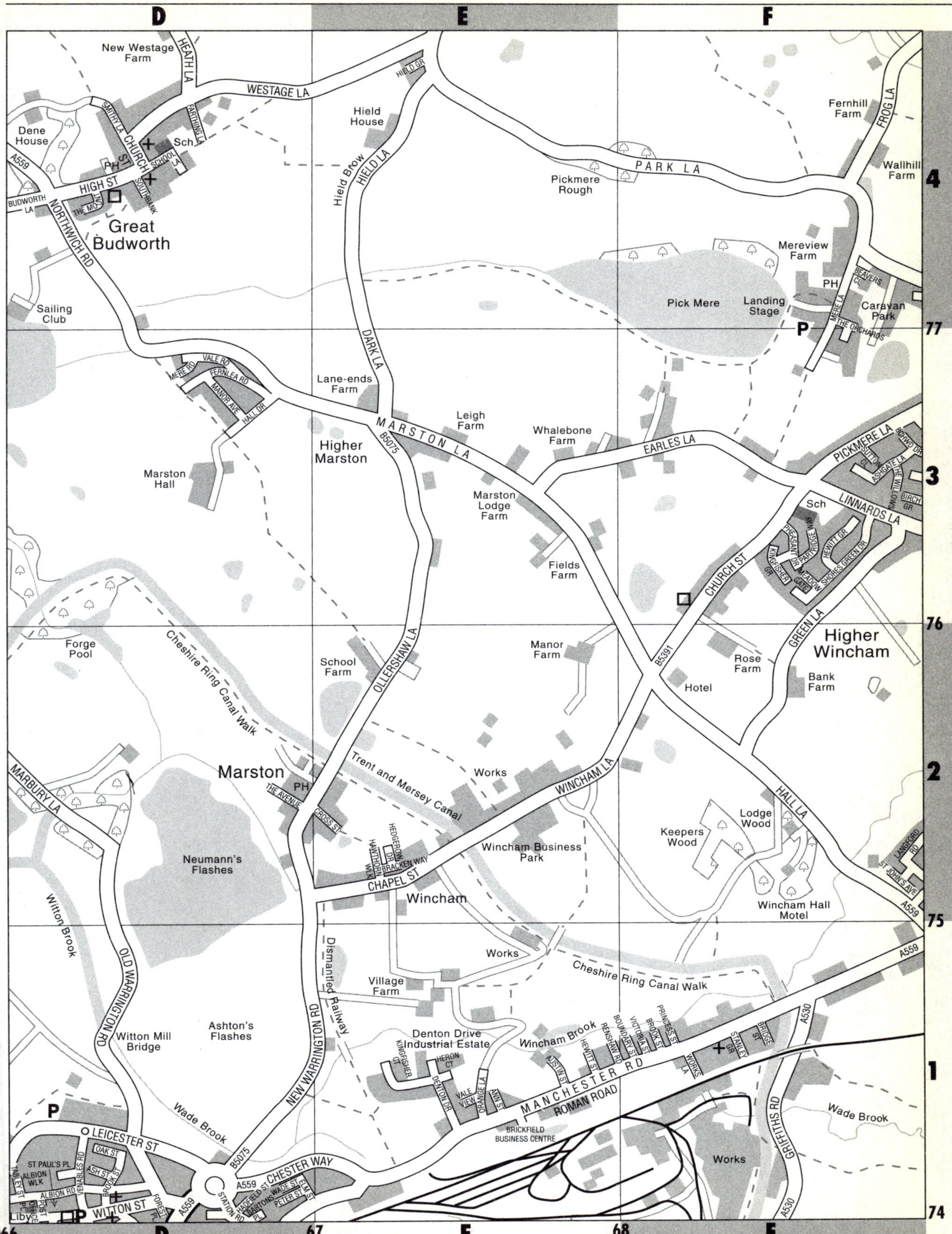
D
E
F
New Westage Farm
HEATH LA
WESTAGE LA
HIELD GR
Dene House
SMITHY LA
FARTHING LA
Sch
CHURCH ST
SCHOOL LA
PH
HIGH ST
SOUTHBANK
A559
BUDWORTH LA
THE MOUNT
NORTHWICH RD
Great Budworth
Sailing Club
Hield House
Hield Brow
HIELD LA
Pickmere Rough
PARK LA
Fernhill Farm
FROG LA
Wallhill Farm
Mereview Farm
PH
BEAVERS CL
Pick Mere
Landing Stage
MERE LA
Caravan Park
P
THE ORCHARDS
DARK LA
VALE RD
MERE RD
FERNLEA RD
MANOR AVE
HALL DR
Lane-ends Farm
Leigh Farm
Whalebone Farm
EARLES LA
MARSTON LA
B5075
Higher Marston
Marston Hall
Marston Lodge Farm
PICKMERE LA
BIRCHWOOD DR
SUTTON CL
ASHGATE LA
THE WILLOWS
BIRCH GR
Sch
LINNARDS LA
PHEASANT DR
PARTRIDGE WAY
HEWITT GR
SHORES GREEN DR
KINGFISHER GR
MEADOW GATE
CHURCH ST
Fields Farm
Forge Pool
Cheshire Ring Canal Walk
School Farm
OLLERSHAW LA
Manor Farm
B5391
Rose Farm
GREEN LA
Higher Wincham
Hotel
Bank Farm
Marston
PH
THE AVENUE
CROSS ST
Trent and Mersey Canal
Works
WINCHAM LA
MARBURY LA
HALL LA
Lodge Wood
Keepers Wood
Neumann's Flashes
HEDGEROW DR
HAWTHORN WLK
BRACKEN WAY
CHAPEL ST
Wincham Business Park
Wincham
LANGFORD RD
ST JOHN'S AVE
A559
Wincham Hall Motel
Witton Brook
OLD WARRINGTON RD
Dismantled Railway
Works
Cheshire Ring Canal Walk
A559
Village Farm
Witton Mill Bridge
Ashton's Flashes
NEW WARRINGTON RD
Denton Drive Industrial Estate
KINGFISHER CT
HERON CT
DENTON DR
VALE VIEW
ORANGE LA
ANN ST
Wincham Brook
AUSTIN ST
HEWITT ST
RENSHAW RD
BOUNDARY ST
VICTORIA ST
BROOK ST
PRINCESS ST
WORKS LA
STANLEY GR
BRIDGE ST
A530
MANCHESTER RD
ROMAN ROAD
BRICKFIELD BUSINESS CENTRE
Wade Brook
GRIFFITHS RD
Wade Brook
Works
P
LEICESTER ST
OAK ST
ST PAUL'S PL
ALBION WLK
ASH ST
BROOK ST
VENABLES RD
ALBION RD
TABLEY ST
POST OFFICE
Liby
P
WITTON ST
FOREST ST
A559
B5075
STATION RD
HADFIELD ST
BARTONS PL
WADE ST
PETER ST
ELM ST
CHESTER WAY
A559
A530
4
77
3
76
2
75
1
74
66
67
68

104
80

79
55

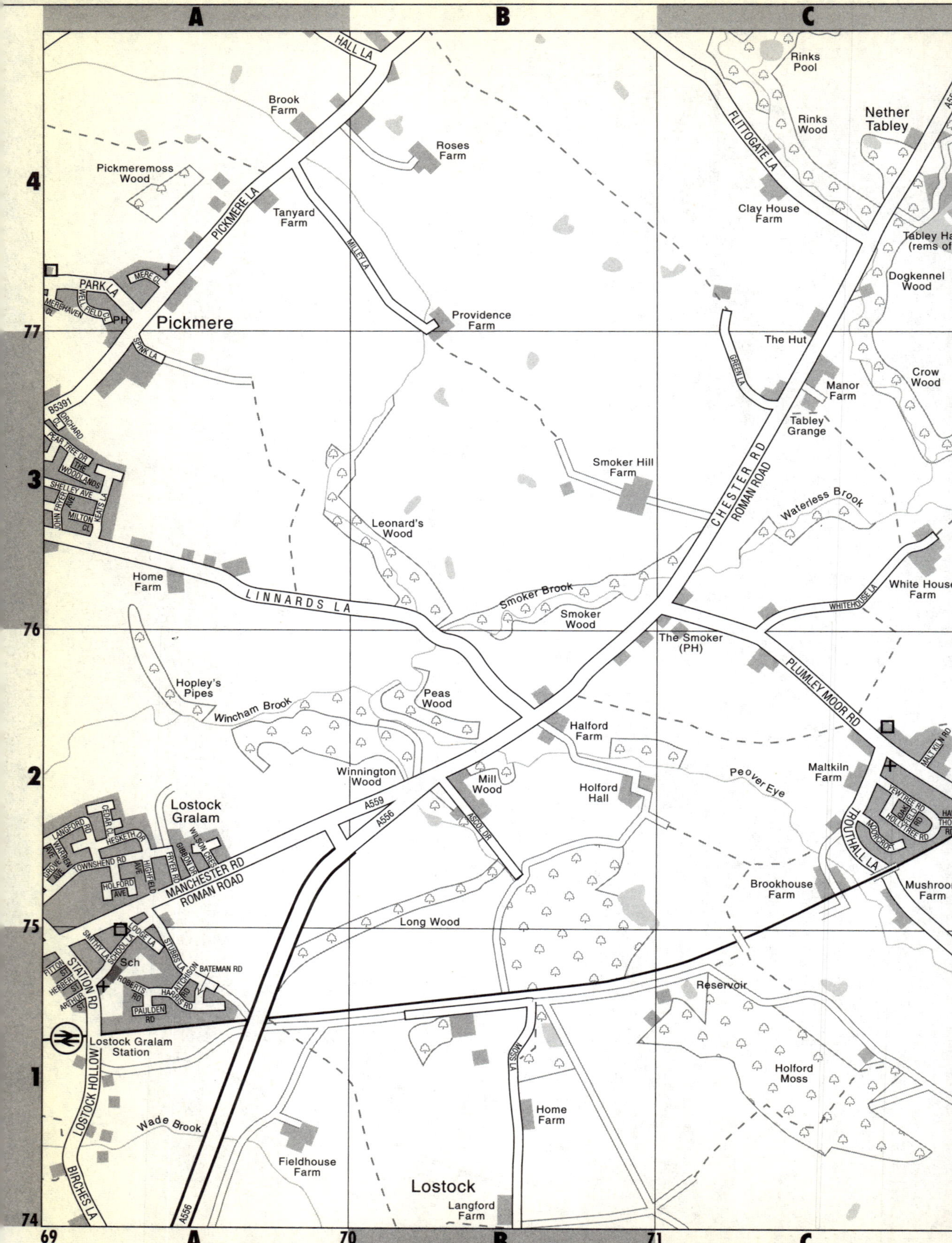
A
B
C
4
3
2
1
77
76
75
74
69
70
71
HALL LA
Brook Farm
Roses Farm
Rinks Pool
Rinks Wood
Nether Tabley
A556
FLITTOGATE LA
Pickmeremoss Wood
PICKMERE LA
Tanyard Farm
MILLEY LA
Clay House Farm
Tabley Hall (rems of)
Dogkennel Wood
PARK LA
MERE CL
WELL FIELD CL
MEREHAVEN CL
PH
Pickmere
Providence Farm
The Hut
SPINK LA
GREEN LA
Manor Farm
Crow Wood
Tabley Grange
B5391
ORCHARD CL
PEAR TREE DR
THE WOODLANDS
SHELLEY AVE
JOHN FRYER AVE
MILTON CL
KEATS LA
Smoker Hill Farm
CHESTER RD
ROMAN ROAD
Waterless Brook
Leonard's Wood
Home Farm
White House Farm
WHITEHOUSE LA
LINNARDS LA
Smoker Brook
Smoker Wood
The Smoker (PH)
PLUMLEY MOOR RD
Hopley's Pipes
Peas Wood
Wincham Brook
Halford Farm
MALT KILN RD
Winnington Wood
Mill Wood
Holford Hall
Peover Eye
Maltkiln Farm
Lostock Gralam
A559
A556
ASCOL DR
YEWTREE RD
OAK RD
HOLLYTREE RD
HAWTHORN RD
MOORCROFT
TROUTHALL LA
CEDAR CL
LANGFORD RD
WILSON CRES
HESKETH DR
WARREN AVE
GROVE AVE
TOWNSHEND RD
GIBBON DR
FRYER RD
HIGHFIELD AVE
HOLFORD AVE
MANCHESTER RD
ROMAN ROAD
Brookhouse Farm
Mushroom Farm
Long Wood
SMITHY LA
SCHOOL LA
LODGE LA
STUBBS LA
Sch
FITTON ST
HEBERT ST
ARTHUR ST
STATION RD
ROBERTS RD
ATCHISON
BATEMAN RD
HARRIS RD
PAULDEN RD
Reservoir
Lostock Gralam Station
MOSS LA
LOSTOCK HOLLOW
Holford Moss
Wade Brook
Home Farm
BIRCHES LA
Fieldhouse Farm
Lostock
Langford Farm
A556

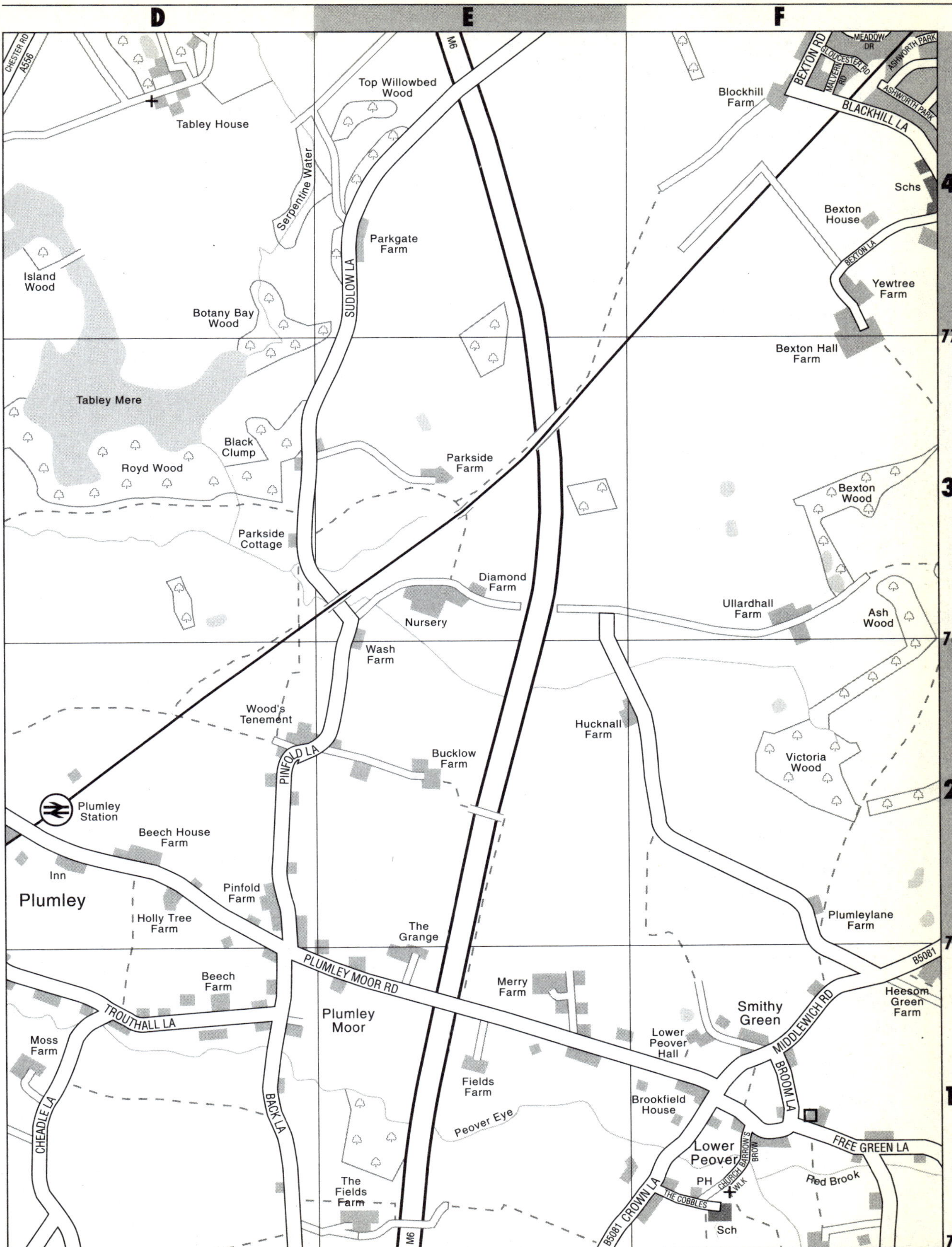
D
E
F
CHESTER RD
A556
Tabley House
Top Willowbed Wood
M6
Blockhill Farm
BEXTON RD
MEADOW DR
GLOUCESTER RD
MALVERN RD
ASHWORTH PARK
BLACKHILL LA
Serpentine Water
Parkgate Farm
Schs
Bexton House
BEXTON LA
Yewtree Farm
Island Wood
SUDLOW LA
Botany Bay Wood
Bexton Hall Farm
Tabley Mere
Black Clump
Parkside Farm
Royd Wood
Bexton Wood
Parkside Cottage
Diamond Farm
Ullardhall Farm
Ash Wood
Nursery
Wash Farm
Wood's Tenement
Hucknall Farm
PINFOLD LA
Bucklow Farm
Victoria Wood
Plumley Station
Beech House Farm
Inn
Plumley
Pinfold Farm
Holly Tree Farm
The Grange
Plumleylane Farm
PLUMLEY MOOR RD
Beech Farm
Merry Farm
Smithy Green
B5081
Heesom Green Farm
TROUTHALL LA
Plumley Moor
MIDDLEWICH RD
Moss Farm
Lower Peover Hall
Fields Farm
BROOM LA
CHEADLE LA
BACK LA
Brookfield House
Peover Eye
FREE GREEN LA
Lower Peover
CHURCH WLK
BARROW'S BROW
PH
Red Brook
The Fields Farm
THE COBBLES
B5081 CROWN LA
Sch
4
77
3
76
2
75
1
74
72
73
74

81
57

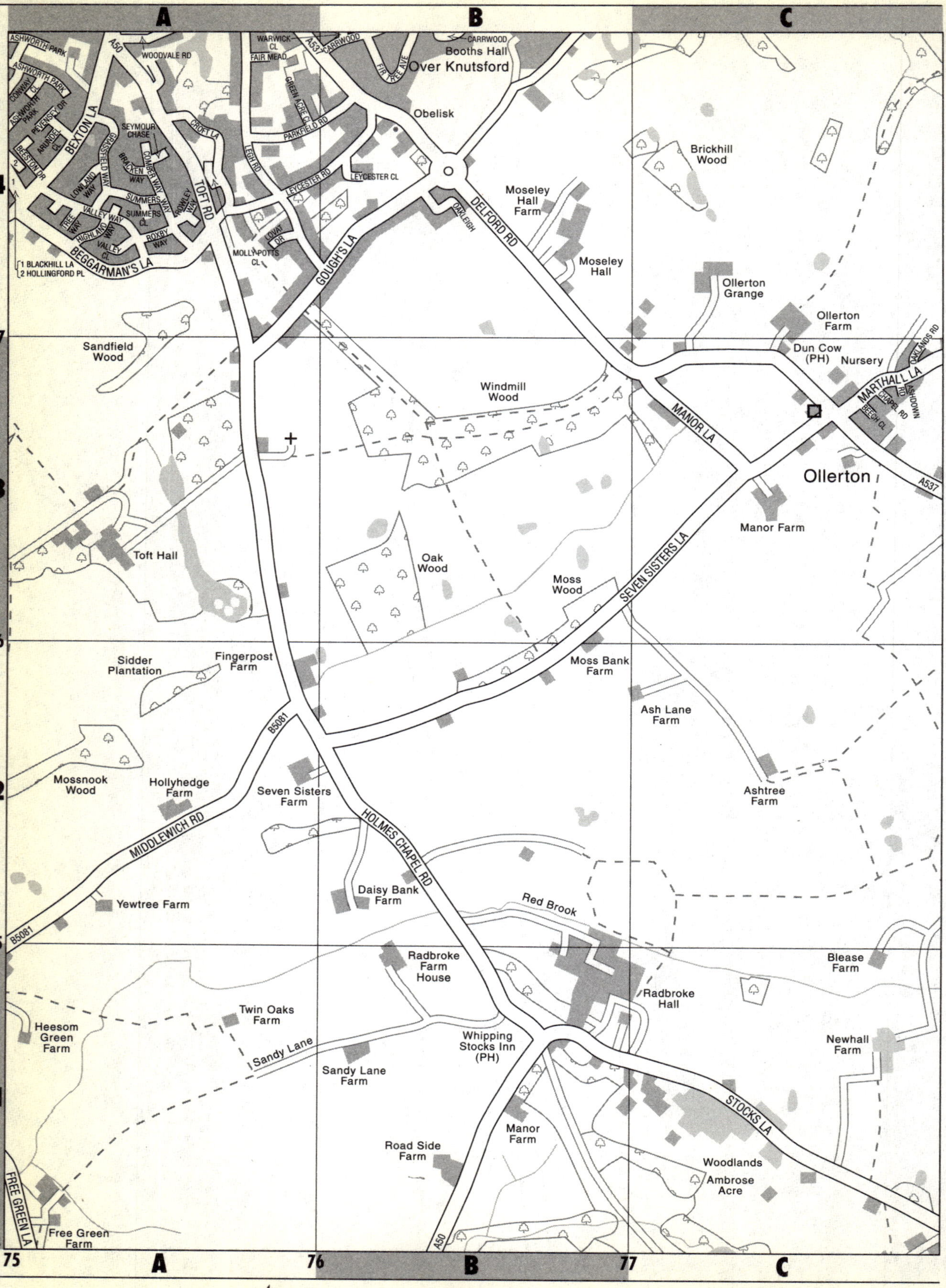
A
B
C
ASHWORTH PARK
A50
WOODVALE RD
WARWICK CL
FAIR MEAD
A537
CARRWOOD
Booths Hall
Over Knutsford
FIR TREE AVE
GREEN ACRE CL
PARKFIELD RD
Obelisk
BEXTON LA
SEYMOUR CHASE
CROFT LA
LEGH RD
LEYCESTER RD
LEYCESTER CL
OAKLEIGH
DELFORD RD
Moseley Hall Farm
Brickhill Wood
TOFT RD
BECKARMAN'S LA
1 BLACKHILL LA
2 HOLLINGFORD PL
MOLLY POTTS CL
LOVAT DR
GOUGH'S LA
Moseley Hall
Ollerton Grange
Ollerton Farm
Dun Cow (PH)
Nursery
OAKLANDS RD
MARTHALL LA
CHAPEL RD
ASHDOWN RD
BEECH CL
Sandfield Wood
Windmill Wood
MANOR LA
Ollerton
A537
Toft Hall
Manor Farm
Oak Wood
SEVEN SISTERS LA
Moss Wood
Sidder Plantation
Fingerpost Farm
Moss Bank Farm
Ash Lane Farm
B5081
Mossnook Wood
Hollyhedge Farm
Seven Sisters Farm
Ashtree Farm
MIDDLEWICH RD
HOLMES CHAPEL RD
Daisy Bank Farm
Yewtree Farm
Red Brook
B5081
Radbroke Farm House
Blease Farm
Radbroke Hall
Heesom Green Farm
Twin Oaks Farm
Sandy Lane
Whipping Stocks Inn (PH)
Newhall Farm
Sandy Lane Farm
STOCKS LA
Manor Farm
Road Side Farm
Woodlands
Ambrose Acre
FREE GREEN LA
Free Green Farm
A50
4
77
3
76
2
75
1
74
75
76
77

81
107

58
84

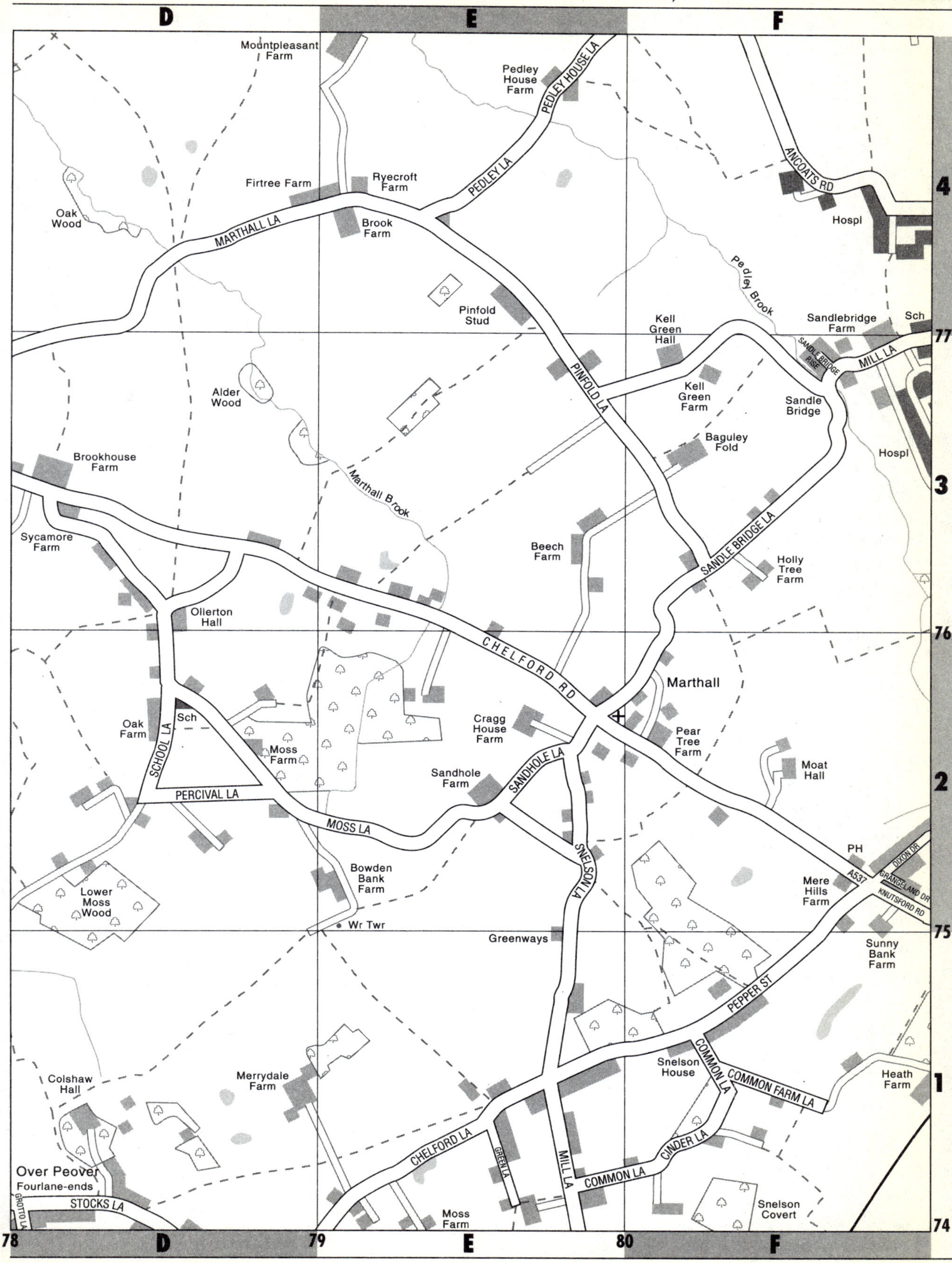
D
E
F
Mountpleasant Farm
Pedley House Farm
PEDLEY HOUSE LA
PEDLEY LA
Firtree Farm
Ryecroft Farm
Oak Wood
MARTHALL LA
Brook Farm
ANCOATS RD
Hospl
Pedley Brook
Pinfold Stud
Kell Green Hall
Sandlebridge Farm
Sch
SANDLE BRIDGE RISE
MILL LA
Alder Wood
PINFOLD LA
Kell Green Farm
Sandle Bridge
Baguley Fold
Hospl
Brookhouse Farm
Marthall Brook
Sycamore Farm
Beech Farm
SANDLE BRIDGE LA
Holly Tree Farm
Ollerton Hall
CHELFORD RD
Marthall
Oak Farm
Sch
SCHOOL LA
Moss Farm
Cragg House Farm
Pear Tree Farm
Moat Hall
Sandhole Farm
SANDHOLE LA
PERCIVAL LA
MOSS LA
PH
DIXON DR
A537
GRANGELAND DR
KNUTSFORD RD
Lower Moss Wood
Bowden Bank Farm
SNELSON LA
Mere Hills Farm
Wr Twr
Greenways
Sunny Bank Farm
PEPPER ST
COMMON LA
Colshaw Hall
Merrydale Farm
Snelson House
COMMON FARM LA
Heath Farm
CHELFORD LA
GREEN LA
MILL LA
CINDER LA
COMMON LA
Over Peover
Fourlane-ends
STOCKS LA
GROTTO LA
Moss Farm
Snelson Covert
4
77
3
76
2
75
1
74
78
79
80
D
E
F

108
84

83
59

A
B
C
4
3
2
1
77
76
75
74
81
82
83
Tanyard Farm
FODEN LA
A535
Golf Course
Oswald Farm
GREEN LA
WARFORD LA
Little Moss Farm
The Moss
Field's Farm
Heathgate Farm
ANCOATS RD
Sandpit Farm
CHELFORD RD
Hospl
PH
Manor Farm
MILL LA
WARFORD CRES
MERRYMAN'S LA
Warford Hall Farm
Dane Ville
ORCHARD CRES
Walton Farm
Hospl
Hospl
Grogram Cottage
Hospl
SOSSMOSS LA
WELSH ROW
Stelfoxes
Dean Green
Sossmoss Wood
SAND LA
Gatley Green Farm
Dog Hole Wood
Peckmill Bottoms
Wyche's Farm
NURSERY LA
Lomas's Bottom
Peck Mill Farm
Sossmoss Hall
Corbishley Bridge
CARTER LA
Corbishley
Heawood Hall Farm
Firtree Farm
Callwood's Moss
Heawood Hall
Line Pits
Roadside Farm
DRUMBLE FIELD
HITCH LOWES
MILLBANK CL
BARNCROFT CL
DIXON DR
BURNT ACRE
WOODLAND END CL
BROOMFIELD CL
MOSS
CLAY HEYS
CHAPEL CT
Sandle Heath
Chandler's Farm
WOODFIN CROFT
ELMSTEAD RD
ASTLE CT
ROBIN LA
OAK RD
WOODLAND CT
ALDERLEY RD
Yarwoods
A537
STATION RD
Chelford Station
PH
Mere Farm
KNUTSFORD RD
Chelford
BOLLINGTON LA
STUBBY LA
Bollington Pits
Sch
George's Wood
Yewtree Cottages
Bloor's Pits
CHELFORD RD
Dumville's Farm
A537
PEOVER LA
Willow Gaff
Knowsley Farm
Fallows Hall Farm
HOLMES CHAPEL RD
A535

83
109

60
86

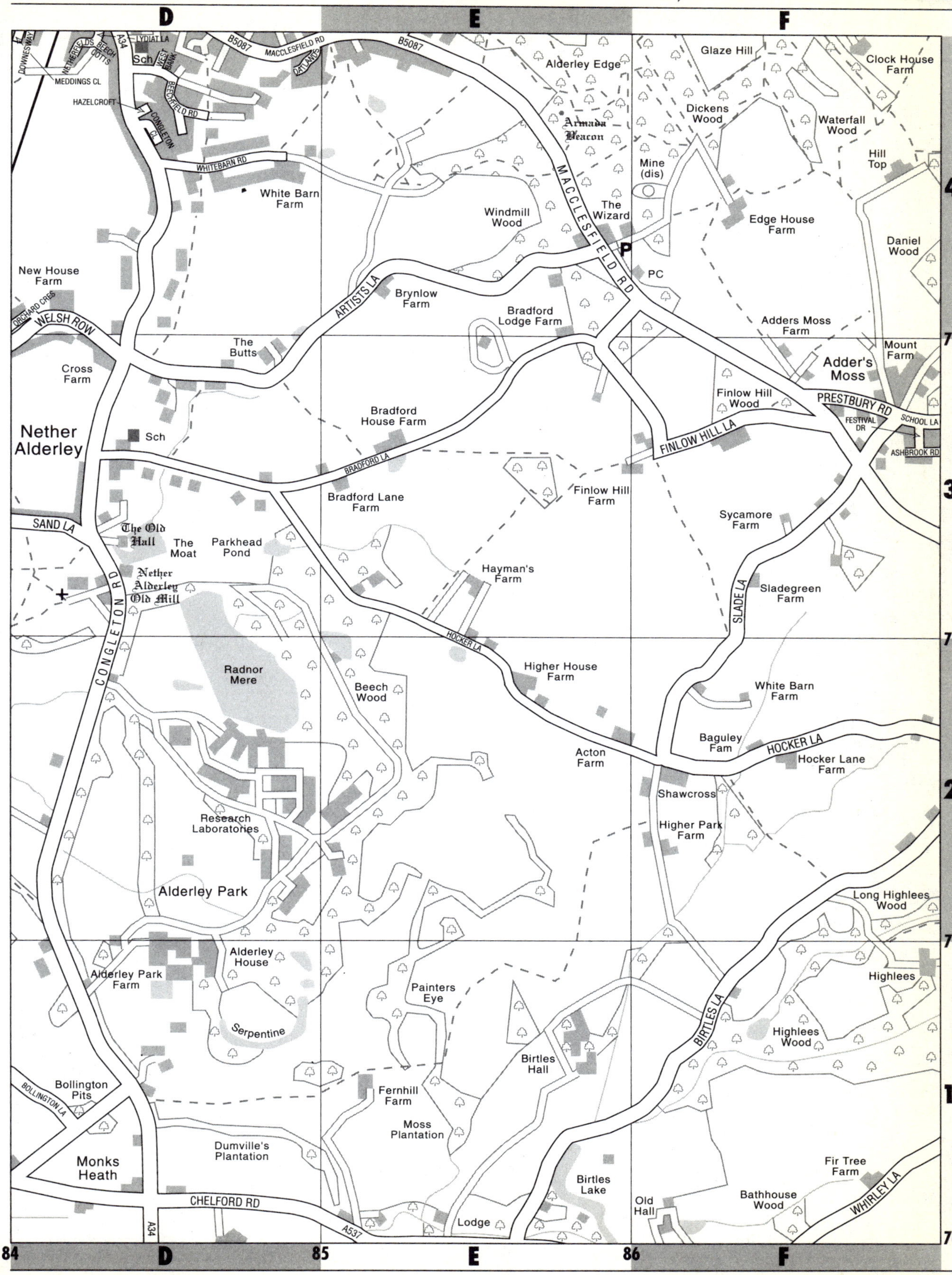
D
E
F
Glaze Hill
Clock House Farm
Alderley Edge
Dickens Wood
Waterfall Wood
Armada Beacon
Hill Top
Mine (dis)
White Barn Farm
Windmill Wood
The Wizard
Edge House Farm
Daniel Wood
New House Farm
Brynlow Farm
PC
Bradford Lodge Farm
Adders Moss Farm
Mount Farm
The Butts
Cross Farm
Adder's Moss
Finlow Hill Wood
Bradford House Farm
Nether Alderley
Sch
Bradford Lane Farm
Finlow Hill Farm
Sycamore Farm
The Old Hall
The Moat
Parkhead Pond
Nether Alderley Old Mill
Hayman's Farm
Sladegreen Farm
Radnor Mere
Higher House Farm
Beech Wood
White Barn Farm
Baguley Fam
Acton Farm
Hocker Lane Farm
Shawcross
Research Laboratories
Higher Park Farm
Alderley Park
Long Highlees Wood
Alderley House
Alderley Park Farm
Painters Eye
Highlees
Serpentine
Highlees Wood
Birtles Hall
Bollington Pits
Fernhill Farm
Moss Plantation
Dumville's Plantation
Monks Heath
Birtles Lake
Fir Tree Farm
Old Hall
Bathhouse Wood
Lodge
LYDIAT LA
Sch
DOWNESWAY
NETHERFIELDS
BEECH COTTS
A34
WEST BANK
MEDDINGS CL
HAZELCROFT
BEECHFIELD RD
CONGLETON CL
B5087
MACCLESFIELD RD
OATLANDS
WHITEBARN RD
MACCLESFIELD RD
ARTISTS LA
ORCHARD CRES
WELSH ROW
PRESTBURY RD
FESTIVAL DR
SCHOOL LA
ASHBROOK RD
FINLOW HILL LA
BRADFORD LA
SAND LA
SLADE LA
CONGLETON RD
HOCKER LA
HOCKER LA
BIRTLES LA
BOLLINGTON LA
CHELFORD RD
A537
A34
WHIRLEY LA
4
77
3
76
2
75
1
74
84
85
86

110
86

85
61

A
B
C
4
3
2
1
77
76
75
74
87
88
89
Goose Green Farm
Allen's Farm
A538
Danielhill
Turner House Farm
Hunter's Pool Farm
SHAWS LA
Greendale Farm
GREENDALE LA
Gadhole Farm
Spittle House
River Bollin
BUTLEY LANES
WILMSLOW RD
Daniel Hill
Read's Wood
Greendale
COACHWAY
BOLLIN GR
Sch
BOLLIN MEWS
Alder Wood
OAK RD
White Gables
CASTLE HILL CT
SADDLEBACK DR
Withinlee Farm
WITHINLEE RD
HOLMLEA WAY
TUDOR DR
CASTLE HILL
SPENCER BROOK
THE VILLAGE A538
ELM RISE
HAWTHORN RISE
MAGNOLIA RISE
PINEHURST
ALDERS WAY
CASTLE RISE
CASTLEGATE MEWS
CASTLEGATE
BIRCH WAY
ROWANSIDE
ARDENBROOK RISE
MACCLESFIELD RD
LARCH RISE
CASTLEFORD DR
SCHOOL LA
Field Bank Farm
Hare Hill
ASHBROOK RD
BEAUMONT CL
COLLAR HOUSE DR
PRESTBURY RD
Withenlee Farm
Dunge Farm
B5087
CHELFORD RD
PACKSADDLE PK
Golf Course
SQUIRRELS CHASE
Greenbank Farm
Spencer Brook
GREYHOUND RD
Broadheath Farm
Harebarrow Farm
CH
MACCLESFIELD RD
DALE HEAD RD
Harebarrowlake
Windmill Farm
Dumber Wood
Vardentown
Walnut Tree Farm
Lower Harebarrow Farm
Big Wood
SUMMERHILL RD
HOCKER LA
BIRTLES LA
Fittontown Farm
Fallibroome Farm
Fleets Farm
ALDERLEY RD
WRIGLEY LA
Whirley Grove
1 SALOP WLK
2 WILTSHIRE WLK
3 STAFFORD WLK
4 NORFOLK WLK
5 LINCOLN PL
6 LINCOLN WLK
7 LANARK WLK
8 ANGUS WLK
PRESTBURY RD
B5087
Highlees Wood
Whirley Farm
SELKIRK CL
BERWICK CL
STIRLING CL
GRANGELANDS
WILSHIRE CL
STAFFORD CL
LINCOLN CL
RENFREW CL
SEVERN CL
SANDY LA
Sch
Sand Pit
CHURCHWAY
EAGLAIS WAY
FRIARS WAY
DONAGH CL
PRIORY LA
Whirley Hall
1 ELGIN AVE
2 WOODSTOCK CL
3 FARWOOD CL
1 DORSET WLK
2 HAMPSHIRE WLK
3 ESSEX WLK
4 KENT WLK
5 WILLOW MEWS
WESTMORLAND CL
BECK LA
BERKSHIRE CL
DURHAM CL
DEVON CL
HEREFORD
KENNEDY AVE
FIR CL
WHIRLEY LA
Birchtree Farm
CORNWALL CL
MILLBANK DR
BATEMILL CL
PORTFORD CL
JUNIPER RISE
SUFFOLK CL
1 COTSWOLD CL
2 HAMBLE WAY
3 BLYTH CL
4 TAMAR CL
Whirleybarn
WHIRLEY RD
ANDERTONS LA
DRUMMOND WAY
RAYLEIGH WAY
BIRCHGATE CL
KEATS DR
UNDERWOOD CL
Sch
LEAMINGTON RD
1 BROOKHOUSE CL
2 MERRYDALE CL
3 ALVESTON CL
4 WELLESBOURNE CL
HOME FARM AVE
BIRCHES CROFT DR
DEERWOOD CL
Hospl
BRACKEN CL
The Mount Farm
BELMONT AVE
BIRTLES RD
FOWEY CL
LANREATH CL
TREEN CL
MADRON AVE
POLPERRO CL
BODMIN AVE
REDRUTH AVE
WEST HOUSE CT
TRURO CL
ST IVES CL
ST AUSTELL AVE
VICTORIA RD
The Mount
Sch
ASHTON AVE
1 HAYLE CL
2 NEWLYN AVE
3 NEWQUAY DR
ST AUSTELL AVE
CAMBORNE AVE
Hospl
FALLIBROOME RD

85
111

62
88

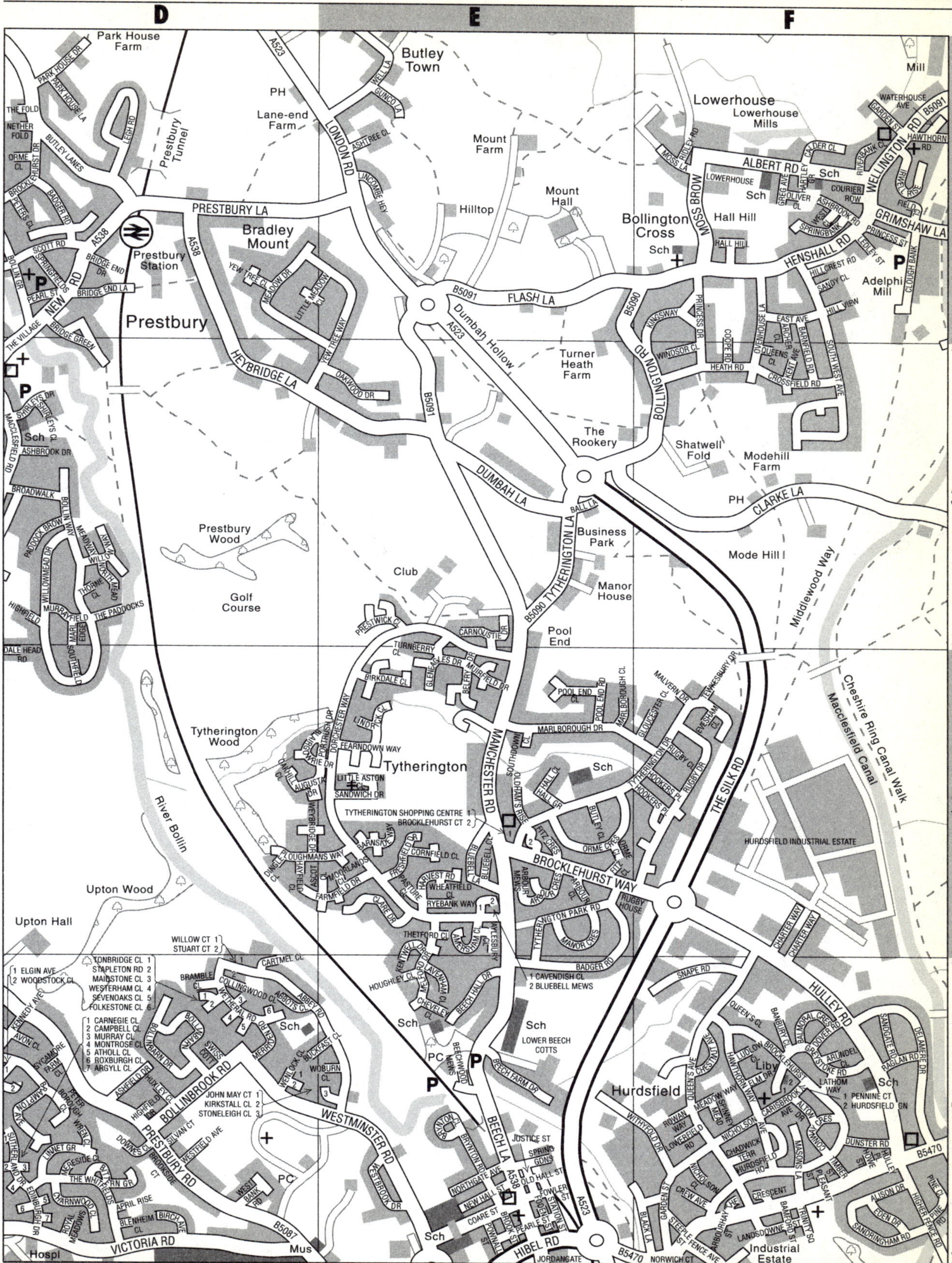
D
E
F
Park House Farm
Butley Town
PH
Lane-end Farm
Prestbury Tunnel
Mount Farm
Mount Hall
Lowerhouse
Lowerhouse Mills
Mill
Hilltop
PRESTBURY LA
Bradley Mount
Prestbury Station
Prestbury
Bollington Cross
Hall Hill
Adelphi Mill
ALBERT RD
HENSHALL RD
WELLINGTON RD
GRIMSHAW LA
MOSS BROW
FLASH LA
B5091
Dumbah Hollow
A523
A538
LONDON RD
HEYBRIDGE LA
Turner Heath Farm
BOLLINGTON RD
B5090
The Rookery
Shatwell Fold
Modehill Farm
PH
CLARKE LA
DUMBAH LA
Business Park
Mode Hill
Middlewood Way
Prestbury Wood
Golf Course
Club
Manor House
Pool End
TYTHERINGTON LA
Tytherington Wood
Tytherington
TYTHERINGTON SHOPPING CENTRE 1
BROCKLEHURST CT 2
MANCHESTER RD
MARLBOROUGH DR
BROCKLEHURST WAY
THE SILK RD
Cheshire Ring Canal Walk
Macclesfield Canal
HURDSFIELD INDUSTRIAL ESTATE
River Bollin
Upton Wood
Upton Hall
WILLOW CT 1
STUART CT 2
1 ELGIN AVE
2 WOODSTOCK CL
TONBRIDGE CL 1
STAPLETON RD 2
MAIDSTONE CL 3
WESTERHAM CL 4
SEVENOAKS CL 5
FOLKESTONE CL 6
1 CARNEGIE CL
2 CAMPBELL CL
3 MURRAY CL
4 MONTROSE CL
5 ATHOLL CL
6 ROXBURGH CL
7 ARGYLL CL
1 CAVENDISH CL
2 BLUEBELL MEWS
JOHN MAY CT 1
KIRKSTALL CL 2
STONELEIGH CL 3
BOLLINBROOK RD
PRESTBURY RD
WESTMINSTER RD
VICTORIA RD
B5087
Hospl
Mus
Sch
LOWER BEECH COTTS
BEECH LA
HULLEY RD
Hurdsfield
1 PENNINE CT
2 HURDSFIELD GN
B5470
Industrial Estate
HIBEL RD
JORDANGATE
NORWICH CT
77
76
75
74
4
3
2
1
90
91
92

112
88

87
63

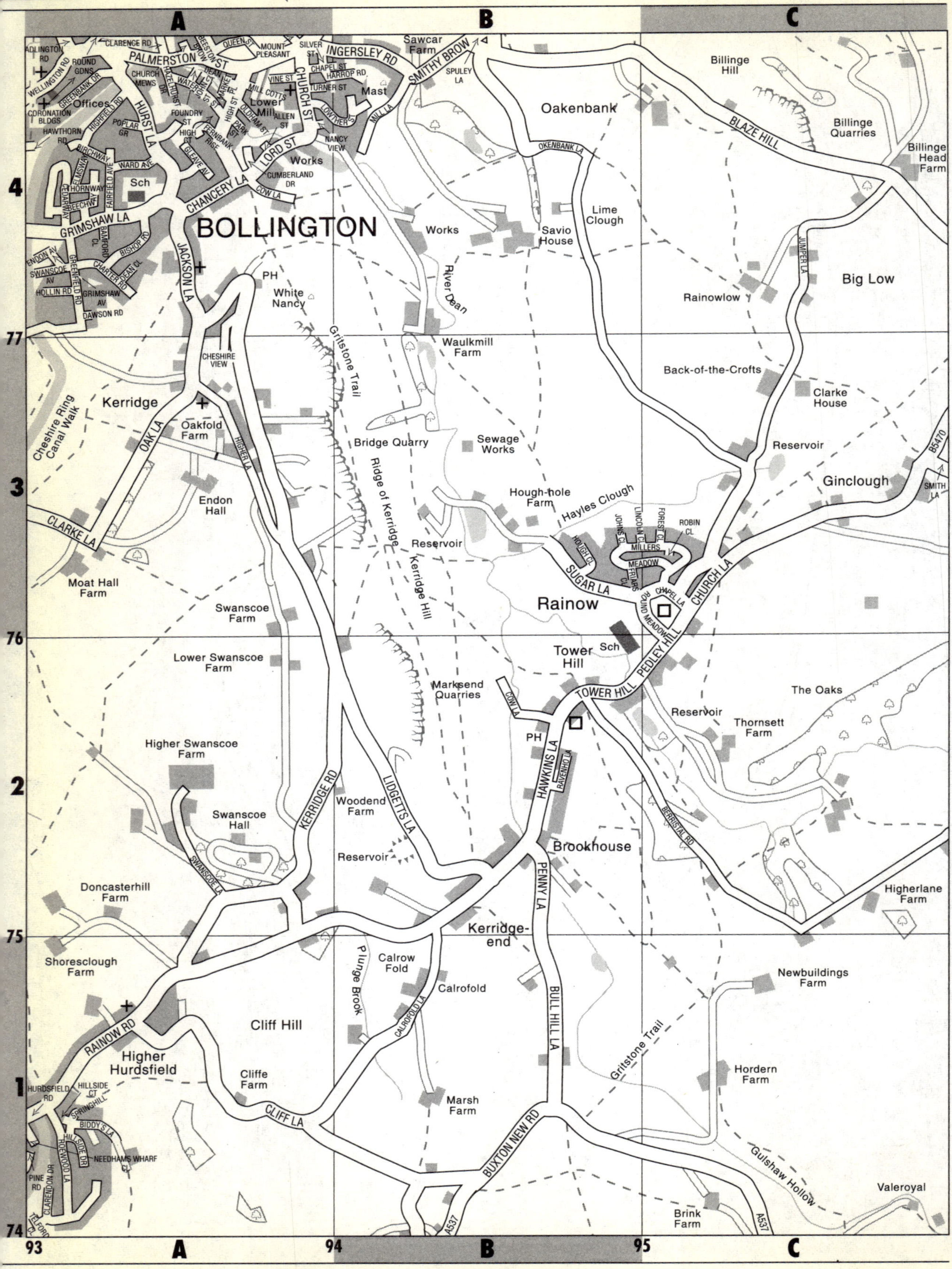
A
B
C
BOLLINGTON
ADLINGTON RD
CLARENCE RD
PALMERSTON ST
QUEEN ST
MOUNT PLEASANT
SILVER ST
INGERSLEY RD
Sawcar Farm
SMITHY BROW
SPULEY LA
ROUND GDNS
WELLINGTON RD
GREENBANK DR
CHURCH MEWS
CHAPEL ST
HARROP RD
VINE ST
CHURCH ST
TURNER ST
Mast
Offices
CORONATION BLDGS
HAWTHORN RD
HIGHFIELD RD
POPLAR GR
HURST LA
Lower Mill
ALLEN ST
LOWTHER ST
MILL LA
FOUNDRY ST
FERNBANK RISE
OLDHAM ST
NANCY VIEW
LORD ST
Works
CUMBERLAND DR
COW LA
WARD AVE
BIRCHWAY
THORNWAY
BEECHWAY
CEDARWAY
FAIRFIELD AVE
Sch
CHANCERY LA
GLEAVE AV
GRIMSHAW LA
BAMFORD CL
BISHOP RD
DEAN CL
CHARTER RD
ENDON AV
SWANSCOE AV
HOLLIN RD
GREENFIELD RD
GRIMSHAW AV
DAWSON RD
JACKSON LA
PH
White Nancy
Oakenbank
OKENBANK LA
BLAZE HILL
Billinge Hill
Billinge Quarries
Billinge Head Farm
Lime Clough
Savio House
Works
River Dean
Big Low
Rainowlow
JUMPER LA
77
Waulkmill Farm
CHESHIRE VIEW
Gritstone Trail
Kerridge
Cheshire Ring Canal Walk
OAK LA
Oakfold Farm
HIGHER LA
Back-of-the-Crofts
Clarke House
Bridge Quarry
Sewage Works
Reservoir
Ridge of Kerridge
B5470
Ginclough
SMITH LA
3
Endon Hall
Hough-hole Farm
Hayles Clough
JOHNS CL
LINCOLN CL
FOREST CL
ROBIN CL
MILLERS
MEADOW
HOUGH CL
FRIARS CL
CLARKE LA
Reservoir
Kerridge Hill
SUGAR LA
CHAPEL LA
CHURCH LA
Moat Hall Farm
Rainow
ROUND MEADOW
Swanscoe Farm
76
Tower Hill
Sch
PEDLEY HILL
Lower Swanscoe Farm
Marksend Quarries
TOWER HILL
COW LA
The Oaks
Reservoir
Thornsett Farm
PH
Higher Swanscoe Farm
HAWKINS LA
RAVENHO LA
2
KERRIDGE RD
LIDGETTS LA
Woodend Farm
Swanscoe Hall
BERRISTAL RD
Brookhouse
Reservoir
SWANSCOE LA
PENNY LA
Doncasterhill Farm
Higherlane Farm
75
Kerridge-end
Shoresclough Farm
Calrow Fold
Plunge Brook
Newbuildings Farm
Calrofold
BULL HILL LA
RAINOW RD
Cliff Hill
CALROFOLD LA
Gritstone Trail
Higher Hurdsfield
1
Cliffe Farm
Hordern Farm
HURDSFIELD RD
HILLSIDE CT
SPRINGHILL
Marsh Farm
BIDDY'S LA
CLIFF LA
HILLSIDE DR
ROEWOOD LA
NEEDHAMS WHARF CL
BUXTON NEW RD
Gulshaw Hollow
PINE RD
CLARENDON DR
Valeroyal
Brink Farm
A537
TELFORD CL
74
93
94
95

87
113

64
90

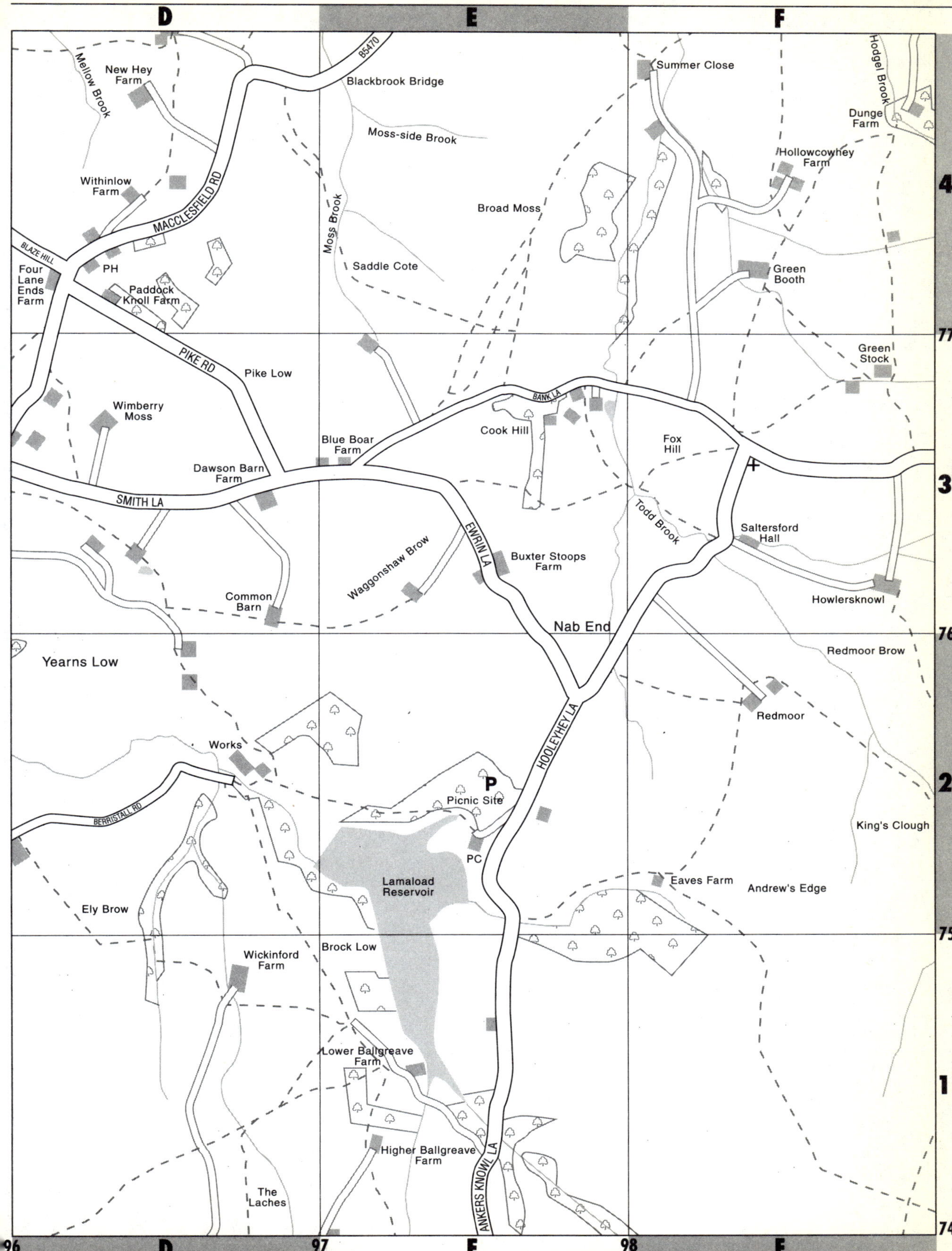
D
E
F
Mellow Brook
New Hey Farm
B5470
Blackbrook Bridge
Summer Close
Hodgel Brook
Dunge Farm
Moss-side Brook
Hollowcowhey Farm
Withinlow Farm
MACCLESFIELD RD
Moss Brook
Broad Moss
4
BLAZE HILL
Four Lane Ends Farm
PH
Saddle Cote
Green Booth
Paddock Knoll Farm
PIKE RD
Pike Low
77
Green Stock
Wimberry Moss
BANK LA
Cook Hill
Blue Boar Farm
Fox Hill
Dawson Barn Farm
SMITH LA
3
Todd Brook
EWRIN LA
Saltersford Hall
Waggonshaw Brow
Buxter Stoops Farm
Common Barn
Howlersknowl
Nab End
76
Yearns Low
Redmoor Brow
Redmoor
HOOLEYHEY LA
Works
P
Picnic Site
2
BERRISTALL RD
King's Clough
PC
Lamaload Reservoir
Eaves Farm
Andrew's Edge
Ely Brow
75
Wickinford Farm
Brock Low
Lower Ballgreave Farm
1
Higher Ballgreave Farm
ANKERS KNOWL LA
The Laches
74
96
D
97
E
98
F

114
90

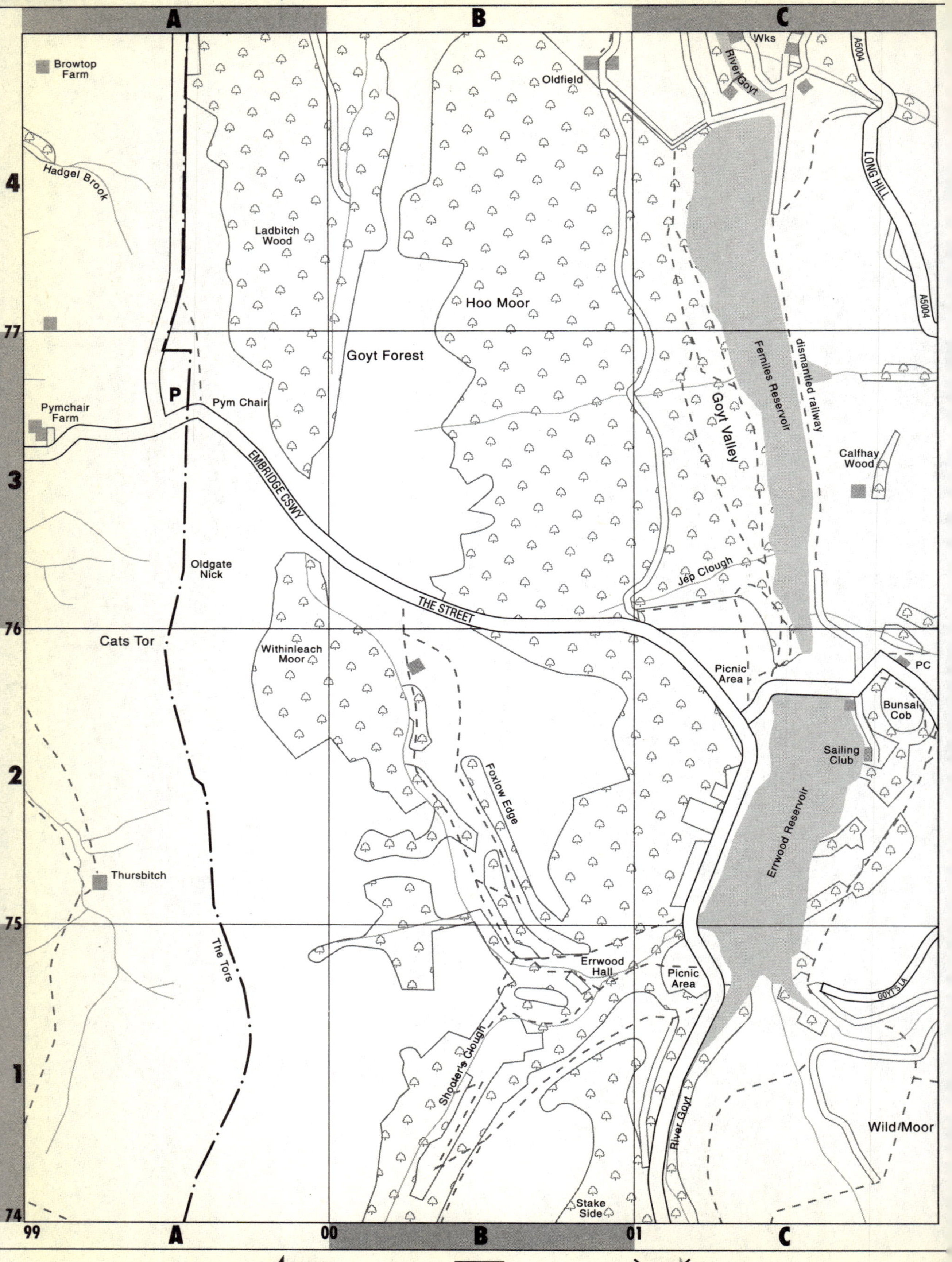
A
B
C
Browtop Farm
Hadgel Brook
Ladbitch Wood
Oldfield
Wks
River Goyt
A5004
LONG HILL
Hoo Moor
Goyt Forest
P
Pym Chair
Pymchair Farm
EMBRIDGE CSWY
Fernilee Reservoir
dismantled railway
Goyt Valley
Calfhay Wood
Oldgate Nick
Jep Clough
THE STREET
Cats Tor
Withinleach Moor
Picnic Area
PC
Bunsal Cob
Sailing Club
Foxlow Edge
Errwood Reservoir
Thursbitch
The Tors
Errwood Hall
Picnic Area
GOYT'S LA
Shooter's Clough
River Goyt
Wild Moor
Stake Side
4
77
3
76
2
75
1
74
99
00
01

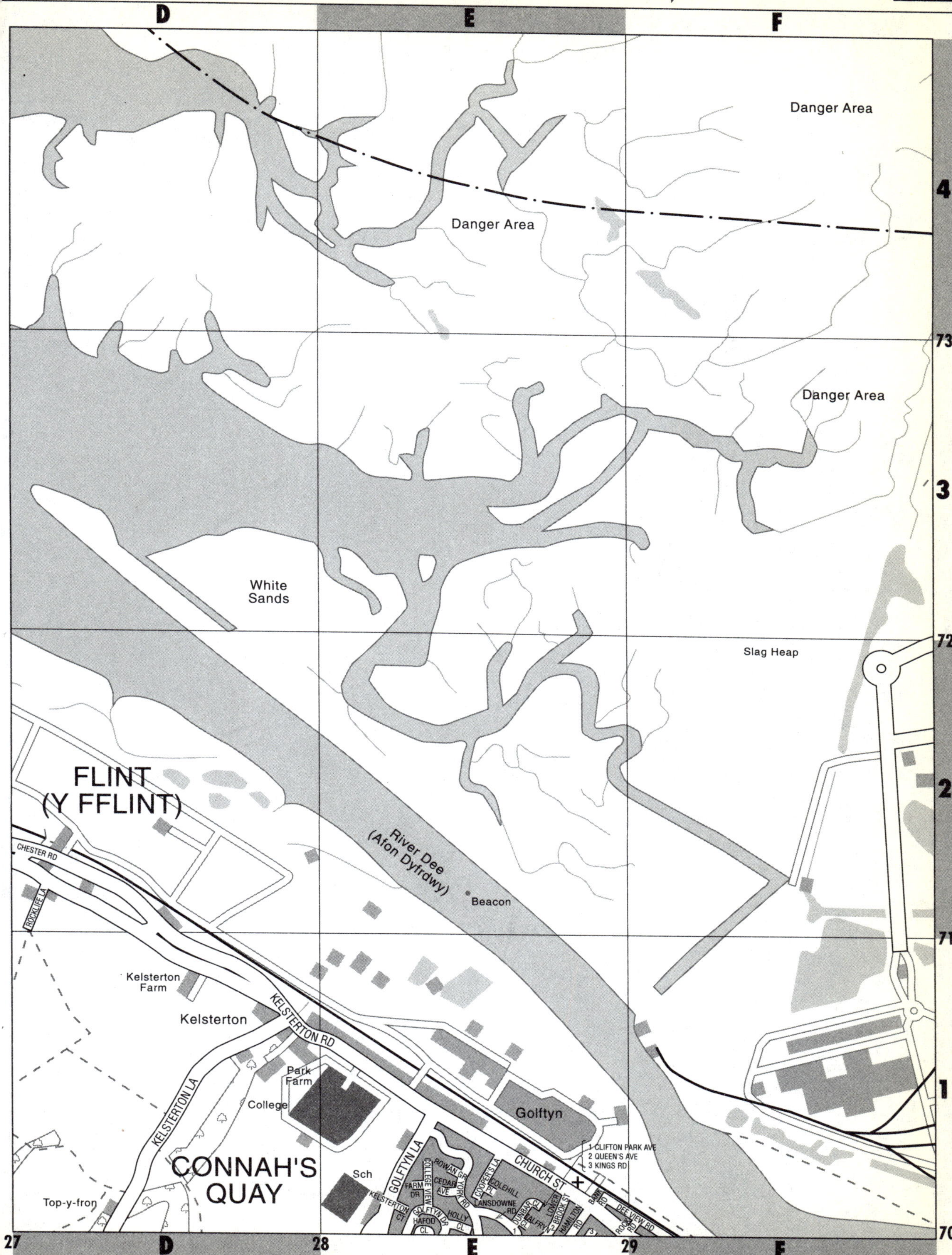
D
E
F
Danger Area
Danger Area
Danger Area
White
Sands
Slag Heap
FLINT
(Y FFLINT)
CHESTER RD
ROCKLIFE LA
River Dee
(Afon Dyfrdwy)
Beacon
Kelsterton
Farm
Kelsterton
KELSTERTON RD
Park
Farm
College
KELSTERTON LA
CONNAH'S
QUAY
Top-y-fron
Sch
Golftyn
GOLFTYN LA
KELSTERTON CT
COLLEGE VIEW
FARM DR
ROWAN GR
CEDAR AVE
YORK RD
GOLFTYN DR
HAFOD CL
HOLLY CL
COOPER'S LA
COLEHILL PL
CHURCH ST
LANSDOWNE RD
DUNBAR CL
TALFRYN
LOWER BROOK ST
HAMILTON RD
BANK RD
ROCK RD
DEE VIEW RD
1 CLIFTON PARK AVE
2 QUEEN'S AVE
3 KINGS RD
4
3
2
1
73
72
71
70
27
28
29

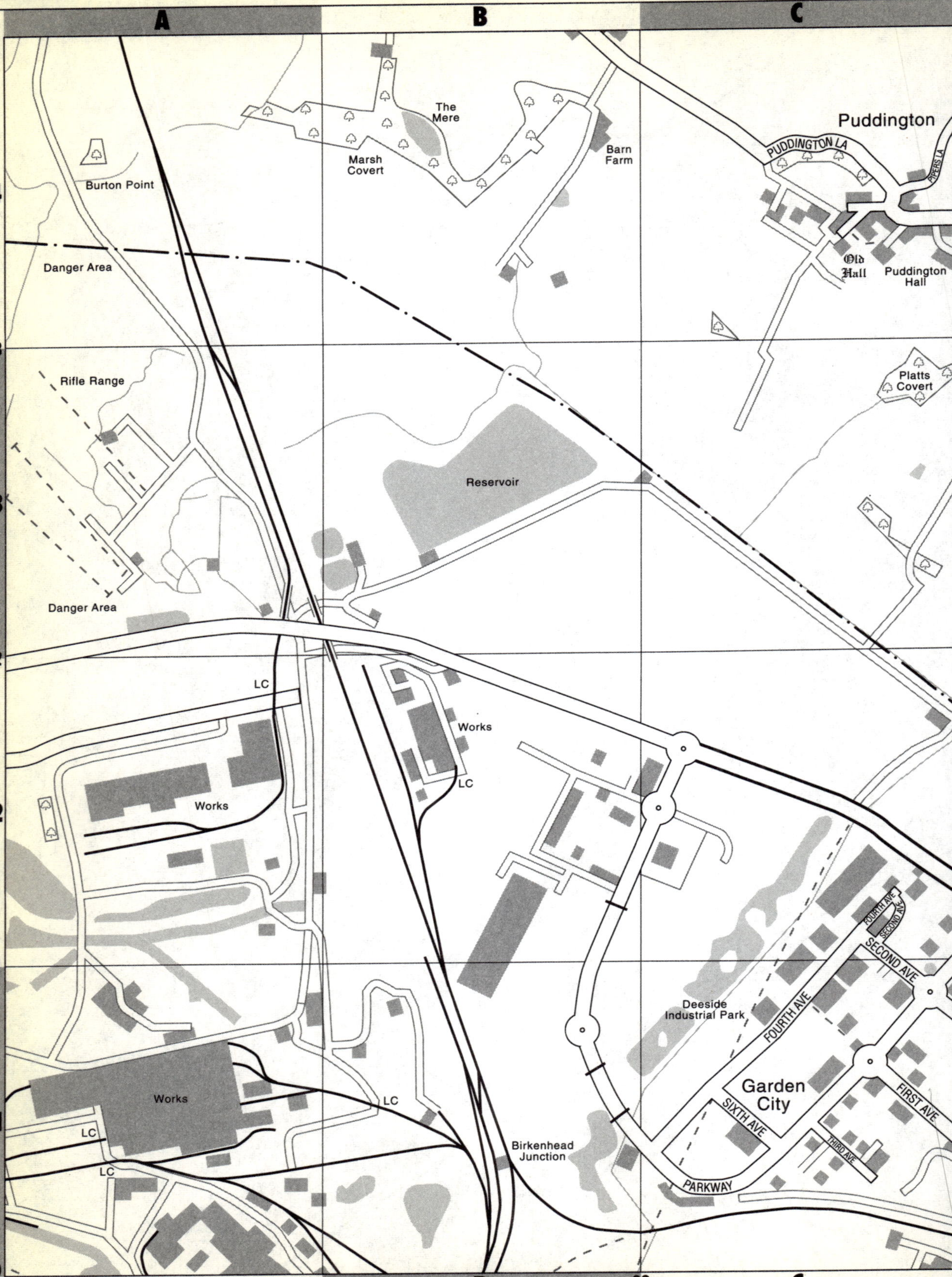
A
B
C
4
73
3
72
2
71
1
70
30
31
32
The Mere
Marsh Covert
Barn Farm
Puddington
PUDDINGTON LA
PIPERS LA
Old Hall
Puddington Hall
Burton Point
Danger Area
Rifle Range
Platts Covert
Reservoir
Danger Area
LC
Works
Works
LC
Works
LC
LC
LC
Birkenhead Junction
Deeside Industrial Park
FOURTH AVE
SECOND AVE
SECOND AVE
FOURTH AVE
Garden City
SIXTH AVE
FIRST AVE
THIRD AVE
PARKWAY

68
94

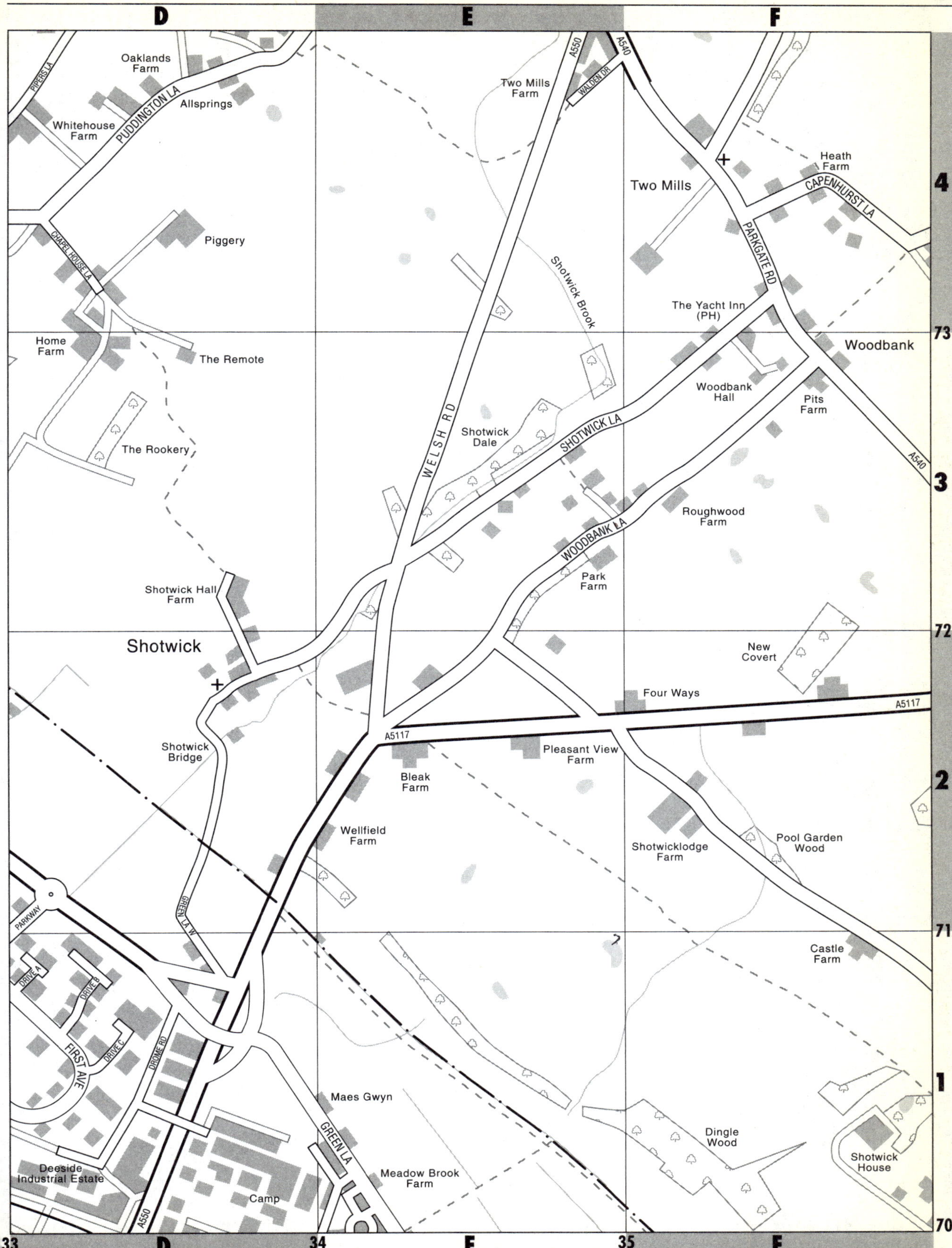
D
E
F
Oaklands Farm
PIPERS LA
PUDDINGTON LA
Allsprings
Whitehouse Farm
Two Mills Farm
A550
A540
WALDEN DR
Heath Farm
Two Mills
CAPENHURST LA
Piggery
CHAPEL HOUSE LA
PARKGATE RD
Shotwick Brook
The Yacht Inn (PH)
Home Farm
The Remote
Woodbank
Woodbank Hall
Pits Farm
WELSH RD
Shotwick Dale
SHOTWICK LA
The Rookery
A540
Roughwood Farm
WOODBANK LA
Park Farm
Shotwick Hall Farm
New Covert
Shotwick
Four Ways
A5117
A5117
Pleasant View Farm
Shotwick Bridge
Bleak Farm
Wellfield Farm
Pool Garden Wood
Shotwicklodge Farm
PARKWAY
GREEN LA W
Castle Farm
DRIVE A
DRIVE B
FIRST AVE
DRIVE C
DROME RD
Maes Gwyn
Dingle Wood
GREEN LA
Shotwick House
Meadow Brook Farm
Deeside Industrial Estate
Camp
A550
4
73
3
72
2
71
1
70
33
34
35
D
E
F

116
94

93
69

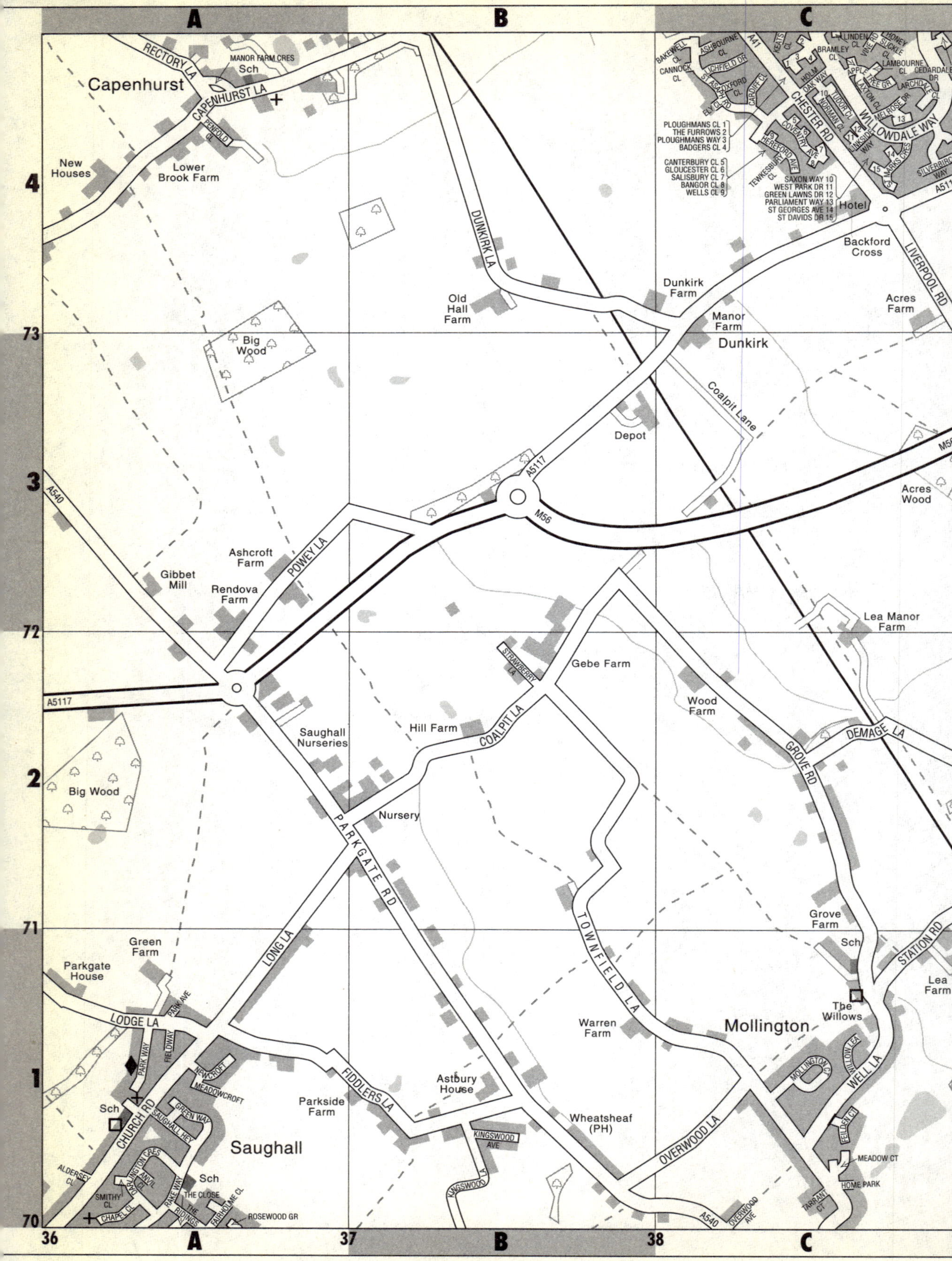
A
B
C
Capenhurst
Sch
MANOR FARM CRES
RECTORY LA
CAPENHURST LA
PENFOLD CL
New Houses
Lower Brook Farm
4
BAKEWELL CL
ASHBOURNE CL
CANNOCK CL
LICHFIELD DR
ST ASAPH RD
OXFORD CL
ELY CL
CARDIFF CL
A41
KEATS CL
HOLM OAK WAY
BRAMLEY CL
LINDEN CL
VINE RD
HONEY SUCKLE CL
LAMBOURNE CL
CEDARDALE DR
APPLE TREE GR
LARCHDALE CL
MELROSE DR
WILLOWDALE WAY
CHESTER RD
NORMAN CL
TUDOR CL
COVENTRY AVE
HEREFORD AVE
TEWKESBURY CL
LINKSIDE WAY
MARKS CRES
SILVERBIRCH WAY
PLOUGHMANS CL 1
THE FURROWS 2
PLOUGHMANS WAY 3
BADGERS CL 4
CANTERBURY CL 5
GLOUCESTER CL 6
SALISBURY CL 7
BANGOR CL 8
WELLS CL 9
SAXON WAY 10
WEST PARK DR 11
GREEN LAWNS DR 12
PARLIAMENT WAY 13
ST GEORGES AVE 14
ST DAVIDS DR 15
Hotel
A5117
Backford Cross
LIVERPOOL RD
DUNKIRK LA
Old Hall Farm
Dunkirk Farm
Manor Farm
Dunkirk
Acres Farm
73
Big Wood
Coalpit Lane
Depot
M56
A5117
3
A540
Acres Wood
POWEY LA
Ashcroft Farm
Gibbet Mill
Rendova Farm
Lea Manor Farm
72
Gebe Farm
STRAWBERRY LA
A5117
Wood Farm
Saughall Nurseries
Hill Farm
COALPIT LA
DEMAGE LA
GROVE RD
2
Big Wood
Nursery
PARKGATE RD
71
Green Farm
Parkgate House
LONG LA
TOWNFIELD LA
Grove Farm
Sch
STATION RD
Lea Farm
The Willows
LODGE LA
PARK AVE
PARK WAY
FIELDWAY
Warren Farm
Mollington
1
NEWCROFT
MEADOWCROFT
GREEN WAY
SAUGHALL HEY
Sch
CHURCH RD
Parkside Farm
FIDDLERS LA
Astbury House
Wheatsheaf (PH)
MOLLINGTON CL
WILLOW LEA
WELL LA
FELLDEN CT
Saughall
KINGSWOOD AVE
OVERWOOD LA
MEADOW CT
HOME PARK
ALDERSEY CL
DARLINGTON CRES
ANVIL CL
Sch
SMITHY CL
RAKE WAY
THE CLOSE
FAIRHOLME CL
THE RIDINGS
CHAPEL CL
ROSEWOOD GR
KINGSWOOD LA
A540
OVERWOOD AVE
TARRANT CT
70
36
37
38

93
117

70
96

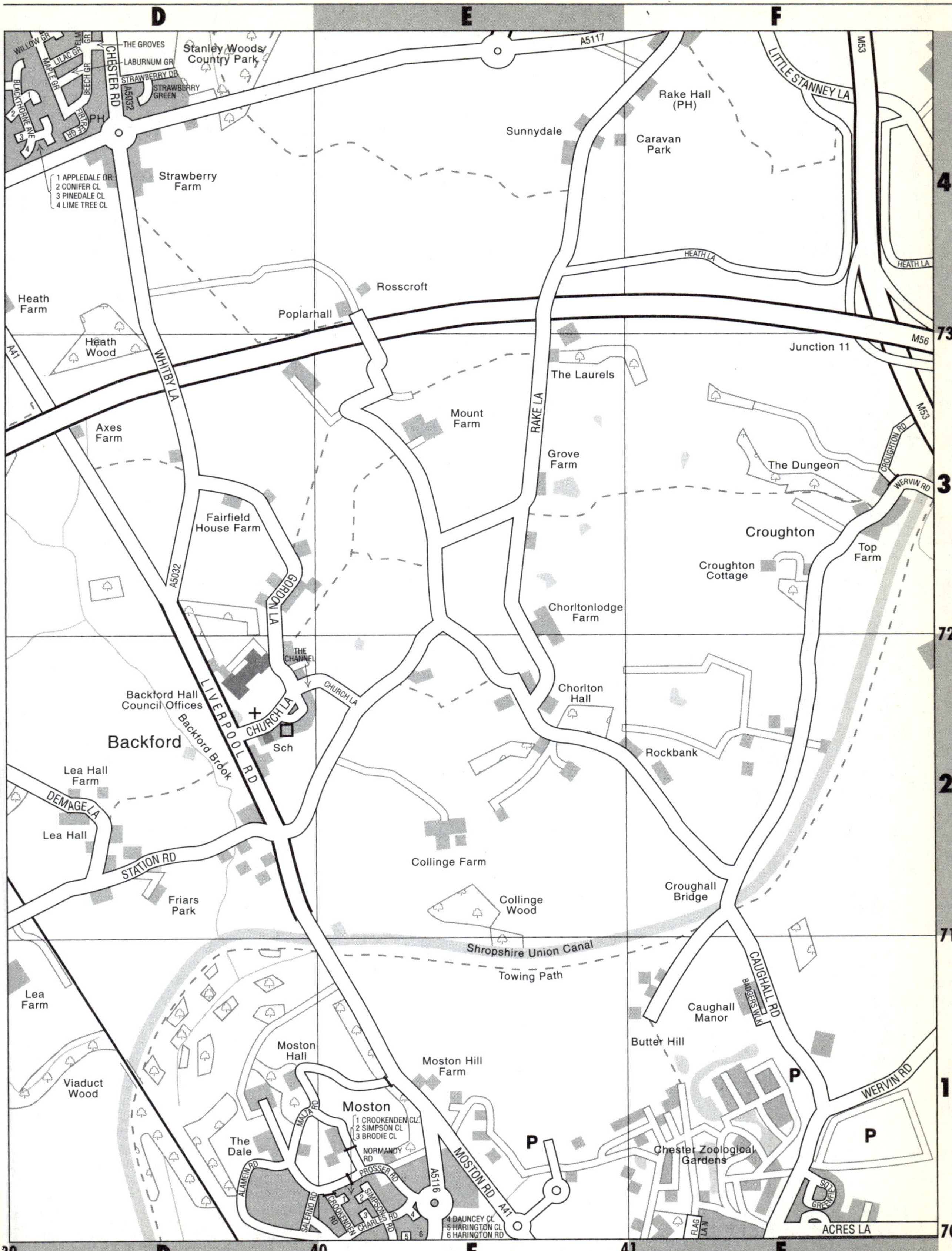
D
E
F
4
73
3
72
2
71
1
70
39
40
41
WILLOW GR
BLACKTHORNE AVE
MAPLE GR
LILAC GR
ELM GR
BEECH GR
FIRTREE GR
PH
THE GROVES
LABURNUM GR
STRAWBERRY DR
STRAWBERRY GREEN
CHESTER RD
A5032
Stanley Woods Country Park
A5117
LITTLE STANNEY LA
M53
Rake Hall (PH)
Sunnydale
Caravan Park
1 APPLEDALE DR
2 CONIFER CL
3 PINEDALE CL
4 LIME TREE CL
Strawberry Farm
HEATH LA
Heath Farm
Rosscroft
Poplarhall
M56
Junction 11
Heath Wood
A41
WHITBY LA
The Laurels
RAKE LA
Mount Farm
Axes Farm
Grove Farm
The Dungeon
CROUGHTON RD
WERVIN RD
Fairfield House Farm
Croughton
Top Farm
Croughton Cottage
GORDON LA
A5032
Chorltonlodge Farm
THE CHANNEL
CHURCH LA
Chorlton Hall
Backford Hall Council Offices
Backford
Backford Brook
LIVERPOOL RD
Sch
Rockbank
Lea Hall Farm
DEMAGE LA
Lea Hall
STATION RD
Collinge Farm
Friars Park
Croughall Bridge
Collinge Wood
Shropshire Union Canal
Towing Path
CAUGHALL RD
BADGERS WLK
Lea Farm
Caughall Manor
Butter Hill
Moston Hall
Moston Hill Farm
Viaduct Wood
Moston
1 CROOKENDEN CL
2 SIMPSON CL
3 BRODIE CL
MALTA RD
NORMANDY RD
P
The Dale
Chester Zoological Gardens
ALAMEIN RD
PROSSER RD
SIMPSON RD
SALERNO RD
CROOKENDEN RD
CHARLES RD
A5116
MOSTON RD
A41
4 DAUNCEY CL
5 HARINGTON CL
6 HARINGTON RD
FLAG LA W
ACRES LA
SOLWAY GREEN

118
96

95
71

A B C

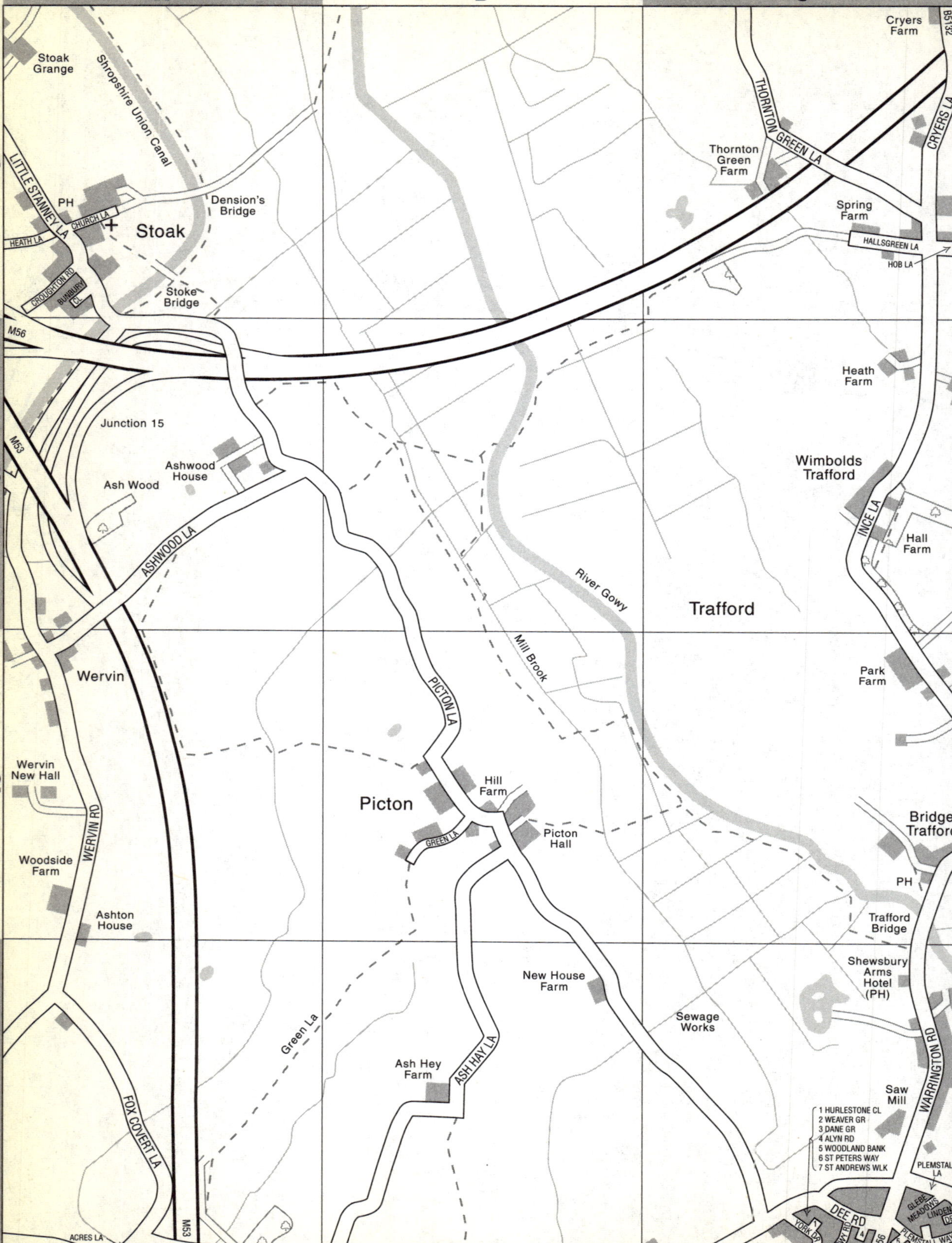

4
73
3
72
2
71
1
70

42 43 44

A B C

95
119

72
98

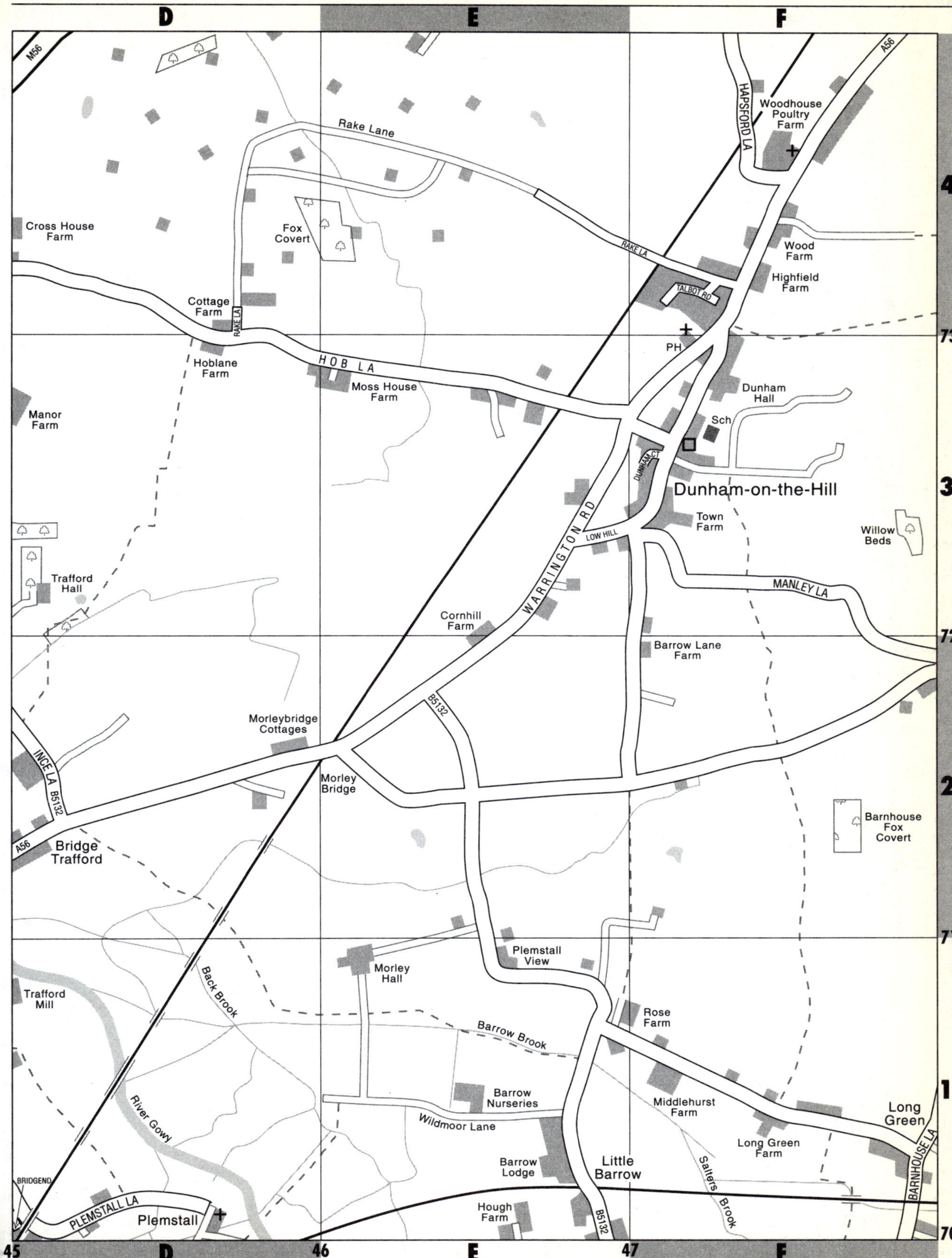
D
E
F
M56
A56
Rake Lane
HAPSFORD LA
Woodhouse
Poultry
Farm
4
Cross House
Farm
Fox
Covert
RAKE LA
Wood
Farm
TALBOT RD
Highfield
Farm
Cottage
Farm
RAKE LA
73
PH
HOB LA
Hoblane
Farm
Moss House
Farm
Dunham
Hall
Manor
Farm
Sch
DUNHAM CT
Dunham-on-the-Hill
3
WARRINGTON RD
Town
Farm
Willow
Beds
LOW HILL
Trafford
Hall
MANLEY LA
Cornhill
Farm
72
Barrow Lane
Farm
B5132
Morleybridge
Cottages
INCE LA
B5132
Morley
Bridge
2
Barnhouse
Fox
Covert
A56
Bridge
Trafford
71
Plemstall
View
Morley
Hall
Trafford
Mill
Back Brook
Rose
Farm
Barrow Brook
1
River Gowy
Barrow
Nurseries
Middlehurst
Farm
Long
Green
Wildmoor Lane
Long Green
Farm
BARNHOUSE LA
Barrow
Lodge
Little
Barrow
Salters
Brook
BRIDGEND
PLEMSTALL LA
Plemstall
Hough
Farm
B5132
70
45
46
47
D
E
F

120
98

97
73

A
B
C
4
3
2
1
73
72
71
70
48
49
50
Church-house Farm
B5393
Alvanley Hall
Golf Course
CH
Greengate Farm
The Green
MANLEY RD
TOWERS LA
PECK MILL LA
Peck Mill Farm
Crabtree Farm
Moor's Brook
Abbot's Clough Farm
Manley Old Hall
Lowerhall Farm
Lower Farm
Rose Farm
COB HALL LA
SUGAR LA
MANLEY LA
Quarry (disused)
New House Farm
Manor Farm
Dunham Heath
Manley House Farm
Manley Hall
MOSS LA
MOSS DR
Siddall's Hill
CHAPEL LA
Rookery Farm
Peckmill Brook
Longster Trail
Grange Farm
Swinford House
MELL LA
BARNHOUSE LA
SMITHY LA
NORTON'S LA
Mouldsworth Hall
Stone House Farm
Mus
Long Wood
The Rookery
GRANGE RD
CHURCH RD
Ashton Brook
CONGAR LA
B5393
Baker Way

97
121

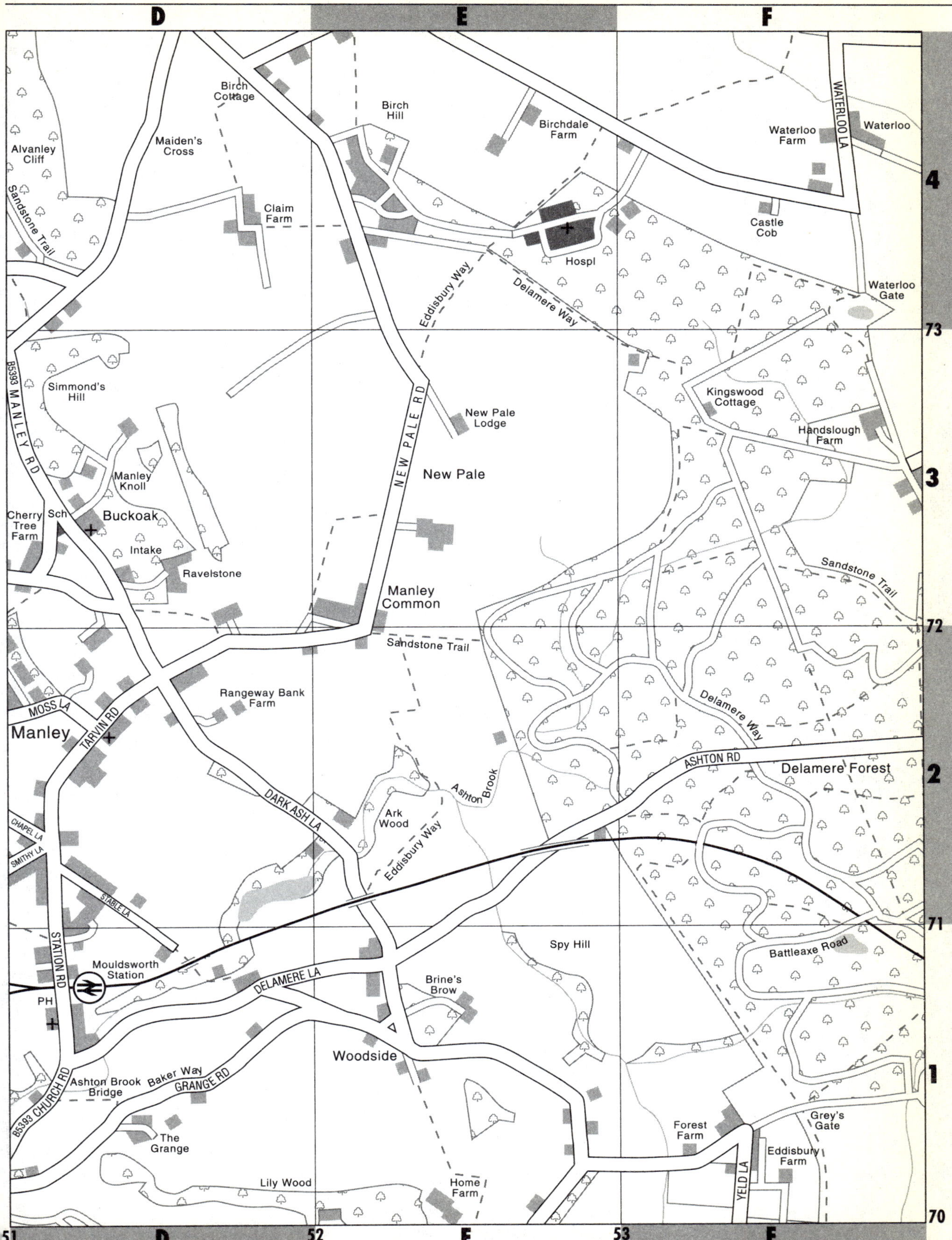
D
E
F
Birch Cottage
Birch Hill
Birchdale Farm
Waterloo Farm
Waterloo
WATERLOO LA
Alvanley Cliff
Maiden's Cross
Claim Farm
Sandstone Trail
Castle Cob
Hospl
Eddisbury Way
Delamere Way
Waterloo Gate
4
73
B5393 MANLEY RD
Simmond's Hill
New Pale Lodge
Kingswood Cottage
Handslough Farm
NEW PALE RD
New Pale
Manley Knoll
3
Cherry Tree Farm
Sch
Buckoak
Intake
Ravelstone
Sandstone Trail
Manley Common
72
Sandstone Trail
Rangeway Bank Farm
MOSS LA
Manley
TARVIN RD
Delamere Way
ASHTON RD
Delamere Forest
2
DARK ASH LA
Ashton Brook
Ark Wood
Eddisbury Way
CHAPEL LA
SMITHY LA
STABLE LA
STATION RD
71
Spy Hill
Battleaxe Road
Mouldsworth Station
DELAMERE LA
Brine's Brow
PH
Woodside
1
Ashton Brook Bridge
Baker Way
GRANGE RD
B5393 CHURCH RD
Grey's Gate
Forest Farm
Eddisbury Farm
The Grange
Lily Wood
Home Farm
YELD LA
70
51
D
52
E
53
F

99
75

A
B
C
4
3
2
1
73
72
71
70
54
55
56
B5152
GUESTS SLACK
TOP RD
Millfield Farm
Commonside
Beech Farm
Big Wood
Crofton Lodge
Dodsley Farm
BEECH LA
Leigh Cottage
The Gorse
Foresthouse Farm
The Paddocks
Town Farm
NORLEY LA
NORLEY RD
TOWN FARM LA
Forestgate
Brownmoss Farm
Norley Hall
NORLEY LA
DELAMERE RD
FOREST LA
Forestgate Farm
Forestgate Farm
HAMBLETTS HOLLOW
Pinewood Farm
Norley
HIGH ST
CRABMILL LA
THE SPINNEY
MADDOCKS HILL
Moy Park Farm
Flaxmere
POST OFFICE LA
SCHOOL LA
HOUGHS LA
FINGER POST LA
Hatch Mere
PC
PH
P
Picnic Area
Delamere Way
ASHTON RD
Hatchmere
BLAKEMERE LA
GALLOWSCLOUGH LA
Sch
PC
P
Hunger Hill
Hotel
Harthill Bank
Barns Bridge Gates
Hart Hill
Claims Farm
Sandstone Trail
Delamere Forest
Blakemere Moss
Delamere Way
Windyhowe Farm
Fir Brook
Linmere Moss
Visitor Centre
Delamere Station
Eddisbury Lodge
P
P
Golf Course
PCs
B5152
Station Cottages
Picnic Area
Relicks Moss
Sandstone Trail
Eddisbury Lodge Cottages
CH
Burnt Wood
STATION RD
Works

99
123

76
102

D E F

4 3 2 1
73 72 71 70

57 D 58 E 59 F

124
102

101
77

101
125

78
104

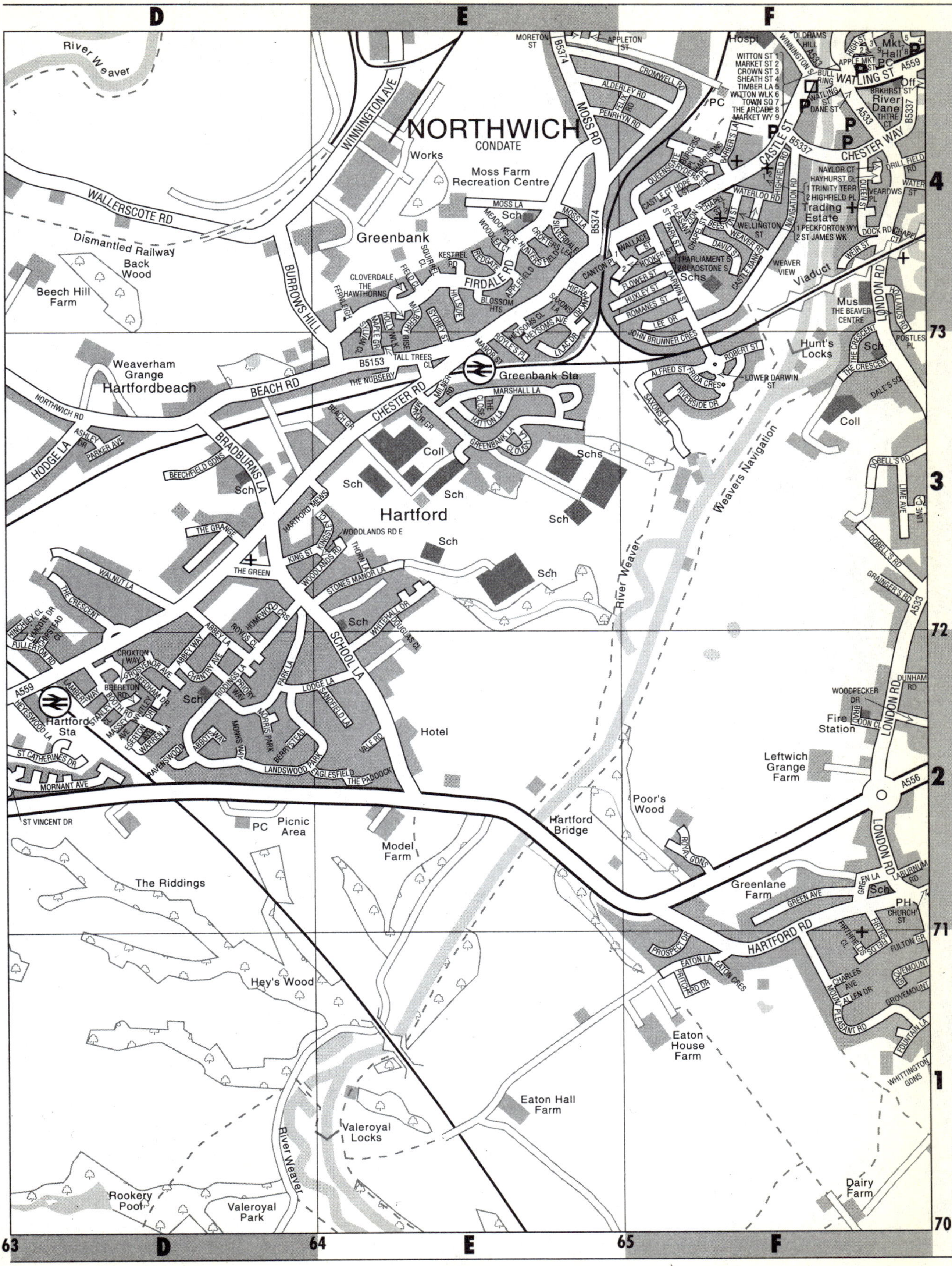

126
104

103
79

103
127

80
106

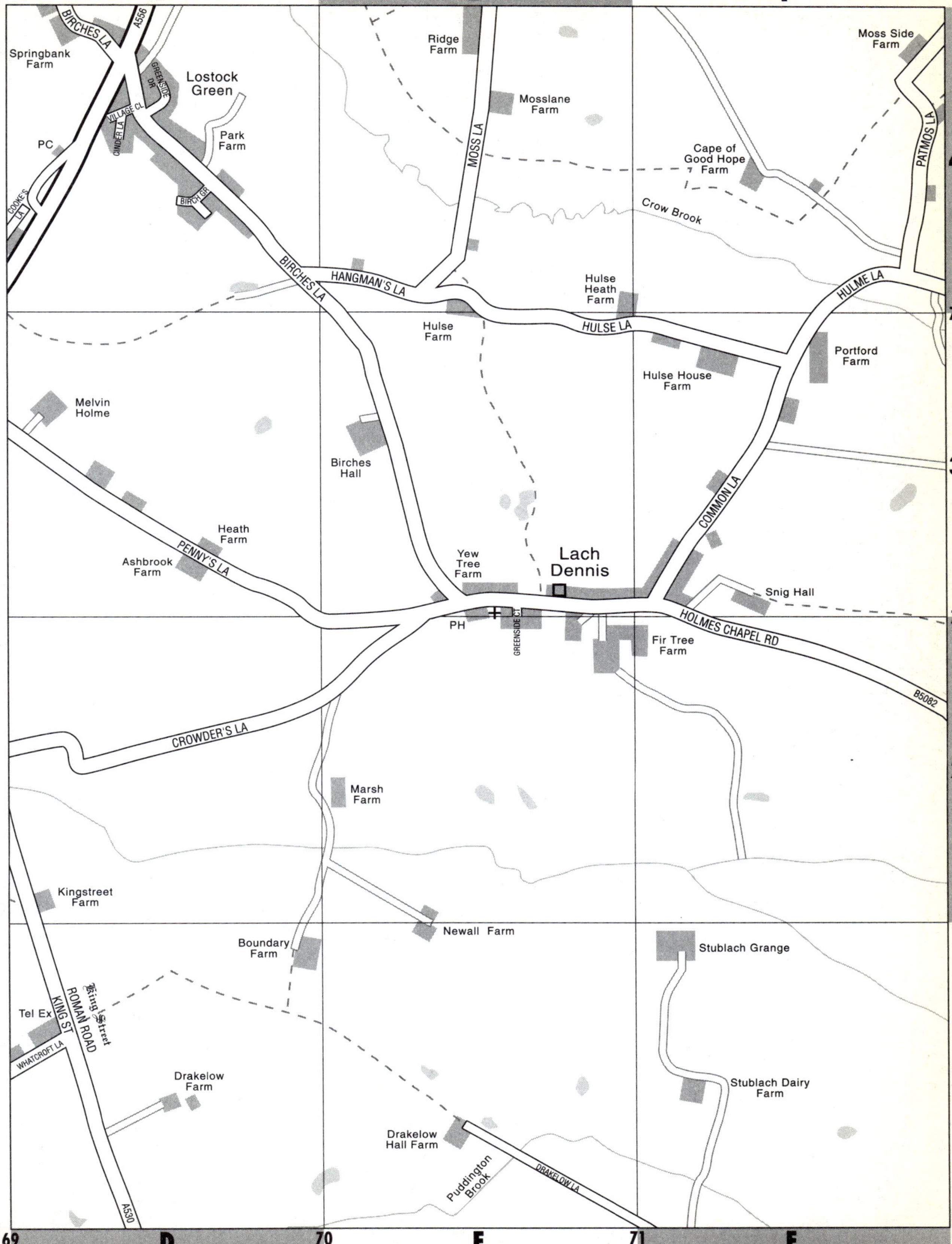
D
E
F
Springbank Farm
Lostock Green
BIRCHES LA
A556
GREENSIDE DR
VILLAGE CL
CINDER LA
PC
COOKE'S LA
Park Farm
BIRCH GR
Ridge Farm
Mosslane Farm
MOSS LA
Moss Side Farm
PATMOS LA
Cape of Good Hope Farm
Crow Brook
HANGMAN'S LA
BIRCHES LA
Hulse Heath Farm
HULME LA
Hulse Farm
HULSE LA
Portford Farm
Hulse House Farm
Melvin Holme
Birches Hall
COMMON LA
Heath Farm
Ashbrook Farm
PENNY'S LA
Yew Tree Farm
Lach Dennis
Snig Hall
PH
GREENSIDE CT
HOLMES CHAPEL RD
Fir Tree Farm
B5082
CROWDER'S LA
Marsh Farm
Kingstreet Farm
Newall Farm
Boundary Farm
Stublach Grange
King Street
ROMAN ROAD
KING ST
Tel Ex
WHATCROFT LA
Drakelow Farm
Stublach Dairy Farm
Drakelow Hall Farm
Puddington Brook
DRAKELOW LA
A530
4
73
3
72
2
71
1
70
69
70
71
D
E
F

105
81

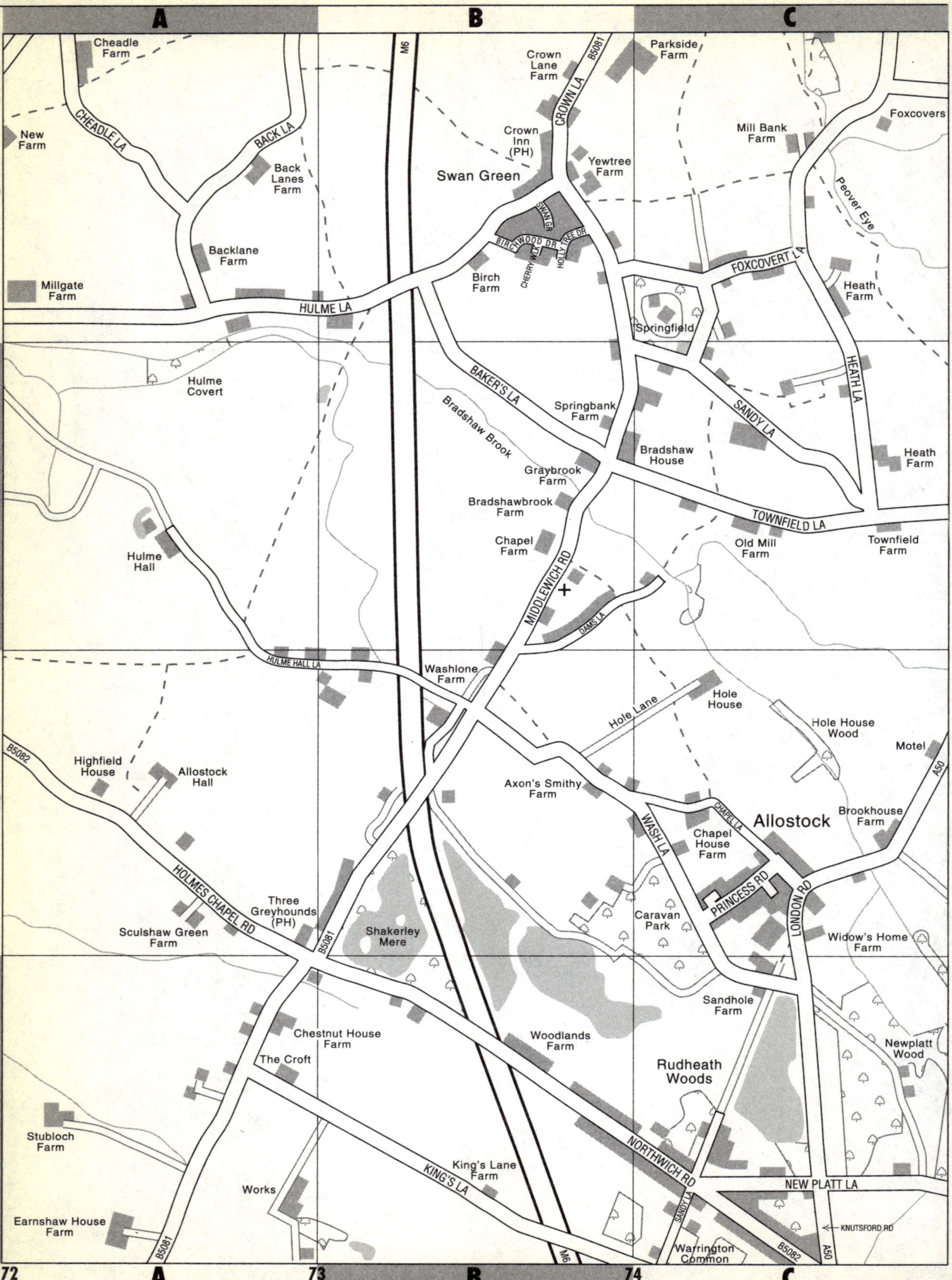

105
129

82
108

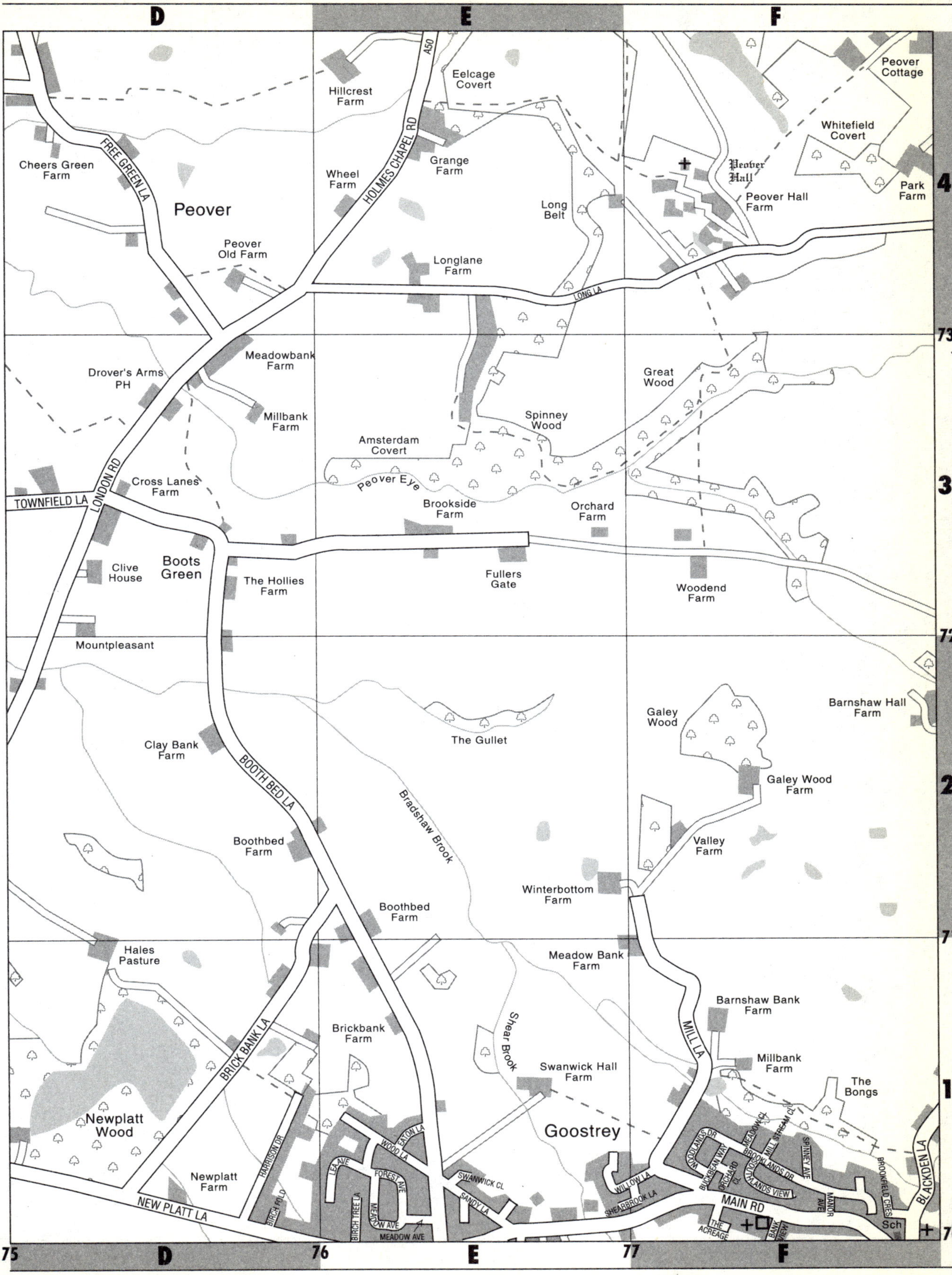

130
108

107
83

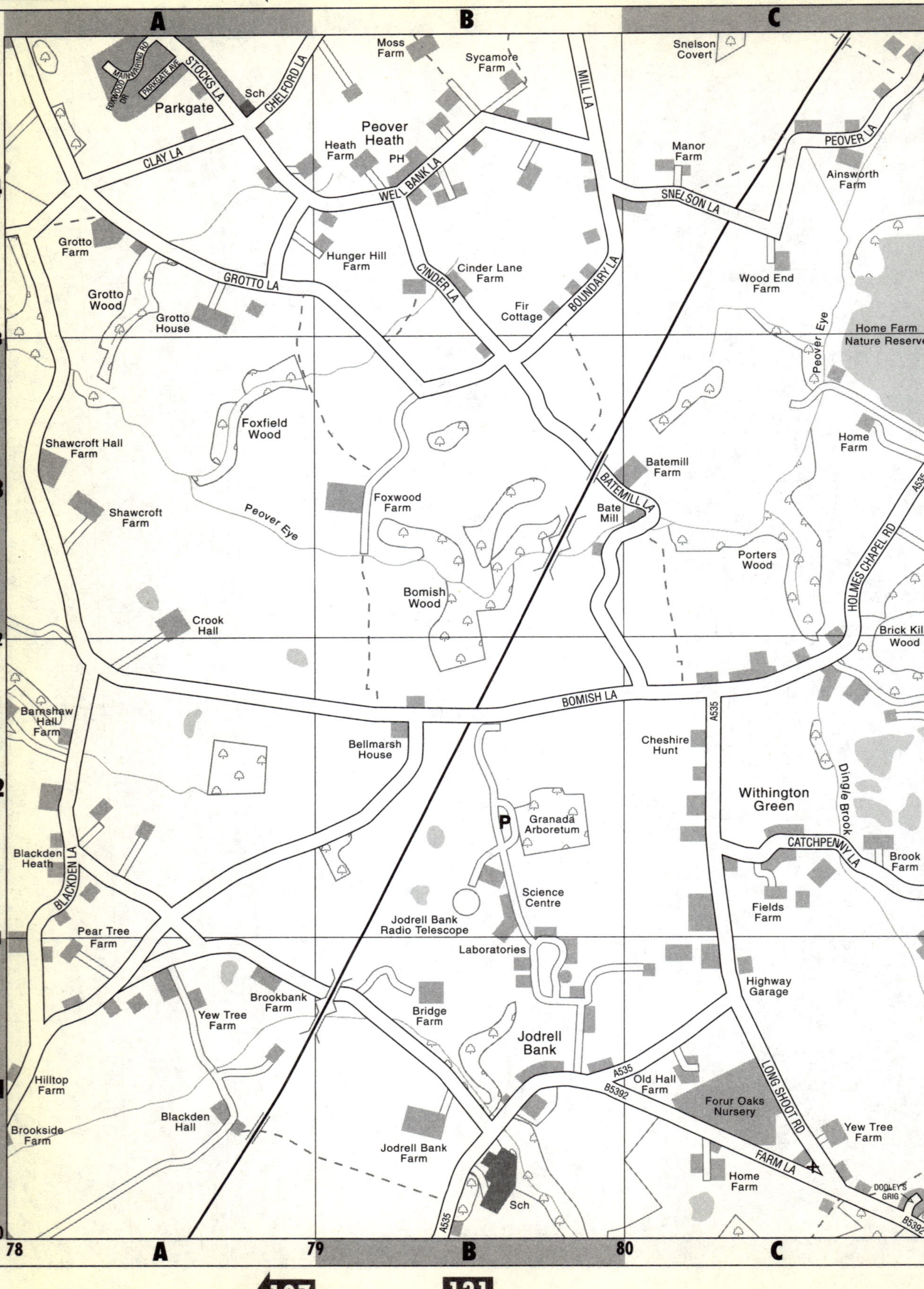

107
131

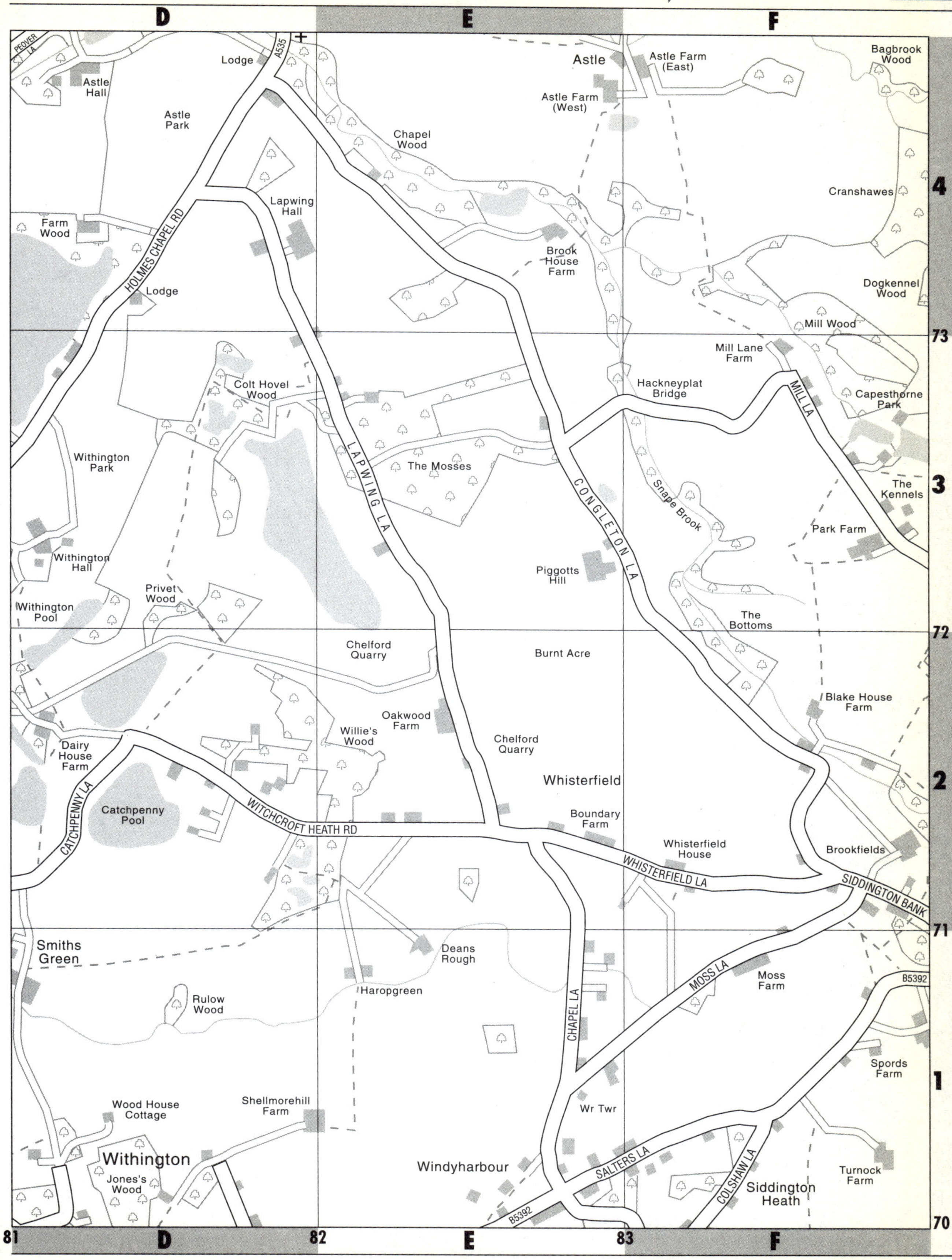
D
E
F
PEOVER LA
Astle Hall
Lodge
A535
Astle
Astle Farm (East)
Bagbrook Wood
Astle Park
Astle Farm (West)
Chapel Wood
Lapwing Hall
Cranshawes
4
Farm Wood
HOLMES CHAPEL RD
Brook House Farm
Lodge
Dogkennel Wood
Mill Wood
73
Mill Lane Farm
Colt Hovel Wood
Hackneyplat Bridge
MILL LA
Capesthorne Park
Withington Park
The Mosses
LAPWING LA
CONGLETON LA
Snape Brook
The Kennels
3
Park Farm
Withington Hall
Piggotts Hill
Privet Wood
Withington Pool
The Bottoms
72
Chelford Quarry
Burnt Acre
Blake House Farm
Oakwood Farm
Willie's Wood
Dairy House Farm
Chelford Quarry
Whisterfield
2
Catchpenny Pool
CATCHPENNY LA
WITCHCROFT HEATH RD
Boundary Farm
Whisterfield House
Brookfields
WHISTERFIELD LA
SIDDINGTON BANK
71
Smiths Green
Deans Rough
MOSS LA
Moss Farm
B5392
Haropgreen
Rulow Wood
CHAPEL LA
Spords Farm
1
Wood House Cottage
Shellmorehill Farm
Wr Twr
Withington
Windyharbour
SALTERS LA
Turnock Farm
Jones's Wood
COLSHAW LA
Siddington Heath
B5392
70
81
D
82
E
83
F

109
85

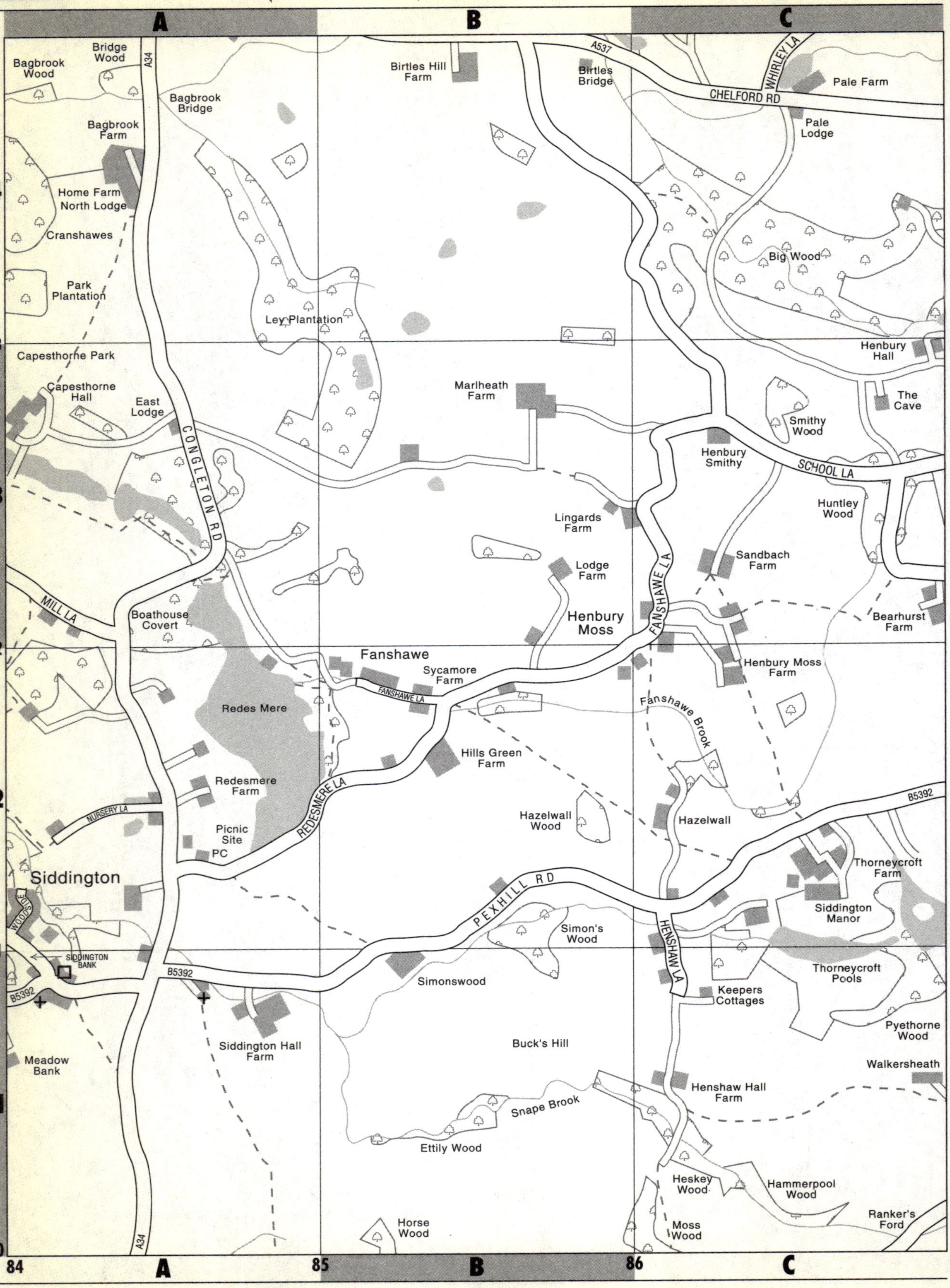

109
133

86
112

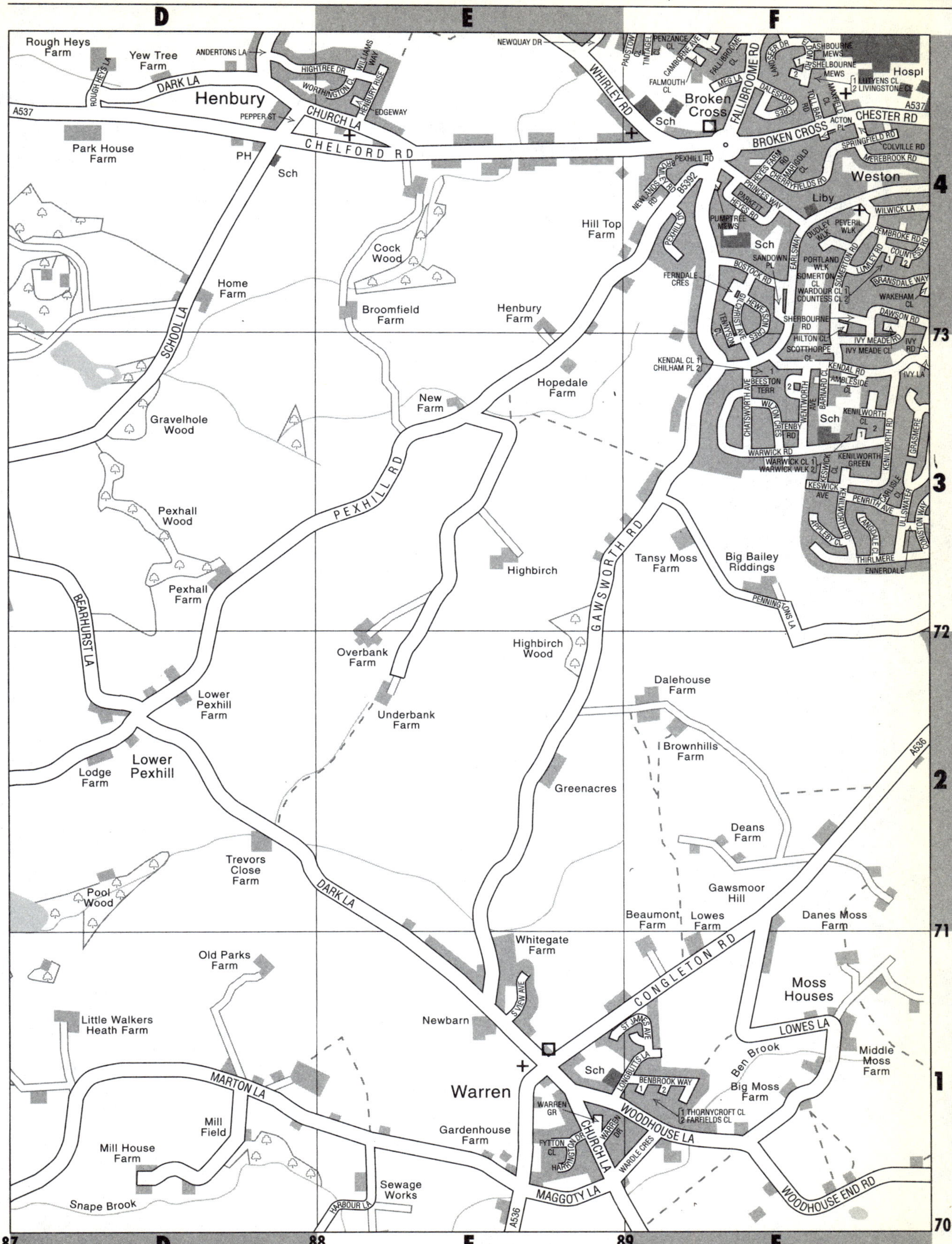

134
112

111
87

A
B
C
MACCLESFIELD
Hospls
Hospl
FIELDBANK
Sch
CHESTER RD
A537
LEA BANK CL
Fire & Amb Sta
IVY RD
ARLINGTON DR
BOX TREE MEWS
BRANSDALE WAY
CHILTERN AVE
AMBERLEY RD
IVY LA
OXFORD RD
B5088
BROOKLANDS AVE
STEVENAGE DR
PARK LA
A536
Offices
College
CONGLETON RD
PARK MOUNT DR
FAIRVIEW RD
TARN MOUNT
THORNTON AVE
PENNINGTONS LA
RISING SUN CL
SURREY RD
MOSS VIEW
THE ROACHES
CRAIG RD
CRAIG CL
MOSS LA
Moss Lane
Danes Moss
WOODHOUSE END RD
BOND ST
PARK VALE
GROVEWOOD MEWS
RYLE'S PARK RD
WESTERN AVE
KNOWSLEY RD
STRATFORD WAY
ROBIN HOOD AVE
LYME AVE
MAYFIELD AVE
RUTLAND RD
CORNBROOK RD
MOORHILL RD
MOSS BOWER RD
STAR LA
TURF LA
HEATHER CL
WINTERTON WAY
Lyme Green Business Park
LONDON RD
A523
Works
GAWEND LA
Moss Head Farm
LYME GREEN SETTLEMENT
ROBIN LA
LINDRUM AVE
MINOR AVE
LIME VIEW
Lyme Green
Lake House Farm
Sutton Reservoir
LEEK OLD RD
BULLOCKS LA
PARVEY LA
WALKER LA
Sutton Lane Ends
Sutton Grange
Symondley Farm
HOLLIN LA
SYMONDLEY RD
HALL LA
JARMAN
Hotel
SELWYN DR
Gurnett
Byrons Wood
Wood's Cut
BYRON'S LA
Cheshire Ring Canal Walk
Golf Course
The Hollins
Club House
HOLLINS RD
BLAKELOW RD
WINDMILL ST
MILL LA
CROSS ST
THE SILK RD
BUXTON RD
FENCE AVE
HIGHER FENCE RD
Schs
BLACK RD
BROOKFIELD LA
LEADBEATERS CL
QUAYSIDE WAY
CANAL SIDE
CUCKSTOOLPIT HILL
A537
COMMERCIAL RD
FENCE AVE IND EST
1 NORWICH CT
2 VICTORIA WLK
3 LICHFIELD CT
4 OXFORD CT
5 CANTERBURY CT
6 ELY CT
7 WINCHESTER CT
8 SALISBURY CT
9 LANCASTER CT
10 YORK CT
1 BUCKLOW WLK
2 KNUTSFORD RD WLK
3 WILMSLOW WLK
4 ALDERLEY WLK
1 ST EDWARDS CL
2 ST BARNABAS CT
3 LINGDALE WLK
4 SQUARE ST
5 HIGGINBOTHAM GN
CHESTERGATE
KING EDWARD ST
CUMBERLAND ST
WATERLOO ST
Mus
PC
Sch
90
91
92
73
72
71
70
4
3
2
1

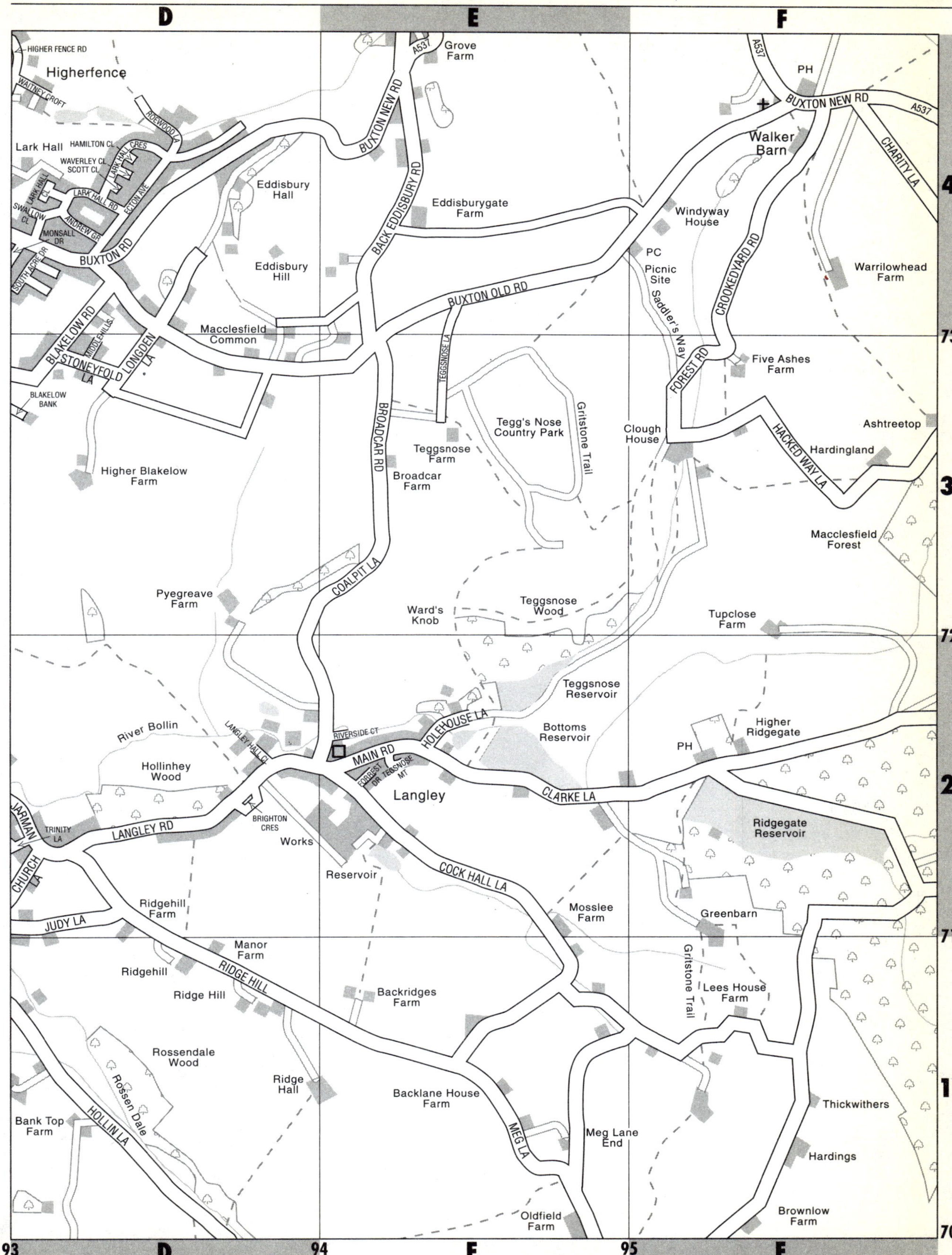
D
E
F
HIGHER FENCE RD
Higherfence
WAITNEY CROFT
ROEWOOD LA
Lark Hall
HAMILTON CL
LARK HALL CRES
WAVERLEY CL
SCOTT CL
LARK HALL CL
LARK HALL RD
ECTON AVE
SWALLOW CL
ANDREW GR
MONSALL DR
SOUTH ACRE DR
BUXTON RD
BLAKELOW RD
MIDDLEHILLS
STONEYFOLD LA
LONGDEN LA
BLAKELOW BANK
Higher Blakelow Farm
Eddisbury Hall
Eddisbury Hill
Macclesfield Common
A537
Grove Farm
BUXTON NEW RD
BACK EDDISBURY RD
Eddisburygate Farm
BUXTON OLD RD
TEGGSNOSE LA
BROADCAR RD
Teggsnose Farm
Broadcar Farm
Tegg's Nose Country Park
Gritstone Trail
COALPIT LA
Pyegreave Farm
Ward's Knob
Teggsnose Wood
A537
PH
BUXTON NEW RD
A537
Walker Barn
CHARITY LA
Windyway House
PC
Picnic Site
Saddler's Way
CROOKEDYARD RD
Warrilowhead Farm
FOREST RD
Five Ashes Farm
Clough House
HACKED WAY LA
Ashtreetop
Hardingland
Macclesfield Forest
Tupclose Farm
River Bollin
Hollinhey Wood
LANGLEY HALL CL
RIVERSIDE CT
MAIN RD
FOREST DR
TEGGSNOSE MT
HOLEHOUSE LA
Teggsnose Reservoir
Bottoms Reservoir
Langley
CLARKE LA
PH
Higher Ridgegate
Ridgegate Reservoir
JARMAN
TRINITY LA
LANGLEY RD
BRIGHTON CRES
Works
CHURCH LA
Reservoir
COCK HALL LA
Ridgehill Farm
JUDY LA
Mosslee Farm
Greenbarn
Manor Farm
Ridgehill
RIDGE HILL
Ridge Hill
Backridges Farm
Gritstone Trail
Lees House Farm
Rossendale Wood
Ridge Hall
Backlane House Farm
Thickwithers
Rossen Dale
Bank Top Farm
HOLLIN LA
MEG LA
Meg Lane End
Hardings
Oldfield Farm
Brownlow Farm
4
73
3
72
2
71
1
70
93
94
95
D
E
F

113
89

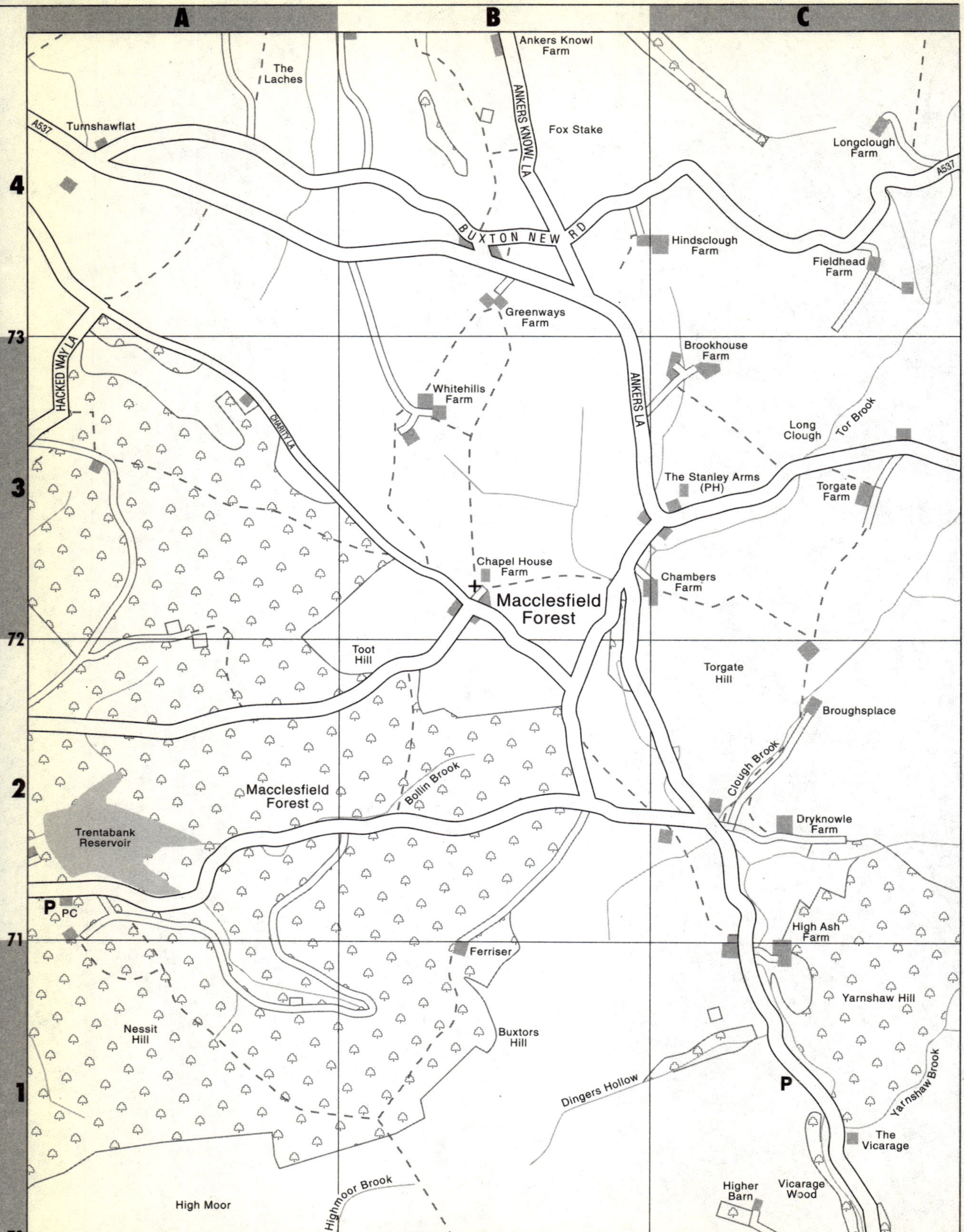

113
137

90

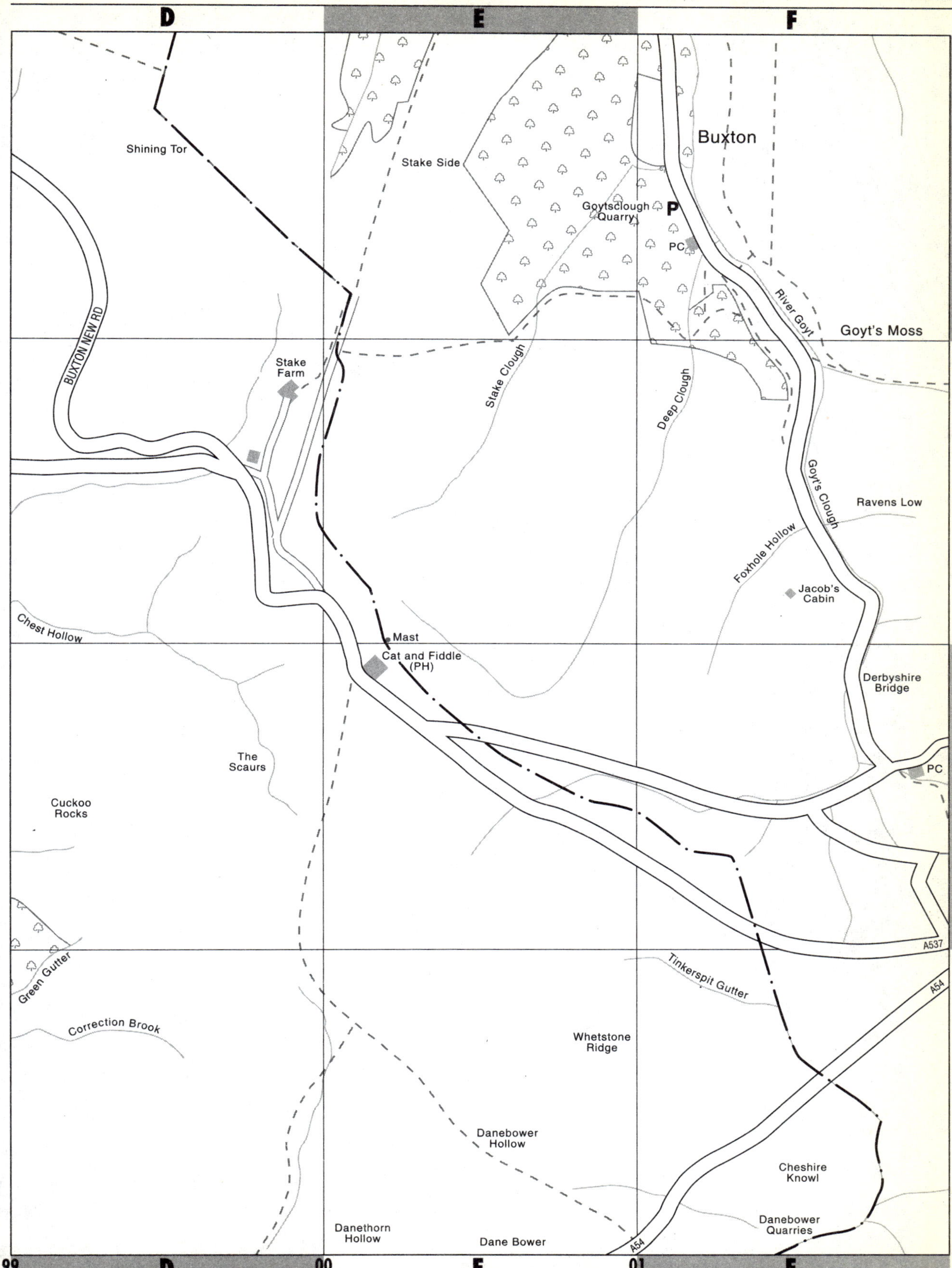
D
E
F
Shining Tor
BUXTON NEW RD
Stake Side
Goytsclough Quarry
P
PC
Buxton
River Goyt
Goyt's Moss
Stake Farm
Stake Clough
Deep Clough
Goyt's Clough
Ravens Low
Foxhole Hollow
Jacob's Cabin
Chest Hollow
Mast
Cat and Fiddle (PH)
Derbyshire Bridge
The Scaurs
PC
Cuckoo Rocks
A537
Green Gutter
Tinkerspit Gutter
A54
Correction Brook
Whetstone Ridge
Danebower Hollow
Cheshire Knowl
Danebower Quarries
Danethorn Hollow
Dane Bower
A54
4
73
3
72
2
71
1
70
99
00
01
D
E
F

138

93

A
B
C
Camp
Old Marsh Farm
Bridge Farm
A494
A548
WELSH RD
HAWTHORN VIEW
CEDAR AVE
DEVA BSNS PK
B5441
RIVERSIDE PK
A494
A548
VILLA RD
Willow Farm
Brookfield Farm
Brook Farm
Home Farm
GREEN LA
SEALAND RD
Waterloo Farm
BARTHOLOMEWS CT
Sealand
SEAHILL RD
CROFTERS WAY
FOX LEA
Seahill Farm
Station Cottages
Church Farm
A548
MANOR RD
MEADOW VIEW
FERRY CL
NORTH GREEN
SOUTH GREEN
EAST GREEN
FOX'S DR
Sealand Manor
Shooting School
DEESIDE CRES
Deeside Cottages
Deeside House
DEESIDE LA
Sealand Nursery
Wood Farm
Engineer Park
River Row Cottages
BABAGE RD
ST IVES PK
FACTORY RD
WHITTLE CL
ALVIS RD
Works
GLENDALE AVE
Works
CLAIR AVE
BERNSDALE CL
HAMILTON AVE
HARRISON GR
CROFTERS PK
RAILWAY TERR
ASIATIC COTTS
PRINCE WILLIAM AVE
River Dee (Afon Dyfrdwy)
EVANSLEIGH DR
LAWRENCE ST
PHOENIX ST
NORTH ST
QUEEN'S AVE
FAIRWAY
WATKIN ST
WOOD ST
PHILIP ST
STATION RD
B5129
Sandycroft
Bridge Inn (PH)
ROSSLYN CL
MOOR LA
CHESTER RD
Hawarden
Rake Cottages
RAKE LA
B5129
B5129
The Beeches
Cop House Farm
4
69
3
68
2
67
1
66
33
34
35
A
B
C

139

D
E
F
4
69
3
68
2
67
1
66
36
37
38
The Paddock
Crabwall Hall
Hotel
Mollington Grange
Hotel
The Poplars
Oulton's Farm
Poplars Farm
Pear Tree Farm
PH
Kingswood Lane
Crabwall Cottage
Sealand Farm
Wash Hall Farm
Yew Tree Farm
Birchen Fields Farm
Cottage Garage
Bank Farm
Point Farm House
Thornleigh Park Farm
Caravan Site
Ferry Lane Farm
Bee's Cottages
Fir Tree Farm
Cop House Farm
River Dee
(Afon Dyfrdwy)
Chester West Employment Park
Sealand Ind Est
Football Ground
Border House Farm
The Stadium Ind Est
Blacon
Sch
Schs
Liby
HERMITAGE RD
KINGSWOOD LA
TOWNFIELD LA
PARKGATE RD
A540
ASPEN GR
GREEN LA
ROSEWOOD GR
THORNBERRY CL
THE RIDINGS
HAYMAKERS WAY
MEADOWS LA
HAKE WAY
THE CLOSE
CHURCH RD
VERNON CL
FOX LEA
WORSLEY AVE
HERMITAGE CT
1 ALDERLY PL
2 HARTHILL RD
3 MOSTYN PL
4 FERNHILL RD
5 LEASIDE RD
6 NORMAN WAY
CAVALIER DR
HADRIAN DR
OWEN CL
CHAUCER CL
BROWNING CL
MILTON RD
THOMAS CL
SHELLEY RD
SAXON WAY
MASEFIELD DR
STAMFORD RD
HATTON RD
NORRIS RD
BURTON RD
THE PARADE
BRENTWOOD RD
CHURCH WAY
WORDSWORTH CRES
CRABWALL PL
KIPLING RD
TENNYSON WLK
GRIFFIN CL
BLAKE CL
BARNES CL
DONNE PL
BLACON AVE
PROVAN WAY
MAYFIELD RD
WILLOW DR
GLENSIDE CL
JONATHAN'S WAY
SAUGHALL RD
CARLISLE RD
WARWICK RD
LINCOLN RD
LICHFIELD RD
EXETER PL
CANTERBURY RD
DURHAM RD
BLACON HALL RD
MALVERN RD
CHURCH HALL CL
THE GLEN
CEDAR MEWS
HIGHFIELD RD
ASHFIELD CRES
HOBART WAY
ONSLOW RD
MELBOURNE RD
CANBERRA WAY
BRISBANE RD
DARWIN RD
MAITLAND WAY
ADELAIDE RD
WESTERN AVE
FOWLER RD
CHEVRON HEY
LLOYD PL
HILLSIDE RD
BELVEDERE DR
SOUTH WAY
ST CHAD'S RD
VENABLE'S RD
SUMNER RD
FISHER RD
DOWNHAM PL
WALTON PL
STRATFORD RD
MORTON RD
CHEVRON CL
CLEAVER RD
GRAHAM CL
COTES PL
STUBBS PL
BRIDGEMAN RD
CLIFTON DR
CHASER CT
GREYHOUND PARK RD
LONGDALE DR
WAVERTREE RD
WOODSIDE RD
OAKFIELD RD
EMBASSY CL
VIRGINIA AVE
IMPERIAL AVE
BRISTOL CL
MELVERLY DR
OVERWOOD LA
SPRINGWOOD CL
WYNDHAM RD
AUCKLAND RD
THE CLOSE
NEVIN RD
PENMON CL
HAFOD CL
TREBORTH RD
REDDINAS CL
TREGELE CL
RHIDDLAN RD
CARMEL CL
CYMAN CL
PHILLIPS RD
DYBERTH RD
CADNANT CL
WILLAN RD
WEMYSS RD
BLACON POINT RD
MUIR RD
RAWSON RD
ASHMUIR CL
1 BIRCHMUIR
2 SILVERMUIR
3 ELMIR
4 BEECHMUIR
SEALAND RD
A548
P
THE QUAD
CHANTRY CT
KNUTSFORD WAY
WINSFORD WAY
HARTFORD WAY
BUMPERS LA
FERRY LA
DEESIDE LA
BURGESS DR
B5129

117 95

A B C

A B C

117 141

96
120

D E F

4
69
3
68
2
67
1
66

42 D 43 E 44 F

142
120

119
97

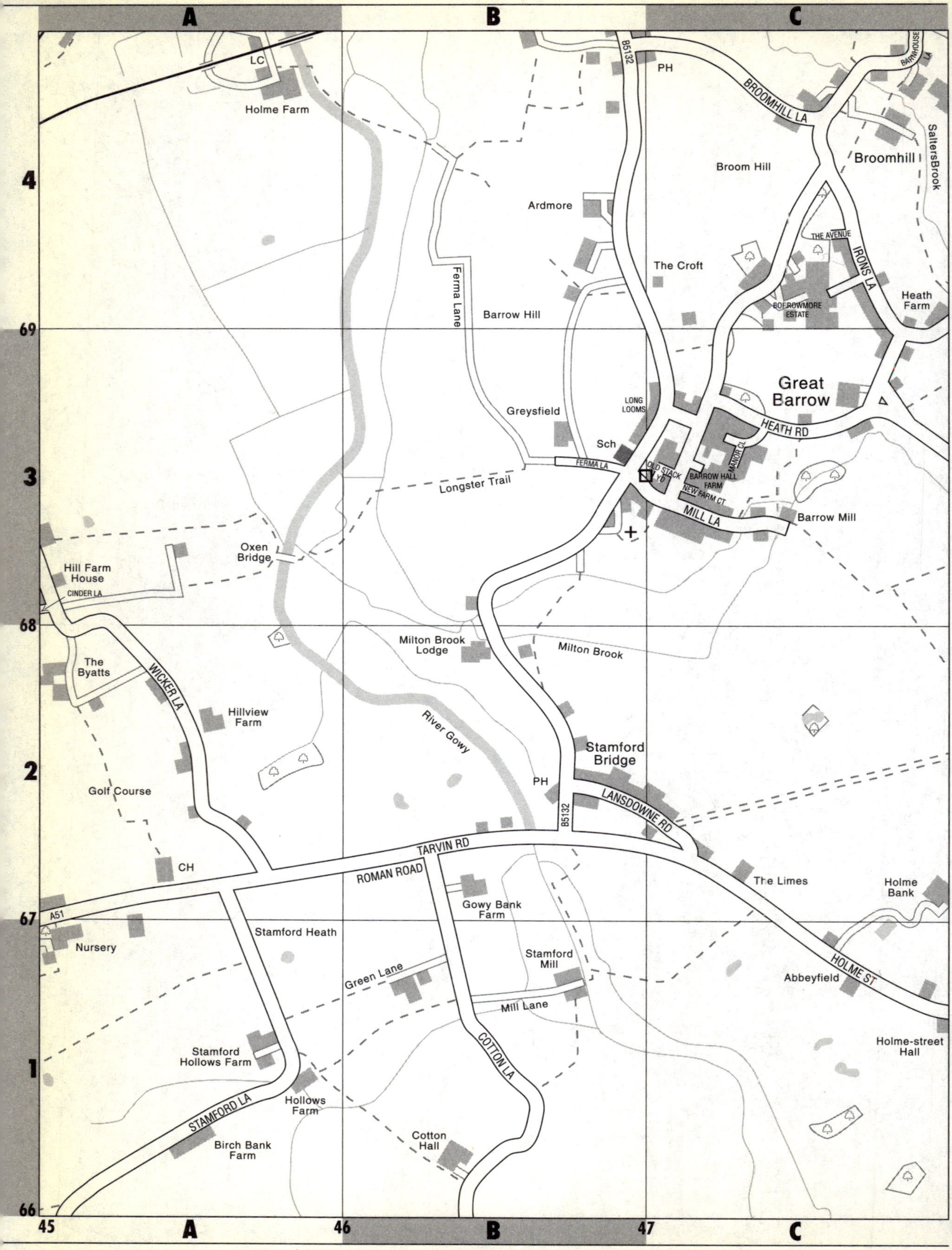

119
143

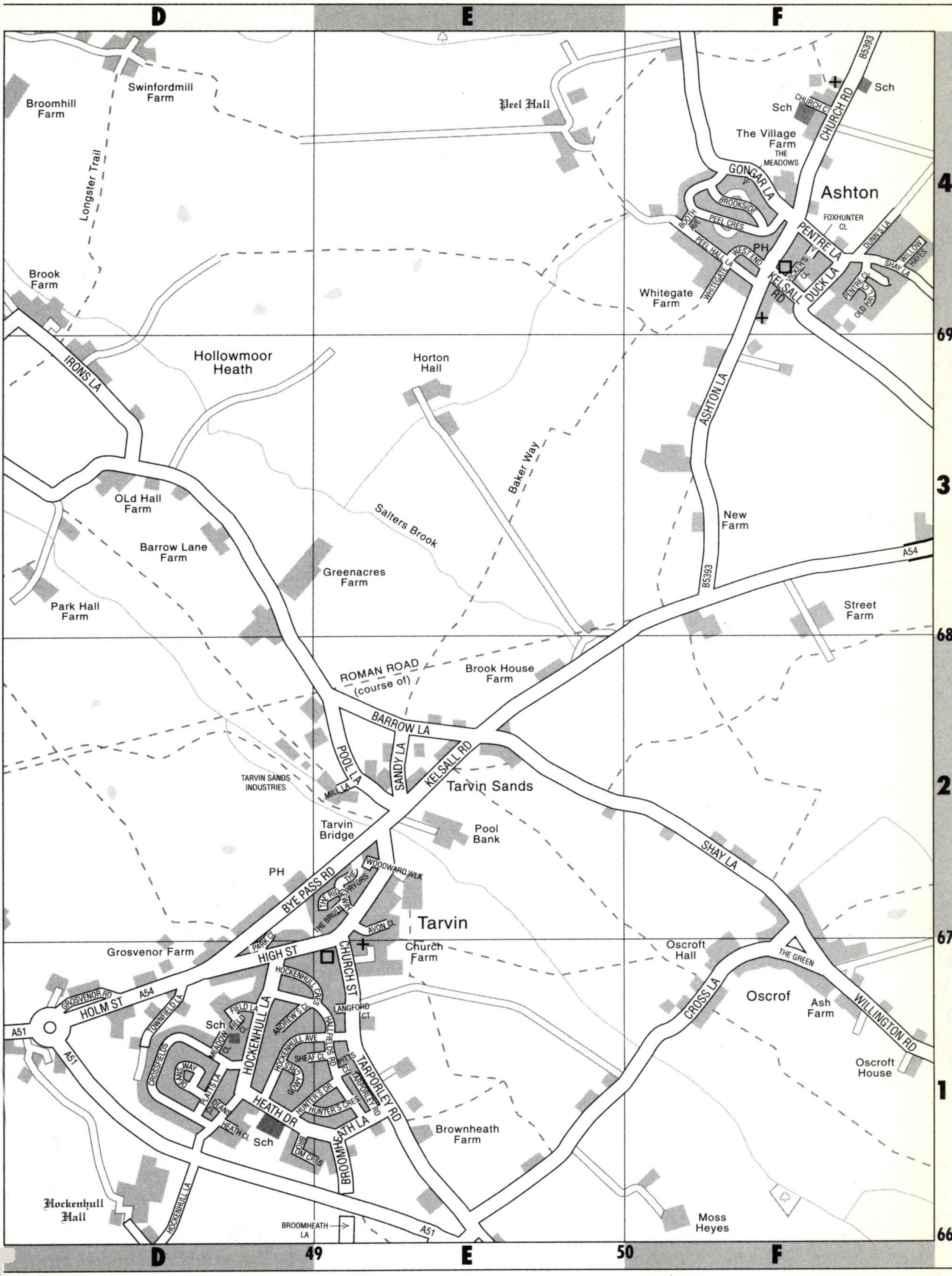
D
E
F
Broomhill Farm
Swinfordmill Farm
Longster Trail
Peel Hall
Sch
Sch
CHURCH CL
CHURCH RD
B5393
The Village Farm
THE MEADOWS
GONGAR LA
BROOKSIDE
PEEL CRES
BOOTH AVE
Ashton
FOXHUNTER CL
PENTRE LA
DUNN'S LA
WILLOW HAYES
SHAY LA
PH
PEEL HALL LA
WEST END
WHITEGATE CL
KELSALL RD
DUCK LA
PENTRE CL
OLD HALL
Whitegate Farm
Brook Farm
Hollowmoor Heath
Horton Hall
IRONS LA
ASHTON LA
Baker Way
OLd Hall Farm
New Farm
Salters Brook
Barrow Lane Farm
Greenacres Farm
A54
B5393
Park Hall Farm
Street Farm
ROMAN ROAD (course of)
Brook House Farm
BARROW LA
POOL LA
SANDY LA
KELSALL RD
TARVIN SANDS INDUSTRIES
MILL LA
Tarvin Sands
Tarvin Bridge
Pool Bank
SHAY LA
PH
BYE PASS RD
WOODWARD WLK
THE PRYORS
THE RIDINGS
THE BRUEN
Tarvin
AVON CL
PARK CL
HIGH ST
CHURCH ST
Church Farm
Grosvenor Farm
Oscroft Hall
THE GREEN
HOCKENHULL CRES
GROSVENOR RD
HOLM ST
A54
A51
TOWNFIELD LA
FIELD LA
ANDREW'S CL
LANGFORD CT
CROSS LA
Oscrof
Ash Farm
WILLINGTON RD
Sch
MEADOW CL
HOCKENHULL LA
HOCKENHULL AVE
HALLFIELDS RD
A51
CROSSFIELDS
SHEAF CL
PITTS CL
DANES WAY
PLATTS LA
TARPORLEY RD
HUNTER'S DR
HUNTER'S CRES
Oscroft House
HEATH DR
HEATH CL
Sch
BROOMHEATH LA
BROOMHEATH CRES
Brownheath Farm
Hockenhull Hall
HOCKENHULL LA
BROOMHEATH LA
A51
Moss Heyes
69
68
67
66
4
3
2
1
D
49
E
50
F

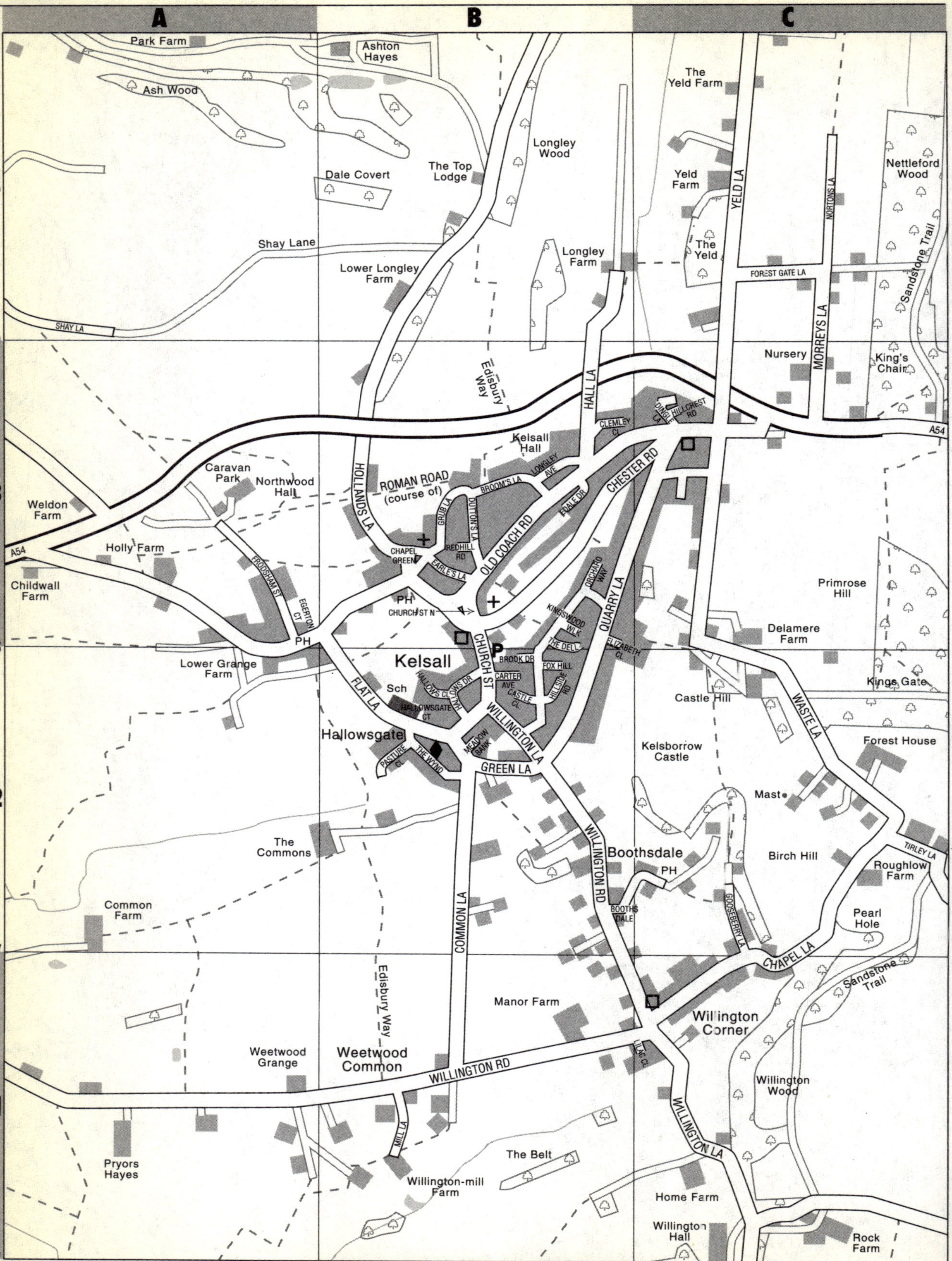
A
B
C
Park Farm
Ashton Hayes
Ash Wood
The Yeld Farm
Longley Wood
The Top Lodge
Dale Covert
Yeld Farm
Nettleford Wood
YELD LA
NORTONS LA
Shay Lane
Longley Farm
The Yeld
Lower Longley Farm
FOREST GATE LA
Sandstone Trail
SHAY LA
MORREYS LA
Nursery
King's Chair
Edisbury Way
HALL LA
DINGLE LA
HILLCREST RD
CLEMLEY CL
A54
Kelsall Hall
LONGLEY AVE
CHESTER RD
Caravan Park
ROMAN ROAD (course of)
BROOM'S LA
Northwood Hall
Weldon Farm
HOLLANDS LA
GRUB LA
DUTTON'S LA
OLD COACH RD
DALE DR
Holly Farm
CHAPEL GREEN
REDHILL RD
EARLE'S LA
ORCHARD WAY
QUARRY LA
Primrose Hill
Childwall Farm
FRODSHAM ST
EGERTON CT
PH
CHURCH ST N
KINGSWOOD WLK
Delamere Farm
THE DELL
ELIZABETH CL
PH
Kelsall
CHURCH ST
BROOK DR
Lower Grange Farm
FOX HILL
CARTER AVE
FLAT LA
HALLOWS CL
HALLOWS DR
CASTLE CL
HILLSIDE RD
Kings Gate
Sch
HALLOWSGATE CT
Castle Hill
WILLINGTON LA
WASTE LA
Hallowsgate
Kelsborrow Castle
Forest House
MEADOW BANK
PASTURE CL
THE WYND
GREEN LA
Mast
The Commons
Boothsdale
Birch Hill
TIRLEY LA
PH
Roughlow Farm
WILLINGTON RD
Common Farm
COMMON LA
BOOTHS DALE
GOOSEBERRY LA
Pearl Hole
CHAPEL LA
Sandstone Trail
Edisbury Way
Manor Farm
Willington Corner
Weetwood Grange
Weetwood Common
LILAC CL
WILLINGTON RD
Willington Wood
MILL LA
WILLINGTON LA
Pryors Hayes
The Belt
Willington-mill Farm
Home Farm
Willington Hall
Rock Farm
4
69
3
68
2
67
1
66
51
52
53
A
B
C

100
124

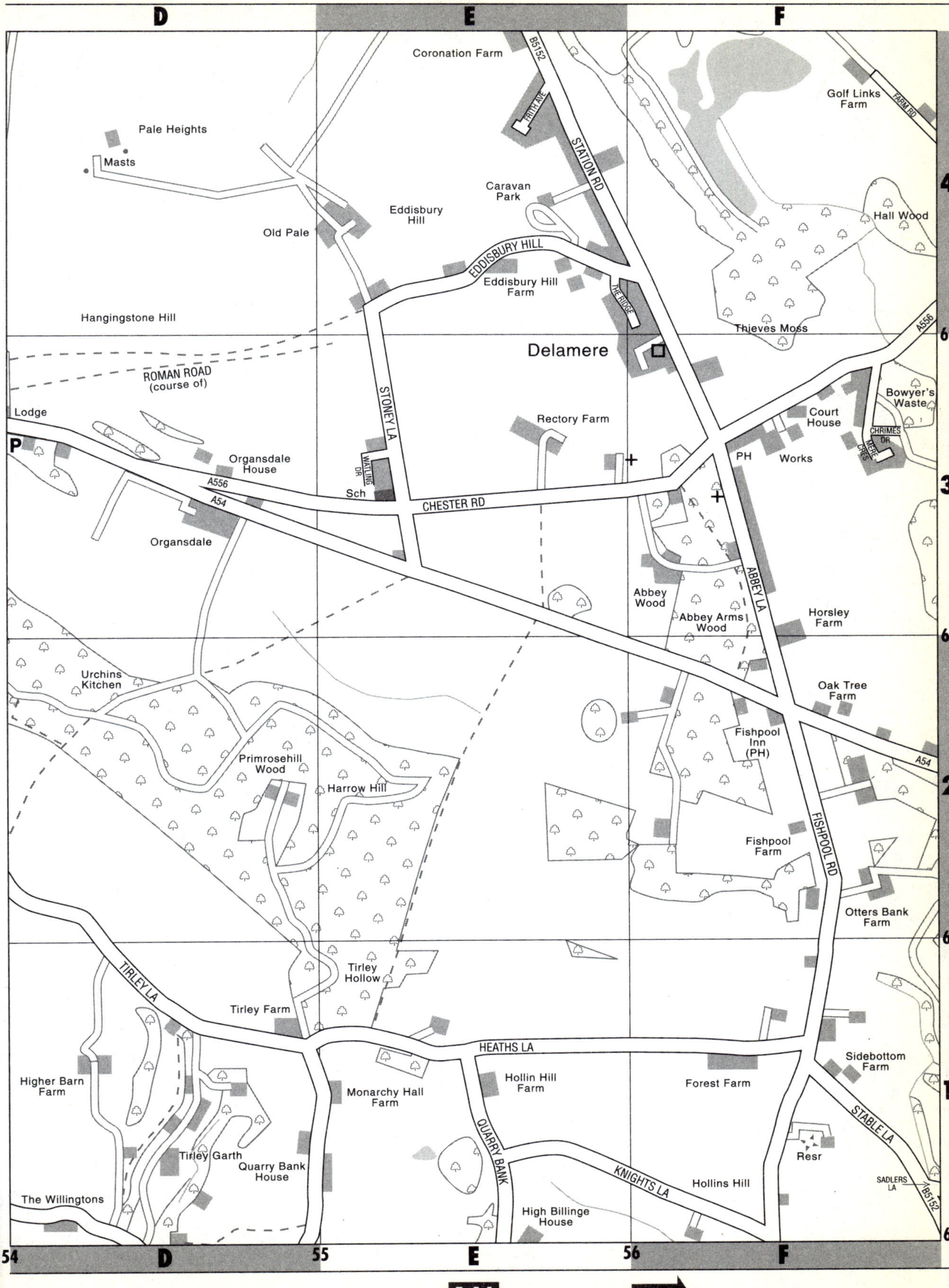

146
124

123
101

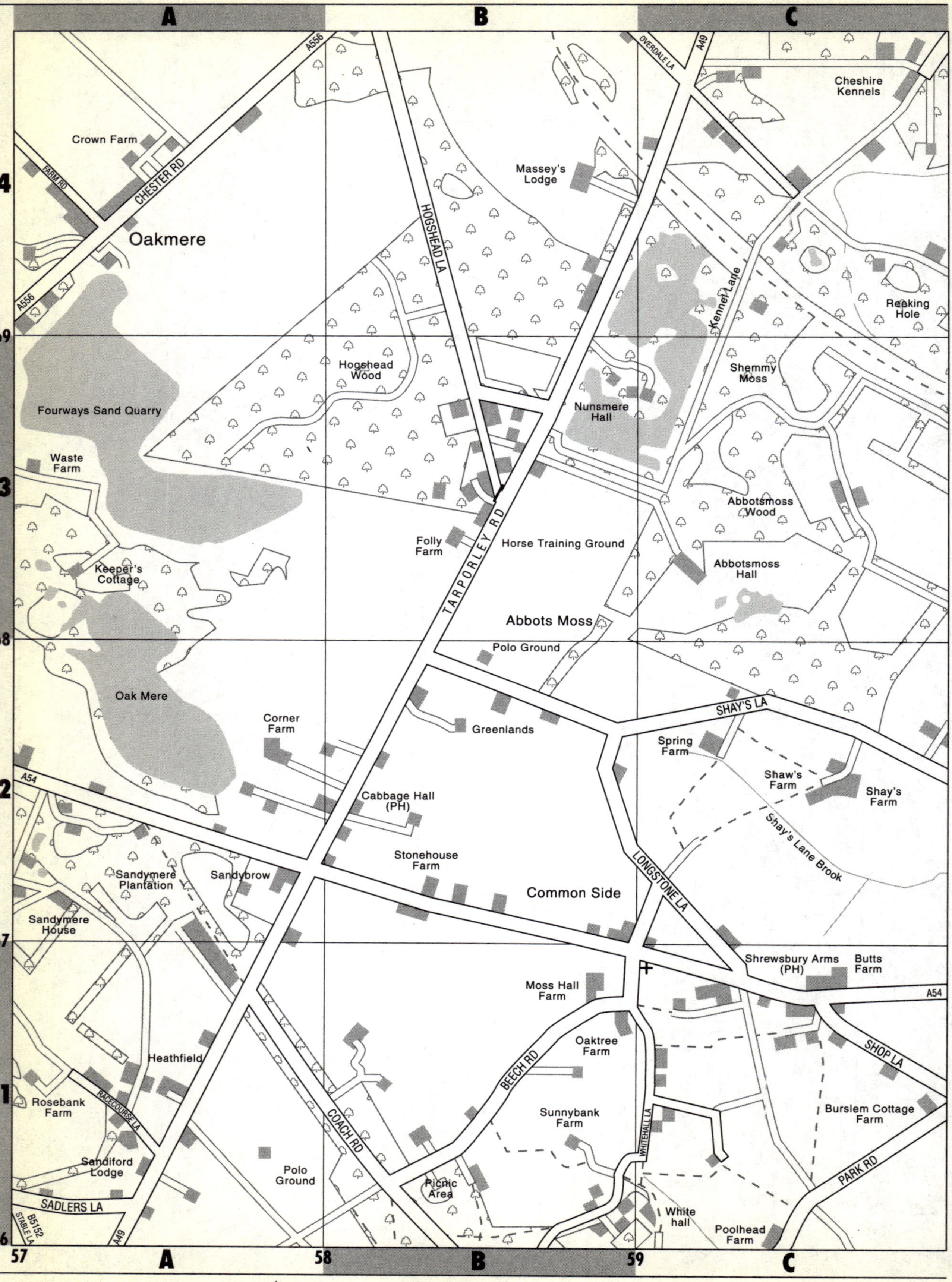

123
147

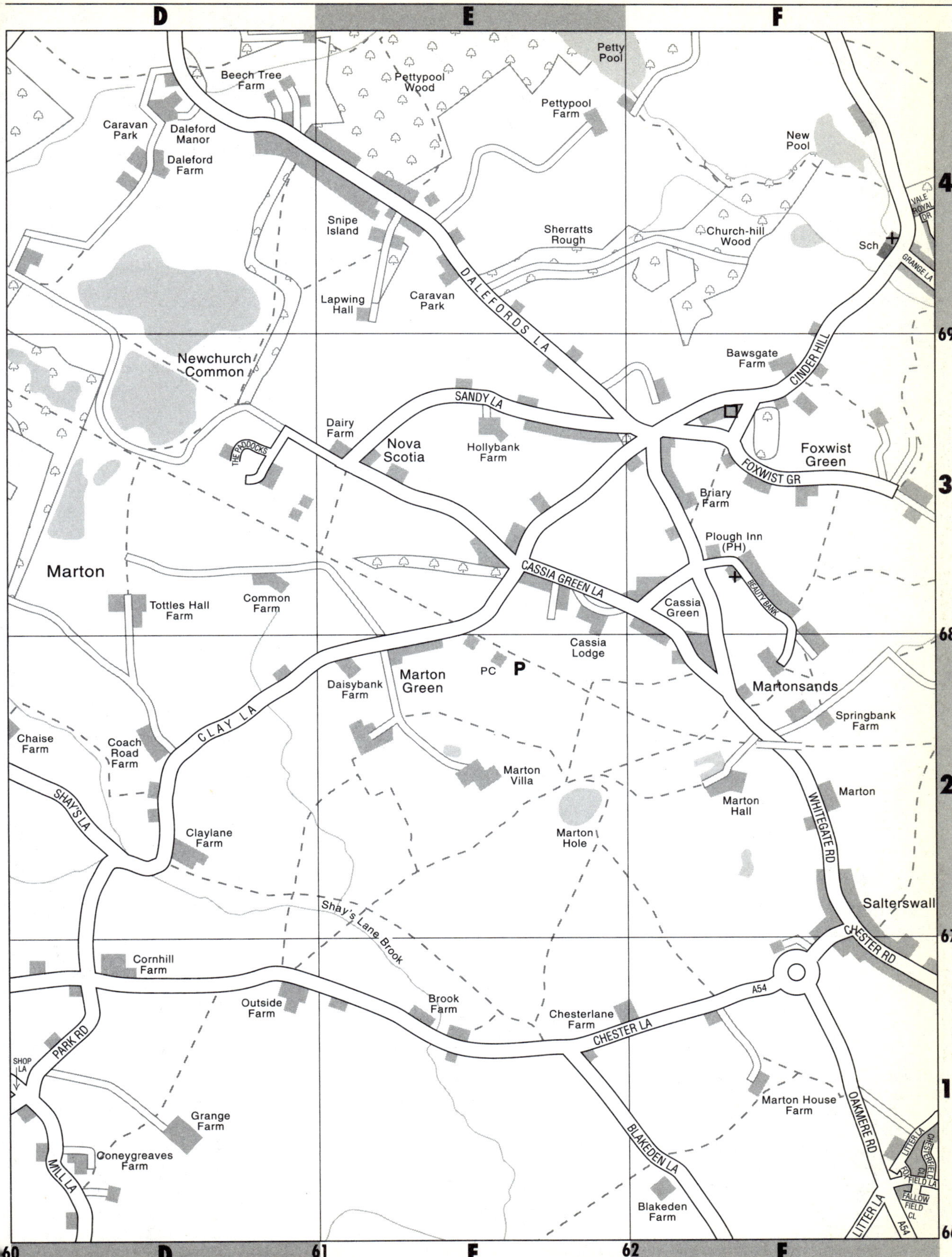
D
E
F
Beech Tree Farm
Pettypool Wood
Petty Pool
Pettypool Farm
Caravan Park
Daleford Manor
Daleford Farm
New Pool
VALE ROYAL DR
Snipe Island
Sherratts Rough
Church-hill Wood
Sch
GRANGE LA
Lapwing Hall
Caravan Park
DALEFORDS LA
4
69
Newchurch Common
Bawsgate Farm
CINDER HILL
SANDY LA
Dairy Farm
Nova Scotia
Hollybank Farm
Foxwist Green
FOXWIST GR
THE PADDOCKS
Briary Farm
3
Plough Inn (PH)
Marton
CASSIA GREEN LA
BEAUTY BANK
Tottles Hall Farm
Common Farm
Cassia Green
Cassia Lodge
68
PC
P
Marton Green
Daisybank Farm
Martonsands
Springbank Farm
Chaise Farm
Coach Road Farm
CLAY LA
Marton Villa
Marton
2
SHAY'S LA
Marton Hall
WHITEGATE RD
Claylane Farm
Marton Hole
Salterswall
Shay's Lane Brook
CHESTER RD
67
Cornhill Farm
A54
Outside Farm
Brook Farm
Chesterlane Farm
CHESTER LA
PARK RD
SHOP LA
1
Marton House Farm
Grange Farm
OAKMERE RD
BLAKEDEN LA
Coneygreaves Farm
LITTER LA
CHESTERFIELD CL
FOX FIELD LA
FALLOW FIELD CL
MILL LA
LITTER LA
Blakeden Farm
A54
66
60
D
61
E
62
F

A
B
C
4
3
2
1
69
68
67
66
63
64
65
Vale Royal
River Weaver
Monk's Well
Valeroyal Park
Eaton Bank Wood
Valeroyal Cut
Whitegate
Quesse Wood
Moulton
Moultonbank Farm
Hillside Farm
Mill Lane Cottages
GRANGE LA
MILL LA
Parkside Farm
Newbridge Wood
MEADOW HOME PARK
Picnic Site
Bark House
Pettypool Brook
Bradford Mill
Bogart Brook
Foxwist Green Farm
Bradford Wood Farm
Meadow House Farm
Meadowbank
SCHOOL RD
Sch
Works
Brook House
Gale Green Farm
BRADFORD RD
Weaver Navigation
Bradfordwood
Catsclough
Cat's Clough
Golf Course
Knight's Grange (Sports Complex)
Sewage Works
WADES LA
SANDRINGHAM CL
Mills
Verdin's Cut
SHEPHERDS FOLD DR
1 LANGDALE CL
2 KESWICK CL
3 STAVELEY DR
4 CARTMEL CL
5 ARNSIDE CL
6 KENTMERE CL
MEADOW CL 1
AMBLESIDE CL 2
ESK DALE CL 3
TURNBERRY CL 4
PRESTWICK CL 5
DALMAHOY CL 6
Roehurst Lane
CHESTER RD
NIXON DR
WINSFORD
Littler
DELAMERE ST
Sch
Guildhall
Coll
Civic Hall
Amb Sta
F Sta
Liby
HIGH ST
Job Cen
Mkt
DINGLE LA
DENE DR
WEAVER ST
River Weaver
NEW RD
WHARTON RD
Stadium
STATION RD
A54
A5018
B5336
MAIN RD
WHITLOW LA
DEAKIN'S RD
NAT LA
WHARTON PARK RD

D
E
F
Peckmill Bridge
LONDON RD
A533
Peckmill Farm
JACK LA B5336
FAIRHOLM RD
RAYLEIGH AV
MERE BANK
WHATCROFT LA
Whatcroft Hall
Dairy Farm
Jack Lane Farm
B5336
Bostockgrange Farm
Sheepsgreen Wood
BRICK KILN LA
Brook House
Bostock Green
Cheshire Ring Canal Walk
4
69
North Lodge
Addashaw Farm
River Dane
JACK LA
Pennel's Wood
Bostock Farm
Hill Wood
3
Bostock Hall School
Trent & Mersey Canal
Industrial Estate
SMOKEHALL LA
Home Farm
Oak Clump
B5336
A5018
68
DEAKIN'S RD
Fiddle Clump
Bull's Wood
BOSTOCK RD
Wharton Green
TIFFILD CT
Oak Wood
BOSTOCK RD
DEAKIN'S RD
South Lodge
2
Wharton Bridge
ECTON CL
CARVER CL
COLLINGTREE AVE
WHARTON PARK RD
WHARTON GDNS
SHAWS LA
Oldhall Farm
ROAD ONE
B5355
Bank Farm
PARK AVE
The Willowbeds
Industrial Estate
Winsford Industrial Estate
Greenhays Farm
GOWY WLK
TAMAR WLK
67
NAT LA
ROAD FOUR
SEVERN WLK
BRADBURY RD
Wharton
DEE WAY
DART WLK
A533
ESK RD
AVON WLK
ROAD FIVE
A54
WEST DR
WHARTON RD
ALT WLK
WILLOW SQUARE
CROOK LA
Liby
BOLLIN AVE
BOLLIN CL
Stanthorne Hall Farm
Sch
LEAF LA
WELLFIELD
ROAD TWO
SCHOOL RD
Schs
NUN HOUSE CL
DOVE PL
BLYTHE
Stanthorne Lodge
BIRCH LA
Sch
PRINCESS ST
NUN HOUSE DR
MAPLE GR
HAWTHORNE GR
DERWENT AVE
AIRE PL
Stanthorne Hall
1
LEDWARD ST
LIME GR
NEWALL CRES
RIBBLE PL
RIBBLE AVE
CLYDE CRES
DANE PL
ROAD THREE
WALNUT DR
CEDAR GR
TRENT CL
MERSEY PL
BIRCH AVE
TRENT AVE
THOMAS PL
ELM GR
LODGE DR
WHEELOCK DR
MIDDLEWICH RD
IOM PATH
PINE GR
GREVILLE DR
Gravel
NUNSMERE CL
Winsford Station
WALLACE CT
COALPIT LA
B5355
CLIVE LA
Clive
STATION RD
DIERDEN ST
GREENFIELDS
ROOKERY RISE
A54
P
SEATON ST
66
66
D
67
E
68
F

127
105

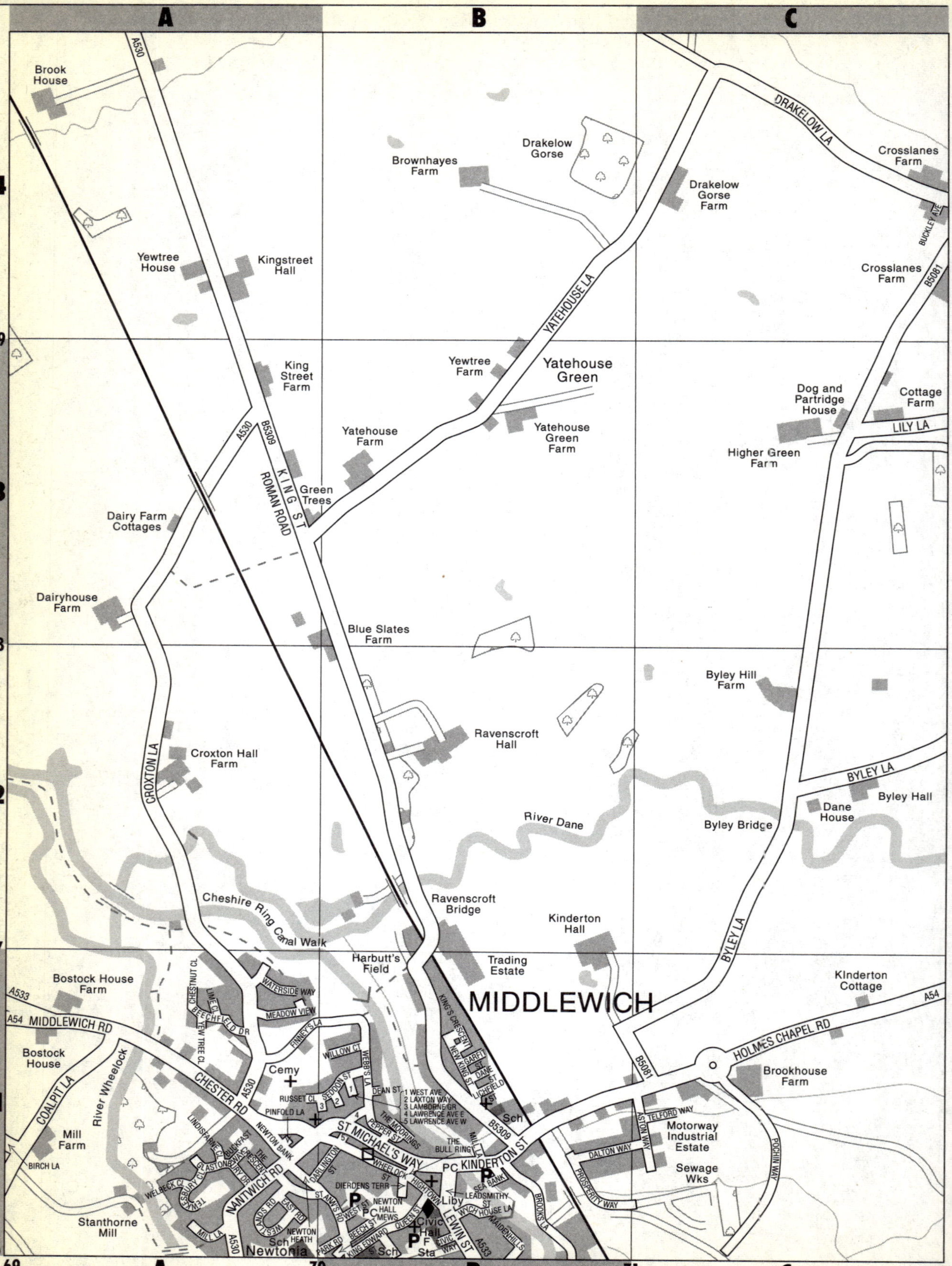

127
151

106
130

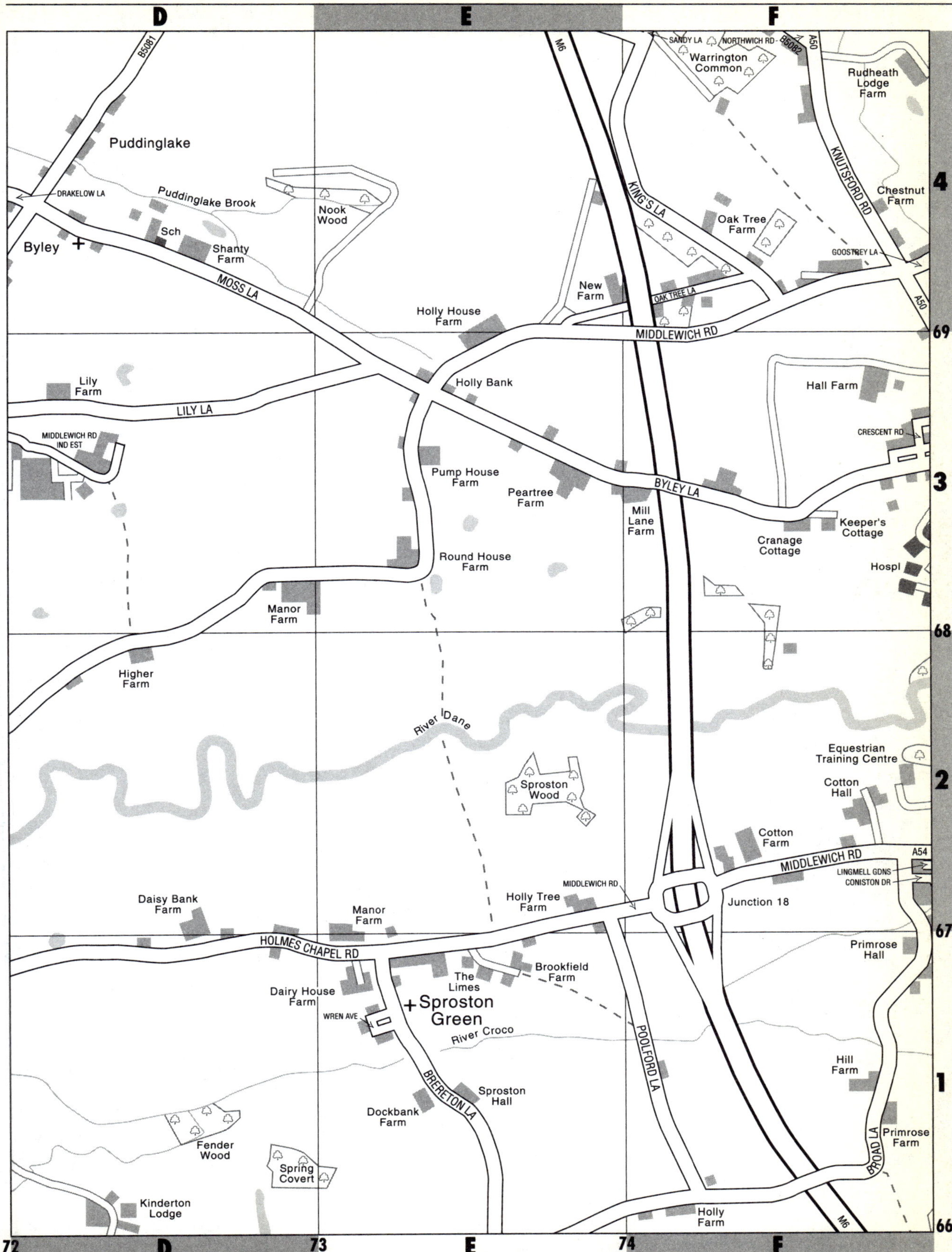

152
130

129
107

A
B
C
4
69
3
68
2
67
1
66
75
76
77
Rudheath Lodge Farm
Racecourse Wood
NEW PLATT LA
MAIN RD
BIRCH TREE LA
BOOTH BED LA
NETHERLEA CT
Caravan Park
Dromedary Lodge
BANK VIEW
MAIN RD
STATION RD
Sch
Shear Brook
GOOSTREY LA
Goostrey Farm
HERMITAGE LA
Hermitage Farm
Mountpleasant
Heyhead Farm
A50
TWEMLOW LA
The Orchards
Blue Slate Farm
CRESCENT RD
BYLEY LA
Cranage
Hollins Farm
Bank Farm
Swan Farm
Hospl
Hermitage Farm
A535
Manor Farm
KNUTSFORD RD
Hermitage
Hermitage Thornes
Saltersford Farm
Twemlow Viaduct
Hotel
Sch
Cemy
River Dane
Sewage Works
Cranage Mill
Holmes Chapel
MACCLESFIELD RD
DANEFIELD RD
ASH CL
ELM DR
Bridge Farm
Cotton Wood
RIVERSIDE CRES
HERMITAGE DR
HAWTHORN CL
CHESTNUT DR
Ryecroft Wood
Saltersford Hall Farm
REES CRES
Sch
Saltersford Hall
PICTON SQ
PC
B5308
A535
SALTERSFORD CNR
MIDDLEWICH RD
P
F Sta
SYCAMORE CL
B5308
CHURCH WLK
Sch
Assembly Rooms
P
Liby
Holmes Chapel Station
Manor Farm
MANOR LA
ST LUKES CL
MAYFIELD CL
EASTGATE RD
BROOKFIELD DR
HILLCREST AVE
OAKFIELD RISE
CARTMEL CL
WEST WAY
CHESTER RD
A54
STATION RD
P
Bellfields Farm
Bayley House
MARDALE CT
GRASMERE DR
RYDAL CL
A54
LINGMELL CL
Sch
VICTORIA AVE
LONDON RD
BROMLEY DR
Works
Marsh Lane House
MARSH LA
ALUM CT
Alum Bridge
River Croco
HOLMES CHAPEL RD
A54
Marsh Lane Farm
Dunkirk Farm
A50
Parkmill Farm

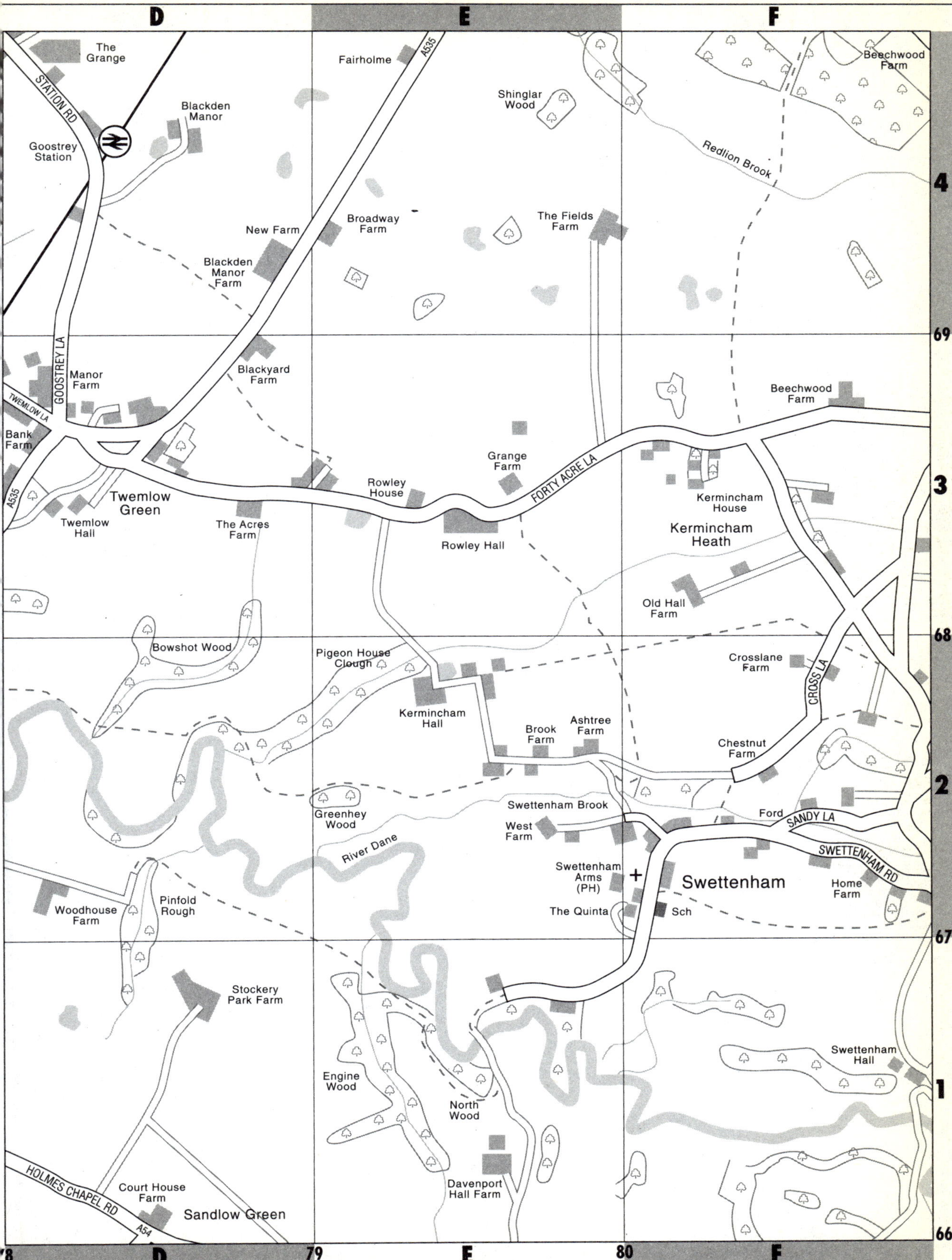
D
E
F
The Grange
Fairholme
A535
Beechwood Farm
STATION RD
Blackden Manor
Shinglar Wood
Goostrey Station
Redlion Brook
4
Broadway Farm
The Fields Farm
New Farm
Blackden Manor Farm
69
GOOSTREY LA
Manor Farm
Blackyard Farm
Beechwood Farm
TWEMLOW LA
Bank Farm
Grange Farm
FORTY ACRE LA
3
A535
Twemlow Green
Rowley House
Kermincham House
Twemlow Hall
The Acres Farm
Rowley Hall
Kermincham Heath
Old Hall Farm
68
Bowshot Wood
Pigeon House Clough
Crosslane Farm
CROSS LA
Kermincham Hall
Ashtree Farm
Brook Farm
Chestnut Farm
2
Greenhey Wood
Swettenham Brook
Ford
SANDY LA
West Farm
River Dane
SWETTENHAM RD
Swettenham Arms (PH)
Swettenham
Home Farm
Pinfold Rough
Woodhouse Farm
The Quinta
Sch
67
Stockery Park Farm
Swettenham Hall
1
Engine Wood
North Wood
Davenport Hall Farm
HOLMES CHAPEL RD
Court House Farm
Sandlow Green
A54
66
78
D
79
E
80
F

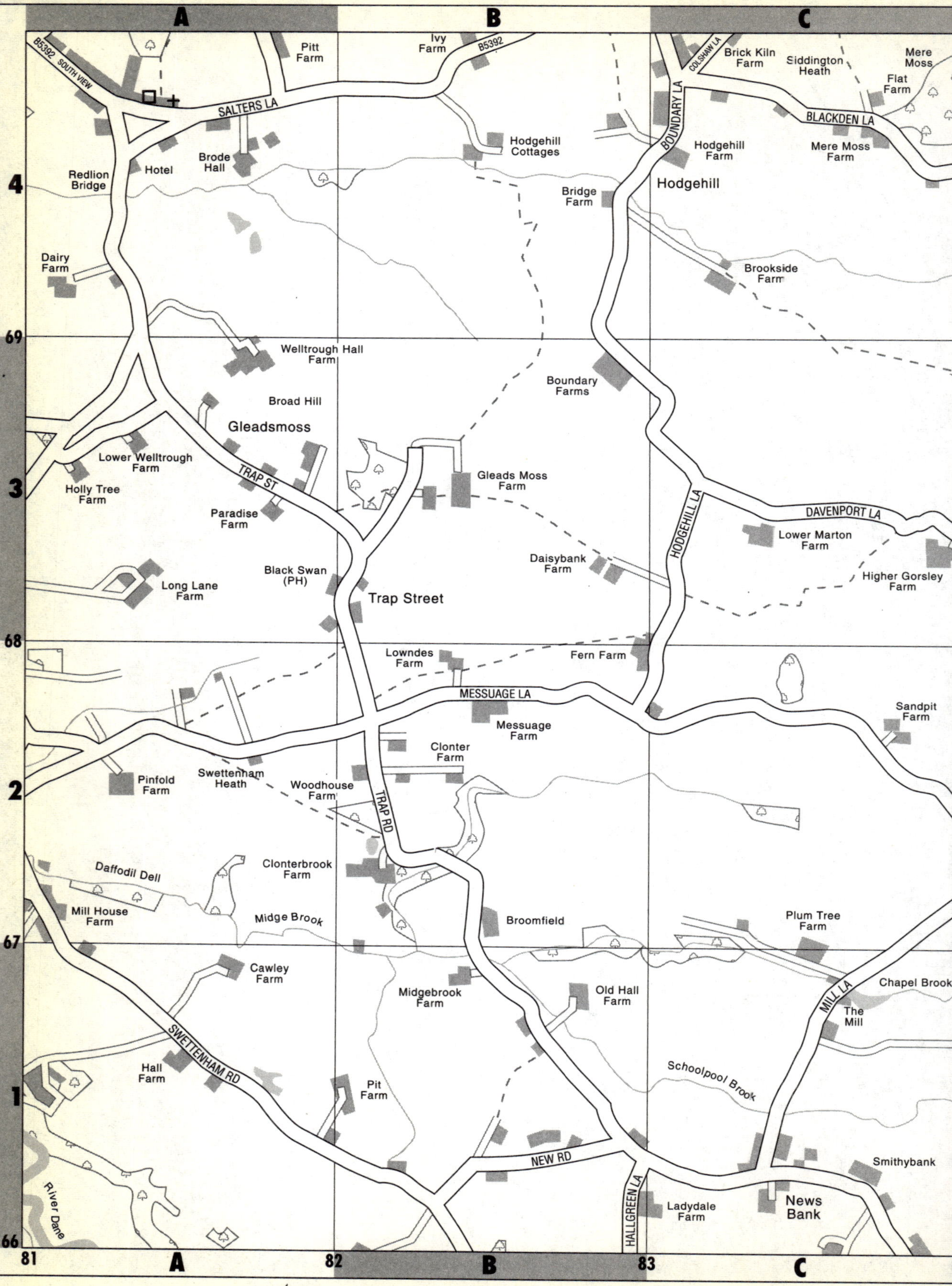
A
B
C
B5392
SOUTH VIEW
Pitt Farm
Ivy Farm
B5392
COLSHAW LA
Brick Kiln Farm
Siddington Heath
Mere Moss
Flat Farm
SALTERS LA
BOUNDARY LA
BLACKDEN LA
Hodgehill Cottages
Hodgehill Farm
Mere Moss Farm
Brode Hall
Hotel
Redlion Bridge
4
Hodgehill
Bridge Farm
Dairy Farm
Brookside Farm
69
Welltrough Hall Farm
Boundary Farms
Broad Hill
Gleadsmoss
Lower Welltrough Farm
Gleads Moss Farm
Holly Tree Farm
TRAP ST
3
HODGEHILL LA
DAVENPORT LA
Paradise Farm
Lower Marton Farm
Daisybank Farm
Higher Gorsley Farm
Black Swan (PH)
Long Lane Farm
Trap Street
68
Lowndes Farm
Fern Farm
MESSUAGE LA
Sandpit Farm
Messuage Farm
Clonter Farm
Pinfold Farm
Swettenham Heath
Woodhouse Farm
2
TRAP RD
Daffodil Dell
Clonterbrook Farm
Mill House Farm
Midge Brook
Broomfield
Plum Tree Farm
67
Cawley Farm
Chapel Brook
Midgebrook Farm
Old Hall Farm
MILL LA
The Mill
SWETTENHAM RD
Hall Farm
Schoolpool Brook
1
Pit Farm
NEW RD
Smithybank
River Dane
HALLGREEN LA
Ladydale Farm
News Bank
66
81
A
82
B
83
C

110
134

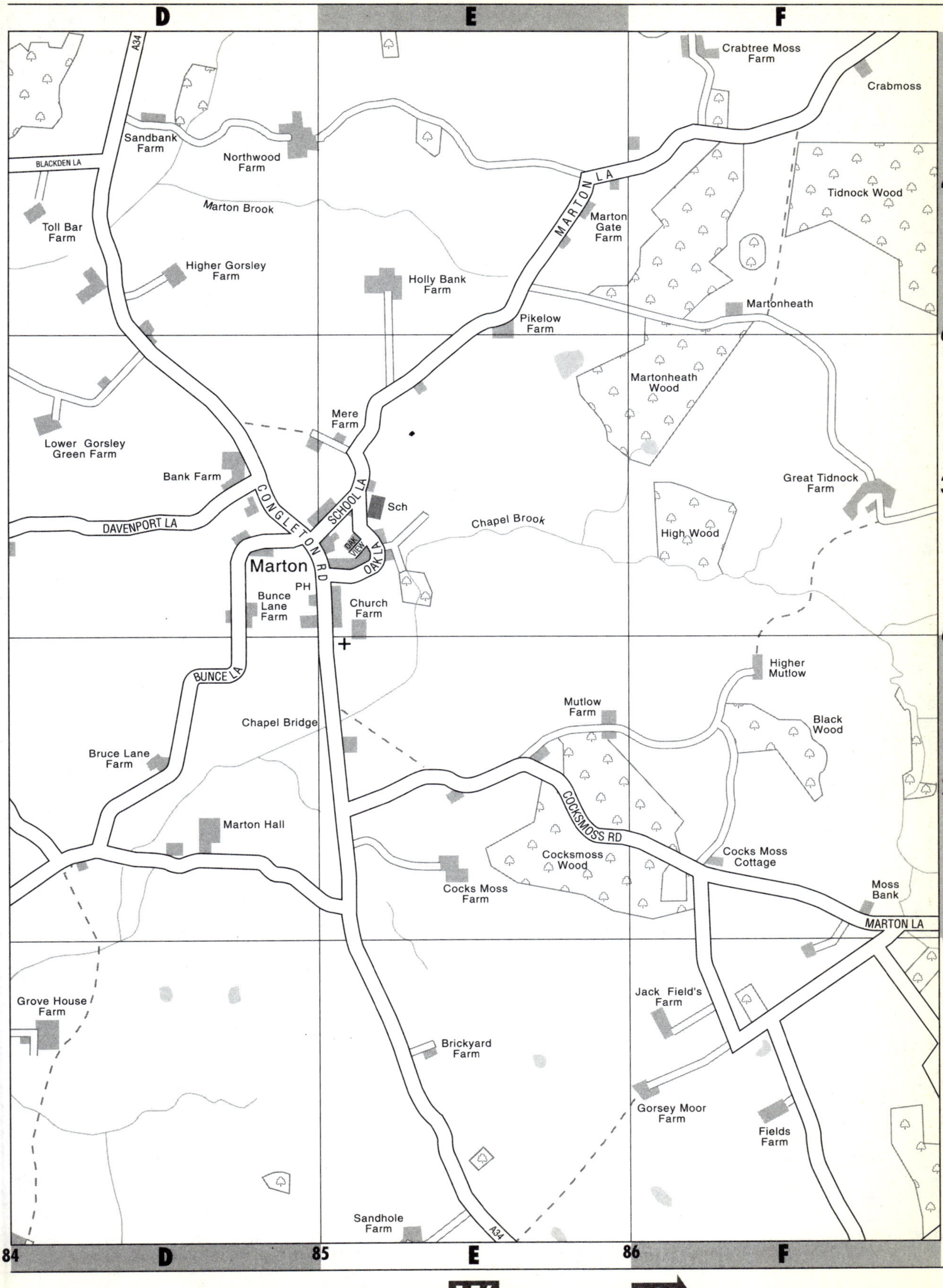

156
134

133
111

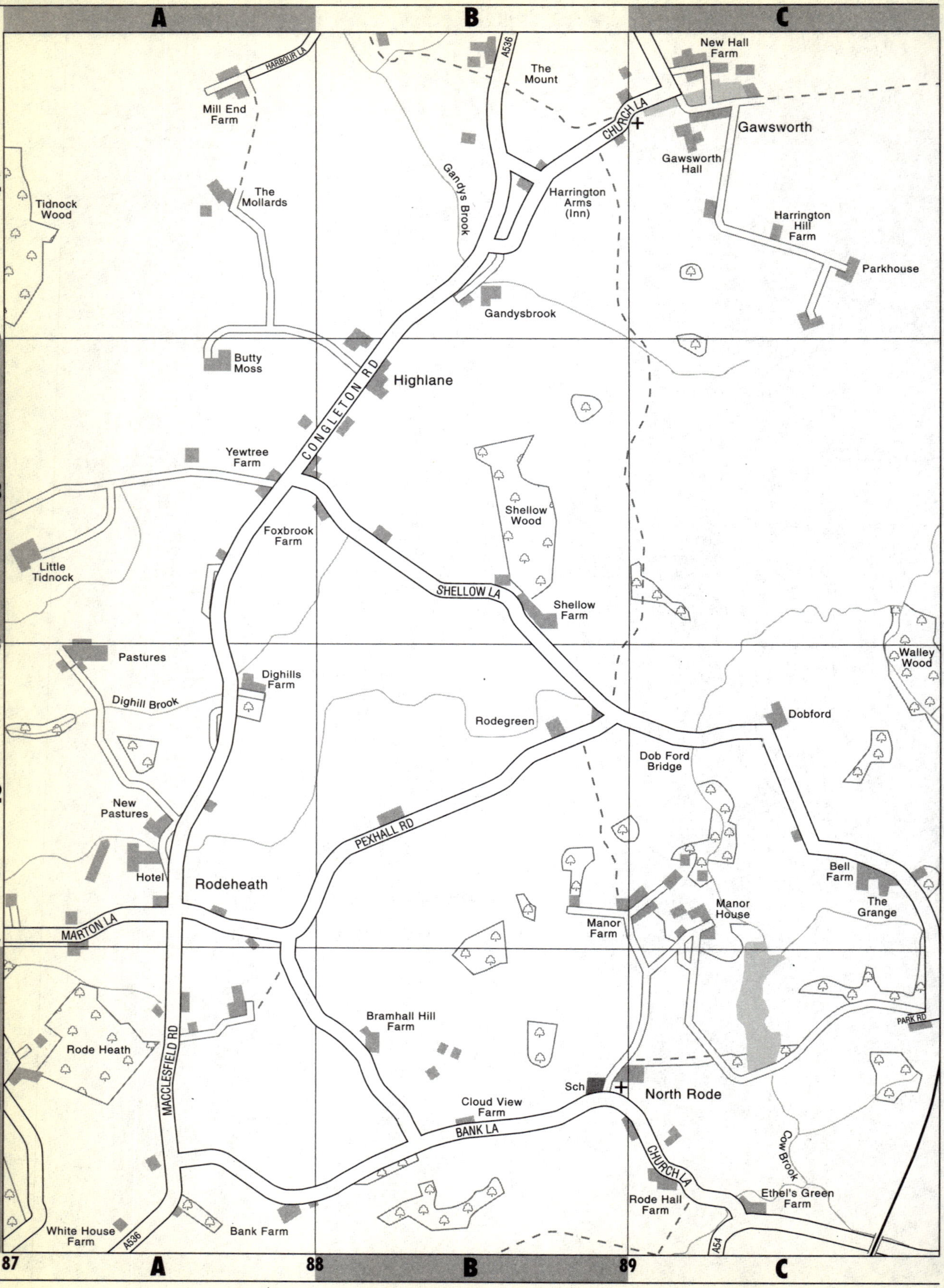

133
157

112
136

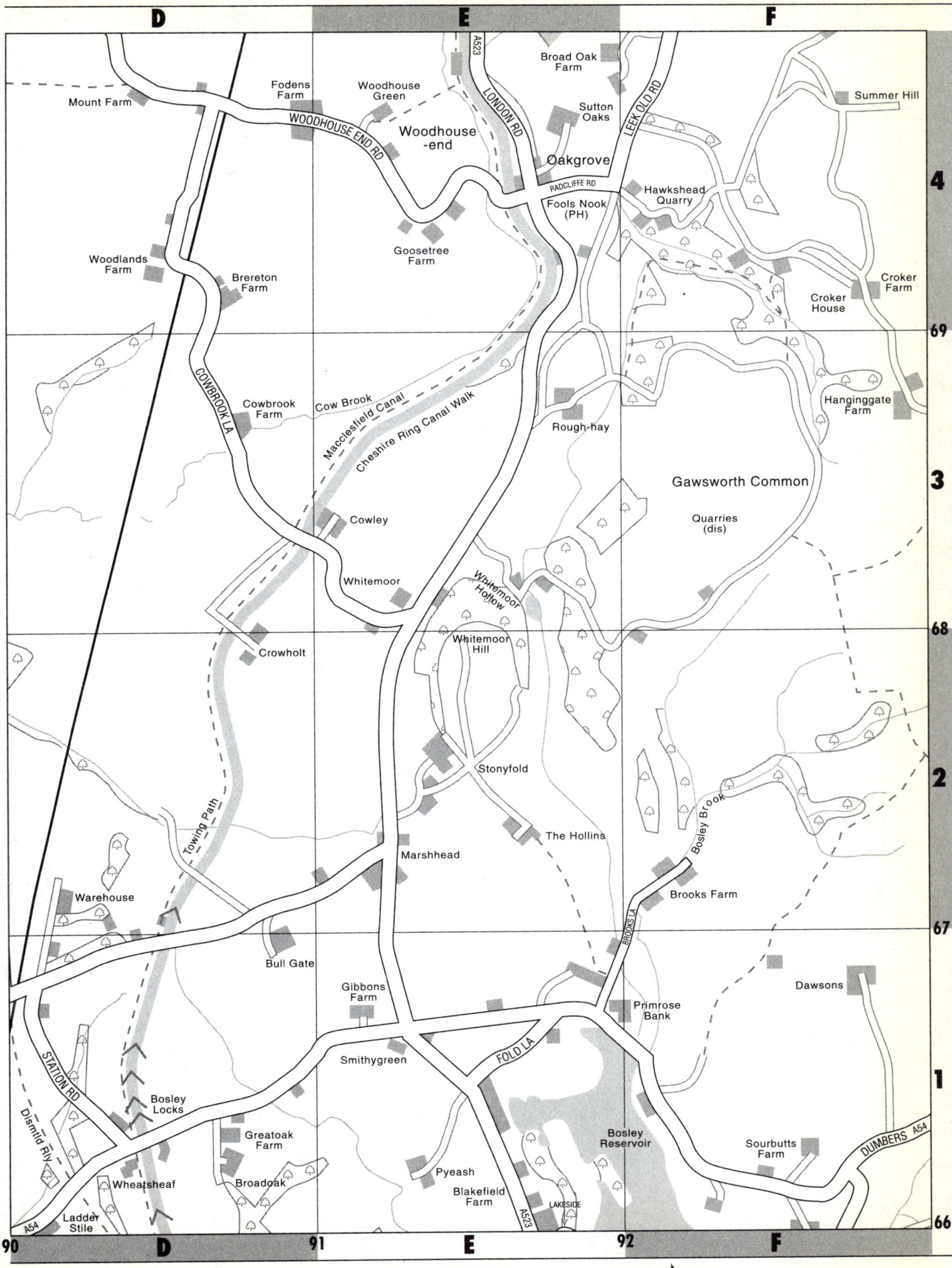

158
136

135
113

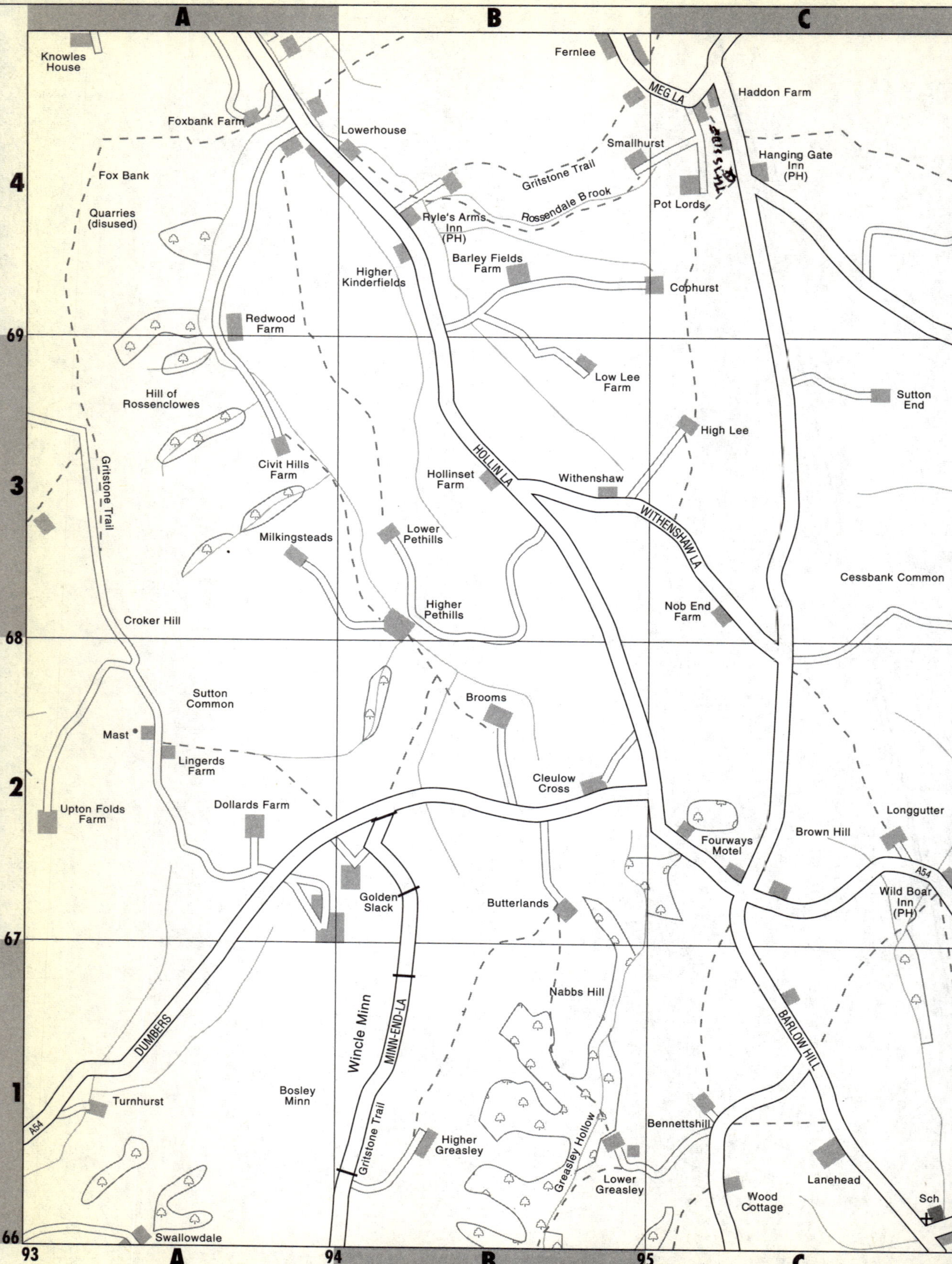

135
159

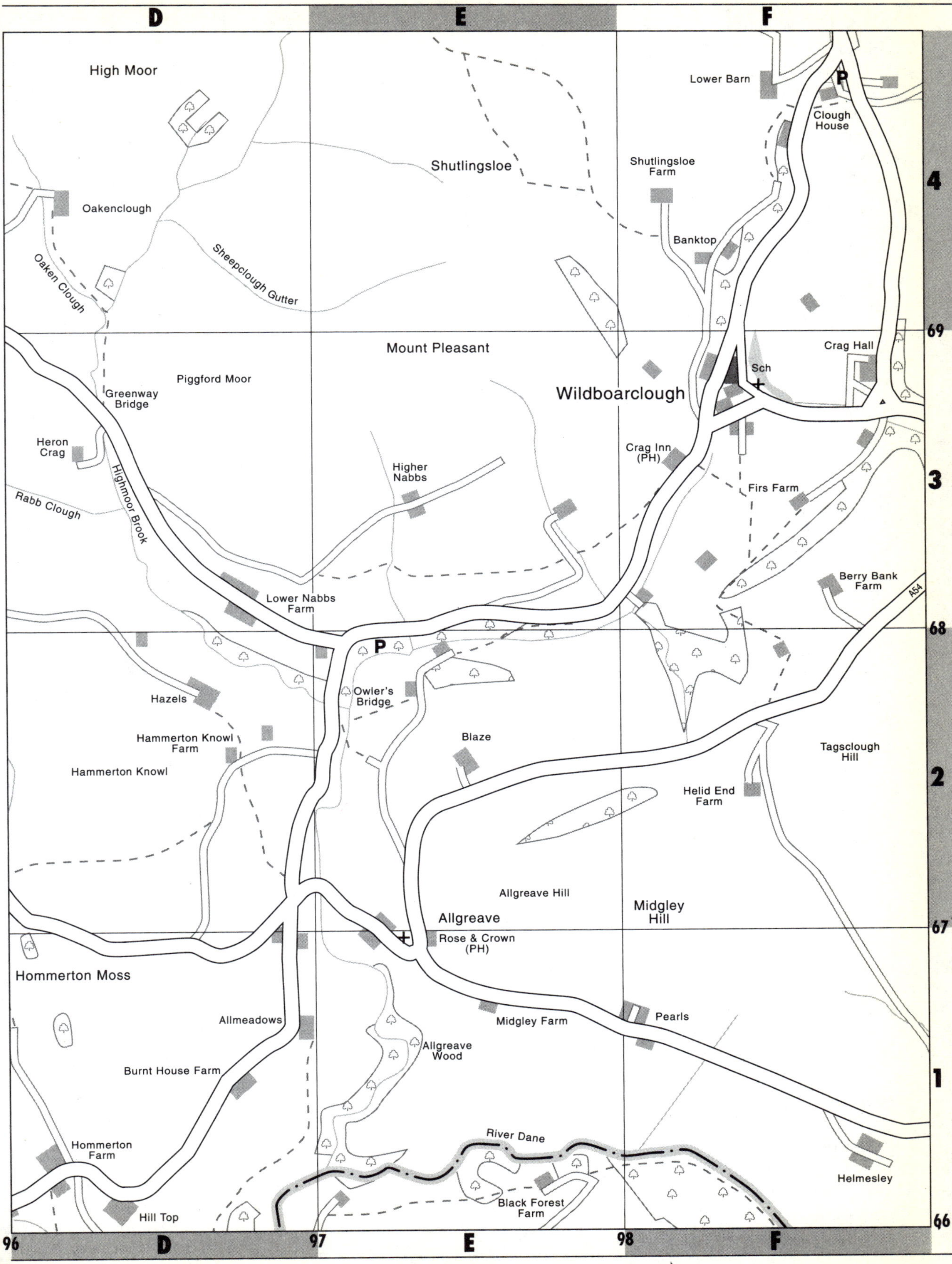
D
E
F
High Moor
Lower Barn
P
Clough House
Shutlingsloe
Shutlingsloe Farm
4
Oakenclough
Banktop
Oaken Clough
Sheepclough Gutter
69
Mount Pleasant
Crag Hall
Sch
Piggford Moor
Greenway Bridge
Wildboarclough
Heron Crag
Crag Inn (PH)
Higher Nabbs
3
Highmoor Brook
Firs Farm
Rabb Clough
Berry Bank Farm
A54
Lower Nabbs Farm
68
P
Hazels
Owler's Bridge
Hammerton Knowl Farm
Blaze
Tagsclough Hill
2
Hammerton Knowl
Helid End Farm
Allgreave Hill
Midgley Hill
Allgreave
67
Rose & Crown (PH)
Hommerton Moss
Allmeadows
Midgley Farm
Pearls
Allgreave Wood
Burnt House Farm
1
River Dane
Hommerton Farm
Helmesley
Black Forest Farm
Hill Top
66
96
D
97
E
98
F

137
115

A
B
C
4
69
3
68
2
67
1
66
99
00
01
Cumberland Cottage
Cumberland Brook
A54
Chy
Wood Moss
Sparbent
Holt
Blackclough
Orchard Farm
Knotbury Common
Leech Wood
Cut-thorn Hill
Three Shire Heads
Panniers Pool
Knotbury Farm
Cut-thorn
Knotbury
Birchenough Hill
Robins Clough
River Dane
Knotbury Lee Farm
Knar
Turn Edge
Far Hole-edge
Hawk's Nest
Flash
Axe Edge Green Farm
Parks
Wicken Walls
Hole-edge
Far Brook
Bennettshitch
Spring Head
Higher Bangs
Lower Bangs
New Cottage
Burntcliff Top
Greens
Wildstone Rock
Midgleygate
Goosetree
P
Manor Farm
The Wash
Greenstitch
Youth Hostel

116
140

161
140

139
117

139
162

118
142

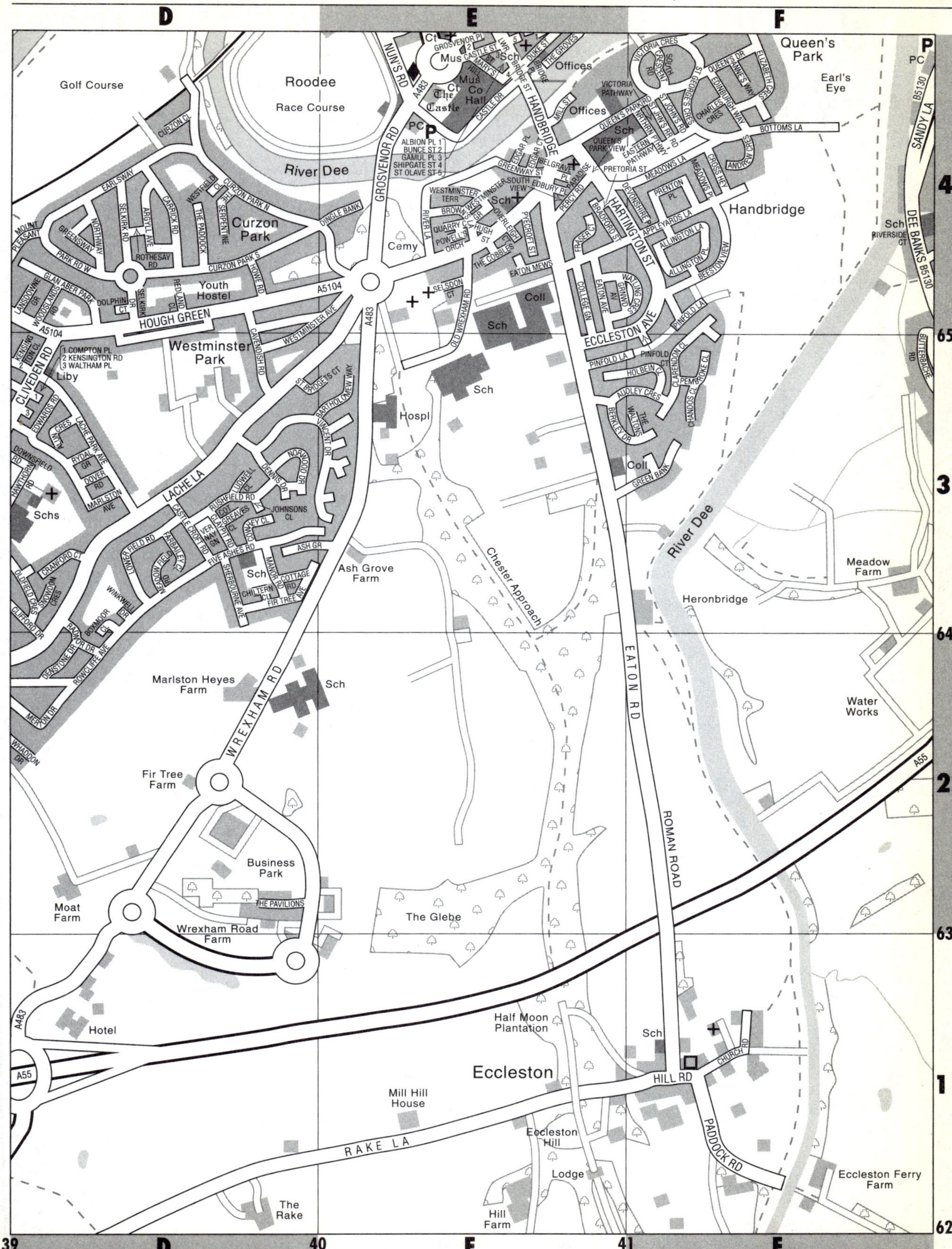
D
E
F
Golf Course
Roodee
Race Course
River Dee
Curzon Park
Youth Hostel
Westminster Park
HOUGH GREEN
A5104
GROSVENOR RD
NUN'S RD
A483
The Castle
Mus
Co Hall
Ct
PC
P
Offices
HANDBRIDGE
Queen's Park
Earl's Eye
BOTTOMS LA
SANDY LA
B5130
DEE BANKS
Handbridge
Sch
Cemy
Coll
Hospl
Liby
Schs
LACHE LA
ECCLESTON AVE
HARTINGTON ST
Ash Grove Farm
Chester Approach
Heronbridge
Meadow Farm
Water Works
Marlston Heyes Farm
WREXHAM RD
EATON RD
ROMAN ROAD
Fir Tree Farm
Business Park
THE PAVILIONS
Moat Farm
Wrexham Road Farm
The Glebe
A55
Hotel
Half Moon Plantation
Eccleston
HILL RD
CHURCH RD
PADDOCK RD
Mill Hill House
RAKE LA
Eccleston Hill
Lodge
Hill Farm
The Rake
Eccleston Ferry Farm
1 COMPTON PL
2 KENSINGTON RD
3 WALTHAM PL
ALBION PL 1
BUNCE ST 2
GAMUL PL 3
SHIPGATE ST 4
ST OLAVE ST 5
4
65
3
64
2
63
1
62
39
40
41

141
119

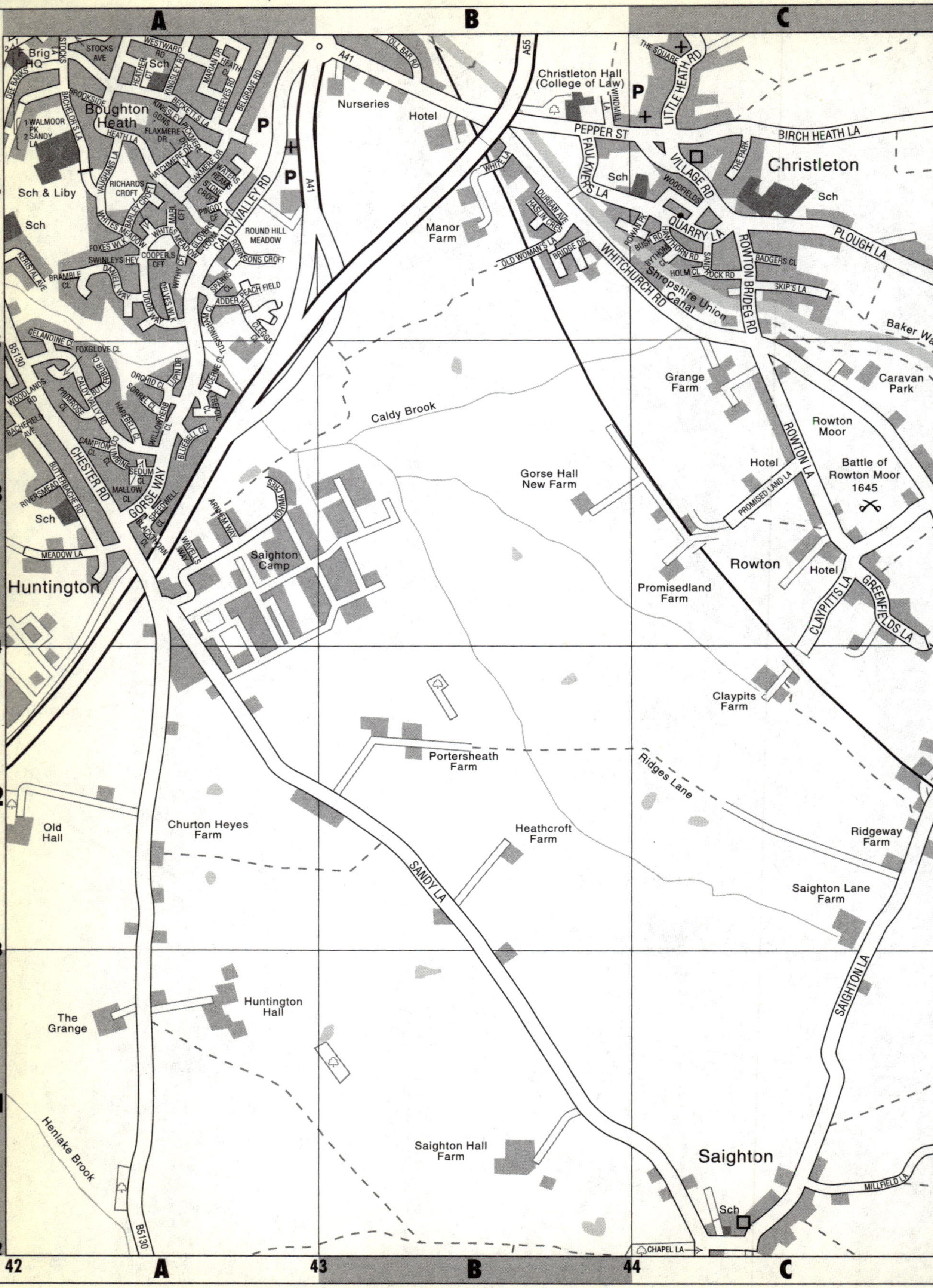

141
164

120
144

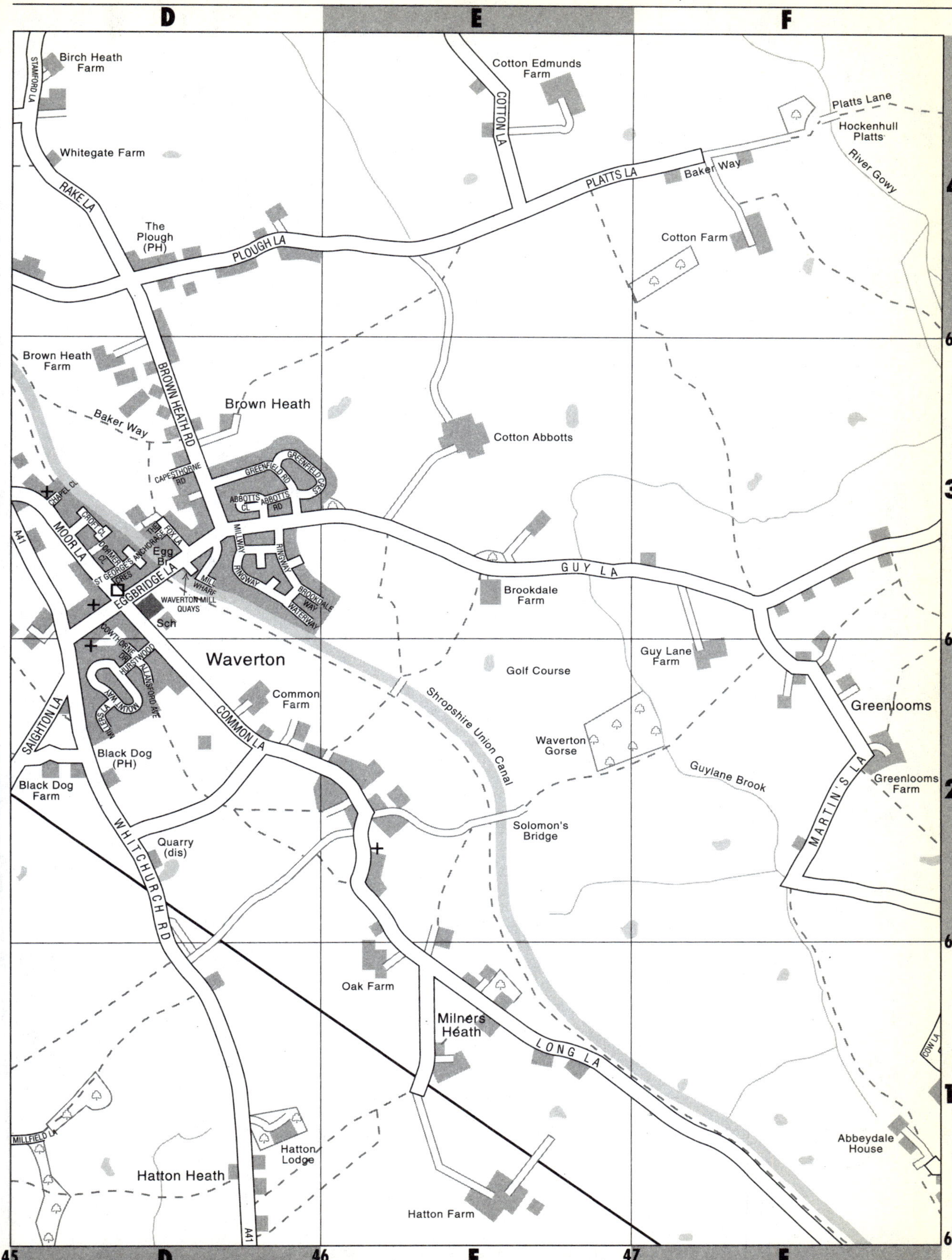

165
144

143
121

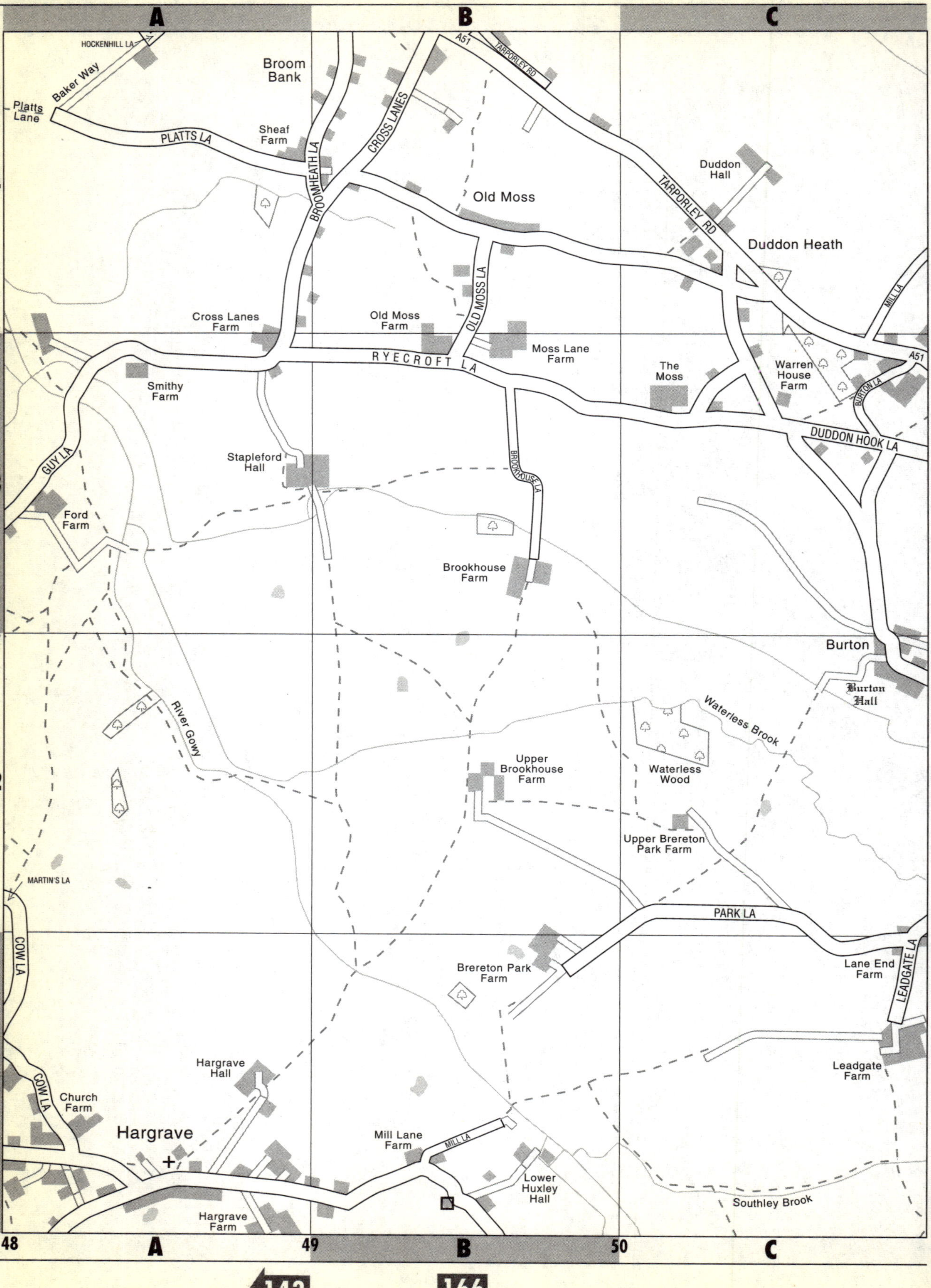

143
166

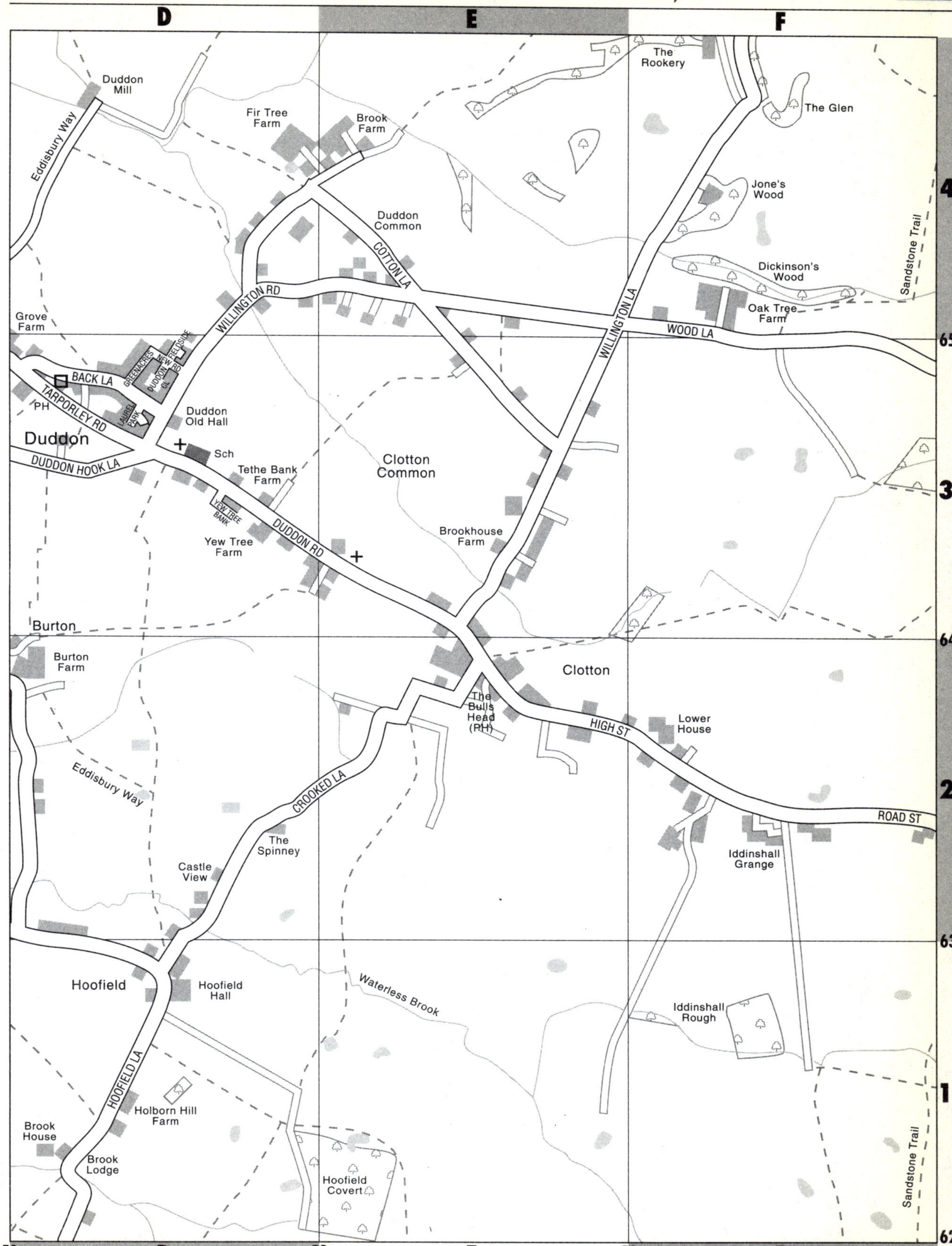
D
E
F
Duddon Mill
Eddisbury Way
Fir Tree Farm
Brook Farm
The Rookery
The Glen
Jone's Wood
Duddon Common
COTTON LA
Dickinson's Wood
Sandstone Trail
Oak Tree Farm
WILLINGTON RD
WILLINGTON LA
WOOD LA
Grove Farm
BACK LA
GREENACRES
FIELDSIDE
NEW RD
DUDDON CL
TARPORLEY RD
LAUREL PARK
PH
Duddon
Duddon Old Hall
Sch
DUDDON HOOK LA
Tethe Bank Farm
Clotton Common
YEW TREE BANK
Yew Tree Farm
DUDDON RD
Brookhouse Farm
Burton
Burton Farm
Clotton
The Bulls Head (PH)
HIGH ST
Lower House
Eddisbury Way
CROOKED LA
ROAD ST
The Spinney
Iddinshall Grange
Castle View
Hoofield
Hoofield Hall
Waterless Brook
Iddinshall Rough
HOOFIELD LA
Holborn Hill Farm
Brook House
Brook Lodge
Hoofield Covert
Sandstone Trail
4
65
3
64
2
63
1
62
51
52
53

145
123

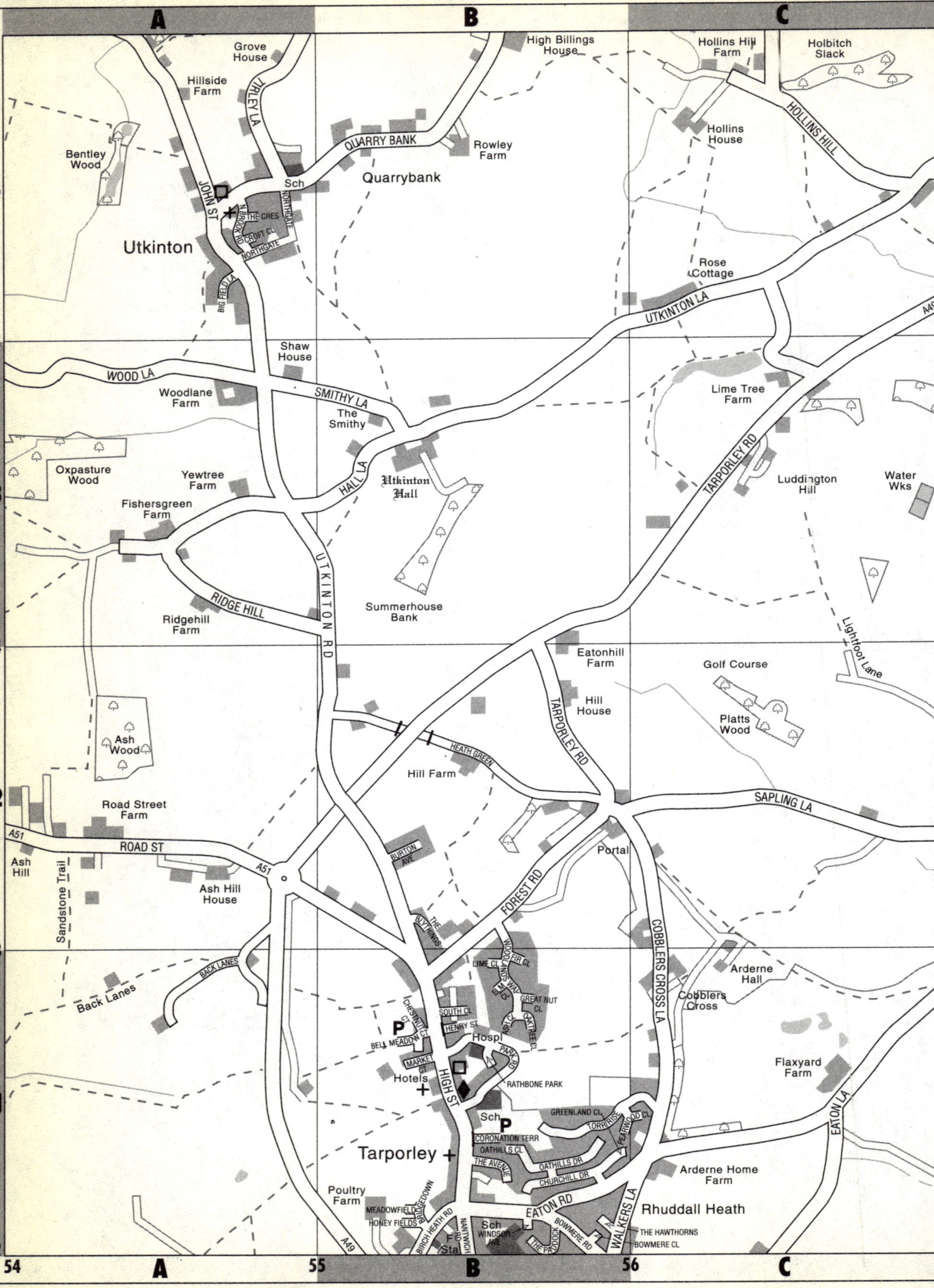

145
168

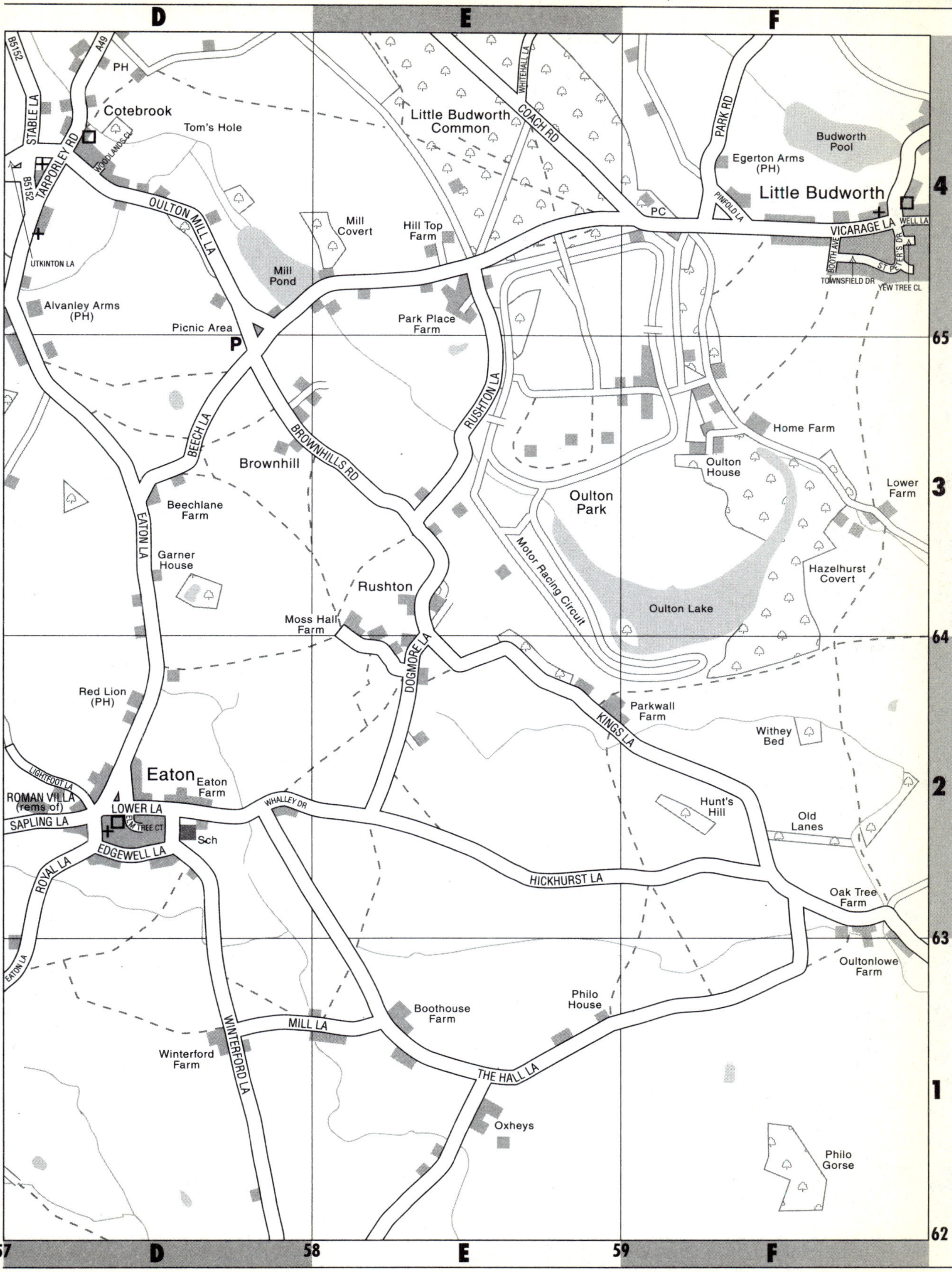
D
E
F
B5152
A49
PH
STABLE LA
Cotebrook
Tom's Hole
TARPORLEY RD
WOODLANDS CL
B5152
OULTON MILL LA
UTKINTON LA
Mill Pond
Alvanley Arms (PH)
Picnic Area
P
Little Budworth Common
WHITEHALL LA
COACH RD
Mill Covert
Hill Top Farm
Park Place Farm
PARK RD
Budworth Pool
Egerton Arms (PH)
PINFOLD LA
PC
Little Budworth
VICARAGE LA
WELL LA
BOOTH AVE
ST PETER'S DR
ST PC
TOWNSFIELD DR
YEW TREE CL
4
65
BEECH LA
BROWNHILLS RD
Brownhill
RUSHTON LA
Home Farm
Oulton House
Oulton Park
Lower Farm
3
Beechlane Farm
EATON LA
Garner House
Motor Racing Circuit
Hazelhurst Covert
Rushton
Oulton Lake
Moss Hall Farm
DOGMORE LA
64
Red Lion (PH)
Parkwall Farm
KINGS LA
Withey Bed
Eaton
Eaton Farm
LIGHTFOOT LA
ROMAN VILLA (rems of)
LOWER LA
SAPLING LA
ELM TREE CT
Sch
EDGEWELL LA
ROYAL LA
WHALLEY DR
Hunt's Hill
Old Lanes
2
HICKHURST LA
Oak Tree Farm
63
EATON LA
Oultonlowe Farm
Philo House
Boothouse Farm
MILL LA
WINTERFORD LA
Winterford Farm
THE HALL LA
1
Oxheys
Philo Gorse
62
57
58
59

147
125

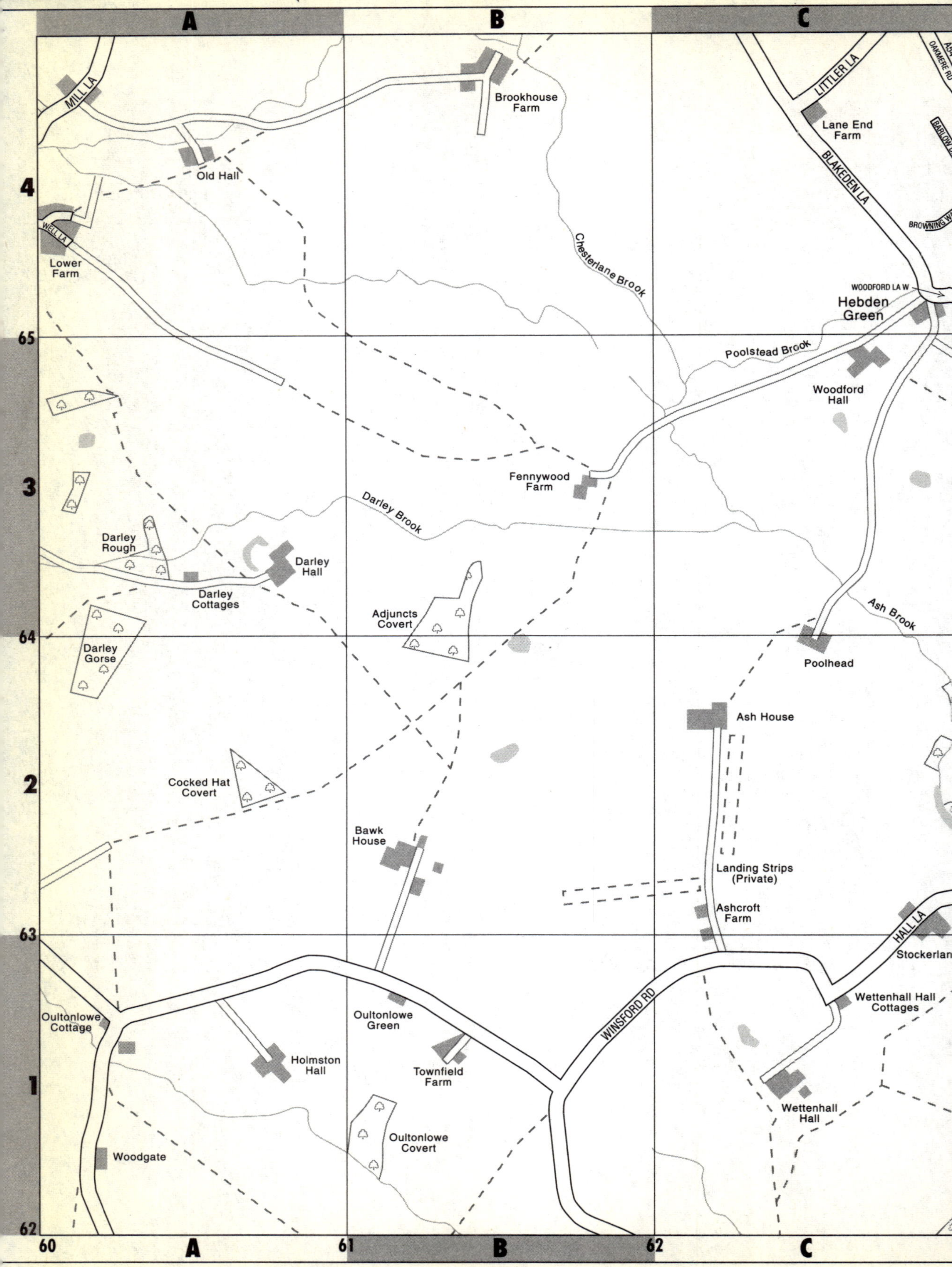

147
170

126
150

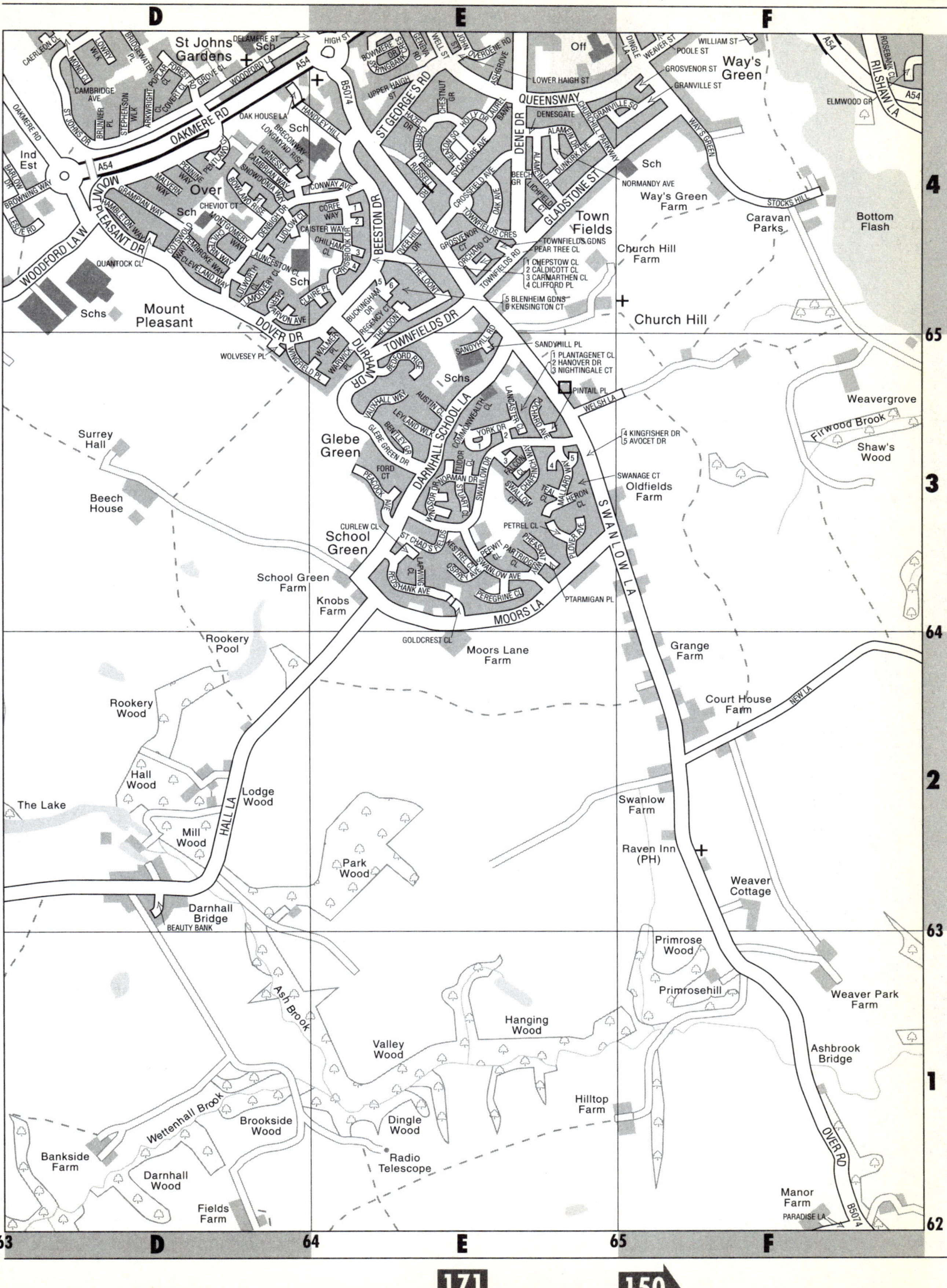

171
150

149
127

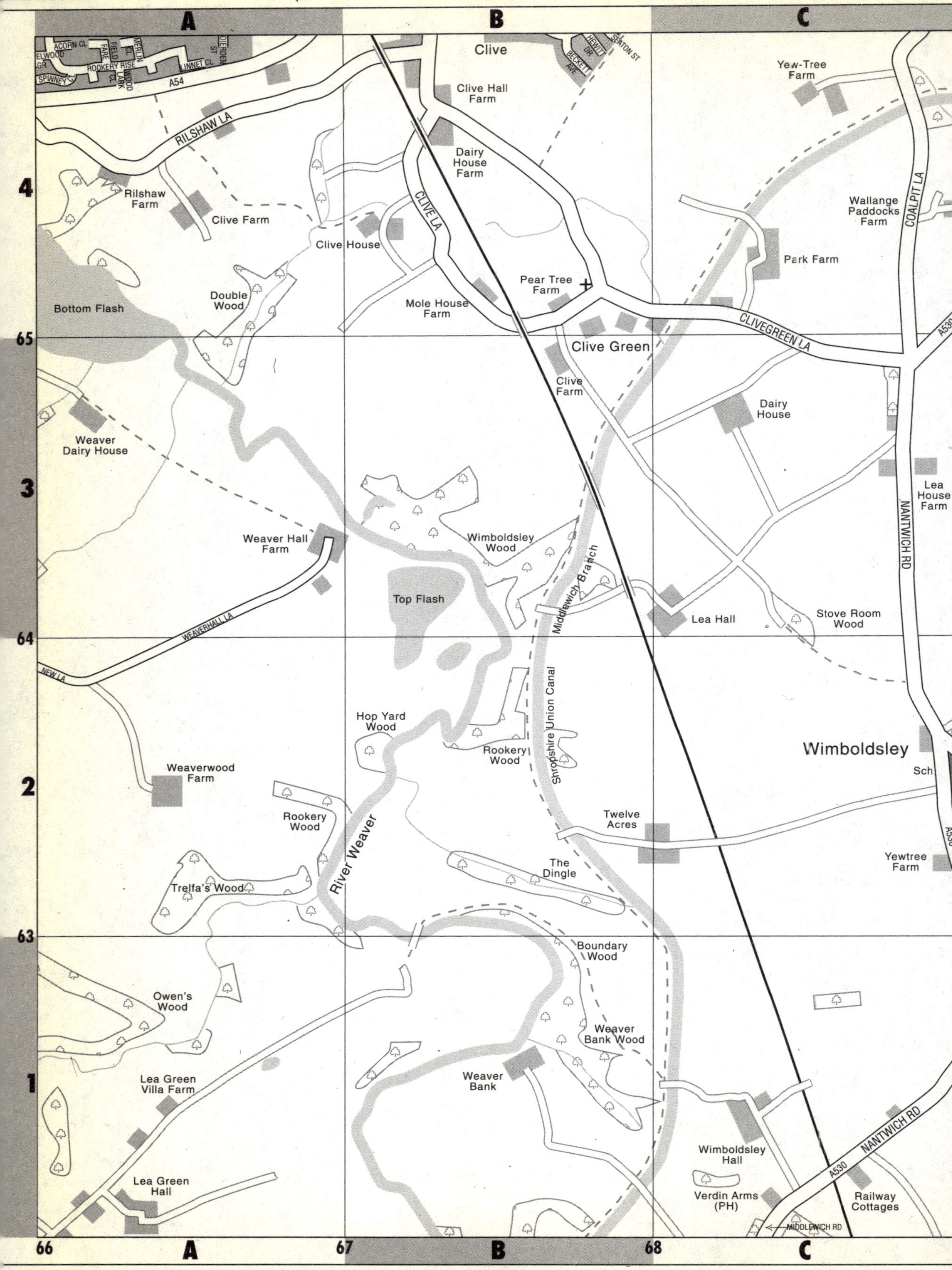

149
172

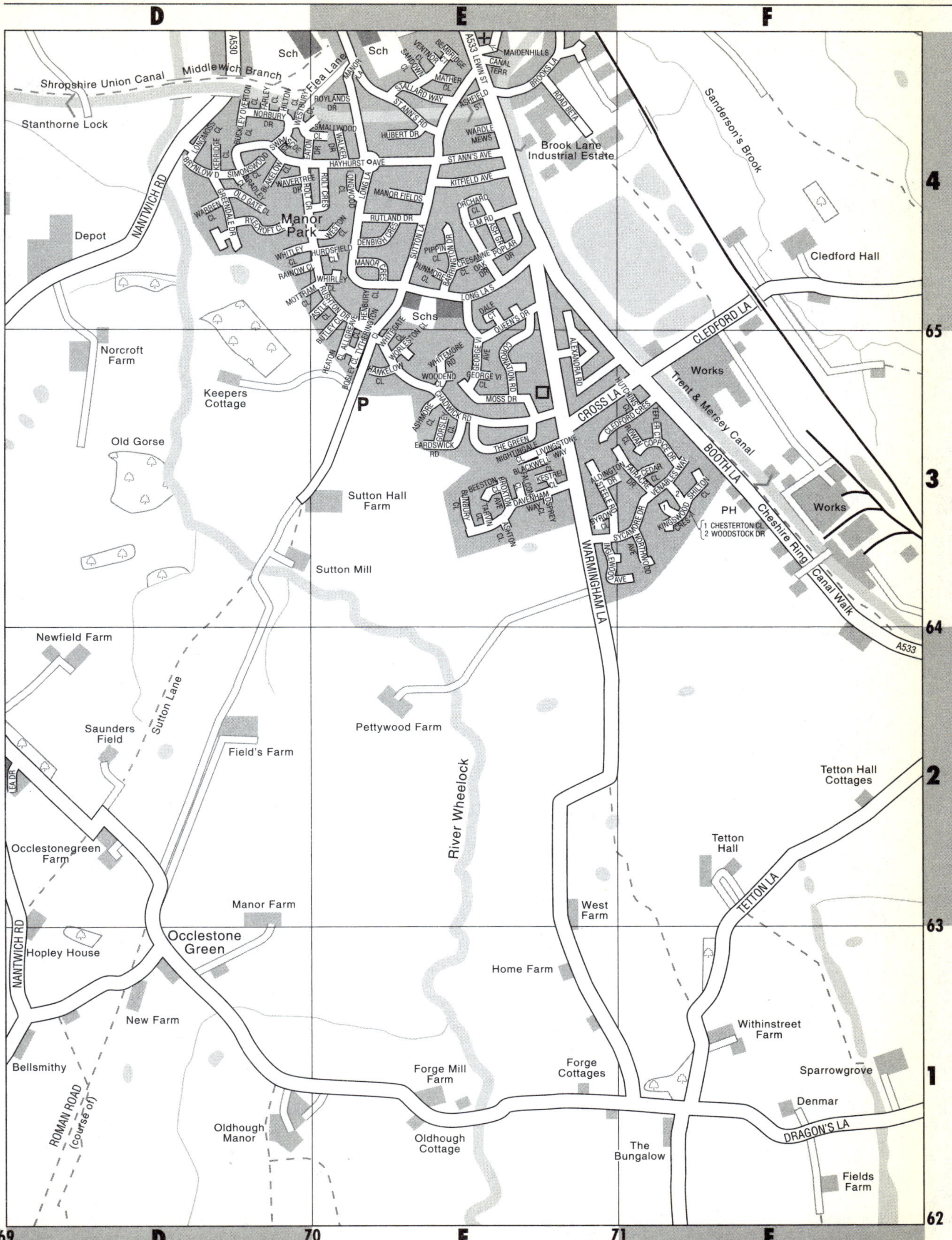
D
E
F
Sch
Sch
A530
A533
Shropshire Union Canal
Middlewich Branch
Flea Lane
Stanthorne Lock
MAIDENHILLS
CANAL TERR
LEWIN ST
BEMBRIDGE CT
VENTNOR CL
SANDOWN CL
MATHER CL
STALLARD WAY
ST ANN'S RD
ASHFIELD ST
BROOKS LA
ROAD BETA
ROYLANDS DR
SMALLWOOD CL
HUBERT DR
WARDLE MEWS
Brook Lane Industrial Estate
HAYHURST AVE
ST ANN'S AVE
KITFIELD AVE
Sanderson's Brook
NANTWICH RD
Depot
Manor Park
MANOR FIELDS
RUTLAND DR
DENBIGH CRES
ORCHARD CL
ELM RD
ASH GR
POPLAR DR
PIPPIN CL
CRESANNE CL
OAK DR
DUNMORE CL
BARRINGTON DR
SUTTON LA
LONG LA S
MANOR CRES
WHIRLEY CL
HURDSFIELD CL
WHITLEY CL
RAINOW CL
WESTON CL
RYECROFT CL
WARREN CL
GREENDALE DR
OLD GATE CL
BRYNLOW D
SIMONSWOOD CL
KERRIDGE CL
LONGMOSS
BUCKLEY CL
OVERTON CL
NORBURY DR
WAVERTREE DR
ROLT CRES
ROLT CR
WALKER DR
LONGWOOD CL
Cledford Hall
CLEDFORD LA
Schs
DALE CT
QUEEN'S DR
ALEXANDRA RD
Norcroft Farm
MOTTRAM CL
HENBURY CL
LYTHERINGTON CL
WHITEGATE CL
WORLESTON CL
WHITEMORE RD
GEORGE VI AVE
GEORGE VI CL
CORONATION RD
HANKELOW CL
WOODEND CL
MOSS DR
Works
Trent & Mersey Canal
Keepers Cottage
P
CROSS LA
HUTCHINS CL
CLEDFORD CRES
TEFLER CL
ROWAN CL
COPPICE DR
CHADWICK RD
ASHMORE CL
GORSLEY CL
EARDSWICK RD
BOOTH LA
Old Gorse
THE GREEN
NIGHTINGALE CL
LIVINGSTONE WAY
BLACKWELL WAY
ALDINGTON DR
FAIRACRE DR
CEDAR CL
VENABLES WAY
SHILTON CL
KESTREL CL
BEESTON CL
BROXTON AVE
DAVENHAM WAY
OSPREY CL
TARTIN CL
BUNBURY CL
ASHTON CL
STEELE RD
BYRON CL
SYCAMORE DR
NORTHWOOD AVE
KINGSWOOD CRES
Sutton Hall Farm
PH
1 CHESTERTON CL
2 WOODSTOCK DR
Cheshire Ring
Works
Canal Walk
Sutton Mill
INGLEWOOD AVE
WARMINGHAM LA
Newfield Farm
A533
Sutton Lane
Saunders Field
Pettywood Farm
Field's Farm
River Wheelock
LEA DR
Tetton Hall Cottages
Occlestonegreen Farm
Tetton Hall
TETTON LA
Manor Farm
West Farm
NANTWICH RD
Occlestone Green
Hopley House
Home Farm
New Farm
Withinstreet Farm
Bellsmithy
Forge Cottages
Forge Mill Farm
Sparrowgrove
ROMAN ROAD (course of)
Denmar
Oldhough Manor
Oldhough Cottage
The Bungalow
DRAGON'S LA
Fields Farm
4
65
3
64
2
63
1
62
69
70
71
D
E
F

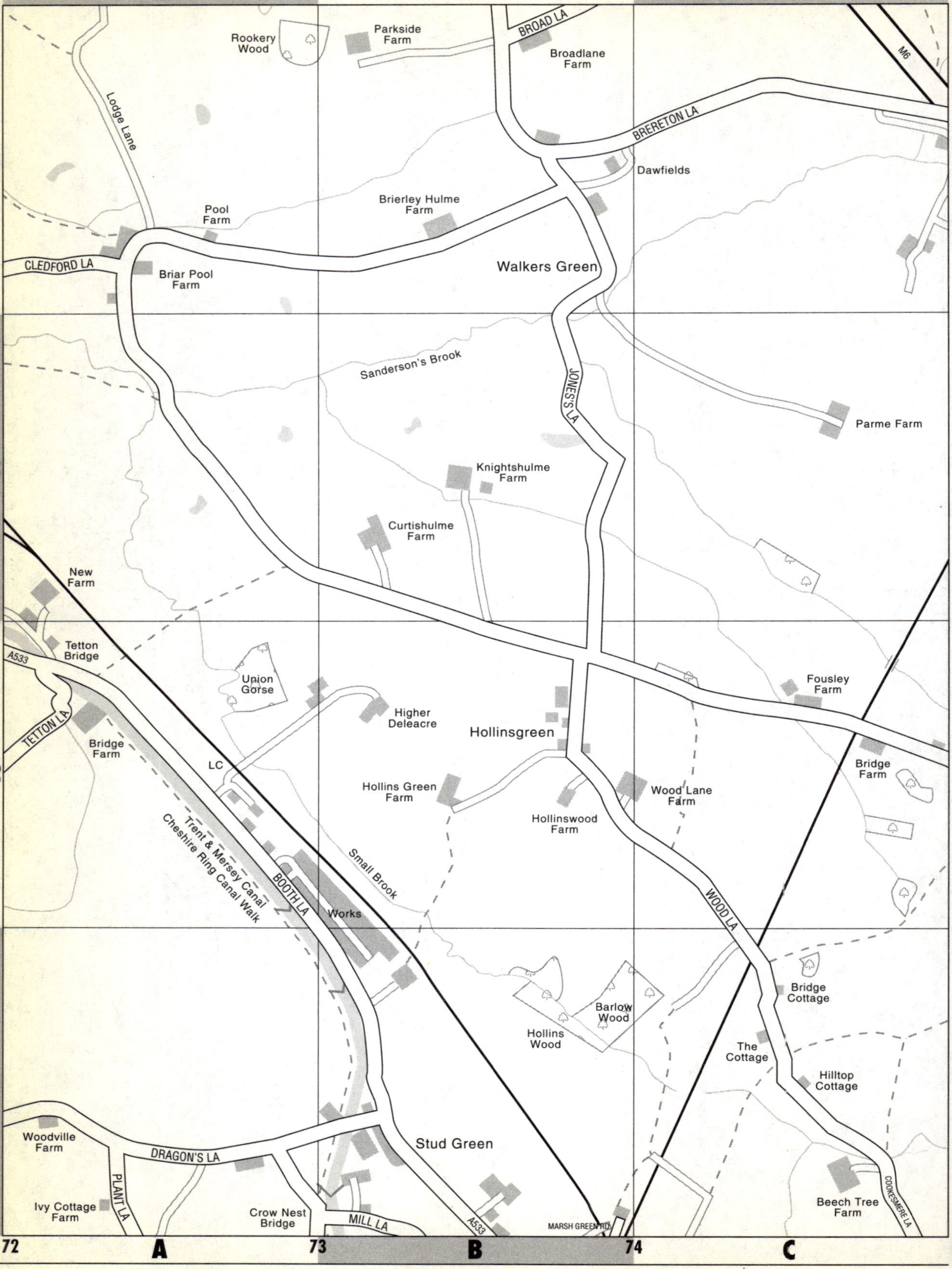
A
B
C
Rookery Wood
Parkside Farm
BROAD LA
Broadlane Farm
M6
Lodge Lane
BRERETON LA
4
Dawfields
Brierley Hulme Farm
Pool Farm
CLEDFORD LA
Briar Pool Farm
Walkers Green
65
Sanderson's Brook
JONES'S LA
Parme Farm
3
Knightshulme Farm
Curtishulme Farm
New Farm
64
Tetton Bridge
A533
Union Gorse
Higher Deleacre
Fousley Farm
TETTON LA
Hollinsgreen
Bridge Farm
2
LC
Hollins Green Farm
Wood Lane Farm
Bridge Farm
Hollinswood Farm
Trent & Mersey Canal
Cheshire Ring Canal Walk
Small Brook
BOOTH LA
WOOD LA
Works
63
Bridge Cottage
Barlow Wood
Hollins Wood
The Cottage
1
Hilltop Cottage
Woodville Farm
Stud Green
DRAGON'S LA
PLANT LA
Ivy Cottage Farm
Crow Nest Bridge
MILL LA
A533
MARSH GREEN RD
Beech Tree Farm
COOKESMERE LA
62
72
73
74

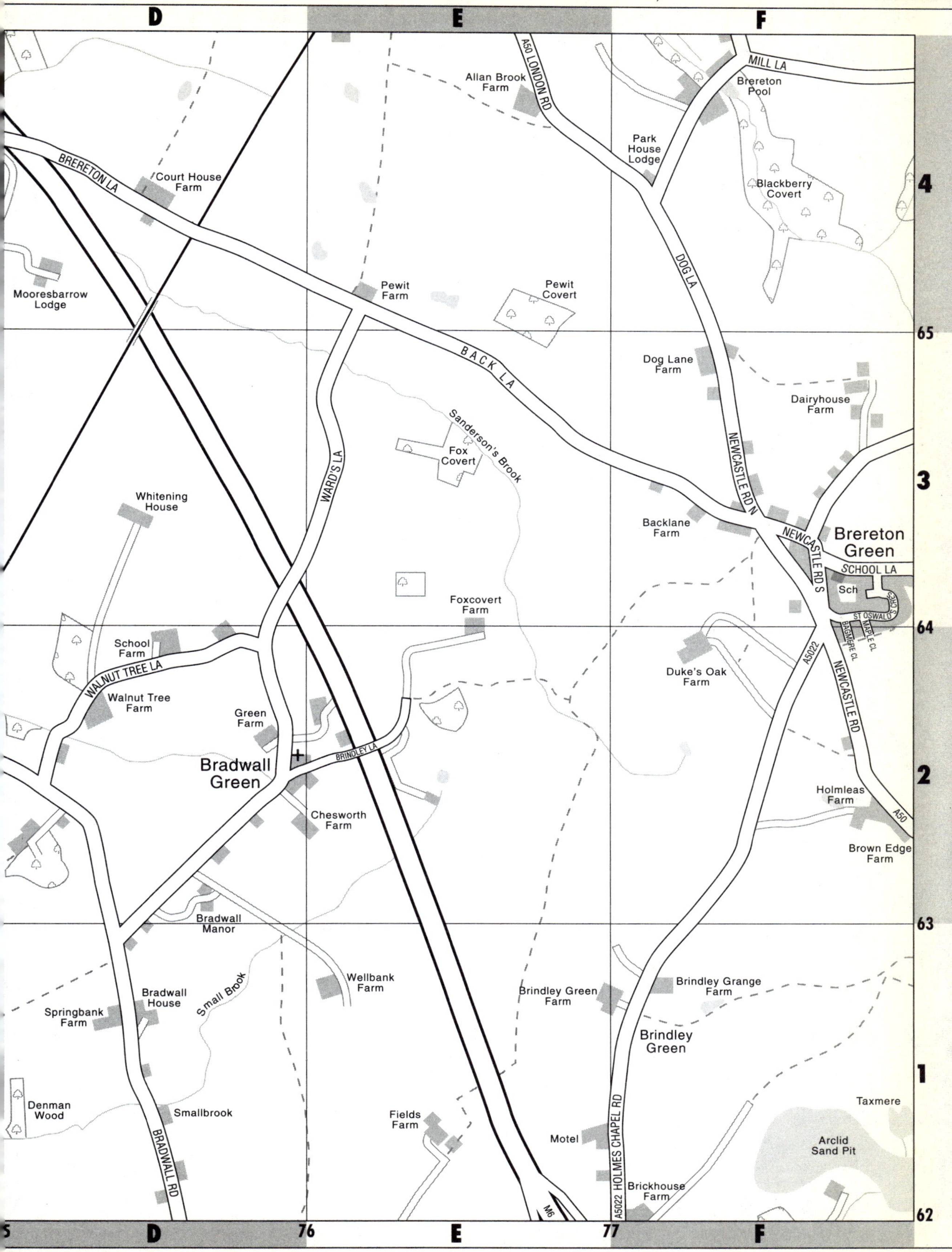
D
E
F
A50 LONDON RD
Allan Brook Farm
MILL LA
Brereton Pool
Park House Lodge
Blackberry Covert
BRERETON LA
Court House Farm
Mooresbarrow Lodge
Pewit Farm
Pewit Covert
DOG LA
4
65
BACK LA
Dog Lane Farm
Dairyhouse Farm
Sanderson's Brook
Fox Covert
NEWCASTLE RD N
3
WARD'S LA
Whitening House
Backlane Farm
NEWCASTLE RD S
Brereton Green
SCHOOL LA
Sch
Foxcovert Farm
64
School Farm
WALNUT TREE LA
Duke's Oak Farm
A5022
NEWCASTLE RD
Walnut Tree Farm
Green Farm
BRINDLEY LA
Bradwall Green
2
Holmleas Farm
Chesworth Farm
A50
Brown Edge Farm
Bradwall Manor
63
Wellbank Farm
Brindley Grange Farm
Bradwall House
Small Brook
Brindley Green Farm
Springbank Farm
Brindley Green
1
Taxmere
Denman Wood
Smallbrook
Fields Farm
Arclid Sand Pit
Motel
A5022 HOLMES CHAPEL RD
BRADWALL RD
Brickhouse Farm
M6
62
76
77

153
131

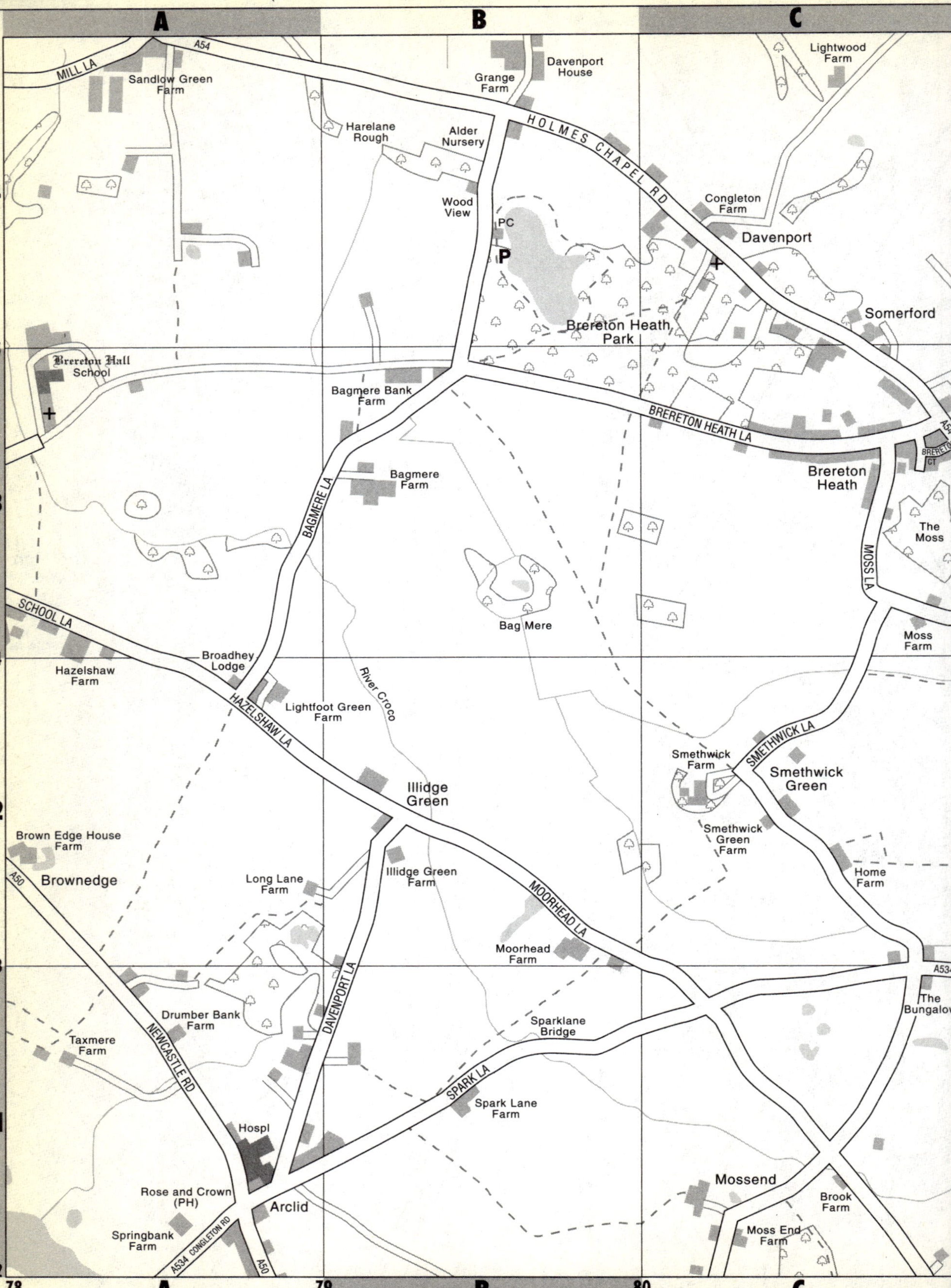

153
176

132
156

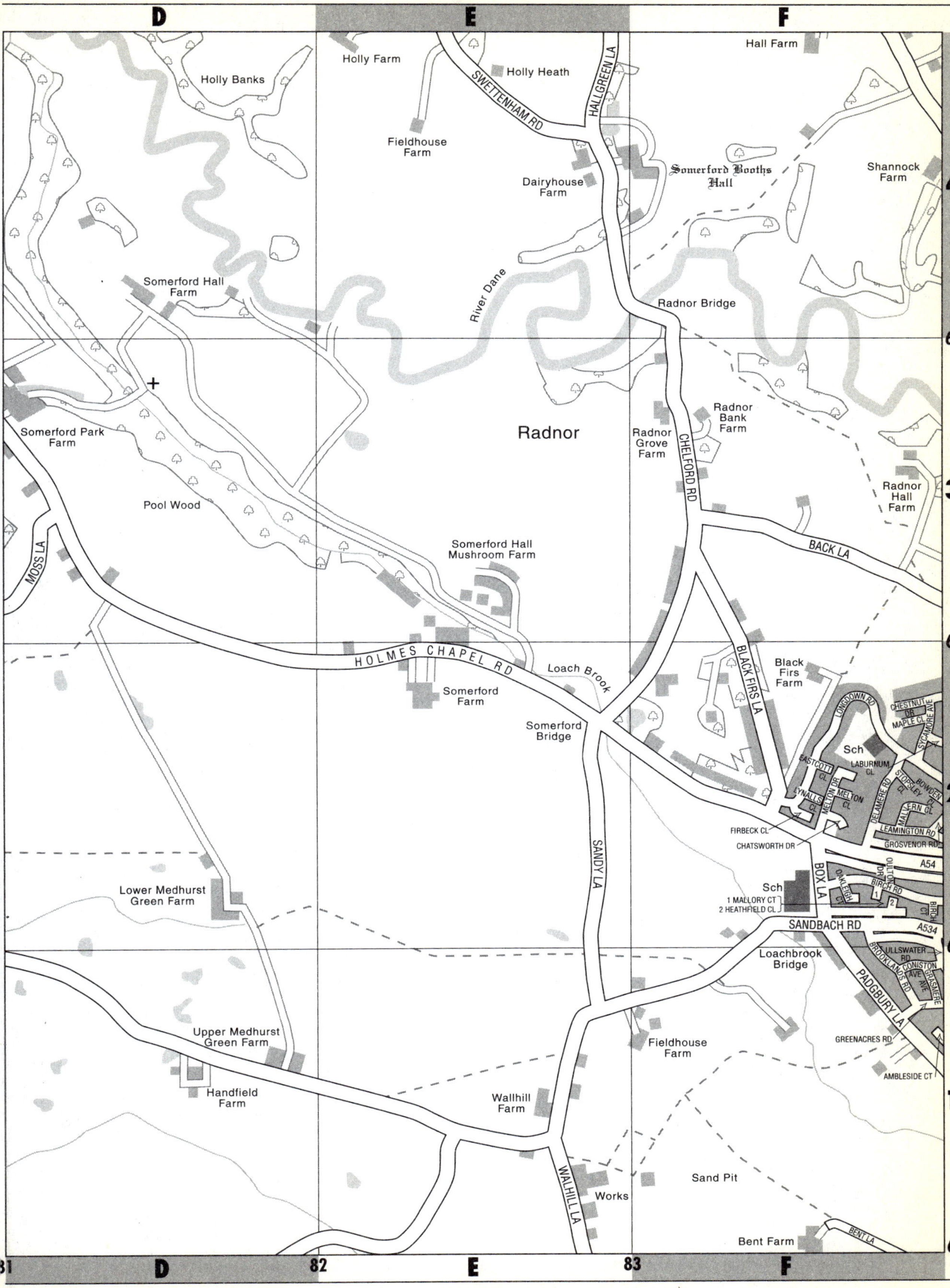

177
156

155
133

155
178

134
158

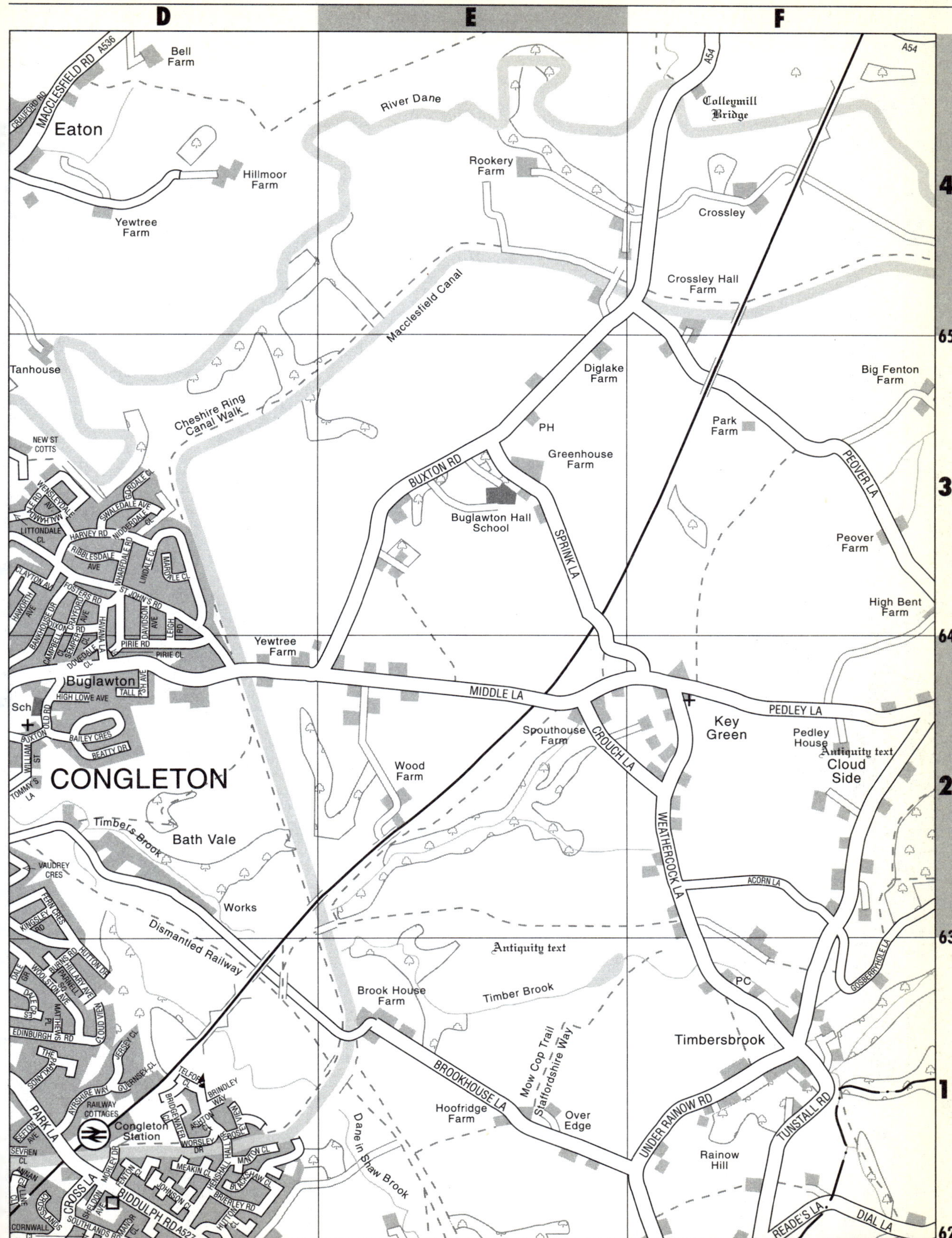
D
E
F
A536
Bell Farm
MACCLESFIELD RD
CRAUFORD RD
Eaton
River Dane
A54
Colleymill Bridge
A54
Hillmoor Farm
Yewtree Farm
Rookery Farm
Crossley
Crossley Hall Farm
Macclesfield Canal
4
65
Tanhouse
Cheshire Ring Canal Walk
Diglake Farm
Big Fenton Farm
NEW ST COTTS
PH
Park Farm
Greenhouse Farm
BUXTON RD
PEOVER LA
3
Buglawton Hall School
SPRINK LA
Peover Farm
High Bent Farm
Yewtree Farm
64
Buglawton
MIDDLE LA
PEDLEY LA
Sch
Key Green
Spouthouse Farm
CROUCH LA
Pedley House
Antiquity text
Cloud Side
CONGLETON
Wood Farm
2
Timbers Brook
Bath Vale
WEATHERCOCK LA
ACORN LA
Works
Dismantled Railway
63
Antiquity text
GOSBERRYHOLE LA
Brook House Farm
Timber Brook
PC
Mow Cop Trail
Staffordshire Way
Timbersbrook
BROOKHOUSE LA
1
Congleton Station
Hoofridge Farm
Over Edge
UNDER RAINOW RD
TUNSTALL RD
Rainow Hill
Dane in Shaw Brook
PARK LA
CROSS LA
BIDDULPH RD A527
READE'S LA
DIAL LA
62
87
88
89
D
E
F

157
135

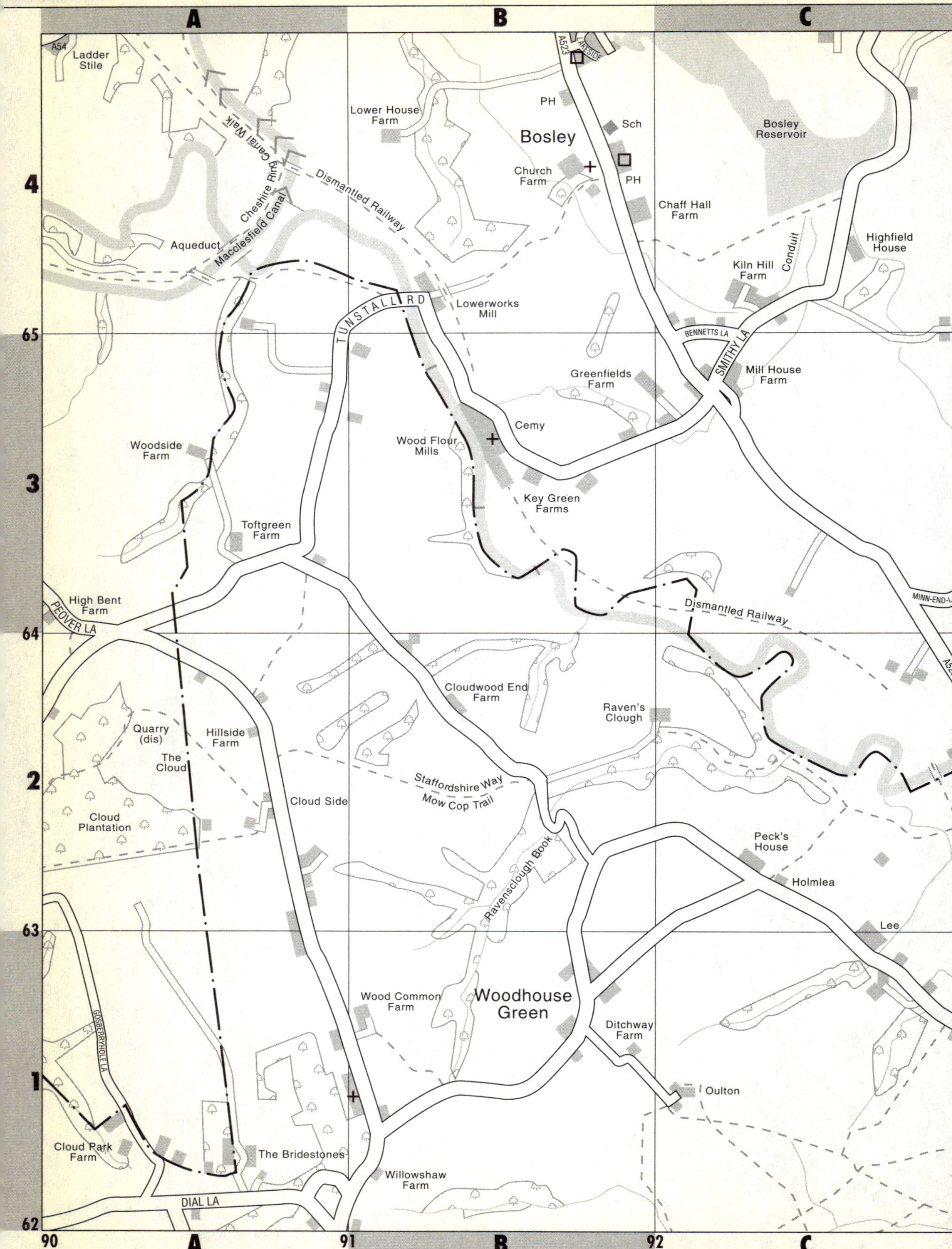
A
B
C
A54
Ladder Stile
Lower House Farm
PH
A523
LAKESIDE
Sch
Bosley
Bosley Reservoir
Church Farm
PH
Chaff Hall Farm
Canal Walk
Cheshire Ring
Macclesfield Canal
Dismantled Railway
Aqueduct
Highfield House
Kiln Hill Farm
Conduit
TUNSTALL RD
Lowerworks Mill
BENNETTS LA
SMITHY LA
Mill House Farm
Greenfields Farm
Cemy
Wood Flour Mills
Woodside Farm
Key Green Farms
Toftgreen Farm
High Bent Farm
PEOVER LA
MINN-END-LA
Dismantled Railway
A523
Cloudwood End Farm
Raven's Clough
Quarry (dis)
Hillside Farm
The Cloud
Staffordshire Way
Mow Cop Trail
Cloud Side
Cloud Plantation
Peck's House
Holmlea
Ravensclough Book
Lee
Wood Common Farm
Woodhouse Green
Ditchway Farm
GOSBERRYHOLE LA
Oulton
Cloud Park Farm
The Bridestones
Willowshaw Farm
DIAL LA
4
65
3
64
2
63
1
62
90
91
92

157

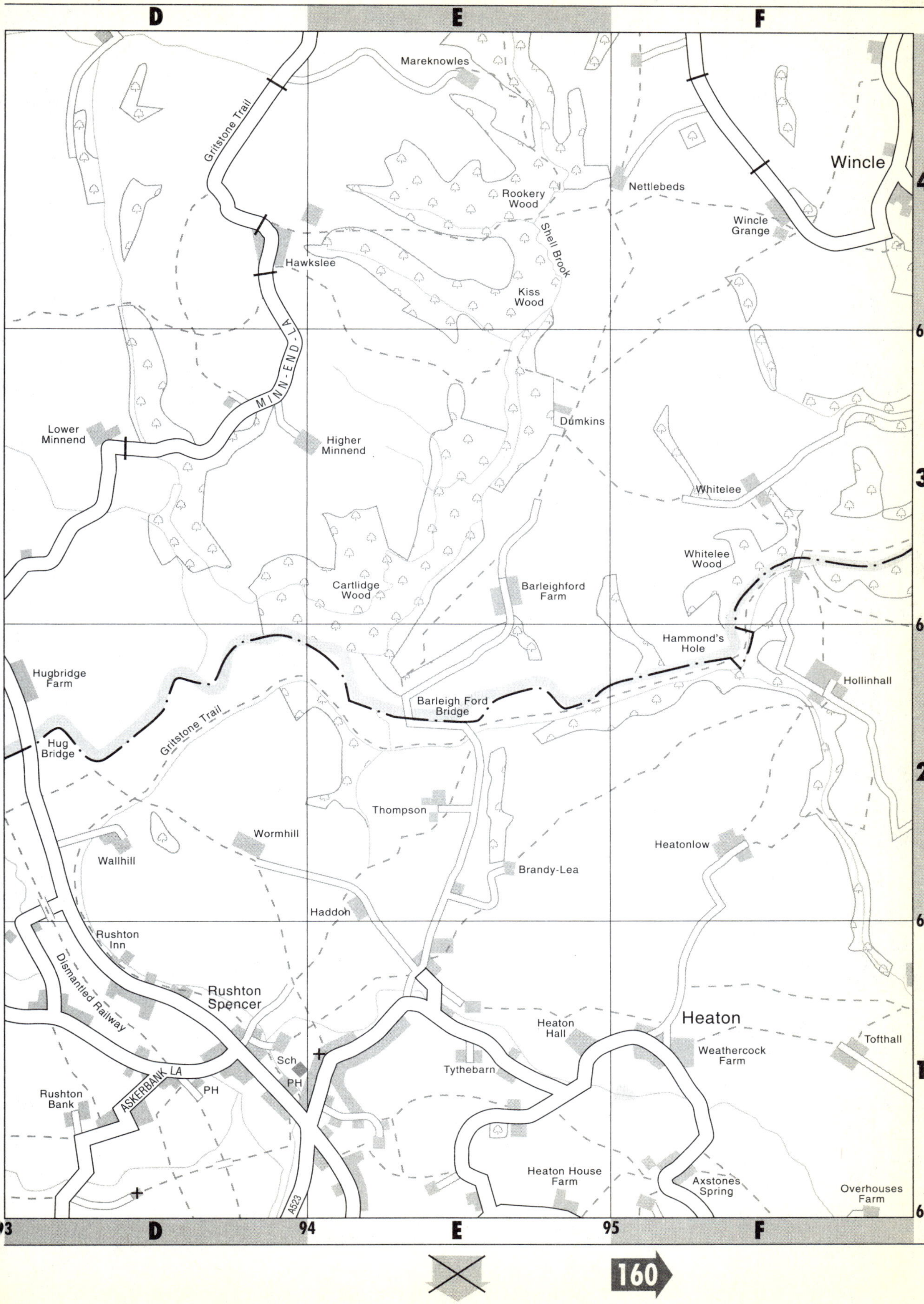
D
E
F
Mareknowles
Gritstone Trail
Rookery Wood
Nettlebeds
Wincle
Wincle Grange
Shell Brook
Hawkslee
Kiss Wood
MINN-END-LA
Lower Minnend
Higher Minnend
Dumkins
Whitelee
Whitelee Wood
Cartlidge Wood
Barleighford Farm
Hammond's Hole
Hugbridge Farm
Hollinhall
Barleigh Ford Bridge
Gritstone Trail
Hug Bridge
Thompson
Wormhill
Wallhill
Heatonlow
Brandy-Lea
Haddon
Rushton Inn
Dismantled Railway
Rushton Spencer
Heaton
Heaton Hall
Tofthall
Weathercock Farm
Sch
PH
Tythebarn
ASKERBANK LA
PH
Rushton Bank
A523
Heaton House Farm
Axstones Spring
Overhouses Farm
4
65
3
64
2
63
1
62
93
94
95
D
E
F

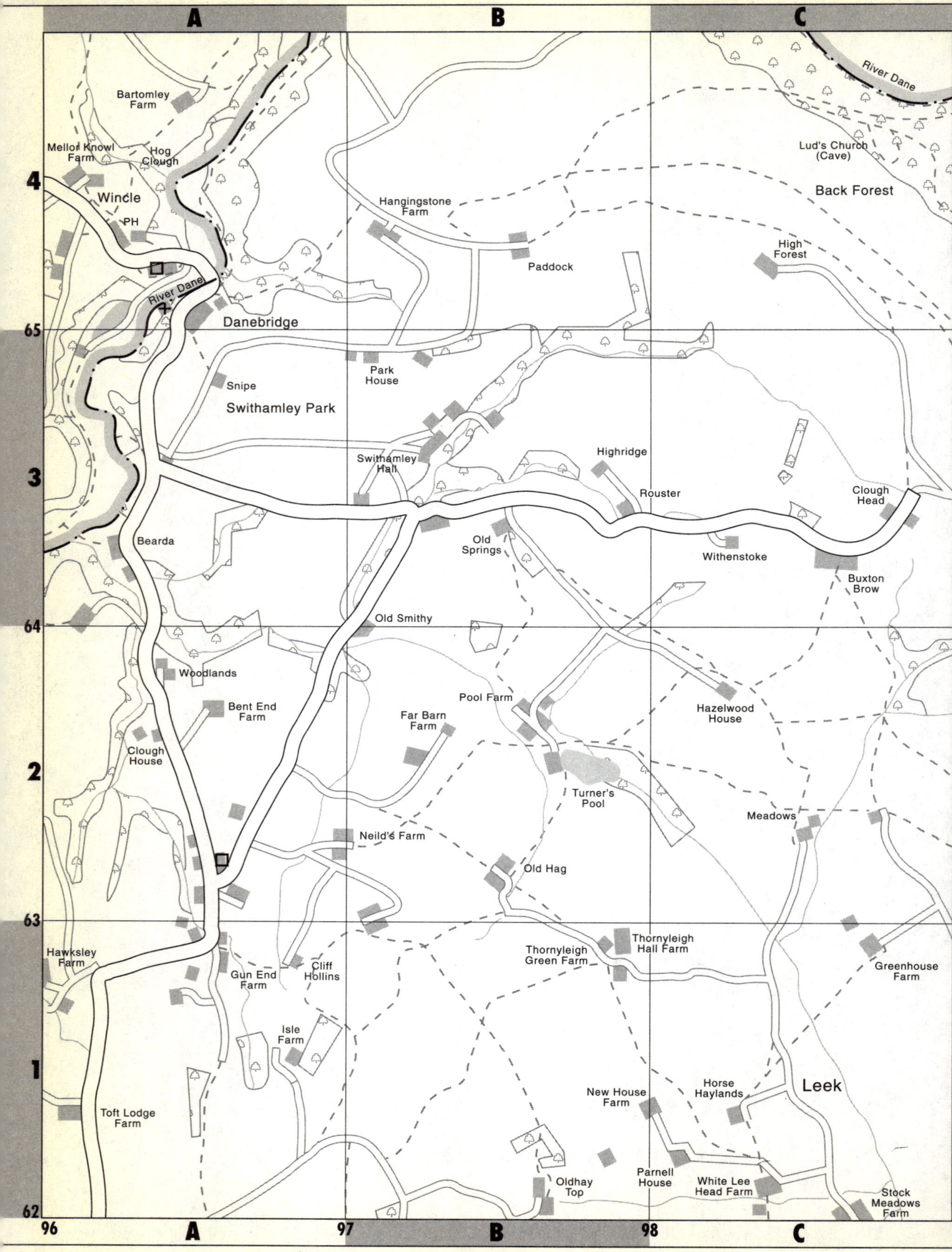
A
B
C
Bartomley Farm
Mellor Knowl Farm
Hog Clough
Wincle
PH
River Dane
Danebridge
Hangingstone Farm
Paddock
Lud's Church (Cave)
Back Forest
High Forest
Park House
Snipe
Swithamley Park
Swithamley Hall
Highridge
Rouster
Clough Head
Bearda
Old Springs
Withenstoke
Buxton Brow
Old Smithy
Woodlands
Bent End Farm
Pool Farm
Far Barn Farm
Hazelwood House
Clough House
Turner's Pool
Meadows
Neild's Farm
Old Hag
Hawksley Farm
Thornyleigh Green Farm
Thornyleigh Hall Farm
Greenhouse Farm
Gun End Farm
Cliff Hollins
Isle Farm
Toft Lodge Farm
New House Farm
Horse Haylands
Leek
Oldhay Top
Parnell House
White Lee Head Farm
Stock Meadows Farm
4
65
3
64
2
63
1
62
96
97
98

139
162

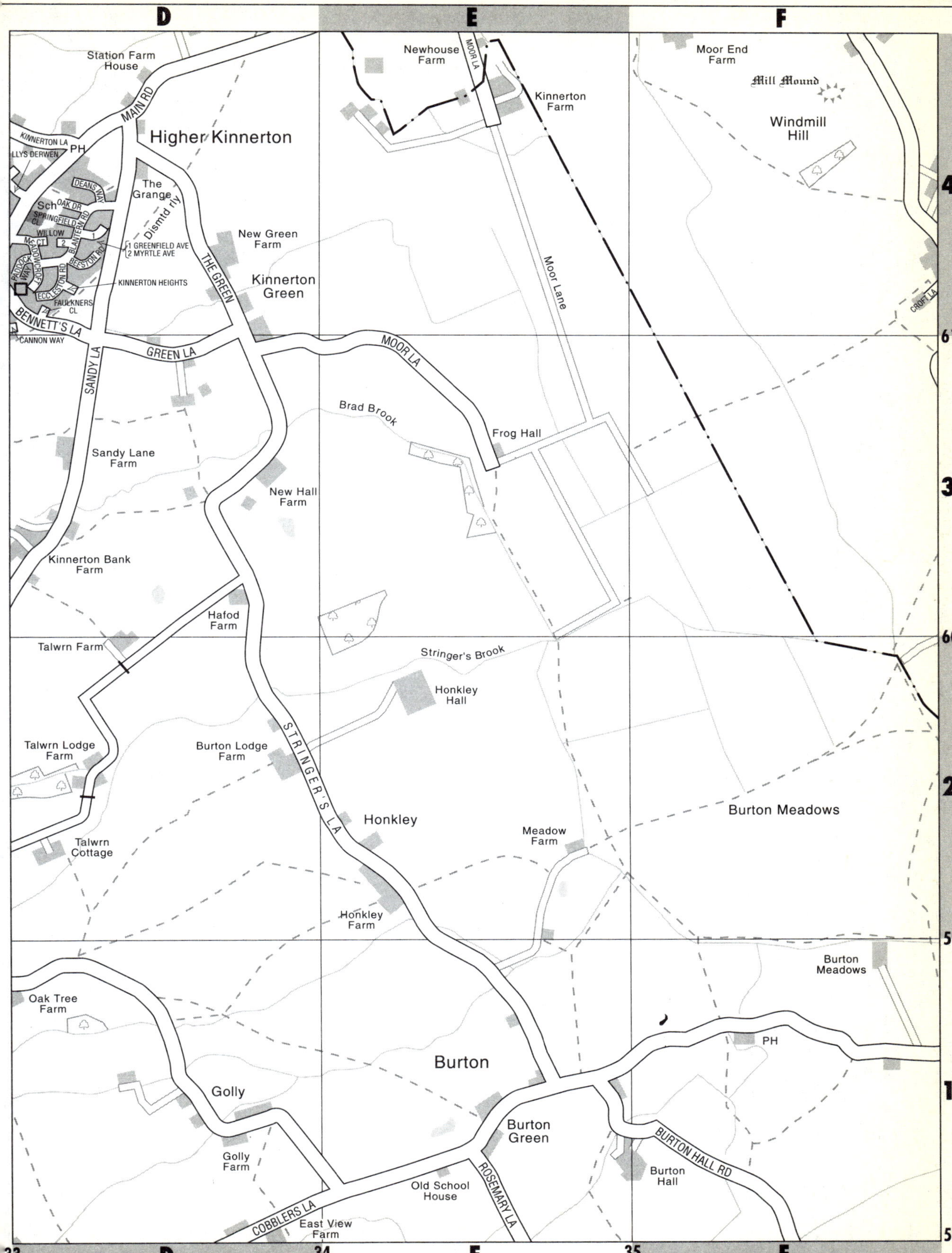
D
E
F
Station Farm House
MAIN RD
Higher Kinnerton
KINNERTON LA
PH
LLYS DERWEN
DEANS WAY
The Grange
Sch
OAK DR
SPRINGFIELD CL
WILLOW
BLANTERN RD
Dismtd rly
BEESTON RD
1 GREENFIELD AVE
2 MYRTLE AVE
PADDOCK WAY
MEADOWCROFT
ECCLESTON RD
KINNERTON HEIGHTS
FAULKNERS CL
BENNETT'S LA
CANNON WAY
THE GREEN
New Green Farm
Kinnerton Green
Newhouse Farm
MOOR LA
Kinnerton Farm
Moor Lane
Moor End Farm
Mill Mound
Windmill Hill
CROFT LA
GREEN LA
SANDY LA
MOOR LA
Brad Brook
Frog Hall
Sandy Lane Farm
New Hall Farm
Kinnerton Bank Farm
Hafod Farm
Talwrn Farm
Stringer's Brook
Honkley Hall
Talwrn Lodge Farm
Burton Lodge Farm
STRINGER'S LA
Honkley
Burton Meadows
Meadow Farm
Talwrn Cottage
Honkley Farm
Burton Meadows
Oak Tree Farm
PH
Burton
Golly
Burton Green
BURTON HALL RD
Golly Farm
Old School House
ROSEMARY LA
Burton Hall
COBBLERS LA
East View Farm
4
61
3
60
2
59
1
58
33
34
35

162

A
B
C
4
61
3
60
2
59
1
58
36
37
38
Black Wood
Belgrave Bridge
RAKE LA
A483
B5445
Balderton Drive
Greenwalls
Dodleston Hall
Dodleston
CROFT LA
Sch
ST MARY'S RD
MALLORY WLK
PENFOLD WAY
BOYDELL WAY
EGERTON WLK
CHURCH CROFT
CASTLE WAY
BELGRAVE CL
Balderton Drive
Belgrave Farm
Belgrave Avenue
Belgrave Cottages
Belgrave Lodge
Belgrave
Moat Farm
PULFORD LA
Works
Oldfields Farm
Cuckoo's Nest
WREXHAM RD
STRAIGHT MILE
Dodleston Lane Farm
The Elms
The Elms
Meadow House Farm
Moorfield Cottages
Lyndale Farm
The Manor
Pulford Crossing
DODLESTON LA
Pulford
FAIRMEADOW
CASTLE CL
PULFORD CT
OLD LA
Pulford Approach
Hotel
Pulford Brook
Broadoak
Pulford Bridge
Broadoak Farm
LC
Brookside Farm
Cam-yr-Alyn Farm
Collynie
CHESTER RD
Sewage Works
Lavister
Llyndir Hall Hotel
LLYNDIR LA
DARLAND LA
A483
B5445

141
164

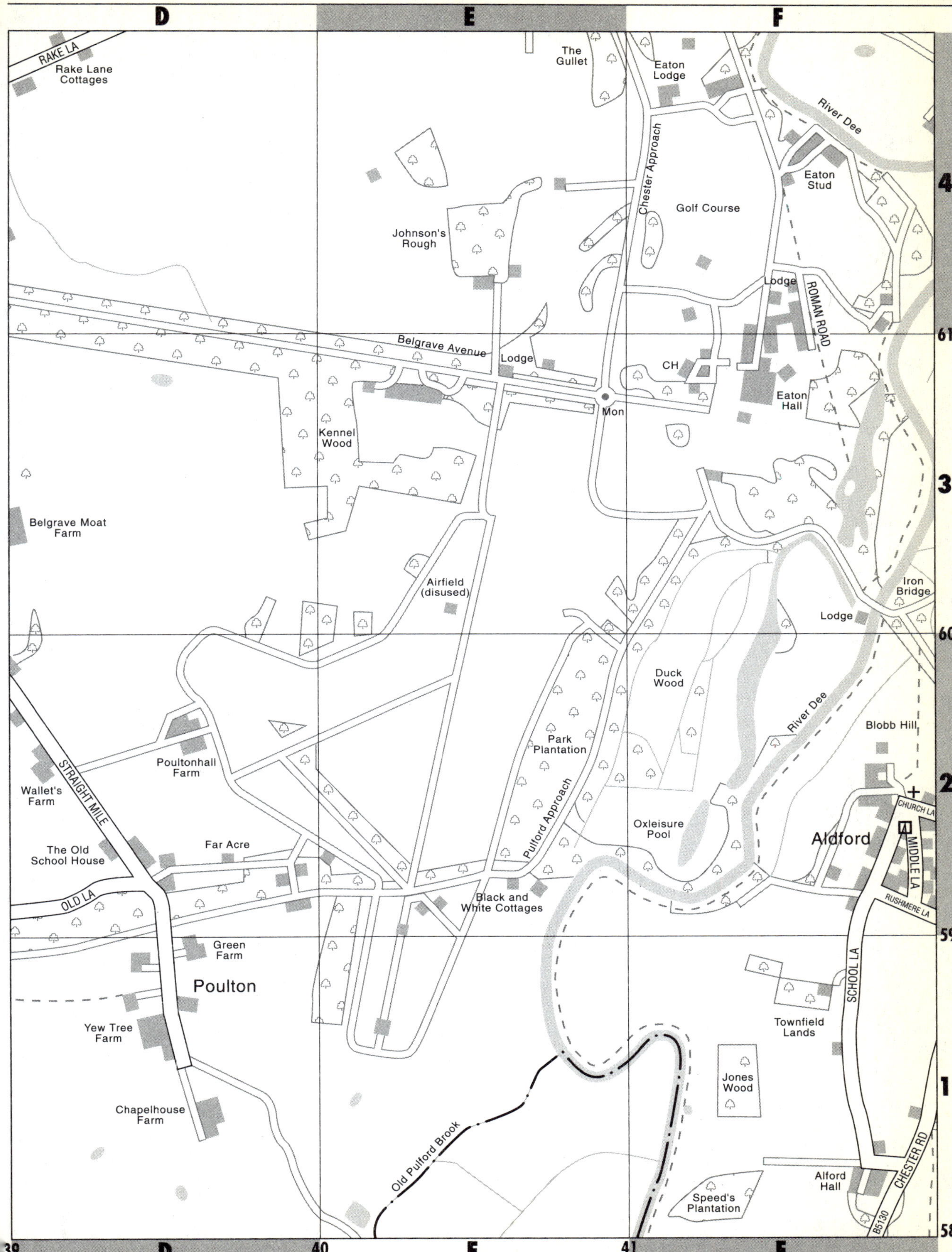

180
164

163
142

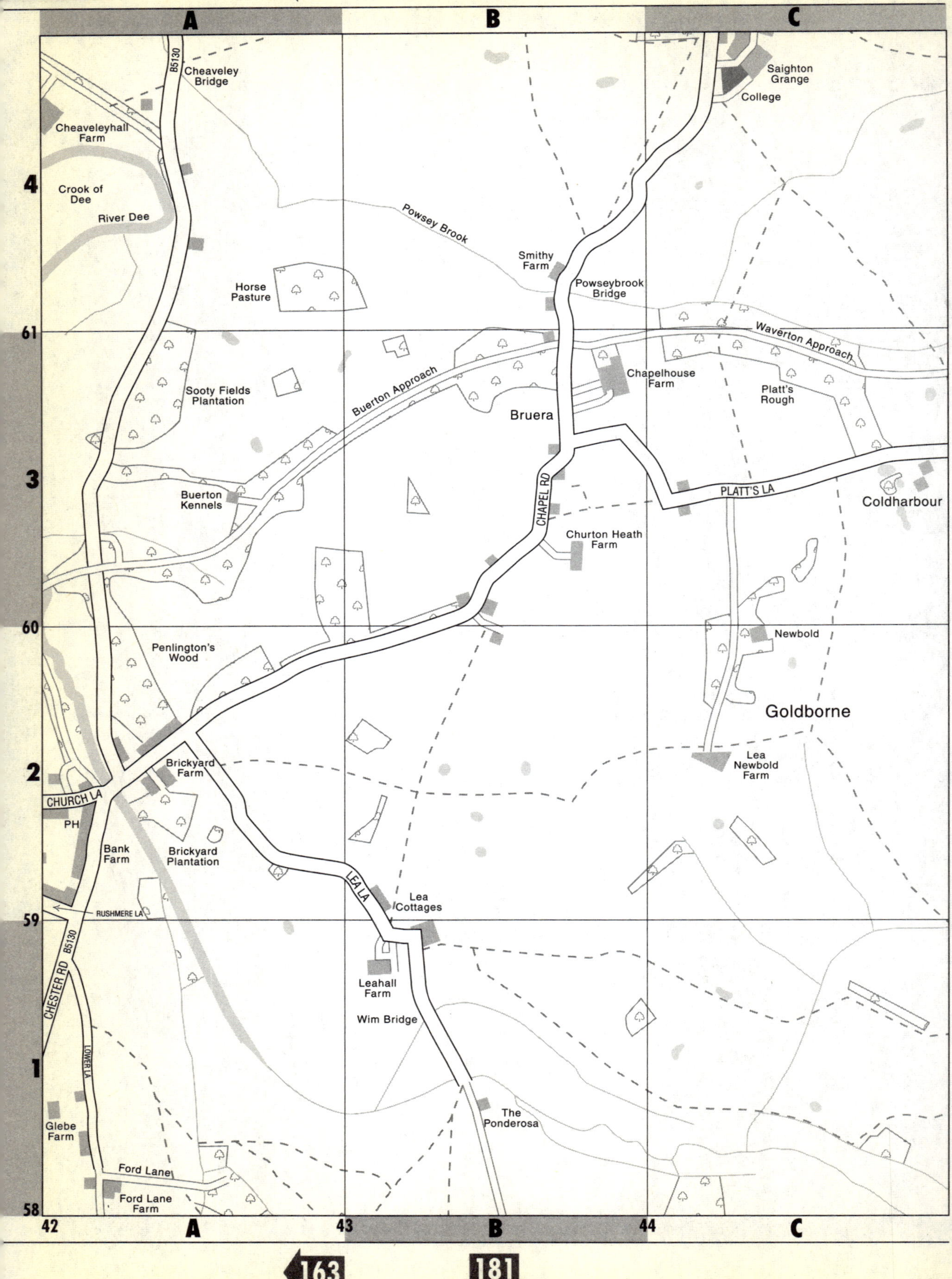

163
181

D
E
F
Lodge Farm
Elm Tree Farm
A41
Hatton Spinney
Shropshire Union Canal
LONG LA
Saighton Gorse
Hatton Heath
4
Hatton House
Hatton Heath Bridge
Lodge
Lake Farm
Hatton Hall
61
Waverton Approach
Dismantled Railway
Hatton Heath Farm
PLATT'S LA
Golborne Manor
Grange Farm
3
NEWTON LA
GATESHEATH LA
CHESTER RD
New Russia Hall
Gatesheath
WHITCHURCH RD
60
Golborne Old Hall
Lordship Cottages
2
Gatesheath Hall Cottages
Golborne Hall
Golborne Brook
Sewage Works
Golborne Bridge
59
Milton Green Farm
Milton Green Farm
Russia Hall
WESTERN AVE
CHAPEL LA
Milton Green
FROG LA
Calveley Hall
Granary
Stonyford Brook
Clayley Hall
Dismantled Railway
1
A41
58
45
46
47

165
144

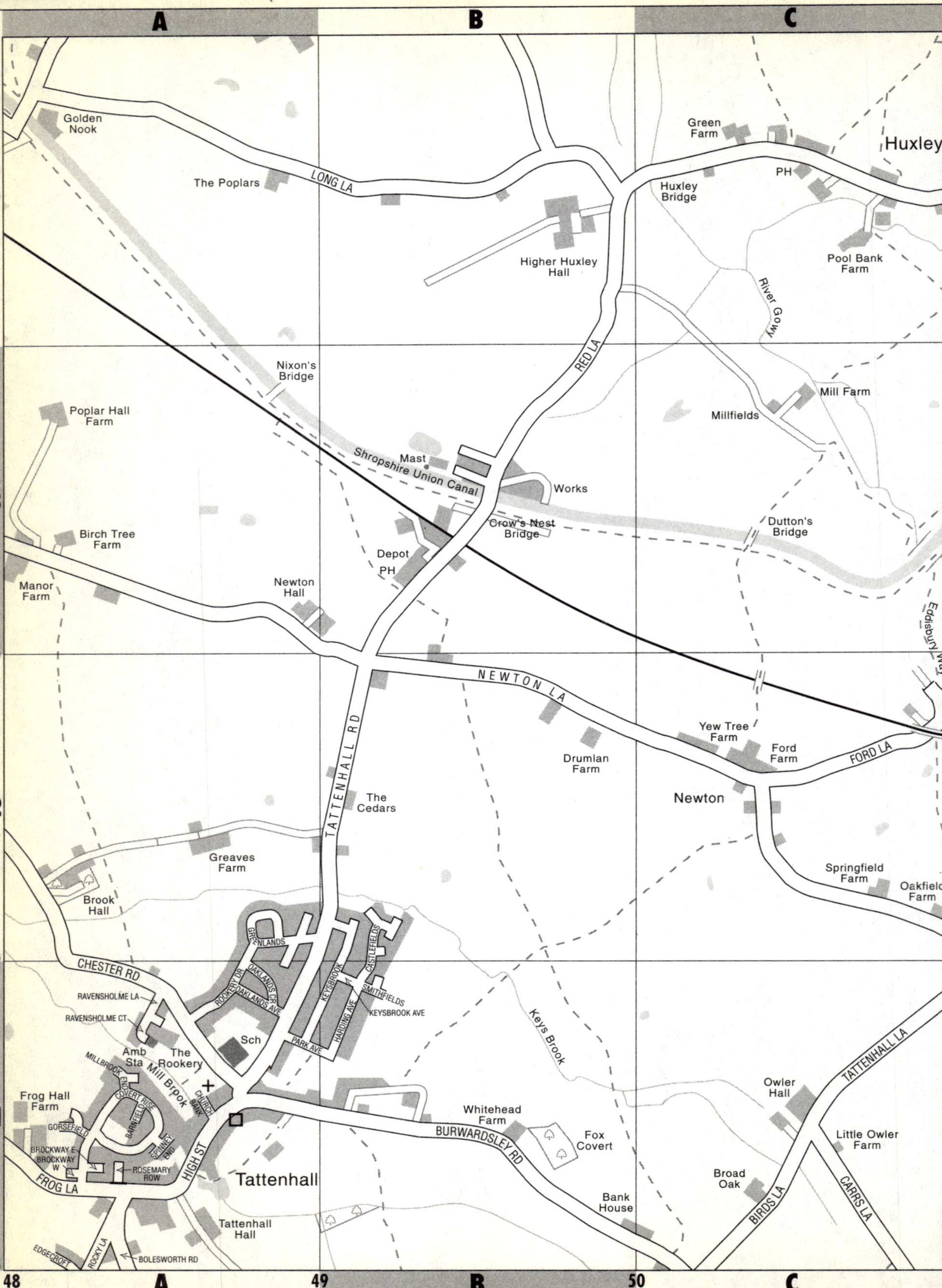
A
B
C
Golden Nook
The Poplars
LONG LA
Green Farm
PH
Huxley
Huxley Bridge
Higher Huxley Hall
Pool Bank Farm
River Gowy
RED LA
Nixon's Bridge
Mill Farm
Millfields
Poplar Hall Farm
Mast
Shropshire Union Canal
Works
Crow's Nest Bridge
Dutton's Bridge
Birch Tree Farm
Depot
PH
Manor Farm
Newton Hall
Eddisbury Way
NEWTON LA
Yew Tree Farm
Ford Farm
FORD LA
Drumlan Farm
TATTENHALL RD
The Cedars
Newton
Greaves Farm
Springfield Farm
Oakfield Farm
Brook Hall
GREENLANDS
CASTLEFIELDS
CHESTER RD
OAKLANDS CR
ROOKERY DR
OAKLANDS AVE
KEYSBROOK
SMITHFIELDS
KEYSBROOK AVE
HARDING AVE
RAVENSHOLME LA
RAVENSHOLME CT
Sch
PARK AVE
Keys Brook
TATTENHALL LA
Amb Sta
The Rookery
Mill Brook
MILLBROOK END
COVERT RISE
CHURCH BANK
Owler Hall
Frog Hall Farm
GORSEFIELD
BARNFIELD
Whitehead Farm
BURWARDSLEY RD
Fox Covert
Little Owler Farm
BROCKWAY E
BROCKWAY W
SPINNEY END
ROSEMARY ROW
HIGH ST
FROG LA
Tattenhall
Broad Oak
Bank House
BIRDS LA
CARRS LA
Tattenhall Hall
EDGECROFT
ROCKY LA
BOLESWORTH RD
4
61
3
60
2
59
1
58
48
49
50

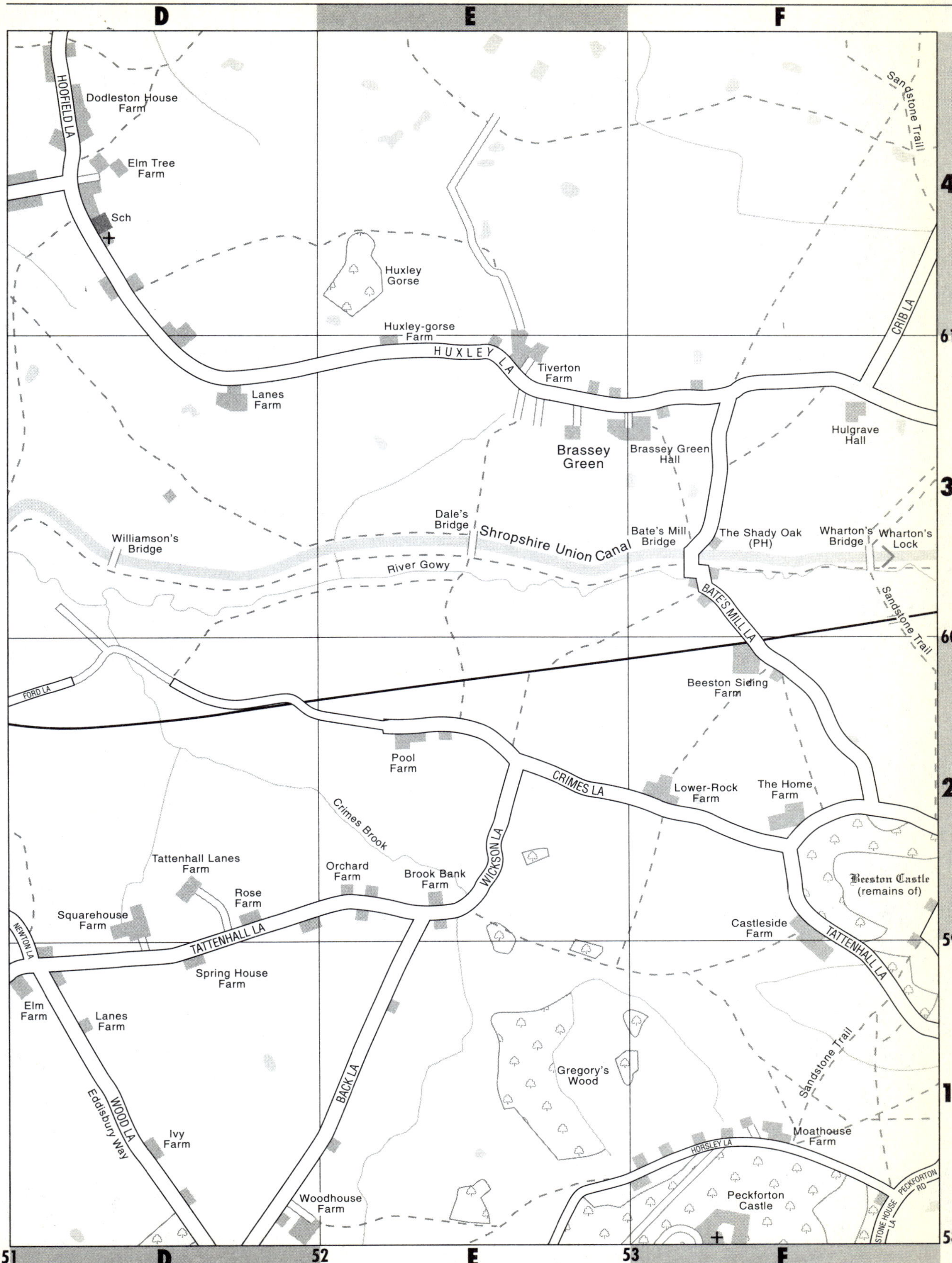
D
E
F
HOOFIELD LA
Dodleston House Farm
Elm Tree Farm
Sch
Huxley Gorse
Huxley-gorse Farm
HUXLEY LA
Tiverton Farm
Lanes Farm
Brassey Green
Brassey Green Hall
Hulgrave Hall
CRIB LA
Sandstone Trail
4
61
3
Dale's Bridge
Shropshire Union Canal
Bate's Mill Bridge
The Shady Oak (PH)
Wharton's Bridge
Wharton's Lock
Williamson's Bridge
River Gowy
BATE'S MILL LA
60
FORD LA
Beeston Siding Farm
Pool Farm
CRIMES LA
Lower-Rock Farm
The Home Farm
2
Crimes Brook
WICKSON LA
Beeston Castle (remains of)
Tattenhall Lanes Farm
Orchard Farm
Brook Bank Farm
Rose Farm
Squarehouse Farm
TATTENHALL LA
Castleside Farm
59
NEWTON LA
Spring House Farm
Elm Farm
Lanes Farm
Gregory's Wood
Sandstone Trail
1
Eddisbury Way
WOOD LA
BACK LA
Ivy Farm
Moathouse Farm
HORSLEY LA
Woodhouse Farm
Peckforton Castle
PECKFORTON RD
STONE HOUSE LA
58
51
52
53
D
E
F

167 146

167 185

147
170

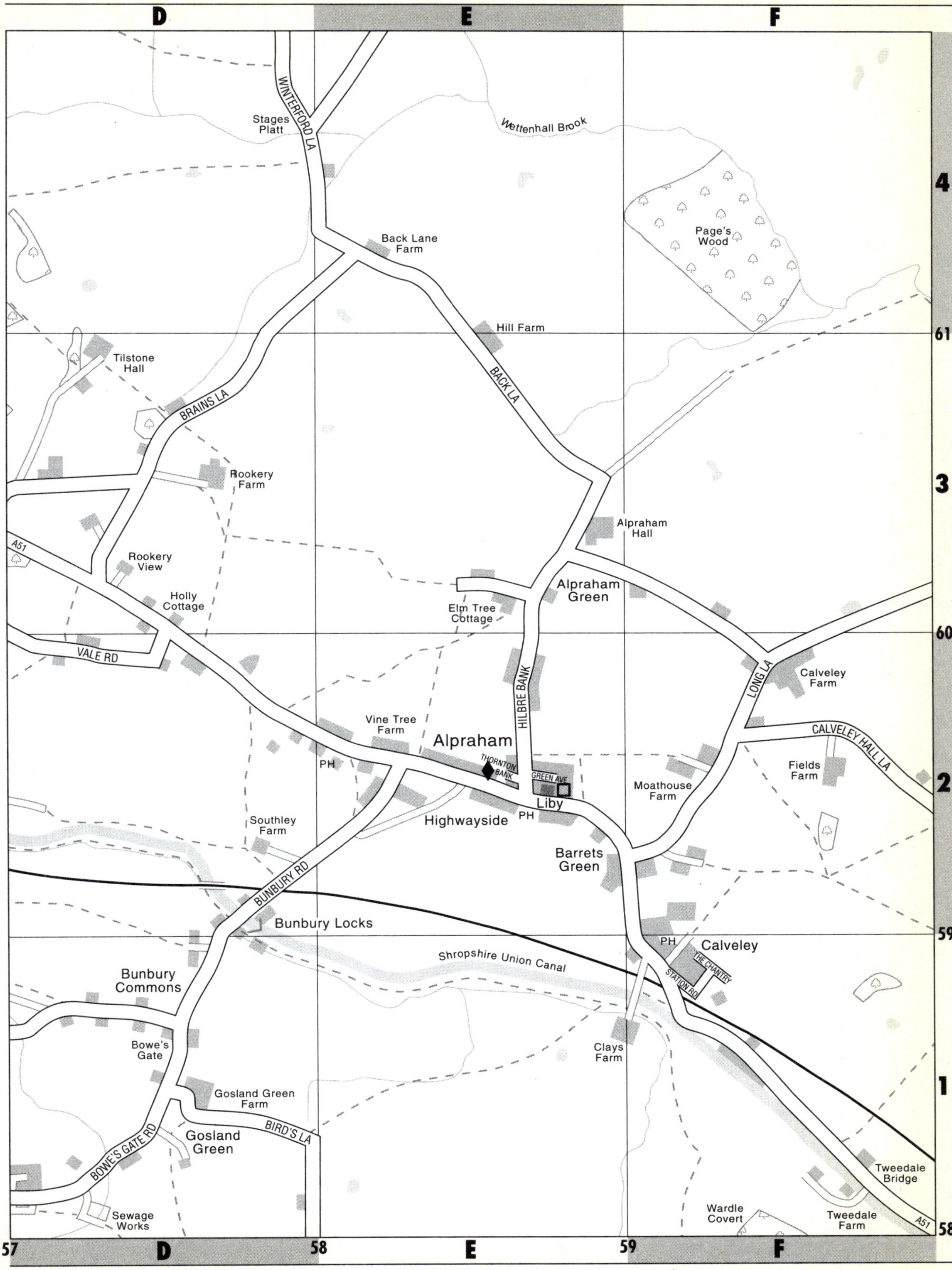

186
170

169
148

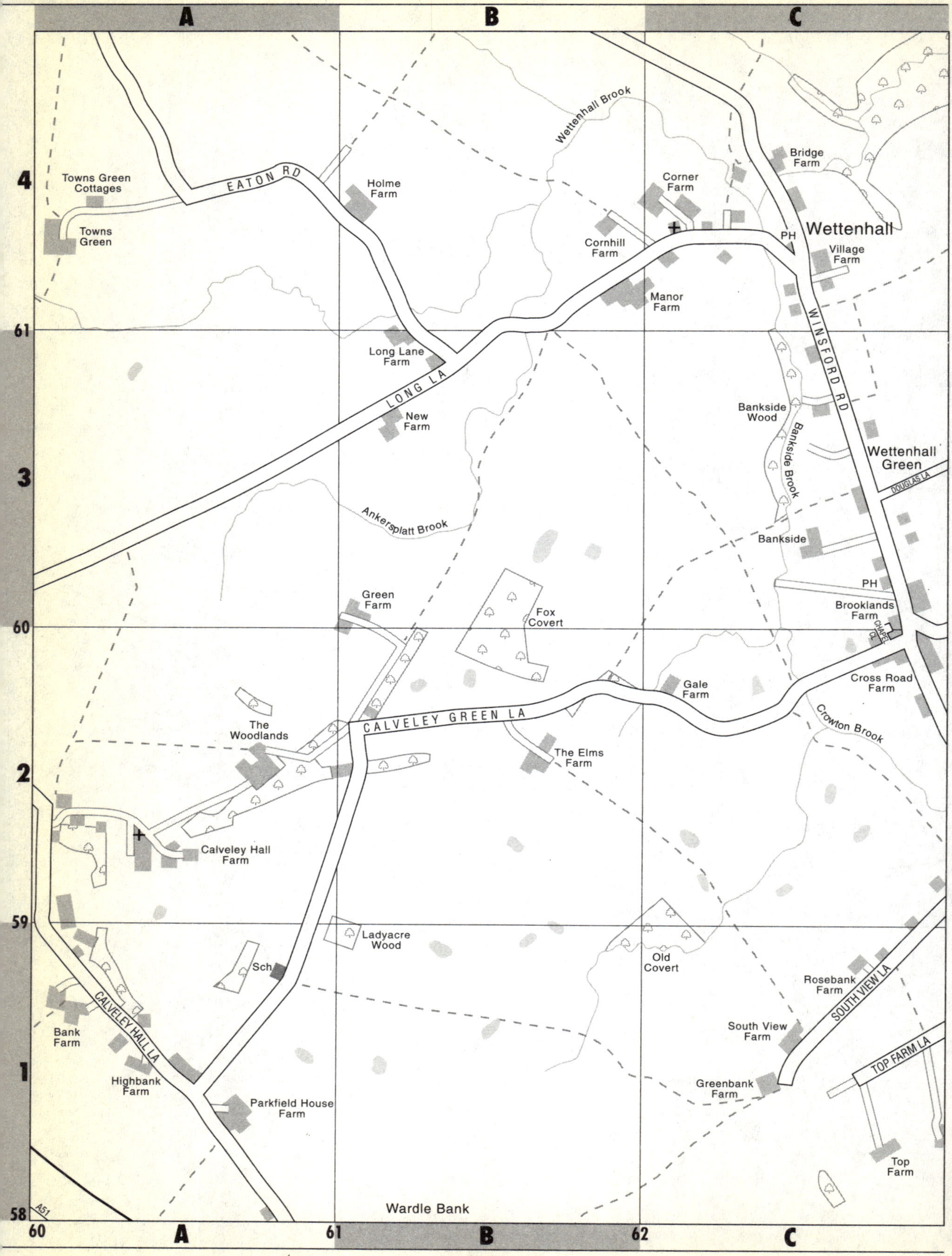

169
187

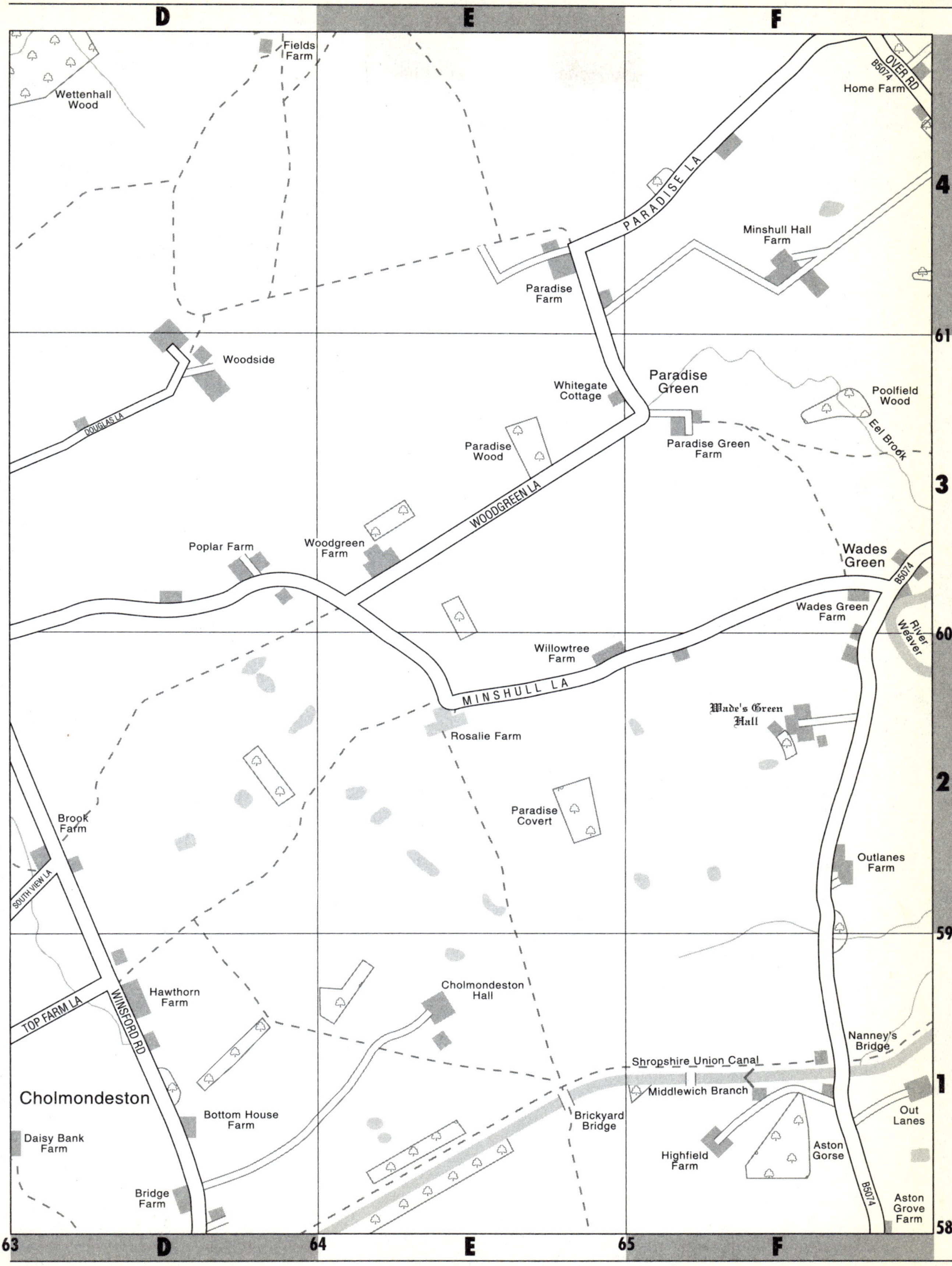
D
E
F
Fields Farm
Wettenhall Wood
PARADISE LA
OVER RD
B5074
Home Farm
4
Minshull Hall Farm
Paradise Farm
61
Woodside
DOUGLAS LA
Whitegate Cottage
Paradise Green
Poolfield Wood
Eel Brook
Paradise Green Farm
Paradise Wood
WOODGREEN LA
3
Poplar Farm
Woodgreen Farm
Wades Green
B5074
Wades Green Farm
River Weaver
60
Willowtree Farm
MINSHULL LA
Wade's Green Hall
Rosalie Farm
2
Paradise Covert
Brook Farm
SOUTH VIEW LA
Outlanes Farm
59
Hawthorn Farm
TOP FARM LA
WINSFORD RD
Cholmondeston Hall
Nanney's Bridge
Shropshire Union Canal
Middlewich Branch
1
Cholmondeston
Bottom House Farm
Brickyard Bridge
Out Lanes
Daisy Bank Farm
Highfield Farm
Aston Gorse
Bridge Farm
B5074
Aston Grove Farm
58
63
D
64
E
65
F

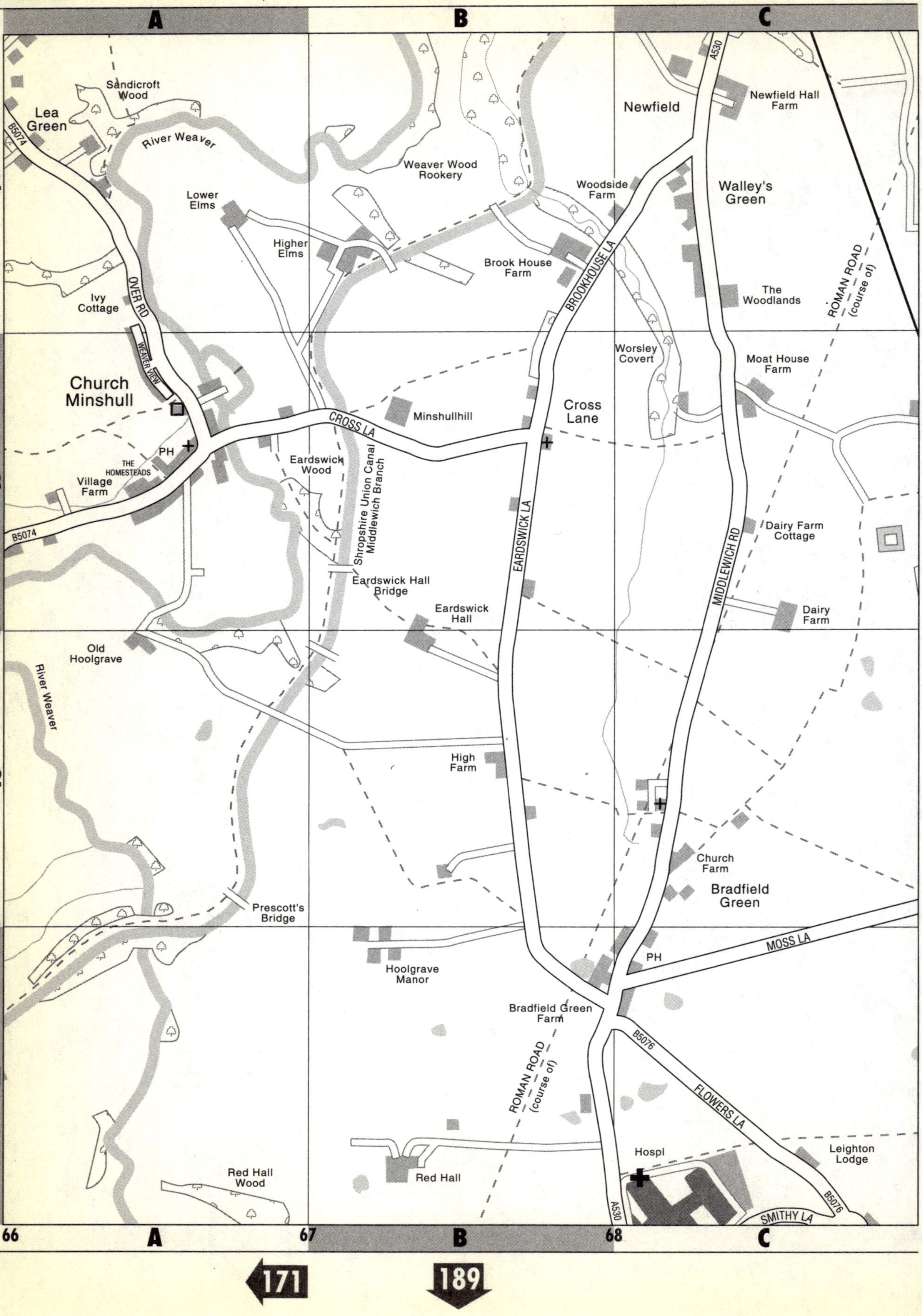
A
B
C
Sandicroft Wood
Lea Green
B5074
River Weaver
Weaver Wood Rookery
Lower Elms
Higher Elms
Newfield
Newfield Hall Farm
A530
Woodside Farm
Walley's Green
Brook House Farm
BROOKHOUSE LA
The Woodlands
ROMAN ROAD (course of)
Ivy Cottage
OVER RD
WEAVER VIEW
Church Minshull
Worsley Covert
Moat House Farm
Minshullhill
CROSS LA
Cross Lane
PH
THE HOMESTEADS
Village Farm
Eardswick Wood
Shropshire Union Canal Middlewich Branch
EARDSWICK LA
Dairy Farm Cottage
MIDDLEWICH RD
Eardswick Hall Bridge
Eardswick Hall
Dairy Farm
Old Hoolgrave
River Weaver
High Farm
Church Farm
Bradfield Green
Prescott's Bridge
MOSS LA
PH
Hoolgrave Manor
Bradfield Green Farm
B5076
ROMAN ROAD (course of)
FLOWERS LA
Hospl
Leighton Lodge
Red Hall Wood
Red Hall
A530
B5076
SMITHY LA
4
61
3
60
2
59
1
58
66
67
68

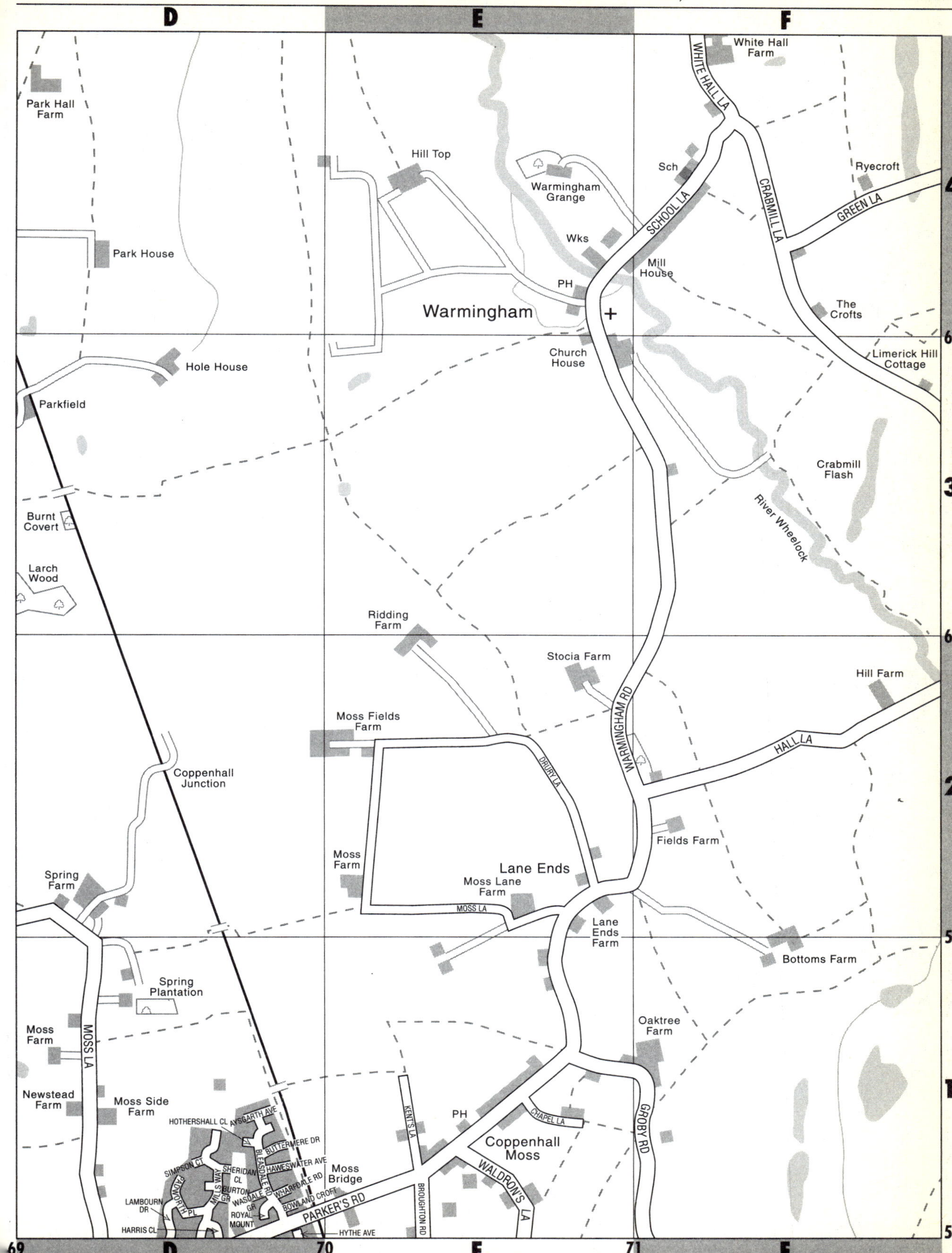
D
E
F
Park Hall Farm
White Hall Farm
WHITE HALL LA
Hill Top
Sch
Ryecroft
Warmingham Grange
SCHOOL LA
CRABMILL LA
GREEN LA
Park House
Wks
Mill House
PH
Warmingham
The Crofts
Hole House
Church House
Limerick Hill Cottage
Parkfield
Crabmill Flash
River Wheelock
Burnt Covert
Larch Wood
Ridding Farm
Stocia Farm
Hill Farm
Moss Fields Farm
WARMINGHAM RD
HALL LA
DRURY LA
Coppenhall Junction
Fields Farm
Moss Farm
Lane Ends
Moss Lane Farm
Spring Farm
MOSS LA
Lane Ends Farm
Bottoms Farm
Spring Plantation
Moss Farm
MOSS LA
Oaktree Farm
Newstead Farm
Moss Side Farm
PH
CHAPEL LA
Coppenhall Moss
GROBY RD
HOTHERSHALL CL
AYSGARTH AVE
BUTTERMERE DR
HAWESWATER AVE
WHARFDALE RD
BOWLAND CROFT
SIMPSON CT
SHERIDAN CL
BURTON GR
WASDALE GR
BLEASDALE RD
ROYAL MOUNT
LAMBOURN DR
HARRIS CL
HYTHE AVE
Moss Bridge
PARKER'S RD
KENT'S LA
BROUGHTON RD
WALDRON'S LA
4
61
3
60
2
59
1
58
69
70
71

173
152

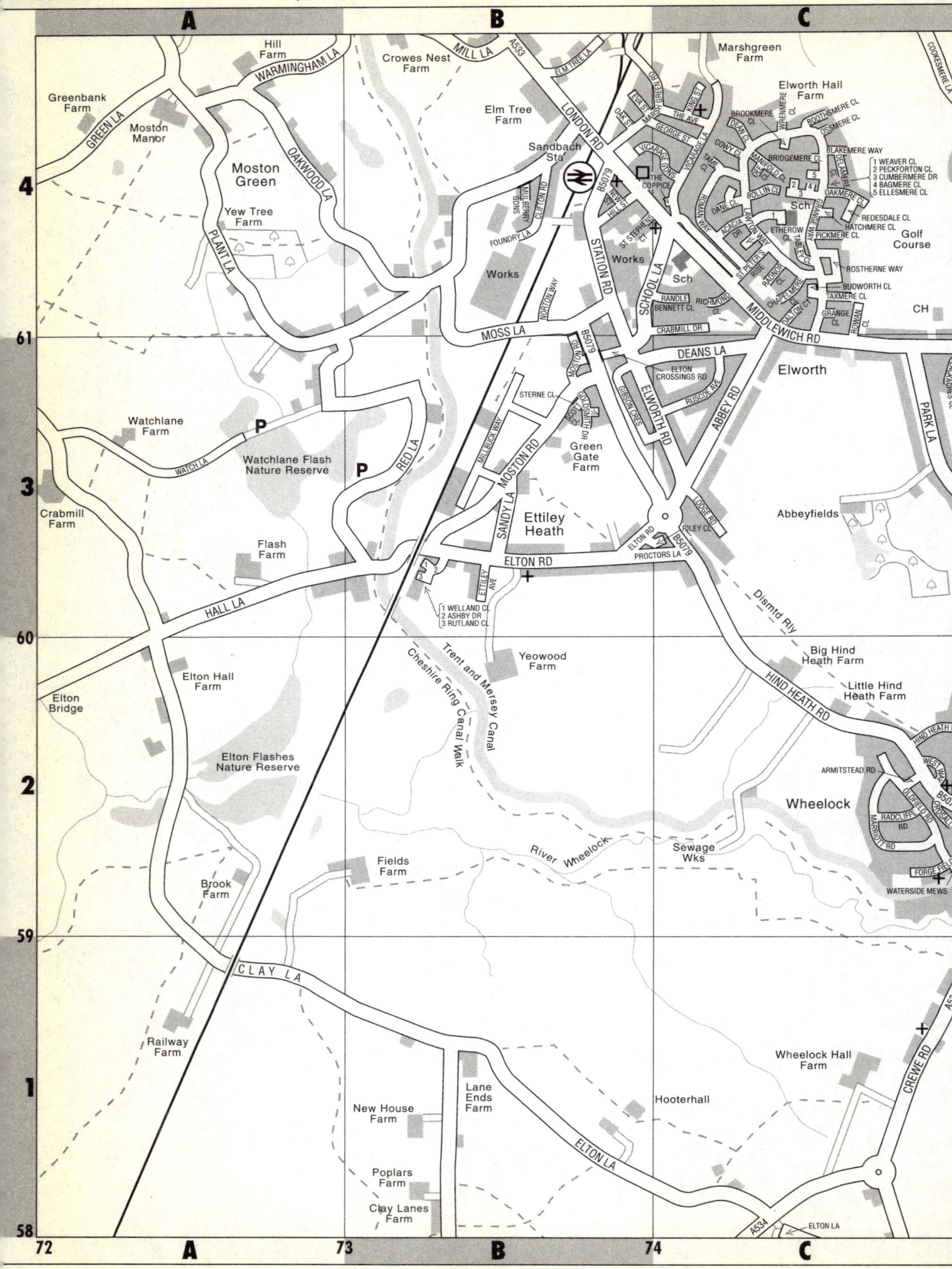

173
191

153
176

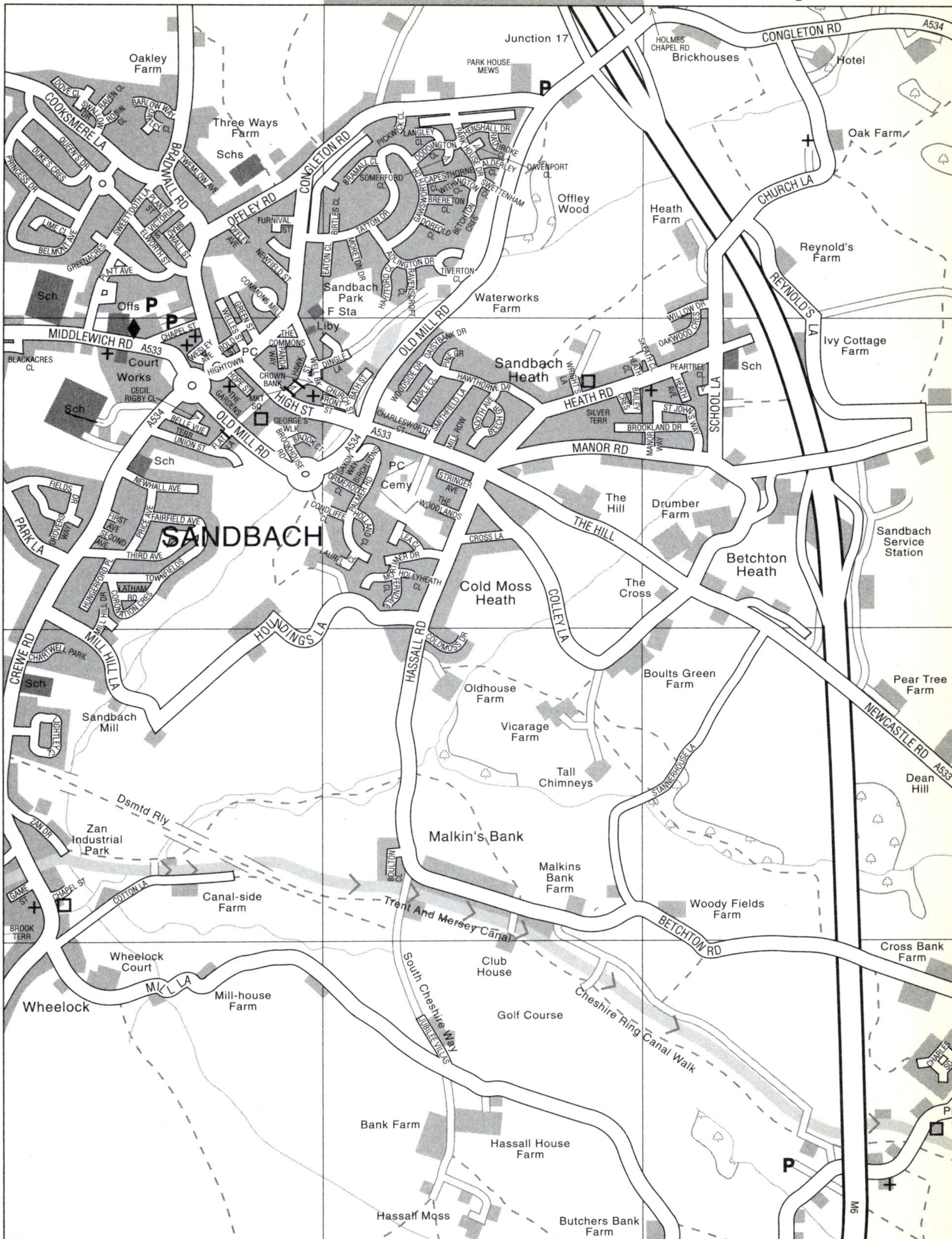

192
176

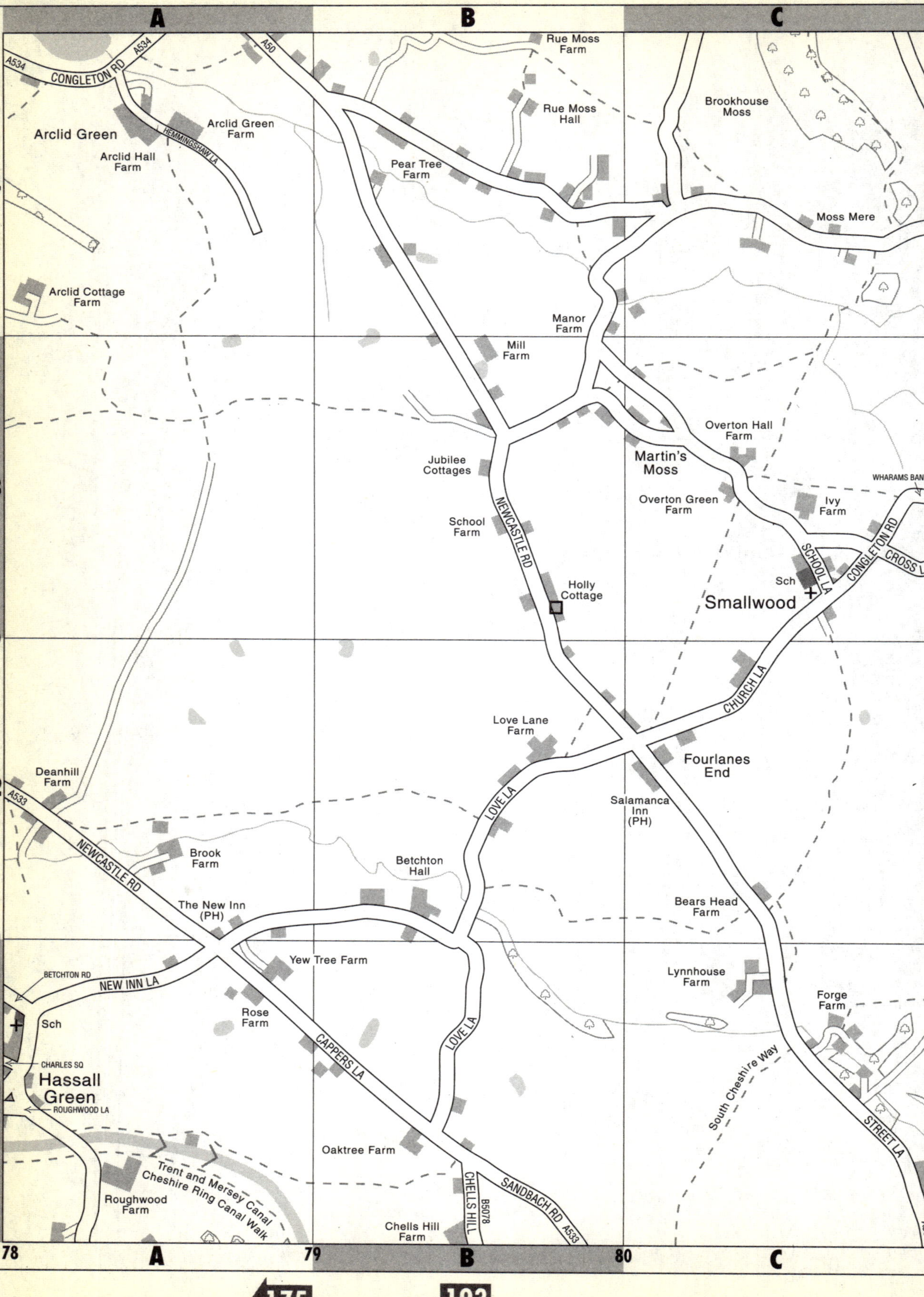
A
B
C
Rue Moss Farm
Brookhouse Moss
A534
CONGLETON RD
A50
Arclid Green
Arclid Green Farm
HEMMINGSHAW LA
Rue Moss Hall
Arclid Hall Farm
Pear Tree Farm
4
Moss Mere
Arclid Cottage Farm
Manor Farm
61
Mill Farm
Overton Hall Farm
Martin's Moss
Jubilee Cottages
3
WHARAMS BANK
Overton Green Farm
Ivy Farm
NEWCASTLE RD
School Farm
SCHOOL LA
CONGLETON RD
CROSS LA
Holly Cottage
Sch
Smallwood
60
CHURCH LA
Love Lane Farm
Fourlanes End
Deanhill Farm
2
A533
Salamanca Inn (PH)
LOVE LA
NEWCASTLE RD
Brook Farm
Betchton Hall
The New Inn (PH)
Bears Head Farm
59
Yew Tree Farm
Lynnhouse Farm
BETCHTON RD
NEW INN LA
Forge Farm
Sch
Rose Farm
CAPPERS LA
LOVE LA
South Cheshire Way
CHARLES SQ
Hassall Green
1
ROUGHWOOD LA
STREET LA
Oaktree Farm
Trent and Mersey Canal
Cheshire Ring Canal Walk
CHELLS HILL
B5078
SANDBACH RD
A533
Roughwood Farm
Chells Hill Farm
A50
58
78
79
80

155
178

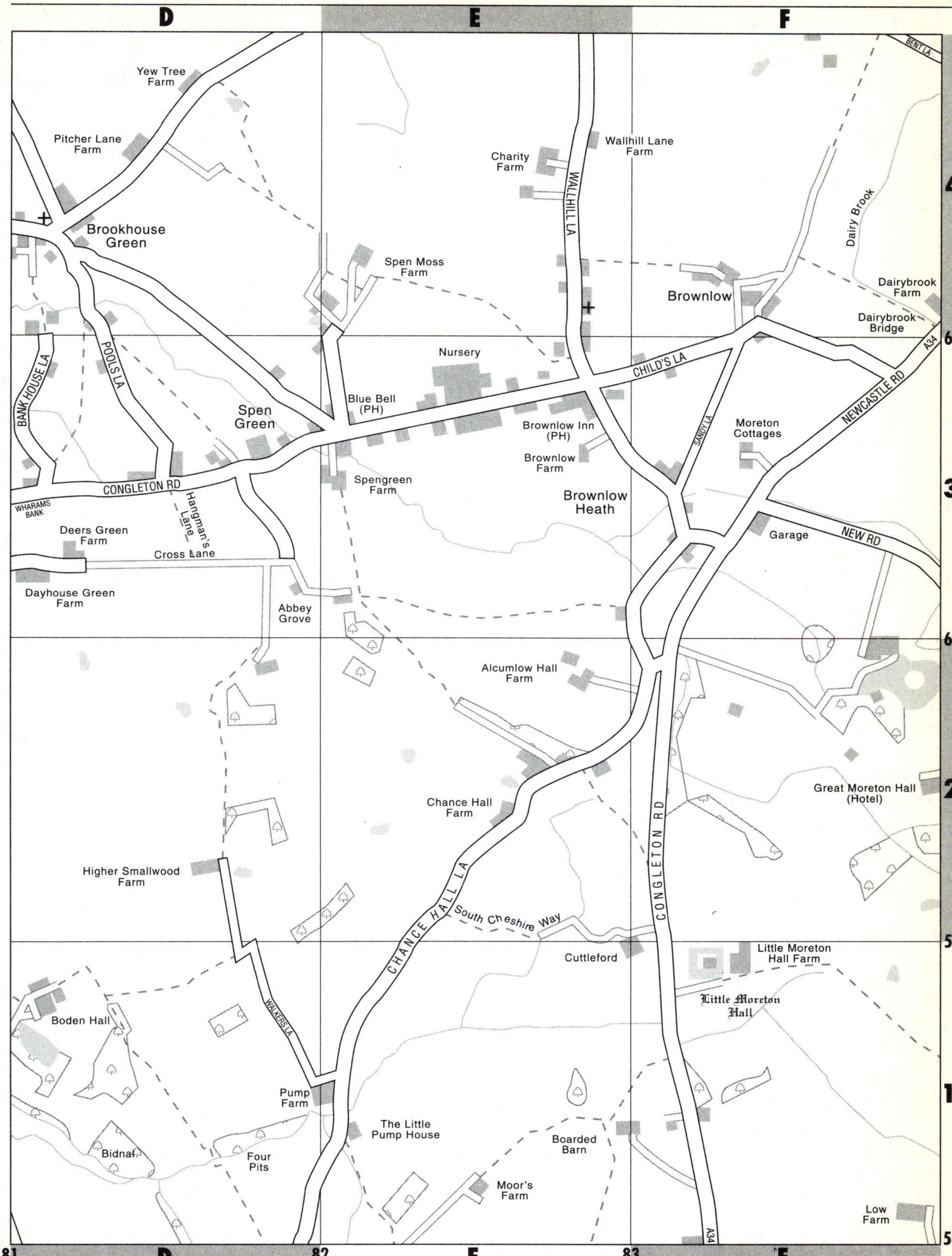

194
178

177
156

177
195

157

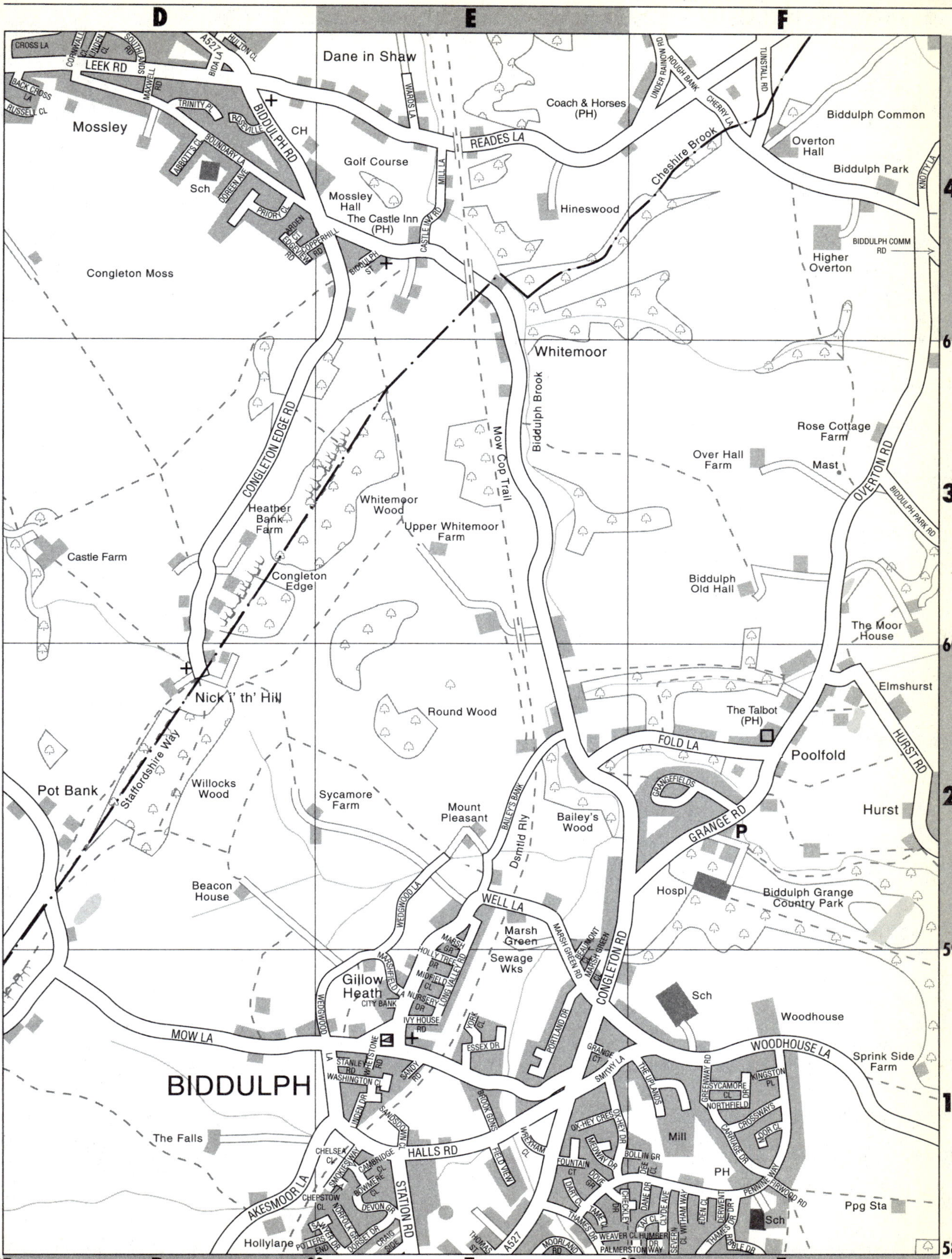
D
E
F
CROSS LA
LEEK RD
A527
HULTON CL
BIDA LA
SOUTHLANDS RD
MAXWELL RD
BACK CROSS LA
RUSSELL CL
Mossley
TRINITY PL
ROSEVILLE
BOUNDARY LA
BIDDULPH RD
CH
ABBOTTS CL
DOREEN AVE
Sch
PRIORY CL
ARDEN CL
EDGEVIEW RD
COPPERHILL RD
BIDDULPH ST
Dane in Shaw
WARDS LA
Golf Course
Mossley Hall
The Castle Inn (PH)
MILL LA
CASTLE INN RD
READES LA
Coach & Horses (PH)
Hineswood
UNDER RAINOW RD
ROUGH BANK
TUNSTALL RD
CHERRY LA
Cheshire Brook
Biddulph Common
Overton Hall
Biddulph Park
KNOTTY LA
BIDDULPH COMM RD
Higher Overton
Congleton Moss
Whitemoor
Biddulph Brook
Mow Cop Trail
CONGLETON EDGE RD
Heather Bank Farm
Whitemoor Wood
Upper Whitemoor Farm
Castle Farm
Congleton Edge
Rose Cottage Farm
Over Hall Farm
Mast
OVERTON RD
BIDDULPH PARK RD
Biddulph Old Hall
The Moor House
Nick i' th' Hill
Round Wood
Elmshurst
The Talbot (PH)
FOLD LA
Poolfold
HURST RD
Pot Bank
Staffordshire Way
Willocks Wood
Sycamore Farm
Mount Pleasant
BAILEY'S BANK
Dsmtld Rly
Bailey's Wood
GRANGEFIELDS
GRANGE RD
P
Hurst
Beacon House
WEDGWOOD LA
WELL LA
Hospl
Biddulph Grange Country Park
Marsh Green
MARSH GR
HOLLY TREE DR
LONG VALLEY RD
MIDFIELD CL
NURSERY DR
MARSHFIELD LA
Sewage Wks
MARSH GREEN RD
BEAUMONT CL
MARSH GREEN CL
CONGLETON RD
Gillow Heath
CITY BANK
IVY HOUSE RD
YORK CL
ESSEX DR
PORTLAND DR
Sch
Woodhouse
MOW LA
WEDGWOOD AVE
GRANGE CT
SMITHY LA
THE UPLANDS
WOODHOUSE LA
GREENWAY RD
SYCAMORE CL
KINGSTON PL
NORTHFIELD DR
Sprink Side Farm
BIDDULPH
STANLEY RD
WHETSTONE RD
WASHINGTON CL
SANDY RD
LINDEN DR
SANDSDOWN CL
BROOK GDNS
WREXHAM CL
OX-HEY CRES
OX-HEY DR
CROSSWAYS
CARRIAGE DR
MOOR CL
Mill
The Falls
HALLS RD
FIELD VIEW
FOUNTAIN CT
MEDWAY DR
BOLLIN GR
DEE CL
PH
CHELSEA CL
SMOKIES WAY
CAMBRIDGE CL
BOWMERE CL
STATION RD
DOVE GR
DART CL
TAME CL
CHECKLEY DR
DANE DR
CLYDE AVE
WITHAM WAY
EDEN CL
DERWENT DR
PENNINE WAY
FIRWOOD RD
Ppg Sta
AKESMOOR LA
CHEPSTOW CL
NORFOLK GR
DEVON GR
CANTERBURY END
POTTERS
DORSET DR
CRAIG SIDE
THOMAS ST
A527
MOORLAND RD
THAMES DR
WEAVER CL
HUMBER DR
TAY CL
SEVERN CL
PALMERSTON WAY
RIBBLE DR
Sch
Hollylane
4
61
3
60
2
59
1
58
87
88
89

157

163

A
B
C
4
57
3
56
2
55
1
54
39
40
41
Pulford Brook
B5130
Sourbutt's Covert
Trevalyn Meadows
Rossett
Ithells Bridge Farm
Almere
Stannage Farm
The White Horse (PH)
WALNUT CROFT
NEW LA
CHESTER RD
KNOWL LA
HOB LA
PUMP LA
PARKER'S ROW
Churton
Knowl Plantation
THE KNOWL
STANNAGE LA
Thornfield
River Dee (Afon Dyfrdwy)
Bowling Alley Plantation
Briarfields
SIBBERSFIELD LA
Mast
Barnston's Monument
TOWNFIELD LA
TOWNFIELD AVE
SPEED'S WAY
CHURTON RD
Sch
OLD SCHOOL CL
Farndon
DEE CRES
DEE VIEW
RIVER LA
PH
HIGH ST
LLOYD CL
BARNSTON CT
MILL FIELD CL
GREENWAY
NIGHTINGALE CL
PLOVER CL
B5130
Plas Devon
Devon Brook
B5102
Works
Brook Lawn
CHURCH CT
Farndon or Holt Bridge
PC
CHURCH LA
RECTORY CL
LIME TREE DR
KINGFISHER CL
HERON CL
STARLING CL
BARTON RD
QUARRY HILL
PARKER DR
QUARRY AVE
INCE DR
PARKER DR S
MEADOW CL
CREWE LA
Cemy
LABURNUM WAY
GREEN ST
CAERLLEW
BRIDGE ST
QUAKERS WAY
CHURCH ST
VICARAGE CT
P
THE GARDENS
Esp Hill
B5102

196

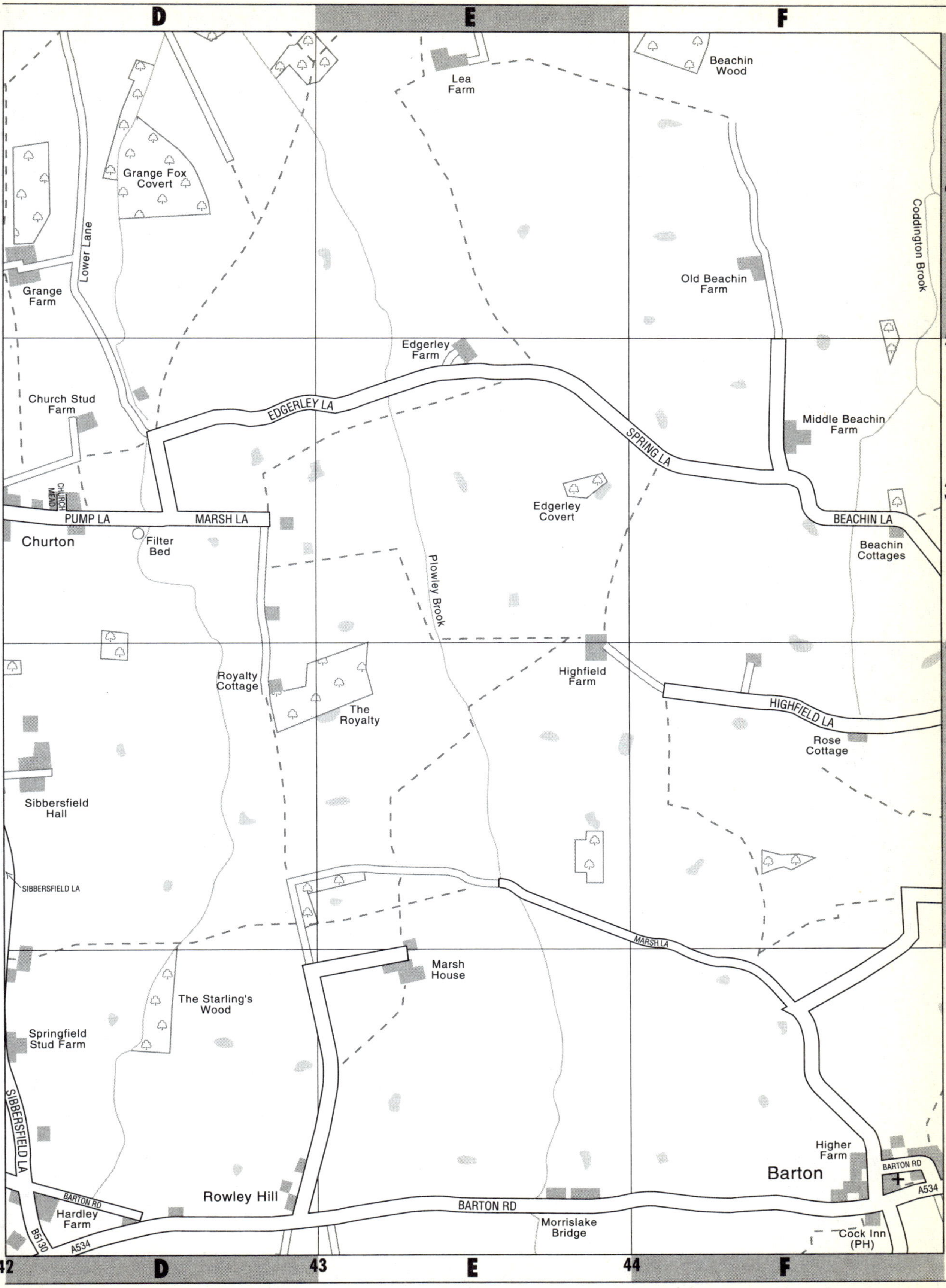
D
E
F
Lea Farm
Beachin Wood
Grange Fox Covert
Lower Lane
Grange Farm
Old Beachin Farm
Coddington Brook
4
Edgerley Farm
57
Church Stud Farm
EDGERLEY LA
SPRING LA
Middle Beachin Farm
CHURCH MEAD
PUMP LA
MARSH LA
Edgerley Covert
BEACHIN LA
3
Churton
Filter Bed
Beachin Cottages
Plowley Brook
56
Highfield Farm
Royalty Cottage
The Royalty
HIGHFIELD LA
Rose Cottage
Sibbersfield Hall
2
SIBBERSFIELD LA
MARSH LA
55
Marsh House
The Starling's Wood
Springfield Stud Farm
1
SIBBERSFIELD LA
Higher Farm
Barton
BARTON RD
A534
BARTON RD
Rowley Hill
BARTON RD
Hardley Farm
B5130
A534
Morrislake Bridge
Cock Inn (PH)
54
42
D
43
E
44
F

181
165

181
198

166
184

199
184

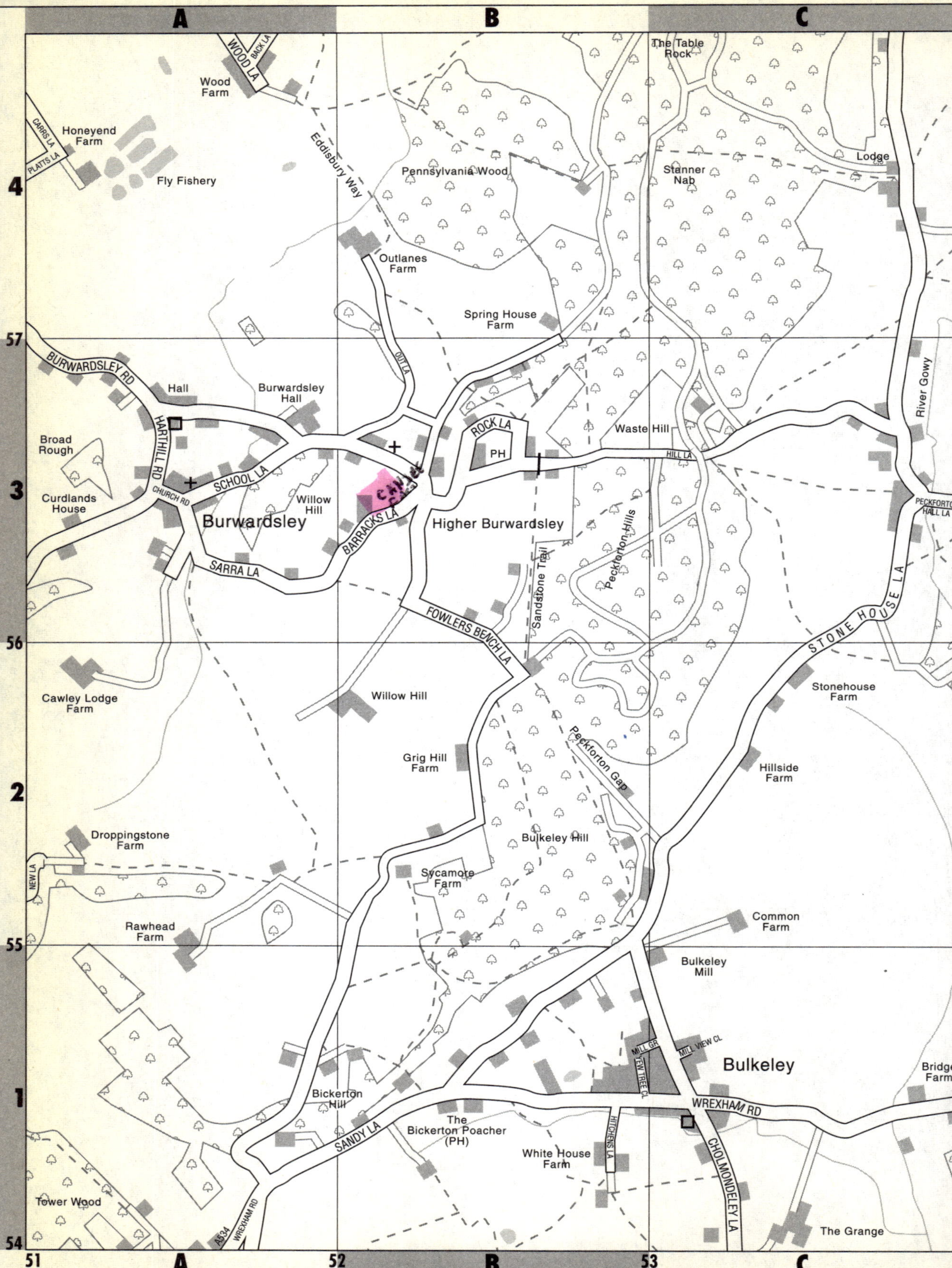
A
B
C
4
3
2
1
57
56
55
54
51
52
53
WOOD LA
BACK LA
Wood Farm
CARRS LA
PLATTS LA
Honeyend Farm
Fly Fishery
Eddisbury Way
Pennsylvania Wood
The Table Rock
Stanner Nab
Lodge
Outlanes Farm
Spring House Farm
River Gowy
BURWARDSLEY RD
Hall
Burwardsley Hall
OUT LA
HARTHILL RD
ROCK LA
PH
Waste Hill
HILL LA
Broad Rough
SCHOOL LA
CHURCH RD
Curdlands House
Willow Hill
Burwardsley
BARRACKS LA
Higher Burwardsley
Peckforton Hills
PECKFORTON HALL LA
SARRA LA
Sandstone Trail
FOWLERS BENCH LA
STONE HOUSE LA
Cawley Lodge Farm
Willow Hill
Stonehouse Farm
Grig Hill Farm
Peckforton Gap
Hillside Farm
Droppingstone Farm
Bulkeley Hill
NEW LA
Sycamore Farm
Rawhead Farm
Common Farm
Bulkeley Mill
MILL GR
MILL VIEW CL
YEW TREE CL
Bulkeley
Bridge Farm
Bickerton Hill
WREXHAM RD
SANDY LA
The Bickerton Poacher (PH)
White House Farm
HITCHENS LA
CHOLMONDELEY LA
Tower Wood
A534
WREXHAM RD
The Grange

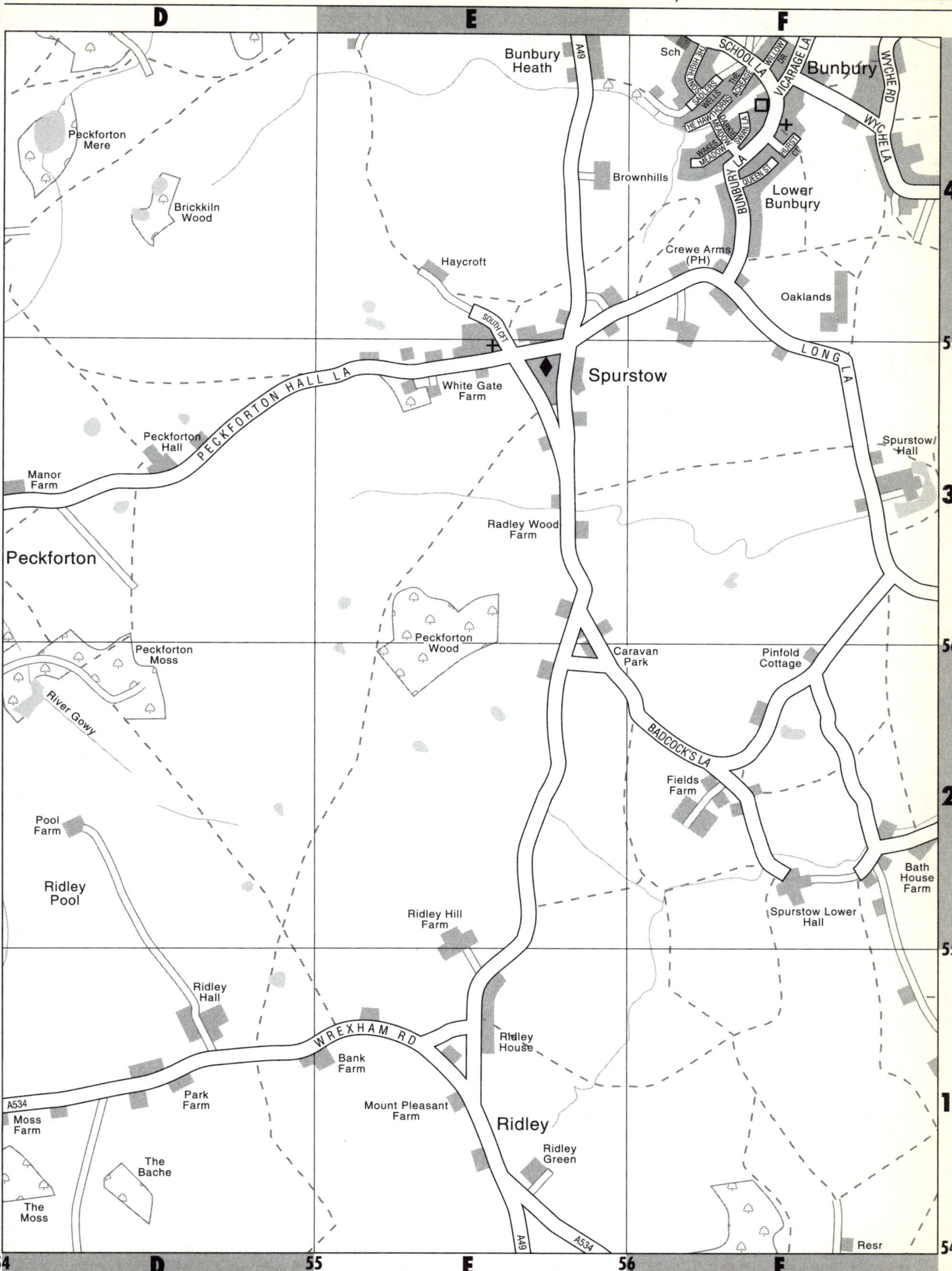
D
E
F
Bunbury Heath
A49
Sch
SCHOOL LA
THE HIGHLANDS
SADLERS WELLS
THE ACREAGE
WILLOW DR
VICARAGE LA
Bunbury
WYCHE RD
WYCHE LA
THE HAWTHORNS
WAKES MEADOW
DARKIE MEADOW
SWAN LA
HURST CT
QUEEN ST
BUNBURY LA
Lower Bunbury
Peckforton Mere
Brickkiln Wood
Brownhills
Crewe Arms (PH)
Haycroft
Oaklands
SOUTH CFT
Spurstow
LONG LA
PECKFORTON HALL LA
White Gate Farm
Peckforton Hall
Manor Farm
Spurstow Hall
Radley Wood Farm
Peckforton
Peckforton Wood
Peckforton Moss
Caravan Park
Pinfold Cottage
River Gowy
BADCOCK'S LA
Fields Farm
Pool Farm
Ridley Pool
Bath House Farm
Spurstow Lower Hall
Ridley Hill Farm
Ridley Hall
WREXHAM RD
Ridley House
Bank Farm
A534
Park Farm
Moss Farm
Mount Pleasant Farm
Ridley
Ridley Green
The Bache
The Moss
A49
A534
Resr
4
57
3
56
2
55
1
54
54
55
56

185
169

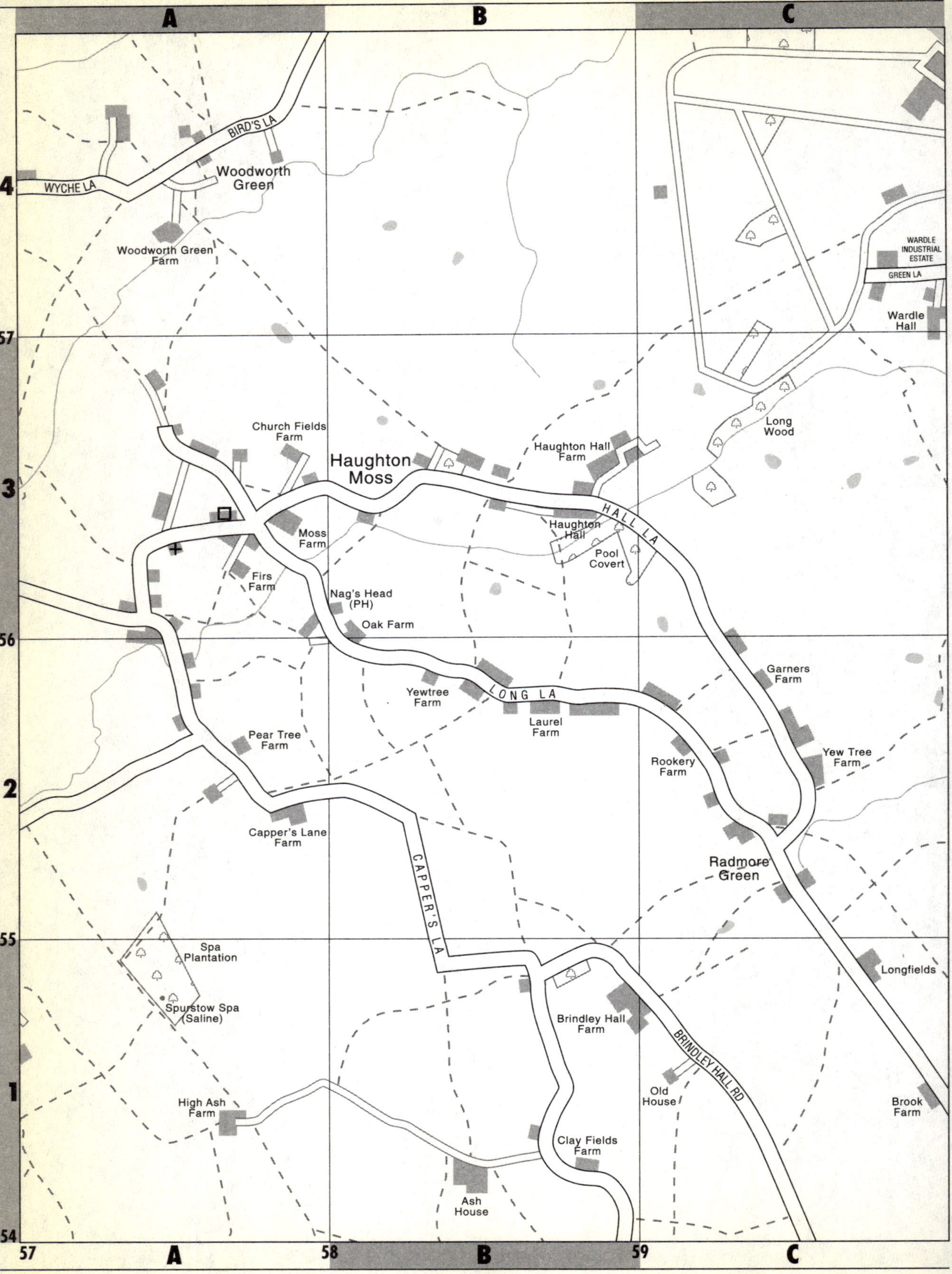

185
202

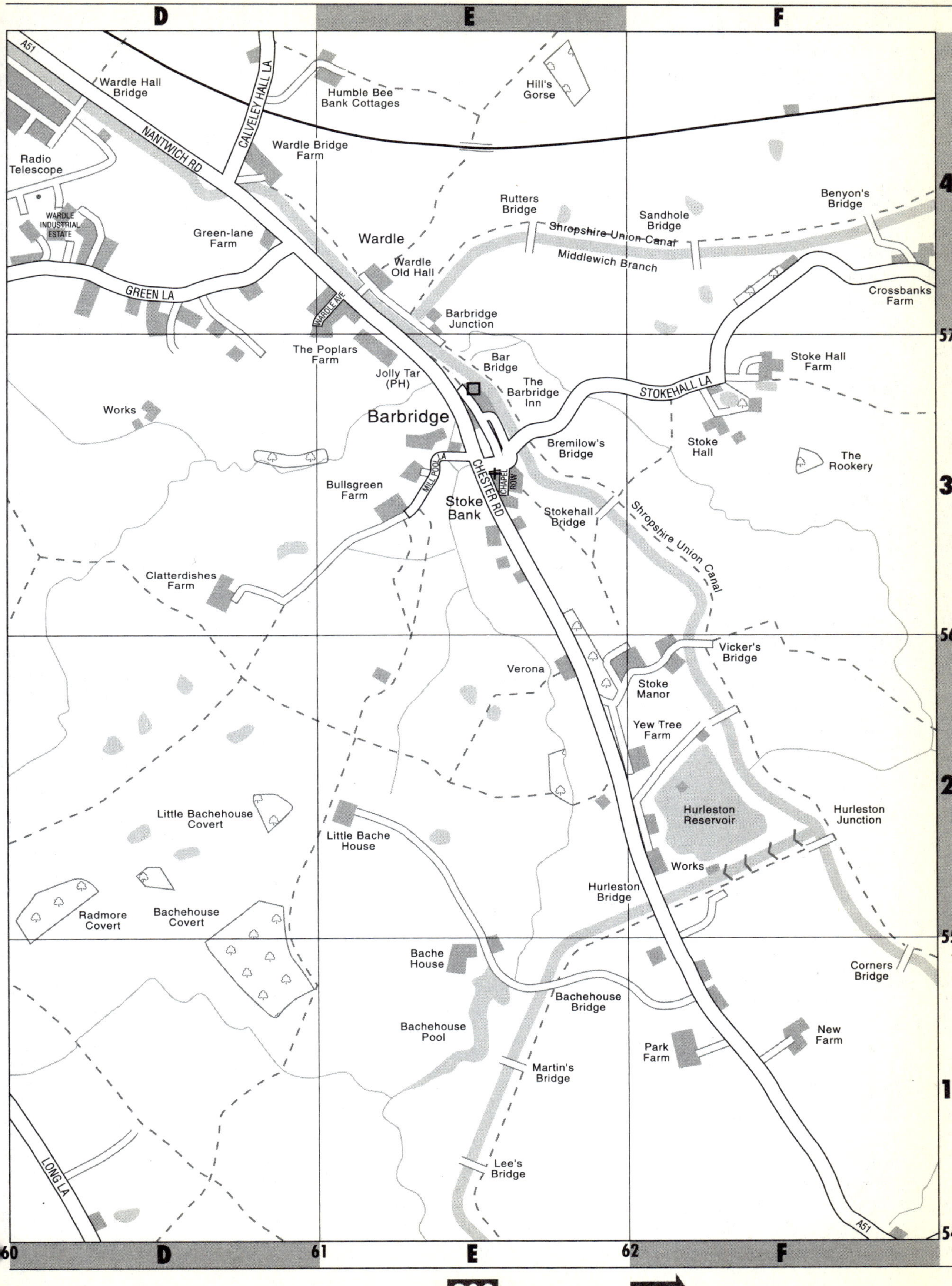
D
E
F
A51
Wardle Hall
Bridge
CALVELEY HALL LA
Humble Bee
Bank Cottages
Hill's
Gorse
NANTWICH RD
Radio
Telescope
Wardle Bridge
Farm
WARDLE
INDUSTRIAL
ESTATE
Green-lane
Farm
Wardle
Rutters
Bridge
Sandhole
Bridge
Benyon's
Bridge
Shropshire Union Canal
Middlewich Branch
Wardle
Old Hall
GREEN LA
WARDLE AVE
Barbridge
Junction
Crossbanks
Farm
4
57
The Poplars
Farm
Jolly Tar
(PH)
Bar
Bridge
The
Barbridge
Inn
STOKEHALL LA
Stoke Hall
Farm
Works
Barbridge
Bremilow's
Bridge
Stoke
Hall
The
Rookery
MILL POOL LA
CHESTER RD
CHAPEL ROW
Bullsgreen
Farm
Stoke
Bank
Stokehall
Bridge
Shropshire Union Canal
3
Clatterdishes
Farm
56
Vicker's
Bridge
Verona
Stoke
Manor
Yew Tree
Farm
2
Hurleston
Reservoir
Hurleston
Junction
Little Bachehouse
Covert
Little Bache
House
Works
Hurleston
Bridge
Radmore
Covert
Bachehouse
Covert
55
Bache
House
Corners
Bridge
Bachehouse
Bridge
Bachehouse
Pool
New
Farm
Park
Farm
Martin's
Bridge
1
Lee's
Bridge
LONG LA
A51
54
60
D
61
E
62
F

187
171

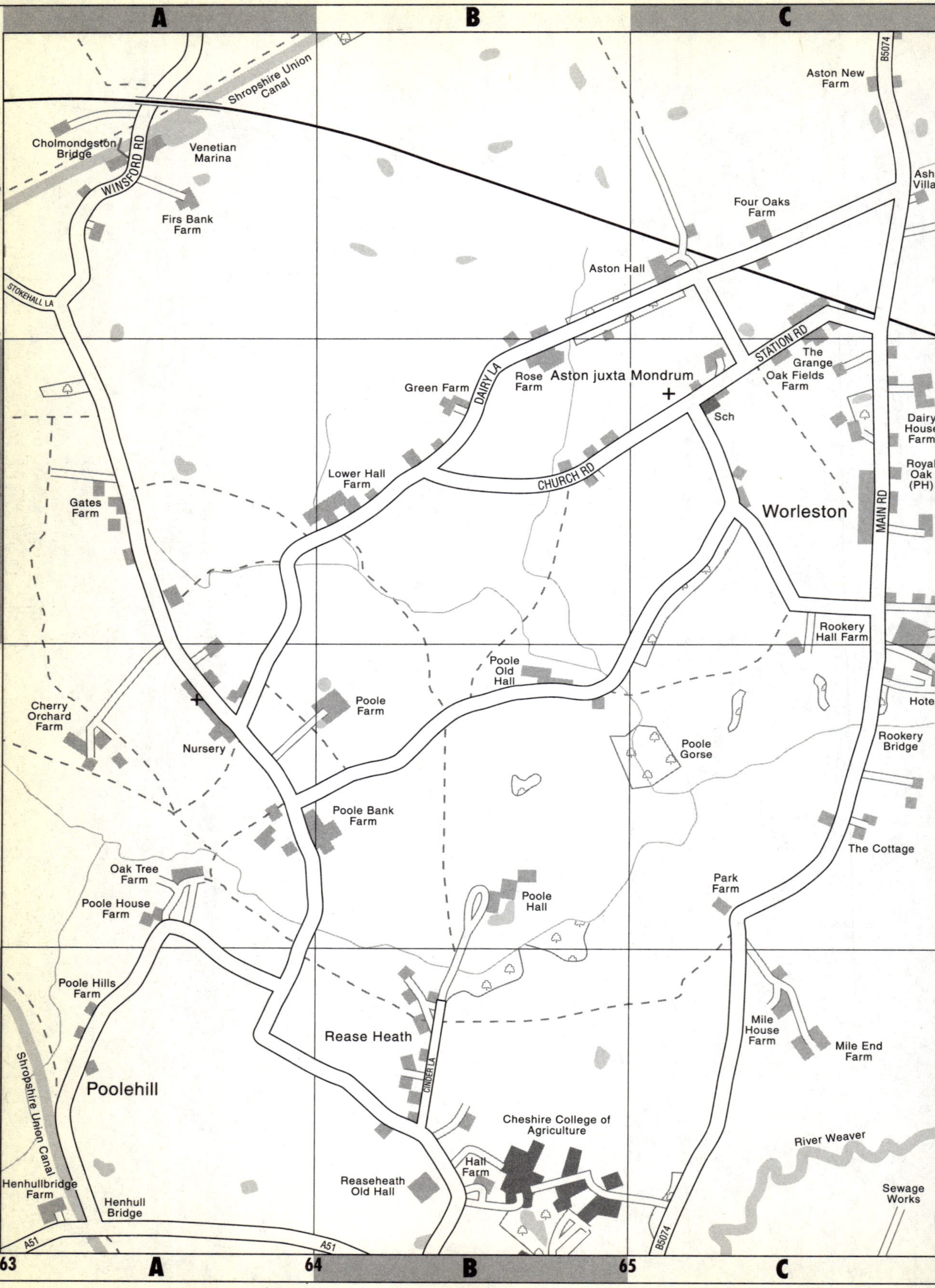

187
204

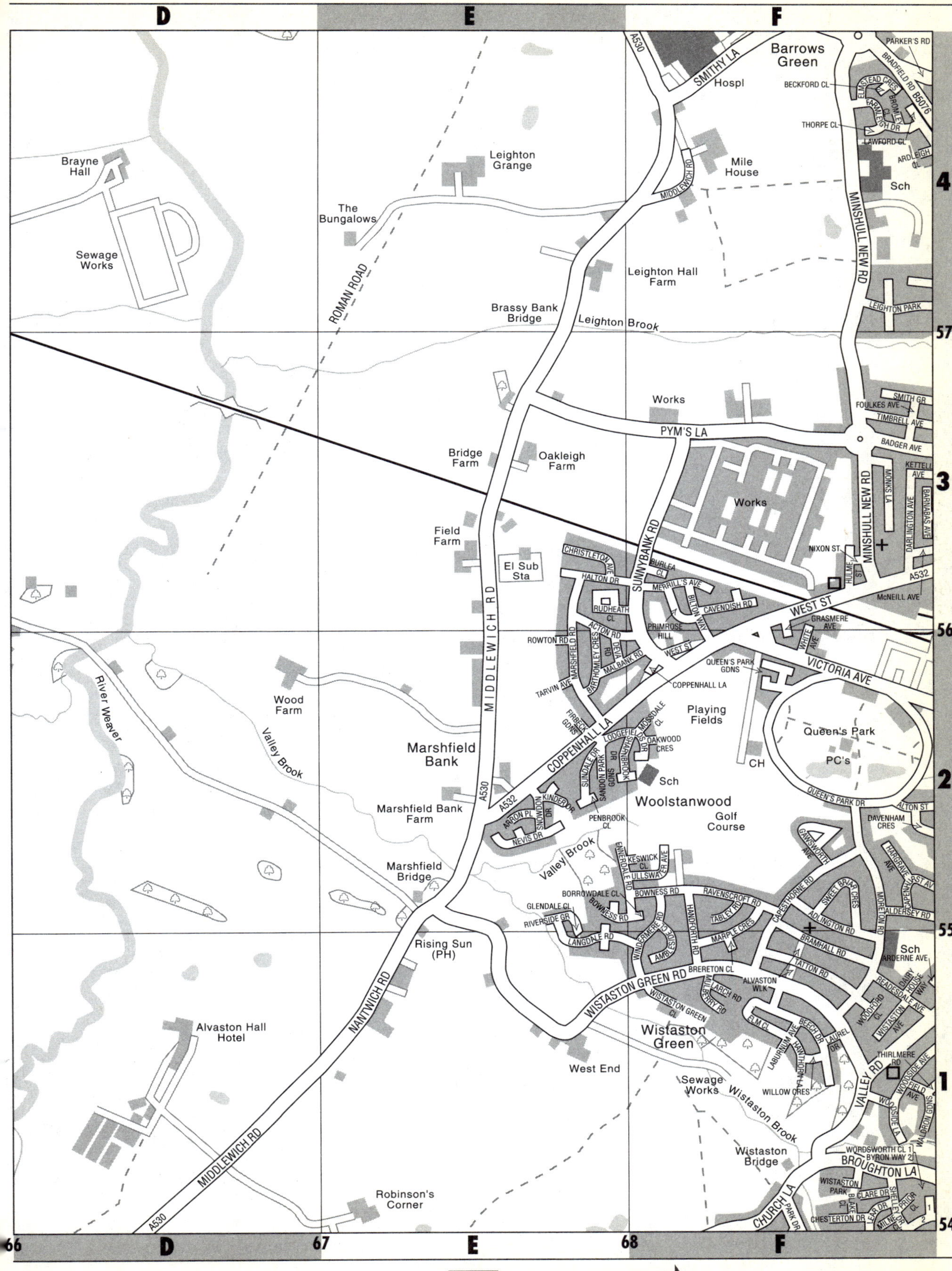
D
E
F
A530
SMITHY LA
Barrows Green
Hospl
PARKER'S RD
BRADFIELD RD B5076
BECKFORD CL
ELMSTEAD CRES
BROMLEY
FARNLEIGH DR
THORPE CL
LAWFORD CL
ARDLEIGH CL
Brayne Hall
Leighton Grange
Mile House
MIDDLEWICH RD
Sch
4
The Bungalows
Sewage Works
MINSHULL NEW RD
Leighton Hall Farm
ROMAN ROAD
Brassy Bank Bridge
Leighton Brook
LEIGHTON PARK
57
Works
SMITH GR
FOULKES AVE
TIMBRELL AVE
PYM'S LA
BADGER AVE
Bridge Farm
Oakleigh Farm
KETTELL AVE
MONKS LA
3
Works
BARNABAS AVE
DARLINGTON AVE
Field Farm
SUNNYBANK RD
El Sub Sta
CHRISTLETON AVE
BURLEA CL
NIXON ST
HULME ST
A532
HALTON DR
MERRILL'S AVE
MCNEILL AVE
RUDHEATH CL
BILTON WAY
CAVENDISH RD
WEST ST
GRASMERE AVE
56
ACTON RD
PRIMROSE HILL
ROWTON RD
DEVA RD
WHITE AVE
MARSHFIELD RD
BARTHOMLEY CRES
MALBANK RD
WEST ST
QUEEN'S PARK GDNS
VICTORIA AVE
TARVIN AVE
COPPENHALL LA
Wood Farm
MIDDLEWICH RD
River Weaver
FIRBECK GDNS
MOSSDALE CL
Playing Fields
Queen's Park
COPPENHALL LA
LODGEFIELD DR
OAKWOOD CRES
Valley Brook
Marshfield Bank
SHARNBROOK DR
SUNDALE DR
SANDON PARK GDNS
CH
PC's
Sch
2
A530
A532
KINDER DR
Woolstanwood
QUEEN'S PARK DR
ALTON ST
ARRON PL
SNOWDON DR
Marshfield Bank Farm
PENBROOK CL
Golf Course
DAVENHAM CRES
NEVIS DR
Valley Brook
GAWSWORTH AVE
HARGRAVE AVE
KESWICK CL
ENNERDALE RD
ULLSWATER AVE
Marshfield Bridge
CAPESTHORNE RD
SWEET BRIAR CRES
BORROWDALE CL
BOWNESS RD
RAVENSCROFT RD
GLENDALE CL
BOWNESS RD
TABLEY RD
ADLINGTON RD
ALDERSEY RD
RIVERSIDE GR
HANDFORTH RD
MARPLE CRES
55
MORETON RD
LANGDALE RD
WINDERMERE RD
AMBLESIDE CL
BRAMHALL RD
Sch
Rising Sun (PH)
ARDERNE AVE
BRERETON CL
TATTON RD
DAIRY HOUSE WAY
WISTASTON GREEN RD
ALVASTON WLK
READESDALE AVE
NANTWICH RD
WISTASTON GREEN CL
MULBERRY RD
LARCH RD
WOODFORD CL
WISTASTON AVE
ELM CL
BEECH DR
LAUREL DR
Alvaston Hall Hotel
Wistaston Green
LABURNUM AVE
HAWTHORN LA
THIRLMERE RD
West End
VALLEY RD
WOODSIDE AVE
1
Sewage Works
Wistaston Brook
WILLOW CRES
WOODSIDE LA
WALDRON GDNS
MIDDLEWICH RD
Wistaston Bridge
WORDSWORTH CL
BYRON WAY
BROUGHTON LA
WISTASTON PARK
CLARE DR
SHELLEY DR
BLAKE CL
PRIOR CL
Robinson's Corner
CHURCH LA
PARK DR
CHESTERTON DR
LEAR DR
MILNE CL
A530
54
66
D
67
E
68
F

189
173

189
206

174
192

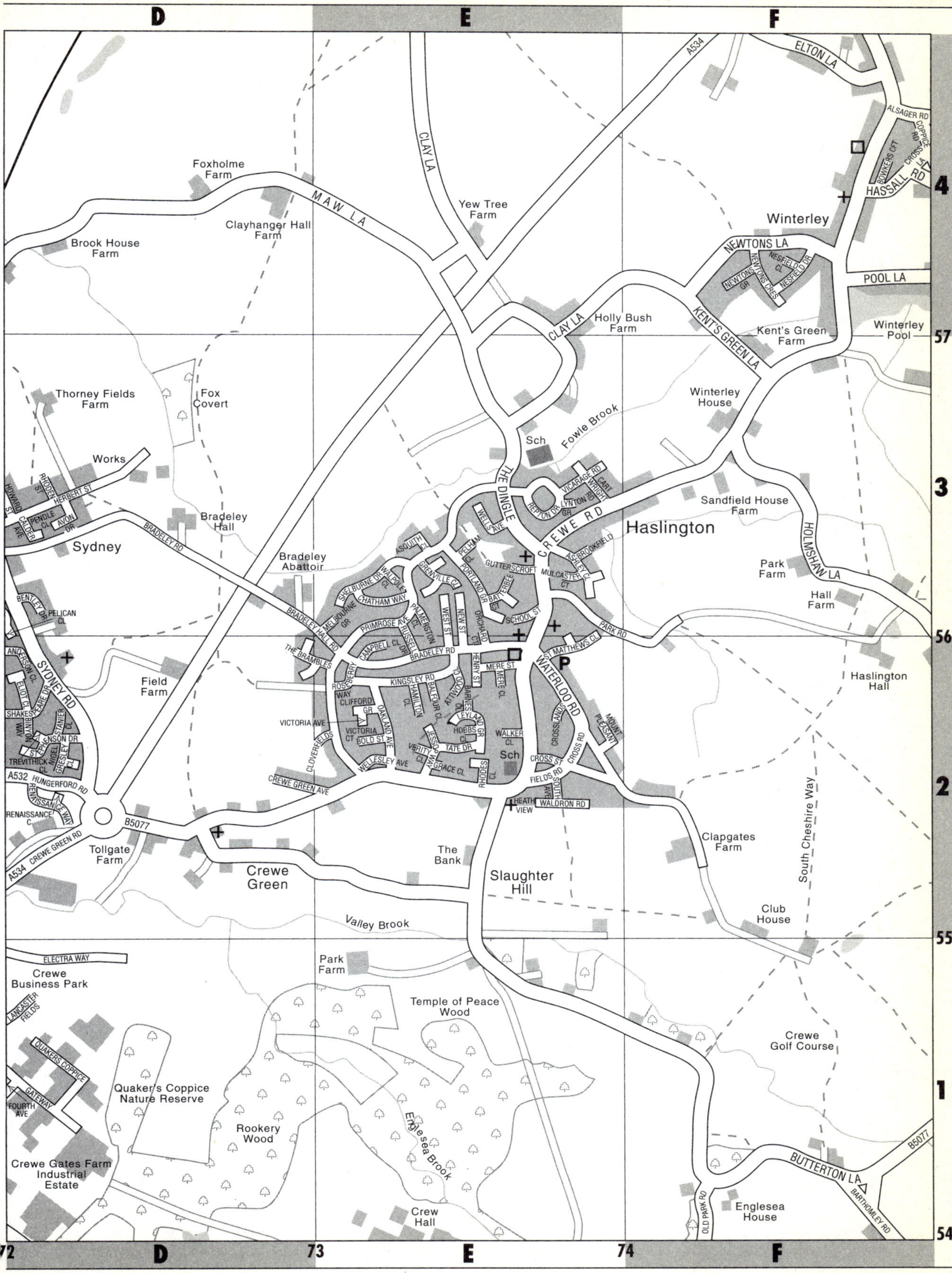
D
E
F
4
3
2
1
57
56
55
54
72
73
74
A534
ELTON LA
ALSAGER RD
COPPICE RD
BOWKERS CFT
CROSS LA
HASSALL RD
CLAY LA
Foxholme Farm
MAW LA
Yew Tree Farm
Clayhanger Hall Farm
Brook House Farm
Winterley
NEWTONS LA
NEWTONS CRES
NEWTONS GR
NESFIELD CL
NESFIELD DR
POOL LA
KENT'S GREEN LA
Holly Bush Farm
Kent's Green Farm
Winterley Pool
Thorney Fields Farm
Fox Covert
Winterley House
Fowle Brook
Sch
Works
HOWARD
RHODEN ST
HERBERT ST
CALDER AVE
PENDLE CL
AVON DR
Bradeley Hall
BRADELEY RD
THE DINGLE
VICARAGE RD
CARTWRIGHT RD
REPTON DR
LYNTON GR
CREWE RD
Sandfield House Farm
Haslington
Sydney
Bradeley Abattoir
ASQUITH CL
WELLS AVE
PELHAM CL
BROOKFIELD
HOLMSHAW LA
Park Farm
Hall Farm
BENTLEY DR
PELICAN CL
GUTTERSCROFT
MULCASTER CT
SHELBURNE DR
WALPOLE CL
GRENVILLE CL
PORTLAND GR
BAYVERBE CT
CHATHAM WAY
MELBOURNE GR
BRADELEY HALL RD
PRIMROSE AVE
PALMERSTON
WEST ST
NEW ST
ORCHARD CT
SCHOOL ST
PARK RD
THE BRAMBLES
CAMPBELL CL
RUSSELL DR
BRADELEY RD
HENRY ST
MERE ST
ST MATTHEWS CL
P
SYDNEY RD
ANDERSON CL
ELIOT CL
SHAKESPEARE DR
BINYON WAY
STEPHENSON DR
STANIER CL
NIGEL GR
GRESLEY CL
TREVITHICK CL
Field Farm
ROSEBERRY WAY
KINGSLEY RD
HAMILTON CL
BALFOUR CL
ATTLEE CL
BARNES CL
MERE CL
WATERLOO RD
Haslington Hall
CLIFFORD GR
VICTORIA AVE
VICTORIA CT
BOLD ST
OAKLAND AVE
LEYLAND GR
HOBBS CL
TATE DR
WALKER CL
CROSSLANDS
MOUNT PLEASANT
CLOVERFIELDS
JESSOP WAY
VERITY CL
GRACE CL
WELLESLEY AVE
RHODES CL
CROSS ST
CROSS RD
FIELDS RD
SOUTH AVE
HEATH VIEW
WALDRON RD
A532
HUNGERFORD RD
RENAISSANCE WAY
RENAISSANCE CT
CREWE GREEN AVE
B5077
A534
CREWE GREEN RD
Tollgate Farm
Crewe Green
The Bank
Slaughter Hill
Clapgates Farm
South Cheshire Way
Club House
Valley Brook
ELECTRA WAY
Crewe Business Park
Park Farm
LANCASTER FIELDS
Temple of Peace Wood
Crewe Golf Course
QUAKERS COPPICE
GATEWAY
FOURTH AVE
Quaker's Coppice Nature Reserve
Rookery Wood
Englesea Brook
Crewe Gates Farm Industrial Estate
BUTTERTON LA
B5077
BARTHOMLEY RD
OLD PARK RD
Englesea House
Crew Hall

A
B
C
4
57
3
56
2
55
1
54
75
76
77
Fingerpost Farm
M6
Whitehall Farm
Wheelockheath Farm
Daisy Bank House
Wheelock Heath
Holly Tree Farm
HASSALL RD
COPPICE RD
SANDY LA
School Farm
ALSAGER RD
Hassall Pond
Day Green
Walnut Tree Farm
POOL LA
Hassall
Hassall Hall
HASSALL RD
Bridgehouse Farm
Bostock House
South Cheshire Way
Moss Cottage
Green Bank Farm
Dunnock's Fold Farm
Castle Farm
DUNNOCKSFOLD RD
Oakhanger Hall
Woodside Farm
Homeshaw Farm
Moss End Farm
WINDSOR DR
SPENCER CL
DERWENT CL
Heathfield Farm
Stockton Farm
DELAMERE CT
CRANBERRY LA
Oakhanger Farm
KENSINGTON CT
BOLLIN CL
Ashfields
CLOSE LA
Gate Farm
VALLEY CL
GOWY CL
Hall o' the Heath
HOLMSHAW LA
NURSERY RD
Rose Tree Farm
Spartan Wood Farm
Peartree Farm
Oakhanger Moss
White Moss Farm
White Moss
BUTTERTON LA
TAYLORS LA
Butterton Lane Farm
CREWE RD B5077
Moss Farm
Oakhanger
B5078
B5077
BUTTERTON LA
RADWAY GREEN RD
LC
Radway Green
MILL LA
Works
B5078
M6

176
194

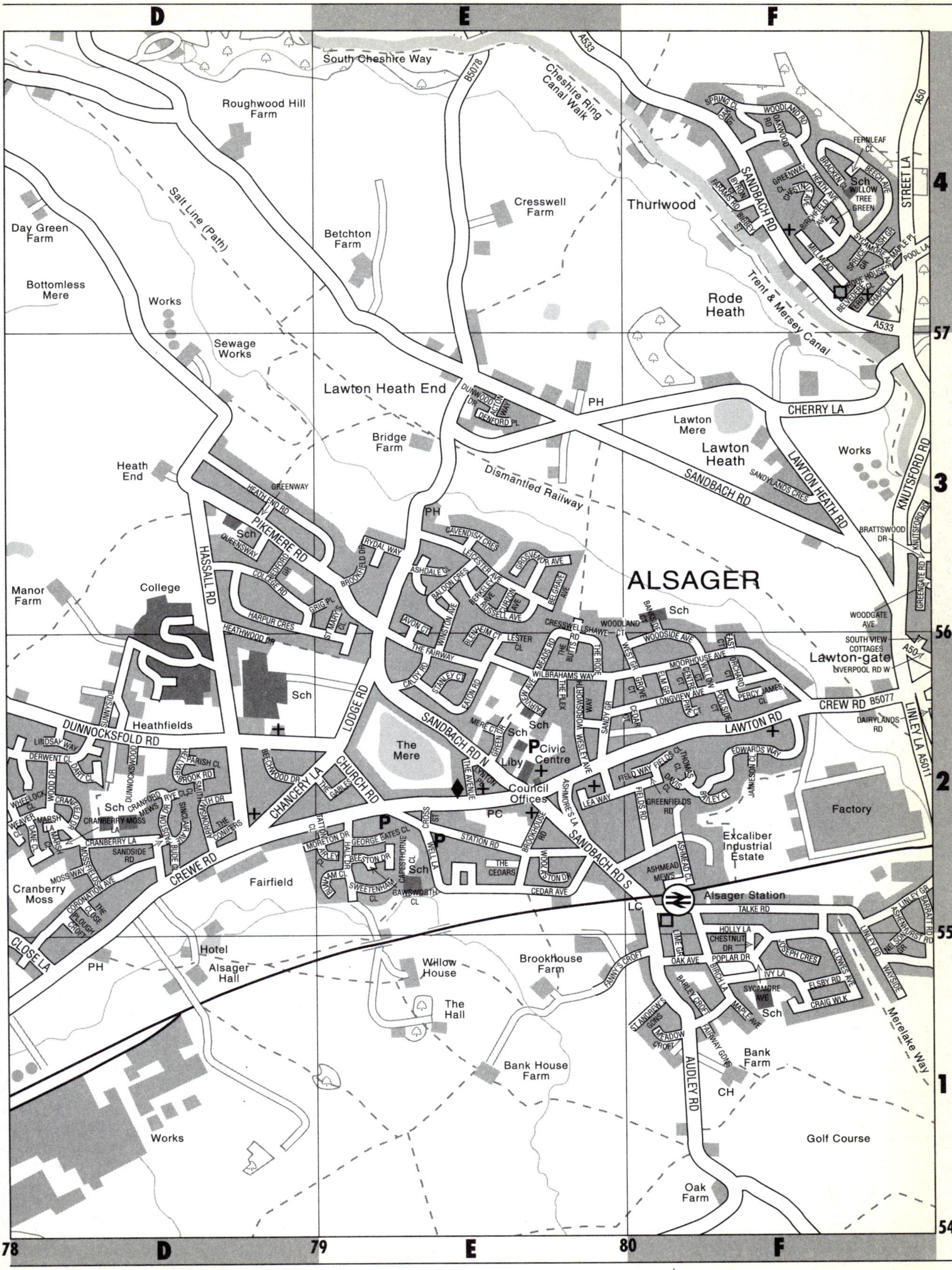

209
194

193
177

193
210

178

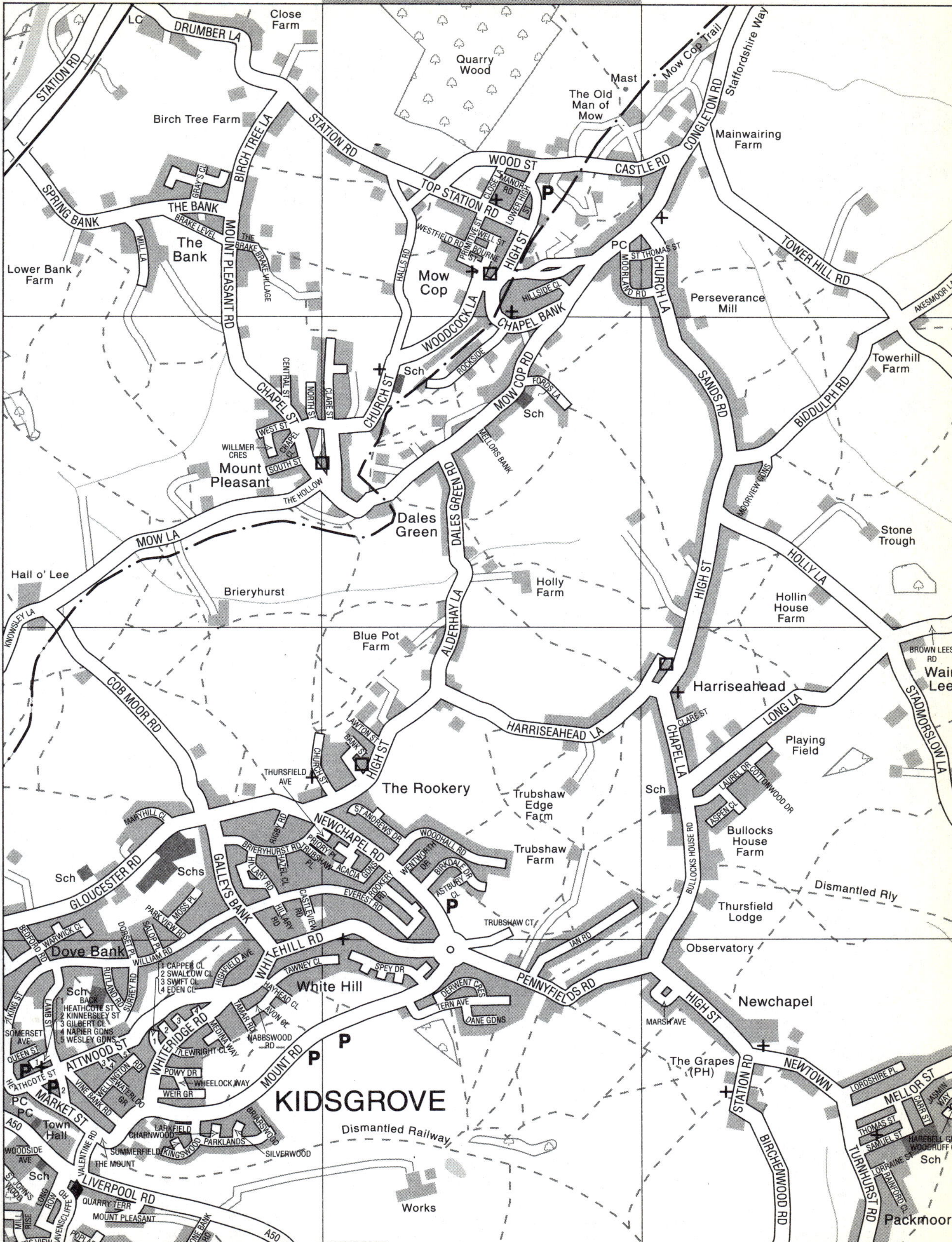
D
E
F
Close Farm
DRUMBER LA
LC
STATION RD
Quarry Wood
Mast
Mow Cop Trail
Staffordshire Way
The Old Man of Mow
CONGLETON RD
Mainwairing Farm
Birch Tree Farm
BIRCH TREE LA
STATION RD
WOOD ST
CASTLE RD
4
SPRING BANK
GRAY'S CL
THE BANK
TOP STATION RD
CLOSE LA
MANOR RD
LOWER HIGH ST
P
BRAKE LEVEL
The Bank
MOUNT PLEASANT RD
THE BRAKE
BRAKE VILLAGE
WESTFIELD RD
PRIMITIVE ST
WELL ST
BOURNE ST
HIGH ST
PC
ST THOMAS ST
MOORLAND RD
CHURCH LA
TOWER HILL RD
Lower Bank Farm
MILL LA
HALLS RD
Mow Cop
HILLSIDE CL
CHAPEL BANK
Perseverance Mill
AKESMOOR LA
57
WOODCOCK LA
ROCKSIDE
Towerhill Farm
CENTRAL ST
NORTH ST
CLARE ST
Sch
CHURCH ST
MOW COP RD
FORDS LA
SANDS RD
BIDDULPH RD
CHAPEL ST
WEST ST
CHAPEL
WILLMER CRES
SOUTH ST
Sch
MELLORS BANK
Mount Pleasant
THE HOLLOW
MOORVIEW GDNS
3
Dales Green
DALES GREEN RD
Stone Trough
MOW LA
HOLLY LA
Hall o' Lee
Brieryhurst
Holly Farm
HIGH ST
Hollin House Farm
KNOWSLEY LA
ALDERHAY LA
Blue Pot Farm
56
BROWN LEES RD
Wain Lee
Harriseahead
COB MOOR RD
LONG LA
STADMORSLOW LA
LAWTON ST
BANK ST
HARRISEAHEAD LA
CLARE ST
Playing Field
CHURCH ST
HIGH ST
CHAPEL LA
THURSFIELD AVE
The Rookery
Trubshaw Edge Farm
Sch
LAUREL DR
COTTONWOOD DR
2
ASPEN CL
MARYHILL CL
RIGBY RD
ST ANDREWS DR
Bullocks House Farm
NEWCHAPEL RD
BULLOCKS HOUSE RD
BRIERYHURST RD
PRIORY PL
TRUBSHAW PL
WOODHALL RD
Trubshaw Farm
HAZEL CL
ACACIA GDNS
WENTWORTH DR
Sch
Schs
GALLEYS BANK
HILLARY RD
ROOKERY
BIRKDALE DR
Dismantled Rly
GLOUCESTER RD
CASTLE VIEW
EVEREST RD
ASTBURY CL
P
Thursfield Lodge
PARK VIEW RD
MOSS PL
HILLARY RD
TRUBSHAW CT
BEDFORD RD
WARWICK CL
DORSET PL
SALOP PL
WHITEHILL RD
IAN RD
55
Dove Bank
WILLIAM RD
Observatory
1 CAPPER CL
2 SWALLOW CL
3 SWIFT CL
4 EDEN CL
HIGHFIELD AVE
TAWNEY CL
SPEY DR
PENNYFIELDS RD
RUTLAND RD
SURREY RD
White Hill
DERWENT CRES
Sch
BACK
1 HEATHCOTE ST
2 KINNERSLEY ST
3 GILBERT CL
4 NAPIER GDNS
5 WESLEY GDNS
HAYHEAD CL
TERN AVE
HIGH ST
Newchapel
KING ST
LAMB ST
TAMAR RD
AVON CL
DANE GDNS
MARSH AVE
SOMERSET AVE
WHITERIDGE RD
MEDINA WAY
NABBSWOOD RD
QUEEN ST
ATTWOOD ST
TELWRIGHT CL
P
P
NEWTOWN
LORDSHIRE PL
The Grapes (PH)
STATION RD
MELLOR ST
P
HEATHCOTE ST
WELLINGTON RD
POWY DR
WATERLOO GR
CARR ST
JASMIN WAY
1
MARKET ST
VINE BANK RD
WHEELOCK WAY
MOUNT RD
WEIR GR
KIDSGROVE
PC
PC
BRIARSWOOD
Town Hall
LARKFIELD
CHARNWOOD
THOMAS ST
SAMUEL ST
HAREBELL GR
WOODRUFF CL
A50
VALENTINE RD
KINGSWOOD
PARKLANDS
Dismantled Railway
BIRCHENWOOD RD
LORRAINE ST
Sch
SUMMERFIELD
WOODSIDE AVE
THE MOUNT
SILVERWOOD
TURNHURST RD
BAINFORD CL
Sch
ST JOHN'S WOOD
LIVERPOOL RD
QUARRY TERR
MOUNT PLEASANT
LONG ROW
RAVENSCLIFFE
Works
MILL RISE
Packmoor
A50
STONE BANK RD
POPLAR DR
MILLERS VIEW
KIDSGROVE BANK
54
84
D
85
E
86
F

180

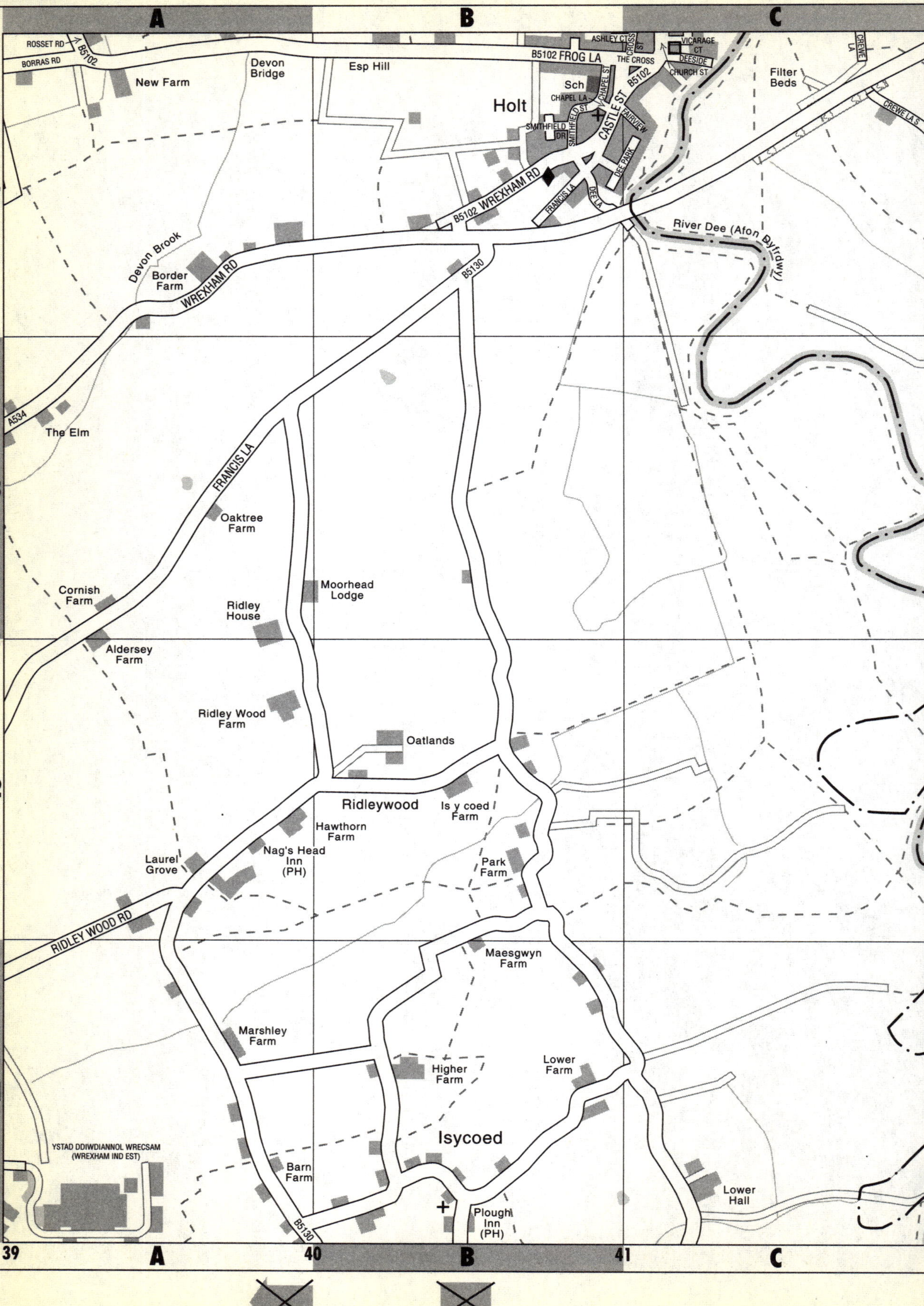
A
B
C
ROSSET RD
BORRAS RD
B5102
New Farm
Devon Bridge
Esp Hill
B5102 FROG LA
ASHLEY CT
CROSS ST
THE CROSS
VICARAGE CT
DEESIDE
CHURCH ST
B5102
Filter Beds
CREWE LA
CREWE LA S
Sch
Holt
CHAPEL LA
CHAPEL ST
SMITHFIELD ST
SMITHFIELD DR
CASTLE ST
FAIRVIEW
DEE PARK
B5102 WREXHAM RD
FRANCIS LA
DEE LA
River Dee (Afon Dyfrdwy)
Devon Brook
Border Farm
WREXHAM RD
B5130
A534
The Elm
FRANCIS LA
Oaktree Farm
Moorhead Lodge
Cornish Farm
Ridley House
Aldersey Farm
Ridley Wood Farm
Oatlands
Ridleywood
Is y coed Farm
Hawthorn Farm
Nag's Head Inn (PH)
Laurel Grove
Park Farm
RIDLEY WOOD RD
Maesgwyn Farm
Marshley Farm
Higher Farm
Lower Farm
Isycoed
YSTAD DDIWDIANNOL WRECSAM (WREXHAM IND EST)
Barn Farm
B5130
Plough Inn (PH)
Lower Hall
4
53
3
52
2
51
1
50
39
40
41

181
198

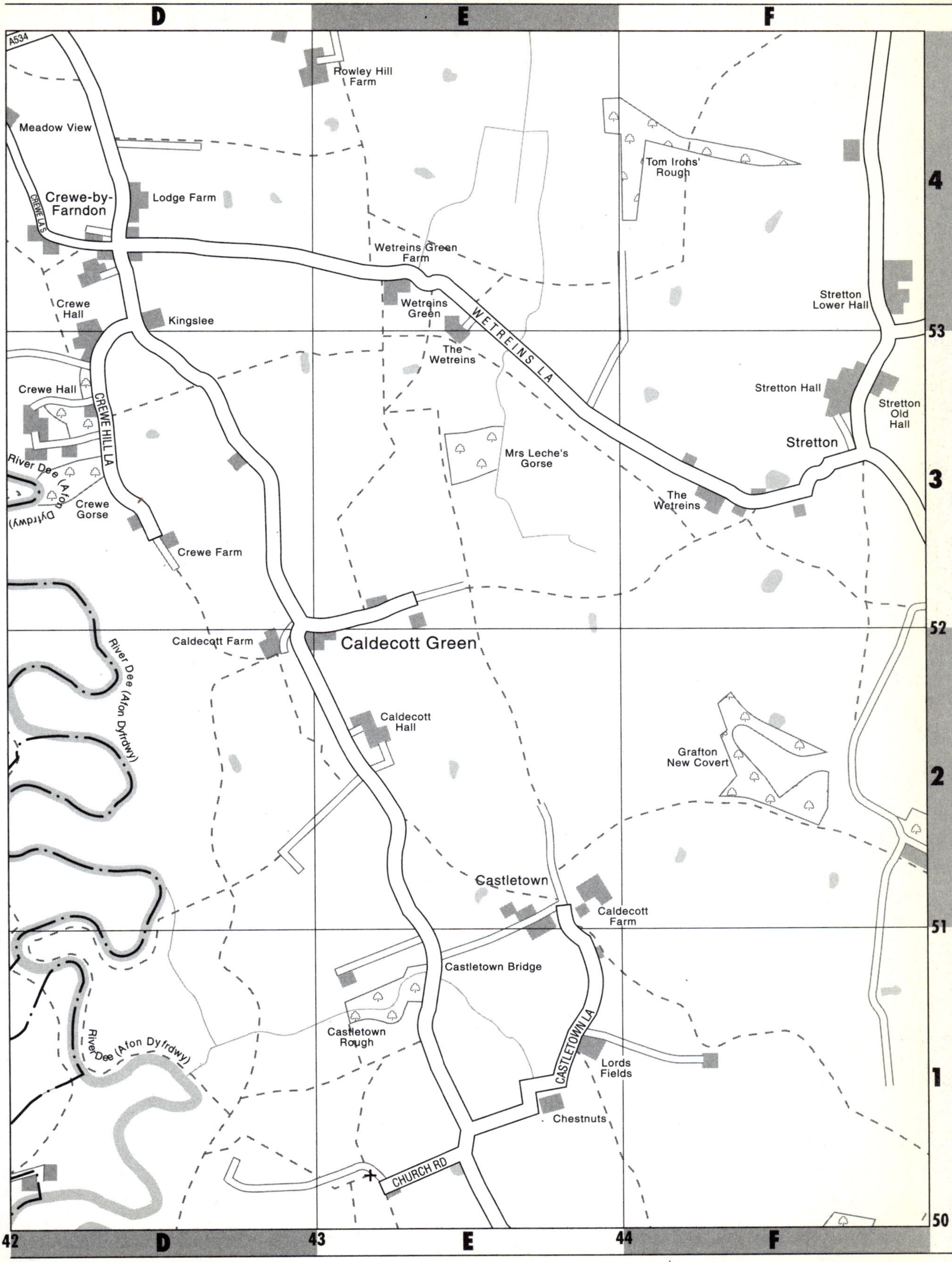

211
198

197
182

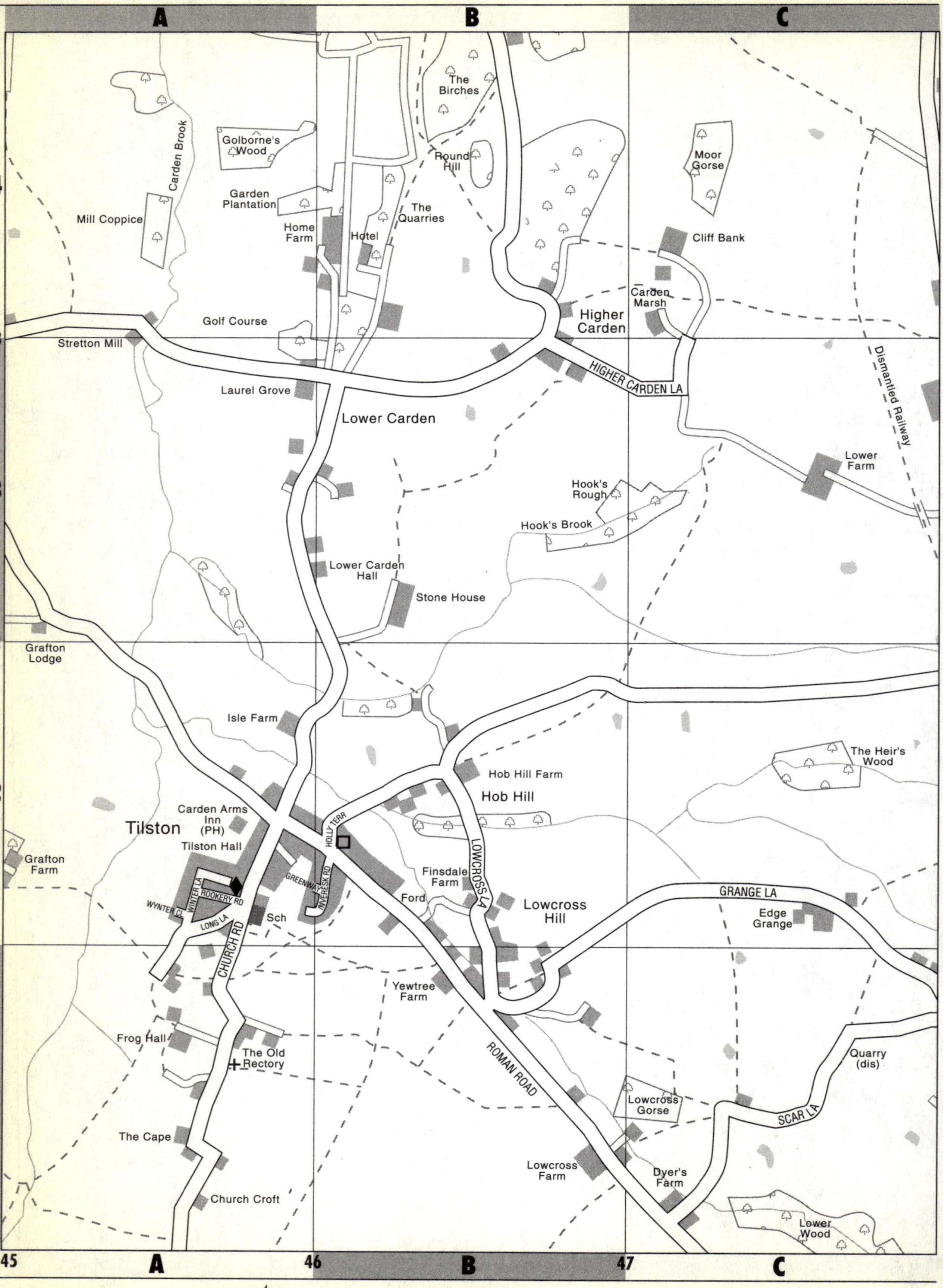

197
212

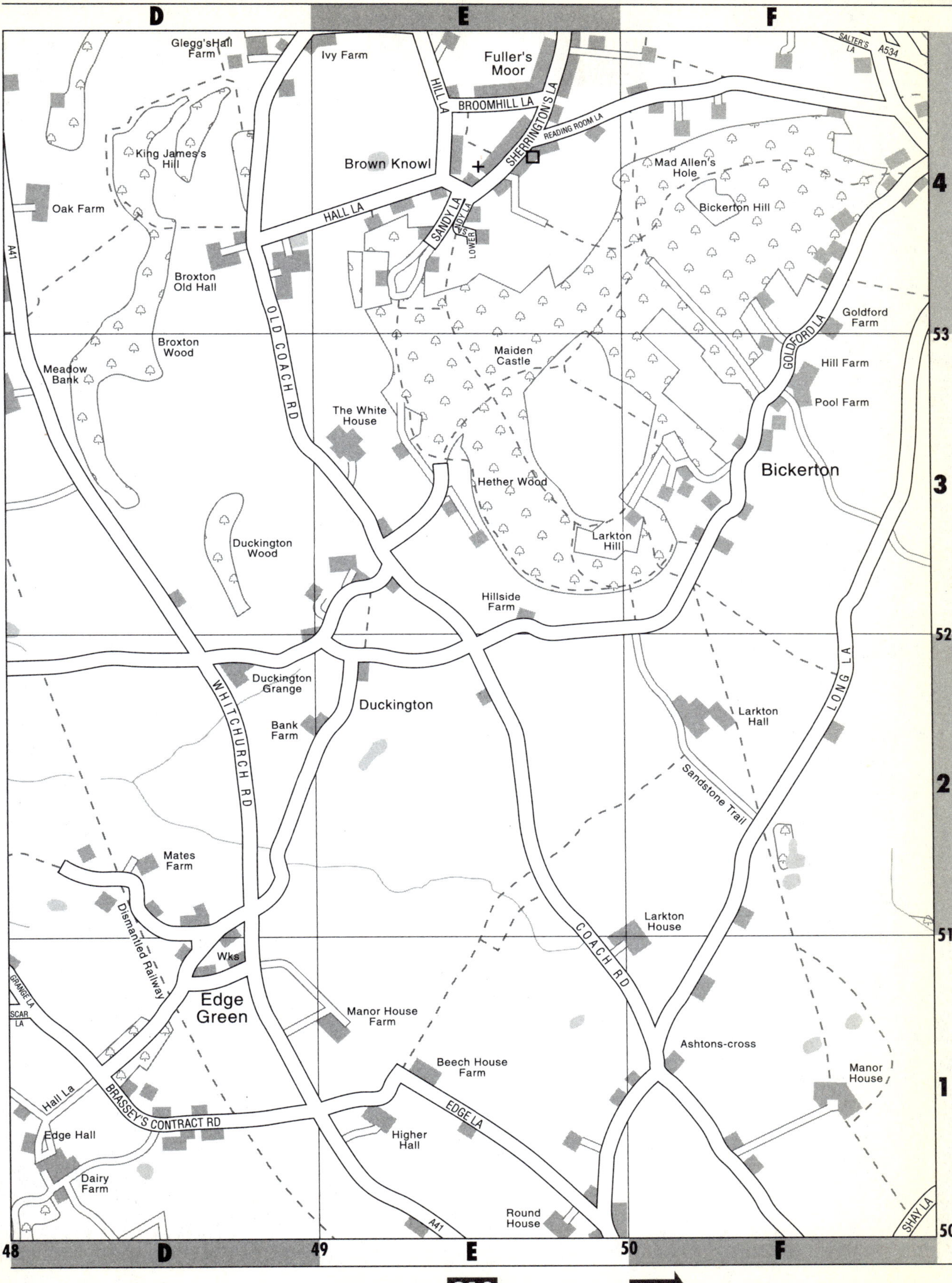
D
E
F
Glegg'sHall Farm
Ivy Farm
Fuller's Moor
HILL LA
BROOMHILL LA
SHERRINGTON'S LA
READING ROOM LA
SALTER'S LA
A534
King James's Hill
Brown Knowl
Mad Allen's Hole
Bickerton Hill
Oak Farm
HALL LA
SANDY LA
LOWER
A41
Broxton Old Hall
OLD COACH RD
Goldford Farm
GOLDFORD LA
Broxton Wood
Maiden Castle
Hill Farm
Meadow Bank
Pool Farm
The White House
Bickerton
Hether Wood
Duckington Wood
Larkton Hill
Hillside Farm
Duckington Grange
WHITCHURCH RD
Duckington
Bank Farm
LONG LA
Larkton Hall
Sandstone Trail
Mates Farm
Dismantled Railway
Larkton House
COACH RD
Wks
GRANGE LA
SCAR LA
Edge Green
Manor House Farm
Ashtons-cross
Beech House Farm
Manor House
Hall La
BRASSEY'S CONTRACT RD
EDGE LA
Edge Hall
Higher Hall
Dairy Farm
Round House
A41
SHAY LA
4
53
3
52
2
51
1
50
48
49
50
D
E
F

199
184

199
214

185
202

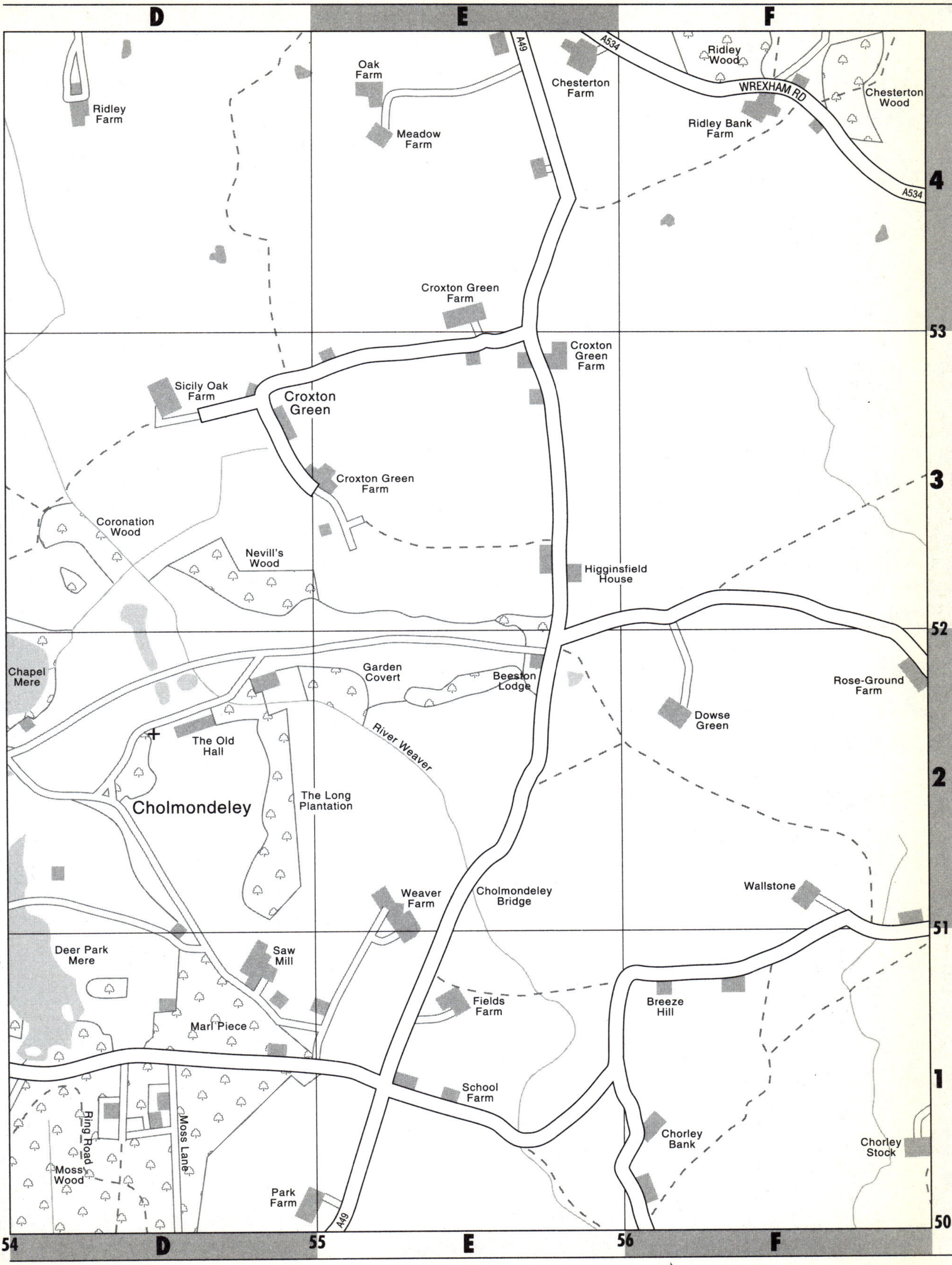

215
202

201
186

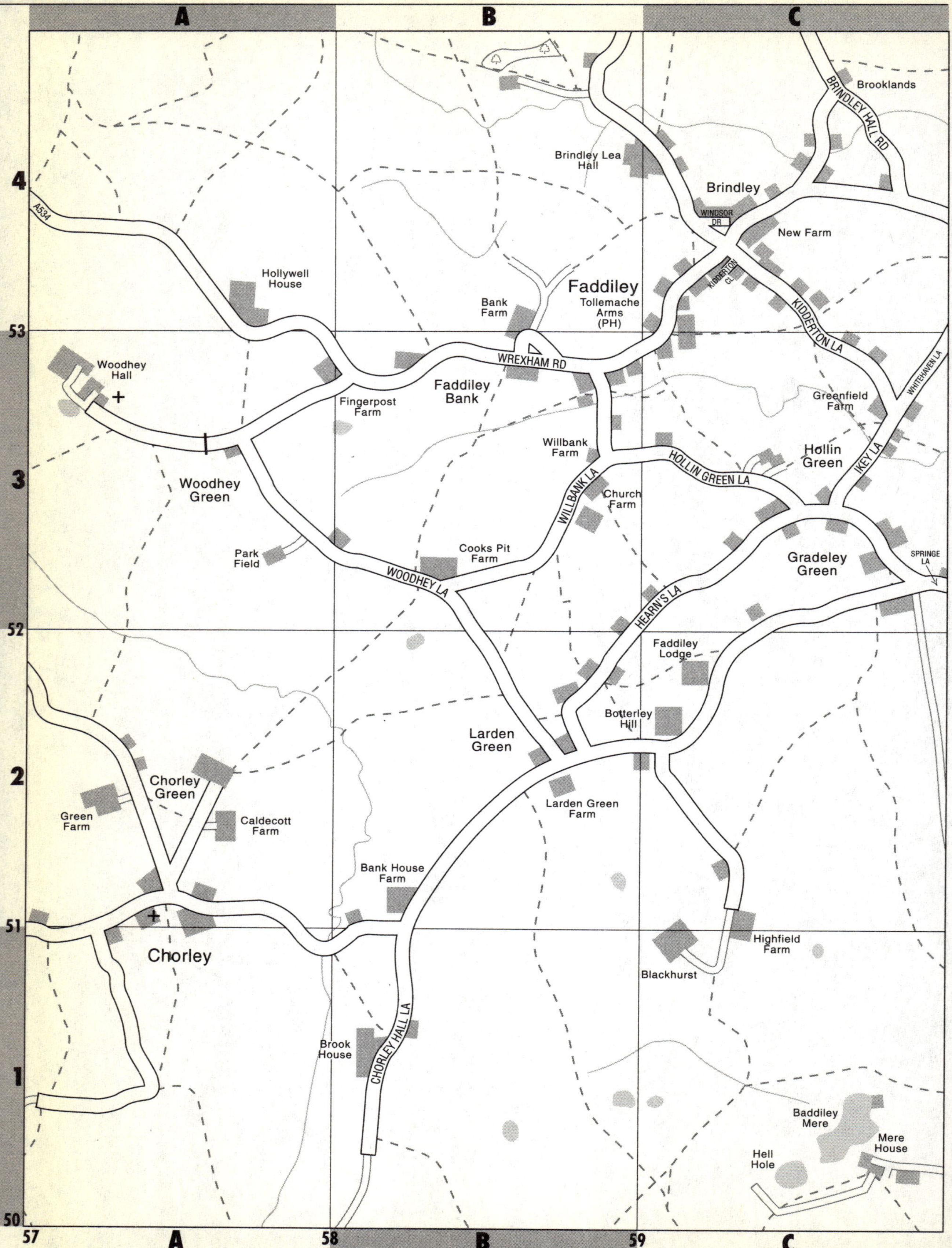

201
216

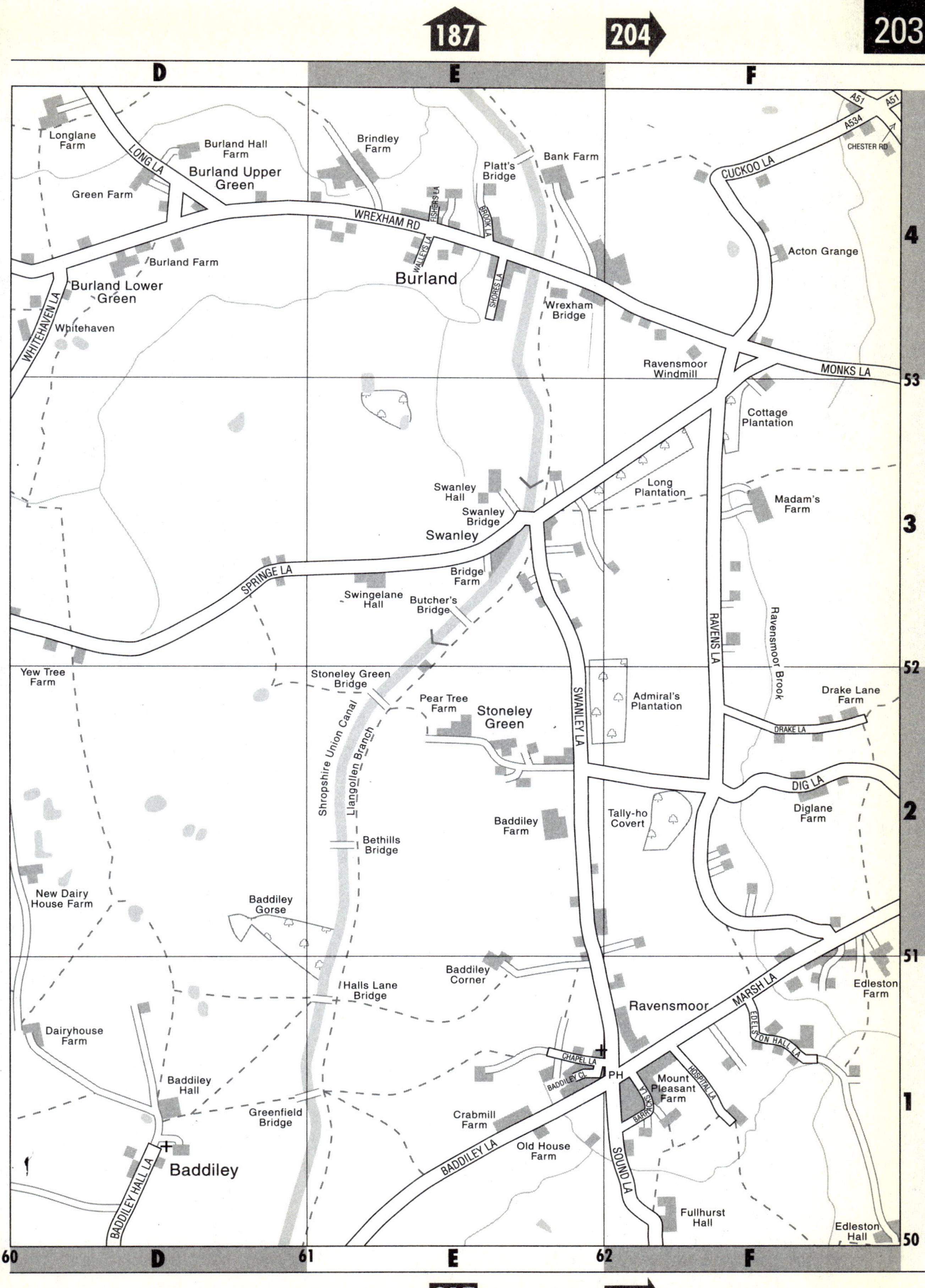
187
204
D
E
F
Longlane Farm
Burland Hall Farm
LONG LA
Burland Upper Green
Green Farm
Brindley Farm
Platt's Bridge
Bank Farm
CUCKOO LA
A51
A534
CHESTER RD
WREXHAM RD
FISHERS LA
BROOK LA
WALLEYS LA
Burland Farm
Burland Lower Green
Burland
SHORES LA
Acton Grange
4
WHITEHAVEN LA
Whitehaven
Wrexham Bridge
Ravensmoor Windmill
MONKS LA
53
Cottage Plantation
Long Plantation
Swanley Hall
Swanley Bridge
Swanley
Madam's Farm
3
SPRINGE LA
Bridge Farm
Swingelane Hall
Butcher's Bridge
RAVENS LA
Ravensmoor Brook
Yew Tree Farm
Stoneley Green Bridge
52
Pear Tree Farm
Stoneley Green
SWANLEY LA
Admiral's Plantation
Drake Lane Farm
DRAKE LA
Shropshire Union Canal
Llangollen Branch
DIG LA
Diglane Farm
Tally-ho Covert
Baddiley Farm
2
Bethills Bridge
New Dairy House Farm
Baddiley Gorse
51
Baddiley Corner
Halls Lane Bridge
Edleston Farm
Ravensmoor
MARSH LA
EDELSTON HALL LA
Dairyhouse Farm
CHAPEL LA
PH
BADDILEY CL
Mount Pleasant Farm
HOSPITAL LA
BARRACKS LA
Baddiley Hall
1
Greenfield Bridge
Crabmill Farm
Old House Farm
BADDILEY LA
BADDILEY HALL LA
Baddiley
SOUND LA
Fullhurst Hall
Edleston Hall
50
60
61
62
217
204

203
188

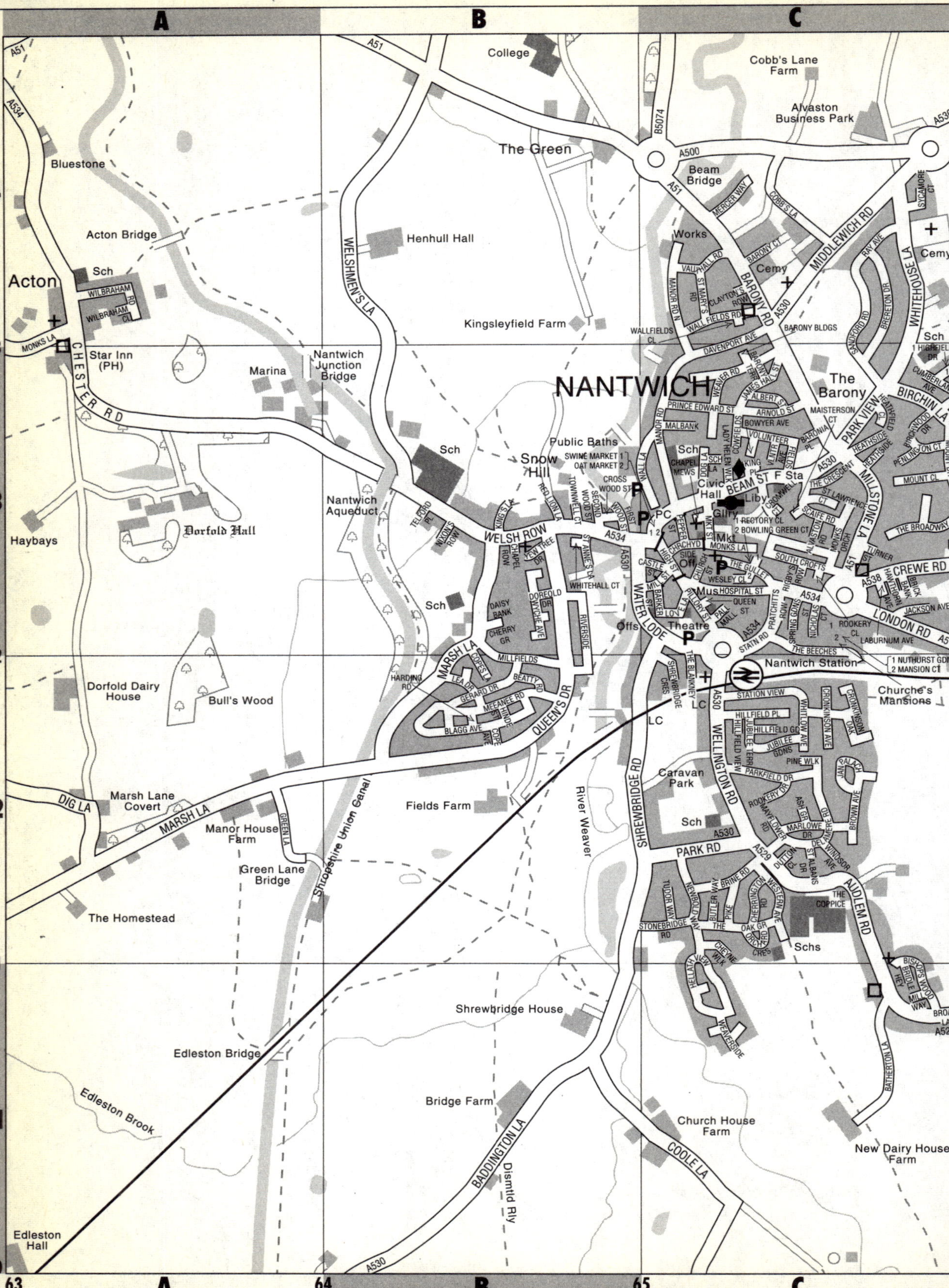
A
B
C
NANTWICH
Acton
Bluestone
Acton Bridge
Sch
Star Inn (PH)
CHESTER RD
MONKS LA
WILBRAHAM RD
Haybays
Dorfold Hall
Marina
Nantwich Junction Bridge
Nantwich Aqueduct
Dorfold Dairy House
Bull's Wood
Marsh Lane Covert
DIG LA
MARSH LA
Manor House Farm
GREEN LA
Green Lane Bridge
Shropshire Union Canal
The Homestead
Edleston Bridge
Edleston Brook
Edleston Hall
College
The Green
Henhull Hall
WELSHMEN'S LA
Kingsleyfield Farm
Sch
Public Baths
Snow Hill
WELSH ROW
Fields Farm
River Weaver
Shrewbridge House
Bridge Farm
BADDINGTON LA
Dismtld Rly
A530
A51
A534
A500
B5074
Cobb's Lane Farm
Alvaston Business Park
Beam Bridge
Works
Cemy
BARONY RD
MIDDLEWICH RD
WHITEHOUSE LA
The Barony
PARK VIEW
BIRCHIN LA
MILLSTONE LA
CREWE RD
LONDON RD
Civic Hall
BEAM ST
F Sta
Liby
Glfry
Mkt
Mus
Theatre
Offs
WATER LODE
Nantwich Station
Church's Mansions
SHREWBRIDGE RD
WELLINGTON RD
Caravan Park
Sch
PARK RD
AUDLEM RD
Schs
THE COPPICE
COOLE LA
Church House Farm
New Dairy House Farm
BATHERTON LA
A529
A538
LC
63
64
65
50
51
52
53
4
3
2
1

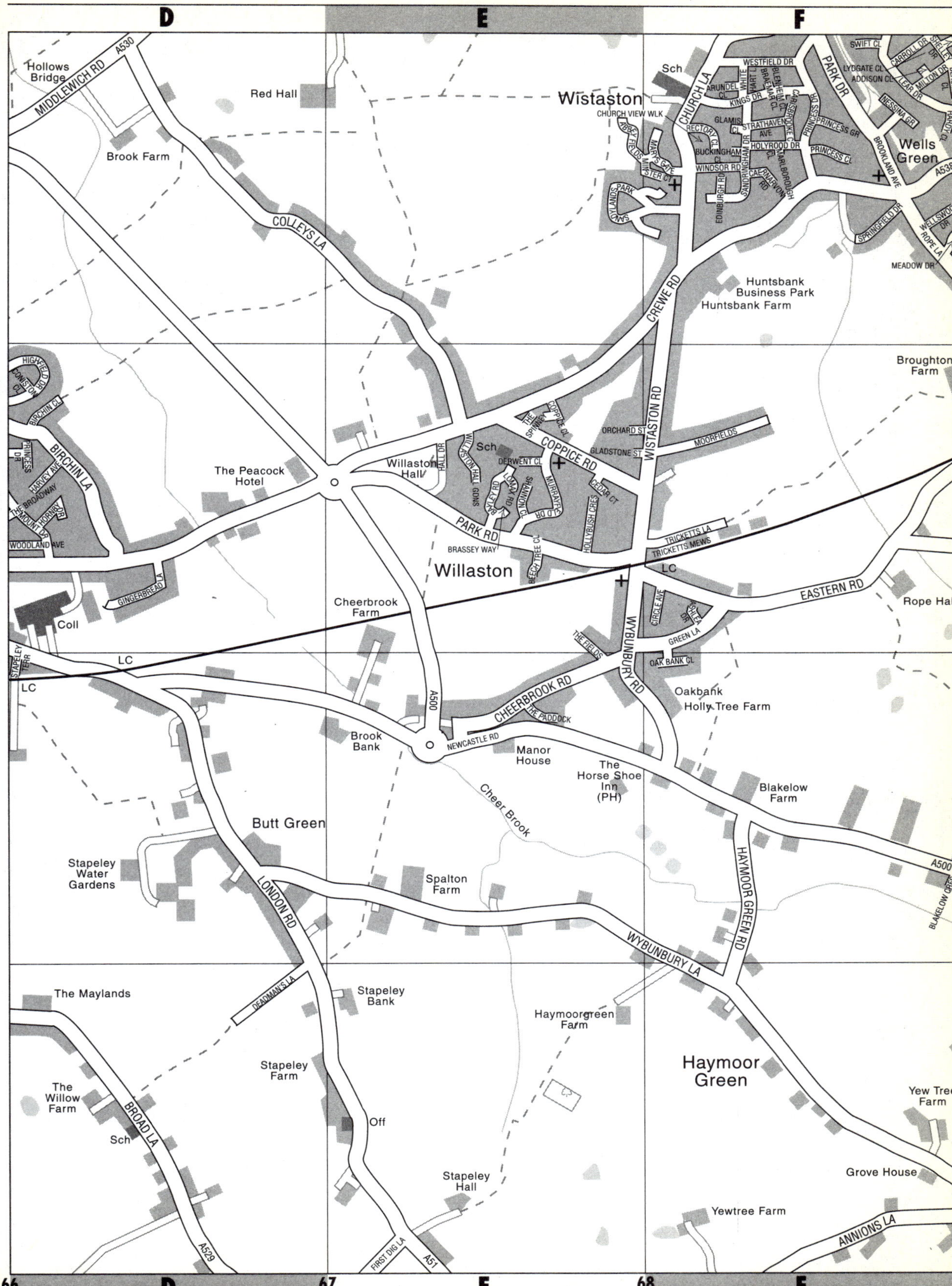
D
E
F
Hollows Bridge
MIDDLEWICH RD
A530
Red Hall
Brook Farm
COLLEYS LA
Sch
Wistaston
CHURCH LA
CHURCH VIEW WLK
WESTFIELD DR
KINGS DR
ARUNDEL CL
GLAMIS CL
STRATHAVEN AVE
HOLYROOD DR
BUCKINGHAM CL
WINDSOR RD
EDINBURGH RD
SANDRINGHAM DR
MARLBOROUGH
PRINCESS DR
PRINCESS GR
PRINCESS CL
PARK DR
SWIFT CL
LYDGATE CL
ADDISON CL
CARROLL DR
MILTON DR
BEAUMONT
NESSINA GR
HARDY CL
BROOKLAND AVE
Wells Green
A538
SPRINGFIELD DR
WELLSWOOD DR
ROPE LA
MEADOW DR
Huntsbank Business Park
Huntsbank Farm
CREWE RD
53
Broughton Farm
HIGHFIELD DR
CONISTON CL
BIRCHIN CL
BIRCHIN LA
PRINCESS DR
HARVEY AVE
THE BROADWAY
HORNBY DR
MOUNT DR
WOODLAND AVE
The Peacock Hotel
Willaston Hall
HALL DR
Sch
THE SPINNEY
COPPICE CL
COPPICE RD
DERWENT CL
ORCHARD ST
GLADSTONE ST
MOORFIELDS
WISTASTON RD
WILLASTON HALL GDNS
MURRAYFIELD DR
SHANNON CL
CEDAR CT
HOLLYBUSH CRES
PARK RD
BRASSEY WAY
BEECH TREE CL
Willaston
TRICKETTS LA
TRICKETTS MEWS
LC
3
EASTERN RD
Rope Hall
GINGERBREAD LA
Cheerbrook Farm
Coll
CIRCLE AVE
GREEN LA
THE FIELDS
OAK BANK CL
WYBUNBURY RD
STAPELEY TERR
LC
LC
52
Oakbank
Holly Tree Farm
A500
CHEERBROOK RD
THE PADDOCK
Brook Bank
NEWCASTLE RD
Manor House
The Horse Shoe Inn (PH)
Blakelow Farm
Cheer Brook
Butt Green
2
Stapeley Water Gardens
LONDON RD
Spalton Farm
HAYMOOR GREEN RD
A500
BLAKELOW CRES
WYBUNBURY LA
51
The Maylands
DEADMAN'S LA
Stapeley Bank
Haymoorgreen Farm
Haymoor Green
Stapeley Farm
The Willow Farm
BROAD LA
Sch
Off
Yew Tree Farm
1
Stapeley Hall
Grove House
Yewtree Farm
ANNIONS LA
A529
FIRST DIG LA
A51
50
66
67
68
D
E
F

205
190

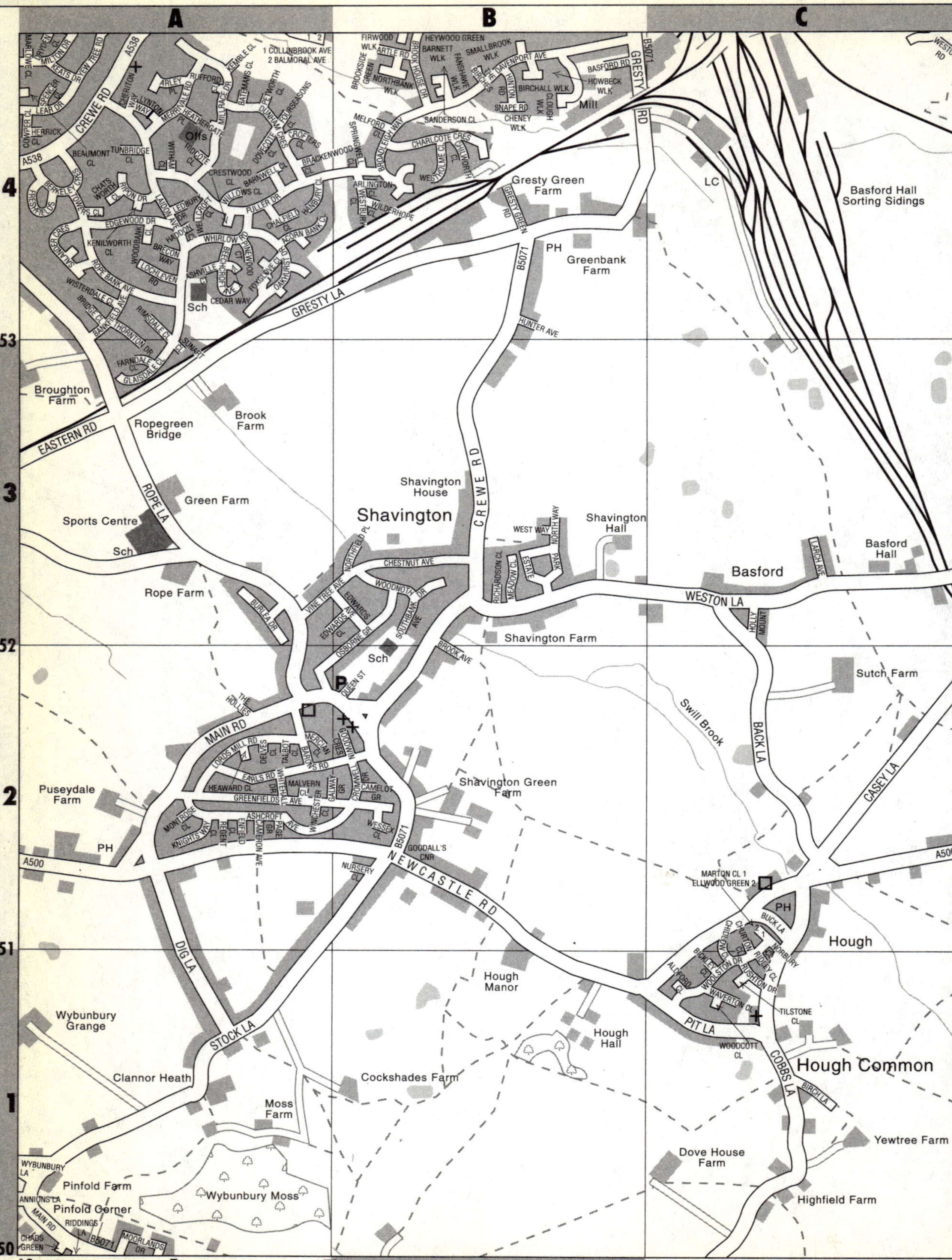
A
B
C
4
53
3
52
2
51
1
50
69
70
71
Basford Hall Sorting Sidings
Gresty Green Farm
Greenbank Farm
PH
LC
GRESTY RD
B5071
GRESTY LA
CREWE RD
A538
EASTERN RD
HUNTER AVE
Broughton Farm
Ropegreen Bridge
Brook Farm
ROPE LA
Green Farm
Sports Centre
Sch
Rope Farm
Shavington House
Shavington
Shavington Hall
Basford Hall
Basford
WESTON LA
CHESTNUT AVE
WEST WAY
NORTH WAY
Shavington Farm
BROOK AVE
Sutch Farm
Swill Brook
BACK LA
CASEY LA
MAIN RD
Puseydale Farm
Shavington Green Farm
PH
A500
GOODALL'S CNR
NEWCASTLE RD
NURSERY CL
MARTON CL 1
ELLWOOD GREEN 2
Hough
Hough Manor
Hough Hall
PIT LA
COBBS LA
Hough Common
BIRCH LA
Yewtree Farm
Dove House Farm
Highfield Farm
DIG LA
STOCK LA
Wybunbury Grange
Clannor Heath
Cockshades Farm
Moss Farm
Wybunbury Moss
Pinfold Farm
Pinfold Corner
WYBUNBURY LA
ANNIONS LA
MAIN RD
RIDDINGS LA
CHADS GREEN
B5071
MOORLANDS DR
Mill
Offs
Sch
P
WESTON RD

191
208

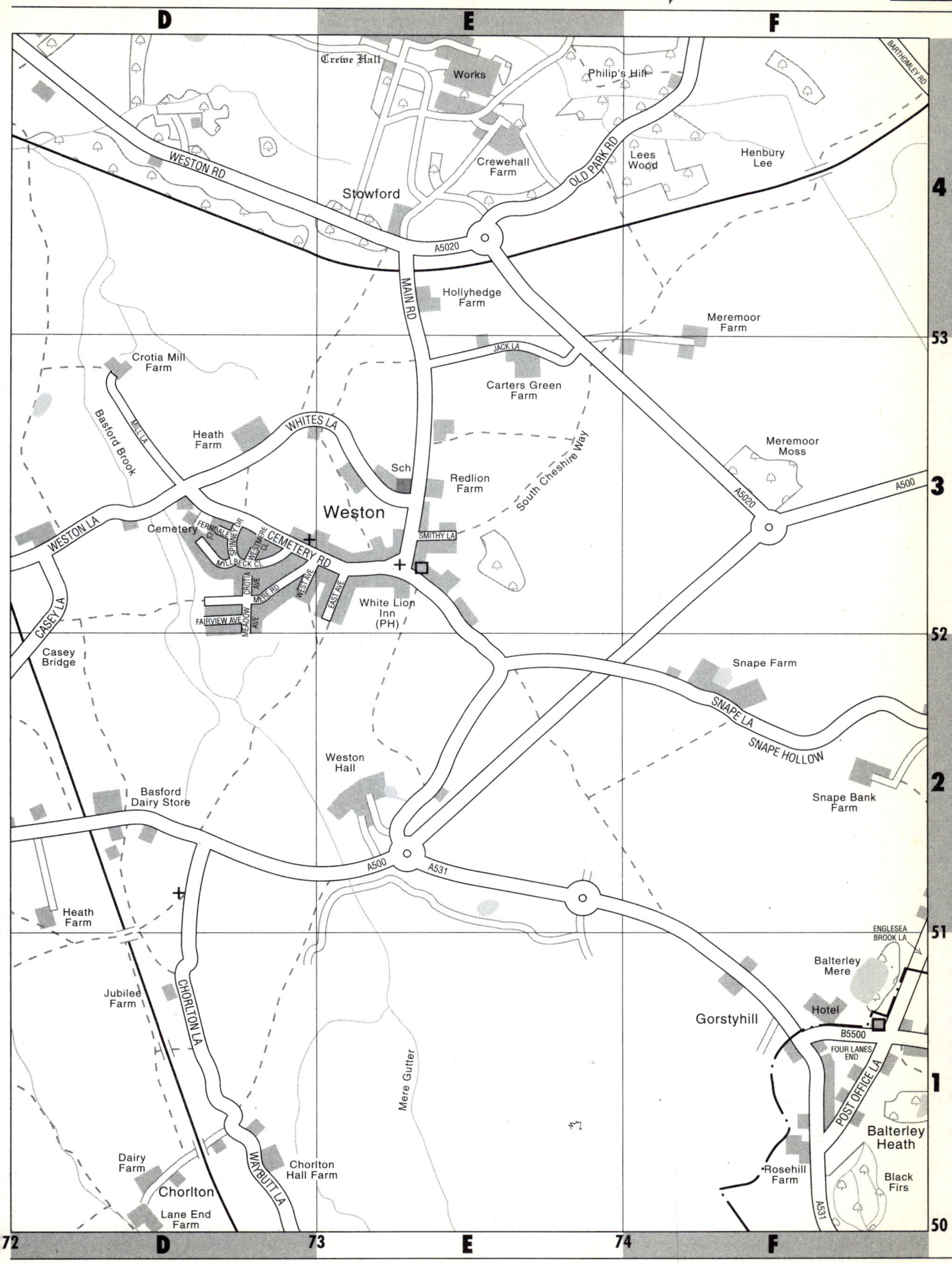

221
208

207
192

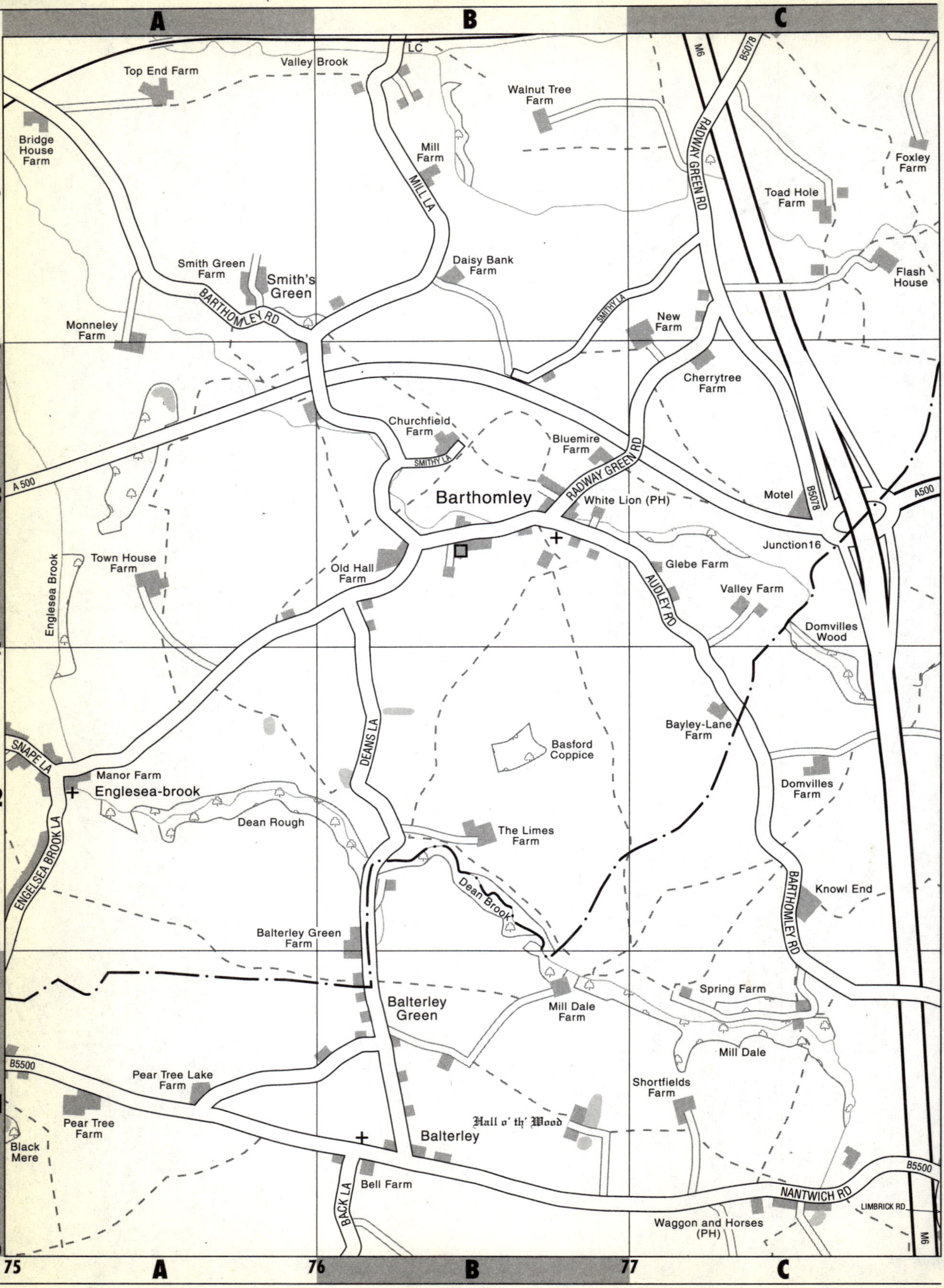
A
B
C
LC
Valley Brook
Top End Farm
Walnut Tree Farm
M6
B5078
Bridge House Farm
Mill Farm
MILL LA
RADWAY GREEN RD
Foxley Farm
Toad Hole Farm
4
Smith Green Farm
Smith's Green
Daisy Bank Farm
Flash House
BARTHOMLEY RD
SMITHY LA
New Farm
Monneley Farm
53
Cherrytree Farm
Churchfield Farm
Bluemire Farm
SMITHY LA
RADWAY GREEN RD
A 500
3
Barthomley
White Lion (PH)
Motel
B5078
A500
Junction16
Town House Farm
Old Hall Farm
Glebe Farm
Englesea Brook
AUDLEY RD
Valley Farm
Domvilles Wood
52
Bayley-Lane Farm
SNAPE LA
Basford Coppice
DEANS LA
Manor Farm
Englesea-brook
Domvilles Farm
2
Dean Rough
The Limes Farm
ENGELSEA BROOK LA
Dean Brook
Knowl End
BARTHOMLEY RD
Balterley Green Farm
51
Spring Farm
Balterley Green
Mill Dale Farm
Mill Dale
B5500
Pear Tree Lake Farm
Shortfields Farm
1
Pear Tree Farm
Hall o' th' Wood
Black Mere
Balterley
B5500
Bell Farm
BACK LA
NANTWICH RD
LIMBRICK RD
Waggon and Horses (PH)
M6
50
75
A
76
B
77
C

207

193

210

D
E
F
Bank Top
AUDLEY RD
4
Lower Foxley
Mosshouse
Foxley
EARDLEYEND RD
Foxley Drumble
Foxley Gorse
Foxley Farm
53
Brockwood Hill Farm
High Foxley Farm
Wrench's Coppice
Eardleyend
Park Manor Farm
3
ALSAGER RD
Eardley Hall
Brockwood Hill
The Fields
Millend
MILLEND LA
HULLOCK'S POOL RD
CROSS LA
A500
Cress Farm
52
Brook Farm
Hullock's Pool
Pool House
Wks
Great Oak Farm
Park Lane Farm
Yewtree Farm
New Farm
GREATOAK RD
Park End
PARK LA
2
Park Farm
Townhouse
BIGNALL END RD
Moat Farm
Pear Tree Farm
EDWARD ST
RAVENS CL
Sch
ALBERT ST
WOOD ST
DIGLAKE ST
Bignall End
Firs Farm
MOAT LA
OLD RD
CHAPEL ST
PC
B5500
RAVEN'S LA
HOPE ST
TIBB ST
NEW RD
WATLANDS RD
BENJAMINS WAY
51
New Peel Farm
WILBRAHAM'S WLK
CHURCH BANK
MCKELLIN CL
RILEYS WAY
GEORGES WAY
IKINS DR
BOYLES HALL RD
GRESLEY WAY
BRIDGE CT
Kent Hill Farm
Liby
WESTLANDS
AARONS DR
BOUGHEY RD
DEAN HOLLOW
Audley
CHESTER RD
CHURCH ST
GREENWAYS
FAIRFIELDS
MONUMENT VIEW
BARTHOMLEY RD
CHAPEL LA
HALL ST
HILL TERR
BRINDLEYS WAY
DELPHSIDE
STEPHENS WAY
The Quarry
VERNON AVE
WESTFIELD AVE
CHERRY TREE RD 1
CEDAR CRES 2
WEDGEWOOD AVE 3
MEADOWSIDE AVE
VERNON CL
1
PEEL HOLLOW
NANTWICH RD
BOOTH ST
HOUGHER WALL RD
Wereton
KELSALL WAY
DURBER CL
BIRCH RD
Old Peel Farm
NEW KING ST
PRINCESS AVE
KING ST
MELLARD ST
GRASSYGREEN LA
Dismtd Rly
BOON HILL RD
ELM TREE DR
QUEEN ST
GEORGE ST
HAWTHORNE AVE
PEAR TREE RD
B5367
Quarry New Farm
WERETON RD
MADDOCK ST
Rye Hills
Boon Hill
CARR LA
LIMBRICK RD
Shraleybrook
Greenbutts House
Ryehill Farm
RYEHILLS
Grange Farm
TOM FIELDS
Sch
50
78
D
79
E
80
F

210

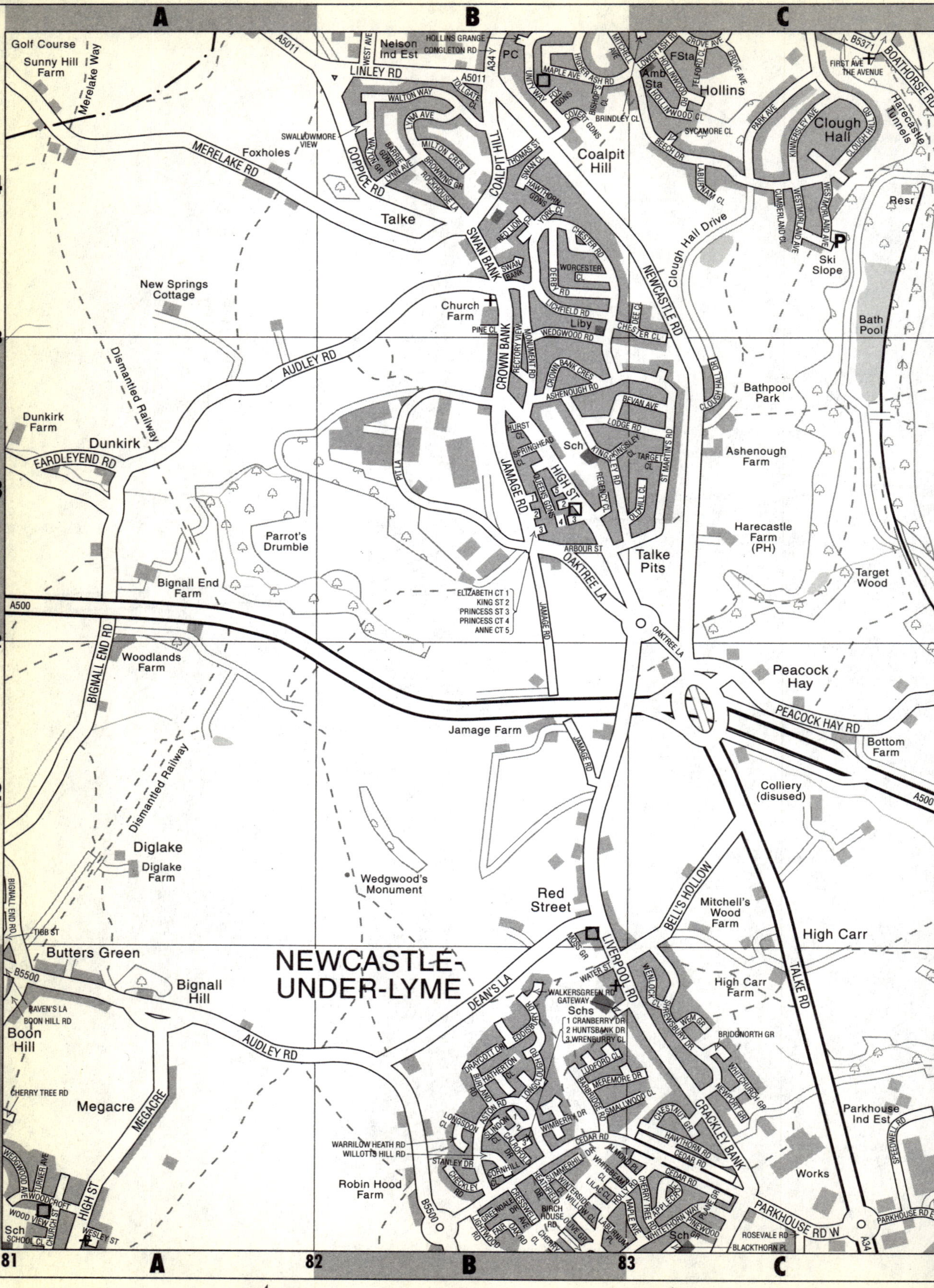
A
B
C
4
53
3
52
2
51
1
50
81
82
83
Golf Course
Sunny Hill Farm
Merelake Way
A5011
Nelson Ind Est
HOLLINS GRANGE
CONGLETON RD
A34
PC
LINLEY RD
WEST AVE
MAPLE AVE
HIGHER ASH RD
LOWER ASH RD
GROVE AVE
FSta
Amb Sta
Hollins
B5371
FIRST AVE
THE AVENUE
BOATHORSE RD
Harecastle Tunnels
Clough Hall
PARK AVE
KINNERSLEY AVE
WALTON WAY
TOLLGATE CL
LYNN AVE
SWALLOWMORE VIEW
MERELAKE RD
Foxholes
COPPICE RD
MILTON CRES
BROWNING GR
ROCKHOUSE LA
COALPIT HILL
THOMAS ST
SWAN CL
HAWTHORN GDNS
Coalpit Hill
BRINDLEY CL
COVERT GDNS
SYCAMORE CL
BEECH DR
LABURNAM CL
CUMBERLAND CL
WESTMORLAND AVE
Resr
Talke
YORK CL
RED LION CL
CHESTER RD
SWAN BANK
WORCESTER CL
DERBY RD
LICHFIELD RD
Clough Hall Drive
NEWCASTLE RD
Ski Slope
P
New Springs Cottage
Church Farm
PINE CL
Liby
DEE CL
CHESTER CL
WEDGWOOD RD
Bath Pool
CROWN BANK
RECTORY VIEW
MONUMENT RD
CROWN BANK CRES
ASHENOUGH RD
AUDLEY RD
Dismantled Railway
CLOUGH HALL DR
Bathpool Park
BEVAN AVE
LODGE RD
Dunkirk Farm
Dunkirk
EARDLEYEND RD
HURST CL
SPRINGHEAD CL
Sch
KINGSLEY CL
TARGET CL
ST MARTIN'S RD
Ashenough Farm
PIT LA
JAMAGE RD
QUEENS GDNS
HIGH ST
REGENCY CL
OLDHILL CL
Parrot's Drumble
Harecastle Farm (PH)
ARBOUR ST
Talke Pits
OAKTREE LA
Bignall End Farm
Target Wood
ELIZABETH CT 1
KING ST 2
PRINCESS ST 3
PRINCESS CT 4
ANNE CT 5
A500
BIGNALL END RD
Woodlands Farm
Peacock Hay
PEACOCK HAY RD
Jamage Farm
Bottom Farm
Colliery (disused)
Diglake
Diglake Farm
Wedgwood's Monument
Red Street
BELL'S HOLLOW
Mitchell's Wood Farm
High Carr
TIBB ST
Butters Green
NEWCASTLE-UNDER-LYME
MOSS GR
LIVERPOOL RD
WATER ST
B5500
Bignall Hill
DEAN'S LA
WALKERSGREEN RD
GATEWAY
Schs
1 CRANBERRY DR
2 HUNTSBANK DR
3 WRENBURRY CL
High Carr Farm
TALKE RD
RAVEN'S LA
BOON HILL RD
Boon Hill
WENLOCK CL
SHREWSBURY DR
WEM GR
BRIDGNORTH GR
EDDISBURY DR
DRAYCOTT DR
HATHERTON CL
BURLAND RD
LUDFORD CL
MEREMORE DR
BARBRIDGE RD
SMALLWOOD CL
WHITCHURCH GR
NEWPORT GR
CHESTNUT GR
CRACKLEY BANK
CHERRY TREE RD
Megacre
MEGACRE
LONGSDON CL
ASTON RD
SLINDON CL
WIMBERRY DR
CEDAR RD
HAWTHORN RD
Parkhouse Ind Est
SPEEDWELL RD
WARRILOW HEATH RD
WILLOTTS HILL RD
STANLEY DR
CHECKLEY RD
CORNHILL CL
SUMMERHILL DR
WINTERSIDE CL
HEATHFIELD
WHITEBEAM CL
ALMOND PL
LILAC CL
CHERRY TREE RD
APPLECROFT
WHITETHORN WAY
PINEWOOD
PLANE GR
Works
Robin Hood Farm
B5500
GREENDALE DR
GRESSWELL RD
BIRCH HOUSE RD
LABURNUM PL
MAPLE AVE
HOLLY RD
Sch
ROSEVALE RD
BLACKTHORN PL
PARKHOUSE RD W
PARKHOUSE RD E
A34
WEDGWOOD AVE
TURNER AVE
WOODCROFT
WOOD VIEW
CHURCH ST
HIGH ST
Sch
SCHOOL CL
WESLEY ST

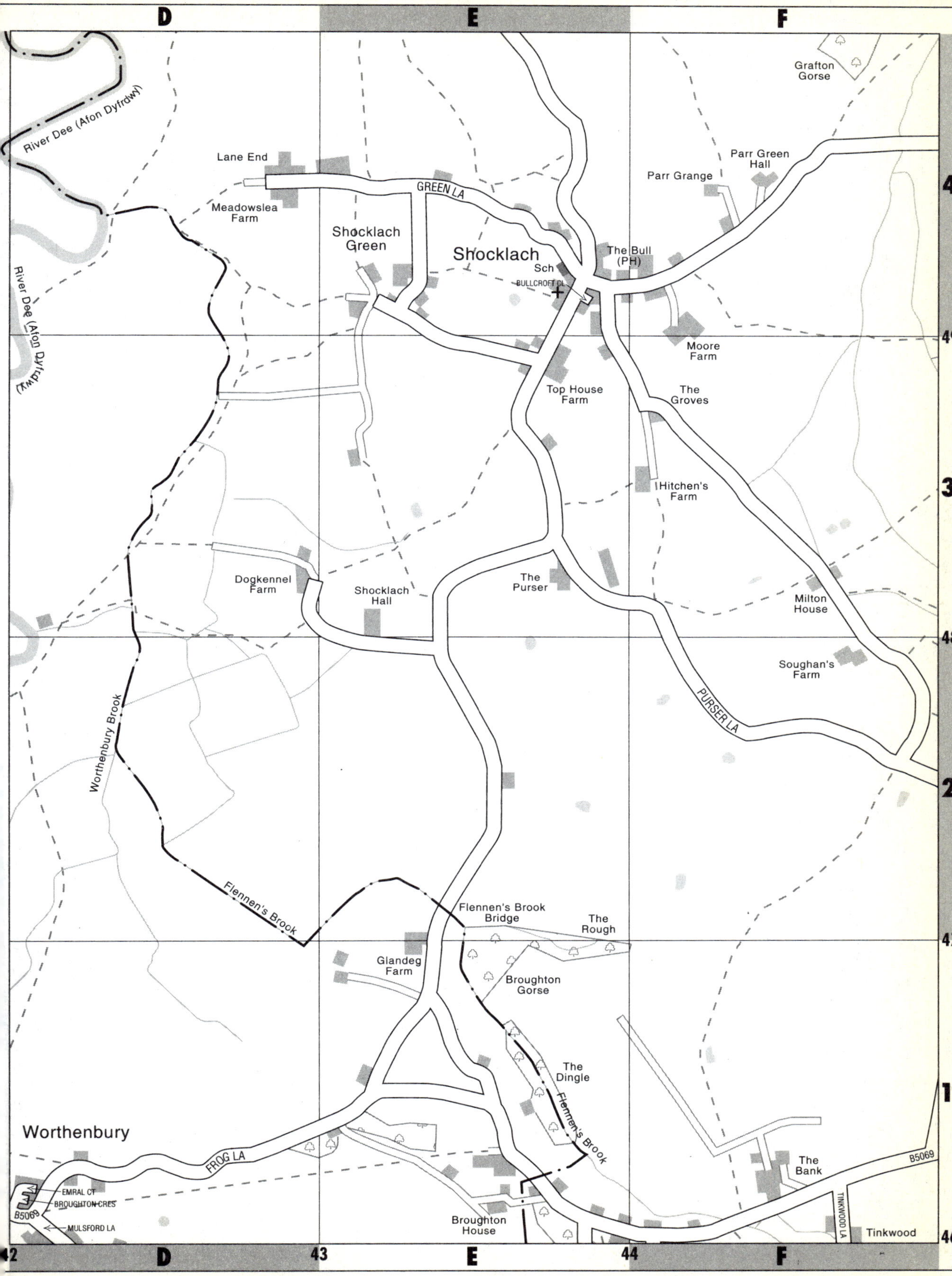
D
E
F
River Dee (Afon Dyfrdwy)
Grafton Gorse
Parr Green Hall
Parr Grange
Lane End
GREEN LA
Meadowslea Farm
Shocklach Green
Shocklach
Sch
BULLCROFT CL
The Bull (PH)
Moore Farm
Top House Farm
The Groves
Hitchen's Farm
The Purser
Dogkennel Farm
Shocklach Hall
Milton House
Soughan's Farm
PURSER LA
Worthenbury Brook
Flennen's Brook
Flennen's Brook Bridge
The Rough
Glandeg Farm
Broughton Gorse
The Dingle
Worthenbury
FROG LA
EMRAL CT
BROUGHTON CRES
B5069
MULSFORD LA
Broughton House
The Bank
TINKWOOD LA
Tinkwood
4
49
3
48
2
47
1
46
42
43
44

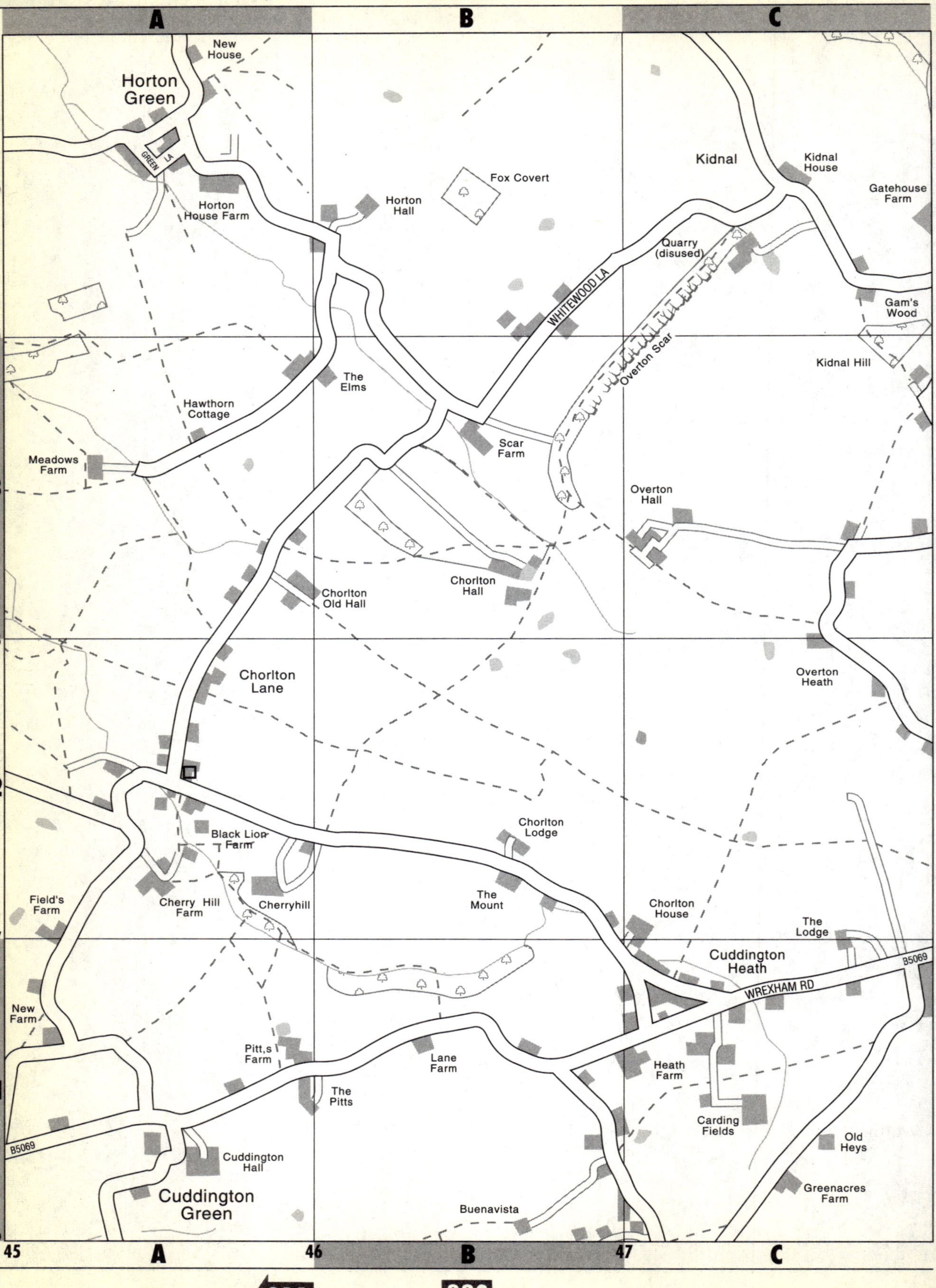
A
B
C
New House
Horton Green
GREEN LA
Horton House Farm
Horton Hall
Fox Covert
Kidnal
Kidnal House
Gatehouse Farm
Quarry (disused)
WHITEWOOD LA
Gam's Wood
Overton Scar
Kidnal Hill
The Elms
Hawthorn Cottage
Meadows Farm
Scar Farm
Overton Hall
Chorlton Hall
Chorlton Old Hall
Chorlton Lane
Overton Heath
Chorlton Lodge
Black Lion Farm
The Mount
Field's Farm
Cherry Hill Farm
Cherryhill
Chorlton House
The Lodge
Cuddington Heath
B5069
WREXHAM RD
New Farm
Pitt,s Farm
Lane Farm
Heath Farm
The Pitts
Carding Fields
Old Heys
B5069
Cuddington Hall
Greenacres Farm
Cuddington Green
Buenavista
4
49
3
48
2
47
1
46
45
46
47

199
214

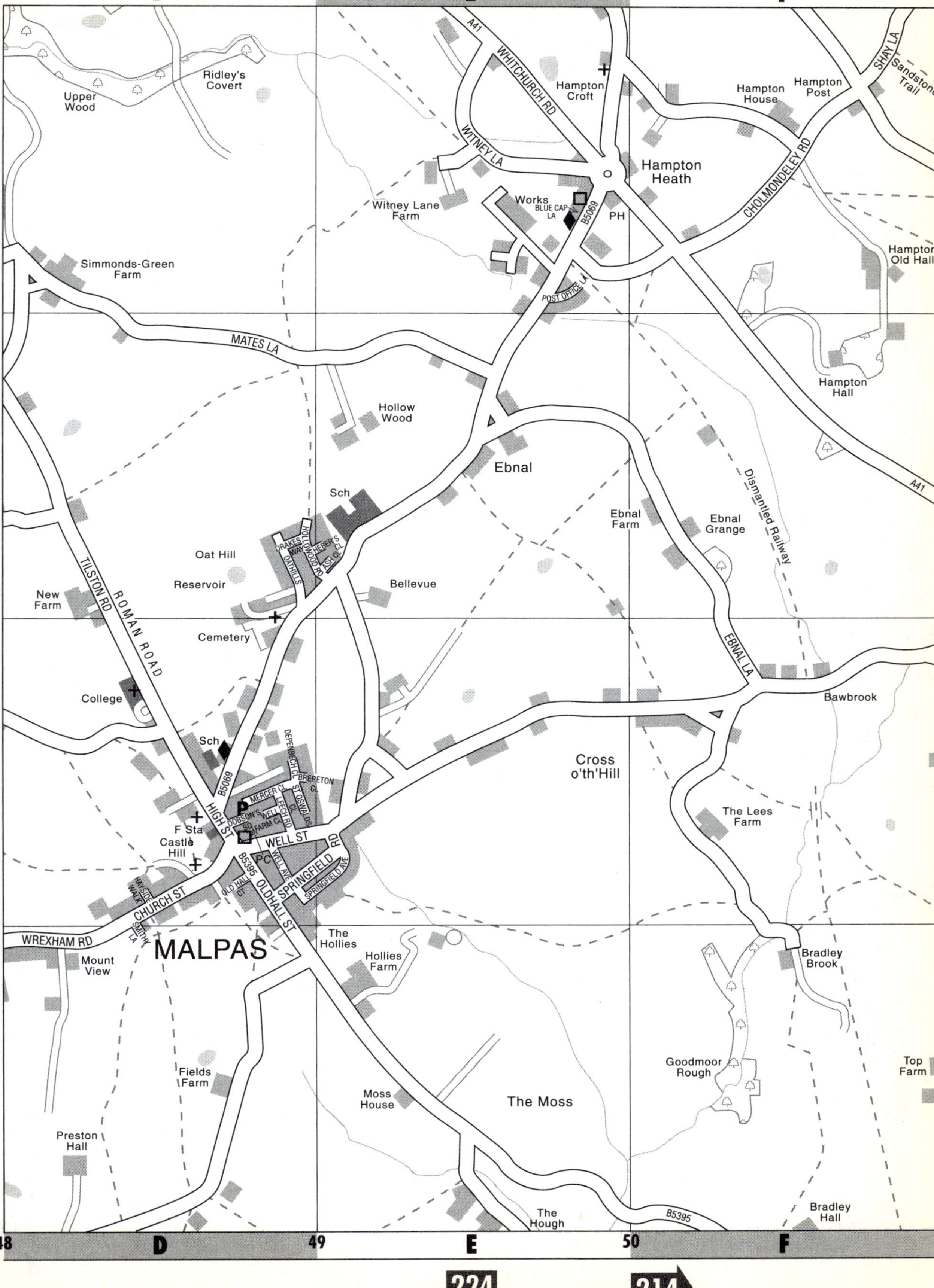

224
214

213
200

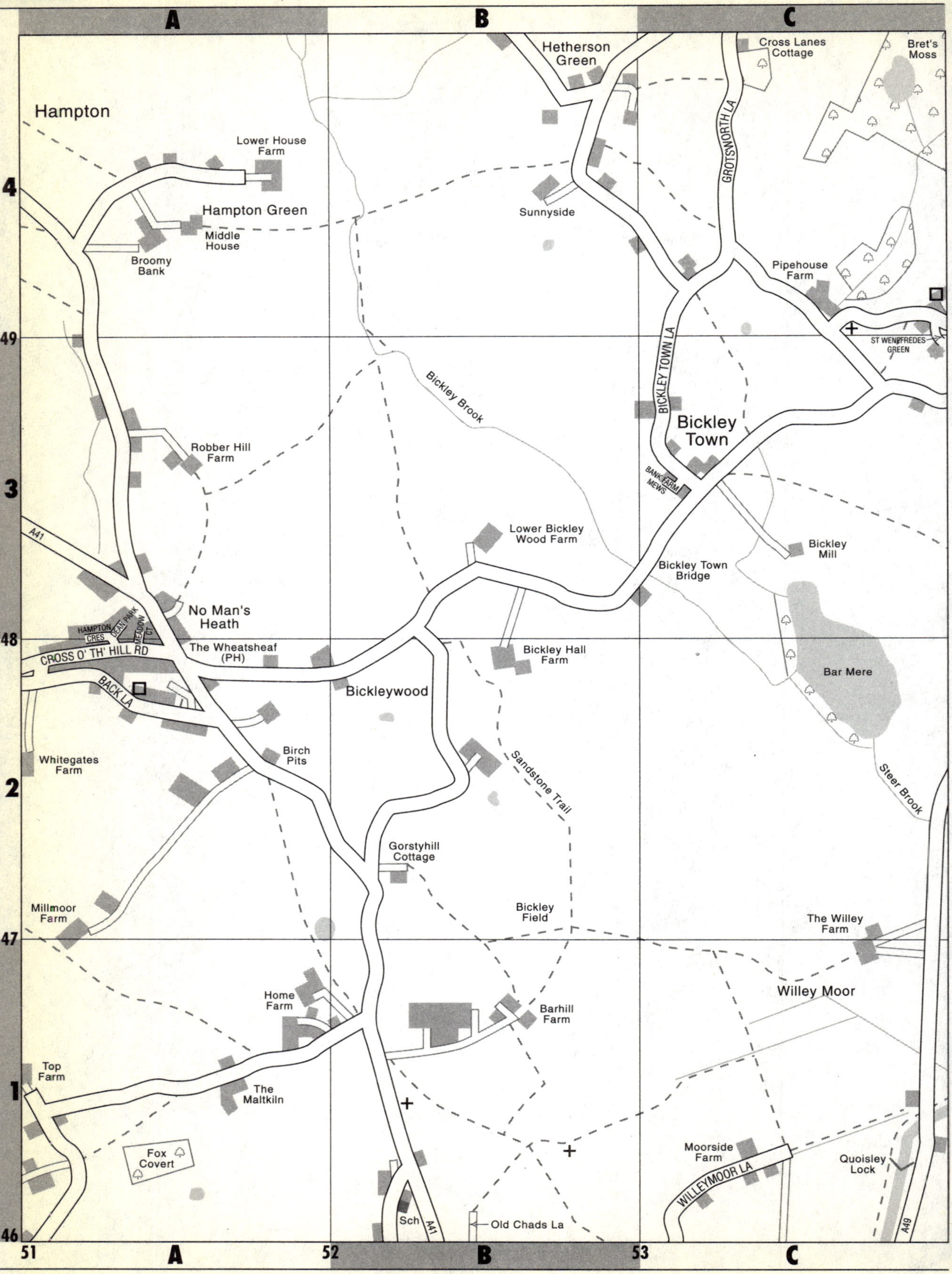
A
B
C
Hetherson Green
Cross Lanes Cottage
Bret's Moss
Hampton
Lower House Farm
GROTSWORTH LA
Hampton Green
Sunnyside
Middle House
Broomy Bank
Pipehouse Farm
ST WENEFREDES GREEN
BICKLEY TOWN LA
Bickley Brook
Bickley Town
Robber Hill Farm
BANK FARM MEWS
A41
Lower Bickley Wood Farm
Bickley Mill
Bickley Town Bridge
No Man's Heath
HAMPTON CRES
DEAN PARK
MEADOW CT
The Wheatsheaf (PH)
CROSS O' TH' HILL RD
Bickley Hall Farm
Bar Mere
BACK LA
Bickleywood
Birch Pits
Whitegates Farm
Sandstone Trail
Steer Brook
Gorstyhill Cottage
Millmoor Farm
Bickley Field
The Willey Farm
Willey Moor
Home Farm
Barhill Farm
Top Farm
The Maltkiln
Fox Covert
Moorside Farm
WILLEYMOOR LA
Quoisley Lock
Sch
A41
Old Chads La
A49
4
49
3
48
2
47
1
46
51
52
53

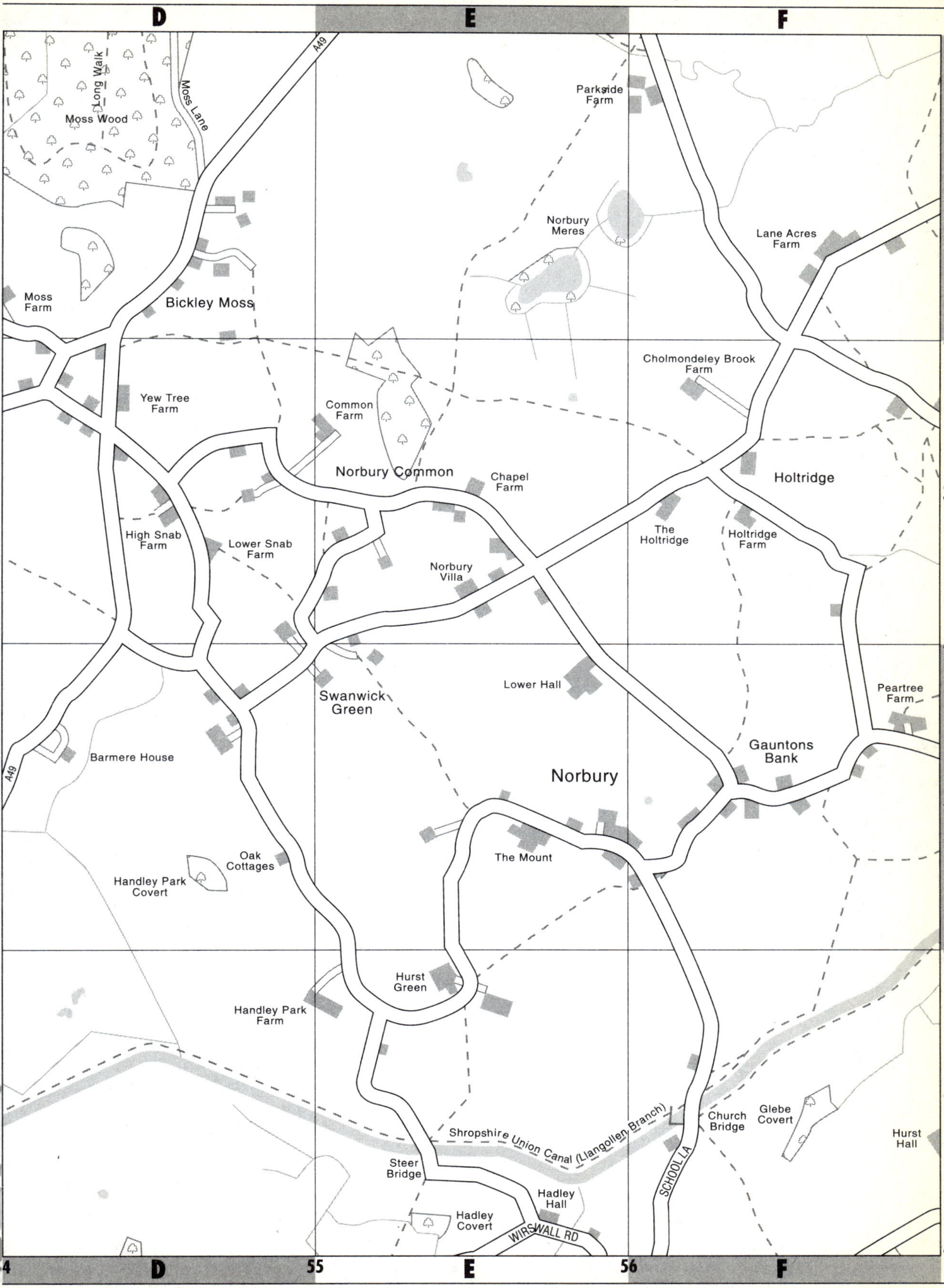
D
E
F
A49
Long Walk
Moss Lane
Moss Wood
Parkside Farm
Norbury Meres
Lane Acres Farm
Moss Farm
Bickley Moss
Cholmondeley Brook Farm
Yew Tree Farm
Common Farm
Norbury Common
Chapel Farm
Holtridge
High Snab Farm
Lower Snab Farm
The Holtridge
Holtridge Farm
Norbury Villa
Lower Hall
Swanwick Green
Peartree Farm
Barmere House
Gauntons Bank
Norbury
A49
The Mount
Oak Cottages
Handley Park Covert
Hurst Green
Handley Park Farm
Shropshire Union Canal (Llangollen Branch)
Church Bridge
Glebe Covert
Hurst Hall
Steer Bridge
SCHOOL LA
Hadley Hall
Hadley Covert
WIRSWALL RD
4
49
3
48
2
47
1
46
4
D
55
E
56
F

215
202

A
B
C
4
49
3
48
2
47
1
46
57
58
59
Chorley Hall
Baddiley Resr
Wrenbury Wood
Frith Green Farm
Frith Farm
New Covert
Wrenburywood
Sprostonwood Farm
Bank Farm
Ivy House Farm
The Heald
Heald Covert
Wrenbury Hall
Sprostonwood House
Spreston Hill Farm
CHALMONDELEY RD
Wrenbury Bridge
Wrenbury Church Bridge
Starkey's Bridge
Porter's Hill
Cotton Arms (PH)
Wrenbury House
Wrenbury
Wrenbury Frith Bridge (Draw-bridge)
Frith-hall Farm
Sch
MARIE CL
NANTWICH RD
PINSLEY VIEW
SANDFIELD CT
SANDFIELD AVE
OAKFIELD AVE
OAKFIELD CL
STATION RD
Shropshire Union Canal (Llangollen Branch)
Thomason's Bridge
Ryebank
Marbury Brook
River Weaver
Sandfield House
South Cheshire Way
Smeaton Hall
Canal Covert
NEW RD
Marbury Heyes
Pinsley Green
PINSLEY GREEN RD
Smeaton Wood Farm
Hurst Hall
Townley Farm
Townley Cottage
Yew Tree Farm
Hewitt's Moss

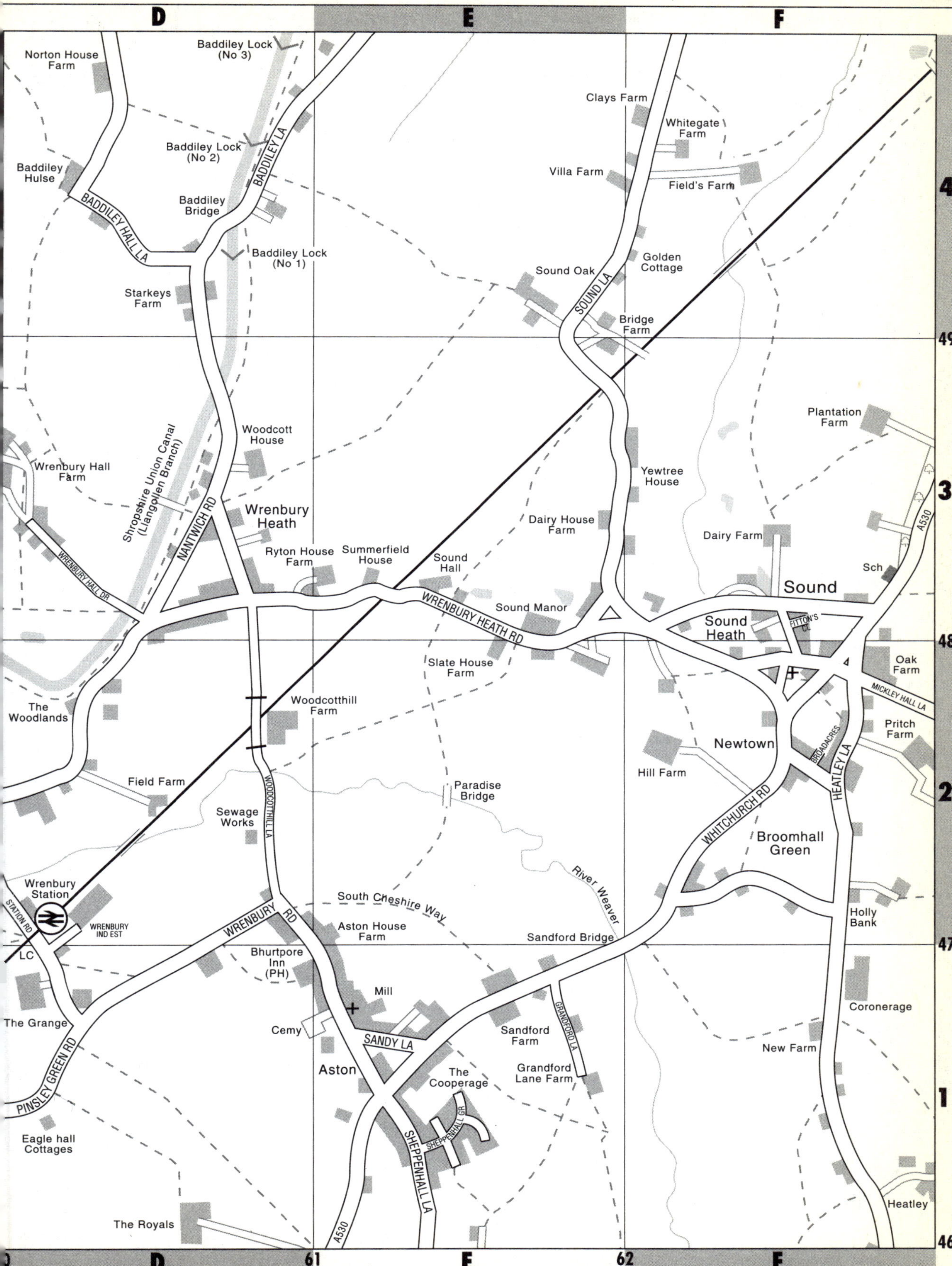
D
E
F
Norton House Farm
Baddiley Lock (No 3)
Baddiley Lock (No 2)
Baddiley Hulse
BADDILEY HALL LA
BADDILEY LA
Baddiley Bridge
Baddiley Lock (No 1)
Starkeys Farm
Clays Farm
Whitegate Farm
Villa Farm
Field's Farm
Golden Cottage
Sound Oak
SOUND LA
Bridge Farm
4
49
Plantation Farm
Woodcott House
Wrenbury Hall Farm
Shropshire Union Canal (Llangollen Branch)
NANTWICH RD
Wrenbury Heath
Yewtree House
3
Dairy House Farm
Dairy Farm
A530
WRENBURY HALL DR
Ryton House Farm
Summerfield House
Sound Hall
Sch
Sound
Sound Manor
WRENBURY HEATH RD
Sound Heath
FITTON'S CL
48
Oak Farm
Slate House Farm
MICKLEY HALL LA
The Woodlands
Woodcotthill Farm
Pritch Farm
Newtown
BROADACRES
HEATLEY LA
Hill Farm
Field Farm
Paradise Bridge
2
Sewage Works
WOODCOTTHILL LA
WHITCHURCH RD
Broomhall Green
River Weaver
Wrenbury Station
South Cheshire Way
Holly Bank
STATION RD
WRENBURY IND EST
WRENBURY RD
Aston House Farm
Sandford Bridge
47
LC
Bhurtpore Inn (PH)
Mill
GRANDFORD LA
Coronerage
The Grange
Cemy
SANDY LA
Sandford Farm
New Farm
PINSLEY GREEN RD
Aston
The Cooperage
Grandford Lane Farm
1
SHEPPENHALL GR
SHEPPENHALL LA
Eagle hall Cottages
Heatley
The Royals
A530
46
61
62

217
204

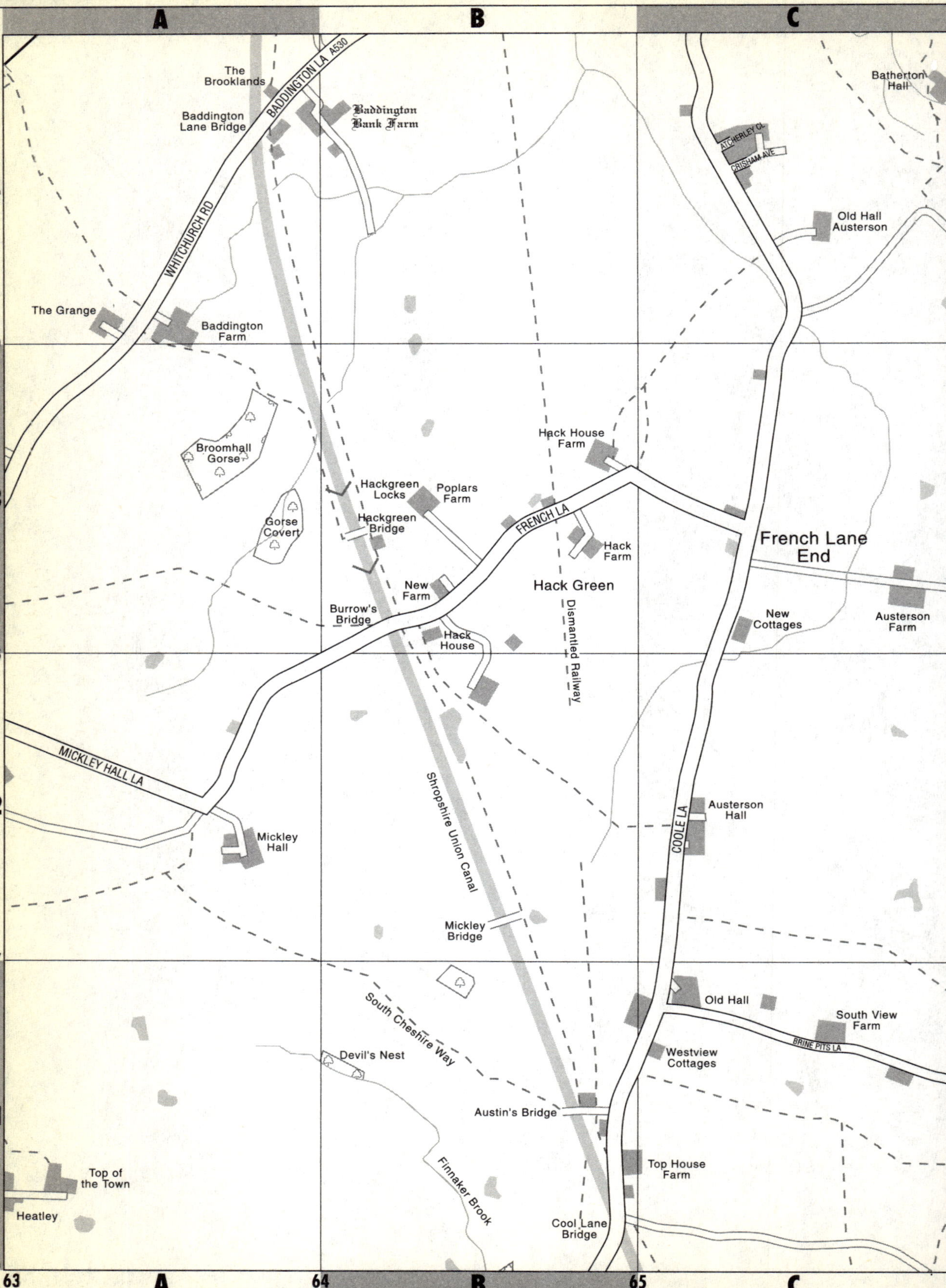

217
229

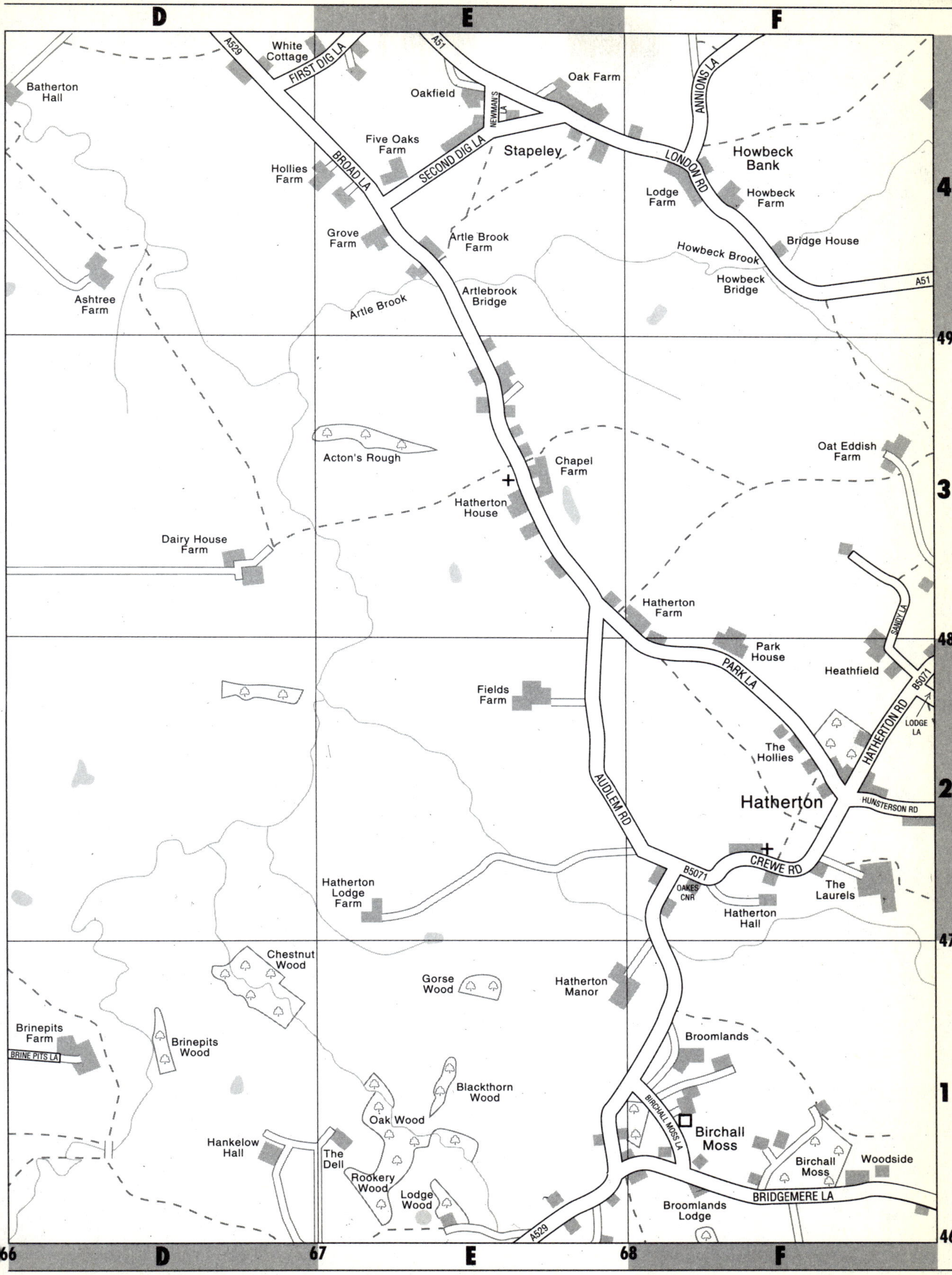
D
E
F
A529
White Cottage
FIRST DIG LA
A51
Oak Farm
ANNIONS LA
Batherton Hall
Oakfield
NEWMAN'S LA
Five Oaks Farm
SECOND DIG LA
Stapeley
LONDON RD
Howbeck Bank
Hollies Farm
BROAD LA
Lodge Farm
Howbeck Farm
4
Grove Farm
Artle Brook Farm
Howbeck Brook
Bridge House
Ashtree Farm
Artle Brook
Artlebrook Bridge
Howbeck Bridge
A51
49
Acton's Rough
Oat Eddish Farm
Chapel Farm
Hatherton House
3
Dairy House Farm
Hatherton Farm
SANDY LA
Park House
48
Heathfield
PARK LA
B5071
Fields Farm
HATHERTON RD
LODGE LA
The Hollies
AUDLEM RD
2
Hatherton
HUNSTERSON RD
CREWE RD
B5071
OAKES CNR
The Laurels
Hatherton Lodge Farm
Hatherton Hall
47
Chestnut Wood
Gorse Wood
Hatherton Manor
Brinepits Farm
Brinepits Wood
BRINE PITS LA
Broomlands
Blackthorn Wood
1
Oak Wood
BIRCHALL MOSS LA
Birchall Moss
Hankelow Hall
The Dell
Rookery Wood
Birchall Moss
Woodside
Lodge Wood
BRIDGEMERE LA
Broomlands Lodge
A529
46
66
D
67
E
68
F

219
206

219
231

207

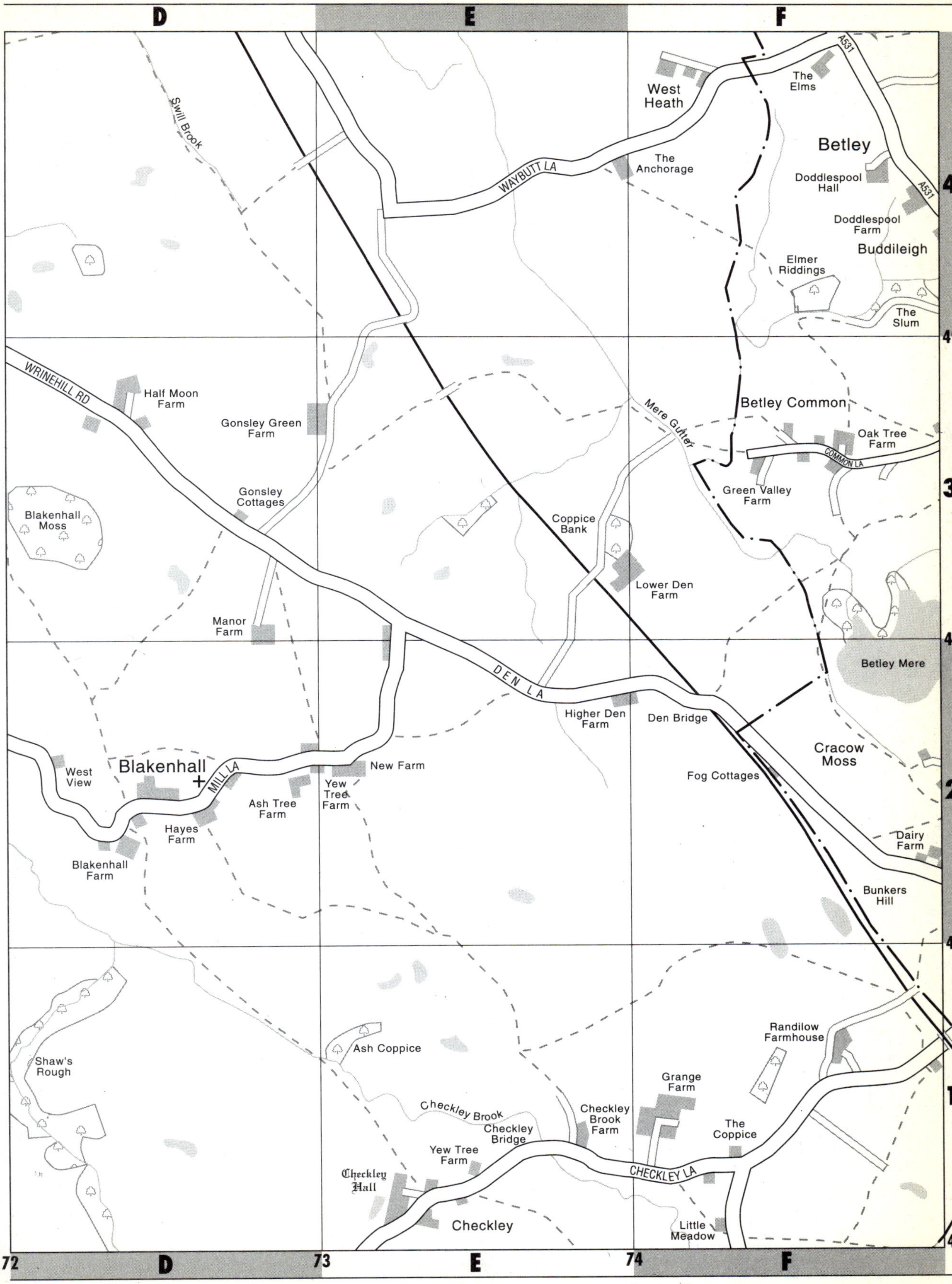

D
E
F
Swill Brook
West Heath
The Elms
A531
Betley
The Anchorage
WAYBUTT LA
Doddlespool Hall
Doddlespool Farm
Buddileigh
Elmer Riddings
The Slum
4
49
WRINEHILL RD
Half Moon Farm
Gonsley Green Farm
Mere Gutter
Betley Common
Oak Tree Farm
COMMON LA
Green Valley Farm
3
Blakenhall Moss
Gonsley Cottages
Coppice Bank
Lower Den Farm
Manor Farm
48
Betley Mere
DEN LA
Higher Den Farm
Den Bridge
Cracow Moss
West View
Blakenhall
MILL LA
New Farm
Yew Tree Farm
Ash Tree Farm
Hayes Farm
Fog Cottages
2
Dairy Farm
Blakenhall Farm
Bunkers Hill
47
Randilow Farmhouse
Ash Coppice
Shaw's Rough
Grange Farm
1
Checkley Brook
Checkley Bridge
Checkley Brook Farm
The Coppice
Yew Tree Farm
Checkley Hall
CHECKLEY LA
Checkley
Little Meadow
46
72
73
74

232

A
B
C
4
45
3
44
2
43
1
42
42
43
44
Sch
Mulsford La
Wood Farm
Chapel La
Barn Rd
Tinkwood La
Sandy La
Dog La
Topwood Farm
Back La
Middle Wood Farm
Upper Threapwood
Caenant Wood
Upper Wood Farm
Windmill (disused)
Threapwood
Emral Brook
Wych Brook
Greaves La
Turpinford Bridge
Lower Threapwood
Mulsford
Sarn Farm
Sarn Bridge
PH
Mulsford Cottage Farm
Greaves Wood
Tallarn Green
Caelica Farm
Warway
Emral Stud
Lower Tallarngreen Farm
Elk View
Cae-li-cae
Sch
The Elms
The Lane
Mulsford Hall
Tallarn Green Bridge
The Pools
Whalebone Cottage
Fields Farm
Oak Farm
Pandy Farm
Pandy Bridge
A525
Burton's Wood
Whalebone Farm
Trowstree Villa
Trowstree
Pandy
The Fields
Roger's Rough
Plassey
Willington Cross
Halghton La
Halghton Lane Farm
Willington
Rock Lane
Charity Farm
Buck Farm
Cherrytree Farm
Penley
Nell Peter's Lane
Bowen's Hall
Cai Lane
Peartree La
A525

D E F

45 D 46 E 47 F

223
213

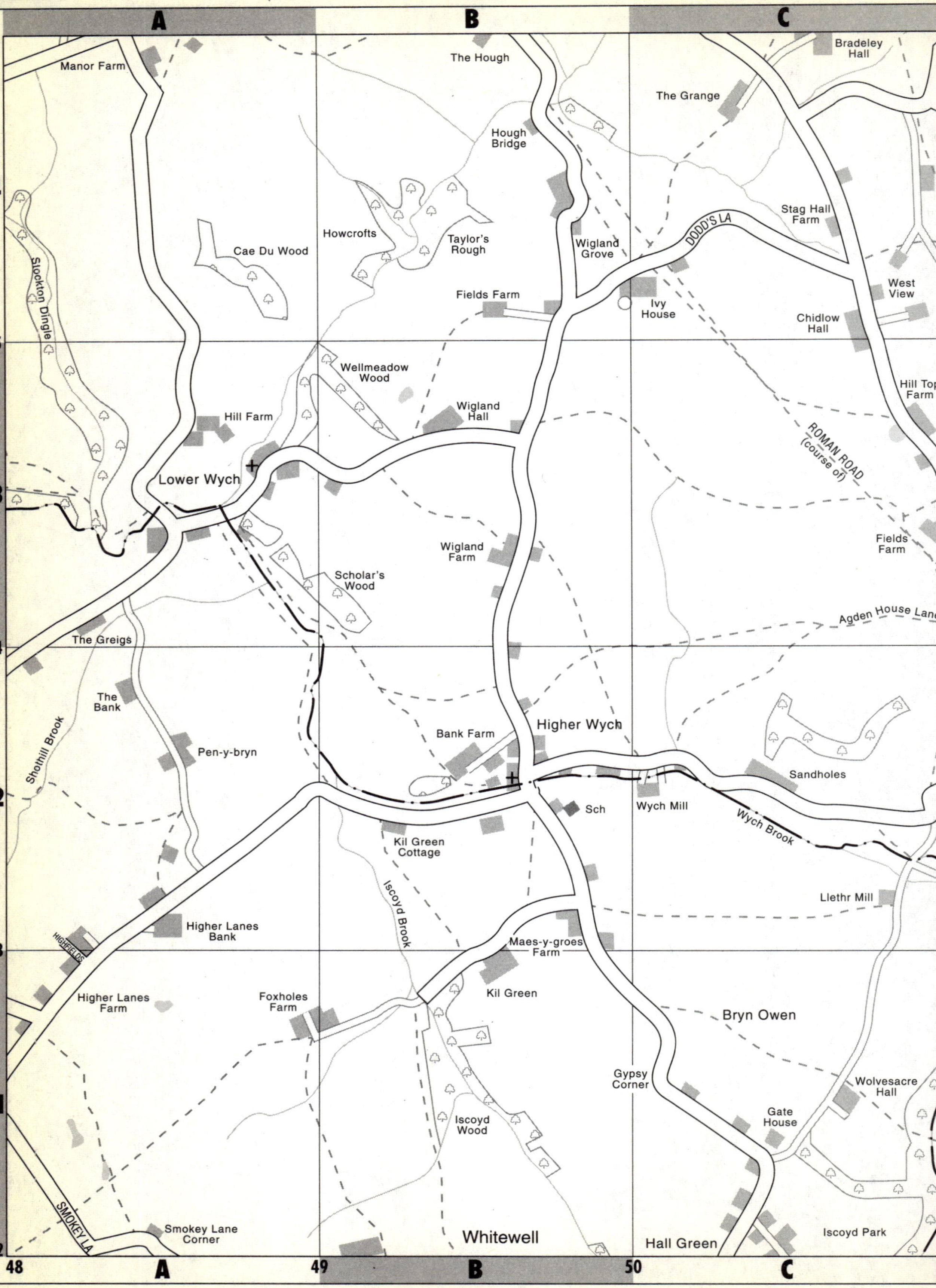
A
B
C
Manor Farm
The Hough
Bradeley Hall
The Grange
Hough Bridge
4
Stockton Dingle
Howcrofts
Cae Du Wood
Taylor's Rough
Wigland Grove
DODD'S LA
Stag Hall Farm
Fields Farm
Ivy House
West View
Chidlow Hall
45
Wellmeadow Wood
Hill Top Farm
Wigland Hall
Hill Farm
ROMAN ROAD (course of)
Lower Wych
3
Wigland Farm
Fields Farm
Scholar's Wood
Agden House Lane
The Greigs
44
The Bank
Higher Wych
Bank Farm
Shothill Brook
Pen-y-bryn
Sandholes
2
Sch
Wych Mill
Wych Brook
Kil Green Cottage
Iscoyd Brook
Llethr Mill
Higher Lanes Bank
HIGHFIELDS
Maes-y-groes Farm
43
Kil Green
Higher Lanes Farm
Foxholes Farm
Bryn Owen
Gypsy Corner
Wolvesacre Hall
1
Iscoyd Wood
Gate House
SMOKEY LA
Smokey Lane Corner
Whitewell
Hall Green
Iscoyd Park
42
48
49
50

223

214
226

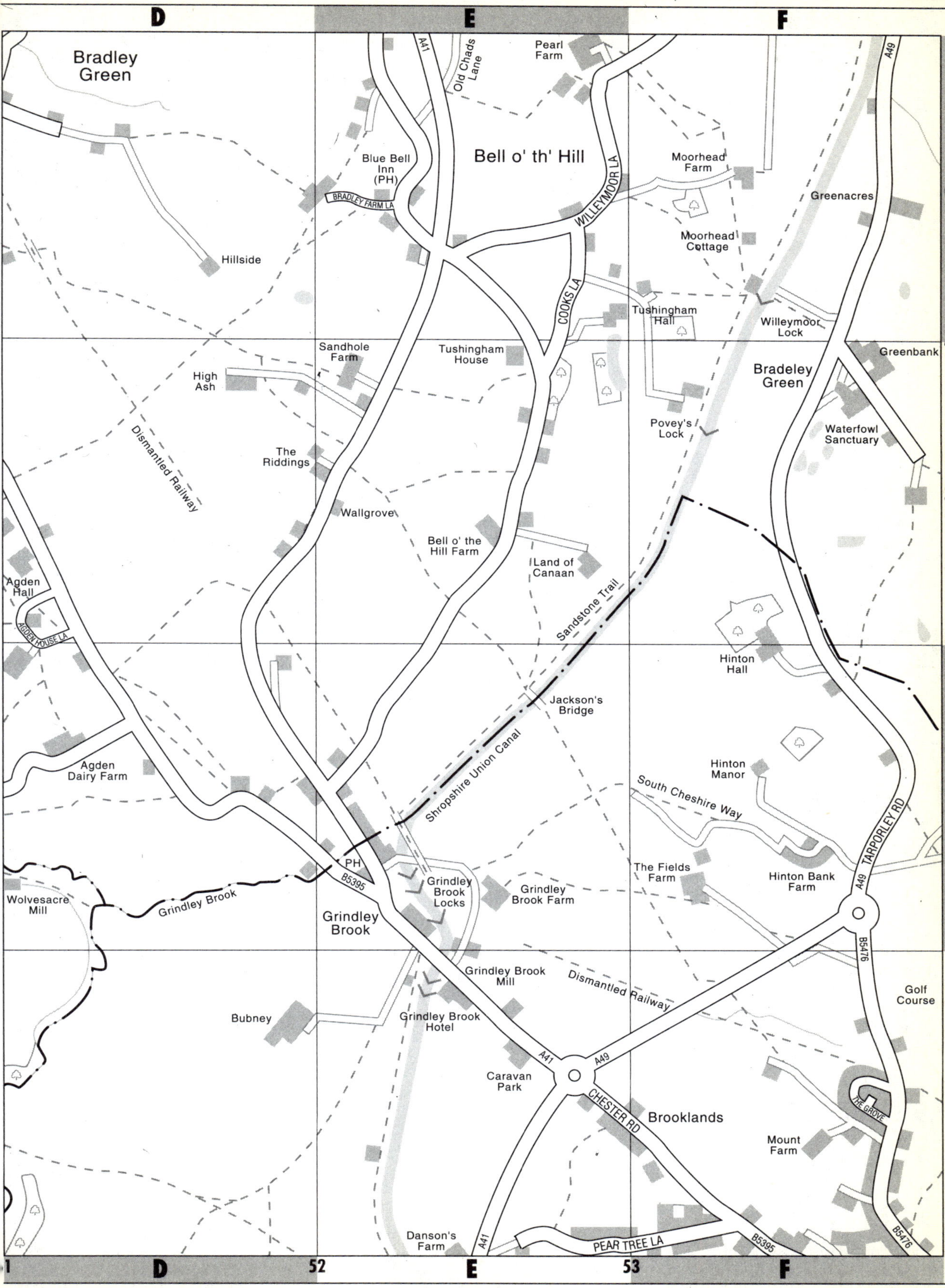
D
E
F
Bradley Green
Pearl Farm
A41
Old Chads Lane
A49
Bell o' th' Hill
Blue Bell Inn (PH)
BRADLEY FARM LA
WILLEYMOOR LA
Moorhead Farm
Greenacres
Moorhead Cottage
Hillside
COOKS LA
Tushingham Hall
Willeymoor Lock
Sandhole Farm
Tushingham House
High Ash
Greenbank
Bradeley Green
Povey's Lock
Waterfowl Sanctuary
Dismantled Railway
The Riddings
Wallgrove
Bell o' the Hill Farm
Land of Canaan
Agden Hall
AGDEN HOUSE LA
Sandstone Trail
Hinton Hall
Jackson's Bridge
Agden Dairy Farm
Shropshire Union Canal
Hinton Manor
South Cheshire Way
TARPORLEY RD
PH
B5395
Grindley Brook Locks
Grindley Brook Farm
The Fields Farm
Hinton Bank Farm
Wolvesacre Mill
Grindley Brook
Grindley Brook
B5476
Grindley Brook Mill
Dismantled Railway
Golf Course
Bubney
Grindley Brook Hotel
Caravan Park
CHESTER RD
Brooklands
THE GROVE
Mount Farm
Danson's Farm
PEAR TREE LA
4
45
3
44
2
43
1
42
52
53

226

225
215

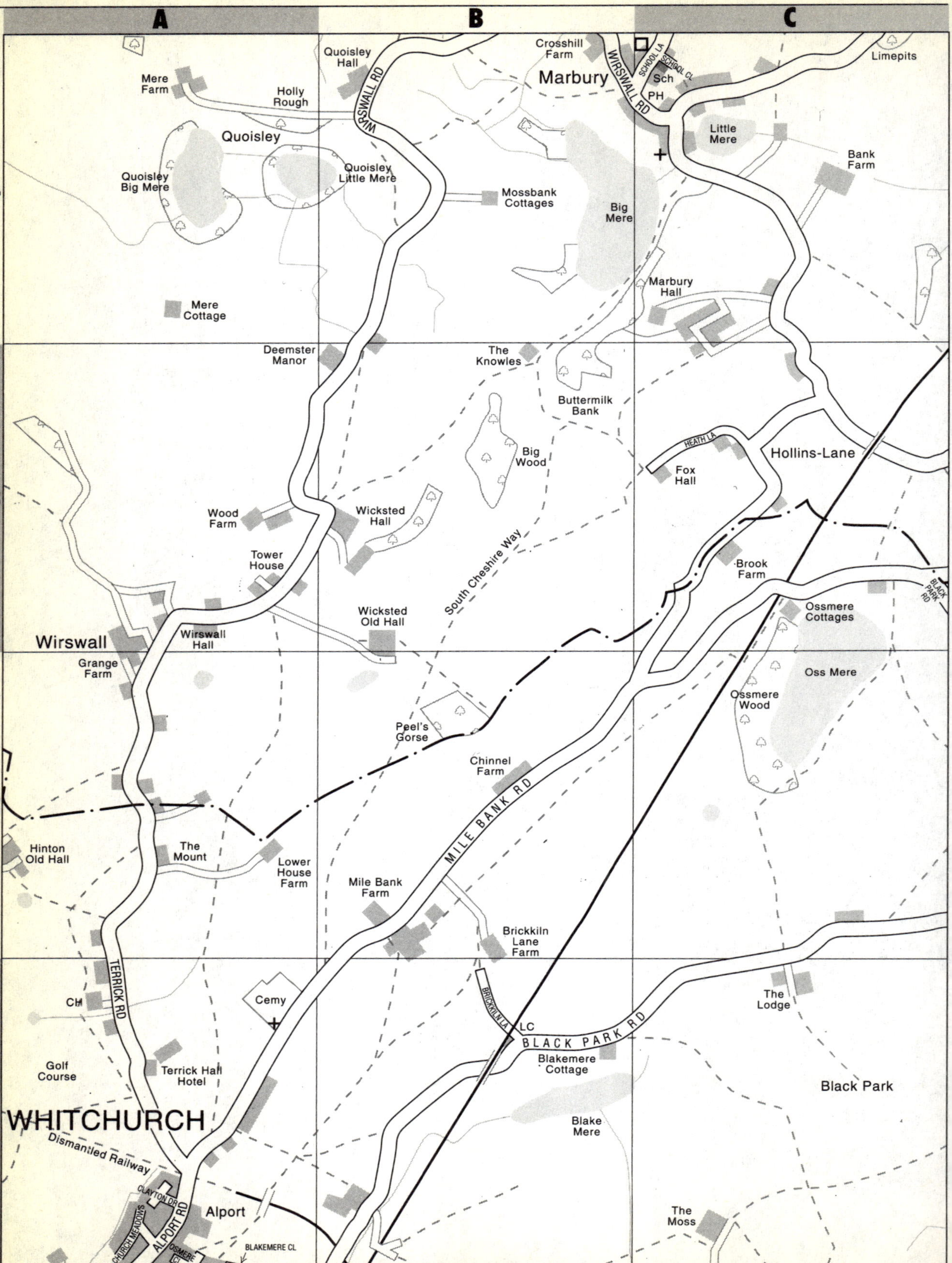
A
B
C
4
45
3
44
2
43
1
42
54
55
56
Mere Farm
Holly Rough
Quoisley Hall
WIRSWALL RD
Crosshill Farm
Marbury
WIRSWALL RD
SCHOOL LA
SCHOOL CL
Sch
PH
Limepits
Quoisley
Quoisley Big Mere
Quoisley Little Mere
Little Mere
Bank Farm
Mossbank Cottages
Big Mere
Marbury Hall
Mere Cottage
Deemster Manor
The Knowles
Buttermilk Bank
HEATH LA
Hollins-Lane
Big Wood
Fox Hall
Wood Farm
Wicksted Hall
Tower House
South Cheshire Way
Brook Farm
BLACK PARK RD
Wicksted Old Hall
Ossmere Cottages
Wirswall
Wirswall Hall
Grange Farm
Oss Mere
Ossmere Wood
Peel's Gorse
Chinnel Farm
MILE BANK RD
Hinton Old Hall
The Mount
Lower House Farm
Mile Bank Farm
Brickkiln Lane Farm
TERRICK RD
Cemy
Ch
The Lodge
BRICKKILN LA
LC
BLACK PARK RD
Blakemere Cottage
Golf Course
Terrick Hall Hotel
Black Park
WHITCHURCH
Blake Mere
Dismantled Railway
CLAYTON DR
Alport
CHURCH MEADOWS
ALPORT RD
OSMERE CL
BLAKEMERE CL
The Moss

225

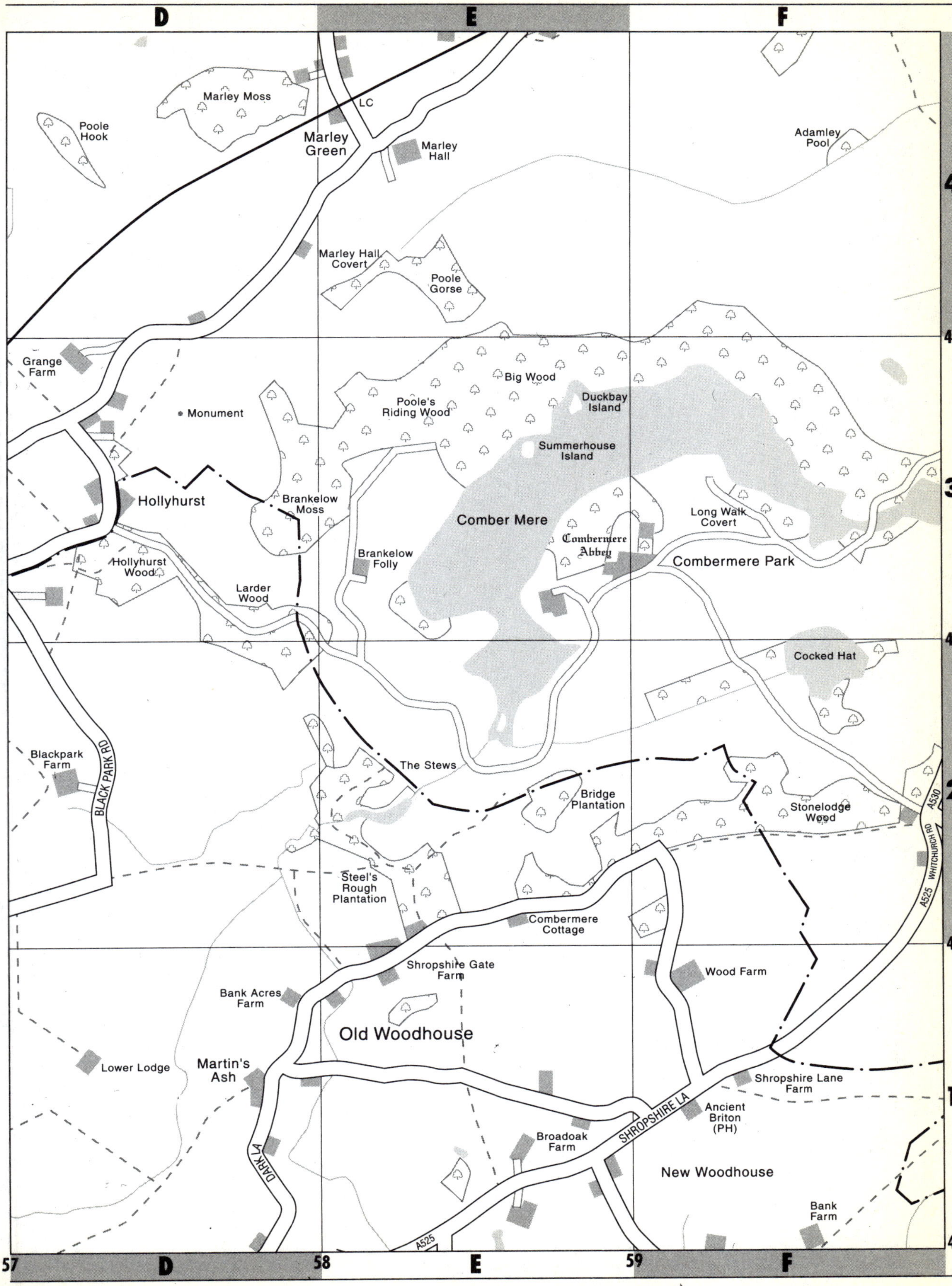
D
E
F
Marley Moss
Poole
Hook
LC
Marley
Green
Marley
Hall
Adamley
Pool
4
Marley Hall
Covert
Poole
Gorse
45
Grange
Farm
Big Wood
Monument
Poole's
Riding Wood
Duckbay
Island
Summerhouse
Island
3
Hollyhurst
Brankelow
Moss
Comber Mere
Long Walk
Covert
Combermere
Abbey
Brankelow
Folly
Combermere Park
Hollyhurst
Wood
Larder
Wood
44
Cocked Hat
Blackpark
Farm
BLACK PARK RD
The Stews
Bridge
Plantation
Stonelodge
Wood
A530
2
WHITCHURCH RD
A525
Steel's
Rough
Plantation
Combermere
Cottage
43
Shropshire Gate
Farm
Wood Farm
Bank Acres
Farm
Old Woodhouse
Lower Lodge
Martin's
Ash
Shropshire Lane
Farm
1
Ancient
Briton
(PH)
SHROPSHIRE LA
Broadoak
Farm
DARK LA
New Woodhouse
Bank
Farm
A525
42
57
D
58
E
59
F

227
217

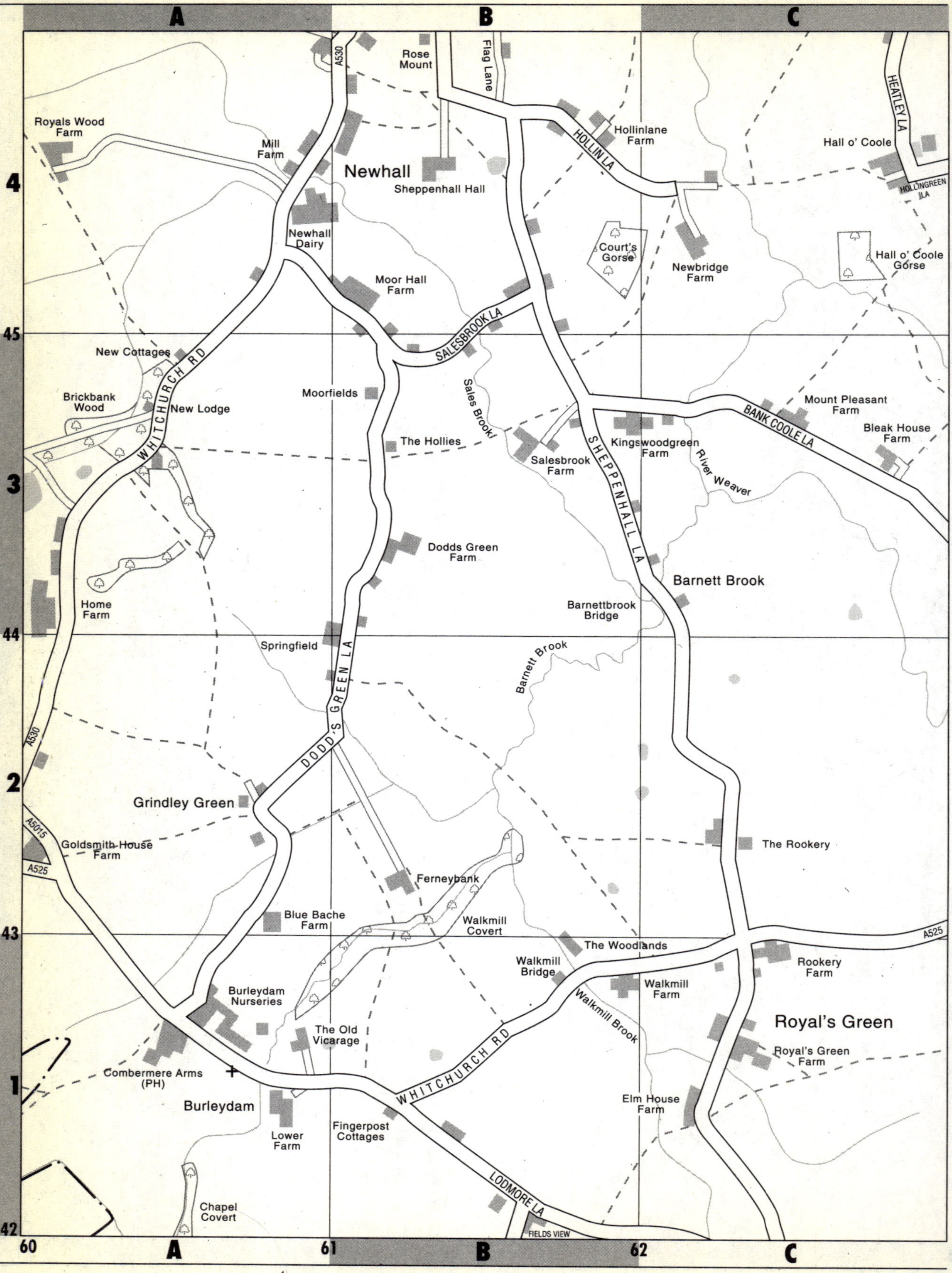

227
233

218
230

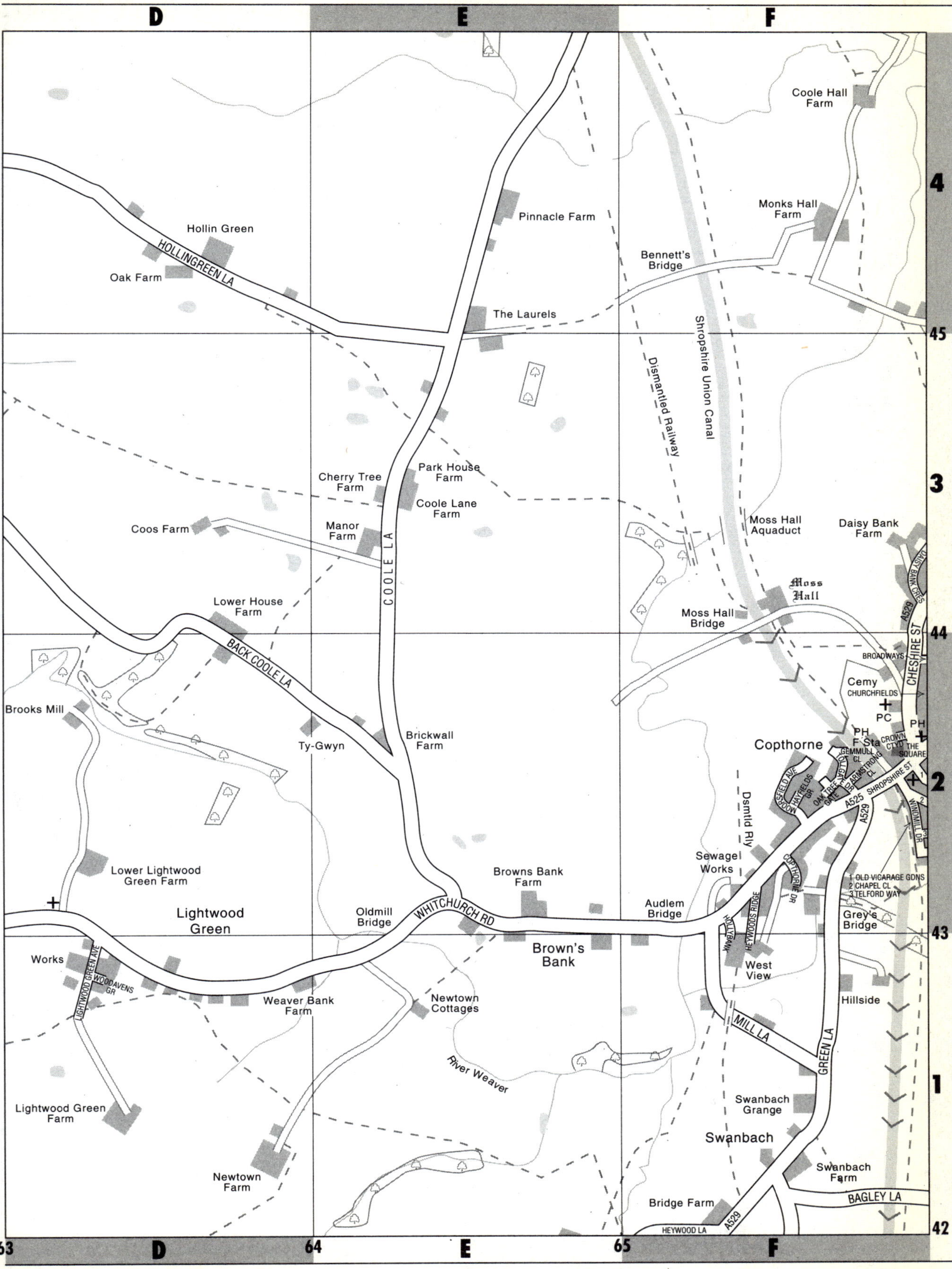

234
230

229
219

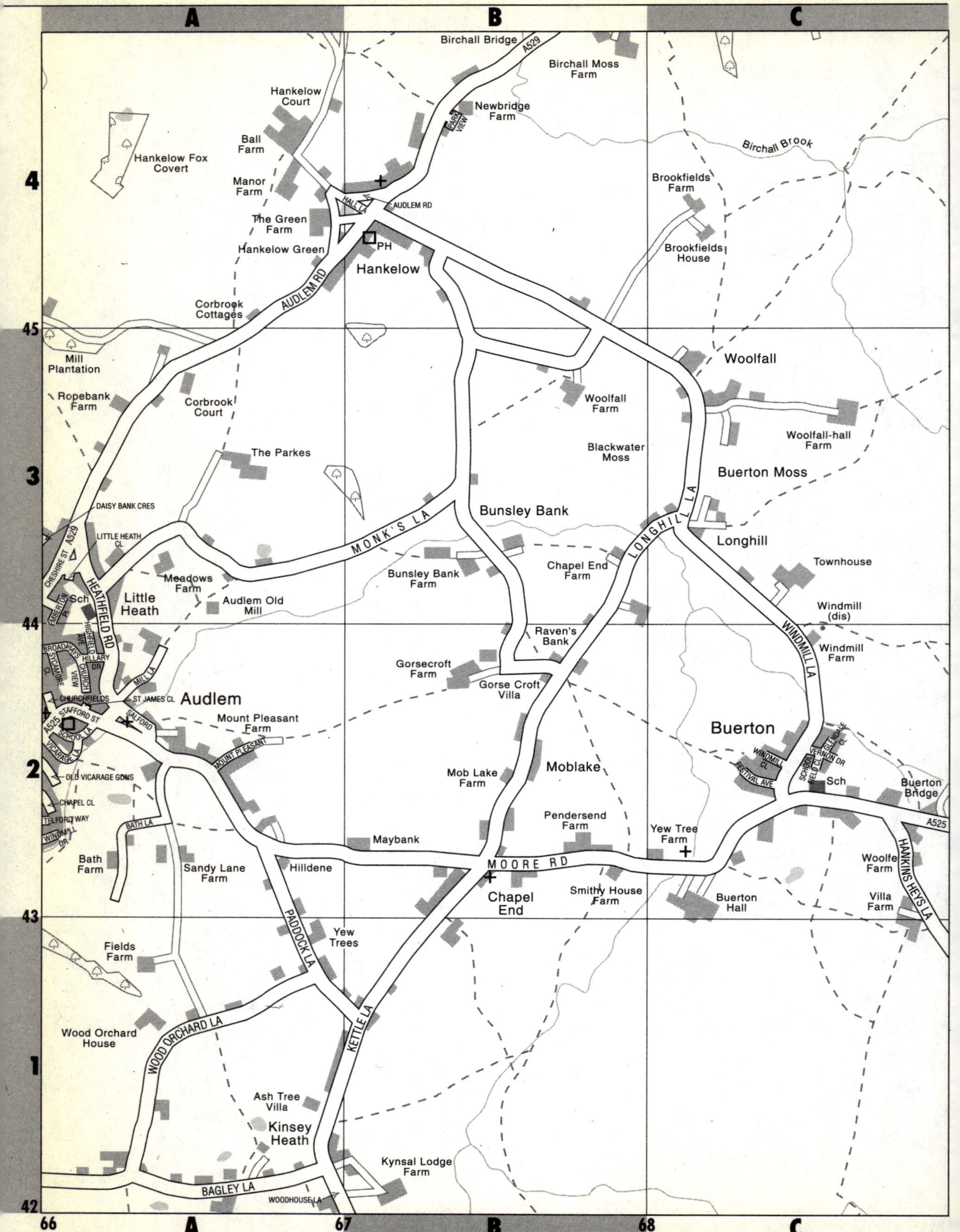

229
235

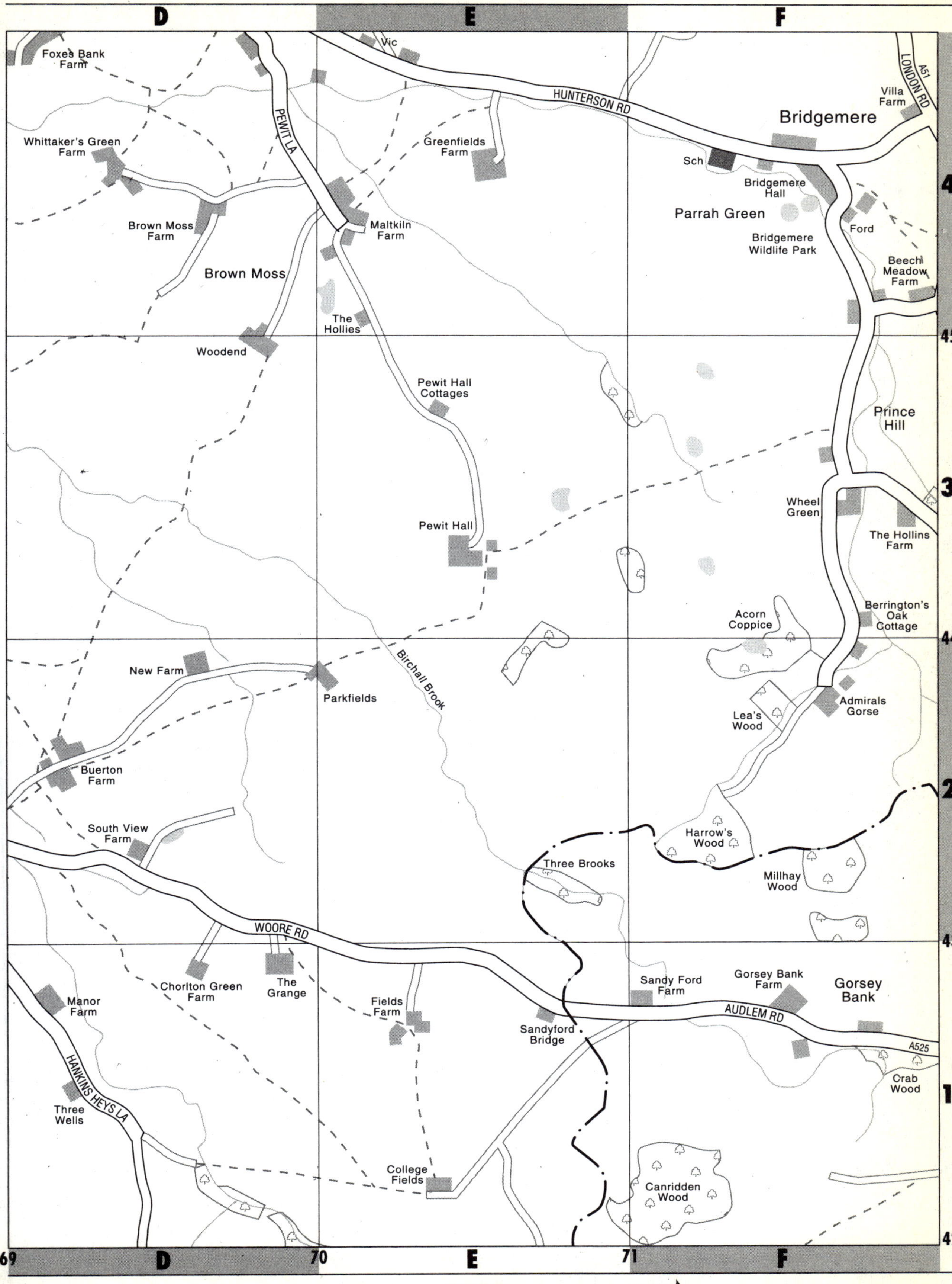
D
E
F
Foxes Bank Farm
Vic
HUNTERSON RD
LONDON RD
A51
Villa Farm
Bridgemere
Whittaker's Green Farm
PEWIT LA
Greenfields Farm
Sch
Bridgemere Hall
Parrah Green
Ford
Brown Moss Farm
Maltkiln Farm
Bridgemere Wildlife Park
Beech Meadow Farm
Brown Moss
The Hollies
Woodend
Pewit Hall Cottages
Prince Hill
Wheel Green
The Hollins Farm
Pewit Hall
Acorn Coppice
Berrington's Oak Cottage
New Farm
Birchall Brook
Parkfields
Admirals Gorse
Lea's Wood
Buerton Farm
South View Farm
Harrow's Wood
Three Brooks
Millhay Wood
WOORE RD
Chorlton Green Farm
The Grange
Sandy Ford Farm
Gorsey Bank Farm
Gorsey Bank
Manor Farm
Fields Farm
AUDLEM RD
Sandyford Bridge
A525
Crab Wood
HANKINS HEYS LA
Three Wells
College Fields
Canridden Wood
4
45
3
44
2
43
1
42
69
70
71

231 221

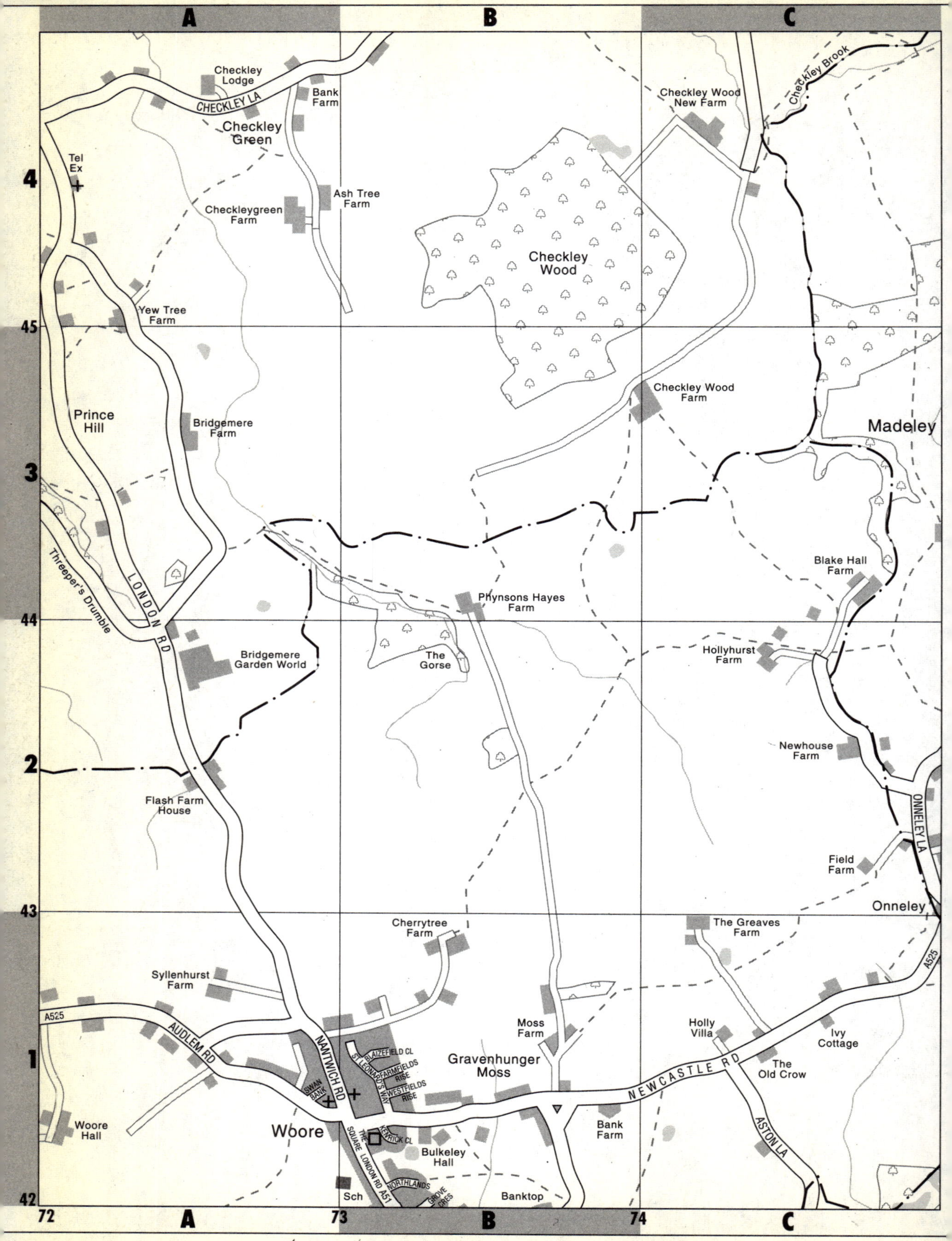
A
B
C
Checkley Lodge
CHECKLEY LA
Checkley Green
Bank Farm
Checkley Wood New Farm
Checkley Brook
Tel Ex
Ash Tree Farm
Checkleygreen Farm
Checkley Wood
Yew Tree Farm
Prince Hill
Bridgemere Farm
Checkley Wood Farm
Madeley
Threeper's Drumble
LONDON RD
Blake Hall Farm
Phynsons Hayes Farm
Bridgemere Garden World
The Gorse
Hollyhurst Farm
Newhouse Farm
Flash Farm House
ONNELEY LA
Field Farm
Onneley
Cherrytree Farm
The Greaves Farm
Syllenhurst Farm
A525
AUDLEM RD
NANTWICH RD
BLAIZEFIELD CL
ST LEONARD'S WAY
FARMFIELDS RISE
WESTFIELDS RISE
SWAN BANK
Moss Farm
Gravenhunger Moss
Holly Villa
Ivy Cottage
The Old Crow
NEWCASTLE RD
Woore Hall
Woore
THE SQUARE
LONDON RD A51
KENRICK CL
Bulkeley Hall
Bank Farm
ASTON LA
NORTHLANDS
GROVE CRES
Sch
Banktop
4
45
3
44
2
43
1
42
72
73
74
A
B
C

231

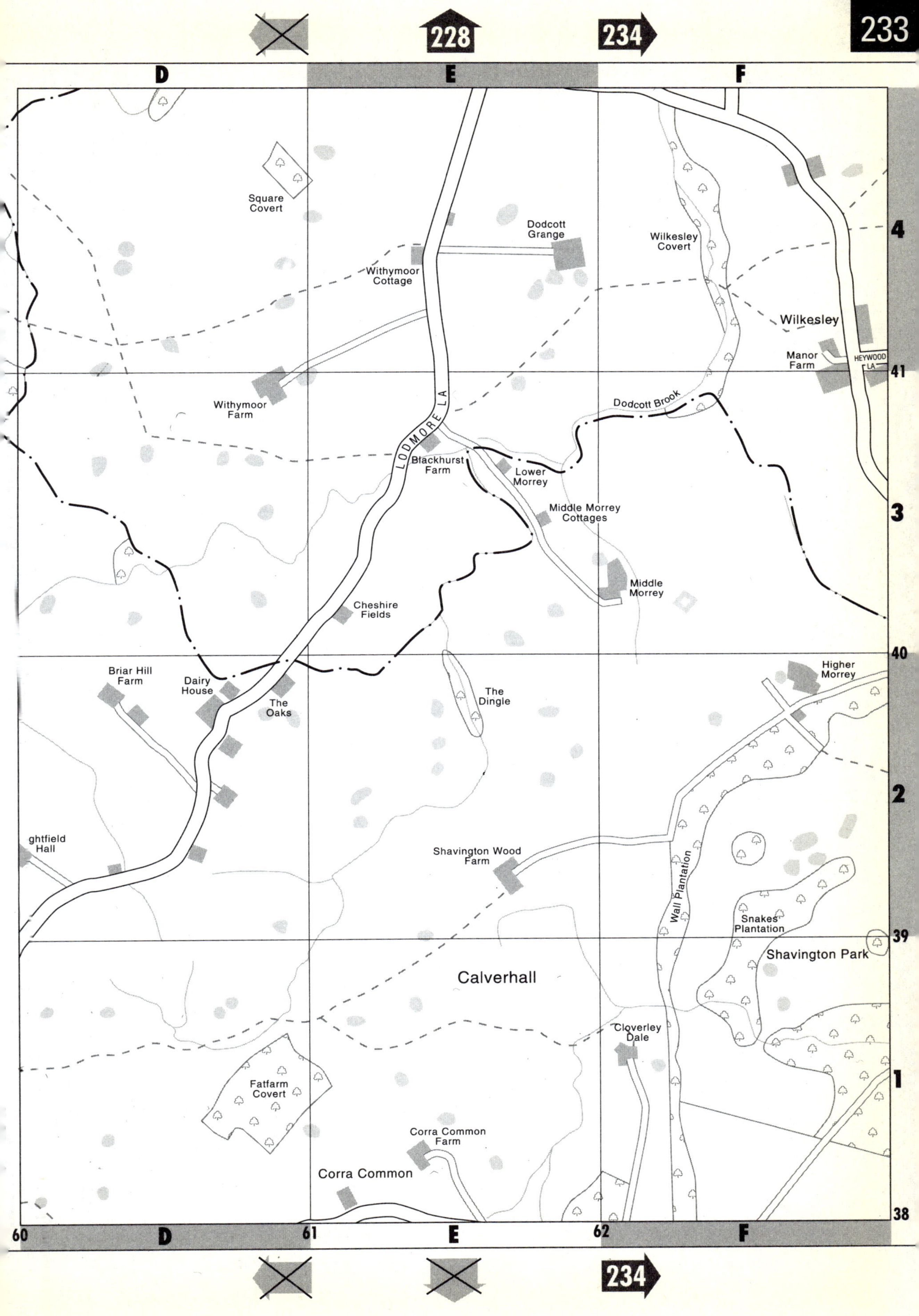

228
234
D
E
F
Square Covert
Dodcott Grange
Wilkesley Covert
Withymoor Cottage
Wilkesley
Manor Farm
HEYWOOD LA
Withymoor Farm
LODMORE LA
Dodcott Brook
Blackhurst Farm
Lower Morrey
Middle Morrey Cottages
Middle Morrey
Cheshire Fields
Briar Hill Farm
Dairy House
The Oaks
The Dingle
Higher Morrey
ghtfield Hall
Shavington Wood Farm
Wall Plantation
Snakes Plantation
Shavington Park
Calverhall
Cloverley Dale
Fatfarm Covert
Corra Common Farm
Corra Common
4
41
3
40
2
39
1
38
60
61
62
234

233
229

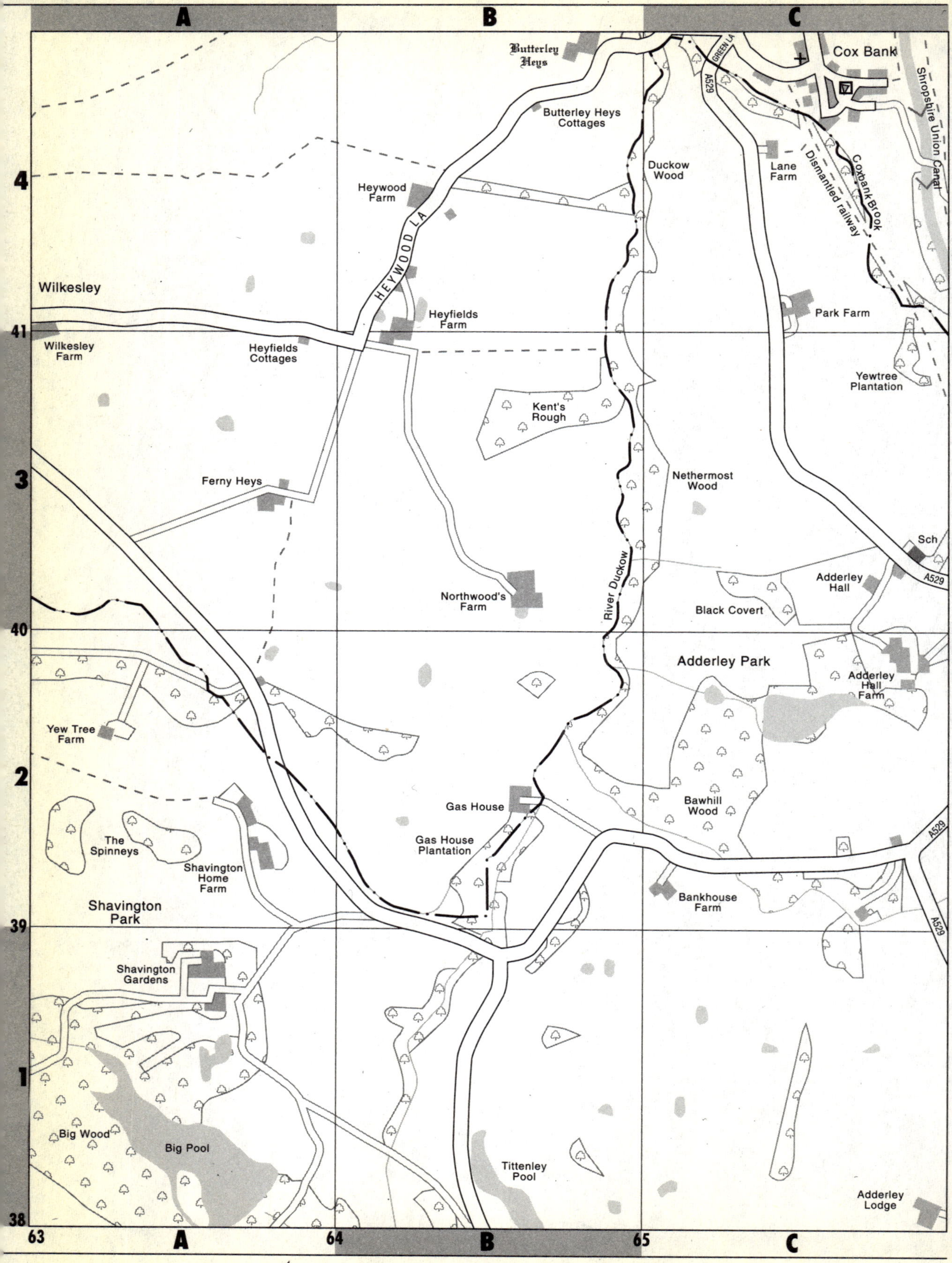
A
B
C
Butterley Heys
Cox Bank
GREEN LA
A529
Shropshire Union Canal
Butterley Heys Cottages
Duckow Wood
Lane Farm
Dismantled railway
Coxbank Brook
4
Heywood Farm
HEYWOOD LA
Wilkesley
Heyfields Farm
Park Farm
41
Wilkesley Farm
Heyfields Cottages
Yewtree Plantation
Kent's Rough
3
Ferny Heys
Nethermost Wood
Sch
Adderley Hall
A529
Northwood's Farm
River Duckow
Black Covert
40
Adderley Park
Adderley Hall Farm
Yew Tree Farm
2
Bawhill Wood
Gas House
A529
Gas House Plantation
The Spinneys
Shavington Home Farm
Bankhouse Farm
Shavington Park
A529
39
Shavington Gardens
1
Big Wood
Big Pool
Tittenley Pool
Adderley Lodge
38
63
64
65

233

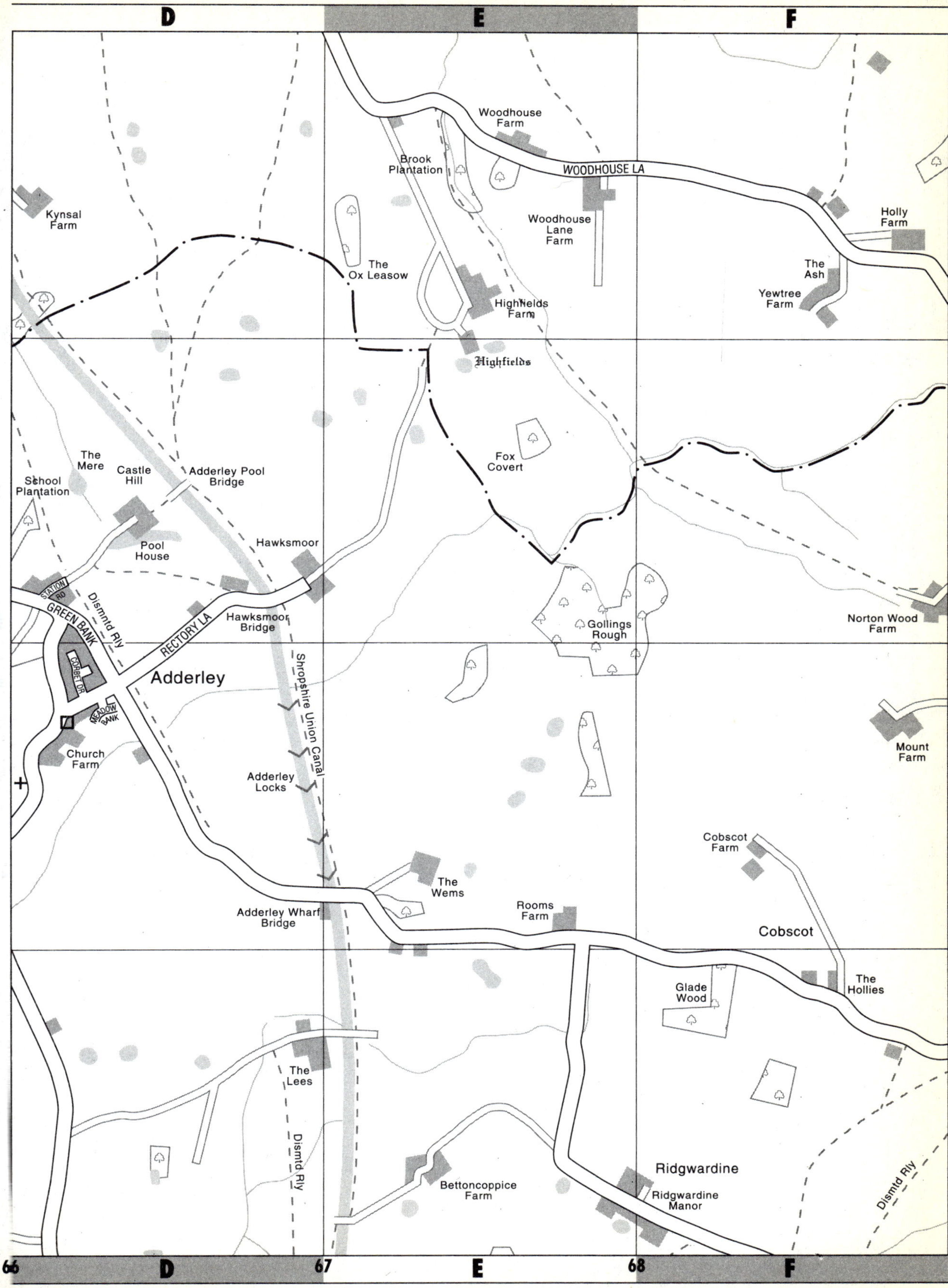
D
E
F
Kynsal Farm
Brook Plantation
Woodhouse Farm
WOODHOUSE LA
Woodhouse Lane Farm
Holly Farm
The Ox Leasow
Highfields Farm
The Ash
Yewtree Farm
Highfields
The Mere
Castle Hill
School Plantation
Adderley Pool Bridge
Fox Covert
Pool House
Hawksmoor
STATION RD
GREEN BANK
Dismntd Rly
Hawksmoor Bridge
RECTORY LA
Gollings Rough
Norton Wood Farm
CORBET DR
Adderley
MEADOW BANK
Shropshire Union Canal
Church Farm
Adderley Locks
Mount Farm
Cobscot Farm
The Wems
Adderley Wharf Bridge
Rooms Farm
Cobscot
Glade Wood
The Hollies
The Lees
Dismtd Rly
Ridgwardine
Bettoncoppice Farm
Ridgwardine Manor
Dismtd Rly
4
41
3
40
2
39
1
38
66
67
68

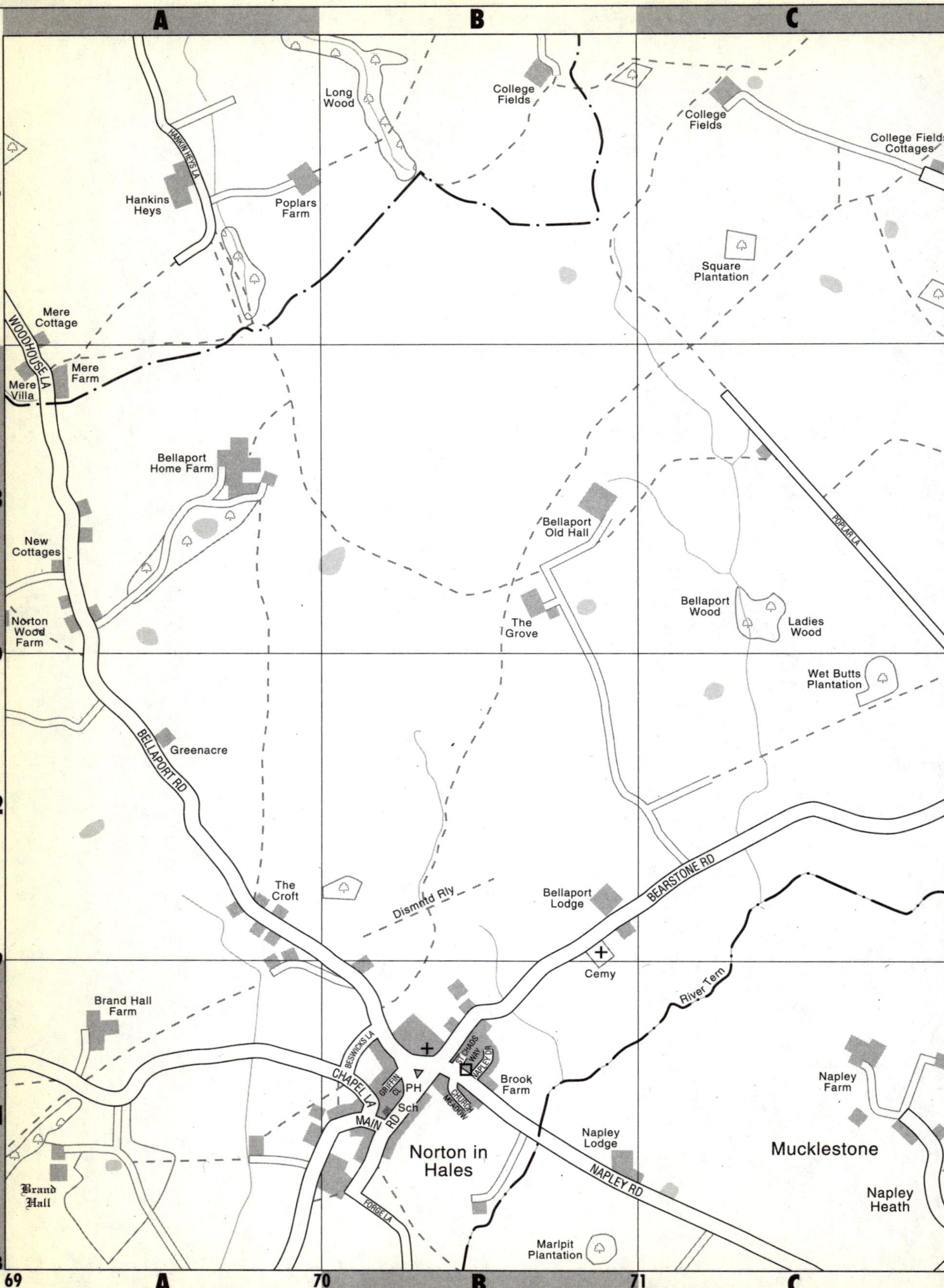
A
B
C
4
41
3
40
2
39
1
38
69
70
71
Long Wood
College Fields
College Fields
College Fields Cottages
HANKIN HEYS LA
Hankins Heys
Poplars Farm
Square Plantation
Mere Cottage
WOODHOUSE LA
Mere Farm
Mere Villa
Bellaport Home Farm
POPLAR LA
Bellaport Old Hall
New Cottages
Bellaport Wood
Ladies Wood
The Grove
Norton Wood Farm
Wet Butts Plantation
BELLAPORT RD
Greenacre
BEARSTONE RD
The Croft
Bellaport Lodge
Dismntd Rly
Cemy
River Tern
Brand Hall Farm
BESWICKS LA
ST CHADS WAY
NAPLEY DR
CHAPEL LA
GRIFFIN CL
PH
Sch
CHURCH MEADOW
Brook Farm
Napley Farm
MAIN RD
Napley Lodge
Norton in Hales
Mucklestone
Brand Hall
NAPLEY RD
FORGE LA
Napley Heath
Marlpit Plantation

USER'S NOTES

EXPLANATION OF THE STREET INDEX REFERENCE SYSTEM

Street names are listed alphabetically and show the locality, the page number and a reference to the square in which the name falls on the map page.

Example:	Simpsons Way. Broug..139 D2
Simpsons Way	This is the full street name, which may have been abbreviated on the map.
Broug	This is the abbreviation for the town, village or locality in which the street falls.
139	This is the page number of the map on which the street name appears.
D2	The letter and figure indicate the square on the map in which the centre of the street falls. The square can be found at the junction of the vertical column carrying the appropriate letter and the horizontal row carrying the appropriate figure.

ABBREVIATIONS USED IN THE INDEX

Road Names

Approach..................................App
Arcade.......................................Arc
Avenue......................................Ave
Boulevard..................................Bvd
Buildings...............................Bldgs
Business Park..................Bsns Pk
Broadway.................................Bwy
By-Pass..................................By-Ps
Causeway...............................Cswy
Circle..Circ
Circus...Cir
Close...Cl
Common.................................Comm
Corner..Cnr
Cottages..................................Cotts
Court..Ct
Courtyard..................................Ctyd
Crescent...................................Cres
Drive..Dri
Drove..Dro
East..E
Embankment............................Emb
Esplanade..................................Espl
Gardens....................................Gdns
Grove...Gr
Heights.......................................Hts
Industrial Estate.................Ind Est
Junction...................................Junc
Lane...La
North..N
Orchard....................................Orch
Parade...Par
Passage.......................................Pas
Place..Pl
Pleasant.....................................Plea
Precinct......................................Prec
Promenade................................Prom
Road...Rd
South..S
Square..Sq
Stairs..Strs
Steps..Stps
Street,Saint....................................St
Terrace.......................................Terr
Walk..Wlk
West...W
Yard..Yd

Key to abbreviations of Town, Village and Rural locality names used in the index of street names.

Locality	Abbreviation	Grid	Page
Acton	Acton	A3	204
Acton Bridge	Act Br	C2	76
Adderley	Adder	D2	235
Adlington	Adlin	B3	62
Alderley Edge	A Edge	B1	60
Aldford	Aldf	F2	163
Allostock	Allos	C2	106
Alpraham	Alpr	E2	169
Alsager	Alsag	E2	193
Altrincham	Altr	E4	31
Alvanley	Alva	E1	73
Antrobus	Antro	E2	53
Appleton	Apple	D3	27
Ashley	Ashl	F3	31
Ashton	Asht	F4	121
Astbury	Astb	A4	178
Aston	Ast	B1	50
Aston	Aston	C1	232
Audlem	Audlem	A2	230
Audley	Audley	E1	209
Backford	Backf	D2	95
Baddiley	Badd	D1	203
Barbridge	Barb	E3	187
Barthomley	Barth	B3	209
Barton	Barton	F1	181
Bate Heath	B Hea	C2	54
Bebington	Beb	F3	43
Beeston	Beest	A1	168
Bell o' th' Hill	B o t H	B4	225
Betley	Betley	F3	221
Bickerton	Bicker	F3	199
Bickley Town	Bic T	C3	214
Biddulph	Bidd	D1	179
Blacon	Blacon	F2	117
Blakenhall	Blake	D2	221
Bold Heath	Bo Hea	F4	13
Bollington	Boll	A4	88
Bosley	Bosl	B4	158
Bradley Green	Brad G	D4	225
Bradwall Green	Bra Gr	D2	153
Bramhall	Bram	F4	35
Brereton Green	Bre Gr	F3	153
Bridgemere	Bridge	F4	231
Broughton	Broug	D2	139
Broxton	Brox	D1	183
Buerton	Buer	C2	230
Bulkeley	Bulk	C1	184
Bunbury	Bun	F4	185
Burland	Burl	E4	203
Burton	Burt	E1	161
Burtonwood	Burton	C3	6
Burwardsley	Burw	A3	184
Buxton	Bux	F4	115
Caldecot Green	Cal Gr	E2	197
Calverhall	Calver	E1	233
Capenhurst	Capen	A4	94
Cheadle	Chea	B4	34
Cheadle Hulme	Ch Hul	E4	35
Chelford	Chelf	A1	84
Chester	Chest	C1	118
Chinley	Chin	F2	39
Cholmondeley	Chol	D2	201
Cholmondeston	Cholm	D1	171
Chorley	Chorl	A2	202
Chowley	Chow	C3	182
Christleton	Christ	C4	142
Church Minshull	Ch Min	A3	172
Clutton	Clutt	B1	182
Coddington	Codd	A2	182
Comberhach	Comb	B4	78
Congleton	Congle	D2	157
Connah's Quay	Con Q	D1	91
Cranage	Cran	A3	130
Crewe	Crewe	C3	190
Croft	Croft	D4	9
Cronton	Cront	B3	12
Crowton	Crow	A1	76
Cuddington	Cudd	F2	101
Cuddington Green	Cudd Gr	A1	212
Culcheth	Cul	D2	5
Daresbury	Dares	D1	25
Davenham	Dave	A1	104
Delamere	Dela	E3	123
Disley	Disley	B3	38
Dodleston	Dodle	A4	162
Duddon	Dudd	D3	145
Dunham Town	Dun T	B2	20
Dunham-on-the-Hill	D-o-t-H	F3	97
Dutton	Dutt	E1	51
Eaton	Eaton	D4	157
Eaton	Eaton	D2	147
Eccleston	Eccles	E1	141
Edge Green	Ed Gr	D1	199
Ellesmere Port	El Por	A3	70
Elton	Elton	B2	72
Faddiley	Fadd	C3	202
Farndon	Farn	C1	180
Flash	Flash	C2	138
Flint	Flint	D2	91
French Lane End	Fr La E	C3	218
Frodsham	Frod	B4	74
Garden City	G Cit	C1	92
Golborne	Golb	C2	164
Goldborne	Gold	E3	3
Goostrey	Goost	E1	107
Great Barrow	Gt Bar	C3	120
Great Budworth	G Bud	D4	79
Great Sankey	Gt San	D3	15
Guilden Sutton	G Sutt	F3	119
Hale	Hale	E1	21
Halewood	Halew	D4	21
Hampton	Hamp	A4	214
Handley	Hand	B4	182
Hargrave	Harg	A1	144
Hartford	Hart	E3	103
Haslington	Hasl	F3	191
Hassall Green	Ha Gr	A1	176
Hatherton	Hather	F2	219
Hatton	Hatt	A1	26
Haughton Moss	H Moss	B3	186
Hawarden	Hawa	A1	116
Haydock	Hay	B3	1
Haymoor Green	Hay Gr	F1	205
Hazel Grove	Haz Gr	B4	36
Heaton	Heat	F1	159
Helsby	Hels	E2	73
Henbury	Henb	D4	111
Heswall	Hes	C3	40
High Lane	H La	F4	37
High Legh	H Legh	D3	29
Higher Kinnerton	H Kin	E4	161
Higher Walton	H Wal	F4	25
Higher Wincham	H Winch	F2	79
Hollins Green	Hol Gr	D1	11
Holmes Chapel	H Chap	C1	130
Holt	Holt	B4	196
Horton Green	Hor Gr	A4	212
Hough Common	Ho Co	C1	206
Huntingdon	Hunt	A3	142
Huxley	Hux	C4	166
Ince	Ince	A3	72
Irlam	Irlam	E4	11
Isycoed	Isyc	B1	196
Kelsall	Kels	B2	122
Kettleshulme	Kettle	C2	64
Kidsgrove	Kids	D1	195
Kingsley	Kings	E1	75
Knutsford	Knuts	D2	57
Lach Dennis	L Den	E3	105
Lawton-gate	Law-g	A2	194
Ledsham	Led	C1	68
Leek	Leek	C1	160
Leigh	Leigh	E4	5
Lindow End	L End	D1	59
Little Bollington	L Boll	A1	20
Little Budworth	L Bud	F4	147
Little Leigh	L Lei	E2	77
Lostock	Lost	B1	80
Lower Kinnerton	L Kin	E1	139
Lyme Handley	L Han	A4	64
Lymm	Lymm	C2	18
Macclesfield	Mfield	A4	112
Macclesfield Forest	Mac For	B3	114
Madeley	Made	C3	232
Malpas	Malpas	D1	213
Manley	Man	D2	99
Marbury	Marb	B4	226
Marston	Mars	D2	79
Marton	Mart	D3	133
Marton	Mar	D3	125
Mere	Mere	A4	56
Mickle Trafford	M Traf	F4	119
Middlewich	Middle	B1	128
Mobberley	Mobb	A3	58
Mollington	Moll	C1	94
Moore	Moore	D3	25
Mottram St Andrew	M St A	D1	61
Mouldsworth	Mould	C1	98
Moulton	Moult	A4	126
Mucklestone	Muck	C1	236
Nantwich	Nant	C3	204
Neston	Nest	B4	66
Nether Alderley	N Ald	D3	85
New Mills	N Mills	E4	39
Newcastle-under-Lyme	N-u-L	B1	210
Newhall	New	B4	228
Newton-le-Willows	N-le-W	B2	2
Norbury	Norb	E2	215
Norley	Norley	C3	100
Northwich	North	E4	103
Norton in Hales	N in H	B1	236
Oakmere	Oak	A4	124
Old Woodhouse	Old W	E1	227
Ollerton	Oller	C3	82
Partington	Part	F1	11
Peckforton	Peckf	D3	185
Penketh	Penk	C2	14
Penley	Penley	A1	222
Peover	Peo	D4	107
Pickmere	Pick	A4	80
Picton	Pict	B2	96
Plumley	Plum	D2	81
Poolehill	Pool	A1	188
Pott Shrigley	Po Shr	E2	63
Poulton	Poul	D1	163
Poynton	Poyn	C2	36
Prestbury	Prest	D4	87
Preston on the Hill	P o t H	D3	51
Puddington	Pudd	C4	92
Pulford	Pulf	B2	162
Radford	Rad	E3	155
Rainow	Rain	C3	88
Ridley	Ridley	E1	185
Rossett	Ross	A3	180
Rostherne	Rosth	C2	30
Royal's Green	Roy Gr	C1	228
Runcorn	Run	F4	49
Saighton	Saigh	C1	142
Sandbach	Sand	D3	175
Saughall	Saug	A1	94
Scholar Green	Sch Gr	C4	194
Sealand	Sea	C3	116
Shavington	Shav	B3	206
Shocklach	Shock	F4	211
Shotwick	Shot	D2	93
Siddington	Sidd	A2	110
Smallwood	Small	C3	176
Sound	Sound	F3	217
Speke	Speke	B4	46
Sproston Green	Sp Gr	E1	129
Spurstow	Spurs	F3	185
St Helens	St Hel	A1	1
Stanlow	Stan	D3	71
Stoak	Stoak	A4	96
Stretton	Stret	C1	26
Sutton	Sutt	A1	50
Sutton Lane Ends	S La E	C1	112
Swettenham	Swett	F2	131
Tabley	Tab	F2	55
Tarbock Green	Tar Gr	F4	21
Tarporley	Tarp	B1	146
Tarvin	Tarv	E2	121
Tattenhall	Tatt	A1	166
Thornton Hough	Thor H	A3	42
Thornton-le-Moors	T-le-M	F1	71
Threapwood	Threap	C4	222
Tilston	Tils	A2	198
Tiverton	Tiver	B3	168
Trafford	Tford	C3	96
Utkinton	Utkin	A4	146
Warmingham	Warm	E4	173
Warren	Warren	E1	111
Warrington	Warr	C3	16
Waverton	Waver	D2	143
Weaverham	Weave	B4	102
Weston	Weston	E3	207
Wettenhall	Wet	C4	170
Whaley Bridge	W Br	E4	65
Whitchurch	Whitch	A1	226
Whitewell	White	B1	224
Whitley	Whit	B2	52
Widnes	Wid	C4	22
Wildboarclough	Wild	F3	137
Willaston	Will	A4	68
Willaston	Willas	E3	205
Willington	Willi	C1	222
Wilmslow	Wilm	A3	60
Wimboldsley	Wimbo	C2	150
Wincle	Winc	F4	159
Winsford	Winsf	C1	126
Winwick	Win	A3	8
Wirswall	Wirsw	A3	226
Wistaston	Wist	F4	205
Withington	With	D1	109
Woodford	Woodf	E1	35
Woodhouse Green	Wd Gr	B1	158
Woore	Woore	A1	232
Worleston	Worles	C3	188
Worthenbury	Worth	D1	211
Wrenbury	Wren	C2	216
Wythenshawe	Wythe	E4	33

Aarons Dr. Audley 209 F1
Abbey Cl. Croft 9 D4
Abbey Cl. Wid 22 B4
Abbey Cl. Winsf 126 A4
Abbey Fields. Wist 205 E4
Abbey Green. Chest 118 B1
Abbey Hey. Run 50 B4
Abbey La. Dela 123 F3
Abbey La. Hart 103 D2
Abbey Pl. Crewe 190 B3
Abbey Rd. Gold 4 B4
Abbey Rd. Hay 1 C4
Abbey Rd. Mfield 87 D1
Abbey Rd. Sand 174 C3
Abbey Rd. Wid 22 B4
Abbey Sq. Chest 118 B1
Abbey St. Chest 118 B1
Abbey Way. Hart 103 D2
Abbeyway N. Hay 2 A4
Abbeyway S. Hay 2 A4
Abbot's Dr. Chest 118 B2
Abbot's Grange. Chest 118 B2
Abbot's Nook. Chest 118 B2
Abbots Cl. Mfield 87 D1
Abbots Keep. Chest 118 B2
Abbots Mews. El Por 70 A3
Abbots Pk. Chest 118 B2
Abbots Way. Hart 103 D2
Abbotsbury Cl. Poyn 36 B3
Abbotsfield Cl. Apple 26 C3
Abbott's Cl. Congle 179 D4
Abbotts Cl. Run 49 D4
Abbotts Cl. Waver 143 D3
Abbotts Rd. Waver 143 D3
Abbotts Way. Winsf 126 A1
Aberdare Cl. Warr 7 F1
Aberdaron Dr. Blacon 117 F2
Aberfeldy Cl. H Chap 130 A1
Abingdon Ave. Warr 17 F4
Abingdon Cres. Chest 140 C3
Abington Cl. Crewe 190 A3
Abington Wlk. Run 50 B3
Abstone Cl. Warr 17 E4
Acacia Av. Wilm 59 F3
Acacia Ave. Knuts 56 C1
Acacia Ave. Warr 17 E4
Acacia Ave. Wid 13 D2
Acacia Cl. Elton 72 B2
Acacia Cres. Crewe 190 C3
Acacia Dr. El Por 69 F1
Acacia Dr. Sand 174 C4
Acacia Gdns. Kids 195 E2
Acacia Gr. Run 49 E4
Acacia St. N-le-W 1 C2
Academy St. Warr 16 A3
Academy Way. Warr 16 A3
Acer Ave. Crewe 190 C4
Achilles Ave. Warr 8 A1
Ack La E. Ch Hul 35 E3
Ack La W. Ch Hul 35 E4
Ackerley Cl. Warr 8 C2
Ackers La. Warr 16 C1
Ackers Rd. Warr 16 C1
Ackersley Ct. Ch Hul 35 D4
Acorn Bank Cl. Wist 206 A4
Acorn Cl. Cudd 101 F1
Acorn Cl. Winsf 150 A4
Acorn Dr. El Por 70 A1
Acorn La. Congle 157 F2
Acorn St. N-le-W 2 B2
Acorn Terr. N Mills 39 D3
Acre La. Beb 43 E4
Acre La. Ch Hul 35 E3
Acre La. Hes 41 E4
Acre Rd. El Por 69 E3
Acreage The. Bun 185 F4
Acreage The. Goost 107 F1
Acrefield Rd. Wid 12 A1
Acres Cres. Kings 75 D1
Acres La. Chest 118 B4
Acreville Gr. Cul 5 E4
Acton Ave. Apple 26 B2
Acton La. Act Br 76 C2
Acton Pl. Mfield 111 F4
Acton Rd. Burton 6 C3
Acton Rd. Crewe 189 E3
Acton Way. Law-g 193 E3
Adam Ave. El Por 69 E2
Adam Cl. El Por 69 E2
Adam St. Warr 16 B4
Adams Cl. N-le-W 2 B1
Adams Cl. Poyn 36 C1
Adams Hill. Knuts 57 D1
Adamson Ct. Warr 17 D1
Adamson St. Warr 16 A2
Adaston Ave. Beb 43 F2
Adder Hill. Chest 142 A4
Adderly Cl. Run 23 E1
Addingham Ave. Wid 22 B4
Addingham Cl. Wid 22 B4
Addison Cl. Wist 205 F4
Addison Sq. Wid 13 D1
Adela Rd. Run 22 C1
Adelaide Rd. Blacon 117 E2
Adelaide Rd. Bram 35 F3
Adelaide St. Crewe 190 B3
Adey Rd. Lymm 19 D3
Adfalent La. Will 68 A4
Adlington Cl. Poyn 36 C1
Adlington Ct. Warr 9 F3
Adlington Dr. North 104 A3
Adlington Dr. Sand 175 E4
Adlington Park. Adlin 36 B1
Adlington Rd. Boll 63 D1
Adlington Rd. Crewe 189 F2
Adlington Rd. Run 24 B1
Adlington Rd. Wilm 60 C4
Adlington St. Mfield 112 B4
Admirals Rd. Warr 9 F2
Adwell Cl. Gold 4 A4
Afton. Wid 12 A1
Agden Brow. L Boll 19 F1
Agden House La. B of H 225 D3
Agden La. L Boll 29 F4
Agden La. Lymm 19 F1
Agden Park La. Lymm 29 E4
Agecroft Rd. North 104 B4
Ainley Cl. Run 50 A3
Ainscough Rd. Warr 9 F2
Ainsdale Cl. Beb 43 E3
Ainsdale Cl. Bram 36 A4
Ainsdale Cl. Penk 14 C2
Ainsworth La. Crow 76 A2
Ainsworth Rd. Weave 77 F1
Aintree Gr. El Por 69 E2
Airdrie Cl. Beb 43 E2
Aire. Wid 12 A1
Aire Cl. El Por 70 A4
Aire Pl. Winsf 127 D1
Airedale Cl. Gt San 14 C4
Airfield View. Broug 139 D3
Aitchison Rd. Lost 80 A1
Ajax Ave. Warr 8 A1
Akesmoor La. Bidd 179 D1
Akesmoor La. Bidd 195 F4
Alamein Cres. Warr 16 B4
Alamein Dr. Winsf 149 E4
Alamein Rd. Chest 95 D1
Alamein Rd. North 78 A2
Alan Dr. Altr 32 A4
Alan St. North 104 A4
Alban Retail Park. Warr 8 A1
Alban St. Crewe 190 B3
Albany Cres. Lymm 18 B2
Albany Gdns. El Por 69 E4
Albany Gr. Lymm 18 B2
Albany Rd. Bram 35 F2
Albany Rd. Lymm 18 B2
Albany Rd. Wilm 59 F3
Albany Terr. Run 23 D1
Albert Dr. Nest 66 B4
Albert Pl. Congle 156 C1
Albert Rd. Boll 87 F4
Albert Rd. Warr 17 D1
Albert Rd. Wid 13 D1
Albert Rd. Wilm 60 A3
Albert Row. Frod 49 D1
Albert Sq. Wid 23 D4
Albert St. Audley 209 F2
Albert St. Chest 118 C1
Albert St. Crewe 190 B3
Albert St. Irlam 11 F3
Albert St. Knuts 56 C1
Albert St. Mfield 112 B4
Albert St. Nant 204 C3
Albert St. Run 23 D1
Albion Pl. Chest 141 E4
Albion Rd. N Mills 39 D3
Albion Rd. North 79 D1
Albion St. Chest 118 B1
Albion St. Crewe 190 A2
Albion Wlk. North 79 D1
Alcock St. Run 23 D2
Aldcliffe. Gold 3 F4
Alder Ave. Poyn 36 C2
Alder Ave. Wid 13 D2
Alder Cres. Warr 16 B4
Alder Dr. El Por 69 F1
Alder Gr. Chest 119 D2
Alder La. Burton 7 E4
Alder La. Cront 12 A3
Alder La. Frod 48 B2
Alder La. Warr 16 A4
Alder La. Win 7 E4
Alder Rd. Gold 3 F4
Alder Rd. Warr 17 E4
Alder Rd. Weave 102 B4
Alder Rise. W Br 65 E4
Alder Root La. Win 7 E4
Alder St. N-le-W 2 B2
Alder Wood Ave. Speke 21 D2
Alderbank Rd. Gt San 15 D3
Alderdale Gr. Wilm 59 F3
Alderfield Dr. Speke 21 D2
Aldergate Ave. Run 50 B4
Alderhay La. Kids 195 E3
Alderley Ave. Gold 3 E4
Alderley Cl. Haz Gr 36 C4
Alderley Cl. Poyn 36 C1
Alderley Cl. Sand 175 E4
Alderley Lodge. Wilm 60 A3
Alderley Rd. Chelf 84 B2
Alderley Rd. M St A 60 C1
Alderley Rd. North 103 F4
Alderley Rd. Prest 86 C2
Alderley Rd. Warr 17 E2
Alderley Rd. Wilm 60 A3
Alderley Wlk. Mfield 112 C4
Alderly Pl. Blacon 117 F3
Alders Rd. H La 38 A4
Alders Way. Prest 86 C3
Aldersey Cl. Run 24 B1
Aldersey Cl. Saug 94 A1
Aldersey La. Codd 182 B3
Aldersey La. Hand 182 B3
Aldersey Rd. Crewe 190 A1
Aldersgate. N Mills 39 D4
Aldersgate Rd. Ch Hul 35 E3
Aldersgreen Ave. H La 37 F4
Alderwood Cl. Warr 10 A3
Aldford Cl. Beb 43 D3
Aldford Cl. Ho Co 206 C1
Aldford Pl. A Edge 59 F1
Aldford Rd. Chest 118 C3
Aldford Way. Winsf 126 A1
Aldgate. El Por 70 A3
Aldington Dr. Middle 151 E3
Aldridge Dr. Burton 6 C4
Aled Way. Brough 140 B3
Alexander Dr. Wid 22 B4
Alexander Gr. Run 23 E1
Alexandra Gr. Irlam 11 F4
Alexandra Pl. Crewe 190 A3
Alexandra Rd. Middle 151 E3
Alexandra Rd. Warr 16 B1
Alexandra Rd. Warr 16 C1
Alexandra St. El Por 70 B4
Alexandra St. Warr 16 C4
Alexandra St. Wid 23 D4
Alexandra St. Winsf 126 B1
Alforde St. Wid 23 D3
Alforde St. Wid 23 D4
Alfred Cl. Wid 23 D4
Alfred Rd. Gold 4 A4
Alfred Rd. Hay 1 C4
Alfred St. Irlam 11 F3
Alfred St. N-le-W 2 C2
Alfred St. North 103 F3
Alfred St. Wid 23 D4
Algernon St. Warr 16 B1
Algernon St. Warr 16 B3
Alice Ct. Wid 23 D2
Alison Dr. Mfield 87 F1
Alistair Dr. Beb 43 E3
All Saints Dr. Warr 17 F2
Allans Cl. Nest 66 C3
Allans Meadow. Nest 66 C4
Allansford Ave. Waver 143 D2
Allcard St. Warr 15 F4
Allen Ave. Cul 5 E2
Allen Dr. Dave 103 F1
Allen Pl. Crewe 190 A3
Allen Rd. Run 48 B4
Allen St. Boll 88 A4
Allen St. Mfield 112 C4
Allen St. Warr 16 A3
Allenby Rd. Irlam 11 E2
Allendale. Run 50 A3
Allerby Way. Gold 3 F4
Allerton Rd. Wid 13 D1
Allgreave Cl. Middle 151 E3
Allington La. Chest 141 F4
Allington Pl. Chest 141 F4
Allotment Rd. Irlam 11 E3
Allport La. Beb 43 E4
Allport Rd. Beb 43 E4
Allports The. Beb 43 E4
Allumbrook Ave. H Chap 130 B2
Allysum Ct. Run 49 F2
Alma Ave. Crewe 190 B3
Alma Cl. Mfield 112 A4
Alma Cl. Sch Gr 194 C4
Alma La. Wilm 60 A4
Alma Rd. Haz Gr 37 D4
Alma St. Chest 118 C1
Alma St. N-le-W 2 A2
Almeda Rd. Speke 21 D1
Almer Dr. Gt San 15 E3
Almond Ave. Crewe 190 C3
Almond Ave. Run 49 E4
Almond Dr. Burton 6 C3
Almond Gr. Warr 17 D4
Almond Gr. Wid 22 B4
Almond Pl. N-u-L 210 C1
Almond Tree Cl. Hale 21 F1
Almond Wlk. Part 11 E1
Alnwick Dr. El Por 70 B1
Alpass Ave. Warr 16 A4
Alpine St. N-le-W 2 A2
Alport Rd. Whitch 226 A1
Alpraham Cres. Chest 118 C3
Alric Wlk. Wythe 33 F4
Alsager Rd. Audley 209 F4
Alsager Rd. Ha Gr 192 B4
Alsager Rd. Hasl 192 B4
Alsfeld Way. N Mills 39 D4
Alt. Wid 12 A1
Alt Wlk. Winsf 127 D1
Alton Dr. Mfield 87 F1
Alton Rd. Wilm 59 F4
Alton St. Crewe 190 A2
Altrincham Rd. Wilm 33 E1
Altrincham Rd. Wilm 33 E2
Alum Ct. H Chap 130 B1
Alun Cres. Chest 141 D3
Alundale Rd. Winsf 126 B2
Alvanley Dr. Hels 73 E1
Alvanley Rd. El Por 69 F2
Alvanley Rd. Hels 73 E1
Alvanley Rise. North 104 A3
Alvanley Terr. Frod 74 A4
Alvanley View. Elton 72 A2
Alvanley Way. El Por 69 F2
Alvaston Rd. Nant 204 C3
Alvaston Wlk. Crewe 189 F1
Alverton Cl. Wid 22 B4
Alveston Cl. Mfield 86 C1
Alvis Rd. Hawa 116 A2
Alwyn Gdns. Chest 118 B4
Alyn Rd. M Traf 96 C1
Alyndale Rd. Brough 140 B3
Amar Rd. Hay 1 B3
Amberleigh Cl. Apple 27 D2
Amberley Dr. Altr 32 A4
Amberley Rd. Mfield 112 A3
Ambleside. Chest 119 D3
Ambleside Cl. Beb 43 F4
Ambleside Cl. Mfield 111 F3
Ambleside Cl. Run 49 F3
Ambleside Cl. Winsf 126 B2
Ambleside Cl. Wist 189 F1
Ambleside Cres. Warr 8 B2
Ambleside Ct. Congle 155 F1
Ambleside Rd. El Por 70 B1
Amelia Cl. Wid 13 D2
Amelia St. Warr 16 B4
Amersham Cl. Mfield 87 E2
Amy St. Crewe 190 B2
Anchor Cl. Run 50 B3
Anchorage The. Nest 66 B4
Anchorage The. Waver 143 D3
Ancoats Rd. L End 83 F4
Anderson Cl. Crewe 191 D2
Anderson Cl. Warr 9 D1
Anderson Ct. Beb 43 E3
Anderson St. Mfield 112 B4
Anderton Way. Wilm 34 B2
Andertons La. Henb 86 A1
Andover Cl. Warr 8 C1
Andrew Cl. Wid 22 B4
Andrew Cres. Chest 141 F4
Andrew Gr. Mfield 113 D4
Andrew La. H La 37 F4
Andrew's Cl. Tarv 121 D1
Andrew's Wlk. Hes 41 D4
Anglesey Dr. Poyn 36 C3
Anglesey Water. Poyn 36 C3
Angus Rd. Beb 43 E3
Angus Wlk. Mfield 86 C1
Ankers Knowl La. Mac For 114 B4
Ankers La. Mac For 114 B3
Ann Cl. El Por 69 E4
Ann St. North 79 E1
Ann St. Run 23 D2
Ann St W. Wid 23 D4
Annable Rd. Irlam 11 F4
Annan Cl. Congle 157 D1
Anne Ct. Kids 210 B3
Anne's Way. Chest 141 F4
Annette Ave. N-le-W 2 A3
Annie St. Warr 16 B3
Annions La. Hay Gr 205 F1
Annis Cl. A Edge 60 A1
Annis Rd. A Edge 60 A1
Ansdell Rd. Wid 13 E1
Anson Cl. Bram 35 F3
Anson Cl. Warr 8 C1
Anson Rd. Poyn 37 D2
Anson Rd. Wilm 34 C1
Anthony Dr. Moult 126 C4
Anthony's Way. Hes 41 D4
Antons Rd. Halew 21 D3
Antony Rd. Warr 16 A1
Antrim Cl. Hay 1 B3
Antrim Dr. El Por 69 F1
Antrim Rd. Warr 8 A1
Antrobus St. Congle 156 B2
Anvil Cl. Saug 94 A1
Apple Market St. North 103 F4
Apple Tree Cl. Hale 21 F1
Apple Tree Gr. El Por 94 C4
Appleby Cl. Mfield 111 F3
Appleby Cl. Wid 22 B4
Appleby Rd. Warr 8 B2
Applecroft. N-u-L 210 C1
Applecross Cl. Warr 10 A3
Appledale Dr. El Por 95 D4
Applefield. North 103 E4
Appleton Cl. Congle 178 C4
Appleton Dr. El Por 69 F2
Appleton Hall Gdns. Apple 26 C3
Appleton Mews. Lymm 18 B2
Appleton Rd. Chest 118 C3
Appleton Rd. Wid 13 D1
Appleton St. North 78 B1
Appleton St. Wid 23 D4
Appleton Thorn
Trading Estate. Apple 27 E3
Appleton Village. Wid 13 D1
Appleton Wlk. Wilm 34 B1
Appletree Gr. Warr 8 C1
Appleyards La. Chest 141 F4
Apprentice La. Wilm 33 F2
April Rise. Mfield 87 D1
Apron Rd. Wythe 33 E3
Aragon Ct. Run 24 B2
Aragon Green. Blacon 117 F3
Aran Cl. Hale 21 E1
Arbour Cl. Mfield 87 E2
Arbour Cres. Mfield 87 E2
Arbour Mews. Mfield 87 E2
Arbour St. Kids 210 B3
Arbourhay St. Mfield 87 F1
Arbury La. Win 8 B3
Arcade The. El Por 70 A3
Arcade The. North 103 F4
Archer Ave. Warr 16 C1
Archer Cl. Boll 87 F4
Archers Way. Blacon 118 A2
Archers Way. El Por 69 F1
Arclid Cl. Wilm 34 C1
Arden. Wid 12 A1
Arden Cl. Chea 34 B4
Arden Cl. Warr 10 A3
Arden Ct. Congle 179 D4
Arden Dr. Nest 66 C3
Arden St. N Mills 39 E4
Ardenbrook Rise. Prest 86 C3
Ardern Lea. Alva 73 E1
Arderne Ave. Crewe 190 A1
Ardleigh Cl. Crewe 189 F4
Argyll Ave. Beb 43 E2
Argyll Ave. Chest 141 D4
Argyll Cl. Mfield 87 D1
Arkenshaw Rd. Croft 9 D4
Arkenstone Cl. Wid 12 B1
Arkle Ave. Wilm 34 C2
Arklow Dr. Hale 21 E1
Arkwright Cl. Winsf 149 D4
Arkwright Ct. Run 23 F2
Arkwright Rd. Run 23 F2
Arley Ave. Warr 26 B4
Arley Cl. Alsag 193 E2
Arley Cl. Chest 118 C3
Arley Cl. Mfield 112 A4
Arley Dr. Wid 12 A1
Arley End. H Legh 29 E2
Arley Mossend La. B Hea 54 B1
Arley Pl. Wist 206 A4
Arley Rd. Antro 54 A4
Arley Rd. Apple 27 E1
Arley Rd. North 104 B4
Arlington Cl. Wist 206 B4
Arlington Cres. Wilm 59 F3
Arlington Dr. Gold 4 B4
Arlington Dr. Mfield 112 A4
Arlington Dr. Penk 14 C2
Arlington Dr. Poyn 36 B2
Arlington Way. Wilm 59 F3
Armett St. Mfield 112 B4
Armitstead Rd. Sand 174 C2
Armour Ave. Warr 8 A1
Armstrong Cl. Audlem 229 F2
Armstrong Cl. Warr 9 E2
Armthorpe Dr. El Por 69 E3
Arncliffe Dr. Burton 6 C3
Arndale. Run 49 F3
Arnhem Cres. Warr 16 B4
Arnhem Way. Hunt 142 A3
Arnold Pl. Wid 22 B4
Arnold St. Nant 204 C3
Arnold's Cres. Broug 139 D2
Arnside Ave. Congle 156 A1
Arnside Ave. Hay 1 A3
Arnside Cl. H La 37 F4
Arnside Cl. Winsf 126 B1
Arnside Gr. Warr 16 A1
Arpley Rd. Warr 16 A2
Arpley St. Warr 16 A2
Arran Cl. H Chap 130 B1
Arran Cl. Warr 9 D1
Arran Dr. Frod 74 B3
Arrivals Way. Wythe 33 D4
Arron Pl. Crewe 189 E2
Arrowcroft Rd. G Sutt 119 F3
Arrowsmith Dr. Alsag 193 D2
Arrowsmith Rd. Hay 1 C4
Arthill La. L Boll 20 A1
Arthog Dr. Altr 31 F4
Arthog Rd. Altr 31 F4
Arthur Ave. El Por 70 B3
Arthur St. Crewe 190 B1
Arthur St. Lost 80 A1
Arthur St. Run 23 D1
Arthur St. Warr 16 A3
Artists La. N Ald 85 E4
Artle Rd. Crewe 206 B4
Arundel Ave. Haz Gr 36 B4
Arundel Cl. Knuts 82 A4
Arundel Cl. Mfield 87 F1
Arundel Cl. Wist 205 F4
Arundel Ct. El Por 70 C2
Arundel Rd. Ch Hul 35 D3
Arundell Cl. Burton 6 C3
Ascol Dr. Plum 80 B2
Ascot Ave. Run 49 D3
Ascot Cl. Congle 156 B2
Ascot Cl. Mfield 87 E2
Ascot Cl. Warr 17 E1
Ascot Cl. Warr 17 F4

Ascot Dr. El Por 69 F2
Ash Ave. Irlam 11 E3
Ash Ave. N-le-W 2 B1
Ash Cl. El Por 69 F1
Ash Cl. H Chap 130 B2
Ash Cl. Malpas 213 E3
Ash Cl. Tarp 146 B1
Ash Gr. Chea 34 A4
Ash Gr. Chest 141 D3
Ash Gr. Congle 156 A2
Ash Gr. El Por 69 E3
Ash Gr. Gold 3 D4
Ash Gr. Knuts 57 E1
Ash Gr. Mfield 112 B2
Ash Gr. Middle 151 E4
Ash Gr. Nant 204 C2
Ash Gr. Run 49 E4
Ash Gr. Sch Gr 193 F4
Ash Gr. Warr 16 B2
Ash Gr. Weave 102 C4
Ash Gr. Wid 22 B4
Ash Gr. Wilm 34 B2
Ash Hay La. Pict 96 B1
Ash House La. L Lei 77 E4
Ash La. Apple 26 C4
Ash La. Wid 22 A4
Ash Lawn Ct. Chest 118 B2
Ash Priors. Wid 12 B2
Ash Rd. Crewe 190 B3
Ash Rd. Cudd 101 F1
Ash Rd. Elton 72 B2
Ash Rd. Hay 1 C4
Ash Rd. Hol Gr 11 D1
Ash Rd. Lymm 18 B2
Ash Rd. Part 11 E2
Ash Rd. Penk 14 C2
Ash Rd. Poyn 36 C2
Ash Rd. Win 8 A3
Ash St. North 79 D1
Ash Terr. Mfield 112 B2
Ash Way. Hes 41 D3
Ashbank. North 104 B4
Ashberry Cl. Wilm 60 B4
Ashberry Dr. Apple 27 D3
Ashbourne Ave. Run 49 D3
Ashbourne Cl. El Por 94 C4
Ashbourne Dr. H La 37 F3
Ashbourne Mews. Mfield 111 F4
Ashbourne Rd. Gt San 15 D3
Ashbourne Rd. Haz Gr 36 C4
Ashbrook Ave. Run 49 F2
Ashbrook Cres. Warr 16 B4
Ashbrook Dr. Prest 87 D3
Ashbrook Rd. Boll 87 F4
Ashbrook Rd. N Ald 85 F3
Ashbury Cl. Run 24 B1
Ashby Dr. Sand 174 B3
Ashby Pl. Chest 118 C2
Ashcroft. Wilm 59 F3
Ashcroft Ave. Shav 206 A2
Ashcroft Rd. Lymm 19 D2
Ashdale Cl. Law-g 193 E3
Ashdene Rd. Wilm 59 F3
Ashdown La. Warr 10 A3
Ashdown Rd. Oller 82 C3
Ashenhurst Rd. Alsag 193 F2
Ashenough Rd. Kids 210 B3
Ashfield Cl. Lymm 19 D2
Ashfield Cres. Beb 43 E4
Ashfield Cres. Blacon 117 E3
Ashfield Dr. Mfield 87 D1
Ashfield Gr. Irlam 11 F3
Ashfield Rd. Beb 43 E4
Ashfield Rd. El Por 70 B3
Ashfield Rd N. El Por 70 B3
Ashford Cl. Wilm 34 B2
Ashford Rd. Wilm 60 A2
Ashford Way. Wid 13 E1
Ashgate La. H Winch 79 F3
Ashgrove. Winsf 149 E4
Ashlands. Frod 74 B4
Ashlea Dr. Willas 205 F3
Ashley Cl. Hasl 191 E3
Ashley Cl. Warr 17 E2
Ashley Ct. Holt 196 B4
Ashley Dr. Ch Hul 35 E3
Ashley Dr. Hart 103 D3
Ashley Gdns. H La 37 E4
Ashley Mill La. Ashl 31 E4
Ashley Mill Rd N. Altr 31 F4
Ashley Rd. Ashl 31 F4
Ashley Rd. Mere 56 B4
Ashley Rd. Rosth 31 E2
Ashley Rd. Run 23 E1
Ashley Rd. Wilm 34 A1
Ashley Way. Wid 23 D4
Ashley Way W. Wid 22 C4
Ashmead Cl. Alsag 193 F2
Ashmead Mews. Alsag 193 F2
Ashmore Cl. Middle 151 E3
Ashmore Cl. Warr 10 A2
Ashmore's La. Alsag 193 E2
Ashmuir Cl. Blacon 117 F2
Ashmuir Cl. Crewe 190 A3
Ashness Dr. Bram 35 F4
Ashridge St. Run 22 C2
Ashton Ave. Mfield 86 B1
Ashton Cl. Beb 43 F2
Ashton Cl. Congle 157 D1
Ashton Cl. Frod 49 E1
Ashton Cl. Middle 151 E3
Ashton Cl. Run 48 C3
Ashton Dr. Frod 49 E1
Ashton La. Asht 121 F3
Ashton Rd. Man 99 F2
Ashton Rd. N-le-W 2 B3
Ashton Rd. Norley 100 A2
Ashton St. Warr 16 A3
Ashtree Cl. Nest 67 D4
Ashtree Cl. Prest 87 E4
Ashtree Croft. Will 68 A4
Ashtree Dr. Nest 67 D4
Ashtree Farm Ct. Will 68 A4
Ashville Ct. Wist 206 A4
Ashville Rd. Run 49 F2
Ashwood. Altr 31 D4
Ashwood Ave. Gold 3 E4
Ashwood Ave. Warr 16 C4
Ashwood Cl. El Por 69 E1
Ashwood Cl. North 78 A2
Ashwood Cres. North 78 A2
Ashwood La. Stoak 96 A3
Ashwood Rd. Disley 38 B3
Ashworth Park. Knuts 81 F4
Askerbank La. Wd Gr 159 D1
Askrigg Ave. El Por 69 D3
Aspen Cl. El Por 69 F1
Aspen Cl. Hes 41 E4
Aspen Cl. Kids 195 F2
Aspen Gr. Saug 117 D4
Aspen Gr. Warr 17 D4
Aspen Way. Chest 119 D2
Aspen Way. H La 38 A4
Aspens The. Cudd 101 E3
Aspinall Cl. Warr 9 D2
Aspull Cl. Warr 9 E2
Asquith Cl. Hasl 191 E3
Assheton Wlk. Hale 21 F1
Astbury Cl. Gold 4 A4
Astbury Cl. Kids 195 E2
Astbury Ct. Congle 156 B1
Astbury Dr. North 78 A2
Astbury La Ends. Congle 178 C4
Astbury St. Congle 156 B1
Aster Cres. Run 49 F3
Aster Rd. Hay 1 C4
Aster Wlk. Part 11 F1
Astle Ct. Chelf 84 A2
Astley Cl. Warr 16 A2
Astley Cl. Wid 12 B2
Astley Ct. Irlam 11 F4
Astley Rd. Irlam 11 F4
Astmoor Bridge La. Run 23 F1
Astmoor East Interchange. Run 24 A2
Astmoor La. Run 23 F1
Aston Ave. Winsf 126 A1
Aston Ct. Warr 9 E1
Aston Fields Rd. Run 50 C2
Aston Green. Run 50 C3
Aston La. Ast 50 C1
Aston La. Run 50 C3
Aston La. Sutt 50 B1
Aston La. Woore 232 C1
Aston La N. Run 50 C2
Aston La S. Run 50 C2
Aston Rd. N-u-L 210 B1
Aston Way. Middle 128 C1
Aston Way. Wilm 34 B3
Astule Dr. Mfield 112 A4
Atcherley Cl. Fr La E 218 C4
Atherton La. Irlam 11 F3
Atherton Rd. El Por 69 F3
Athey St. Mfield 112 B4
Athlone Rd. Warr 8 A1
Athol Cl. Beb 43 F3
Athol Dr. Beb 43 F3
Athol Rd. Ch Hul 35 E3
Atholl Ave. Crewe 190 B1
Atholl Cl. Mfield 87 D1
Athy Cl. N-le-W 1 C2
Atlanta Ave. Wythe 33 D4
Atterbury Cl. Wid 12 B1
Attlee Ave. Cul 5 D2
Attwood Cl. Hasl 191 E2
Attwood St. Kids 195 D1
Aubourn Cl. Wid 12 B2
Auckery Ave. El Por 69 E2
Auckland Rd. Blacon 117 E2
Audlem Cl. Run 49 F2
Audlem Dr. North 104 A3
Audlem Rd. Audlem 230 A4
Audlem Rd. Hather 219 E2
Audlem Rd. Nant 204 C2
Audlem Rd. Woore 232 A1
Audley Cres. Chest 141 F3
Audley Rd. Alsag 193 F1
Audley Rd. Audley 210 A1
Audley Rd. Barth 208 C3
Audley Rd. Kids 210 A3
Audley Rd. N-u-L 210 A1
Audley St. Crewe 190 B3
Audley St W. Crewe 190 B3
Audre Cl. Gt San 14 B3
Aughton Way. Broug 139 E2
Augusta Dr. Mfield 87 D2
Austell Rd. Wythe 33 E4
Austin Cl. Winsf 149 E3
Austin St. North 79 E1
Austral Ave. Warr 17 E4
Australia La. Apple 17 E1
Autumn Ave. Knuts 57 E1
Avebury Cl. Gold 3 F4
Avebury Cl. Wid 13 F2
Avens Rd. Part 11 F2
Avenue The. A Edge 60 A1
Avenue The. Alsag 193 E2
Avenue The. Altr 31 F4
Avenue The. Beb 43 E4
Avenue The. Comb 78 B4
Avenue The. Gt Bar 120 C4
Avenue The. H Legh 29 E3
Avenue The. Kids 194 C1
Avenue The. Lymm 18 B1
Avenue The. Mars 79 D2
Avenue The. N-le-W 2 B2
Avenue The. Sand 174 C4
Avenue The. Tarp 146 B1
Avery Cl. Warr 8 C1
Avery Cres. Hay 1 B4
Avery Rd. Hay 1 B4
Avery Sq. Hay 1 B4
Aviemore Dr. Warr 9 D2
Avocet Cl. N-le-W 2 B2
Avocet Cl. Warr 8 B2
Avocet Dr. Winsf 149 E3
Avon. Wid 12 A1
Avon Ave. Penk 14 C2
Avon Cl. Kids 195 D1
Avon Cl. Mfield 87 D1
Avon Cl. Nest 66 C3
Avon Cl. Tarv 121 E2
Avon Ct. Alsag 193 E3
Avon Dr. Congle 156 C1
Avon Dr. Crewe 191 D3
Avon Rd. Altr 31 F4
Avon Rd. Chea 34 B4
Avon Rd. Cul 5 D1
Avon Wlk. Winsf 127 D1
Avondale. El Por 70 A1
Avondale Ave. Beb 43 F3
Avondale Dr. Wid 12 A1
Avondale Rd. Hay 1 B4
Avonlea Cl. Chest 140 C3
Avonside Way. Mfield 112 B3
Avro Way. Wythe 32 C4
Axminster Wlk. Bram 35 F4
Aycliffe Wlk. Wid 22 B4
Aylesbury Cl. El Por 69 E2
Aylesbury Cl. Mfield 87 E2
Aylesby Cl. Knuts 57 D1
Aylsham Cl. Wid 12 B2
Ayrshire Way. Congle 157 D1
Aysgarth Av. Crewe 173 D1
Azalea Gr. Run 49 F2

Babage Rd. Hawa 116 A2
Babbacombe Rd. Penk 14 C2
Bache Ave. Chest 118 B3
Bache Dr. Chest 118 B3
Bache Hall Ct. Chest 118 B3
Bache Hall Est. Chest 118 B3
Bachefield Ave. Hunt 142 A3
Bachelor's La. Chest 142 A4
Back Legh St. N-le-W 2 A2
Back Booth St. N-le-W 2 A2
Back Bridge St. N-le-W 2 A2
Back Brook Pl. Warr 16 C2
Back Crosland Terr. Hels 73 D1
Back Cross La. Congle 179 D4
Back Eastford Rd. Warr 16 A1
Back Eddisbury Rd. Mfield 113 E4
Back Eddisbury Rd. Rain 113 E4
Back Heathcote St. Kids 195 D1
Back High St. Run 23 D1
Back Jodrell St. N Mills 39 D4
Back La. Alpr 169 E3
Back La. Alva 73 E1
Back La. Antro 54 B4
Back La. Ashl 32 A2
Back La. B Hea 54 B4
Back La. Beest 167 E1
Back La. Betley 208 B1
Back La. Bic T 214 A2
Back La. Bre Gr 153 E3
Back La. Burton 6 B4
Back La. Congle 156 A2
Back La. Dudd 145 D3
Back La. Dun T 20 B3
Back La. H Legh 29 F3
Back La. Hay Gr 220 B3
Back La. Penk 14 A2
Back La. Peo 106 A4
Back La. Plum 81 D1
Back La. Rad 155 F3
Back La. Shav 206 C2
Back La. Threap 222 C4
Back La. Whit 52 C2
Back Lanes. Tarp 146 A1
Back Lawrence St. N-le-W 2 A2
Back Market St. N-le-W 2 A2
Back Paradise St. Mfield 112 B4
Back Park St. Congle 156 C1
Back Queen St. Chest 118 B1
Back River St. Congle 156 B2
Back Union Rd. N Mills 39 E4
Back Wallgate. Mfield 112 B4
Backford Cl. Run 50 B3
Badcock's La. Spurs 185 F2
Baddiley Cl. Badd 203 E1
Baddiley Hall La. Badd 217 D4
Baddiley La. Badd 203 E1
Baddington La. Fr La E 204 B1
Badger Ave. Crewe 190 A3
Badger Bait. Nest 66 C3
Badger Cl. Run 50 A3
Badger Rd. Mfield 87 E1
Badger Rd. Prest 87 D4
Badgers Cl. Christ 142 C4
Badgers Cl. El Por 94 C4
Badgers Cl. Winsf 126 A1
Badgers Park. Nest 66 C3
Badgers Set. Cudd 101 E3
Badgers Wlk. Chest 95 F1
Badgersrake La. El Por 68 C3
Badgersrake La. Led 68 B2
Badgersrake La. Pudd 68 B2
Bag La. Crow 101 F4
Bag La. Cudd 101 F4
Bagley La. Audlem 230 A1
Bagmere Cl. Bre Gr 153 F2
Bagmere Cl. Sand 174 C4
Bagmere La. Bre Gr 154 A3
Bagnall Cl. Gt San 15 E3
Bagot Ave. Warr 15 F4
Bagstock Ave. Poyn 36 C1
Baguley Ave. Wid 22 A3
Bahama Cl. Hay 1 B4
Bahama Rd. Hay 1 B4
Bailey Ave. El Por 69 F3
Bailey Cl. Crewe 190 B4
Bailey Cres. Congle 157 D2
Bailey Cres. Sand 175 E3
Bailey Ct. Alsag 193 F2
Bailey La. Part 11 F2
Bailey Wlk. Altr 31 E4
Bailey's Bank. Bidd 179 E2
Bailey's La. Hale 21 D1
Baileys Cl. Wid 13 D3
Baileys La. Halew 21 D4
Baines Ave. Irlam 11 F4
Baker Dr. El Por 69 F2
Baker Rd. Run 48 B4
Baker St. Mfield 112 B4
Baker's Ct. Winsf 126 C1
Baker's La. Winsf 126 C1
Bakestondale Rd. Po Shr 63 F2
Bakestonedale Rd. Rain 64 A2
Bakewell Cl. El Por 94 C4
Bakewell Rd. Burton 7 D4
Bakewell Rd. Haz Gr 36 C4
Bala Cl. Warr 7 F1
Baldock Cl. Warr 17 E2
Baldon Cres. Alsag 193 E3
Balfour Cl. Hasl 191 E2
Balham Cl. Wid 13 D2
Ball La. Boll 87 E3
Ball La. Crow 75 F2
Ball La. Kings 75 F2
Ballater Cres. Chest 119 D1
Ballater Dr. Warr 8 C2
Balliol Cl. S La E 112 C2
Balmoral Ave. Crewe 190 A1
Balmoral Ave. North 104 A3
Balmoral Cl. Knuts 57 D1
Balmoral Cl. Winsf 126 B2
Balmoral Cres. Mfield 87 F1
Balmoral Dr. H Chap 130 A1
Balmoral Dr. H La 37 F4
Balmoral Dr. Hels 73 D2
Balmoral Dr. Poyn 36 B2
Balmoral Gdns. El Por 70 B2
Balmoral Pk. Blacon 118 A2
Balmoral Rd. Warr 16 C1
Balmoral Way. Wilm 60 A3
Bamburgh Ct. El Por 70 C2
Bamford Cl. Chea 34 B4
Bamford Cl. Run 49 E4
Bamford St. Mfield 87 F1
Banbury Cl. Mfield 87 F1
Banbury Dr. Gt San 15 E3
Banbury St. Kids 194 B1
Bancroft. Act Br 76 C2
Bancroft Rd. Wid 13 E1
Bandon Cl. Hale 21 E1
Banff Ave. Beb 43 E3
Bangor Cl. El Por 94 C4
Bank Cl. Chest 118 C3
Bank Cl. Mfield 112 C4
Bank Cl. Nest 67 D3
Bank Coole La. New 228 C3
Bank Farm Mews. Bic T 214 C3
Bank Gdns. Penk 14 C2
Bank House La. Hels 73 E2
Bank House La. Small 177 D3
Bank La. Eaton 134 B1
Bank La. Rain 89 E3
Bank Mews. Hels 73 E2
Bank Rd. Con Q 91 E1
Bank Side. Weave 77 E1
Bank Sq. Wilm 60 A4
Bank St. Congle 156 C1
Bank St. Gold 3 D4
Bank St. Hol Gr 11 D3
Bank St. Kids 195 E2
Bank St. Mfield 112 C4
Bank St. N-le-W 1 C2
Bank St. Warr 16 A3
Bank St. Wid 23 D2
Bank The. Sch Gr 195 D4
Bankes' La. Run 48 C3
Bankfield Ave. Irlam 11 E3
Bankfield Ave. Wist 206 A4
Bankfield Rd. Wid 12 B1
Bankfields Dr. Beb 44 A3
Bankhall La. Altr 31 F4
Bankhey. Nest 66 C3
Bankhouse Dr. Congle 157 D3
Banklands Cl. Irlam 11 E3
Banks Cl. Congle 156 B2
Banks Cres. Warr 16 C2
Banks Rd. Hes 40 B4
Banks View. Goost 107 F1
Bankside. Altr 32 B3
Bankside. Run 50 C4
Bankside Cl. Wilm 34 B1
Bankside Ct. Alsag 193 F3
Banky Fields. Congle 156 B1
Barbauld St. Warr 16 A3
Barber Dr. Sch Gr 194 C4
Barber St. Mfield 112 C3
Barber's La. Antro 53 E3
Barber's La. North 103 F4
Barberry Wlk. Part 11 F1
Barbondale Cl. Gt San 14 C4
Barbridge Rd. N-u-L 210 B1
Barclay Rd. Poyn 36 C1
Bardell Cl. Poyn 36 B1
Bardsley Ave. Warr 7 F1
Barford Cl. G San 7 D1
Barford Dr. Gold 4 A4
Barham Ct. Warr 9 E2
Barington Dr. Run 50 C4
Baristow Cl. Chest 118 B2
Bark St. Congle 156 C1
Barker St. Crewe 190 B1
Barker St. Nant 204 C3
Barker's Hollow Rd. P-o-t-H 51 D3
Barkhill Rd. Chest 119 D4
Barley Castle Cl. Apple 27 D2
Barley Croft. Alsag 193 F1
Barley Croft. Chest 142 A4
Barley Dr. Bram 35 F4
Barley Rd. Warr 17 E2
Barleycastle La. Apple 27 E2
Barleycroft Terr. Sch Gr 194 C4
Barlow Dr. Winsf 148 C4
Barlow Gr. St Hel 1 A1
Barlow Hill. Winc 136 C1
Barlow Rd. Moult 126 C4
Barlow Rd. Wilm 34 A1
Barlow Way. Sand 175 D4
Barmouth Cl. Warr 7 F1
Barn Croft. Hels 73 E2
Barn Croft Rd. Halew 21 D4
Barn Ct. Clutt 182 B1
Barn La. Gold 2 C4
Barn Meadow. North 78 C1
Barn Rd. Congle 156 B2
Barn Rd. Threap 222 B4
Barn St. Wid 23 D3
Barn Way. N-le-W 2 A2
Barnabas Ave. Crewe 189 F3
Barnaby Rd. Poyn 36 B1
Barnack Cl. Warr 17 D4
Barnacre Dr. Nest 41 D1
Barnard Cl. Mfield 111 F3
Barnard St. Warr 15 E2
Barnbridge Cl. Sch Gr 194 C4
Barnbrook Cl. Winsf 126 A1
Barncroft. Run 50 B4
Barncroft Cl. Chelf 84 A2
Barnes Ave. Warr 9 D1
Barnes Cl. Blacon 117 F3
Barnes Cl. Gt San 15 D3
Barnes Cl. Hasl 191 E2
Barnes Cl. Wid 13 E1
Barnes Rd. Wid 13 E1
Barneston Rd. Wid 13 F2
Barnett Ave. N-le-W 1 C2
Barnett St. Mfield 112 A4
Barnett Wlk. Crewe 206 B4
Barnfield. Tatt 166 A1
Barnfield Ave. Run 50 B3
Barnfield Rd. Boll 87 F3
Barnfield Rd. Warr 17 E4
Barnham Cl. Gold 3 D4
Barnhill Farm Cotts. Bot H 214 B1
Barnhill Grange. Brox 183 D2
Barnhill Rd. Brox 183 D1
Barnhouse La. Gt Bar 98 A2
Barns La. Dun T 20 A3
Barns Pl. Altr 32 B4
Barnside Way. Mfield 87 E2
Barnside Way. Moult 126 C4
Barnstaple Way. Penk 14 C2
Barnston Ct. Farn 180 C1
Barnston Rd. Hes 41 D4
Barnston Towers Cl. Hes 41 E4
Barnswood Cl. Warr 17 E1

Barnton Cl. Gold 3 E4
Barnwell Ave. Cul 4 B2
Barnwell Cl. Wist 206 A4
Baron Cl. Warr 17 E4
Baron's Cl. Wid 22 B4
Baronet Rd. Warr 16 A1
Baronia Pl. Nant 204 C3
Barons Cl. Run 23 F1
Barons Quay Rd. North 78 C1
Barons Rd. Shav 206 A2
Barony Bldgs. Nant 204 C3
Barony Ct. Nant 204 C4
Barony Rd. Nant 204 C4
Barony Terr. Nant 204 C3
Barony Way. Chest 140 C3
Barracks La. Burl 203 F1
Barracks La. Burw 184 B3
Barracks La. Mfield 112 C4
Barracks Sq. Mfield 112 A3
Barrastitch La. Cudd 101 F3
Barratt Rd. Alsag 193 F2
Barrel Well Hill. Chest 118 C1
Barrie Gdns. Kids 210 B4
Barrow Green. Chea 34 B4
Barrow Hall Farm. Gt Bar 120 C3
Barrow Hall La. Gt San 14 C4
Barrow La. Altr 32 A4
Barrow La. N-le-W 3 E1
Barrow La. Tarv 121 E2
Barrow Meadow. Chea 34 C4
Barrow's Brow. Peo 81 F1
Barrow's Green La. Wid 13 F2
Barrow's Row. Wid 13 D2
Barrowdale Rd. Gold 3 D4
Barrows Cl. Crewe 190 A4
Barrule Cl. Apple 26 B4
Barry St. Warr 16 B2
Barrymore Ave. Warr 16 C2
Barrymore Cres. Comb 78 B4
Barrymore Ct. Warr 17 D1
Barrymore Rd. Run 49 D4
Barrymore Rd. Warr 17 D1
Barrymore Rd. Weave 77 F1
Barrymore Way. Beb 43 D3
Bars The. Chest 118 C1
Barsbank Cl. Lymm 18 B2
Barsbank La. Lymm 18 B2
Barston Ave. El Por 69 F3
Bartegate. Run 50 A3
Bartholomew Way. Chest 141 E3
Bartholomews Ct. Sea 116 C3
Barthomley Cres. Crewe 189 E2
Barthomley Rd. Audley 209 D1
Barthomley Rd. Barth 208 A4
Barthomley Rd. Betley 208 C2
Barton Ave. Warr 17 D1
Barton Cl. Run 50 B4
Barton Cl. Wilm 34 B1
Barton Ct. Winsf 126 C1
Barton Rd. Barton 181 E1
Barton Rd. Congle 156 C2
Barton Rd. Farn 180 C1
Barton St. Gold 3 D4
Barton St. Mfield 112 B3
Bartons Pl. North 79 D1
Barwood Ave. Law-g 194 A3
Basford Rd. Crewe 206 B4
Basford Way. Winsf 126 A1
Baskervyle Cl. Hes 41 D3
Baskervyle Rd. Hes 41 D3
Baslow Dr. Chea 34 B4
Bate's Mill La. Beest 167 F3
Bate's Mill La. Tiver 167 F3
Bateman Rd. Lost 80 A1
Batemans Cl. Wist 206 A4
Batemill Cl. Mfield 86 C1
Batemill La. Peo 108 B3
Batemill La. With 108 B3
Bates La. Hels 73 E2
Bath Cres. Ch Hul 35 D3
Bath La. Audlem 230 A2
Bath St. Chest 118 C1
Bath St. Sand 175 E3
Bath St. Warr 16 A3
Batherton Cl. Wid 23 D4
Batherton La. Fr La E 204 C1
Bathwood Dr. Nest 66 C3
Batterbee Ct. Hasl 191 E3
Battersby La. Warr 16 B3
Battery La. Warr 17 F4
Bawtry Ct. Warr 8 C1
Baxter Cl. Run 50 B4
Baxter St. Warr 15 F3
Baycliffe. Lymm 18 B1
Baycliffe Cl. Run 49 E3
Bayley Rd. Willas 205 E3
Baytree Cl. El Por 69 F1
Bayvil Cl. Run 50 C4
Beach Gr. Hart 103 E3
Beach House La. Mobb 32 A1
Beach Rd. Hart 103 D3
Beach Rd. North 103 D3
Beachin La. Codd 182 A2
Beacon Hill View. Run 48 B4
Beacon La. Hes 41 D4
Beaconsfield Cres. Wid 13 D2
Beaconsfield Gr. Wid 13 D2
Beaconsfield Rd. Run 22 C1
Beaconsfield Rd. Wid 13 D2
Beaconsfield St. Chest 118 C1
Beadnell Dr. Penk 14 C2
Beaford Dr. Wythe 33 F4
Beagle Point. Winsf 126 A1
Beagle Wlk. Wythe 33 F4
Beam St. Nant 204 C3
Beamont St. Wid 23 D2
Beard Cres. N Mills 39 E4
Beardsmore Dr. Gold 3 F4
Bearhurst La. Henb 111 D2
Bearstone Rd. N in H 236 C2
Bearstone Rd. Woore 236 C2
Beasley Cl. El Por 69 E2
Beatrice St. Warr 16 B2
Beatty Ave. Warr 8 B1
Beatty Dr. Congle 157 D2
Beatty Rd. Nant 204 B2
Beaufort Chase. Wilm 34 C1
Beaufort Cl. A Edge 60 A1
Beaufort Cl. Gt San 15 D3
Beaufort Cl. Run 49 D4
Beaufort St. Warr 15 F2
Beaulieu Ave. Winsf 126 C1
Beaumaris Cres. Haz Gr 36 B4
Beaumaris Dr. El Por 70 B1
Beaumont Cl. Bidd 179 E2
Beaumont Cl. Prest 86 C3
Beaumont Cl. Wist 205 F4
Beauty Bank. Mar 125 F3
Beauty Bank. Winsf 149 D2
Beaver Centre The. North 103 F4
Beaverbrook Ave. Cul 5 D2
Beavers Cl. Pick 79 F4
Bebington Rd. El Por 69 E2
Becconsall Cl. Crewe 190 A4
Becconsall Dr. Crewe 190 A4
Beck La. Mfield 86 C1
Beckett Ave. Winsf 150 B4
Beckett Dr. Part 19 D4
Beckett,s La. Chest 142 A4
Beckford Cl. Crewe 189 F4
Bedells La. Wilm 60 A3
Bedford Ave. El Por 70 A1
Bedford Ave E. El Por 70 A1
Bedford Ct. Crewe 190 B1
Bedford Gdns. Crewe 190 B1
Bedford Gr. Alsag 193 D3
Bedford Gr. Irlam 11 D3
Bedford Pl. Crewe 190 B1
Bedford Rd. Kids 195 D2
Bedford Rd. Mfield 112 A4
Bedford Rise. Winsf 149 E3
Bedford St. Crewe 190 B1
Bedford St. Warr 26 B4
Bedward Row. Chest 118 B1
Beech Ave. Cul 5 D2
Beech Ave. Frod 74 B4
Beech Ave. Gold 3 F4
Beech Ave. Hay 1 C4
Beech Ave. Mobb 57 F3
Beech Ave. Penk 14 B2
Beech Ave. Sch Gr 193 F4
Beech Ave. Warr 17 E2
Beech Cl. A Edge 60 A2
Beech Cl. Congle 156 A2
Beech Cl. Cudd 101 F1
Beech Cl. Oller 82 C3
Beech Cl. Part 11 F1
Beech Cotts. A Edge 85 D4
Beech Cres. Poyn 36 C2
Beech Ct. Croft 4 C1
Beech Dr. Kids 210 C4
Beech Dr. Knuts 57 E1
Beech Dr. Wist 189 F1
Beech Farm Dr. Mfield 87 E1
Beech Gr. Chest 119 D2
Beech Gr. Crewe 190 C3
Beech Gr. El Por 95 D4
Beech Gr. Lymm 18 A1
Beech Gr. Mfield 112 C3
Beech Gr. Sand 175 E3
Beech Gr. Warr 16 B2
Beech Gr. Warr 17 D4
Beech Gr. Weave 102 B4
Beech Gr. Wilm 60 A3
Beech Gr. Winsf 149 E4
Beech Hall Dr. Mfield 87 E1
Beech Hey La. Will 43 D1
Beech Heyes Cl. Weave 102 C4
Beech Heyes Dr. Weave 102 C4
Beech La. Eaton 147 D3
Beech La. Mfield 87 E1
Beech La. Norley 75 F1
Beech La. North 78 A2
Beech La. Wilm 60 A3
Beech Rd. A Edge 60 A2
Beech Rd. H La 37 F4
Beech Rd. Hes 41 E4
Beech Rd. L Bud 124 B1
Beech Rd. Run 49 E4
Beech Rd. Sutt 50 A2
Beech Rd. W Br 65 F4
Beech Rd. Warr 26 B4
Beech Rise. Crow 76 A1
Beech Rise. Crow 76 B1
Beech Rise. W Br 65 E3
Beech St. Middle 128 B1
Beech St W. Crewe 190 B2
Beech Tree Cl. Willas 205 E3
Beech View Rd. Kings 75 E1
Beechcroft Ave. Wist 206 A4
Beechcroft Dr. El Por 70 A1
Beeches The. Chest 119 D3
Beeches The. Hels 73 E2
Beeches The. Nant 204 C3
Beechfield. Moult 126 C4
Beechfield Ave. Wilm 59 F3
Beechfield Cl. Hes 41 D4
Beechfield Dr. Middle 128 A1
Beechfield Gdns. Hart 103 D3
Beechfield Rd. A Edge 85 D4
Beechfield Rd. Ch Hul 35 D4
Beechfield Rd. El Por 70 A3
Beechfield Rd. Warr 17 D1
Beechlands Ave. Chest 119 D1
Beechmill Dr. Cul 4 C2
Beechmoore. Moore 25 D3
Beechmuir. Blacon 117 F2
Beechtree Farm Cl. H Legh 29 E4
Beechtree La. H Legh 29 D4
Beechway. Boll 88 A4
Beechway. Chest 118 B3
Beechway. H La 37 F4
Beechway. Wilm 60 A3
Beechways. Apple 26 B3
Beechways Dr. Nest 66 B4
Beechwood. Knuts 57 E1
Beechwood Ave. Gt San 14 C3
Beechwood Ave. N-le-W 2 B2
Beechwood Ave. Run 49 F3
Beechwood Ave. Warr 16 C4
Beechwood Dr. Alsag 193 D2
Beechwood Dr. Eaton 156 C4
Beechwood Dr. H Winch 79 F3
Beechwood Dr. Wilm 60 C4
Beechwood Gr. Ch Hul 35 D4
Beechwood La. Cul 4 B2
Beechwood Mews. Mfield 87 E1
Beechwood Rd. Beb 43 E4
Beechwood Rd. Brough 140 C3
Beecroft Cl. Warr 7 E1
Beeston Brow. Boll 88 A4
Beeston Cl. Boll 63 E1
Beeston Cl. H Chap 130 A2
Beeston Cl. Middle 151 E3
Beeston Cl. Warr 9 E2
Beeston Ct. Run 24 B2
Beeston Dr. Alsag 193 E2
Beeston Dr. Knuts 82 A4
Beeston Dr. Winsf 149 E4
Beeston Gn. El Por 69 F3
Beeston Mount. Boll 63 E1
Beeston Rd. Broug 139 D2
Beeston Rd. H Kin 161 D4
Beeston Rd. Wilm 34 B3
Beeston St. North 103 F4
Beeston Terr. Mfield 111 F3
Beeston View. Chest 141 F4
Beggarman's La. Knuts 82 A4
Belfry Cl. Wilm 60 B4
Belfry Dr. Mfield 87 E2
Belgrave Ave. Alsag 193 E3
Belgrave Ave. Brough 140 C3
Belgrave Ave. Congle 156 B2
Belgrave Ave. Warr 16 C4
Belgrave Cl. Dodle 162 A3
Belgrave Cl. Gold 4 B4
Belgrave Cl. Wid 13 F2
Belgrave Cres. Crewe 190 A1
Belgrave Dr. El Por 69 F3
Belgrave Pl. Chest 141 E4
Belgrave Rd. Chest 142 A4
Belgrave Rd. Irlam 11 E3
Belgrave Rd. Mfield 112 B2
Belgrave Rd. North 104 A2
Belgrave St. Chest 118 C1
Bell Ave. S La E 112 C2
Bell House Rd. Wid 13 E1
Bell La. Warr 17 F2
Bell Meadow Ct. Tarp 146 B1
Bellaport Rd. N in H 236 A2
Bellard Dr. Chest 119 D2
Belle Vue Terr. Sand 175 D3
Bellemonte Rd. Frod 74 B3
Belleville Ave. Wythe 33 F4
Bellhouse La. H Wal 25 E4
Bellhouse La. Warr 17 E1
Bellingham Dr. Run 49 D4
Bellvue La. G Sutt 119 F2
Belmont Ave. Mfield 86 B1
Belmont Ave. Sand 175 D4
Belmont Ave. Warr 16 C2
Belmont Cres. Gt San 15 D3
Belmont Rd. Bram 35 F3
Belmont Rd. G Bud 53 F1
Belmont Rd. North 104 B4
Belmont Rd. Wid 13 E1
Belvedere Cl. Frod 49 E1
Belvedere Dr. Blacon 117 F2
Belvedere Rd. N-le-W 2 A3
Belvedere Terr. Sch Gr 193 F4
Belvoir Rd. Warr 26 A4
Belvoir Rd. Wid 13 D1
Bembridge Cl. Wid 12 C2
Bembridge Ct. Middle 151 E4
Benbrook Gr. Wilm 34 B1
Benbrook Way. Warren 111 F1
Bendee Ave. Nest 67 D4
Bendee Rd. Nest 67 D4
Benja Fold. Ch Hul 35 F3
Benjamins Way. Audley 209 F1
Bennet Cl. Will 68 A4
Bennet Rd. North 104 B3
Bennett Ave. Warr 16 C3
Bennett St. Warr 16 A3
Bennett's La. H Kin 161 D4
Bennett's La. Wid 13 F1
Bennetts La. Bosl 158 C3
Benson Rd. Warr 9 E2
Benson Wlk. Wilm 34 B1
Bent La. Astb 178 A4
Bent La. Crow 101 E4
Bent La. Cul 5 D1
Bent La. Part 19 E4
Bentham Ave. Warr 8 B2
Bentham Rd. Cul 5 D1
Bentinck St. Run 22 C2
Bentley Dr. Crewe 191 D3
Bentley Gr. Winsf 149 E3
Bentley's Farm La. Whit 52 C3
Bentside Rd. Disley 38 B3
Benty Heath La. Thor H 42 C2
Benty Heath La. Will 43 D2
Beresford St. Warr 16 C4
Berkeley Ave. Alsag 193 E3
Berkeley Cl. Gold 4 B4
Berkeley Cres. Wist 206 A4
Berkeley Ct. Run 24 B2
Berkley Dr. Chest 141 E3
Berkshire Cl. Mfield 86 C1
Berkshire Dr. Congle 156 B2
Berkshire Dr. Irlam 11 E3
Berkshire Dr. Warr 17 F4
Bernard Ave. Apple 26 B4
Bernisdale Rd. Mobb 57 F2
Bernsdale Cl. Hawa 116 A2
Berristal Rd. Rain 88 C2
Berry Cl. El Por 69 E2
Berry Dr. El Por 69 E2
Berry Rd. Wid 12 B1
Berrystead. Hart 103 D2
Bertram St. N-le-W 2 A2
Berwick Ave. Beb 43 F2
Berwick Cl. Mfield 86 C1
Berwick Cl. Warr 17 F3
Berwick Ct. H Chap 130 A1
Berwick Gdns. El Por 69 D3
Berwick Gr. El Por 69 D3
Berwick Rd. El Por 69 D3
Berwyn Cl. El Por 69 D3
Berwyn Gr. St Hel 1 A2
Bessancourt. H Chap 130 B2
Bessemer Rd. Irlam 11 F3
Beswick St. Mfield 112 A4
Beswicks La. L End 59 E2
Beswicks La. N in H 236 B1
Beswicks Rd. North 78 C1
Betchton Cres. Sand 175 E4
Betchton Rd. Ha Gr 175 F1
Betchworth Cres. Run 49 E3
Betjeman Cl. Warr 16 C2
Betjeman Way. Crewe 190 C3
Betley Cl. North 104 A3
Betley St. Crewe 190 B2
Betsyfield Dr. Croft 9 D4
Bettisfield Ave. Beb 43 E3
Betty's La. Beest 168 B1
Bevan Ave. Kids 210 C3
Bevan Cl. Gt San 15 E3
Beverley Ave. Apple 26 B4
Beverley Dr. Hes 41 D3
Beverley Rd. Gt San 15 E3
Beverley Way. El Por 69 D4
Bevin Ave. Cul 5 D2
Bevyl Rd. Nest 41 D1
Bewsey Farm Rd. Gt San 15 E4
Bewsey Rd. Warr 15 F3
Bewsey St. Warr 16 A3
Bexhill Ave. Warr 8 A2
Bexington Dr. Crewe 190 A4
Bexton Ave. Winsf 126 A1
Bexton La. Knuts 82 A4
Bexton Rd. Knuts 56 C1
Bibbey St. Sch Gr 193 F4
Bibby Ave. Warr 16 C3
Bickerton Ave. Frod 74 B4
Bickerton Cl. Warr 9 E2
Bickley Cl. Ho Co 206 C1
Bickley Cl. Run 23 E1
Bickley Cl. Warr 8 C2
Bickley Town La. Bic T 214 C3
Bicknell Cl. Gt San 15 D4
Bida La. Congle 179 D4
Biddulph Comm Rd. Bidd 179 F4
Biddulph Park Rd. Bidd 179 F3
Biddulph Rd. Bidd 195 F3
Biddulph Rd. Congle 179 D4
Biddulph Rd. Kids 195 F3
Biddulph St. Congle 179 E4
Biddy's La. Mfield 88 A1
Bideford Rd. Penk 14 C2
Bidston Cl. Chest 118 B3
Bidston Dr. Wilm 34 C1
Bidston Gn. El Por 69 E2
Bidvale Way. Crewe 190 B4
Big Field La. Utkin 146 A4
Biggin Ct. Warr 8 C1
Bignall End Rd. Audley 210 A2
Billington Ave. N-le-W 2 B3
Billington Rd. Wid 12 A2
Bilton Cl. Wid 13 F1
Bilton Way. Crewe 189 F3
Bings Rd. W Br 65 F4
Bingswood Ave. W Br 65 F4
Bingswood Rd. W Br 65 F4
Binney Rd. North 104 A4
Binyon Way. Crewe 191 D2
Birch Ave. Crewe 190 C3
Birch Ave. Irlam 11 E3
Birch Ave. Mfield 87 D1
Birch Ave. Warr 8 A2
Birch Ave. Wilm 59 F3
Birch Ave. Winsf 127 D1
Birch Brook Rd. Lymm 19 D3
Birch Cl. Crewe 190 C3
Birch Cres. N-le-W 1 C2
Birch Ct. Congle 155 F2
Birch Fold. Allos 107 D1
Birch Gdns. Sand 175 E3
Birch Gr. El Por 70 A1
Birch Gr. H Winch 79 F3
Birch Gr. Knuts 57 E1
Birch Gr. Lost 105 D4
Birch Gr. Warr 16 B2
Birch Gr. Warr 16 C4
Birch Heath La. Christ 142 C4
Birch Heath Rd. Tarp 168 B4
Birch House Rd. N-u-L 210 B1
Birch La. Alsag 193 F1
Birch La. Ho Co 206 C1
Birch La. Winsf 127 F1
Birch Rd. Audley 209 F1
Birch Rd. Chest 140 C3
Birch Rd. Congle 155 F2
Birch Rd. Hay 1 C4
Birch Rd. Part 11 E2
Birch Rd. Poyn 36 C1
Birch Rd. Run 49 E4
Birch Rd. Wid 13 D2
Birch Rise. Chest 118 B3
Birch Tree Ave. Haz Gr 37 D4
Birch Tree Ct. Chest 118 C2
Birch Tree La. Goost 107 E1
Birch Tree La. Sch Gr 195 D4
Birch Tree Rd. Gold 3 F4
Birch Way. Prest 86 C3
Birchall Ave. Cul 4 C2
Birchall Moss La. Hather 219 F1
Birchall St. Croft 9 D4
Birchall Wlk. Crewe 206 B4
Birchdale Cres. Apple 26 B4
Birchdale Rd. Apple 26 B4
Birchdale Rd. Warr 17 D4
Birchen Rd. Halew 21 D4
Birchenwood Rd. Kids 195 F1
Birches Cl. Hes 41 D4
Birches Croft Dr. Mfield 86 C1
Birches La. L Den 105 D4
Birches La. Lost 105 D4
Birches The. Broug 139 D2
Birches The. Crewe 206 B4
Birches The. Nest 41 F1
Birchfield Ave. Sch Gr 193 F4
Birchfield Ave. Wid 13 D1
Birchfield Rd. Gt San 15 D3
Birchfield Rd. Lymm 19 D2
Birchfield Rd. Wid 13 D2
Birchgate Cl. Mfield 86 C1
Birchin Cl. Nant 205 D3
Birchin La. Nant 205 D3
Birchinall Cl. Mfield 112 A4
Birchmuir. Blacon 117 F2
Birchmuir Cl. Crewe 190 A3
Birchway. Boll 88 A4
Birchway. Ch Hul 35 E4
Birchway. H La 37 F4
Birchway. Hes 41 E3
Birchways. Apple 26 C3
Birchwood Bvd. Warr 9 E1
Birchwood Dr. Nant 204 C3
Birchwood Dr. Peo 106 B4
Birchwood Dr. Wilm 60 B4
Birchwood Park Ave. Warr 9 E3
Bird's La. Bun 186 A4
Birds La. Tatt 166 C1
Birdwell Dr. Gt San 15 D3
Birkdale Ave. Beb 43 E3
Birkdale Cl. Bram 35 F4
Birkdale Cl. Mfield 87 E2
Birkdale Ct. North 104 A4
Birkdale Dr. Kids 195 E2
Birkdale Rd. Penk 14 C2
Birkdale Rd. Wid 13 D3
Birkenhead Rd. Will 42 C1
Birkenhead St. North 104 B4
Birkett Ave. El Por 70 B1
Birkin Cl. Knuts 57 E2
Birkinheath La. Rosth 31 D2
Birley St. N-le-W 2 B2
Birtles Cl. Sand 175 E4
Birtles La. N Ald 85 F1

Birtles Rd. Mfield 86 B1
Birtles Way. Wilm 34 B3
Birtwistle Rd. North 104 B3
Bishop Rd. Boll 88 A4
Bishop Reeves Rd. Hay 1 C4
Bishop St. Chest 118 C2
Bishop's Cl. Kids 210 B4
Bishopdale Cl. Gt San 14 C4
Bishops Ct. Broug 139 E2
Bishops Ct. Warr 7 F2
Bishops Gdns. El Por 70 A3
Bishops Way. Wid 13 E2
Bishops Wood. Nant 204 C1
Bishopsfield Ct. Chest 118 C2
Bispham Rd. Gt San 15 D2
Bittern Cl. Poyn 36 A2
Bittern Cl. Warr 8 B2
Bittern Gr. Mfield 87 D1
Black Denton's Pl. Wid 13 E1
Black Diamond St. Chest 118 B2
Black Firs La. Rad 155 F2
Black Friars. Chest 118 B1
Black La. Mfield 87 F1
Black Lion La. El Por 69 E3
Black Moss Rd. Dun T 20 C4
Black Park Rd. Whitch 226 B1
Black Rd. Mfield 112 C4
Blackacres Cl. Sand 174 C3
Blackboards La. El Por 69 D4
Blackbrook Cl. Wid 12 B2
Blackbrooke Ave. Warr 8 C1
Blackburn Cl. Gold 3 F4
Blackburne Ave. Wid 22 A3
Blackburne Cl. Warr 9 E1
Blackcroft Ave. North 78 A1
Blackden La. Goost 108 A2
Blackden La. Sidd 132 C4
Blackden Wlk. Wilm 34 B1
Blackdown Cl. El Por 69 D3
Blackeys La. Nest 66 C4
Blackhill La. Knuts 81 F4
Blackhurst Brow. M St A 61 D1
Blackhurst St. Warr 16 A3
Blackledge Cl. Warr 9 D2
Blackshaw Cl. Congle 157 D1
Blackshaw Dr. G San 7 D1
Blackshaw La. A Edge 59 F1
Blackshaw St. Mfield 112 B4
Blackthorn Cl. Broug 139 D2
Blackthorn Cl. Hunt 142 A3
Blackthorn Pl. N-u-L 210 C1
Blackthorn Wlk. Part 11 E1
Blackthorne Ave. El Por 95 D4
Blackwell Cl. Middle 151 E3
Blacon Ave. Blacon 118 A3
Blacon Hall Rd. Blacon 117 F3
Blacon Point Rd. Blacon 117 F2
Blagg Ave. Nant 204 B2
Blair Cl. Haz Gr 36 B4
Blair Dr. Wid 12 A2
Blairgowrie Dr. Mfield 87 D2
Blaizefield Cl. Woore 232 B1
Blake Cl. Blacon 117 F3
Blake Cl. Wist 189 F1
Blake La. Cudd 102 A1
Blake St. Congle 156 B2
Blakeacre Rd. Halew 21 D3
Blakeden La. Mar 125 F1
Blakeden La. Winsf 148 C4
Blakeley Brow. Beb 43 D3
Blakeley Ct. Beb 43 D4
Blakeley Dene. Beb 43 D4
Blakeley Rd. Beb 43 D3
Blakelow Bank. Mfield 112 C3
Blakelow Cl. Middle 151 D4
Blakelow Cres. Hay Gr 205 F2
Blakelow Rd. Mfield 112 C3
Blakely La. Mobb 58 C4
Blakemere Cl. Whitch 226 A1
Blakemere Ct. El Por 70 B4
Blakemere La. Norley 100 B2
Blakemere Way. Sand 174 C4
Blandford Rd. Gt San 15 D3
Blankney The. Nant 204 C2
Blantern Rd. H Kin 161 D4
Blantyre St. Run 22 C2
Blaze Hill. Rain 88 C4
Bleasdale Rd. Crewe 173 D1
Bleeding Wolf La. Sch Gr 194 C3
Blenheim Cl. Mfield 87 D1
Blenheim Cl. Poyn 36 C2
Blenheim Cl. Warr 8 C1
Blenheim Cl. Wilm 60 B4
Blenheim Cl. Wist 205 F4
Blenheim Ct. Alsag 193 E3
Blenheim Gdns. Winsf 149 E4
Blossom Hts. North 103 E4
Blossom Rd. Part 11 F1
Blossoms La. Ch Hul 35 D1
Blossoms La. Wilm 35 D1
Blue Cap La. Hamp 213 E4
Blue Hatch. Frod 74 B4
Bluebell Ave. Hay 1 C4
Bluebell Cl. Hunt 142 A3
Bluebell Cl. Mfield 87 E2
Bluebell Ct. Run 49 F2
Bluebell La. Mfield 87 E2
Bluebell Mews. Mfield 87 E2
Bluecoat St. Warr 16 A4
Blundell Rd. Wid 22 B4
Blyth Cl. Mfield 86 C1
Blyth Cl. Run 50 B3
Blyth Rd. Beb 43 E4
Blythe Ave. Ch Hul 35 E3
Blythe Ave. Congle 156 A1
Blythe Ave. Wid 13 D3
Blythe Pl. Winsf 127 D1
Blythings The. Tarp 146 B2
Boat Stage. Lymm 18 C2
Boathorse Rd. Kids 210 C4
Boathouse La. Nest 41 E2
Bob's La. Irlam 11 E2
Boden St. Mfield 112 B4
Bodiam Ct. El Por 70 C1
Bodmin Ave. Mfield 86 C1
Bodmin Cl. Run 50 A3
Bodmin Dr. Bram 35 F4
Bodnant Cl. Crewe 190 A4
Bold Cross. Bo Hea 13 F4
Bold La. Bo Hea 6 B4
Bold La. Burton 6 B4
Bold Pl. Chest 118 B1
Bold Sq. Chest 118 C1
Bold St. Hasl 191 E2
Bold St. Run 23 D2
Bold St. Sand 175 D3
Bold St. Warr 16 A3
Bold St. Wid 23 D4
Bolesworth Hill Rd. Brox 183 E2
Bolesworth Rd. Brox 183 E4
Bolesworth Rd. Chest 118 C3
Bolesworth Rd. Tatt 183 E4
Boleyn Cl. Blacon 117 F3
Boleyn Ct. Run 24 B2
Boleynwood Ct. Wilm 34 A1
Bolland's Ct. Chest 118 B1
Bollin Ave. Altr 31 D4
Bollin Ave. Winsf 127 D1
Bollin Cl. Alsag 192 C2
Bollin Cl. Cul 5 D1
Bollin Cl. Lymm 19 D2
Bollin Cl. Sand 174 C4
Bollin Cl. Winsf 127 D1
Bollin Dr. Congle 156 C1
Bollin Dr. Lymm 19 D2
Bollin Gr. Bidd 179 F1
Bollin Hill. Wilm 60 A4
Bollin Mews. Prest 86 C4
Bollin Way. Prest 87 D3
Bollin Wlk. Wilm 60 A4
Bollinbarn. Mfield 87 D1
Bollinbarn Dr. Mfield 87 D1
Bollinbrook Rd. Mfield 87 D1
Bollington Ave. North 104 A3
Bollington La. N Ald 84 C1
Bollington Rd. Boll 87 F3
Bollinway. Altr 32 A4
Bollinwood Chase. Wilm 60 B4
Bolshaw Farm La. Chea 34 B3
Bolshaw Rd. Chea 34 B3
Bolton Ave. Ch Hul 35 D3
Bolton Ave. Warr 16 C2
Bolton Cl. Gold 4 A4
Bolton Cl. Poyn 36 B2
Bomish La. With 108 B2
Bond Cl. Warr 15 E2
Bond St. Mfield 112 B4
Bond St. North 78 B1
Bonis All La. Prest 61 F2
Boon Hill Rd. Audley 209 F1
Booth Ave. Asht 121 F4
Booth Ave. L Bud 147 F4
Booth Ave. Sand 175 E3
Booth Bed La. Allos 107 D2
Booth Bed La. Goost 107 D2
Booth La. Middle 151 F3
Booth La. Sand 151 F3
Booth Rd. Hart 103 D2
Booth Rd. Wilm 34 A1
Booth St. Audley 209 E1
Booth St. Congle 156 B1
Booth St. N-le-W 2 A2
Booth St. Warr 15 F2
Booth's Hill Cl. Lymm 18 B2
Booth's Hill Rd. Lymm 18 B2
Booth's La. Lymm 18 A1
Boothbank La. Rosth 30 A3
Boothby St. Mfield 112 B4
Boothfields. Knuts 57 E1
Booths La. Whit 52 C3
Boothsdale. Dela 122 B2
Boothsmere Cl. Sand 174 C4
Border Rd. Hes 41 D4
Border Way. Chest 119 E1
Borough Rd. Congle 156 C2
Borras Rd. Holt 196 A4
Borron Rd. N-le-W 2 A3
Borrowdale Ave. Warr 8 B2
Borrowdale Cl. Crewe 189 F2
Borrowdale Cl. Frod 74 B4
Borrowdale Rd. Wid 12 B4
Borrowmore Estate. Gt Bar 120 C4
Bosden Cl. Wilm 34 B3
Bosley Cl. Middle 151 E3
Bosley Cl. Wilm 34 B1
Bosley Dr. Poyn 37 D2
Bosley View. Congle 157 D1
Bostock Gn. El Por 69 F3
Bostock Rd. Mfield 111 F4
Bostock Rd. Moult 127 E2
Bostock Rd. Winsf 127 D2
Bostock St. Warr 15 F3
Boston Ave. Run 23 E1
Boston Cl. Ch Hul 35 E4
Boston Cl. Cul 4 C2
Boswell Ave. Warr 16 A1
Boteler Ave. Warr 15 F4
Bottoms La. Chest 141 F4
Boughey Rd. Audley 209 F1
Boughton. Chest 118 C1
Boughton Hill Ave. Chest 119 D1
Boughton Hill Dr. Chest 119 D1
Boulevard The. Broug 139 E2
Boulevard The. El Por 69 F2
Boulton Cl. Sand 175 E2
Boundary La. Chest 140 C3
Boundary La. Congle 179 D4
Boundary La. Hes 41 D4
Boundary La. Peo 108 A4
Boundary La. Sidd 132 C4
Boundary La N. Cudd 101 F1
Boundary La S. Cudd 101 F1
Boundary Park. Nest 66 B4
Boundary St. North 79 F1
Boundary St. Warr 16 C4
Bourne Ave. Gold 3 E4
Bourne Rd. Kids 194 C1
Bourne St. Sch Gr 195 E4
Bourne St. Wilm 59 F3
Bournemouth Cl. Run 50 B3
Bouverie St. Chest 118 B2
Boverton Cl. Warr 7 F1
Bow Green Rd. Altr 20 C1
Bow La. Altr 31 D4
Bowden Cl. Congle 156 A2
Bowden Cl. Cul 4 C2
Bowden Cl. Warr 16 C4
Bowden Cres. N Mills 39 E4
Bowden Dr. North 104 B4
Bowden View La. Mere 29 F1
Bowe's Gate Rd. Bun 169 D1
Bowen Cl. Bram 35 F3
Bowen Cooke Ave. Crewe 190 A3
Bowen St. Crewe 190 A2
Bower Cres. Stret 26 B1
Bower Rd. Hes 41 E4
Bower St. Wid 13 E1
Bowerfield Ave. Haz Gr 36 B4
Bowerfield Cres. Haz Gr 36 C4
Bowery Ave. Ch Hul 34 C3
Bowfell Cl. Beb 43 E2
Bowfell Dr. H La 37 F4
Bowkers Cft. Hasl 191 F4
Bowland Cl. Run 49 F3
Bowland Cl. Warr 10 A3
Bowland Croft. Crewe 173 D1
Bowland Rise. Winsf 149 D4
Bowling Green Ct. Nant 204 C3
Bowling Green Ct. North 78 C1
Bowman Ave. Warr 17 D3
Bowmere Cl. Bidd 179 E1
Bowmere Cl. Tarp 146 B1
Bowmere Dr. Winsf 149 E4
Bowmere Rd. Tarp 146 B1
Bowness Ave. Beb 43 E3
Bowness Ave. Irlam 11 E2
Bowness Ave. Warr 8 B1
Bowness Ct. H Chap 130 A2
Bowness Ct. Congle 156 A1
Bowness Rd. Crewe 189 E2
Bowood Ct. Warr 8 A2
Bowring Dr. Nest 41 D1
Bowyer Ave. Nant 204 C3
Box La. Congle 155 F2
Box Tree Mews. Mfield 112 A4
Box Wlk. Part 11 E1
Boxmoor Cl. Chest 141 D3
Boydell Ave. Warr 16 C2
Boydell Ave. Warr 17 D1
Boydell Way. Dodle 162 A3
Boyle Ave. Warr 8 C1
Boyles Hall Rd. Audley 209 F1
Bracken Cl. Broug 139 E2
Bracken Cl. Mfield 86 C1
Bracken Cl. Sch Gr 193 F4
Bracken Cl. Warr 9 E3
Bracken Rd. El Por 69 F2
Bracken Way. Comb 78 B4
Bracken Way. Frod 74 B3
Bracken Way. H Winch 79 E2
Bracken Way. Knuts 82 A4
Bracken Way. North 78 B2
Brackendale. Elton 72 A2
Brackendale. Run 49 E4
Brackenwood Cl. Wist 206 A4
Brackenwood Mews. Warr 17 E1
Brackenwood Mews. Wilm 60 C4
Brackle St. Run 22 C2
Brackley Ave. Irlam 11 E3
Brackley St. Warr 16 B1
Bradburn Rd. Irlam 11 F4
Bradburns La. Hart 103 D3
Bradbury Rd. Winsf 127 D1
Braddon Cl. North 103 F2
Bradeley Hall Rd. Hasl 191 E3
Bradeley Rd. Hasl 191 D3
Bradfield Rd. Crewe 190 A4
Bradford La. N Ald 85 E2
Bradford Rd. Winsf 126 C2
Bradford St. Chest 141 E4
Bradgate Ave. Chea 34 B4
Brading Wlk. Wythe 33 F4
Bradlegh Rd. N-le-W 2 A1
Bradley Cl. Middle 151 D4
Bradley Farm La. B of H 225 E4
Bradley La. Burton 2 A1
Bradley La. Frod 74 B3
Bradley La. N-le-W 1 C1
Bradley St. Mfield 112 C3
Bradshaw Ave. Brough 140 A4
Bradshaw Hall La. Chea 34 C4
Bradshaw La. Lymm 19 E2
Bradshaw La. Warr 17 D2
Bradshaw Pl. Congle 156 C1
Bradshaw St. Wid 13 D1
Bradwall Rd. Sand 175 D4
Bradwall St. Sand 175 D4
Bradwell Cl. El Por 70 A2
Bradwell Dr. Chea 34 B4
Bradwell Gr. Congle 156 C2
Bradwell Rd. Gold 3 F4
Bradwell Rd. Haz Gr 36 C4
Braemar Ave. North 104 B4
Braemar Cl. H Chap 130 B1
Braemar Cl. Warr 9 D2
Braemar Cl. Wist 205 F4
Braemar Ct. El Por 70 C2
Braeside Cl. El Por 69 E3
Braeside Cl. Mfield 112 C3
Braham Cres. Irlam 11 E2
Braidwood Ave. Knuts 57 E2
Brains La. Alpr 169 D3
Braintree Rd. Wythe 33 F4
Brairwood. Wilm 60 B4
Braithwaite Cl. Run 49 E3
Brake Level. Sch Gr 195 D4
Brake The. Sch Gr 195 D4
Brake Village. Sch Gr 195 D4
Brakeley Rd. L-Lei 77 E2
Bramall Cl. Sand 175 E4
Bramble Cl. Chest 142 A4
Bramble Cl. Mfield 87 D1
Bramble Cl. Penk 14 C2
Bramble Cl. Winsf 126 B2
Bramble Way. Run 49 F2
Brambles The. Hasl 191 D2
Brambling Cl. Run 49 F3
Bramhall Centre The.
Ch Hul 35 F3
Bramhall Cl. Winsf 126 A1
Bramhall Dr. Beb 43 F2
Bramhall Dr. H Chap 130 A2
Bramhall La S. Bram 35 F4
Bramhall Rd. Crewe 189 F1
Bramhall St. Warr 15 F3
Bramley Cl. Bram 35 F3
Bramley Cl. El Por 94 C4
Bramley Cl. Wilm 59 E2
Bramley Dr. Bram 35 F3
Bramley Rd. Bram 35 F3
Bramley Wlk. Hels 73 D1
Brampton Ave. Mfield 87 D1
Brampton Ct. St Hel 1 A2
Bramway. Ch Hul 35 E4
Bramway. H La 37 F4
Brancepth Ct. El Por 70 B2
Brancote Gdns. Beb 43 E4
Branden Dr. Knuts 57 D1
Brandon. Wid 12 A1
Brandwood Ave. Warr 8 A1
Bransdale Way. Mfield 111 F4
Brantfield Ct. Warr 8 C1
Brassey St. Chest 118 C1
Brassey Way. Willas 205 E3
Brassey's Contract Rd.
Ed Gr 199 D1
Brathwaite Rd. Gold 3 E4
Brattswood Dr. Law-g 194 A3
Bray Cl. Crewe 190 C3
Bray Cl. Run 49 E3
Bray Rd. Chest 140 C3
Bread St. Mfield 112 B4
Breamar Cl. Chest 119 E2
Breck Rd. Wid 13 D1
Breck The. El Por 69 F4
Brecon Dr. El Por 69 F1
Brecon Way. Wist 206 A4
Breconway. Winsf 149 D4
Bredon Cl. El Por 69 D3
Breezehill Cl. Nest 66 C4
Breezehill Park. Nest 66 C4
Breezehill Rd. Nest 66 C4
Brendon Ave. Warr 8 A2
Brendon Gr. St Hel 1 A2
Breninall Cl. Gt San 15 E3
Brent Cl. Poyn 36 A2
Brentfield. Wid 12 B1
Brenton Ct. Chea 34 C4
Brentwood Ave. Irlam 11 E3
Brentwood Rd. Blacon 117 F3
Brereton Cl. Crewe 189 F1
Brereton Cl. Malpas 213 D2
Brereton Cl. Run 50 A4
Brereton Cl. Sand 175 E4
Brereton Ct. Bre Gr 154 C3
Brereton Dr. Nant 204 C4
Brereton Gr. Irlam 11 F3
Brereton Heath La. Bre Gr 154 C3
Brereton La. Bra Gr 152 C4
Brereton La. Bre Gr 153 D4
Brereton La. Sp Gr 129 E1
Brereton Rd. Hart 103 D2
Brereton Rd. Wilm 34 C2
Bretton Ct Mews. Broug 139 F2
Bretton Dr. Broug 139 D2
Bretton La. Broug 139 F3
Bretton Rd. Broug 139 F2
Brian Ave. Warr 16 B4
Brian Ave. Warr 16 C1
Briar Ave. Hol Gr 11 D1
Briar Cl. Knuts 57 D2
Briar Dr. Hes 41 D4
Briar La. Weave 102 C4
Briar Rd. Gold 3 D4
Briardale Gdns. El Por 69 E3
Briardale Rd. El Por 69 E3
Briardale Rd. Will 43 D1
Briarfield Ave. Wid 12 A1
Briarfield Rd. El Por 70 A3
Briarfield Rd. Hes 41 D4
Briarlands Cl. Ch Hul 35 E3
Briarstead Cl. Ch Hul 35 E4
Briarswood. Kids 195 D1
Briarwood Ave. Mfield 112 B3
Briarwood Ave. Warr 16 C4
Brick Bank. Nant 204 C3
Brick Bank La. Allos 107 D1
Brick Kiln La. Moult 127 D4
Brick St. N-le-W 1 C2
Brick St. Warr 16 B3
Brickfield
Business Centre. North 79 E1
Brickfield La. Chest 119 F1
Brickhill La. Ashl 32 A2
Brickhurst Way. Warr 17 D4
Brickkiln La. Dun T 20 B2
Brickkiln La. Whitch 226 B1
Bridge Ave. Altr 32 B3
Bridge Ave. Warr 16 C2
Bridge Ave E. Warr 16 C3
Bridge Cl. Audley 209 F1
Bridge Cl. Cudd 102 A2
Bridge Cl. Lymm 19 D2
Bridge Cl. Wist 206 A4
Bridge Ct. Chest 119 D1
Bridge Ct. Nest 66 C4
Bridge Dr. Christ 142 B4
Bridge Dr. Wilm 34 B2
Bridge End Dr. Prest 87 D4
Bridge End La. Prest 87 D4
Bridge Foot. Warr 16 A2
Bridge Green. Prest 87 D4
Bridge La. Apple 26 C4
Bridge La. Cudd 101 F2
Bridge La. Frod 49 E1
Bridge La. Warr 17 E4
Bridge Meadow. El Por 69 F1
Bridge Pl. Chest 141 E4
Bridge Rd. Warr 17 E4
Bridge Row. Congle 156 C2
Bridge St. Brough 140 B4
Bridge St. Chest 118 B1
Bridge St. Gold 3 D4
Bridge St. Hay Gr 220 B4
Bridge St. Holt 180 C1
Bridge St. Mfield 112 B4
Bridge St. N-le-W 2 A2
Bridge St. Nest 66 C4
Bridge St. North 79 F1
Bridge St. Run 23 D2
Bridge St. W Br 65 F4
Bridge St. Warr 16 A3
Bridge St Row. Chest 118 B1
Bridge Terr. Chest 119 D1
Bridge View Close. Wid 23 D2
Bridgedown. Tarp 146 B1
Bridgefield Ave. Wilm 34 B1
Bridgeman Rd. Blacon 117 F2
Bridgeman St. Warr 15 E2
Bridgemere Cl. Sand 174 C4
Bridgemere La. Bridge 220 A1
Bridgemere La. Hather 219 F1
Bridgend. M Traf 97 D1
Bridges Rd. Stan 70 C3
Bridgeside Dr. Hels 73 D2
Bridgestones. Congle 156 B1
Bridgewater Ave. Warr 16 C2
Bridgewater Cl. Chea 34 B4
Bridgewater Cl. Congle 157 D1
Bridgewater Dr. Chest 119 E1
Bridgewater Mews. Warr 226 B4
Bridgewater Pl. Winsf 126 A1
Bridgewater St. Lymm 18 C2
Bridgewater St. Run 23 D1
Bridgeway East. Run 24 B1
Bridgeway West. Run 24 B1
Bridgfield Cl. H La 37 F4
Bridgnorth Gr. N-u-L 210 C1
Bridle Cl. Beb 43 F4
Bridle Hey. Nant 204 C1

Bridle Park. Beb 43 F4
Bridle Rd. Beb 43 F3
Bridle Rd. Crewe 190 A2
Bridle Rd. Woodf 35 F1
Bridle Way. El Por 69 E2
Bridle Way. Woodf 35 F1
Bridlemere Ct. Warr 16 C4
Brierley Rd. Congle 157 D1
Brierley St. Crewe 190 B2
Briers Cl. Warr 8 C2
Brieryhurst Rd. Kids 195 D2
Briggs Ave. Crewe 190 B1
Bright St. Crewe 190 A3
Brighton Cres. S La E 113 D2
Brighton St. Warr 15 F3
Brimelow Cres. Penk 14 C2
Brimstage Cl. Hes 41 E4
Brimstage Green. Hes 41 E4
Brimstage Rd. Hes 41 E4
Brindley Ave. Warr 16 C2
Brindley Ave. Winsf 126 B1
Brindley Cl. Kids 194 C1
Brindley Gr. Wilm 34 C1
Brindley Hall Rd. Burl 202 C4
Brindley Hall Rd. Fadd 186 C1
Brindley La. Bra Gr 153 E2
Brindley Rd. Run 23 F2
Brindley St. Run 22 C2
Brindley Way. Congle 157 D1
Brindleys Way. Audley 209 F1
Brine Pits La. Fr La E 218 C1
Brine Rd. Nant 204 C2
Brinell Dr. Irlam 11 F3
Brinley Cl. Beb 43 E3
Brinton Cl. Wid 22 C4
Brisbane Cl. Bram 35 F3
Brisbane Rd. Blacon 117 E2
Bristol Ave. Run 50 C3
Bristol Cl. Blacon 117 F3
Bristow Cl. Gt San 15 D4
Brittania Dr. North 104 C4
Brittania Gdns. Hels 73 D1
Brittania Rd. Hels 73 D1
Brixham Ave. Chea 34 C4
Brixham Wlk. Bram 35 F4
Broad La. Altr 32 A4
Broad La. Apple 27 E4
Broad La. Burton 1 B1
Broad La. H Chap 129 F1
Broad La. Hay Gr 205 D1
Broad La. Hes 40 B4
Broad La. Sp Gr 129 F1
Broad Oak Ave. Broug 139 D2
Broad Oak Ave. Hay 1 A3
Broad Oak Ave. Penk 14 C2
Broad St. Crewe 190 B3
Broad Wlk. Wilm 59 F4
Broadacre. Comb 78 B3
Broadacres. Sound 217 F2
Broadbent Ave. Warr 16 C2
Broadcar Rd. Mfield 113 E3
Broadheys La. H Legh 28 B3
Broadhurst Ave. Cul 4 C1
Broadhurst Ave. Warr 15 E2
Broadhurst La. Congle 156 B2
Broadlake. Will 67 F4
Broadland Gdns. El Por 69 F1
Broadland Rd. El Por 69 F1
Broadleigh Way. Wist 206 B4
Broadley Ave. Gold 3 E4
Broadmead. Chest 119 E1
Broadmead. Hes 41 E4
Broadoak La. H Legh 29 E3
Broadoak La. Mobb 57 F3
Broadwalk. Prest 87 D3
Broadway. Altr 32 A4
Broadway. North 78 A2
Broadway. Wid 12 A1
Broadway. Wilm 60 A3
Broadway E. Chest 118 C3
Broadway The. Nant 204 C3
Broadway W. Chest 118 B2
Broadways. Audlem 230 A2
Broadwood Cl. H La 37 F4
Brock Gdns. Hale 21 F1
Brock Rd. Warr 9 E2
Brockhurst St. North 104 A4
Brockhurst Way. North 104 A3
Brocklehurst Ave. Mfield 87 F1
Brocklehurst Ct. Mfield 87 E2
Brocklehurst Dr. Prest 87 D4
Brocklehurst Way. Mfield 87 E2
Brockway E. Tatt 166 A1
Brockway W. Tatt 166 A1
Brodie Cl. Chest 95 E1
Brogden Ave. Cul 4 C2
Broken Banks. Mfield 112 B4
Broken Cross. Mfield 111 F4
Brokencross Pl. North 104 C4
Bromborough Village Rd. Beb 43 F4
Bromley Ave. Gold 3 E4
Bromley Cl. Crewe 189 F4
Bromley Cl. Hes 40 C4
Bromley Cl. Warr 8 C2
Bromley Dr. H Chap 130 B1
Bromley Rd. Congle 156 C2
Bromley Rd. Mfield 111 F4
Brompton Way. El Por 69 F1
Bronington Ave. Beb 43 E3
Broockhouse La. Whit 52 A1
Brook Ave. Shav 206 B3
Brook Ave. Warr 16 C1
Brook Ave. Warr 16 C3
Brook Ave. Wilm 34 B2
Brook Bottom Rd. N Mills 39 D4
Brook Cl. Crewe 190 C2
Brook Cl. Cront 12 B3
Brook Ct. Sand 175 D3
Brook Dr. Ch Hul 35 D4
Brook Dr. Gt San 15 D3
Brook Dr. Kels 122 B2
Brook End. St Hel 1 A1
Brook Furlong. Frod 48 C1
Brook Gdns. Bidd 179 E1
Brook Hey. Nest 41 D1
Brook House Dr. Crewe 206 B4
Brook La. A Edge 59 F2
Brook La. Broug 139 E4
Brook La. Burl 203 E4
Brook La. Chest 118 C2
Brook La. Knuts 57 D1
Brook La. North 104 B4
Brook La. Warr 18 A4
Brook Pl. Warr 16 C2
Brook Rd. El Por 69 E3
Brook Rd. Lymm 18 B2
Brook Rd. Tarp 168 B4
Brook Side. Weave 102 B4
Brook St. Chest 118 B1
Brook St. Congle 156 C2
Brook St. Crewe 190 B2
Brook St. Gold 3 D4
Brook St. Knuts 57 D1
Brook St. Mfield 87 E1
Brook St. Mfield 112 B4
Brook St. Mfield 112 C4
Brook St. Nest 66 C4
Brook St. North 79 D1
Brook St. North 79 F1
Brook St. Run 23 D1
Brook St. Wid 13 D1
Brook Terr. Sand 175 D2
Brook Way. Gt San 15 D3
Brook Well. Nest 66 C3
Brookdale. Wid 12 A2
Brookdale Ave. Knuts 57 E1
Brookdale Way. Waver 143 D3
Brooke Ave. Chest 118 B4
Brooke Dr. Wilm 34 B2
Brooke Way. Wilm 34 B2
Brookes Ave. Broug 139 D2
Brookfield. Hasl 191 E3
Brookfield Ave. Poyn 36 B2
Brookfield Ave. Run 23 F1
Brookfield Cl. Lymm 18 B2
Brookfield Cl. Tarp 168 B4
Brookfield Cres. Goost 107 F1
Brookfield Dr. Alsag 193 E3
Brookfield Dr. Chest 118 C2
Brookfield Dr. H Chap 130 A2
Brookfield La. Mfield 112 C4
Brookfield Park. Warr 17 D1
Brookfield Rd. Comb 78 B4
Brookfield Rd. Cul 4 B2
Brookfield Rd. Lymm 18 B2
Brookfield St. N-le-W 2 A2
Brookhouse Cl. Mfield 86 C1
Brookhouse La. Ch Min 172 B4
Brookhouse La. Congle 157 E1
Brookhouse La. Dudd 144 B3
Brookhouse Rd. Alsag 193 E2
Brookhouse Rd. Sand 175 D3
Brookhurst Ave. Beb 43 E3
Brookhurst Cl. Beb 43 E3
Brookhurst Rd. Beb 43 E3
Brookkash Rd. Wythe 34 A4
Brookland Ave. Wist 205 F4
Brookland Dr. Sand 175 F3
Brookland La. St Hel 1 A1
Brookland St. Warr 16 C4
Brooklands Ave. Mfield 112 A4
Brooklands Dr. Goost 107 E1
Brooklands Dr. North 104 A2
Brooklands Gr. Crewe 190 A3
Brooklands Rd. Congle 155 F1
Brooklands Rd. Nest 41 E1
Brookledge La. Adlin 62 C3
Brooklyn Dr. El Por 69 F3
Brooklyn Dr. Lymm 18 C2
Brooklyn St. Crewe 190 B1
Brookmere Cl. Sand 174 C4
Brooks Dr. Altr 32 B4
Brooks La. Bosl 135 F1
Brooks La. Middle 128 B1
Brookside. Asht 121 F4
Brookside. Chest 142 A4
Brookside. Cudd 101 F2
Brookside. Kings 75 E1
Brookside Ave. Gt San 15 D2
Brookside Ave. Lymm 18 B2
Brookside Ave. Poyn 36 C2
Brookside Ave. S La E 112 C1
Brookside Ave. Warr 16 B1
Brookside Cl. Hay 1 A4
Brookside Ct. Mfield 87 D1
Brookside Green. Crewe 206 B4
Brookside La. H La 37 F4
Brookside Rd. Congle 156 B2
Brookside Terr. Chest 118 C2
Brookside View. Hay 1 A4
Brookside Way. Hay 1 A4
Brookvale Ave N. Run 50 A3
Brookvale Ave S. Run 50 A3
Brookvale Cl. Burton 6 C3
Brookway La. St Hel 1 A1
Brookwood Cl. Warr 26 A4
Broom Ave. Apple 26 C3
Broom Cres. Tarv 121 D1
Broom Field Cl. Wilm 60 C4
Broom La. Peo 81 F1
Broom Rd. Part 11 F1
Broom St. Crewe 190 A3
Broom's La. Kels 122 B3
Broome Ct. Run 50 A3
Broomehouse Ave. Irlam 11 F4
Broomfield Cl. Chelf 84 A2
Broomfields Rd. Apple 26 B4
Broomheath La. Dudd 144 B4
Broomheath La. Tarv 121 E1
Broomheath La. Tarv 144 B4
Broomhill La. Brox 199 E4
Broomhill La. Gt Bar 120 C4
Broomlands. Hes 40 C4
Broomsfield La. North 78 A2
Broseley Ave. Cul 4 B2
Broseley La. Gold 4 B3
Brotherton Cl. Beb 43 E4
Brough St W. Mfield 112 B4
Broughton Ave. Gold 3 E4
Broughton Cres. Worth 211 D1
Broughton Hall Rd. Broug 139 E2
Broughton La. Wist 189 F1
Broughton Mills Rd. Broug 139 F3
Broughton Rd. Adlin 62 B3
Broughton Rd. Crewe 190 B4
Brow La. Antro 53 E3
Brow La. Hes 40 C4
Brow The. Kings 75 E1
Browmere Dr. Croft 9 D4
Brown Ave. Law-g 194 A3
Brown Ave. Nant 204 C2
Brown Heath Rd. Christ 143 D3
Brown Heath Rd. Waver 143 D3
Brown Lees Cl. Crewe 190 A1
Brown Lees Rd. Kids 195 F2
Brown St. A Edge 60 A1
Brown St. Congle 156 C2
Brown St. Mfield 112 B4
Brown St. Warr 16 A3
Brown St. Wid 23 E4
Brown's La. Chest 141 E4
Brown's La. Wilm 60 C4
Brownhill Dr. Warr 16 C4
Brownhills Rd. Eaton 147 E3
Browning Ave. Wid 22 C4
Browning Cl. Blacon 117 F3
Browning Dr. El Por 69 F2
Browning Gr. Kids 210 B4
Browning Green. El Por 69 F2
Browning St. Crewe 190 B2
Browning Way. Winsf 149 D4
Brownlow Cl. Poyn 36 C1
Broxton Ave. Middle 151 E3
Broxton Cl. Wid 12 B2
Broxton Dr. Crewe 190 A1
Broxton Rd. Brox 182 B1
Broxton Rd. Clutt 182 B1
Broxton Rd. El Por 69 F3
Bruce Ave. Warr 8 B1
Bruce Cres. Beb 43 E3
Bruce Dr. El Por 69 E2
Bruche Ave. Warr 16 C4
Bruche Dr. Warr 16 C4
Bruche Heath Gdns. Warr 17 D4
Bruen The. Tarv 121 E2
Bruera Rd. El Por 69 F2
Brunner Bsns Centre. North 78 B1
Brunner Pl. Winsf 149 D4
Brunner Rd. Wid 23 D4
Brunswick Cres. El Por 69 F2
Brunswick Hill. Mfield 112 B4
Brunswick Rd. N-le-W 1 C2
Brunswick St. Mfield 112 B4
Brunswick St. St Hel 1 A2
Brunswick Terr. Mfield 112 B4
Bruntleigh Ave. Warr 17 D2
Bryant Ave. Warr 16 C3
Brymau Four Estate. Brough 140 B4
Brymau One Estate. Brough 140 C4
Brymau Three Estate. Brough 140 B4
Brymau Two Estate. Brough 140 C4
Brynlow Dr. Middle 151 D4
Brynn St. Wid 23 D4
Brynton Cl. Mfield 87 E1
Brynton Rd. Mfield 87 E1
Buchan Cl. Gt San 15 D4
Buchan Gr. Crewe 190 A2
Buck La. Ho Co 206 C2
Buckbean Way. Goost 107 F1
Buckden Way. Mfield 112 B4
Buckfast Ave. Hay 2 A4
Buckfast Cl. Ch Hul 35 D3
Buckfast Cl. Mfield 87 E1
Buckfast Cl. Penk 14 C2
Buckfast Ct. Poyn 36 B3
Buckfast Way. Middle 128 A1
Buckingham Ave. Chest 119 D1
Buckingham Ave. Wid 13 D2
Buckingham Cl. Wist 205 F4
Buckingham Dr. Gt San 15 E2
Buckingham Dr. Knuts 57 D1
Buckingham Dr. Winsf 149 E4
Buckingham Rd. El Por 70 B1
Buckingham Rd. Irlam 11 E3
Buckingham Rd. Poyn 36 B2
Buckingham Rd. Wilm 59 F3
Buckland Cl. Wid 22 B4
Buckley Ave. Middle 128 C4
Buckley Cl. Middle 151 D4
Buckley St. Mfield 112 B4
Buckley St. Warr 16 A3
Bucklow Ave. Mobb 58 A2
Bucklow Ave. Part 11 F2
Bucklow Wlk. Mfield 112 C4
Bucklowhill La. Mere 30 A2
Buckton St. Warr 16 B4
Bude Cl. Alsag 193 D2
Bude Cl. Bram 35 F4
Bude Cl. Crewe 190 A4
Bude Rd. Wid 12 C1
Budworth Ave. Warr 16 C2
Budworth Ave. Wid 12 B1
Budworth Cl. Run 49 E4
Budworth Cl. Sand 174 C4
Budworth Heath La. B Hea 54 B1
Budworth La. Comb 78 C4
Budworth La. G Bud 78 C4
Budworth Rd. B Hea 54 C1
Budworth Rd. El Por 69 F1
Budworth Rd. Tab 55 E1
Budworth Wlk. Wilm 34 C1
Buffs La. Hes 41 D4
Buggen La. Nest 66 B4
Buildings Rd. Nest 41 F1
Bulkeley Rd. Poyn 36 C2
Bulkeley Rd. Wilm 34 B2
Bulkeley St. Chest 119 D1
Bull Hill. Nest 66 C3
Bull Hill La. Rain 88 B1
Bull Ring. North 103 F4
Bull Ring The. Middle 128 B1
Bullcroft Cl. Shock 211 E4
Bullocks House Rd. Kids 195 F2
Bullocks La. Mfield 112 C2
Bullocks La. S La E 112 C2
Bumper's La. Blacon 117 F1
Bunbury Cl. Middle 151 E3
Bunbury Cl. North 104 A3
Bunbury Cl. Stoak 96 A4
Bunbury Dr. Run 49 E3
Bunbury Gr. El Por 70 B1
Bunbury La. Bun 185 F4
Bunbury Rd. Alpr 169 E2
Bunce La. Mart 133 D2
Bunce St. Chest 141 E4
Bunham Cl. Alsag 193 E2
Buntingford Rd. Warr 17 E2
Bunts La. Congle 156 C1
Burdett Rd. El Por 69 F1
Burfield Dr. Apple 26 B4
Burford Ave. Ch Hul 35 E3
Burford Cl. Wilm 59 F3
Burford Cres. Wilm 59 F3
Burford La. Lymm 19 E1
Burgamot La. Comb 78 B4
Burges St. Chest 118 C2
Burgess Ave. Warr 16 A1
Burgess Dr. Sea 117 D3
Burgess Pl. North 103 F4
Burgess St. Mfield 112 C4
Burjen Way. Crewe 190 A3
Burkhardt Dr. N-le-W 2 C2
Burland Cl. Run 22 C1
Burland Gr. Winsf 126 A1
Burland Rd. N-u-L 210 B1
Burlea Cl. Crewe 189 F3
Burlea Dr. Shav 206 A3
Burley La. Apple 27 E2
Burleyhurst La. Mobb 58 C3
Burnell Rd. El Por 70 C2
Burnet Cl. Warr 9 E1
Burnfell. Gold 3 F4
Burnham Cl. Cul 4 C2
Burnham Cl. Penk 14 C3
Burnham Cl. Wid 12 B2
Burnham Rd. Chest 140 C3
Burns Cl. El Por 69 F2
Burns Cres. Wid 22 C4
Burns Dr. Crewe 190 C2
Burns Gr. Warr 8 B1
Burns Rd. Congle 157 D1
Burns Way. Blacon 117 F3
Burnsall Ave. Gold 3 F4
Burnsall Dr. Wid 12 B2
Burnside. Altr 32 B4
Burnside Ave. Warr 16 B1
Burnt Acre. Chelf 84 A2
Burran Rd. Wythe 33 E4
Burrough Cl. Warr 9 F2
Burrows Hill. North 103 D4
Burrows St. Hay 1 A3
Burrows The. Cudd 101 E3
Burslam St. Congle 156 C1
Burton Ave. Tarp 146 B2
Burton Cl. Cul 4 C2
Burton Dr. Poyn 36 B2
Burton Gn. El Por 69 E2
Burton Gr. Crewe 173 D1
Burton Hall Rd. Burt 161 F1
Burton La. Dudd 144 C3
Burton Rd. Blacon 117 F3
Burton Rd. Nest 66 C3
Burton Rd. Warr 8 B1
Burtonwood Rd. Burton 7 D1
Burtonwood Rd. Gt San 15 D4
Burwardsley Rd. Tatt 166 B1
Bush Rd. Christ 142 C4
Bush Rd. Wid 22 C3
Bushell Cl. Nest 66 C4
Bushell Rd. Nest 66 C4
Bushway. Hes 40 B4
Butler Way. Nant 204 C2
Butley Cl. Mfield 87 E2
Butley Cl. Middle 151 E4
Butley Lanes. Prest 61 F1
Butter Ave. Warr 7 F1
Butterbache Rd. Hunt 142 A3
Butterbur Cl. Hunt 142 A3
Buttermarket St. Warr 16 A3
Buttermere Ave. El Por 70 B2
Buttermere Ave. Warr 8 B2
Buttermere Cl. Frod 74 B4
Buttermere Ct. Congle 156 A1
Buttermere Dr. Altr 32 B3
Buttermere Dr. Crewe 173 D1
Buttermere Gr. Run 49 E3
Buttermere Rd. Part 11 F2
Buttermere Rd. Winsf 126 B1
Butterton La. Crew 192 B1
Butterton La. Hasl 192 B1
Button Field. Winsf 126 A4
Butts The. Alsag 193 E2
Butts The. Run 23 F1
Buxton Ave. Crewe 190 C2
Buxton New Rd. Mac For 114 B4
Buxton New Rd. Rain 88 B1
Buxton Old Rd. Congle 157 D2
Buxton Old Rd. Disley 38 C2
Buxton Old Rd. Mfield 113 E4
Buxton Old Rd. Rain 113 E4
Buxton Rd. Congle 157 E3
Buxton Rd. Disley 38 C3
Buxton Rd. H La 37 E4
Buxton Rd. Haz Gr 37 E4
Buxton Rd. Mfield 112 C4
Buxton Rd. N Mills 39 E2
Buxton Rd. W Br 39 E2
Buxton Rd West. Disley 38 A3
Bye La. H Wal 25 E3
Bye Pass Rd. Tarv 121 D2
Bye Pass The. Chest 119 F1
Byland Ave. Ch Hul 35 D3
Bylands Cl. Poyn 36 B2
Byley La. Cran 129 E3
Byley La. Middle 128 C2
Byley La. Sp Gr 128 C2
Byley Way. Winsf 126 A1
Byng Ave. Irlam 11 E2
Byron Cl. Blacon 117 F3
Byron Cl. Crewe 190 C2
Byron Cl. Middle 151 E3
Byron Cl. Sch Gr 193 F4
Byron Ct. Warr 8 B1
Byron St. Run 23 D1
Byron Way. Wist 190 A1
Byron's La. Mfield 112 C3
Byrons St. Mfield 112 B3
Bythom Cl. Christ 142 C4

Cabot Cl. Warr 7 E1
Cabul Cl. Warr 16 B4
Cadnant Cl. Blacon 117 E2
Cadshaw Cl. Warr 9 E3
Caerleon Cl. Winsf 149 D4
Caerllew. Holt 180 C1
Caernarvon Ave. Winsf 149 D4
Caernarvon Cl. Run 23 F1
Caernarvon Ct. El Por 70 B1
Caernarvon Rd. Wist 205 F4
Caesars Cl. Run 23 F1
Cairns Cres. Blacon 117 E2
Cairo St. Warr 16 A3
Caister Way. Winsf 149 E4
Caithness Ct. Run 23 D1
Calamine St. Mfield 112 C3
Calday Gr. Hay 1 A4
Caldbeck Ave. Warr 8 B1
Caldene Terr. W Br 65 F4
Calder Ave. Crewe 191 D3
Calder Cl. Boll 87 F4
Calder Cl. Poyn 36 B1
Calder Cl. Wid 13 F2
Calder Way. El Por 69 E3
Calderfield Cl. Warr 26 A4
Caldicott Ave. Beb 43 E4

Caldicott Cl. Winsf 149 E4
Caldwell Rd. Wid 23 D4
Caldwell's Gate La. Antro 54 A4
Caldy Cl. Chest 118 B3
Caldy Dr. El Por 69 E2
Caldy Rd. Alsag 193 E2
Caldy Rd. Wilm 34 B2
Caldy Valley Rd. Chest 142 A4
Caldy Valley Rd. Hunt 142 A4
Caldy Way. Winsf 126 A1
Callands Rd. Warr 7 E1
Calrofold Dr. N-u-L 210 B1
Calrofold La. Rain 88 B1
Calstock Cl. Penk 14 C2
Calveley Ave. Beb 43 F2
Calveley Green La. Alpr 170 B2
Calveley Green La. Wet 170 B2
Calveley Hall La. Alpr 170 A1
Calver Rd. Warr 8 A2
Calverly Cl. Run 50 B3
Calvers. Run 23 F1
Camamile Wlk. Part 11 F1
Camberley Cl. Bram 36 A4
Camborne Ave. Mfield 111 F4
Camborne Cl. Run 50 B3
Cambourne Cl. Congle 178 C4
Cambourne Rd. Burton 6 C3
Cambrai Ave. Warr 16 B1
Cambrian Ave. Chest 119 D1
Cambrian Way. Winsf 149 D4
Cambridge Ave. Mfield 112 A4
Cambridge Ave. Wilm 59 F4
Cambridge Ave. Winsf 126 A1
Cambridge Cl. Bidd 179 E1
Cambridge Cl. Warr 26 A4
Cambridge Gdns. Apple 26 B3
Cambridge Gdns. Hels 73 E2
Cambridge Rd. Beb 43 F4
Cambridge Rd. Chest 118 C3
Cambridge Rd. El Por 70 B3
Cambridge Rd. Mfield 112 A4
Cambridge St. Run 23 E1
Cambridge St. Wid 23 D4
Camden Rd. El Por 70 A3
Camden St. Crewe 190 B2
Camelot Cl. N-le-W 1 C2
Camelot Gr. Shav 206 B2
Camelot Way. Run 50 A4
Cameron Ave. Run 48 C4
Cameron Ave. Shav 206 A2
Cameron Ct. Warr 8 A2
Cameron Rd. Wid 23 D4
Camm St. Crewe 190 B1
Campbell Ave. Run 49 D4
Campbell Cl. Congle 157 D2
Campbell Cl. Hasl 191 E2
Campbell Cl. Mfield 87 D1
Campbell Cres. Gt San 14 C3
Campden Way. Wilm 34 B2
Campion Cl. Hunt 142 A3
Campion Cl. Warr 9 E3
Campsey Ash. Wid 12 C2
Camrose Cl. Run 49 E3
Camsley La. Lymm 18 A2
Canaan. Gold 4 B4
Canada Cl. Warr 9 D1
Canadian Ave. Chest 119 D2
Canal Ct
Trading Est. El Por 70 B4
Canal Rd. Congle 156 C1
Canal Reach. Run 24 B1
Canal Side. Apple 17 E1
Canal Side. Chest 118 B1
Canal Side. Mfield 112 C4
Canal Side. Moore 25 E3
Canal Side. North 78 A1
Canal Side. P-o-t-H 50 C3
Canal Side. Run 48 B4
Canal St. Chest 118 B1
Canal St. Congle 156 C1
Canal St. Mfield 112 C4
Canal St. N-le-W 1 C2
Canal St. Run 23 D1
Canal St. W Br 65 F4
Canal Terr. Middle 151 E4
Canalside. Stan 70 B3
Canberra Ave. Warr 8 B2
Canberra Rd. Bram 35 F3
Canberra Sq. Warr 8 B1
Canberra Way. Blacon 117 E2
Candelan Way. H Legh 29 E2
Candleston Cl. Warr 7 F1
Canford Cl. Crewe 190 A4
Canford Cl. Gt San 15 E3
Cann La. Apple 26 C2
Cann La. B Hea 55 D3
Cannel Ct. Run 50 A3
Cannell St. Warr 15 E2
Canning St. Chest 118 B1
Canniswood Rd. Hay 1 A3
Cannock Cl. El Por 94 C4
Cannon St. El Por 70 A3
Cannon Way. H Kin 161 D4
Canon St. Run 23 D2
Canon Wilson Cl. Hay 1 B3
Canons Rd. Gt San 15 E3
Canterbury Cl. El Por 94 C4
Canterbury Ct. Mfield 112 C4
Canterbury Rd. Blacon 117 F3
Canterbury Rd. Wid 22 B4
Canterbury St. Warr 16 B2
Cantley Cl. Run 49 E3
Canton Pl. North 103 E4
Canton St. Mfield 112 B3
Canton Wlks. Mfield 112 B3
Canute Pl. Knuts 57 D1
Capeland Cl. Chest 140 C3
Capenhurst Ave. Crewe 190 A2
Capenhurst Ave. Warr 9 D1
Capenhurst La. Capen 94 A4
Capenhurst La. El Por 69 F2
Capenhurst La. El Por 70 A2
Capesthorne Cl. Alsag 193 E2
Capesthorne Cl. H Chap 130 A2
Capesthorne Cl. Haz Gr 36 C4
Capesthorne Cl. Sand 175 E4
Capesthorne Rd. Crewe 189 F2
Capesthorne Rd. H La 37 F4
Capesthorne Rd. Haz Gr 36 C4
Capesthorne Rd. Warr 8 C1
Capesthorne Rd. Waver 143 D3
Capesthorne Rd. Wilm 59 F3
Capitol Wlk. Congle 156 B1
Capper Cl. Kids 195 D1
Capper's La. Fadd 186 B2
Capper's La. Spurs 186 B2
Cappers La. Ha Gr 176 B1
Car St. Chest 118 C1
Carden Cl. Warr 9 E2
Cardenbrook Gr. Wilm 34 B1
Cardeston Cl. Run 49 F2
Cardiff Cl. El Por 94 C4
Cardigan Cl. Mfield 112 A4
Cardigan Cl. Warr 7 E1
Carey St. Wid 13 D1
Carisbrook Ave. Mfield 87 F1
Carisbrook Dr. Winsf 149 E4
Carisbrooke Cl. Wist 205 F4
Carleton Rd. Poyn 37 E2
Carlett Bvd. Beb 43 F3
Carlingford Rd. Warr 26 A4
Carlisle Cl. Mfield 111 F3
Carlisle Cl. Mobb 58 A2
Carlisle Cl. Winsf 126 A1
Carlisle Rd. Blacon 117 F3
Carlisle St. A Edge 60 A1
Carlisle St. Crewe 190 A1
Carlisle St. Warr 26 B4
Carlow Cl. Hale 21 E1
Carlton Ave. Brough 140 B3
Carlton Ave. Ch Hul 35 E3
Carlton Ave. Run 23 E1
Carlton Ave. Wilm 34 B1
Carlton Cl. M Traf 119 F4
Carlton Cl. Nest 41 E1
Carlton Cres. El Por 69 F4
Carlton Pl. Chest 119 D2
Carlton Rd. Lymm 19 D3
Carlton Rd. North 104 A4
Carlton St. Warr 26 B4
Carlton St. Wid 23 D4
Carlton Way. Hol Gr 11 E3
Carlyle Cres. El Por 69 F2
Carmarthen Cl. Warr 7 E1
Carmarthen Cl. Winsf 149 E4
Carmel Cl. Blacon 117 E2
Carmel Ct. Wid 13 D2
Carmel Mews. Wilm 34 A1
Carmenna Dr. Bram 35 F4
Carmichael Cl. Part 11 F2
Carnegie Cl. Mfield 87 D1
Carnoustie Cl. Wilm 60 B4
Carnoustie Dr. Mfield 87 E3
Carol Dr. Hes 41 E4
Carol St. Warr 16 B2
Caroline St. Irlam 11 F4
Caroline St. Wid 23 D4
Carpenter Gr. Warr 9 D1
Carr Brow. H La 37 F4
Carr Brow. H La 38 A4
Carr La. Audley 209 D1
Carr La. Gold 4 A4
Carr La. Hale 21 F2
Carr La. L End 59 E1
Carr La. Wid 21 F2
Carr St. Kids 195 F1
Carr Wood Ave. Bram 35 F4
Carrgreen La. Part 19 F3
Carriage Dr. Bidd 179 F1
Carriage Dr. Frod 74 A3
Carrick Dr. El Por 70 A1
Carrick Rd. Chest 141 D4
Carrington Cl. Warr 9 E2
Carrington Way. Crewe 190 A4
Carroll Dr. Wist 205 F4
Carrs La. Tatt 166 C1
Carrwood. Altr 32 A4
Carrwood. Knuts 57 E1
Carrwood Rd. Wilm 59 F4
Carsdale Rd. Wythe 33 F4
Carter Ave. Kels 122 B2
Carter La. Chelf 84 A2
Carter St. Chest 118 C1
Cartier Cl. G San 7 E1
Cartier Cl. Gt San 15 E4
Cartledge Cl. Cudd 102 A2
Cartmel Ave. Warr 8 B2
Cartmel Cl. H Chap 130 A2
Cartmel Cl. Mfield 87 D1
Cartmel Cl. Warr 7 F1
Cartmel Cl. Winsf 126 B1
Cartmel Dr. El Por 69 F1
Cartmell Cl. Run 49 D3
Cartridge La. Apple 27 F3
Cartwright Rd. Hasl 191 E3
Cartwright St. Run 23 E1
Cartwright St. Warr 15 F3
Carver Cl. Winsf 127 D2
Case Rd. Hay 1 B3
Casey La. Shav 206 C2
Cassia Green La. Mar 125 E3
Cassley Rd. Speke 21 D2
Casson St. Crewe 190 A3
Castle Bank. North 103 F4
Castle Cl. Broug 139 D3
Castle Cl. Kels 122 B2
Castle Cl. Pulf 162 B1
Castle Croft Rd. Chest 141 D3
Castle Ct. North 103 F4
Castle Dr. Chest 141 E4
Castle Dr. El Por 70 A2
Castle Dr. Hes 40 C4
Castle Green. Warr 7 D1
Castle Hill. N-le-W 2 C2
Castle Hill. Prest 86 C3
Castle Hill Ct. Prest 86 C4
Castle Inn Rd. Congle 179 E4
Castle Mill La. Ashl 32 A3
Castle Rd. Kids 195 E4
Castle Rd. Run 49 F4
Castle Rise. Prest 86 C3
Castle Rise. Run 23 E1
Castle St. Chest 141 E4
Castle St. Crewe 190 B2
Castle St. Holt 196 B4
Castle St. Mfield 112 B4
Castle St. Nant 204 C3
Castle St. North 103 F4
Castle St. Wid 13 E1
Castle St Mall. Mfield 112 B4
Castle Way. Altr 32 B4
Castle Way. Dodle 162 A3
Castlefields. Tatt 166 B2
Castlefields Ave E. Run 24 A1
Castlefields Ave N. Run 23 F1
Castlefields Ave S. Run 24 A1
Castleford Dr. Prest 86 C3
Castlegate. Prest 86 C3
Castlegate Mews. Prest 86 C3
Castlemere Dr. Crewe 190 B4
Castleton Dr. H La 37 F3
Castletown La. Shock 197 E1
Castleview Rd. Kids 195 D2
Catchpenny La. With 108 C2
Cateford Cl. Wid 12 B1
Catford Green. Speke 21 D2
Catfoss Cl. Warr 8 C1
Cathcart Green. G Sutt 119 F3
Catherine St. Chest 118 A1
Catherine St. Crewe 190 B1
Catherine St. Mfield 112 B4
Catherine St. Warr 15 F4
Catherine St. Warr 16 A4
Catherine St. Wid 23 D4
Catherine Way. N-le-W 2 A1
Catterall Ave. Warr 8 B1
Caughall Rd. Chest 95 F1
Caunce Ave. Gold 3 D4
Caunce Ave. Hay 1 A3
Causeway Ave. Warr 16 B2
Cavalier Dr. Blacon 117 F3
Cavell Dr. El Por 70 A2
Cavendish Cl. Gt San 15 E4
Cavendish Cl. Mfield 87 E2
Cavendish Cres. Alsag 193 E3
Cavendish Farm Rd. Run 49 D3
Cavendish Gdns. El Por 70 A2
Cavendish Mews. Wilm 60 A3
Cavendish Rd. Chest 141 D3
Cavendish Rd. Crewe 189 F3
Cavendish Rd. Haz Gr 36 C4
Cavendish St. Run 22 C1
Caversham Cl. Apple 26 C3
Cawdor Dr. Chest 119 D1
Cawdor St. Run 22 C2
Cawdor St. Warr 26 B4
Cawfield Ave. Wid 12 B1
Cawley Ave. Cul 4 C2
Cawley St. Mfield 112 C4
Cawley St. Run 23 D1
Cawood Cl. El Por 69 D3
Cawthorne Ave. Warr 17 D1
Caxton Cl. El Por 69 F2
Caxton Cl. Wid 12 B2
Cecil Rigby Cl. Sand 175 D3
Cecil St. Chest 119 D1
Cedar Ave. Alsag 193 E2
Cedar Ave. Con Q 91 E1
Cedar Ave. El Por 69 E3
Cedar Ave. G Cit 116 A4
Cedar Ave. Gold 3 F4
Cedar Ave. Kids 194 B1
Cedar Ave. Run 49 E4
Cedar Ave. Sutt 50 A2
Cedar Ave. Wid 13 D1
Cedar Cl. Lost 80 A2
Cedar Cl. Middle 151 F3
Cedar Cl. Poyn 36 C2
Cedar Cres. Audley 209 F1
Cedar Cres. N-le-W 2 B1
Cedar Ct. Alsag 193 F2
Cedar Ct. Congle 178 C4
Cedar Ct. Croft 4 C1
Cedar Ct. Willas 205 E3
Cedar Dr. Chest 119 D2
Cedar Dr. North 78 A2
Cedar Gr. Chest 119 D2
Cedar Gr. Hay 1 C4
Cedar Gr. Mfield 112 B3
Cedar Gr. Nest 66 C4
Cedar Gr. Warr 16 B2
Cedar Gr. Warr 17 D4
Cedar Gr. Winsf 127 D1
Cedar Mews. Blacon 117 F2
Cedar Park. Chest 119 E1
Cedar Rd. Gt San 14 B4
Cedar Rd. N-u-L 210 B1
Cedar Rd. Part 11 F2
Cedar Rd. Weave 102 B4
Cedar Way. Wist 206 A4
Cedardale Dr. El Por 94 C4
Cedarfield Rd. Lymm 19 D2
Cedars The. Alsag 193 E2
Cedarway. Hes 41 D3
Cedarway. Wilm 59 F2
Cedarways. Apple 26 B3
Cedarwood. Cudd 101 E3
Celandine Cl. Hunt 142 A3
Celyn Cres. Brough 140 B3
Cement Pl. Chest 118 B1
Cemetery Rd. Weston 207 D3
Cemlyn Cl. Blacon 117 F2
Central Ave. El Por 70 B2
Central Ave. Warr 16 A2
Central Ave. Warr 16 B4
Central Dr. Chea 34 B4
Central Dr. Hay 1 A3
Central Dr. North 78 A2
Central Expressway. Run 49 F4
Central Gr. North 104 B4
Central Rd. North 104 B4
Central Rd. Part 11 F2
Central Rd. Wythe 33 E3
Central St. Sch Gr 195 D3
Central Trading Estate.
Brough 140 C4
Centre Ct. Alsag 193 F2
Centre Park Sq. Warr 16 A2
Centurion Cl. Warr 9 E2
Centurion Row. Run 23 F1
Chads Green. Hay Gr 206 A1
Chadwick Ave. Croft 9 D4
Chadwick Ave. Warr 16 C1
Chadwick Rd. Middle 151 E3
Chadwick Rd. Run 23 F2
Chadwick Terr. Mfield 87 F1
Chaffinch Cl. Warr 9 F2
Chaffinch Way. Winsf 149 E3
Chain Maker's Row.
Brough 140 C4
Chalfield Ave. El Por 69 E3
Chalfield Cl. El Por 69 E3
Chalfield Cl. Wist 206 A4
Chalfont Cl. Apple 26 C3
Chalgrave Cl. Wid 13 F2
Chalkwell Dr. Hes 41 E4
Challinor St. Chest 119 D1
Chalmondeley Rd. Wren 216 A3
Chamber Brook La. Kings 75 E1
Chambers St. Crewe 190 B1
Chance Hall La. Astb 177 E2
Chance Hall La. Sch Gr 177 E2
Chancel La. Wilm 60 A4
Chancery La. Alsag 193 D2
Chandos Cl. Chest 141 F3
Change La. Will 68 A4
Channel The. Back 95 D2
Chantler Ave. Warr 16 C2
Chantry Ave. Hart 103 D2
Chantry Cl. Disley 38 C3
Chantry Ct. Blacon 117 F1
Chantry Ct. Crewe 190 B2
Chantry Ct. Mfield 112 B3
Chantry Fold. Disley 38 C3
Chantry Rd. Disley 38 B3
Chantry The. Alpr 169 F1
Chantry Wlk. Hes 41 D3
Chapel Ave. Kings 75 E1
Chapel Bank. Kids 195 E3
Chapel Cl. Audlem 229 F2
Chapel Cl. Cholm 170 C2
Chapel Cl. Comb 78 B4
Chapel Cl. El Por 70 B4
Chapel Cl. Saug 94 A1
Chapel Cl. Sch Gr 195 D3
Chapel Cl. Waver 143 D3
Chapel Cross Rd. Warr 9 D1
Chapel Ct. Chelf 84 A2
Chapel Ct. North 103 F4
Chapel Dr. Altr 32 B4
Chapel Green. Kels 122 B3
Chapel House La. Pudd 93 D4
Chapel La. Act Br 76 C2
Chapel La. Allos 106 C2
Chapel La. Altr 32 B4
Chapel La. Apple 27 D2
Chapel La. Audley 209 E1
Chapel La. Badd 203 E1
Chapel La. Burton 6 C3
Chapel La. Chest 119 D1
Chapel La. Crewe 173 E1
Chapel La. Cront 12 B2
Chapel La. Dela 122 C1
Chapel La. Dutt 77 D4
Chapel La. Hand 165 D1
Chapel La. Hol Gr 10 C1
Chapel La. Holt 196 B4
Chapel La. Kids 195 F2
Chapel La. Kings 75 E1
Chapel La. Man 98 C2
Chapel La. Mere 30 A2
Chapel La. Moult 126 C4
Chapel La. N in H 236 B1
Chapel La. Part 11 F1
Chapel La. Rain 88 C3
Chapel La. Sch Gr 193 F4
Chapel La. Threap 222 C4
Chapel La. Warr 26 B4
Chapel La. Wilm 60 A3
Chapel La. With 109 E1
Chapel Mews. El Por 70 A2
Chapel Mews. Nant 204 C3
Chapel Rd. A Edge 60 A1
Chapel Rd. Aldf 164 B3
Chapel Rd. Oller 82 C3
Chapel Rd. Penk 14 C2
Chapel Rd. Saigh 164 B3
Chapel Rd. W Br 65 F3
Chapel Rd. Winsf 126 C1
Chapel Row. Barb 187 E3
Chapel Row. Nant 204 B3
Chapel St. A Edge 60 A1
Chapel St. Audley 209 F2
Chapel St. Boll 88 A4
Chapel St. Chest 118 C1
Chapel St. Congle 156 B1
Chapel St. Crewe 190 B2
Chapel St. H Winch 79 E2
Chapel St. Hay 1 C3
Chapel St. Holt 196 B4
Chapel St. Kids 194 B1
Chapel St. Mfield 112 B3
Chapel St. Moult 126 C4
Chapel St. N Mills 39 D3
Chapel St. N-le-W 2 A2
Chapel St. North 103 F4
Chapel St. Sand 175 D2
Chapel St. Sand 175 D3
Chapel St. Sch Gr 195 D3
Chapel St. W Br 65 F4
Chapel St. Weave 77 E1
Chapel St. Wid 23 D4
Chapel Wlks. Ch Hul 35 D3
Chapel Wlks. Lymm 19 E1
Chapel Yd. Warr 16 A3
Chapelmere Cl. Sand 174 C4
Chapelmere Ct. Crewe 190 B4
Charcoal Rd. Dun T 20 C2
Charity La. Mac For 114 A3
Charlcote Cres. Wist 206 B4
Charlecote Rd. Poyn 36 C2
Charles Ave. Dave 103 F1
Charles Ave. Gt San 14 B4
Charles Cres. Chest 141 F4
Charles Price Gdns. El Por 70 B3
Charles Rd. Chest 95 E1
Charles Sq. Ha Gr 175 F1
Charles St. Chest 118 B1
Charles St. Chest 118 C2
Charles St. Crewe 190 B2
Charles St. Gold 3 D4
Charles St. Irlam 11 F3
Charles St. Wid 23 D4
Charlesworth Cres. W Br 39 E2
Charlesworth Ct. Sand 175 E3
Charlesworth Rd. W Br 39 E2
Charlesworth St. Crewe 190 B3
Charlook Wlk. Part 11 F1
Charlotte Ct. Chest 118 B1
Charlotte St. Chest 118 A1
Charlotte St. Mfield 112 B4
Charlotte St W. Mfield 112 B4
Charlotte Wlk. Wid 23 D4
Charlton Cl. Run 50 A4
Charlton St. Mfield 112 B4
Charlton St. Warr 16 C2
Charminster Cl. Gt San 15 D3
Charnock Ave. N-le-W 1 C2
Charnock Rd. Cul 4 C2
Charnwood. Kids 195 D1
Charnwood Cl. Mfield 87 D1
Charnwood Cl. Warr 10 A3
Charnwood Cres. Haz Gr 36 B4
Charter Ave. Warr 16 A4
Charter Cres. El Por 69 F2
Charter Rd. Boll 88 A4
Charter Way. Mfield 87 F2
Charterhall Dr. Chest 118 C1
Chartwell Park. Sand 175 D2
Chase Dr. El Por 69 F1

Chase The. Beb 43 E3
Chase Way. El Por 69 F1
Chaser Ct. Blacon 117 F2
Chatburn Ct. Cul 4 C1
Chatfield Dr. Warr 9 F2
Chatham St. Mfield 112 B4
Chatham Way. Hasl 191 E3
Chatsworth Ave. Cul 4 C2
Chatsworth Ave. Mfield 111 F3
Chatsworth Cl. El Por 69 E3
Chatsworth Cl. Wist 206 A4
Chatsworth Dr. Chest 119 D3
Chatsworth Dr. Congle 155 F2
Chatsworth Dr. Wid 12 B2
Chatsworth Rd. H La 37 F3
Chatsworth Rd. Haz Gr 36 C4
Chatsworth Rd. Wilm 59 F2
Chatterton Dr. Run 50 C4
Chatwell Gdns. Apple 26 C3
Chaucer Cl. Blacon 117 F3
Chaucer Pl. Warr 16 C2
Chaucer St. Run 23 D1
Cheadle La. Peo 106 A4
Cheadle La. Plum 81 D1
Checkley Dr. Bidd 179 E1
Checkley La. Bridge 221 F1
Checkley Rd. N-u-L 210 B1
Chedlee Dr. Chea 34 C4
Chedworth Dr. Wid 12 B2
Cheerbrook Rd. Willas 205 E2
Cheese Hill La. Norley 101 D2
Chelford Ave. Gold 3 E4
Chelford Ct. Wilm 34 C3
Chelford La. Peo 83 E1
Chelford Rd. Chelf 83 E2
Chelford Rd. Chelf 84 B1
Chelford Rd. Henb 110 C4
Chelford Rd. Mfield 111 E4
Chelford Rd. N Ald 84 B4
Chelford Rd. N Ald 85 D1
Chelford Rd. Prest 86 B3
Chelford Rd. Rad 155 F3
Chelford Rd. Wilm 34 B3
Chell St. Crewe 190 A3
Chells Hill. Ha Gr 176 B1
Chelsea Cl. Bidd 179 E1
Chelston Dr. Chea 34 B3
Cheltenham Cl. Gt San 15 D4
Cheltenham Cres. Crewe 190 A4
Cheltenham Cres. Run 49 D3
Cheltenham Rd. El Por 70 B2
Chemical St. N-le-W 2 A2
Cheney Wlk. Crewe 206 B4
Chepstow Cl. Bidd 179 E1
Chepstow Cl. Winsf 149 E4
Cherington Cl. Wilm 34 C2
Cherington Cres. Mfield 112 A4
Cheriton Way. Wist 206 A4
Cherrington Rd. Nant 204 C2
Cherry Blossom Rd. Run 49 F2
Cherry Cl. N-le-W 1 C2
Cherry Cl. N-u-L 210 B1
Cherry Cl. Will 67 E4
Cherry Cres. Winsf 149 E4
Cherry Gr. El Por 70 A1
Cherry Gr. Nant 204 B3
Cherry Grove Rd. Chest 119 D1
Cherry La. Congle 179 F4
Cherry La. Cudd 101 F1
Cherry La. Law-g 193 F3
Cherry La. Lymm 28 A4
Cherry La. Weave 102 B4
Cherry Rd. Chest 119 D1
Cherry Tree Ave. Law-g 194 A3
Cherry Tree Ave. Lymm 18 B1
Cherry Tree Ave. North 78 A2
Cherry Tree Ave. Penk 14 C2
Cherry Tree Ave. Poyn 36 C2
Cherry Tree Ave. Run 49 E4
Cherry Tree Cl. Hale 21 F1
Cherry Tree Cl. Hay 1 A3
Cherry Tree Cl. Wilm 60 C4
Cherry Tree Dr. Haz Gr 37 D4
Cherry Tree Dr. St Hel 1 A1
Cherry Tree Rd. Audley 209 F1
Cherry Tree Rd. Crewe 190 C3
Cherry Tree Rd. Gold 3 F4
Cherry Tree Rd. N-u-L 210 C1
Cherry Wlk. Ch Hul 35 E4
Cherry Wlk. Part 11 E1
Cherry Wlk. Peo 106 B4
Cherryfields Rd. Mfield 111 F4
Cherrysutton. Wid 12 A2
Cherrywood Cres. North 78 A2
Cherwell Cl. Ch Hul 35 D4
Cheryl Ct. Cudd 102 A2
Cheryl Dr. Wid 13 E1
Chesford Grange. Warr 17 F4
Chesham Cl. Wilm 59 F2
Chesham Rd. Wilm 59 F2
Chesham St. Chest 118 C1
Cheshire Cl. N-le-W 2 C2
Cheshire St. Audlem 229 F2
Cheshire View. Boll 88 A3
Cheshyre Dr. Run 23 F1
Cheshyre's La. Run 48 C4
Chessington Cl. Apple 26 C3
Chest Nut Cl. Tarp 146 B1
Chester Ave. Gold 3 E4
Chester Cl. Irlam 11 E3
Chester Cl. Kids 210 C4
Chester Cl. Run 24 A1
Chester Cl. Wilm 34 C1
Chester High Rd. Will 67 E4
Chester La. Mar 125 E1
Chester La. Winsf 125 E1
Chester New Rd. H Wal 25 F4
Chester Rd. Acton 204 A3
Chester Rd. Aldf 180 C3
Chester Rd. Audley 209 E1
Chester Rd. Barb 187 E3
Chester Rd. Broug 139 E3
Chester Rd. Dares 25 D1
Chester Rd. Dela 123 E3
Chester Rd. El Por 69 E2
Chester Rd. El Por 70 A1
Chester Rd. Farn 180 C3
Chester Rd. Flint 91 D2
Chester Rd. Frod 74 A4
Chester Rd. Golb 165 F3
Chester Rd. H Chap 130 A1
Chester Rd. H Wal 25 E3
Chester Rd. Hart 102 C2
Chester Rd. Hart 103 E3
Chester Rd. Hawa 116 A1
Chester Rd. Haz Gr 36 B4
Chester Rd. Hes 41 E3
Chester Rd. Hunt 142 A3
Chester Rd. Kels 122 B3
Chester Rd. Kids 210 B4
Chester Rd. Knuts 56 A3
Chester Rd. Mere 56 A3
Chester Rd. Mfield 112 A4
Chester Rd. Middle 128 A1
Chester Rd. Nest 66 C4
Chester Rd. North 103 E3
Chester Rd. Oak 124 A4
Chester Rd. Plum 80 C3
Chester Rd. Poyn 36 B2
Chester Rd. Ross 162 B1
Chester Rd. Rosth 30 B3
Chester Rd. Run 50 C3
Chester Rd. Sutt 50 A2
Chester Rd. Tab 56 A1
Chester Rd. Tatt 166 A1
Chester Rd. Warr 17 D1
Chester Rd. Weave 102 B2
Chester Rd. Whitch 225 E1
Chester Rd. Winsf 125 F1
Chester Rd. Woodf 36 B2
Chester Row. N-le-W 7 E4
Chester Sq. Crewe 190 B2
Chester St. Chest 140 C4
Chester St. Crewe 190 B2
Chester St. Warr 16 A3
Chester St. Wid 13 D1
Chester Way. North 104 A4
Chesterfield Cl. Winsf 125 F1
Chesterfield Rd. Beb 43 E2
Chestergate. Mfield 112 B4
Chestergate Mall. Mfield 112 B4
Chesterton Cl. Middle 151 F3
Chesterton Dr. Wist 189 F1
Chestnut Ave. El Por 69 F1
Chestnut Ave. Gt San 14 B4
Chestnut Ave. Irlam 11 E3
Chestnut Ave. Mfield 87 F1
Chestnut Ave. Sch Gr 193 F4
Chestnut Ave. Shav 206 B3
Chestnut Ave. Wid 13 D1
Chestnut Cl. Chest 119 D2
Chestnut Cl. Cudd 101 F1
Chestnut Cl. Middle 128 A1
Chestnut Cl. Wilm 60 C4
Chestnut Ct. Tarp 146 B1
Chestnut Dr. Congle 156 A2
Chestnut Dr. H Chap 130 B2
Chestnut Dr. Poyn 36 C2
Chestnut Gr. Beb 43 E4
Chestnut Gr. Crewe 190 C3
Chestnut Gr. Gold 3 F4
Chestnut Gr. N-u-L 210 C1
Chestnut Gr. North 78 A2
Chestnut Gr. Winsf 149 E4
Chestnut La. Frod 73 F2
Chestnut Wlk. Part 11 E1
Chetham Ct. Warr 8 A2
Chetton Dr. Run 50 C4
Chetwode Mews. Whit 52 B1
Chetwode St. Crewe 190 B3
Chetwood Dr. Wid 12 C2
Cheveley Cl. Mfield 87 E1
Chevin Gdns. Bram 36 A4
Cheviot Ave. Warr 8 A2
Cheviot Cl. El Por 69 D3
Cheviot Ct. Winsf 149 D4
Chevron Cl. Blacon 117 F2
Chevron Hey. Blacon 117 F2
Cheyne Wlk. Nant 204 C2
Cheyney Rd. Blacon 118 A2
Cheyney Rd. Chest 118 A2
Chicago Ave. Wythe 33 D4
Chichester Cl. Run 50 B3
Chichester St. Chest 118 B1
Chidlow Cl. Ho Co 206 C2
Chidlow Cl. Wid 23 D3
Child's La. Astb 177 F3
Childer Cres. El Por 69 D4
Childer Gdns. El Por 69 D4
Childwall Ct. El Por 69 F4
Childwall Gdns. El Por 69 F4
Childwall Rd. El Por 69 F4
Chilham Cl. Winsf 149 E4
Chilham Pl. Mfield 111 F3
Chilington Ave. Wid 22 B4
Chiltern Ave. Mfield 112 A4
Chiltern Ave. Warr 8 A2
Chiltern Cl. Chest 141 D3
Chiltern Cl. Cudd 102 A1
Chiltern Cres. Warr 8 A2
Chiltern Pl. Warr 8 A2
Chiltern Rd. Cul 4 C2
Chiltern Rd. St Hel 1 A2
Chiltern Rd. Warr 8 A2
Chiltern Way. Winsf 149 D4
Chilton Dr. El Por 69 F1
Chilworth Cl. Wist 206 B4
China La. Warr 16 B1
Chines The. Cudd 101 E3
Chippingdall Cl. Gt San 15 E3
Chipstead Cl. Hart 103 D2
Chirk Cl. Chest 118 C3
Chirk Pl. Winsf 126 A1
Chiswick Cl. Run 50 B4
Chiswick Gdns. Apple 26 C3
Chollerton Cl. H Legh 29 E2
Cholmondeley La. Bulk 200 C4
Cholmondeley Rd. El Por 69 F2
Cholmondeley Rd. Hamp 213 F4
Cholmondeley Rd. Run 49 E2
Cholmondeley St. Wid 23 D2
Cholmondely St. Mfield 112 B3
Chorley Hall Cl. A Edge 59 F1
Chorley Hall La. A Edge 60 A1
Chorley Hall La. Chorl 202 B1
Chorley St. Warr 16 A3
Chorley's La. Wid 13 F2
Chorlton Cl. Run 24 B1
Chorlton La. Ho Co 207 D1
Chowley Oak La. Chow 182 C3
Chrimes Dr. Oak 123 F3
Christchurch Ave. Wist 190 A1
Christie Cl. El Por 44 A1
Christie St. Wid 13 E1
Christleton Ave. Crewe 189 E3
Christleton Ct. Run 24 B2
Christleton Dr. El Por 69 F3
Christleton Rd. Chest 119 D1
Christleton Way. Wilm 34 B3
Christopher Dr. Beb 44 A3
Church Bank. Audley 209 E1
Church Bank. Tatt 166 A1
Church Bk. W Br 65 E4
Church Cl. Weave 77 E1
Church College Cl. Chest 118 A2
Church Croft. Dodle 162 A3
Church Ct. Asht 121 F4
Church Ct. Farn 180 C1
Church Dr. Warr 9 D1
Church End. Hale 21 E1
Church Farm Ct. Hes 40 C4
Church Green. Part 19 D4
Church Hall Cl. Blacon 117 F2
Church Hill. Knuts 57 D1
Church La. Aldf 163 F2
Church La. Apple 17 D1
Church La. Back 95 D2
Church La. Beb 44 A2
Church La. Chest 118 B4
Church La. Cul 4 C2
Church La. El Por 69 E2
Church La. Elton 72 B1
Church La. Farn 180 C1
Church La. G Sutt 119 F3
Church La. Gold 3 E4
Church La. Henb 111 E4
Church La. Kids 195 F4
Church La. Mobb 58 B3
Church La. N Mills 39 E4
Church La. Nest 66 C4
Church La. Rain 88 C3
Church La. S La E 112 C2
Church La. Sand 175 F4
Church La. Sch Gr 194 B4
Church La. Small 176 C2
Church La. Stoak 96 A4
Church La. Warren 134 B4
Church La. Warren 134 C1
Church La. Weave 77 E1
Church La. Wist 205 F4
Church La. Woodf 35 E1
Church Mead. Aldf 181 D3
Church Meadow. N in H 236 B1
Church Meadow La. Hes 40 C4
Church Meadows. L Lei 77 E3
Church Meadows. Whitch 226 A1
Church Mews. Boll 88 A4
Church Mews. Knuts 57 D1
Church Par. El Por 70 B3
Church Rd. Alsag 193 E2
Church Rd. Asht 121 F4
Church Rd. Broug 139 E2
Church Rd. Burw 184 A3
Church Rd. Ch Hul 35 D4
Church Rd. Eccles 141 F1
Church Rd. Frod 74 B4
Church Rd. Hale 47 F4
Church Rd. Halew 21 D4
Church Rd. Hay 1 C4
Church Rd. L Lei 77 E2
Church Rd. Lymm 18 C1
Church Rd. N Mills 39 E4
Church Rd. North 78 A1
Church Rd. North 104 A4
Church Rd. Saug 94 A1
Church Rd. Shock 197 E1
Church Rd. Thor H 42 A3
Church Rd. Tils 198 A2
Church Rd. Wilm 34 B2
Church Rd. Wilm 59 F2
Church Rd. Worles 188 B3
Church St. Audley 210 A1
Church St. Boll 88 A4
Church St. Chest 118 B2
Church St. Con Q 91 E1
Church St. Dave 104 A2
Church St. El Por 70 B3
Church St. Farn 180 C1
Church St. Frod 74 A4
Church St. G Bud 79 D4
Church St. H Winch 79 F3
Church St. Holt 180 C1
Church St. Kels 122 B2
Church St. Kids 194 B1
Church St. Kids 195 D2
Church St. Malpas 213 D2
Church St. Mfield 112 B4
Church St. Moult 126 C4
Church St. N-le-W 2 C2
Church St. Nant 204 C3
Church St. Run 23 D2
Church St. Sand 175 E3
Church St. Sch Gr 195 E3
Church St. Tarv 121 E1
Church St. Warr 16 B3
Church St. Weave 77 E1
Church St. Wid 23 D3
Church St. Wilm 60 A4
Church St. Winsf 126 C1
Church St N. Kels 122 B3
Church St W. Mfield 112 B4
Church Terr. Wilm 34 B2
Church View. Audlem 230 A2
Church View. Kings 75 D1
Church View. Knuts 57 D1
Church View. Lymm 19 D2
Church View Terr. S La E 112 C2
Church View Wlk. Wist 205 F4
Church Way. Blacon 117 F3
Church Wk. Win 8 A3
Church Wlk. H Chap 130 B2
Church Wlk. Knuts 57 D1
Church Wlk. North 104 A4
Church Wlk. Peo 81 F1
Church Wlk. Wilm 59 F3
Churchfield Rd. Frod 74 B4
Churchfields. Audlem 230 A2
Churchfields. Croft 9 D4
Churchfields. Cudd 102 A1
Churchfields. Hels 73 E2
Churchfields. Knuts 57 E1
Churchfields. North 78 A2
Churchfields. Wid 13 D3
Churchill Ave. Cul 5 D2
Churchill Cl. Congle 156 A2
Churchill Dr. Tarp 146 B1
Churchill Parkway. Winsf 149 E4
Churchill Way. Mfield 112 B4
Churchill Way. Nest 66 C4
Churchmere Cl. Crewe 190 B4
Churchside. Mfield 112 B4
Churchside Wlk. Chest 140 C4
Churchward Cl. Chest 118 B2
Churchway. Alva 73 E1
Churchway. Mfield 86 C1
Churchway Rd. Speke 21 D1
Churchyard Side. Nant 204 C3
Churton Cl. Ho Co 206 C2
Churton Rd. Chest 119 D1
Churton Rd. Farn 180 C1
Churton St. Chest 119 D1
Cicely Mill La. Rosth 30 B2
Cinder Cl. G Sutt 119 F3
Cinder Hill. Winsf 125 F3
Cinder Hill La. Sch Gr 194 C4
Cinder La. Apple 17 F1
Cinder La. Chelf 83 F1
Cinder La. G Sutt 119 F3
Cinder La. Lost 105 D4
Cinder La. Peo 108 B4
Cinder La. Worles 188 B1
Cinnamon Brow. Warr 8 C2
Cinnamon La N. Warr 8 C2
Circle Ave. Willas 205 F3
Circle The. Crewe 190 B1
Circle The. Mere 30 B1
Circuit The. A Edge 60 A2
Circuit The. Ch Hul 35 D4
Circuit The. Wilm 59 E3
Circular Dr. Chest 140 C2
City Bank. Bidd 179 E1
City Rd. Chest 118 C1
City Walls Rd. Chest 118 B1
Civic Way. El Por 70 A2
Civic Way. Middle 128 B1
Clair Ave. Hawa 116 A2
Claire Pl. Winsf 149 E4
Clamhunger La. Mere 56 B4
Clamley Ct. Speke 21 D2
Clanfield Ave. Wid 12 B2
Clap Gate Cres. Wid 22 A3
Clap Gates Cres. Warr 15 F4
Clap Gates Rd. Warr 15 F4
Clare Ave. Chest 119 D2
Clare Ave. Wilm 34 B2
Clare Dr. El Por 70 A1
Clare Dr. Mfield 87 E2
Clare Dr. Wist 189 F1
Clare St. Kids 195 F2
Clare St. Sch Gr 195 E3
Claremont Ave. Wid 13 E2
Claremont Dr. Wid 13 D2
Claremont Rd. Ch Hul 35 D4
Claremont Rd. Crewe 190 A1
Claremont Rd. Cul 4 B2
Claremont Rd. Run 23 D1
Clarence Ave. Chest 119 D1
Clarence Ave. Wid 13 D2
Clarence Ct. Wilm 60 A3
Clarence Gr. Crewe 190 A3
Clarence Rd. Boll 63 D1
Clarence Rd. Warr 17 D1
Clarence St. N-le-W 1 C2
Clarence St. Run 22 C2
Clarence St. Warr 16 C4
Clarence Terr. Boll 63 D1
Clarence Terr. Run 23 D2
Clarendon Cl. Chest 141 F3
Clarendon Cl. Run 50 B4
Clarendon Ct. Warr 7 F2
Clarendon Dr. Mfield 88 A1
Clarendon Rd. Irlam 11 F4
Clares Farm Cl. Warr 17 F4
Clarke Ave. Cul 5 D2
Clarke Ave. Warr 16 B1
Clarke La. Boll 87 F3
Clarke La. S La E 113 E2
Clarke Terr. Mfield 112 B3
Clarks Terr. Run 48 B4
Clary Meadow. North 78 C1
Clatterbridge Rd. Thor H 42 B4
Claude St. Warr 16 B3
Claughton Ave. Crewe 190 B1
Claverton Cl. Run 49 D3
Clay Heys. Chelf 84 A2
Clay La. Burton 6 C3
Clay La. Hasl 174 A1
Clay La. Mar 125 D2
Clay La. Peo 108 A4
Clay La. Sand 174 A1
Clay La. Wilm 34 B3
Clay La. Wilm 59 E3
Clayhill Gn. El Por 69 E4
Claypit Rd. Chest 141 D3
Claypitts La. Waver 142 C3
Clayton Av. Congle 157 D3
Clayton Ave. Gold 3 F4
Clayton Cres. Run 22 C1
Clayton Cres. Wid 12 C1
Clayton Dr. Whitch 226 A1
Clayton Rd. Warr 9 F3
Clayton's Row. Nant 204 C4
Clayton-by-pass. Congle 156 B2
Cleave Rd. Weave 77 E1
Cleaver Rd. Blacon 117 F2
Cledford Cres. Middle 151 F3
Cledford La. Middle 151 F4
Cleethorpes Rd. Run 50 B4
Cleeve Way. Ch Hul 35 D3
Clegg St. Mfield 112 C4
Clegge St. Warr 16 A4
Cleggs Cl. Chest 142 A4
Clelland St. Warr 16 B2
Clemley Cl. Kels 122 B3
Clerewood Ave. Chea 34 A4
Clevedon Cl. Mfield 112 A4
Cleveland Dr. El Por 69 D3
Cleveland Dr. Gold 3 E4
Cleveland Rd. Warr 8 A2
Cleveland Way. Winsf 149 D4
Cleveleys Ave. Wid 13 E1
Cleveleys Rd. Gt San 15 D2
Cleves Cl. Blacon 117 E3
Cliff La. Act Br 76 B2
Cliff La. Apple 17 E1
Cliff La. Lymm 28 A3
Cliff La. Mfield 88 A1
Cliff La. Rain 88 A1
Cliff Rd. Act Br 76 C2
Cliff Rd. Wilm 60 A4
Cliff Side. Wilm 60 A4
Cliff View. Frod 74 A4
Cliffbrook Gr. Wilm 34 B1
Cliffe Rd. Apple 26 B4
Cliffe Rd. Crewe 190 A4
Cliffe Rd. Nest 66 C3
Cliffe St. Warr 16 A3
Cliffe St. Wid 13 E1
Clifford Dr. Chest 140 C3
Clifford Gr. Hasl 191 E2

Clifford Pl. Winsf 149 E4
Clifford Rd. Mfield 112 A4
Clifford Rd. Penk 15 D2
Clifford Rd. Poyn 36 B2
Clifford Rd. Wilm 59 F3
Clifton Ave. Beb 43 F2
Clifton Ave. Crewe 190 A2
Clifton Ave. Cul 4 B2
Clifton Cl. Warr 17 E4
Clifton Cres. Frod 49 E1
Clifton Dr. Blacon 117 F2
Clifton Dr. North 104 A3
Clifton Dr. Wilm 59 F2
Clifton Gdns. El Por 70 B2
Clifton La. Run 49 F2
Clifton Park Ave. Con Q 91 E1
Clifton Rd. Run 49 D3
Clifton Rd. Run 49 F2
Clifton Rd. Sand 174 B4
Clifton St. A Edge 60 A1
Clifton St. Crewe 190 A2
Clifton St. Warr 16 B2
Cliftonville Rd. Warr 17 E3
Clincton Cl. Wid 22 A4
Clincton Cl. Wid 22 A4
Clincton View. Wid 22 A4
Clipsley Cres. Hay 1 A4
Clipsley La. Hay 1 A3
Clitheroe Rd. Weave 77 F1
Clive Ave. Warr 8 B1
Clive La. Winsf 150 B4
Cliveden Rd. Chest 140 C3
Clivegreen La. Winsf 150 C4
Clock Face Rd. Bo Hea 13 F4
Clomley Gdns. Hale 21 F1
Close La. Alsag 192 C2
Close La. Sch Gr 195 E4
Close The. Alsag 193 D2
Close The. Blacon 117 E2
Close The. North 103 E3
Close The. Saug 94 A1
Closeburn Ave. Hes 40 C3
Cloud View. Congle 157 D1
Cloudberry Wlk. Part 11 F1
Clough Ave. Warr 8 A1
Clough Ave. Wilm 34 A1
Clough Bank. Boll 87 F4
Clough Hall Dr. Kids 210 C3
Clough Hall Rd. Kids 210 C4
Clough La. North 103 E3
Clough Rd. Winsf 126 C1
Clough The. Run 23 F1
Clough Wlk. Crewe 206 B4
Cloughside. Disley 38 C3
Clovelly Ave. Gt San 14 C4
Clovelly Gr. Run 50 B3
Clover Ave. Frod 74 B4
Clover Ct. Run 50 A3
Clover Dr. Winsf 126 B2
Clover La. Chest 140 C3
Clover Pl. Chest 140 C3
Cloverdale. North 103 E4
Cloverdale Rd. Mfield 112 A3
Cloverfield. Run 50 B4
Cloverfield Gdns. El Por 69 E4
Cloverfields. Hasl 191 E2
Clowes Ave. Alsag 193 F1
Clowes St. Mfield 112 A4
Clumber Cl. Poyn 36 C2
Clumber Rd. Poyn 36 C2
Clwyd Cl. Broug 139 D3
Clyde Ave. Bidd 179 F1
Clyde Cres. Winsf 127 D1
Clyde Gr. Crewe 190 A2
Clydesdale. El Por 70 A2
Clydesdale Ave. Crewe 190 A2
Clydesdale Rd. Apple 26 B4
Coach Rd. Bicker 199 E1
Coach Rd. Chow 183 D2
Coach Rd. Ed Gr 199 E1
Coach Rd. Hamp 199 E1
Coach Rd. L Bud 147 E4
Coachway. Prest 86 C4
Coalbrookdale Rd. Nest 41 F1
Coalpit Hill. Kids 210 B4
Coalpit La. Moll 94 B2
Coalpit La. S La E 113 E3
Coalpit La. Winsf 127 F1
Coare St. Mfield 87 E1
Coastguard La. Nest 41 D1
Cob Hall La. Man 98 B3
Cob Moor Rd. Kids 195 D2
Cob Moor Rd. Law-g 195 D2
Cobal Ct. Frod 74 A4
Cobb's La. Nant 204 C4
Cobbett's Way. Wilm 59 F2
Cobblers Cross La. Tarp 146 C1
Cobblers La. Burt 161 D1
Cobbles The. Chest 141 E4
Cobbles The. Cudd 101 E2
Cobbles The. Peo 81 F1
Cobbs La. Apple 26 C4
Cobbs La. Ho Co 206 C1
Cobden St. N-le-W 2 B2
Cobden St. Warr 16 A3
Cock Hall La. S La E 113 E2
Cock La. G Bud 78 C4
Cockhedge Centre. Warr 16 A3
Cockhedge La. Warr 16 B3
Cockhedge Way. Warr 16 A3
Cockington Cl. North 104 A2
Cocklade La. Hale 21 E1
Cockpit La. Cudd 102 A1
Cocksheadhey Rd. Boll 63 E1
Cocksmoss Rd. Mart 133 E2
Coe La. Rosth 30 B4
Coerdon Dr. Apple 17 E1
Cogshall La. Comb 78 A4
Cogshall La. L Lei 77 F4
Cogshall La. North 78 B3
Colborne St. N-le-W 2 C2
Colchester Sq. Chest 140 C3
Coldmoss Dr. Sand 175 E2
Coldstream Cl. Warr 8 C2
Cole Ave. N-le-W 2 B2
Colebrook Cl. Warr 10 A2
Coleclough Pl. Cul 4 C2
Colehill Bank. Congle 156 C1
Colehill Pl. Con Q 91 E1
Coleridge Cl. Blacon 118 A3
Coleridge Way. Crewe 190 C3
Colinwood Ave. Broug 139 D2
Collar House Dr. Prest 86 C3
College Cl. Warr 16 B3
College Cl. Wilm 59 F4
College Fields. Wist 190 A1
College Gn. Chest 141 E4
College La. Bun 168 C1
College Rd. Alsag 193 D3
College View. Con Q 91 E1
Colley La. Ha Gr 175 E3
Colley La. Sand 175 E3
Colleys La. Nant 205 E4
Colleys La. Willas 205 E4
Collier St. Run 22 C2
Collier's Row. Run 48 C4
Colliers La. B Hea 54 C1
Colliery Green Cl. Nest 66 C3
Colliery Green Cl. Nest 66 C3
Colliery Green Dr. Nest 66 C3
Collin St. Warr 15 F3
Collinbrook Ave. Crewe 190 A1
Collingham Green. El Por 69 D3
Collingham Way. Winsf 126 B1
Collingtree Ave. Winsf 127 D2
Collingwood Cl. Mfield 87 D1
Collingwood Cl. Poyn 37 D2
Collingwood Rd. N-le-W 2 A2
Collins Green Rd. Burton 1 C1
Collins St. Crewe 190 A2
Collinson Ct. Frod 74 A4
Colmere Ct. El Por 70 B4
Colne Rd. Burton 6 C3
Colshaw Dr. Wilm 34 B1
Colshaw La. Sidd 109 F1
Colshaw Wlk. Wilm 34 B1
Columbine Cl. Hunt 142 A3
Columbine Cl. Wid 12 A2
Columbine Wlk. Part 11 F1
Colveley Way. Winsf 126 A1
Colville Ct. Warr 8 A2
Colville Rd. Mfield 111 F4
Colwyn Cl. Warr 7 F1
Colwyn Rd. Bram 35 F4
Comber Way. Knuts 82 A4
Comboy Dr. North 104 B3
Combs Cl. N Mills 39 D4
Commercial Ave. Wilm 34 C3
Commercial Rd. Mfield 112 C4
Common Farm La. Chelf 83 F1
Common La. Betley 221 F3
Common La. Chelf 83 F1
Common La. Cul 4 C2
Common La. Kels 122 B2
Common La. L Den 105 F3
Common La. Stret 52 C4
Common La. Tarv 122 B2
Common La. Warr 16 C1
Common La. Waver 143 D2
Common Rd. N-le-W 1 C2
Common St. N-le-W 1 C2
Common The. Run 49 F4
Commonhall St. Chest 118 B1
Commons Mill. Sand 175 D4
Commons The. Sand 175 D3
Commonside. Alva 73 F1
Commonwealth Cl. Winsf 149 E3
Company's Cl. Run 48 C3
Compass Cl. Run 50 B3
Compton Pl. Chest 141 D3
Compton Pl. El Por 70 A3
Concord Pl. Warr 8 B1
Condliffe Cl. Sand 175 E3
Conery Cl. Hels 73 E2
Coney Gr. Run 50 A3
Congar La. Mould 98 C1
Congleton Cl. A Edge 85 D4
Congleton Edge Rd. Congle 179 D3
Congleton La. Sidd 109 E3
Congleton La. With 109 E3
Congleton Rd. A Edge 85 D3
Congleton Rd. Astb 177 F2
Congleton Rd. Bidd 178 C1
Congleton Rd. Bidd 179 E1
Congleton Rd. Broug 139 E2
Congleton Rd. Kids 194 B1
Congleton Rd. Mart 133 D3
Congleton Rd. Mfield 112 A3
Congleton Rd. N Ald 85 D3
Congleton Rd. Sand 175 D4
Congleton Rd. Sch Gr 177 F2
Congleton Rd. Sidd 110 A3
Congleton Rd. Small 176 A4
Congleton Rd. Small 176 C3
Congleton Rd. Small 177 D3
Congleton Rd. Warren 111 F1
Congleton Rd N. Law-g 194 C3
Congleton Rd N. Sch Gr 194 C3
Congleton Rd S. Law-g 194 B2
Conifer Cl. El Por 95 D4
Conifer Gr. Gt San 14 C4
Conifer Wlk. Part 11 E1
Conifers The. Alsag 193 D2
Coniston Ave. Beb 43 E2
Coniston Ave. Congle 155 F1
Coniston Ave. Penk 14 B2
Coniston Ave. Winsf 126 B1
Coniston Cl. El Por 44 A1
Coniston Cl. Nant 205 D3
Coniston Cl. Run 49 E3
Coniston Dr. Frod 74 B4
Coniston Dr. H Chap 130 A2
Coniston Dr. Wilm 34 B2
Coniston Rd. Chest 118 C3
Coniston Rd. H La 37 E4
Coniston Rd. Nest 66 C3
Coniston Rd. Part 11 F2
Coniston Way. Mfield 111 F3
Connaught Ave. Warr 16 C4
Connaught Cl. Wilm 60 B4
Connaught Dr. N-le-W 2 B1
Conroy Way. N-le-W 7 E4
Constable Dr. Wilm 60 C4
Constables Cl. Run 24 A1
Constance Rd. Part 11 F2
Constance Way. Wid 23 D3
Convamore Rd. Ch Hul 35 E4
Conway Ave. Irlam 11 F4
Conway Ave. Warr 7 F1
Conway Ave. Winsf 149 E4
Conway Cl. Brough 140 B3
Conway Cl. Crewe 190 B4
Conway Cl. Gt San 14 C3
Conway Cl. Knuts 82 A4
Conway Cres. Mfield 87 F1
Conway Ct. El Por 70 B2
Conway Dr. N-le-W 2 C2
Coogee Ave. Gt San 14 C4
Cook Ave. Hay 1 C4
Cook St. El Por 70 B3
Cooke's La. North 104 C3
Cooks La. B of H 225 E4
Cooksmere La. Sand 175 D4
Coole La. Fr La E 218 C2
Coole La. New 229 E3
Coombe Dr. Run 49 D4
Coombe Park. El Por 69 E3
Coope Rd. Boll 87 F3
Cooper Ave. N-le-W 1 C2
Cooper Ave. Warr 8 A1
Cooper La. Hay 1 B3
Cooper St. Congle 156 C2
Cooper St. Run 23 D2
Cooper St. Wid 13 D1
Cooper's La. Con Q 91 E1
Cooper,s Cft. Chest 142 A4
Cop Meadow. S La E 112 C1
Cope Ave. Nant 204 B2
Copeland Gr. Run 49 F3
Copeland Rd. Warr 16 A1
Copes La. Nant 204 B2
Copeswood Cl. Broug 139 E2
Copgrove Wlk. Wythe 33 F4
Coppenhall La. Crewe 189 E2
Copper Beach Cl. Broug 139 E2
Copper St. Mfield 112 C3
Copper Wood. Cudd 101 F3
Copperfield Cl. Warr 9 E3
Copperfield Rd. Ch Hul 35 D3
Copperfield Rd. Poyn 36 B1
Copperfields. Wilm 60 B4
Copperhill Rd. Congle 179 D4
Coppice. Cudd 101 E3
Coppice Cl. Disley 38 A3
Coppice Cl. Run 24 A1
Coppice Cl. Willas 205 E3
Coppice Dr. Disley 38 A3
Coppice Dr. Middle 151 F3
Coppice Green. Warr 7 D1
Coppice La. Disley 38 A3
Coppice Rd. Hasl 192 A4
Coppice Rd. Kids 210 B4
Coppice Rd. Poyn 37 D2
Coppice Rd. Willas 205 E3
Coppice Rise. Mfield 112 B3
Coppice The. Altr 32 A4
Coppice The. Nant 204 C2
Coppice The. Sand 174 C4
Coppice The. W Br 65 F3
Coppins Cl. Chest 119 D1
Coppins Cl. Hels 73 D2
Coppins The. Warr 8 B1
Coppins The. Wilm 59 F2
Copse The. Altr 32 B4
Copse The. N-le-W 2 A2
Copse The. Run 50 A3
Copthorne Cl. Congle 156 C1
Copthorne Dr. Audlem 229 F2
Corbet Ave. Warr 16 A4
Corbet Dr. Adder 235 D2
Corbet St. Warr 16 A4
Corfe Way. Winsf 149 E4
Coridor Rd. Stan 71 D3
Corks La. Disley 38 C3
Cormorant Cl. Crewe 190 C2
Cormorant Dr. Run 22 C1
Cornbrook Rd. Mfield 112 B2
Corner Croft. Wilm 60 A2
Corners The. Weave 102 C4
Cornfield Cl. El Por 69 F1
Cornfield Cl. Mfield 87 E2
Cornhill Cl. N-u-L 210 B1
Cornish Way. Wythe 33 E4
Cornishway Ind Est. Wythe 33 E4
Cornubia Rd. Wid 23 E4
Cornwall Ave. Run 23 D1
Cornwall Cl. Congle 157 D1
Cornwall Cl. H La 37 F4
Cornwall Cl. Mfield 86 C1
Cornwall Cl. Run 23 F1
Cornwall Gr. Crewe 190 A3
Cornwall Rd. Chea 34 A4
Cornwall Rd. Chest 118 B4
Cornwall Rd. Irlam 11 E3
Cornwall Rd. Wid 13 D2
Cornwall St. Chest 118 B2
Cornwall St. Warr 16 C4
Cornwell Cl. Wilm 60 B4
Coronation Ave. Alsag 193 D2
Coronation Ave. Cul 5 E4
Coronation Ave. Warr 17 E1
Coronation Ave. Winsf 126 C1
Coronation Bldgs. Boll 88 A4
Coronation Cres. Crewe 190 C3
Coronation Cres. Kids 194 C1
Coronation Cres. Sand 175 D3
Coronation Dr. Frod 49 E1
Coronation Dr. Hay 2 A4
Coronation Dr. Penk 14 C2
Coronation Dr. Wid 22 A4
Coronation Gr. North 78 A2
Coronation Rd. Broug 139 D2
Coronation Rd. Congle 156 C2
Coronation Rd. El Por 70 B2
Coronation Rd. Middle 151 E3
Coronation Rd. Run 23 D1
Coronation Rd. Run 50 C3
Coronation St. Chest 140 C4
Coronation St. Crewe 190 B3
Coronation St. Mfield 112 B3
Coronation Terr. Tarp 146 B1
Coroner's La. Wid 13 D2
Coronet Way. Wid 22 A4
Correction Brow. Poyn 37 E3
Corstons La. Nest 67 D3
Corwen Cl. Warr 7 F1
Cossack Ave. Warr 8 A1
Cotebrook Dr. Chest 118 B4
Cotebrook Rd. North 104 B3
Cotes Pl. Blacon 117 F2
Cotesmore Dr. Hes 41 E4
Cotgreaves Cl. Chest 141 D3
Cotswold Ave. Gold 3 E3
Cotswold Cl. Chest 118 C3
Cotswold Cl. Cudd 102 A1
Cotswold Cl. Mfield 86 C1
Cotswold Gr. St Hel 1 A2
Cotswold Rd. Warr 8 A2
Cotswold Way. Winsf 149 D4
Cottage Cl. Beb 43 E3
Cottage Cl. Nest 66 C4
Cottage Dr East. Hes 40 C3
Cottage Dr West. Hes 40 C3
Cottage La. Hes 40 C3
Cottage La. Mfield 112 C4
Cottage Rd. Chest 141 D3
Cottage St. Mfield 112 A4
Cottam Dr. Warr 9 D2
Cotterill. Run 49 E4
Cotterill Dr. Warr 17 E4
Cotterill St. Crewe 190 B1
Cottesmore Gdns. Altr 32 B4
Cotton La. Dudd 145 E4
Cotton La. Run 49 E4
Cotton La. Sand 175 D2
Cottonwood Dr. Kids 195 F2
Cottrell Rd. Altr 32 B4
Coulton Rd. Wid 13 F2
Counce Ave. N-le-W 2 B1
Countess Ave. Wilm 34 C3
Countess Cl. Mfield 111 F4
Countess Rd. Mfield 112 A4
Countess Way. Chest 118 B2
Counting House Rd. Disley 38 C3
Courier Row. Boll 87 F4
Courtney Green. Wilm 34 B1
Courtney Rd. Chest 140 C2
Cousens Way. Chest 118 A2
Coventry Ave. El Por 94 C4
Coverdale Cl. Gt San 14 B4
Covert Cl. Winsf 149 D4
Covert Gdns. Kids 210 B4
Covert Rise. Tatt 166 A1
Cow La. Ashl 31 F3
Cow La. Harg 144 A1
Cow La. Mfield 112 B3
Cow La. Norley 101 D3
Cow La. Rain 88 B2
Cowanway. Wid 12 C3
Cowbrook La. Warren 135 D3
Cowdell St. Warr 16 A4
Cowfields. Nant 204 C3
Cowhey Cl. Chest 141 D3
Cowper Cl. Wist 206 A4
Cowthorne Dr. Waver 143 D2
Cowy Cl. Sand 174 C4
Coyt Rd. W Br 65 F3
Crab La. Warr 9 D2
Crabmill Dr. Sand 174 C4
Crabmill La. Norley 100 C3
Crabmill La. Warm 173 F4
Crabtree Ave. Altr 32 B4
Crabtree Ave. Disley 38 C3
Crabtree Gr. Crewe 190 C3
Crabtree La. H Legh 29 D3
Crabwall Pl. Blacon 117 F3
Cradley. Wid 12 B1
Craig Cl. Mfield 112 A3
Craig Dr. W Br 65 F3
Craig Gdns. El Por 69 F4
Craig Rd. Congle 156 C2
Craig Rd. Mfield 112 A3
Craig Wlk. Alsag 193 F1
Craigleigh Gr. Beb 43 F2
Craigside. Bidd 179 E1
Craithe Rd. Chest 119 D1
Crampton Dr. Altr 32 B4
Cranage Cl. Run 49 E4
Cranage Rd. Crewe 190 A2
Cranage Way. Wilm 34 B3
Cranberry Dr. N-u-L 210 B1
Cranberry La. Alsag 193 D2
Cranberry Moss La. Alsag 193 D2
Cranberry Rd. Part 11 F2
Cranborne Rd. Crewe 190 B3
Cranborne Rd. Warr 16 A1
Cranebrook Cl. Crewe 190 A4
Cranfield Dr. Alsag 193 D2
Cranford Ave. Knuts 56 C1
Cranford Ave. Mfield 112 C4
Cranford Cl. Beb 43 F2
Cranford Ct. Chest 141 D3
Cranford Ct. Warr 17 F4
Cranford Mews. Alsag 193 D2
Cranford Rd. Wilm 34 A1
Cranham Ave. Gold 3 F4
Cranleigh Cl. Warr 26 A4
Cranleigh Cres. Blacon 118 A2
Cranleigh Dr. Haz Gr 37 D4
Cranmere Cl. North 104 A2
Cranshaw La. Wid 13 D3
Cranswick Gn. El Por 69 E3
Crantock Dr. Chea 34 B4
Cranwell Ave. Cul 4 C2
Crauford Rd. Eaton 157 D4
Craven Ave. Gold 3 F4
Craven Ct. Warr 7 F2
Crawford Ave. Wid 12 A1
Crawford Pl. Run 49 D3
Crawford's Wlk. Chest 118 C2
Crawley Ave. Warr 8 A2
Crayford Ave. Congle 157 D3
Cresanne Cl. Middle 151 E4
Crescent Dr. Hels 73 D2
Crescent Dr. W Br 39 E1
Crescent Rd. A Edge 60 A1
Crescent Rd. Congle 156 B1
Crescent Rd. Cran 129 F3
Crescent Rd. El Por 70 B3
Crescent Rd. Rosth 30 A2
Crescent The. Chest 118 B2
Crescent The. Congle 156 B1
Crescent The. El Por 69 F3
Crescent The. Hart 103 D3
Crescent The. Lymm 18 C1
Crescent The. M St A 61 D1
Crescent The. Mfield 87 F1
Crescent The. Middle 128 A1
Crescent The. N Mills 39 D4
Crescent The. Nant 204 C3
Crescent The. North 103 F3
Crescent The. Rosth 30 A2
Crescent The. Utkin 146 A4
Crescent The. Weave 77 F1
Cressbrook Rd. Warr 16 B1
Cressington Gdns. El Por 70 B3
Cresswell Ave. N Mills 39 E4
Cresswell Ave. N-u-L 210 B1
Cresswell Cl. Warr 7 E1
Cresswell St. N Mills 39 E4
Cresta Dr. Run 48 C3
Crestwood Cl. Wist 206 A4
Crew Ave. Mfield 87 F1
Crew Rd. Alsag 193 F2
Crewe Green Ave. Hasl 191 E2
Crewe Green Rd. Crewe 191 D2
Crewe Hill La. Cal Gr 197 D3
Crewe La. Farn 180 C1
Crewe La S. Cal Gr 197 D4

Crewe Rd. Alsag 193 D2
Crewe Rd. Crewe 190 C1
Crewe Rd. Hasl 191 E3
Crewe Rd. Hather 219 F2
Crewe Rd. Nant 205 E3
Crewe Rd. Sand 175 D2
Crewe Rd. Shav 206 B3
Crewe Rd. Willas 205 E3
Crewe Rd. Wist 205 E3
Crewe St. Chest 118 C1
Crewe St. Crewe 190 B2
Crewood Common Rd.
Crow 76 A2
Crib La. Tiver 168 A4
Criccieth Ct. El Por 70 B1
Crimes La. Beest 167 E2
Crisham Ave. Fr La E 218 C4
Critchley Rd. Speke 21 D2
Croasdale Dr. Run 49 F3
Crocus St. North 78 A2
Croesmere Dr. El Por 69 E1
Croft Cl. Altr 32 B3
Croft Cl. Utkin 146 A4
Croft Cl. Waver 143 D3
Croft Ct. El Por 70 C2
Croft La. Dodle 162 A4
Croft La. Knuts 82 A4
Croft Rd. Wilm 59 F2
Croft St. Gold 3 D4
Croft St. Wid 23 D3
Croft The. Chest 118 B3
Croft The. Run 23 F1
Croften Dr. Nest 66 C3
Crofters Cl. El Por 69 F1
Crofters Cl. Wist 206 A4
Crofters Ct. H Chap 130 B2
Crofters Gn. Wilm 59 F3
Crofters Heath. El Por 69 F1
Crofters Lea. North 103 E4
Crofters Pk. Hawa 116 A2
Crofters Way. Saug 116 C4
Crofton Cl. Apple 27 E3
Crofton Gdns. Cul 4 C2
Crofton Rd. Run 22 C1
Croftside. Warr 17 F4
Croftsway. Hes 40 B4
Cromer Dr. Crewe 190 A4
Cromford Ct. W Br 65 F3
Cromley Rd. H La 37 F3
Crompton Rd. Mfield 112 B4
Cromwell Ave. Gt San 15 D4
Cromwell Ave. Warr 7 E2
Cromwell Ave S. Gt San 15 E2
Cromwell Ct. Irlam 11 F4
Cromwell Ct. Nant 204 C3
Cromwell Dr. Shav 206 B2
Cromwell Rd. Ch Hul 35 E3
Cromwell Rd. El Por 70 B3
Cromwell Rd. Irlam 11 F4
Cromwell Rd. North 103 F4
Cromwell St. Wid 23 D3
Cronkinson Ave. Nant 204 C2
Cronkinson Oak. Nant 204 C2
Cronton La. Wid 12 C3
Cronton Park Ave. Cront 12 B3
Cronton Park Cl. Cront 12 B3
Cronton Rd. Cront 12 B3
Cronulla Dr. Gt San 14 B4
Crook La. Winsf 127 D1
Crook St. Chest 118 B1
Crooked La. Dudd 145 E2
Crookedyard Rd. Mac For 113 F4
Crookenden Cl. Chest 95 E1
Crookenden Rd. Chest 95 E1
Croppers Rd. Warr 8 C2
Crosby Ave. Warr 16 A4
Crosby Gr. Will 68 A4
Crosfield St. Warr 16 A3
Cross Green. Chest 118 C3
Cross Hey. Chest 141 F4
Cross La. Audley 209 F3
Cross La. Ch Min 172 B3
Cross La. Congle 157 D1
Cross La. Croft 9 E4
Cross La. Frod 73 D4
Cross La. Hasl 191 F4
Cross La. Middle 151 E3
Cross La. N-le-W 2 A2
Cross La. Nest 66 C3
Cross La. Sand 175 E3
Cross La. Small 176 C3
Cross La. Swett 131 F2
Cross La. Tarv 121 F1
Cross La. Warr 17 D2
Cross La. Wilm 60 C4
Cross Lane E. Part 11 F2
Cross Lane W. Part 11 F1
Cross Lanes. Tarv 144 B4
Cross O' Th' Hill Rd. Bic T 214 A2
Cross Rd. Chea 34 A4
Cross Rd. Hasl 191 E2
Cross St. Alsag 193 E2
Cross St. Chest 118 C1
Cross St. Congle 156 B2
Cross St. Crewe 190 B2
Cross St. Gold 3 D4
Cross St. Hasl 191 E2
Cross St. Holt 196 C4
Cross St. Mars 79 E2
Cross St. Mfield 112 C3
Cross St. N Mills 39 E4
Cross St. Nest 66 C4
Cross St. North 78 A2
Cross St. Run 23 D2
Cross St. Warr 16 A4
Cross St. Wid 13 E1
Cross The. Holt 196 C4
Cross The. Lymm 18 C2
Cross Wood St. Nant 204 B3
Crossall St. Mfield 112 B4
Crossdale Rd. Beb 43 E3
Crossfield Ave. Cul 4 C1
Crossfield Rd. Boll 87 F3
Crossfield Rd. Wilm 34 B2
Crossfields. Tarv 121 D1
Crossings The. N-le-W 2 B2
Crossland Terr. Hels 73 D1
Crosslands. Congle 157 D1
Crosslands. Hasl 191 E2
Crossledge. Congle 156 A2
Crossley Ave. El Por 69 F3
Crossley Cres. Chest 119 D3
Crossley Dr. Hes 40 B4
Crossley St. Warr 16 B3
Crossway. Bram 35 F3
Crossway. Crewe 190 B3
Crossway. Wid 22 B4
Crossway The. Thor H 42 B2
Crossways. Bidd 179 F1
Crossways Rd. Law-g 194 A2
Crosthwaite Ave. Beb 43 F2
Croston Cl. A Edge 60 B1
Croston Cl. Wid 12 B2
Crotia Ave. Weston 207 D3
Crouch La. Congle 157 E2
Crouchley La. Lymm 18 C1
Croughton Ct. El Por 69 F4
Croughton Rd. El Por 69 F4
Croughton Rd. Stoak 95 F3
Croughton Rd. Stoak 96 A4
Crow Gdns. N-le-W 2 A2
Crow La E. N-le-W 2 B2
Crow La W. N-le-W 2 A2
Crow Wood Pl. Wid 13 E2
Crowbrook Gr. Wilm 34 B1
Crowder's La. L Den 105 D2
Crowland Gdns. Ch Hul 35 D3
Crowley La. H Legh 28 A2
Crown Ctyd. Audlem 229 F2
Crown Ave. Wid 22 A4
Crown Bank. Sand 175 D3
Crown Bank Cres. Kids 210 B3
Crown Fields Cl. N-le-W 2 A3
Crown Gate. Run 49 F4
Crown Green. Lymm 19 D2
Crown La. Peo 106 B4
Crown Park Dr. N-le-W 2 A3
Crown St. N-le-W 2 A2
Crown St. North 103 F4
Crown St. Warr 16 A3
Crown St W. Mfield 112 B4
Crownest La. G Bud 78 C4
Croxton La. Middle 128 A2
Croxton Way. Hart 103 D2
Croyde Cl. Wythe 33 F4
Croyde Rd. Speke 21 D2
Crum Hill. North 104 A4
Cryers La. Elton 72 A1
Cryers La. T-le-M 96 C4
Cuckoo La. Nest 67 E4
Cuckoo La. Pool 203 F4
Cuckstoolpit Hill. Mfield 112 C4
Cuddington La. Cudd 101 E2
Cuddington Way. Wilm 34 B3
Cuerdley Green. Penk 14 A1
Cuerdley Rd. Penk 14 B2
Culbin Cl. Warr 10 A3
Culcheth Hill Dr. Cul 4 C2
Culford Cl. Run 24 B1
Culland St. Crewe 190 B1
Cullen Cl. Beb 43 E2
Cullen Rd. Run 48 B4
Cumber Dr. Wilm 59 E2
Cumber La. Wilm 59 E2
Cumberland Ave. Irlam 11 E3
Cumberland Ave. Nant 204 C3
Cumberland Cl. Crewe 190 B3
Cumberland Cl. Kids 210 C4
Cumberland Cres. Hay 1 A3
Cumberland Dr. Altr 31 D4
Cumberland Dr. Boll 88 A4
Cumberland Gr. El Por 69 E2
Cumberland Rd. Congle 156 A2
Cumberland Rd. Part 11 F1
Cumberland St. Mfield 112 B4
Cumberland St. Warr 16 B2
Cumbermere Dr. Sand 174 C4
Cumbers Dr. Nest 67 D3
Cumbers La. Nest 67 D3
Cuncliffe Cl. Run 50 A4
Cundiff Cl. Mfield 112 C3
Cunliffe Ave. N-le-W 2 A3
Cunningham Cl. Gt San 14 B4
Cunningham Dr. Beb 43 E4
Cunningham Dr. Run 22 C1
Cunningham Dr. Wythe 34 A4
Cunningham Rd. Wid 22 B4
Cuppin St. Chest 118 B1
Curlender Way. Hale 21 F1
Curlew Cl. Winsf 149 E3
Curlew Gr. Warr 9 F2
Currans Rd. Warr 8 A1
Curzon Ave. Alsag 193 E3
Curzon Cl. Chest 141 D4
Curzon Gr. Winsf 126 C1
Curzon Mews. Wilm 60 A3
Curzon Park N. Chest 141 D4
Curzon Park S. Chest 141 D4
Curzon Rd. Chea 34 A4
Curzon Rd. Poyn 36 C1
Curzon St. Chest 140 C4
Curzon St. Run 22 C1
Cygnet Cl. El Por 69 E2
Cyman Cl. Blacon 117 E2
Cynthia Ave. Warr 17 D4
Cynthia Rd. Run 22 C1
Cypress Ave. El Por 69 F1
Cypress Ave. Wid 13 D1
Cypress Cl. Warr 17 F4
Cypress Gr. Run 49 E4
Cyprus Way. H La 38 A4
Cyril Bell Cl. Lymm 18 C2
Cyril St. Warr 16 A4
Daffodil Cl. Wid 13 F2
Dagnall Ave. Warr 7 F1
Daintry St. Mfield 112 C4
Daintry Terr. Mfield 112 C4
Dairy Farm Cl. Lymm 18 C2
Dairy House La. Ch Hul 35 D2
Dairy House La. Wilm 35 D2
Dairy House Way. Crewe 189 F1
Dairy La. Worles 188 B3
Dairybrook Gr. Wilm 34 B1
Dairyground Rd. Bram 35 F4
Dairylands Rd. Alsag 193 F2
Daisy Ave. N-le-W 2 B1
Daisy Bank. Nant 204 B3
Daisy Bank Cres. Audlem 229 F3
Daisy Bank La. North 78 B2
Daisy Bank Rd. Lymm 18 B2
Daisy Bank Rd. Penk 14 C2
Daisy Way. H La 37 F4
Daisybank Dr. Congle 156 B2
Daisybank Dr. Sand 175 E3
Dalby Cl. Warr 10 A3
Dalby Ct. L Den 104 C3
Dale Ave. Beb 43 E4
Dale Ave. Bram 35 F4
Dale Ave. El Por 69 E3
Dale Cl. Warr 15 F2
Dale Cl. Wid 22 A4
Dale Cres. Congle 156 C1
Dale Ct. Middle 151 E4
Dale Dr. Chest 118 B4
Dale Dr. El Por 69 F3
Dale Gdns. El Por 70 A2
Dale Gr. Congle 157 D1
Dale Gr. Irlam 11 F3
Dale Head Rd. Prest 86 C2
Dale Hey. El Por 70 F1
Dale House Fold. Poyn 37 D2
Dale La. Apple 26 C4
Dale Rd. Beb 43 E3
Dale Rd. Gold 3 D4
Dale Rd. N Mills 39 E4
Dale St. Chest 119 D1
Dale St. Mfield 112 C4
Dale St. Run 23 D1
Dale The. Gt San 14 C3
Dale The. Nest 66 C3
Dale The. Tiver 168 B3
Dale View. N-le-W 2 C2
Dale's Sq. North 103 F3
Dalecroft. D-o-t-H 72 C1
Dalefords La. Cudd 102 A1
Dalefords La. Mar 125 E4
Dales Green Rd. Kids 195 E3
Dalesford Cl. Gold 4 B4
Dalesford Cres. Mfield 111 F4
Daleside. Chest 118 B4
Dalesway. Hes 40 C4
Dalewood Cres. Elton 72 A2
Dalham La. Warr 16 A3
Dalmahoy Cl. Winsf 126 B1
Dalston Dr. Ch Hul 35 E3
Dalton Bank. Warr 16 B3
Dalton Ct. Run 23 F2
Dalton Ct. Sand 174 C4
Dalton St. Run 23 E1
Dalton Way. Middle 128 B1
Dalwood Cl. Run 50 C4
Dam Head La. Hol Gr 11 D3
Dam La. Croft 8 C4
Dam La. Hol Gr 11 D2
Dam La. Mobb 58 B2
Dam La. Warr 17 E4
Dame Hollow. Chea 34 B4
Damery Ct. Bram 35 F4
Damery Rd. Bram 35 F4
Damhead La. Will 67 F4
Damian Dr. N-le-W 2 A3
Dams La. Allos 106 B3
Damson La. Mobb 58 A2
Damson Wlk. Part 11 E1
Danby Cl. Run 49 E3
Dane Ave. Part 11 F2
Dane Bank Ave. Congle 156 C2
Dane Bank Ave. Crewe 190 A1
Dane Bank Dr. Disley 38 B3
Dane Bank Rd. North 104 A4
Dane Cl. Alsag 193 D2
Dane Cl. Sand 174 C4
Dane Dr. Bidd 179 F1
Dane Dr. Wilm 60 B3
Dane Gdns. Kids 195 E1
Dane Gr. M Traf 119 F4
Dane Hill Cl. Disley 38 B3
Dane Pl. Winsf 127 D1
Dane St. Congle 156 B2
Dane St. Middle 128 B1
Dane St. North 103 F4
Danebank Rd. Lymm 18 B2
Danebank Rd E. Lymm 18 B2
Danefield Ct. Chea 34 B4
Danefield Rd. H Chap 130 B2
Danefield Rd. North 104 A4
Danes Sq. Mfield 112 B3
Danescroft. Wid 12 A2
Daneside
Business Park. Congle 156 C2
Daneswell Rd. Speke 21 D1
Daniel Adamson Ave. Part 11 E2
Daniel Cl. Warr 10 A2
Daniell Way. Chest 142 A4
Dans Rd. Wid 13 F1
Dappleheath Rd. Crewe 190 A1
Darent Rd. Hay 1 A4
Daresbury Cl. H Chap 130 A2
Daresbury Expressway.
Dares 25 D2
Daresbury Expressway.
Run 24 B2
Daresbury La. Dares 25 E1
Darian Ave. Wythe 33 E4
Dark Ash La. Asht 99 D2
Dark Ash La. Man 99 D2
Dark La. Henb 111 D4
Dark La. Henb 111 E2
Dark La. Kings 75 D1
Dark La. Mars 79 E3
Dark La. Old W 227 D1
Dark La. Tatt 183 F4
Dark La. Warren 111 E2
Dark La. Whit 52 B3
Darkie Meadow. Bun 185 F4
Darland La. Ross 162 B1
Darley Ave. Crewe 190 A2
Darley Cl. Wid 12 A2
Darley Rd. Haz Gr 36 C4
Darleydale Dr. Beb 43 F3
Darlington Ave. Crewe 189 F3
Darlington Cres. Saug 94 A1
Darlington St. Middle 128 B1
Darnaway Cl. Warr 10 A3
Darnhall School La. Winsf 149 E3
Dart Cl. Alsag 193 D2
Dart Cl. Bidd 179 E1
Dart Wlk. Winsf 127 D1
Dartnall Cl. H La 38 A3
Darwin Gr. Bram 35 F3
Darwin Rd. Blacon 117 E2
Darwin St. North 103 F4
Daryl Rd. Hes 41 D4
Daten Ave. Warr 9 F3
Dauncey Cl. Chest 95 E1
Davehall Ave. Wilm 60 A4
Daven Rd. Congle 156 C1
Davenham Ave. Warr 16 C4
Davenham Cres. Crewe 190 A2
Davenham Ct. Dave 104 A2
Davenham Rd. Dave 104 C2
Davenham Rd. L Den 104 C2
Davenham Rd. Wilm 34 B2
Davenham Way. Middle 151 E3
Davenport Av. Wilm 59 F2
Davenport Ave. Crewe 206 B4
Davenport Ave. Nant 204 C4
Davenport Ave. Warr 16 C3
Davenport Cl. Sand 175 E4
Davenport La. Bre Gr 154 B1
Davenport La. Mart 132 C3
Davenport La. Mobb 58 B3
Davenport Rd. Hes 40 C4
Davenport Row. Run 49 E4
Davenport St. Congle 156 B1
Davenport St. Crewe 190 B3
Davenport St. Mfield 112 C4
Davey La. A Edge 60 A1
Davey La. A Edge 60 A1
Daveylands. Wilm 60 B4
David Rd. Lymm 18 B2
David St. North 103 F4
David's Ave. Gt San 15 D3
Davidson Ave. Congle 157 D3
Davies Ave. Chea 34 A3
Davies Ave. N-le-W 2 B2
Davies Ave. Warr 16 C2
Davies Cl. Wid 23 D2
Davies Way. Lymm 18 B2
Davis Cl. Alsag 193 F2
Davy Rd. Run 23 F2
Dawlish Ave. Chea 34 C4
Dawlish Cl. Bram 35 F4
Dawlish Cl. Hol Gr 11 D2
Dawn Cl. Nest 67 D3
Dawn Gdns. El Por 70 A2
Dawpool Cl. Chest 118 B3
Dawpool Dr. Beb 43 E4
Dawson Dr. Chest 118 B2
Dawson Rd. Boll 88 A4
Dawson Rd. Chea 34 B4
Dawson Rd. Mfield 111 F4
Dawstone Rd. Hes 41 D4
De Lacy Row. Run 24 A1
Deacon Rd. Wid 13 D1
Deacon Trading Est. N-le-W 2 A1
Deacons Cl. Croft 9 D4
Deadman's La. Hay Gr 205 D1
Deakin's Rd. Winsf 127 D2
Dean Bank. Beest 168 B2
Dean Cl. Boll 88 A4
Dean Cl. Part 11 F2
Dean Cl. Sand 174 C4
Dean Cl. Wid 23 D4
Dean Cl. Wilm 34 B1
Dean Cres. Warr 8 A1
Dean Ct. Boll 88 A4
Dean Dr. Wilm 34 B1
Dean Hollow. Audley 209 E1
Dean La. Haz Gr 36 C4
Dean Meadow. N-le-W 2 B2
Dean Park. Hamp 214 A3
Dean Rd. Gold 3 D4
Dean Rd. Irlam 11 F3
Dean Rd. Wilm 34 C2
Dean Row Rd. Wilm 34 B1
Dean St. Middle 128 B1
Dean St. North 104 B4
Dean St. Wid 23 D4
Dean St. Winsf 126 B1
Dean's La. N-u-L 210 B1
Deanery Cl. Chest 118 B2
Deans Cl. Chest 118 B3
Deans Cl. Tarv 121 D1
Deans La. Barth 208 B2
Deans La. Sand 174 C3
Deans La. Warr 17 F2
Deans Rd. Stan 70 C2
Deans Way. H Kin 161 D4
Deans Way. Tarv 121 D1
Deansgate. El Por 70 A3
Deansway. Wid 22 B4
Deanwater Cl. Warr 9 E2
Deanwater Ct. Chea 34 B4
Deanway. Wilm 34 B1
Dearnford Ave. Beb 43 E3
Dearnford Cl. Beb 43 E3
Debra Cl. El Por 69 E2
Debra Rd. El Por 69 E2
Dee Banks. Chest 141 F4
Dee Cl. Bidd 179 F1
Dee Cl. Kids 210 C4
Dee Cl. Sand 174 C4
Dee Cres. Farn 180 C1
Dee Fords Ave. Chest 119 D1
Dee Hills Pk 118 C1
Dee La. Chest 118 C1
Dee La. Holt 196 B4
Dee Park. Holt 196 B4
Dee Park Cl. Hes 41 D3
Dee Park Rd. Hes 41 D3
Dee Side. Hes 40 B4
Dee View. Farn 180 C1
Dee View Rd. Con Q 91 E1
Dee View Rd. Hes 40 C4
Dee Way. Winsf 127 D1
Deepdale. Wid 12 B2
Deer Park Ct. Run 49 F3
Deerwood Cl. El Por 69 E4
Deerwood Cl. Mfield 86 C1
Deerwood Cres. El Por 69 E4
Deeside. El Por 70 A2
Deeside. Holt 196 C4
Deeside Cl. El Por 70 A1
Deeside Cres. Sea 116 C3
Deeside La. Sea 116 C2
Deirdre Ave. Wid 13 D1
Delafield Cl. Warr 8 C2
Delamere Ave. Beb 43 F2
Delamere Ave. El Por 69 F3
Delamere Ave. Gold 3 F3
Delamere Ave. Wid 12 B1
Delamere Cl. Beb 43 F2
Delamere Cl. Sand 174 C4
Delamere Ct. Alsag 192 C2
Delamere Ct. Beb 43 F2
Delamere Dr. El Por 69 F3
Delamere Dr. Mfield 87 F1
Delamere Gn. El Por 69 F2
Delamere La. Asht 99 D1
Delamere Park Way E.
Cudd 101 E3
Delamere Park Way W.
Cudd 101 E3
Delamere Rd. Congle 155 F2
Delamere Rd. Nant 204 C2
Delamere Rd. Norley 100 A3
Delamere Rd. Wilm 34 C2
Delamere Rise. Winsf 126 A1

Delamere St. Chest 118 B1
Delamere St. Crewe 190 B2
Delamere St. Warr 15 F3
Delamere St. Winsf 126 A1
Delamore's Acre. Will 68 A4
Delavor Cl. Hes 40 C4
Delavor Rd. Hes 40 C4
Delenty Dr. Warr 9 F2
Delery Dr. Warr 16 C4
Delford Rd. Knuts 82 B4
Delfur Rd. Bram 35 F4
Delhi Rd. Irlam 11 F4
Dell Cl. Beb 43 D3
Dell Dr. Warr 9 D1
Dell La. Hes 41 D4
Dell The. Cudd 101 E3
Dell The. G Sutt 119 F3
Dell The. Kels 122 B2
Delmar Rd. Knuts 57 E1
Delph La. Dares 25 D1
Delph La. Warr 8 C3
Delph La. Win 7 F3
Delph La. Win 8 C3
Delphfield. Run 50 B4
Delphfields Rd. Apple 26 B4
Delphside. Audley 209 F1
Delta Ct. Brough 140 A3
Delves Ave. Warr 15 F4
Delves Cl. Shav 206 A2
Delves Wlk. Chest 142 A4
Delvine Dr. Chest 118 B3
Demage Dr. El Por 69 E2
Demage La. Backf 94 C2
Demage La. Chest 118 B4
Demage La S. Chest 118 B4
Den La. Blake 221 E2
Denbigh Cl. Haz Gr 36 B4
Denbigh Cl. Hels 73 D1
Denbigh Cres. Middle 151 E4
Denbigh Ct. El Por 70 B2
Denbigh Dr. Winsf 149 D4
Denbigh Gdns. El Por 70 B2
Denbigh St. Chest 118 A2
Denbury Ave. Warr 16 C1
Dene Ave. N-le-W 1 C2
Dene Dr. Winsf 149 E4
Denehurst Park Way.
Cudd 101 E3
Denesgate. Winsf 149 E4
Deneside Ave. Crewe 190 B3
Deneway. Ch Hul 35 E4
Deneway. H La 37 F4
Denewood Ct. Wilm 60 A3
Denford Cl. Broug 139 E2
Denford Pl. Law-g 193 E3
Denhall Cl. Chest 118 C3
Denhall La. Nest 67 D1
Denham Ave. Gt San 15 D3
Denham Dr. Ch Hul 35 E4
Denise Ave. Penk 14 C3
Denison Rd. Haz Gr 36 C4
Dennett Cl. Warr 17 F3
Dennis Dr. Chest 141 D3
Dennis Rd. Wid 23 E4
Dennison Rd. Ch Hul 35 D4
Densham Ave. Warr 8 A1
Denston Cl. Crewe 190 A1
Denstone Dr. Chest 141 D2
Dentith Dr. Blacon 117 F3
Denton Cl. Winsf 126 B1
Denton Dr. North 79 E1
Denton St. Wid 13 E1
Denver Ave. Crewe 190 A2
Depenbech Cl. Malpas 213 D2
Depmore La. Kings 75 D1
Derby Cl. Irlam 11 E3
Derby Cl. N-le-W 2 A2
Derby Cl. Nest 66 C2
Derby Dr. Warr 16 C4
Derby Pl. Chest 118 C2
Derby Rd. Gold 3 E4
Derby Rd. Kids 210 B4
Derby Rd. Warr 16 B1
Derby Rd. Wid 13 E2
Derby Row. N-le-W 7 E4
Derby St. Congle 156 B2
Derby St. Crewe 190 A3
Derby St. N-le-W 2 A2
Derbyshire Hill Rd. St Hel 1 A1
Derbyshire Rd. Part 11 E1
Derbyshire Rd. Poyn 37 E3
Derek Ave. Warr 8 C1
Derrington Ave. Crewe 190 B2
Derwent Ave. Winsf 127 D1
Derwent Cl. Alsag 193 D2
Derwent Cl. Cul 5 D1
Derwent Cl. H Chap 130 A2
Derwent Cl. Mfield 112 A3
Derwent Cl. Part 11 F2
Derwent Cl. Willas 205 E3
Derwent Cres. Kids 195 E1
Derwent Dr. Bidd 179 F1
Derwent Dr. Ch Hul 35 E3
Derwent Dr. Congle 156 C1
Derwent Dr. El Por 44 A1
Derwent Dr. Wilm 34 B3
Derwent Rd. Chest 118 C3
Derwent Rd. H La 37 F4
Derwent Rd. Warr 16 A1
Derwent Rd. Wid 12 B1
Derwent Way. Nest 66 C4
Desoto Rd. Wid 22 C3
Desoto Rd E. Wid 22 C3
Desoto Rd W. Wid 22 C3
Deva Ave. Brough 140 B3
Deva Bsns Pk. G Cit 116 A4
Deva Cl. Poyn 36 A2
Deva La. Chest 118 B3
Deva Rd. Crewe 189 E2
Deva Terr. Chest 118 C1
Devon Cl. Mfield 86 C1
Devon Gr. Bidd 179 E1
Devon Pl. Congle 156 C2
Devon Pl. Wid 13 D2
Devon Rd. Chest 118 C3
Devon Rd. Irlam 11 E3
Devon Rd. Part 11 F1
Devonshire Dr. A Edge 60 A1
Devonshire Gdns. N-le-W 2 B1
Devonshire Pl. Chest 141 F4
Devonshire Pl. Run 23 D1
Devonshire Rd. Broug 139 E2
Devonshire Rd. Haz Gr 36 C4
Devonshire Rd. Warr 16 C4
Dewar Ct. Run 23 F2
Dewes St. Crewe 190 A3
Dewhurst Rd. Warr 9 E1
Dial La. Bidd 158 A1
Dial Rd. Altr 32 B4
Dial St. Warr 16 B3
Dibbins Green. Beb 43 D4
Dibbinsdale Rd. Beb 43 D4
Dickens Cl. Ch Hul 35 D3
Dickens La. Poyn 36 C1
Dickenson St. Warr 16 B4
Dickinson Cl. Hay 1 A3
Dickson Cl. Wid 23 D4
Dickson St. Wid 23 D4
Dicksons Dr. Chest 118 B2
Dierden St. Winsf 127 D1
Dierdens Terr. Middle 128 B1
Dig La. Acton 203 F2
Dig La. Burl 203 F2
Dig La. Frod 74 A4
Dig La. Hay Gr 206 A2
Diglake St. Audley 209 F2
Diglee Rd. W Br 39 E2
Dinas Cl. Blacon 117 E2
Dingle Av. L End 59 E2
Dingle Ave. N-le-W 1 C1
Dingle Bank. Chest 141 E4
Dingle Bank Cl. Lymm 18 C2
Dingle Cl. Mfield 87 D2
Dingle La. Apple 26 C3
Dingle La. Kels 122 C3
Dingle La. Sand 175 E3
Dingle La. Winsf 126 B1
Dingle The. Hasl 191 E3
Dingle The. Lymm 18 C2
Dingle The. North 78 A2
Dingle Way. Cudd 101 F3
Dingle Wlk. Winsf 126 B1
Dinglebrook Gr. Wilm 34 C1
Dingleway. Apple 26 B4
Dinmor Rd. Wythe 33 E4
Dirty La. Rosth 30 C3
Ditchfield La. H Legh 29 E2
Ditchfield Pl. Wid 22 A4
Ditchfield Rd. Penk 14 C2
Ditchfield Rd. Wid 22 A4
Ditton Rd. Wid 22 B3
Ditton Rd. Wid 23 D3
Dixon Ave. N-le-W 2 B3
Dixon Cl. Hay 2 A4
Dixon Dr. Chelf 84 A2
Dixon Rd. Congle 157 D3
Dixon St. Irlam 11 F4
Dixon St. Warr 16 A3
Dobb Hedge Cl. Altr 32 B3
Dobell's Rd. North 103 F3
Dobers La. Frod 74 B2
Dobers La. Kings 74 B2
Dobson's Sq. Malpas 213 D2
Dock Rd. North 103 F4
Dock St. El Por 70 B4
Dock St. Wid 23 D3
Dock Yard Rd. Stan 70 C3
Docks Rd. Wid 22 C3
Dodd's Green La. New 228 A2
Dodd's La. Apple 27 D3
Dodd's La. Brad G 224 C4
Doddington Cl. Sand 175 E4
Doddington Rd. Crewe 190 A2
Dodds La. Astb 178 B3
Doddswood Dr. Congle 156 C2
Dodgsley Dr. Kings 75 E1
Dodleston La. Dodle 162 B2
Dodleston La. Pulf 162 B2
Doe's Meadow Rd. Beb 43 D4
Doeford Cl. Cul 4 C3
Dog La. Bre Gr 153 F4
Dog La. Chow 182 A2
Dog La. Codd 182 B2
Dog La. Nant 204 C3
Dog La. Threap 223 E4
Dogmore La. Eaton 147 E2
Dolly La. Chin 39 F2
Dolphin Cres. El Por 69 F1
Dolphin Ct. Chest 141 D4
Dombey Rd. Poyn 36 B1
Domestic App. Wythe 33 E4
Domville Cl. Lymm 18 C2
Don Wlk. El Por 70 A4
Donagh Cl. Mfield 86 C1
Donkey La. Wilm 60 A3
Donne Pl. Blacon 117 F3
Donnington Way. Chest 140 C4
Dooley's Grig. With 92 C1
Dooley's La. Wilm 33 E1
Dorac Ave. Chea 34 B4
Dorchester Cl. Wilm 60 B4
Dorchester Park. Run 24 C2
Dorchester Rd. Chest 140 C3
Dorchester Rd. Gt San 15 E3
Dorchester Way. Burton 6 C3
Dorchester Way. Mfield 87 E2
Doreen Ave. Congle 179 D4
Doreold Dr. Nant 204 B3
Dorfold St. Crewe 190 B2
Dorfold Way. Chest 118 A4
Doric Ave. Frod 74 B4
Dormer Cl. Waver 143 D3
Dorney Cl. Apple 26 C3
Dornoch Ct. H Chap 130 A1
Dorothea St. Warr 16 B4
Dorric Way. Crewe 190 B4
Dorrington Cl. Run 50 B4
Dorrit Cl. Poyn 36 C1
Dorset Cl. Congle 156 C2
Dorset Ct. Run 50 A3
Dorset Dr. Bidd 179 E1
Dorset Pl. Chest 119 D3
Dorset Pl. Kids 195 D1
Dorset Rd. Chest 118 B4
Dorset Rd. Irlam 11 E3
Dorset Way. Warr 17 D4
Dorset Wlk. Mfield 86 C1
Douglas Ave. Bo Hea 6 A3
Douglas Cl. Hart 103 E3
Douglas Cl. Wid 13 F2
Douglas La. Wet 171 D3
Douglas Pl. Brough 140 C3
Doune Ct. El Por 70 B2
Dounrey Cl. Warr 9 D1
Dove Cl. El Por 70 A4
Dove Cl. Hels 73 E3
Dove Cl. Sand 175 D4
Dove Cl. Warr 9 F2
Dove Gr. Bidd 179 E1
Dove Pl. Winsf 127 D1
Dovecote Cl. Wist 206 A4
Dovedale Cl. Beb 43 F3
Dovedale Cl. Congle 157 D2
Dovedale Cl. H La 37 F4
Dover Cl. Run 50 C3
Dover Ct. El Por 70 B1
Dover Dr. El Por 70 B1
Dover Dr. Winsf 149 D4
Dover Rd. Chest 141 D3
Dover Rd. Mfield 87 F1
Dover Rd. Warr 17 D2
Dovesmead Rd. Hes 41 E4
Doward St. Wid 13 E1
Downes Cl. Mfield 87 D1
Downesway. A Edge 59 F1
Downham Ave. Cul 4 C1
Downham Dr. Hes 41 D4
Downham Pl. Blacon 117 F2
Downham Rd S. Hes 41 D4
Downing Cl. S La E 112 C2
Downs End. Knuts 57 E1
Downs Rd. Run 23 D1
Downs The. Cudd 101 E3
Downsfield Rd. Chest 141 D3
Downside. Wid 12 A2
Downswood Ct. Chest 118 B2
Downswood Dr. Chest 118 B2
Downway La. St Hel 1 A1
Dragon Yd. Wid 13 D2
Dragon's La. Middle 152 A1
Drake Ave. Irlam 11 F3
Drake Cl. Warr 7 E1
Drake La. Acton 203 F2
Drake La. Burl 203 F2
Drake Rd. Nest 41 F1
Drakelow La. L Den 128 C4
Drakelow La. Middle 128 C4
Drakes Way. Malpas 213 D3
Draxford Ct. Wilm 60 A3
Draycott Dr. N-u-L 210 B1
Drayton Ave. Chea 34 A4
Drayton Cl. Run 22 C1
Drayton Cres. Crewe 190 C3
Drenfell Rd. Sch Gr 194 C4
Drill Field Rd. North 103 F4
Drive A. G Cit 93 D1
Drive B. G Cit 93 D1
Drive C. G Cit 93 D1
Drive The. Altr 32 B4
Drive The. H Chap 130 B1
Drive The. Lymm 19 E1
Drome Rd. G Cit 93 D1
Drovers Way. Sand 175 D3
Drumber La. Sch Gr 195 D4
Drumber The. Winsf 126 B1
Drumble Field. Chelf 84 A2
Drummond Ave. El Por 69 E2
Drummond Way. Mfield 86 C1
Druridge Dr. Penk 14 C2
Drury Cl. Crewe 190 C3
Drury La. Knuts 57 D1
Drury La. Warm 173 E2
Dryden Cl. Wist 190 A1
Dryden Pl. Warr 8 B1
Dryhurst Dr. Disley 38 B3
Dryhurst La. Disley 38 B3
Dublin Croft. El Por 69 F1
Duck La. Asht 121 F4
Duckworth Gr. Warr 9 D1
Duddon Cl. Dudd 145 D3
Duddon Hook La. Dudd 144 C3
Duddon Rd. Dudd 145 D3
Dudleston Rd. El Por 69 D3
Dudley Ave. Run 23 E1
Dudley Cres. Beb 44 A2
Dudley Rd. El Por 70 A3
Dudley Rd. Irlam 11 E2
Dudley St. Warr 16 A4
Dudley Wlk. Mfield 111 F4
Dudlow Green Rd. Apple 26 C3
Dufton Wlk. Wythe 33 F4
Duke Ave. Ch Hul 34 C3
Duke Ave. Cul 5 E4
Duke St. A Edge 60 A1
Duke St. Chest 141 E4
Duke St. Congle 156 B1
Duke St. Crewe 190 B2
Duke St. Mfield 112 B4
Duke St. N-le-W 2 A2
Duke's Cres. Sand 175 D4
Dukesway. Chest 118 C4
Dulas Ct. Chest 118 B4
Dulverton Ave. Chest 119 E1
Dumbah La. Boll 87 E3
Dumbers. Bosl 136 A1
Dunbar Cl. Con Q 91 E1
Dunbar Cl. El Por 69 E3
Dunbar Cl. H Chap 130 B1
Duncan Ave. N-le-W 2 B3
Duncan Ave. Run 23 E1
Duncan St. Warr 16 B4
Duncansby Cres. Gt San 14 C3
Duncansby Dr. Beb 43 E2
Dundalk Rd. Wid 22 C4
Dundee Cl. Warr 8 C2
Dundee Ct. El Por 70 C2
Dundonald Ave. Warr 16 B1
Dundonald Rd. Ch Hul 35 D4
Dundrennan Cl. Poyn 36 B3
Dunham Cl. Beb 43 F2
Dunham Cres. Wist 206 A4
Dunham Ct. D-o-t-H 97 F3
Dunham Rd. Altr 20 C1
Dunham Rd. North 104 A2
Dunham Rd. Part 19 F4
Dunham Rd. Wilm 34 B3
Dunham Way. Chest 118 C3
Dunkirk Ave. Winsf 149 E4
Dunkirk Dr. El Por 70 A1
Dunkirk La. Capen 94 B4
Dunkirk La. El Por 70 A1
Dunley Cl. Warr 10 A3
Dunlin Ave. N-le-W 2 B2
Dunlin Cl. Poyn 36 A2
Dunlin Cl. Run 49 F3
Dunlin Cl. Warr 8 C2
Dunlop St. Warr 16 A2
Dunmore Cl. Middle 151 E4
Dunmore Cres. El Por 69 D3
Dunmore Rd. El Por 69 D3
Dunmow Rd. Warr 17 E2
Dunn's La. Asht 121 F4
Dunnock Cl. Warr 8 C2
Dunnock Gr. Warr 9 F2
Dunnocksfold Rd. Alsag 193 D2
Dunnockswood. Alsag 193 D2
Dunoon Cl. H Chap 130 A1
Dunraven Rd. Nest 67 D4
Dunscar Cl. Warr 9 E3
Dunsford. Wid 12 B2
Dunstan La. Nest 67 F2
Dunster Cl. North 104 A2
Dunster Gr. Hes 41 D4
Dunster Rd. Mfield 87 F1
Dunwood Dr. Law-g 193 E3
Durban Ave. Christ 142 B4
Durber Cl. Audley 209 E1
Durham Cl. Mfield 86 C1
Durham Cl. Warr 17 F4
Durham Ct. El Por 70 C2
Durham Dr. Winsf 149 E3
Durham Gr. Irlam 11 E3
Durham Rd. Blacon 117 F3
Durham Rd. Wid 13 D2
Durlston Cl. Wid 12 B1
Dutton Cl. Nant 204 C2
Dutton Green. Stan 70 C2
Dutton La. Crow 101 E3
Duxford Ct. Warr 8 C1
Dyar Terr. North 78 B1
Dyberth Rd. Blacon 117 E2
Dye House La. N Mills 39 E4
Dyer St. Gold 2 C4
Dyers Cl. Lymm 19 D2
Dyers La. Lymm 19 D2
Dykin Cl. Wid 13 F2
Dykin Rd. Wid 13 F2

Eadie Gr. Crewe 190 A4
Eaglaisway. Mfield 86 C1
Eagland Pl. Congle 156 C2
Eagle Brow. Lymm 18 B2
Eagle La. El Por 69 E4
Eagles Way. Run 49 F3
Eaglesfield. Hart 103 E2
Ealing Rd. Gt San 15 D3
Eanlewood La. Run 50 B4
Eardley Cres. Congle 156 C2
Eardswick Cl. Chest 118 B2
Eardswick La. Ch Min 172 B3
Eardswick Rd. Middle 151 E3
Earl Rd. Ch Hul 34 C3
Earl Rd. Wilm 34 C3
Earl St. Warr 16 A4
Earle Cl. N-le-W 1 C2
Earle Cres. Nest 41 E1
Earle Dr. Nest 41 E1
Earle Rd. Wid 23 E4
Earle St. Crewe 190 B2
Earle St. N-le-W 2 A2
Earle's La. Kels 122 B3
Earles La. H Winch 79 F3
Earles La. Mars 79 F3
Earls Gdns. El Por 70 A3
Earls Oak. Chest 118 B4
Earls Rd. Shav 206 A2
Earlston Ct. Chest 118 C1
Earlsway. Chest 141 D4
Earlsway. Mfield 111 F4
Earndale. Wid 13 D3
Easby Cl. Ch Hul 35 D3
Easby Cl. Poyn 36 B2
Easenhall Cl. Wid 13 E3
East Ave. Boll 87 F4
East Ave. Chea 34 B4
East Ave. Gt San 15 D2
East Ave. North 104 B3
East Ave. Warr 16 B1
East Ave. Warr 16 B4
East Ave. Weston 207 E3
East Ct. Alsag 193 F2
East Dam Wood Rd. Speke 21 D1
East Dudley St. Winsf 126 C1
East Green. Sea 116 A3
East La. Cudd 102 A2
East La. Run 49 F4
East Lancashire Rd. Gold 3 E3
East Lancashire Rd. Hay 1 B4
East Mains. Speke 21 D2
East Millwood Rd. Speke 21 D2
East Park Rd. Mfield 112 A3
East Rd. Halew 21 D3
East Rd. Middle 128 A1
East Rd. Wythe 33 E4
East St. Wid 13 E1
East View. Warr 17 E1
Eastbury Cl. Wid 13 E3
Eastcott Cl. Congle 155 F2
Eastdale Rd. Warr 17 D4
Eastern Pathway. Chest 141 F4
Eastern Rd. Shav 205 F3
Eastern Rd. Willas 205 F3
Eastfields Gr. Saug 117 D4
Eastford Rd. Warr 16 A1
Eastgate Rd. H Chap 130 B2
Eastgate Row N. Chest 118 B1
Eastgate St. Chest 118 B1
Eastham Rake. Beb 43 F2
Eastham Rake. Will 43 F2
Eastham Village Rd. Beb 44 A2
Eastham Way. Wilm 34 B3
Eastward Ave. Wilm 59 F3
Eastway. El Por 69 E4
Eastway. Wid 12 B1
Eastwood. Run 24 B1
Eastwood Ave. N-le-W 2 C2
Eastwood Rd. Burton 6 C4
Eaton Ave. Chest 141 E4
Eaton Bank. Congle 156 C2
Eaton Cl. Broug 139 E2
Eaton Cl. Poyn 37 D2
Eaton Cl. Sand 175 E4
Eaton Cres. Dave 103 F1
Eaton Dr. A Edge 59 F1
Eaton Dr. Middle 151 D4
Eaton Gr. Brough 140 C3
Eaton La. Dave 103 F1
Eaton La. Eaton 146 C1
Eaton La. Goost 107 E1
Eaton La. Mfield 112 B3
Eaton La. Tarp 168 C4
Eaton Mews. Chest 141 E4
Eaton Rd. Alsag 193 E2
Eaton Rd. Chest 141 F2
Eaton Rd. Eccles 141 F2
Eaton Rd. Tarp 146 B1
Eaton Rd. Wet 170 B4
Eaton St. Crewe 190 B2
Eaton St. Run 23 D1
Eaton View. Moult 126 C4

Eaves Brow Rd. Croft 9 D4
Eaves Knoll Rd. N Mills 39 D4
Ebnal La. Malpas 213 F2
Eccles Cl. W Br 65 E4
Eccles Rd. W Br 65 F3
Eccleston Ave. Beb 43 E4
Eccleston Ave. Chest 141 E3
Eccleston Ave. El Por 69 F3
Eccleston Cl. Warr 9 E3
Eccleston Dr. Run 23 E1
Eccleston Rd. H Kin 161 D4
Eccleston Way. Wilm 34 B2
Ecton Ave. Mfield 113 D4
Ecton Cl. Winsf 127 D2
Edale Cl. Beb 43 F3
Edale Cl. Chea 34 B4
Edale Dr. Kels 122 B3
Edbury Pl. Chest 141 E4
Eddisbury Cl. Mfield 112 C4
Eddisbury Dr. N-u-L 210 B1
Eddisbury Hill. Dela 123 E4
Eddisbury Rd. El Por 69 F1
Eddisbury Sq. Frod 74 A4
Eddisbury Terr. Mfield 112 C4
Edelsten St. Warr 15 F3
Edelston Hall La. Burl 203 F1
Eden Ave. Cul 5 E2
Eden Ave. H La 37 F4
Eden Ave. Winsf 126 C1
Eden Cl. Bidd 179 F1
Eden Cl. El Por 69 E3
Eden Cl. Kids 195 D1
Eden Cl. Wilm 59 F3
Eden Dr. Mfield 87 F1
Edendale. Wid 12 A1
Edenfield Cl. Mobb 58 A2
Edenfield Rd. Mobb 58 A2
Edenhall Cl. H Chap 130 A2
Edgar Ct. Chest 141 E4
Edgar Pl. Chest 141 E4
Edgars Dr. Warr 9 D1
Edge Gr. Chest 118 C1
Edge La. Ed Gr 199 E1
Edge View La. L End 59 D1
Edgecroft. Tatt 166 A1
Edgehill Chase. Wilm 60 C4
Edgerley La. Aldf 181 E3
Edgerley La. Farn 181 E3
Edgerton Rd. Gold 3 F4
Edgerton St. Run 22 C2
Edgeview Rd. Congle 179 D4
Edgeway. Henb 111 E4
Edgeway. Wilm 60 A3
Edgewell La. Eaton 147 D2
Edgewood Dr. Beb 43 E3
Edgewood Dr. Wist 206 A4
Edgworth St. Warr 16 A3
Edinburgh Ct. El Por 70 B2
Edinburgh Dr. Mfield 87 D1
Edinburgh Pl. Congle 156 C1
Edinburgh Rd. Congle 156 C1
Edinburgh Rd. Wid 22 A4
Edinburgh Rd. Wist 205 F4
Edinburgh Way. Chest 141 F4
Edison Rd. Run 23 E2
Edith St. Run 22 C2
Edleston Rd. Crewe 190 B2
Edlestone Gr. Wilm 34 C1
Edna St. Chest 118 C2
Edward Gdns. Warr 17 F3
Edward Rd. Gt San 14 B3
Edward St. Audley 209 F2
Edward St. Crewe 190 B1
Edward St. El Por 70 B4
Edward St. Hay 1 A3
Edward St. Mfield 112 A4
Edward St. North 104 B4
Edward St. Wid 13 E1
Edwards Ave. Shav 206 B3
Edwards Cl. Shav 206 B3
Edwards Rd. Chest 141 D3
Edwards Way. Alsag 193 F2
Edwards Way. Wid 22 B4
Edwin St. Wid 13 E1
Egdon Cl. Wid 13 F1
Egerton. H Legh 29 E3
Egerton Ave. Hart 103 D2
Egerton Ave. Part 19 E4
Egerton Ave. Warr 16 C4
Egerton Ct. Kels 122 A3
Egerton Dr. Chest 118 B3
Egerton Moss. Ashl 31 F3
Egerton Rd. Blacon 117 E3
Egerton Rd. Lymm 18 B1
Egerton Rd. Wilm 34 A1
Egerton Sq. Knuts 57 D1
Egerton St. Chest 118 C1
Egerton St. Congle 156 B1
Egerton St. El Por 70 B3
Egerton St. Run 23 D2
Egerton St. Warr 16 B1
Egerton St. Warr 16 B3
Egerton Wlk. Dodle 162 A4
Eggbridge La. Waver 143 D3
Egypt St. Warr 16 A3
Egypt St. Wid 22 C4
Elaine Cl. El Por 69 E2
Elaine Cl. El Por 69 E2
Elaine Cl. Wid 13 E1
Elaine St. Warr 16 B4
Elcombe Ave. Gold 3 F4
Elder Dr. Chest 140 C3
Elderberry Way. Wilm 60 C4
Elderberry Wlk. Part 11 E1
Eldon Rd. Mfield 111 F4
Eldon St. Warr 16 B3
Eldon Terr. Nest 66 C4
Eleanor St. El Por 70 B3
Eleanor St. Wid 23 D4
Electra Way. Crewe 191 D1
Electricity St. Crewe 190 B2
Elgar Ave. Beb 43 F3
Elgar Cl. El Por 69 F2
Elgin Ave. H Chap 130 A1
Elgin Ave. Mfield 87 D1
Elgin Ave. Warr 16 A1
Elgin Cl. Chest 119 D2
Eliot Cl. Crewe 191 D2
Elizabeth Ave. Disley 38 B3
Elizabeth Cl. Kels 122 B3
Elizabeth Cres. Chest 141 F4
Elizabeth Ct. Kids 210 B3
Elizabeth Ct. Wid 23 D4
Elizabeth Dr. Warr 17 D4
Elizabeth Rd. Hay 1 C4
Elizabeth Rd. Part 11 F2
Elizabeth St. Congle 156 B1
Elizabeth St. Crewe 190 A3
Elizabeth St. Mfield 112 B4
Elizabethan Way. North 104 C3
Elk View. Willi 222 C3
Elkan Cl. Wid 13 F1
Elkan Rd. Wid 13 F1
Ella Gr. Knuts 57 D1
Elland Dr. El Por 69 E3
Ellen Brook Rd. Wythe 33 E4
Ellen St. Warr 15 F4
Ellerby Cl. Run 50 C4
Ellerton Ave. El Por 69 E3
Ellerton Cl. Wid 12 B2
Ellesmere Ave. Broug 139 E2
Ellesmere Ave. Chest 118 B3
Ellesmere Cl. Sand 174 C4
Ellesmere Pl. Crewe 190 A3
Ellesmere Rd. Cul 4 C2
Ellesmere Rd. North 104 A2
Ellesmere Rd. Warr 16 A1
Ellesmere St. Run 23 D1
Ellesmere St. Warr 16 B3
Ellesworth Cl. Gt San 15 E4
Elliot St. Wid 23 D4
Ellis La. Frod 49 E1
Ellis St. Crewe 190 A3
Ellis St. Wid 23 D4
Ellison St. Warr 16 B1
Ellison St. Warr 16 B3
Elloway Rd. Speke 21 D2
Ellwood Green. Ho Co 206 C2
Elm Ave. N-le-W 2 B1
Elm Ave. Wid 13 D1
Elm Beds Rd. Poyn 37 E1
Elm Cl. Part 11 F1
Elm Cl. Poyn 36 C2
Elm Cl. Tarp 146 B1
Elm Cl. Wist 189 F1
Elm Cres. A Edge 60 A2
Elm Dr. Crewe 190 C3
Elm Dr. H Chap 130 B2
Elm Dr. Mfield 87 F1
Elm Gr. A Edge 60 A1
Elm Gr. Alsag 193 F2
Elm Gr. Brough 140 C3
Elm Gr. El Por 70 A1
Elm Gr. Warr 16 C4
Elm Gr. Wilm 34 B2
Elm Gr. Winsf 127 D1
Elm Green. Will 67 F4
Elm Rd. Congle 156 A2
Elm Rd. H La 37 F4
Elm Rd. Hay 1 C4
Elm Rd. Hol Gr 11 D1
Elm Rd. Middle 151 E4
Elm Rd. Penk 14 C2
Elm Rd. Run 49 E4
Elm Rd. Warr 8 A2
Elm Rd. Weave 102 B4
Elm Rd. Will 67 F4
Elm Ridge Dr. Altr 32 B4
Elm Rise. Frod 74 B4
Elm Rise. Prest 86 C3
Elm Sq. Chest 140 C3
Elm St. El Por 70 B4
Elm St. North 79 D1
Elm Tree Ave. Lymm 18 B1
Elm Tree Ave. Warr 16 C4
Elm Tree Ct. Eaton 147 D2
Elm Tree Dr. Audley 209 F1
Elm Tree La. Sand 174 B4
Elm Tree Rd. Gold 3 F4
Elm Tree Rd. Lymm 18 B1
Elmfield Cl. A Edge 60 A1
Elmfield Rd. A Edge 60 A2
Elmir. Blacon 117 F2
Elmore Cl. H Chap 130 A2
Elmore Cl. Run 24 B1
Elms The. Run 22 C1
Elmstead Cres. Crewe 189 F4
Elmstead Rd. Chelf 84 A2
Elmsway. Altr 32 A4
Elmsway. Boll 88 A4
Elmsway. Ch Hul 35 E4
Elmsway. H La 37 F3
Elmwood Ave. Chest 118 C2
Elmwood Ave. Warr 16 C4
Elmwood Cl. Law-g 194 A2
Elmwood Gr. Winsf 149 F4
Elmwood Rd. North 78 A2
Elnor Ave. W Br 65 F3
Elnor La. W Br 65 F2
Elsby Rd. Alsag 193 F1
Elston Ave. N-le-W 2 B3
Elstree Ave. Chest 119 D2
Elswick Ave. Bram 35 F4
Eltham Cl. Wid 13 F2
Eltham Wlk. Wid 13 F2
Elton Cl. Beb 43 F2
Elton Cl. Gold 3 F4
Elton Cl. Warr 9 E2
Elton Crossings Rd. Sand 174 B3
Elton Dr. Haz Gr 36 B4
Elton La. Elton 72 C2
Elton La. Hasl 174 B1
Elton Lordship La. Frod 73 D4
Elton Rd. Sand 174 B3
Elvington Cl. Run 49 F2
Elworth Ave. Wid 13 D3
Elworth Rd. Sand 174 C3
Elworth St. Sand 175 D4
Elworth Way. Wilm 34 B2
Elwyn Dr. Halew 21 D4
Ely Cl. El Por 94 C4
Ely Ct. Mfield 112 C4
Embassy Cl. Blacon 117 E2
Emberton Pl. Audlem 230 A3
Embleton Ct. Run 49 E3
Embridge Cswy. Bux 90 A3
Emerald Rd. Wythe 33 F4
Emily St. Wid 23 D4
Emmerdale Ave. Warr 8 A2
Emmett St. North 78 A2
Empress Dr. Crewe 190 A2
Emral Ct. Worth 211 D1
Emslie Ct. Nest 66 B4
Enderby Rd. Chest 118 B1
Endon Av. Boll 88 A4
Endsleigh Cl. Chest 118 B4
Endsleigh Gdns. Chest 118 B4
Enfield Cl. Shav 206 A2
Enfield Park Rd. Warr 9 D2
Enfield Rd. El Por 70 A3
Engelsea Brook La.
Weston 208 A2
Englefield Ave. Brough 140 B3
Englefield Cl. Crewe 190 A4
Englesea Gr. Crewe 190 A1
Ennerdale. Chest 118 C3
Ennerdale. Mfield 111 F3
Ennerdale Ave. Beb 43 F2
Ennerdale Cl. Winsf 126 B2
Ennerdale Dr. Congle 156 A1
Ennerdale Dr. Frod 74 B4
Ennerdale Rd. Crewe 189 E2
Ennerdale Rd. Part 11 F2
Ennis Cl. Hale 21 E1
Enticott Rd. Irlam 11 E3
Enville St. Warr 16 B2
Epping Dr. Warr 17 E4
Epsom Ave. Wilm 34 C2
Epsom Gdns. Apple 26 C4
Epworth Cl. Burton 6 C4
Eric Ave. Warr 16 C4
Eric St. Wid 13 E1
Ermine Rd. Chest 118 C2
Ernest St. Crewe 190 B1
Errington Ave. El Por 70 B3
Errwood Cl. Hale 21 F1
Erskine Rd. Part 11 F1
Erwood St. Warr 16 A3
Esk Dale Cl. Winsf 126 B1
Esk Rd. Winsf 127 D1
Eskdale. El Por 70 A2
Eskdale Ave. Ch Hul 35 E3
Eskdale Ave. Warr 8 B2
Eskdale Cl. Beb 43 F3
Eskdale Cl. Run 49 E3
Essex Cl. Congle 156 C3
Essex Dr. Bidd 179 E1
Essex Dr. Kids 194 C1
Essex Gdns. Irlam 11 E2
Essex Rd. Chest 119 D3
Essex Wlk. Mfield 86 C1
Esther St. Wid 13 D1
Esthers La. Weave 102 B4
Ethelda Dr. Chest 119 D3
Etherow Cl. Sand 174 C4
Eton Dr. Thor H 41 F3
Eton Rd. El Por 70 B2
Etterick Park. Chest 119 D1
Ettiley Ave. Sand 174 B3
Euclid Ave. Warr 17 D1
Europa Bvd. Warr 7 E2
Europa Way. El Por 70 B3
Eustace St. Warr 16 A3
Eva St. Sand 174 B4
Evans Cl. Hay 1 C4
Evans Pl. Warr 16 B2
Evans St. Crewe 190 B3
Evansleigh Dr. Hawa 116 A2
Evelyn St. Warr 15 E2
Everest Cl. El Por 69 F2
Everest Rd. Kids 195 E2
Everglade Cl. Mfield 112 A3
Everite Rd. Wid 22 A4
Eversley. Wid 12 A1
Eversley Cl. Apple 26 C3
Eversley Cl. Frod 74 B3
Eversley Ct. Chest 118 B2
Eversley Pk. Chest 118 B2
Evesham Cl. Mfield 87 F2
Evesham Cl. Warr 26 B4
Ewart St. Brough 140 A4
Ewloe Ct. El Por 70 B1
Ewrin La. Rain 89 E3
Excalibur Way. Irlam 11 F4
Exchange Cl. Mfield 112 B4
Exchange St. Mfield 112 B4
Exeter Cl. Chea 34 C4
Exeter Pl. Blacon 117 F3
Exeter Rd. El Por 70 B3
Exeter Wlk. Bram 35 F4
Exit Rd W. Wythe 33 D4
Exmouth Cres. Run 50 C3
Exmouth Way. Burton 6 C3
Exton Pk. Chest 118 B2
Eyam Rd. Haz Gr 36 C4
Eyebrook Rd. Altr 20 C1

Factory La. Disley 38 C4
Factory La. Wid 13 D2
Factory Rd. Hawa 116 A2
Fair Haven's Ct. Wid 23 D4
Fair Mead. Knuts 82 A4
Fair Oak Rd. N-u-L 210 B1
Fair View Cl. North 77 F2
Fairacre Dr. Middle 151 F3
Fairacres Rd. H La 37 F4
Fairbourne Av. Wilm 59 F2
Fairbourne Ave. A Edge 60 A2
Fairbourne Cl. Warr 7 F2
Fairbourne Cl. Wilm 59 F2
Fairbourne Dr. Wilm 59 F2
Fairbrother Cres. Warr 8 B1
Fairburn Cl. Wid 13 F2
Fairclough Ave. Warr 16 B2
Fairclough Cres. Hay 1 A3
Fairclough St. Burton 6 C3
Fairclough St. N-le-W 2 A2
Fairfax Dr. Run 23 E1
Fairfax Dr. Wilm 59 F2
Fairfield Ave. El Por 70 A1
Fairfield Ave. Sand 175 D3
Fairfield Gdns. Warr 16 C1
Fairfield Rd. Broug 139 D2
Fairfield Rd. Chest 119 D2
Fairfield Rd. Irlam 11 E3
Fairfield Rd. Lymm 18 C2
Fairfield Rd. North 104 A2
Fairfield Rd. Warr 16 C1
Fairfield Rd. Wid 13 D1
Fairfield St. Warr 16 B3
Fairfields. Audley 209 F1
Fairford Rd. Chest 140 C3
Fairford Way. Wilm 60 B4
Fairhaven Cl. Bram 35 F4
Fairhaven Cl. Gt San 15 D2
Fairhaven Dr. Beb 43 E3
Fairhaven Rd. Wid 13 E1
Fairhills Rd. Irlam 11 F4
Fairholm Rd. Dave 127 D4
Fairholme Ave. Nest 41 E1
Fairholme Cl. Saug 94 A1
Fairlawn Cl. Beb 43 D3
Fairmeadow. Pulf 162 B1
Fairoak Ct. Run 50 C2
Fairoak La. Run 50 C2
Fairview. Holt 196 C4
Fairview Ave. Alsag 193 E2
Fairview Ave. Weston 207 D3
Fairview Rd. El Por 70 A1
Fairview Rd. Mfield 112 A3
Fairway. Ch Hul 35 E3
Fairway. Hawa 116 A1
Fairway Gdns. Alsag 193 F1
Fairway The. Alsag 193 E2
Fairways. Apple 26 B3
Fairways. Frod 74 B4
Fairways Dr. El Por 69 E4
Fairywell Cl. Wilm 34 B1
Falcon Cl. Middle 151 E3
Falcon Cl. N Mills 39 E4
Falcon Cl. Winsf 149 E3
Falcon Dr. Crewe 190 A4
Falcon Rd. El Por 69 F2
Falcondale Rd. Win 8 A3
Falconers Green. Warr 7 D1
Falcons Way. Run 49 F3
Fallibroome Cl. Mfield 111 F4
Fallibroome Rd. Mfield 111 F4
Fallowfield. Run 23 E1
Fallowfield Cl. Winsf 125 F1
Fallowfield Ct. Crewe 190 A3
Fallowfield Gr. Warr 9 D1
Falmouth Cl. Mfield 111 F4
Falmouth Dr. Penk 14 C2
Falmouth Pl. Run 50 C3
Falmouth Rd. Congle 178 C4
Falmouth Rd. Crewe 190 A3
Falstone Cl. Warr 10 A3
Falstone Dr. Run 50 C4
Fanner's La. H Legh 28 B3
Fanny's Croft. Alsag 193 E1
Fanshawe La. Henb 110 C3
Fanshawe Wlk. Crewe 206 B4
Faraday Rd. El Por 70 A2
Faraday Rd. Run 23 E2
Faraday St. Warr 9 F2
Farams Rd. Sch Gr 193 F4
Farbailey Cl. Chest 141 D3
Farfields Cl. Warren 111 F1
Faringdon Rd. Win 8 A3
Farley Cl. Middle 151 D4
Farm Cl. Weave 77 E1
Farm Dr. Con Q 91 E1
Farm La. Apple 26 C4
Farm La. Disley 38 A3
Farm La. With 108 C1
Farm Rd. North 104 C4
Farm Rd. Oak 124 A4
Farm Rd. Weave 77 E1
Farmdale Dr. Elton 72 A2
Farmer's La. Burton 7 D3
Farmers Heath. El Por 69 E1
Farmfield Dr. Mfield 87 E2
Farmfields Rise. Woore 232 B1
Farmleigh Dr. Crewe 189 F4
Farmstead Way. El Por 69 F1
Farndale Cl. Wist 206 A3
Farndon Cl. Broug 139 E2
Farndon Cl. Cudd 102 A2
Farndon Rd. El Por 69 F3
Farnham Ave. Mfield 112 A3
Farnham Cl. Ch Hul 35 D4
Farnhill Cl. Run 50 B4
Farnley Cl. Run 24 B1
Farnworth Cl. Wid 13 D2
Farnworth Rd. Penk 14 B2
Farnworth St. Wid 13 D2
Farr Hill Dr. Hes 40 C4
Farr Hill Rd. Hes 40 C4
Farrant St. Wid 23 D4
Farrell Rd. Warr 26 B4
Farrell St. Warr 16 B3
Farriers Way. Winsf 126 A1
Farthing La. G Bud 79 D4
Farwood Cl. Mfield 86 C1
Faulkner's La. L End 58 C1
Faulkner's La. Mobb 58 C1
Faulkners Cl. H Kin 161 D4
Faulkners La. Christ 142 B4
Fawns Keep. Wilm 60 B4
Fawns Leap. Cudd 101 F3
Fearndown Way. Mfield 87 E2
Fearnhead La. Warr 9 D1
Fearnley Way. N-le-W 2 B1
Feather La. Hes 40 C4
Feilden Ct. Moll 94 C1
Felix Rd. North 103 F4
Felskirk Rd. Wythe 33 E4
Fence Ave. Mfield 112 C4
Fence Ave Ind Est. Mfield 112 C4
Fence La. Astb 178 B2
Fenham Dr. Penk 14 C2
Fennel St. Warr 16 B3
Fenton Cl. Congle 157 D1
Fenton Cl. Wid 12 B2
Fenwick La. Run 49 E3
Fenwick Rd. El Por 69 F1
Ferguson Ave. El Por 69 F3
Ferguson Dr. Warr 8 B1
Ferma La. Gt Bar 120 B3
Fern Ave. N-le-W 2 B1
Fern Cl. Warr 9 E2
Fern Cres. Congle 157 D2
Fern Ct. Crewe 190 C2
Fern Lea Dr. Mfield 112 A4
Fern Rd. El Por 70 A1
Fern Way. Weave 77 E1
Fernbank Cl. Crewe 190 C2
Fernbank Rise. Boll 88 A4
Fernbankcl. Warr 9 F2
Ferndale Av. Elton 72 A2
Ferndale Cl. Bo Hea 13 F4
Ferndale Cl. Sand 175 E3
Ferndale Cl. Warr 17 E4
Ferndale Cl. Weston 207 D3
Ferndale Cres. Mfield 111 F4
Fernhill Rd. Blacon 117 F3
Fernhurst. Run 49 E4
Fernlea Rd. Hes 41 D4
Fernlea Rd. Mars 79 D3
Fernleaf Cl. Sch Gr 193 F4
Fernleigh. North 103 E4
Fernwood Gr. Wilm 60 B4
Ferry Cl. Sea 116 A3
Ferry La. Sea 117 E1
Ferry La. Warr 17 F2
Ferry Rd. Beb 44 A3
Ferryview Wlk. Run 23 F1
Festival Ave. Buer 230 C2
Festival Ave. Warr 8 B1

Festival Cres. Warr 8 B1
Festival Dr. N Ald 85 F3
Festival Hill. Congle 156 C1
Festival Rd. El Por 69 F3
Festival Way. Run 49 E4
Fiddler's Ferry Rd. Wid 13 E1
Fiddlers La. Saug 94 B1
Field Ave. Wist 189 F1
Field Cl. Boll 87 F4
Field Cl. Ch Hul 35 E2
Field Cl. North 103 E4
Field Cl. Tarv 121 D1
Field Hey La. Will 43 D1
Field La. Apple 26 B3
Field La. Tarv 121 D1
Field View. Bidd 179 E1
Field View Cl. Mfield 112 C3
Field Way. Alsag 193 F2
Field Wlk. Part 11 E1
Fieldbank. Mfield 112 A4
Fieldbank Rd. Mfield 112 A4
Fieldfare. Winsf 150 A4
Fieldfare Cl. Warr 9 F2
Fieldgate. Wid 22 A4
Fieldhead Mews. Wilm 60 C4
Fieldhead Rd. Wilm 60 C4
Fieldhouse Row. Run 49 E4
Fielding Ave. Poyn 36 C1
Fieldmuir Cl. Warr 9 D2
Fields Cl. Alsag 193 F2
Fields Cres. Congle 156 B1
Fields Dr. Sand 175 D3
Fields Rd. Alsag 193 F2
Fields Rd. Congle 178 C4
Fields Rd. Hasl 191 E2
Fields The. Willas 205 E3
Fields View. Roy Gr 228 B1
Fieldsend Dr. Gold 4 B4
Fieldside. Dudd 145 D3
Fieldsway. Run 49 D3
Fieldview Dr. Warr 8 B1
Fieldway. Chest 118 C2
Fieldway. El Por 69 D4
Fieldway. Frod 74 B4
Fieldway. Saug 94 A1
Fieldway. Weave 77 E1
Fieldway. Wid 13 E1
Fife Rd. Warr 16 C4
Fifth Ave. Kids 194 C1
Fifth Ave. Run 49 F4
Fiji St. Warr 15 F3
Filkin's La. Chest 119 D1
Finch La. Halew 21 D4
Finchdale Gdns. Gold 4 A4
Finchett Dr. Chest 118 A2
Findlay Cl. N-le-W 2 A1
Finlan Rd. Wid 23 D4
Finlow Hill La. N Ald 85 F3
Finney Cl. Wilm 34 B1
Finney Dr. Wilm 34 B1
Finney Gr. Hay 1 C3
Finney La. Chea 34 A4
Finney La. Wythe 34 A4
Finney's La. Middle 128 A1
Finningley Ct. Warr 8 C1
Finsbury Park. Wid 13 E3
Fir Ave. Bram 35 F4
Fir Ave. Halew 21 D4
Fir Cl. Halew 21 D4
Fir Cl. Poyn 36 C2
Fir Cl. Tarp 146 B1
Fir Ct. Mfield 86 C1
Fir Gr. Mfield 112 B3
Fir Gr. Warr 16 C4
Fir Gr. Weave 102 C4
Fir La. Cudd 102 A1
Fir Rd. Bram 35 F4
Fir St. Irlam 11 E3
Fir St. Wid 13 E1
Fir Tree Ave. Chest 141 D3
Fir Tree Ave. Gold 3 F4
Fir Tree Ave. Knuts 82 B4
Fir Tree Cl. Stret 26 B1
Fir Tree La. Burton 7 D4
Fir Tree La. Chest 119 F1
Fir Way. Hes 41 D3
Firbank. Elton 72 B2
Firbank Cl. Run 24 B1
Firbeck Cl. Broug 139 D2
Firbeck Cl. Congle 155 F2
Firbeck Gdns. Crewe 189 E2
Firdale Rd. North 103 E4
Firemans Sq. Chest 118 B1
Firman Cl. Gt San 15 D4
Firs La. Apple 26 A3
First Ave. Adlin 36 B1
First Ave. Crewe 190 C1
First Ave. G Cit 93 D1
First Ave. Kids 194 C1
First Ave. Sand 175 D3
First Dig La. Hay Gr 219 E4
First Wood St. Nant 204 B3
Firthfields Cl. Dave 103 F1
Firths Fields. Dave 103 F1
Firtree Ave. Warr 17 D4
Firtree Cl. North 78 A2
Firtree Gr. El Por 95 D4
Firwood Rd. Bidd 179 F1
Firwood Wlk. Crewe 190 B1
Fisher Rd. Blacon 117 F2
Fisher St. Run 23 D2
Fisherfield Dr. Warr 10 A3
Fishers La. Burl 203 E4
Fishpool Rd. Dela 123 F2
Fistral Ave. Chea 34 B4
Fitton St. Lost 80 A1
Fitton's Cl. Sound 217 F3
Fitz Cl. Mfield 87 E2
Fitz Cres. Mfield 87 E2
Fitz Walter Rd. Warr 17 E4
Fitzherbert St. Warr 16 B4
Fitzwilliam Ave. S La E 112 C2
Fitzwilliam Wlk. Run 24 A1
Five Ashes Rd. Chest 141 D3
Fiveways Par. Haz Gr 36 C4
Flag La. Crewe 190 B2
Flag La. Nest 66 C4
Flag La N. Chest 118 C4
Flag La S. Chest 118 B4
Flander Cl. Wid 12 B1
Flash La. Antro 53 F3
Flash La. Boll 87 E4
Flashes La. Nest 67 D3
Flat La. Kels 122 B2
Flat La. Sand 175 D3
Flatt La. El Por 70 A3
Flatts La. Kettle 64 C2
Flaxley Cl. Warr 10 A3
Flaxmere Dr. Chest 142 A4
Fleet La. St Hel 1 A1
Fleet St. El Por 70 A3
Fleetwood Cl. Gt San 15 D2
Fleetwood Wlk. Run 50 B3
Fleming St. El Por 70 B3
Flers Ave. Warr 16 B2
Fletcher Dr. H La 37 F3
Fletcher Gr. North 104 B3
Fletcher St. Crewe 190 A3
Fletcher St. Warr 16 A2
Fletchers La. Lymm 18 C2
Fletsand Rd. Wilm 60 B3
Flint Cl. Nest 66 C3
Flint Ct. El Por 70 B1
Flint Dr. Nest 66 C3
Flint Gr. Irlam 11 E3
Flint Meadow. Nest 66 C4
Flint St. Mfield 112 C4
Flittogate La. Plum 80 C4
Flixton Dr. Crewe 190 A1
Florence St. Warr 16 B2
Flower St. North 103 F4
Flowers La. Crewe 172 C1
Fluin La. Frod 74 B4
Foden Ave. Alsag 194 A2
Foden La. L End 59 E1
Foden La. Woodf 35 E2
Foden St. Mfield 87 E1
Foden Wlk. Wilm 34 B1
Fogg's La. Antro 53 D3
Fol Hollow. Congle 156 A1
Fold La. Bidd 179 F2
Fold La. Bosl 135 E1
Fold The. Prest 87 D4
Folds The. Thor H 42 A3
Foley Wlk. Wythe 33 F4
Folkestone Cl. Mfield 87 D1
Folkstone Way. Run 50 B4
Folly La. Warr 15 F4
Forbes Cl. Warr 9 F2
Forbes Park. Bram 35 E4
Ford Cl. Crewe 190 A3
Ford Ct. Winsf 149 E3
Ford La. Crewe 190 A3
Ford La. Tatt 166 C2
Ford St. Warr 16 B3
Ford's La. Ch Hul 35 E3
Fordington Rd. Gt San 15 D3
Fords La. Kids 195 E3
Foregate St. Chest 118 B1
Forest Ave. Goost 107 E1
Forest Cl. Cudd 101 F2
Forest Cl. Rain 88 C3
Forest Dr. Broug 139 D2
Forest Gate La. Dela 122 C4
Forest Gdns. Part 11 E2
Forest La. Norley 100 B3
Forest Pl. North 79 D1
Forest Rd. Cudd 101 F2
Forest Rd. El Por 69 F4
Forest Rd. Hes 41 D4
Forest Rd. Mfield 113 F3
Forest Rd. Tarp 146 B2
Forest Rd. Winsf 149 D4
Forest St. Chest 118 C1
Forest St. Weave 102 B4
Forester Ave. Knuts 57 E1
Foresters Cl. Norley 101 D3
Forge Cl. Cront 12 B3
Forge Fields. Sand 174 C2
Forge La. Congle 156 A2
Forge La. N in H 236 B1
Forge Rd. El Por 69 E3
Forge Rd. Gt San 14 C3
Forge Rd. W Br 65 F4
Forge Shopping Centre
The. Warr 16 B1
Forge St. Crewe 190 B2
Forge Way. Chest 140 C2
Formby Cl. Penk 14 C2
Formby Dr. Chea 34 A4
Forrest Dr. S La E 113 E2
Forshaw St. Warr 16 B4
Forshaw's La. Burton 6 C4
Forster Ave. Weave 102 C4
Forster St. Warr 16 A4
Forsythia Wlk. Part 11 E1
Forty Acre La. Cran 131 E3
Forty Acre La. Swelt 131 E3
Forum The. Chest 118 B1
Forwood Rd. Beb 43 E4
Foster St. Wid 13 D1
Fosters Rd. Congle 157 D3
Fothergill St. Warr 16 B4
Fotheringay Ct. El Por 70 B1
Foulkes Ave. Crewe 189 F3
Foundary Bank. Congle 156 C2
Foundry Ct. Mfield 112 B4
Foundry La. Sand 174 B4
Foundry La. Sch Gr 194 C4
Foundry La. Wid 22 B3
Foundry St. Boll 88 A4
Foundry St. N-le-W 2 A2
Foundry St. Warr 16 A3
Fountain Cl. Poyn 36 B2
Fountain Ct. Bidd 179 E1
Fountain Ct. Winsf 126 B1
Fountain La. Dave 103 F1
Fountain La. Frod 74 A4
Fountain Sq. Disley 38 B3
Fountain St. Congle 156 B1
Fountain St. Mfield 112 C4
Fountains Ave. Hay 1 C4
Fountains Cl. Run 50 B3
Fountains Rd. Ch Hul 35 E3
Fountains Wlk. Gold 4 A4
Four Lanes End. Betley 207 F1
Fourseasons Cl. Wist 206 A4
Fourth Ave. Crewe 190 C1
Fourth Ave. G Cit 92 C1
Fourth Ave. Kids 194 C1
Fourth Ave. Run 49 F4
Fowey Cl. Mfield 86 B1
Fowler Rd. Blacon 117 E2
Fowler St. Mfield 87 E1
Fowlers Bench La. Burw 184 B3
Fowley Common La. Cul 5 D3
Fox Bench Cl. Ch Hul 35 E3
Fox Cover. G Sutt 119 F3
Fox Covert. Run 50 B4
Fox Covert La. Pict 96 A1
Fox Covert La. Stoak 96 A1
Fox Gdns. Kids 210 B4
Fox Gdns. Lymm 18 B2
Fox Gr. Knuts 57 E1
Fox Hill. Kels 122 B2
Fox La. Clutt 182 B1
Fox La. Waver 143 D3
Fox Lea. Saug 117 D4
Fox St. Congle 156 C2
Fox St. Run 23 D1
Fox St. Warr 15 F3
Fox's Dr. Sea 116 A3
Foxall Way. El Por 69 E1
Foxcote. Wid 12 A1
Foxcover Rd. Hes 41 E4
Foxcovert La. Peo 106 C4
Foxdale Ct. Apple 26 B4
Foxes Hey. Cudd 101 E3
Foxes Fold. North 78 C1
Foxes Wlk. Chest 142 A4
Foxfield Cl. Warr 8 C2
Foxfield La. Winsf 126 A1
Foxglove Cl. Hunt 142 A3
Foxglove Cl. Wist 206 A4
Foxglove Ct. Frod 74 B4
Foxglove Way. Nest 66 C3
Foxglove Wlk. Part 11 F1
Foxhill Gr. Hels 73 E2
Foxhills Cl. Stret 26 B2
Foxhunter Cl. Asht 121 F4
Foxlea. Comb 78 B4
Foxley Cl. Lymm 19 D1
Foxwist Cl. Chest 118 B2
Foxwist Gr. Winsf 125 F3
Foxwood Dr. Peo 108 A4
Frances St. Crewe 190 B1
Frances St. Irlam 11 F3
Frances St. Mfield 112 A4
Francis Cl. Wid 22 B4
Francis Ct. Chest 118 C1
Francis La. Holt 196 A3
Francis Rd. Frod 49 E1
Francis Rd. Irlam 11 F4
Francis Rd. Warr 16 B1
Francis St. Chest 118 C1
Frank Bott Ave. Crewe 190 A4
Frank Perkins Way. Irlam 11 F4
Frank St. Wid 13 E1
Frank Webb Ave. Crewe 190 A3
Franklin Cl. Gt San 15 E4
Fraser Ct. Chest 141 E4
Fraser Rd. Gt San 14 B3
Frawley Ave. N-le-W 2 B3
Freckleton Cl. Gt San 15 D2
Frederick St. Warr 16 C2
Frederick St. Wid 23 D4
Fredric Pl. Run 23 D2
Free Green La. Peo 107 D4
French La. Fr La E 218 B3
French La. Sound 218 B3
French St. Wid 13 E1
Freshfield. Chea 34 A4
Freshfield Dr. Mfield 87 E2
Freshfields. Comb 78 B4
Freshfields. Wist 206 A4
Freshfields Dr. Warr 9 E1
Freshmeadow La. Hels 73 D1
Freshwater Cl. Gt San 14 B4
Friars Cl. Rain 88 B3
Friars Gate. Warr 16 A2
Friars La. Warr 16 A2
Friars Way. Mfield 86 C1
Frida Cres. North 103 F3
Friends La. Gt San 14 B3
Frith Ave. Dela 123 E4
Frith Terr. Mfield 112 B2
Frobisher Rd. Nest 66 C4
Froda Ave. Frod 74 A4
Frodsham Rd. Alva 73 E1
Frodsham St. Chest 118 B1
Frodsham St. Kels 122 A3
Frodsham Way. Wilm 34 C2
Frog La. Golb 165 F1
Frog La. Hand 165 F1
Frog La. Holt 196 A4
Frog La. Pick 55 D1
Frog La. Tatt 166 A1
Frog La. Worth 211 D1
Froghall La. H Legh 29 E4
Froghall La. Warr 16 A3
Frome Ct. El Por 70 A4
Front St. Sand 175 E3
Frosts Mews. El Por 70 A3
Fryer Rd. Lost 80 A2
Fuchsia Cl. El Por 69 F1
Fulbeck. Wid 12 B1
Fulbrook Dr. Ch Hul 35 D3
Fuller Dr. Wist 206 A4
Fullerton Rd. Hart 103 D2
Fulmar Cl. Poyn 36 A2
Fulmards Cl. Wilm 60 B4
Fulshaw Ave. Wilm 60 A3
Fulshaw Cross. Wilm 60 A3
Fulshaw Ct. Wilm 60 A3
Fulshaw Park. Wilm 60 A3
Fulshaw Park S. Wilm 60 A2
Fulton Gr. Dave 103 F1
Fulwood Gdns. El Por 69 E3
Fulwood Mews. El Por 69 E3
Fulwood Rd. El Por 69 E3
Fulwood Rd. Gold 3 F4
Furber St. Crewe 190 B3
Furne Rd. Blacon 117 F2
Furness Cl. H Chap 130 A2
Furness Cl. Poyn 36 B2
Furness Cl. Winsf 149 D4
Furness Lodge Cl. W Br 39 E2
Furness Rd. Ch Hul 35 E3
Furness Row. W Br 39 E2
Furnival St. Crewe 190 B1
Furnival St. Sand 175 D4
Furrocks Cl. Nest 66 C3
Furrocks La. Nest 66 C3
Furrocks Way. Nest 66 C3
Furrows The. El Por 94 C4
Fylde Ave. Chea 34 B4
Fytton Cl. Warren 111 E1

Gable Wlk. Wilm 60 A4
Gables Cl. Warr 8 C2
Gables The. Alsag 193 E2
Gabriel Bank. Crow 76 A1
Gadbrook
Business Centre. L Den 104 B3
Gadbrook Park. L Den 104 B3
Gadbrook Rd. L Den 104 B3
Gail Cl. A Edge 60 A1
Gainford Cl. Wid 12 B2
Gainsborough Cl. Wilm 60 C4
Gainsborough Ct. Wid 12 A1
Gainsborough Rd. Crewe 190 A2
Gainsborough Rd. Warr 16 A1
Gairloch Cl. Warr 8 C2
Gaisgill Ct. Wid 12 B1
Gala Cl. Broug 139 E2
Gale Rd. N Mills 39 E4
Galleys Bank. Kids 195 D2
Gallowsclough La. Norley 100 C2
Gallowsclough La. Oak 100 C2
Galway Gr. Shav 206 A2
Game St. Sand 175 D2
Gamul Pl. Chest 141 E4
Ganton Cl. Wid 13 D2
Garden Ave. Winsf 126 A1
Garden Ct. Chest 118 B1
Garden La. Burw 183 F2
Garden La. Chest 118 B1
Garden Rd. Knuts 56 C2
Garden St. Boll 87 F4
Garden St. Congle 156 B2
Garden St. Mfield 87 F1
Garden Terr. Chest 118 B1
Garden Terr. Chest 118 C1
Garden Wlk. Part 11 E1
Gardens The. Holt 180 C1
Gardens The. Sand 175 D3
Garfit St. Middle 128 B1
Garigill Cl. Wid 13 E3
Garner St. Warr 16 B4
Garnets La. Wid 22 A2
Garnett Ave. Warr 17 D2
Garrett Field. Warr 9 E3
Garside Ave. Gold 3 E4
Garth Dr. Chest 118 B3
Garth Hts. Wilm 60 B4
Garton Dr. Gold 3 F4
Garven Pl. Warr 16 A3
Garwood Cl. Gt San 15 E4
Gas Rd. Mfield 112 B4
Gaskell Ave. Knuts 56 C1
Gaskell Ave. Warr 17 D2
Gaskell St. Warr 16 B1
Gatcombe Mews. Wilm 60 A3
Gate Warth St. Warr 15 E2
Gateacre Cl. El Por 69 F4
Gatefield St. Crewe 190 B2
Gatesheath Dr. Chest 118 B4
Gatesheath La. Golb 165 F3
Gateway. Crewe 190 C1
Gateway. Crewe 191 D1
Gaunts Way. Run 49 F3
Gavin Rd. Wid 22 A4
Gawend La. S La E 112 B1
Gawer Pk. Chest 118 B2
Gawesworth Way. Wilm 34 C2
Gawsworth Ave. Crewe 189 F2
Gawsworth Cl. Alsag 193 E2
Gawsworth Cl. Bram 35 F3
Gawsworth Cl. H Chap 130 A2
Gawsworth Cl. North 104 A2
Gawsworth Cl. Poyn 36 C1
Gawsworth Dr. Sand 175 E4
Gawsworth Rd. El Por 69 F3
Gawsworth Rd. Mfield 111 E3
Gawsworth Rd. Warren 111 E3
Gayhurst Ave. Warr 8 C1
Gaymoore Cl. Chest 118 B2
Gaynor Ave. Hay 1 C4
Gayton Cl. Chest 118 C3
Gayton Farm Rd. Hes 41 D3
Gayton La. Hes 41 D3
Gayton Parkway. Hes 41 E3
Gayton Rd. Hes 41 D3
Gemmull Cl. Audlem 229 F2
General St. Warr 16 B3
Geneva Rd. Winsf 126 B1
George Bates Cl. Alsag 193 E2
George Rd. Gt San 15 E2
George St. A Edge 60 A1
George St. Audley 209 E1
George St. Chest 118 B1
George St. El Por 70 B4
George St. Knuts 57 D1
George St. Mfield 112 B4
George St. N-le-W 2 A2
George St. North 78 A2
George St. Sand 174 C4
George St. W Br 65 F4
George St. Winsf 126 C1
George St W. Mfield 112 B4
George VI Ave. Middle 151 E3
George VI Cl. Middle 151 E3
George's Cl. Poyn 36 C2
George's La. B Hea 54 B1
George's Rd E. Poyn 36 C2
George's Rd W. Poyn 36 C2
George's Wlk. Sand 175 D3
Georges Cres. Warr 17 D1
Georges Way. Audley 209 F1
Gerard Dr. Nant 204 B2
Gerosa Ave. Win 8 A4
Gerrard Ave. El Por 69 E2
Gerrard Ave. Warr 15 F4
Gerrard Dr. Weave 77 E1
Gerrard Rd. Croft 9 D4
Gerrard St. Wid 23 D4
Gerrards Ave. Chest 119 D1
Giantswood La. Congle 156 B3
Giantswood La. Eaton 156 B3
Gibb Hill. Antro 53 E1
Gibbon Dr. Lost 80 A2
Gibson Cres. Sand 174 B3
Gibson St. Warr 16 B1
Gibson St. Warr 16 B3
Gig La. Warr 17 F4
Gigg La. Moore 25 D3
Gilbert Cl. Kids 195 D1
Gilchrist Ave. Mfield 111 F4
Gilchrist Rd. Irlam 11 F3
Gilderdale Cl. Warr 10 A3
Gill Bent Rd. Ch Hul 35 D4
Gillan Cl. Run 50 B3
Gillow Cl. Crewe 190 A4
Giltbrook Cl. Wid 12 C2
Gilwell Cl. Warr 17 E1
Gingerbread La. Nant 205 D3
Girton Cl. El Por 70 B2
Girton Rd. El Por 70 B2
Girvin Dr. Nest 66 C3
Gladstone Ave. Chest 118 A1

Gladstone Rd. Broug 139 D2
Gladstone Rd. Chest 118 A2
Gladstone Rd. Nest 66 C4
Gladstone St. Crewe 190 B2
Gladstone St. North 103 F4
Gladstone St. Warr 16 A3
Gladstone St. Wid 23 D4
Gladstone St. Willas 205 E3
Gladstone St. Winsf 149 E4
Glaisdale Cl. Wist 206 A3
Glamis Cl. Chest 119 D1
Glamis Cl. Wist 205 F4
Glan Aber Park. Chest 141 D4
Glandon Dr. Ch Hul 35 E4
Glastonbury Ave. Ch Hul 35 E3
Glastonbury Ave. Chest 118 B4
Glastonbury Ave. Gold 4 B4
Glastonbury Cl. Run 24 C2
Glastonbury Dr. Middle 128 A1
Glastonbury Dr. Poyn 36 B3
Glazebrook La. Hol Gr 11 D3
Glazebrook St. Warr 16 B3
Glaziers La. Croft 4 A1
Glaziers La. Croft 4 B1
Gleadmere. Wid 12 B1
Gleave Av. Boll 88 A4
Gleave Rd. Burton 6 C3
Glebe Ave. Warr 17 E1
Glebe Green Dr. Winsf 149 E3
Glebe La. Wid 13 D3
Glebe Meadows. M Traf 96 C1
Glebe Rd. Cudd 102 A2
Glebe St. Kids 194 B1
Glebe The. Run 23 F1
Glebecroft Av. Elton 72 A2
Glebeland. Cul 4 C2
Glebelands Rd. Knuts 57 D1
Glen Aber Dr. Chest 140 C4
Glen Cl. Hol Gr 11 D1
Glen Rd. El Por 69 E2
Glen The. Blacon 117 F3
Glen The. Run 49 F3
Glenathol Rd. El Por 69 E2
Glenbourne Park. Ch Hul 35 E3
Glenburn Ave. Beb 43 F2
Glencoe Cl. H Chap 130 B1
Glencoe Rd. El Por 69 E2
Glencourse Rd. Wid 13 D3
Glendale Av. Elton 72 A2
Glendale Ave. Hawa 116 A2
Glendale Cl. Buer 230 C2
Glendale Cl. Crewe 189 E2
Glendene Ave. Ch Hul 35 E3
Glendyke Rd. El Por 69 E2
Gleneagles Cl. Bram 36 A4
Gleneagles Cl. Chest 119 D2
Gleneagles Cl. Wilm 60 B4
Gleneagles Dr. H Chap 130 A1
Gleneagles Dr. Hay 1 A3
Gleneagles Dr. Mfield 87 E2
Gleneagles Dr. Wid 13 D3
Gleneagles Dr. Winsf 126 B1
Gleneagles Rd. El Por 69 E2
Glenesk Rd. El Por 69 E2
Glenfield Dr. Poyn 36 B2
Glenholme Rd. Ch Hul 35 E4
Glenmaye Rd. El Por 69 E2
Glenn Pl. Wid 12 C1
Glenorchy Cl. H Chap 130 B1
Glenside Cl. Blacon 117 E3
Glenton Park. Nest 66 C3
Glenville Cl. Run 49 D3
Glenwood Cl. El Por 69 E3
Glenwood Gdns. El Por 69 E3
Glenwood Rd. El Por 69 E3
Gleyve. H Legh 29 E3
Gloucester Ave. Gold 3 D4
Gloucester Cl. El Por 94 C4
Gloucester Cl. Mfield 87 F2
Gloucester Cl. Warr 17 E4
Gloucester Rd. Chea 34 B4
Gloucester Rd. Kids 194 C1
Gloucester Rd. Knuts 81 F4
Gloucester Rd. Poyn 36 B2
Gloucester Rd. Wid 13 D2
Gloucester St. Chest 118 B2
Glover Rd. Warr 9 E2
Glover St. Crewe 190 A3
Glover St. N-le-W 2 B2
Glovers Loom. Chest 142 A4
Glyn Ave. Beb 43 F4
Goathland Way. Mfield 112 B3
Goddard Rd. Run 23 F2
Goddard St. Crewe 190 A3
Godfrey St. Warr 16 B4
Godscroft La. Frod 73 F3
Godstall La. Chest 118 B1
Godward Rd. N Mills 39 D4
Golborne Dale Rd. N-le-W 3 D2
Golborne Rd. Gold 3 E4
Golborne Rd. Win 8 A4
Golborne St. Warr 16 A3
Goldborne La. H Legh 28 C1
Goldcliffe Cl. Warr 7 E2
Goldcrest Cl. Run 49 F3
Goldcrest Cl. Winsf 149 E3
Golden Sq. Warr 16 A3
Goldfinch La. Warr 9 F2
Goldford La. Bicker 199 F3
Goldsmith Dr. Sand 174 B3
Golftyn Dr. Con Q 91 E1
Golftyn La. Con Q 91 E1
Gonsley Cl. Chest 118 B2
Gonville Ave. S La E 112 C2
Gooch Dr. N-le-W 2 B1
Goodall St. Mfield 112 C4
Goodall's Cnr. Shav 206 B2
Goodrington Rd. Wilm 34 C2
Goodwood Cl. Chest 118 A1
Goodwood Cl. North 78 A2
Goodwood Gr. El Por 69 F2
Goose La. Hatt 26 A1
Gooseberry La. Kels 122 C2
Goosebrook Cl. Comb 78 B4
Goosebrook La. Antro 52 C1
Goosetrey Cl. Wilm 34 C1
Goostrey La. Cran 130 A4
Goostrey Rd. Goost 130 A4
Gordale Cl. Congle 157 D3
Gordon Ave. Beb 43 F4
Gordon Ave. Hay 1 C4
Gordon Ave. Warr 17 D4
Gordon La. Back 95 D3
Gore La. L End 59 E1
Gorse Bank Rd. Altr 32 B4
Gorse Covert Rd. Warr 10 A3
Gorse La. Astb 178 B3
Gorse Sq. Part 11 E2
Gorse Stacks. Chest 118 B1
Gorse The. Altr 31 D4
Gorse Way. Hunt 142 A3
Gorsefield. Tatt 166 A1
Gorsefield Ave. Beb 43 E3
Gorsefield Cl. Beb 43 E3
Gorsefield Hey. Wilm 60 C4
Gorselands. Ch Hul 35 D3
Gorsewood Rd. Run 50 B3
Gorsey Bank Cres. Hay Gr 220 A4
Gorsey La. Bo Hea 6 B3
Gorsey La. Part 20 A4
Gorsey La. Warr 16 B4
Gorsey La. Wid 13 F1
Gorsey Rd. Wilm 59 F4
Gorseywell La. Run 50 C3
Gorsley Cl. Middle 151 E3
Gorstage La. Weave 102 B4
Gorston Wlk. Wythe 33 E4
Gosberryhole La. Congle 158 A1
Gosforth Pl. Chest 118 C2
Gosling Cl. Hatt 26 A1
Gosling Rd. Croft 9 D4
Gosport Dr. Warr 8 C1
Goss St. Chest 118 B1
Gothurst Ct. Wid 22 B4
Gough Ave. Warr 8 A1
Gough's La. Knuts 82 B4
Goulden St. Crewe 190 A3
Goulden St. Warr 15 F3
Goulders Ct. Run 50 A3
Gowy Cl. Alsag 192 C2
Gowy Cl. Wilm 34 C1
Gowy Cres. Tarv 121 D1
Gowy Ct. El Por 69 F4
Gowy Rd. M Traf 96 C1
Gowy Wlk. Winsf 127 D2
Goyt Pl. W Br 65 F4
Goyt Rd. Disley 38 B3
Goyt Rd. N Mills 39 E3
Goyt View. N Mills 39 D3
Goyt's La. Bux 90 C1
Grace Ave. Warr 16 A4
Grace Cl. Hasl 191 E2
Grafton Mews. Chest 118 B2
Grafton Rd. El Por 70 B4
Grafton St. N-le-W 2 A2
Grafton St. Warr 15 F3
Graham Ave. El Por 69 E3
Graham Cl. Wid 12 B1
Graham Dr. Disley 38 B3
Graham Dr. Halew 21 D4
Graham Rd. Blacon 117 F2
Graham Rd. Wid 22 B4
Grainger's Rd. North 103 F3
Grammar School Rd. Warr 16 C2
Grammer School Rd. Lymm 18 C1
Grampian Way. Beb 43 F2
Grampian Way. Nest 66 C3
Grampian Way. Winsf 149 D4
Granby Cl. Run 50 B3
Granby Rd. Ch Hul 35 D4
Granby Rd. Warr 26 A4
Grandford La. New 217 E1
Grange Ave. North 78 A2
Grange Ave. Warr 16 C2
Grange Cl. Crewe 190 C2
Grange Cl. Gold 3 E3
Grange Cl. Sand 174 C4
Grange Cres. El Por 44 A1
Grange Ct. Bidd 179 E1
Grange Dr. Penk 15 D2
Grange Dr. Thor H 42 A4
Grange Dr. Wid 12 B1
Grange La. Ed Gr 198 C2
Grange La. Tils 198 C2
Grange La. Weave 102 A4
Grange La. Winsf 126 A2
Grange Park Ave. Run 23 E1
Grange Park Ave. Wilm 60 A4
Grange Rd. Asht 99 D1
Grange Rd. Bidd 179 F2
Grange Rd. Chest 118 B2
Grange Rd. Chest 119 E1
Grange Rd. Cudd 101 F1
Grange Rd. El Por 70 B2
Grange Rd. Hay 1 B3
Grange Rd. Mfield 112 B3
Grange Rd. North 78 A2
Grange Rd. North 104 B3
Grange Rd. Run 23 E1
Grange Rd W. Chest 119 E1
Grange The. Hart 103 D3
Grange Valley. Hay 1 B3
Grange Way. Sand 174 C4
Grangebrook Dr. Winsf 126 B2
Grangefields. Bidd 179 F2
Grangeland Dr. Chelf 83 F2
Grangelands. Mfield 86 C1
Grangemoor. Run 49 E4
Grangeside. Chest 118 B4
Grangeway. Run 49 E4
Grangeway. Wilm 34 B2
Grangeway Ct. Run 49 E4
Granston Cl. Warr 7 F1
Grant Cl. Warr 7 E1
Grant St. N-le-W 2 A2
Grantham Ave. Warr 16 C4
Grantham Ave. Warr 26 A4
Grantham Cl. North 104 B4
Granville Dr. El Por 69 D4
Granville Rd. Chest 118 A2
Granville Rd. North 104 A3
Granville Rd. Wilm 59 F3
Granville Sq. Winsf 149 F4
Granville St. Run 23 D2
Granville St. Warr 16 B3
Granville St. Winsf 149 F4
Grapes St. Mfield 112 B4
Grappenhall La. Apple 27 F3
Grappenhall Rd. El Por 69 F2
Grappenhall Rd. Warr 16 B1
Grasmere. Mfield 111 F3
Grasmere Ave. Congle 155 F1
Grasmere Ave. Crewe 189 F3
Grasmere Ave. Warr 8 C2
Grasmere Cres. Bram 35 F4
Grasmere Dr. H Chap 130 A2
Grasmere Dr. Run 49 E3
Grasmere Rd. A Edge 60 A1
Grasmere Rd. Chest 118 C3
Grasmere Rd. El Por 70 B1
Grasmere Rd. Frod 74 B4
Grasmere Rd. Lymm 18 C2
Grasmere Rd. Nest 66 C3
Grasmere Rd. Part 11 F2
Grason Ave. Wilm 34 B1
Grassfield Way. Knuts 82 A4
Grassmere Cres. H La 37 F4
Grassmoor Cl. Beb 43 F4
Grassygreen La. Audley 209 F1
Gratrix Rd. Beb 43 E4
Gravel La. Wilm 59 F3
Graveyard La. Mobb 58 C3
Gray Ave. Hay 1 B3
Gray's Cl. Sch Gr 195 D4
Graylag Cl. Run 49 F3
Greasby Dr. El Por 69 F2
Great Ashfield. Wid 12 B2
Great King St. Mfield 112 B4
Great Queen St. Mfield 112 B4
Great Riding. Run 50 B4
Greatoak Rd. Audley 209 F2
Greaves La. Threap 222 C4
Grebe Cl. Knuts 57 D2
Grebe Cl. Poyn 36 A2
Greeba Ave. Warr 16 A2
Greek St. Run 22 C2
Green Acre Cl. Knuts 82 A4
Green Ave. Alpr 169 E2
Green Ave. Dave 103 F2
Green Ave. North 78 A2
Green Bank. Adder 235 D3
Green Bank. Chest 141 F3
Green Bridge Cl. Run 24 A1
Green Coppice. Run 50 B4
Green Dr. Alsag 193 E2
Green Dr. Wilm 34 B1
Green Hall Mews. Wilm 60 A3
Green Jones Brow. Burton 6 C3
Green La. A Edge 59 F1
Green La. Acton 204 A2
Green La. Apple 27 D3
Green La. Audlem 229 F1
Green La. Barb 187 D4
Green La. Boll 63 D1
Green La. Burton 6 C4
Green La. Chest 119 D2
Green La. Chest 140 C2
Green La. Chow 182 C3
Green La. Dave 103 F2
Green La. Disley 38 B2
Green La. El Por 69 E2
Green La. El Por 70 B2
Green La. H Kin 161 D3
Green La. H Winch 79 F2
Green La. Hor Gr 212 A4
Green La. Irlam 11 F3
Green La. Kels 122 B2
Green La. Knuts 56 B2
Green La. L End 84 C4
Green La. Peo 83 E1
Green La. Pict 96 B2
Green La. Plum 80 C3
Green La. Poyn 37 E2
Green La. Sand 173 F4
Green La. Saug 117 E4
Green La. Sea 116 B4
Green La. Shock 211 E4
Green La. Warr 17 D4
Green La. Wid 12 C1
Green La. Willas 205 F3
Green La. Wilm 60 A4
Green La. Win 8 A4
Green La Cl. Win 8 A4
Green La W. G Cit 93 D2
Green Lawns Dr. El Por 94 C4
Green Meadows. Gold 3 F3
Green Oaks Path. Wid 23 E4
Green Park. Weave 102 C4
Green Rd. Part 11 F2
Green St. A Edge 60 A1
Green St. Holt 180 C1
Green St. Knuts 57 D1
Green St. Mfield 112 C4
Green St. Sand 175 D4
Green St. Warr 15 F3
Green The. Burw 183 F2
Green The. Chea 34 C4
Green The. El Por 70 A1
Green The. H Kin 161 D4
Green The. Hart 103 D3
Green The. Law-g 194 A2
Green The. Middle 151 E3
Green The. Nest 66 B4
Green The. Nest 66 C3
Green The. Tarv 121 F1
Green The. Thor H 42 B2
Green The. Wilm 34 C2
Green View. Lymm 19 D3
Green Villa Pk. Wilm 59 F2
Green Way. Saug 94 A1
Green Wlk. Cudd 102 A2
Green Wlk. Part 11 E1
Greenacre Dr. Beb 43 E4
Greenacre Rd. Chest 140 C2
Greenacres. Crewe 190 B3
Greenacres. Dudd 145 D3
Greenacres. Frod 74 B3
Greenacres. Sand 175 D4
Greenacres Cl. Gold 4 A4
Greenacres Rd. Congle 155 F1
Greenall Ave. Penk 14 B2
Greenall Rd. North 104 A4
Greenalls Ave. Warr 16 B1
Greenbank Ave. El Por 69 E4
Greenbank Dr. Boll 88 A4
Greenbank Gdns. Warr 16 C1
Greenbank La. North 103 E3
Greenbank Rd. Chest 119 D2
Greenbank Rd. Warr 16 C1
Greenbank St. Warr 16 B1
Greenbridge Rd. Run 24 A1
Greendale Dr. Middle 151 D4
Greendale Dr. N-u-L 210 B1
Greendale La. M St A 86 A4
Greenfield Ave. H Kin 161 D4
Greenfield Cl. N Mills 39 D4
Greenfield Cres. Waver 143 D3
Greenfield Gdns. Elton 72 A2
Greenfield La. Chest 119 D3
Greenfield La. Frod 49 D1
Greenfield Rd. Boll 88 A4
Greenfield Rd. Broug 139 E2
Greenfield Rd. Congle 156 A2
Greenfield Rd. El Por 69 D4
Greenfield Rd. Waver 143 D3
Greenfield Way. Cudd 102 A2
Greenfields. Chest 95 F1
Greenfields. Winsf 127 D1
Greenfields Ave. Apple 26 B4
Greenfields Ave. Beb 43 E4
Greenfields Ave. Shav 206 A2
Greenfields Cl. N-le-W 2 B2
Greenfields Cl. Nest 66 C3
Greenfields Cl. Warr 17 E4
Greenfields Cres. Beb 43 E4
Greenfields Croft. Nest 66 C3
Greenfields Dr. Nest 66 C3
Greenfields Rd. Alsag 193 F2
Greengate Rd. Law-g 193 F3
Greengates Cres. Nest 66 C3
Greenhill La. Whit 52 A3
Greenhill Wlk. Disley 38 B3
Greenhills Cl. Mfield 112 C4
Greenhouse Farm Rd. Run 50 A4
Greenhythe Rd. Chea 34 B3
Greenland Cl. Tarp 146 B1
Greenlands. Tatt 166 A2
Greenlea Cl. El Por 70 A1
Greenore Dr. Hale 21 E1
Greensbridge La. Halew 21 D4
Greenshall La. Disley 38 C3
Greenshank Cl. N-le-W 2 B2
Greenside Ave. Frod 74 B4
Greenside Ct. L Den 105 E3
Greenside Dr. Lost 105 D4
Greensway. Chest 141 D4
Greenway. Alsag 193 D3
Greenway. Apple 26 B4
Greenway. Ch Hul 35 E3
Greenway. Congle 156 A2
Greenway. Crewe 190 B4
Greenway. Farn 180 C1
Greenway. Gt San 14 C4
Greenway. Tils 198 B2
Greenway. Warr 16 C4
Greenway. Wilm 60 A3
Greenway Cl. Hels 73 D2
Greenway Cl. Sch Gr 193 F4
Greenway Dr. North 104 B4
Greenway Rd. Bidd 179 F1
Greenway Rd. Chea 34 B3
Greenway Rd. Run 23 D1
Greenway Rd. Speke 21 D2
Greenway Rd. Wid 13 D1
Greenway St. Chest 141 E4
Greenway Wlk. North 104 B4
Greenways. Audley 209 F1
Greenwell Rd. Hay 1 B3
Greenwood Ave. Chest 141 E4
Greenwood Ave. Congle 156 C2
Greenwood Cl. Croft 4 C1
Greenwood Cl. Weave 77 E1
Greenwood Cres. Warr 8 C1
Greenwood Dr. N-le-W 2 B1
Greenwood Dr. Wilm 60 B4
Greenwood Rd. Lymm 18 C1
Greg Ave. Boll 87 F4
Greg Mews. Wilm 34 A1
Gregory Cl. Gt San 15 E4
Gregson Rd. Wid 13 E1
Grenfell Cl. Nest 41 E1
Grenfell Park. Nest 41 E1
Grenfell St. Wid 23 D4
Grenville Cl. Hasl 191 E3
Grenville Cres. Beb 43 E4
Grenville Rd. Nest 41 F1
Gresford Ave. Chest 118 C2
Gresford Cl. Warr 7 F1
Gresley Way. Audley 209 F1
Gresty Green Rd. Shav 206 B4
Gresty La. Shav 206 A4
Gresty Rd. Crewe 190 B1
Gresty Terr. Crewe 190 C2
Greta Ave. Chea 34 B3
Greville Dr. Winsf 127 D1
Grey Friars. Chest 118 B1
Grey St. Warr 16 B3
Greyhound Park Rd.
Blacon 117 F2
Greyhound Rd. N Ald 86 A3
Greymarsh Dr. Poyn 36 C1
Greymist Ave. Warr 17 E4
Greys Ct. Warr 9 E1
Greystoke Dr. A Edge 60 A1
Greystoke Rd. Mfield 87 F1
Greystone Park. Crewe 190 B2
Greystone Rd. Penk 14 C2
Greystones. El Por 69 E2
Greystones Rd. Chest 119 E1
Grice St. Warr 16 B1
Griffin Cl. Blacon 117 F3
Griffin Cl. N in H 236 B1
Griffin Cl. N Mills 39 E3
Griffin Mews. Wid 13 D2
Griffiths Dr. North 104 B3
Griffiths Rd. Lost 79 F1
Griffiths Rd. North 104 C4
Griffiths St. Warr 16 C2
Grig Pl. Alsag 193 E3
Grimsditch La. Dares 52 A3
Grimsditch La. Whit 52 A3
Grimshaw Ave. Boll 88 A4
Grimshaw La. Boll 88 A4
Grindley Bank. M Traf 119 F4
Grindley Gdns. El Por 70 B1
Grisedale Ave. Warr 8 A2
Grisedale Cl. Run 49 F3
Grisedale Rd. Beb 43 F4
Grisedale Way. Mfield 112 A3
Grizedale. Wid 12 C2
Groarke Dr. Penk 14 B3
Groby Rd. Crewe 190 C4
Grosvenor Ave. Alsag 193 E3
Grosvenor Ave. Gold 3 E4
Grosvenor Ave. Hart 103 D2
Grosvenor Ave. Warr 16 C4
Grosvenor Cl. Gt San 15 E3
Grosvenor Cl. Wilm 60 A2
Grosvenor Ct. Chest 118 C1
Grosvenor Ct. Winsf 149 E4
Grosvenor Dr. Poyn 36 B2
Grosvenor Gdns. N-le-W 2 B1
Grosvenor Pk Rd. Chest 118 C1
Grosvenor Pk Terr. Chest 118 C1
Grosvenor Pl. Chest 141 E4
Grosvenor Prec The.
Chest 118 B1
Grosvenor Rd. Chest 141 E4
Grosvenor Rd. Congle 156 A2
Grosvenor Rd. Hay 1 A4

Grosvenor Rd. Tarv 121 D1
Grosvenor Rd. Wid 13 D2
Grosvenor St. Chest 118 B1
Grosvenor St. Crewe 190 A3
Grosvenor St. Mfield 112 B4
Grosvenor St. Run 23 D2
Grosvenor St. Winsf 149 F4
Grotsworth La. Bic T 214 C4
Grotto La. Peo 108 A4
Grounds St. Warr 16 A4
Grove Ave. Chest 119 D2
Grove Ave. Kids 194 C1
Grove Ave. Law-g 194 A2
Grove Ave. Lost 80 A2
Grove Ave. Lymm 18 B2
Grove Ave. Wilm 60 A4
Grove Cl. Winsf 149 D4
Grove Cres. Woore 232 B1
Grove Ct. Alsag 193 F2
Grove Gdns. Chest 119 F1
Grove La. Ch Hul 35 D3
Grove Park. Knuts 57 D1
Grove Park Ave. Law-g 194 A2
Grove Rd. Backf 94 C2
Grove Rise. Lymm 18 C2
Grove St. N Mills 39 D4
Grove St. Run 22 C2
Grove St. Warr 16 B2
Grove St. Wilm 60 A3
Grove The. Ch Hul 35 D3
Grove The. Knuts 57 E2
Grove The. Law-g 194 A2
Grove The. Penk 14 C2
Grovemount. Dave 103 F1
Groves The. Chest 118 B1
Groves The. El Por 95 D4
Grove The. Whitch 225 F1
Grovewood Mews. Mfield 112 B3
Grub La. Kels 122 B3
Grundy St. Gold 3 D4
Guardian St. Warr 15 F3
Guernsey Cl. Apple 26 B4
Guernsey Cl. Congle 157 D1
Guernsey Dr. El Por 70 B1
Guernsey Rd. Wid 13 F2
Guest St. Run 23 D4
Guests Slack. Kings 100 A4
Guilden Green. G Sutt 119 F2
Guilden Sutton La. Chest 119 E3
Guildford Ave. Ch Hul 35 D3
Guildford Cl. Warr 9 D1
Guildford Rd. Chest 140 C3
Guillemot Cl. Crewe 190 C3
Gull Cl. Poyn 36 A2
Gullet The. Nant 204 C3
Gulls Way. Hes 40 C4
Gunco La. Mfield 112 C3
Gunco La. Prest 87 E4
Gunn Gr. Nest 66 C4
Gutterscroft. Hasl 191 E3
Gutticar Rd. Wid 12 A1
Guy La. Harg 143 E3
Guy La. Waver 143 E3

Hacked Way La. Mac For 113 F3
Haddon Cl. A Edge 59 F1
Haddon Cl. H Chap 130 A2
Haddon Cl. H La 37 F3
Haddon Cl. Mfield 112 A3
Haddon Cl. Wist 206 A4
Haddon Dr. Wid 12 B2
Haddon La. Nest 67 E2
Haddon Rd. Chea 34 B4
Haddon Rd. Nest 67 E1
Hadfield Cl. Wid 13 F1
Hadfield St. North 79 D1
Hadley Ave. Beb 43 E4
Hadlow La. Will 67 F4
Hadlow Rd. Will 67 F3
Hadrian Dr. Blacon 117 F3
Hadrian Way. Cudd 102 A1
Hafod Cl. Blacon 117 E2
Hafod Cl. Con Q 91 E1
Hag Bank La. Disley 38 B4
Hague Bar Rd. N Mills 39 D4
Hague Fold. N Mills 38 C4
Haig Ave. Gt San 15 D3
Haig Ave. Irlam 11 E2
Haig Ct. Knuts 57 E2
Haig Rd. Knuts 57 E2
Haig Rd. Wid 13 D1
Hale Ave. Poyn 36 B1
Hale Bank Rd. Wid 21 F3
Hale Gate Rd. Hale 21 F1
Hale Gate Rd. Wid 22 A2
Hale Gr. Gt San 15 D3
Hale Rd. Altr 32 B4
Hale Rd. Hale 21 D1
Hale Rd. Wid 22 B4
Hale St. Warr 16 A4
Hale View. Run 48 C4
Hale View Rd. Hels 73 E2
Halewood La Ends. Halew 21 D4
Haley Rd N. Burton 6 C3
Haley Rd S. Burton 6 C3
Half St. Mfield 112 B3
Halfacre La. Apple 17 F1
Halghton La. Penley 222 A1
Halifax Cl. Warr 8 B1
Halkett Cl. Chest 140 C3
Halkyn Rd. Chest 118 C2
Hall Ave. Wid 12 A1
Hall Cl. Mfield 87 E2
Hall Cl. Mfield 87 E2
Hall Dr. Alsag 193 E2
Hall Dr. Apple 26 B3
Hall Dr. Mars 79 D3
Hall Dr. Willas 205 E3
Hall Gr. Mfield 87 E2
Hall Hill. Boll 87 F4
Hall La. Antro 53 D1
Hall La. Apple 27 D4
Hall La. Audlem 230 B4
Hall La. Bo Hea 6 A2
Hall La. Brox 199 E4
Hall La. Cront 12 B4
Hall La. Dares 25 E1
Hall La. H Moss 186 B3
Hall La. H Winch 79 F2
Hall La. Kels 122 B3
Hall La. L Lei 77 F4
Hall La. Lost 79 F2
Hall La. Mobb 58 B2
Hall La. Part 11 F2
Hall La. Pick 55 D1
Hall La. S La E 112 C2
Hall La. Sand 174 A3
Hall La. Stret 52 C4
Hall La. Utkin 146 B3
Hall La. Warm 173 F2
Hall La. Winsf 149 D2
Hall La The. Eaton 147 E1
Hall Moss La. Ch Hul 35 E2
Hall Nook. Penk 14 C2
Hall O'shaw St. Crewe 190 C2
Hall Rd. Hay 1 C4
Hall Rd. Warr 17 E4
Hall Rd. Wilm 34 C2
Hall Rd. Wilm 60 A4
Hall St. Audley 209 E1
Hall St. Mfield 112 B4
Hall St. N Mills 39 D4
Hall St. Warr 16 B3
Hall Terr. Gt San 14 C4
Hall Wood Rd. Wilm 34 B2
Hall Wood Rd. Wilm 34 C1
Halla Way. Warr 16 C2
Hallastone Rd. Hels 73 E2
Hallcroft. Part 11 F2
Hallcroft Pl. Warr 17 D1
Hallefield Cres. Mfield 112 C4
Hallefield Dr. Mfield 112 C4
Hallefield Rd. Mfield 112 C4
Hallfield Dr. Elton 72 A2
Hallfield Park. El Por 69 E2
Hallfields Rd. Tarv 121 E1
Hallfields Rd. Warr 16 B4
Hallgreen La. Rad 155 E4
Halliday Cl. Warr 9 F2
Halliwell's Brow. H Legh 29 D2
Hallows Ave. Warr 16 B4
Hallows Cl. Kels 122 B2
Hallows Dr. Kels 122 B2
Hallowsgate Ct. Kels 122 B2
Halls Rd. Bidd 179 E1
Halls Rd. Sch Gr 195 E4
Hallsgreen La. Tford 96 C4
Hallshaw Ave. Crewe 190 C3
Hallwood Cl. Run 49 D3
Hallwood Dr. Will 68 B2
Hallwood Link Rd. Run 49 F3
Halsall Ave. Warr 16 B4
Halsall Cl. Run 50 B3
Halstone Av. Wilm 59 F2
Halton Brook Ave. Run 23 E1
Halton Cres. El Por 69 F1
Halton Ct. Run 23 E1
Halton Dr. Crewe 189 E3
Halton Link Rd. Run 49 F4
Halton Lodge Ave. Run 49 E4
Halton Rd. Chest 118 C3
Halton Rd. El Por 69 F1
Halton Rd. Gt San 14 B4
Halton Rd. Run 23 E1
Halton St. Hay 1 C3
Halton Station Rd. Run 49 F2
Halton View Rd. Wid 13 E1
Halton Way. El Por 69 F1
Hamble Dr. Penk 15 D2
Hamble Way. Mfield 86 C1
Hambledon Cl. El Por 69 D3
Hambleton Cl. Wid 12 B2
Hambleton Rd. Chea 34 B4
Hambleton Way. Winsf 149 D4
Hambletts Hollow. Norley 100 C3
Hamilton Ave. Hawa 116 A2
Hamilton Ave. Irlam 11 E2
Hamilton Cl. Hasl 191 E2
Hamilton Cl. Mfield 113 D4
Hamilton Cl. Nest 41 D1
Hamilton Pl. Chest 118 B1
Hamilton Rd. Con Q 91 E1
Hamilton Rd. Lymm 18 B2
Hamilton St. Chest 118 C2
Hammond St. Crewe 190 B2
Hamnet Ct. Warr 9 F2
Hampshire Cl. Congle 156 B2
Hampshire Rd. Part 11 E1
Hampshire Wlk. Mfield 86 C1
Hampson Ave. Cul 4 C2
Hampson Cres. Wilm 34 B2
Hampton Cl. Nest 66 C3
Hampton Cl. Wid 13 F2
Hampton Cres. Hamp 214 A2
Hampton Cres. Nest 66 C3
Hampton Ct. Run 24 B2
Hampton Dr. Cront 12 B3
Hampton Dr. Gt San 15 E2
Hampton Gdns. El Por 70 A3
Hampton Rd. Chest 140 C3
Hampton Rd. Irlam 11 E2
Hamsterley Cl. Warr 10 A3
Hanbury Cl. Wist 206 A4
Hancock Rd. Congle 156 C2
Hand St. Mfield 112 A4
Handbridge. Chest 141 E4
Handford Ave. Beb 43 F3
Handford Rd. Chest 118 C3
Handforth Cl. Warr 17 E2
Handforth La. Run 49 E3
Handforth Rd. Crewe 189 F2
Handforth Rd. Wilm 34 C1
Handley Hill. Winsf 149 E4
Handley St. Run 22 C2
Hangman's La. Lost 105 E4
Hankelow Cl. Chest 118 B2
Hankelow Cl. Middle 151 E3
Hankey St. Run 22 C1
Hankins Heys La. Buer 231 D1
Hankinson Cl. Part 11 F1
Hanley Cl. Disley 38 B3
Hanley Cl. Wid 12 B1
Hanley Rd. Wid 12 B1
Hanns Hall Rd. Will 67 E4
Hanover Dr. Winsf 149 E3
Hanover St. Warr 16 A2
Hapsford Cl. Warr 9 E2
Hapsford La. D-o-t-H 97 F4
Hapsford La. Elton 72 B2
Hapsford La. Elton 72 C1
Harbord St. Warr 16 B2
Harbour Cl. Run 50 B3
Harbour La. Warren 111 E1
Harburn Wlk. Wythe 33 F4
Harcourt Cl. Warr 9 F2
Harden Park. Wilm 60 A2
Harding Ave. Tatt 166 B1
Harding Ave. Warr 8 C1
Harding Rd. Chest 118 A4
Harding Rd. Nant 204 B2
Hardingswood Rd. Kids 194 C1
Hardknott Rd. Beb 43 F4
Hardwick Cl. H La 37 F3
Hardwick Dr. Mfield 112 A3
Hardwick Grange. Warr 17 F4
Hardwick Rd. Run 23 E2
Hardwicke Rd. Poyn 36 C2
Hardy Cl. El Por 69 F2
Hardy Cl. Wist 205 F4
Hardy Dr. Ch Hul 35 E4
Hardy Rd. Lymm 18 B1
Hardy St. Warr 16 A3
Hardy St. Warr 16 A4
Hare La. Chest 119 E2
Hare's La. Frod 73 F4
Harebell Cl. Hunt 142 A3
Harebell Gr. Kids 195 F1
Harecastle Ave. Kids 194 C1
Harefield Dr. Wilm 60 A3
Harefield Rd. Wilm 34 C2
Harewood Ave. El Por 69 E2
Harewood Cl. Winsf 126 A1
Harewood Way. Mfield 112 A3
Harfield Gdns. El Por 69 E3
Hargrave Ave. Crewe 189 F2
Hargrave Dr. El Por 69 F3
Hargrave La. Thor H 42 C3
Hargreaves Ct. Wid 13 E1
Hargreaves Rd. North 104 B4
Harington Cl. Chest 95 E1
Harington Rd. Chest 118 B4
Harlech Cl. Warr 7 F1
Harlech Ct. El Por 70 B2
Harlech Way. El Por 70 B2
Harlow Cl. Warr 17 E2
Harlyn Ave. Bram 35 F4
Harn The. El Por 69 E2
Harold Rd. Hay 1 C4
Harper Cl. Mfield 112 B3
Harper Gr. Congle 156 C2
Harpers Rd. Warr 9 D1
Harpur Cres. Alsag 193 D3
Harraps Pl. Mfield 112 A3
Harriet St. Crewe 190 C2
Harriet St. Irlam 11 F3
Harrington Dr. Warren 111 E1
Harris Cl. Crewe 173 D1
Harris Rd. Lost 80 A1
Harris St. Wid 13 E1
Harriseahead La. Kids 195 E2
Harrison Dr. Allos 107 D1
Harrison Dr. Hay 1 A3
Harrison Gr. Hawa 116 A2
Harrison Sq. Warr 7 F1
Harrison St. Wid 22 A3
Harrison Way. N-le-W 2 B2
Harrisons Pl. North 103 F4
Harrogate Cl. Beb 43 E2
Harrogate Rd. Beb 43 E2
Harrop Rd. Boll 88 B4
Harrop Rd. Run 23 D1
Harrow Cl. Apple 26 C3
Harrow Dr. Run 23 F1
Harrow Gr. Beb 43 F4
Harrow Rd. El Por 70 B2
Hartford Av. Wilm 59 F3
Hartford
Business Centre. Hart 102 C2
Hartford Cl. Sand 175 E4
Hartford Dr. El Por 69 F2
Hartford Mews. Hart 103 E3
Hartford Rd. Dave 103 F1
Hartford Way. Blacon 118 A1
Harthill La. Burw 183 F2
Harthill Rd. Blacon 117 F3
Harthill Rd. Burw 184 A3
Hartington Dr. Haz Gr 36 C4
Hartington Rd. Bram 35 F3
Hartington Rd. Chea 34 B4
Hartington Rd. H La 37 F4
Hartington St. Chest 141 F4
Hartland Cl. Poyn 36 B3
Hartland Cl. Wid 13 D3
Hartley Cl. Lymm 18 C2
Hartley Gr. Boll 87 F4
Harty Rd. Hay 1 A3
Harvard Cl. Run 24 B1
Harvard Ct. Warr 8 A2
Harvest Cl. Moult 126 C4
Harvest Rd. Mfield 87 E2
Harvey Ave. N-le-W 1 C2
Harvey Ave. Nant 205 D3
Harvey La. Gold 3 D4
Harvey Rd. Congle 157 D3
Harwood Gdns. Warr 17 D1
Haryngton Ave. Warr 15 F4
Haseley Cl. Poyn 36 C3
Haslemere Ave. Altr 32 B3
Haslemere Dr. Penk 14 B2
Haslemere Way. Crewe 190 B3
Haslin Cres. Christ 142 B4
Hassall Rd. Alsag 193 D3
Hassall Rd. Ha Gr 192 A4
Hassall Rd. Hasl 192 A4
Hassall Rd. Sand 175 E2
Hassall Way. Wilm 34 C3
Hastings Ave. Warr 8 A2
Hasty La. Altr 32 C4
Hasty La. Wythe 32 C4
Hatchery Cl. Apple 27 D2
Hatchings The. Lymm 18 C1
Hatchmere Cl. Sand 174 C4
Hatchmere Cl. Warr 15 F3
Hatchmere Dr. Chest 142 A4
Hatfield Ct. H Chap 130 A2
Hathaway Dr. Mfield 112 B3
Hatherton Cl. N-u-L 210 B1
Hatherton Rd. Hather 220 A3
Hatherton Way. Chest 118 B2
Hatley La. Frod 73 F4
Hatter St. Congle 156 C2
Hatton Ave. Beb 43 F2
Hatton La. Apple 26 A1
Hatton La. Hatt 26 A1
Hatton La. North 103 E3
Hatton La. Stret 26 A1
Hatton Rd. Blacon 117 F3
Hatton St. Mfield 112 B4
Havana La. Congle 157 D3
Havannah La. Eaton 156 C3
Havannah La. St Hel 1 A2
Havannah St. Congle 156 C2
Haven The. Crewe 190 B4
Havergal St. Run 22 C1
Havisham Cl. Warr 9 E3
Hawarden Gdns. El Por 70 B1
Haweswater Av. Crewe 173 D1
Haweswater Ave. Hay 1 A3
Haweswater Cl. Run 50 A3
Haweswater Dr. Winsf 126 B1
Hawk Rd. N Mills 39 F4
Hawk St. Sand 175 D3
Hawker Cl. Broug 139 E2
Hawkins La. Rain 88 B2
Hawkins Rd. Nest 41 F1
Hawks Ct. Run 49 F3
Hawks Way. Hes 40 C4
Hawkshaw Cl. Warr 9 E2
Hawkshead Rd. Burton 6 C3
Hawkstone Gr. Hels 73 E2
Hawley Dr. Altr 32 A4
Hawley La. Altr 32 A4
Hawley's Cl. Warr 7 F1
Hawley's La. Warr 8 A1
Haworth Ave. Congle 157 D3
Haworth Cl. Mfield 112 A3
Hawthorn Ave. N-le-W 2 B2
Hawthorn Ave. Nant 204 C3
Hawthorn Ave. Run 23 D1
Hawthorn Ave. Wid 13 D1
Hawthorn Ave. Wilm 60 A4
Hawthorn Bank. N Mills 39 D3
Hawthorn Cl. H Chap 130 B2
Hawthorn Cl. Winsf 126 B2
Hawthorn Dr. Irlam 11 E3
Hawthorn Gdns. Kids 210 B4
Hawthorn Gr. Ch Hul 35 E3
Hawthorn Gr. Crewe 190 B4
Hawthorn Gr. Warr 16 B1
Hawthorn Gr. Warr 16 B2
Hawthorn Gr. Wilm 60 A4
Hawthorn La. Beb 43 E4
Hawthorn La. Wilm 60 A4
Hawthorn La. Wist 189 F1
Hawthorn Park. Wilm 60 A4
Hawthorn Rd. Boll 87 F4
Hawthorn Rd. Chest 140 C3
Hawthorn Rd. Christ 142 C4
Hawthorn Rd. El Por 69 E3
Hawthorn Rd. N-u-L 210 C1
Hawthorn Rd. Nest 41 E1
Hawthorn Rd. Plum 80 C2
Hawthorn Rd. Weave 102 B4
Hawthorn Rise. Prest 86 C3
Hawthorn St. Wilm 60 A3
Hawthorn Terr. Wilm 60 A3
Hawthorn View. G Cit 116 A4
Hawthorn View. Wilm 60 A4
Hawthorn Way. Mfield 87 F1
Hawthorn Wlk. H Winch 79 E2
Hawthorn Wlk. Part 11 E1
Hawthorn Wlk. Wilm 60 A4
Hawthorne Ave. Audley 209 F1
Hawthorne Ave. Cul 5 E2
Hawthorne Ave. Gt San 15 D3
Hawthorne Ave. Warr 17 D4
Hawthorne Cl. Congle 156 A2
Hawthorne Cl. Hay 1 A3
Hawthorne Dr. Sand 175 E3
Hawthorne Dr. Will 43 D1
Hawthorne Gr. North 77 F2
Hawthorne Gr. Poyn 37 E2
Hawthorne Gr. Warr 16 C4
Hawthorne Gr. Winsf 127 D1
Hawthorne Rd. Warr 26 B4
Hawthorne St. Warr 16 A4
Hawthorns The. Bun 185 F4
Hawthorns The. North 103 E4
Hawthorns The. Tarp 146 B1
Hay Croft. Chea 34 C4
Haycastle Cl. Warr 7 F1
Haycroft Cl. El Por 69 E1
Haydock Cl. Chest 118 A1
Haydock La. Hay 1 B4
Haydock St. N-le-W 2 A2
Haydock St. Warr 16 A3
Haye's Rd. Irlam 11 F3
Hayes Cres. Frod 49 E1
Hayes Dr. North 78 B2
Hayes Pk. Chest 118 B2
Hayfield Cl. Mfield 87 D2
Hayfield Rd. N Mills 39 E4
Hayfield Rd. Warr 17 E4
Hayfields. Knuts 57 E2
Hayfields Gr. Audlem 229 F2
Hayhead Cl. Kids 195 D1
Hayhurst Ave. Middle 151 E4
Hayhurst Cl. North 103 F4
Hayle Cl. Mfield 86 B1
Hayling Cl. Crewe 190 A4
Haymakers Cl. Chest 140 C2
Haymakers Way. Saug 117 D4
Haymoor Green Rd.
Hay Gr 205 F2
Hayside Walk. Malpas 213 D2
Hayton St. Knuts 56 C1
Haywood Cres. Run 24 B1
Hazel Ave. Mfield 112 A3
Hazel Ave. Run 48 C4
Hazel Cl. El Por 69 F1
Hazel Cl. Kids 195 D2
Hazel Dr. Lymm 18 C1
Hazel Dr. Poyn 36 C2
Hazel Dr. Weave 102 B4
Hazel Dr. Winsf 149 E4
Hazel Dr. Wythe 34 A4
Hazel Gr. Alsag 194 A2
Hazel Gr. Crewe 190 B4
Hazel Gr. Gold 3 D4
Hazel Gr. Warr 17 D4
Hazel Rd. Chest 140 C3
Hazel St. Warr 16 B4
Hazel Wlk. Part 11 E1
Hazelbadge Cl. Poyn 36 B2
Hazelbadge Rd. Poyn 36 B2
Hazelborough Cl. Warr 10 A3
Hazelcroft. A Edge 85 D4
Hazelehurst Rd. Frod 74 B3
Hazelhurst Dr. Boll 88 A4
Hazelshaw La. Bre Gr 154 A2
Hazelwood Mews. Warr 17 E1
Hazelwood Rd. North 78 A2
Hazelwood Rd. Wilm 60 B4
Hazlemere Ave. Mfield 112 A3
Headland Cl. Gold 3 F3
Headlands The. Chest 118 C1
Heald St. N-le-W 1 C2
Healey Cl. Crewe 190 A4
Hearn's La. Burl 202 C3
Hearn's La. Fadd 202 C3

Heary St. Mfield 112 C3
Heath Ave. El Por 70 A1
Heath Ave. Sand 175 F3
Heath Ave. Sch Gr 193 F4
Heath Bank. Chest 119 E3
Heath Cl. Chest 142 A4
Heath Cl. Sand 175 E3
Heath Cl. Tarv 121 D1
Heath Ct. El Por 69 D3
Heath Dr. Run 49 D4
Heath Dr. Tarv 121 D1
Heath End Rd. Alsag 193 D3
Heath Gr. El Por 69 D4
Heath Green. Tarp 146 B2
Heath La. Allos 106 C3
Heath La. Chest 142 A4
Heath La. Croft 4 A1
Heath La. El Por 68 B4
Heath La. G Bud 54 A1
Heath La. Gold 3 E3
Heath La. H Legh 28 B3
Heath La. L Lei 77 D4
Heath La. Marb 226 C3
Heath La. Peo 106 C3
Heath La. Stoak 95 F4
Heath La. Will 68 B4
Heath Rd. Boll 87 F3
Heath Rd. Chest 118 B4
Heath Rd. Congle 156 A1
Heath Rd. Gt Bar 120 C3
Heath Rd. Penk 14 C3
Heath Rd. Run 23 D1
Heath Rd. Sand 175 E3
Heath Rd. Weave 77 F1
Heath Rd. Wid 12 C1
Heath Rd S. Run 48 C3
Heath St. Crewe 190 B2
Heath St. Gold 3 D4
Heath St. Warr 26 B4
Heath Terr. Chest 118 B4
Heath Way. Tarp 168 B4
Heathbank Rd. Chea 34 C4
Heathbrook. North 104 C4
Heathcote Gdns. North 104 B4
Heathcote St. Kids 195 D1
Heather Ave. Irlam 11 E3
Heather Brae. N-le-W 2 A2
Heather Cl. El Por 69 F2
Heather Cl. Mfield 112 B2
Heather Cl. Run 49 F2
Heather Cl. Warr 9 E3
Heather Ct. Chest 142 A4
Heather Wlk. Part 11 E1
Heatherfield Ct. Wilm 60 C4
Heathergate Pl. Wist 206 A4
Heathfield. Wilm 60 A3
Heathfield Ave. Crewe 190 B2
Heathfield Cl. Congle 155 F2
Heathfield Cl. Nant 204 C3
Heathfield Dr. N-u-L 210 B1
Heathfield Park. Warr 17 D1
Heathfield Rd. Audlem 230 A3
Heathfield Rd. El Por 70 A3
Heathfield Sq. Knuts 56 C1
Heathfields Cl. Chest 118 B2
Heathgate Ave. Speke 21 D1
Heathlands Rd. El Por 69 D4
Heathmoor Ave. Gold 3 E3
Heaths La. Utkin 123 E1
Heathside. Nant 204 C3
Heathview. Hasl 191 E2
Heathview Cl. Wid 22 A3
Heathview Rd. Wid 22 A3
Heathway. Hes 41 D4
Heathwood Dr. Alsag 193 D3
Heathwood Gr. Warr 17 D4
Heatley La. Sound 217 F2
Heatley Way. Wilm 34 B2
Heaton Cl. Middle 151 E3
Heaton Ct. Warr 9 F3
Heaton Sq. Winsf 149 E4
Heaward Cl. Shav 206 A2
Hebden Ave. Cul 5 D2
Heber's Cl. Malpas 213 E3
Hedge Hey. Run 24 A1
Hedge Row. Rain 63 E1
Hedgerow Dr. H Winch 79 E2
Heights The. Hels 73 E2
Helena Cl. Knuts 57 E1
Helford St. Congle 156 B2
Hellath View. Nant 204 C1
Hellyar-Brook Rd. Alsag 193 D2
Helmsdale. Gt San 15 E3
Helmsdale Cl. Crewe 190 A3
Helsby Ave. Beb 43 F2
Helsby Rd. Alva 73 E1
Helsby St. Warr 16 B3
Helsby Way. Wilm 34 B2
Helston Cl. Bram 35 F4
Helston Cl. Penk 14 C3
Helston Cl. Run 50 A3
Helston Gr. Chea 34 B4
Helton Cl. H Chap 130 A2
Hemlegh Vale. Hels 73 D1
Hemming St. North 78 B1
Hemmingshaw La. Small 176 A4
Hemsworth Ave. El Por 69 E3
Henbury Cl. Middle 151 E4
Henbury La. Ch Hul 34 C3
Henbury Pl. Run 49 D3
Henbury Rd. Wilm 34 B2
Henbury Rise. Henb 111 E4
Henderson Cl. Gt San 14 B3
Henderson Rd. Wid 22 C4
Henderson St. Mfield 112 B4
Hendon Cl. Crewe 190 C3
Henley Ave. Irlam 11 F3
Henley Cl. Apple 26 C3
Henley Cl. Nest 66 C3
Henley Ct. Run 23 E1
Henley Dr. Winsf 126 C1
Henley Rd. Chest 140 C3
Henley Rd. Nest 66 C3
Henrietta St. Congle 156 B2
Henry Pl. Chest 118 B1
Henry Rd. Crewe 190 B3
Henry St. Hasl 191 E2
Henry St. Lymm 18 C2
Henry St. Tarp 146 B1
Henry St. Warr 16 A3
Henry St. Wid 13 E1
Henshall Ave. Warr 16 C2
Henshall Dr. Sand 175 E4
Henshall Hall Dr. Congle 157 D1
Henshall La. Dun T 20 B3
Henshall Rd. Boll 87 F4
Henshall St. Chest 118 B2
Henshaw La. Sidd 110 C1
Hepherd St. Warr 15 E2
Hepley Rd. Poyn 37 D2
Herald Park. Crewe 190 C2
Heralds Cl. Wid 22 A4
Herbert St. Burton 6 C3
Herbert St. Congle 156 C2
Herbert St. Crewe 191 D3
Herbert St. Lost 80 A1
Herberts La. Hes 40 C4
Herdman St. Crewe 190 B1
Hereford Ave. El Por 94 C4
Hereford Ave. Gold 3 D4
Hereford Cl. Mfield 86 C1
Hereford Cl. Warr 17 E4
Hereford Dr. Wilm 34 C2
Hereford Pl. Blacon 118 A3
Hereward Rd. Chest 119 D1
Hermitage Ct. Saug 117 D4
Hermitage Dr. H Chap 130 B2
Hermitage Green La. Win 3 D1
Hermitage La. Cran 130 B4
Hermitage La. Goost 130 B4
Hermitage Rd. Saug 117 D4
Hermitage The. Hes 40 C4
Heron Cl. Broug 139 D2
Heron Cl. Farn 180 C1
Heron Cl. Knuts 57 D2
Heron Cl. Winsf 149 E3
Heron Cres. Crewe 190 C3
Heron Ct. Nest 66 B4
Heron Ct. North 79 E1
Heron Dr. Poyn 36 A2
Heron Pl. Chest 118 B2
Herrick Cl. Wist 206 A4
Hertford Cl. Congle 156 C2
Hertford Cl. Warr 17 F4
Hertford Gr. Irlam 11 E3
Hesketh Cl. Penk 14 C2
Hesketh Croft. Crewe 190 A4
Hesketh Dr. Lost 80 A2
Hesketh Meadow La. Gold 3 F4
Hesketh Rd. Hale 21 F1
Hesketh St N. Warr 15 E2
Hesnall Cl. Leigh 5 E4
Hessle Dr. Hes 40 C4
Heswall Ave. Cul 4 C2
Heswall Rd. El Por 69 E2
Hewitt Dr. Winsf 150 B4
Hewitt Gr. H Winch 79 F3
Hewitt St. Chest 118 C2
Hewitt St. Crewe 190 B1
Hewitt St. North 79 E1
Hewitt St. Warr 16 B2
Hewood Cl. N-le-W 7 E4
Hey Lock Cl. N-le-W 7 E4
Hey Shoot La. Cul 5 E3
Heybridge La. Prest 87 D3
Heyes Ave. Hay 1 B3
Heyes Dr. Lymm 18 B1
Heyes Farm Rd. Mfield 111 F4
Heyes La. A Edge 60 B2
Heyes La. Apple 26 C4
Heyes Park. Hart 102 C2
Heyes Rd. Wid 22 B4
Heyeswood La. Hart 103 D2
Heyfield Park Rd. El Por 69 D4
Heys Ave. Beb 43 E4
Heys The. Run 23 F1
Heysbank Rd. Disley 38 B3
Heysham Cl. Run 50 B3
Heysoms Ave. North 103 E4
Heysoms Cl. North 103 E4
Heythrop Dr. Hes 41 E4
Heywood Cl. A Edge 60 A1
Heywood Green. Crewe 206 B4
Heywood La. Roy Gr 234 B4
Heywood Rd. A Edge 60 A1
Heywood Rd. El Por 69 E3
Heywood St. Congle 156 B1
Heywoods Ridge. Audlem 229 F2
Hibbert St. N Mills 39 D3
Hibbert St. Wid 23 D4
Hibel Rd. Mfield 87 E1
Hickhurst La. Eaton 147 E2
Hickmore Heys. G Sutt 119 F3
Hickory Cl. Warr 17 F4
Hickson St. North 78 A2
Hidcote Cl. Wist 206 A4
Hield Gr. B Hen 79 E4
Hield La. B Hen 79 E4
Higginbotham Gn. Mfield 112 C3
High Bank Cl. Irlam 11 E3
High Bent Ave. Ch Hul 35 D3
High Cross. Clutt 182 B1
High Ct. Boll 88 A4
High Elm Dr. Altr 32 B4
High Elm Rd. Altr 32 B4
High Elms. Ch Hul 35 D3
High Field. L Boll 20 A1
High Hill Rd. N Mills 39 E4
High Lea Rd. N Mills 39 D4
High Legh Rd. Lymm 29 E4
High Lowe Ave. Congle 157 D2
High Meadow. Chea 34 C4
High St. Audley 210 A1
High St. Boll 88 A4
High St. Brough 140 C4
High St. Congle 156 B1
High St. Crewe 190 B2
High St. Dudd 145 E2
High St. Farn 180 C1
High St. Frod 49 D1
High St. G Bud 79 D4
High St. Gold 3 D4
High St. Hale 21 E1
High St. Kids 195 E2
High St. Kids 195 F1
High St. Kids 195 F3
High St. Kids 210 B3
High St. Malpas 213 D2
High St. Mfield 112 B3
High St. N Mills 39 E4
High St. N-le-W 2 B2
High St. Nant 204 C3
High St. Nest 66 C4
High St. Norley 100 C3
High St. North 103 F4
High St. Run 23 D1
High St. Sand 175 D3
High St. Sch Gr 195 E4
High St. Tarp 146 B1
High St. Tarv 121 E4
High St. Tatt 166 A1
High St. Warr 16 B3
High St. Weave 77 E1
High St. Winsf 126 B1
High View. Hels 73 E2
Higham Ave. Warr 7 F1
Highbank Cl. North 78 A2
Highbank Rd. Kings 75 E1
Highbank Rd. North 103 E4
Highcliffe Ave. Blacon 118 A2
Highcroft Ave. Congle 156 C1
Higher Ash Rd. Kids 210 B4
Higher Ashton. Wid 12 C2
Higher Carden La. Clutt 198 B3
Higher Downs. Knuts 57 E1
Higher Fence Rd. Mfield 87 F1
Higher Ferry. Sea 140 A4
Higher Heyes Dr. Kings 75 E1
Higher La. Boll 88 A3
Higher La. Dutt 51 E2
Higher La. L Han 64 C3
Higher La. Lymm 19 D1
Higher Rd. Halew 21 D3
Higher Rd. Wid 21 E3
Highfield. Elton 72 A2
Highfield. Prest 87 D3
Highfield Ave. Apple 26 B2
Highfield Ave. Audlem 230 A2
Highfield Ave. Gold 2 C4
Highfield Ave. Gt San 15 D3
Highfield Ave. Kids 195 D1
Highfield Ave. Lost 80 A2
Highfield Cl. Nest 66 C4
Highfield Cres. Wid 13 D1
Highfield Cres. Wilm 34 B1
Highfield Dr. Lymm 18 B1
Highfield Dr. Mfield 87 D1
Highfield Dr. Nant 205 D3
Highfield Estate. Wilm 34 B1
Highfield La. Codd 181 F2
Highfield La. Win 8 B4
Highfield Parkway. Ch Hul 35 E2
Highfield Pl. North 103 F4
Highfield Rd. Blacon 117 E3
Highfield Rd. Boll 88 A4
Highfield Rd. Chea 34 C4
Highfield Rd. Congle 156 C1
Highfield Rd. El Por 69 D3
Highfield Rd. El Por 70 B3
Highfield Rd. Lymm 18 B1
Highfield Rd. Mfield 112 B4
Highfield Rd. Nest 66 C4
Highfield Rd. North 103 F4
Highfield Rd. Poyn 36 A2
Highfield Rd. Wid 13 D1
Highfield Rd N. El Por 70 B3
Highfield Terr. N Mills 39 E4
Highfields. White 224 A1
Highgate Cl. Crewe 190 A4
Highgrove Mews. Wilm 60 A3
Highland Way. Knuts 82 A4
Highlands Rd. Run 48 C4
Highlands The. Bun 185 F4
Hightown. Crewe 190 B2
Hightown. Middle 128 B1
Hightown. Sand 175 D3
Hightree Dr. Henb 111 E4
Highwood Rd. Apple 26 B4
Hignett Ave. St Hel 1 A1
Hilary Ave. Chea 34 B4
Hilary Cl. Chest 119 D1
Hilary Cl. Gt San 14 B3
Hilary Cl. Wid 13 F2
Hilary Rd. Beb 43 F3
Hilary Wlk. Wythe 33 E4
Hilbre Bank. Alpr 169 E2
Hilden Rd. Warr 8 C1
Hill Cl. Nest 67 D3
Hill Cliffe Rd. Warr 26 A4
Hill Ct. Nest 67 D3
Hill Dr. Wilm 34 C2
Hill Farm Cl. Warr 8 C2
Hill Fields Cl. Congle 156 B2
Hill La. Brox 199 E4
Hill La. Burw 184 C3
Hill La. Peckf 184 C3
Hill Rd. Eccles 141 F1
Hill Rd N. Hels 73 E2
Hill Rd S. Hels 73 E2
Hill St. Crewe 190 B2
Hill St. Mfield 112 B3
Hill St. Run 23 D1
Hill St. Sand 174 B4
Hill St. Winsf 126 C1
Hill Terr. Audley 209 E1
Hill The. Ha Gr 175 E3
Hill The. Sand 175 E3
Hill Top. Altr 32 A4
Hill Top. North 78 A1
Hill Top Ave. Ch Hul 35 D4
Hill Top Ave. Wilm 60 A4
Hill Top Ave. Winsf 126 B1
Hill Top La. Hes 41 D4
Hill Top La. Nest 67 D3
Hill Top Rd. Act Br 76 C1
Hill Top Rd. Dutt 51 E1
Hill Top Rd. Warr 16 C1
Hill Top Rd. Warr 17 E4
Hill Top Rise. W Br 65 E4
Hill View. Boll 87 F4
Hill View. W Br 65 E4
Hill View. Wid 12 C3
Hill View Ave. Hels 73 D1
Hillary Ave. Congle 157 D1
Hillary Dr. Audlem 230 A2
Hillary Rd. Kids 195 D2
Hillberry Cres. Warr 16 A2
Hillbre Ave. Hes 40 C3
Hillbre Way. Wilm 34 B2
Hillbrook Rd. Ch Hul 35 E3
Hillcourt Rd. H La 37 F4
Hillcrest. Congle 156 B2
Hillcrest Ave. H Chap 130 A2
Hillcrest Dr. El Por 69 D3
Hillcrest Rd. Boll 87 F4
Hillcrest Rd. El Por 69 D3
Hillcrest Rd. Kels 122 C3
Hillcrest Rd. Warren 112 A2
Hillfield. Frod 74 A4
Hillfield. Run 50 B4
Hillfield Gdns. Nant 204 C2
Hillfield Pl. Nant 204 C2
Hillfield Rd. El Por 69 E4
Hillfield View. Nant 204 C2
Hillfields. Congle 156 B2
Hillfoot Cres. Warr 26 A4
Hillfoot La. Kings 74 C2
Hillingden Ave. Halew 21 D4
Hillock La. Warr 17 E4
Hillsboro Ave. Frod 74 B4
Hillside. North 103 E4
Hillside Ave. N-le-W 1 C1
Hillside Ave. Run 48 C4
Hillside Cl. Bram 36 A4
Hillside Cl. Disley 38 B3
Hillside Cl. Kids 195 E4
Hillside Ct. Mfield 88 A1
Hillside Dr. Crewe 190 C3
Hillside Dr. El Por 69 F4
Hillside Dr. Mfield 88 A1
Hillside Gr. Penk 14 C2
Hillside La. Moult 126 C4
Hillside Park. Knuts 57 E1
Hillside Rd. Apple 26 B2
Hillside Rd. Blacon 117 F2
Hillside Rd. Frod 74 B4
Hillside Rd. Hes 41 D4
Hillside Rd. Kels 122 B2
Hillside Rd. Knuts 57 D1
Hillside View. N Mills 39 D4
Hilltop Rd. G Sutt 119 F3
Hilltop Rd. Lymm 18 B1
Hillview Rise. North 78 C1
Hilton Ave. Gt San 15 D3
Hilton Cl. Mfield 111 F4
Hilton Cl. Middle 151 D4
Hilton Dr. Irlam 11 E3
Hilton Rd. N Mills 38 A4
Hilton Rd. Poyn 37 E3
Hinchley Cl. Hart 103 D2
Hind Heath La. Sand 174 C2
Hind Heath Rd. Sand 174 C2
Hinde St. Nant 204 B2
Hinderton Dr. Hes 40 C3
Hinderton La. Nest 67 D4
Hinderton Rd. Nest 66 C4
Hindle Ave. Warr 7 F1
Hindley Cres. North 78 A2
Hinton Cres. Apple 26 C4
Hinton Rd. Crewe 206 B4
Hinton Rd. Run 23 D1
Hitch Lowes. Chelf 84 A2
Hitchen's Cl. Run 50 B4
Hitchens La. Bulk 184 B1
Hob Hey La. Cul 4 B2
Hob La. D-o-t-H 97 E3
Hob La. Farn 180 C3
Hob La. Tford 97 E3
Hobart Cl. Bram 35 F2
Hobart Way. Blacon 117 E2
Hobb La. H Wal 25 E3
Hobbs Cl. Hasl 191 E2
Hobbs Hill La. H Legh 28 C1
Hobcroft La. Mobb 58 A4
Hobson St. Mfield 112 B3
Hockenhull Ave. Tarv 121 D1
Hockenhull Cres. Tarv 121 E1
Hockenhull La. Tarv 121 D1
Hocker La. N Ald 85 E2
Hockerley Ave. W Br 65 E4
Hockerley Cl. W Br 65 E4
Hockerley La. W Br 65 E4
Hockley Cl. Poyn 37 D2
Hockley Rd. Poyn 37 D2
Hodge La. Hart 103 D3
Hodge La. Weave 102 B3
Hodgehill La. Mart 132 C3
Hodgkingson Ave. Warr 7 F1
Hoghton Rd. Hale 21 F1
Hogshead La. Oak 124 B4
Holbein Cl. Chest 141 F3
Holbury Cl. Crewe 190 A4
Holcombe Ave. Gold 3 E4
Holcroft La. Cul 5 E1
Holden Pl. Warr 16 C4
Hole House La. L Lei 77 F2
Holehouse La. Adlin 62 B1
Holehouse La. S La E 113 E2
Holehouse La. Sch Gr 194 B4
Holes La. Warr 17 D4
Holford Ave. Lost 80 A2
Holford Ave. Warr 15 F4
Holford Cres. Knuts 57 D1
Holford Way. N-le-W 2 C2
Holgrave Cl. H Legh 29 E2
Holker Cl. Poyn 36 C2
Holland Cl. Sand 175 E3
Holland Rd. Bram 35 F4
Holland St. Crewe 190 A3
Holland St. Mfield 112 B4
Hollands La. Kels 122 B3
Hollands Pl. Mfield 112 C4
Hollands Rd. North 103 F4
Hollies La. Wilm 60 C4
Hollies Rd. Halew 21 D4
Hollies The. Moult 126 C4
Hollies The. Run 49 E4
Hollies The. Shav 206 A2
Hollin Green La. Burl 202 C3
Hollin Green La. Fadd 202 C3
Hollin La. New 228 B4
Hollin La. S La E 136 B3
Hollin La. Wilm 33 F3
Hollin Rd. Boll 88 A4
Hollingford Pl. Knuts 82 A4
Hollingreen La. New 229 D4
Hollins Cres. Kids 194 C1
Hollins Dr. Win 8 A3
Hollins Grange. Kids 210 B4
Hollins Hill. Utkin 146 C4
Hollins La. Antro 53 F2
Hollins La. Win 7 F3
Hollins Rd. Mfield 112 C3
Hollins Terr. Mfield 112 C3
Hollins Way. Wid 22 A3
Hollinshead Cl. Sch Gr 194 C4
Hollinwood Cl. Kids 210 C4
Hollinwood Rd. Disley 38 B3
Hollinwood Rd. Kids 210 C4
Hollow Dr. Warr 16 C1
Hollow La. Kings 75 D2
Hollow La. Knuts 57 D1
Hollow Oak La. Cudd 101 E2
Hollow The. Sch Gr 195 D3
Holloway. Run 22 C1
Hollowood Rd. Malpas 213 D3
Holly Ave. N-le-W 2 B2
Holly Bank Rd. Wilm 34 A1
Holly Bush La. Hol Gr 10 B1
Holly Cl. Con Q 91 E1

Holly Cl. Hale 21 E1
Holly Cl. M Traf 119 F4
Holly Ct. Hels 73 E3
Holly Dr. Winsf 149 E4
Holly Gr. Tab 56 A2
Holly Gr. Warr 17 D4
Holly La. Alsag 193 F2
Holly La. Kids 195 F3
Holly La. Wilm 33 F3
Holly Mount. Shav 206 C3
Holly Rd. Ch Hul 35 F3
Holly Rd. Chest 140 C3
Holly Rd. El Por 70 B3
Holly Rd. Gold 3 E4
Holly Rd. H La 37 F4
Holly Rd. Hay 1 A3
Holly Rd. Lymm 19 D3
Holly Rd. Mfield 112 A4
Holly Rd. N-u-L 210 C1
Holly Rd. Penk 14 C3
Holly Rd. Poyn 36 C2
Holly Rd. Weave 102 B4
Holly Rd N. Wilm 60 A3
Holly Rd S. Wilm 60 A3
Holly Terr. Penk 14 C3
Holly Terr. Tils 198 B2
Holly Tree Dr. Bidd 179 E1
Holly Tree Dr. Peo 106 B4
Holly Wlk. North 103 E4
Holly Wlk. Part 11 E1
Hollybank. Audlem 229 F2
Hollybank. Moore 25 D3
Hollybank Rd. Run 49 F4
Hollybush Cres. Willas 205 E3
Hollyfield Rd. El Por 70 A3
Hollyheath Cl. Sand 175 E3
Hollythorn Ave. Ch Hul 35 E4
Hollytree Rd. Plum 80 C2
Holm Cl. Christ 142 C4
Holm Dr. Elton 72 B2
Holm Oak Way. El Por 94 C4
Holme St. Tarv 120 C1
Holmes Chapel Rd. Allos 106 A2
Holmes Chapel Rd. Bre Gr 154 B4
Holmes Chapel Rd. Congle 156 A2
Holmes Chapel Rd. L Den 105 F2
Holmes Chapel Rd. Middle 128 C1
Holmes Chapel Rd. Oller 82 B2
Holmes Chapel Rd. Peo 82 B2
Holmes Chapel Rd. Rad 155 E2
Holmes Chapel Rd. Sand 153 F1
Holmes Chapel Rd. Sp Gr 129 E1
Holmes Chapel Rd. With 108 C3
Holmes Chapel Rd. With 109 D4
Holmes Ct. Warr 9 E2
Holmesville Ave. Congle 156 A2
Holmfield Ave. Run 23 E1
Holmfield Dr. Ch Hul 35 D4
Holmfield Dr. El Por 69 E2
Holmlea Dr. Crewe 190 C2
Holmlea Way. Prest 86 B3
Holmsfield Rd. Warr 16 B3
Holmshaw La. Hasl 192 A2
Holmwood Dr. El Por 70 A1
Holt Hey. Nest 67 D3
Holt La. Run 49 F4
Holt St. Crewe 190 A2
Holt's La. Wilm 33 F2
Holyhead Cl. Warr 7 E2
Holyrood Ave. Wid 13 D2
Holyrood Dr. Wist 205 F4
Holyrood Way. Chest 119 D1
Holywell Cl. Nest 41 D1
Holywell La. Clutt 182 B1
Home Farm Ave. Mfield 86 C1
Home Park. Moli 94 C1
Homecrofts. Nest 66 C3
Homestead Ave. Hay 1 C3
Homestead Rd. Disley 38 B3
Homesteads The. Ch Min 172 A3
Homeway. Hels 73 D1
Homewood Cres. Hart 103 D3
Honey Fields. Tarp 146 B1
Honey Suckle Cl. El Por 94 C4
Honeysuckle Cl. Broug 139 E2
Honeysuckle Cl. Wid 13 D2
Hong Kong Ave. Wythe 33 D4
Honister Ave. Warr 8 B1
Honiton Way. Penk 14 C2
Hood La. Gt San 15 E2
Hood La N. Gt San 15 E3
Hood Rd. Wid 12 C1
Hoofield La. Dudd 145 D1
Hoofield La. Hux 167 D4
Hoogreen La. H Legh 29 F1
Hoogreen La. Mere 29 F1
Hooker St. North 103 F4
Hookers Pl. Mfield 87 F2
Hookstone Dr. El Por 69 E3
Hoole Gdns. Chest 119 D2
Hoole La. Chest 119 D2
Hoole Rd. Chest 119 D2
Hooleyhey La. Mac For 89 E2
Hooleyhey La. Rain 89 E2
Hoolpool La. Hels 72 C3
Hooton Green. El Por 44 A1
Hooton La. El Por 44 A1
Hooton Rd. El Por 43 E1
Hooton Rd. Will 43 E1
Hooton Way. El Por 44 A1
Hooton Way. Wilm 34 B3
Hope Ave. Wilm 34 B2
Hope Croft. El Por 69 F1
Hope Farm Prec. El Por 69 F1
Hope Farm Rd. El Por 69 F1
Hope Green Way. Adlin 36 B1
Hope La. Adlin 36 B1
Hope La. Adlin 36 C1
Hope Rd. Broug 139 D2
Hope St. Audley 209 F2
Hope St. Chest 140 C4
Hope St. Crewe 190 B1
Hope St. Mfield 112 C4
Hope St. N-le-W 2 A2
Hope St. North 103 F4
Hope St. Sand 175 D3
Hope St W. Mfield 112 B4
Hopefield Rd. Lymm 19 D2
Hopwood St. Warr 16 B3
Horace Black Gdns. El Por 70 B3
Horace Lawton Ct. Congle 156 B2
Horbury Gdns. El Por 69 E3
Hornbeam Ave. El Por 69 F1
Hornbeam Cl. Run 24 B1
Hornbeam Rd. Halew 21 D4
Hornby Dr. Nant 205 D3
Hornby La. Win 8 A3
Horridge Ave. N-le-W 2 B3
Horrocks La. Warr 16 A3
Horrocks Rd. Chest 118 C3
Horsemarket St. Warr 16 A3
Horseshoe Cl. Kings 75 D1
Horseshoe Cres. Warr 8 C2
Horseshoe La. A Edge 60 A1
Horsley La. Beest 167 F1
Horstone Cres. El Por 69 F1
Horstone Gdns. El Por 70 A1
Horstone Rd. El Por 69 F1
Hospital La. Burl 203 F1
Hospital St. Crewe 190 B3
Hospital St. Nant 204 C3
Hospital Way. Run 49 F4
Hotel Rd. Wythe 33 E4
Hotel St. N-le-W 2 A2
Hothershall Cl. Crewe 173 D1
Hough Cl. Rain 88 B3
Hough Green. Ashl 31 F3
Hough Green. Chest 141 D4
Hough Green Rd. Wid 12 B2
Hough La. A Edge 60 B2
Hough La. Comb 78 A2
Hough La. North 78 A2
Hough La. Wilm 60 B2
Hough's La. H Wal 26 A3
Hougher Wall Rd. Audley 209 E1
Houghley Cl. Mfield 87 E1
Houghs La. Norley 100 C3
Houghton Cft. Cront 12 B3
Houghton Cl. Chest 118 C2
Houghton Cl. N-le-W 2 A2
Houghton St. N-le-W 2 A2
Houghton St. Warr 16 A3
Houghton St. Wid 13 E1
Houndings La. Sand 175 D3
Housesteads Dr. Chest 118 C2
Housman Cl. Blacon 118 A3
Hove Cl. Crewe 190 A4
Hove The. Run 50 B3
Hover Prec. N-le-W 2 A1
Howard Ave. Beb 43 E4
Howard Ave. Lymm 19 D2
Howard Ct. Run 24 B2
Howard Rd. Brough 140 B3
Howard Rd. Cul 5 D1
Howard St. Crewe 191 D3
Howards Way. Nest 67 D3
Howarth Ct. Run 23 D1
Howbeck Cres. Hay Gr 220 A4
Howbeck Wlk. Crewe 206 B4
Howe Rd. Chest 141 D4
Howe St. Mfield 87 F1
Howells Ave. El Por 69 E2
Howey Hill. Congle 156 B1
Howey La. Congle 156 B1
Howey La. Frod 74 A4
Howey Rise. Frod 74 A4
Howley La. Warr 16 C3
Howson Rd. Warr 8 B2
Howty Cl. Wilm 34 B1
Hoylake Cl. Run 50 B3
Hoyle St. Warr 15 F4
Hubert Dr. Middle 151 E4
Hudson Cl. Warr 15 E4
Hugh St. Chest 141 E4
Hughes Ave. Warr 8 B1
Hughes Pl. Warr 8 B1
Hughes St. Warr 16 B2
Hulley Pl. Mfield 87 F1
Hulley Rd. Mfield 87 F1
Hullock's Pool Rd. Audley 209 F3
Hulme Hall Ave. Ch Hul 35 D4
Hulme Hall Cres. Ch Hul 35 D4
Hulme Hall La. Allos 106 A2
Hulme Hall Rd. Ch Hul 35 D4
Hulme La. Allos 106 B4
Hulme La. Peo 106 B4
Hulme Sq. Mfield 112 B3
Hulme St. Crewe 189 F3
Hulse La. L Den 105 E3
Hulseheath La. Mere 30 A2
Humber Cl. Wid 13 F2
Humber Dr. Bidd 179 F1
Humber Rd. El Por 69 F1
Humber Rd. Warr 8 C1
Hume St. Warr 16 B3
Humphrey's Cl. Run 50 B4
Hungerford Ave. Crewe 190 C2
Hungerford Pl. Sand 175 D3
Hungerford Rd. Crewe 190 C2
Hungerford Terr. Crewe 190 C2
Hunsterson Rd. Bridge 220 A2
Hunsterson Rd. Hather 220 A2
Hunt Rd. Hay 1 C3
Hunter Ave. Shav 206 B4
Hunter Ave. Warr 8 A2
Hunter St. Chest 118 B1
Hunter's Cres. Tarv 121 E1
Hunter's Dr. Tarv 121 E1
Hunters Cl. Wilm 34 C1
Hunters Ct. Hels 73 E2
Hunters Ct. Run 49 F3
Hunters Field. North 103 E4
Hunters Hill. Kings 75 E1
Hunters Hill. Weave 77 E1
Hunters Mews. Wilm 60 B4
Hunters Rise. Winsf 126 B1
Hunters Way. Nest 66 B4
Hunters Wlk. Chest 118 B1
Hunterson Rd. Bridge 231 E4
Huntley St. Gt San 15 E2
Huntly Chase. Wilm 60 B4
Hunts Cl. Chest 119 D1
Hunts La. Warr 16 C1
Huntsbank Dr. N-u-L 210 B1
Huntsman Dr. Irlam 11 F4
Hurdsfield Cl. Middle 151 E4
Hurdsfield Green. Mfield 87 F1
Hurdsfield Ho. Mfield 87 F1
Hurdsfield Industrial Estate. Mfield 87 F2
Hurford Ave. El Por 69 F2
Hurlbote Cl. Wilm 34 B3
Hurlestone Cl. M Traf 96 C1
Hurley Cl. Gt San 15 E3
Hurn Cl. Crewe 190 A4
Hurst Ave. Ch Hul 35 E3
Hurst Cl. Kids 210 B3
Hurst Ct. Bun 185 F4
Hurst La. Boll 88 A4
Hurst La. Cul 5 D4
Hurst Lea Rd. N Mills 39 E4
Hurst Mews. Kings 75 E1
Hurst Mill La. Leigh 5 E4
Hurst Rd. Bidd 179 F2
Hurst St. Wid 23 D2
Hurst The. Kings 75 E1
Hursthead Rd. Ch Hul 35 D4
Hurstwood. Waver 143 D2
Hutchins' Cl. Middle 151 F3
Hutchinson St. Wid 23 D3
Huttfield Rd. Speke 21 D2
Hutton Cl. Congle 157 D1
Hutton Cl. Cul 4 C3
Hutton Dr. Congle 157 D1
Huxley Cl. Bram 35 F4
Huxley Cl. Mfield 87 D1
Huxley Ct. El Por 69 F4
Huxley Dr. Bram 35 F4
Huxley La. Hux 167 E3
Huxley La. Tiver 167 E3
Huxley St. North 103 F4
Hyacinth Cl. Hay 1 C3
Hyde Bank Rd. N Mills 39 E4
Hyde Cl. El Por 69 F2
Hyde Cl. Run 49 E3
Hylton Ct. El Por 70 C1
Hylton Dr. Bram 35 E4
Hythe Ave. Crewe 190 A4
Ian Rd. Kids 195 E1
Ikey La. Burl 202 C3
Ikins Dr. Audley 209 F1
Ilex Ave. Win 8 A4
Ilford Gdns. Apple 26 B2
Imperial Ave. Blacon 117 E2
Imperial Mews. El Por 70 A3
Ince Ave. Beb 43 F2
Ince Dr. Farn 180 C1
Ince La. Elton 72 A2
Ince La. Tford 96 C3
Ince Orch. Elton 72 A2
Ingersley Rd. Boll 88 B4
Ingham Ave. N-le-W 2 B1
Ingham Cl. Chest 119 D1
Ingham Rd. Wid 12 C2
Inglegreen. Hes 41 D4
Inglenook Rd. Penk 14 C2
Ingleton Cl. H Chap 130 A2
Ingleton Gr. Run 49 E3
Inglewood Ave. Middle 151 E3
Inglewood Cl. Warr 10 A3
Inman Ave. St Hel 1 A1
Innisfree Cl. El Por 69 E3
Insall Rd. Warr 8 C1
Intack La. H Legh 28 A2
Intake Cl. Will 68 A4
Inveresk Rd. Tils 198 B2
Ion Path. Winsf 127 E1
Irby Cl. El Por 69 F2
Ireland Rd. Hale 21 F1
Ireland Rd. Hay 1 B3
Ireland St. Warr 16 A4
Ireland St. Wid 13 E1
Iris Cl. Wid 12 B1
Iris Wlk. Part 11 F1
Ironbridge Dr. H Chap 130 B1
Irons La. Gt Bar 120 C4
Irvine Dr. Wythe 34 A4
Irving's Cres. Brough 140 C3
Irwell Gr. Warr 16 A1
Irwell La. Run 23 D2
Irwell Rise. Boll 87 F4
Irwell St. Wid 23 D2
Irwin Dr. Wilm 34 B3
Isherwood Cl. Warr 8 C2
Isis Cl. Congle 156 C1
Iveagh Cl. Run 50 A4
Iver Cl. Chest 118 C4
Iver Cl. Cront 12 B3
Iver Rd. Chest 118 B4
Ivy Dr. Cudd 102 A1
Ivy Farm Dr. Nest 66 C3
Ivy Farm Rd. Brox 183 E1
Ivy Gdns. Congle 156 B1
Ivy House Rd. Bidd 179 E1
Ivy La. Alsag 193 F1
Ivy La. Mfield 112 A3
Ivy Meade Cl. Mfield 111 F4
Ivy Meade Rd. Mfield 111 F3
Ivy Mews. Chest 119 D3
Ivy Rd. Gold 3 D4
Ivy Rd. Mfield 112 A4
Ivy Rd. Poyn 36 C2
Ivy Rd. Warr 17 F4
Ivy St. Run 23 D1
Ivy Wlk. Part 11 E1
Ivychurch Mews. Run 23 E1
Jack La. Moult 127 D3
Jack La. Weston 207 E3
Jackson Ave. Cul 4 C2
Jackson Ave. Nant 204 C3
Jackson Ave. Warr 16 C3
Jackson La. Boll 88 A4
Jackson Rd. Congle 156 C3
Jackson St. Burton 6 C3
Jackson St. Hay 1 A4
Jackson St. Mfield 112 B3
Jackson's La. Haz Gr 36 B4
Jacksons Edge Rd. Disley 38 A3
Jamage Rd. Kids 210 B3
James Ave. El Por 69 E2
James Cl. Wid 23 D2
James Hall St. Nant 204 C3
James Pl. Chest 118 C1
James Rd. Hay 1 C4
James St. Chest 118 B1
James St. Mfield 112 B3
James St. North 104 B4
James St. Warr 16 A3
Jamieson Cl. Alsag 193 F2
Jamieson Cl. Chest 119 D1
Jan Palach. Nant 204 C2
Jarman. S La E 112 C2
Jasmin Way. Kids 195 F1
Jasmine Gr. Wid 22 B4
Jasmine Wlk. Part 11 F1
Jay Cl. Warr 10 A2
Jays Cl. Run 50 C4
Jedburgh Ave. El Por 68 C3
Jellicoe Ave. Irlam 11 F3
Jennet's La. Leigh 5 E4
Jenny La. Woodf 35 F2
Jensen Ct. Run 23 E2
Jersey Ave. El Por 70 B1
Jersey Cl. Congle 157 D1
Jervis Cl. Warr 9 D2
Jesmond Cres. Crewe 190 A1
Jesmond Rd. Chest 118 A1
Jessop Way. Hasl 191 E2
Jockey St. Warr 16 A4
Jodrell Cl. H Chap 130 A2
Jodrell Cl. Mfield 112 C4
Jodrell Meadow. W Br 65 F4
Jodrell Rd. W Br 65 E4
Jodrell St. Mfield 112 C4
Jodrell St. N Mills 39 D4
John Brunner Cres. North 103 F3
John Fryer Ave. H Winch 80 A3
John Lloyd Cl. Irlam 11 F4
John May Ct. Mfield 87 E1
John Middleton Cl. Hale 21 F1
John Nicholas Cres. El Por 70 B3
John Rd. Lymm 18 B2
John St. Boll 88 A4
John St. Congle 156 B1
John St. Crewe 190 B2
John St. Crewe 190 B3
John St. El Por 70 A3
John St. Gold 3 D4
John St. Irlam 11 F3
John St. Mfield 112 B3
John St. Utkin 146 A4
John St. Warr 16 A3
John St. Winsf 126 B1
Johns Ave. Hay 1 C4
Johns Ave. Run 48 C4
Johns Cl. Rain 88 B3
Johnson Ave. N-le-W 2 A3
Johnson Cl. Congle 157 D1
Johnson St. W Br 65 F4
Johnson's La. Wid 23 F4
Johnsons Cl. Chest 141 D3
Jolley St. Warr 16 A3
Jonathan's Way. Blacon 117 F3
Jones's La. Bra Gr 152 B3
Jones's La. Sp Gr 152 B3
Jonson Rd. Nest 66 C4
Jordangate. Mfield 112 B4
Joseph Cres. Alsag 193 F1
Joseph St. Wid 13 E1
Joy La. Bo Hea 6 B2
Joyce Ave. Winsf 126 B1
Jubilee Ave. Crewe 190 A2
Jubilee Ave. Penk 14 C2
Jubilee Ave. Warr 16 C4
Jubilee Cres. Hay 1 C4
Jubilee Gdns. N Mills 39 E4
Jubilee Gdns. Nant 204 C2
Jubilee Gr. Lymm 18 B2
Jubilee Rd. Congle 156 C1
Jubilee St. N Mills 39 E4
Jubilee Terr. Nant 204 C2
Jubilee Villas. Ha Gr 175 E1
Jubilee Way. Wid 12 C1
Jubilee Way. Winsf 126 B1
Jubits La. Bo Hea 13 D4
Juddfield St. Hay 1 A4
Judy La. S La E 113 D2
Julian Way. Wid 12 C2
Jumper La. Rain 88 C4
Junction La. N-le-W 2 A2
June Ave. Beb 43 F4
Juniper Dr. El Por 69 F1
Juniper Gr. El Por 69 F1
Juniper La. Warr 18 A4
Juniper Rise. Mfield 86 C1
Justice St. Mfield 87 E1
K Edward Rd. Knuts 57 D1
Karen Cl. N-le-W 7 D3
Karen Way. El Por 69 E2
Kay La. H Legh 29 D4
Kaye Ave. Cul 4 C2
Keats Cl. El Por 94 C4
Keats Dr. Mfield 86 C1
Keats Dr. Wist 206 A4
Keats Gr. Warr 8 B1
Keats La. H Winch 80 A3
Keats Terr. Blacon 118 A3
Keble St. Wid 23 D4
Keckwick La. Dares 25 D2
Keckwick La. Run 24 C2
Keele Cres. Mfield 112 A3
Keeper's La. Weave 102 C4
Keepers Cl. Knuts 57 E2
Keepers La. Antro 53 E2
Keepers Wlk. Run 23 F1
Keith Ave. Gt San 14 C3
Keith Dr. Beb 43 E3
Kelburn Ct. Warr 9 F3
Kelsall Ave. Beb 43 F2
Kelsall Cl. Beb 43 F2
Kelsall Cl. Warr 9 E2
Kelsall Cl. Wid 12 B1
Kelsall Rd. Asht 121 F4
Kelsall Rd. Tarv 121 E2
Kelsall St. Congle 156 C2
Kelsall Way. Audley 209 E1
Kelsall Way. Wilm 34 B3
Kelsterton Ct. Con Q 91 E1
Kelsterton La. Con Q 91 D1
Kelsterton Rd. Con Q 91 D1
Kelvin Cl. Warr 9 E3
Kelvin Gr. Chest 118 C2
Kemberton Dr. Wid 13 D3
Kemble Cl. Wist 206 A4
Kemmel Ave. Warr 16 B2
Kempsell Way. Halew 21 D4
Kempton Ave. Crewe 190 B4
Kempton Cl. Chest 118 A1
Kempton Cl. N-le-W 2 B3
Kempton Cl. Run 49 E3
Kendal Ave. Warr 8 B1
Kendal Cl. Chest 119 D3
Kendal Cl. El Por 69 E1
Kendal Cl. Mfield 111 F3
Kendal Ct. Congle 156 A1
Kendal Dr. Ch Hul 35 E3
Kendal Dr. El Por 69 F1
Kendal Rd. Mfield 111 F3
Kendal Rd. Wid 12 B1
Kendal Rise. Run 49 E3
Kendrick St. Warr 16 A3
Kenilworth Ave. Knuts 57 E1
Kenilworth Ave. Run 49 D4
Kenilworth Ave. Wilm 34 B2
Kenilworth Cl. Mfield 111 F3
Kenilworth Cl. Wist 206 A4

Kenilworth Ct. El Por 70 C1
Kenilworth Dr. Haz Gr 36 B4
Kenilworth Dr. Warr 16 C4
Kenilworth Gdns. N-le-W 2 B1
Kenilworth Green. Mfield 111 F3
Kenilworth Rd. Gold 3 F4
Kenilworth Rd. Mfield 111 F3
Kenilworth Rd. Nest 66 C3
Kenley Ave. Cront 12 B3
Kenmare Bank. North 104 A3
Kenmore Gr. Irlam 11 E3
Kennedy Ave. Mfield 86 C1
Kennedy Cl. Chest 119 D3
Kennel La. Cudd 102 A1
Kennelwood Rd. Comb 78 B4
Kennerley's La. Wilm 60 A4
Kennet Dr. Congle 156 C1
Kennet Rd. Hay 1 B3
Kenneth Rd. Wid 22 B4
Kenrick Cl. Woore 232 B1
Kensington Ave. Warr 17 E1
Kensington Cl. Chest 141 D3
Kensington Cl. Alsag 192 C2
Kensington Ct. Wilm 60 A3
Kensington Ct. Winsf 149 E4
Kensington Green. Chest 140 C3
Kensington Rd. Chest 141 D3
Kensington Rd. El Por 70 A3
Kent Ave. Boll 87 F3
Kent Cl. Beb 43 D4
Kent Gr. Run 23 D1
Kent Rd. Chest 118 C3
Kent Rd. Gt San 15 E2
Kent Rd. Irlam 11 E3
Kent Rd. Part 11 F1
Kent St. Warr 16 B2
Kent St. Wid 13 D1
Kent Wlk. Mfield 86 C1
Kent Wlk. N-le-W 2 B1
Kent's Green La. Hasl 191 F4
Kent's La. Crewe 173 E1
Kentmere Ave. Winsf 126 B1
Kenton Rd. Halew 21 D4
Kentridge Dr. El Por 69 E2
Kentwell Dr. Mfield 87 E2
Kenview Cl. Wid 22 A2
Kenwood Ave. Ch Hul 35 E3
Kenyon Ave. Penk 14 C3
Kenyon La. Croft 3 F2
Kenyon's La. Hay 1 C4
Kerfoot St. Warr 16 A4
Keristal Ave. Chest 142 A4
Kerridge Cl. Middle 151 D4
Kerridge Rd. Mfield 88 A2
Kerry Cft. El Por 69 F1
Kershaw St. Wid 12 B1
Kestrel Ave. Knuts 57 D2
Kestrel Cl. Middle 151 E3
Kestrel Cl. Winsf 149 E3
Kestrel Dr. Crewe 190 A4
Kestrel La. Warr 9 F2
Kestrel Rd. Hes 41 E4
Kestrel Rd. North 103 E4
Kestrels Way. Run 49 F3
Keswick Ave. Beb 43 E2
Keswick Ave. Mfield 111 F3
Keswick Ave. Warr 8 B1
Keswick Cl. Chest 119 D3
Keswick Cl. Crewe 189 F2
Keswick Cl. Irlam 11 E2
Keswick Cl. Mfield 111 F3
Keswick Cl. Wid 12 B1
Keswick Cl. Winsf 126 B1
Keswick Cres. Warr 8 B1
Keswick Ct. Congle 156 A1
Keswick Dr. Ch Hul 35 E3
Keswick Dr. Frod 74 B4
Keswick Rd. H La 37 F4
Ketlan Ct. Brough 140 C4
Kettell Ave. Crewe 190 A3
Kettle La. Audlem 230 B1
Kettleshulme Way. Poyn 37 D2
Kettleshulme Wlk. Wilm 34 C1
Keyes Cl. Warr 9 F2
Keyes Gdns. Warr 9 F2
Keysbrook. Tatt 166 B1
Keysbrook Ave. Tatt 166 B1
Kidderton Cl. Fadd 202 C4
Kidderton La. Burl 202 C4
Kidderton La. Fadd 202 C4
Kidsgrove Bank. Kids 195 D1
Kilbuck La. Hay 2 A4
Kilburn Ave. Beb 43 F3
Kilburn Cl. Chea 34 A4
Kildare Cl. Hale 21 E1
Kildonnan Rd. Warr 17 D1
Kilford Cl. Warr 7 F1
Killingworth La. Warr 10 A3
Kilmorey Pk. Chest 118 C2
Kilmorey Pk Ave. Chest 118 C2
Kilmorey Pk Rd. Chest 118 C2
Kiln La. Hay Gr 220 A4
Kilncroft. Run 50 A3
Kilsby Dr. Wid 13 F1
Kilshaw Rd. Burton 6 C3
Kilsyth Cl. Warr 8 C2
Kimberley Dr. Warr 16 B1
Kimberley St. Warr 15 F3
Kimberley Terr. Chest 118 C1
Kinder Dr. Crewe 189 E2
Kinder View. N Mills 39 E4
Kinderton Cl. H Legh 29 E2
Kinderton St. Middle 128 B1
King Arthur's Wlk. Run 24 A1
King Edward Rd. Mfield 112 B4
King Edward St. Mfield 112 B4
King Edward St. Middle 128 B1
King Edward St. Warr 16 C4
King George Ave. North 104 A4
King George Cres. Warr 16 C4
King George Rd. Hay 2 A4
King James Ct. Run 49 F3
King Pl. Nant 204 C3
King St. Audley 209 E1
King St. Chest 118 B1
King St. Congle 156 C2
King St. Crewe 190 B2
King St. El Por 70 B3
King St. Hart 103 D3
King St. Kids 195 D1
King St. Kids 210 B3
King St. Knuts 57 D1
King St. L Den 104 C3
King St. Mfield 112 C4
King St. Middle 128 A3
King St. N-le-W 2 A2
King St. North 104 C3
King St. Run 23 D2
King St. Sand 174 C4
King's Ave. Gold 3 F4
King's Cres. Middle 128 B1
King's Cres E. Chest 119 D1
King's Cres W. Chest 119 D1
King's La. Cran 106 B1
King's La. L Den 106 B1
King's La. Nant 204 B3
King's Rd. Wilm 59 F4
Kingfisher Cl. Farn 180 C1
Kingfisher Cl. Run 49 F3
Kingfisher Cl. Warr 9 F2
Kingfisher Ct. North 79 E1
Kingfisher Dr. Winsf 149 E3
Kingfisher Gr. H Winch 79 F3
Kingham Cl. Wid 13 E1
Kings Cl. Chest 140 C3
Kings Cl. Wilm 60 A3
Kings Ct. Run 24 B2
Kings Dr. Hels 73 D2
Kings Dr. Wist 205 F4
Kings La. Eaton 147 E2
Kings Meadow. Run 50 B4
Kings Rd. Con Q 91 E1
Kings Rd. El Por 69 E4
Kings Rd. Gold 3 D4
Kings Rd. Irlam 11 F3
Kings Rd. Warr 9 D1
Kingsdale Rd. Gt San 14 C4
Kingsdale Rd. Gt San 15 D4
Kingshead Cl. Run 24 A1
Kingsley Ave. Beb 43 F2
Kingsley Ave. Wilm 34 B1
Kingsley Cl. Hart 103 E3
Kingsley Cl. Kids 210 B3
Kingsley Cres. Run 23 D1
Kingsley Dr. Apple 26 B4
Kingsley Dr. North 104 A3
Kingsley Gdns. Chest 142 A4
Kingsley Green. Kings 74 C3
Kingsley Rd. Chest 142 A4
Kingsley Rd. Congle 157 D2
Kingsley Rd. Crow 76 A1
Kingsley Rd. El Por 70 B3
Kingsley Rd. Frod 74 C2
Kingsley Rd. Hasl 191 E2
Kingsley Rd. Kids 210 B3
Kingsley Rd. Kings 74 C2
Kingsley Rd. Run 23 D1
Kingsley Wlk. Winsf 126 A1
Kingsmead. Chest 118 B4
Kingsmead Ct. Croft 9 D4
Kingston Ave. Gt San 14 C3
Kingston Ave. Mfield 112 C4
Kingston Cl. Run 23 F1
Kingston Pl. Bidd 179 F1
Kingston Rd. Wilm 34 B3
Kingsway. Boll 87 F4
Kingsway. Chest 118 C3
Kingsway. Crewe 190 A1
Kingsway. Frod 74 A4
Kingsway. Hes 41 E3
Kingsway. N-le-W 2 B1
Kingsway. North 104 A4
Kingsway. Wid 13 D1
Kingsway. Winsf 126 C1
Kingsway N. Warr 16 C3
Kingsway S. Warr 16 C2
Kingsway W. Chest 118 C2
Kingswood. Kids 195 D1
Kingswood. Poyn 36 C2
Kingswood Ave. Saug 94 B1
Kingswood Cres. Middle 151 F3
Kingswood La. Saug 94 B1
Kingswood Rd. Warr 7 D1
Kingswood Wlk. Kels 122 B3
Kinloch Cl. Crewe 190 A3
Kinloch Cl. Halew 21 D4
Kinnerley Rd. El Por 70 A2
Kinnersley Ave. Kids 210 C4
Kinnersley St. Kids 195 D1
Kinnerton Cl. Brough 140 C3
Kinnerton Heights. H Kin 161 D4
Kinnerton La. H Kin 161 D4
Kinnock Parr. Burton 6 C3
Kinross Cl. Warr 8 C2
Kinsale Dr. Warr 9 E2
Kinsey Rd. El Por 70 B1
Kinsey St. Congle 156 C1
Kintore Cl. Beb 43 E2
Kintore Dr. Gt San 14 B3
Kipling Ave. Warr 8 B1
Kipling Cres. Wid 22 C4
Kipling Rd. Blacon 117 F3
Kipling Way. Crewe 190 C2
Kirby Cl. Chest 118 B3
Kircaldy Ave. Gt San 14 B3
Kirkacre Ave. N-le-W 7 E4
Kirkby Rd. Cul 4 C2
Kirkfell Dr. H La 37 F4
Kirkham Ave. Gold 3 F3
Kirkham Cl. Gt San 15 D2
Kirkham Rd. Chea 34 B4
Kirkham Rd. Wid 13 E1
Kirkstall Cl. Mfield 87 D1
Kirkstall Dr. Poyn 36 B2
Kirkstead Rd. Ch Hul 35 E3
Kirkstone Ave. Warr 8 B1
Kirkstone Cres. Run 50 A2
Kirkstone Ct. Congle 156 A1
Kirkwall Dr. Penk 15 D2
Kirkwood Cl. Chest 119 D1
Kishfield La. Kettle 65 D3
Kitchen St. Chest 118 A1
Kitchener Ave. Irlam 11 E2
Kitfield Ave. Middle 151 E4
Kitt's Moss La. Ch Hul 35 E3
Knap The. Hes 41 D3
Knight Rd. Burton 6 C3
Knight St. Mfield 112 C4
Knight's Cl. Mfield 112 C4
Knights La. Utkin 123 F1
Knights Meadow. Winsf 126 B2
Knights Way. Shav 206 A2
Knightsbridge Ave. Warr 17 E1
Knightwake Rd. N Mills 39 D4
Knole Ave. Poyn 36 C2
Knoll St. N Mills 39 D4
Knoll The. Run 49 F4
Knottingley Dr. El Por 69 E3
Knotty La. Bidd 179 F4
Knowe The. Will 68 A4
Knowl Hey Rd. Halew 21 D3
Knowl La. Farn 180 C3
Knowl The. Farn 180 C3
Knowle Cl. El Por 69 F2
Knowle Green. Wilm 34 B2
Knowle Park. Wilm 34 B2
Knowles St. Wid 13 E1
Knowsley Ave. Gold 3 E4
Knowsley La. Law-g 194 C2
Knowsley Rd. Chest 118 C2
Knowsley Rd. Haz Gr 36 C4
Knowsley Rd. Mfield 112 B3
Knutsford Rd. Antro 53 E2
Knutsford Rd. Apple 27 F4
Knutsford Rd. Chelf 84 A1
Knutsford Rd. Cran 130 A3
Knutsford Rd. G Bud 54 A1
Knutsford Rd. H Chap 130 A3
Knutsford Rd. L End 59 E1
Knutsford Rd. Law-g 193 F3
Knutsford Rd. Mobb 57 F2
Knutsford Rd. Mobb 58 C2
Knutsford Rd. Sch Gr 193 F3
Knutsford Rd. Warr 16 B2
Knutsford Rd. Wilm 59 F2
Knutsford Rd Wlk. Mfield 112 C4
Knutsford View. Altr 32 B4
Knutsford Way. Blacon 117 F1
Kohima Cres. Hunt 142 A3
Kronsbec Ave. El Por 69 E3
Kynaston Dr. Brough 140 A4

Labelia Wlk. Part 11 E1
Labernum Farm Cl. Nest 67 D3
Laburnam Cl. Congle 156 A2
Laburnam Cl. Kids 210 C4
Laburnum Ave. Nant 204 C3
Laburnum Ave. Warr 17 E4
Laburnum Ave. Wist 189 F1
Laburnum Cres. North 78 A2
Laburnum Gr. Brough 140 C3
Laburnum Gr. Crewe 190 B3
Laburnum Gr. El Por 95 D4
Laburnum Gr. Run 49 E4
Laburnum Gr. Weave 102 B4
Laburnum La. Altr 31 F4
Laburnum La. Penk 14 B3
Laburnum Pl. N-u-L 210 B1
Laburnum Rd. Dave 103 F2
Laburnum Rd. Gold 3 F4
Laburnum Rd. Irlam 11 E3
Laburnum Rd. Mfield 112 C3
Laburnum Rd. North 104 B3
Laburnum Way. Holt 180 B1
Lacey Ave. Wilm 34 A1
Lacey Ct. Wid 23 D4
Lacey Ct. Wilm 34 A1
Lacey Gr. Wilm 34 B1
Lacey Green. Wilm 34 A1
Lacey St. Wid 23 D4
Lache Hall Cres. Chest 140 C2
Lache La. Chest 141 D3
Lache La. Dodle 140 C2
Lache Park Ave. Chest 141 D3
Ladies Mile. Knuts 56 C1
Ladies Walk. Nest 66 C4
Lady Helen Wlk. Nant 204 C3
Lady La. Croft 9 E4
Lady Lane. Mobb 58 B4
Ladybarn Cr. Bram 35 F3
Ladybrook Gr. Wilm 34 B1
Ladycroft Cl. Warr 17 F4
Ladyfield St. Wilm 60 A4
Ladyfield Terr. Wilm 60 A4
Ladypit Rd. N Mills 39 F2
Ladypool. Hale 21 E1
Ladys Cl. Poyn 36 C2
Ladythorn Cres. Bram 35 F3
Ladythorn Gr. Bram 35 F4
Ladythorn Rd. Bram 35 F3
Ladywood Rd. Warr 7 E1
Lagos Gr. Winsf 126 C1
Laira St. Warr 16 B4
Lake House Cl. Weave 77 E1
Lake La. Whit 52 C3
Lake View. Congle 156 A1
Lakelands Cl. Mfield 112 C4
Lakeside. Bosl 158 B4
Lakeside Cl. Wid 22 A4
Lakeside Dr. Poyn 36 C3
Lakeside Dr. Warr 16 A2
Lakeside Rd. Lymm 18 B1
Laleston Cl. Wid 22 C4
Lamb La. Ashl 31 E3
Lamb St. Kids 195 D1
Lambert Ct. Wid 23 D4
Lambert Way. Hart 103 D2
Lambert's La. Congle 156 C1
Lamborne Gr. Middle 128 B1
Lambourn Ave. Cront 12 B3
Lambourn Cl. Poyn 36 B2
Lambourn Dr. Crewe 173 D1
Lambourne Cl. El Por 94 C4
Lambourne Cl. Wythe 33 E4
Lambourne Gr. St Hel 1 A2
Lambs La. Warr 17 D4
Lambsickle Cl. Run 48 C3
Lambsickle La. Run 49 D3
Lampeter Cl. Warr 7 F1
Lamport Cl. Wid 13 F2
Lanark Wlk. Mfield 86 C1
Lancashire Rd. Part 11 F1
Lancaster Ave. Gold 3 E4
Lancaster Ave. Run 48 C4
Lancaster Ave. Wid 12 A1
Lancaster Cl. Haz Gr 36 B4
Lancaster Cl. N-le-W 1 C2
Lancaster Cl. Winsf 149 E3
Lancaster Ct. Mfield 112 C4
Lancaster Dr. Chest 119 D1
Lancaster Fields. Crewe 191 D1
Lancaster Gdns. El Por 70 B2
Lancaster Park. Broug 139 D2
Lancaster Rd. Irlam 11 E3
Lancaster Rd. Wid 13 D2
Lancaster Rd. Wilm 34 C1
Lancaster St. Warr 15 F3
Lancelyn Dr. Wilm 60 B4
Lancer Ct. Run 23 F2
Lancers Cft. El Por 69 F1
Lancing Ave. Warr 8 A2
Lancing Rd. El Por 70 B2
Land Cut La. Warr 9 E2
Land La. Wilm 60 B3
Lander Cl. Gt San 15 E4
Landscape Dean. Hels 73 E2
Landsdowne St. Mfield 87 F1
Landseer Ave. Nest 66 C4
Landseer Ave. Warr 16 A1
Landseer Dr. Mfield 111 F4
Landswood Park. Hart 103 D2
Lane Head Ave. Gold 3 F4
Lane Head Rd. W Br 65 E3
Lane The. White 223 E2
Lane The. Willi 223 E2
Laneside Rd. N Mills 39 F4
Langcliffe Cl. Cul 4 C2
Langdale Ave. Lymm 18 C2
Langdale Cl. H La 37 F4
Langdale Cl. Mfield 111 F3
Langdale Cl. Warr 8 C1
Langdale Cl. Wid 22 B4
Langdale Cl. Winsf 126 B1
Langdale Ct. Congle 156 A1
Langdale Rd. Ch Hul 35 E3
Langdale Rd. Part 11 F2
Langdale Rd. Run 23 D1
Langdale Way. Frod 49 E1
Langfield. Gold 3 F4
Langfield Gr. Beb 43 E3
Langford. Hale 21 E1
Langford Ct. Tarv 121 E1
Langford Rd. Lost 80 A2
Langford St. Mfield 112 B4
Langland Cl. Warr 7 F1
Langley Ave. N-le-W 2 B1
Langley Cl. Gold 3 E4
Langley Cl. Sand 175 E4
Langley Ct. El Por 70 C2
Langley Dr. Wilm 34 C2
Langley Hall Cl. S La E 113 D2
Langley Rd. North 104 A3
Langley Rd. S La E 113 D2
Langport Dr. Chest 119 E1
Langton Cl. Wid 12 A2
Langton Green. Warr 17 E4
Langwell Cl. Warr 10 A3
Lanham Wlk. Wythe 33 E4
Lanreath Cl. Mfield 86 B1
Lansdown Cl. Ch Hul 35 E4
Lansdown Rd. Broug 139 D2
Lansdowne. Cul 4 C2
Lansdowne. Frod 74 B3
Lansdowne Gr. Chest 141 D4
Lansdowne Rd. Con Q 91 E1
Lansdowne Rd. Crewe 190 C3
Lansdowne Rd. Gt Bar 120 B2
Lapwing Cl. Winsf 149 E3
Lapwing Gr. Run 50 A3
Lapwing La. Penk 25 D4
Lapwing La. With 109 E3
Larch Ave. Mfield 112 A3
Larch Ave. N-le-W 2 B1
Larch Ave. Penk 14 C3
Larch Ave. Shav 206 C3
Larch Ave. Wid 13 D1
Larch Cl. Gold 3 F3
Larch Cl. Poyn 36 C2
Larch Cl. Run 49 E4
Larch Cl. Weave 102 B4
Larch Rd. Hay 1 C4
Larch Rd. Part 11 F2
Larch Rd. Run 49 E4
Larch Rd. Wist 189 F1
Larch Rise. Prest 86 B3
Larch Way. Brough 140 C3
Larchdale Cl. El Por 94 C4
Larchfields. Saug 117 D4
Larchtree Cl. North 78 A2
Larchway. Ch Hul 35 E4
Larchway. H La 37 F4
Larchways. Apple 26 B3
Larchwood Dr. Wilm 60 C4
Lark Hall Cl. Mfield 113 D4
Lark Hall Cres. Mfield 113 D4
Lark Hall Rd. Mfield 113 D4
Larkfield. Kids 195 D1
Larkfield Ave. Warr 17 D3
Larkspur Cl. Chest 140 C2
Larkspur Cl. Run 49 F2
Larkstoke Cl. Apple 26 C3
Larksway. Hes 41 D4
Lasky La. Warr 17 F2
Latchford Rd. Hes 41 D3
Latchford St. Warr 17 D2
Latham Ave. Hels 73 D1
Latham Ave. N-le-W 2 B2
Latham Ave. Run 23 E1
Latham Ave. Warr 16 A4
Latham Rd. Sand 175 D3
Latham St. Winsf 126 B1
Lathom Rd. Irlam 11 F4
Lathom Way. Mfield 87 F1
Launceston Cl. Run 50 B3
Launceston Cl. Winsf 149 D4
Launceston Dr. Ram 35 F4
Launceston Dr. Penk 14 C2
Laura St. Crewe 190 B1
Laurel Ave. N-le-W 2 B2
Laurel Ave. Warr 17 E4
Laurel Bank. Warr 17 E1
Laurel Bank. Wid 13 D2
Laurel Bank. Winsf 149 E4
Laurel Cl. North 78 A2
Laurel Cl. Sand 175 E3
Laurel Dr. El Por 70 A1
Laurel Dr. Gold 3 E4
Laurel Dr. Kids 195 F2
Laurel Dr. Will 43 D1
Laurel Dr. Wist 189 F1
Laurel Gr. Chest 119 D2
Laurel Park. Dudd 145 D3
Laurel Way. Ch Hul 35 E4
Laurel Wlk. Part 11 F1
Laureston Ave. Crewe 190 C2
Lavender Cl. Run 23 E1
Lavender Dr. North 104 C4
Lavender Wlk. Part 11 E1
Lavenham Cl. Haz Gr 36 C4
Lavenham Cl. Mfield 87 E1
Law St. Chest 118 C2
Lawford Cl. Crewe 189 F4
Lawford Dr. Hes 41 E4
Lawn Ave. Warr 16 C4
Lawn Dr. Chest 118 B4
Lawns Ave. Beb 43 D3
Lawnsdale. Cudd 101 E3
Lawnswood Gr. Elton 72 A2
Lawrence Ave. Moult 126 C4
Lawrence Ave E. Middle 128 B1

Lawrence Ave W. Middle 128 B1
Lawrence Pl. Poyn 36 B1
Lawrence St. Crewe 190 B2
Lawrence St. Hawa 116 A2
Lawrence St. N-le-W 2 A2
Lawson Cl. Warr 17 F4
Lawton Ave. Bram 35 F4
Lawton Ave. Law-g 194 B2
Lawton Coppice. Law-g 194 C2
Lawton Heath Rd. Law-g 193 F3
Lawton Rd. Alsag 193 F2
Lawton St. Congle 156 C1
Lawton St. Crewe 190 B2
Lawton St. Kids 195 E2
Lawton Way. Sand 174 C4
Lawtongate Estate. Law-g 194 A2
Laxey Ave. Warr 17 E3
Laxton Cl. El Por 94 C4
Laxton Way. Middle 128 B1
Layland Ave. Cul 4 C2
Layton Cl. Warr 9 F2
Lea Ave. Crewe 190 C2
Lea Ave. Goost 107 E1
Lea Bank Cl. Mfield 112 A4
Lea Cl. Sand 175 E3
Lea Cross Gr. Wid 12 B2
Lea Dr. Nant 204 B2
Lea Dr. Wimbo 151 D2
Lea La. Golb 164 B2
Lea St. N Mills 39 D4
Lea Way. Alsag 193 E2
Leacroft Rd. Warr 10 A3
Leadbeaters Cl. Mfield 112 C4
Leadbeaters Rd. Mfield 112 C4
Leadgate La. Hux 144 C1
Leadsmithy St. Middle 128 B1
Leadworks La. Chest 118 C1
Leaf La. Winsf 127 D1
Leafield Dr. Ch Hul 34 C3
Leafield Rd. Disley 38 B3
Leafy Way. Weave 102 B4
Leahurst Cl. Chest 118 C2
Leamington Ave. N-le-W 2 B1
Leamington Cl. Gt San 15 D4
Leamington Cl. Nest 66 C3
Leamington Rd. Congle 155 F2
Leamington Rd. Mfield 86 C1
Lear Dr. Wist 205 F4
Leas Cl. El Por 69 E3
Leaside. Run 23 E1
Leaside Rd. Blacon 117 F3
Leatham Cl. Warr 9 F2
Leathers La. Halew 21 D4
Ledbury Dr. Wist 206 A4
Ledge Ley. Chea 34 C4
Ledger Rd. Hay 1 A3
Ledley St. Boll 87 F4
Ledsham Cl. Warr 9 E2
Ledsham Hall La. Led 68 C2
Ledsham La. Led 68 C2
Ledsham Park Dr. El Por 69 D3
Ledsham Rd. El Por 69 D3
Ledston Cl. Run 24 B1
Ledward St. Winsf 127 D1
Ledyard Cl. Gt San 15 E4
Lee Dr. North 103 F4
Lee Cl. Knuts 56 C1
Lee St. Chest 118 C1
Leech Rd. Malpas 213 D2
Leek Old Rd. S La E 112 C1
Leek Rd. Congle 179 D4
Leen La. Chest 118 B1
Lees La. El Por 70 C2
Lees La. M St A 61 D4
Lees La. Nest 67 D4
Lees La. Stan 70 C2
Lees Rd. Ch Hul 35 E3
Legh Gdns. Knuts 57 D1
Legh Rd. Adlin 62 B3
Legh Rd. Hay 1 A3
Legh Rd. Knuts 82 A4
Legh Rd. Prest 87 D4
Legh St. Gold 3 D4
Legh St. Lymm 18 C2
Legh St. N-le-W 2 A2
Legh St. Warr 16 A3
Leicester Ave. Alsag 193 E3
Leicester St. North 79 D1
Leicester St. Warr 15 F3
Leigh Ave. Knuts 57 E2
Leigh Ave. Wid 13 D1
Leigh Green Cl. Wid 22 B4
Leigh La. L Lei 77 E3
Leigh Rd. Congle 157 D3
Leigh Rd. Disley 38 A3
Leigh Rd. Wilm 59 E3
Leigh St. Mfield 112 C4
Leigh Way. Weave 77 E1
Leigh's Brow. North 77 F2
Leighstone Ct. Chest 118 B2
Leighton Chase. Nest 41 E1
Leighton Dr. Gold 4 A4
Leighton Park. Crewe 189 F4
Leighton Park. Nest 66 B4
Leighton Rd. Nest 41 E1
Leighton St. Crewe 190 A3
Leighton View. Crewe 190 A4
Leightons The. Nest 66 B4
Leinster Gdns. Run 22 C2
Leinster St. Run 22 C2
Lenfield Dr. Hay 1 A3
Lenthall Ave. Congle 178 C4
Leon Cl. Gt San 14 B4
Leonard St. Blacon 118 A2
Leonard St. Run 48 B4
Leonard St. Warr 16 B1
Leonard St. Warr 16 B4
Leslie Rd. Winsf 149 D4
Lessingham Rd. Wid 12 C2
Lester Cl. Alsag 193 E2
Leven Ave. Winsf 126 C1
Leven Wlk. El Por 70 A4
Levens Way. Wid 22 B4
Leveret Rd. Speke 21 D2
Lewin St. Middle 128 B1
Lewis Ave. Warr 7 F1
Lewis Cres. Wid 23 D4
Lewis Gr. Wid 12 B1
Lewis St. Crewe 190 B2
Lexden St. Warr 15 F3
Leycester Cl. Knuts 82 B4
Leycester Rd. Knuts 82 A4
Leycester Rd. Mobb 57 F4
Leyfield Ct. Chest 140 C3
Leygate View. N Mills 39 D4
Leyland Dr. Brough 140 B3
Leyland Gr. Hasl 191 E2
Leyland Gr. Hay 1 A3
Leyland Wlk. Winsf 149 E3
Leyton Cl. Run 49 D3
Libson Cl. Warr 9 D2
Lichfield Ave. Gold 3 E4
Lichfield Cl. Knuts 57 E1
Lichfield Ct. Mfield 112 C4
Lichfield Ct. Winsf 149 E4
Lichfield Dr. El Por 94 C4
Lichfield Rd. Blacon 117 F3
Lichfield Rd. Kids 210 B4
Lichfield St. Middle 128 B1
Lidgetts La. Rain 88 B2
Liebig St. Wid 23 D4
Light Alders La. Disley 38 A3
Light Oaks Rd. Leigh 5 E3
Lightburn St. Run 22 C1
Lightfoot Cl. Hes 41 D4
Lightfoot La. Eaton 147 D2
Lightfoot La. Hes 41 D4
Lightfoot St. Chest 118 C1
Lighthouse Rd. Hale 47 F4
Lightley Cl. Sand 175 D2
Lightwood Green Ave.
Roy Gr 229 D1
Lightwood Rd. N-u-L 210 B1
Lilac Ave. Gt San 15 D3
Lilac Ave. Knuts 56 C1
Lilac Ave. Wid 13 D1
Lilac Cl. N-u-L 210 B1
Lilac Cl. Tarv 122 C1
Lilac Cres. Run 49 E4
Lilac Dr. North 103 E3
Lilac Gr. El Por 95 D4
Lilac Gr. Warr 16 C1
Lilac Wlk. Part 11 E1
Lilford Ave. Warr 15 F4
Lilford Dr. Gt San 14 C3
Lilford Sq. Mfield 112 B3
Lilford St. Warr 15 F4
Lillyfield. Hes 40 C3
Lily Ave. N-le-W 2 B1
Lily La. Cran 129 D3
Lily La. Middle 129 D3
Lime Ave. Frod 74 B4
Lime Ave. North 103 F3
Lime Ave. Weave 102 B4
Lime Cl. Hol Gr 11 D1
Lime Cl. Middle 128 A1
Lime Cl. Sand 175 D4
Lime Cl. Tarp 146 B1
Lime Ct. North 103 F3
Lime Gr. Alsag 193 F1
Lime Gr. Brough 140 B3
Lime Gr. Chest 119 D2
Lime Gr. Elton 72 A2
Lime Gr. Gold 3 F3
Lime Gr. Mfield 112 C4
Lime Gr. Run 49 E4
Lime Gr. Winsf 127 D1
Lime Kiln La. Kids 194 B1
Lime St. Congle 156 B1
Lime St. Crewe 190 B3
Lime St. El Por 70 B4
Lime Tree Ave. Congle 156 A2
Lime Tree Ave. Crewe 190 C3
Lime Tree Cl. El Por 95 D4
Lime Tree Dr. Farn 180 C1
Lime Tree Gr. Hes 41 E4
Lime Tree La. H Legh 29 E3
Lime View. S La E 112 B1
Lime Wlk. Part 11 E1
Lime Wlk. Wilm 34 B1
Limehurst Gr. Beb 43 E3
Limekiln La. Burton 6 C2
Limekiln Row. Run 50 A4
Limes La. Whit 52 B3
Limes The. Cul 4 C2
Limetree Ave. Warr 16 C1
Limetree Ave. Warr 17 D4
Limewood Cres. North 78 A2
Limewood Gr. North 78 A2
Lincoln Ave. Chea 34 A4
Lincoln Ave. Irlam 11 E2
Lincoln Cl. Gold 4 B4
Lincoln Cl. Mfield 86 C1
Lincoln Cl. Rain 88 C3
Lincoln Cl. Run 49 E3
Lincoln Cl. Warr 17 F3
Lincoln Dr. Chest 119 D3
Lincoln Pl. Mfield 86 C1
Lincoln Rd. Blacon 117 F3
Lincoln Rd. El Por 69 E2
Lincoln Rd. Kids 194 C1
Lincoln Rd. Wilm 34 C1
Lincoln Sq. Wid 13 D1
Lincoln St. Crewe 190 A3
Lincoln Wlk. Mfield 86 C1
Lincombe Hey. Prest 87 E4
Lincombe Rd. Wythe 33 E4
Lindale Cl. Congle 157 D3
Linden Cl. Congle 179 D4
Linden Cl. El Por 94 C4
Linden Cl. Warr 17 E4
Linden Ct. Wid 12 C2
Linden Dr. Bidd 179 E1
Linden Dr. Crewe 190 C2
Linden Dr. Hels 73 D1
Linden Dr. M Traf 96 C1
Linden Gr. Brough 140 B3
Linden Gr. Ch Hul 35 E2
Linden Gr. Chest 119 D2
Linden Way. H La 38 A4
Linden Way. Wid 12 C2
Lindfield Cl. Moore 25 D3
Lindi Ave. Warr 17 E1
Lindisfarne Ave. Gold 4 B4
Lindisfarne Cl. Middle 128 A1
Lindisfarne Dr. Poyn 36 B2
Lindley Ave. Warr 16 C2
Lindop Cl. Knuts 57 E1
Lindow Fold Dr. Wilm 59 E3
Lindow La. Wilm 59 F3
Lindow Par. Wilm 59 F3
Lindrick Cl. Mfield 87 E2
Lindrum Ave. S La E 112 B1
Linds Worth Cl. Gt San 15 E3
Lindsay Way. Alsag 193 D2
Lindsay Wlk. Cudd 102 A2
Linear View. N-le-W 2 B1
Linen Hall Pl. Chest 118 B1
Lines Rd. Irlam 11 F4
Linfield Est N. Wilm 60 A3
Lingdale Wlk. Mfield 112 B3
Lingefield Rd. Run 48 C4
Lingfield Dr. Crewe 190 B4
Lingfield Est S. Wilm 60 A3
Lingley Green Ave. Gt San 14 B4
Lingley Rd. Gt San 14 B3
Linglongs Ave. W Br 65 E3
Linglongs Rd. W Br 65 E3
Lingmell Gdns. H Chap 129 F2
Lingwood Rd. Gt San 14 C3
Link The. Wilm 34 B2
Links Ave. El Por 69 E4
Links Cl. Beb 43 D3
Links Rd. Wilm 59 F2
Linkside Ave. Win 8 A3
Linkside Way. El Por 94 C4
Linksway. Chest 118 B4
Linksway. Congle 178 C4
Linksway Cl. Congle 178 C4
Linkway. Run 49 E4
Linley Gr. Alsag 193 F2
Linley La. Alsag 194 A1
Linley Rd. Alsag 193 F1
Linley Rd. Ch Hul 35 D4
Linley Rd. Kids 210 B4
Linnards La. H Winch 80 A3
Linnards La. Plum 80 A3
Linnet Cl. N-le-W 2 B2
Linnet Cl. Warr 8 B2
Linnet Cl. Winsf 150 A4
Linnet Gr. Mfield 87 D1
Linnet Gr. Warr 9 F2
Linnets Way. Hes 40 C4
Linton Cl. Knuts 57 E1
Linton Gdns. Apple 26 B2
Linwood Ave. Apple 26 B4
Linwood Cl. Run 50 B3
Lion St. Congle 156 B1
Liskeard Cl. Run 50 A3
Liskeard Dr. Bram 35 F4
Lismore Wlk. Wythe 33 F4
Lister Rd. Run 23 E2
Litter La. Winsf 125 F1
Little Abbey Gateway.
Chest 118 B1
Little Aston Cl. Mfield 87 E2
Little Gn. El Por 69 E2
Little Heath Cl. Audlem 230 A3
Little Heath Rd. Chest 119 F1
Little Heath Rd. Christ 142 C4
Little La. Nest 41 D1
Little Meadow Cl. Prest 87 D4
Little Moss Cl. Sch Gr 194 C3
Little Moss La. Sch Gr 194 C3
Little Roodee. Hawa 139 D4
Little St. Congle 156 B1
Little St. Mfield 112 B4
Little St John St. Chest 118 B1
Little Stanney La. Stoak 95 F4
Little Wissage. El Por 69 F1
Littlebourne. Run 50 C4
Littlecote Ave. Apple 26 B2
Littledale Rd. Gt San 14 B4
Littledales La. Weave 102 C2
Littlegate. Run 49 F4
Littler Grange Ct. Winsf 126 A1
Littler Rd. Hay 1 A3
Littlestone Cl. Wid 13 D2
Littleton Cl. Gt San 15 E2
Littleton La. Chest 119 F1
Littondale Cl. Congle 157 D3
Liverpool Pl. Wid 12 B1
Liverpool Rd. Back 95 D2
Liverpool Rd. Chest 118 B3
Liverpool Rd. Gt San 15 E2
Liverpool Rd. Hay 1 A4
Liverpool Rd. Irlam 11 F3
Liverpool Rd. Kids 195 D1
Liverpool Rd. N-u-L 210 B1
Liverpool Rd. Nest 41 F1
Liverpool Rd. Warr 15 E2
Liverpool Rd. Wid 12 B1
Liverpool Rd. Will 41 F2
Liverpool Rd E. Kids 194 C1
Liverpool Rd E. Law-g 194 C1
Liverpool Rd W. Law-g 194 A2
Liverpool Row. N-le-W 7 E4
Liverpool St. North 104 B4
Livingstone Cl. Gt San 15 E4
Livingstone Cl. Mfield 111 F4
Livingstone Rd. El Por 70 B4
Livingstone Way. Middle 151 E3
Llandaff Cl. El Por 69 F1
Llandovery Cl. Winsf 149 D4
Llne Cl. Congle 157 D1
Lloyd Cl. Farn 180 C1
Lloyd Cres. N-le-W 1 C2
Lloyd Pl. Blacon 117 F2
Llyndir La. Ross 162 A1
Llys Derwen. H Kin 161 D4
Loachbrook Ave. Congle 156 A1
Lobelia Gr. Run 49 F3
Loch St. Run 23 D2
Lochinvar Ave. El Por 68 C3
Lochleven Rd. Wist 206 A4
Lochmaben Cl. H Chap 130 A1
Lock La. Part 11 F2
Lock Rd. Beb 44 A4
Lock Rd. Warr 16 C3
Locker Ave. Warr 8 A1
Lockerbie Cl. Warr 8 C2
Lockett Rd. Wid 13 D2
Lockett St. Warr 16 C2
Lockgate East. Run 24 B1
Lockgate West. Run 24 A1
Locking Stumps La. Warr 9 D2
Lockitt St. Crewe 190 B2
Lodge Brow. Adlin 63 D1
Lodge Cl. Lymm 19 D2
Lodge Dr. Moult 126 C4
Lodge Dr. Winsf 127 D1
Lodge Hollow. Hels 73 D2
Lodge La. Antro 54 A3
Lodge La. Cront 12 A2
Lodge La. Dult 76 B4
Lodge La. Hart 103 D2
Lodge La. Hather 220 A2
Lodge La. Lost 80 A1
Lodge La. N-le-W 2 A4
Lodge La. N-le-W 2 B4
Lodge La. Run 49 F4
Lodge La. Saug 94 A1
Lodge La. Warr 15 F4
Lodge Rd. Alsag 193 E2
Lodge Rd. Kids 210 B3
Lodge Rd. Knuts 57 E2
Lodge Rd. Sand 174 C3
Lodge Rd. Wid 22 A4
Lodgefields Dr. Crewe 189 F2
Lodmore La. Roy Gr 233 E3
Lofthouse Gate. Wid 12 C2
Lomas Sq. Mfield 112 B3
Lomax Rd. Willas 205 E3
Lomond Gr. El Por 69 F2
London Rd. A Edge 60 A1
London Rd. Adlin 62 B3
London Rd. Allos 107 D3
London Rd. Apple 26 B3
London Rd. Blake 220 B3
London Rd. Bre Gr 130 B1
London Rd. Bridge 232 A3
London Rd. Dave 104 A1
London Rd. Frod 74 A4
London Rd. H Chap 130 B1
London Rd. Hather 220 B3
London Rd. Hay Gr 205 D2
London Rd. Mfield 112 B2
London Rd. Nant 204 C3
London Rd. North 103 F4
London Rd. North 104 A1
London Rd. Prest 62 A1
London Rd. S La E 112 B2
London Rd. Sand 174 B4
London Rd. Warr 26 B3
London Rd. Woore 232 A3
London Rd S. Poyn 36 B2
London Rd Terr. Mfield 112 B3
London Row. N-le-W 7 E4
Loney St. Mfield 112 B4
Long Acre. Weave 77 E1
Long Acres Rd. Nest 41 F1
Long Barn La. Warr 17 E4
Long Croft La. Chea 34 C4
Long Hill. W Br 65 F1
Long La. Alpr 169 F2
Long La. Bicker 199 F2
Long La. Boll 63 D1
Long La. Burl 203 D4
Long La. Chest 119 D3
Long La. Fadd 186 B2
Long La. H Moss 186 B2
Long La. Harg 143 E1
Long La. Hux 166 B4
Long La. Kids 195 F2
Long La. Middle 151 E4
Long La. Saug 94 A1
Long La. Spurs 186 B2
Long La. Tils 198 A2
Long La. W Br 65 F2
Long La. Warr 8 A1
Long La. Waver 143 E1
Long La. Wet 170 B3
Long La S. Middle 151 E4
Long Lane. Peo 107 E4
Long Looms. Gt Bar 120 C3
Long Meadow. Hes 40 C3
Long Row. Kids 195 D1
Long Shoot Rd. With 108 C1
Long Spinney. Run 50 B4
Long Valley Rd. Bidd 179 E1
Long Wlk. Part 11 E1
Longacre St. Mfield 112 B4
Longacres Rd. Altr 32 B4
Longbarn Bvd. Warr 9 E1
Longburgh Cl. Chest 118 C2
Longbutt La. Lymm 18 C1
Longbutts La. Warren 111 F1
Longclough Rd. N-u-L 210 B1
Longdale Dr. Blacon 117 E3
Longden Ct. Bram 35 F3
Longden La. Mfield 113 D3
Longden St. Mfield 112 C4
Longdin St. Warr 16 C2
Longdown Rd. Congle 155 F2
Longfield Ave. Chea 34 B4
Longfield Ave. Chest 118 B4
Longfield Gdns. Irlam 11 E2
Longford St. Crewe 190 B1
Longford St. Warr 16 A4
Longhill La. Audlem 230 C3
Longlands Dr. N Mills 39 D4
Longlands Rd. N Mills 39 D4
Longley Ave. Kels 122 B3
Longlooms Rd. El Por 70 B1
Longmeade Gdns. Wilm 60 B3
Longmeadow. Ch Hul 35 E4
Longmeadow. Weave 102 B4
Longmoss Cl. Middle 151 D4
Longmynd Rise. Winsf 149 D4
Longnor Rd. Chea 34 B4
Longnor Rd. Haz Gr 36 C4
Longridge. Knuts 57 E2
Longridge
Trading Estate. Knuts 57 E2
Longsdon Cl. N-u-L 210 B1
Longshaw St. Warr 7 F1
Longsides Rd. Altr 32 B4
Longsight La. Ch Hul 34 C3
Longston Ave. Gold 3 E4
Longstone La. L Bud 124 C2
Longview Ave. Alsag 193 F2
Longwood Cl. Middle 151 E4
Longwood Rd. Apple 26 C3
Longwood Rd. Stret 26 C3
Lonsdale Cl. Wid 22 B4
Looe Cl. Wid 12 C1
Looms The. Nest 41 D1
Loont The. Winsf 149 E4
Lord Nelson St. Warr 16 B3
Lord St. Boll 88 A4
Lord St. Chest 118 C1
Lord St. Crewe 190 B2
Lord St. Croft 9 D4
Lord St. Mfield 112 B4
Lord St. N-le-W 2 A2
Lord St. Run 22 C2
Lord St. Warr 16 A2
Lord's St. Irlam 11 E3
Lords La. Warr 9 E2
Lords Mill Rd. Shav 206 A2
Lordship La. Frod 73 D4
Lordshire Pl. Kids 195 F1
Lorne St. Chest 118 B1
Lorraine St. Kids 195 F1
Lostock Ave. Warr 15 F4
Lostock Hall Rd. Poyn 36 A2
Lostock Hollow. Lost 80 A1
Lostock Rd. Poyn 36 B1
Lostock Way. Wilm 34 B2
Louise St. Chest 118 B1

Loushers La. Warr 16 B1
Lovage Cl. Warr 9 E1
Lovat Dr. Knuts 82 A4
Love La. Ha Gr 176 B2
Love La. Nant 204 C3
Love St. Chest 118 B1
Lovel Terr. Wid 22 A3
Lovely La. Warr 15 F3
Low Hill. D-o-t-H 97 E3
Low Leighton Rd. N Mills 39 E4
Low Meadow. W Br 65 E4
Lowcross La. Tils 198 B2
Lowe Ave. Congle 156 C1
Lowe Ave. Warr 16 C2
Lowe Cres. Antro 53 E2
Lowe Dr. Knuts 57 D1
Lowe St. Gold 3 D4
Lowe St. Mfield 112 B4
Lower Ash Rd. Kids 194 C1
Lower Bank St. Mfield 112 C4
Lower Beech Cotts. Mfield 87 E1
Lower Bridge St. Chest 141 E4
Lower Brook St. Con Q 91 E1
Lower Church St. Wid 23 D3
Lower Cl. Halew 21 D4
Lower Darwin St. North 103 F3
Lower Exchange St. Mfield 112 B4
Lower Field Rd. Chest 141 D3
Lower Greenshall La. Disley 38 C3
Lower Hague. N Mills 38 C4
Lower Haigh St. Winsf 149 E4
Lower Hall La. Clutt 182 B1
Lower Hall Mews. Clutt 182 B1
Lower Heath. Congle 156 C2
Lower Heath Ave. Congle 156 C2
Lower High St. Sch Gr 195 E4
Lower House La. Wid 22 C4
Lower La. Eaton 147 D2
Lower Macclesfield Rd.
W Br 65 F3
Lower Mersey St. El Por 70 B4
Lower Park Cres. Poyn 36 B3
Lower Park Rd. Chest 118 C1
Lower Park Rd. Poyn 36 A3
Lower Park St. Congle 156 C2
Lower Rake La. Hels 73 D2
Lower Rd. Halew 21 E4
Lower Rd. Wid 21 E3
Lower Robin Hood La. Hels 73 D2
Lower Sandy La. Brox 199 E4
Lower Wash La. Warr 16 C2
Lowerfield Rd. Mfield 87 F1
Lowerhouse. Boll 87 F4
Lowerlea. Disley 38 B3
Lowes La. Warren 111 F1
Loweswater Cres. Hay 1 A3
Lowfield Gdns. Cul 5 E4
Lowfields Ave. Beb 43 F2
Lowfields Cl. Beb 43 F2
Lowland Way. Knuts 82 A4
Lowlands Rd. Run 22 C1
Lowry Cl. Gt San 15 E3
Lowry Wlk. Winsf 149 D4
Lowther Ave. Cul 4 C2
Lowther St. Boll 88 B4
Lowton Gdns. Gold 3 D3
Lowton Rd. Gold 3 E4
Loxdale Dr. El Por 69 F2
Loxley Cl. Gt San 15 D4
Loyola Hey. Cront 12 C4
Lucerne Cl. Hunt 142 A3
Ludford Cl. N-u-L 210 B1
Ludford St. Crewe 190 B3
Ludlow Ave. Crewe 190 C2
Ludlow Cl. Mfield 87 F1
Ludlow Cl. Winsf 149 D4
Ludlow Cres. Run 49 D4
Ludlow Dr. El Por 70 C2
Ludlow Rd. Blacon 118 A3
Ludwell Cl. Chest 141 D3
Lugsdale Rd. Wid 23 D4
Luke's Ave. Gold 3 E4
Lulworth Cl. Winsf 149 D4
Lumb Brook Rd. Apple 26 C4
Lumb Cl. Bram 35 F3
Lumb La. Bram 35 F3
Lumber La. Burton 6 C4
Lumley Pl. Chest 118 B1
Lumley Rd. Chest 118 B2
Lumley Rd. Mfield 111 F4
Lumley Wlk. Hale 21 F1
Lumpy St. Congle 156 B2
Lune Way. Wid 12 B1
Lunehurst. Gold 3 F4
Lunt Ave. Crewe 190 B1
Lunts Heath Rd. Wid 13 D3
Lupin Dr. Hay 1 C3
Lupin Dr. Hunt 142 A3
Lupus Way. El Por 69 F2
Luscombe Cl. Halew 21 D4
Luther Gr. St Hel 1 A1
Luton Rd. El Por 70 A3
Luton St. Wid 23 D4
Lutyens Cl. Mfield 111 F4
Lyceum Cl. Crewe 190 A4
Lyceum Way. Crewe 190 A4
Lychgate. H Wal 25 F4
Lycroft Cl. Run 49 D3
Lydbury Cl. Warr 7 E1
Lydden Rd. El Por 70 A4
Lydgate Cl. Wist 205 F4
Lydial La. A Edge 60 A1
Lydiate La. Run 48 B4
Lydiate La. Will 42 C1
Lydiate The. Hes 40 C4
Lydney Ave. Chea 34 B4
Lydstep Ct. Warr 7 F1
Lydyett La. North 78 A2
Lymcote Dr. Hart 103 D2
Lyme Ave. Mfield 112 B3
Lyme Ave. Wilm 34 A1
Lyme Gr. Lymm 18 B1
Lyme Green
Settlement. S La E 112 B1
Lyme Rd. Disley 38 A3
Lyme Rd. Poyn 37 E2
Lyme St. Hay 1 C3
Lyme St. N-le-W 1 C2
Lymewood Dr. Disley 38 B3
Lymewood Dr. Wilm 60 C4
Lymm Rd. L Boll 20 A1
Lymm Rd. Warr 17 F2
Lymmhay La. Lymm 18 C2
Lymmington Ave. Lymm 18 B2
Lynalls Cl. Congle 155 F2
Lynbrook Rd. Crewe 190 C2
Lyncastle Rd. Apple 27 E2
Lyncastle Way. Apple 27 E2
Lyncombe Cl. Ch Hul 35 D3
Lyndale Ave. Beb 43 F2
Lyndale Ave. Warr 16 B4
Lyndhurst Cl. Wilm 59 E3
Lyndon Gr. Run 49 D4
Lyngard Cl. Wilm 34 C1
Lynham Ave. Gt San 15 D3
Lynn Ave. Kids 210 B4
Lynn Cl. Run 49 E4
Lynn Gr. Mfield 112 B3
Lynndene. El Por 69 E4
Lynneal Ave. El Por 69 E1
Lynthorpe Ave. Irlam 11 E3
Lynton Ave. Irlam 11 F3
Lynton Cl. Hes 41 D3
Lynton Cl. Penk 14 C2
Lynton Cres. Wid 12 C1
Lynton Gr. Hasl 191 E3
Lynton La. A Edge 60 A1
Lynton Park Rd. Chea 34 C4
Lynton Pl. Alsag 193 E2
Lynton Pl. Broug 139 D2
Lynton Way. Wist 206 A4
Lynwood. Altr 32 A4
Lynwood Ave. Gold 3 E3
Lynwood Rd. Blacon 117 F3
Lyon St. Chest 118 B1
Lyon St. Crewe 190 B2
Lyon St. Mfield 112 B4
Lyon St. Warr 16 C2
Lyon's La. Apple 26 C3
Lyons Rd. Penk 15 D2
Lyster Cl. Warr 9 F2
Lytham Dr. Bram 36 A4
Lytherton Ave. Irlam 11 E2
Lythgoes La. Warr 16 A3

Mabledon Cl. Chea 34 B4
Mablins La. Crewe 190 A4
Macclesfield Rd. A Edge 85 E4
Macclesfield Rd. Congle 156 C3
Macclesfield Rd. Eaton 134 A1
Macclesfield Rd. Eaton 156 C3
Macclesfield Rd. H Chap 130 C2
Macclesfield Rd. Haz Gr 36 C4
Macclesfield Rd. Kettle 64 B2
Macclesfield Rd. L Han 64 B2
Macclesfield Rd. N Ald 85 E4
Macclesfield Rd. Prest 86 C2
Macclesfield Rd. Rain 89 D4
Macclesfield Rd. W Br 65 E3
Macclesfield Rd. Wilm 60 B3
Macdermott Rd. Wid 22 C3
Macdonald Rd. Irlam 11 F4
Macon Ct. Crewe 190 C2
Macon Way. Crewe 190 C2
Maddock St. Audley 209 E1
Maddocks Hill. Norley 100 C3
Madeley Cl. Altr 31 F4
Madeley Cl. Broug 139 E2
Madeley St. Crewe 190 B1
Madeline McKenna Ct. Wid 12 B2
Madron Ave. Mfield 86 B1
Maelor Cl. Beb 43 E3
Mag La. H Legh 28 C3
Magdala Pl. North 104 B4
Maggoty La. Warren 111 E1
Magnolia Cl. El Por 69 F1
Magnolia Cl. Warr 17 F4
Magnolia Dr. Run 49 F2
Magnolia Rise. Prest 86 C3
Magnolia Wlk. Part 11 E1
Maidenhills. Middle 128 B1
Maidstone Cl. Mfield 87 D1
Main Cl. Hay 1 A3
Main La. Croft 3 F2
Main Rd. Broug 139 D2
Main Rd. Goost 107 F1
Main Rd. H Kin 161 D4
Main Rd. Hay Gr 220 A4
Main Rd. Moult 126 C4
Main Rd. N in H 236 B1
Main Rd. S La E 113 E2
Main Rd. Shav 206 A2
Main Rd. Weston 207 E4
Main Rd. Worles 188 C3
Main St. Frod 74 A4
Main St. Run 49 F4
Maintree Cres. Speke 21 D2
Mainwaring Dr. Brough 140 B4
Mainwaring Dr. Wilm 60 B4
Mainwaring Rd. Peo 108 A4
Mairesfield Ave. Warr 17 D1
Maisterson Ct. Nant 204 C3
Maitland Way. Blacon 117 E2
Maitland Wood Cl. North 104 B4
Major Cross St. Wid 23 D4
Makepeace Cl. Chest 119 E2
Malaga Ave. Wythe 33 D4
Malam Dr. North 104 B3
Malbank. Nant 204 C3
Malbank Rd. Crewe 189 F2
Malcolm Ave. Warr 8 B1
Malcolm Cres. Beb 43 E3
Malcolm St. Run 23 D1
Malhamdale Rd. Congle 157 D3
Malin Cl. Hale 21 E1
Maliston Rd. Gt San 15 D3
Mallaig Cl. H Chap 130 B1
Mallard Cl. Knuts 57 D1
Mallard Cl. Run 49 F3
Mallard Cl. Warr 8 B2
Mallard Cres. Poyn 36 A2
Mallard La. Warr 9 F2
Mallard Way. Winsf 149 E3
Mallory Ct. Congle 155 F2
Mallory Rd. El Por 70 A2
Mallory Wlk. Dodle 162 A4
Mallow Cl. Hunt 142 A3
Mallow Wlk. Part 11 F1
Mallowdale Cl. Beb 43 F3
Malmesbury Ave. Ch Hul 35 D3
Malmesbury Cl. Poyn 36 B2
Malory Cl. Crewe 190 C3
Malpas Cl. North 104 B4
Malpas Cl. Wilm 34 C1
Malpas Dr. Gt San 15 E2
Malpas Rd. El Por 69 F2
Malpas Rd. North 104 B4
Malpas Rd. Run 49 E4
Malpas Way. Gt San 15 E2
Malt Kiln Rd. Plum 80 C2
Malt St. Knuts 57 D1
Malta Rd. Chest 95 D1
Maltmans Rd. Lymm 18 B2
Malton Ave. Gold 3 F4
Malton Cl. Cront 12 B3
Malton Dr. Haz Gr 36 B4
Malvern Ave. El Por 70 B2
Malvern Cl. Congle 155 F2
Malvern Cl. Gt San 15 D4
Malvern Cl. Shav 206 A2
Malvern Dr. Mfield 87 F2
Malvern Rd. Blacon 118 A3
Malvern Rd. Knuts 81 F4
Malvern Rd. St Hel 1 A2
Malvern Way. Winsf 149 D4
Manchester Bridge. Crewe 190 C2
Manchester New Rd. Part 11 F2
Manchester Rd. Congle 156 C3
Manchester Rd. Hol Gr 11 D1
Manchester Rd. Knuts 56 C2
Manchester Rd. Lost 79 E1
Manchester Rd. Mfield 87 E2
Manchester Rd. North 79 E1
Manchester Rd. Part 11 F2
Manchester Rd. Warr 16 C4
Manchester Rd. Warr 17 E4
Manchester Rd. Warr 18 A4
Manchester Rd. Wilm 34 B1
Manchester Row. N-le-W 7 E4
Mancroft Cl. Warr 17 F4
Manifold Cl. Sand 174 C4
Manifold Dr. H La 37 F3
Manley Cl. H Chap 130 A2
Manley Cl. North 104 A3
Manley Gdns. Warr 15 F3
Manley Gr. Bram 35 F3
Manley La. D-o-t-H 97 F3
Manley La. Man 98 B2
Manley Rd. Alva 98 C4
Manley Rd. Frod 74 A2
Manley Rd. Man 99 D3
Manley Rd. Warren 112 A3
Manley View. Elton 72 B2
Manners La. Hes 40 C3
Manning La S. Chest 119 D3
Manning St. Crewe 190 B1
Mannings La. Chest 119 D3
Manor La. H Chap 130 B2
Manor Ave. Crewe 190 A1
Manor Ave. Gold 3 E4
Manor Ave. Goost 107 F1
Manor Ave. Mars 79 D3
Manor Ave. N-le-W 1 C2
Manor Cl. Bram 35 E4
Manor Cl. Broug 139 E4
Manor Cl. Congle 157 D1
Manor Cl. Gt Bar 120 C3
Manor Cl. Nest 66 B4
Manor Cl. Warr 17 E4
Manor Cl. Wilm 59 F4
Manor Cres. Broug 139 E4
Manor Cres. Knuts 57 D1
Manor Cres. Mfield 87 E2
Manor Cres. Middle 151 E4
Manor Ct. Crewe 190 A1
Manor Ct. Gold 3 E4
Manor Dr. Chest 119 E1
Manor Dr. Elton 72 B2
Manor Dr. North 78 A1
Manor Dr. North 104 B4
Manor Farm Cl. M Traf 119 F4
Manor Farm Cres. Capen 94 A4
Manor Farm Ct. Broug 139 D4
Manor Farm Rd. Run 24 B2
Manor Fields. Middle 151 E4
Manor Gdns. Wilm 60 B4
Manor Gr. Hart 103 E3
Manor La. Broug 139 D4
Manor La. Dave 104 B1
Manor La. El Por 69 E2
Manor La. Middle 151 E4
Manor La. Oller 82 C3
Manor Park Ave. Run 24 B2
Manor Park N. Knuts 57 E1
Manor Park S. Knuts 57 E1
Manor Rd. Beb 43 F3
Manor Rd. Chest 141 D3
Manor Rd. Cudd 101 F1
Manor Rd. Frod 49 E1
Manor Rd. Hay 1 C4
Manor Rd. Lymm 18 C1
Manor Rd. Nant 204 C3
Manor Rd. Run 23 E1
Manor Rd. Sand 175 E3
Manor Rd. Sch Gr 195 E4
Manor Rd. Sea 116 A3
Manor Rd. Thor H 42 A4
Manor Rd. W Br 65 F3
Manor Rd. Wid 12 A1
Manor Rd. Wilm 59 F4
Manor Rd N. Nant 204 C4
Manor St. North 103 E3
Manor Way. Crewe 190 B1
Manor Way. Sand 175 F3
Manora Rd. North 104 A4
Manorfield Cl. Capen 69 D1
Manorial Rd. Nest 66 B4
Manse Field Rd. Kings 75 D1
Manse Gdns. N-le-W 2 B2
Mansell Cl. Wid 13 E3
Mansfield Cl. Warr 10 A2
Mansfield Rd. El Por 70 A1
Mansion Ct. Nant 204 C3
Mansion Dr. Knuts 57 D1
Manston Rd. Penk 14 C2
Manx St. Warr 16 A2
Maori Dr. Frod 74 A4
Maple Ave. Alsag 193 F1
Maple Ave. Disley 39 D3
Maple Ave. El Por 69 E3
Maple Ave. Gold 3 F4
Maple Ave. Hay 1 A4
Maple Ave. Kids 210 B4
Maple Ave. Mfield 112 B3
Maple Ave. N-le-W 2 B1
Maple Ave. N-u-L 210 C1
Maple Ave. Poyn 36 C2
Maple Ave. Run 49 E4
Maple Ave. Sutt 50 A2
Maple Ave. Wid 13 D1
Maple Cl. Bre Gr 153 F2
Maple Cl. Congle 155 F2
Maple Cl. Sand 175 E3
Maple Cres. Penk 14 C2
Maple Gr. Beb 43 E4
Maple Gr. Brough 140 B3
Maple Gr. Chest 119 D2
Maple Gr. Crewe 190 C4
Maple Gr. El Por 95 D4
Maple Gr. North 78 A2
Maple Gr. North 103 E4
Maple Gr. Warr 16 B2
Maple Gr. Winsf 127 D1
Maple La. Cudd 101 F1
Maple Pl. Sch Gr 193 F4
Maple Rd. A Edge 60 A2
Maple Rd. Bram 35 F3
Maple Rd. Part 11 F2
Maple Rd. Warr 17 F4
Maple Rd. Win 8 A3
Mapleton Dr. Run 49 F2
Maplewell Cres. Gt San 15 D3
Maplewood Gr. Saug 117 D4
Maplewood Rd. Wilm 60 C4
Marble Arch. Knuts 57 D1
Marbury Gdns. El Por 69 F3
Marbury La. Mars 78 C3
Marbury Rd. Chest 119 E1
Marbury Rd. Comb 78 B3
Marbury Rd. Mars 78 B3
Marbury Rd. North 78 B3
Marbury Rd. Wilm 34 A1
Marbury St. Warr 16 B2
March St. Crewe 190 C2
Marchwiel Rd. El Por 70 B2
Marcliff Gr. Knuts 57 D1
Marcross Cl. Warr 7 F1
Mardale Ave. Warr 8 B2
Mardale Cl. Congle 157 D3
Mardale Cres. Lymm 18 C2
Mardale Ct. H Chap 130 A1
Mardon Cl. Knuts 57 E2
Marfords Ave. Beb 43 E4
Margaret Ave. Warr 17 D4
Margaret Ct. Wid 23 D4
Margaret's La. El Por 69 D4
Margery Ave. Sch Gr 194 C4
Marian Dr. Chest 142 A4
Marian Rd. Hay 1 C4
Marie Cl. Wren 216 C2
Marie Dr. Apple 17 E1
Marigold Cl. Mfield 111 F4
Marina Ave. Gt San 15 E2
Marina Cl. Wilm 34 B3
Marina Dr. Chest 118 C4
Marina Dr. El Por 70 A3
Marina Dr. Warr 8 B1
Marina Gr. Run 23 D1
Marina La. Run 50 C4
Marina Village. Run 50 C4
Marina Wlk. El Por 70 A3
Marine Ave. Part 11 E2
Marine Dr. Hes 40 B4
Mariner Cl. Run 50 B3
Marion Dr. Run 48 C3
Maritime Cl. N-le-W 2 B3
Mark Ave. El Por 69 E2
Mark Cl. Chest 118 C1
Mark Rake. Beb 43 E4
Market Centre The. Crewe 190 B2
Market Ct. Tarp 146 B1
Market Gate. Warr 16 A3
Market Pl. Boll 88 A4
Market Pl. Mfield 112 B4
Market Pl. Winsf 126 C1
Market Sq. Chest 118 B1
Market Sq. Congle 156 C1
Market Sq. Crewe 190 B2
Market Sq. Sand 175 D3
Market St. Congle 156 B1
Market St. Crewe 190 B2
Market St. Crewe 190 B3
Market St. Disley 38 B3
Market St. Kids 195 D1
Market St. N Mills 39 D4
Market St. N-le-W 2 A2
Market St. Nant 204 C3
Market St. North 103 F4
Market St. W Br 65 F4
Market St. Wid 23 D4
Market Way. North 103 F4
Marl Cft. Chest 142 A4
Marl Edge. Prest 87 D3
Marl Heys. Chest 118 C4
Marlborough Ave. A Edge 60 A1
Marlborough Ave. Winsf 126 B2
Marlborough Cl. Knuts 57 E2
Marlborough Cl. Mfield 87 E2
Marlborough Cl. Wist 205 F4
Marlborough Cres. Warr 16 C1
Marlborough Cres. Wid 13 D3
Marlborough Ct. Mfield 112 B4
Marlborough Dr. Hels 73 D1
Marlborough Dr. Mfield 87 E2
Marlborough Rd. El Por 70 B2
Marlborough Wlk. El Por 70 B2
Marley Ave. Crewe 190 A4
Marley Rd. Poyn 36 C1
Marley Way. Brough 140 C4
Marlfield Rd. Altr 32 B4
Marlfield Rd. Warr 17 D1
Marline Ave. Beb 43 E3
Marling Cl. Frod 74 B3
Marling Park. Wid 12 A1
Marlow Ave. Chest 118 B4
Marlow Cl. Warr 9 E3
Marlow Dr. Altr 20 C1
Marlow Dr. Wilm 34 B3
Marlowe Cl. Blacon 118 A3
Marlowe Ct. Mfield 112 B3
Marlowe Dr. Nant 204 C2
Marlowe Rd. Nest 66 C4
Marlston Ave. Chest 141 D3
Marlston Pl. Run 49 D3
Marple Cres. Crewe 189 F2
Marple Rd. North 104 B4
Marquis Dr. Chea 34 B4
Marriott Rd. Sand 174 C2
Marron Ave. Warr 8 A1
Marsden Ave. Warr 17 D2
Marsden Terr. Mfield 112 B4
Marsh Ave. Kids 195 F1
Marsh Cl. Alsag 193 D2
Marsh Gr. Bidd 179 E2
Marsh Green Cl. Bidd 179 E1
Marsh Green Rd. Bidd 179 E1
Marsh Green Rd. Sand 174 C4
Marsh Hall Rd. Wid 13 D2
Marsh House La. Warr 16 B4
Marsh La. Acton 204 A2

Marsh La. Alsag 193 D2
Marsh La. Burl 203 F1
Marsh La. Codd 181 F2
Marsh La. Crow 101 D4
Marsh La. Dutt 51 F2
Marsh La. Elton 72 A2
Marsh La. Farn 181 D3
Marsh La. Frod 74 A4
Marsh La. H Chap 130 C1
Marsh La. Mere 30 C2
Marsh La. N Mills 39 E3
Marsh La. Nant 204 B3
Marsh La. Penk 14 B1
Marsh La. Run 23 F2
Marsh Rd. Apple 27 D2
Marsh St. Warr 16 B4
Marsh St. Wid 23 D3
Marshall Ave. Warr 7 F1
Marshall La. North 103 E3
Marshall Rd. Warr 17 E4
Marshfield La. Bidd 179 E1
Marshfield Rd. Crewe 189 E2
Marshgate. Wid 22 A3
Marshlands Rd. Nest 66 C3
Marson St. Warr 16 A3
Marston Cl. Beb 43 F2
Marston La. Mars 79 E3
Marten Ave. Beb 43 E4
Martens Rd. Irlam 11 F3
Marthall La. Chelf 83 D4
Marthall La. Oller 82 C3
Marthall Way. Wilm 34 C3
Martham Cl. Warr 17 D2
Martin Ave. N-le-W 1 C2
Martin Ave. N-le-W 2 B3
Martin Ave. Warr 8 C1
Martin Cl. Chest 118 B4
Martin Cl. Cul 4 C2
Martin Cl. Run 50 A4
Martin Rd. Chest 118 B4
Martin Rd. Frod 74 A4
Martin St. Crewe 190 C2
Martin's La. Harg 143 F2
Martindale Gr. Run 49 E3
Martland Ave. Gold 3 E4
Martlet Ave. Disley 38 B3
Marton Cl. Congle 156 C3
Marton Cl. Ho Co 206 C2
Marton La. Eaton 134 A2
Marton La. Mart 133 E4
Marton La. Warren 111 D1
Marton Rd. Broug 139 E2
Marton Way. Wilm 34 C3
Mary St. Crewe 190 C3
Mary St. Wid 23 E4
Maryhill Cl. Kids 195 D2
Maryhill Rd. Run 49 D4
Marys Gate. Wist 205 F4
Masefield Ave. Wid 22 C4
Masefield Dr. Blacon 117 F3
Masefield Dr. Crewe 190 C2
Maskery Pl. Congle 156 B2
Mason Ave. Warr 16 C4
Mason Ave. Wid 13 D2
Mason Cl. El Por 69 E1
Mason St. Chest 118 B1
Mason St. Run 23 E2
Mason St. Warr 16 B3
Masons La. Mfield 87 F1
Massey Ave. Hart 103 D2
Massey Ave. Lymm 18 A1
Massey Ave. Warr 7 F1
Massey Ave. Winsf 126 C1
Massey Brook La. Lymm 18 A1
Massey St. A Edge 60 A1
Masseyfield Rd. Run 50 A3
Mates La. Ed Gr 213 D3
Mather Ave. Gold 3 F3
Mather Ave. Run 48 B4
Mather Cl. Middle 151 E4
Mather Dr. Comb 78 B4
Mather Dr. North 104 B4
Mathers Cl. Warr 9 D2
Mathieson Rd. Wid 22 C3
Matlock Dr. Haz Gr 36 C4
Matlock Rd. Chea 34 B4
Matterdale Cl. Frod 74 B4
Matthew Cl. Chest 118 C1
Matthews Pl. Congle 157 D1
Matthews St. Warr 16 B4
Matty's La. Frod 74 A4
Mavor Ct. Crewe 190 A2
Maw Green Rd. Crewe 190 C4
Maw La. Hasl 191 E4
Mawdsley Ave. Warr 17 F4
Mawson Cl. Warr 15 E4
Maxfield Cl. Mfield 111 F4
Maxwell Cl. El Por 70 A1
Maxwell Rd. Congle 179 D4
Maxwell St. Crewe 190 B2
May Ave. Ch Hul 35 D3
May Rd. Hes 41 D4
May Wlk. Part 11 E1
Mayberry Gr. Warr 9 D1
Maybrook Pl. Warr 16 C2
Maydews Pas. Mfield 112 B4
Maydor Ave. Brough 140 B4
Mayfair Cl. Gt San 14 B4
Mayfair Gr. Wid 12 B1
Mayfield Ave. Mfield 112 B3
Mayfield Ave. Wid 12 A1
Mayfield Cl. H Chap 130 B2
Mayfield Dr. Beb 44 A3
Mayfield Dr. Cudd 102 A2
Mayfield Dr. Gold 4 B4
Mayfield Gdns. Nest 41 F1
Mayfield Gr. Cudd 102 A2
Mayfield Gr. Wilm 59 F3
Mayfield Rd. Blacon 117 E3
Mayfield Rd. Bram 35 F2
Mayfield Rd. Mobb 57 F2
Mayfield Rd. North 104 B4
Mayfield Rd. Warr 17 D1
Mayfield Terr. Mfield 112 B3
Mayfield View. Lymm 18 C1
Mayflower Rd. Nant 204 C2
Maythorn Ave. Croft 9 D4
Maytree Ave. Chest 119 D1
McCarthy Cl. Warr 10 A2
McClellan Pl. Wid 13 D1
McGarva Way. El Por 70 B2
Mckee Ave. Warr 8 A1
Mckellin Cl. Audley 209 F1
McLaren St. Crewe 190 B4
McMinnis Ave. St Hel 1 A1
McNeill Ave. Crewe 190 A3
Mead Ave. Sch Gr 194 C4
Mead Cl. Knuts 56 C1
Mead Rd. Warr 17 D4
Meade The. Wilm 60 B4
Meadow Ave. Congle 156 B1
Meadow Ave. Goost 107 E1
Meadow Ave. Goost 107 E1
Meadow Ave. Warr 16 A1
Meadow Ave. Weston 207 D3
Meadow Bank. Adder 235 D2
Meadow Bank. Kels 122 B2
Meadow Brow. A Edge 60 A1
Meadow Cl. Cudd 102 A2
Meadow Cl. Farn 180 C1
Meadow Cl. Goost 107 F1
Meadow Cl. H La 37 F4
Meadow Cl. Hels 73 D2
Meadow Cl. N-le-W 1 C2
Meadow Cl. Nest 66 C3
Meadow Cl. Shav 206 B3
Meadow Cl. Tarv 121 D1
Meadow Cl. W Br 65 E4
Meadow Cl. Will 67 F4
Meadow Cl. Wilm 59 F2
Meadow Cl. Winsf 126 B2
Meadow Croft. Alsag 193 F1
Meadow Croft. Will 67 F4
Meadow Ct. Bic T 214 A2
Meadow Ct. Moll 94 C1
Meadow Dr. Knuts 81 F4
Meadow Dr. North 78 A2
Meadow Dr. Prest 87 D4
Meadow Dr. Wist 205 F4
Meadow Field Rd. Chest 141 D3
Meadow Gate. H Winch 79 F3
Meadow Gr. North 104 A3
Meadow Gr. Winsf 126 C3
Meadow Home Park. Winsf 126 B3
Meadow La. Disley 38 B3
Meadow La. El Por 70 B3
Meadow La. Hunt 142 A3
Meadow La. Moult 126 C4
Meadow La. Warr 9 D1
Meadow La. Will 42 C1
Meadow Rd. Broug 139 E2
Meadow Rd. Weave 102 C4
Meadow Rise. Winsf 126 A1
Meadow Row. Run 24 A1
Meadow St. N Mills 39 E4
Meadow St. North 104 A4
Meadow View. Elton 72 A2
Meadow View. Middle 128 A1
Meadow View. Sea 116 A3
Meadow View Dr. Frod 74 A4
Meadow Way. Law-g 194 A3
Meadow Way. Mfield 87 F1
Meadow Wlk. Part 11 E1
Meadowbank Gdns. Cul 5 E4
Meadowcroft. H Kin 161 D4
Meadowfield. Tarp 146 B1
Meadowfield. W Br 65 E4
Meadows La. Chest 141 F4
Meadows La. Saug 117 D4
Meadows Pl. Chest 141 F4
Meadows Rd. Chea 34 C4
Meadows Rd. Kids 194 C1
Meadows The. Asht 121 F4
Meadows The. Congle 156 C2
Meadows The. Irlam 11 F3
Meadows The. Nest 66 C3
Meadowside. Adlin 63 D4
Meadowside. Disley 39 D3
Meadowside. North 103 E4
Meadowside. W Br 65 E4
Meadowside Ave. Audley 209 E1
Meadowside Rd. Beb 43 E4
Meadowsway. Chest 118 B4
Meadowsweet Rd. Mobb 57 F2
Meads Rd. Alsag 193 E2
Meadscroft Dr. A Edge 59 F1
Meadway. Bram 35 F3
Meadway. El Por 69 D4
Meadway. Gold 3 E4
Meadway. H La 37 F4
Meadway. Hes 40 C3
Meadway. Prest 87 D3
Meadway. Run 49 F4
Meadway. Wid 12 A1
Meakin Cl. Congle 157 D1
Meal St. N Mills 39 E4
Meddings Cl. A Edge 85 D4
Medina Ave. Winsf 126 C1
Medina Way. Kids 195 D1
Medway Cl. Gold 4 B4
Medway Cl. Warr 8 C1
Medway Dr. Bidd 179 E1
Medway Rd. Cul 5 D1
Mee St. Mfield 112 C3
Meeanee Rd. Nant 204 B2
Meeting La. Penk 14 C3
Meg La. Mfield 111 F4
Meg La. S La E 113 E1
Megacre. Audley 210 A1
Melbourne Ave. Wythe 33 D4
Melbourne Gr. Hasl 191 E3
Melbourne Rd. Blacon 117 E2
Melbourne Rd. Bram 35 F3
Melbury Ct. Warr 9 F3
Melbury Rd. Ch Hul 35 D3
Melchett Cres. North 104 B4
Melford Cl. Wist 206 B4
Melford Ct. Warr 17 E4
Melford Dr. Mfield 87 E1
Melford Dr. Run 23 E1
Meliden Gr. Hels 73 D1
Melkridge Cl. Chest 119 D2
Melksham Cl. Mfield 112 A4
Mell La. Man 98 C2
Mell La. Mould 98 C2
Mellard St. Audley 209 E1
Mellock Cl. Nest 66 C3
Mellock La. Nest 66 C4
Mellor Cl. Run 24 B1
Mellor Cres. Knuts 56 C1
Mellor St. Crewe 190 B3
Mellor St. Kids 195 F1
Mellors Bank. Kids 195 E3
Melrose Ave. Apple 26 B4
Melrose Ave. Burton 6 C4
Melrose Ave. Chest 119 D1
Melrose Dr. Crewe 190 A4
Melrose Dr. El Por 94 C4
Melton Ave. Warr 26 A4
Melton Cl. Congle 155 F2
Melton Dr. Congle 155 F2
Melton Rd. Run 49 E4
Melverly Dr. Blacon 117 E2
Melville Cl. Warr 16 A4
Melville Cl. Wid 13 E1
Melville Rd. Irlam 11 E3
Mendell Cl. Beb 43 F4
Mendip Ave. Warr 8 A2
Mendip Cl. Chea 34 A4
Mendip Cl. El Por 69 F2
Menin Ave. Warr 16 B2
Menlow Cl. Warr 17 E1
Mentmore Gdns. Apple 26 C3
Meols Cl. El Por 69 F2
Meols Cl. Hale 21 F1
Mercer Cl. Malpas 213 D2
Mercer Rd. Hay 1 B3
Mercer St. Burton 6 C3
Mercer St. N-le-W 2 B2
Mercer Way. Chest 140 C3
Mercer Way. Nant 204 C4
Mercian Cl. Shav 206 A2
Mere Ave. Beb 43 D3
Mere Bank. Dave 127 D4
Mere Brook Wlk. Crewe 190 B1
Mere Cl. El Por 69 E1
Mere Cl. Hasl 191 E2
Mere Cl. Pick 80 A4
Mere Cres. Oak 123 F3
Mere Ct. Alsag 193 E2
Mere La. Cudd 102 A1
Mere La. Pick 79 F4
Mere Rd. Mars 79 D3
Mere Rd. N-le-W 2 C2
Mere Rd. Warr 9 D1
Mere Rd. Weston 207 D3
Mere St. Hasl 191 E2
Merebank Rd. Crewe 190 A1
Merebrook Rd. Mfield 111 F4
Merecroft. Chest 119 D1
Meredith Ave. Warr 17 D1
Meredith St. Crewe 190 B3
Merehaven Cl. Pick 80 A4
Mereheath La. Knuts 56 C3
Mereheath La. Mere 56 C3
Mereheath Park. Knuts 56 C2
Merelake Rd. Alsag 210 A4
Merelake Rd. Kids 210 A4
Meremore Dr. N-u-L 210 B1
Mereside Ave. Congle 156 A2
Mereside Cl. Mfield 87 D1
Mereside Rd. Mere 30 B1
Merevale Cl. Run 49 F3
Meriton Rd. Wilm 34 B2
Merlin Ave. Knuts 57 D2
Merlin Cl. Run 24 A1
Merlin Cl. Winsf 150 A4
Merlin Way. Crewe 190 A4
Merridale The. Altr 32 A4
Merriden Rd. Mfield 87 D1
Merrill's Ave. Crewe 189 F3
Merriman Ave. Knuts 57 E2
Merrivale Rd. Wist 206 A4
Merrydale Cl. Mfield 86 C1
Merryman's La. L End 84 A4
Mersey Pl. Winsf 127 D1
Mersey Rd. Run 23 D2
Mersey Rd. Wid 23 D2
Mersey St. Run 23 D2
Mersey St. St Hel 1 A2
Mersey St. Warr 16 A3
Mersey View. Run 48 B4
Mersey View Rd. Wid 22 A2
Mersey Wlk. Warr 16 C3
Merseyton Rd. El Por 70 B4
Merton Ave. Haz Gr 36 C4
Merton Cl. Nest 66 C3
Merton Dr. Chest 141 D2
Merton Rd. Beb 44 A2
Merton Rd. El Por 69 F2
Mertoun Rd. Warr 16 A1
Mervyn Rd. Weave 77 F1
Merwood Ave. Chea 34 B4
Messuage La. Mart 132 B2
Meteor Cres. Warr 8 B1
Mevagissey Rd. Run 50 B3
Mevril Rd. W Br 65 F3
Mews The. North 78 A1
Mews The. Tarp 168 B4
Meynell Cl. Wist 190 A1
Meynell Pl. Blacon 118 A3
Micawber Rd. Poyn 36 C1
Micklegate. Run 50 B4
Micklewright Ave. Crewe 190 B3
Mickley Hall La. Sound 218 A2
Middle Wlk. Knuts 57 D1
Middle La. Aldf 163 F2
Middle La. Congle 157 E2
Middle La. Kings 74 C1
Middle La. Part 11 E1
Middle Wlk. Frod 74 A4
Middlecroft. G Sutt 119 F3
Middlehills. Mfield 113 D3
Middlehurst Ave. Weave 102 C4
Middlehurst Rd. Warr 17 D1
Middlewich Rd. Allos 106 B3
Middlewich Rd. Ch Min 172 C3
Middlewich Rd. Cran 129 F2
Middlewich Rd. Cran 129 F3
Middlewich Rd. Crewe 189 E2
Middlewich Rd. H Chap 130 A2
Middlewich Rd. Nant 204 C4
Middlewich Rd. North 104 B4
Middlewich Rd. Oller 82 A2
Middlewich Rd. Peo 81 F1
Middlewich Rd. Peo 106 B3
Middlewich Rd. Sand 174 C4
Middlewich Rd. Winsf 127 F1
Middlewich Rd. Worles 189 E2
Middlewich Rd Ind Est. Middle 129 D3
Middlewich St. Crewe 190 B3
Middlewood. Gold 3 F4
Middlewood Rd. H La 37 E4
Middlewood Rd. Poyn 37 E3
Middlewood View. H La 37 E4
Midfield Cl. Bidd 179 E1
Midhurst Cl. Chea 34 C4
Midland St. Wid 13 D1
Midland Terr. N Mills 39 E4
Midway. Ch Hul 35 D3
Milborne Cl. Chest 118 C3
Mile Bank Rd. Whitch 226 B2
Miles Cl. Warr 9 F2
Milk St. Congle 156 B2
Mill Ave. Gt San 14 C4
Mill Bank. Nest 67 D3
Mill Brow. Wid 13 E1
Mill Cl. Chest 118 B3
Mill Cl. Knuts 57 E2
Mill Cl. Warr 8 C2
Mill Cotts. Boll 88 A4
Mill Field Cl. Farn 180 C1
Mill Gr. Bulk 184 C1
Mill Green. Congle 156 B2
Mill Green. Will 67 F4
Mill Green La. Wid 13 F3
Mill Hill Ave. Haz Gr 36 B4
Mill Hill Dr. Sand 175 D3
Mill Hill La. Sand 175 D2
Mill Hill Rd. Haz Gr 36 B4
Mill La. Adlin 62 A3
Mill La. Audlem 229 F1
Mill La. Audlem 230 A2
Mill La. Barth 208 B4
Mill La. Blake 221 D2
Mill La. Bo Hea 13 E3
Mill La. Bre Gr 153 F4
Mill La. Chest 118 B3
Mill La. Congle 179 E4
Mill La. Cront 12 B3
Mill La. Crow 75 F2
Mill La. Cudd 101 F3
Mill La. Dudd 145 D4
Mill La. Eaton 147 E1
Mill La. El Por 69 F3
Mill La. Goost 107 F1
Mill La. Gt Bar 120 C3
Mill La. H Wal 25 F4
Mill La. Haz Gr 36 C4
Mill La. Hes 41 D4
Mill La. Hux 144 B1
Mill La. Kings 75 F2
Mill La. L Bud 125 D1
Mill La. L End 84 A4
Mill La. Lymm 19 E2
Mill La. M St A 61 E3
Mill La. Mfield 112 B4
Mill La. Middle 128 A1
Mill La. Middle 128 B1
Mill La. Mobb 58 A2
Mill La. N-le-W 2 C2
Mill La. Nest 67 E1
Mill La. Nest 67 E3
Mill La. Peo 108 B4
Mill La. Prest 61 F3
Mill La. Rad 132 C1
Mill La. Sand 174 B4
Mill La. Sch Gr 195 D4
Mill La. Sidd 109 F3
Mill La. Small 175 D1
Mill La. Sutt 49 F1
Mill La. Tarv 121 E2
Mill La. Tarv 122 B1
Mill La. Warr 7 F3
Mill La. Warr 8 C2
Mill La. Warr 16 C1
Mill La. Weston 207 D3
Mill La. Will 42 C1
Mill La. Win 7 F3
Mill La. Winsf 126 A3
Mill La. Wythe 32 C2
Mill Park Dr. Beb 43 F2
Mill Pool La. Barb 187 E3
Mill Rd. Mfield 112 B3
Mill Rise. Kids 195 D1
Mill Row. Sand 175 E3
Mill St. Chest 141 E4
Mill St. Congle 156 B2
Mill St. Congle 156 C2
Mill St. Crewe 190 B2
Mill St. Gold 3 D4
Mill St. Mfield 112 B4
Mill St. Nest 66 B4
Mill St. Warr 16 A3
Mill St. Wilm 60 A4
Mill St Mall. Mfield 112 B4
Mill Stream Cl. Goost 107 F1
Mill View Cl. Bulk 184 C1
Mill Way. Nant 204 C1
Mill Wharf. Waver 143 D3
Millar Cres. Wid 23 D4
Millbank. Lymm 18 C2
Millbank Cl. Chelf 84 A2
Millbank Dr. Mfield 86 C1
Millbeck Cl. Weston 207 D3
Millbrook End. Tatt 166 A1
Millbrook Gr. Wilm 34 B1
Millbuck Way. Sand 174 B3
Milldale Rd. Gold 4 A4
Millend La. Audley 209 E3
Miller St. Warr 16 B2
Millers La. Lymm 19 D3
Millers La. Waver 143 D2
Millers Meadow. Rain 88 C3
Millers View. Kids 195 D1
Millersdale Cl. Beb 43 F3
Millersdale Gr. Run 49 E3
Milley La. Pick 80 B4
Millfield La. Hay 1 C4
Millfield La. Saigh 142 C1
Millfield Rd. Wid 13 E1
Millfield Terr. El Por 69 E4
Millfields. Nant 204 B2
Millhouse Ave. Warr 16 B1
Millhouse La. Croft 9 D3
Millhouse La. Warr 9 D3
Millingfield The. H Chap 130 B1
Millingford Ind Est. Gold 3 D4
Millington Cl. Run 49 F2
Millington Hall La. Rosth 30 A3
Millington La. Rosth 30 A3
Millington La. Weave 102 A3
Millrace Dr. Wist 206 A4
Mills Way. Crewe 173 D1
Millstone Ave. Kids 194 C1
Millstone Cl. Poyn 36 C3
Millstone La. Nant 204 C3
Millstone Pas. Mfield 112 C3
Millway. Altr 32 B4
Millway. Waver 143 D3
Millway Rd. Speke 21 D2
Millwood Ct. Speke 21 D2
Milne Cl. Wist 189 F1
Milner Cop. Hes 41 D4
Milner Rd. Hes 41 D4
Milner Rd. North 103 E3
Milner St. Warr 15 F3
Milnthorpe Rd. Burton 6 C3
Milton Ave. Irlam 11 F3

Milton Ave. N-le-W 2 A2
Milton Ave. Wid 22 C4
Milton Cl. H Winch 80 A3
Milton Cres. Kids 210 B4
Milton Dr. Poyn 36 B2
Milton Dr. Wist 206 A4
Milton Gr. Hels 73 D1
Milton Gr. Poyn 36 B2
Milton Gr. Warr 16 B2
Milton Rd. Blacon 117 F3
Milton Rd. Bram 35 F4
Milton Rd. El Por 70 B2
Milton Rd. Gold 3 E4
Milton Rd. Wid 23 D4
Milton Rough. Act Br 76 C1
Milton St. Chest 118 B1
Milton St. Wid 23 D3
Milvain Dr. Warr 8 B1
Milverton Dr. Ch Hul 35 D3
Mine Way. Hay 1 C4
Miners Way. Speke 21 D2
Miners Way. Wid 23 D4
Minerva Cl. Warr 16 B1
Minn-end-la. Bosl 159 D3
Minn-end-la. Winc 159 D3
Minor Ave. S La E 112 B2
Minor Cl. Lymm 18 C1
Minshull La. Ch Min 171 E2
Minshull La. Wet 171 D3
Minshull New Rd. Crewe 189 F4
Minshull St. Knuts 57 D1
Minster Ct. Run 48 C4
Minster Ct. Wist 205 F4
Minster Dr. Altr 31 D4
Minton Cl. Congle 157 D1
Minton Way. Wid 13 D3
Mirfield Cl. Gold 3 E4
Mirion St. Crewe 190 B2
Misty Cl. Wid 12 B1
Mitchell Ave. Burton 6 C3
Mitchell Ave. Kids 194 B1
Mitchell Dr. Kids 194 B1
Mitchell St. Gold 3 D4
Mitchell St. Warr 26 B4
Mithril Cl. Wid 13 F2
Moat House Dr. Crewe 190 A1
Moat La. Audley 209 D2
Moat La. Hol Gr 10 C1
Mobberley Cl. Warr 17 E2
Mobberley Rd. Ashl 31 F2
Mobberley Rd. Knuts 57 E2
Mobberley Rd. Wilm 33 E1
Moelfre Dr. Ch Hul 35 E4
Mold Rd. Broug 139 D2
Mollington Ct. Moll 94 C1
Molly Potts Cl. Knuts 82 A4
Molyneux Ave. Warr 15 F4
Mona Ave. Chea 34 B4
Mond Cl. Winsf 149 D4
Mond Rd. Wid 23 D4
Mond St. North 78 A2
Monica Dr. Wid 13 D3
Monk St. Crewe 190 A3
Monk's La. Audlem 230 B3
Monks Gr. El Por 70 A3
Monks La. Acton 203 F4
Monks La. Crewe 189 F3
Monks La. Nant 204 C3
Monks Orch. Nant 204 C3
Monks St. Warr 15 F3
Monks Way. Hart 103 D2
Monkswood Cl. Warr 7 F1
Monmouth Cl. Warr 17 F4
Monroe Cl. Warr 17 D4
Monsall Cl. Mfield 112 C4
Monsall Dr. Mfield 112 C4
Montclare Cres. Warr 16 C1
Montcliffe Cl. Warr 9 E3
Montgomery Cl. Knuts 57 E2
Montgomery Rd. Wid 22 B4
Montgomery Way. Winsf 149 D4
Montmorency Rd. Knuts 57 E2
Montpelier Ave. Run 49 D3
Montrose Cl. Mfield 87 D1
Montrose Cl. Shav 206 A2
Montrose Cl. Warr 8 C2
Montrose Ct. Chest 140 C4
Montrose Ct. H Chap 130 A1
Monument Rd. Kids 210 B3
Monument View. Audley 209 F1
Mood Gdns. A Edge 60 A1
Moody St. Congle 156 B1
Moon St. Wid 23 D4
Moor Cl. Bidd 179 F1
Moor Cres. L Kin 139 E1
Moor La. Elton 72 C1
Moor La. Frod 74 A4
Moor La. H Kin 161 E3
Moor La. H Kin 161 E4
Moor La. Hawa 116 A1
Moor La. Hes 40 C4
Moor La. Waver 143 D3
Moor La. Wid 23 D4
Moor La. Wilm 59 F3
Moor La. Woodf 35 F2
Moor La S. Wid 22 C4
Moor St. Congle 156 C1
Moorcroft. Plum 80 C2
Moorcroft Ave. Chest 119 D1
Moorcroft Cres. G Sutt 119 E2
Moorcroft Mews. Brough 140 B3
Moordale Rd. Knuts 57 D1
Moorditch La. Frod 48 B1
Moore Ave. St Hel 1 A2
Moore Ave. Warr 17 E2
Moore Cl. Wid 13 E1
Moore Dr. Hay 1 C3
Moore Gr. Lymm 19 D3
Moore La. Moore 25 E3
Moore Rd. Audlem 230 B2
Moore Rd. Buer 230 B2
Moorfield Cres. Gold 4 A4
Moorfield Dr. Nest 41 E1
Moorfield Dr. Wilm 59 F3
Moorfield Rd. Wid 13 E2
Moorfields. Willas 205 F3
Moorfields. Wist 205 F3
Moorhead La. Bre Gr 154 B2
Moorhill Rd. Mfield 112 B2
Moorhouse Ave. Alsag 193 F2
Moorhouse Cl. Chest 118 B3
Mooring Cl. Run 50 B3
Moorings. Congle 156 C1
Moorings Cl. Nest 41 D1
Moorings The. Disley 38 C3
Moorings The. Hes 40 B4
Moorings The. Middle 128 B1
Moorland Cl. Hes 41 D4
Moorland Dr. Chea 34 C4
Moorland Dr. Run 50 C4
Moorland Park. Hes 41 D4
Moorland Rd. Bidd 179 E1
Moorland Rd. El Por 69 F4
Moorland Rd. Kids 195 E4
Moorlands Ave. Cudd 102 A2
Moorlands Cl. Mfield 87 E2
Moorlands Dr. Hay Gr 206 A1
Moorlands Park. Cudd 102 A2
Moors La. Winsf 149 E3
Moorsbrook Gr. Wilm 34 C1
Moorsfield Ave. Audlem 229 F2
Moorside. Knuts 57 D1
Moorside Ave. Nest 66 B4
Moorside Ct. Wid 22 C4
Moorside La. Nest 66 B4
Moorside La. Po Shr 63 F2
Moorson Ave. Sch Gr 194 C4
Moorview Gdns. Kids 195 F3
Moorway. Hes 41 D4
Moran Cres. Mfield 112 A4
Moran Rd. Mfield 112 A4
Moresby Cl. Run 50 C4
Moreton Ave. Bram 35 F3
Moreton Dr. Alsag 193 E2
Moreton Dr. H Chap 130 A2
Moreton Dr. Sand 175 E4
Moreton Dr. Wilm 34 C2
Moreton Rd. Crewe 189 F2
Moreton St. North 78 B1
Moreton Terr. Frod 74 A4
Morgan Cl. Blacon 117 F3
Morland Ave. Beb 43 E3
Morland Ave. Nest 66 C4
Morley Cl. M Traf 119 F4
Morley Dr. Congle 157 D1
Morley Green. Wilm 33 E1
Morley Rd. Run 23 D1
Morley Rd. Warr 16 A1
Morley St. Warr 16 B3
Mornant Ave. Hart 103 D2
Mornington Ave. El Por 70 B2
Morphany La. Dares 51 F3
Morreys La. Dela 122 C4
Morris Ave. Warr 16 C2
Morris Cl. Hay 1 A3
Morris Dr. Weave 77 E1
Morris Park. Hart 103 D2
Morrison Cl. Gt San 15 D3
Mort Ave. Warr 17 D2
Mortimer Ave. Warr 16 A4
Mortimer Dr. Sand 175 E3
Mortlake Cl. Wid 12 B2
Mortlake Cres. Chest 119 D1
Morton Ave. Hels 73 D1
Morton Cl. Gt San 15 E4
Morton Dr. Poyn 36 C2
Morton Dr. S La E 112 C2
Morton Rd. Blacon 117 F2
Morton Rd. Run 50 B4
Morval Cres. Run 49 E4
Morven Cl. Warr 8 C2
Mosedale Gr. Run 49 F3
Moseley Ave. Warr 17 D2
Moss Bank. Ch Hul 35 E3
Moss Bank. Chest 118 B2
Moss Bank. Winsf 126 B1
Moss Bank Rd. Wid 23 E4
Moss Bower Rd. Mfield 112 B2
Moss Brow. Boll 87 F4
Moss Brow La. H Legh 28 B2
Moss Cl. Warr 16 C1
Moss Cl. Will 68 A4
Moss Croft. Crewe 190 A4
Moss Dr. Man 98 C2
Moss Dr. Middle 151 E3
Moss Gate. Warr 10 A3
Moss Gr. Brough 140 B3
Moss Gr. Lymm 19 D2
Moss Green Way. St Hel 1 A1
Moss La. A Edge 60 A1
Moss La. Boll 87 F4
Moss La. Bre Gr 154 C3
Moss La. Ch Hul 35 E3
Moss La. Ch Min 172 C1
Moss La. Cran 129 D4
Moss La. Crewe 173 D1
Moss La. Cudd 102 A2
Moss La. Eaton 156 C3
Moss La. H Legh 28 B2
Moss La. H Legh 29 F3
Moss La. Hol Gr 10 C3
Moss La. Irlam 11 E3
Moss La. Knuts 56 B3
Moss La. Law-g 194 C2
Moss La. Leigh 5 F3
Moss La. Lost 105 E4
Moss La. M St A 61 D1
Moss La. Man 99 D2
Moss La. Mfield 112 B2
Moss La. Middle 129 D4
Moss La. Mobb 58 C2
Moss La. Moore 25 D3
Moss La. Norley 101 D3
Moss La. North 103 E4
Moss La. Oller 83 E2
Moss La. Part 11 F1
Moss La. Part 11 F2
Moss La. Part 20 A4
Moss La. Sand 174 B4
Moss La. Sidd 109 F1
Moss La. St Hel 1 A1
Moss La. Warm 173 E2
Moss La. Wilm 33 F3
Moss Pl. Kids 195 D2
Moss Rd. A Edge 60 B1
Moss Rd. Astb 178 C4
Moss Rd. Congle 178 C4
Moss Rd. Irlam 11 E4
Moss Rd. North 103 E4
Moss Rd. Warr 17 D2
Moss Rose. A Edge 60 A1
Moss Side La. Antro 53 E4
Moss Side La. Hol Gr 10 C2
Moss Side La. Penk 24 C4
Moss Side Rd. Irlam 11 F3
Moss Sq. Crewe 190 B2
Moss Sq. Mfield 112 B2
Moss St. Weave 77 E1
Moss St. Wid 23 E4
Moss Terr. North 78 B1
Moss Terr. Warren 112 A3
Moss The. Comb 78 B4
Moss View Rd. Warren 112 A2
Moss Way. Alsag 193 D2
Mossdale Cl. Crewe 189 F2
Mossfields. Alsag 193 D2
Mossford Ave. Crewe 190 A4
Mosshall La. Stret 26 C1
Mosslands Cl. El Por 69 F1
Mossley Ave. Beb 43 E4
Mossley Ct. Congle 178 C4
Mossvale. El Por 69 E4
Mosswood Rd. Wilm 34 C1
Moston Gr. Lymm 18 B2
Moston Rd. Chest 95 E1
Moston Rd. Chest 118 B4
Moston Rd. Sand 174 B3
Moston Way. El Por 69 F2
Mostyn Ave. Hes 40 B4
Mostyn Gdns. Nest 41 E1
Mostyn Pl. Blacon 117 F3
Mottershead Rd. Wid 23 D4
Mottram Cl. Middle 151 D4
Mottram Rd. A Edge 60 B1
Moughland La. Run 49 D4
Moulders La. Warr 16 A2
Moulton Cl. Knuts 57 E1
Moulton Cl. Run 49 F2
Mount Ave. Hes 40 C4
Mount Hall Mews. Hes 40 C4
Mount Pleasant. Audlem 230 A2
Mount Pleasant. Chest 140 C4
Mount Pleasant. Crewe 190 A3
Mount Pleasant. Elton 72 A2
Mount Pleasant. Hasl 191 E2
Mount Pleasant. Kids 195 D1
Mount Pleasant. Wid 13 D1
Mount Pleasant. Wilm 60 A4
Mount Pleasant Ave. St Hel 1 A2
Mount Pleasant Dr. Winsf 149 D4
Mount Pleasant Rd. Dave 103 F1
Mount Pleasant Rd. Sch Gr 195 D4
Mount Rd. Kids 195 D1
Mount Rd. Run 49 F4
Mount St. Wid 13 D1
Mount Terr. Mfield 112 C4
Mount The. Altr 32 B4
Mount The. Chest 118 C1
Mount The. Congle 156 A1
Mount The. G Bud 79 D4
Mount The. Hes 40 C4
Mount The. Kids 195 D1
Mount The. Sch Gr 194 C4
Mount Way. Waver 143 D2
Mountain View. Brough 140 C3
Mountain View. Hels 73 D2
Mountbatten Way. Congle 156 B2
Mountfield Rd. Bram 35 F3
Mourne Cl. El Por 69 D3
Mow Cop Rd. Kids 195 E3
Mow La. Bidd 179 D1
Mow La. Sch Gr 195 D3
Mowcroft La. Penk 14 A2
Mowpen Brow. H Legh 29 D3
Moxon Ave. Warr 16 C3
Mudhouse La. Nest 67 F1
Mudhurst La. Disley 38 C1
Muir Rd. Blacon 117 F2
Muirfield Cl. Wilm 60 B4
Muirfield Dr. Mfield 87 E2
Muirfield Dr. Winsf 126 B1
Mulberry Ave. Gold 3 F4
Mulberry Cl. Chea 34 B4
Mulberry Cl. Elton 72 B2
Mulberry Cl. Warr 17 F3
Mulberry Gdns. Sand 174 B4
Mulberry Rd. Wist 189 F1
Mulberry Rise. North 103 E4
Mulcaster Ct. Hasl 191 E3
Mullen Cl. Warr 7 F1
Mullins Ave. N-le-W 2 B3
Mullion Gr. Warr 9 D1
Mulsford La. Worth 222 A4
Murdishaw Ave. Run 50 B3
Muriel Cl. Gt San 14 B3
Murray Cl. Mfield 87 D1
Murrayfield. Prest 87 D3
Murrayfield Dr. Willas 205 E3
Museum St. Warr 16 A2
Music Hall Pass. Chest 118 B1
Myddleton La. Win 8 B3
Myrica Gr. Chest 119 D2
Myrtle Ave. H Kin 161 D4
Myrtle Ave. Hay 1 A4
Myrtle Ave. N-le-W 2 B1
Myrtle Gr. Chest 119 D2
Myrtle Gr. Warr 16 B2
Myrtle Gr. Wid 22 B4
Myrtle Rd. Part 11 E2
Myrtle St. El Por 70 B4
Mythholme Ave. Irlam 11 E2

N Brook Rd. Utkin 146 A4
Nab Cl. Boll 63 E1
Nab La. Boll 63 E1
Nabbswood Rd. Kids 195 D1
Nairn Ave. H Chap 130 A1
Nairn Cl. Beb 43 E2
Nairn Cl. Warr 9 D2
Nancy View. Boll 88 A4
Nansmoss La. Wilm 33 E1
Nantwich Rd. Audley 209 D1
Nantwich Rd. Barb 187 D4
Nantwich Rd. Betley 208 C1
Nantwich Rd. Brox 183 E1
Nantwich Rd. Crewe 190 B1
Nantwich Rd. El Por 69 F2
Nantwich Rd. Middle 151 D4
Nantwich Rd. Tarp 168 B4
Nantwich Rd. Tiver 168 B4
Nantwich Rd. Wimbo 150 C3
Nantwich Rd. Winsf 151 D4
Nantwich Rd. Woore 232 A1
Nantwich Rd. Worles 189 E1
Nantwich Rd. Wren 217 D3
Nantwich Way. Wilm 34 C3
Naomi Cl. Blacon 117 E3
Napier Gdns. Kids 195 D1
Napier Rd. Chest 118 B4
Napier St. Warr 16 B3
Napley Dr. N in H 236 B1
Napley Rd. Muck 236 B1
Napley Rd. N in H 236 B1
Nares Cl. Warr 7 E1
Narrow La. Adlin 37 D1
Naseby Rd. Congle 156 A2
Nat La. Winsf 126 C1
Naughton Lea. Cront 12 B2
Naughton Rd. Wid 23 D4
Navigation Cl. Run 50 B3
Navigation Rd. North 103 F4
Navigation St. Warr 16 B3
Naylor Ave. Gold 3 D4
Naylor Ct. North 103 F4
Naylor Rd. Wid 13 E1
Naylor St. Warr 16 A3
Neal Ave. Chea 34 A4
Neath Cl. Poyn 36 B3
Needham Dr. Hart 103 D2
Needhams Wharf Cl. Mfield 88 A1
Neil St. Wid 13 D1
Neills Rd. Bo Hea 6 A3
Nelson Ave. Poyn 37 D2
Nelson Cl. Poyn 37 D2
Nelson Dr. Irlam 11 F3
Nelson Gr. Alsag 193 F1
Nelson Rd. El Por 70 B4
Nelson St. Chest 118 C1
Nelson St. Congle 156 B1
Nelson St. Crewe 190 B1
Nelson St. Mfield 112 B4
Nelson St. N-le-W 2 A2
Nelson St. Run 23 D2
Nelson St. Wid 23 D1
Nemos Cl. Hels 73 E1
Neptune Cl. Run 50 B4
Nesfield Cl. Hasl 191 F4
Nesfield Dr. Hasl 191 F4
Nessina Gr. Wist 205 F4
Neston Dr. Chest 118 C3
Neston Gn. El Por 69 E2
Neston Rd. Nest 67 D2
Neston Rd. Thor H 41 F3
Neston Rd. Will 67 F4
Neston Way. Wilm 34 B2
Nether Fold. Prest 87 D4
Netherfield. Wid 22 B4
Netherfields. A Edge 85 D4
Netherlea Ct. Goost 130 B4
Netherley Rd. Tar Gr 12 A1
Netherpool Rd. El Por 69 F4
Netherton Dr. Frod 74 A4
Neumann St. North 104 A4
Neville Ave. St Hel 1 A1
Neville Ave. Warr 8 B1
Neville Cres. Penk 15 D2
Neville Dr. Chest 119 D1
Neville Rd. Beb 43 F4
Neville Rd. Chest 119 D1
Neville St. Crewe 190 B1
Neville St. N-le-W 2 A2
Nevin Cl. Bram 36 A4
Nevin Rd. Blacon 117 E2
Nevis Dr. Crewe 189 E2
New Bank Rd. Wid 12 A1
New Barnet. Wid 12 C2
New Cane Bank. Chest 118 A1
New Chester Rd. Beb 43 F3
New Crane St. Chest 118 A1
New Cut La. Warr 17 E4
New Farm Ct. Gt Bar 120 C3
New Grosvenor Rd. El Por 70 A4
New Hall Ave. Chea 34 A4
New Hall La. Croft 4 C1
New Hall La. Cul 5 D1
New Hall St. Mfield 87 E1
New Hey La. Will 68 A3
New Horwich Rd. W Br 65 F4
New Inn La. Ha Gr 176 A1
New King St. Audley 209 E1
New King St. Middle 128 B1
New La. Aldf 180 C3
New La. Apple 27 D3
New La. Burw 183 F2
New La. Croft 9 D4
New La. Winsf 149 F2
New Manchester Rd. Warr 17 D4
New Manor Rd. P-o-t-H 51 D3
New Moss Rd. Irlam 11 E3
New Pale Rd. Man 99 E3
New Platt La. Goost 130 B4
New Rd. Antro 27 E1
New Rd. Astb 178 A2
New Rd. Audley 209 F2
New Rd. Chin 39 F1
New Rd. Dudd 145 D3
New Rd. El Por 69 D4
New Rd. Lymm 18 C2
New Rd. Mere 30 C2
New Rd. North 78 B2
New Rd. Prest 87 D4
New Rd. Rad 132 B1
New Rd. W Br 65 F3
New Rd. Warr 16 B2
New Rd. Winsf 126 C1
New Rd. Wren 216 C2
New Scool La. El Por 44 A1
New St. Congle 156 C1
New St. Hasl 191 E3
New St. N Mills 39 E4
New St. Nest 66 C3
New St. Run 23 D1
New St. Sand 174 B4
New St. Wilm 59 F3
New St Cotts. Eaton 157 D3
New Warrington Rd. North 79 D1
New York Ave. Wythe 33 D4
Newall Cres. Winsf 127 D1
Newbold Way. Nant 204 C2
Newbridge Cl. Run 50 B3
Newbridge Cl. Warr 7 E1
Newbridge Rd. Stan 70 C2
Newburgh Cl. Run 24 B1
Newbury Ave. Crewe 190 B4
Newbury Cl. Ch Hul 35 D3
Newbury Cl. Wid 13 D2
Newbury Rd. Chea 34 B4
Newbury Rd. Chest 140 C3
Newby Ct. Congle 156 A1
Newcastle Rd. Astb 178 A4
Newcastle Rd. Bre Gr 153 F2
Newcastle Rd. Congle 156 A1
Newcastle Rd. Ha Gr 176 A2
Newcastle Rd. Hay Gr 205 E2
Newcastle Rd. Ho Co 206 B2
Newcastle Rd. Kids 210 C4
Newcastle Rd. Shav 206 B2
Newcastle Rd. Small 176 B3
Newcastle Rd. Woore 232 C1
Newcastle Rd N. Bre Gr 153 F3

Newcastle Rd S. Bre Gr 153 F3
Newcastle St. Crewe 190 A3
Newchapel Rd. Kids 195 E2
Newchurch La. Cul 4 C1
Newcombe Ave. Warr 16 C4
Newcroft. Saug 94 A1
Newdigate St. Crewe 190 B2
Newdigate St. Crewe 190 B3
Newfield Dr. Crewe 190 C3
Newfield St. Sand 175 D4
Newgate. Mfield 112 B4
Newgate. Wilm 59 E4
Newgate St. Chest 118 B1
Newhall Ave. Sand 175 D3
Newhall Ct. Chest 118 C3
Newhall Rd. Chest 118 C3
Newham Cl. S La E 112 C2
Newhaven Rd. Warr 8 A2
Newland Cl. Wid 12 B2
Newlands Ave. Bram 35 F4
Newlands Ave. Ch Hul 35 D4
Newlands Cl. Ch Hul 35 D4
Newlands Cl. Frod 74 B3
Newlands Dr. Gold 3 E4
Newlands Dr. Wilm 59 F3
Newlands Rd. Mfield 111 F4
Newlands Rd. Warr 16 C1
Newlyn Ave. Congle 178 C4
Newlyn Ave. Mfield 86 B1
Newlyn Cl. Run 50 A3
Newlyn Gdns. Penk 14 B2
Newman St. Warr 16 C2
Newman's La. Hay Gr 219 E4
Newmoore La. Run 24 C2
Newnham Dr. El Por 70 B2
Newplatt La. Allos 107 D1
Newplatt La. Cran 107 D1
Newport Gr. N-u-L 210 C1
Newquay Cl. Run 50 A3
Newquay Ct. Congle 178 C4
Newquay Dr. Bram 35 F4
Newquay Dr. Mfield 111 E4
Newry Pk. Chest 118 B2
Newry Pk E. Chest 118 B2
Newsham Cl. Wid 12 A2
Newsholme Cl. Cul 4 C2
Newstead Cl. Poyn 36 B3
Newton Bank. Middle 128 A1
Newton Gr. Warr 8 C2
Newton Hall Ct. Chest 118 C3
Newton Hall Dr. Chest 118 C3
Newton Hall La. Mobb 58 C3
Newton Hall Mews. Middle . 128 B1
Newton Heath. Middle 128 A1
Newton Hollow. Kings 74 B1
Newton La. Chest 118 C2
Newton La. Dares 51 F4
Newton La. Golb 166 B2
Newton La. N-le-W 2 C3
Newton La. Tatt 166 B2
Newton Park Dr. N-le-W 2 C2
Newton Park View. Chest .. 118 B3
Newton Pl. Congle 156 C1
Newton Rd. El Por 70 B3
Newton Rd. Gold 3 E3
Newton Rd. St Hel 1 A2
Newton Rd. Warr 8 A3
Newton Rd. Wilm 34 A1
Newton Rd. Win 8 A3
Newton St. Crewe 190 B3
Newton St. Mfield 112 B4
Newtons Cres. Hasl 191 F4
Newtons Gr. Hasl 191 F4
Newtons La. Hasl 191 F4
Newtown. Kids 195 F1
Newtown. Nest 66 C4
Newtown Cl. Chest 118 B1
Nicholas Ave. North 104 B3
Nicholas Ct. Chest 118 B1
Nicholas Rd. Weave 77 E1
Nicholas Rd. Wid 22 B4
Nicholas St. Chest 118 B1
Nicholas St Mews. Chest ... 118 B1
Nicholls St. Warr 17 D1
Nicholson Ave. Mfield 87 F1
Nicholson Cl. Mfield 87 F1
Nicholson St. Warr 15 F3
Nickelby Rd. Poyn 36 C2
Nickolson Cl. M Traf 119 F4
Nicol Ave. Warr 17 F4
Nidderdale Cl. Congle 157 D3
Niddries La. Moult 126 C4
Nield Ct. Chest 118 B4
Nigel Gresley Cl. Crewe 191 D2
Nigel Rd. Hes 41 E4
Nigel Wlk. Run 24 A1
Nightingale Cl. Farn 180 C1
Nightingale Cl. Middle 151 E3
Nightingale Cl. Run 49 F3
Nightingale Cl. Warr 9 F2
Nightingale Cl. Wilm 34 A1
Nightingale Ct. Winsf 149 E3
Nile St. Crewe 190 B1
Nixon Dr. Winsf 126 A1
Nixon Rd. Cudd 101 F2
Nixon St. Crewe 189 F3
Nixon St. Mfield 112 A4
Noahs Ark La. L End 58 C1
Noble Cl. Warr 9 F2
Nook La. Antro 53 F3
Nook La. Gold 3 D4
Nook La. Warr 9 D1
Nook La. Warr 17 D2
Nook The. Brough 140 C3
Nook The. Ch Hul 35 E3
Nook The. Chest 118 C2
Nook The. G Sutt 119 E2
Noon Ct. N-le-W 2 A1
Nora St. Warr 16 B3
Norbreck Ave. Crewe 190 A1
Norbreck Dr. Gt San 15 D2
Norbury Ave. Warr 16 B4
Norbury Cl. Ho Co 206 C2
Norbury Cl. Knuts 57 E2
Norbury Cl. Wid 13 F1
Norbury Dr. Congle 156 C2
Norbury Dr. Middle 151 D4
Norbury Hollow Rd. Haz Gr . 37 D4
Norbury St. Mfield 112 B4
Norbury St. North 104 A4
Norbury Way. Wilm 34 B3
Norcott Ave. Warr 16 C1
Norcott Dr. Burton 6 C3
Norden Cl. Warr 9 E3
Norfolk Cl. Irlam 11 E3
Norfolk Dr. Gt San 14 C3
Norfolk Gr. Bidd 179 E1
Norfolk Pl. Wid 22 B4
Norfolk Rd. Chest 118 C2
Norfolk Rd. Congle 156 C2
Norfolk Rd. El Por 70 B3
Norfolk Rd. Kids 194 C1
Norfolk St. Run 23 D2
Norfolk Wlk. Mfield 86 C1
Norgrove Cl. Run 50 B4
Norland St. Wid 13 E1
Norland's La. Cront 12 C4
Norland's La. Wid 12 C4
Norleane Cres. Run 49 D4
Norley Ave. Beb 43 F2
Norley Ave. El Por 69 F3
Norley Dr. Chest 119 E1
Norley La. Crow 76 A1
Norley La. Norley 101 D4
Norley Rd. Cudd 101 F2
Norley Rd. Kings 75 D1
Norley Rd. Kings 100 B4
Norley Rd. Norley 100 B4
Norman Ave. Hay 2 A4
Norman Ave. N-le-W 2 C2
Norman Cl. El Por 94 C4
Norman Dr. Winsf 149 E3
Norman Rd. Run 23 D1
Norman St. Warr 16 A3
Norman Way. Blacon 117 F3
Norman's La. Whit 52 C3
Normandy Ave. Winsf 149 E4
Normandy Rd. Chest 95 E1
Norreys Ave. Warr 15 F4
Norris Rd. Blacon 117 F3
Norris St. Warr 16 B4
North Ave. Warr 16 A4
North Downs. Knuts 57 E1
North Dr. H Legh 29 E2
North Dr. Hes 41 D4
North Dr. North 104 C4
North Fields. Knuts 57 E2
North Florida Rd. Hay 1 C4
North Green. Sea 116 A3
North Mead. Prest 87 D3
North Parade. Nest 41 D1
North Park Brook Rd. Warr 7 F1
North Rd. Altr 32 A4
North Rd. El Por 44 C1
North Rd. El Por 70 A4
North Rd. Halew 21 D3
North Rd. Wythe 33 E3
North St. Brough 140 A4
North St. Chest 119 D1
North St. Congle 156 B2
North St. Crewe 190 B4
North St. Hawa 116 A2
North St. Hay 1 C3
North St. Sch Gr 195 D3
North Stafford St. Crewe 190 B2
North View. Crewe 190 A3
North View. Gt San 14 C4
North Way. H Chap 130 B2
North Way. Shav 206 B3
Northbank Wlk. Crewe 206 B4
Northbury Rd. El Por 69 F1
Northcote Rd. Bram 35 F4
Northdale Rd. Warr 17 D4
Northern La. Wid 12 A2
Northern Pathway. Chest 141 F4
Northern Rise. El Por 69 F2
Northfield Dr. Bidd 179 F1
Northfield Dr. Wilm 60 B4
Northfield Pl. Shav 206 B3
Northgate. Utkin 146 A4
Northgate Ave. Chest 118 B2
Northgate Ave. Mfield 87 E1
Northgate Row. Chest 118 B1
Northgate St. Chest 118 B1
Northlands. Woore 232 B1
Northolt Ct. Warr 8 C1
Northumberland Rd. Part 11 F1
Northward Rd. Wilm 59 F3
Northway. Chest 141 D4
Northway. Lymm 18 B2
Northway. North 78 B1
Northway. Run 49 F4
Northway. Warr 8 A1
Northway. Wid 12 B1
Northwich Rd. Antro 53 D3
Northwich Rd. Cran 106 C1
Northwich Rd. Dutt 51 D1
Northwich Rd. G Bud 78 C4
Northwich Rd. Knuts 56 B1
Northwich Rd. Run 50 B3
Northwich Rd. Run 50 C2
Northwich Rd. Stret 52 C4
Northwich Rd. Tab 56 B1
Northwich Rd. Weave 102 C4
Northwich Rd. Whit 52 C3
Northwood Ave. Middle 151 F3
Northwood Ave. N-le-W 2 C2
Northwood La. H Legh 28 C1
Northwood Rd. Run 23 F1
Norton Ave. Brough 140 B3
Norton Ave. Penk 14 C3
Norton Gate. Run 50 B4
Norton Hill. Run 24 B1
Norton La. Run 50 A4
Norton Rd. Chest 119 E1
Norton Station Rd. Run 50 B4
Norton View. Run 50 A4
Norton Village. Run 24 B1
Norton Way. Sand 174 B4
Norton's La. Gt Bar 98 A1
Norton's La. Mould 98 A1
Nortons La. Dela 122 C4
Nortonwood La. Run 24 B1
Norville. El Por 69 E4
Norwich Ave. Gold 3 E4
Norwich Ct. Mfield 112 C4
Norwood Ave. Ch Hul 35 E3
Norwood Ave. Gold 3 F4
Norwood Ave. H La 37 E4
Norwood Dr. Chest 141 D3
Nottingham Cl. Warr 17 F3
Nun House Cl. Winsf 127 D1
Nun House Dr. Winsf 127 D1
Nun's Rd. Chest 141 E4
Nuns Rd. Chest 118 B1
Nunsmere Cl. Winsf 127 D1
Nursery Ave. Altr 31 F4
Nursery Cl. Shav 206 B2
Nursery Cl. Wid 13 E2
Nursery Dr. Bidd 179 E1
Nursery La. Congle 156 C1
Nursery La. N Ald 84 B3
Nursery La. Sidd 110 A2
Nursery La. Wilm 59 F3
Nursery Rd. Hasl 192 C2
Nursery Rd. North 78 A2
Nursery Rd. Sch Gr 194 C3
Nursery The. North 103 E3
Nutfield Ave. Crewe 190 A4
Nuthurst Gdns. Nant 204 C3
Nuttall Ct. Warr 9 E2
Nuttall St. Irlam 11 F3

Oak Ave. Alsag 193 F1
Oak Ave. Disley 39 D3
Oak Ave. Gold 3 D4
Oak Ave. Hay 1 C4
Oak Ave. Irlam 11 E3
Oak Ave. Mfield 112 A3
Oak Ave. N-le-W 2 B2
Oak Ave. Wilm 59 F3
Oak Ave. Winsf 149 E4
Oak Bank. Disley 39 D3
Oak Bank Cl. Willas 205 F2
Oak Bank Dr. Boll 63 D1
Oak Bank La. Chest 119 E3
Oak Cl. Wilm 59 F3
Oak Cottages. Wilm 33 F2
Oak Dr. Ch Hul 35 E4
Oak Dr. H Kin 161 D4
Oak Dr. Middle 151 E4
Oak Dr. Run 49 E4
Oak Gr. El Por 70 A2
Oak Gr. Nant 204 C2
Oak Gr. Poyn 36 B2
Oak House La. Winsf 149 D4
Oak La. Boll 88 A3
Oak La. Cudd 101 F1
Oak La. Mart 133 E3
Oak La. Wilm 59 F3
Oak Lea Ave. Wilm 60 A3
Oak Mews. Wilm 34 B1
Oak Rd. Chelf 84 A2
Oak Rd. Chest 140 C3
Oak Rd. El Por 43 F1
Oak Rd. Lymm 18 B2
Oak Rd. M St A 86 A4
Oak Rd. Part 11 E1
Oak Rd. Penk 14 C2
Oak St. Crewe 190 B2
Oak St. Croft 9 D4
Oak St. El Por 70 B4
Oak St. North 79 D1
Oak St. Sand 174 B4
Oak St. Sch Gr 193 F4
Oak Tree Cl. Crewe 190 C3
Oak Tree Dr. Crewe 190 C3
Oak Tree Gate. Audlem 229 F2
Oak Tree La. Cran 129 F4
Oak View. Knuts 57 E1
Oak View. Mart 133 E3
Oak View. Speke 21 D2
Oak Wood Rd. Mere 29 F1
Oakdale Ave. Warr 16 B1
Oakdale Cl. Broug 139 D2
Oakdene Ave. Chea 34 A4
Oakdene Ave. El Por 69 E3
Oakdene Ave. Warr 17 E4
Oakdene Cl. Beb 43 E3
Oakdene Way. Tarp 168 B4
Oakenclough Cl. Wilm 34 B1
Oakes Cnr. Hather 219 F2
Oakfield Ave. Chest 118 B4
Oakfield Ave. Knuts 57 E2
Oakfield Ave. Wren 216 C2
Oakfield Cl. A Edge 60 A2
Oakfield Cl. Wren 216 C2
Oakfield Dr. Chest 118 B4
Oakfield Dr. Wid 22 A4
Oakfield Rd. A Edge 60 A1
Oakfield Rd. Beb 43 E4
Oakfield Rd. Blacon 117 E2
Oakfield Rd. El Por 68 C4
Oakfield Rd. Plum 80 C2
Oakfield Rd. Poyn 36 C2
Oakfield Rise. H Chap 130 A2
Oakhill Cl. Mfield 87 D2
Oakhurst Chase. A Edge 60 A1
Oakhurst Dr. Wist 206 A4
Oakland Ave. Hasl 191 E2
Oakland St. Warr 16 C4
Oakland St. Wid 23 D2
Oaklands. G Sutt 119 F2
Oaklands Ave. Tatt 166 A1
Oaklands Cl. Wilm 34 C1
Oaklands Cres. Tatt 166 A1
Oaklands Dr. Lymm 18 B1
Oaklands Rd. Gold 3 F4
Oaklands Rd. Oller 82 C3
Oaklea Ave. Chest 118 C2
Oakleigh. Knuts 82 B4
Oakleigh Ct. Congle 155 F2
Oakleigh Rise. North 78 C1
Oakley Cl. Sand 175 D4
Oakley St. Crewe 190 B3
Oakmere Cl. Sand 174 C4
Oakmere Dr. Chest 142 A4
Oakmere Dr. El Por 69 F1
Oakmere Dr. Penk 14 C2
Oakmere Rd. Wilm 34 B3
Oakmere Rd. Winsf 125 F1
Oakmere St. Run 23 D1
Oaks Dr The. Chest 118 B4
Oaks The. Beb 43 E4
Oaksdean Ct. Wilm 34 A1
Oaksway. Hes 41 E3
Oaktree Cl. North 78 A2
Oaktree Cl. Tarp 146 B1
Oakways. Apple 26 B3
Oakwood Ave. Warr 16 C4
Oakwood Ave. Wilm 59 F3
Oakwood Cres. Crewe 189 F2
Oakwood Cres. Sand 175 F3
Oakwood Ct. Altr 31 D4
Oakwood Dr. Prest 87 E3
Oakwood Gate. Warr 9 E2
Oakwood La. Altr 31 D4
Oakwood La. North 78 A1
Oakwood La. Sand 174 A4
Oakwood Rd. Disley 38 B3
Oakwood Rd. Sch Gr 193 F4
Oat Market. Nant 204 C3
Oathills. Malpas 213 D3
Oathills Cl. Tarp 146 B1
Oathills Dr. Tarp 146 B1
Oatlands. A Edge 85 D4
Oban Dr. Hes 41 D4
Oban Gr. Warr 9 D2
O'Connell Cl. Hay 1 B3
Offley Ave. Sand 175 D4
Offley Rd. Sand 175 D4
Ogden Rd. Ch Hul 35 E3
Oglet La. Speke 46 C4
Oil Sites Rd. Stan 71 E3
Okell St. Run 23 D1
Old Boston. Hay 2 A4
Old Brickworks
Industrial Estate. Po Shr 63 F2
Old Butt La. Kids 194 B1
Old Chester Rd. El Por 69 E2
Old Chester Rd. H Wal 25 F4
Old Chester Rd. Hels 73 E2
Old Church Cl. El Por 70 B4
Old Coach Rd. Brox 199 D3
Old Coach Rd. Ed Gr 199 D3
Old Coach Rd. Kels 122 B3
Old Farm Cl. Will 68 A4
Old Gate Cl. Middle 151 D4
Old Hall Ave. W Br 65 F2
Old Hall Cl. Warr 26 A4
Old Hall Cres. Wilm 34 C2
Old Hall Ct. Asht 121 F4
Old Hall Ct. Malpas 213 D2
Old Hall Dr. El Por 70 A2
Old Hall Gdns. Chest 118 C2
Old Hall La. Elton 72 A2
Old Hall La. Knuts 56 A2
Old Hall La. Tab 55 F2
Old Hall La. Woodf 61 E4
Old Hall Park. G Sutt 119 F3
Old Hall Pl. Chest 118 B1
Old Hall Rd. Gt San 15 E4
Old Hall Rd. North 104 A3
Old Hall St. Mfield 87 E1
Old Hey Wlk. N-le-W 2 B1
Old Higher Rd. Wid 21 E3
Old Hutte La. Hale 21 D3
Old La. Act Br 76 C2
Old La. Antro 53 E2
Old La. Dave 104 B1
Old La. Poul 162 C1
Old La. Pulf 162 C1
Old Market Pl. Knuts 57 D1
Old Mill Cl. Hes 41 D4
Old Mill Ct. Chest 118 B3
Old Mill La. Haz Gr 37 D4
Old Mill La. Mfield 112 C3
Old Mill La. Whit 52 C2
Old Mill Rd. Sand 175 E3
Old Moss La. Leigh 5 F3
Old Moss La. Tarv 144 B4
Old Orchard. Wilm 60 A4
Old Orchard The. Antro 53 E2
Old Park Rd. Crewe 207 E4
Old Pearl La. Chest 119 D1
Old Quay Cl. Nest 66 B4
Old Quay La. Nest 66 B4
Old Quay St. Wid 23 D2
Old Rd. Audley 209 D1
Old Rd. North 78 B2
Old Rd. W Br 39 E2
Old Rd. W Br 65 F2
Old Rd. W Br 65 F3
Old Rd. Warr 16 A2
Old Rd. Wilm 34 B2
Old Rd. Wilm 60 A4
Old School Cl. Farn 180 C1
Old School House La. Win 8 A4
Old Smithy La. Lymm 18 B1
Old Stack Yd. Gt Bar 120 C3
Old Vicarage Gdns.
Audlem 229 F2
Old Vicarage Rd. Will 68 A4
Old Wargrave Rd. N-le-W 2 B2
Old Warrington Rd. North 79 D1
Old Whint Rd. Hay 1 A3
Old Woman's La. Christ 142 B4
Old Wrexham Rd. Chest 141 E4
Oldfield Cres. Chest 140 C3
Oldfield Dr. Chest 119 E1
Oldfield Dr. Mobb 58 A2
Oldfield La. Dun T 20 C2
Oldfield Rd. El Por 70 A3
Oldfield Rd. Lymm 18 B2
Oldfield Rd. Sand 174 C2
Oldgate. Wid 22 B4
Oldhall St. Malpas 213 D2
Oldham St. Boll 88 A4
Oldham St. Warr 16 B2
Oldham's Rise. Mfield 87 E2
Oldhams Hill. North 78 C1
Oldhill Cl. Kids 210 C3
O'Leary St. Warr 16 B4
Olive Dr. Nest 66 C4
Olive Gr. N-u-L 210 B1
Olive Rd. Nest 66 C4
Oliver Cl. Boll 87 F4
Oliver La. El Por 69 E2
Oliver St. Warr 16 A3
Ollersett Ave. N Mills 39 E4
Ollershaw La. Mars 79 E2
Ollerton Rd. Wilm 34 B3
Ollier St. Wid 23 D4
108 Steps. Mfield 112 B4
One Oak La. Wilm 60 C4
Onneley La. Made 232 C2
Onslow Rd. Blacon 117 E2
Onston La. Crow 101 F4
Openshaw La. Irlam 11 F3
Orange Gr. Warr 8 C1
Orange La. North 79 E1
Orchard Ave. Act Br 76 C2
Orchard Ave. Lymm 18 C2
Orchard Ave. Part 11 F2
Orchard Ave. W Br 65 E4
Orchard Brow. Hol Gr 11 D1
Orchard Cl. Ch Hul 35 E4
Orchard Cl. Chest 118 B3
Orchard Cl. El Por 69 F1
Orchard Cl. Frod 74 A3
Orchard Cl. Goost 107 F1
Orchard Cl. H Winch 80 A3
Orchard Cl. Mfield 112 A3
Orchard Cl. Middle 151 E4
Orchard Cl. North 78 A2
Orchard Cl. Poyn 36 C2
Orchard Cl. Weave 77 E1
Orchard Cl. Wilm 59 F3
Orchard Cl. Winsf 149 E4
Orchard Cres. Kids 194 B1

Orchard Cres. N Ald 84 C3
Orchard Cres. Nant 204 C2
Orchard Croft. G Sutt 119 F3
Orchard Ct. Alsag 193 F2
Orchard Ct. Chest 119 D1
Orchard Ct. Hasl 191 E2
Orchard Dene. Cudd 101 E3
Orchard Dr. L Lei 77 E3
Orchard Dr. Nest 66 C3
Orchard Dr. Wilm 34 C1
Orchard Green. A Edge 60 A1
Orchard Haven. El Por 69 F1
Orchard La. El Por 69 D4
Orchard Park La. Elton 72 B2
Orchard Pl. Hels 73 E2
Orchard Rd. El Por 70 A1
Orchard Rd. Lymm 19 D3
Orchard Rd. W Br 65 E4
Orchard St. Chest 118 B1
Orchard St. Crewe 190 B3
Orchard St. North 104 A4
Orchard St. Warr 9 D1
Orchard St. Warr 16 B3
Orchard St. Warr 26 B4
Orchard St. Willas 205 E3
Orchard Way. Congle 156 A2
Orchard Way. Kels 122 B3
Orchard Way. Wid 12 A2
Orchards The. Brough 140 B3
Orchards The. Pick 79 F3
Orchid Cl. Hunt 142 A3
Orchid Cl. Irlam 11 F4
Ordnance Ave. Warr 9 F2
Ordsall Cl. Sand 174 C2
Orford Ave. Disley 38 B3
Orford Ave. Warr 16 B4
Orford Cl. H La 37 F4
Orford Cl. Hale 21 F1
Orford Green. Warr 8 B1
Orford La. Warr 16 A4
Orford Rd. Warr 16 C4
Orford St. Warr 16 A3
Orkney Cl. El Por 70 B1
Orkney Cl. Wid 13 F2
Orme Cl. Mfield 87 E2
Orme Cl. Prest 87 D4
Orme Cres. Mfield 87 E2
Ormerod Cl. Sand 175 E3
Ormesby Gr. Beb 43 D3
Ormonde Rd. Chest 118 B2
Ormonde St. Chest 118 C1
Ormston Ave. N-le-W 2 A3
Orrell Cl. Gt San 15 D3
Osborne Ave. Warr 8 B1
Osborne Gr. Shav 206 B3
Osborne Rd. Gold 3 F4
Osborne Rd. Warr 16 A1
Osmere Cl. Whitch 226 A1
Osprey Ave. Winsf 149 E3
Osprey Cl. Middle 151 E3
Osprey Cl. Run 49 F3
Osprey Cl. Warr 8 C2
Osprey Dr. Wilm 60 B4
Ossmere Cl. Sand 174 C4
Ostler's La. Mobb 58 C4
Otters Bank. Winsf 126 A1
Oughtrington Cres. Lymm 19 D2
Oughtrington La. Lymm 19 D1
Oughtrington View. Lymm 19 D2
Oulton Ave. Chest 118 B4
Oulton Dr. Congle 155 F2
Oulton Mill La. Eaton 147 D4
Oulton Mill La. Utkin 147 D4
Oulton Pl. Chest 118 B1
Out La. Burw 184 B3
Outwood Dr. Chea 34 A4
Outwood La. Wythe 33 D4
Outwood Rd. Chea 34 A4
Oval The. Chea 34 A4
Oval The. El Por 70 B2
Ovenhouse La. Boll 87 F4
Over Hill Dr. Winsf 149 E4
Over Rd. Ch Min 172 A4
Overdale La. Oak 101 E1
Overdale Rd. Disley 38 C3
Overdale Rd. Will 43 D1
Overdene Rd. Winsf 149 E4
Overfields. Knuts 57 E2
Overhill Dr. Wilm 60 C4
Overhill La. Wilm 60 C4
Overhill Rd. Wilm 60 B4
Overleigh Ct. Chest 141 E4
Overpool Gdns. El Por 69 F2
Overpool Rd. El Por 69 F3
Overton Cl. Congle 156 B2
Overton Cl. Middle 151 D4
Overton Dr. Frod 74 B3
Overton Rd. Bidd 179 F3
Overton Way. Wilm 34 B3
Overway. Winsf 126 C1
Overwood Ave. Moll 94 C1
Overwood La. Blacon 117 E2
Overwood La. Moll 94 B1
Ovington Cl. Run 49 F2
Owen Cl. Blacon 117 F3
Owen St. Crewe 190 B1
Owen St. Warr 16 A4
Owley Wood Rd. Weave 77 F1
Ox-Hey Cres. Bidd 179 E1
Ox-Hey Dr. Bidd 179 E1
Oxborough Cl. Wid 12 C2
Oxenham Rd. Warr 8 A2
Oxford Cl. El Por 94 C4
Oxford Ct. Mfield 112 C4
Oxford Dr. Halew 21 D4
Oxford Dr. Thor H 41 F3
Oxford Gr. Irlam 11 E3
Oxford Rd. Chest 140 C3
Oxford Rd. Mfield 112 A4
Oxford Rd. Run 49 D4
Oxford St. Crewe 190 A3
Oxford St. N-le-W 2 A2
Oxford St. Warr 16 B2
Oxford St. Wid 23 D4
Oxmead Cl. Warr 9 D1
Oxmoor Cl. Run 50 A3
Oxton Cl. Wid 12 B2
Oxton Gn. El Por 69 E2

Packsaddle Pk. Prest 86 C3
Padam Cl. Brough 140 B3
Paddington Bank. Warr 16 C3
Paddock Brow. Prest 87 D3
Paddock Chase. Poyn 36 C3
Paddock Dr. Nest 41 E1
Paddock Hill. L End 59 D1
Paddock La. Audlem 230 A1
Paddock La. Dun T 20 A3
Paddock La. Kettle 64 C2
Paddock La. Part 19 E4
Paddock La. W Br 65 F3
Paddock Rd. Eccles 141 F1
Paddock Rise. Run 49 F2
Paddock The. Chest 141 D4
Paddock The. El Por 69 E2
Paddock The. Elton 72 A2
Paddock The. Hart 103 E2
Paddock The. Hels 73 E1
Paddock The. Hes 41 E4
Paddock The. Lymm 19 E2
Paddock The. Tarp 146 B1
Paddock The. W Br 65 F3
Paddock The. Willas 205 E2
Paddock The. Wilm 34 B2
Paddock Way. H Kin 161 D4
Paddock Wlk. Cudd 101 E3
Paddockhill La. Mobb 59 D2
Paddocks Green. Congle 178 C4
Paddocks The. Mar 125 D3
Paddocks The. Prest 87 D3
Padgate La. Warr 16 C4
Padgbury Cl. Congle 156 A1
Padgbury La. Congle 156 A1
Padston Dr. Alsag 193 D2
Padstow Cl. Crewe 190 B4
Padstow Cl. Mfield 111 F4
Padstow Cl. Penk 14 C2
Padstow Dr. Bram 35 F4
Padstow Sq. Run 50 A3
Padworth Pl. Crewe 173 D1
Page Gr. Shav 206 B3
Page La. Wid 13 E1
Paignton Cl. Penk 14 C2
Painswick Rd. El Por 69 F1
Paisley Ave. Beb 43 F2
Palace Fields Ave. Run 50 A4
Palace Fields
Local Centre. Run 50 A3
Palace Hey. Nest 67 D3
Palatine Cl. Blacon 117 E3
Palgrave Cl. Blacon 118 A3
Palin Dr. Gt San 14 B4
Pall Mall. Nant 204 C3
Pallard Ave. Frod 74 B4
Palliser Cl. Warr 10 A2
Palm Gr. El Por 70 A1
Palmer Cres. Warr 15 E4
Palmer Rd. Sand 175 E3
Palmerston Cl. Hasl 191 E3
Palmerston Rd. Mfield 112 A4
Palmerston St. Boll 88 A4
Palmerston Way. Bidd 179 E1
Palmerstone Cl. Blacon 118 A2
Palmyra Sq N. Warr 16 A3
Palmyra Sq S. Warr 16 A3
Panda Way. Sand 175 D3
Pangbourne Cl. Apple 26 C3
Panton Pl. Chest 118 C2
Panton Rd. Chest 118 C2
Parade Rd. Wythe 33 E4
Parade The. Blacon 117 F3
Parade The. Nest 41 D1
Paradise. Chest 141 E4
Paradise La. Ch Min 171 F4
Paradise St. Mfield 112 B4
Paragon Cl. Wid 13 D3
Parbold Ct. Wid 22 B4
Parchments The. N-le-W 2 B2
Parish Cl. Alsag 193 D2
Park Ave. Brough 140 C3
Park Ave. Ch Hul 35 E3
Park Ave. Hay 1 A3
Park Ave. Kids 210 C4
Park Ave. Poyn 36 C2
Park Ave. Saug 94 A1
Park Ave. Tatt 166 A1
Park Ave. W Br 39 E2
Park Ave. Warr 16 B2
Park Ave. Weave 77 E1
Park Ave. Wid 13 D1
Park Ave. Wilm 60 B4
Park Ave. Winsf 127 D2
Park Ave N. N-le-W 2 B1
Park Ave S. N-le-W 2 B1
Park Bank. Congle 156 C1
Park Brook Rd. Mfield 112 A4
Park Bvd. Warr 16 A2
Park Cl. Tarv 121 D1
Park Cres. Apple 26 B3
Park Cres. Cudd 101 F2
Park Cres. W Br 39 E2
Park Cres. Wilm 34 A1
Park Ct. Frod 74 A4
Park Ct. Run 49 D4
Park Dr. Chest 119 D2
Park Dr. El Por 70 A2
Park Dr. Wist 205 F4
Park Dr S. Chest 119 D2
Park Estate. Shav 206 B3
Park Gn. Mfield 112 B4
Park House Dr. Prest 87 D4
Park House Dr. Sand 175 E4
Park House La. Prest 87 D4
Park House Mews. Sand 175 E4
Park La. Apple 26 A3
Park La. Audley 209 D2
Park La. B Hen 79 F4
Park La. Congle 156 C1
Park La. Frod 74 A4
Park La. H Wal 25 F3
Park La. Harg 144 C2
Park La. Hart 103 D2
Park La. Hather 219 F2
Park La. L Boll 20 A1
Park La. Mfield 112 B3
Park La. Moult 126 C4
Park La. Pick 79 F4
Park La. Poyn 36 C2
Park La. Sand 174 C3
Park Mount Cl. Mfield 112 A3
Park Mount Dr. Mfield 112 A3
Park Pl. Warr 16 A3
Park Rd. Beb 43 F3
Park Rd. Congle 156 C2
Park Rd. Disley 38 A3
Park Rd. Eaton 134 C1
Park Rd. El Por 70 B2
Park Rd. Gold 3 D4
Park Rd. Gt San 14 B4
Park Rd. H La 37 F3
Park Rd. Hasl 191 E3
Park Rd. Hes 41 D4
Park Rd. L Bud 124 C1
Park Rd. Lymm 29 E4
Park Rd. Mfield 112 B3
Park Rd. Middle 128 B1
Park Rd. N Mills 39 E4
Park Rd. Nant 204 C2
Park Rd. North 78 B1
Park Rd. Part 19 E4
Park Rd. Run 49 D4
Park Rd. T-le-M 71 F1
Park Rd. Tarp 146 B1
Park Rd. W Br 65 E3
Park Rd. Warr 8 B1
Park Rd. Wid 13 D1
Park Rd. Wid 13 E1
Park Rd. Will 68 A4
Park Rd. Willas 205 E3
Park Rd. Wilm 59 F4
Park Rd N. N-le-W 2 C2
Park Rd S. N-le-W 2 B1
Park Rd W. Chest 141 D4
Park St. Boll 88 A4
Park St. Chest 118 B1
Park St. Congle 156 C1
Park St. Hay 1 A3
Park St. Mfield 112 B4
Park St. Nest 66 C4
Park St. North 103 F4
Park Terr. Chest 118 C1
Park The. Christ 142 C4
Park The. Penk 14 B2
Park Vale Rd. Mfield 112 B3
Park View. Audlem 230 B4
Park View. Beb 43 E4
Park View. L Boll 20 A1
Park View Rd. Kids 195 D2
Park Way. Saug 94 A1
Park West. Hes 40 C4
Park Wlk. Chest 118 C2
Parkdale Rd. Warr 17 D4
Parker Ave. Hart 103 D3
Parker Dr. Farn 180 C1
Parker Dr S. Farn 180 C1
Parker St. Mfield 112 C4
Parker St. Run 23 D2
Parker St. Warr 16 A3
Parker's Rd. Crewe 190 A4
Parker's Row. Aldf 180 C3
Parkers Ct. Run 49 F3
Parkett Heyes Rd. Mfield 111 F4
Parkfield. El Por 70 A1
Parkfield Ave. Warr 17 D2
Parkfield Dr. El Por 70 A2
Parkfield Dr. Hels 73 D2
Parkfield Dr. Nant 204 C2
Parkfield Rd. Broug 139 E2
Parkfield Rd. Knuts 82 A4
Parkfield Rd. North 104 B4
Parkfields La. Warr 8 C1
Parkgate. Knuts 57 E2
Parkgate Ave. Peo 108 A4
Parkgate Ct. Chest 118 A2
Parkgate La. Knuts 57 E2
Parkgate La. Thor H 41 F3
Parkgate Rd. Chest 118 A2
Parkgate Rd. Mfield 112 B2
Parkgate Rd. Moll 117 F4
Parkgate Rd. Nest 66 B4
Parkgate Rd. Pudd 68 B1
Parkgate Rd. Saug 94 B2
Parkgate Rd. Shot 93 F4
Parkgate Rd. Warr 16 B1
Parkgate Way. Run 50 B4
Parkgate Way. Wilm 34 B2
Parkhill Ct. Knuts 57 D1
Parkhouse Rd E. N-u-L 210 C1
Parkhouse Rd W. N-u-L 210 C1
Parkland Cl. Apple 27 D2
Parkland Dr. Elton 72 A2
Parklands. El Por 69 E3
Parklands. Kids 195 D1
Parklands. Wid 12 B2
Parklands Dr. Elton 72 B2
Parklands Dr. Hes 41 E3
Parklands Gdns. El Por 69 E3
Parklands The. Congle 157 D1
Parklands View. El Por 69 E3
Parklands Way. Poyn 36 C2
Parklea. El Por 69 E3
Parkside. H La 37 E4
Parkside Cl. H La 37 E4
Parkside Rd. N-le-W 3 D1
Parkside Rd. Win 3 D1
Parkstone Dr. Crewe 190 A4
Parksway. Warr 17 E4
Parkway. G Cit 92 C1
Parkway. Wilm 60 A3
Parkwood Cl. Beb 43 F4
Parkwood Cl. Lymm 18 B1
Parliament St. North 103 F4
Parliament Way. El Por 94 C4
Parlington Cl. Wid 22 B4
Parnell Sq. Congle 157 D1
Parr Gr. Hay 1 A3
Parr St. Mfield 112 B4
Parr St. Warr 16 B2
Parr St. Wid 13 E1
Parry Dr. Warr 17 F2
Parson St. Congle 156 B1
Parsonage Green. Wilm 60 A4
Parsonage Rd. Wid 23 D2
Parsonage St. Mfield 112 B4
Parsonage Way. Gt San 15 D3
Parsons La. Chest 118 A4
Partridge Cl. Warr 9 F2
Partridge Cl. Winsf 149 E3
Partridge Way. H Winch 79 F3
Parvey La. S La E 112 C1
Pasture Cl. Kels 122 B2
Pasture Cl. Mfield 87 E2
Pasture Dr. Croft 9 D4
Pasture La. Warr 9 D1
Patch La. Ch Hul 35 E3
Patmos La. Peo 105 F4
Patrivale Cl. Warr 16 C3
Patten La. Warr 16 A3
Patterdale Ave. Warr 8 B1
Patterdale Rd. Part 11 F2
Patterson Cl. Warr 9 F2
Patterson St. N-le-W 2 A2
Paul Cl. Gt San 14 B3
Paul St. Warr 16 A3
Paulden Rd. Lost 80 A1
Pavement La. Mobb 57 F2
Pavilions The. Eccles 141 D2
Paxford Pl. Wilm 60 A3
Payne Cl. Gt San 15 E3
Peach Field. Chest 142 A4
Peach Gr. Hay 1 C4
Peach Tree Cl. Hale 21 F1
Peacock Ave. Chea 34 A3
Peacock Ave. Warr 16 C3
Peacock Ave. Winsf 149 E3
Peacock Hay Rd. Kids 210 C2
Peacock La. H Legh 29 F3
Peacock Way. Wilm 34 B3
Peak Rd. N Mills 39 E4
Pear Tree Ave. Crewe 190 A4
Pear Tree Ave. Run 49 E4
Pear Tree Cl. Frod 49 E1
Pear Tree Cl. Hale 21 F1
Pear Tree Cl. Winsf 149 E4
Pear Tree Dr. H Winch 80 A3
Pear Tree Farm Cotts.
L Den 104 C2
Pear Tree La. Act Br 76 C2
Pear Tree La. Whitch 225 E1
Pear Tree Rd. Audley 209 F1
Pear Tree Way. Chest 118 C3
Pear Tree Way. El Por 69 F1
Pearl La. Chest 119 D1
Pearl St. Prest 87 D4
Pearle St. Mfield 87 E1
Pearlings The. Chest 119 D1
Pearson Ave. Warr 16 B1
Pearson St. Mfield 112 C4
Peartree Cl. Sand 175 F3
Peartree La. Penley 222 B1
Peartree Pl. Warr 16 B2
Pearwood Cl. Tarp 146 B1
Peasley Cl. Warr 9 D1
Peck Mill La. Alva 98 A4
Peckfield Cl. Run 50 A3
Peckforton Cl. Sand 174 C4
Peckforton Dr. El Por 69 F2
Peckforton Dr. Run 49 F2
Peckforton Hall La. Peckf 185 D3
Peckforton Hall La. Spurs 185 D3
Peckforton Rd. Beest 168 A1
Peckforton Way. Chest 118 C3
Peckforton Way. North 103 F4
Peckmill Cl. Wilm 34 C1
Pedley Hill. Adlin 62 C4
Pedley Hill. Rain 88 C2
Pedley House La. L End 58 C1
Pedley La. Chelf 83 E4
Pedley La. Congle 157 F2
Pedley St. Crewe 190 B1
Peebles Cl. El Por 68 C3
Peebles Cl. H Chap 130 A1
Peel Cres. Asht 121 F4
Peel Dr. Astb 178 A4
Peel Hall La. Asht 121 F4
Peel Hollow. Audley 209 D1
Peel House La. Wid 13 D1
Peel La. Astb 178 B4
Peel Sq. Crewe 190 A3
Peel St. Crewe 190 A3
Peel St. Mfield 112 B3
Peel St. N-le-W 2 A2
Peel St. Run 22 C1
Peerswood Ct. Nest 66 C3
Peewit Cl. Winsf 149 E3
Peggie's La. Adlin 62 B1
Pelham Cl. Hasl 191 E3
Pelham Rd. Warr 17 E2
Pelican Cl. Crewe 191 D3
Pemberton Cl. Will 68 A4
Pemberton Rd. Chest 118 B1
Pembridge Ct. El Por 70 C2
Pembridge Gdns. El Por 70 C2
Pembroke Cl. Chest 141 F3
Pembroke Ct. Run 24 B3
Pembroke Dr. El Por 70 A2
Pembroke Gdns. Apple 26 B2
Pembroke Gr. Irlam 11 E3
Pembroke Rd. Mfield 111 F4
Pembroke Way. Winsf 149 D4
Pemston Ct. El Por 69 F4
Penbrook Cl. Crewe 189 E2
Pendine Cl. Warr 7 E1
Pendle Cl. Crewe 191 D3
Pendlebury St. Warr 17 D2
Penfold Cl. Capen 94 A4
Penfold Hey. Chest 118 B4
Penfold Way. Dodle 162 A4
Penfolds. Run 23 E1
Penistone Dr. El Por 69 D3
Penkeith's La. Run 23 D2
Penketh Ave. Warr 15 F4
Penketh Ct. Run 23 D1
Penketh Rd. Gt San 15 D2
Penkford La. Burton 1 B1
Penlington Ct. Nant 204 C3
Penmann Cres. Halew 21 D4
Penmark Cl. Warr 7 E1
Penmon Cl. Blacon 117 E2
Penn Gdns. El Por 70 A3
Penn House Cl. Bram 35 F4
Penn La. Run 22 C1
Pennant Cl. Warr 10 A2
Pennine Ct. Mfield 87 F1
Pennine Rd. Warr 8 C1
Pennine Way. Bidd 179 F1
Pennine Way. Winsf 149 D4
Pennine Wlk. El Por 69 D3
Pennington Gn. El Por 69 E2
Pennington La. Burton 1 B1
Penningtons La. Warren 111 F3
Penny La. Burton 1 B1
Penny La. Cront 12 A3
Penny La. Hay 2 A4
Penny La. Rain 88 B2
Penny's La. L Den 105 D3
Penny's La. North 104 C4
Pennyfields Rd. Kids 195 E1
Pennypleck La. Antro 28 A1
Penrhyn Cres. Haz Gr 36 B4
Penrhyn Cres. Run 49 D4
Penrhyn Rd. North 103 F4
Penrith Ave. Mfield 111 F3
Penrith Cl. Frod 49 E1
Penrith Cl. Part 11 F2
Penry Ave. Irlam 11 F3
Penryn Cl. Penk 14 C2
Pensarn Gdns. Warr 7 E1
Pensby Ave. Chest 118 B3
Pensby Dr. El Por 69 E2

Pensby Rd. Hes 40 C4
Pentland Ave. Warr 8 A2
Pentland Cl. Chest 119 D1
Pentland Cl. Winsf 149 D4
Pentland Pl. Warr 8 A2
Pentre Cl. Asht 121 F4
Pentre La. Asht 121 F4
Penzance Cl. Mfield 111 F4
Peover La. Chelf 108 C4
Peover La. Congle 157 F3
Peover Rd. Wythe 34 C3
Pepper St. Apple 27 D2
Pepper St. Chelf 83 F1
Pepper St. Chest 118 B1
Pepper St. Christ 142 B4
Pepper St. Hale 21 E1
Pepper St. Henb 111 D4
Pepper St. Lymm 18 C2
Pepper St. Middle 128 B1
Pepper St. Mobb 31 F1
Pepper St. Nant 204 C3
Peppers The. Lymm 18 C2
Percival Cl. Chest 118 B4
Percival La. Oller 83 D2
Percival La. Run 22 C1
Percival Rd. Chest 118 B4
Percival Rd. El Por 70 A3
Percival St. Warr 16 B3
Percy James Cl. Alsag 193 F2
Percy Rd. Chest 141 E4
Percy St. North 104 A4
Percy St. Warr 15 F3
Peregrine Cl. Winsf 149 E3
Perimeter Rd. Elton 72 B3
Perrey St. Run 23 D1
Perrin Ave. Run 48 C4
Perrins Rd. Burton 6 C3
Perth Cl. Bram 35 F3
Perth Cl. H Chap 130 A1
Perth Cl. Warr 8 C2
Peter House Rd. S La E 112 C2
Peter Pl. Crewe 190 A3
Peter St. Gold 3 D4
Peter St. Mfield 112 B4
Peter St. North 79 D1
Peter St W. Mfield 112 B4
Peterborough Cl. Mfield 87 D1
Peters Cl. Prest 87 D4
Petersgate. Run 50 B4
Petersham Dr. Apple 26 C3
Peterstone Cl. Warr 7 E1
Petrel Ave. Poyn 36 A2
Petrel Cl. Winsf 149 E3
Petunia Cl. Mfield 112 A3
Petworth Ave. Warr 8 A2
Petworth Cl. Wist 206 A4
Pevensey Dr. Knuts 82 A4
Peveril Cl. Apple 26 B4
Peveril Dr. Haz Gr 36 C4
Peveril Gdns. Disley 39 D3
Peveril Mews. Disley 39 D3
Peveril Wlk. Mfield 111 F4
Pewit La. Bridge 231 D4
Pewterspear La. Apple 26 C2
Pexhall Rd. Eaton 134 B2
Pexhill Dr. Mfield 111 F4
Pexhill Rd. Henb 111 E3
Pexhill Rd. Mfield 111 E3
Pexhill Rd. Sidd 110 B2
Pexhill Rd. Warren 111 E3
Pheasant Cl. Warr 9 F2
Pheasant Dr. H Winch 79 F3
Pheasant Field. Hale 21 E1
Pheasant Way. Winsf 149 E3
Pheasant Wlk. H Legh 29 E2
Philip Rd. Wid 22 A4
Philip St. Hawa 116 A1
Philips Dr. Gt San 14 B4
Philips La. El Por 69 E2
Phillip St. Chest 118 C2
Phillips Rd. Blacon 117 E2
Phillips Way. Hes 40 C4
Phipps' La. Burton 6 C4
Phoenix Ave. Warr 7 F1
Phoenix St. Hawa 116 A2
Phythian Cres. Penk 14 C2
Pichael Nook. Warr 17 D2
Pickering Cres. Warr 17 E2
Pickering Rd. Wid 22 A3
Pickering St. Chest 118 C2
Pickerings Cl. Run 49 E3
Pickford St. Mfield 112 B4
Pickmere Cl. Sand 174 C4
Pickmere Dr. Beb 43 F2
Pickmere Dr. Chest 142 A4
Pickmere Dr. Run 50 B3
Pickmere La. H Winch 79 F3
Pickmere La. Pick 55 E1
Pickmere La. Tab 55 E1
Pickmere Rd. Wilm 34 B3
Pickmere St. Warr 15 F3
Pickwick Cl. Sand 175 E4
Pickwick Pl. Kids 194 B1
Pickwick Rd. Poyn 36 B2
Picow Farm Rd. Run 22 C1
Picow St. Run 23 D1
Picton Ave. El Por 70 B3
Picton Ave. Run 23 D1
Picton Cl. Beb 43 F2
Picton Cl. Warr 9 E2
Picton Dr. Wilm 34 C1
Picton Dr. Winsf 126 A1
Picton Gorse La. Chest 119 D4
Picton Gorse La. Pict 119 D4
Picton La. M Traf 96 B2
Picton La. Pict 96 B2
Picton La. Stoak 96 B2
Picton Sq. H Chap 130 B2
Piele Rd. Hay 1 C4
Pierce St. Mfield 112 B4
Pierpoint La. Chest 118 B1
Pierpoint St. Gold 3 D4
Pierpoint St. Warr 15 F4
Pigot Pl. Warr 16 C3
Pike La. Kings 75 D2
Pike Rd. Rain 89 D3
Pike St. Warr 16 B1
Pike The. Nant 204 C2
Pikemere Rd. Alsag 193 D3
Pikenall La. Act Br 76 B2
Pilgrim Cl. Win 8 A3
Pillmoss La. Hatt 52 A4
Pillory St. Nant 204 C3
Pimblett Rd. Hay 1 C4
Pimblett St. Gold 3 D4
Pincot Rd. N Mills 39 E4
Pine Ave. N-le-W 2 B1
Pine Ave. Wid 13 D1
Pine Cl. Hay 1 B3
Pine Cl. Mfield 87 F1
Pine Ct. Alsag 193 F2
Pine Gdns. Chest 118 B3
Pine Gr. Chest 119 D2
Pine Gr. El Por 70 A1
Pine Gr. Gold 3 E4
Pine Gr. Sand 175 E3
Pine Gr. Warr 17 D4
Pine Gr. Winsf 127 D1
Pine Rd. Bram 35 F4
Pine Rd. Hes 41 E4
Pine Rd. Mfield 87 F1
Pine Rd. Poyn 36 C2
Pine Rd. Run 49 E4
Pine Tree Cl. Broug 139 E2
Pine Trees. Mobb 57 F4
Pine Wlk. Nant 204 C2
Pinedale Cl. El Por 95 D4
Pinehey. Nest 41 E1
Pinehurst. Prest 86 C3
Pinetree Cl. North 78 A2
Pineways. Apple 26 B3
Pinewood Ave. Warr 16 C4
Pinewood Cl. Elton 72 B2
Pinewood Ct. Wist 206 A4
Pinewood Dr. Hes 41 D4
Pinewood Gr. N-u-L 210 C1
Pinewood Rd. Burton 7 D4
Pinewood Rd. Wilm 60 C4
Pinfold Ct. Chest 141 F3
Pinfold La. Chelf 83 E3
Pinfold La. Chest 141 F4
Pinfold La. L Bud 147 F4
Pinfold La. Middle 128 A1
Pinfold La. Plum 81 D2
Pinfold La. Wythe 32 C3
Pinfold St. Mfield 112 B4
Pinfold Way. Weave 77 E1
Pingard's La. Crow 101 E3
Pingate Dr. Ch Hul 35 D3
Pingate La. Ch Hul 35 D3
Pingate La S. Ch Hul 35 D3
Pingot Croft. Chest 142 A4
Pinmill Brow. Frod 74 A4
Pinmill Cl. Frod 74 B4
Pinners Brow. Warr 16 A3
Pinsley Green Rd. New 216 C1
Pinsley View. Wren 216 C2
Pintail Pl. Winsf 149 E3
Pinwood Ct. Wilm 34 C1
Pipe La. Warr 9 E1
Piper's Cl. Hes 40 B4
Piper's End. Hes 40 B4
Piper's La. Hes 40 B4
Pipers Ash. Winsf 126 A1
Pipers Ct. Chest 119 D2
Pipers La. Chest 119 D2
Pipers La. Pudd 93 D4
Pipers The. Gold 3 F4
Pipit Ave. N-le-W 2 B2
Pipit La. Warr 9 F2
Pippin Cl. Middle 151 E4
Pippits Row. Run 49 F2
Pirie Cl. Congle 157 D2
Pirie Rd. Congle 157 D2
Pit La. Ho Co 206 C1
Pit La. Kids 210 B3
Pit La. Wid 13 D2
Pitt St. Mfield 112 B3
Pitt St. Wid 23 D3
Pitts Cl. Tarv 121 E1
Pitville Terr. Wid 22 B4
Plane Gr. N-u-L 210 C1
Plane Tree Dr. Crewe 190 C3
Plane Tree Gr. Hay 2 A4
Plane Tree Rd. Part 11 E2
Plant La. Sand 174 A4
Plant St. Sand 175 D4
Plantagenet Cl. Winsf 149 E3
Plantation Cl. Run 24 A1
Plantation Dr. El Por 69 F4
Plas Newton La. Chest 118 C3
Platt Ave. Sand 175 D4
Platt's La. Saigh 164 C3
Platts La. Christ 143 E4
Platts La. Tarv 121 D1
Platts La. Tarv 144 A4
Platts La. Tatt 183 F4
Platts St. Hay 1 A3
Pleasance Way. N-le-W 2 B2
Pleasant St. Mfield 87 F1
Pleasant St. North 103 F4
Pleasant Way. Ch Hul 35 E3
Pleck Rd. El Por 70 A1
Plemstall Cl. M Traf 119 F4
Plemstall La. M Traf 97 D1
Plemstall Way. M Traf 96 C1
Plex The. Alsag 193 E2
Plinston Ave. Warr 16 C2
Plough La. Christ 143 D4
Ploughmans Cl. El Por 94 C4
Ploughmans Way. El Por 94 C4
Ploughmans Way. Mfield 87 D2
Plover Ave. Winsf 149 E3
Plover Cl. Farn 180 C1
Plover Cl. N-le-W 2 B2
Plovers La. Hels 73 E3
Plum Terr. Chest 118 B1
Plumbs Fold. North 78 A1
Plumley Cl. Chest 119 E1
Plumley Moor Rd. Plum 81 E1
Plumley Rd. Wilm 34 B3
Plumpstons La. Frod 49 D1
Plumtre Ave. Warr 15 F4
Plymouth Cl. Run 50 C3
Plymouth Dr. Bram 35 F4
Plymyard Ave. Beb 43 E3
Plymyard Cl. Beb 43 E3
Plymyard Copse. Beb 43 E3
Poachers La. Warr 16 C2
Pochard Ave. Winsf 149 E3
Pochard Dr. Poyn 36 A2
Pochin Way. Middle 128 C1
Pocket Nook La. Gold 4 A4
Pocklington Ct. Warr 8 C1
Pole La. Antro 53 F1
Polperro Cl. Mfield 86 B1
Polperro Cl. Penk 14 C2
Pond St. Gold 4 A4
Pond View Cl. Hes 41 E4
Pond Wlk. St Hel 1 A1
Pool End Cl. Mfield 87 E2
Pool End Rd. Mfield 87 E2
Pool House Rd. Poyn 37 E3
Pool La. Hasl 192 A4
Pool La. Ince 71 F2
Pool La. Lymm 18 A2
Pool La. Run 23 D2
Pool La. T-le-M 71 F1
Pool La. Tarv 121 E2
Pool La. Warr 16 A1
Pool Rd. Hol Gr 11 D2
Pool Side. Sch Gr 194 A4
Pool St. Mfield 112 C3
Pool St. Wid 23 D4
Poole Ave. Warr 8 A1
Poole Hall La. El Por 69 F4
Poole Hall Rd. El Por 69 F4
Poolford La. Sp Gr 129 E1
Pools La. Small 177 D3
Pools Platt La. Antro 53 F3
Poolside Ct. Alsag 193 F2
Poolside Rd. Run 23 D1
Pooltown Rd. El Por 69 F3
Poplar Av. Wilm 59 F3
Poplar Ave. Cul 4 C1
Poplar Ave. Moult 126 C4
Poplar Ave. N-le-W 2 B2
Poplar Ave. Penk 14 C2
Poplar Ave. Run 49 E4
Poplar Cl. Congle 156 A2
Poplar Cl. Cudd 102 A2
Poplar Cl. Run 49 E4
Poplar Cl. Winsf 149 D4
Poplar Dr. Alsag 193 F1
Poplar Dr. Kids 195 D1
Poplar Dr. Middle 151 E4
Poplar Gr. Boll 88 A4
Poplar Gr. Crewe 190 C3
Poplar Gr. Elton 72 A2
Poplar Gr. Hay 1 B3
Poplar La. Woore 236 C3
Poplar Rd. Chest 140 C3
Poplar Rd. Hay 1 B3
Poplar Rd. Mfield 112 B3
Poplar Rd. Weave 102 B4
Poplar Way. H La 38 A4
Poplars Ave. Warr 8 B2
Poplars The. Gold 4 B4
Poplor Weint. Nest 66 C4
Popular Gr. Irlam 11 E3
Popular Wlk. Part 11 E1
Porlock Cl. Hes 41 D3
Porlock Cl. Penk 14 C2
Porter Ave. N-le-W 2 B3
Porter Dr. North 104 B3
Porter St. Run 23 E1
Porter Way. North 104 B3
Porters Croft. G Sutt 119 F3
Portford Cl. Mfield 86 C1
Porthcawl Cl. Wid 12 B2
Portland Dr. Bidd 179 E1
Portland Dr. Sch Gr 194 C3
Portland Gr. Hasl 191 E3
Portland Pl. Hels 73 E2
Portland St. N-le-W 1 C2
Portland St. Run 22 C2
Portland Wlk. Mfield 111 F4
Portleven Rd. Run 50 A3
Portloe Rd. Chea 34 A4
Portola Cl. Warr 17 E1
Portree Dr. H Chap 130 A1
Portrush Dr. Mfield 87 E2
Portside. Run 50 C4
Portsmouth Pl. Run 50 C3
Post Office La. Betley 207 F1
Post Office La. Hamp 213 E4
Post Office La. Norley 100 C3
Post Office La. Run 48 B4
Post Office Pl. North 79 D1
Postles Pl. North 103 F3
Potters End. Bidd 179 E1
Potters La. Wid 21 F3
Poulton Cres. Warr 17 E4
Poulton Dr. Wid 22 B4
Poulton Hill Rd. Beb 43 D4
Poulton Rd. Beb 43 D4
Pound Rd. El Por 69 E4
Povey Rd. Warr 8 B1
Powell Ave. Warr 9 F2
Powell St. Warr 16 C2
Powell's Orch. Chest 141 E4
Powey La. Moll 94 A3
Powey La. Saug 94 A3
Pownall Ave. Bram 35 F4
Pownall Ct. Wilm 59 F4
Pownall Rd. Wilm 59 F4
Pownall Sq. Mfield 112 B4
Pownall St. Mfield 87 E1
Powy Dr. Kids 195 D1
Powys St. Warr 15 F3
Poynton St. Mfield 112 B4
Pratchitts Row. Nant 204 C3
Preece Ct. Crewe 190 A3
Preesall Ave. Chea 34 A4
Prenton Pl. Chest 141 F4
Prescot Rd. Wid 12 B1
Prescot St. Chest 118 C2
Prescott Rd. Wilm 34 A1
Prescott St. Warr 16 C2
Prestbury Dr. Warr 17 E2
Prestbury La. Prest 87 D4
Prestbury Rd. Mfield 87 D1
Prestbury Rd. Mfield 112 B4
Prestbury Rd. N Ald 85 F3
Prestbury Rd. N Ald 86 A3
Prestbury Rd. Wilm 60 C3
Preston Ave. Irlam 11 F4
Preston On The Hill. P-o-t-H 50 C3
Preston St W. Mfield 112 A3
Prestwich Ave. Cul 4 C2
Prestwick Cl. Mfield 87 E3
Prestwick Cl. Winsf 126 B1
Prestwood Ct. Warr 10 A4
Pretoria St. Chest 141 E4
Price Ave. Sand 175 D3
Price Gr. St Hel 1 A1
Priest La. M St A 61 D1
Priestfield Rd. El Por 70 B3
Priestley St. Warr 15 F3
Priestner Dr. Hels 73 D2
Priestway La. Nest 67 F1
Priesty Ct. Congle 156 B1
Priesty Fields. Congle 156 B1
Primitive St. Sch Gr 195 E4
Primrose Ave. Hasl 191 E3
Primrose Ave. Mfield 112 A3
Primrose Cl. Hunt 142 A3
Primrose Cl. Run 50 A4
Primrose Cl. Warr 8 B1
Primrose Cl. Wid 12 C1
Primrose Gr. Hay 1 C4
Primrose Hill. Crewe 189 F3
Primrose Hill. Cudd 101 F2
Primrose La. Hels 73 D1
Prince Albert St. Crewe 190 B2
Prince Edward St. Nant 204 C3
Prince Henry Sq. Warr 16 A3
Prince Rd. Poyn 37 E3
Prince William Ave. Hawa 116 A2
Prince's St. Wid 23 D4
Princes Ave. Beb 43 F3
Princes Ave. Chest 118 C1
Princes Ave. North 104 A4
Princes Cl. Run 23 F1
Princes Park. North 78 A1
Princes Pl. Wid 12 C1
Princes Rd. El Por 70 A3
Princes St. N-le-W 2 A2
Princes Way. Mfield 111 F4
Princess Ave. Audley 209 E1
Princess Ave. Gt San 14 C4
Princess Ave. Hay 2 A4
Princess Ave. Warr 16 C3
Princess Ave. Warr 17 D4
Princess Cl. Wist 205 F4
Princess Cres. Middle 151 E3
Princess Cres. Warr 16 C3
Princess Ct. Kids 210 B3
Princess Dr. Boll 87 F4
Princess Dr. Nant 205 D3
Princess Dr. Sand 175 D4
Princess Dr. Wist 205 F4
Princess Gr. Wist 205 F4
Princess Rd. Lymm 18 B2
Princess St. Boll 87 F4
Princess St. Chest 118 B1
Princess St. Congle 156 B2
Princess St. Crewe 190 B3
Princess St. Kids 210 B3
Princess St. Knuts 57 D1
Princess St. North 79 F1
Princess St. Run 23 D2
Princess St. Warr 15 E2
Princess St. Winsf 127 D1
Princess Wlk. Bram 36 A4
Princeway. Frod 74 A4
Prior Cl. Wist 189 F1
Priory Cl. Chest 118 B2
Priory Cl. Congle 179 D4
Priory Cl. Crewe 190 A4
Priory Cl. Run 24 A1
Priory Cl. Winsf 126 B2
Priory Dr. Mfield 86 C1
Priory La. Mfield 86 C1
Priory Pl. Chest 118 B1
Priory Pl. Kids 195 E2
Priory Rd. Altr 31 D4
Priory Rd. Run 24 B1
Priory Rd. Wilm 59 F4
Priory St. Altr 31 E4
Priory St. North 104 A4
Priory St. Warr 16 A2
Priory The. Win 8 A4
Priory Way. Hart 103 D2
Priscilla St. Crewe 190 C2
Pritchard Dr. Dave 103 F1
Proctors Cl. Wid 13 E1
Proctors La. Sand 174 C3
Proffits La. Hels 73 F2
Promised Land La. Waver 142 C3
Prospect Ave. Irlam 11 F3
Prospect Dr. Altr 32 B4
Prospect Dr. Dave 103 F1
Prospect La. Hol Gr 10 B2
Prospect Rd. Irlam 11 F3
Prospect St. Congle 156 B1
Prosperity Way. Middle 128 B1
Prosser Rd. Chest 95 E1
Provan Way. Blacon 117 E3
Provident St. St Hel 1 A2
Prunus Rd. Crewe 190 C3
Pryors The. Tarv 121 E2
Ptarmigan Pl. Winsf 149 E3
Public Hall St. Run 23 D2
Pudding La. Tiver 168 A4
Puddington La. Nest 92 C4
Puddington La. Pudd 93 D4
Puffin Ave. Poyn 36 A2
Pulford Ct. Run 49 F3
Pulford Ct. Pulf 162 B1
Pulford La. Dodle 162 A3
Pulford Rd. Blacon 117 F3
Pulford Rd. El Por 69 F2
Pulford Rd. Winsf 126 B1
Pullman Cl. Hes 41 E4
Pump La. Farn 181 D3
Pump La. Run 49 F4
Pumptree Mews. Mfield 111 F4
Purdy Cl. Warr 7 E1
Purley Dr. Irlam 11 E3
Purser La. Shock 211 F2
Pye Cl. Hay 2 A4
Pye Rd. Hes 41 D4
Pyecroft Cl. Gt San 14 B3
Pyecroft Rd. Gt San 14 B3
Pyecroft St. Chest 141 E4
Pym's La. Crewe 189 F3
Pyrus Ave. Crewe 190 C3
Pyrus Gr. Hels 73 E2

Quad The. Blacon 117 F1
Quadrant Cl. Run 50 B3
Quail Cl. Warr 8 B2
Quakers Coppice. Crewe 191 D1
Quakers Way. Holt 180 C1
Quantock Cl. El Por 69 D3
Quantock Cl. Winsf 149 D4
Quarry Ave. Farn 180 C1
Quarry Bank. Utkin 146 B4
Quarry Bank Rd. Wilm 33 F2
Quarry Cl. Chest 141 E4
Quarry Cl. Run 23 E1
Quarry Hill. Farn 180 C1
Quarry La. Apple 26 B3
Quarry La. Christ 142 C4
Quarry La. Kels 122 B3
Quarry Rd. N Mills 39 E4
Quarry Rd. Will 42 B1
Quarry Terr. Kids 195 D1
Quay Fold. Warr 15 F3

Quay Pl. Run 50 C4
Quay Side. Frod 49 E1
Quay The. Frod 49 E1
Quayside. Congle 156 C1
Quayside. Nest 66 C3
Quayside Mews. Lymm 18 C2
Quayside Way. Mfield 112 C4
Queastybirch La. Hatt 52 A4
Quebec Rd. Warr 16 B4
Queen St. Audley 209 E1
Queen St. Boll 88 A4
Queen St. Bun 185 F4
Queen St. Chest 118 B1
Queen St. Congle 156 B1
Queen St. Congle 156 C2
Queen St. Crewe 190 C3
Queen St. El Por 70 B4
Queen St. Gold 3 D4
Queen St. Kids 195 D1
Queen St. Knuts 56 C1
Queen St. Mfield 112 B4
Queen St. Middle 128 B1
Queen St. N-le-W 2 A2
Queen St. Nant 204 C3
Queen St. North 103 F4
Queen St. Shav 206 B2
Queen Victoria St. Mfield 112 B4
Queen's Ave. Chest 118 C1
Queen's Ave. Con Q 91 E1
Queen's Ave. Cul 5 E4
Queen's Ave. Hawa 116 A2
Queen's Ave. Mfield 87 F1
Queen's Ave. Wid 22 A4
Queen's Cl. Mfield 87 F1
Queen's Cl. Run 22 C1
Queen's Dr. Chest 141 F4
Queen's Dr. Middle 151 E4
Queen's Dr. Nant 204 B2
Queen's Dr. Sand 175 D4
Queen's Par. Winsf 126 B1
Queen's Park Gdns. Crewe 189 F2
Queen's Park Rd. Chest 141 E4
Queen's Park View. Chest 141 E4
Queen's Rd. Chest 118 C1
Queen's Rd. Run 22 C1
Queen's Rd. Wilm 60 A3
Queen's Way. Broug 139 D2
Queens Ave. El Por 70 A2
Queens Ave. Warr 16 C4
Queens Cl. Boll 87 F3
Queens Cres. Chest 118 C4
Queens Cres. Warr 17 D4
Queens Ct. Winsf 126 B1
Queens Dr. Gold 3 E4
Queens Dr. Hels 73 D2
Queens Dr. Hes 40 C4
Queens Dr. N-le-W 2 B3
Queens Dr. Warr 17 D1
Queens Gdns. El Por 70 A3
Queens Gdns. Kids 210 B3
Queens Pl. Chest 118 B1
Queens Rd. Chest 119 D2
Queens Rd. El Por 69 E4
Queens Rd. Hay 2 A4
Queensgate. Bram 35 F3
Queensgate. North 103 F4
Queensway. Alsag 193 D3
Queensway. Chea 34 B4
Queensway. Chest 118 C3
Queensway. Crewe 190 B2
Queensway. Frod 74 A4
Queensway. Hes 41 E3
Queensway. Knuts 56 C2
Queensway. Poyn 36 B2
Queensway. Run 22 C2
Queensway. Wid 22 C3
Queensway. Winsf 149 E4
Quillet The. Nest 66 C4
Quinn St. Wid 23 D4
Quinta Rd. Congle 156 A2

Raby Ave. Beb 43 D3
Raby Cl. Beb 43 D4
Raby Cl. Hes 40 C4
Raby Cl. Wid 13 F1
Raby Dr. Beb 43 D3
Raby Gdns. Nest 66 C4
Raby Hall Rd. Beb 43 D3
Raby Hall Rd. Thor H 42 C3
Raby Mere Rd. Beb 42 C4
Raby Mere Rd. Thor H 42 B3
Raby Park Cl. Nest 66 C4
Raby Park Rd. Nest 66 C4
Raby Rd. Nest 66 C4
Raby Rd. Thor H 42 A3
Race The. Wilm 34 B1
Racecourse La. Dela 124 A1
Racecourse Pk. Wilm 59 F3
Racefield Cl. Lymm 18 C2
Racefield Rd. Knuts 56 C1
Radcliffe Ave. Cul 4 C2
Radcliffe Rd. S La E 135 E4
Radcliffe Rd. Sand 174 C2
Raddel La. Whit 52 B3
Raddle Wharf. El Por 70 B4
Radford Cl. Wid 22 B4
Radlett Cl. Penk 14 C2
Radley Dr. Thor H 41 F3
Radley La. Warr 8 C2
Radnor Cl. Congle 156 A2
Radnor Cl. Sand 174 C4
Radnor Dr. Chest 141 D2
Radnor Dr. Wid 12 B1
Radnor Park
Trading Estate. Congle 156 A2
Radway Gn. El Por 69 F3
Radway Green Rd. Barth 208 C4
Raeburn Ave. Beb 43 F3
Raeburn Ave. Nest 66 C4
Raglan Ct. Warr 9 F3
Raglan Rd. Mfield 87 F1
Ragley Cl. Poyn 36 C2
Railbrook Ct. Crewe 190 B1
Railton Ave. Crewe 190 A4
Railway Cottages. Congle 157 D1
Railway St. Crewe 190 B1
Railway St. N-le-W 2 A2
Railway Terr. Hawa 116 A2
Railway View. Burton 1 B1
Rainbow Cl. Wid 12 B2
Rainbow St. Crewe 190 B2
Rainford Cl. Kids 195 F1
Rainow Cl. Middle 151 D4
Rainow Rd. Mfield 88 A1
Rainow Rd. Rain 88 A1
Rainow View. Boll 63 E1
Rainow Way. Wilm 34 C1
Rake La. Back 95 E3
Rake La. Christ 143 D4
Rake La. D-o-t-H 97 D4
Rake La. D-o-t-H 97 F4
Rake La. Eccles 141 E1
Rake La. Frod 72 C3
Rake La. Hawa 139 D4
Rake La. Hels 73 D3
Rake La. Hels 73 E2
Rake La. Stoak 95 E3
Rake The. Beb 43 E4
Rake The. Nest 67 E1
Rake Way. Saug 94 A1
Raleigh Cl. Warr 7 E1
Raleigh Rd. Nest 41 F1
Ramp Rd E. Wythe 33 E4
Ramp Rd S. Wythe 33 E4
Ramp Rd W. Wythe 33 D4
Rampit Cl. Hay 1 C4
Ramsbottom St. Crewe 190 A3
Ramsbrook La. Hale 21 E2
Ramsbrook La. Wid 21 E2
Ramsdale Rd. Bram 35 F4
Ramsden Ct. Chest 140 C2
Ramsey Cl. Warr 9 F2
Ramsey Cl. Wid 13 F2
Ramsfield Rd. Speke 21 D2
Randle Bennett Cl. Sand 174 C4
Randle Meadow. El Por 69 F1
Rangemoor Cl. Warr 10 A3
Rannoch Cl. El Por 69 F2
Ranworth Rd. Gt San 14 C3
Rappax Rd. Altr 32 A4
Rathbone Park. Tarp 146 B1
Rathbone St. N-le-W 2 A2
Rathlin Cl. Wid 13 F2
Rathmell Cl. Cul 4 C2
Raven Cl. Sand 175 D4
Raven's La. Audley 209 F2
Ravenfield Dr. Wid 12 B2
Ravenho La. Rain 88 B2
Ravenoak Park Rd. Ch Hul 35 D4
Ravenoak Rd. Ch Hul 35 D4
Ravens Cl. Audley 209 F2
Ravens La. Acton 203 F3
Ravens La. Burl 203 F3
Ravenscliffe Rd. Kids 195 D1
Ravenscroft. H Chap 130 A2
Ravenscroft Cl. Sand 175 E4
Ravenscroft Rd. Crewe 189 F2
Ravensfield. Cudd 101 E2
Ravensholme Ct. Tatt 166 A1
Ravensholme La. Tatt 166 A1
Ravenswood. Hart 103 D2
Ravenswood Dr. Ch Hul 35 D4
Ravenswood Rd. Wilm 59 F2
Ravenwood Dr. Altr 32 B4
Rawcliffe Cl. Wid 12 C2
Rawdon Cl. Run 50 A4
Rawlings Cl. Warr 9 F2
Rawlinson Cres. Halew 21 D4
Rawson Rd. Blacon 117 F2
Ray Ave. Nant 204 C4
Rayleigh Ave. Dave 127 D4
Rayleigh Way. Mfield 86 C1
Raymond Ave. Warr 16 B1
Raymond St. Chest 118 B1
Raymond Way. Nest 67 D4
Rays Brow. North 78 A1
Reades La. Congle 179 E4
Readesdale Ave. Crewe 189 F1
Reading Room La. Brox 199 E4
Reaper Cl. Gt San 15 E3
Reay St. Wid 13 E1
Rectory Ave. Gold 3 E4
Rectory Cl. Farn 180 C1
Rectory Cl. Hes 40 C4
Rectory Cl. Nant 204 C3
Rectory Cl. Wist 205 F4
Rectory La. Adder 235 D3
Rectory La. Capen 94 A4
Rectory La. Hes 40 C4
Rectory La. Led 68 C1
Rectory La. Lymm 18 C2
Rectory View. Kids 210 B3
Red Bank Ave. N-le-W 2 C1
Red Brow La. P-o-t-H 50 C4
Red Brow La. Run 50 C4
Red Cow Yd. Knuts 57 D1
Red Ct. El Por 69 E4
Red House La. Dun T 20 B4
Red La. Apple 26 B4
Red La. Disley 38 B3
Red La. Frod 74 B4
Red La. Hux 166 B3
Red La. Sand 174 B3
Red La. Warr 26 B4
Red La. Whit 52 B1
Red Lion Cl. Kids 210 B4
Red Lion La. El Por 69 E4
Red Lion La. Nant 204 B3
Red Pike. El Por 69 E4
Red Stone Hill. Hels 73 E2
Redacre. Poyn 36 C3
Redbourne Dr. Wid 12 A2
Redbrook Cl. Beb 43 E3
Redbrook Gr. Wilm 34 B1
Redbrook Rd. Part 11 F1
Redbrook Way. Adlin 62 B3
Redcar Dr. Beb 43 E3
Reddish Ave. W Br 65 E3
Reddish Cres. Lymm 18 C2
Reddish La. Lymm 19 D3
Reddish La. W Br 65 E3
Reddish Rd. W Br 65 E3
Reddy La. Rosth 30 A4
Redesdale Cl. Sand 174 C4
Redesdale Cl. Warr 8 C1
Redesmere Cl. North 104 A3
Redesmere Dr. A Edge 60 A1
Redesmere La. Sidd 110 A2
Redesmere Rd. Wilm 34 B3
Redfern Dr. Congle 156 C2
Redgate. North 103 E4
Redhill Rd. Chest 140 C3
Redhill Rd. Kels 122 B3
Redhills Mews. El Por 70 A3
Redhouse La. Disley 38 C3
Redland Cl. Chest 141 D4
Redmayne Cl. N-le-W 2 A2
Redmere Dr. Hes 41 E4
Redmoor La. Disley 39 D2
Redmoor La. N Mills 39 D3
Redpoll La. Warr 9 F2
Redruth Ave. Mfield 86 C1
Redruth Cl. Run 50 B3
Redshank Ave. Winsf 149 E3
Redshank Cl. N-le-W 2 B2
Redshank La. Warr 9 F2
Redvales Ct. Warr 9 E2
Redvers Ave. El Por 44 A1
Redway La. Boll 88 A4
Redwood Cl. Brough 140 C3
Redwood Cl. North 78 A2
Redwood Cl. Warr 17 F4
Redwood Dr. El Por 69 F1
Reece Cl. M Traf 119 F4
Reed La. Antro 53 E3
Reedgate La. Antro 27 F1
Reedsmere Cl. Warr 16 C1
Reedsmere Walk. Comb 78 B4
Reel Cl. Warr 17 E3
Reeman Ct. Wilm 34 A1
Rees Cres. H Chap 130 B2
Reeve St. Gold 4 A4
Reeves Rd. Chest 142 A4
Regal Cl. El Por 69 F2
Regal Cres. Wid 22 A4
Regency Cl. Kids 210 B3
Regency Ct. Winsf 149 E4
Regent Ave. Hay 1 A4
Regent Ave. Mfield 112 A3
Regent Ave. Warr 17 D4
Regent Bk. Wilm 59 F3
Regent Cl. Bram 35 E2
Regent Cl. Shav 206 A2
Regent Cl. Wilm 59 F3
Regent Rd. Wid 13 D1
Regent St. El Por 70 A3
Regent St. Moult 126 C4
Regent St. N-le-W 2 A2
Regent St. Run 23 D2
Regent St. Warr 16 A3
Regents Cl. Chest 119 D1
Reid Ave. Warr 15 F4
Reid St. Crewe 190 B3
Remer St. Crewe 190 C4
Renaissance Ct. Crewe 191 D2
Renaissance Way. Crewe 191 D2
Rendel Cl. N-le-W 2 B1
Rendlesham Cl. Warr 10 A3
Renfrew Ave. Beb 43 F3
Renfrew Cl. Mfield 86 C1
Renown Cl. Warr 9 E2
Renshaw Rd. North 79 E1
Rensherds Pl. H Legh 29 E3
Renton Ave. Run 23 E1
Repton Cl. H Legh 29 E2
Repton Dr. Hasl 191 E3
Repton Rd. El Por 70 B2
Reservoir Rd. W Br 65 E4
Reservoir Terr. Chest 118 C1
Retreat The. Crewe 190 B3
Rex Buildings. Wilm 60 A3
Reynold's La. Sand 175 F3
Reynolds Ave. St Hel 1 A1
Reynolds Mews. Wilm 60 C4
Reynolds St. Warr 16 C2
Rhoden St. Crewe 191 D3
Rhodes Cl. Hasl 191 E2
Rhodes St. Warr 16 B4
Rhodesway. Hes 41 D4
Rhona Cl. Beb 43 E2
Rhona Dr. Gt San 14 C3
Rhuddlan Ct. El Por 70 B1
Rhuddlan Rd. Blacon 117 E2
Rhyl St. Wid 22 C4
Ribble Ave. Winsf 127 D1
Ribble Cl. Cul 4 C1
Ribble Cl. Wid 13 F2
Ribble Dr. Bidd 179 F1
Ribble Pl. Winsf 127 D1
Ribblesdale. El Por 70 A2
Ribblesdale Ave. Congle 157 D3
Ribblesdale Cl. Beb 43 F3
Ribchester Gdns. Cul 5 D2
Richard Cl. Run 24 A1
Richard Moon St. Crewe 190 A2
Richard St. Crewe 190 A3
Richard St. North 104 B4
Richards Croft. Chest 142 A4
Richardson Cl. Shav 206 B3
Richardson St. Warr 16 B4
Richmond Ave. Hay 1 A4
Richmond Ave. Run 23 F1
Richmond Ave. Warr 17 D2
Richmond Ave. Warr 17 E2
Richmond Ave. Wilm 34 B2
Richmond Cl. Cul 4 B2
Richmond Cl. Lymm 19 D2
Richmond Cl. Sand 174 C4
Richmond Cres. Chest 119 E1
Richmond Ct. El Por 70 B2
Richmond Dr. Lymm 19 D2
Richmond Dr. North 104 A2
Richmond Hill. Knuts 57 D1
Richmond Hill. Mfield 112 C3
Richmond Pl. Mfield 112 C3
Richmond Rd. Crewe 190 C3
Richmond St. Warr 17 D2
Richmond St. Wid 13 E1
Rickaby Cl. Beb 43 E4
Ridding La. Run 50 A3
Riddings La. Hart 103 D2
Riddings La. Hay Gr 220 A4
Ridge Hill. S La E 113 D1
Ridge Hill. Utkin 146 A3
Ridge Park. Ch Hul 35 E3
Ridge The. Dela 123 E4
Ridge View. Mfield 112 B3
Ridgeborne Cl. Warr 7 E1
Ridgeway. Alva 74 A1
Ridgeway. Gold 3 F4
Ridgeway. Wilm 60 C4
Ridgeway Gdns. Lymm 18 B2
Ridgeway The. Cront 12 B3
Ridgeway The. Disley 38 B3
Ridgeway The. Hes 41 D4
Ridgeway The. Run 50 B3
Ridgeway The. Tarv 121 E2
Ridgewell Ave. Gold 3 E4
Ridgmont Rd. Bram 35 F3
Ridgway St. Warr 16 B4
Ridgway St. Crewe 190 B3
Ridings The. Saug 117 D4
Ridley Cl. Ho Co 206 C1
Ridley Dr. Gt San 15 E2
Ridley Rd. Boll 87 F4
Ridley Wood Rd. Isyc 196 A2
Ridsdale. Wid 22 B4
Rigby Ave. Crewe 190 A4
Rigby Rd. Kids 195 D2
Rigby St. Gold 3 D4
Rigby's Row. Nant 204 C3
Rigg St. Crewe 190 A3
Riley Cl. Sand 174 C3
Riley Dr. Run 49 D4
Rileys Way. Audley 209 F1
Rilshaw La. Winsf 150 A4
Rilston Ave. Cul 4 B2
Rimington Cl. Cul 4 C2
Rimsdale Cl. Wist 206 A4
Ring Rd. Chest 119 E2
Ring-o-bells La. Disley 38 B3
Ringsfield Rd. Speke 21 D1
Ringstone Way. W Br 65 E4
Ringway. El Por 69 F2
Ringway. Nest 41 F1
Ringway. Waver 143 D3
Ringway Rd. Run 23 E1
Ringway Rd. Wythe 33 E4
Ringwood Cl. Warr 10 A3
Ripley Ave. Ch Hul 35 D3
Ripley Cl. Haz Gr 36 C4
Ripley St. Warr 15 F3
Ripon Ave. El Por 69 E3
Ripon Ave. Gold 3 E4
Ripon Cl. N-le-W 2 B3
Ripon Dr. Wist 206 A4
Ripon Row. Run 49 E3
Rise The. W Br 65 E3
Riseley St. Mfield 112 B4
Riseley's Pas. Mfield 112 B4
Rising Sun Cl. Warren 112 A3
Rising Sun Rd. Warren 112 A2
Risley Rd. Warr 9 F3
Rivacre Brow. El Por 69 F4
Rivacre Rd. Beb 44 A2
Rivacre Rd. El Por 44 B1
River La. Brough 140 C4
River La. Chest 141 E4
River La. Farn 180 C1
River La. Part 11 F2
River Rd. Warr 16 A2
River St. Congle 156 B2
River St. Mfield 112 C3
River St. Wilm 60 A4
River View. Winsf 126 C1
Riverbank Cl. Boll 87 F4
Riverbank Cl. Hes 40 C3
Riverbank Rd. Hes 40 C3
Riverdane Rd. Congle 156 C2
Rivermead Ave. Altr 32 B4
Riversdale. Frod 49 E1
Riversdale. Warr 17 F4
Riversdale Rd. Run 49 F4
Rivershill Gdns. Altr 32 B3
Riverside. Nant 204 B3
Riverside. North 104 A3
Riverside Cl. Warr 16 B2
Riverside Cres. H Chap 130 B2
Riverside Ct. Chest 141 F4
Riverside Ct. S La E 113 E2
Riverside Dr. North 103 F3
Riverside Gr. Crewe 189 E2
Riverside Pk. G Cit 116 A4
Riverside Wlk. Nest 66 B3
Riversmead. Hunt 142 A3
Riverview Rd. Nest 66 C3
Rivington Ct. Warr 17 F4
Rivington Gr. Irlam 11 E3
Rivington Rd. El Por 70 B3
Rivington Rd. Run 50 C2
Rixton Ave. Warr 15 F4
Roaches The. Mfield 112 A3
Road Beta. Middle 151 E4
Road Five. Winsf 127 E1
Road Four. Winsf 127 D1
Road One. Winsf 127 D2
Road St. Tarp 146 A2
Road Three. Winsf 127 E1
Road Two. Winsf 127 D1
Roadside Ct. Gold 3 E4
Roan Ct. Mfield 112 C4
Roan House Way. Mfield 112 C4
Roan Mews. Mfield 112 C4
Rob Rd. N-le-W 2 C3
Robert Moffat. H Legh 29 E3
Robert St. North 103 F3
Robert St. Run 23 E1
Robert St. Warr 15 F3
Robert St. Wid 13 D1
Robert's Terr. Chest 118 A1
Roberts Ave. Hay 1 A3
Roberts Ct. Run 49 F3
Roberts Dr. North 104 B3
Roberts Rd. Lost 80 A1
Robin Cl. Rain 88 C3
Robin Cl. Run 50 B4
Robin Cl. Sand 175 D4
Robin Cres. S La E 112 B1
Robin Hood Ave. Mfield 112 B3
Robin Hood La. Hels 73 D1
Robin La. Chelf 84 A2
Robin La. S La E 112 B1
Robin's La. Bram 35 F4
Robin's La. Ch Hul 35 E4
Robins Cft. El Por 69 F1
Robins Cl. Bram 35 F4
Robins La. Croft 4 B1
Robinsbay Rd. Wythe 33 F4
Robinsons Croft. Chest 142 A4
Robson St. Warr 16 B3
Roby Gr. Gt San 15 D3
Roche Gdns. Ch Hul 35 D3
Rochester Cl. Gold 3 D4
Rochester Cl. Gt San 15 E3
Rochester Cres. Crewe 190 C3
Rochester Dr. El Por 70 B2
Rochford Ave. Wythe 33 E4
Rock Bank. W Br 65 F3
Rock Dr. Frod 49 E1
Rock Farm Cl. Nest 67 D3
Rock Farm Dr. Nest 67 D3
Rock Farm Gr. Nest 67 D3
Rock La. Burw 184 B3
Rock La. Chest 118 B2
Rock La. Wid 12 C2
Rock Rd. Con Q 91 F1
Rock St. N Mills 39 E4
Rock The. Hels 73 E1
Rockfield Dr. Hels 73 E1
Rockford Lodge. Knuts 57 E1

Rockhouse La. Kids 210 B4
Rockingham Cl. Warr 10 B3
Rocklands La. Thor H 42 B4
Rocklee Gdns. Nest 67 D3
Rocklife La. Flint 91 D2
Rocksavage Expressway. Run 49 E3
Rockside. Kids 195 E3
Rockwood Ave. Crewe 190 A2
Rocky La. Hes 40 C4
Rocky La. Tatt 182 C4
Rocky La S. Hes 41 D4
Roddy La. Kings 75 F1
Rode House Cl. Sch Gr 193 F4
Rode The. Alsag 193 E2
Rodeheath Cl. Wilm 60 B4
Rodepool Cl. Wilm 34 B1
Rodgers Cl. Frod 49 D1
Rodney St. Mfield 112 B4
Rodney St. Warr 16 A3
Roe Park. Astb 178 C1
Roe St. Congle 156 C1
Roe St. Mfield 112 B4
Roebuck St. Crewe 190 B3
Roeburn Way. Penk 14 B2
Roedean Wlk. Crewe 190 B3
Roehurst La. Winsf 126 B1
Roemarsh Ct. Run 49 F3
Roewood La. Mfield 88 A1
Roewood La. Mfield 113 D4
Roften Ind Est. El Por 43 E1
Rokeby Ct. Run 24 B3
Rokeden. N-le-W 2 B2
Roland Ave. Run 22 C1
Rolands Wlk. Run 23 F1
Rolleston St. Warr 16 A3
Rolls Ave. Crewe 190 A4
Rolt Cres. Middle 151 D4
Roman Cl. Run 23 F1
Roman Ct. Nest 66 C4
Roman Dr. Blacon 117 E3
Roman Rd. Warr 16 B1
Roman Rd. Wid 22 C3
Roman Rise. North 78 A2
Roman Way. Sand 174 C4
Romanes St. North 103 F4
Romiley Rd. El Por 69 F3
Romney Cl. Nest 66 C4
Romney Croft. Nest 66 C4
Romney Way. Nest 66 C4
Romsey Dr. Ch Hul 35 E3
Ronald Dr. Warr 9 D1
Ronaldshay. Wid 13 F1
Ronaldsway. Halew 21 D4
Ronaldsway. Hes 40 C3
Rood Hill. Congle 156 B2
Rood La. Congle 156 C2
Rook Rd. Warr 16 C2
Rook St. Crewe 190 B1
Rookery Cl. Nant 204 C3
Rookery Dr. Nant 204 C2
Rookery Dr. Tatt 166 A1
Rookery Rd. Kids 195 E2
Rookery Rd. Tils 198 A2
Rookery Rise. Winsf 127 D1
Rookery Rise. Winsf 150 A4
Rookery The. Broug 139 D2
Rookery The. N-le-W 2 B2
Rookerypool Cl. Wilm 34 B1
Rooks Way. Hes 40 C4
Roome St. Warr 16 B4
Rope Bank Ave. Wist 206 A4
Rope La. Shav 206 A3
Rope La. Wist 206 A3
Rope Wlk. Congle 156 B2
Ropewalk The. Nest 66 B4
Rosam Ct. Run 49 F3
Roscoe Ave. N-le-W 2 C2
Roscoe Ave. Warr 16 B4
Roscoe Cres. Run 48 C4
Roscoe Rd. Irlam 11 F4
Roscote Cl. Hes 40 C4
Roscote The. Hes 40 C4
Rose Ave. Hay 1 C3
Rose Ave. Irlam 11 F4
Rose Bank. Lymm 18 C2
Rose Cl. Run 50 B3
Rose Cres. Wid 22 C4
Rose Gdns. Nest 66 C3
Rose Lea Cl. Wid 13 D2
Rose St. Wid 22 C4
Rose Terr. Crewe 190 B3
Rose View Ave. Wid 13 D1
Rose Wlk. Part 11 E1
Roseacre Dr. Chea 34 B4
Rosebank Cl. Winsf 149 F4
Rosebank Rd. Irlam 11 E2
Rosebank Walk. North 78 A2
Roseberry Way. Hasl 191 E2
Rosedale Ave. Gold 3 E4
Rosedale Ave. Warr 17 E4
Rosefield Ave. Lymm 18 C2
Roseheath Dr. Halew 21 D3
Rosehill Ave. Bo Hea 6 A3
Rosehill Rd. Crewe 190 A1
Rosemary Ave. Run 49 F2
Rosemary Ave. Warr 16 C1
Rosemary Cl. Broug 139 E2
Rosemary Cl. Gt San 15 E3
Rosemary La. Burt 161 E1
Rosemary Row. Tatt 166 A1
Rosemary Wlk. Part 11 F1
Rosemoor Gdns. Apple 26 C3
Rosendale Dr. Warr 10 A3
Rosevale Rd. N-u-L 210 C1
Roseville Dr. Congle 179 D4
Rosewood Ave. Chest 118 B3
Rosewood Ave. Frod 74 B4
Rosewood Ave. Warr 16 C4
Rosewood Cl. Crewe 190 C3
Rosewood Gr. Saug 117 D4
Ross Cl. Gt San 15 E4
Ross Dr. El Por 69 E3
Ross Rd. El Por 70 A3
Ross St. Wid 13 D1
Rossall Cl. Hale 21 F1
Rossall Dr. Bram 35 F3
Rossall Gr. El Por 69 E3
Rossall Rd. Gt San 15 D2
Rossall Rd. Wid 13 E1
Rossbank Rd. El Por 70 A4
Rosscliffe Rd. El Por 70 A3
Rossenclough Rd. Wilm 34 B1
Rossendale Rd. Chea 34 B4
Rossett Ave. Wythe 33 E4
Rossett Cl. Warr 7 F1
Rossett Rd. Holt 180 A1
Rossfield Rd. El Por 70 A3
Rosslyn Cl. Hawa 116 A1
Rosslyn La. Cudd 102 A2
Rosslyn Rd. Chest 119 D2
Rossmill La. Altr 32 A4
Rossmore Gdns. El Por 69 E3
Rossmore Rd E. El Por 69 F4
Rossmore Rd W. El Por 69 E4
Rossmount Rd. El Por 70 A3
Rosswood Rd. El Por 70 A3
Rostherne Ave. El Por 69 F2
Rostherne Ave. Gold 3 E4
Rostherne Ave. H La 37 F4
Rostherne Cl. Warr 15 E2
Rostherne Cres. Wid 12 B1
Rostherne Rd. Wilm 59 F2
Rostherne Way. Sand 174 C4
Rothay Dr. Penk 14 B2
Rothbury Cl. Run 49 E3
Rother Dr. El Por 70 A4
Rothesay Cl. Run 23 F1
Rothesay Dr. Beb 43 F2
Rothesay Rd. Chest 141 D4
Rough Bank. Congle 179 F4
Rough Heys La. Henb 111 D4
Roughlea Ave. Cul 4 B2
Roughley Ave. Warr 15 E2
Roughlyn Cres. Dodle 140 C1
Roughwood La. Ha Gr 176 A1
Round Gdns. Boll 88 A4
Round Hill Meadow. Chest 142 A4
Round Meadow. Rain 88 C3
Round Thorn. Croft 9 D4
Round Way. N Mills 39 E4
Roundabout The. Cront 12 B3
Roundhey. Chea 34 B4
Roundway. Ch Hul 35 E3
Routledge St. Wid 13 D1
Rowan Ave. Gold 3 F4
Rowan Cl. Gt San 14 B4
Rowan Cl. Middle 151 F3
Rowan Cl. N-le-W 2 B1
Rowan Cl. Run 49 E4
Rowan Cl. Sand 174 C4
Rowan Cl. Winsf 126 B2
Rowan Dr. Ch Hul 35 E4
Rowan Gr. Con Q 91 E1
Rowan Pk. Christ 142 C4
Rowan Pl. Chest 119 D2
Rowan Rd. Weave 102 B4
Rowan Way. Mfield 87 F1
Rowan Wlk. Part 11 E1
Rowans The. Broug 139 D2
Rowanside. Prest 86 C3
Rowanside Dr. Wilm 60 C4
Rowcliffe Ave. Chest 141 D2
Rowe St. Warr 16 A3
Rowland Cl. Warr 9 D2
Rowley Bank La. H Legh 29 D1
Rowley Rd. Haz Gr 36 C4
Rowley Way. Knuts 82 A4
Rowson Dr. Irlam 11 E3
Rowthorn Cl. Wid 22 C4
Rowton Brideg Rd. Christ 142 C4
Rowton La. Waver 142 C3
Rowton Rd. Crewe 189 E2
Roxbo Rough Cl. Burton 7 D3
Roxburgh Cl. Mfield 87 D1
Roxburgh Rd. El Por 68 C3
Roxby Way. Knuts 82 A4
Roxholme Wlk. Wythe 33 E4
Royal Ave. Wid 12 B1
Royal Gdns. North 103 F2
Royal La. Eaton 147 D2
Royal Meadows. Mfield 87 D1
Royal Mews. L Den 104 B3
Royal Mount. Crewe 173 D1
Royal Pl. Wid 22 A4
Royal Rd. Disley 38 B3
Royden Ave. Irlam 11 F4
Royden Ave. Run 49 D4
Royds Cl. Hart 103 D2
Roylands Dr. Middle 151 E4
Royle St. Congle 156 B2
Royle St. North 104 A4
Royle St. Winsf 126 C1
Royle's Pl. North 103 E3
Royleen Dr. Frod 74 B3
Royston Ave. Warr 17 D4
Royston Cl. El Por 69 F2
Royston Cl. Gold 3 F4
Rozel Cres. Gt San 15 D3
Ruby Ct. El Por 70 B2
Rudd Ave. St Hel 1 A1
Rudheath Cl. Crewe 189 E3
Rudloe Ct. Warr 8 C1
Rudstone Cl. El Por 69 D3
Rue De Bohars. Tarp 168 B4
Rufford Cl. Wist 206 A4
Rufford Ct. Warr 17 F4
Rugby Cl. Mfield 87 F2
Rugby Dr. Mfield 87 F2
Rugby House. Mfield 87 E2
Rugby Rd. El Por 70 B2
Ruislip Ct. Warr 8 C1
Runcorn Docks Rd. Run 22 C1
Runcorn Rd. L Lei 77 E3
Runcorn Rd. Moore 25 E3
Runcorn Rd. North 78 A1
Runcorn Spur Rd. Run 49 E4
Runger La. Wythe 32 C4
Runnell The. Nest 41 E2
Runnymede. Warr 17 E4
Runnymede Dr. Hay 1 A3
Ruscoe Ave. Sand 174 C3
Ruscolm Cl. Gt San 14 B4
Rushey Cl. Altr 32 B4
Rushfield Cres. Run 50 A3
Rushfield Rd. Ch Hul 35 D3
Rushfield Rd. Chest 141 D3
Rushgreen Rd. Lymm 19 D2
Rushmere La. Aldf 163 F2
Rushmore Gr. Warr 17 D4
Rushside Rd. Ch Hul 35 D3
Rushton Ave. N-le-W 2 A2
Rushton Cl. North 104 B4
Rushton Dr. Chest 118 B4
Rushton Dr. Ho Co 206 C1
Rushton Dr. Middle 151 E4
Rushton Fold. M St A 61 D1
Rushton La. Eaton 147 E3
Rushton La. L Bud 147 E3
Rushton Rd. Ch Hul 35 D3
Ruskin Ave. N-le-W 2 B2
Ruskin Ave. Warr 8 B1
Ruskin Ct. Knuts 57 D1
Ruskin Dr. El Por 70 B2
Ruskin Rd. Congle 156 B1
Ruskin Rd. Crewe 190 B1
Ruskin Way. Knuts 57 D2
Russell Ave. Alsag 193 E3
Russell Ave. H La 37 F4
Russell Cl. Congle 179 D4
Russell Ct. Wid 13 D2
Russell Dr. Hasl 191 E2
Russell Rd. Run 48 C4
Russell Rd. Winsf 149 E4
Russell St. Chest 118 C1
Russet Cl. Middle 128 A1
Russet Rd. Weave 102 B4
Ruthin Ct. El Por 70 B2
Ruthin Wlk. Hels 73 D1
Rutland Ave. Gold 3 E4
Rutland Ave. Halew 21 D4
Rutland Ave. Warr 26 A4
Rutland Cl. Congle 156 C2
Rutland Cl. Sand 174 B3
Rutland Dr. Middle 151 E4
Rutland Dr. Weave 77 E1
Rutland Pl. Chest 119 D3
Rutland Rd. Haz Gr 36 C4
Rutland Rd. Irlam 11 E3
Rutland Rd. Kids 195 D1
Rutland Rd. Mfield 112 B2
Rutland Rd. Part 11 F1
Rutland St. Run 22 C1
Ryburn Rd. Mfield 112 A3
Rydal Ave. H La 37 F4
Rydal Ave. Warr 16 A1
Rydal Cl. El Por 70 B1
Rydal Cl. H Chap 130 A1
Rydal Cl. Nest 66 C3
Rydal Cl. Winsf 126 B2
Rydal Ct. Congle 156 A1
Rydal Dr. Altr 32 B4
Rydal Gr. Chest 141 D3
Rydal Gr. Hels 73 D1
Rydal Gr. Run 49 D4
Rydal Pl. Mfield 112 A3
Rydal St. N-le-W 2 B2
Rydal Way. Alsag 193 E3
Rydal Way. Wid 12 B1
Ryde Cl. Crewe 190 A4
Ryder Rd. Warr 17 E4
Ryder Rd. Wid 13 D3
Ryders St. North 103 F4
Rye Cl. Alsag 193 D2
Ryebank Ave. Crewe 190 A4
Ryebank Way. Mfield 87 E2
Ryecroft. Elton 72 A2
Ryecroft Cl. Middle 151 D4
Ryecroft La. Dudd 144 B3
Ryecroft La. Mobb 57 F2
Ryecroft Rd. Hes 41 E4
Ryehills. Audley 209 F1
Rylands St. Warr 16 A3
Rylands St. Wid 23 D4
Ryle St. Mfield 112 B3
Ryle's Park Rd. Mfield 112 B3
Ryles Cl. Mfield 112 B3
Ryles Cres. Mfield 112 B3
Ryleys La. A Edge 59 F1

S Bank Cl. A Edge 60 A1
S View Ave. Warren 111 E1
S View Rd. Chest 118 A1
Sabre Cl. Run 50 B4
Sack La. B Hea 54 C3
Saddleback Dr. Prest 86 C4
Saddlers Rise. Run 50 B4
Sadler Cl. Winsf 126 B1
Sadler Rd. Winsf 126 B1
Sadler St. Wid 13 E1
Sadler's Cl. H Chap 130 A2
Sadlers La. Dela 124 A1
Sadlers Wells. Bun 185 F4
Safferon Cl. Warr 9 D1
Saffron Wlk. Part 11 F1
Sagars Rd. Wilm 34 B2
Sage Cl. Warr 9 E1
Saighton La. Saigh 142 C1
Saighton La. Waver 142 C1
St Alban Rd. Penk 14 C3
St Albans Cl. Hay 2 A4
St Albans Dr. Nant 204 C2
St Albans Pl. N Mills 39 E4
St Albans St. N Mills 39 E4
St Ambrose Rd. Wid 13 E1
St Andrew's Gdns. Alsag 193 F1
St Andrew's Rd. El Por 70 C2
St Andrew's Rd. Mfield 112 A4
St Andrews Cl. North 104 C4
St Andrews Cl. Warr 9 D2
St Andrews Dr. H Chap 130 A1
St Andrews Dr. Kids 195 E2
St Andrews Wlk. M Traf 96 C1
St Andrews Wlk. N Mills 39 E4
St Ann's Ave. Middle 151 E4
St Ann's Rd. Middle 151 E4
St Ann's Rd S. Chea 34 B4
St Ann's Sq. Chea 34 B4
St Anne St. Chest 118 B1
St Anne's La. Nant 204 B3
St Anne's Rd. Wid 13 D1
St Annes Ave. Warr 17 D1
St Annes Ave E. Warr 17 D1
St Asaph Dr. Warr 7 F2
St Asaph Rd. El Por 94 C4
St Augustine's Ave. Warr 16 C2
St Austel Cl. Penk 14 C2
St Austell Ave. Mfield 86 C1
St Austell Cl. Mfield 86 C1
St Austell Cl. Run 50 A3
St Austell Dr. Chea 34 A4
St Austins La. Warr 16 A2
St Barnabas Ct. Mfield 112 B3
St Barnabas Pl. Warr 15 F3
St Bede's Ave. Weave 77 E1
St Benedicts Cl. Warr 16 A4
St Brannocks Rd. Ch Hul 35 D4
St Brides Cl. Penk 14 C2
St Bridgets Cl. Warr 8 C2
St Bridgets Ct. Chest 141 D3
St Catherines Dr. Hart 103 D2
St Chad's Fields. Winsf 149 E3
St Chad's Rd. Blacon 117 F2
St Chads Cl. Hay Gr 220 A4
St Chads Way. N in H 236 B1
St Christophers Cl. Chest 118 B4
St Clairs St. Crewe 190 B1
St David Rd. Beb 44 A3
St David's Terr. Brough 140 B3
St Davids Dr. El Por 94 C4
St Davids Dr. Warr 7 F1
St Edwards Cl. Mfield 112 B3
St Elmo Park. Poyn 37 E2
St Elphins Cl. Warr 16 B3
St George's Cres. Chest 141 F4
St George's Cres. Waver 143 D3
St George's Ct. Wid 22 B4
St George's Pl. Mfield 112 B4
St George's Rd. Winsf 149 E4
St George's St. Mfield 112 B3
St George's Way. Thor H 42 A3
St Georges Ave. El Por 94 C4
St Georges Rd. N Mills 39 E4
St Helens Cl. Hol Gr 11 D2
St Helens Rd. Gold 4 A4
St Helens Rd. North 104 A4
St Hilda's Dr. Frod 49 E1
St Ives Cl. Mfield 86 C1
St Ives Pk. Hawa 116 A2
St James Ave. Chest 118 B4
St James Ave. Congle 156 B1
St James Ave. Warren 111 F1
St James Cl. Audlem 230 A2
St James Cl. Frod 49 E1
St James Wlk. North 103 F4
St James' Dr. Wilm 60 A3
St James' Sq. N Mills 39 E4
St James' Way. Ch Hul 34 C3
St John Ave. Warr 16 A1
St John St. Chest 118 B1
St John St. N-le-W 2 A2
St John's Ave. Knuts 56 C1
St John's Ave. Lost 79 F2
St John's Cl. North 104 C4
St John's La. Wilm 59 F2
St John's Rd. Beb 44 A3
St John's Rd. Chest 141 F4
St John's Rd. Congle 156 C3
St John's Rd. Knuts 57 D1
St John's Rd. Mfield 112 B4
St John's Rd. Wilm 59 F2
St John's Rear Rd. Chest 141 F4
St John's St. Run 23 D2
St John's Way. Cudd 102 A1
St John's Way. Sand 175 F3
St John's Wood. Kids 194 C1
St Johns Dr. Winsf 149 D4
St Joseph's Cl. Penk 14 C3
St Katherines Way. Warr 16 B3
St Lawrence Ct. Nant 204 C3
St Lawrence Rd. Frod 74 A4
St Leonard's Way. Woore 232 B1
St Luke's Cres. Wid 13 D2
St Luke's Way. Frod 49 D1
St Lukes Cl. H Chap 130 B2
St Margaret's Ave. Warr 8 B1
St Mark's St. Hay 1 A3
St Marks Cres. El Por 94 C4
St Marks Rd. Chest 140 C3
St Martin's Rd. Kids 210 C3
St Martin's Way. Chest 118 B1
St Martins Dr. El Por 69 E1
St Martins La. Run 50 B4
St Mary's Ave. Weave 77 E1
St Mary's Cl. Alsag 193 E3
St Mary's Cl. Apple 26 B3
St Mary's Hill. Chest 141 E4
St Mary's Rd. Disley 38 B3
St Mary's Rd. Dodle 162 A4
St Mary's Rd. N Mills 39 D4
St Mary's Rd. Nant 204 C4
St Mary's Rd. Penk 14 C3
St Mary's Rd. Run 23 F1
St Mary's Rd. Wid 23 D2
St Mary's St. Crewe 190 B2
St Mary's St. Warr 16 B2
St Marys Cl. Hale 21 F1
St Matthews Cl. Apple 26 B4
St Matthews Cl. Hasl 191 E2
St Mawes Cl. Wid 12 C1
St Mawgan Ct. Warr 8 C1
St Michael's Ave. Bram 35 F4
St Michael's Cl. L Lei 77 E3
St Michael's Cl. Wid 22 B4
St Michael's Rd. Wid 22 B4
St Michael's View. Crewe 190 A3
St Michael's Way. Middle 128 B1
St Monicas Cl. Apple 26 B4
St Nicholas Ct. Nant 204 C3
St Nicholas Rd. Gold 4 A4
St Olave St. Chest 141 E4
St Oswald's Cres. Bre Gr 153 F3
St Oswalds Cl. Malpas 213 D2
St Oswalds Cl. Win 8 A3
St Oswalds Way. Chest 118 B1
St Paul's Cl. Crewe 190 B2
St Paul's Pl. North 79 D1
St Paul's Rd. Mfield 112 C4
St Paul's Rd. Wid 23 D4
St Paul's St. Crewe 190 B2
St Pauls Gdns. El Por 69 D4
St Peter's Ave. Knuts 56 C1
St Peter's Cl. Hes 40 C4
St Peter's Cl. Lymm 19 D2
St Peter's Dr. L Bud 147 F4
St Peter's Rise. Sand 174 C4
St Peter's Way. Warr 16 A3
St Peters Rd. Congle 156 C1
St Peters Way. M Traf 119 F4
St Saviour's St. Kids 194 B1
St Stephen Rd. Penk 14 C3
St Stephen's Ave. Warr 8 A2
St Stephens Cl. Hes 41 E3
St Stephens Ct. Sand 174 B4
St Thomas Ct. Wid 12 C1
St Thomas St. Kids 195 F4
St Vincent Dr. Hart 102 C2
St Vincent Rd. Penk 14 C3
St Wenefredes Green. Bic T 214 C3
St Werburgh Mount. Chest 118 B1
St Werburgh St. Chest 118 B1
St Wilfred's Dr. Warr 17 E1
Salander Cres. Wist 206 A4
Salerno Rd. Chest 95 D1
Salesbrook La. New 228 B3
Salford. Audlem 230 A2
Salford Pl. Congle 156 C2
Salisbury Ave. Brough 140 C3
Salisbury Ave. Crewe 190 B1

Salisbury Cl. Crewe 190 B1
Salisbury Cl. El Por 94 C4
Salisbury Ct. Mfield 112 C4
Salisbury Rd. Hay 1 C4
Salisbury St. Blacon 118 A2
Salisbury St. Gold 3 D4
Salisbury St. Run 23 D1
Salisbury St. Warr 16 B3
Salisbury St. Wid 23 D4
Salkeld St. North 104 A4
Salop Pl. Kids 195 D2
Salop Wlk. Mfield 86 C1
Saltash Cl. Run 50 A3
Salter's La. Bicker 183 F1
Salter's La. Bicker 199 F4
Salter's La. Brox 183 F1
Salter's La. Pict 119 E4
Salters La. Sidd 109 F1
Salters La. With 132 A4
Saltersbrook Gr. Wilm 34 C1
Saltersford Cnr. H Chap 130 C2
Saltersgate. El Por 69 F1
Saltney Ferry Rd. Brough 140 A4
Saltwood Dr. Run 50 B3
Samuel St. Chest 118 C1
Samuel St. Crewe 190 A3
Samuel St. Kids 195 F1
Samuel St. Mfield 112 B4
Samuel St. Warr 15 F2
Sanbec Gdns. Cront 12 B3
Sand La. N Ald 84 C3
Sandbach Rd. Congle 156 A2
Sandbach Rd. Ha Gr 176 B1
Sandbach Rd. Law-g 193 F3
Sandbach Rd. Sch Gr 193 F4
Sandbach Rd N. Alsag 193 E2
Sandbach Rd S. Alsag 193 E2
Sanderling Rd. N-le-W 2 B2
Sanders Hey Cl. Run 50 A3
Sanders Sq. Mfield 112 B3
Sanderson Cl. Crewe 206 B4
Sanderson Cl. Gt San 14 B3
Sandfield Ave. Wren 216 C2
Sandfield Cl. Gold 3 F4
Sandfield Cres. Cul 5 E4
Sandfield Ct. Frod 74 A4
Sandfield Ct. Wren 216 C2
Sandfield La. Act Br 76 C1
Sandfield La. Hart 103 E2
Sandfield Park. Hes 40 B4
Sandfields. Frod 74 A4
Sandford Rd. Nant 204 C4
Sandgate Rd. Mfield 87 F1
Sandham Gr. Hes 41 E4
Sandham Rd. Speke 21 D2
Sandheys. Nest 41 E1
Sandhole La. Chelf 83 E2
Sandhole La. Crow 101 D4
Sandhurst Ave. Wist 190 A1
Sandhurst St. Warr 16 C2
Sandicroft Cl. Warr 9 E3
Sandiford Rd. H Chap 130 B2
Sandileigh. Chest 118 C2
Sandileigh Ave. Knuts 56 C1
Sandiway. Beb 43 E3
Sandiway. Knuts 57 D1
Sandiway Ave. Wid 12 A1
Sandiway Cl. Cudd 102 A1
Sandiway La. Antro 53 D1
Sandiway Park. Weave 102 C2
Sandiway Rd. Crewe 190 A4
Sandiway Rd. Wilm 34 B3
Sandle Bridge La. Chelf 83 F3
Sandle Bridge Rise. L End 83 F3
Sandon Cres. Nest 66 C3
Sandon Park Gdns. Crewe 189 E2
Sandon Pl. Wid 13 E1
Sandon Rd. Chest 118 C2
Sandon St. Crewe 190 B2
Sandown Cl. Cul 4 C2
Sandown Cl. Middle 151 E4
Sandown Cl. Run 49 E3
Sandown Cl. Wilm 60 A4
Sandown Cres. Cudd 102 A2
Sandown Dr. Altr 32 B3
Sandown Pl. Mfield 111 F4
Sandown Rd. Crewe 190 B4
Sandpiper Cl. N-le-W 2 B2
Sandra Dr. N-le-W 2 B2
Sandringham Ave. Chest 119 D1
Sandringham Ave. Hels 73 D2
Sandringham Cl. Winsf 126 B2
Sandringham Dr. Gt San 15 E2
Sandringham Dr. Poyn 36 B2
Sandringham Dr. Wist 205 F4
Sandringham Gdns. El Por 70 B1
Sandringham Rd. Wid 13 D2
Sandrock Rd. Christ 142 C4
Sands Rd. Kids 195 F3
Sandsdown Cl. Bidd 179 E1
Sandside Rd. Alsag 193 D2
Sandstone Wlk. Hes 41 D4
Sandwich Dr. Mfield 87 E2
Sandwood Ave. Broug 139 D2
Sandy Brow La. Gold 3 F1
Sandy Cl. Boll 87 F4
Sandy Gr. Alsag 193 E2
Sandy La. Allos 106 C3
Sandy La. Astb 177 F3
Sandy La. Bicker 184 B1
Sandy La. Bo Hea 14 A3
Sandy La. Brough 140 B3
Sandy La. Brox 199 E4
Sandy La. Chest 119 D1
Sandy La. Congle 156 A1
Sandy La. Croft 9 D4
Sandy La. Cront 12 B3
Sandy La. Gold 2 C4
Sandy La. Gold 4 A4
Sandy La. Goost 107 E1
Sandy La. H Kin 161 D3
Sandy La. Hasl 192 A4
Sandy La. Hather 219 F3
Sandy La. Hunt 142 B2
Sandy La. Lymm 19 D2
Sandy La. Mar 125 E3
Sandy La. Mfield 86 B1
Sandy La. Nest 67 D3
Sandy La. New 217 E1
Sandy La. Penk 15 D2
Sandy La. Rad 155 E2
Sandy La. Run 48 C4
Sandy La. Run 50 C3
Sandy La. Saigh 142 B2
Sandy La. Sand 174 B3
Sandy La. Swett 131 F2
Sandy La. Tarv 121 E2
Sandy La. Threap 222 C4
Sandy La. Warr 8 B1
Sandy La. Warr 26 B4
Sandy La. Weave 77 E1
Sandy La. Wid 12 B3
Sandy La. Wilm 59 F4
Sandy La W. Warr 8 A2
Sandy Moor La. Run 24 B2
Sandy Rd. Bidd 179 E1
Sandyhill Pl. Winsf 149 E3
Sandyhill Rd. Winsf 149 E3
Sandylands Cres. Law-g 193 F3
Sandylands Park. Wist 205 E4
Sankey St. Gold 3 D4
Sankey St. N-le-W 2 A2
Sankey St. Warr 16 A3
Sankey St. Wid 23 D3
Sankey Valley
Ind Est. N-le-W 2 A1
Sankey Way. Gt San 15 E3
Sankey Way. Warr 15 E3
Sanky La. Hatt 25 F1
Santon Dr. Gold 3 F4
Sapling La. Eaton 146 C2
Sarra La. Burw 184 A3
Sarsfield Ave. Gold 3 E4
Saughall Hey. Saug 94 A1
Saughall Rd. Blacon 117 F3
Saunders St. Crewe 190 A2
Saundersfoot Cl. Warr 7 F1
Saville Ave. Warr 15 F4
Saville St. Mfield 112 C3
Sawley Cl. Cul 5 D1
Sawley Cl. Run 50 C4
Sawley Dr. Ch Hul 35 E3
Sawpit St. Part 20 A3
Sawyer Dr. Bidd 179 E1
Saxon Crossway. Winsf 126 A1
Saxon Rd. Run 23 E1
Saxon Terr. Wid 13 D1
Saxon Way. Blacon 117 F3
Saxon Way. El Por 94 C4
Saxon Way. Sand 175 E3
Saxons La. North 103 E4
Saxons La. North 103 F3
Sayce St. Wid 13 D1
Scafell Ave. Warr 8 B2
Scafell Cl. Beb 43 E2
Scafell Cl. H La 37 F4
Scaife Rd. Nant 204 C3
Scaliot Cl. N Mills 39 D4
Scar La. Ed Gr 198 C1
Sceptre Cl. N-le-W 2 A2
School Ave. Nest 66 C3
School Bank. Norley 101 D3
School Brow. Warr 16 B3
School Cl. Audley 210 A1
School Cl. Knuts 56 C1
School Cl. Marb 226 C4
School Cl. Poyn 36 C2
School Cres. Crewe 190 C2
School Field Cl. Buer 230 C2
School Green. Clutt 182 B1
School Hill. Hes 40 C4
School La. Aldf 163 F1
School La. Antro 53 E2
School La. Astb 178 A4
School La. Audlem 230 A2
School La. Bo Hea 13 F4
School La. Bre Gr 153 F3
School La. Bun 168 C1
School La. Burw 184 A3
School La. Ch Hul 35 D4
School La. Cudd 102 A1
School La. Dun T 20 B3
School La. Eaton 156 C4
School La. El Por 69 D4
School La. Elton 72 A2
School La. Frod 74 B4
School La. G Bud 79 D4
School La. G Sutt 119 F3
School La. Hart 103 E2
School La. Henb 111 D3
School La. Hol Gr 11 D1
School La. Irlam 11 E3
School La. Lost 80 A1
School La. M Traf 119 F4
School La. Marb 215 F1
School La. Mart 133 E3
School La. Moult 126 C4
School La. N Ald 86 A3
School La. Nant 204 C3
School La. Nest 41 D1
School La. Nest 66 C3
School La. Norley 100 B3
School La. Oller 83 D2
School La. Poyn 36 C2
School La. Run 49 F4
School La. Sand 174 B4
School La. Sand 175 F3
School La. Small 176 C3
School La. Warm 173 F4
School La. Warr 10 B3
School La. Whit 52 C3
School La. Will 42 A1
School Rd. El Por 70 A3
School Rd. L Den 104 B3
School Rd. Wilm 34 B2
School Rd. Winsf 126 C3
School Rd. Winsf 127 D1
School Rd N. North 104 C3
School Rd S. L Den 104 C3
School St. Chest 118 C2
School St. Gold 3 D4
School St. Hasl 191 E3
School St. N-le-W 2 A2
School St. Warr 16 A2
School Way. North 104 A4
School Way. Wid 13 E2
Schooner Cl. Run 50 B3
Scotch Hall La. Antro 53 D2
Scotland Rd. Warr 16 A3
Scott Ave. Crewe 190 C2
Scott Ave. Wid 22 C4
Scott Cl. Mfield 113 D4
Scott Cl. Sand 174 B3
Scott Rd. Prest 87 D4
Scott Rd. Warr 16 B3
Scott Wlk. N-le-W 2 B1
Scotthorpe Cl. Mfield 111 F3
Scotton Ave. El Por 69 D3
Scretton Green
Distribution Park. Apple 27 E2
Scroggins La. Part 11 F2
Sea Bank. Middle 128 B1
Sea La. Run 23 E1
Sea View. Nest 66 C2
Seabank Rd. Hes 40 C3
Seabury St. Warr 17 D2
Seacombe Dr. El Por 69 F2
Seafield Ave. Hes 40 C3
Seaford Cl. Run 24 B1
Seaford Pl. Warr 8 A2
Seagull Cl. Crewe 190 C3
Seahill Rd. Saug 116 C4
Seal Rd. Bram 35 F4
Sealand Rd. Blacon 117 E2
Sealand Rd. Chest 118 A1
Sealand Rd. Sea 116 B3
Sealand Way. Wilm 34 B2
Seathwaite Cl. Run 49 F3
Seaton Cl. Crewe 190 A4
Seaton St. Winsf 127 E1
Seaview Ave. Beb 44 A3
Seaville St. Chest 118 C1
Secker Ave. Warr 16 B1
Secker Cl. Warr 16 B1
Second Ave. Adlin 36 B1
Second Ave. Crewe 190 C1
Second Ave. G Cit 92 C2
Second Ave. Kids 194 C1
Second Ave. Run 49 F4
Second Ave. Sand 175 D3
Second Dig La. Hay Gr 219 E4
Second Wood St. Nant 204 B3
Sedbergh Gr. Run 49 F3
Sedburgh Cl. H Chap 130 A2
Seddon St. Middle 128 B1
Sedgefield Rd. Chest 118 A1
Sedgewick Cres. Burton 6 C3
Sedgmere Ave. Crewe 190 A4
Sedum Cl. Hunt 142 A3
Sefton Ave. Congle 157 D1
Sefton Ave. Wid 13 D2
Sefton Dr. Wilm 34 B1
Sefton Rd. Chest 119 D2
Sefton St. N-le-W 1 C2
Selby Cl. Poyn 36 B3
Selby Gdns. Ch Hul 35 E3
Selby Gn. El Por 69 D3
Selby St. Warr 15 F3
Selkirk Ave. Beb 43 F2
Selkirk Ave. Warr 17 D2
Selkirk Cl. El Por 68 C3
Selkirk Cl. Mfield 86 C1
Selkirk Dr. Chest 141 D4
Selkirk Dr. H Chap 130 A1
Selkirk Rd. Chest 141 D4
Seller St. Chest 118 C1
Selsdon Ct. Chest 141 E4
Selsey Cl. Crewe 190 A4
Selworthy Dr. Crewe 190 A4
Selworthy Dr. Warr 17 E2
Selwyn Dr. Ch Hul 35 E4
Selwyn Dr. S La E 112 C2
Semper Cl. Congle 157 D2
Seneschal Ct. Run 49 F3
Senna La. Antro 53 D1
Senna La. Comb 78 B4
Sennen Cl. Run 50 B3
Sephton Ave. Cul 4 C2
Serpentine The. Chest 141 D4
Servite Cl. El Por 69 F3
Sett Cl. N Mills 39 D4
Seven Sisters La. Oller 82 C3
Sevenoaks Cl. Mfield 87 D1
Severn Cl. Bidd 179 F1
Severn Cl. Congle 156 C1
Severn Cl. Mfield 86 C1
Severn Cl. Warr 8 C1
Severn Cl. Wid 13 F2
Severn Dr. Ch Hul 35 E3
Severn Rd. Cul 4 C1
Severn Wlk. Winsf 127 D1
Severnvale. El Por 70 A2
Sewell St. Run 23 D1
Sextant Cl. Run 50 B3
Sexton Ave. St Hel 1 A1
Seymour Chase. Knuts 82 A4
Seymour Ct. Run 24 B2
Seymour Dr. El Por 69 F3
Seymour Dr. Warr 17 D4
Seymour Rd. Ch Hul 35 D4
Shackleton Cl. Warr 15 E4
Shadewood Cres. Warr 17 D1
Shadewood Rd. Mfield 112 A3
Shadowmoss Rd. Wythe 33 F4
Shady Brook La. Weave 77 E1
Shaftesbury Ave. Chest 119 E1
Shaftesbury Ave. Penk 14 C1
Shaftesbury Way. Burton 6 C4
Shaftway Cl. Hay 1 C4
Shakerley Ave. Congle 156 C2
Shakespeare Dr. Crewe 191 D2
Shakespeare Gr. Warr 8 B1
Shakespeare Rd. Nest 41 F1
Shakespeare Rd. Wid 13 D1
Shalford Ave. Wythe 33 E4
Shallacres. El Por 69 F4
Shallcross Ave. W Br 65 F2
Shallcross Cres. W Br 65 F2
Shallcross Rd. W Br 65 F2
Shanklin Cl. Gt San 14 B3
Shannon Cl. Chest 140 C3
Shannon Cl. Willas 205 E3
Sharnbrook Dr. Crewe 189 E2
Sharon Park Cl. Warr 17 E1
Sharp St. Warr 16 B4
Sharp St. Wid 23 D4
Sharpley St. Mfield 112 B4
Sharston Cres. Knuts 57 D1
Shavington Ave. Chest 118 C2
Shaw Dr. Knuts 57 E2
Shaw St. Cul 5 D2
Shaw St. Hay 1 C3
Shaw St. Mfield 112 B4
Shaw St. Run 22 C1
Shaw St. Warr 16 A3
Shaw's Ave. Warr 16 B4
Shawell Ct. Wid 13 F1
Shaws La. M St A 86 B4
Shaws La. Winsf 126 C2
Shaws La. Winsf 127 D2
Shay La. Asht 122 A4
Shay La. Hamp 200 A1
Shay La. Tarv 121 F2
Shay's La. Mar 124 C2
Sheaf Cl. Tarv 121 E1
Shearbrook La. Goost 107 F1
Sheardhall Ave. Disley 38 C3
Sheath St. North 104 A4
Shed La. Chest 119 D1
Sheepfield Cl. El Por 69 E4
Sheerwater Cl. Warr 16 C4
Sheffield Cl. Gt San 15 E3
Sheffield Row. N-le-W 7 E4
Sheilings The. Gold 3 F4
Shelagh Ave. Wid 13 D1
Shelbourne Mews. Mfield 111 F4
Shelburne Dr. Hasl 191 E3
Sheldon Ave. Chest 119 D1
Sheldon Ave. Congle 157 D1
Sheldon Rd. Haz Gr 36 C4
Sheldrake Dr. Nest 66 C3
Shellbrook Gr. Wilm 34 B1
Shelley Ave. H Winch 80 A3
Shelley Cl. Crewe 190 C2
Shelley Dr. Wist 189 F1
Shelley Gr. Warr 16 C2
Shelley Rd. Blacon 117 F3
Shelley Rd. Wid 13 D1
Shellow La. Warren 134 B3
Shellway Rd. Stan 71 D2
Shelton Cl. Wid 13 F2
Shepcroft La. Apple 26 B2
Shepherd's La. Chest 118 B3
Shepherds Fold Dr. Winsf 126 B2
Shepherds Row. Run 23 F1
Shepley Cl. Haz Gr 36 B4
Sheppard Cl. Crewe 190 B3
Sheppenhall Gr. New 217 E1
Sheppenhall La. New 228 B3
Sheppenhall La. Roy Gr 228 B3
Shepperton Cl. Apple 26 C3
Shepsides Cl. El Por 69 E2
Shepton Rd. El Por 69 F1
Sherborne Cl. Run 24 C2
Sherborne Rd. Crewe 190 B3
Sherbourne Ave. Chest 141 D3
Sherbourne Cl. Ch Hul 35 D3
Sherbourne Rd. El Por 70 B2
Sherbourne Rd. Mfield 111 F4
Sherbourne Way. Burton 6 C3
Sherbrook Rise. Wilm 60 B3
Sherbrooke Rd. Disley 38 B3
Sheri Dr. N-le-W 2 B1
Sheridan Ave. Gold 3 E4
Sheridan Cl. Crewe 173 D1
Sheringham Cl. Chest 140 C3
Sheringham Dr. Crewe 190 A4
Sheringham Rd. Gt San 14 C3
Sherlock Ave. Hay 1 C4
Sherratt Cl. Congle 156 C1
Sherrington's La. Brox 199 E4
Sherwin St. Crewe 190 B1
Sherwood Cl. Wid 12 B1
Sherwood Cres. Burton 6 C3
Sherwood Gr. Hels 73 D2
Sherwood Rd. Mfield 112 B3
Shetland Cl. Warr 8 C2
Shetland Cl. Wid 13 F2
Shetland Dr. Beb 43 F4
Shetland Dr. El Por 70 B1
Shevington Cl. Wid 13 F2
Shevington Wlk. Wid 13 F2
Shiggins Cl. Gt San 15 E3
Shillingford Cl. Apple 26 C3
Shilton Cl. Middle 151 F3
Ship St. Frod 49 E1
Shipbrook Rd. Chest 118 C3
Shipbrook Rd. L Den 104 A2
Shipbrook Rd. North 104 B3
Shipgate St. Chest 141 E4
Shipton Cl. Gt San 15 D4
Shipton Cl. Wid 12 B2
Shirley Dr. Warr 17 D1
Shirleys Cl. Prest 87 D3
Shirleys Dr. Prest 87 D3
Shocklach Rd. Chest 118 C3
Shones Croft. Nest 67 D3
Shop La. L Bud 124 C1
Shopping Precinct The.
Elton 72 A2
Shoreham Dr. Penk 15 D2
Shores Green Dr. H Winch 79 F3
Shores La. Burl 203 E4
Short St. Hay 1 C3
Short St. Mfield 112 B4
Short St. N-le-W 1 C2
Short St. Wid 23 D3
Shotwick La. Shot 93 F3
Shrewbridge Cres. Nant 204 C2
Shrewbridge Rd. Nant 204 B2
Shrewsbury Dr. N-u-L 210 C1
Shrewsbury Gdns. Ch Hul 35 E3
Shrewsbury Rd. El Por 70 B3
Shrewsbury St. Warr 16 B2
Shrewsbury Way. Chest 140 C3
Shrigley Cl. Wilm 34 B1
Shrigley Rd. Boll 63 D3
Shrigley Rd. Po Shr 63 D3
Shrigley Rd. Poyn 37 E2
Shrigley Rd N. Poyn 37 E2
Shrigley Rise. Boll 63 E1
Shropshire Cl. Warr 17 F3
Shropshire La. New 227 F1
Shropshire La. Old W 227 F1
Shropshire Rd. Stan 70 C2
Shropshire St. Audlem 229 F2
Shurlach Rd. North 104 B3
Shutley La. L Lei 77 E3
Sibbersfield La. Farn 180 C2
Sibell St. Chest 118 C1
Siddall St. North 104 A4
Siddeley Cl. Broug 139 E2
Siddeley Dr. N-le-W 1 C2
Siddington Ave. North 104 A2
Siddington Bank. Sidd 109 F2
Siddington Rd. Poyn 36 C1
Siddington Rd. Wilm 34 B3
Siddon St. Winsf 126 C1
Side End La. Kettle 64 C2
Sidlaw Cl. El Por 69 D3
Sidmouth Cl. Penk 14 C2
Sidmouth Gr. Chea 34 C4
Sidney Rd. Nest 41 F1
Siemens Rd. Irlam 11 F3
Silcock St. Gold 3 D4
Silk Hill. W Br 65 F4
Silk Mill St. Knuts 57 D1
Silk Rd The. Boll 87 F2
Silk Rd The. Mfield 87 F2
Silk St. Congle 156 B1

Silsden Ave. Gold 4 A4
Silvan Ct. Mfield 87 D1
Silver Ave. Hay 1 A3
Silver La. Croft 9 F4
Silver La. Warr 10 B3
Silver St. Boll 88 A4
Silver St. Congle 156 C1
Silver St. Warr 16 A3
Silver Terr. Sand 175 E3
Silverbirch Croft. Broug 139 D2
Silverbirch Way. El Por 94 C4
Silverdale. North 103 E4
Silverdale Cl. Frod 74 B4
Silverdale Cl. H La 37 F4
Silverdale Dr. Wilm 60 A2
Silverdale Rd. N-le-W 2 A2
Silverdale Rd. Warr 16 A1
Silvergate Ct. Congle 178 C4
Silvermuir. Blacon 117 F2
Silverne Dr. El Por 70 A1
Silverwood. Kids 195 D1
Simons La. Frod 74 A3
Simonside. Wid 12 B1
Simonstone Rd. Broug 139 E2
Simonswood Cl. Middle 151 D4
Simpkin Ave. Warr 16 C2
Simpson Cl. Chest 95 E1
Simpson Ct. Crewe 173 D1
Simpson La. Po Shr 63 E4
Simpson Rd. Chest 95 E1
Simpson St. Wilm 59 F3
Simpsons Way. Broug 139 D2
Sinclair Ave. Alsag 193 D2
Sinclair Ave. Warr 8 A1
Sinclair Ave. Wid 23 D4
Sinderland La. Dun T 20 C4
Singapore Ave. Wythe 33 D4
Singleton Ave. Crewe 190 B3
Singleton Rd. El Por 69 F2
Six Acre Gdns. Moore 25 D3
Six Acre La. Moore 25 D3
Sixpenny Wlk. Warr 16 B3
Sixth Ave. G Cit 92 C1
Skeath Cl. Sand 175 F3
Skellern St. Kids 194 B1
Skiddaw Cl. Run 50 A2
Skip's La. Christ 142 C4
Skipton Cl. Haz Gr 36 B4
Skipton Dr. El Por 69 E3
Skye Cl. Wid 13 F2
Slack St. Mfield 112 C3
Slacken La. Kids 194 B1
Slade La. Mobb 58 A4
Slade La. N Ald 85 F3
Slade St. North 104 A4
Slag La. Gold 3 E4
Slag La. Hay 1 A4
Slag La. Hay 1 B4
Slater St. Mfield 112 B3
Slater St. Warr 16 B2
Slindon Cl. N-u-L 210 B1
Slutchers La. Warr 16 A2
Small Ave. Warr 8 B1
Small Cres. Warr 8 B1
Small La. Mobb 58 A4
Smallbrook Wlk. Crewe 206 B4
Smallman Rd. Crewe 190 B1
Smallwood Cl. Middle 151 E4
Smallwood Cl. N-u-L 210 B1
Smethwick La. Bre Gr 154 C2
Smith Cl. Alsag 193 D2
Smith Cres. Warr 16 B4
Smith Dr. Warr 16 B4
Smith Gr. Crewe 190 A3
Smith La. Mobb 57 F3
Smith La. Rain 89 D3
Smith Rd. Wid 22 C4
Smith St. Mfield 112 B3
Smith St. Warr 16 A3
Smith's La. Weave 77 E1
Smithfield Dr. Holt 196 B4
Smithfield La. Sand 175 E3
Smithfield St. Holt 196 B4
Smithfields. Tatt 166 B1
Smithills Cl. Warr 9 E3
Smiths Lawn. Wilm 60 A3
Smithy Brow. Croft 8 C4
Smithy Brow. Rain 88 B4
Smithy Brow. Rain 88 B4
Smithy Cl. Cront 12 B3
Smithy Cl. Saug 94 A1
Smithy Cl. Will 67 D2
Smithy Green. Ch Hul 35 D4
Smithy Hill. Thor H 42 A3
Smithy La. Bidd 179 E1
Smithy La. Bosl 158 C3
Smithy La. Brox 183 E1
Smithy La. Crewe 189 F4
Smithy La. Croft 9 D4
Smithy La. Cront 12 B3
Smithy La. Cudd 102 A3
Smithy La. Dun T 20 B2
Smithy La. Eaton 156 B4
Smithy La. El Por 69 E3
Smithy La. G Bud 79 D4
Smithy La. Hels 73 E3
Smithy La. Kings 75 D1
Smithy La. L Lei 77 D3
Smithy La. Lost 80 A1
Smithy La. M St A 61 E1
Smithy La. Malpas 213 D2
Smithy La. Mould 98 C1
Smithy La. Part 11 F2
Smithy La. Utkin 146 B3
Smithy La. Weston 207 E3
Smithy La. Will 68 A4
Smithy Pathway. Chest 140 C2
Smokehall La. Moult 126 C3
Smokey La. White 224 A1
Smokies Way. Bidd 179 E1
Smyth Rd. Wid 13 E1
Snab La. Nest 66 C2
Snabwood Cl. Nest 66 C3
Snaefell Rise. Apple 26 B4
Snape Hollow. Weston 207 F2
Snape La. Weston 207 F2
Snape Rd. Crewe 206 B4
Snape Rd. Mfield 87 F1
Snapebrook Gr. Wilm 34 C1
Snelson La. Chelf 83 E2
Snelson La. Chelf 108 C4
Snipe Cl. Poyn 36 A2
Snow Hill. Mfield 112 C3
Snowberry Cl. Wid 13 F2
Snowberry Wlk. Part 11 E1
Snowdon Cl. El Por 69 D3
Snowdon Cl. Gt San 14 B4
Snowdon Cres. Chest 141 D3
Snowdon Dr. Crewe 189 E2
Snowdon St. North 77 F2
Snowdonia Way. Winsf 149 D4
Snowdrop Cl. Run 49 F2
Solly Cres. Congle 156 A1
Solway Cl. Warr 8 C2
Solway Gr. Run 49 E3
Solway Rd. North 78 B1
Somerford Ave. Crewe 190 A2
Somerford Cl. Sand 175 E4
Somerford Rd. Broug 139 E2
Somerford Wlk. Wid 13 F2
Somerley Cl. Crewe 190 A4
Somerset Ave. Kids 194 C1
Somerset Cl. Congle 156 B2
Somerset Cl. Irlam 11 E3
Somerset Rd. Chest 118 C3
Somerset St. Chest 118 B2
Somerset Way. Warr 17 D4
Somerton Cl. Mfield 111 F4
Somerton Rd. Mfield 111 F4
Somerville Cl. Beb 43 D3
Somerville Cl. H Legh 29 E2
Somerville Cl. Nest 66 C3
Somerville Cres. El Por 70 B2
Somerville Rd. Wid 22 B4
Somerville St. Crewe 190 A1
Soot Hill. North 78 B2
Sorbus Cl. Elton 72 B2
Sorbus Dr. Crewe 190 C3
Sorby Rd. Irlam 11 F4
Sorrel Cl. Hunt 142 A3
Sorrel Cl. Warr 9 E1
Sossmoss La. N Ald 84 B3
Sound La. Burl 203 F1
Sound La. Sound 217 E4
Souter's La. Chest 118 B1
South Acre Dr. Mfield 113 D4
South Acre Dr. Wilm 34 B2
South Ave. Chest 118 C2
South Ave. Hasl 191 E2
South Ave. Warr 16 A4
South Ave. Warr 16 B1
South Bank. Chest 118 B2
South Bank Gr. Congle 156 C1
South Bank Terr. Run 22 C2
South Cft. Spurs 185 E3
South Cl. Tarp 146 B1
South Cl. Wilm 59 F3
South Crescent Rd. Chest 141 F4
South Crofts. Nant 204 C3
South Dale. Penk 14 C3
South Downs. Knuts 57 E1
South Downs Dr. Altr 31 E4
South Downs Rd. Altr 31 F4
South Dr. Hes 41 D4
South Dr. North 104 B3
South Gr. A Edge 60 A1
South Green. Sea 116 A3
South La. Wid 13 F2
South La Entry. Bo Hea 13 F3
South Mead. Poyn 36 A3
South Meadway. H La 37 F4
South Oak La. Wilm 59 F3
South Par. Run 48 B4
South Park Dr. Poyn 36 C3
South Park Rd. Mfield 112 B4
South Pier Rd. Stan 70 B4
South Rd. Altr 31 F4
South Rd. El Por 70 B2
South Rd. Run 48 B4
South Rd. Speke 21 D2
South Rd. Stan 70 C2
South St. A Edge 60 A1
South St. Chest 119 D1
South St. Congle 156 B2
South St. Crewe 190 B1
South St. Sch Gr 195 D3
South St. Wid 23 D4
South View. Chest 141 E4
South View. N Mills 39 D4
South View. With 132 A4
South View Cottages. Alsag 193 F2
South View La. Cholm 170 C1
South Way. Blacon 117 F2
South West Ave. Boll 87 F3
Southampton Way. Run 50 C3
Southbank. G Bud 79 D4
Southbank Ave. Shav 206 B3
Southdale Rd. Warr 17 D4
Southdown Cl. Mfield 87 E2
Southdown Cres. Chea 34 C4
Southern St. Warr 16 B1
Southfield. Prest 87 D2
Southfield Cl. Wilm 34 B2
Southfield Rd. El Por 69 E3
Southfields. Knuts 57 E2
Southfields Ave. Gt San 14 C3
Southlands. H Chap 130 B1
Southlands Ave. Penk 14 C2
Southlands Mews. Run 22 C1
Southlands Rd. Congle 179 D4
Southlands View. Goost 107 F1
Southport St. St Hel 1 A2
Southward Rd. Hay 2 A4
Southway. Run 49 F4
Southway. Wid 22 B4
Southway Ave. Apple 26 B4
Southwell Cl. Gold 3 E4
Southwood Ave. Run 24 B1
Southworth Ave. Warr 15 F4
Southworth La. Croft 8 C4
Southworth La. Win 8 C4
Southworth Rd. N-le-W 2 C2
Sovereign Cl. North 104 C3
Sovereign Cl. Run 50 B4
Sovereign Ct. Warr 9 E2
Spark Hall Cl. Stret 26 C1
Spark La. Run 23 F1
Spark La. Small 154 B1
Sparks Cl. Chest 142 A4
Sparrow La. Knuts 57 D1
Sparrowhawk Cl. Run 50 A4
Spath La. Wilm 34 C3
Spath La E. Ch Hul 35 D3
Spath Wlk. Ch Hul 35 D3
Spawell Cl. Gold 3 F4
Speakman Ave. N-le-W 2 B3
Speakman St. Run 22 C2
Speed's Way. Farn 180 C1
Speedwell Cl. Hes 41 E4
Speedwell Cl. Hunt 142 A3
Speedwell Dr. Hes 41 E4
Speedwell Rd. N-u-L 210 C1
Speke Bvd. Halew 21 D2
Speke Bvd. Speke 21 D2
Speke Rd. Wid 22 B4
Spencer Brook. Prest 86 C3
Spencer Cl. Alsag 192 C2
Spencer Cl. Wist 206 A4
Spencer Rd. Nest 41 F1
Spencer St. North 78 A2
Spenlow Cl. Poyn 36 C1
Spey Cl. Winsf 126 C1
Spey Dr. Kids 195 E1
Spindle St. Congle 156 C1
Spink La. Pick 80 A3
Spinnaker Cl. Run 50 B3
Spinner Cres. Comb 78 B4
Spinney. Cudd 101 E3
Spinney Ave. Goost 107 F1
Spinney Ave. Wid 12 A1
Spinney Cl. Wilm 34 B2
Spinney Cl. Winsf 150 A4
Spinney Dr. El Por 69 E1
Spinney Dr. Weston 207 D3
Spinney End. Tatt 166 A1
Spinney La. Knuts 56 C2
Spinney Mead. Mfield 87 F1
Spinney The. Hes 41 E3
Spinney The. Law-g 194 C2
Spinney The. Nest 41 E1
Spinney The. Norley 100 C3
Spinney The. Willas 205 E3
Spinney Wlk. Run 24 A1
Spital Wlk. Chest 118 C1
Spodegreen La. L Boll 30 B4
Spout La. Mobb 58 A2
Spragg St. Congle 156 C2
Spring Ave. El Por 69 E3
Spring Bank. Sch Gr 195 D4
Spring Bank Rd. N Mills 39 E4
Spring Cl. Sch Gr 193 F4
Spring Ct. Run 23 D1
Spring Gdns. Crewe 190 C3
Spring Gdns. El Por 69 E3
Spring Gdns. Mfield 87 E1
Spring Hill. Tarp 168 B4
Spring La. Codd 181 F3
Spring La. Croft 9 D3
Spring La. Lymm 19 F2
Spring Meadow. North 78 C1
Spring Mount. N Mills 39 E4
Spring Rd. Poyn 36 C1
Spring St. Congle 156 C1
Spring St. Wid 23 D3
Spring St. Wilm 60 A4
Springbank. Boll 87 F4
Springbank Cl. Run 49 D3
Springbank Cres. Winsf 149 E4
Springbourne. Frod 74 B3
Springcroft. Nest 41 E1
Springe La. Badd 203 D3
Springfield Ave. Gold 2 C4
Springfield Ave. Hels 73 D2
Springfield Ave. Lymm 19 D3
Springfield Ave. Malpas 213 E2
Springfield Ave. Warr 17 D2
Springfield Ave. Warr 17 D4
Springfield Cl. H Kin 161 D4
Springfield Cres. North 77 F2
Springfield Dr. Chest 118 C2
Springfield Dr. Wilm 59 E3
Springfield Dr. Wist 205 F4
Springfield Park. Hay 1 B4
Springfield Rd. Malpas 213 D2
Springfield Rd. Mfield 111 F4
Springfield Rd. Mobb 57 F2
Springfield Rd. Wid 22 A4
Springfield St. Warr 16 A3
Springfields. Cudd 101 E2
Springfields. Knuts 57 E2
Springfields. M Traf 119 F4
Springfields. Prest 87 D4
Springfields Dr. Congle 156 B2
Springhead Cl. Kids 210 B3
Springhill. Mfield 88 A1
Springhill Ave. Beb 43 E3
Springholm Dr. Apple 26 B2
Springmount. Gold 3 F4
Springwell Cl. Wist 206 B4
Springwood Ave. Knuts 57 E2
Springwood Cl. Blacon 117 E2
Sprink La. Congle 157 E3
Spruce Ave. Cudd 102 A2
Spruce Cl. Gold 3 F4
Spruce Cl. Warr 17 F4
Spruce Gr. Sch Gr 193 F4
Spuley La. Po Shr 63 E1
Spuley La. Rain 63 E1
Spunhill Ave. El Por 69 E1
Spurlong Rd. Burton 6 C3
Spurston Cl. H Legh 29 E2
Square St. Mfield 112 C3
Square The. Altr 32 B4
Square The. Audlem 229 F2
Square The. Christ 142 C4
Square The. Ince 72 A3
Square The. Nest 41 D1
Square The. Woore 232 B1
Squires Ave. Wid 23 D4
Squirrel Cl. North 103 E4
Squirrel's Jump. A Edge 60 B1
Squirrels Chase. Prest 86 C3
Stable La. Mould 99 D2
Stablings The. Wilm 60 A3
Stadium Way. Chest 118 A2
Stadmorslow La. Kids 195 F2
Stafford Cl. Mfield 86 C1
Stafford Gdns. El Por 70 A3
Stafford Rd. Warr 16 B1
Stafford St. Audlem 230 A2
Stafford St. Crewe 190 B3
Stafford Wlk. Mfield 86 C1
Stage La. Lymm 19 E2
Staines Cl. Apple 26 C3
Stainmore Cl. Warr 10 A3
Staithes Rd. Wythe 33 E4
Stalbridge Rd. Crewe 190 B1
Stallard Way. Middle 151 E4
Stalmine Ave. Chea 34 A4
Stamford Ave. Crewe 190 B2
Stamford Cl. Mfield 112 B2
Stamford Ct. Chest 119 E1
Stamford Ct. Lymm 18 C2
Stamford Ct. Mfield 112 B3
Stamford La. Christ 120 B1
Stamford Rd. A Edge 60 A1
Stamford Rd. Blacon 117 F3
Stamford Rd. L Boll 20 A1
Stamford Rd. Mfield 112 B2
Stamford Rd. Wilm 34 A1
Stamford St. El Por 70 A3
Stamore Rd. Run 23 E1
Stamp Ave. Crewe 190 B3
Standford Dr. North 104 A3
Stanhope Ave. Crewe 190 C2
Stanhope Cl. Wilm 60 B4
Stanier Cl. Crewe 191 D2
Stanlaw Rd. El Por 70 B2
Stanley Ave. Gt San 14 B4
Stanley Ave. Warr 16 C1
Stanley Bank Rd. Hay 1 A4
Stanley Cl. Hart 103 D2
Stanley Cl. Wid 13 E1
Stanley Ct. Alsag 193 E2
Stanley Dr. N-u-L 210 B1
Stanley Gr. North 79 F1
Stanley Hall La. Disley 38 B3
Stanley La. Beb 43 F2
Stanley Park Dr. Chest 140 C3
Stanley Pl. Chest 118 B1
Stanley Pl. Warr 16 C1
Stanley Rd. Bidd 179 E1
Stanley Rd. Ch Hul 34 C3
Stanley Rd. Chea 34 C3
Stanley Rd. El Por 70 B4
Stanley Rd. Knuts 56 C1
Stanley Rd Ind Est. Knuts 57 D1
Stanley St. Chest 118 B1
Stanley St. Crewe 190 B2
Stanley St. N-le-W 2 A2
Stanley St. North 104 B4
Stanley St. Run 23 D2
Stanley St. Warr 16 A2
Stannage La. Farn 180 C3
Stanner Cl. Warr 7 E1
Stannerhouse La. Ha Gr 175 F2
Stanney Cl. Beb 43 F2
Stanney Cl. Nest 66 C4
Stanney La. El Por 70 B2
Stanney La. Stoak 70 C1
Stanney Mill La. El Por 70 C1
Stanney Mill La. Stan 70 C1
Stanney Mill Rd. El Por 70 C1
Stanney Woods Ave. El Por 70 B1
Stanneylands Cl. Wilm 34 B1
Stanneylands Dr. Wilm 34 A1
Stanneylands Rd. Wilm 34 A2
Stansfield Ave. Warr 16 C3
Stanstead Ave. Penk 14 C2
Stanthorne Ave. Crewe 190 A2
Stanton Cl. Hay 1 B3
Stanton Ct. Nest 66 C4
Stanton Dr. Chest 118 B3
Stanton Rd. Warr 17 E2
Stapeley Terr. Nant 205 D2
Stapleford Ct. El Por 69 F4
Stapleton Ave. Warr 16 B4
Stapleton Rd. Mfield 87 D1
Stapleton Way. Wid 22 A3
Stapley Cl. Run 22 C1
Star La. Lymm 18 B2
Star La. Mfield 112 B2
Starbeck Dr. El Por 69 D3
Starkey Gr. Warr 16 C2
Starling Cl. Farn 180 C1
Starling Cl. Run 50 B4
Start La. W Br 65 D4
Statham Ave. Lymm 18 B2
Statham Ave. Warr 8 B1
Statham Cl. Lymm 18 B2
Statham Dr. Lymm 18 B2
Statham La. Lymm 18 A3
Statham St. Mfield 112 B4
Station Ave. El Por 69 E4
Station Ave. Hels 73 D2
Station Cl. Nest 66 C4
Station Gn. El Por 69 E4
Station Hill. Act Br 76 C1
Station La. G Sutt 119 F4
Station Rd. Act Br 77 D1
Station Rd. Adder 235 D3
Station Rd. Alpr 169 F1
Station Rd. Alsag 193 E2
Station Rd. Astb 178 A1
Station Rd. Back 95 D2
Station Rd. Bidd 179 E1
Station Rd. Chelf 84 A1
Station Rd. Chest 118 C1
Station Rd. Crow 76 B1
Station Rd. Dela 123 E4
Station Rd. Dun T 20 A3
Station Rd. Eaton 135 D1
Station Rd. El Por 69 E4
Station Rd. El Por 70 B3
Station Rd. Elton 72 A2
Station Rd. Goost 131 D4
Station Rd. Gt San 14 B4
Station Rd. H Chap 130 B1
Station Rd. Hawa 116 A1
Station Rd. Hay 1 B3
Station Rd. Hes 40 C3
Station Rd. Ince 72 A3
Station Rd. Irlam 11 F4
Station Rd. Kids 194 C1
Station Rd. Kids 195 F1
Station Rd. Lost 80 A1
Station Rd. Mobb 57 F4
Station Rd. Mould 99 D2
Station Rd. N Mills 39 D4
Station Rd. Nant 204 C3
Station Rd. Nest 66 B4
Station Rd. Nest 66 C4
Station Rd. Nest 67 D1
Station Rd. North 79 D1
Station Rd. Run 22 C1
Station Rd. Sand 174 B4
Station Rd. Sch Gr 195 D4
Station Rd. Sch Gr 195 E4
Station Rd. Sutt 50 A2
Station Rd. W Br 39 E2
Station Rd. Warr 9 D1
Station Rd. Warr 16 C1
Station Rd. Weave 77 D1
Station Rd. Wilm 34 A2
Station Rd. Wilm 34 B2
Station Rd. Wilm 60 A4
Station Rd. Winsf 127 D1
Station Rd. Worles 188 C3
Station Rd. Wythe 33 E4

Station Rd N. Warr 9 D1
Station Rd S. Warr 9 D1
Station St. Mfield 87 E1
Station View. Chest 118 C1
Station View. Nant 204 C2
Staveley Dr. Winsf 126 B1
Steam Mill St. Chest 118 C1
Stearns Cl. Blacon 118 A3
Steel St. Warr 16 C4
Steele Rd. Middle 151 E3
Steele St. Chest 118 B1
Steeple Ct. Nest 66 C4
Steeple St. Mfield 87 F1
Stenhills Cres. Run 23 E1
Step Hill. Mfield 112 B4
Stephen St. Warr 16 B3
Stephen's Gr. Hels 73 D1
Stephens Gdns. El Por 69 D3
Stephens Terr. El Por 69 D3
Stephens Way. Audley 209 F1
Stephenson Dr. Crewe 191 D2
Stephenson Wlk. Winsf 149 D4
Sterne Cl. Sand 174 B3
Stetchworth Rd. Warr 16 A1
Steven Ct. Chest 118 C1
Stevenage Cl. Mfield 112 A4
Stevenage Dr. Mfield 112 A4
Stevens Rd. Hes 41 E4
Stevens St. A Edge 60 A1
Steventon. Run 24 C2
Steward's Ave. Wid 22 C4
Stewart St. Crewe 190 A2
Stile End. M Traf 119 F4
Stiles The. Cudd 101 E3
Stirling Cl. Chest 119 D1
Stirling Cl. Mfield 86 C1
Stirling Cl. Warr 17 F4
Stirling Ct. El Por 70 B2
Stirling Ct. H Chap 130 A1
Stirrup Cl. Warr 9 D2
Stock La. Hay Gr 206 A1
Stock La. Ho Co 206 A1
Stockham Cl. Run 50 A4
Stockham La. Run 50 A4
Stockley La. Whit 52 C4
Stockport Rd. Warr 17 F2
Stocks Ave. Chest 119 D1
Stocks Hill. Winsf 149 F4
Stocks La. Chest 119 D1
Stocks La. Penk 14 B3
Stocks La. Peo 82 C1
Stockswell Rd. Tar Gr 12 A2
Stockton La. Apple 16 C1
Stockton Rd. Wilm 59 F2
Stoke Abbott Cl. Bram 35 F4
Stoke Cl. Beb 43 F2
Stoke Gdns. El Por 70 B2
Stokehall La. Barb 187 F3
Stokehall La. Cholm 187 F3
Stokesay Ct. El Por 70 C2
Stone Barn La. Run 50 A3
Stone Chair La. Sch Gr 194 C4
Stone Croft. Chest 142 A4
Stone Cross La. Gold 3 E4
Stone Heyes La. North 77 F3
Stone House La. Peckf 184 C3
Stone House La. Ridley 184 C3
Stone Mead Ave. Altr 32 B4
Stone Pit La. Croft 3 F1
Stone Pl. Chest 118 C2
Stonebank Dr. Nest 67 D3
Stonebridge Rd. Nant 204 C2
Stonechat Cl. Run 49 F3
Stonecrop Cl. Run 49 F2
Stonecrop Cl. Warr 9 E2
Stonehaven Dr. Warr 9 D2
Stoneheads Rise. W Br 65 E4
Stonehill Cl. Apple 26 B2
Stonehills La. Run 23 E1
Stonehouse Green. Congle 156 B2
Stonelea. Run 24 A1
Stoneleigh Cl. Mfield 87 E1
Stoneleigh Gdns. Apple 17 E1
Stoneley Ave. Crewe 190 B4
Stoneley Rd. Crewe 190 B4
Stones Manor La. Hart 103 E3
Stoney Holt. Run 50 B4
Stoney La. Dela 123 E3
Stoney La. Wilm 59 F3
Stoneyfold La. Mfield 113 D3
Stoneyland Dr. N Mills 39 D4
Stony La. Congle 156 B1
Stopsley Cl. Congle 155 F2
Stour Ct. El Por 70 A4
Straight Length. Frod 73 F4
Straight Mile. Eccles 162 C3
Straight Mile. Poul 163 D2
Straker Ave. El Por 69 F3
Stratford Rd. Blacon 117 F2
Stratford Rd. Nest 66 B3
Stratford Sq. Chea 34 B4
Stratford Way. Mfield 112 B3
Strathaven Ave. Wist 205 F4
Strathclyde Cl. H Chap 130 A1
Strathearn Rd. Hes 40 C4
Stratton Cl. Run 50 A3
Stratton Rd. Gt San 15 D3
Strawberry Cl. Warr 9 E2
Strawberry Dr. El Por 95 D4
Strawberry Green. El Por 95 D4
Strawberry La. Act Br 76 C2
Strawberry La. Moll 94 B2
Strawberry La. Wilm 59 F3
Street Hey Lane. Will 43 D1
Street La. Adlin 62 B4
Street La. Sch Gr 176 C1
Street La. Whit 52 B2
Street The. Bux 90 B3
Street The. Chest 119 E4
Street The. M Traf 119 E4
Stretton Ave. Gold 3 E4
Stretton Cl. Beb 43 F2
Stretton Rd. Stret 26 C1
Stretton Way. Wilm 34 B3
Stringer Ave. Sand 175 E3
Stringer Cres. Warr 16 C2
Stringer's La. Burt 161 D2
Strumness Cl. Warr 9 D2
Stuart Cl. Chest 119 E2
Stuart Cl. Winsf 149 E3
Stuart Cl. Mfield 87 D1
Stuart Dr. Warr 16 C1
Stuart Pl. Chest 118 B1
Stuart Rd. Run 24 B2
Stubbs La. Lost 80 A1
Stubbs La. Mobb 58 C2
Stubbs Pl. Blacon 117 F2
Stubbs Terr. Mfield 112 C4
Stubby La. N Ald 84 C1
Styal Rd. Wilm 34 A1
Styal Rd. Wythe 33 F4
Styal View. Wilm 34 A1
Sudbury Dr. Chea 34 B4
Sudbury Rd. Haz Gr 36 C4
Sudlow La. Knuts 56 B1
Sudlow La. Plum 81 E4
Suez St. N-le-W 2 A2
Suez St. Warr 16 A3
Suffolk Ave. El Por 69 F3
Suffolk Cl. Congle 156 B2
Suffolk Cl. Mfield 86 C1
Suffolk Cl. Warr 17 F3
Suffolk Dr. Wilm 34 B1
Suffolk Pl. Wid 22 B4
Suffolk St. Run 22 C2
Sugar La. Adlin 63 D1
Sugar La. Man 98 C3
Sugar La. Rain 88 B3
Sugar Pit La. Knuts 56 C2
Sulby Ave. Warr 16 A2
Sulgrave Ave. Poyn 36 C2
Summer Cl. Run 23 F1
Summer La. Dares 51 E4
Summer La. Run 23 F1
Summerfield. Kids 195 D1
Summerfield Ave. Warr 7 F1
Summerfield Dr. Moult 126 C4
Summerfield Pl. Wilm 60 A3
Summerfield Rd. G Sutt 119 F3
Summerfield Rd. Mobb 57 F2
Summerfields. Knuts 57 E2
Summerhill Dr. N-u-L 210 B1
Summerhill Rd. Prest 86 C2
Summerlea. Ch Hul 35 D4
Summers Cl. Knuts 82 A4
Summers Way. Knuts 82 A4
Summertrees Rd. El Por 69 F2
Summerville Gdns. Warr 16 C1
Summit Cl. Stret 26 C1
Sumner Rd. Blacon 117 F2
Sumner St. Hay 1 A3
Sumpter Pathway. Chest 118 C2
Sunart Cl. Wist 206 A3
Sunbank La. Altr 32 C3
Sunbeam St. N-le-W 2 B2
Sunbury Cres. Chest 140 C3
Sunbury Gdns. Apple 26 C4
Suncroft Cl. Warr 17 F4
Suncroft Rd. Hes 41 E4
Sundale Dr. Crewe 189 E2
Sunderland St. Mfield 112 B4
Sundown Cl. N Mills 39 D4
Sunfield Cl. El Por 69 E2
Sunningdale Ave. Wid 12 A1
Sunningdale Cl. Burton 6 C4
Sunningdale Cl. North 104 C4
Sunningdale Dr. Beb 43 D3
Sunningdale Dr. Bram 36 A4
Sunningdale Rd. Ch Hul 35 D4
Sunningdale Rd. Mfield 112 A3
Sunningdale Way. Nest 66 C2
Sunny Bank. Wilm 59 E2
Sunny Bank. Wilm 60 A3
Sunny Bank Cl. Mfield 112 B3
Sunny Bank Rd. Altr 31 E4
Sunnybank Cl. N-le-W 2 B2
Sunnybank Rd. Crewe 189 F3
Sunnyside. Alsag 193 D2
Sunnyside. Gt San 14 B4
Surrey Dr. Congle 156 C3
Surrey Rd. Chest 119 D3
Surrey Rd. Kids 195 D1
Surrey Rd. Warren 112 A2
Surrey St. Crewe 190 C2
Surrey St. Run 23 D1
Surrey St. Warr 16 B2
Surridge. H Legh 29 E3
Susan Dr. Penk 14 B3
Susan St. Wid 13 E1
Sussex Ave. Warren 112 A3
Sussex Dr. Kids 194 C1
Sussex Pl. Congle 156 C3
Sussex Rd. Chest 118 C2
Sussex Rd. Irlam 11 E3
Sussex Rd. Part 11 F1
Sussex St. Wid 13 E1
Sussex Way. Chest 118 C2
Sutherland Ct. Run 23 D1
Sutherland Dr. Beb 43 E2
Sutherland Dr. Mfield 87 D1
Sutherland Way. Chest 119 D2
Sutton Ave. Cul 4 C2
Sutton Ave. Nest 66 C3
Sutton Causeway. Sutt 49 F1
Sutton Cl. Beb 43 F2
Sutton Cl. H Winch 79 F3
Sutton Cl. M Traf 119 F4
Sutton Cl. Mfield 112 B3
Sutton Dr. Chest 118 C3
Sutton Hall Dr. El Por 69 D3
Sutton Hall Gdns. El Por 69 D3
Sutton La. Middle 151 E4
Sutton Rd. A Edge 59 F1
Sutton Rd. Poyn 37 D1
Sutton St. Run 23 D1
Sutton St. Warr 16 B2
Sutton Way. El Por 69 F2
Sutton Way. Wilm 34 C3
Sutton's La. Wid 23 D4
Swale Rd. El Por 70 A4
Swaledale Ave. Congle 157 D3
Swaledale Cl. Beb 43 F3
Swaledale Cl. Gt San 14 B4
Swallow Cl. Kids 195 D1
Swallow Cl. Mfield 113 D4
Swallow Cl. Warr 9 F2
Swallow Ct. Winsf 149 E3
Swallow Dr. Sand 175 D4
Swan Ave. St Hel 1 A1
Swan Bank. Congle 156 B1
Swan Bank. Kids 210 B4
Swan Bank. Woore 232 A1
Swan Cl. El Por 69 F2
Swan Cl. Kids 210 B4
Swan Cl. Poyn 36 A2
Swan Ct. Crow 101 F4
Swan Gr. Peo 106 B4
Swan La. Bun 185 F4
Swan La. Ch Hul 35 D4
Swan Rd. Hay 1 C2
Swan St. Congle 156 B1
Swan St. Wilm 60 A4
Swanage Cl. Warr 16 C1
Swanage Ct. Winsf 149 E3
Swanley La. Acton 203 E2
Swanlow Ave. Winsf 149 E3
Swanlow Dr. Winsf 149 E3
Swanlow La. Winsf 149 F3
Swanscoe Av. Boll 88 A4
Swanscoe Cl. Middle 151 D4
Swanscoe La. Mfield 88 A2
Swanwick Cl. Goost 107 E1
Sweet Briar Cres. Crewe 189 F2
Sweet Brier Cl. North 78 A2
Sweetenham Cl. Alsag 193 E2
Sweetfield Gdns. El Por 69 E4
Sweetfield Rd. El Por 69 E4
Sweettooth La. Sand 175 D4
Swettenham Cl. Sand 175 E4
Swettenham Rd. Somer 132 A1
Swettenham Rd. Swett 132 A1
Swettenham Rd. Wilm 34 B3
Swettenham St. Mfield 112 C4
Swift Cl. Kids 195 D1
Swift Cl. Warr 8 C2
Swift Cl. Wist 205 F4
Swinburne Dr. Crewe 190 C2
Swindale Ave. Warr 8 A2
Swinden Cl. Run 24 B1
Swine Market. Nant 204 C3
Swineyard La. H Legh 28 B2
Swinford Ave. Wid 13 F1
Swinley Chase. Wilm 34 C1
Swinleys Hey. Chest 142 A4
Swinnerton St. Crewe 190 B1
Swinton Sq. Knuts 57 D1
Swireford Rd. Hels 73 D1
Swiss Cott. Mfield 87 D1
Swiss Hill. A Edge 60 A1
Swithin Rd. Wythe 33 F4
Swynnerton Way. Wid 13 D3
Sycamore Ave. Alsag 193 F1
Sycamore Ave. Congle 155 F2
Sycamore Ave. Crewe 190 B3
Sycamore Ave. Hay 1 A3
Sycamore Ave. N-le-W 2 B2
Sycamore Ave. Sch Gr 193 F4
Sycamore Ave. Wid 13 D1
Sycamore Ave. Winsf 149 E4
Sycamore Cl. Audlem 230 A2
Sycamore Cl. Bidd 179 F1
Sycamore Cl. H Chap 130 B2
Sycamore Cl. Kids 210 C4
Sycamore Cl. Wilm 34 A1
Sycamore Cres. Hol Gr 11 D1
Sycamore Cres. Mfield 112 A4
Sycamore Cres. North 78 A2
Sycamore Ct. Nant 204 C4
Sycamore Dr. Chest 140 C3
Sycamore Dr. El Por 70 A1
Sycamore Dr. Lymm 18 B2
Sycamore Dr. Middle 151 F3
Sycamore Dr. Sutt 50 A2
Sycamore Farm Cl. Mfield 87 D1
Sycamore Gr. Broug 139 D2
Sycamore La. Gt San 15 D3
Sycamore Rd. Part 11 F2
Sycamore Rd. Run 49 E4
Sycamore Rise. Mfield 112 A3
Syddal Cr. Ch Hul 35 E2
Syddal Green. Ch Hul 35 E3
Syddall Ave. Chea 34 B4
Sydney Ave. Wythe 33 D4
Sydney Rd. Blacon 118 A2
Sydney Rd. Bram 35 F3
Sydney Rd. Crewe 190 C3
Sydney St. North 103 E4
Sydney St. Run 48 B4
Sylvan Av. Wilm 59 F3
Sylvan Cl. North 103 E4
Symondley Rd. S La E 112 C1
Synge St. Warr 16 B4
Sytch Croft. Nest 66 C4
Tabley Ave. Wid 12 B1
Tabley Cl. Knuts 56 C2
Tabley Cl. Sand 174 C4
Tabley Gr. Knuts 56 C1
Tabley Hill La. Knuts 56 A1
Tabley Hill La. Tab 56 A1
Tabley Rd. Crewe 189 F2
Tabley Rd. Knuts 56 C2
Tabley Rd. Wilm 34 B3
Tabley St. North 79 D1
Tabor St. Mfield 112 C3
Tadgers La. Frod 73 E4
Talbot Ave. Nest 66 C3
Talbot Cl. Nest 66 C3
Talbot Cl. Shav 206 A2
Talbot Cl. Warr 9 F2
Talbot Gdns. Nest 66 C3
Talbot Rd. A Edge 60 A1
Talbot Rd. D-o-t-H 97 F4
Talbot Rd. El Por 69 F2
Talbot St. Chest 118 B2
Talbot St. Gold 3 D4
Talfryn Cl. Con Q 91 E1
Talisman Cl. Run 50 B4
Talke Rd. Alsag 193 F2
Talke Rd. Audley 210 C1
Tall Ash Ave. Congle 157 D2
Tall Trees Cl. North 103 E3
Tamar Cl. Congle 156 C1
Tamar Cl. Mfield 86 C1
Tamar Rd. Kids 195 D1
Tamar Wlk. Winsf 127 D1
Tame Cl. Bidd 179 E1
Tame Cl. Sand 174 C4
Tame Wlk. Wilm 34 B1
Tamworth Cl. Haz Gr 36 B4
Tamworth St. N-le-W 2 A2
Tan House La. Burton 7 D3
Tan House La. Wid 23 E4
Tankersley Gr. Gt San 15 D3
Tanner St. Congle 156 C1
Tanner's La. Gold 3 D4
Tanners La. Warr 16 A3
Tannery La. Nest 66 C4
Tannery La. Penk 14 B2
Tanyard Dr. Altr 32 B4
Tanyard La. Ashl 32 A3
Tapley Ave. Poyn 36 C1
Taplow Cl. Apple 26 C3
Target Cl. Kids 210 C3
Target Rd. Hes 40 B4
Tarn Cl. Winsf 126 B1
Tarn Ct. Warr 17 F4
Tarn Mount. Mfield 112 A3
Tarnway. Gold 3 F4
Tarparley Wlk. Wilm 34 C1
Tarporley Rd. Dudd 145 D3
Tarporley Rd. El Por 69 F2
Tarporley Rd. L Bud 124 B3
Tarporley Rd. L Lei 52 A1
Tarporley Rd. Mar 124 B3
Tarporley Rd. Stret 52 B4
Tarporley Rd. Tarv 121 E1
Tarporley Rd. Utkin 146 C3
Tarporley Rd. Whit 52 B2
Tarporley Rd. Whitch 225 F2
Tarrant Ct. Moll 94 C1
Tarvin Ave. Crewe 189 E2
Tarvin Cl. El Por 70 B2
Tarvin Cl. Gold 3 F4
Tarvin Cl. Middle 151 E3
Tarvin Cl. Run 49 E3
Tarvin Rd. Alva 73 F2
Tarvin Rd. Beb 43 F2
Tarvin Rd. Chest 119 D1
Tarvin Rd. Chest 119 F1
Tarvin Rd. Christ 120 B2
Tarvin Rd. Frod 73 F2
Tarvin Rd. Man 99 D2
Tarvin Rd. Tarv 120 C2
Tarvin Sands Industries.
Tarv 121 D2
Tarvin Way. Wilm 34 B3
Tasman Cl. Gt San 15 E4
Tate Dr. Hasl 191 E2
Tattenhall La. Beest 167 D1
Tattenhall La. Beest 167 F1
Tattenhall La. Tatt 167 D1
Tattenhall Rd. Tatt 166 B2
Tatton Cl. Alsag 193 E2
Tatton Cl. Chest 140 C3
Tatton Cl. Winsf 126 B1
Tatton Dr. Sand 175 E4
Tatton Lodge. Knuts 57 D1
Tatton Rd. Crewe 189 F1
Tatton Rd. Wythe 34 C3
Tatton St. Knuts 57 D1
Tatton Stile. Mobb 58 A2
Tavener Cl. Beb 43 E3
Tavistock Rd. Penk 14 C2
Tavlin Ave. Warr 7 F1
Tawney Cl. Kids 195 D1
Taxal Moor Rd. W Br 65 E2
Taxi Rd. Wythe 33 D4
Taxmere Cl. Sand 174 C4
Tay Cl. Bidd 179 F1
Taylor Rd. Altr 20 C3
Taylor Rd. Hay 1 C4
Taylor St. Warr 16 A1
Taylor St. Wid 13 E1
Taylor's Lane. Penk 14 A1
Taylors La. Hasl 192 B1
Taylors Row. Run 23 E1
Teal Ave. Knuts 57 D1
Teal Cl. Warr 8 C2
Teal Cl. Warr 9 F2
Teal Cl. Winsf 149 E3
Teals Way. Hes 40 C4
Tebay Rd. Beb 43 F4
Tedder Dr. Wythe 33 F4
Tedder Sq. Wid 22 B4
Teddington Cl. Apple 26 C3
Tees Ct. El Por 70 A4
Teesdale Rd. Hay 1 B4
Tefler Ct. Middle 151 F3
Teggsnose La. Mfield 113 E3
Tegid Way. Brough 140 B3
Tegsnose Mt. S La E 113 E2
Telegraph Rd. Hes 41 D4
Telford Cl. Congle 157 D1
Telford Cl. Kids 210 C4
Telford Cl. Mfield 88 A1
Telford Pl. Nant 204 B3
Telford Rd. El Por 70 C2
Telford Way. Audlem 229 F2
Telford Way. Chest 140 C3
Telford Way. Middle 128 C1
Telford's Quay. Stan 70 B4
Tempest Rd. A Edge 60 B1
Tenby Cl. Warr 7 F1
Tenby Dr. Run 23 E1
Tenby Rd. Mfield 111 F3
Tennyson Ave. Crewe 190 C2
Tennyson Cl. Mfield 111 F3
Tennyson Cl. Wist 190 A1
Tennyson Dr. Warr 8 B1
Tennyson Rd. El Por 70 A2
Tennyson Rd. Wid 13 D1
Tennyson Wlk. Blacon 118 A3
Terence Ave. Warr 16 C3
Terminal Rd E. Wythe 33 D4
Terminal Rd N. Wythe 33 E4
Tern Ave. Kids 195 E1
Tern Cl. Wid 13 D2
Tern Dr. Poyn 36 A2
Terrace Rd. Wid 23 D3
Terrick Rd. Whitch 226 A1
Tetchill Cl. El Por 69 E1
Tetton La. Middle 151 F2
Tewkesbury Cl. Ch Hul 35 D3
Tewkesbury Cl. Chest 118 B4
Tewkesbury Cl. El Por 94 C4
Tewkesbury Cl. Middle 128 A1
Tewkesbury Cl. Poyn 36 B2
Tewkesbury Dr. Mfield 87 F2
Tewkesbury Rd. Gold 3 D4
Thackeray Dr. Chest 119 E2
Thames Cl. Congle 156 C1
Thames Cl. Warr 8 B1
Thames Dr. Bidd 179 E1
Thames Gdns. El Por 70 A2
Thames Rd. Cul 4 C1
Thames Side. El Por 70 A2
Thamesdale. El Por 70 A2
Thaxstead Wlk. Wythe 33 E4
Theatre Ct. North 103 F4
Thelwall La. Warr 17 D2
Thelwall New Rd. Warr 17 E2
Thelwall Rd. El Por 69 F2
Thetford Cl. Mfield 87 E2
Thetford Rd. Gt San 14 C3
Thewlis St. Warr 15 F3
Third Ave. Adlin 36 B1
Third Ave. Crewe 190 C1
Third Ave. G Cit 92 C1
Third Ave. Kids 194 C1

Third Ave. Run 49 F4
Third Ave. Sand 175 D3
Thirlmere. Mfield 111 F3
Thirlmere Ave. Warr 8 B2
Thirlmere Cl. A Edge 59 F1
Thirlmere Cl. Frod 49 E1
Thirlmere Cl. H Chap 130 A2
Thirlmere Ct. Congle 156 A1
Thirlmere Dr. Lymm 18 C2
Thirlmere Rd. Chest 119 D3
Thirlmere Rd. El Por 70 A1
Thirlmere Rd. Nest 66 C3
Thirlmere Rd. Part 11 F2
Thirlmere Rd. Wist 190 A1
Thirlmere Way. Wid 22 B4
Thirsk Cl. Run 49 E3
Thistle Sq. Part 11 F1
Thistle Wlk. Part 11 E1
Thistlewood Dr. Wilm 60 B4
Thomas Cl. Alsag 193 F2
Thomas Cl. Blacon 117 F3
Thomas Cl. El Por 70 A1
Thomas Cl. M Traf 119 F4
Thomas Pl. Winsf 127 D1
Thomas St. Bidd 179 E1
Thomas St. Congle 156 C2
Thomas St. Crewe 190 B2
Thomas St. Gold 3 D4
Thomas St. Kids 195 F1
Thomas St. Kids 210 B4
Thomas St. Run 23 D2
Thomas St. Wid 23 D4
Thompson Ave. Cul 4 C2
Thompson Cl. N-le-W 2 B1
Thompson St. Warr 9 F2
Thoresway Rd. Wilm 59 F3
Thoriby Rd. Cul 4 C2
Thorley Gr. Crewe 190 A1
Thorley La. Wythe 33 D4
Thorley Mews. Bram 35 F4
Thorn Cl. Penk 14 C2
Thorn Cl. Run 49 E4
Thorn Dr. Wythe 34 A4
Thorn Gr. Ch Hul 35 D4
Thorn La. Hart 103 E3
Thorn Rd. Ch Hul 35 F3
Thorn Rd. Run 49 E4
Thorn Rd. Warr 17 D4
Thorn Tree Cl. Hale 21 F1
Thorn Wlk. Part 11 E1
Thornberry Cl. Saug 117 D4
Thornbury Ave. Gold 3 F4
Thornbush Cl. Gold 3 F4
Thorne Cl. Prest 87 D3
Thorne Dr. El Por 69 D2
Thorney Dr. Ch Hul 35 E3
Thorneyholme Dr. Knuts 57 D1
Thornfield Cl. Gold 3 E4
Thornfield Hey. Wilm 60 C4
Thorngrove Dr. Wilm 60 B3
Thorngrove Hill. Wilm 60 B3
Thorngrove Rd. Wilm 60 B3
Thornhills. Wid 12 A2
Thornleigh Ave. Beb 43 F2
Thornleigh Dr. El Por 69 F3
Thornley Rd. Lymm 18 B2
Thornsgreen Rd. Wythe 33 E4
Thornton. Wid 22 C4
Thornton Ave. Mfield 112 A3
Thornton Bank. Alpr 169 E2
Thornton Common Rd. Beb 43 D4
Thornton Common Rd. Thor H 42 B4
Thornton Cres. Hes 41 D3
Thornton Dr. Chest 118 B3
Thornton Dr. Wilm 34 B2
Thornton Dr. Wist 206 A4
Thornton Green La. T-le-M 96 C4
Thornton Mews. El Por 69 D4
Thornton Rd. Chea 34 B4
Thornton Rd. El Por 70 C2
Thornton Rd. Gt San 15 D2
Thornton Sq. Mfield 112 A3
Thorntree Green. Apple 27 D3
Thornway. Boll 88 A4
Thornway. Ch Hul 35 E4
Thornway. H La 37 F4
Thornwythe Gr. El Por 69 F2
Thornycroft. Winsf 126 A1
Thornycroft Cl. Warren 111 F1
Thornycroft St. Mfield 112 C4
Thorp St. Mfield 112 B4
Thorpe Cl. Crewe 189 F4
Thowler La. Rosth 30 A3
Threaphurst La. Haz Gr 37 E4
Three Fields Cl. Congle 156 A2
Threeways. Cudd 101 E2
Thurlow. Gold 3 F4
Thursfield Ave. Kids 195 D2
Thurstaston Rd. Hes 40 C4
Thurston Cl. Gt San 15 E3
Thurston Green. A Edge 60 A1
Thurston Rd. Chest 140 C3
Thynne St. Warr 16 A2
Tibb St. Audley 209 F1
Tibbs Cross La. Bo Hea 13 E4
Tidal La. Warr 16 C4
Tideswell Cl. Chea 34 B4
Tideswell Rd. Haz Gr 36 C4
Tidnock Ave. Congle 156 C3
Tiffild Ct. Winsf 127 D2
Tilbury Pl. Run 50 C3
Tildsley Cres. Run 48 C3
Tile La. Cront 12 A3
Tilewright Cl. Kids 195 D1
Tilley St. Warr 16 B3
Tilman Cl. Gt San 15 D4
Tilston Ave. Warr 17 D2
Tilston Rd. Ed Gr 213 D3
Tilston Rd. Malpas 213 D3
Tilston Wlk. Wilm 34 C1
Tilstone Cl. Ho Co 206 C1
Tilstone Cl. North 104 A3
Timber La. North 103 F4
Timber St. Mfield 87 F1
Timberfields Rd. Saug 117 D4
Timberley Ave. Warr 17 D2
Timbersbrook Gr. Wilm 34 B1
Timberscombe Gdns. Warr 17 F3
Timbrell Ave. Crewe 190 A3
Timmis Cl. Warr 9 D2
Timmis Cres. Wid 13 D1
Timperley St. Wid 23 D4
Tinkwood La. Cudd Gr 211 F1
Tinsley St. Warr 16 C2
Tintagel Cl. Mfield 111 F4
Tintagel Cl. Run 50 A3
Tintern Ave. Chest 118 C3
Tintern Cl. Warr 7 F1
Tintern Rd. Ch Hul 35 D3
Tirley La. Utkin 123 D1
Tithebarn Cl. Hes 40 C4
Tithebarn Dr. Nest 41 D1
Tithebarn Rd. Altr 32 B4
Tithings The. Run 23 F1
Tiverton Cl. Chest 118 C3
Tiverton Cl. Sand 175 E4
Tiverton Cl. Wid 12 B2
Tiverton Sq. Penk 14 C2
Tobermory Cl. Hay 1 A3
Todbrook Cl. W Br 65 E3
Toft Cl. Chest 140 C3
Toft Rd. Knuts 82 A4
Toft Way. Wilm 34 C2
Toll Bar Ave. Mfield 112 C4
Toll Bar Rd. Christ 142 B4
Toll Bar Rd. Mfield 111 F4
Toll Bar Rd. Warr 8 A2
Tolland La. Altr 31 F4
Tollard Cl. Ch Hul 35 D3
Tollemache Dr. Crewe 190 A4
Tollemache Terr. Chest 118 C1
Tollgate Cl. Kids 210 B4
Tollgate Dr. Audlem 229 F2
Tollitt St. Crewe 190 B2
Tom Fields. Audley 209 F1
Tom La. Rosth 30 C3
Tomkinson St. Chest 118 C2
Tomlinson Ave. Warr 16 B4
Tommy's La. Congle 156 C2
Tommy's La. Crewe 190 C1
Tonbridge Cl. Mfield 87 D1
Toogood Cl. M Traf 119 F4
Top Farm La. Cholm 170 C1
Top Rd. Frod 74 B3
Top Rd. Kings 75 D1
Top Station Rd. Sch Gr 195 E4
Topgate Cl. Hes 41 D4
Topping Ct. Warr 9 D2
Torbrook Gr. Wilm 34 B1
Torkington Rd. Wilm 60 B3
Toronto Ave. Wythe 33 D4
Torr Rd. Mfield 112 B2
Torr Rise. Tarp 146 B1
Torr Top St. N Mills 39 E4
Torridon Gr. El Por 69 F2
Torrvale Rd. N Mills 39 D4
Totland Gr. Chest 118 C2
Totton Ct. Warr 9 E1
Tower Ct. Warr 15 F4
Tower Hill. Rain 88 B2
Tower Hill Rd. Bidd 195 F4
Tower La. Run 50 B4
Tower La. Weave 77 D1
Tower Rd. Chest 118 A1
Tower Way. Crewe 190 B2
Towers Cl. Poyn 36 C3
Towers Cl. Wist 206 A4
Towers La. Alva 98 B4
Towers Rd. Poyn 36 C3
Towfield La. Part 19 D4
Town Farm La. Norley 100 C4
Town Hill. Warr 16 A3
Town La. Hale 21 E1
Town La. Mobb 58 A2
Town La. Nest 66 C3
Town Sq. North 103 F4
Town Well. Kings 75 E1
Towneley Ct. Wid 13 D1
Townfield Ave. Farn 180 C1
Townfield Cl. Kids 194 B1
Townfield Ct. North 78 A2
Townfield La. Allos 106 C3
Townfield La. Farn 180 B1
Townfield La. Frod 74 B4
Townfield La. Moll 94 B1
Townfield La. North 78 A2
Townfield La. Tarv 121 D1
Townfield Rd. Mobb 58 A2
Townfield View. Run 24 B1
Townfields. Knuts 57 E1
Townfields. Sand 175 D3
Townfields Cres. Winsf 149 E4
Townfields Dr. Winsf 149 E4
Townfields Gdns. Winsf 149 E4
Townfields Rd. Winsf 149 E4
Townley Pl. Mfield 112 B4
Townley St. Mfield 112 B4
Townsend La. Sch Gr 194 A4
Townsend Rd. Congle 156 C1
Townsfield Dr. L Bud 147 F4
Townshend Rd. Lost 80 A2
Township Cl. Clutt 182 B1
Townwell Ct. Nant 204 B3
Tracy Dr. N-le-W 2 C2
Trafalgar Ave. Poyn 37 D2
Trafalgar Cl. Poyn 37 D2
Trafalgar Ct. Wid 23 D3
Trafford Ave. Warr 15 F4
Trafford Cres. Run 49 E3
Trafford Rd. A Edge 60 A1
Trafford Rd. Wilm 34 A1
Trafford St. Chest 118 B1
Tragan Dr. Penk 14 B2
Tramway Rd. Irlam 11 F4
Tramway St. Chest 118 C1
Tranmere Dr. Wilm 34 C1
Trap Rd. Swett 132 B2
Trap St. With 132 A3
Traver's Entry. Bo Hea 6 A4
Travis St. Wid 23 D4
Treborth Rd. Blacon 117 E2
Tree Bank Cl. Run 49 D4
Tree Tops. Nest 66 C2
Tree Way. Knuts 82 A4
Treen Cl. Mfield 86 B1
Trefoil Cl. Hunt 142 A3
Trefoil Cl. Warr 9 E3
Tregele Cl. Blacon 117 E2
Trenance Cl. Run 50 B3
Trenchard Dr. Wythe 33 F4
Trent Ave. Winsf 127 D1
Trent Cl. Ch Hul 35 E3
Trent Cl. Wid 13 D2
Trent Cl. Winsf 127 D1
Trent Way. Hes 41 D3
Trentdale. El Por 70 A2
Trentham Cl. Wid 13 D2
Trentham St. Run 22 C2
Trevithick Cl. Crewe 191 D2
Trevone Cl. Knuts 57 D1
Tricketts La. Willas 205 F3
Tricketts Mews. Willas 205 F3
Trinity Cl. Wist 190 A1
Trinity Ct. Warr 9 F3
Trinity La. S La E 112 C2
Trinity Pl. Congle 179 D4
Trinity Pl. Wid 23 D4
Trinity Sq. Mfield 87 F1
Trinity St. Chest 118 B1
Trinity St. Run 23 D2
Trinity Terr. North 103 F4
Troon Cl. Beb 43 E3
Troon Cl. Bram 36 A4
Troon Cl. H Chap 130 B1
Troon Cl. Hay 1 A3
Trossach Cl. Warr 8 C1
Troutbeck Ave. Warr 15 F4
Troutbeck Ave. Congle 156 A1
Troutbeck Ave. N-le-W 1 C2
Trouthall La. Plum 81 D1
Trubshaw Ct. Kids 195 E2
Trubshaw Pl. Kids 195 D2
Trumans La. El Por 69 E4
Truro Cl. Bram 35 F4
Truro Cl. Congle 178 C4
Truro Cl. Mfield 86 C1
Truro Cl. Run 50 B3
Truro Cl. Warr 17 D4
Tudor Cl. El Por 94 C4
Tudor Cl. North 104 C3
Tudor Cl. Warr 17 D1
Tudor Cl. Winsf 149 E3
Tudor Green. Blacon 117 F3
Tudor Green. Wilm 34 C1
Tudor Rd. Run 24 B2
Tudor Rd. Wilm 34 C1
Tudor Way. Chest 142 A4
Tudor Way. Congle 156 B1
Tudor Way. Nant 204 C2
Tudorway. Hes 41 D4
Tulip Rd. Hay 1 C3
Tulip Rd. Part 11 F1
Tully Ave. N-le-W 1 C2
Tunbridge Cl. Wist 206 A4
Tunnel Rd. North 78 A1
Tunnicliffe Rd. S La E 112 C2
Tunnicliffe St. Mfield 112 B4
Tunstall Rd. Bosl 158 B4
Tunstall Rd. Congle 157 F1
Tunstall Rd. Wd Gr 158 B4
Turf La. Mfield 112 B2
Turnall Rd. Wid 22 A4
Turnberry Cl. Lymm 18 B2
Turnberry Cl. Mfield 87 E2
Turnberry Cl. North 104 C4
Turnberry Cl. Winsf 126 B1
Turnberry Dr. Wilm 60 B4
Turner Ave. Audley 210 A1
Turner Cl. Wid 12 B2
Turner St. Boll 88 A4
Turner St. Nant 204 C3
Turner St. Warr 16 A3
Turnhurst Rd. Kids 195 F1
Turnock St. Mfield 112 C4
Turnstone Ave. N-le-W 2 B2
Turret Hall Dr. Gold 3 F4
Turriff Dr. Beb 43 E2
Turrocks Cl. Nest 66 C3
Turrocks Croft. Nest 66 C3
Turton Cl. Hale 21 F1
Turton Cl. Warr 9 E3
Turton St. Gold 3 D4
Tuscan Cl. Wid 13 D3
Tushingham Cl. Chest 142 A4
Tuson Dr. Wid 12 C3
Tweedsmuir Cl. Warr 9 D2
Twemlow Ave. Sand 175 D4
Twemlow La. Cran 130 B3
Twenty Acre Rd. Gt San 15 E4
Twinnies Ct. Wilm 34 A1
Twinnies Rd. Wilm 34 A1
Twiss Green Dr. Cul 4 C2
Twiss Green La. Cul 4 C2
Twist Ave. Gold 3 E4
Two Acre Gr. El Por 69 F1
Twyford Cl. Wid 13 D3
Twyford La. Wid 13 E3
Tyler St. A Edge 60 A1
Tyne Cl. Warr 8 C1
Tynedale Ave. Crewe 190 B1
Tynemouth Rd. Run 50 B3
Tynesdale. El Por 70 A2
Tynwald Cres. Wid 12 C3
Tynwald Dr. Apple 26 B4
Tyrer Rd. N-le-W 7 E4
Tytherington Dr. Mfield 87 F2
Tytherington La. Mfield 87 E3
Tytherington Park Rd. Mfield 87 E2
Tytherington Shopping Centre. Mfield 87 E2
Ullapool Cl. El Por 68 C3
Ullswater. Mfield 111 F3
Ullswater Ave. Crewe 189 F2
Ullswater Ave. Warr 8 B2
Ullswater Ave. Winsf 126 B1
Ullswater Cres. Chest 119 D3
Ullswater Gr. Run 49 E3
Ullswater Rd. Congle 156 A1
Ullswater Rd. El Por 70 B1
Ullswater Rd. Wilm 34 B2
Ulverston Ave. Warr 8 A2
Ulverston Cl. Hay 1 A3
Ulviet Gate. H Legh 29 E2
Under Rainow Rd. Congle 157 F1
Underbridge La. H Wal 25 E3
Underway The. Run 49 F4
Underwood Cl. Mfield 86 C1
Underwood Ind Pk. Crewe 190 A3
Underwood La. Crewe 190 A3
Underwood Rd. A Edge 60 B1
Unicorn Gateway. Mfield 112 B4
Union Cl. Congle 156 B2
Union Rd. Mfield 112 C4
Union Rd. N Mills 39 E4
Union St. Chest 118 C1
Union St. Congle 156 B2
Union St. Crewe 190 B2
Union St. Mfield 112 B4
Union St. Run 23 D1
Union St. Sand 175 D3
Union St. Warr 16 A3
Union Terr. Chest 118 B1
Union Wlk. Chest 118 B1
Upcast La. L End 59 E2
Upcast La. Wilm 59 F2
Uplands. Cudd 101 E2
Uplands Rd. North 78 C2
Uplands The. Bidd 179 F1
Uplands The. Run 50 A4
Upper Cambrian Rd. Chest 118 A1
Upper Haigh St. Winsf 149 E4
Upper Mersey Rd. Wid 23 D3
Upper Mersey St. El Por 70 B4
Upper Northgate St. Chest 118 B1
Upper Raby Rd. Will 42 A1
Upton Ave. Ch Hul 35 D4
Upton Bridle Path. Wid 12 C2
Upton Cl. Gold 3 E4
Upton Dr. Chest 118 B3
Upton Dr. Penk 14 C3
Upton La. Chest 118 B4
Upton La. Wid 12 C2
Upton Rd. El Por 69 E2
Upton Way. Wilm 34 B3
Upwood Rd. Gold 3 E4
Ure Ct. El Por 70 A4
Utkinton La. Utkin 146 C4
Utkinton Rd. Tarp 146 B3
Utkinton Rd. Utkin 146 B3
Vahler Terr. Run 23 E1
Vale Ave. Warr 16 A4
Vale Cl. Broug 139 E2
Vale Ct. Dutt 51 D2
Vale Gdns. El Por 70 A2
Vale Gdns. Hels 73 D2
Vale Head. Wilm 34 B1
Vale Owen Rd. Warr 8 B1
Vale Rd. Alpr 169 D2
Vale Rd. El Por 70 A2
Vale Rd. Hart 103 E2
Vale Rd. Mars 79 D3
Vale Rd. Tiver 168 C3
Vale Rd. Wilm 59 F4
Vale Royal Dr. Winsf 126 A4
Vale View. North 79 E1
Valebrook Dr. Hay Gr 220 A4
Valentine Rd. Kids 195 D1
Valentine Rd. N-le-W 1 C2
Valiant Cl. Warr 8 C1
Valley Cl. Alsag 192 C2
Valley Cl. Knuts 82 A4
Valley Ct. Warr 8 C1
Valley Dr. Chest 118 B3
Valley Dr. El Por 69 E3
Valley Dr. Wilm 34 B2
Valley La. Cudd 101 F2
Valley Rd. Beb 43 E4
Valley Rd. Bram 35 F4
Valley Rd. Crewe 190 A1
Valley Rd. Mfield 112 A3
Valley Rd. Weave 77 E1
Valley Rd. Wist 189 F1
Valley View. El Por 69 E3
Valley View. North 104 B4
Valley Way. Knuts 82 A4
Vanguard Ct. Warr 9 E2
Vardon Dr. Wilm 60 B3
Varey Rd. Congle 156 C2
Vaudrey Cres. Congle 156 C2
Vaudrey Dr. Warr 17 E4
Vaughan Rd. W Br 65 F3
Vaughans La. Chest 142 A4
Vauxhall Cl. Penk 14 C2
Vauxhall Rd. Nant 204 C4
Vauxhall Way. Winsf 149 E3
Vearows Pl. North 103 F4
Venable's Rd. Blacon 117 F2
Venables Rd. North 79 D1
Venables Way. H Legh 29 E2
Venables Way. Middle 151 F3
Venns Rd. Warr 16 B4
Ventnor Cl. Gt San 14 B4
Ventnor Cl. Middle 151 E4
Verbena Cl. Part 11 F2
Verbina Cl. Run 49 F2
Verdin Ave. North 78 C1
Verdin Cl. Moult 126 C4
Verdin Cl. Winsf 126 B1
Verdin Ct. Crewe 190 A4
Verdin St. North 104 B4
Vere St. Crewe 190 B3
Verity Cl. Hasl 191 E2
Vernay Gn. Chest 141 D3
Vernon Ave. Audley 209 E1
Vernon Ave. Congle 178 C4
Vernon Ave. El Por 44 A1
Vernon Cl. Audley 209 E1
Vernon Cl. Poyn 36 B1
Vernon Cl. Saug 117 D4
Vernon Dr. Buer 230 C2
Vernon Rd. Chest 118 A1
Vernon Rd. Poyn 36 C1
Vernon St. Crewe 190 A3
Vernon St. Mfield 112 C4
Vernon St. Warr 16 A2
Vernon Way. Crewe 190 B2
Veronica Way. El Por 69 E4
Vetch Cl. Hol Gr 11 D3
Vetches The. G Sutt 119 F3
Viaduct St. N-le-W 2 A2
Vicar's La. Chest 118 B1
Vicarage Ave. Ch Hul 35 D4
Vicarage Cl. G Sutt 119 F3
Vicarage Cl. Hale 21 F1
Vicarage Ct. Holt 196 C4
Vicarage Dr. Hay 1 A4
Vicarage Gdns. Sand 174 C4
Vicarage Hill. Hels 73 E2
Vicarage La. Audlem 230 A2
Vicarage La. Bun 168 C1
Vicarage La. Frod 74 B4
Vicarage La. Hels 73 E2
Vicarage La. L Bud 147 F4
Vicarage La. Nest 67 E1
Vicarage La. Poyn 36 C3
Vicarage La. Sand 174 C4
Vicarage Rd. Chest 118 C2
Vicarage Rd. Hasl 191 E3
Vicarage Rd. Hay 1 A4
Vicarage Rd. North 104 A4
Vicarage Rd. Wid 23 D4
Vicarage Row. Beb 44 A3
Vicarage Wlk. North 104 A4
Vicars Cross Rd. Chest 119 E1
Vicker's Cl. Asht 121 F4
Vickers Rd. Wid 22 C2
Vickers Way. North 104 A4

Victoria Ave. Crewe 190 A2
Victoria Ave. Gt San 14 B3
Victoria Ave. H Chap 130 B1
Victoria Ave. Hasl 191 E2
Victoria Ave. Hes 41 D3
Victoria Ave. Kids 194 C1
Victoria Ave. Warr 17 D1
Victoria Ave. Wid 13 D2
Victoria Centre. Crewe 190 B2
Victoria Cl. Ch Hul 35 E3
Victoria Cres. Chest 118 B2
Victoria Cres. Chest 141 F4
Victoria Ct. Chest 118 B2
Victoria Ct. Hasl 191 E2
Victoria Gr. Wid 13 D2
Victoria Park. North 78 C1
Victoria Pathway. Chest 141 F4
Victoria Pl. Chest 118 B1
Victoria Pl. Warr 16 B1
Victoria Rd. Brough 140 B3
Victoria Rd. Chest 118 B1
Victoria Rd. Chest 118 B2
Victoria Rd. El Por 70 B3
Victoria Rd. Gt San 15 D2
Victoria Rd. N-le-W 2 B2
Victoria Rd. Nest 67 D3
Victoria Rd. North 104 A4
Victoria Rd. Penk 14 B2
Victoria Rd. Run 23 D1
Victoria Rd. Warr 16 B1
Victoria Rd. Warr 16 C1
Victoria Rd. Wid 23 D3
Victoria Rd. Wilm 60 A3
Victoria Sq. Warr 16 B1
Victoria St. Crewe 190 B2
Victoria St. Knuts 56 C1
Victoria St. N Mills 39 D3
Victoria St. North 79 F1
Victoria St. Sand 175 D4
Victoria St. Warr 16 B3
Victoria St. Wid 23 D4
Victoria Way. Ch Hul 35 E3
Victoria Wlk. Mfield 112 C4
Victory Rd. Irlam 11 E4
Viewlands Dr. Wilm 34 B1
Villa Rd. Sea 116 A4
Villagate La. Apple 27 E3
Village Cl. Lost 105 D4
Village Cl. Run 50 A4
Village Cl. Warr 17 F2
Village La. Whit 52 B2
Village Rd. Christ 142 C4
Village Rd. Hes 40 C4
Village The. Astb 178 A4
Village The. Nest 67 E1
Village The. Prest 86 C3
Villars St. Warr 16 B3
Vincent Cl. Gt San 15 E4
Vincent Dr. Chest 141 E3
Vincent St. Crewe 190 C2
Vincent St. Mfield 112 B4
Vine Bank Rd. Kids 195 D1
Vine Cl. Mfield 112 A3
Vine Cres. Gt San 14 B4
Vine Rd. El Por 69 F1
Vine St. Boll 88 A4
Vine St. Run 23 D1
Vine St. Wid 23 D4
Vine Tree Ave. Crewe 190 A1
Vine Tree Ave. Shav 206 A3
Violet Cl. Warr 9 E3
Violet St. Wid 23 D4
Virginia Dr. Blacon 117 E2
Viscount Dr. Chea 34 B4
Vista Ave. N-le-W 2 A2
Vista Rd. Hay 2 A3
Vista Rd. N-le-W 2 A3
Vista Rd. Run 49 D4
Vista The. Irlam 11 E2
Volunteer Ave. Nant 204 C3
Volunteer Fields. Nant 204 C3
Volunteer St. Chest 118 B1
Volunteer St. Frod 49 E1
Vose Cl. Gt San 15 E3
Vulcan Cl. N-le-W 2 B1
Vulcan Cl. Warr 8 C1
Vyrnwy Rd. Brough 140 B3

W Lorne St. Chest 118 B1
Waddington Cl. Gold 3 F4
Waddington Cl. Warr 8 C1
Wade Cres. North 78 A2
Wade St. North 79 D1
Wadebrook Gr. Wilm 34 B1
Wades La. Winsf 126 B2
Wadeson Way. Croft 9 D4
Wadsworth Cl. Wilm 34 C2
Wagg St. Congle 156 B1
Waggs Rd. Congle 156 B1
Wagon La. Hay 1 A3
Waine St. Crewe 190 B3
Waitney Croft. Mfield 113 D4
Wakefield Rd. El Por 69 F1
Wakefield St. Gold 3 D4
Wakeham Cl. Mfield 111 F4
Wakes Meadow. Bun 185 F4
Walden Cl. Warr 17 E2
Walden Dr. Pudd 93 E4
Waldon Rd. Mfield 112 A3
Waldron Gdns. Wist 189 F1
Waldron Rd. Hasl 191 E2
Waldron's La. Crewe 173 E1
Walfield Ave. Congle 156 B3
Walford Ave. Crewe 190 A2
Walgrove Cl. Congle 156 A2
Walker Cl. Hasl 191 E2
Walker Dr. Middle 151 E4
Walker La. S La E 112 C1
Walker St. Chest 118 C2
Walker St. Crewe 190 A3
Walker St. Mfield 112 B4
Walker St. Warr 16 A3
Walkers La. El Por 69 E3
Walkers La. Penk 14 C2
Walkers La. Sch Gr 177 D1
Walkers La. Tarp 146 B1
Walkersgreen Rd. N-u-L 210 B1
Wall Fields Rd. Nant 204 C4
Wall Hill Way. Act Br 76 C2
Wall La. Nant 204 C3
Wallace Ct. Winsf 127 E1
Wallace St. North 103 F4
Wallace St. Wid 23 D4
Wallcroft. Will 68 A4
Waller St. Mfield 112 C3
Wallerscote Rd. Weave 102 C4
Walleys La. Burl 203 E4
Wallfields Cl. Nant 204 C4
Wallhill La. Astb 177 E4
Wallingford Rd. Wilm 34 B3
Wallis St. Crewe 190 B2
Wallis St. Warr 16 A2
Wallrake. Hes 40 C4
Walls Ave. Chest 118 A1
Wallworth's Bank. Congle 156 C1
Walmer Pl. Winsf 149 E3
Walmoor Park. Chest 119 D1
Walmsley St. N-le-W 2 B2
Walmsley St. Wid 23 E4
Walnut Ave. Weave 102 B4
Walnut Cl. Chest 118 B4
Walnut Cl. Warr 17 F4
Walnut Croft. Aldf 180 C3
Walnut Dr. Winsf 127 D1
Walnut Gr. El Por 70 A1
Walnut La. Hart 103 D3
Walnut Rd. Part 11 E2
Walnut Rise. Congle 156 A1
Walnut Tree La. Bra Gr 153 D2
Walpole Cl. Hasl 191 E3
Walpole Gr. Warr 8 B1
Walpole Rd. Run 49 E3
Walpole St. Chest 118 B2
Walsh Cl. N-le-W 2 B3
Walsingham Rd. Penk 14 C3
Walter St. Chest 118 B2
Walter St. Warr 16 C4
Walter St. Wid 13 E1
Walthall St. Crewe 190 B1
Waltham Ave. Cul 5 E4
Waltham Dr. Ch Hul 35 D3
Waltham Pl. Chest 141 D3
Walton Lea Rd. Warr 26 A4
Walton Ave. Penk 14 C3
Walton Gr. Kids 210 B4
Walton Heath Rd. Warr 16 A1
Walton Lea Rd. H Wal 25 F4
Walton New Rd. Warr 26 A4
Walton Pl. Blacon 117 F2
Walton Rd. Cul 4 C2
Walton Rd. Warr 26 B4
Walton St. Run 23 D1
Walton Way. Kids 210 B4
Waltons The. Chest 141 F3
Wansfell Pl. Warr 8 A2
Warburton Bridge Rd. Hol Gr 11 D1
Warburton Cl. Altr 32 B3
Warburton Cl. Lymm 19 D2
Warburton Dr. Altr 32 B3
Warburton La. Part 11 F1
Warburton Rd. Wilm 34 B2
Warburton St. Warr 16 B1
Warburton View. Hol Gr 11 D1
Ward Ave. Boll 88 A4
Ward Cl. G San 7 D1
Ward La. Disley 38 C2
Ward's La. Bra Gr 153 E3
Ward's Terr. Chest 118 C2
Wardle Ave. Barb 187 E4
Wardle Cres. Warren 111 F1
Wardle Industrial Estate. Barb 187 D4
Wardle Mews. Middle 151 E4
Wardley Rd. Warr 16 A1
Wardour Cl. Mfield 111 F4
Wardour St. Warr 15 F3
Wards La. Congle 179 E4
Wareham Cl. Warr 17 E4
Wareham Dr. Crewe 190 A4
Warford Ave. Poyn 37 D1
Warford Cres. L End 84 A4
Warford La. L End 59 D1
Wargrave Mews. N-le-W 2 B1
Wargrave Rd. N-le-W 2 A2
Wargrave Rd. N-le-W 2 B1
Warham St. Wilm 60 A4
Waring Ave. St Hel 1 A1
Waring Ave. Warr 16 C3
Warington La. Lymm 19 F2
Warkworth Cl. Wid 12 B2
Warkworth Ct. El Por 70 C2
Warmingham La. Middle 151 E3
Warmingham La. Sand 174 A4
Warmingham Rd. Crewe 173 E2
Warmingham Rd. Sand 173 E2
Warren Ave. Hes 40 B4
Warren Ave. Knuts 56 C1
Warren Ave. Lost 80 A2
Warren Cl. Knuts 56 C1
Warren Cl. Middle 151 D4
Warren Cl. Poyn 36 A2
Warren Croft. Run 50 B4
Warren Ct. El Por 69 E2
Warren Ct. Frod 74 B3
Warren Dr. Altr 32 B4
Warren Dr. Apple 26 B4
Warren Dr. Broug 139 D2
Warren Dr. El Por 69 F4
Warren Dr. N-le-W 2 C2
Warren Dr. Warren 111 E1
Warren Gr. Warren 111 E1
Warren La. Hart 103 D2
Warren La. Warr 17 E4
Warren Lea. Poyn 36 C3
Warren Rd. Apple 26 B4
Warren Rd. Warr 8 B1
Warren The. Cudd 101 E3
Warren Way. Tarp 168 B4
Warren Way. Wilm 60 C4
Warrilow Heath Rd. N-u-L 210 B1
Warrington Ave. Crewe 190 B3
Warrington Ave. El Por 70 A1
Warrington Rd. Bo Hea 13 E4
Warrington Rd. Comb 78 B4
Warrington Rd. Croft 9 F4
Warrington Rd. Cront 12 C4
Warrington Rd. Cudd 102 A3
Warrington Rd. Cul 5 E3
Warrington Rd. D-o-t-H 97 E3
Warrington Rd. Gold 3 D3
Warrington Rd. Hatt 25 F2
Warrington Rd. L Lei 77 D3
Warrington Rd. Lymm 18 A2
Warrington Rd. M Traf 119 F4
Warrington Rd. Mere 56 B4
Warrington Rd. Penk 14 C2
Warrington Rd. Run 23 F1
Warrington Rd. Run 24 A2
Warrington Rd. Warr 9 E2
Warrington Rd. Warr 9 F4
Warrington Rd. Wid 13 E1
Warrington Rd. Wid 23 E4
Warton Cl. Bram 36 A4
Warton Cl. Penk 15 D2
Warwick Ave. Gt San 14 B4
Warwick Ave. N-le-W 2 B1
Warwick Ave. Warr 15 F4
Warwick Cl. Kids 195 D2
Warwick Cl. Knuts 57 E1
Warwick Cl. Mfield 111 F3
Warwick Cl. Nest 66 C3
Warwick Ct. El Por 70 C1
Warwick Dr. Haz Gr 36 B4
Warwick Pl. Winsf 149 E3
Warwick Rd. Blacon 117 F3
Warwick Rd. Irlam 11 E3
Warwick Rd. Mfield 111 F3
Warwick Wlk. Mfield 111 F3
Wasdale Gr. Crewe 173 D1
Wash La. Allos 106 C2
Wash La. Warr 16 C2
Washington Cl. Bidd 179 E1
Wasley Cl. Warr 8 C2
Waste La. Cudd 101 F2
Waste La. Kels 122 C2
Watch La. Sand 174 A3
Water La. Wilm 60 A4
Water Lode. Nant 204 C3
Water St. Boll 88 A4
Water St. Mfield 112 B4
Water St. N-le-W 2 B2
Water St. N-u-L 210 B1
Water St. North 104 A4
Water St. Run 23 D2
Water St. Wid 23 D3
Water Tower Rd. Nest 41 F1
Water Twr St. Chest 118 B1
Waterbridge Ct. Apple 26 B4
Waterfoot La. W Br 65 E3
Waterford Dr. Nest 67 D4
Waterford Way. Run 50 B3
Watergate Row. Chest 118 B1
Watergate Sq. Chest 118 B1
Watergate St. Chest 118 B1
Waterhouse Ave. Boll 87 F4
Waterloo Cl. El Por 70 B3
Waterloo Gr. Kids 195 D1
Waterloo La. Kings 74 C1
Waterloo Rd. Bram 35 F4
Waterloo Rd. Chest 118 B2
Waterloo Rd. Hasl 191 E2
Waterloo Rd. North 103 F4
Waterloo Rd. Poyn 37 D1
Waterloo Rd. Run 22 C1
Waterloo Rd. Run 22 C2
Waterloo Rd. Wid 23 D3
Waterloo St W. Mfield 112 B4
Waters Gn. Mfield 112 B4
Waters Reach. Poyn 36 C3
Waters Reams. Chest 142 A4
Watersfield Cl. Chea 34 C4
Waterside. Apple 26 B4
Waterside. Mfield 112 C4
Waterside La. Wid 22 B3
Waterside Mews. Sand 174 C2
Waterside Rd. Disley 38 C4
Waterside Rd. N Mills 38 C4
Waterside View. North 104 C3
Waterside Way. Middle 128 A1
Watertower View. Chest 118 C1
Waterway. Waver 143 D3
Waterways. Gt San 15 E3
Waterworks La. El Por 68 C4
Waterworks La. Win 8 A4
Watery La. Astb 178 B3
Watery La. Win 7 F3
Watkin St. Hawa 116 A1
Watkin St. Warr 16 A4
Watking Ave. N-le-W 1 C2
Watlands Rd. Audley 209 F1
Watling Cres. Chest 141 F4
Watling Ct. Chest 119 E1
Watling Dr. Dela 123 E3
Watling St. North 103 F4
Watson's Cl. Broug 139 E2
Watton Cl. Warr 17 E2
Wavell Ave. Wid 22 B4
Wavells Way. Hunt 142 A3
Waverley Ave. Apple 26 B4
Waverley Cl. Mfield 113 D4
Waverley Dr. Ch Hul 35 D4
Waverley Terr. Chest 118 C2
Waverton Cl. Ho Co 206 C1
Waverton Mill Quays. Waver 143 D3
Waverton Rd. El Por 69 F3
Wavertree Ave. Sch Gr 194 C4
Wavertree Ave. Wid 23 D4
Wavertree Ct. El Por 69 F4
Wavertree Dr. Middle 151 D4
Wavertree Rd. Blacon 117 E3
Way's Green. Winsf 149 F4
Waybutt La. Betley 221 E4
Waybutt La. Ho Co 221 E4
Wayfarers Dr. N-le-W 2 C1
Wayford Cl. Frod 49 D1
Wayside. Alsag 193 F1
Wayside Cl. Lymm 18 B1
Wayside Ct. M Traf 119 F4
Wayside Dr. Poyn 36 B2
Wayside Rd. Mfield 112 C4
Waywell Cl. Warr 8 C2
Weal Stone La. Chest 118 C3
Wealstone Ct. Chest 118 C3
Weaste La. Apple 17 F1
Weates Cl. Wid 13 F2
Weathercock La. Congle 157 F2
Weaver Cl. Alsag 193 D2
Weaver Cl. Bidd 179 E1
Weaver Cl. Sand 174 C4
Weaver Cres. Frod 49 E1
Weaver Ct. Mfield 112 B4
Weaver Gr. M Traf 119 F4
Weaver Gr. St Hel 1 A2
Weaver Grange. Moult 126 C4
Weaver La. Frod 49 D1
Weaver Park Ind Est. Sutt 49 E1
Weaver Rd. Cul 5 D1
Weaver Rd. El Por 70 B1
Weaver Rd. Frod 49 E1
Weaver Rd. Moult 126 C4
Weaver Rd. Nant 204 C3
Weaver Rd. North 103 F4
Weaver Rd. Run 49 D3
Weaver St. Chest 118 B1
Weaver St. Winsf 126 C1
Weaver View. Ch Min 172 A3
Weaver View. North 103 F4
Weaver View. Weave 77 E1
Weaver Way. North 78 C1
Weaver's La. Ch Hul 35 E3
Weaverhall La. Winsf 150 A2
Weaverham Rd. Cudd 102 A2
Weaverham Rd. Weave 102 A3
Weaverham Way. Wilm 34 C2
Weaverside. Nant 204 C1
Weaverside Ave. Run 49 F2
Webb Dr. Burton 6 C3
Webb's La. Middle 128 B1
Webster Cl. Broug 139 E2
Websters La. El Por 69 F1
Weddell Cl. Gt San 15 E4
Wedge Ave. Hay 1 A3
Wedgwood Ave. Audley 210 A1
Wedgwood Dr. Wid 13 D2
Wedgwood La. Bidd 179 E1
Wedgwood Rd. Kids 210 B4
Wednesbury Dr. Gt San 14 C3
Weedon Ave. N-le-W 2 A3
Weir Gr. Kids 195 D1
Weir La. Warr 17 F3
Weir St. North 103 F4
Weir St. Warr 16 A1
Welbeck Cl. Middle 128 A1
Welford Ave. Gold 3 E4
Welford Cl. Wilm 60 C4
Well Ave. Malpas 213 D2
Well Bank. Sand 175 D3
Well Bank La. Peo 108 B4
Well Cl. Nest 67 E3
Well Farm Cl. Malpas 213 D2
Well Field Cl. Pick 80 A4
Well La. Alsag 193 E2
Well La. Antro 53 D2
Well La. Bidd 179 E2
Well La. Chest 118 C3
Well La. Hes 41 D3
Well La. Kings 75 E1
Well La. L Bud 147 F4
Well La. Moll 94 C1
Well La. Nest 66 C3
Well La. Penk 14 C2
Well La. Prest 87 E4
Well La. Stret 52 C4
Well La. Weave 77 E1
Well St. Malpas 213 D2
Well St. N Mills 39 D4
Well St. Sch Gr 195 E4
Well St. Winsf 126 B1
Welland Cl. Sand 174 B3
Wellbrook Cl. Run 50 B3
Wellcroft Cl. Wist 206 A4
Weller Ave. Poyn 36 B1
Weller Cl. Poyn 36 B1
Welles St. Sand 175 D3
Wellesbourne Cl. Mfield 86 C1
Wellesbourne Cl. Nest 66 B3
Wellesley Ave. El Por 70 B3
Wellesley Ave. Hasl 191 E2
Wellesley Wlk. El Por 70 B3
Wellfield. Wid 13 D2
Wellfield. Winsf 127 D1
Wellfield Rd. Cul 4 C2
Wellington Cl. El Por 70 B3
Wellington Cl. Knuts 57 E2
Wellington Gdns. N-le-W 2 A2
Wellington Pl. Chest 118 B1
Wellington Rd. Boll 87 F4
Wellington Rd. Broug 139 D2
Wellington Rd. El Por 70 B2
Wellington Rd. El Por 70 B3
Wellington Rd. Haz Gr 37 D4
Wellington Rd. Kids 195 D1
Wellington Rd. Nant 204 C2
Wellington Rd N. El Por 70 B3
Wellington St. Mfield 112 B4
Wellington St. N-le-W 2 A2
Wellington St. North 103 F4
Wellington St. Run 23 D2
Wellington St. Warr 16 B3
Wellington St. Wid 23 D3
Wells Ave. Hasl 191 E3
Wells Cl. Chea 34 B4
Wells Cl. El Por 94 C4
Wells Cl. M Traf 119 F4
Wells Cl. Warr 17 D4
Wellswood Dr. Wist 205 F4
Wellswood Rd. El Por 69 F4
Welsby Cl. Warr 8 C2
Welsh La. Winsf 149 E3
Welsh Rd. El Por 68 C2
Welsh Rd. G Cit 93 E3
Welsh Rd. Led 68 C2
Welsh Rd. Pudd 93 E3
Welsh Rd. Shot 93 E3
Welsh Row. N Ald 84 C3
Welsh Row. Nant 204 B3
Welshampton Cl. El Por 69 E1
Welshmen's La. Nant 204 B4
Welshpool Cl. Warr 7 E1
Welton Cl. Wilm 59 F2
Welton Dr. Wilm 59 F2
Welwyn Cl. Warr 17 E2
Wemyss Rd. Blacon 117 E2
Wenger Rd. Wid 13 D3
Wenlock Cl. Mfield 87 D1
Wenlock Cl. N-u-L 210 C1
Wenlock Gdns. El Por 69 F1
Wenlock La. El Por 69 F1
Wenlock Rd. Run 50 A2
Wenlock Way. Chest 140 C3
Wensley Dr. Haz Gr 36 B4
Wensley Rd. Gold 3 F4
Wensleydale Av. Congle 157 D3
Wensleydale Ave. Beb 43 F3
Wentworth Ave. Mfield 111 F3
Wentworth Ave. Warr 17 D4
Wentworth Cl. North 104 C4
Wentworth Cl. Wid 13 D3
Wentworth Dr. Beb 43 E3
Wentworth Dr. Bram 36 A4
Wentworth Dr. Kids 195 E2
Wereton Rd. Audley 209 E1
Wervin Rd. Chest 96 A2
Wervin Rd. Stoak 96 A2
Wesley Ave. Alsag 193 E2
Wesley Ave. Hay 1 C4
Wesley Ave. Sand 175 D3
Wesley Ct. Congle 156 B1

Wesley Cl. Nant 204 C3
Wesley Cl. Nest 66 B4
Wesley Ct. Winsf 126 C1
Wesley Gdns. Kids 195 D1
Wesley Pl. Crewe 190 B1
Wesley Pl. North 104 A4
Wesley St. Audley 210 A1
Wessex Cl. Shav 206 B2
Wessex Cl. Warr 17 F4
Wessex Dr. North 104 B3
West Ave. Crewe 190 A2
West Ave. Kids 194 B1
West Ave. Middle 128 B1
West Ave. North 104 B4
West Ave. Warr 16 A4
West Ave. Warr 16 B1
West Ave. Weston 207 D3
West Bank. A Edge 85 D4
West Bank. Chest 118 B2
West Bank Rd. Mfield 87 D1
West Bank St. Wid 23 D3
West Bond St. Mfield 112 B4
West Cl. Boll 87 F4
West Dr. Gt San 15 D2
West Dr. Hes 41 D4
West Dr. Nest 66 C3
West Dr. Winsf 127 D1
West Dudley St. Winsf 126 C1
West End. Asht 121 F4
West End Cotts. Congle 156 B1
West End Gr. Hay 1 A3
West End Rd. Hay 1 A3
West Gate. Wid 22 A4
West Gr. Alsag 193 F2
West Gr. Hes 40 C4
West Heath Gr. Lymm 18 B2
West Heath
Shopping Centre. Congle 156 A2
West House Ct. Mfield 86 C1
West Hyde. Lymm 18 B2
West La. Cudd 101 F2
West La. H Legh 29 E3
West La. Run 49 F4
West Mains. Speke 21 D2
West Park Ave. Poyn 36 A2
West Park Dr. El Por 94 C4
West Quay Rd. Warr 7 F2
West Rd. Congle 156 B2
West Rd. El Por 70 B2
West Rd. Run 48 B4
West Rd. Weave 77 D1
West Side Ave. Hay 1 A3
West St. A Edge 60 A1
West St. Chest 118 C2
West St. Congle 156 B2
West St. Crewe 189 F3
West St. Crewe 190 A3
West St. Hasl 191 E3
West St. Mfield 112 A4
West St. Middle 128 B1
West St. Sch Gr 195 D3
West St. Warr 16 A4
West Vale. Nest 66 C3
West View. Warr 9 D1
West View Rd. Norley 101 D3
West Way. H Chap 130 A2
West Way. Sand 174 C2
West Way. Shav 206 B3
Westage La. B Hen 79 D4
Westage La. G Bud 79 D4
Westbourne Ave. Crewe 190 A3
Westbourne Rd. Blacon 118 A2
Westbourne Rd. Warr 26 A4
Westbrook Ave. Warr 16 B1
Westbrook Centre. Warr 7 E1
Westbrook Cres. G San 7 D1
Westbrook Cres. Warr 7 D1
Westbrook Dr. Mfield 87 E1
Westbrook Rd. Kings 75 D1
Westbrook Way. Warr 7 D1
Westbury Cl. Middle 151 D4
Westbury Cl. Wist 206 B4
Westbury Dr. Mfield 112 A4
Westbury Way. Chest 140 C3
Westby Cl. Bram 36 A4
Westdale Rd. Warr 17 D4
Westenra Ave. El Por 69 F3
Westerham Cl. Mfield 87 D1
Western App. Chest 118 C2
Western Ave. Blacon 117 E2
Western Ave. El Por 69 F4
Western Ave. Hand 165 E1
Western Ave. Mfield 112 B3
Western Ave. Nant 204 C2
Western Ct. Chest 118 C2
Western Dr. Mfield 112 B3
Westfield Ave. Audley 209 E1
Westfield Ave. Mfield 87 D1
Westfield Cl. Chest 141 D4
Westfield Cres. Run 22 C1
Westfield Dr. Knuts 56 C1
Westfield Dr. Willas 205 F4
Westfield Gr. North 77 F2
Westfield Mews. Run 22 C1
Westfield Rd. Chea 34 C4
Westfield Rd. North 104 A4
Westfield Rd. Run 22 C1
Westfield Rd. Sch Gr 195 E4
Westfields. Altr 31 F4
Westfields Rise. Woore 232 B1
Westford Rd. Warr 16 A1
Westgate. Wilm 60 A3
Westgate Ave. Winsf 126 A1
Westholme Cl. Wist 206 B4
Westhouse Cl. Beb 43 E3
Westlands. Audley 209 F1
Westlands Cl. Nest 41 F1
Westlands Rd. Middle 128 A1
Westlands The. Congle 156 B1
Westmere Cl. Weston 207 D3
Westminster Ave. Chest 141 D3
Westminster Cl. Warr 17 E1
Westminster Cl. Wid 22 A4
Westminster Dr. Beb 43 E4
Westminster Dr. Ch Hul 35 D3
Westminster Dr. Hay 1 C4
Westminster Dr. Wilm 60 A2
Westminster Gr. Chest 141 E4
Westminster Gr. El Por 70 B3
Westminster
Industrial Park. El Por 69 F3
Westminster Pl. Warr 16 A3
Westminster Rd. Broug 139 D2
Westminster Rd. Chest 118 C2
Westminster Rd. El Por 70 B3
Westminster Rd. Mfield 87 E1
Westminster St. Crewe 190 B1
Westminster St. Mfield 112 B4
Westminster Terr. Chest 141 E4
Westmoreland Cl. Altr 31 D4
Westmorland Ave. Kids 210 C4
Westmorland Ave. Wid 13 D1
Westmorland Ave. Wid 13 D1
Westmorland Cl. Mfield 86 C1
Westmorland Rd. Part 11 F1
Westmorland Terr. H Chap 130 A2
Weston Cl. Middle 151 E4
Weston Cres. Run 49 D3
Weston Ct. Run 48 C4
Weston Gr. Chest 118 B4
Weston La. Shav 206 C3
Weston Point Expressway.
Run 49 D3
Weston Rd. Crewe 190 C1
Weston Rd. Run 48 C4
Weston Rd. Weston 207 D4
Weston Rd. Wilm 60 C3
Westover Rd. Warr 16 C4
Westrees. Cudd 101 E3
Westville Dr. Congle 156 A1
Westward Rd. Chest 142 A4
Westward Rd. Wilm 59 F3
Westway. Hes 40 C3
Westway Cres. Warr 10 A3
Westwood. Run 24 B1
Westwood Ct. Nest 41 F1
Westwood Rd. Chea 34 A4
Westy La. Warr 16 C2
Wet Gate La. Lymm 19 E2
Wetheral Rd. Mfield 87 D1
Wetherby Cl. Chest 118 A1
Wetherby Cl. N-le-W 2 B3
Wetherby Way. El Por 69 E3
Wetreins La. Barton 197 E3
Wetreins La. Farn 197 E3
Wetton La. Act Br 76 C2
Wexford Ave. Hale 21 E1
Wey Gates Dr. Altr 32 B4
Weybridge Cl. Apple 26 C4
Weybridge Dr. Mfield 87 D2
Weymouth Cl. Run 50 C3
Weymouth Rd. Burton 6 C3
Whaddon Dr. Chest 140 C2
Whaley La. W Br 65 E4
Whalley Ave. Cul 5 E4
Whalley Dr. Eaton 147 D2
Whalley Gr. Wid 13 E2
Whalley Hayes. Mfield 112 B4
Whalley Rd. North 104 A4
Whalley St. Warr 16 B3
Wharams Bank. Small 176 C3
Wharf La. Astb 178 A2
Wharf Rd. N-le-W 1 C1
Wharf Rd. W Br 65 F4
Wharf St. Warr 16 B2
Wharf The. P-o-t-H 50 C3
Wharfdale Cl. Gt San 15 D4
Wharfdale Dr. Beb 43 F3
Wharfdale Rd. Congle 157 D3
Wharfdale Rd. Crewe 173 D1
Wharfe Cl. Congle 156 C1
Wharfe La. El Por 70 A4
Wharfedale. Run 50 A3
Wharmby Rd. Hay 1 C3
Wharton Gdns. Winsf 127 D2
Wharton Park Rd. Winsf 126 C1
Wharton Rd. Winsf 127 D1
Whatcroft Cl. Run 49 E3
Whatcroft La. Dave 104 C1
Whatcroft La. L Den 104 C1
Wheat Croft Cl. Gt San 15 E3
Wheat Moss. Chelf 84 A2
Wheatfield Cl. Mfield 87 E2
Wheatfield Cl. North 78 A2
Wheatfield Rd. Cront 12 B3
Wheatland Rd. Hes 41 E4
Wheatlands. Run 23 F1
Wheatley Ave. N-le-W 2 B3
Wheatley Rd. Crewe 190 C3
Wheatsheaf La. Antro 53 D2
Wheatsheaf Rd. W Br 65 F3
Wheelman Rd. Crewe 190 A4
Wheelock Cl. Alsag 193 D2
Wheelock Cl. Wilm 34 B1
Wheelock Dr. Winsf 127 D1
Wheelock St. Middle 128 B1
Wheelock Way. Kids 195 D1
Wheldon Cl. Chest 118 B4
Wheldrake Cl. El Por 69 D3
Whernside. Wid 12 B2
Whetstone Hey. El Por 69 E3
Whetstone Rd. Bidd 179 E1
Whimbrel Ave. N-le-W 2 B2
Whimbrel Cl. Run 49 F3
Whinchat Ave. N-le-W 2 B2
Whinchat Dr. Warr 9 F2
Whinfell Gr. Run 49 F3
Whipcord La. Chest 118 A1
Whirley La. Henb 85 F1
Whirley Rd. Mfield 86 B1
Whirlow Rd. Wist 206 A4
Whisterfield La. Sidd 109 F2
Whiston St. Mfield 112 B4
Whitbarrow Rd. Lymm 18 B2
Whitby Ave. Chest 118 B3
Whitby Ave. Warr 8 B1
Whitby Cl. Crewe 190 A4
Whitby Cl. Poyn 36 B2
Whitby La. Back 95 D3
Whitby Rd. El Por 70 B3
Whitby Rd. Run 23 D1
Whitby's La. Winsf 126 A1
Whitchurch Gr. N-u-L 210 C1
Whitchurch Rd. Audlem 229 E2
Whitchurch Rd. Brox 199 D2
Whitchurch Rd. Chest 119 D1
Whitchurch Rd. Chow 183 D2
Whitchurch Rd. Christ 142 C4
Whitchurch Rd. Ed Gr 199 D2
Whitchurch Rd. Fr La E 218 A4
Whitchurch Rd. Golb 165 E2
Whitchurch Rd. Hand 165 E2
Whitchurch Rd. Hand 182 B4
Whitchurch Rd. New 229 E2
Whitchurch Rd. Roy Gr 228 B1
Whitchurch Rd. Saigh 165 E2
Whitchurch Rd. Sound 217 F2
Whitchurch Rd. Waver 143 D2
Whitchurch Way. Run 49 E4
White Ave. Crewe 189 F2
White Broom. Lymm 19 D2
White Field Ave. N-le-W 2 C1
White Friars. Chest 118 B1
White Hall La. Warm 173 F4
White Hall Rd. Kids 194 C1
White Hart La. Wist 205 F4
White House Cl. Hay 1 A3
White House Dr. Warr 17 F4
White La. Christ 142 B4
White Lodge Cl. Beb 43 E3
White Lodge Mews. Cudd 102 A2
White St. Mfield 112 B3
White St. Warr 16 A3
White St. Warr 16 B1
White St. Wid 23 D3
Whitebarn Rd. A Edge 85 D4
Whitebeam Ave. El Por 69 F1
Whitebeam Cl. N-u-L 210 B1
Whitebeam Cl. Run 24 B1
Whitecroft Rd. El Por 69 F1
Whitecross Rd. Warr 15 F3
Whitefield Ave. Warr 16 C4
Whitefield Cl. Gold 3 D4
Whitefield Cl. Lymm 19 D3
Whitefield Ct. Croft 4 C1
Whitefield Gr. Lymm 19 D2
Whitefield Rd. Warr 26 A4
Whitefields. Elton 72 A2
Whitefriars Wlk. Wythe 33 E4
Whitegate. Asht 121 F4
Whitegate Ave. Cul 4 C1
Whitegate Cl. Middle 151 E3
Whitegate Rd. Winsf 125 F2
Whitegates Cl. Will 42 C1
Whitegates Cres. Will 67 F4
Whitehall Ave. Kids 194 C1
Whitehall Cl. North 78 A2
Whitehall Cl. Wilm 60 A3
Whitehall Ct. Nant 204 B3
Whitehall Dr. Hart 103 E3
Whitehall Dr. Shav 206 A2
Whitehall La. L Bud 124 C1
Whitehall Pl. Frod 74 A4
Whitehaven La. Burl 203 D4
Whitehaven Rd. Ch Hul 35 E3
Whitehill Rd. Kids 195 D1
Whitehouse Dr. Altr 32 A4
Whitehouse Expressway.
Run 50 A3
Whitehouse La. Dun T 20 B4
Whitehouse La. Nant 204 C4
Whitehouse La. Plum 80 C3
Whitehouse Rd. Mere 30 A2
Whiteleas Rd. W Br 65 E2
Whitemere Ct. El Por 70 B4
Whitemore Rd. Middle 151 E3
Whiteridge Rd. Kids 195 D1
Whites La. Weston 207 D3
Whites Meadow. Chest 142 A4
Whitesands Rd. Lymm 18 B2
Whiteside Rd. Hay 1 A3
Whitethorn Ave. Gt San 14 B4
Whitethorn Way. N-u-L 210 C1
Whitewood La. Hor Gr 212 B4
Whitfield Gr. Hay 1 A3
Whitfields The. Mfield 87 D1
Whitley Ave. North 78 A2
Whitley Ave. Warr 17 D2
Whitley Cl. Middle 151 D4
Whitley Cl. Run 48 C4
Whitley Dr. Hart 103 D2
Whitley La. H Legh 55 D4
Whitlow Ave. Nant 204 C2
Whitlow La. Moult 126 C4
Whittaker Ave. Warr 8 B1
Whittington Gdns. Dave 104 A1
Whittle Ave. Gt San 15 D4
Whittle Ave. Hay 1 A3
Whittle Cl. Hawa 116 A2
Whittle Hall La. Gt San 14 B4
Whittlewood Cl. Warr 10 A3
Whitton Dr. Chest 118 C3
Wicker La. Altr 32 B4
Wicker La. G Sutt 120 A2
Wicklow Cl. El Por 69 D3
Wickson La. Beest 167 E2
Wicksten Dr. Run 23 E1
Widgeon Cl. Poyn 36 A2
Widgeons Covert. Thor H 41 F3
Widnes Rd. Wid 23 D4
Wiend The. Chest 118 B2
Wight Cl. El Por 70 B1
Wightman Ave. N-le-W 2 B3
Wigmore Cl. Warr 10 A3
Wigsey La. Part 19 D4
Wigshaw La. Cul 4 C2
Wilbraham Cl. Acton 204 A4
Wilbraham Rd. Acton 204 A4
Wilbraham Rd. Congle 156 C2
Wilbraham Rd. Weave 77 F1
Wilbraham's Wlk. Audley 209 E1
Wilbrahams Way. Alsag 193 E2
Wilcott Dr. Wilm 59 F2
Wildcote Cl. Wid 13 E2
Wilderhope Cl. Wist 206 B4
Wilderspool Cres. Warr 16 A1
Wilderspool Cswy. Warr 16 B2
Wilding Ave. Run 23 D1
Wilding St. Crewe 190 C2
Wildings Old La. Croft 9 D4
Wildwood Gr. Warr 17 D4
Wilkin Croft. Chea 34 C4
Wilkins La. Wilm 33 F3
Wilkinson Ave. Warr 16 C3
Wilkinson Cl. Wid 23 D3
Wilkinson St. El Por 70 B3
Wilkinson St. Warr 16 B4
Wilkinson St N. El Por 70 B3
Willan Rd. Blacon 117 E2
Willaston Hall Gdns. Willas 205 E3
Willaston Rd. Thor H 42 B3
Willaston Way. Wilm 34 B3
Willbank La. Fadd 202 B3
Willcock Rd. Hay 2 A4
Willeymoor La. B of H 225 E4
William Johnson Gdns.
El Por 70 B3
William Penn Cl. Penk 14 C3
William Rd. Hay 1 A3
William Rd. Kids 195 D1
William St. Chest 118 B1
William St. Chest 118 C2
William St. Congle 157 D2
William St. Crewe 190 C2
William St. Mfield 112 C4
William St. North 104 A4
William St. Wid 13 E1
William St. Winsf 126 C1
Williams Ave. N-le-W 2 B3
Williams Way. Henb 111 E4
Williamson Cres. W Br 65 E4
Williamson Rd. W Br 65 E4
Willington Ave. Beb 43 F2
Willington La. Dudd 145 F4
Willington La. Kels 122 B2
Willington Rd. Dudd 145 D4
Willington Rd. Kels 122 B2
Willington Rd. Tarv 122 B1
Willis St. Warr 16 B3
Willmer Cres. Sch Gr 195 D3
Willotts Hill Rd. N-u-L 210 B1
Willoughby Cl. Warr 7 E1
Willow Ave. N-le-W 2 C2
Willow Ave. Wid 13 D1
Willow Bank. Ch Hul 35 D3
Willow Bank Est. N-le-W 2 C2
Willow Cl. Chest 118 B4
Willow Cl. Lymm 18 C2
Willow Cl. N-u-L 210 B1
Willow Cl. Poyn 36 C2
Willow Cl. Run 49 E4
Willow Cl. Winsf 126 B2
Willow Cres. Chest 119 D2
Willow Cres. Warr 17 D4
Willow Cres. Wist 189 F1
Willow Ct. Alsag 193 F2
Willow Ct. H Kin 161 D4
Willow Ct. Mfield 87 D1
Willow Ct. Middle 128 B1
Willow Dr. Blacon 117 E3
Willow Dr. Bun 185 F4
Willow Dr. Sand 175 F4
Willow Dr. Warr 16 C1
Willow Dr. Wilm 34 B2
Willow Gr. Chest 119 D2
Willow Gr. El Por 95 D4
Willow Gr. Elton 72 A2
Willow Gr. North 78 A2
Willow Green. Knuts 56 C2
Willow Green. Weave 102 B4
Willow Hayes. Asht 121 F4
Willow La. Apple 26 B2
Willow La. Goost 107 F1
Willow La. Thor H 42 B2
Willow Lea. Moll 94 C1
Willow Mews. Mfield 86 C1
Willow Rd. Chest 140 C3
Willow Rd. H La 37 F4
Willow Rd. Hay 1 C4
Willow Rd. N-le-W 2 C2
Willow Rd. Part 11 F1
Willow Square. Winsf 127 D1
Willow St. Congle 156 C2
Willow Tree Gn. Sch Gr 193 F4
Willow Way. Broug 139 D2
Willow Way. Ch Hul 35 E4
Willow Way. Prest 87 D3
Willoway Rd. Chest 119 D1
Willowbrow Rd. Thor H 42 B2
Willowdale Way. El Por 94 C4
Willowgreen La. L Lei 77 D3
Willowherb Cl. Hunt 142 A3
Willowmead Dr. Prest 87 D3
Willows Cl. Wist 206 A4
Willows The. Frod 74 B4
Willows The. H Winch 79 F3
Willows The. Part 11 F2
Wilmere La. Wid 13 D3
Wilmot Ave. Gt San 14 B4
Wilmslow Ave. El Por 69 F3
Wilmslow Cres. Warr 17 F2
Wilmslow Dr. El Por 69 F3
Wilmslow Old Rd. M St A 61 D1
Wilmslow Old Rd. Wythe 32 C3
Wilmslow Park Rd. Wilm 60 B4
Wilmslow Rd. A Edge 60 A2
Wilmslow Rd. Chea 34 B3
Wilmslow Rd. M St A 61 D2
Wilmslow Rd. M St A 61 E3
Wilmslow Rd. M St A 86 A4
Wilmslow Rd. Prest 61 E3
Wilmslow Rd. Wilm 34 B3
Wilmslow Rd. Woodf 35 E1
Wilmslow Rd. Wythe 32 C3
Wilmslow Wlk. Mfield 112 C4
Wilsden Rd. Wid 12 A1
Wilson Cl. Warr 17 E2
Wilson Cres. Lost 80 A2
Wilson Dr. Moult 126 C4
Wilson Patten St. Warr 16 A2
Wilson St. Warr 16 A4
Wilsons La. El Por 70 A2
Wilton Ave. Chea 34 B4
Wilton Cres. A Edge 59 F1
Wilton Cres. Mfield 111 F3
Wilton Dr. Altr 32 B4
Wilton La. Gold 4 A3
Wiltshire Cl. Mfield 86 C1
Wiltshire Cl. Warr 17 E4
Wiltshire Dr. Congle 156 C2
Wiltshire Rd. Part 11 F1
Wiltshire Wlk. Mfield 86 C1
Wilwick La. Mfield 111 F4
Wimberry Dr. N-u-L 210 B1
Wincham La. H Winch 79 E2
Winchester Ave. El Por 70 B2
Winchester Ave. Gt San 15 E3
Winchester Cl. Shav 206 A2
Winchester Cl. Wilm 59 F3
Winchester Ct. Mfield 112 C4
Winchester Pl. Wid 22 B4
Winchester Sq. Chest 140 C3
Wincle Ave. Poyn 36 C1
Wincroft Cl. Wid 22 B4
Wincroft Rd. Wid 22 B4
Windemere Ave. Chest 119 D3
Windemere Dr. Congle 156 A1
Windermere Ave. Warr 8 B2
Windermere Ave. Wid 13 D2
Windermere Cl. Nest 66 C4
Windermere Dr. A Edge 59 F1
Windermere Rd. El Por 70 B1
Windermere Rd. H La 37 F4
Windermere Rd. Hay 1 A3
Windermere Rd. Wilm 34 B2
Windermere Rd. Winsf 126 B1
Windermere Rd. Wist 189 F1
Windermere St. Wid 13 D2
Windfield Gdns. El Por 69 E4
Windle Ct. Nest 41 F1

Windle Ct. Warr 9 E2
Windlehurst Rd. H La 37 E4
Windmill Cl. Apple 26 B3
Windmill Cl. Buer 230 C2
Windmill Dr. Audlem 229 F2
Windmill Hill Ave. Run 24 B1
Windmill Hill Ave E. Run 24 B1
Windmill Hill Ave N. Run 24 B2
Windmill Hill Ave S. Run 24 B1
Windmill Hill Ave W. Run 24 B1
Windmill La. Apple 26 B3
Windmill La. Boll 88 A3
Windmill La. Buer 230 C2
Windmill La. Christ 142 B4
Windmill La. P-o-t-H 51 D3
Windmill La. Penk 14 C3
Windmill Rise. Chest 118 B4
Windmill St. Mfield 112 C3
Windmill St. Run 23 D1
Windscale Rd. Warr 9 D1
Windsor Av. Wilm 59 F4
Windsor Ave. Crewe 190 A3
Windsor Ave. N-le-W 2 B1
Windsor Ave. Nant 204 C2
Windsor Ave. Tarp 146 B1
Windsor Cl. Boll 87 F3
Windsor Cl. Cudd 101 F2
Windsor Cl. Poyn 36 B2
Windsor Dr. Alsag 192 C2
Windsor Dr. Broug 139 D2
Windsor Dr. El Por 70 A2
Windsor Dr. Fadd 202 C4
Windsor Dr. Hay 2 A4
Windsor Dr. Hels 73 D1
Windsor Dr. Warr 17 D2
Windsor Dr. Winsf 149 E3
Windsor Gr. Chea 34 C4
Windsor Gr. Run 49 D4
Windsor Pl. Congle 156 C1
Windsor Rd. Chest 140 C3
Windsor Rd. Gold 3 E4
Windsor Rd. Wid 13 D2
Windsor Rd. Wist 205 F4
Windsor Sq. Mfield 112 B2
Windsor St. Warr 15 F3
Windsor Way. Knuts 56 C1
Windways. El Por 69 E4
Windy Bank Ave. Gold 3 F4
Winfrith Rd. Warr 9 D1
Wingate Rd. Beb 43 F3
Wingfield Ave. Wilm 59 F3
Wingfield Dr. Wilm 59 F3
Wingfield Pl. Winsf 149 D3
Winifred St. Warr 16 B4
Winkwell Dr. Chest 141 D3
Winmarith Dr. Altr 32 B4
Winmarleigh St. Warr 16 A2
Winnington Ave. North 103 E4
Winnington St. North 78 B1
Winnington St. Winsf 126 C1
Winnows The. Run 23 E1
Winscombe Dr. Chest 119 E1
Winsfield Rd. Haz Gr 36 C4
Winsford Cl. Hay 1 C4
Winsford Dr. Burton 6 C4
Winsford Gr. El Por 69 E2
Winsford Rd. Cholm 171 D1
Winsford Rd. Wet 170 C3
Winsford Way. Blacon 117 F1
Winslow Cl. Run 50 B4
Winstanley Cl. Gt San 15 E3
Winstanley Ind Est. Warr 8 A1
Winstanley Rd. Nest 66 C3
Winston Ave. Alsag 193 E3
Winston Ave. N-le-W 2 B2
Winston Ave. St Hel 1 A1
Winston Ct. Chest 119 D3
Winter Gr. St Hel 1 A2
Winter La. Tils 198 A2
Winterbottom La. Mere 55 F4
Winterford La. Eaton 147 D1
Wintergreen Wlk. Part 11 F1
Winterside Cl. N-u-L 210 B1
Winterton Way. Mfield 112 B2
Winton Gr. Run 24 B1
Winton Rd. Gold 3 F3
Winwick La. Croft 3 F2
Winwick La. Gold 3 F2
Winwick Link Rd. Win 8 B3
Winwick Rd. N-le-W 2 C1
Winwick Rd. Warr 8 A1
Winwick St. Warr 16 A3
Winwick View. Burton 1 B1
Wirksmoor Rd. N Mills 39 D4
Wirral Cl. Cul 4 C2
Wirral Cres. Nest 66 C3
Wirswall Rd. Marb 226 B4
Wisenholme Cl. Run 49 F3
Wistaston Ave. Wist 189 F1
Wistaston Green Cl. Wist 189 F1
Wistaston Green Rd. Wist 189 F1
Wistaston Park. Wist 189 F1
Wistaston Rd. Crewe 190 B2
Wistaston Rd. Willas 205 F3
Wistaston Rd. Wist 205 F3
Wisterdale Cl. Wist 206 A4
Witchcroft Heath Rd. With 109 D2
Witham Cl. Wist 206 A4
Witham Way. Bidd 179 F1
Withens Cl. Weave 102 B4
Withens La. Weave 102 B4
Wither's La. H Legh 28 B3
Withers Ave. Warr 16 B4
Within Way. Hale 47 F4
Withington Ave. Cul 5 D2
Withington Cl. North 104 A3
Withington Cl. Sand 175 E4
Withinlee Rd. M St A 86 B3
Withins Rd. Cul 4 C2
Withins Rd. Hay 1 C4
Withy Cft. Chest 142 A4
Withy Cl. Frod 74 B4
Withycombe Rd. Penk 14 C2
Withyfold Dr. Mfield 87 F1
Witney La. Ed Gr 213 E4
Witt Rd. Wid 23 D4
Witter Pl. Chest 118 C1
Wittering La. Hes 40 B4
Witterings The. Nest 41 F1
Witton St. North 79 D1
Witton Wlk. North 103 F4
Wivern Pl. Run 23 D2
Woburn Ave. N-le-W 2 B1
Woburn Cl. Hay 1 C4
Woburn Cl. Mfield 87 E1
Woburn Ct. Poyn 36 C2
Woburn Dr. Chest 118 B4
Woburn Dr. Cront 12 B3
Woking Rd. Ch Hul 35 D4
Wolfe Cl. Knuts 57 E2
Wolstanholme Cl. Congle 156 C1
Wolverham Rd. El Por 70 B2
Wolverton Dr. Run 24 B1
Wolvesey Pl. Winsf 149 D3
Wood Croft. G Sutt 119 F2
Wood End La. Nest 67 F2
Wood La. Apple 26 C4
Wood La. Bra Gr 152 C2
Wood La. Broug 139 D2
Wood La. Dudd 145 F4
Wood La. Goost 107 E1
Wood La. Mobb 58 B4
Wood La. Nest 66 B4
Wood La. Nest 67 E1
Wood La. Part 11 E1
Wood La. Run 49 F2
Wood La. Run 50 B3
Wood La. Tatt 167 D1
Wood La. Utkin 146 A3
Wood La. Weave 102 C4
Wood La. Will 43 D1
Wood La E. Adlin 63 D4
Wood La N. Adlin 63 D4
Wood La S. Adlin 63 D4
Wood La W. Adlin 63 D4
Wood Orchard La. Audlem 230 A1
Wood St. Audley 209 F2
Wood St. Congle 156 B2
Wood St. Crewe 190 B1
Wood St. Gold 3 D4
Wood St. Hawa 116 A1
Wood St. Mfield 112 B4
Wood St. N Mills 39 D4
Wood St. Sch Gr 195 E4
Wood St. Warr 16 B3
Wood St. Wid 13 E1
Wood View. Audley 210 A1
Wood's La. Crow 101 E3
Woodacre Gr. El Por 69 F4
Woodacre Rd. El Por 69 F4
Woodall Dr. Run 23 D1
Woodavens Gr. Roy Gr 229 D1
Woodbank Cl. Wist 206 A4
Woodbank La. Shot 93 F3
Woodbank Rd. El Por 70 A1
Woodbank Rd. Penk 15 D2
Woodbine Ave. Irlam 11 E2
Woodbine Rd. Lymm 19 D2
Woodbourne Rd. N Mills 39 D3
Woodbrook. W Br 65 F4
Woodbrook Ct. W Br 65 F4
Woodbrook Rd. A Edge 60 B1
Woodburn Dr. Hes 40 C3
Woodchurch La. El Por 69 F3
Woodclose. El Por 44 A1
Woodcock La. Sch Gr 195 E3
Woodcote Ave. El Por 70 B1
Woodcote Cl. Warr 8 B1
Woodcote View. Wilm 34 C1
Woodcotes The. Beb 43 E3
Woodcott Ave. Winsf 126 A1
Woodcott Cl. Ho Co 206 C1
Woodcott Gr. Wilm 34 C1
Woodcotthill La. Wren 217 D2
Woodcroft. Audley 210 A1
Woodend. Run 50 C4
Woodend Cl. Middle 151 E3
Woodend La. Hol Gr 10 B1
Woodend La. Mobb 58 C4
Woodend Rd. El Por 69 F3
Woodfall Cl. Nest 67 D3
Woodfall Gr. Nest 67 D3
Woodfall La. Nest 67 D3
Woodfield Gr. Chest 119 D3
Woodfield Rd. Ch Hul 35 D4
Woodfield Rd. El Por 70 B3
Woodfield Rd N. El Por 70 B3
Woodfields. Christ 142 C4
Woodfin Croft. Chelf 84 A2
Woodford Ave. Gold 3 E4
Woodford Cl. Crewe 189 F1
Woodford Cl. Hels 73 D1
Woodford Cl. Run 49 D3
Woodford Cl. Warr 17 E2
Woodford La. Prest 61 E4
Woodford La. Winsf 149 D4
Woodford La W. Winsf 149 D4
Woodford Rd. Bram 35 F2
Woodford Rd. Poyn 36 A3
Woodford Rd. Wilm 61 D4
Woodford Rd. Woodf 35 F2
Woodgate Ave. Law-g 194 A3
Woodgreen La. Ch Min 171 E3
Woodhall Cl. Woodf 35 F2
Woodhall Rd. Kids 195 E2
Woodham Gr. Nest 66 C3
Woodhatch Rd. Run 50 A3
Woodhey La. Fadd 202 B3
Woodhouse Cl. Warr 9 F2
Woodhouse End Rd. Warren 135 D4
Woodhouse La. Bidd 179 F1
Woodhouse La. Buer 235 E4
Woodhouse La. Dun T 20 B2
Woodhouse La. Warren 111 F1
Woodhouse La. Wythe 33 E4
Woodhouse Rd. Wythe 33 E4
Woodland Ave. Crewe 190 C2
Woodland Ave. Lymm 19 D1
Woodland Ave. N-le-W 2 C2
Woodland Ave. Nant 205 D3
Woodland Ave. Wid 12 C1
Woodland Bank. M Traf 96 C1
Woodland Cl. Chelf 84 A2
Woodland Ct. Alsag 193 E2
Woodland Dr. Lymm 19 D1
Woodland End. Chelf 84 A2
Woodland Gdns. Crewe 190 B3
Woodland Rd. El Por 70 A1
Woodland Rd. Sch Gr 193 F4
Woodland Walk. Beb 43 E4
Woodland Wlk. Run 24 A1
Woodlands Ave. Chest 118 A2
Woodlands Ave. Congle 156 B2
Woodlands Ave. Kids 194 B1
Woodlands Cl. Nest 66 B4
Woodlands Cl. Utkin 147 D4
Woodlands Cres. H Legh 29 E2
Woodlands Dr. Chest 118 C2
Woodlands Dr. Goost 107 F1
Woodlands Dr. Knuts 57 D1
Woodlands Dr. Warr 17 F2
Woodlands Gr. North 77 F2
Woodlands La. Chest 119 D1
Woodlands Rd. Disley 38 A3
Woodlands Rd. Hart 103 D3
Woodlands Rd. Hunt 142 A3
Woodlands Rd. Mfield 112 B3
Woodlands Rd. N Mills 39 D4
Woodlands Rd. Nest 66 B4
Woodlands Rd. Wilm 33 F1
Woodlands Rd. Wilm 34 C2
Woodlands Rd E. Hart 103 E3
Woodlands The. H Winch 80 A3
Woodlands The. North 78 C1
Woodlands The. Sand 175 E3
Woodlands Way. Tarp 146 B1
Woodlark Cl. Winsf 150 A4
Woodlea Ave. Chest 118 B4
Woodlea Cl. Beb 43 E3
Woodlea Ct. North 103 E4
Woodley Fold. Penk 14 C2
Woodnoth Dr. Shav 206 B3
Woodpecker Cl. Warr 9 F2
Woodpecker Dr. North 103 F2
Woodridge. Run 24 B1
Woodrow Way. Irlam 11 F4
Woodruff Cl. Kids 195 F1
Woodruff Wlk. Part 11 F1
Woods Gr. Ch Hul 35 D4
Woods La. Ch Hul 35 D4
Woods Rd. Irlam 11 F4
Woodsfin La. Tatt 183 F4
Woodshutt's St. Kids 194 C1
Woodside. El Por 70 B1
Woodside. Knuts 57 D1
Woodside. Law-g 194 C2
Woodside. Sidd 110 A2
Woodside Ave. Alsag 193 F2
Woodside Ave. Frod 74 B4
Woodside Ave. Kids 195 D1
Woodside Ave. Wist 189 F1
Woodside Ct. Chest 118 B2
Woodside Dr. H La 37 F4
Woodside Dr. Sand 175 E3
Woodside La. Poyn 36 C2
Woodside La. Wist 189 F1
Woodside Rd. Blacon 117 E3
Woodside Rd. Gt San 14 B4
Woodside Rd. Hay 1 C4
Woodside Rd. Lymm 19 D1
Woodside St. N Mills 39 D3
Woodside Terr. North 104 A2
Woodslands Rd. Chest 141 D4
Woodsome Cl. El Por 70 A1
Woodsome Dr. El Por 70 A1
Woodstock Ave. Ch Hul 35 D4
Woodstock Ave. N-le-W 2 B1
Woodstock Cl. Mfield 87 D1
Woodstock Dr. Middle 151 F3
Woodvale Cl. Warr 8 C1
Woodvale Rd. El Por 69 E3
Woodvale Rd. Knuts 82 A4
Woodview Rd. Wid 22 A4
Woodville Pl. Wid 12 B1
Woodward St. Weave 77 E1
Woodward Wlk. Tarv 121 E2
Woolacombe Cl. Warr 16 B1
Woolaston Dr. Alsag 193 E2
Woolden Rd. Irlam 11 D4
Woolley Ave. Poyn 36 B1
Woolmer Cl. Warr 10 A3
Woolston Ave. Congle 157 D1
Woolston Dr. Ho Co 206 C1
Woolston Grange Ave. Warr 9 E1
Woolton Ct. El Por 69 F4
Worcester Ave. Gold 3 D4
Worcester Cl. Gt San 15 E3
Worcester Cl. Kids 210 B4
Worcester Pl. Blacon 118 A2
Worcester St. El Por 70 B3
Worcester Wlk. El Por 70 B3
Wordsworth Ave. Warr 16 A1
Wordsworth Ave. Wid 22 C4
Wordsworth Cl. Wist 189 F1
Wordsworth Cres. Blacon 118 A3
Wordsworth Dr. Crewe 190 C2
Wordsworth Way. Alsag 193 E2
Wordsworth Way. El Por 69 F1
Works La. North 79 F1
World Way. Wythe 33 D4
Worleston Cl. Middle 151 E3
Worrall St. Congle 156 C2
Worsborough Ave. Gt San 15 D3
Worsley Ave. Saug 117 D4
Worsley Ave. Warr 16 C2
Worsley Dr. Congle 157 D1
Worsley Rd. Warr 16 A1
Worsley St. Gold 3 D4
Worsley St. Warr 15 F4
Worthing St. North 104 B4
Worthington Ave. Part 11 F2
Worthington Cl. Henb 111 E4
Worthington Cl. Run 50 A4
Wrekin Way. Chest 140 C3
Wren Ave. Sp Gr 129 E1
Wren Cl. Mfield 87 D1
Wren Cl. Run 50 A3
Wren Cl. Warr 9 F2
Wrenburry Cl. N-u-L 210 B1
Wrenbury Hall Dr. Wren 217 D3
Wrenbury Heath Rd. Sound 217 E3
Wrenbury Ind Est. Wren 217 D2
Wrenbury Rd. New 217 D2
Wrenmere Cl. Sand 174 C4
Wrenshot La. H Legh 29 E3
Wrexham Cl. Bidd 179 E1
Wrexham Cl. Warr 7 F1
Wrexham Ind Est. Isyc 196 A1
Wrexham Rd. Bicker 200 A4
Wrexham Rd. Bulk 184 C1
Wrexham Rd. Burl 203 E4
Wrexham Rd. Chest 141 D2
Wrexham Rd. Cudd Gr 212 C1
Wrexham Rd. Dodle 141 D2
Wrexham Rd. Eccles 162 C3
Wrexham Rd. Fadd 202 B3
Wrexham Rd. Holt 196 A4
Wrexham Rd. Malpas 212 C1
Wrexham Rd. Pulf 162 C3
Wrexham Rd. Ridley 185 E1
Wright Ave. North 104 B3
Wright Cres. Wid 23 D3
Wright St. Kids 194 B1
Wright Tree Villas. Irlam 11 E3
Wright's La. Burton 6 C2
Wright's La. Sand 175 E3
Wrights Lane. Penk 14 A1
Wrigley La. N Ald 86 A2
Wrigley Rd. Hay 1 C3
Wrinehill Rd. Blake 220 C4
Wrinehill Rd. Hay Gr 220 C4
Wroxham Cl. Chest 118 B2
Wroxham Cl. Hels 73 D2
Wroxham Rd. Gt San 14 B4
Wrynose Rd. Beb 43 F4
Wt Bear Yd. Knuts 57 D1
Wybersley Rd. H La 38 A4
Wybunbury La. Hather 220 A4
Wybunbury La. Hay Gr 205 F2
Wybunbury Rd. Willas 205 E3
Wych House La. Middle 128 B1
Wych La. Adlin 62 B3
Wyche Ave. Nant 204 B3
Wyche La. Bun 185 F4
Wyche Rd. Bun 185 F4
Wychelm Rd. Part 11 F2
Wychwood Ave. Lymm 18 B2
Wycliffe Ave. Wilm 60 A4
Wycliffe Rd. El Por 69 F2
Wycliffe Rd. Hay 1 C4
Wyedale. El Por 70 A2
Wyedale Rd. Hay 1 B3
Wyncroft Cl. El Por 70 A2
Wynd The. Kels 122 B2
Wyndham Cl. Bram 35 F4
Wyndham Cres. El Por 69 F1
Wyndham Rd. Blacon 117 E2
Wynfield Ave. Wythe 33 F4
Wyngate Rd. Altr 31 F4
Wynnstay Rd. Broug 139 E2
Wynter Cl. Tils 198 A2
Wythburn Gr. Run 49 F3
Wythens Rd. Chea 34 A4

Yardley Ave. Warr 15 F4
Yarmouth Rd. Gt San 14 C3
Yarrow Cl. Broug 139 E2
Yarwoodheath La. Rosth 30 C4
Yatehouse La. L Den 128 B4
Yatehouse La. Middle 128 B4
Yates Cl. Gt San 15 E3
Yates Rd. N Mills 39 E4
Yates Rd. T-le-M 71 F1
Yates St. Crewe 190 B1
Yeald Brow. Lymm 18 A2
Yeardsley Ave. W Br 39 E2
Yeardsley Green. W Br 65 E4
Yeardsley La. W Br 39 E2
Yeld La. Dela 122 C4
Yeoman Way. El Por 69 F1
Yeovil Cl. Warr 17 E4
Yerburgh St. Chest 118 B2
Yew Tree Ave. N-le-W 2 A2
Yew Tree Bank. Dudd 145 D3
Yew Tree Cl. Broug 139 E2
Yew Tree Cl. Bulk 184 B1
Yew Tree Cl. L Bud 147 F4
Yew Tree Cl. Mfield 112 A3
Yew Tree Cl. Middle 128 A1
Yew Tree Cl. Prest 87 D4
Yew Tree Cl. T-le-M 71 F1
Yew Tree Cl. Wilm 60 B4
Yew Tree Dr. Nant 204 B3
Yew Tree Dr. North 78 A2
Yew Tree La. Apple 27 E3
Yew Tree La. Astb 178 B2
Yew Tree Park Rd. Ch Hul 35 D3
Yew Tree Rd. Adlin 37 D1
Yew Tree Rd. Wist 206 A4
Yew Tree Way. Prest 87 E3
Yew Wlk. Part 11 E1
Yewdale Dr. El Por 69 F1
Yewlands. Cudd 101 E3
Yewlands Dr. Knuts 57 E1
Yewtree Cl. Nest 66 C4
Yewtree La. Poyn 36 C2
Yewtree Rd. Plum 80 C2
York Ave. Cul 4 C1
York Ave. Gt San 14 C4
York Cl. Bidd 179 E1
York Cres. Wilm 60 B4
York Ct. Mfield 112 C4
York Dr. M Traf 96 C1
York Dr. Warr 17 D1
York Dr. Winsf 149 E3
York Pl. Run 23 D1
York Rd. Con Q 91 E1
York Rd. El Por 70 B3
York Rd. Warr 17 D1
York Rd. Wid 22 B4
York St. Chest 118 B1
York St. Mfield 112 C4
York St. Run 23 D1
York St. Warr 16 B2
Yorkshire Rd. Part 11 F1
Ystad Ddiwdiannol Wrecsam. Isyc 196 A1

Zan Dr. Sand 175 D2
Zinnia Dr. Irlam 11 F4
Zion St. North 103 F4

STREET ATLASES ORDER FORM

T502N99C	Hardback QUANTITY TOTAL	Softback QUANTITY TOTAL	Pocket QUANTITY TOTAL
	£12.99	£8.99	£4.99
Berkshire	ISBN 0-540-05992-7	ISBN 0-540-05993-5	ISBN 0-540-05994-3
Buckinghamshire	ISBN 0-540-05989-7	ISBN 0-540-05990-0	ISBN 0-540-05991-9
East Essex	ISBN 0-540-05848-3	ISBN 0-540-05866-1	ISBN 0-540-05850-5
West Essex	ISBN 0-540-05849-1	ISBN 0-540-05867-X	ISBN 0-540-05851-3
North Hampshire	ISBN 0-540-05852-1	ISBN 0-540-05853-X	ISBN 0-540-05854-8
South Hampshire	ISBN 0-540-05855-6	ISBN 0-540-05856-4	ISBN 0-540-05857-2
Hertfordshire	ISBN 0-540-05995-1	ISBN 0-540-05996-X	ISBN 0-540-05997-8
East Kent	ISBN 0-540-06026-7	ISBN 0-540-06027-5	ISBN 0-540-06028-3
West Kent	ISBN 0-540-06029-1	ISBN 0-540-06031-3	ISBN 0-540-06030-5
Nottinghamshire	ISBN 0-540-05858-0	ISBN 0-540-05859-9	ISBN 0-540-05860-2
Oxfordshire	ISBN 0-540-05986-2	ISBN 0-540-05987-0	ISBN 0-540-05988-9
Surrey	ISBN 0-540-05983-8	ISBN 0-540-05984-6	ISBN 0-540-05985-4
East Sussex	ISBN 0-540-05875-0	ISBN 0-540-05874-2	ISBN 0-540-05873-4
West Sussex	ISBN 0-540-05876-9	ISBN 0-540-05877-7	ISBN 0-540-05878-5
	£12.99	£9.99	£4.99
Bristol and Avon	ISBN 0-540-06140-9	ISBN 0-540-06141-7	ISBN 0-540-06142-5
Cheshire	ISBN 0-540-06143-3	ISBN 0-540-06144-1	ISBN 0-540-06145-X
Derbyshire	ISBN 0-540-06137-9	ISBN 0-540-06138-7	ISBN 0-540-06139-5
Staffordshire	ISBN 0-540-06134-4	ISBN 0-540-06135-2	ISBN 0-540-06136-0
	£10.99		
Warwickshire	ISBN 0-540-05642-1		

Name ______________________

Address ______________________

____

______________________ *Postcode*

◆ ***Free postage and packing*** ◆ *All available titles will normally be dispatched within 5 working days of receipt of order but please allow up to 28 days for delivery*

☐ *Please tick this box if you do not wish your name to be used by other carefully selected organisations that may wish to send you information about other products and services*

I enclose a cheque / postal order, for a ***total*** *of* ☐

made payable to ***Reed Book Services****, or please debit my*

☐ *Access* ☐ *American Express* ☐ *Visa*

account by ☐

Account no ☐☐☐☐ ☐☐☐☐ ☐☐☐☐ ☐☐☐☐

Expiry date ☐☐ ☐☐

Signature ______________________

Registered office: Michelin House, 81 Fulham Road, London SW3 6RB. Registered in England No 1974080